ARCTIC OC

Barents Sea

25,000

Bering Sea

EUROPE
000

ASIA

PACIFIC
OCEAN

45,000

0

65,000–
55,000

Arabian
Sea

South
China
Sea

Equator

INDIAN
OCEAN

OCEANIA

800–
700*

Tasman
Sea

45,000

OUTHERN OCEAN

ANTARCTICA

THE WORLD

Also by Simon Sebag Montefiore

Nonfiction

Catherine the Great and Potemkin
Stalin: The Court of the Red Tsar
Young Stalin
Jerusalem: The Biography
The Romanovs: 1613–1918
Titans of History: The Giants Who Made Our World
Written in History: Letters That Changed the World
Voices of History: Speeches That Changed the World

Fiction

Sashenka
One Night in Winter
Red Sky at Noon

Children's fiction (with Santa Montefiore)
The Royal Rabbits of London series

THE WORLD

A FAMILY HISTORY OF HUMANITY

Simon Sebag Montefiore

Alfred A. Knopf
New York
2023

Library of Congress Cataloging-in-Publication Data
Names: Sebag Montefiore, Simon, [date] author.
Title: The world : a family history / Simon Sebag Montefiore.
Description: First edition. | New York : Alfred A. Knopf, 2023. | Includes
bibliographical references and index.
Identifiers: LCCN 2022033250 | ISBN 9780525659532 (hardcover) |
ISBN 9780525659549 (ebook)
Subjects: LCSH: Royal houses—Anecdotes | World history—Anecdotes |
Upper class—Biography—Anecdotes
Classification: LCC D107 .S43 2023 | DDC 929.7—dc23/eng/20220720
LC record available at https://lccn.loc.gov/2022033250

Jacket design and illustration by Helen Crawford-White

Manufactured in India
Second Printing, February 2023

TO MY DARLING SON,

SASHA

In memory of my parents,
Stephen & April

If a kingdom be a great family, a family likewise is a little kingdom, torn with factions and exposed to revolutions.

Samuel Johnson

The world is a mountain and our deeds, voices;
The voices have echoes; to us they will return.

Rumi

Until the lions have their own historians, the history of the hunt will always glorify the hunter.

Chinua Achebe

Truth never yet fell dead in the streets; it has such an affinity with the soul of man, the seed however broadcast will catch somewhere and produce its hundredfold.

Theodore Parker

So many wars, so many shapes of crime . . .
Unholy Mars bends all to his mad will;
The world is like a chariot run wild.

Virgil

The whole question is: who controls whom.

Lenin

He who believes that by studying isolated histories, he can acquire a fairly just view of history as a whole, is like the person who, after looking at the severed limbs of an animal once alive and beautiful, fancies he has seen the creature alive in all its action and grace . . . It is only indeed by study of the interconnection of all the particulars, their resemblances and differences, that we are enabled at least to make a general survey, and thus derive both benefit and pleasure from history.

Polybius

Midway on life's journey, I found myself in a dark wood, for the straight path was lost.

Dante Alighieri

CONTENTS

ACT TWO

ACT THREE

ACT NINE

ACT TEN

ACT TWELVE

ACT FIFTEEN

Trumps and Xis, Sauds, Assads and Kims

PREFACE AND ACKNOWLEDGEMENTS

This is a world history that I wrote during the menacing times of Covid lockdown and Russian invasion of Ukraine. There are a million ways to do such a thing; hundreds of historians, starting in ancient times, have done it their way; most universities now have professors of world history and scores of such works are published annually, many of them brilliant, and I have tried to read them all. No book is easy to write, world history harder than most. 'Words and ideas pour out of my head,' wrote Ibn Khaldun composing his world history, 'like cream into a churn.' There has been much cream and much churning in the writing of this.

I have always wanted to write an intimate, human history like this, in some ways a new approach, in some ways a traditional one, which is the fruit of a lifetime of study and travels. I have been lucky enough to visit many of the places in this history, to witness wars and coups that play a part in it, and to have conversations with a few characters who have played roles on the world stage.

When I was eleven, my father, a thoughtful medical doctor, gave me an abridged version of the now pungently unfashionable Arnold Toynbee's *A Study of History*. 'Maybe one day,' he said, 'you'll write something like this,' and I spent hours reading histories of places and times that were not taught at my English school, where study of the Tudors and Nazis dominated.

This book has given me the greatest satisfaction of my writing life, and presented the most daunting challenge. But I have suffered much less than many other historians. Ibn Khaldun saw both his parents perish of the plague. Sir Walter Raleigh wrote his *History of the World* while waiting to be executed, a condition that surely fostered the required perspective. But he was beheaded before finishing (an unbearable thought). History has a special, almost mystic power to shape (and, if abused, to distort) the present: that's what makes history-writing an essential and noble – but dangerous – profession. Sima Qian, the Chinese world historian (born circa 145 BC), was accused of defaming the emperor and given a choice between execution and becoming a palace eunuch. He opted for castration so that he could complete his history: 'before I had finished my rough manuscript, I met with this calamity . . . If it may be handed down to men who will appreciate it, and penetrate to the villages and great cities, then though I should suffer a thousand mutilations, what regret should I have?' Every historian, every writer shares that dream. Sima Qian was in my thoughts as I wrote . . .

Among living historians, a galaxy of distinguished, brilliant scholars have read, discussed and corrected all or part of this book: thank you to Dominic Lieven, Professor of International History, LSE; Peter Frankopan, Professor of Global History, Oxford; Olivette Otele, Professor of the Legacies and Memory of Slavery, SOAS; Thomas Levenson, Professor of Science Writing, MIT; Sir Simon Schama, Professor of History and Art History, Columbia Univeristy; David Abulafia, Professor Emeritus of Mediterranean History, Cambridge University; Abigail Green, Professor of Modern European History, Oxford.

Dr Henry Kissinger, US Secretary of State 1973–7, read his period; I had the honour to talk about the creation of the internet with Sir Tim Berners-Lee and Rosemary Berners-Lee. Thanks to Ben Okri.

Thanks to the following for correcting these specific subjects:

Africa: Luke Pepera.

Americas: (USA) Annette Gordon-Reed, Charles Warren Professor of American Legal History, Harvard Law School; Andrew Preston, Professor of American History, Cambridge University; (Mesoamerica/South America) Matthew Restall, Edwin Erle Sparks Professor of Colonial Latin American History, Penn State College of Liberal Arts; (Brazil) Lilia Schwarcz, Professor of Anthropology, University of São Paulo.

China: (early) Michael Nylan, Professor, East Asian Studies, Berkeley University; (Qin onwards) Mark C. Elliott, Mark Schwartz Professor of Chinese and Inner Asian History, Harvard University.

Genetics/DNA: Dr Adam Rutherford.

Greeks: Roderick Beaton, Emeritus Koraes Professor of Modern Greek & Byzantine History, King's College, London.

India/South Asia: Tirthankar Roy, Professor in Economic History, LSE; Dr Tripurdaman Singh, Institute of Commonwealth Studies, School of Advanced Studies, London University; William Dalrymple; Dr Sushma Jansari, Curator, South Asia Collections, British Museum; Dr Imma Ramos, Curator, South Asia Collections, British Museum; Dr Katherine Schofield, Senior Lecturer in South Asian Music and History, King's College London.

Iran: Lloyd Llewellyn-Jones, Professor in Ancient History, Cardiff University.

Japan: Dr Christopher Harding, Senior Lecturer, Asian History, Edinburgh University.

Ukraine: Serhii Plokhy, Mykhailo Hrushevsky Professor of Ukrainian History, Harvard University

My thanks to the following for their corrections in subjects presented chronologically:

Prehistory: Professor Chris Stringer, Research Leader, Human Evolution, Natural History Museum; (Sumeria/Mesopotamia) Augusta McMahon, Professor of Mesopotamian Archaeology, Cambridge; Dr John MacGinnis, Department of Middle East, British Museum.

Ancient Egypt: Salima Ikhram, Professor of Egyptology, American University in Cairo.

Ancient Rome: Greg Woolf, Ronald J. Mellor Chair of Ancient History at University of California.

Silk Roads: Peter Frankopan.

Byzantium: Jonathan Harris, Professor of the History of Byzantium, Royal Holloway, University of London; Peter Frankopan.

Vikings: Neil Price, Professor of Archaeology, University of Uppsala.

Kyivan Rus/Muscovy: Dr Sergei Bogatyrev, Associate Professor, University College London (author of a forthcoming book on familial memory in Kyivan Rus).

Medieval Europe/Normans: Robert Bartlett, Emeritus Professor, St Andrews University.

Mongols: Timothy May, Professor of Central Eurasian History, University of North Georgia.

Incas and Aztecs: Matthew Restall, Edwin Erle Sparks Professor of Colonial Latin American History, Penn State College of Liberal Arts.

Ethiopia: Dr Mai Musié, postdoctoral researcher in Race and Ethnicity in the ancient Graeco-Roman world, Oxford University; Dr Verena Krebs, Ruhr-University Bochum; Dr Adam Simmons, Nottingham Trent University; Dr Bar Kribus, Hebrew University, Jerusalem.

Khmer/Cambodia: Ashley Thompson, Professor in Southeast Asian Art, SOAS.

Portugal/Portuguese empire: Malyn Newitt, Charles Boxer Professor of History, King's College London; Zoltán Biedermann, Professor of Early Modern History, SELCS, University College London.

Spain/Spanish Empire: Dr Fernando Cervantes, University of Bristol.

Seventeenth-century England: Ronald Hutton, Professor of History, University of Bristol.

Brazil: Lilia Schwarcz.

Hawaii: Nicholas Thomas, Professor of Social Anthropology, Cambridge.

France: Robert Gildea, Professor of Modern History, Worcester College, Oxford.

Saint-Domingue/Haiti: Dr Sudhir Hazareesingh, Balliol College, Oxford; John D. Garrigus, Professor of History at the University of Texas at Arlington.

Netherlands/Dutch Empire: David Onnekink, Assistant Professor of History at Utrecht University.

Germany: Katja Hoyer.

Cold War: Sergey Radchenko, Distinguished Professor at the Johns Hopkins School of Advanced International Studies.

Dr N. Zaki translated Arabic texts. Keith Goldsmith read US sections. Jago Cooper, Kate Jarvis and Olly Boles helped in the early sections. Jonathan Foreman spent many hours discussing world history.

Lives are made by great teachers and inspirational mentors: thank you to the late majestic Professor Isabel de Madariaga who taught me how to write history in my first book *Catherine the Great & Potemkin*; Jeremy Lemmon, the late Stuart Parsonson, Howard Shaw, Hugh Thompson.

Thanks to the team who have sustained me: Dr Marcus Harbord for health; Rino Eramo of Café Rino and Ted 'Longshot' Longden at The Yard for blood-pumping cortados; Carl van Heerden and Dominique Felix for Spartan fitness sessions; Akshaya Wadhwani for high-tech. Thanks to dear friends Samantha Heyworth, Robert Hardman; Aliai Forte; Tamara Magaram; Marie-Claude Bourrely and Eloise Goldstein for their help on Côte d'Ivoire.

Thanks to my publishers at Hachette, David Shelley, Maddy Price, Elizabeth Allen; the heroic Jo Whitford; and to the brilliant Peter James, the king of editors; my former editor Bea Hemming; in the USA, the late Sonny Mehta, to Reagan Arthur and Edward Kastenmeier at Knopf; and to my superlative agents Georgina Capel, Rachel Conway, Irene Baldoni, Simon Shaps.

I dedicate this to my late parents Stephen and April. I thank my wife Santa, daughter Lilochka and son Sasha for tolerating three years of hermetic focus with laughter, love and tolerance: 'One for all and all for one.'

Simon Sebag Montefiore
London

NOTE

This is a work of synthesis, the product of a lifetime's reading, using primary sources wherever possible. Each subject here has a vast historiography, so to save space I list in the Bibliography the main works used in each section.

Names matter: 'things in actual fact', suggested Confucius, 'should be made to accord with the implications attached to them by names'. The traditional academic style is to Hellenize eastern dynasties, e.g. Genghis Khan's Genghizids. Unless they are actually Greek (Seleucids), I try to use their own names for themselves: I call Persian Achaemenids, Haxamanishiya; the Abbasids, Abbasiya. I try to avoid neologisms – mostly using Romaioi instead of Byzantines, Hattian instead of Hittite. I try to avoid anglicizing everything: French kings are François, Spanish kings Enrique. But if they are well known, I use the familiar: Cyrus, not Kouresh, Pompey, not Pompeius. In Ottoman times, I generally use Turkish rather than Arabic: Mehmed Ali instead of Muhammad Ali, even though this will displease Egyptians. I use Türkiye instead of Turkey: if ever there was an example of Eurocentric misspelling, it is that. For Chinese rulers, I use either their given name (Liu Che) or their posthumous title (Emperor Wu or Wudi); for the Ming and Qing, I use era names (the Kangxi Emperor, thereafter Kangxi).

For geographical context, I cite modern states, but this can be confusing: the Kingdom of Dahomey was in today's Republic of Benin (not the Republic of Dahomey); the Kingdom of Benin was in Nigeria (not the Republic of Benin).

The chrononyms of world history are world-sized – Stone, Dark and Axial Ages, Great Opening and Renaissance, and a lot of revolutions; many now seem reductionist, old-fashioned and clichéd. But it is the historian's job to classify and some of these are clichés because they are largely true.

Apologies for all inconsistencies.

INTRODUCTION

As the tide fell, the footsteps emerge. The footsteps of a family walking on the beach of what is now a small village in eastern England, Happisburgh. Five sets of footprints. Probably a male and four children, dating from between 950,000 and 850,000 years before the present. These, discovered in 2013, are the oldest family footprints ever found. They are not the first: even older footprints have been found in Africa, where the human story started. But these are the oldest traces of a *family*. And they are the inspiration for this history of the world.

There have been many histories of the world, but this one adopts a new approach, using the stories of families across time to provide a different, fresh perspective. It is one that appeals to me because it offers a way of connecting great events with individual human drama, from the first hominins to today, from the sharpened stone to the iPhone and the drone. World history is an elixir for troubled times: its advantage is that it offers a sense of perspective; its drawback is that it involves too much distance. World history often has themes, not people; biography has people, not themes.

The family remains the essential unit of human existence – even in the age of AI and galactical warfare. I have woven history together telling the stories of multiple families in every continent and epoch, using them to tether the onward rush of the human story. It is a biography of many people instead of one person. Even if the span of these families is global, their dramas are intimate – birth, death, marriage, love, hate; they rise; they fall; rise again; they migrate; they return. In every family drama, there are many acts. That is what Samuel Johnson meant when he said every kingdom is a family and every family a little kingdom.

Unlike many of the histories that I grew up with, this is a genuine world history, not unbalanced by excessive focus on Britain and Europe but rather giving Asia, Africa and the Americas the attention they deserve. The focus on family also makes it possible to pay more attention to the lives of women and children, both of whom were slighted in the books I read as a schoolboy. Their roles – like the shape of family itself

– change through the arc of time. My aim is to show how the fontanelles of history grew together.

The word family has an air of cosiness and affection, but of course in real life families can be webs of struggle and cruelty too. Many of the families that I follow are power families in which the intimacy and warmth of nurture and love are at once infused and distorted by the peculiar and implacable dynamics of politics. In power families, danger comes from intimacy. 'Calamity,' as Han Fei Tzu warned his monarch in second-century BC China, 'will come to you from those you love.'

'History is something very few people were doing,' writes Yuval Noah Harari, 'when everyone else was ploughing fields and carrying water buckets.' Many of the families I choose are ones that exercise power, but others encompass enslaved persons, doctors, painters, novelists, executioners, generals, historians, priests, charlatans, scientists, tycoons, criminals – and lovers. Even a few gods.

Some will be familiar, many will not: here we follow the dynasties of Mali, Ming, Medici and Mutapa, Dahomey, Oman, Afghanistan, Cambodia, Brazil and Iran, Haiti, Hawaii and Habsburg; we chronicle Genghis Khan, Sundiata Keita, Empress Wu, Ewuare the Great, Ivan the Terrible, Kim Jong-un, Itzcoatl, Andrew Jackson, King Henry of Haiti, Ganga Zumba, Kaiser Wilhelm, Indira Gandhi, Sobhuza, Pachacuti Inca and Hitler alongside Kenyattas, Castros, Assads and Trumps, Cleopatra, de Gaulle, Khomeini, Gorbachev, Marie Antoinette, Jefferson, Nader, Mao, Obama; Mozart, Balzac and Michelangelo; Caesars, Mughals, Saudis, Roosevelts, Rothschilds, Rockefellers, Ottomans.

The lurid coexists with the cosy. There are many loving fathers and mothers but also 'Fatso' Ptolemy IV dismembers his son and sends the parts to the child's mother; Nader Shah and Empress Iris blind their sons; Queen Isabella tortures her daughter; Charlemagne possibly sleeps with his; Ottoman power mother Kösem orders the strangling of her son and in turn is strangled on the orders of her grandson; Valois potentate Catherine de' Medici orchestrates a massacre at the wedding of her daughter whose rape by her sons she seems to have condoned; Nero sleeps with his mother, then murders her. Shaka kills his mother, then uses it as a pretext to launch a massacre. Saddam Hussein unleashes his sons against his sons-in-law. The killing of brothers is endemic – even now: Kim Jong-un has recently murdered his brother in a very modern way using a reality-show stunt as cover, a nerve agent as poison.

We follow the tragedies too of teenaged daughters, dispatched by cold parents to marry strangers in faraway lands where they then die in childbirth: sometimes their marriages facilitated affinities between states; more often, their sufferings achieved little since family connections were totally trumped by interests of state. We also follow enslaved women who rise to rule empires; here is Sally Hemings, enslaved half-sister of Thomas Jefferson's late wife, secretly bearing the president's children; here is Razia of the Delhi sultanate who seizes power as sovereign but is destroyed by her relationship with an African general; in al-Andalus, a caliph's daughter, Wallada, becomes poetess and libertine. Following our chosen families through pandemics, wars, floods and booms, we chart the lives of women from the village to the throne to the factory and the premiership, from catastrophic maternal mortality and legal impotence to the rights to vote, to abortion and contraception; and the trajectory of children from devastating child mortality to industrialized labour and the modern cult of childhood.

This is a history that focuses on individuals, families and coteries. There are many other ways of approaching history with this span. But I am a historian of power and geopolitics is the engine of world history. I have spent most of my career writing about Russian leaders, and this is the sort of history I have always enjoyed reading – it encompasses passions and furies, the realm of the imagination and senses, and the grit of ordinary life in a way missing from pure economics and political science. The centrality of this human connection is a way of telling the global story that shows the impact of political, economic and technical changes while revealing how families too have evolved. This is another bout in the long struggle between structure and agency, impersonal forces and human character. But these are not necessarily exclusive. 'Men make their own history,' wrote Marx, 'but they don't make it as they please; they don't make it under self-selected circumstances, but under circumstances existing already, given and transmitted from the past.' So often history is presented as a staccato series of events, revolutions and paradigms, experienced by neatly categorized, narrowly identified people. Yet the lives of real families reveal something different – idiosyncratic, singular people living, laughing, loving over decades and centuries in a layered, hybrid, liminal, kaleidoscopic world that defies the categories and identities of later times.

The families and characters I follow here tend to be exceptional – but they also reveal much about their era and place. It is a way of looking at how kingdoms and states evolved, at how the interconnectivity of peoples developed, and at how different societies absorbed outsiders and merged with others. In this multifaceted drama, I hope that the simultaneous, blended yet single narrative catches something of the messy unpredictability and contingency of real life in real time, the feeling that much is happening in different places and orbits, the mayhem and the confusion of a dizzying, spasmodic, bare-knuckle cavalry charge, often as absurd as it is cruel, always filled with vertiginous surprises, strange incidents and incredible personalities that no one could foresee. That's why the most successful leaders are visionaries, transcendent strategists but also improvisers, opportunists, creatures of bungle and luck. 'Even the shrewdest of the shrewd,' admitted Bismark 'goes like a child into the dark.' History is made by the interplay of ideas, institutions and geopolitics. When they come together in felicitous conjunction, great changes happen. But even then, it is personalities who roll the dice . . .

A book of this scale has many themes: one is the shaping of nations by migration. We follow stable families and we follow families in movement or formed by movement: the great mass movements of families – migrations and conquests – that created every race and nation.

We follow both inner families and wider power families, often expanded to clans and tribes. The inner family is a reality for all of us in terms of biology, and for many of us in terms of parental care, however flawed; wider dynasties are constructs that use trust and lineage as a glue to preserve power, protect wealth and share perils. Yet all of us instinctively understand both of these: in many ways we are all members of dynasties, and this family history is a chronicle of all of us. It is just that the means of ruling families and what is at stake for them are more lethal.

In Europe and the USA, we tend to think of family as a small unit that is no longer of political importance in the age of individualism, mass politics, industrialization and high-tech – and that we no longer need families as much as we used to. There is truth in that, and in the later centuries, family takes on a different aspect, particularly in the west. When there are not prominent families, I continue to use character and connection to tether a complex narrative, but it turns out that, in our individualistic, supposedly rational world, dynasties have evolved but not vanished. Far from it.

During the American revolution, Tom Paine insisted that 'A hereditary monarch is as absurd a position as a hereditary doctor,' but doctors, like many other professions, were then often hereditary. One cannot write about dynasty without religion: rulers and dynasties governed as sacred monarchies, agents and sometimes personifications of divine will, a conviction that dovetailed with family to make hereditary succession seem natural, a reflection of the natural organization of society through lineage. After 1789, sacred dynasty evolved to fit new national and popular paradigms and after 1848, mass politics. Traditional religion – bells and smells – is less predominant today, yet our so-called secular societies are just as religious as those of our forefathers and our orthodoxies are just as rigid and absurd as the old religions. An overarching theme then is the human need for religiosity and soteriology, providing every individual, family, nation with a righteous mission that gives meaning and shape to existence. 'He who has a *why* to live for,' says Nietzsche, 'can tolerate any *how*.'

In today's liberal democracies, we pride ourselves on pure, rational politics without clan, kin and connection. Certainly, family matters much less. But most politics remains as much about personality and patronage as about policy. Modern states, even liberal democracies in north America and western Europe, are more complex and less rational than we like to pretend: formal institutions are often bypassed by informal networks and personal courts that include family: in democracies or semi-democracies, one only has to think of Kennedys and Bushes, Kenyattas and Khamas, Nehrus, Bhuttos and Sharifs, Lees and Marcoses, demo-dynasties who represent reassurance and continuity but have to be elected (and can be unelected too). Research in today's USA, India and Japan reveals that national dynasties are replicated locally among congressional and state lineages. And then there is the growing number of hereditary rulers in Asia and Africa who – behind the cosplay of republican institutions – are in effect monarchs.

'Kinship and family remain a force to be reckoned with,' writes Jeroen Duindam, the doyen of dynastic historians. 'Personalised and enduring forms of leadership in politics and in business tend to acquire semi-dynastic traits even in the contemporary world.'

While family has had different shapes at different times and power is always in flux, there is an opposite phenomenon to which it is linked and to which this book pays much attention: slavery. In the form of household slaves, slavery was an ever-present feature of family from the start, but this was the family not of the enslaved but of the slave master. Slavery shattered families; it was an anti-family institution. The enslaved families that did exist – in Roman households or Islamic harems or those like Sally Hemings and Jefferson in slave-owning America – encompassed coercion without choice, and often outright rape. One theme of this history: family for many can be a privilege.

This book is written at a time of exciting and long-overdue developments in history writing that are reflected here: an emphasis on peoples in Asia and Africa; the interconnectedness of polities, languages, cultures; a focus on the role of women and racial diversity. But history has become a sparkwheel, its moral power instantly igniting torches of knowledge and dumpster-fires of ignorance. One has only to glance at the hellscapes of Twitter and Facebook, hear their borborygmi of prejudices and conspiracies, to see that history is ever more fissile thanks to digital distortion. Part-science, part-literature, part-mysticism, part-ethics, History has always been important because the past, whether gold-speckled splendour or heroic suffering, however imagined, possesses a legitimacy and an authenticity, even a sanctity, that is built into us – and often expressed through the stories of families and nations. It can move multitudes, create nations, justify slaughter and heroism, tyranny and freedom, with the silent power of a thousand armies. That is why at its best, its pursuit of truth is essential. Every ideology, religion and empire has sought to control the hallowed past to legitimize whatever they are doing in the present. There are plenty of attempts today in east and west to force history into an ideology.

The old childish history of 'goodies' and 'baddies' is back in fashion, albeit with different 'goodies' and 'baddies'. Yet as James Baldwin pointed out, 'An invented past can never be used; it cracks and crumbles under the pressures of life like clay in the season of drought.' The best clue is the use of tangled jargon. As Foucault wrote, ideological jargon is a sign of coercive ideology: 'it tends to exert a sort of pressure and something like a power of constraint on other discourses', for the jargon conceals the lack of factual basis, intimidates dissidents and allows collaborators to flaunt their virtuous conventionality. 'What is at stake,' asked Foucault, so often on point, 'in the will to truth, in the will to utter this "true" discourse, if not desire and power?' Baldwin warned, 'Nobody's more dangerous than he who imagines himself pure in heart: for his purity, by definition, is unassailable.' Ideologies of history rarely survive contact with the messiness, nuance and complexity of real life: 'The individual which power has constituted,' noted Foucault, 'is at the same time its vehicle.'

Of necessity, there is much focus on the dark matter of history – war, crime, violence and oppression – because they are facts of life and they are engines of change. History is 'the slaughter bench,' wrote Hegel, 'on which the happiness of peoples are sacrificed'. War is always an accelerant: 'The sword tells more truth than books, its edge is parting wisdom from vanity,' writes Abu Tammam ibn Aws, poet of ninth-century Iraq. 'Knowledge is found in the sparkle of lances.' And every army, wrote Trotsky, 'is a copy of society and suffers from all its diseases, usually at a higher temperature'. Empires – polities of centralized rule, continental mass, geographical span, diverse peoples – are omnipresent in many forms; the steppe empires of nomadic horsemen that menaced sedentary societies for many millennia are very different from the European transoceanic empires that dominated the world between 1500 and

1960. Some were the work of a single conqueror or vision but most were conquered and ruled ad hoc, haphazardly and multifariously. Today's world contenders are 'empire nations' – led by China, America, Russia – which combine the cohesion of nation and the span of empire with awesome, often continental, mass. In Moscow, imperialists, fortified by a new ultra-nationalism, control the world's largest empire nation – with lethal results. The tournament of geopolitics – what Pope Julius II called 'the World Game' – is implacable; success is always temporary, and the human cost is always too high.   .

Many crimes have been neglected and concealed, and they must be covered in full. In this book, my aim is to write a nuanced history that shows humans and their polities as the complicated, flawed, inspiring entities they really are. The best medicine for the crimes of the past is to cast the brightest light upon them; and, once those crimes are beyond the reach of punishment, this illumination is the truest redemption, the only one that counts. This book aims to cast that light: achievements and crimes are chronicled, whoever the perpetrators were. I try to tell the stories of as many of the innocents killed, enslaved or repressed as I can: everyone counts or no one counts.

Today we are blessed with exciting new scientific methods – carbon-dating, DNA, glottochronology – that allow us to discover more about the past and to chart the damage humans are doing to their earth through global warming and pollution. Yet even with all these new tools, at its essence history is still about people. My last trip before writing this was to Egypt: when I saw the animated faces of the tomb portraits of Fayum, I thought how much these people in the first century looked like us. They and their families do share many characteristics with us today, but the differences are as great. In our own lives, we often scarcely understand people we know well. The first rule of history is to realize how little we know about people in the past, how they thought, how their families worked.

It is a challenge to avoid teleology, writing history as if its outcome was known all along. Historians are bad prophets but good at prophesying the future when they already know what happened. But historians are often not so much chroniclers of the past or seers of the future as simply mirrors of their own present. The only way to understand the past is to shake off the present: our job is to seek what facts we can to chronicle the lives of earlier generations – high and low and as broad as the world – using everything we know.

A world historian, wrote al-Masudi in ninth-century Baghdad, is like 'a man who, having found pearls of all kinds and colours, gathers them together into a necklace and makes them into an ornament that its possessor guards with great care'. That is the kind of world history I want to write.

The familial footsteps on Happisburgh beach were rapidly destroyed by the tides – but it would be several hundreds of thousands of years before the beginning of what we call history.

ACT ONE
WORLD POPULATION:

70,000 BC: 150,000
10,000 BC: 4 million
5000 BC: 5 million
2000 BC: 27 million
1000 BC: 50 million

Houses of Sargon and Ahmose:
Ziggurats and Pyramids

Four thousand years ago, Enheduanna was at the height of her splendour when a raider invading the empire attacked her city, seized her and evidently raped her. Not only did she survive but she was restored to power – and recovered by writing about her ordeal. Enheduanna was the first woman whose words we can hear, the first named author, male or female, the first victim of sexual abuse who wrote about her experiences, and a female member of the first dynasty whom we can know as individuals. She was as privileged as you can get in the 2200s BC – a princess of the Akkadian empire (based in Iraq), high priestess of the moon goddess and favourite daughter of the first conqueror that we know of: Sargon. But like every empire, it all depended on power and violence – and when the empire tottered it was she, a woman, who endured that downfall in the form of sexual violence.

She was probably in her thirties, politically experienced as the long-serving high priestess of the moon goddess Nanna or Sin, and potentate of the city of Ur, but still young enough to bear children. Brought up at the court of her father, Sargon, king of the Four Quarters of the World, from the Mediterranean to the Persian Gulf, daughter of his favourite queen Tashlultum, she believed passionately in her patron goddess but she also enjoyed the luxury of royalty: she appears on a disk wearing a fluted robe and cap and tightly plaited hair, performing a ritual at her temple. She presided over a huge staff – as testified by the seals of 'Adda, estate manager of Enheduanna' and 'Sagadu the scribe' – but fashion and hairstyle were also important: one seal reads 'Ilum Palilis hairdresser of Enheduanna child of Sargon'. In her temple complex, Enheduanna had her hair plaited by Ilum Palilis – the first named fashionista in history – as she dictated orders to Sagadu about her estates, the temple herds and her poetry. Her hymns praised the goddess – 'when she speaks heaven shakes' – and of course her father, 'my King'. But then some time after his death, when his sons and grandsons struggled to hold the empire together, a raider, or a rebel known as Lugal (king), launched a coup and somehow seized the princess-priestess-poetess herself. Possessing her won him the prestige of Sargon the Great; if he could father a child by her, he might found a dynasty, ennobled by the blood of Sargon. Enheduanna knew what she faced: 'Oh moon god Sin, is this Lugal my destiny?' she wrote. 'Tell heaven to set me free of it!' It sounds as if she was raped by this upstart: 'That man has defiled the rites decreed by holy heaven ... Forcing his way in as if he was an equal, he dared approach me in his lust.' She remembered it viscerally as any woman would: 'a slobbery hand was laid across my honeyed mouth'. And he removed her from her beloved temple: 'When Lugal stood paramount, he expelled me from the temple, flying out of the window like a swallow.'

But she was lucky: the empire struck back. Her brother or nephew routed Lugal and reconquered the Akkadian empire, thus liberating Enheduanna and restoring her as high priestess. How did she grieve for her pain and celebrate her survival? She did what writers do: she wrote. And she wrote proudly: 'I am Enheduanna, let me speak to you! My prayer, my tears flowing like some sweet intoxicant. I went towards the shade. It shrouded me in swirling dust.'

The exact date and precise details of this episode are obscure but we know she existed and we know her words: in her survival as a woman, not to speak of her record as author and ruler, she represents the experience of women throughout history, as ruler, writer, victim, whose survival she herself celebrates unforgettably as a goddess 'in a queenly robe . . . riding on leashed lions', slashing 'her enemies to pieces' – quite an image and a voice both astonishingly modern and very much of the twenty-third century BC.

Enheduanna lived a long time ago, yet the human family was already very old in her time. It probably started in Africa. We do not know how exactly humans evolved and we probably never shall. All we know is that all humans were originally Africans, that the nurturing of children required teams that we call families and that the story of humanity from the beginning to the twenty-first century AD is an invincibly exciting and complicated drama. Historians have long debated when history began.* It is easy to point to footprints, chiselled tools, dusty walls and bone fragments, but for the purposes of this book history started when war, food and writing coalesced to allow a potentate, usually a male one like Sargon but sometimes a female like Enheduanna, to harness power and promote his or her children in order to keep it.

---

* Archaeologists have not: they identify the start of history as the point when writing was invented.

Seven to ten million years ago, while our planet, itself four to five billion years old, was in the grip of ice ages that receded and returned, hominins of a currently unknown genus separated from chimpanzees. By about two million years ago, in east Africa, a creature who walked upright on two feet had evolved. This was *Homo erectus*, who lasted most of the next two million years – the longest period of human existence – and who lived by foraging and hunting. Soon afterwards, some of these creatures migrated out of Africa into Europe and Asia, where different climates caused them to develop into different branches to which scientists have given Latin names such as *antecessor*, *neanderthalensis* and *heidelbergensis* after the places where their bones were discovered. DNA suggests most were dark-skinned with dark eyes. They already used stone axes. By 500,000 years ago, from South Africa to China, they were hunting large animals and perhaps using fire to cook, and there is evidence of both caring and violence from the start: some disabled individuals lived to a good age, suggesting social care, while on the other hand several skulls found in a northern Spanish cave had head injuries inflicted 430,000 years ago – the first confirmed murders. Some 300,000 years ago, they started to make offsite fires, changing landscapes for the first time, and using wooden spears and traps to hunt large animals.

Hominin brains nearly tripled in size, requiring an ever-richer diet. Larger-headed babies were harder for females to deliver: the tightness of the female pelvis – a compromise between the form necessary to walk upright and that needed to deliver a baby – made childbirth dangerous for both the mother and the baby, a vulnerability that helped shape the family in history. We guess this meant that they needed a group of related people to help raise their babies – and, if correct, these small blood-related communities became the defining unit of human history, the family that we still need today even though we are masters of the planet, dominators of every other species and the creators of remarkable new technologies. Anthropologists love to project that families were a certain size, that men did one task, women another, but all this is guesswork.

Most likely, there was a mosaic of many different-looking hominin species, coexisting, sometimes isolated from each other, sometimes interbreeding, sometimes fighting. By about 120,000 years ago, as earth was in a warming period (so warm that hippopotami were bathing in the Thames), modern humans – *Homo sapiens*, wise man – emerged in Africa. Sixty thousand years later, some of these humans migrated into Asia (Europe came later), where they encountered the other hominin species on the way eastwards. The reasons for their travels are mysterious, but most likely they were a combination of quests for food and land, climate and environmental changes, spasms of disease, religious rites and love of adventure. Crossing seas as wide as 100 miles in boats, they reached Indonesia, Australia and the Philippines between 65,000 and 35,000 years ago. Then they ventured into the Pacific, island by island.

Sapiens coexisted with the other hominin families: over 100,000 years, they fought and killed some Neanderthals and raised families with others. Today Europeans, Chinese and Native Americans are 2 per cent Neanderthal in their DNA while some indigenous Australians, Melanesians and Filipinos have an additional 6 per cent of DNA, inherited from an enigmatic, ancient Asian population first identified from fragmentary fossils and DNA recovered from the Denisova Cave in Siberia. This pattern of migrating, settling and conquering – the mass movement of existing families and the generation of new ones by competition (sometimes murderous), nurturing and mixing – is the perpetual dance of human creation and destruction: it started early, is repeated throughout history and continues today. The humans who emerged were almost uniform – gracile faces, globular skulls, little noses, biologically almost identical. Yet the tiniest differences have justified centuries of conflict, oppression and racism.

By 40,000 years ago, *Homo sapiens* had outcompeted, killed or absorbed other hominins, and wiped out many large animals. Long before this, they had developed vocal cords that allowed them to talk, and brains that sparked the wish and ability to tell stories. Somehow the appetite for comfort, the need for safety, the instinct to raise children and perhaps even the enjoyment of companionship encouraged people to settle in clusters of families. They lived by hunting and gathering, worshipping the spirits of nature, expressing their beliefs through paintings in caves – the earliest in Indonesia and Australia dating from over 40,000 years ago – carving figures of curvaceous women and lion-headed men, and ritualistically burying some people in graves with jewels and beads. They made the first linen cloth, which replaced animal skins as clothing; bows and arrows improved hunting; dogs were trained for hunting and then domesticated. These hunter-gatherers were tall and fit, their teeth strong, undecayed by grain or sugar. But throughout history the fate of an individual was decided by geography and timing: some lived in lush abundance, some eked out meagre lives in icy tundras.

Sixteen thousand years ago, the climate began to warm, the ice to recede, grasses and legumes along with herds of deer and cattle became more plentiful in some regions. Some bands of these hunter-gatherers crossed the icy land bridge between Asia and Alaska and entered the Americas, where in a glimpse of perilous existence, 13,000 years ago, the footsteps of a woman in New Mexico show her holding a child, sometimes putting it down and lifting it up again, as she was stalked by sabre-toothed tigers. Her footsteps came back alone. The tigers may have devoured the child.

Humans started to build first wooden then stone structures: in Russia and Ukraine, close to the edge of the ice, they raised wooden enclosures sometimes embellished with mammoth tusks and bones, possibly to celebrate hunts. They buried a few people in elaborate graves, many of them with physical deformities, perhaps regarded as sacred. The people of the Amazon used ochre to paint their world of mastodons, giant sloths and horses; those of Australia depicted bilbies and dugongs. In Japan, people made pottery; in China, they fired their pottery so that they could cook over fires. These were now fully formed people, not apes. Their families, like ours, probably shared sacred rituals and useful knowledge while nursing hatred for their close relatives and distant rivals. It is tempting to impose our wishful thinking that women for example were powerful, but actually we know virtually nothing about them.

The thawing of the ice accelerated 11,700 years ago; this marked the dawn of a warm age that is still continuing, and the rising waters cut off America and Australia from Asia, and Britain from continental Europe. Now there were perhaps four million people on earth. After most of the ice had melted, around 9000 BC, a few lucky ones found that they lived in regions where they could cultivate animals and plants. But even by 8000 human hunting and management of forests started to drive the large mammals – mammoths, mastodons, indigenous horses in America – to extinction. For several millennia, many people still lived seasonally, hunting game in one season, gathering grasses and fruits in another. Yet even before agriculture was fully organized, people across the world – from Japan to Finland and the Americas – were raising monumental structures that were both sacred and social. The temples acted as calendars linked to celestial bodies, and people possibly just gathered there to celebrate successful harvests, then returned to their hunting-foraging life. In south-east Türkiye, at Göbekli Tepe, structures that looked like temples, pillars topped with sculpted foxes, snakes and scorpions, were built by hunter-gatherers who did not yet farm yet already shared religious rites. Nearby, at Karahan Tepe, they built another monumental temple embellished with sculptures of people – including a small room featuring eleven statues of *phalloi*. Starting around 9500

BC the temples, built 4,500 years before Stonehenge, were used for over 1,500 years.

People started settling in villages – one of the earliest was at Jericho in Canaan (Palestine) – before agriculture became their chief source of nourishment: they still foraged and hunted. Contrary to the traditional image of a 'revolution', there was no sudden switch: many peoples moved back and forth between agriculture and hunting, fishing and foraging. Even though it only takes between 30 and 200 years to domesticate a crop, it took 3,000 years (the difference between today and the pharaohs) from the beginnings of cultivating cereals to full agriculture, and another 3,000 before the real emergence of states – while in most parts of the world such states never developed at all.

At first, this meant the diet of most individuals was worse, not better: these agrarian planters were shorter, weaker, more anaemic, their teeth worse. Women worked with the men, developing strong upper arms – along with deformed knees and bent toes – from working the land and grinding grain. Life may have been better before farming, but it worked because it was more efficient for the species. Competition was ferocious; farmer villages vanquished hunter bands who coveted their food stores. For unknown reasons, the Göbekli and Karahan Tepe temples were filled in and buried. In Jericho, the thousand inhabitants built the first walls to protect themselves. Under their houses, they buried their dead and sometimes, after removing the flesh, they remoulded the faces with plaster and placed stones in the eye sockets – skull portraits that were popular from Israel to Iraq, more confirmation that humans could mentalize supernatural and magical beings and recognize the difference between body and spirit.

Starting around 7500 BC, the villagers of Çatalhöyük (central Türkiye) – which housed over 5,000 inhabitants – lived by planting cereals and rearing sheep while starting to hammer copper into useful tools. Near Raqqa, Syria, villagers in Tell Sabi Abyad built granaries for their food stores and used clay tokens to record how much they possessed. The oldest intact cloth, found in Çayönü, (Türkiye) dates to 7000 BC. Safe in walled villages, women had more children who could be weaned and fed porridge, but 50 per cent of them died young because they lived in intimate proximity to people and animals which made them prey to diseases: then as now, epidemics were symptoms of the species' success, not its failure. But they required more settlements to organize the growing of more food: between 10,000 and 5000 BC, the world population scarcely grew from four million to five million. For most of history – the next eight and a half millennia – life expectancy was around thirty.

Small towns developed in Iraq, Egypt and China, followed by Pakistan/India where fecund, moist riverine soils along with the most useful breeds of domesticated animals gave these four regions a boost in the formation of sophisticated societies that would grant them supremacy over Eurafrica for many millennia.

All over the world, people started to raise megalithic stone structures, often in circles: around 7000 BC, Nubians – not Egyptians but sub-Saharan Africans – pulled huge stones from far away and raised them at Nabta Playa in circles linked to the observance of stars. The first commodities and luxuries were traded or exchanged: from Iran to Serbia, copper, gold and silver were mined and crafted; lapis lazuli was used in burials; and in the Yangtze Valley, the Chinese started to make silk.

In Malta, Germany, Finland and later England, communities moved gigantic stones across long distances to build structures that were – possibly – temples to follow the sun, to predict rain, to sacrifice humans, to celebrate fertility. Faith was interlinked with power and family: both men and women did the hunting and farming, but the latter probably raised the children and spun textiles: the oldest cotton has been found in the Jordan Valley. In Africa, where families weaved raffia and bark cloth these clans may have been run by women with power descending through the female line.* In Eurasia, the value of female skills began to be calculated: fathers charged a bride price to future husbands who if powerful could keep several women and protect their children. Originally families honoured both male and female lineages, but to avoid conflicts over land or grain they at some point started to favour the male lineage, though genetically all descendants were identical – a tradition that still endures in many places into the age of iPhones. Yet even in Iraq women could rise to power.

---

* In the Andes, in 7000 BC, a female teenaged warrior was found buried with her spear; out of twenty-seven buried hunters discovered in south America from this period, eleven were female. Women may have led and fought as well as nurtured and nursed, or the burials could be merely ritualistic.

KUBABA: FIRST QUEEN

At Eridu, on a lagoon in Iraq near the mouth of the Euphrates River on the Persian Gulf, around 5400 BC, fishermen and shepherds founded a village where they raised a temple to the god Enki. So rich was this environment that other cities were built nearby, so close that they could almost see other. The invention of the spindle whorl – a sphere with a hole – to make cloth may have been the first gadget, developed as early as pottery and agriculture, with consequences far beyond its immediate usefulness. Difficult to create, cloth was essential but expensive: societies were arranged around food, war and cloth. Eridu was one of the first towns in Sumeria, followed by Ur and Uruk, where a terraced platform was built to Anu, the sky god, topped off with a temple – a ziggurat.

Their leaders were both patriarchs and priests. Their gods were partly playful hucksters, but they evolved into harsher judges who threatened rule-breakers and then policed something altogether greater still: the afterlife. The gods got bigger as the rulers and communities got bigger and the competition with others became fiercer.*

It is not known how Uruk, now home to over 20,000 people, was organized – there were no palaces and there is mention of 'the people' – but there were priest-kings and the temples controlled the wealth: the idea of property probably started with reference to special treasure and artefacts set aside for the sacred within these temples.

To the north, on the Eurasian steppes, horses – the animals that would help humans dominate the terrestrial until the nineteenth century – were being domesticated. Around 3500 BC, horses were fitted with bits so they could be ridden. Soon, the wheel was developed in Ukraine/ Russia, where the first linguistic references to wheels appear. It is likely the wheel reached Iraq before the horses: the earliest wagons were pulled not by horses but by another member of the equid family, the kunga – a sturdy cross between female donkey and Syrian ass, the first example of human interbreeding of animals – depicted in art pulling early four-wheeled wagons. The remains of one was recently discovered in Syria. The new technology spread to India; kungas vanished; and the horse empowered shepherds to become ferocious, nomadic cavalry and families to move across vast distances to settle in new lands. War already drove technology: wagons were weaponized as chariots, so prestigious that warband chiefs fielded charioteer armies. When they died, they

---

* Competition was brutal: in Europe around 5500 BC, the villages of early farmers were annihilated by invasions or wars, with unknown enemies leaving mass graves of tortured, scalped, cannibalized bodies.

were buried with horse and chariot. The steppe peoples found copper reserves too: at Sintasha, north of the Aral Sea, bronze was created by mixing copper and tin from Bactria (Afghanistan), used for weapons and decorations.

These horsemen were soon led by sword-swinging warlords who built strongholds with high audience chambers, perhaps the first palaces – one stands at Arslantepe (eastern Türkiye) – and buried heroic male warriors in extravagant tombs with food, swords and jewellery.

Around 3100, the people of Uruk – which meant the Place – may have invented writing, initially pictograms, but then took to marking clay with the wedge-end of a reed, a process that we call cuneiform, which means wedge-shaped. The first named people in history are an accountant, a slave master and two enslaved persons. The first receipt, confirmed by the first signature of the first named person – the accountant – reads:

'29,086 measures barley. 37 months. Kushim.'

Another records the ownership of En-pap X and Sukkalgir, the first named enslaved people. These were slave-owning societies. We do not know when slavery started, but it was probably at the same time as organized fighting. Most enslaved people were war captives or debtors. Royal taxes paid for soldiers who captured the slaves who now built the cities or toiled within family households: a history of family is also a history of slavery.

Towards 2900, kings – starting as Big Men, Lugalene in Sumerian – appear as rulers of all the Iraqi cities that now engaged in vicious wars: 'Kish was defeated and the kingship taken to Uruk. Then Uruk was defeated and the kingship taken to Ur.' Kingship 'descended from heaven' and it soon became hereditary. The crown was not inherited by eldest sons; kings had many children by chief wives and junior women. They chose the most able – or the more ferocious son killed his brothers. What they gained in ability they lost in stability for the children fought for power, and often destroyed the very realm they coveted. As people in Britain celebrated their rites at Stonehenge,* one of the first family rulers, around 2500, was Kubaba of Kish, the world's first female potentate that we know of, who owned taverns and brewed beer, and who was succeeded by her son and grandson. We know nothing else about them but a lot about their world.

These kings now built palaces alongside the rich temples; they ruled

---

* Around 3000 BC, at Waun Mawn, in Wales, the inhabitants created a circle henge of bluestones, some of which were later dragged a long way to build a new and larger circle at Stonehenge.

with a hierarchy of courtiers, generals, tax collectors. Writing was a tool for ruling, recording the ownership of property, transactions in grain and promulgation of laws. The Sumerians created pictures of themselves, men and women, not just praying but also drinking – and loving. They recorded recipes, and both men and women celebrated their enjoyment of sex; they drank beer through straws and imbibed opium. Later they studied mathematics and astronomy.

Thousands of cuneiform texts survive to reveal a world where taxes, war and death were certain, but so were the prayers of the priests to ensure that the sun would shine and rain would fall, crops would grow, sheep would make more sheep, the palm trees would be beautiful at dawn, the canals full of fish.

Uruk and the Sumerian cities were neither unique nor isolated. Cities became the marketplaces, information exchanges, marriage agencies, sexual carousels, fortresses, laboratories, courts and theatres of human community, but there were compromises: city folk had to conform; they could not feed themselves, having lost the skills of the wild and the thrills of the steppe. If the harvests failed, they starved; in epidemics, they died in droves. Sumeria was already in contact with other worlds. Lapis lazuli, the first international luxury commodity, tells the story: mined in Afghanistan, it was traded via the cities of India/Pakistan, to Sumer – mentioned in *The Epic of Gilgamesh** – then on to Mari in Syria and all to the way to Egypt, where objects were made with lapis, found in the Abdju temple city.

Around 3500 BC, the villages of Egypt started to consolidate into larger polities. Fifty years later, the king of the south, Tjeni, who was known as Narmer – Catfish – united Egypt under one crown, celebrating his victory with religious festivals, where sacred beer was quaffed, and com-memorated in objects: a palette, used to grind and mix male and female cosmetics, shows him killing his enemies with a raised mace, watched

---

* One of the rulers of Uruk named in its king list was Gilgamesh, whose mythical story – *The Epic of Gilgamesh*, written down around 2000 BC and known by most Sumerians – recounts the rise of a single family and the development of cities. Gilgamesh is part god, part man, who travels with his wild friend Enkidu in search of eternal life. Such travels reflect early trading that allowed flint and obsidian to reach Sumer from Anatolia. Enkidu, creature of nature, is seduced by a divine harlot, Shamhat, but their sexual passion depletes his savage power and he settles in the dazzling city of Uruk. In *The Epic of Gilgamesh*, a flood threatens all mankind, revealing a theme of world history: the ever-present fear of the world's end felt as strongly then as today. Only the family of Utnapishtim/Ziusudra, a Noah-like figure, survives – the definition of an elite family. The story, which inspired many sacred books, ends with the gods teaching Gilgamesh the limits of human supremacy, a lesson that Sapiens still struggles to learn: 'You were given the kingship, such was your destiny; everlasting life was not your destiny.'

by a cow goddess, while on its other side Narmer, shown as a powerful sacred bull, tramples rebels under hoof. Nearby, Narmer marches to view his fallen enemies, who have been beheaded, their penises sliced off. Our first real glimpse of the refinement and brutality of Egypt is a cosmetics artefact – and a pile of penises.

KHUFU AND MOTHER: THE PYRAMID BUILDERS

Egypt was the first African kingdom that we can observe: Egyptian kingship reflected a life where everything depended on the Nile and the sun. Its towns and villages were spread along the thread of the river which gave the soil its richness. The sun crossing the sky every day was regarded as a god, and all life was played out in that daily journey. Kings travelled up and down the Nile – and to the underworld – on splendid boats.

Narmer and his family lived in mudbrick palaces and were buried in mudbrick tombs in the desert at Abdju, where large mudbrick enclosures contained boats to carry them across the sky on their journey to join the sun.

The Egyptian kings thought deeply about life and death and believed in their sacred role, affirmed by a network of temples and priests. Originally different gods were revered in different towns that were gradually agglomerated into a single story symbolizing the union of the two kingdoms – upper and lower Egypt – and the life of the monarch before and after death. Like so many sacred narratives, it was a story of family love, sex and hatred.*

When they died, the kings did not really perish but instead became Osiris while their heirs became Horus. The power of the kings was absolute, demonstrated at this time by human sacrifice. The tomb of the third king of Narmer's dynasty, Djer, was surrounded by 318 sacrificed courtiers.

Around 2650, King Djoser, also known as Netjerikhet, added a

---

* Different versions of the Osiris myth were favoured during different periods. Osiris ruled the earth, but his brother Seth seized power and murdered him. Isis, the sister and wife of Osiris, found his body and resurrected him – perhaps the origin of mummification. His death and revival were linked to the annual flooding of the life-giving Nile. He impregnated Isis but, barely alive, fell to Duat, the underworld, which he then ruled. The world was inherited by their son, Horus, god of the sun, moon and stars, the personification of life and power. There were thousands of gods in the Egyptian pantheon, but the kings were protected by Horus; in some ways they were themselves Horus. Like Osiris they could marry their sisters.

novelty to his tomb: instead of separating the tomb and enclosure, he built them on top of one another to create the step pyramid, six steps high – and it still stands. His minister, the *tjati*, possessed the vision of his master: his name was Imhotep, so trusted by the king that on the statue base in the entrance both of their names appear. Most probably the minister of the king was also his doctor because, later, Imhotep was worshipped as a god of medicine.

The new king Sneferu, succeeding in 2613, signalled his swagger by his Horus name, *neb Maat*, lord of truth, righteousness and the sacred order of the universe – and that was not all. His other name, *netjer nefer*, meant Perfect God. A story in a later papyrus implies Sneferu's hedonism – he had himself rowed out on to a palace lake by twenty girls wearing just fishing nets – and his aggression, noting that he sent a 170-foot ship *Praise-of-the-Two-Lands* to raid Nubia where he enslaved captives and seized 200,000 cattle.

Sneferu ordered the building of the Meidum Pyramid, built like all pyramids on an east–west axis, associating the king with the daily journey of the sun. When he attempted an even bigger pyramid at Dahshur, he demanded a steep angle of inclination of 60 degrees, but disaster struck: the foundations were not strong enough and cracks suddenly appeared as the pyramid collapsed in on itself. Now Perfect God ordered a perfect pyramid and it was built fast while the Bent Pyramid was finished (and it still stands 4,000 years later). The Red Pyramid, Sneferu's third, was completed in record time. Sneferu was surely buried there: a body was found in modern times – but lost.

His widow Hetepheres, daughter, wife and now mother of kings, smoothed the succession of her son Khufu, who built the Great Pyramid at Giza, designed to outdo even his father's works. She gloried in titles Mother of the Dual King, Follower of Horus, Director of the Ruler, suggesting that if Khufu respected anyone it was her.

Khufu must have been obsessed with his pyramid. It is still perhaps the greatest building of world history: 2.3 million blocks. Its height of 481 feet made it the tallest building on earth until the Eiffel Tower. His workers were arranged in teams which adopted playful names such as King's Drunkards, perhaps just 10,000 in all, living in a special workers' village beside the site, with food and medical care provided. He added little pyramids too for his female relations.*

---

* Khufu's favourite dwarf and jester Perniankhu, with his short twisted legs, lived in the Great Palace with him, nicknamed 'One who delights his lord every day, the king's dwarf'. His royal favour was underlined by his tomb close to the Great Pyramid itself and he may have achieved great wealth – and have been a member of a dwarf dynasty. Another court

When Khufu's mother was buried, her tomb was packed with import-ed treasures, real and depicted. Turquoise came from Sinai, cedarwood from Lebanon, lapis from Afghanistan, ebony and carnelian from Nubia, myrrh and frankincense from Punt (Eritrea/Ethiopia/Somalia, perhaps Yemen) probably brought on ships from Sumer, where a con-queror founded the first empire: his name was Sargon.

MY FATHER I KNEW NOT: SARGON KING-SMASHER

Sargon was a boy abandoned in a basket, rescued and nurtured. 'My mother was a priestess; my father I knew not,' he declared in a poetical inscription that may capture his own voice. After all, they were a family of poets as well as potentates. Sargon was born in the northern steppes, 'the highlands of Azupiranu', speaking a Semitic language like those that became Phoenician, Hebrew, Arabic, instead of Sumerian from the south. 'My mother conceived me in secret, she gave birth to me in hiding.' He was a self-creation. 'She set me in a basket of rushes, she sealed the lid with tar. She cast me into the river but it did not rise over me.' His enchanted birth, mysterious paternity, obscure concealment, charmed rise – to be repeated in the myths of many world changers, Moses, Cyrus, Jesus – explained the mystical process of how exceptional leaders, throughout history, could rise to power from nowhere.

'A water carrier Akki rescued him,' raised him as his own son and ap-pointed him 'his gardener': in a society where all prosperity was based on irrigation and rainfall, the river, the water carrier and the garden all represent purity and holiness. Through Akki, young Sargon found service with the king of Kish, Ur-Zababa, descendant of Queen Kubaba, rising to become cupbearer. Power is always personal; proximity is influence; the more personal and absolute the power, the closer to the body the better: cupbearers, physicians, bodyguards and bearers of the royal chamberpot shared its glow. Inanna (later known as Ishtar), the

---

dwarf, Seneb, who served Khufu's son King Djedefre, was buried at Giza very near Per-niankhu: it is possible Seneb was Perniankhu's son. Seneb was a high court official with many titles, owned thousands of cattle and was married to a well-born priestess, who was not a dwarf, with whom he had children. A beautiful statue shows them together. Next to the Great Pyramid, Khufu buried a barque, 140 feet long and made of Lebanese cedar, for his voyage into the underworld. When he died in 2525 BC, Khufu was succeeded in turn by two sons Djedefre and Khafra. Neither attempted to outdo their father, but Khafra built a funeral pyramid that was smaller but on a higher site. It contained twenty-five statues of himself sitting on his throne with the falcon Horus behind his head in white stone. But his masterpiece was the sculpture of a recumbent lion with Khafra's own face: the Sphinx.

goddess of love, sex and war, appeared to Sargon in a terrifying dream in which he was covered in blood. When he told the king, Ur-Zababa sensed that the blood was his own and ordered his assassination, but Inanna warned him. Sargon reappeared as if nothing had happened, 'solid as a mountain. Ur-Zababa was afraid,' unsure if Sargon knew of his duplicity. But then came alarming news.

The most aggressive king in Iraq, Lugalzaggesi of Umma, was marching on Kish: Ur-Zabada sent Sargon to negotiate with him. But his letter asked Lugalzaggesi to kill Sargon. Lugalzaggesi contemptuously revealed the request and unleashed Sargon, who seized Uruk. But then he routed Lugalzaggesi and around 2334 surges into history in his own inscriptions, taking the regnal name Rightful King – Sharrumkin.* He paraded the fallen Lugalzaggesi through the Temple of Enlil, where he smashed his skull with a mace.

Sargon galloped south 'to wash his weapons in the sea' – the Persian Gulf – then eastwards. 'Sargon King of Kish,' reads the inscription on his tablets, 'triumphed in thirty-four battles,' invading the kingdom of Elam in Iran and, after advancing northwards, defeating the nomadic Amorites and taking the cities of Ashur and Nineveh, before turning west into Syria and Türkiye. He was now calling himself King of the Four Quarters of the World, and a later legend praises his fighting prowess in an unforgettable metaphor:

> The writhing ranks will writhe back and forth,
> Two women in labour, bathed in their own blood!

Sargon created the first power family which we can know personally: it was his daughter Enheduanna, who was the first poetess. But naturally she was also a connoisseur of paternal power: 'My King, something's been created here that no one's created before.' She meant empire.

ENHEDUANNA'S REVENGE

It was no coincidence that Sargon appointed his daughter Enheduanna as high priestess of the moon god of Uruk. Temples were rich complexes at the centre of Akkadian cities. Sargon himself may have been the first ruler to maintain a standing army – 5,400 men ate daily at his table in Akkad. He enforced law that was a mixture of reason and

---

* This was mistranslated by the Jewish authors of the Bible as 'Sargon' – though they were referring to the much later king Sargon II, Neo-Assyrian king circa 720–705 BC.

magic: water ordeals decided difficult cases. At her temple, Enheduanna presided over thousands of employees and estates. The relationship between the temples and the royal family was close: Sargon believed that Inanna (Ishtar) and her divine husband Dagan were his special protectors.

When Sargon died he left Enheduanna in charge of her temple, but the new king, her brother Rimush, immediately faced rebellions and invasions. These he defeated, killing 23,000 people, torturing, enslaving and deporting others, then he invaded Elam (Iran), and returned with gold, copper and more slaves. Rimush died in a special way, assassinated by killer scribes, stabbed either with the reeds used for writing or the copper pins used to attach the cylinder seals – the first death by bureaucracy! The Sargons lived by conquest: it was Sargon's grandson, Enheduanna's nephew Naram-Sin, who probably faced the revolt of Lugal – and the capture and rape of his aunt. Naram-Sin smashed the usurper and restored the high priestess to her temple. We do not know when she died, but Naram-Sin ruled for thirty-seven years, carrying out sorties into Iran to smash the Lullubi raiders, boasting of killing 90,000 and claiming that he ruled lands as far away as Lebanon. On his Victory Stele, Naram-Sin is a muscular, bare-chested warrior wearing a divine horned helmet and tight kilt, holding a spear and bow and crushing his enemies in Iran, with nothing between him, the Mighty, and the sun and stars: the first mortal to be depicted as equal to a goddess.

The capital Akkad flourished under House Sargon. Its location is unknown, but standing somewhere on the Tigris it became a new sort of city. 'Its population dine on the best of food, draw the best of drinks, make merry in the courtyard and throng the festival grounds,' recounts *The Epic of Gilgamesh*, probably referring to Akkad.* 'Acquaintances dine together. Monkeys, mighty elephants . . . dogs, lions, ibexes and sheep jostle each other in public places . . .', while its stores were packed with 'gold and silver, copper, tin and blocks of lapis'. Grandees dressed richly, both men and women wearing cosmetics and taking trouble with their hair. Fashions changed as quickly as they do today – Sargon had worn a shaggy coat; the Naram-Sin elite preferred a robe tied with a pin at the shoulder. Akkadians consulted diviners – using extispicy, the reading of animal entrails – to advise on their decisions. There was a culinary cult: tablets record the variety of food eaten, from sheep and pigs to

---

* Some scholars argue that this is a description of Akkad; others insist it depicts Babylon, the greatest city when later versions of *The Epic of Gilgamesh* were written down.

deer, rabbits, fieldmice, jerboas and hedgehogs. Beer was the favourite drink, enjoyed by men and women, made from fermented barley, drunk through a straw, at taverns run by independent women. Elite girls attended school and could write both Sumerian and Akkadian. In glimpses of family life, women gave birth in a seated position; children are shown playing with rattles, wheeled sheep and mini-wagons. Love spells were common: girls wore love charms around their thighs.

Foreigners wandered its streets, admiring its wonders. '*Tigi* drums, flutes and *zamzam* instruments resounded,' says *The Epic*: 'its harbours where ships moored were full of joy,' trading with the entire Indian Ocean: 'at the wharf . . . ships moor from Meluhha [India/Pakistan], Magan [Yemen/Oman] and Dilmun [Bahrain]'. Amorites, Meluhhans, Elamites bore goods there 'like laden donkeys', traders paying for their goods in barley or silver: there were so many Meluhhans that they lived together in their own village.

Meluhha – land of ivory – was centred around two cities, Harappa and Mohenjo-daro, on the Indus (Pakistan but extending into India and Afghanistan), so well planned that they were built in grids with standardized bricks and even boasted public rubbish bins, and public lavatories and sewers that London would not possess until the nineteenth century and that are not universal in south Asia today. Using their own (still undeciphered) script, their workshops made jewellery in ivory, gold, carnelian, as well as textiles and ceramics. Mohenjo-daro may have housed as many as 85,000 people, the biggest city in the world, but its largest building was a public bath – no palaces, no ziggurats.

These Indian cities were not ruled by single kings; more likely they were governed by councils – perhaps Pakistan/India invented democracy – but the bathhouse stood in a sequestered citadel which might suggest it was the precinct of a priestly elite. Versions of urban life were being sampled simultaneously on several continents. In China, there were towns on the Yellow River and in the north, at Shimao (Shaanxi). In Ukraine, Taljanky, containing 10,000 people, was larger and maybe even earlier than the first city at Uruk. In America, long since separated from Asia, people in Mexico and Guatemala were building towns with as many as 10,000 inhabitants and pyramidal mounds that reflected their sacred calendar, using a form of writing, storing surplus maize in storehouses, and sculpting giant heads, probably of their rulers, who seem to be sporting helmets worn for their ballgames.* On the Mississippi,

---

* Their rulers lived in plastered palaces with large basalt columns and their ordinary people in wattle houses on massive terraces. They pierced their bodies with thorns; they may have practised ritual bleeding and sacrifices; and they used rubber to make the balls used in

people were raising monumental earthworks that somehow linked stars and calendar: the inhabitants of the largest of these – now called Poverty Point – were not farmers but nomadic hunters who somehow came together to build massive structures.

In west Asia, the Sargon family illustrated a paradox of empire. The bigger it grew, the more borders had to be defended; the richer it was, the more tempting a target it became for less settled neighbours – and the greater was the incentive for destructive family feuds. Drought brought hunger; nomads swooped on the cities. In 2193 BC, the Sargons lost control: 'Who was king?' asks the Sumerian king list. 'Who was *not* king?' By 1800, west Asia was in turmoil – even Egypt ceased to be a player in the most humiliating and gruesome way. It started with a row about hippopotami.

THE SHATTERED HEAD OF SEQENENRE THE BRAVE

The king stood no chance. His hands were tied behind his back. He was likely to be kneeling. Seqenenre Taa, ruler of southern Egypt, had been captured in battle and now Apophis, Asiatic ruler of northern Egypt, was leading the squad of killers. There were at least five of them. The first blow of the Asiatic axe smashed into Seqenenre's royal face, severing his left cheek, a wound that would have opened his entire face. A second slash shattered the back of the skull before a javelin penetrated his forehead just above the eye.

It was the sacred hippos of Thebes who provided the pretext. Apophis told Seqenenre that their grunting far away in Thebes was keeping him awake in Avaris (Hutwaret): he ordered them killed, a declaration of war. Seqenenre seized the gauntlet and marched north, leading his troops from the front. But something went wrong. Seqenenre was captured and Apophis devised his public demolition. A final fifth blow from a sword sliced straight into the brain. For those who looked upon the shattered body of the king – as we still can today – it must have seemed as if his family and Egypt itself were finished. In fact, this nadir was the moment the recovery started.

In 1558 BC, when Seqenenre the Brave, son of Senakhtenre Ahmose and his commoner queen Tetisheri, succeeded his father as king in Thebes, Egypt was already broken. The chaos was accelerated

---

their ritualistic games. We do not know the name of the city – we call it San Lorenzo – nor of the people. Much later the Mexica called them Olmecs – the Rubber People.

by stampede migrations where the movement of one people forced others to advance. Tribes of pale-skinned, dark-eyed, aquiline people on the Black Sea steppes migrated from their pasturelands, driven by changing climate, the lust for conquest and the pressure of other tribes behind them. Speaking an Indo-European language, they were cattle-breeders who had become expert horsemen. Three pieces of technology made them deadly adversaries: the bronze bit meant horses could be controlled; swift chariots with bladed wheels added a heavy punch to their charges; and they could fire composite bows – new killing machines made of laminated wood, sinew and horn – from the saddle at the gallop.

These horsemen galloped westwards into the Balkans and eastwards towards India. They shattered established kingdoms but also settled into them. In Iran, this horde – whom scholars later called Aryans – brought their Avestan language and holy scriptures, the *Avesta*; in India, the Aryans may have overwhelmed the Indus cities and then settled, merging the Indus Valley culture with their own rituals and language, and formulating the stories, prayers and poems of the *Vedas* written in what became Sanskrit. Their warlords and priests imposed a hierarchy of castes, the *varnas*.* This culture long afterwards formed the *Sanatana Dharma* – Eternal Way – later called Hinduism by Europeans. Some tribes rode southwards through the Caucasus into eastern Türkiye where they founded the kingdom of Hatti – the Hittites of the Bible – while others hit Canaan, stampeding its peoples, known as the Hyksos, to invade Egypt.

Around 1630, an Asiatic warlord Apophis, whose tribes had invaded Egypt, ruled the north from his capital Hutwaret in the Nilotic delta, while Seqenenre held Thebes in the south. Just four years into his reign, Seqenenre was in his prime, tall, athletic, with a head of thick curly black hair (that is still on the skull of his mummy today). Not only did he face Asiatics to the north, a new southern kingdom of Kush had

---

* The rise of Aryan culture occurs between 1500 and 500 BC, though there may be more continuity between the Aryan and Indus Valley cultures than was previously supposed. Three millennia later, in Europe, Nazi ideologues commandeered the word Aryan for their racist ideology. At the same time, Reza Shah, whom we will meet later, changed the name of Persia to Iran (Aryan). In today's India, Hindu nationalists reject the idea that Indian, especially Hindu, faith or race can possibly have European origins. But in central Asia, long known as the Aryavarta – Abode of the Aryans – this concerns not race but language and culture: Old Persian (Avestan) and Sanskrit are still closely linked; the stories and rituals of the Persian *Avesta* are similar to those of the Indian *Rigveda* and other Vedic stories, and to the *Ramayana* with its tales of ideal kings and families. The latest DNA research in India reveals that most Indians are descended from a mixture of the original southern Indians, the Harappans, and steppe peoples related to Iranians.

subjugated the Nubian city states. Based at Kerma (Sudan), its kings co-opted the old Egyptian gods, even worshipping Osiris and Horus, as well as Egyptian kings.

Kush left vast monuments. Enriched by their gold mines, ostrich feathers, leopard furs and spices, its kings built massive royal tombs in which hundreds of courtiers and relatives were killed with them. Kushite fortresses were impressive and their main shrine, in Kerma, was a colossal pre-Kushite temple built of mudbrick that still survives.

Somehow the Egyptians reclaimed the carved-up body of Seqenenre, but there was no time to mummify him to the usual standards. His brother Kamose the Strong mourned him: 'Why do I ponder my strength while . . . I sit squeezed between an Asiatic and a Nubian, each holding a portion of Egypt?' But Kamose had a mission: 'No man can be calm, when despoiled by the taxes of the Asiatic: I will grapple with him. I'll rip open his belly! My wish is to rescue Egypt and to kill the Asiatic!' Kamose attacked his enemies in both directions.

His heir was his young nephew Ahmose, just ten years old, who adored his grandmother. 'His love for her was greater than anything,' he declared on the stela he raised at Abdju. But his mother Ahhotep was even more important – King's Daughter, King's Great Wife, King's Mother, she was a commander and international arbiter. Her title 'The Mistress of the Shores of Hau-nebut whose reputation is high over every foreign land' suggests she cultivated links with Aegean peoples.

Egyptian kings had already launched expeditions to 'hack up Asia', raiding 'Iwa' (Türkiye) and 'Iasy' (Cyprus), but Hau-nebut was Crete, with which the Egyptian family had a special relationship. Knossos, Crete's capital, and its other cities boasted unfortified palatial complexes decorated with ecstatic, playful frescoes of naked male athletes leaping over sacred bulls and bare-chested women in patterned skirts.* A maze in Knossos was surely the basis for the legend of the monstrous Minotaur said to demand the sacrifice of children, but it was not just a legend: children's bones found with cooking pots suggest these stories were based on reality; and Labyrinthos, the name of the maze, may have been the name of the city itself. For around 250 years, between 1700 and 1450 BC, these Cretans traded throughout the Mediterranean. They brought home Egyptian artefacts, and Cretan griffins and bull-leaping

* Though nineteenth-century historians named it after a mythic king, Minos, there is no evidence of a monarchy and its 'throne room' may have been a council chamber or a temple for rituals. Cretans may have worshipped goddesses portrayed on their frescoes. Some suggest these were female rulers, but there's no evidence either way. Their language has still not been deciphered.

frescoes decorated the palace at Hutwaret. Ahmose may have married a Cretan princess.

Some time around 1500, a volcanic eruption at Thera, the Greek island of Santorini – the most explosive catastrophe in world history, more powerful than the hydrogen bombs, a boom heard thousands of miles away – shot clouds of poisonous sulphur dioxide into the atmosphere and sent a tsunami across the Mediterranean, drowning tens of thousands. It changed the climate, blighted harvests and devastated kingdoms. Crete was wounded by Thera, but regained its vigour for a while before warlords from mainland Greece took control. Egypt recovered.

As soon as he came of age, in 1529, Ahmose married his own sister Ahmose-Nefertari and marched on Hutwaret, finishing off the Asiatics then pursuing them across Sinai. When he faced uprisings, his mother Ahhotep crushed the rebels. 'Give praise to the Lady of the Land,' Ahmose wrote on his stela at the Temple of Amun at Ipetsut. 'She has pacified Upper Egypt.' Ahhotep's grave goods included a necklace of golden flies – for courage in battle. When Ahmose died in his thirties, his sister-wife Ahmose-Nefertari ruled for their son, Amenhotep, who also married his sister: these incestuous marriages intensified the sanctity of the family and emulated the gods. But ultimately interbreeding was disastrous, destroying the very family they were meant to strengthen.* The Ahmoses faced extinction, a problem they solved by adoption: they chose a general, Thutmose, as heir.

Thutmose had crushed the Nubians and invaded Syria, a hoary but tough commoner who married a daughter of Ahmose, though he

---

* If the Egyptians did not grasp the dangers of incestuous marriage, they did produce guides to medicine and gynaecology, written on papyrus, which together with other papyri reveal how much they knew – and how little. Illness was caused by demons and bad spirits that were cured by both magic and treatment. Doctors, often also priests, were specialized, ranging from 'Physician of the Eyes' to 'Shepherd of the Anus'; Djoser had Hesy-Ra, a 'Chief of Dentists and Doctors', in 2700 BC, and there was a chief female doctor Peseshet in 2400. Babies were delivered with the mothers in a kneeling position, supervised by female midwives. Their physicians believed channels led from the heart to the rest of the body. Pain was treated with opium, burns with aloe, epilepsy with camphor; wounds were bound with bandages. Tests for pregnancy used female urine on barley and emmer seeds; if they grew the woman was pregnant; if it was barley, it would be a boy, if emmer a girl. Fertility was tested with an onion in the vagina; if the woman's breath smelled in the morning, she was fertile. Other measures are more sensible: if the perineum was 'very swollen due to childbirth you should prepare for her: oil to be soaked into vagina'. Contraceptives for females included pessaries of sour milk, honey, natron or acacia gum, the latter a known spermicide. Crocodile dung would have acted as an indirect contraceptive. After rape: 'Instructions for a woman suffering in her vagina and limbs having been beaten . . . You should prepare for her: oil to be eaten until she is well.'

retained his non-royal wife Ahmes, mother of his favourite daughter, Hatshepsut.

'Enraged like a panther', Thutmose was determined to 'destroy unrest throughout the foreign lands, to subdue the rebels of the desert region', and invaded Kush. This was no raid but the deliberate devastation of a kingdom and culture: the king, accompanied by his wife and daughter Hatshepsut, led the army himself. While former kings had been stopped by the rapids on the Nile, Thutmose built a fleet and had the boats, including his personal yacht the *Falcon*, dragged overland. He defeated Kush in battle, burning the splendid capital Kerma – a triumph celebrated in his inscription boasting of 'extending the frontiers' on the sacred rock of the Kushites.

The real prize was the gold mines. It was Nubian gold that funded armies, built temples and crafted the sumptuous funerary regalia for the tombs of royalty, to be worn in the afterlife – and it was Nubian prisoners who worked the mines. Thutmose expanded the temple of Ipet-isut (Karnak) and prepared a new location for the royal tomb in the Valley of Kings. Before he returned home, he hunted down the ruler of Kush, whom he killed personally with his bow; then he hung him upside down on the bow of the *Falcon*, leaving him to decay in the sun, an arrow still stuck in his chest.

Thutmose loved his first non-royal wife, Ahmes, most – she was his chief consort and no doubt their daughter Hatshepsut grew up with the confidence of the favourite child of the favourite wife of a warrior king. But his marriage into the royal family, to Mutneferet, King's Daughter, was no less important. This had produced an heir, a young Thutmose, whom the king married to his beloved Hatshepsut.

The old paladin died in 1481, and Thutmose II followed him soon afterwards, leaving his half-sister/wife Hatshepsut in charge of a baby stepson. Taking the regency, Hatshepsut – Foremost of Noblewomen – was exceptional in all things.

HATSHEPSUT:
FOREMOST OF THE WOMEN – FIRST PHARAOH

She believed she was born to rule. 'The God's Wife Hatshepsut conducted the affairs of the land, the Two Lands being in her counsels,' read one of her inscriptions from her regency. 'She is served; Egypt bows the head.' After seven years, she declared herself king in her own right. But it was a challenge to fit her vision of herself within the traditions of male kingship and she solved it in a bewildering display of sexual fluidity that the twenty-first century should find understandable: she presented herself first as male, King Maatkare, even appearing as a man, though often with female epithets, sometimes as a beautiful woman with a broad intelligent face but a male body; at other times she depicts herself in traditional male kilt and headdress but with breasts. The word for palace – *peraa* – was used to describe Egypt's sovereign: Hatshepsut became the first 'pharaoh'.

She adored her father, projecting herself as the King's First-Born Daughter but simultaneously as the daughter of Amun (originally the god of air, increasingly the senior deity), who was Thutmose too. Her father had declared that Hatshepsut would make a better king than a weak son. 'Then His Majesty said to them: "This daughter of mine, Hatshepsut – may she live! – I have appointed as my successor,"' she claimed in her mortuary temple. '"She shall direct the people . . . Obey her."'

She was not alone. Her intimate adviser was one of her father's courtiers, Senenmut, who climbed from obscurity to Steward of the King's Daughter – tutor to Hatshepsut's daughter, Neferure, a position that gave him access to the queen. When she herself was promoted to king, he became High Steward of Amun and Overseer of the King's Works, mentioning himself in inscriptions at royal temples.* Rumours spread that he was her lover – partly a reflection of the chauvinistic belief that behind a clever woman there must be a cleverer man. Ministers often boasted that they were 'beloved of the King', but he went further: 'I entered into the mysteries of the Lady of the Two Lands.' At their greatest monument, cheeky Theban workmen drew graffiti of a figure penetrating a slim woman from behind, presumed to be Senenmut having sex with Hatshepsut.

Assisted by Senenmut, Hatshepsut built monuments all over the empire, from Nubia to Sinai, dispatching an expedition in 1463 BC to the Land of God – the Egyptian name for Punt – to procure materials for her buildings and festivals, including incense, ebony, cosmetics and pet monkeys. Five ships, each with a crew of 210 including marines and 30 oarsmen, were led by her keeper of the seal, Nehsi, a Nubian. In a world that now boasted around 30 millions, there was a regular trade route down the Red Sea to east Africa and probably another to

---

* The titles reveal the complexity of the court – Royal Seal Bearer, Gentleman of the Bedchamber, Fan Bearer of the Lord of Two Lands – but security was vital: Master of the Secrets was 'Eyes of the King'. The royal bodyguards were made up of Nubian but also Mycenaeans from the Aegean. The police were often Nubian.

west Africa where, over the next centuries, the Nok people would create exquisite terracotta statues, later using furnaces to make iron, and a third route through the Gulf to India. Nehsi met the rulers of Punt, King Parahu and his enormously proportioned wife Ati, and returned with frankincense and thirty-one myrrh trees, which Hatshepsut replanted at her temples.

At Karnak, already expanded by her father,* she created a national shrine to Amun-Ra, the god associated with her father, adding a mud-brick palace designated 'The Royal Palace – I am not far from him'.†

As Thutmose III grew up, Hatshepsut felt the pressure to hand over power to her stepson/nephew, whom she married to her daughter. As she entered her fifties, suffering arthritis, then diabetes and cancer (revealed by a mummy recently identified as her), after twenty successful years in power, she must have reluctantly watched Thutmose III develop into a vigorous pharaoh with the courtiers increasingly turning to the rising sun. When Hatshepsut was dead, Thutmose III defaced her monuments, but she had laid the foundations for his successes. Every year he campaigned in Canaan and Syria, eighteen campaigns altogether, defeating the Syrian kingdom Mitanni and its Canaanite allies at Megiddo, where he addressed his troops with the words, 'Be steadfast, be steadfast! Be vigilant! Be vigilant!', returning with booty of 2,000 horses and chariots, 1,796 male slaves and uncounted females, among them three Syrian girls who became special for him. The Ahmoses were bombastic, militaristic monarchs who were expected to look and live

---

* The definition of life after death had changed since the days of Sneferu. Then, only kings had been worthy of afterlife; now high officials too inscribed their tombs with the sacred texts to achieve divinity and resurrection. The new royal family promoted the cult of Osiris, god of earth and the lord of the underworld, who oversaw the rebirth after death assisted by Ra and Horus, the two gods of the sky. The Egyptians embraced different concepts of the soul of the dead: the *ba* existed in parallel to the individual, but in death by day travelled with the sun and by night rejoined the mummified body with Osiris. The *ka* was a deathless spirit that needed food to survive and allowed the dead to travel to the underworld for judgement by Osiris, a terrifying voyage that, according to the so-called Coffin Texts, led them to the Field of Offering. There they faced fearsome alternatives between eternal life and damnation to hell where they had to eat excrement and drink urine. But if chosen, they entered a paradisiacal world. All of this depended on the survival of the mummy in the grave: just in case, Egyptians were now buried with a *shabti*, a burial figurine, to serve as a substitute in case the mummy was destroyed, so the *ba* could return every night.

† On the base of one of the three pairs of obelisks, which Senenmut chose and transported from Aswan, she inscribed her rationale for accession: 'I have done this with a love for my father Amun . . . I call this to the attention of people who live in the future who shall consider this monument that I made for my father . . . He [Amun] will say, "How like her it is, loyal to her father!" For I am his daughter.' No daughter has ever loved a father so splendidly. But her masterpiece was Dkjeser Djeseru, Holy of Holies, her mortuary temple, a complex of terraces cut into the rock face.

the part: Thutmose III's son Amenhotep II was the model of the athletic prince of a martial empire: he rode faster than anyone else, rowed harder than 200 rowers and could shoot an arrow through a copper target one palm thick.

BOY RACER, MARKSMAN, HORSE WHISPERER, BULL BREAKER: AMENHOTEP

Amenhotep and other royal children were brought up in the Family Palace next to the main palace where the royal wives resided with the pharaoh. Marriage in Egypt was a sacred bond, based on pragmatic arrangements, but divorce was permitted and ex-wives could remarry. Most Egyptians were not polygamous, but pharaohs had multiple wives, led by the Great Royal Wife, and thousands of concubines. Foreign conquests increased the number of royal wives, their sanctuary run by an Overseer of the Family Palace, which itself adjoined the Royal Nursery where ordinary children were brought up with the princes and princesses. The key carer of a royal baby was the 'great nurse who brought up the god', whose own children were brought up with the family; these Children of the Nursery were likely to become ministers in adulthood.

Princesses were taught weaving, singing and reading. They were never sent abroad to marry foreign kings, as they were too superior for foreigners. Princes were taught to read first Egyptian by the Scribe of the House of the Royal Children, using pen ink on papyrus, then Babylonian cuneiform, the language of diplomacy. Their tutors and nannies were – like childhood mentors through the ages – well positioned to become trusted advisers. Princes hunted bulls, lions and elephants – and they were obsessed with horses, introduced into Egypt by the Hyksos. Out near the Geza pyramids, Prince Amenhotep – who 'loved his horses . . . [was] strong-willed in breaking them in; he raised horses without equal' – practised shooting his bow and then went hunting: 'His Majesty appeared again in the chariots. The number of wild bulls he took: 40.' Hunting was always training for war: the spearhead of his army was a fifty-strong corps of chariots, each manned by a team of three, an officer with a composite bow, a driver and a guard with a shield.

As pharaoh, the horse-crazy marksman Amenhotep II expanded his domain eastwards towards Iraq, while in the Mediterranean Egypt traded with the Mycenaean peoples of Arzawa (Greece) and Alashiya

(Cyprus). In 1424, after crushing local kings at Kadesh (Syria), he killed seven of them personally and hung their corpses upside down. Troops were rewarded by the tally of penises and hands heaped at the feet of pharaohs or skewered on spears like kebabs. Amenhotep II returned after one Syrian expedition with three-quarters of a ton of gold, fifty-four tons of silver, 210 horses, 300 chariots and 90,000 prisoners. Only the best was ever good enough for the sardonic, exacting Amenhotep II,* pharaoh for twenty-six years, who said: 'If you lack a gold battleaxe inlaid with bronze, why make do with a wooden club?'

Not everyone could be so ferociously macho: his grandson Amenhotep III was more fixated on a religious vision that changed Egypt, a vision he shared with one remarkable woman. To call it a love match would be an understatement.

MISTRESS OF EGYPT: GOLD, WIVES AND DIPLOMACY

When he was a teenager, Amenhotep III married Tiye, aged thirteen, who became the most prominent wife in Egyptian history. She was not his sister but the daughter of a cavalry officer. Great Royal Wife Tiye was tiny, four foot nine, with long hair, still lustrous on her mummy, and her portraits show her beauty. Married for thirty-five years, the couple had nine children together.

Amenhotep promoted the state religion in processions of barques and statues, and ever more gigantist temples where his inscriptions described how Amun-Ra himself had crept into the bedchamber of the Great Wife: 'She awoke because of the god's scent and cried out with pleasure.' And the god announced, 'Amenhotep is the name of the child I have placed in your womb.' Amenhotep III was himself a god and Tiye was his divine partner, enthroned beside him on colossal statues, known to the ancients as the Colossi of Memnon. Presented as the equal of her husband, Tiye corresponded with foreign monarchs from the Greeks of Arzawa to Babylon. 'Tiye knows all the words I spoke with your father Amenhotep,' wrote King Tushrata of Mitanni to their son,

---

* It is rare to hear the actual voice of a pharaoh. Amenhotep II witheringly mocked the louche entourage of his Nubian viceroy: 'You, in faraway Nubia, a charioteering hero who brought booty from every foreign country, are now master of a wife from Babylon, a servant girl from Byblos [Lebanon], a young girl from Alalakh, a hag from Arapkha. These Syrians are worthless – what are they good for?' When the viceroy was too trusting of his Nubian subjects, he was told: 'Don't trust the Nubians, beware their people and witchcraft. Beware that servant whom you've promoted . . .'

suggesting, 'Enquire carefully of Tiye.' He even wrote directly to the 'Mistress of Egypt'.*

Tiye was a female potentate, but the next queen, Nefertiti, would be even more powerful and her husband, Amenhotep IV, was not like anyone else: if the portraits of the couple are accurate they were an extraordinary pair and their eccentricities would almost destroy the empire.

---

* Some 380 letters discovered in the House of the Pharaonic Correspondence in the city of Akhetaten reveal the fascinating correspondence, written in Babylonian in cuneiform, with the powers of west Asia. The Great Kings of the time gloried in their membership of the club of world arbiters – rather like today's G7 – who called each other 'brother'. Like today, all were very touchy about their status. Egypt and Hatti were the leading powers.

Houses of Hattusa and Rameses

SUN MANIA: NEFERTITI AND THE KING OF HATTI

The new pharaoh, Amenhotep IV, had a strange slit-eyed, angular face with an elongated head and extended torso with androgynous breasts, a potbelly and short legs – or at least was shown this way. Nefertiti, who may have been his first cousin, Tiye's niece, appeared as his equal everywhere – even in an inscription of her killing foreign prisoners on the royal barge. Nefertiti's beauty was striking, but here too there was a kink: her statues suggest an elongated skull. Did this new fashion in royal statues express Amenhotep's divinity or was he presenting his bizarre looks as evidence of divinity?

The cone-headed pharaoh was absorbed by religious matters, as Egyptian power in Syria was being challenged by a rising empire: an aggressive and gifted warrior, Suppiluliuma, was the king of Hatti, whose people were superb charioteers descended from Aryan invaders and who now ruled from the Aegean to the Euphrates. Suppiluliuma, scion of the greatest dynasty of the time, that ruled for almost 500 years, had crushed Greek kingdoms in the west; now he tested Egyptian power by taking Kadesh in northern Syria.

The pharaoh failed to get Kadesh back, but the wars had unleashed hordes of Habiru* – brigands – who attacked Egyptian allies in Canaan. 'I'm at war . . . Send archers!' begged Abdi-Heba, king of a small belea-guered fortress. 'If no archers, the king will have no lands.' The fortress was Jerusalem, making its first appearance in history.

As the Hattians advanced into Canaan and the Habiru marauded, Amenhotep IV launched a religious revolution. He embraced one sun god, Aten, and changed his own name to Akhenaten – Effective for Aten; Nefertiti became Neferneferuaten-Nefertiti – Beauteous are the Joys of Aten (and everyone else had to change their names from Amun to Akhen too). Then he founded a new capital, Akhetaten – Horizon

* These Habiru could be the first mention of 'Hebrews', who would emerge later as the Jews.

of Aten – between Memphis, the ancient capital, and Thebes.* The
new theology, known sinisterly as the Teaching, downgraded not just
Amun but all the other gods popular with the elite and the people, to
elevate one god, an idea that may have influenced the writers of the
Bible and the religions to come. Even the word 'gods' was changed to its
singular form. The divine partnership of Akhenaten and Nefertiti had
a cosy intimacy to it: illuminated and joined by the rays of the divine
sun, they appeared in engravings with three children on their laps.
It was the first appearance of a nuclear family as a political–religious
statement.

In 1342, the royal family, starred in a spectacular jubilee 'seated upon
the great palanquin of electrum to receive the tribute of Syria and Kush,
the West and the East . . . even the islands in the midst of the sea [the
Greeks], presenting tribute'. The foreigners were unimpressed by this
sun cult: 'Why,' wrote King Ashuruballit of Assyria, 'should my messen-
gers be made to stay constantly outside to die under the sun?' The sun
was about to lose its dazzle, and its eclipse would bring the most famous
of all pharaohs to the throne.

TRANSITIONING: THE MALE NEFERTITI, TUTANKHAMUN'S WIFE AND THE PRINCE OF HATTI

A new male co-pharaoh was named as Neferneferuaten-Nefertiti, who
was probably the queen transitioning into a male king. But the sun cult
depended on one man – and in 1336 Akhenaten died, to be succeeded
by a mysterious pharaoh named Smenekhkara, most likely Nefertiti
in male guise, who ruled with her own daughter Meritaten as King's
Great Wife. But courtiers were enraged by the sun cult, and knives were
out: Nefertiti died – or was killed. Her replacement was a nine-year-old
son of Akhenaten by one of his secondary wives: Tutankhaten – Living
Image of Aten – who was swiftly married to another of the daughters of
Akhenaten and Nefertiti, Ankhesenpaaten.

The vanishing of Nefertiti heralded a counter-revolution to undo

---

* The capital's centrepiece was the House of Aten next to the Pharaoh's House and the state
department, the House of Pharaoh's Correspondence, guarded by colossi of Akhenaten
and Nefertiti. Every day the royal family rode in ceremonial chariots from palace to temple,
accompanied by priests and protected by baton-wielding bodyguards. The royal artist, 'The
King's Favourite and Master of Works, the Sculptor Thutmose', set up a studio, specializing
in Nefertitis, sculpting both his famously beautiful teen-queen, her eyes of black painted
quartz held in place by beeswax, wearing her blue crown, and the naked adult woman and
mother.

the Atenists and restore Amun-Ra. The capital returned to Memphis, the new city abandoned; Tutankhaten became Tutankhamun, his wife Ankhesenamun.

The pharaoh, five foot six, was not strong – he may have fractured his leg in a chariot accident; he also suffered from malaria and it sounds as if he had a temper. Now he consulted 'with Amun', which meant his powerful advisers, Ay, his great-uncle, and the top general Horemheb, who boasted that Tutankhamun promoted him to 'Lord of the Land'. The boy-pharaoh declared ,'The temples of the gods and goddesses had fallen into ruin . . .' but he himself 'drove away chaos'. The royal couple were half-siblings, the queen was barely pubescent and two daughters were stillborn (their tiny mummies buried with Tutankhamun, his paternity proved by their DNA). The pharaoh faced the relentless advance of the Hattian king Suppiluliuma. 'If armies were sent east,' admitted Tutankhamun, 'they had no success.' He sent an army northwards. Suppiluliuma's chariots routed it.

In 1322, Tutankhamun died at the age of nineteen – whether as a result of malaria, some other infection or murder – but his tomb was not ready, so his entombed regalia was paltry compared to the treasures prepared for kings who died in predictable old age.

Only one of House Ahmose was left: Queen Ankhesenamun, also nineteen, was alone in a vicious court at the mercy of Great-Uncle Ay who was angling to marry her and become pharaoh himself. Overseer of the Army Horemheb had, he claimed, been designated as heir, but he was campaigning in Syria. In a desperate move, the daughter of Nefertiti turned to the other great dynasty.

Great King Suppiluliuma was at war, besieging Carchemish (Türkiye). In a letter, included in *The Deeds of Suppiluliuma*, an account written by his heir and found among the ruins of Hattusa, teenaged queen Ankhesenamun wrote: 'My husband has died and I have no son. They say that you have many sons. You might give me one of your sons to become my husband. I would not wish to take one of my subjects [she meant Ay] as husband . . . I am afraid.'

Suppiluliuma sent a son, Prince Zannanza, through Canaan towards Egypt. But he was too late. The journey took a long time; the old minister Ay was acclaimed pharaoh and married the young queen. But Zannanza was still on his way. We do not know what happened, but Horemheb surely intercepted and murdered him. It was a favour Pharaoh Ay did not forget. No one knows for how long Ankhesenamun survived, but Ay soon died, leaving the throne to Horemheb.

Suppiluliuma was incensed – 'Oh gods, the people of Egypt did this to me' – sending his charioteers to ravage Egyptian Canaan. But the soldiers and their prisoners returned with a plague, always a symptom of an interlinked world. Soon afterwards, Suppililiuma died and the crown prince, leaving his domineering Babylonian queen Tawananna ruling an empire beset by rebellion. In 1321, Mursili II, son of Suppiluliuma, grieved: 'O gods, what have you done? You've let plague into Hatti and everyone is dying.' The pandemic decimated the capital, Hattusa. Out of the chaos in Egypt and Hatti, two potentates emerged who would now clash in the greatest battle of the ancient world.

The day began with a surprise.

CLASH OF THE CHARIOTEERS: RAMESES AND MUWATALLI

In May 1274, north of Kadesh, Rameses II, aged twenty-five, five foot seven, fair-skinned with ginger wavy hair, the monarch of a new dynasty, rode out of his camp in a golden chariot wearing his full regalia, followed by his army of over 20,000 divided into four divisions. His mission: retake Kadesh, a walled city surrounded by water. But his manoeuvres were more leisurely parade than vigilant advance.

The capture and interrogation of two Bedouin confirmed that the Hattian army under King Muwatalli was 120 miles away near Aleppo. Closer to his home base, the Great King of Hatti deployed a much larger force of 47,500, including 3,500 chariots – but they were far away.

Fording the Orontes, the Egyptians set up a new forward camp to begin the siege. Just five years on the throne, Rameses, slim, fit, aquiline, was energetic and confident like his father. The family were new: Tutankhamun's general Horemheb had had no children: he appointed a commoner as King's Deputy, Paramessu, a general, whom he then promoted to King's Son. Paramessu took the regnant name Rameses, but it was his son Seti, another tough, athletic general – still impressive as a mummy – who restored the empire with parvenu vigour. Even while his father was still alive, Seti was storming up the coast of Canaan, where he forced the rulers of Lebanon to cut timber for his navy then seized Kadesh. But the Hattians, now under the impressive team of Muwatalli and his brother, Hattusili, grandsons of Suppiluliuma, seized it back.

When Rameses II succeeded his father – taking the throne name Usermaatra (Ozymandias) – Kadesh was his first priority. Rameses was flamboyant and narcissistic, engraving his name on more monuments than anyone else. He had already begun to build a capital, Per-Rameses – House of Rameses. His tomb builders lived in a workers' village at Deir el-Medina, proud of their speciality – 'I am a craftsman,' wrote one, 'who excels in his art at the forefront of knowledge.' In his works, Rameses would define the very word pharaonic.

Maestro of bow and chariot, Rameses first defeated the fleets of the Sherden, raiders of the eastern Mediterranean. Then he turned to Kadesh.

As Rameses set up camp, Muwatalli's spies were watching, but they were spotted, captured and tortured to reveal alarming news: the Hattians were very close, poised to attack. Rameses was outraged by his generals' incompetence. He took personal charge, sending the royal princes out of the battle zone, dispatching his vizier to bring up the Ptah division. Before they were ready, the Hattians ambushed them, their chariots smashing into the Amun division commanded by Rameses, who sent out the call: 'His Majesty is all alone.' Then they hit the Ra division as it crossed the river. Thousands of chariots crashed into each other. Commanded by Muwatalli, Hattian chariots broke the Egyptian lines with their flimsier chariots; the Egyptians fled. It was a desperate fight in which the pharaoh himself, riding his chariot and firing his bow, was almost killed, only rescued by his Greek guards resplendent in horned helmets and hacking swords. There is no reason to doubt Rameses' claims that his own personality saved the day. He was lucky: the Children of Hatti started plundering the pharaonic camp. As chariot reinforcements arrived in the nick of time, Rameses, shouting orders from his chariot, rallied his forces for Muwatalli's charge. Rameses' counter-attack broke the Hattian lines.

Night fell over the battlefield as the last Egyptian divisions arrived to consolidate the line. At dawn the two kings ordered their frayed armies into a savage frontal combat that ended in stalemate. Rameses withdrew his men; Muwatalli offered negotiations. Yet Muwatalli had won: Kadesh remained Hattian. Once he got home, Rameses transformed the desperate pandemonium of the Hattian ambush into a heroic legend. In no fewer than five massive monuments, he recast Kadesh as a triumph.*

Rameses shared this glory with one person – Great Wife Nefertari,

---

* The brash grandiloquent gigantism of his vision endures today in all five – above all his spectacular masterpiece, the Temple of Rameses United with Thebes, eleven acres in size, crowned with a colossus of Rameses. These works expressed not just the plenitude of his power but his apotheosis as a living god.

who now played a special role in making peace between enemies,* just as in China a queen commanded chariot armies in battle.

WAR QUEENS: LADY HAO OF SHANG, PUDEHEPA OF HATTUSA AND NEFERTARI OF EGYPT

As the charioteers of Rameses and Muwatalli clashed in Syria, the new weaponry had reached north-western China, where Wuding had inherited a realm around the Yellow River gradually built by his family, the Shang, over a few hundred years. Legends depict an earlier Chinese king Yu 'who controlled the flood' of the Yellow River, but real history starts with the Shang.

Wuding, the twenty-first of his lineage, was a warrior king who around 1250 BC expanded Shang influence by conquest and marriage: many of his sixty-four wives were princesses of conquered fiefdoms. A favourite wife, Fu Hao, rose within his household to become a commander and high priestess. Wuding expanded into north-eastern China, fighting the other fiefdoms but also the northern peoples, the Guifang – Border Demons – from whom he had learned the arts of crossbow and chariot. Overseeing an agricultural society that also produced bronze crafts, weaponry and silk, the Shang ruled from Yin (near Anyang, Henan Province), aided by scribes who used the earliest Chinese writing from which today's language derives. While worshipping a supreme god, Di, who may have been the supreme ancestor of the Shang, along with a lesser pantheon, they revered their ancestors as intermediaries and they daily consulted court diviners who used scapulimancy, the cracks on burned ox bones or turtle shells, to answer all the essential questions of life – from the imminence of natural disasters to health, harvest and family.

The bones and shells were burned and the diviners interpreted the cracks, their comments written on the bones, thousands of which survive. Scapulimancy helped people cope with a dangerous, unpredictable world, but the divinations were frustratingly vague.

War was waged partly in order to capture humans to sacrifice and

---

* Just at this time, a court scribe, Any, wrote advice to his son on how to live, giving a glimpse of Egyptian conservative family values: 'Truth is sent by God,' 'Keep away from rebels' and 'Scorn the woman of ill repute, don't try to sleep with her,' alongside 'Give back in abundance the bread your mother gave you: support her as she supported you.' But the soul and eternity are always on an Egyptian's mind: 'Don't lose yourself in the exterior world to the extent that you neglect the place of your eternal rest.'

so ensure a serene afterlife: the Shang – contemporary with Rameses in Egypt* – were buried in a family necropolis of tombs cut into the loess soil, with bronze artefacts and weapons. 'Offerings to Da Ding', reads one inscription. 'Da Jia and Zu Yi, 100 cups of wine, 100 Qiang prisoners, 300 cattle . . .'. When Shang potentates died, hundreds were killed and buried with them.

Lady Fu Hao, mentioned in 170 oracle bones, may have started as a court diviner, but became the king's partner. When the king appointed Lady Hao, he consulted the diviners and they confirmed the appointment. Hao won four successive campaigns, mainly against barbarians, but when she died at the age of thirty-three she was buried with sixteen sacrificed slaves and her favourite pets, six dogs.† The king missed her bitterly, regularly asking her advice in the afterlife.

In 1045, the Shang were said to have been destroyed by their own perverted corruption: King Zhou and his wife Daji floated on pleasure boats on a lake of booze, cavorting with concubines while devising vicious tortures for their enemies, the worst being the Cannon Burning Torment in which victims were fried alive on red-hot metal. Yet these excesses are likely to be the propaganda of the Zhou, a rising dynasty from the west, who destroyed them. At the battle of Muye, they were defeated by King Wu of Zhou. After the Shang couple had committed suicide in the ruins of their burning palace, Wu hunted down the Shang, family and troops, collecting 177,779 ears, then amid the rituals of chanting, bells and flutes he 'beheaded and sacrificed their little prince and master of the cauldron [and] the leaders of their forty families', scalping them. The Zhou family now ruled for several centuries, developing the first bureaucracy, the Grand Secretariat. Wu's son Cheng was challenged by rebellious nobles but was rescued by that rare phenomenon, a benign uncle, Dan, *gong* (duke) of Zhou.

Once Cheng came of age, the duke of Zhou surrendered power – and later came to define responsible rule and the idea of the Mandate of Heaven: if a dynasty ruled well, they would ensure order, blessed by

---

* We know much less about Europe, but it was a violent world: Celtic peoples migrated from the east and settled in central Europe. Around this time, 1,400 people including women and children were killed in the Tollense Valley (German–Polish border) in what appears to have been the ambush of a merchant caravan, executed by having their skulls smashed.

† Their bones were placed around her lacquered coffin along with an array of bronze vessels, some engraved with her name, 560 hairpins, 700 pieces of jade, opal and ivory carved into figurines of dragons, phoenixes and elephants, and among 130 weapons her favourite battleaxes. She was not the only female commander of Wuding's armies, and women commanded Chinese armies at least until the Tang in the seventh century.

heaven, but if they abused power, they would lose the Mandate and be replaced.

Back in Syria, a less virtuous uncle, Hattusili, seized the Hattian throne from his nephew. After occupying Dimasqu (Damascus), he stopped to pray at a shrine to Ishtar, where he met and married the priest's daughter Puduhepa, one of the first women of power whose voices we can hear. The Egyptian war went on until King Hattusili and Queen Puduhepa negotiated a peace treaty with Rameses – the first surviving treaty – that, like many such carve-ups right up to our own times, split Canaan–Syria – and then arranged a marriage between their children. It was Queen Puduhepa who did much of the negotiating while her husband galloped westwards to scourge a vassal, the Mycenaean kingdom of Ahhiyawa. The two had fallen out over Hattusili's small ally, Wilusa – also known as Ilios or Troy.

In 1250, Hattusili negotiated with the king of Ahhiyawa, Tawagalawa (Eteocles), and in a letter only part of which survives wrote: 'Now as we have come to an agreement about Wilusa over which we went to war . . .'. The timing is roughly right for a war in which the Trojans, backed by their Hattian allies, fought the Mycenaeans, possibly descendants of Aryan invaders. Based at Mycenae in the Peloponnese, they were ruled by kings and sword-swinging, chariot-riding warrior aristocrats who wassailed in the draughty halls of fortresses. They now worshipped male and female gods, and their battle-scarred bodies sporting golden masks were buried with bronze swords. But they were also Eurasian traders.*

The war ended in the burning of Troy, confirmed by archaeological excavations. The backing of Hatti explains why little Troy could defy a coalition of Greeks. But these Hattian letters suggest that the 'Trojan war', later celebrated in *The Iliad*, was, if it happened at all, a sideshow in Hatti's long struggle to control the Greeks.

Fifteen years after Kadesh, Rameses II and Hattusili III signed an 'Eternal Peace', pledging 'great peace and great brotherhood between themselves for ever', co-signed by Queen Puduhepa. She not only mediated between the many offspring of the king by concubines, officiated at religious festivals and sat as a judge, but – always acute, sarcastic, haughty – also negotiated the marriage of her daughter to Rameses. Nefertari sent her 'sister' a golden twelve-strand necklace and

---

* Mycenaeans traded tin from Afghanistan, amber from the Baltic, plying the seas from Greece to Italy and Spain. One of the earliest shipwrecks dated around 1300 BC – studied by the historical science that we might call naufragiology – contains goods from as far away as Babylon and Italy, showing that a Eurasian network already existed.

a luxurious dyed garment. But Puduhepa negotiated very frankly with Rameses.

'My sister, you promised to give me your daughter,' wrote Rameses. 'That's what you wrote. But you've withheld her and are angry with me. Why?'

'I've indeed withheld my daughter,' replied Puduhepa. 'And you will certainly approve of my reasons. The treasure house of Hatti was burned [by rebels].' Puduhepa teased Rameses: 'Does my brother possess nothing at all? . . . My brother, you seek to enrich yourself at my expense. That's not worthy of your reputation or your status.' No one else in the world would speak to Rameses the Great like that. Then she boasted of her daughter's charms: 'With whom shall I compare the daughter of heaven and earth whom I shall give to my brother?' But 'I want her made superior to all the other daughters of Great Kings.'

In 1246 BC, Rameses and Puduhepa were ready. 'Wonderful, wonderful is this situation,' exclaimed Rameses. 'The Sun God and the Storm God, the gods of Egypt and Hatti, have granted our two countries peace for ever!' Puduhepa set off with her daughter, accompanied by a trove of 'gold, silver, much bronze, slaves, horses without limit, cattle, goats, rams by the myriad!' Puduhepa bade her daughter goodbye at the frontier and thereafter Rameses 'loved her more than anything', but when no children appeared, her father blamed Rameses. 'You've sired no son with my daughter,' wrote Hattusili. 'Isn't it possible?' Since Rameses had sired over a hundred children, this cast an unfair aspersion. At the apogee of their empires, the super-monarchs were discussing a summit. 'Though we Great Kings are brothers, one has never seen the other,' wrote Puduhepa to Rameses, so they decided to meet in Canaan. But the summit never happened. Hattusili faced challenges from the Aegean to the Euphrates, and Rameses ruled for far too long, sixty-seven years, and by the time he died at ninety, twisted by arthritis, tormented with dental problems (all revealed by his mummy), his elderly son had to cope with attacks on all his frontiers* but especially on the Mediterranean, where all the powers now faced a catastrophe. No one knows what caused it, but it is probable that a synchronicity of climate, natural disaster, pandemics, greed and systemic implosion sparked movements on some faraway steppe that unleashed a stampede migration in which maritime marauders shattered the rich cities of the Mediterranean and western Asia. The raiders sound like

* The son, Merneptah, dealt with rebellions in Libya, Nubia and Canaan where, among the vanquished Canaanite tribes listed on his inscription, he cites 'Israel', the first definite mention of the Jewish people.

Greeks, the Egyptians called them 'Sea Peoples' but they came by land too, sporting new iron breastplates and leg greaves, wielding stabbing swords and shields, all made by the smelting of iron ore and meteoric iron to make a stronger metal. Iron had been known for a long time and it is likely that the smelting process developed slowly in many places, starting in India and spreading via the sophisticated blacksmiths of Hatti to Europe and Africa.*

Egypt and Hatti fought back. Hattusili's son, Tudaliya IV, attacked the raiders in Alishiya (Cyprus), but he was soon struggling to hold back the horses of the apocalypse. 'If nobody is left to yoke the horses,' Tudaliya wrote forlornly, 'you must show even more support. If the charioteer jumps from the chariot and the valet flees the chamber, and not even a dog is left, your support for your king must be all the greater.' In Egypt Rameses III claimed to have defeated these invaders in the Nile delta, a triumph celebrated by his gigantist temple-palace – the Mansion of a Million Years of King Rameses – in which enemy penises are depicted, heaped at his feet. But his gravebuilders, living with their families in their special village at Deir el-Medina, were no longer paid: they refused to work and launched a sit-in at the temples – the first strike.

'Barbarians conspired in their islands,' wrote Rameses III, 'no land could withstand their weaponry.' The Rameses family disintegrated; Egypt fell to Libyan chieftains; Hatti was broken; in Europe, Celts advanced into the west; in the Mediterranean, Greek-speaking peoples settled Aegean coasts. In western Asia, Semitic peoples, many speaking Aramaic, founded new kingdoms: in Canaan, they built thriving trading cities on the coast; in the interior, they formed a kingdom around Damascus, while further south one Semitic tribe, speaking an early version of Hebrew, settled and coalesced into a people who called themselves 'Israel'. They may already have worshipped a peculiar notion – one deity – who did not reside in a single temple but travelled with them in a mobile shrine.† Yet these were all tiny peoples. The mayhem was

---

* The division of early history into Stone, Bronze and Iron Ages was devised in 1825 by the Danish historian Christian Jürgensen Thomsen. Sub-Saharan Africa did not experience a prehistoric Bronze Age: tools were made of stone. Then they were made from iron. For some, the sudden influx of iron-working technology supports the argument that the technology reached Africa from outside the continent. But more recently it has been argued that iron-working technology developed independently in one or more centres, possibly Nok (Nigeria) or Kush (Sudan).

† The Israelites immigrated to Canaan from servitude in Egypt many centuries earlier – according to the Bible. Contrary to the biblical story of conquest, it is likely they conquered some local peoples and intermarried with others.

also the opportunity for a northern Iraqi city to build the first empire to dominate all of western Asia: the city was Ashur and the spectacular cruelties of Assyria would terrify the known world.

The Nubian Pharaohs and Great Kings of Ashur:
House Alara versus House Tiglath-Pileser

In 853 BC, at Qarqar in northern Syria, the kings of Israel and ten other kingdoms prepared to fight the most powerful monarch of his day, Shalmaneser III of Assyria, who was advancing to destroy them.

Ashur was an old city founded around 2600, home of the god Ashur, worshipped in his ziggurat tower and temple, where Assyrian kings were crowned. For a long time, Assyria was just a minor city state in a region dominated by Akkad and Babylon, but around 1300 its kings, descended from the semi-mythical Adasi, started to conquer northern Iraq. After its expansion had been checked by Hatti and Babylon, Assyria – Assurayu in Assyrian (a dialect of Akkadian) – exploited the predations of the Sea Peoples to shatter both powers: Shalmaneser routed the king of Hatti, whose empire was fatally undermined by the attacks of Kassite nomads; Hattusa was abandoned. The Assyrian king captured the Babylonian king, on whom he 'trod with my feet upon his lordly neck as a footstool', and then struck at the kingdom of Elam (Iran), invading Arabia, seizing entrepôts in Dilmun (Bahrain) and Meluhha (India), calling himself King of the Upper and Lower Seas and King of Kings. After seizing power in 1114, Tiglath-Pileser I, tempted by the riches of Canaan, plundered the kingdoms of Damascus and Tyre, Sidon and Beirut, celebrating, he claimed, by harpooning a 'seahorse' – surely a whale – in the Mediterranean. When Assyria was crippled by the strife among his heirs, a small people in southern Canaan took the opportunity to expand their own kingdom.

Around 1000, the Israelites were united under elected kings, first Saul and then David, a warlord who made his name fighting the Philistine tribes of the coast. David, whose existence as the founder of a kingdom called the House of David is confirmed by a stele found at Tel Dan, chose a small Canaanite stronghold and shrine as his capital: Jerusalem. On Mount Moriah, David's son Solomon built a temple to the one god idiosyncratically worshipped by the Israelites, who disdained Baal and the Canaanite pantheon of gods. There is no evidence for Solomon's existence except the Bible,* but there is plenty of evidence for the Jewish Temple that existed soon afterwards. The united Israelite kingdom quickly broke up: the House of David ruled the southern part, Judah – the origin of the word Jew – based around the richly endowed Jerusalem Temple that was raided by one of the Libyan pharaohs of Egypt, who mentioned it in his inscriptions. The northern half of Canaan was ruled by a larger, more formidable kingdom, Israel, built up by a general, Omri, who seized the throne, founded a new capital, Samaria, where the ivory artefacts of his splendid palace have been found, and made it a regional power, building his own temple, conquering Moab across the Jordan and marrying his son Ahab to a princess of Sidon: Jezebel.

Israel was close to the Canani† and their rich coastal city states, like Tyre, Byblos and Acre (Lebanon/Israel), traders in purple dye, cedarwood, carved ivory and ebony (imported from Africa) and glass artefacts, united together at this time under a priest-king Ithobaal of Sidon, Jezebel's father. Worshipping Baal, Astarte and other gods, the Canani – also known as the Phoenicians – voyaging in ships powered by rows of enslaved oarsmen, were already founding colonies in Sicily, Sardinia, Spain (Cadiz), trading and seeking new sources of iron, tin and silver, even passing into the Atlantic to found Mogador in Morocco. In the process, they spread their written language, an alphabet of 22 consonants, just at the time the Tyrians founded their New City, Qart Hadasht – Carthage (Tunisia). Assyrian kings furnished their palaces with Canaanite ivories; Omri's palace in Samaria was filled with the Canani's ivory carvings and treasures.

The marriage of Ahab to Jezebel linked Omri's family to this sophisticated Eurasian network, very far from the puritanical priests of remote Jerusalem. Many of the achievements assigned by the Bible to Solomon may describe Omri, who built the port-fortress at Tel Kheleifah on the Red Sea between Elath and Aqaba, to trade spices and ivory, via the kingdom of Sheba (Yemen/Eritrea), with Africa, Arabia and India. But when Omri died in 873, Ahab and Jezebel faced an imminent threat: Assyria was back.

Shalmaneser III, portrayed on his steles gripping a royal mace and wearing the crown, robes and braided long beard of an Assyrian

---

* The Bible is a library of different sacred texts written by anonymous Jewish authors much later, during the Babylonian exile from the religiously pure monotheistic point of view of the kingdom of Judah. It was biased against the more cosmopolitan kingdom of Israel. Like all sacred texts, it is filled with obscurities, but it is also sometimes a historical source, sometimes mythological.

† These peoples called themselves 'Canani' but the Greeks called them 'Phoenicians', after their top brand, the purple dye phoenix, derived from the *Murex* mollusc.

monarch, blessed by his god Ashur, reconquered Iraq, attacked into Persia – boasting that he received the tribute of the Paruwash (the first mention of the Persians) – then struck westwards, demanding the tribute of Israelites and Canani.

Ahab of Israel and Hadanezer of Aram-Damascus refused and massed their armies, joined by the 1,000 cameleers of King Gindibu of the Arabs, their first appearance in history, and the first recorded use of camels in battle.*

Shalmaneser marched south. Jews and Arabs, Aramaeans and Phoenicians drew their swords.

TIGLATH-PILESER AND FAMILY: THE WORLD-CONQUERING ASSYRIANS

Shalmaneser, fielding 100,000 men that day, defeated the Israelite– Aramaean–Arab alliance, killing 14,000 of them, but a rebellion called him home. As soon as he was gone, the allies fell out among themselves: Ahab returned to his alliance with his compatriots in Jerusalem, marrying his daughter Athaliah to its heir. But he was killed by Hadanezer. Jezebel oversaw the succession of her family in Jerusalem and Samaria, but in 825, 'Jehu of the House of Omri' – as the Assyrians called him – assassinated both kings and then trapped Queen Mother Jezebel in her Samarian palace, where she faced down the rebels dressed in her royal jewels and regalia, only for three court eunuchs, suborned by the rebels, to toss her out of the window. Jehu trampled the queen with his horse, her body torn apart by dogs – and paid tribute to Shalmaneser.

The sole survivor of this family massacre was Queen Mother Athaliah of Judah who seized power in Jerusalem and ruled in her own right – that rare phenomenon, a queen regnant. But Athaliah was – like her mother Jezebel – a homicidal megalomaniac who slaughtered the royal family to retain power. Only one Davidic prince was hidden from her killers. Once his survival was known, the courtiers assassinated Athaliah. Israel was an Assyrian vassal but tiny Judah survived as Assyria itself faltered.[†]

---

* Camels, two-humped in Bactria and one-humped in Arabia, had been domesticated for milking in the fourth to third millennium BC, then used as pack animals and ridden mounts. They were already central to the life of the Arabs as currency, transport and food: when an Arab chieftain died, his favourite camel was buried with him or left hobbled by his grave to die. Arab chieftains had already fought the Assyrians, but their troops were also in demand as mercenaries. Camels transported Arab fighters, who then switched mounts and galloped on horseback into battle.

† Shalmaneser III died facing a rebellion by his sons, one of whom emerged as King

In 754 Urartu, a mountain kingdom famed for its military ferocity and bronze craftsmanship, situated in the mountains of north-western Iran, Azerbaijan and Armenia, shattered the Assyrians. The downfall seemed final, but one man changed everything: his real name was Pulu, a prince who governed the Assyrian capital Kahlu (Nimrud). In 745, taking the name Tiglath-Pileser III, he created a new Assyria, diminishing the overmighty nobility, recruiting a professional army and specialized auxiliaries, all funded by his efficient tax collecting, directed though a cabinet of seven; his orders stamped with the imperial seal of the king killing a lion were conveyed along royal roads by special couriers. Tiglath-Pileser was voracious and tireless, in perpetual motion, scourging Elam, climbing with his men into the mountains to defeat Urartu* and routing an Arab queen. When Damascus and Israel besieged Jerusalem, King Ahaz of Judah unwisely invited Tiglath-Pileser to help: '"I'm your servant . . . Come and save me," and the King of Assyria came.'

Tiglath-Pileser made Judah a vassal and reduced Israel to a rump, whose king in 727 desperately sought a way to escape Assyrian rule: he appealed to Egypt, but its pharaohs no longer counted. The unthinkable was about to happen: Kush was about to take Egypt.

ALARA OF KUSH: FIRST AFRICAN EMPIRE

In 727 BC, Piye, king of Kush, galloped northwards into Egypt. Kush had existed for millennia alongside Egypt, its twin riverine civilization. Around 800, a local ruler called Alara, who later assumed the title of king, united a realm based in Napata, a city founded by Thutmose III, close to the holy cobra mountain of Jebel Barkal, which was governed by a literate court – with secretaries of the archives and chief treasurers. Kush fielded crack archers and formidable cavalry, all funded by

---

Shamsi-Adad. His queen was Shammuramat, a Babylonian princess, whom the Greeks called Semiramis. When Shamsi-Adad died in 811 BC, their son Adad-Nirari III was a child, so Semiramis took power, describing herself as 'King of the Universe, King of Assyria, Daughter-in-Law of Shalmaneser, King of the Four Regions of the World' – and winning the respect of the martial Assyrians. Like a real king of Assyria, she led her armies into Iran and died in battle. But thanks to the queen, Assyria retained its power.

* The name of Mount Ararat is a rare geographical hint of Urartu's existence, but there are many excavations of Urartian cities in Türkiye and Armenia. Elam was also a powerful realm; its people spoke a language unlike any other in the region; its capital Susa was a famous walled city while its chief temple was the ziggurat 174 feet high at Choga Zanbil which, writes Lloyd Llewellyn-Jones, is 'the best-preserved ziggurat in existence, a monument to Elamite ingenuity and might'.

trade between the Mediterranean, inland Africa and, via the Red Sea, India.

Alara oversaw a hybrid Egyptian–Kushite religion. Originally Kushites buried their dead beneath circular mounds at el-Kurru near their capital Kerma, accompanied by droves of relatives or servants, sacrificed by being buried alive. Then their kings started to build pyramids for their burials: 200 pyramids still stand in Sudan, almost double those of Egypt. Like a pharaoh, Alara called himself Son of Amun and married his sister. Alara's brother Kashta succeeded him just as the instability in Egypt, particularly a conflict in Thebes between a king and his Amun priests, forced the latter to seek asylum in Napata, the new Kushite capital, where they encouraged Kashta to see himself as the legitimate guardian of Amun – and of Egypt.

In 760, Kashta raided Thebes where he forced the Egyptians to accept his daughter as God's Wife of Amun and proclaimed himself King of the Two Lands. Kashta and his heirs claimed to be protectors of ancient gods, but the dynasty never presented themselves as Egyptian: in her statue at Karnak, Kashta's daughter, Amenirdis, depicted as God's Wife of Amun, is dressed like an Egyptian but her face in unmistakably Kushite.

Fifteen years later, Kashta's son King Piye, invited by one of the Egyptian factions to intervene, advanced into Egypt, presenting himself as more Egyptian than the Egyptians, respectfully honouring Amun. Kings made obeisance to him in Thebes as pharaoh – as he boasted on Jebel Barkal. Married to a cousin, and to his own sister, Piye was content to leave his Egyptian vassals to rule on his behalf until challenged by the rulers of Memphis. In 729, he personally led the storming of Memphis. All the potentates of the delta submitted to him, promising to 'open our treasuries and bring you the choice of our studs and the best of our horses'. He loved horseflesh more than jewels or women: 'The king's wives and daughters came to him and paid honour but His Majesty did not pay them attention. Instead he went off to the stables where he saw that the horses were hungry.' In a city stinking of dead bodies, he could barely tolerate any cruelty to animals. 'It's more painful to me,' he wrote on his pyramid in Napata, 'that my horses should be hungry than every ill deed you have done.' When he died, he was buried in his Napata pyramid with his favourite squadron of horses.

His brother Shabaka did not stay in Napata but marched north, enforcing direct rule and religious purity by burning one of his opponents alive, installing his son as high priest and female cousins as God's Wives of Amun. House Alara now ruled all of modern Egypt and Sudan, at least 2,100 miles of the Nile – one of the largest African empires of world history. The royal archives at Nineveh show friendly contacts between Shabaka and Assyria, but the titans were bound to clash. Shabaka was unlikely to be threatened by the new Assyrian king, who was said to be a weakling. But first impressions can be deceptive.

His name was Sennacherib. When the news spread that Sennacherib was king, the entire Assyrian empire flickered into rebellion – and Hezekiah, king of Judah, asked for Shabaka's help.

In 701, the pharaoh's army of Kushites and Egyptians under Prince Taharqo, younger son of Piye, marched north across Sinai just as Sennacherib fought his way south-west towards Jerusalem. The two greatest families, one Asian, one African, were now to fight for the world.

AFRICA VERSUS ASIA: SHABAKA VERSUS SENNACHERIB

It was hard to be Sennacherib: his father was Sargon II, a triumphant warlord who had conquered Cyprus, Phoenicia and the rest of Israel, ethnically cleansing it and deporting 29,000 of its elite to Assyria, before turning to Urartu. In a spectacular exploit, Sargon had led his army into the mountains to destroy the kingdom before returning to the heartland to found his own new capital, Dur Sharrukin – Fort Sargon – where he declared himself King of the World. But predators can never rest. Now old, but drawn to one last campaign in Tabal (Türkiye) in 705, he was killed during an enemy raid on his camp, his sacred body lost.*

Sennacherib must have loathed the old monster: he never praised or mentioned his father. But he possessed all the atrocious grandeur of his father and grandfather, lashing out at Babylon, independent-minded city state of the god Marduk, whose blessing the Assyrians could never quite ignore. Then Sennacherib hacked his way southwards, consuming Phoenicia and Judah, city by city.

As the King of the World approached Jerusalem, the House of David prayed for deliverance from God and for a relieving army from Egypt. The Kushite Prince Taharqo, aged twenty, raced towards Jerusalem.

---

* His grandfather was (probably) the conqueror Tiglath-Pileser, but some scholars argue that Sargon was a usurper. The mission of the Assyrian kings was to expand the territory of the god Ashur, legislate and rule justly, enrich the homeland and serve all their gods. Their palace reliefs and historical annals describe the battles and killing, but this is exaggerated for effect. Their deportations were intended to disrupt rebellions and populate core Assyria.

Kushite prince and Assyrian king met at Eltekeh near Ashdod; the Kushites were defeated and pursued back to Egypt. Sennacherib besieged Jerusalem but then, paid off with Temple gold, he withdrew, returning laden with booty to pay for the embellishment of his capital, Nineveh, sacred to the goddess of love and war, Ishtar. Building massive walls, with eighteen gates, decorated with winged apotropaic bulls, and a new palace, Sennacherib was surprisingly green-fingered for a blood-soaked conqueror: he prided himself on the city's gardens, irrigated by fifty-five miles of viaducts and canals to bring water from the mountains; his own in his palace contained rare plants, while he promised every Ninevite an allotment garden. Supernatural protection was essential at all times in a world threatened by evil spirits. Like the city gates, his palaces were magically protected by pairs of human-headed winged bulls – lamassus – weighing thirty tons – 'a wonder to behold', said Sennacherib. Sennacherib's city, with its 120,000 inhabitants, was so big it is only partly covered by modern Mosul.

Blessed with at least seven children, he placed his eldest on the Babylonian throne, but a Babylonian faction arrested the boy and sold him to the king of Elam, who hated the Assyrians and executed him. Now it was personal: 'I put on my coat of mail . . . my helmet,' Sennacherib recorded. 'I hurriedly mounted my great battle chariot' and 'stopped their advance, decimated them with arrow and spear. I slashed their throats, cut off their precious lives as one cuts a string.' In 689, he destroyed Babylon. 'Like the waters of a storm, I made the contents of their gullets and entrails slither along the earth,' he wrote with macabre Assyrian glee. 'My prancing steeds plunged into their blood. The wheels of my chariot . . . were spattered with blood . . . Their testicles I cut off; I ripped out their genitals like seeds of summer cucumbers.'

Sennacherib was supreme: yet it is one of the ironies of power that kings of the world struggle to cope with their own children.

DEPRESSION OF A WORLD KING:
ESARHADDON AND TAHARQO

Sennacherib first favoured one of his surviving sons, Ardamullisi, then changed his mind and appointed the younger Esarhaddon: 'This is the son who shall succeed me.' But 'Jealousy overcame my brothers,' recorded Esarhaddon, 'plotting evil.'

Ardamullisi decided to assassinate his father and brother. Oblivious,

Sennacherib was praying at a Nineveh temple, kneeling, when his eldest son hacked him to death. But Esarhaddon exterminated his brothers and their entire families, though by the standards of House Tiglath-Pileser he was a milksop: the stress took its toll. He suffered fevers, loss of appetite, blisters and paranoia – what we would call depression. 'Is one day not enough for the king to mope and eat nothing?' wrote his doctors. 'This is already the third day!'

In Nineveh, he trained his youngest son, the remarkable Ashurbanipal, who now moved into the heir's residence, the House of Succession. 'I cantered on thoroughbreds, rode stallions raring to go,' recalled Ashurbanipal. 'I held a bow . . . I threw quivering lances; I took the reins of a chariot and made the wheels spin.' But he also studied. Even the most brutish dynasties become cultivated in the end. 'I learned . . . the hidden and secret lore of all the scribal arts. I'm able to recognize celestial and terrestrial omens and can discuss them with an assembly of scholars.' Ashurbanipal was also trained in vigilance and security by his grandmother, Naqia. Now he watched his father's back, as Esarhaddon marched against Egypt. Pharaoh Taharqo, son of Piye, was preparing to restore Egyptian power over Judah.

Just as this Nubian ruled the cradle of civilization, migrations were starting that would change the continent. Most of Africa had long been the domain of Khoesan hunter-foragers, but in the west – today's Nigeria, Niger and Cameroon – Bantu-speaking peoples farmed beans, sorghum and millet, herded cattle and sheep, forged weapons from iron ore and traded with the north. Now, for reasons we may never know, the Bantu started to migrate slowly southwards, settling the best land, killing, conquering and marrying into the Khoesan, whom they slowly drove into more marginal regions. Their warlords probably conquered kingdoms, but since they left no pyramids or inscriptions to equal Kush, we can track them only by the march of their Bantu language.

To their north, Taharqo trained his army Assyrian-style: on a sixty-mile all-night run, 'the king himself was on horseback to see his army running when he exercised with them in the desert behind Memphis in the ninth hour of the night. They reached the Great Lake at sunrise.' Then he led them into Judah and Phoenicia, agreeing treaties with Jerusalem and Tyre, both of them keen to escape the Assyrian yoke.

In 674, Esarhaddon invaded Egypt. Taharqo defeated him, but three years later Esarhaddon, after destroying Tyre, swooped across Sinai and besieged Memphis. Taharqo retreated to Kush, leaving his treasury and his women behind. Yet he returned. If he thought Esarhaddon's death had saved him, he was wrong. In 667, the young scholar-king

Ashurbanipal finally woke the Kush empire: 'I made Egypt and Nubia feel my weapons bitterly.'*

ASHURBANIPAL AND GRANDMOTHER: A POWER PARTNERSHIP

The security chief and top adviser of Ashurbanipal was his grandmother, Naqia. It was she who backed his succession and orchestrated the oaths of allegiance across the empire. This history has a cast of female potentates but few equal Naqia, who ordered, 'Whether plotters are bearded or half-men [eunuchs] or royal princes, kill them and bring them to Zakutu [Naqia] and Ashurbanipal King of Assyria your lord.'

Ashurbanipal was a scholar who proudly wore a pen as well as a sword, but the Assyrian empire was surprisingly bureaucratic: scribes were constantly present with their hinged writing boards to record taxes, booty, royal orders. Some 32,000 cuneiform tablets survive. But Ashurbanipal was also the first collector of literature, creating a library of scholarly texts, oracular requests and reports and buying other collections from Babylon, the home of high culture, and he was contemptuous of his coarse forefathers who knew nothing of books. Yet, however fastidious he was, warfare was an essential part of being a world king. Lions were hunted† – and so were people.

Ashurbanipal turned eastwards to strike Elam, whose king, Teumman, was shot with an arrow in the back and beheaded, the head brought back to Nineveh. Ashurbanipal poured libations from his trophy as prisoners paraded around the city wearing decapitated heads around their necks. In the royal pleasure park, the king and chief queen Libbalisharrat, sitting on thrones facing each other, relaxed at parties and played board games, as servants fanned them and served pomegranates and grapes, eunuchs officiated, lyres and harpists played and tame lions were walked. This inscription presents a scene of serene splendour, yet

---

* The House of Alara, still using pharaonic titles and burying their kings in pyramids, ruled Kush for several centuries more, finally moving the capital deeper into Sudan to Meroe to be safer from Egyptian invasion.

† Lion killing was the motif of Assyrian monarchy. Iraqi lions were smaller than those in Africa, but the beasts were corralled by armies of beaters, and driven towards the king by eunuchs holding mastiffs, watched by huge crowds. It was religious, it was sport and it was training for warfare. After the hunt, the king celebrated: 'I, Ashurbanipal, king of the universe, king of the land of Ashur, whom Ashur and Ninlil endowed with supreme strength, who killed lions with the terrible bow of Ishtar, lady of battle: I offered a libation of wine over them.'

there is a very Assyrian touch: the head of King Teumman hangs upside down in a tree next to the picnic like a gruesome fruit.

Ashurbanipal's victories did not alleviate the tensions within his own family. He was a control freak who interfered in his brother's subordinate kingdom: 'My faithless brother Shamashshumukin, whom I treated well and established as king of Babylon, forgot this kindness – and planned evil,' assembling a coalition of Babylonians, Elamites, Arabs and Aramaeans. After four years of war, his brother threw himself into the flames of his palace. Ashurbanipal ordered tongues to be slit or ripped out, prisoners were flayed, and in the temple 'between the colossi where they had cut down Sennacherib, my grandfather, I cut them down as an offering to his soul. Their dismembered bodies I fed to dogs, swine, fish of the deep . . .' Elam was sacked, yet the family war weakened Assyria, and the constant campaigns in Iran failed to declaw the dynamic peoples of the steppe who regarded Ashurbanipal's empire as prey.

Just after these victories, Ashurbanipal got a nasty shock: an army of sheepskin-clad nomadic horsemen, Medes and Persians, led by a Mede khan Dia-oku, rode into Assyria right up to the walls of Nineveh. These Parsa (Persians) and Mada (Medes), the most successful of the Aryan peoples of the Iranian plateau, rode tough little Nisean horses, lived in portable *ger*, tents, and tended their herds of horses – 160,000 of them – enjoying themselves raiding, feasting, gambling, storytelling and horseracing.*

To defeat these barbarians he hired other barbarians, the Scythians, Aryan horsemen who ranged across the steppes of central Asia. The Mede khan's son was killed. The son of one Persian khan – who also called himself king of Anshan – Kurosh, sent his son to Ashurbanipal's court as a hostage. The other Persian khan was Haxamanis (Achaemenes). As these shaggy horsemen galloped ignominiously back

---

* The Medes and Persians, guided by a class of priestly diviners, the magi (from whom we get the word magic), saw the world as an endless duel between light and darkness, truth and lies, ruled by the fire-giving god of light, wisdom and truth, Ahura-Mazda. They were inspired by an Aryan prophet, Zoroaster, who may have lived in Bactria during the second millennium – or much later in the time of Cyrus or Darius. Only fragments of his life were preserved: his birth as a baby that laughed rather than bawled; his vision at the age of thirty in which he saw a being of lightness who revealed the truth of Ahura-Mazda (Wise Lord), who represented *asha* – order and truth – while fighting the darkness of Angra Mainyu (Destructive Spirit), who represented *druj* – the chaos and the lie. Much of Zoroastrianism, expressed in the Persian sacred text the *Avesta*, is linked to Indian Hindu religion, referring as it does to Indian gods such as Mithra, thus showing a shared Indo-Iranian origin. Unlike Jesus Christ but like Muhammad, Zoroaster married and had children; like Jesus, he died violently aged seventy-seven by an assassin's dagger.

to their herds, who would have believed that these two khans were the progenitors of the world-conquering Persian greats, Cyrus and Darius?

Ashurbanipal was exhausted. 'Let the king apply this lotion and perhaps the fever will abate,' advised his doctor. 'I'm sending ointment.' But when, after forty-two years of war and refinement, Ashurbanipal died at the age of sixty, it looked as if Assyria would rule for ever.

Yet, just fifteen years later, Nineveh would fall and out of a story of cannibalism, burning cities and vines growing out of royal vaginas rose the family that would rule an empire on three continents.

ACT TWO
100 MILLION

Haxamanis and Alcmaeon:
Houses of Persia and Athens

NEBUCHADNEZZAR, HIS QUEEN AND THE
WHORE OF BABYLON

In 612 BC, the armies of Assyria's enemies surrounded Nineveh, trapping the king, Ashurbanipal's son Sinsharishkun, within the doomed city. The seven and a half miles of walls were reinforced, the broad gates narrowed, but the very size of this capital of the world made it almost impossible to defend. Attracted to the prizes of this now lame giant, new predators arrived to feast on the body.

A Babylonian potentate, Nabopolassar, had seized the throne there in 626. Determined to regain Babylon, Sinsharishkun called in Egyptian help, but in 616 Nabopolassar defeated the once invincible Assyrians.

Yet it took the Median cavalry to bring them down. The Median king, Uvaxštra (Cyaxares in Greek) – son of Fravartis, who had been killed by Ashurbanipal – was based in his mountain capital of Ecbatana, a city of seven circular walls fortified with bastions painted in bright colours. As he grew up, Scythians had taken over most of Iran. When he was ready, Uvaxštra invited the Scythian chieftains to a banquet and, when they were drunk, killed them all. He then united the Median tribes of western Iran, and allied with Nabopolassar of Babylon to carve up Assyria. In 612, 'the King of Babylon mobilized his army and the King of the Medes joined him. They advanced along the Tigris towards Nineveh.' The siege lasted three months, during which Scythians arrived to join the mayhem. In August, the attackers smashed the dykes, and the flooding enabled them to breach the walls. The fighting was savage – at the Halzi Gate, skeletons of men and women, even a baby, struck by arrows, lay tangled for many centuries where they fell. 'A great slaughter was made of the people,' recounts the *Babylonian Chronicles*. 'Horsemen charging, flashing sword, and glittering spear, hosts of slain, heaps of corpses, dead without end, they stumble over the bodies.' At the palace Sinsharishkun – last of House Tiglath-Pileser – perished in the flames.

Nabopolassar commandeered the Assyrian kingdom for his Babylonian empire; Uvaxštra, who had been little more than a horse-breeding chieftain two years earlier, ruled from northern Iran westwards into Türkiye. Uvaxštra gave his daughter Amartis to Nabopolassar's son, Crown Prince Nebuchadnezzar. But Egypt, invited in by the Assyrians, was not yet finished.

Pharaoh Necho rode up the Levantine coast to defeat the Babylonians. On the way north, he was challenged by Josiah, king of Judah, who sensed an opportunity for glorious independence, a moment of exhilaration captured in the Bible. But Necho routed the Judeans at Megiddo – the biblical origin of Armageddon – and then conquered Syria.

In 605, Nebuchadnezzar halted the Egyptians at Carchemish and 'inflicted such a defeat on them that none returned home'. Then, learning that his father was dying, he literally galloped home – 620 miles – to be crowned twenty-two days later.

Nebuchadnezzar spent most of his long reign suppressing rebellions, successfully on the Phoenician coast, less so in Canaan. In 586, Zedekiah of Judah defied him: Nebuchadnezzar stormed Jerusalem and destroyed the city, deporting most of the Jews to his capital: Babylon became a huge building site as he constructed eleven miles of walls with an inner royal city entered by the colossal Ishtar Gate glazed in deep blue and decorated with Ishtar's lions, Adad's bulls and Marduk's dragons. This led to the Processional Way known as May the Arrogant Not Flourish and so to the temple of Esagila and a ziggurat tower known as The House That Is the Border between Heaven and Earth, the centrepiece of the city. Home to 250,000 people – Babylonians, Scythians, Greeks, Medes, Jews – Babylon was notorious for its wild pleasures. The Jews denounced the king as 'destroyer of nations' and wrote holy books in a distinctive monotheistic voice. Refusing to vanish like other defeated peoples, the Jews dreamed of a return to their sacred city Zion amid the sun-blistered wilderness of Judah: Jerusalem. It was a longing that defined them: religions and peoples are formed by shared experiences of suffering, lived and relived as inherited stories. 'By the rivers of Babylon,' they sang, 'they sat down and remembered Zion.'

Everyone enjoyed the metropolis – except those few austere Jews who called it the Whore of Babylon.* But in the palace the Median queen was

---

* Their books were collated into the Bible – exceptional because it records the unique survival of the Jewish people and faith in the face of political and physical destruction. But it became a book of universal significance because the founder of Christianity, Jesus, was a practising Jew who revered and fulfilled its prophecies. In turn, Muhammad, the founder of Islam, studied and revered both Old and New Testaments, which he often cited in his own sacred text, the Quran, making them also sacred for Islam. There is slim evidence that the biblical story of the Tower of Babel might have been influenced by the Babylon ziggurat, but there is no evidence that the Jews deported to Babylonia hated the ziggurat or called

homesick. Nebuchadnezzar supposedly built the Hanging Gardens of Babylon to comfort her.

Her father Uvaxštra advanced into Anatolia until he was stopped by a regional potentate, Alyattes, who, based in Sardis, ruled Lydia, a rich realm extending to the Aegean, trading between Babylon and Greece. Alyattes was the first to cast coins, money that gleamed with electrum, an alloy of silver and gold. The Lydians invented coins at the same time as they appeared in India and China.

Uvaxštra's army was made up of Medes, Persians and Scythians; the latter were training his young men in their unsurpassed ability to shoot bows on the gallop, skills aided by first the bit, then foot supports, which gradually improved from a length of rope into wooden and eventually iron stirrups. Together these innovations meant they could control their mounts while shooting their bows. But when Uvaxštra insulted these Scythians, they killed the boys, cooked them in a stew and fed them to the king before seeking asylum with Alyattes, who refused to surrender the cannibalistic gourmets. Their armies met in May 585 on the River Halys when suddenly 'the day became night' – a solar eclipse – which so amazed both sides that they stopped fighting and made peace: Uvaxštra married his son Rishtivaiga (Spearthrower, Astyages) to Alyattes' daughter Aryenis.

When both kings died, Rishtivaiga found himself at the centre of a family network as brother-in-law to Nebuchadnezzar of Babylon and the new king Croesus of Lydia, who boasted that he was the world's richest king. To keep his tribal federacy together, Rishtivaiga married his daughter Mandana to a Persian khan, king of Anshan, Cambyses (Kabūjiya).* When their baby, named Cyrus – Koresh – half Mede, half Persian, was born, he was brought up like all Persian khans until he was six by his mother Mandana, who still at this stage churned milk, made bread, spun cloth. Then he was handed over to his father Cambyses to be trained in horsemanship and marksmanship, wearing trousers and leather chaps.† When Cambyses died, Cyrus donned the cowhide coat,

---

it anything other than 'the temple of Marduk'. Babylon may have influenced the Book of Revelation, but the Whore is probably a much later metaphor for the Roman empire.

* According to the Greek historian Herodotos writing a century later, Astyages (Rishtivaiga) suffered a nightmare about Mandana in which she urinated a golden jet that flooded his empire. But when Mandana became pregnant, Astyages dreamed that a vine grew out of her vagina until it was entwined around the whole of Asia: the child would unite the Medes and Persians.

† The Persians and Medes 'introduced trouser-wearing to the world', writes Lloyd Llewellyn-Jones. In Egypt, Greece and Iraq, people mainly wore robes of light cloth. In 2008 the mummified body of a boy from 500 BC was discovered in an Iranian salt mine wearing a tunic and baggy 'harem' trousers. Herodotos was horrified by the vulgarity of trousers: 'The Athenians were the first Greeks to endure the sight of Persian clothing.' Yet the trousers caught on.

the *gaunaka*, of kings of Anshan and started to plan the destruction of his grandfather Rishtivaiga, who had alienated his khans by adopting fancy court ritual and bureaucratic controls. One of them, Arbaku, sent an appeal to Cyrus sewn inside the body of a hare: 'The Median nobles will join you.' Cyrus extended his power by marrying a khan's daughter, Cassandane, from the respected Haxamanishiya (Achaemenid) clan, with whom he had two sons. But he also negotiated with the king of Babylon, Nabunid (Nabonidus), against their mutual Median enemy.

When Rishtivaiga cavorted with a concubine, she sang about a 'lion who had a wild boar in his power but let him into his lair'.

'Who is this wild boar?' asked Rishtivaiga.

'Cyrus,' she replied. But before Rishtivaiga could break Cyrus, the Persian gathered his khans at Pathragarda, his capital near Shiraz: 'I'm the man destined to undertake your liberation; you're the match of the Medes. Fling off the yoke of Rishtivaiga!' Cyrus marched against his grandfather: in 550 at Pasargadae, the Persians broke before the Median charges, but their women opened their robes and flashed their vulvas at their men, shouting, 'Where are you off to, quitters? Do you want to crawl back into where you came from?' The Persians turned and fought, Cyrus seized Rishtivaiga, took his capital Ecbatana and married his daughter.

Next, Cyrus came up against the richest man in the world, Croesus.

CYRUS AND QUEEN TOMYRIS: CONQUEROR TO GOBLET

Croesus claimed he was descended from the Greek god Herakles (Hercules) and regularly consulted the ancient Greek oracle at Delphi – but he was not Greek himself. Yet as master of Eurasian trade, whose currency was widely used, he was as at home with the people of the Aegean as with those of the Euphrates (he was after all brother-in-law of Nebuchadnezzar, cousin of Cyrus). But now Cyrus had to be stopped, so Croesus turned to the Greeks, recruiting two Greek city states, Sparta and Athens, to join Babylon and Egypt.

Croesus' fixer on Greek matters was an Athenian nobleman named Alcmaeon, descended from the half-divine king Nestor, and member of one of the richest families in the city. Alcmaeon did so well that Croesus offered to pay him as much as he could carry from the Lydian treasury. In a story that illustrated his family's voracity, Alcmaeon turned up in Sardis wearing loose clothes filled with pockets and wide boots that he filled with Croesian coins, adding to the family fortune. The story of

Alcmaeon was not just that of Athens but of the Greeks themselves.

After the chaos of 1200, when the Mycenaean kingdoms were over-thrown, the Greeks gathered in villages that coalesced into small cities (*poleis*) – the process known as synoecism – where they developed a con-cept of communal self-government. Their Greekness centred on their language, developed from the Phoenicians whom they encountered around the Mediterranean: Phoenicians only used consonants; the Greeks added vowels to develop the first alphabetic system of writing. Then came their stories. Around 850, writing and reading started to spread.* *Rhapsodes* – song-stitchers – recited poems at festivals. Drama, developing out of religious festivals, became popular. It was not so much that Greeks placed humanity at the centre of their world; all people did that. What was new was their consciousness of this self-focus.† Their sculptors developed the skill to fashion human likeness out of marble. Their religion was a set of rituals rather than a system of beliefs, concerned with living rather than afterlife. They worshipped a pantheon of flawed, greedy gods, led by Zeus, and treasured stories of half-divine supermen, like Hercules, and god-blessed travellers, like Odysseus, whose global exploits reflected the voyages of Greek sailors.‡ 'Are you here on business,' asks a character in *The Odyssey*, 'or traversing the seas as reckless raiders?' The Greeks, like their rivals the Phoenicians, were seafarers, traders and pirates, colonizing the Mediterranean they called the Great Sea in ships powered by rows of oars.

Yet not all their cites were naval: Sparta was a land-based monarchy, more precisely a diarchy ruled by two kings from rival dynasties, de-scended from Hercules, elected to rule with a twenty-eight-man council

---

* Greeks had started to write captions on their drinking cups. Around 750 BC, one of the earliest examples, at the Greek settlement on Ischia in the Bay of Naples, a Greek named Nestor etched three lines on to his drinking cup that combined verse, storytelling, theology, sex and drinking: 'Nestor's hearty-drinking cup am I. He who drinks this cup will soon take fire with fair-crowned Aphrodite's hot desire.'

† They saw the world as a system that could be studied by lovers of wisdom, *philosophoi*. Around 500 BC, the contrarian philosopher Heraklitos of Ephesus first used the word cosmos – order – to mean the universe. 'All things come into being by conflict of opposites,' he said, 'and everything flows' in a constant evolution: 'No man ever steps in the same river twice.' His view of the infallibility of gods and kings is always relevant: 'Eternity is a child moving counters in a game; the power of kings is like a child's game.' Finally he was the first to define war as one of the engines of human development: 'War is the father of all and king of all; and some he shows as gods, others as men, some he makes slaves, others free.'

‡ Between 750 and 650, a group of writers, later personalized as 'Homer', wrote two epic poems, *The Iliad* and *The Odyssey*, channelling ancient Mycenaean tales. Homer called the Greeks 'Argives' or 'Achaeans', but a common ancestor named Hellen was invented in a poem *Catalogue of Women* to give them a name for themselves: Hellenes. It was the Romans who much later called them Graeci, after the first Greek-speaking tribe they encountered.

of Elders, assuming command in times of war. The Peloponnesian city was organized around a small citizenry of Spartiates who did not trade but served as soldiers in order to overawe a conquered subject population of serfs – the helots, benighted inhabitants of Helos. Spartiates were trained by living in a barracks, not with their families; they dined with their soldier messmates and maintained their martial ferocity and the obedience of the underclass by sending squads of adolescent Spartiates annually into the countryside to kill a certain number of serfs; they were also spurred by wargames such as missions to steal cheeses, and by having ephebophilic relationships with twenty-something men.* They married in their twenties, but did not live with their families until they were thirty and only ceased military service at sixty. Deformed children were exposed – that is, abandoned to the elements. They prided themselves on manners and control, and were so curt that the word laconic comes from Laconia, the Spartan homeland. Yet Spartiate women, famed for fitness, blondeness and morality, trained in tiny tunics, nicknamed 'thigh-flashers' by prudish Athenians.

Dominated by a martial nobility, Greek society was macho, social and competitive: men exercised naked at *gymnasia*; at *symposia* dinners, they drank mixed wine and water out of a shared bowl, symposiasts told stories and had sex with pipe-playing *hetairai* – courtesans – or cupbearer boys. Their peasant farmers served as infantrymen, hoplites, wearing iron cuirasses, greaves, plumed helmets, and they fought together in a *phalanx*, guarded by their interlinked shields; nobles fought on horseback – all of them much in demand as mercenaries. In distant Babylon, Nebuchadnezzar employed Greek auxiliaries.

The Greeks prided themselves on their involvement in governing the *polis* – politics based on good governance, *eunomia*, and freedom, *eleutheria*. Yet their *poleis* were dominated by aristocracies and often ruled by tyrants, sometimes by benign autocrats, who were supported by middle and lower classes against overweening nobles.

Alcmaeon and his Athenian family were typical of these aristocrats. Athens had developed as an aristocracy in which an elected council of nine archons ruled, presenting their ideas to an assembly of male citizens. A mythical Alcmaeonid was said to have been the first archon in the eighth century BC, and in the 630s the clan leader Megacles and his

---

* This was common to all societies in ancient Greece: there was no concept of sexual identity. The relationship between an older man – the *erastes* – and a youth, generally fifteen to nineteen – the *eromenos* – was a normal stage in male life; most men married and had children as well as intimate friendships with other men. But the virile man took the position of sexual superiority.

son Alcmaeon ruled as archons. In 621, a nobleman Drakon drafted the first laws in his own blood, but his draconian code scarcely restrained the aristocratic faction fights that often led to massacres: eighty skeletons with bound wrists were found in one mass grave. Around 593, Solon, an archon, established a constitution that turned the poor into full citizens, but its system still favoured the Alcmaeonids and other clans. When another Megacles murdered his opponents, the entire family were expelled from Athens, even down to the bones of their ancestors. Yet they rose again.

The Athenian rivalry with Sparta started early: in 510, when Athens was ruled by a tyrant, the Alcmaeonids, now led by Cleisthenes, appealed for help to the Spartans who, seeing the chance to make Athens a client state, drove out the autocrat. Instead Cleisthenes dispensed with the Spartans and then promised new powers to the people who had supported him. Athens depended on its navy; its triremes needed rowers; and that meant the people had to be consulted. Cleisthenes devised the rule of the people – democracy – by an assembly (*ecclesia*) of all the male citizens (excluding women and slaves).* Real democracy was regarded as election by lottery: the ruling Council of Five Hundred was chosen by lot. Only the ten commanders – *strategoi* – were chosen annually by a show of hands or by a vote using pebbles. Devised by a member of the most ambitious family in Athens, people power was never quite as democratic as it seemed – not with the Alcmaeonids involved.†

In 547, as he negotiated his anti-Cyrus alliance, Croesus thrice consulted Pyphia, high priestess of the Delphic Oracle, via his Athenian ally Alcmaeon, focusing on war with Persia. Her oracular reply was a masterpiece of ambiguity: if he attacked Persia, he would destroy a great empire. Cyrus marched immediately. In 546, when the kings fought, Cyrus placed his dromedaries, which carried his supplies, at the front, thereby panicking Croesus' cavalry. Croesus was executed, and Cyrus dispatched Arbaku to mop up the Greek cities of Ionia, the Aegean coast.

Only Babylon held out, but its empire was mired in crisis. In 539, Cyrus routed the Babylonians. Now King of the World, he paraded into Babylon on a white stallion accompanied by his son Cambyses and held a durbar for the princes of his vast new empire at which the ex-king Nabonidus was executed. Now he showed respect for the Babylonian

---

* At the apogee of Athens, a third of its people were enslaved.

† There was another type of Greek state. In the wild, mountainous north, closer to the peoples of the Balkans and the Eurasian steppe, Greek kingdoms Macedonia and Epiros were *ethne*, semi-tribal states that had evolved into military monarchies.

elite – including the top banking family, the Egibi* – and careful reverence for Marduk in his temple of Esgila where he buried a clay cylinder
that recast his career of conquest and killing as the liberation of Babylon
and all his subject peoples.†

Yet his empire would be different from that of Tiglath-Pileser and Nebuchadnezzar. All deportees could return home. All could worship their
own gods and manage local affairs – provided they absolutely obeyed
the King of the World and paid his taxes. In 537, 40,000 Jews returned
to Jerusalem to rebuild their Temple: no wonder some regarded Cyrus
as the anointed one, the Messiah.

Now finally he could relax in his new palace and gardens – *pairidaeza*,
origin of the word paradise‡ – at his capital at Pathragarda (Pasargadae).
His empire was now the largest the world had seen, but could he keep it
together? Cyrus accepted no limits. Egypt was next, but in the east a Scythian queen based on the steppes between Turkmenistan and Kazakhstan
was raiding his lands. She too had to be destroyed. Summoning his sons,
he appointed Cambyses, king of Babylon, as his successor and assigned
the second boy Bardis to rule Bactria before he himself set off.

The queen's name was Tomyris (Tahmirih), which simply means
brave. Women leaders were much more common among the nomadic
tribes of Scythians§ in the north and the Arabs in the south than among

* The Egibi family were the first known business dynasty in history: they dealt in property,
land, slaves, trading and lending, surviving adeptly through dynasties and conquests. An
archive of 1,700 clay tablets reveals their dealings over five generations from about 600
to 480 BC, referencing promissory notes and divisions of land. They married their sons
to the daughters of other rich families. Dowries included land, silver, slaves and entire
businesses. Starting as land managers under Nebuchadnezzar II and rising to become
judges under Nabonidus, they now switched to serving Cyrus and would prosper even
more under his successor (but one) Darius. They progressed from lending to rulers to
becoming officials for the Great Kings.
† The cylinder is surely the most successful PR document of ancient times and its reputation as the 'first declaration of human rights' is absurd: Cyrus and his times had no concept
of human rights.
‡ The Jewish writers of the Bible based their idea of the Garden of Eden on the Persian
pairidaeza.
§ The Scythians were skilled horsemen but also exquisite craftsmen. Like their fellow
Aryans, the Persians, they revered fire as the senior of their seven gods, whose relations
with men were mediated by transgender shamans. 'Their favoured intoxicants,' wrote
Herodotos, 'were hashish with fermented mare's milk.' Scythians cherished silver and
gold artefacts, beautifully worked, but they were a civilization that ritualized aggression.
They crucified and beheaded their enemies, scalped them (scalping developed simultaneously in the Old and New Worlds), flayed them and used their skins to cover their quivers,
their blood as a drink and their heads, sliced below the eyebrows, as drinking cups. Every
hundredth prisoner of war was sacrificed. As for their own dead, Scythians removed their
brains and guts, which they ate, and interred them in burial chambers, filled with gold
artefacts, sacrificed slaves and relatives and horses, all covered by mounds.

the settled peoples, because their women fought alongside the men on equal terms: 37 per cent of Scythian warriors found in tombs were women with bodies trained to ride and fire arrows, wearing armour and golden headdresses, lying beside horses in golden trappings – just like the men. The Greek myth of the one-breasted she-warriors, the Amazons, was based on the Scythians.

These were the people that Cyrus now pursued, but somehow the septuagenarian world conqueror was himself killed. Tomyris crucified and beheaded him in the Scythian manner, stuffing his head into a wineskin filled with blood with the words, 'I warned you I'd quench your thirst for blood, and so I shall.'*

She made a cup out of his head.

At a king's death, the sacred fires were extinguished. In 529 BC, the Persians brought back what was left of Cyrus, but a royal funeral in which the waxed body was borne on a golden chariot was impossible.†

DARIUS AND BUDDHA: THE WHEEL

The news that Cyrus had 'gone away from the throne' shook the empire. Cyrus' son, Cambyses II, underwent the ritual investiture that combined sacred blessing and tribal glory at the shrine of the goddess Anahita (the Persian equivalent of Ishtar) in Pasargadae. A Great King underwent a metamorphosis, throwing aside his own clothes and choosing a throne name, donning the robe of Cyrus, drinking magical (and intoxicating) elixirs of sacred terebinth and distilled milk cooked up by the magi, taking the sceptre, then being crowned with the *kidaris* or royal tiara, before all the courtiers threw themselves to their knees in obeisance.

Cambyses planned to finish his father's work and take Egypt. He had to prove himself fast. First he married his two elder sisters, Atossa and Roxane, to prevent them marrying anyone else, appointing his strapping brother Bardiya, a muscled bowman extraordinaire known as Strongbody, as satrap of Bactria – and culling all opposition. Accompanied by Strongbody and a well-connected young courtier Darius, and raising a force that reflected his family's astonishing multinational empire,

---

* Herodotos is our only source for this Scythian story, wherein Cyrus's death reflects the Greek view of Persian kings as voracious, effeminate tyrants.
† The Persians buried the giblets in a golden sarcophagus in Cyrus' simple Lydian-style temple that still stands near his paradise of Pasargadae.

pointy-hatted Scythians, Medes, Persians and a Phoenician navy, he conquered Egypt and killed the pharaoh yet treated Egyptian traditions respectfully. He planned to attack Carthage (a plan vetoed by his Phoenician sailors, who refused to attack their compatriots) and instead marched down the Nile and into Nubia and Ethiopia. His successes were remarkable, yet he did not inspire loyalty.* Jealous of Strongbody, Cambyses sent him back to Persia, then, tormented by stories of his treason, ordered his killing. In 522, Strongbody declared himself king, while in Cambyses' own retinue a cabal of seven respected khans, all related to the dynasty, plotted against him. The youngest of them was Darius (Dārayavauš, or Holder of Good), aged twenty-two, grandson of the khan of the Haxamanishiya clan who had served Cyrus as quiver bearer and was now Cambyses' lance bearer. Even though he was the junior member, he was tall, charismatic, athletic and remarkably confident: he emerged as the candidate for king.

As Cambyses rushed home, he met with an unfortunate accident: dismounting from his horse, he cut himself with his dagger and died of gangrene. Darius later wrote that Cambyses 'died his own death' – whatever that means. One has to wonder if the Seven quietly killed him. Now they galloped for home, where Strongbody had married his surviving sister Atossa but alienated his own nobles. The Seven arrived at his fortress near the sacred mountain Bisitun, where Strongbody was cavorting with a concubine. A eunuch let the hit squad into the royal chamber where the half-naked Strongbody put up such a fight with a stool that it took all Seven to subdue him. Darius' brother Artafarna delivered the fatal stab. The Seven met at dawn on horseback to decide who was to be king. Whosever horse neighed first would be he. Darius ordered his groom to dip his fingers into a mare's vulva first and then, just as sun rose, to wave them temptingly under the nose of his stallion, which then neighed. The other six fell to their knees before the prince, who now adopted the throne name Darius. More likely he had been the king-designate from the start.† The Seven agreed that the rest of them

---

* According to Herodotos and other Greek sources, he was alleged to be 'half mad', and it was said that he slaughtered the sacred Egyptian bull Apis, used humans for target practice, killed his wife, buried twelve noblemen upside down and taught justice to a corrupt judge by skinning him, tanning him and using the leather to make a chair which he then offered to his victim's son and successor as judge: 'Remember,' he said, 'on what you sit.'
† Herodotos and the court doctor-historian Ctesias both tell this story, implying that Darius somehow cheated his way to the throne – very Persian behaviour in Greek eyes. The story of Darius' equine vaginal gambit reflected the importance of horses in Persian–Median culture. A horse was regularly sacrificed in honour of Cyrus. The story was based on the Persian practice, hippomancy, divination using the behaviour of horses.

could always have access to Darius even if he was in bed with a girl.

The empire was in ruins; nine contenders rose to claim the throne. But blessed with irrepressible energy and invincible luck, claiming to be the warrior of Truth, manifestation of Ahura-Mazda, and aided by his six compadres, within two years Darius defeated all contenders, whom he dubbed 'agents of the Lie', definition of evil in Zarathustrianism. They were skinned and stuffed, crucified and rectally impaled on the walls of Ecbatana near Mount Bisitun. There, on a blood-red cliff-face, with a winged Ahura-Mazda, chief god of truth, order and war, hovering above him, Darius himself appears, brandishing his bow, sporting the *kidaris*, the bejewelled robe, and a square-cut plaited beard scented with oil, as he crushes a pretender beneath his foot – 'I cut off his nose, ears, tongue and tore out one eye' – while the others writhe in chains awaiting their impalement. The message, in three languages, was pure fake news, obscuring the killings of Cambyses and Strongbody and the usurping of the throne and merging his ancestry with that of Cyrus: 'I am Darius, King of Kings ... a Haxamanishiya. Whoever helped my family, I favoured; whoever was hostile, I eliminated.'

Darius the Great was that most unusual phenomenon, a warlord of panache and stamina who was both visionary and master of detail, so much so that his subjects nicknamed him the Trader. He launched an imperial currency, the daric, but he was also a master of security: his spies – King's Ears – reported any treason to his secret-police boss entitled the King's Eye. Constantly travelling in splendour, a maestro of colossal projects, tolerant of other religions (helping the Jews rebuild the Temple in Jerusalem), he built a new capital at Parsa (Persepolis) with enormous throne halls and a ceremonial staircase designed to be ascended, probably by Darius, on horseback, all built with 'the gold of Sardis and Bactria, lapis and carnelian of Sogdiana, silver and ebony from India, friezes from Ionia, ivory from Ethiopia and India'. As a young man he had married the daughter of one of the Seven, with whom he had three sons, but now he married all the wives and daughters of Cyrus, Cambyses and Strongbody, having children with each. Atossa, Cyrus' daughter, now married her third Great King. In a marital history brimming with blood and betrayal, both her brother-kings had likely been murdered by her new husband Darius. It was enough either to crush a woman's spirit or, in her case, to fortify it for she became the mother of three sons, including Xerxes, and a political force.*

---

* When she was older, Atossa found a tumour in her breast. Most of Darius' doctors were Egyptians, but Darius had captured a Greek doctor, Democedes, who had set the king's broken ankle. Democedes lived splendidly as royal doctor but longed to return home. Now

Darius' women and children resided in a protected household: women were invisible in the inscriptions of court life; indeed, since the court was frequently on the road, women travelled in special giant curtained carriages which in camp were placed together to create a familial compound. Yet royal women were potentates who ran their own estates. The family court, protected by trusted eunuchs – African and Colchian (Georgian) boys seized or bought in childhood and then castrated – was run by Darius' mother Irdabama, who ruled when he was away.

Darius was restless: when he travelled, the courtiers and their wives and families – 15,000 people – went with him. The sacred fire was borne ahead of him, pulled by eight white horses, then came the magi, followed by the empty carriage of Ahura-Mazda, then the crack royal bodyguard the Immortals and the top courtiers, led by the Master of the Thousand, and the Royal Companions, followed in turn by the queen's household. Wherever he stopped, a palatial round tent would be erected at the centre of a resplendent tented capital.

The empire was a family business, with Darius' brother, Artafarna, King Stabber, ruling as satrap of Greek Ionia, and most commanders being relatives or descendants of the Seven. But inevitably at least one of the Seven would resent that sacred kingship of their old messmate. Vidafarnâ (Intraphrenes) was outraged when one day refused entry to the royal apartments and cut the ears off the guards. When the rest of the Seven all wisely disavowed him, Darius executed Vidafarnâ and his family. Recalling the death of Cyrus in battle, Darius considered the succession: his sons were raised as warrior princes, growing up in the harem, awoken at dawn by trumpets, tutored by Greek eunuchs and magi, hardened by iced baths, practising horsemanship with spear and bow to enable them to accompany their father on lion hunts and to war. Even the princesses were taught bow shooting, riding and history. Among his many sons, Xerxes (Khshayarsha – He Who Rules Over Heroes) was handsome, brave in war and in the hunt. Male beauty was evidence of Ahura-Mazda's favour: slaves were trained as beauticians; Persian men wore make-up and eyeliner; false beards and hairpieces were so valuable that they were taxed; beards were curled and anointed with perfumed oil. Getting dressed in the morning was a special ritual.

Darius, like Cyrus, recognized no limits. Once he was secure, the Trader ordered the building of a canal between the Nile and the Red

---

he operated successfully on Atossa's tumour, the first recorded mastectomy. Allowed to join a Persian embassy to Greece, he escaped and returned home.

Sea, opening Mediterranean trade to Arabia and India. Then in 516 he invaded Afghanistan and India.

As Darius conquered provinces that his successors would rule for centuries – seven satrapies covered modern Afghanistan – the news of his invasion would have reached a prince living in the kingdom of Magada, one of the sixteen *mahajanapadas*, principalities of north-east India, dominated by high castes, Brahmin priests and *kshatriya* kings and nobles according to the Vedic rituals of what later became Hinduism.* But many of the cities were republics ruled by *sanghas*, popular assemblies. The prince's teachings both challenged and dovetailed with these existing religions to found what would become the first world religion.

Siddartha Gautama, the son of a minor ruler, a *kshatriya*, elder of the Shakya clan, and his wife, a princess of neighbouring Koliya (Nepal), enjoyed the noble lifestyle, at sixteen marrying his first cousin Yasodhara, with whom he had a son Rahula. 'I lived a spoilt, a very spoilt life.' But already he contemplated life and death, and was uneasy with his own pleasure-loving existence, deciding to seek enlightenment by embracing asceticism. Following Rahula's birth, he left his marital home to travel with two friends as a *sramana* – a seeker.

After studying meditation, he rejected extreme asceticism when he accepted food from a village girl named Sujata. Instead he embraced a Middle Way. Sitting to meditate beneath a pipal tree in a deer park at Sarnath, he awoke with knowledge that human life is frustrating and desperate, cursed with ambition and appetites, but this could be mitigated by the Four Noble Truths and understanding of the *dharma*, a path of duty that to him meant the cosmic truth that led, after a lifetime of contemplation and suffering following his programme of the Noble Eightfold Path, to nirvana, freedom from endless rebirth. 'We are what we think,' preached Gautama. 'All that we are arises with our thoughts. With our thoughts, we make the world.'

Now he formed the first *sangha*, a coterie of monks who believed they were witnessing the wheel-turning revelations of an exceptional human: the imagery of a chariot wheel turning to change consciousness and power was already part of Indian culture, used in the early Indus cities. They called Gautama's version the wheel of *dharma* – the *dharmachakra*

---

* Hinduism itself is composed of different beliefs, practices and scriptures. Many of its traditions emerged out of the divinely revealed *Vedas* (the 'knowledge', composed *c.* 1500–500 BC) and its later sacred Vedic texts including the *Puranas* ('old' or 'ancient', composed from around AD 300). The *Vedas* include liturgical hymns and guidance for Brahmins (priests). Only Brahmins had the authority to use the *Vedas* in rituals.

– and hailed him as Buddha, Enlightened One, though he never called himself that, preferring the modest Tathagata, the One Who's Here. His teachings channelled Vedic ethics and meditations, yet he also threatened the dominance of the Brahmins.

Settling in Kosala, now surrounded by many followers, Buddha was joined by his son Rahula, who became a monk. But Buddha experienced betrayal from within his own family: his cousin Devadatta tried to seize control and kill him. When that failed, Devadatta spun off his own sect.

As he aged, Buddha advised the *sangha* to 'meet in harmony, don't fall prey to worldly desires' and to 'preserve their personal mindfulness', but he refused to appoint an heir: 'I've taught the *dharma*, making no distinction of inner and outer . . . If there is anyone who thinks: "I'll take charge of the Order" . . . the Tathagata [himself] does not think in such terms. Why should the Tathagata make arrangements for the Order? I'm now old, worn out.'

In Kushinagar, he achieved in bodily death the elevated state of *parinirvana*, after which his adepts cremated him and distributed his bones and relics among his followers, who started to build domed stupas in which to store and revere them. Buddha left no writings, but his son Rahula and the *sangha* preserved his teachings until a council started to organize his order. Buddha did not claim to be a god, merely a sage, and did not wish to create a structured religion, leaving a metaphysical worldview instead. His popularity revealed the human need for a higher mission, to mitigate the terrifying unpredictability of life and the inevitability of death but also to share values and rituals across oceans and peoples: its power was that it offered salvation to all.*

After his death his followers formalized his ideas and rituals, and Buddha himself was soon regarded as divine, his very fingernails

---

* At the same time, in China, divided into warring kingdoms, a philosopher created his own moral order, founded on an ethical vision of China as a realm of families, a hierarchy starting with the ruler and extending down to the father's rule over his family. Kong Qiu, later known as Master Kong (latinized by seventeenth-century Jesuits into Confucius), was a pragmatist and an enthusiast, not merely a bloodless ascetic – 'Why didn't you say how passionate I am?' he used to ask his followers – and he liked to ride and hunt. But, faced with interminable wars and power plays, he advocated an ethical path, 'the Way': 'When the Way prevails under Heaven', there would be order; without it there would be chaos. Yet he also preached kindness: 'Is there one word to guide a person throughout life?' asked a follower. 'How about "reciprocity"?' suggested Confucius. 'Never impose on others what you would not choose for yourself.' It was a fourth-generation disciple, Mengzi (Mencius), who developed and structured his ideas. Confucius' *Analects*, written before 200 BC, proposed orderly realms, ruled by kings guided by virtue and advised by scholars like himself; prayer would win divine harmony in the cosmos which would in turn deliver moral harmony on earth.

revered. Yet it needed a wheel-turning political leader to transform the movement into a world religion. It took time – but the wheel was turning.

Darius never made it to Buddha's north-eastern India but he conquered Gandhara and Kamboya in the west, recruiting Indian troops who later served in the Persian armies that attacked Greece. He was curious enough to appoint a Greek sea captain, Scylas of Caryanda, to sail from the Red Sea to explore the Indian coast. Then, after a Scythian raid, he ordered his Greek allies, expert seamen, to build a pontoon bridge of boats, lashed together, across the Bosphoros – and invaded Russia and Ukraine.

The Alexandrians and the Haxamanishiya:
Eurasian Duel

QUEEN AMESTRIS AND THE MUTILATION OF ARTAYNTE

Darius disappeared into the vastness of Russia and Ukraine, chasing the Scythians. Like later invaders, he was bewildered by the scale of the steppes, tormented by the freezing winter and frustrated by elusive enemies who avoided pitched battle and withdrew, drawing him deeper into hostile territory. Whatever disasters befell him here, he survived and in 511 BC made it back to Persia, lucky not to have become a drinking goblet. He left 80,000 troops under Bagavazdā, his cousin, who swerved southwards towards Macedonia; its king, Amyntas, submitted. But the Persian envoys abused Macedonian women: the king's son Alexander killed the offenders and the feud was healed only when Amyntas married his daughter to Bagavazdā's son.

This was the beginning of the duel between the two families that would define the next three centuries. Amyntas' Argeads, who claimed descent from Macedon, a nephew of Hellen, founder of Greece, and from Hercules, had ruled their realm since about 650. The Macedonians, rough, bearded mountaineers living in a state of perpetual feud in forested highlands under a semi-barbaric monarchy, were not regarded by Athenians and Spartans as fully Greek. Later when Amyntas' son Alexander tried to compete in the Olympic Games, reserved for true Greeks, his qualifications were challenged; he was forced to cite his mythical genealogy – and then went on to win the race.

Darius had conquered the richer Greeks of Ionia; only Sparta and a sprinkling of city states, led by Athens, remained independent. The Ionian Greeks, who provided much of the Persian fleet but smarted under Darius' taxes, now rebelled and burned Sardis. They were suppressed, but the western Greeks had helped them.

In 491, Darius, now in his sixties, dispatched his son-in-law Mrduniya (Mardonius), son of the greatest of the Seven,[*] to conquer Greece.

---

[*] Mrduniya was son of the Great King's nephew as well as his son-in-law, husband of Darius' daughter, Artozostra. In one of the few family tablets found in royal archives, Darius dictates: 'Darius the King commands "Give 100 sheep in my estate to my daughter Artozostra. April 506."' The letter, written not in the Persian of his royal inscriptions but

Mrduniya crossed the Hellespont in command of 600 ships and an army, co-opting King Alexander I of Macedon. The Persians were surprised when Athens and Sparta, feeling perhaps for the first time the bond of Greekness, combined to resist. When Mrduniya was wounded in Thrace, Darius promoted his other nephew Artafarna. Landing on the Marathon Plain, the Persians faced only the hoplites of Athens – the Spartans were late – but the Greeks routed them. After Marathon, the Athenians instituted a novelty to control the dominance of their paladins: voters could secretly write a politician's name on a pottery shard (*ostrakon*) to sentence him to exile – ostracism – for ten years, providing at least 6,000 votes were cast.

Marathon was a minor setback for Darius who at sixty-four decided to lead a second invasion – while promoting Xerxes, who boasted, 'Darius my father made me the greatest after himself.' In October 486, Xerxes smoothly succeeded his father, then, advised by Alexander of Macedon among others, crossed the Hellespont on a bridge of ships to invade Greece with 800 ships and 150,000 troops, including Indians, Ethiopians and many Greeks. The Athenians abandoned Athens and led by the Spartan king Leotychidas retreated southwards to defend the Corinthian Isthmus – but they left a rearguard under the other Spartan king, Leonidas, whose allies persuaded him to delay the Persians at the narrow pass of Thermopylae with 300 Spartans – and several thousand Phocians and helots (forgotten in most accounts). Xerxes watched as his Immortals were slaughtered in the narrow defile, until a Greek traitor revealed a path round the Greek rear. The Persians surprised Leonidas at dawn. 'Eat a good breakfast,' said jaunty Leonidas, 'for tonight we eat in the underworld' – and then they fought to the death.* Xerxes advanced towards deserted Athens, its people evacuated to Salamis island by their fleet. Xerxes' fleet closed in on the Greek ships moored between Salamis and the mainland. His Greek vassal, Queen Artemisia of Halicarnassus, a woman who commanded her own fleet, warned against fighting Athenian sailors in a confined space and advised a blockade. But convinced that the enemy navy would disperse and that anyway victory was inevitable, Xerxes ordered an assault, his fleet soon lured into the narrows. Seated on a silver throne, he watched admiringly as the Ionian Greeks smashed the Spartan ships with swashbuckling Artemisia in the thick of the fighting – 'My women are men, my men are

in Elamite, reveals how he gave orders orally that were then written on to tablets by his courtiers and dispatched.

* 'Go tell the Spartans, passer-by,' read the poignant inscription, 'that here obedient to their laws we lie.'

women,' he exclaimed – but the Athenians, commanded by Xanthippos, one of the Alcmaeonids, then broke out, destroying 200 ships. Xerxes had to watch one of his brothers killed and cast into the sea. Furiously he executed his Phoenician admirals. But Salamis was not decisive. His army was undefeated, 600 ships battle ready. 'Return to Sardis,' Mrduniya advised Xerxes, 'and take the greater part of the army. Leave me to complete the enslavement of the Greeks.' After burning Athens, Mrduniya advanced on the allied forces, which he harassed with cavalry.

As the Greeks retreated, covered by the Spartans, Mrduniya, astride his white horse, charged at the head of a thousand Immortals. The training of the Spartans and the advantage given by their armour broke the lightly armed Persians. A Spartan killed Mrduniya with a slung stone, and the Persians fled. Their undefeated second army tried to retire through Thrace to Asia, but Alexander of Macedon switched sides and massacred many of their troops. The conquest was over* – but Xerxes had burned Athens, and Persia overshadowed Greece for another 150 years.

While the Greek navy defeated the Persians, commanded by Xerxes' brother Masišta, at Mycale off Ionia, Xerxes' love life was destroying his court. First he had fallen in love with Masišta's wife. In order to spend more time with her, he married his son, Crown Prince Darius, to the daughter of Masišta, Artaynte, but, dropping the mother, he fell wildly in love with the teenager. The queen then uncovered a planned coup by Masišta and his family. At the Nowruz (new year's) feast, when the king asked her to choose a gift she demanded the Masišta family. Xerxes, his follies exposed, withdrew. The queen ordered a traitor's death for Masišta's wife, whose nose, ears, tongue and breasts were cut off and thrown to dogs.

Unsurprisingly Xerxes had lost his mystique: in 465, courtiers

---

* Soon after Salamis, a Greek of good family was born in Halicarnassus (Bodrum) in Ionia, Persian territory, later moving to Athens, whence he travelled the Eurasian world, visiting Egypt (possibly with an Athenian fleet), Tyre and Babylon before settling in an Athenian colony in Calabria, Italy. When he was thirty-five, he started to write what he called 'the demonstration of an enquiry' whose purpose was 'to prevent the traces of human events from being erased by time, and to preserve the fame of the important and remarkable achievements'. He was Herodotos; enquiry in Greek was *historie* and he called the book *Historiai*, inventing history prose as a genre, history as a science of evidence – some of his stories were outlandish but much has been confirmed as fact – but also as a cultural weapon. Even though as many Greeks had fought for the Persians as against them, his history helped create a narrative of western – Hellenic – superiority over barbarous Persian autocracy. Herodotos' tales were typical of the Greek version of Persian history that influenced all western historiography up to the eighteenth and nineteenth centuries when Europeans traced their cultural superiority over Asians and others to the ancient Greeks.

murdered him in his bedroom. In the ensuing conspiracy, Darius was outplayed by his brother Artaxerxes (Artaxšaça) who, as Great King, turned again to Greek matters, offering to fund any Greek power that would challenge the empire of Athens, now led to its zenith by the most gifted of all of the Alcmaeon family.

PERICLES, ASPASIA AND THE PLAGUE OF ATHENS

In 431 BC, Pericles, the 'foremost man in the Athenian democracy', stood up in the Assembly to recommend war against the city's rival Sparta. Born in 495, Pericles grew up during the Persian War – his father had defeated the Persians at Mycale. His mother Agariste was an Alcmaeon, niece of the creator of democracy, Cleisthenes, so Pericles was brought up as a prince of democracy in a family mansion, studying philosophy, literature and music, the height of Athenian culture and haughtiness. His wide forehead earning him the nickname Squillhead; he cultivated an air of self-control and reliability in the Assembly. In the early 460s, in his mid-thirties, Pericles backed full democracy. Success in Athenian politics required oratory but also military talent since the most prestigious offices were now the ten *strategoi*. Pericles excelled at both, annually re-elected to wear the helmet of a *strategos*, which he did for thirty years.

As a young man, Pericles married a relative with whom he had two children, but they also raised an orphaned Alcmaeonid, Alcibiades, who grew up to be a handsome and gifted youth and who would one day dominate Athens. At home Pericles held a salon,* attended by the young philosopher Socrates. But in the 440s, when he was in his political prime, he fell in love with a *hetaira*, a courtesan, one of the cultivated entertainers who performed at *symposia*, and regarded as very different from the city's many *pornai*, street prostitutes. Aspasia of Miletos, the Greek city in Ionia, was a beautiful intellectual, her conversation so fine that wives of Socrates' friends came to listen to her talk. The Athenians had long outlawed polygamy so when Aspasia moved in, Pericles divorced his wife, allowing him to remarry. But their two sons were infuriated and Pericles was criticized for his love of Aspasia, with whom he went on to have another son.

Pericles praised Athenian democracy, but it went hand in hand with

---

* He launched the play *The Persians* by Aeschylus, the first instance of the literature that promoted the legend of Greek superiority over Persian despotism.

a new sort of empire. Since Salamis, Sparta in the Peloponnese and Athens on the Aegean had been increasingly vicious rivals for hegemony over Greece, each building a league of allied cities. Pericles expanded the huge fleet that had defeated the Great King, creating the Delian League of tribute-paying cities, using the revenues to embellish the Acropolis with the Temple of Athena known as the Parthenon and to extend the city walls to enclose the Piraeus harbour: Athens was almost impregnable as long as grain arrived via the Black Sea, from Scythia (Ukraine was already the bread-basket of the eastern Mediterranean). By the 450s, Athens had developed such confidence – other Greeks would call it overweening arrogance – that it believed its democracy, empire and culture made it the natural leader of the civilized world. Yet it also led to the rise of slavery. Athenians disdained farm work and toil in the navy. Since the enslaved worked the farms, silver mines, triremes and households, they needed to be replenished in war: some were from Scythia but others must have been Greek.* Athens's thalassocracy placed the metropolis, the mother city, on a collision course with the land power Sparta. Love of its power – and fear of losing it – led Athens to bully smaller cities that defied it. The more powerful it became, the more Sparta feared and loathed it.

In 451 the Athenians again defeated the Persians in Cyprus. Finally King Artaxerxes agreed a truce with the Greeks – but the removal of the ancestral enemy undermined Hellenic solidarity and led to war with Sparta.

After Sparta had invaded Attica, Pericles bribed the Spartans to withdraw and negotiated a treaty. But the rivalry was exacerbated by clashes between smaller allies of the chief players. In 431, the Spartans dispatched an ultimatum: expel Pericles and the Alcmaeonids and halt Athens's heavy-handed measures to enforce economic control – or fight! Pericles advocated war since it was inevitable and Athens was stronger and could win. The Spartans returned to Attica, but Pericles brought Attican farmers inside the city walls. 'Remain quiet,' he advised, 'take care of the fleet, refrain from putting the city in danger,' while he led raids against the Peloponnese. After the first year, he honoured Athenian dead in resounding if hubristic style. But within a year the very span of Athenian naval power rebounded on the city: an illness, a symptom of Afro-Eurasian trade networks though we do not know its origins, reached the metropolis through sailors. Life expectancy was

---

* Enslaved persons were often manumitted (freed) – 'slaves more than freemen,' wrote Xenophon later, 'need hope' – and children of masters and enslaved women were born free (unlike in Atlantic slavery).

already low: the mean age at death for men was forty-four, for women thirty-six; now this disease, probably a haemorrhagic fever, its symptoms ranging from fever and dysentery to vomiting and a bleeding throat, was exceedingly infectious and those who cared for the sick were the most likely to die. Some people, including an aristocrat and general, the thirty-year-old Thucydides, recovered and sensing that they were now immune (though immunity was not understood) they looked after the sick: later Thucydides wrote the history of all he had seen. A third of the city, 100,000 Athenians, died. Soon there were so many bodies that pyres were lit, on which random people would just throw loved ones. Pericles organized mass graves: one has been found containing 240 bodies with ten children.

The plague undermined confidence. 'The catastrophe,' wrote Thucydides, 'was so overwhelming that men, not knowing what would happen to them next, became indifferent to every rule of religion or law,' and it stretched the limits of early government, impairing the ability to feed the city and undermining its religious system that was designed to keep natural disasters at bay. The Spartans withdrew, a move which saved them: the plague did not hit the Laconian homeland. The disease respected no elites. Pericles was blamed, deposed as general and fined. Aspasia was denounced, and Pericles wept in public. But he was not out for long. Within months, the people recalled him, but his two legitimate sons died of the plague and he asked the Assembly to grant citizenship to his illegitimate son by Aspasia.

Then came the ultimate blow.

ALCIBIADES AND SOCRATES

Pericles himself contracted the plague.

Already dying, in a last speech he declared that the role of the statesman is 'to know what must be done and be able to explain it; to love one's country and be incorruptible'. He died disappointed but claiming, 'I have never caused an Athenian to put on mourning clothes.' The plague eased, but a second wave hit in 426 BC, three years after Pericles' death. Athens took the war to the Peloponnese, fostering a helot revolt, while Sparta captured the silver mines that funded Athens. In 421, both sides agreed to a truce, by which time another extraordinary leader had emerged from the Alcmaeonids.

The boy brought up in Pericles' house, Alcibiades, now thirty years old, had grown up so uncannily beautiful that 'he was hunted by many women of noble family' and 'sought after by men too'. He was a fearless soldier: in an early war against Corinth, he was almost killed but was saved by Socrates, his sometime lover. Tutored by Socrates, Alcibiades was a superb speaker – even his lisp was charming – and he was a born showman, rich enough to lay on choruses for the people. He was also a prince of democracy. Socrates taught him that 'Ethical virtue is the only thing that matters.' But Alcibiades turned out to be a very bad pupil.

Growing up spoiled by birth and nature, Alcibiades, now elected *strategos* by a fascinated people, was sybaritic, wilful and narcissistic. He used his vanity as an argument for his own ambition. 'It is perfectly fair,' he explained to the people, 'for a man who has a high opinion of himself not to be put on the same level as everyone else.' If there was envy 'for the magnificence in which I live my life', that lifestyle was just a way to project Athenian glory. To announce his emergence into public life, 'I entered seven chariots for the [Olympic] chariot race (more than any private individual before).'

In 416, *strategos* Alcibiades advocated a return to an even more ruthless war against Sparta: 'If we don't rule others, others will rule us.' An appeal for help from a city in Sicily inspired him to demand the dispatch of an expedition. 'This is the way we won our empire,' he said. 'We've reached a stage where we are forced to plan new conquests to hold on to what we have got' – how every empire justifies its expansion. 'We shall increase our power!' The Athenians agreed.

Just before he left for Sicily, Athenians awoke to find the *phalloi* of the city's Hermes statues smashed – sacrilege that was blamed on Alcibiades. He was recalled to stand trial. Realizing that he would be found guilty, he defected to Sparta. Without his talents, the Sicilian expedition was a catastrophe and Alcibiades swore vengeance on Athens. 'I'll let them know I am alive,' he muttered. Democracy was 'an obvious absurdity'. He conceived a devastating strategy for the Spartans: they built a fortress near Athens that made it impossible for Attican farmers to feed the city; all food had to be imported. But while in Sparta, Alcibiades seduced the wife of King Agis and, when exposed, he promised to negotiate a treaty with Persia to fund the war against Athens. Persia held the key.

Leading a Spartan fleet to Ionia, Alcibiades appealed to the Persian king Darius II, who had come to the throne after a spasm of familial homicide, aided by Parysatis, his sister-wife. When the Spartans ordered his killing, Alcibiades defected to Darius and advised him to wait out the war. His plan was to engineer his return to Athens , where a noble coup had temporarily overthrown democracy.

The Athenian navy, headquartered in Samos, more loyal to democracy, took power in Athens which then elected Alcibiades as commander. In 410, at Cyzicus, he won a total victory over the Spartans. After a streak of victories including the capture of Byzantion on the Bosphoros, vital for the supply of grain, Alcibiades returned in glory to Athens. He was pardoned, and elected *strategos autokrator*.

In 408, Darius II, faced with a victorious Athens, backed Sparta, funding its new fleet in return for a free hand in Asia Minor.

The Spartans routed the Athenian fleet when Alcibiades was visiting a nearby island. The Athenians blamed the insouciant playboy, who then fled to his castles on the Hellespont. The restored democracy was now desperate. The Spartans, having secured Persian cash and Macedonian timber, denying both to Athens, could now build a new fleet. When they sank Athens's last fleet and cut off its grain, the metropolis was forced to surrender.

There was one loose end: Alcibiades was living in a Hellespontine castle with his mistress. The Spartans sent a hit squad, and he died fighting – the last of the Alcmaeonids.

THE POISON CONTEST OF PERSIA AND THE LITERARY HALITOSIS PLOT OF MACEDONIA

Spartan ascendancy was short. Athens restored its democracy, launching investigations into the military and moral disasters of the war. In this vicious showdown, the Athenians arrested Socrates, once tutor of Alcibiades. Socrates believed all humans must aspire to *arete* – virtuous excellence – while the alternative, 'the unexamined life', is 'not worth living'. But those who insist on telling the truth to everyone are often unbearable. Perhaps Athenian potentates did not want their follies to be overexamined by this loquacious curmudgeon, and Socrates was tried and sentenced to death.* The city swiftly recovered. Meanwhile Sparta dared to intervene in the politics of Persia, now dominated by one of the sharpest potentates produced by House Haxamanishiya.

* Socrates used this trial to promote his ideas. He was ordered to take poison. Socrates' student Plato preserved the master's sayings and proposed an ideal state in his *Republic*. Their quest for virtue was part of the evolving Greek focus on humanity: his contemporary Protagoras argued that 'Man is the measure of all things,' while on Kos a doctor, Hippocrates – whose father and sons were physicians too – started to categorize and diagnose diseases caused by nature and not gods: he was said to have noted that the swelling of fingers could be a sign of heart disease. One of the diseases these doctors identified was called *karkinos* – the crab – which was later known as cancer.

Queen Parysatis guided the dynasty for decades. In 423, she had helped her husband-brother Darius II win the throne, overcoming a challenge from another brother whom she had killed using a special Persian method: suffocation in cold ashes that were heaped inside a specially built tower into which the victim was placed. She and Darius had successfully increased Persian power over Greece, but she had a weakness: mother of thirteen children, she passionately loved her son Cyrus, whom she had appointed as satrap of the west: there he fell in love with an enslaved golden-haired Greek girl, Aspasia, whose chastity and beauty dazzled him. While Parysatis favoured Cyrus, Darius groomed another son, Artaxerxes, for the throne – and he too fell in love. But his choice was dangerous for Parysatis: Stateira was the daughter of a powerful clan. When her father and brothers crossed the king and Parysatis, they ordered the entire clan buried alive. But Artaxerxes successfully begged for his wife Stateira to be allowed to live. Naturally she remembered the killing of her family. For twenty years, the two women watched one another.

In 404, when Darius died, the gentle Artaxerxes, married to Stateira, succeeded, while the queen mother groomed her favourite son Cyrus, then aged twenty-two, who sounds like a charismatic sociopath, to seize the throne. Two years later, Cyrus hired 12,000 Greek mercenaries under an Athenian aristocratic adventurer, Xenophon, and marched on Persia, but when the brothers met in battle the young challenger was unhorsed and then beheaded.* Parysatis watched the killers present her darling's head and hand to Artaxerxes.

Parysatis never got over Cyrus' death, and awaited her vengeance: she won Cyrus' killers in games of dice. One was skinned; another forced to drink molten lead; and the third was killed by scaphism, in which the victim was enclosed between two boats while force-fed honey and milk until maggots, rats and flies infested their living faecal cocoon, eating them alive.

Artaxerxes inherited his brother's breathtakingly beautiful Greek lover, Aspasia, who was brought to him gagged and tied. He had her freed and rewarded: he waited many years for her to finish grieving for Cyrus.

* The Persian and Greek worlds were thoroughly interlinked. While Greek writers promoted Greek superiority, half the Greeks lived in the Persian empire. Even the victor of the battle of Salamis, the Athenian strategos Themistocles, had ended up serving Xerxes; Alcibiades was as at home with Persian satraps as he was with Spartan kings. Young Cyrus' commander, Xenophon, now had to fight his way back to Greece, an exploit he recounted in his *Anabasis*, the first soldier's memoir – while our source for the Persian court is the Greek royal doctor, Ctesias.

His mother Parysatis vied with his wife Stateira, who as the mother of three sons was growing in prestige. Stateira cultivated popularity by appearing in a carriage with the curtains open, delighting the public, and made clear that she despised the many cruelties of the old queen. While Artaxerxes fathered 115 children by his concubines, he really loved a beautiful eunuch. When the youth died of natural causes, he asked Aspasia to wear his robes; his grief touched her. 'I come, O King,' she said, 'to comfort your grief.' They become lovers, finally.

The queen mother and the queen respectfully circled one another, watched by the king: both were extremely vigilant of poison. All autocracies – from the courts of ancient Persia to those of twenty-first-century dictators – run on personal power and access that make competition among the first circle both intimate and vicious. Poison is the ideal weapon at such close quarters, measured and ambiguous – killing the family way. The Persian court was especially watchful, the cupbearer and food taster key positions at court, while the punishment for poisoning was grinding a culprit's face and head between two stones until they were reduced to jelly. For special occasions, the king kept a rare Indian poison – and its antidote.

Stateira's rising power may have been the catalyst for Parysatis, who doubtless regarded herself as guarding the king and dynasty from a deep threat: the two queens often dined together with extreme caution.

Now, in her Susa palace, Parysatis served Stateira a roast fowl, and had her female slave smear the Indian poison on one side of the carving knife so that when she carved the roasted bird, she was able safely to eat her own half. Stateira, reassured, then ate hers and died in agony, able to recount what had happened to the outraged king, whose antidote presumably failed to work. After torturing the servants and grinding the slave to jelly, Artaxerxes exiled his nonagenarian mother.

Artaxerxes turned his attention to Greece, playing off Sparta and Athens until in 387 he imposed the King's Peace which recognized Greek autonomy but established him as the ultimate arbiter of the Hellenic world. Artaxerxes had succeeded where Xerxes and Darius had failed, ruling with an iron will from Egypt and India to the Greek world – where no power was so influenced by Persia as Macedonia.

The Argeads of Macedonia had thrived in the interplay of Persia, Athens and Sparta: King Archelaos leveraged their appetite for shipbuilding timber to build his mountainous, goat-infested fiefdom into a regional force for the first time, aided by his gold and silver mines. But in 399 when Archelaos was out hunting, three courtiers stabbed him to death.

This was the sort of brutishness that civilized Greeks expected of the wild Macedonians. Their dialect was almost incomprehensible. They worked their own fields instead of using slaves like most Greeks; the polygamy of their kings was uncouth and often led to queens and princes killing each other for the crown; their drinking unmixed wine led to oafish royal drunkenness and brawls. Macedonia was usually divided between settled towns in the south, ungovernable northern tribes and predatory outsiders from Persia to Athens whose patronage had allowed Archelaos to transform the kingdom, moving the capital from Agae, which remained the location for royal weddings and burials, to a colonnaded new capital at Pella, where the uncouth goat-chaser played the Greek king.

Archelaos proudly invited a literary celebrity, Euripides, to stay and was infuriated when one of his lovers mocked the poet's halitosis. Archelaos had him thrashed. The boy plotted against the king along with two other embittered lovers. The literary halitosis plot led to Archelaos' assassination. In 393 his nephew Amyntas III restored order. Amyntas had three sons: all three would be kings. The youngest would be the greatest Greek of his time.

ONE-EYED PHILIP AND QUEEN OLYMPIAS

Like all Greeks, the three princes were raised on Homer, but in Macedonia they also fought, hunted and spent days recovering from hard-drinking *symposia*. Most unusually for a Macedonian king, Amyntas died old and in his bed, leaving the throne to the eldest boy, Alexander II, who was defeated by the city of Thebes, then the leading Greek power, which forced him to surrender fifty hostages.

The king sent his youngest brother, the thirteen-year-old Philip. Spending three years in Thebes, Philip was taught a lifestyle of vegetarianism, celibacy and pacifism (all of which he later ignored), but he stayed in the house of the Theban general who was his mentor, probably also his lover, and studied the tactics of the Sacred Band, the elite corps of 300 (supposedly 150 male couples) whose victories had won Thebes its supremacy.

At home, both his elder brothers died violently, leaving a baby as King Amyntas IV. But in 359 BC the Macedonians, facing an invasion from their aggressive neighbours, the Illyrians, acclaimed Philip II, who immediately killed as many of his surviving brothers as he could get his hands on, then divided and played his enemies – by bribery, trickery and marriage (his own, to an Illyrian princess). Influenced by Persian guests, he imitated the Great Kings by creating an inner court of Royal Companions. Then he relentlessly drilled a new army, coordinating cavalry led by his Companions with a remodelled infantry, armed with *xiphos* stabbing swords and fourteen-foot *sarissa* pikes that allowed them to form wedges invulnerable to cavalry.

In 358, Philip first defeated the Illyrians and northern Macedonians, doubling the size of his kingdom and recruiting his best general Parmenion, then making marriage alliances with Thessaly and Epiros, marrying first Princess Philinna who soon gave birth to a son Arrhidaios, then his fourth wife, Princess Polyxena, a daughter of the king of Molassia, part of Epiros. In 356, Polyxena gave birth to a boy named Alexander and later to a daughter, Cleopatra. When Philip learned his team had won the Olympics, Polyxena changed her name to Olympias to celebrate. But they were never close, and soon Olympias found she positively disliked him. Vigilant and feral in her political instincts, Olympias, an adept of Dionysian mystery cults, nurtured a menagerie of sacred snakes that slept in her bed with her and frightened her menfolk – and that surely included Philip, who was afraid of virtually nothing else. Besides, he was very rarely at home.

In twenty years of harsh campaigning and silken diplomacy, Philip defeated all his threatening neighbours, then intervened in Greece proper to defend the neutrality of sacred Delphi and crush the resurgent democracy, Athens, where the orator Demosthenes rallied the resistance to the Macedonian 'despot', mocking Macedonia as 'a place not even able to provide a slave worth buying'. Philip led from the front, and that was a dangerous game. An arrow hit him in the right eye, a wound he survived thanks to his doctor; on another occasion, he was stabbed in the leg. Philip's skull and body have been found in his tomb at Agae and reconstructed, giving us a sense of this fearsomely compact and pugilistic warlord, scarred, limping, one-eyed – yet ever vigilant.

His firstborn, Arrhidaios, epileptic or autistic, was incapable of ruling. The younger one, Alexander, aged thirteen in 343 BC, was avidly reading Homer and Euripedes, and training for war – but he was also learning about Persia. Philip gave asylum to a Persian rebel satrap, Artabazus, who brought his daughter Barsine: she befriended Alexander, who regularly cross-examined Persian visitors. The two would meet again.

Alexander barely knew his father but was close to his mother Olympias, one of the few not afraid to confront Philip – and protect her son. In 342, Philip hired the thirty-seven-year-old Athenian philosopher Aristotle to tutor Alexander. When Philip faced war with Athens, he appointed

Alexander as regent. Alexander always kept under his pillow Aristotle's copy of *The Iliad* and a dagger, two objects that symbolized his two contradictory facets: the cultured Greek and the ferocious Macedonian.

In his father's absence, Alexander showed his mettle by defeating rebel tribes. As Athens gathered a coalition of Greek states to stop Philip, they sent envoys to Artaxerxes III of Persia.

ROULETTE: DARIUS III AND ALEXANDER III

It was the perfect moment to approach the Great King. The impressive Artaxerxes III was keen to intervene in Greece. He had crushed Sidon, Egypt and Ionia, aided by two exceptional henchmen, a Greek freebooter Mentor and a Persian eunuch Bogoas, in whom the absence of testicles was no bar to military brutality. When Artaxerxes returned to his capital after fifteen years of war, he promoted Bogoas to Commander of the Thousand, chief minister. But, alarmed by the rise of Philip, he funded Athens and sent a unit to harass the Macedonians in Thrace, a decision that would have world-changing consequences.

Philip summoned his son Alexander, by now aged eighteen, for the battle of Greece. In the summer of 338 BC on the field of Chaeronea. Philip fielded 30,000 infantry and 2,000 cavalry, giving Alexander command of the Companion cavalry on the left flank, against the coalition led by Athens that fielded double the number of cavalry. But nothing could equal Philip's generalship nor his army's experience: on his own right flank, he deliberately fell back while on the left Alexander led a charge that annihilated the Sacred Band of Thebes to the last man. When Philip saw the dead Sacred Band, remembering his youth in Thebes he wept and erected the Lion of the Chaeronea, a statue under which were later found the bones of 254 men (the Macedonians cremated their dead; Greeks were buried). Now the ruler of Greece – entitled hegemon of the Council of the Greeks – received important news from Persia: a wave of mutual poisonings had decimated the royal family.

Artaxerxes, aged sixty, had planned to dismiss the eunuch Bogoas, who instead poisoned the king and then one by one eliminated his sons, finally summoning a heroic general and royal relative, Artashaiyata, who had made his name by winning a series of single combats. Bogoas crowned him Darius III. Inevitably the new king longed to rid himself of the eunuch.

A deadly game of poison roulette ensued as each of them tried to kill the other. Bogoas poured the king a glass of poisoned wine and the king, for once better informed, insisted the eunuch drink his own cup. The poisoner died by poison. Regardless of the habitual spasms of murderous intrigue at the top, the empire, restored by Artaxerxes III and now led by a confident, capable soldier-king Darius III, was the un-challenged superpower – and likely to remain so for centuries to come.

At the age of forty-eight, the grizzled one-eyed Philip, hegemon of Greece, fell in love with a teenage girl, never a good look. In 337 BC, Philip announced a Hellenic expedition against Persia, officially to avenge Xerxes' burning of Athens but really to replenish his coffers with Ionian treasure and chasten Persia for backing Macedonian enemies in Thrace – 'You,' Alexander later wrote to the Great King, 'sent troops into Thrace which we control.' As he mustered his vanguard, Philip announced that he was marrying again. After six diplomatic marriages to foreigners, including Olympias of Epiros, who had brought him possession of Molassia, he announced he was marrying the teenaged Macedonian, Cleopatra, niece of a nobleman, Attalos. His infatuation destabilized his crowded polygamous household: Olympias was infu-riated. Already surrounded by a coterie of young supporters led by a kinsman Ptolemy, who may have been an illegitimate son of the king, Alexander was alarmed.

At the marriage feast, the Macedonians drank hard and fought fast. The king's new uncle-in-law Attalos mocked Alexander, who was only half-Macedonian: 'Now surely there'll be born for us true-bred kings – not bastards!' Alexander threw his goblet at Attalos, who threw his back. Philip ordered Alexander to apologize. His son refused and the soused father drew a sword and lurched towards him, but tripped, fell over, then passed out.

'The man ready to cross from Europe to Asia,' sneered Alexander, 'can't make it from one table to another.' After dinner, Olympias and Alexander escaped into the night. Philip summoned Alexander back, but when a Persian satrap offered his daughter to the prince, the king refused and exiled Alexander's henchman Ptolemy. Soon afterwards the Macedonian vanguard left for Asia.

In July 336, at Aegae, the family was again together for the wedding of Alexander's sister Cleopatra to his mother's brother, Alexander of Epiros (the clan had a lot of Cleopatras and Alexanders). Philip was exuberant: his new wife had just given birth to a daughter. The day after the wedding, he presided over games, then entered a theatre to watch a show accompanied by the two Alexanders, acknowledging the cheers of the crowd. Suddenly one of his Bodyguards Pausanias lunged and stabbed him in the heart. Attended by Alexander, he died as Pausanias was chased by the guards. Pausanias' motives are mysterious. He had been Philip's lover, but when the king moved on to another youth Pausanias had mocked the new boy as a 'hermaphrodite'. The new lover had complained to his friend Attalus, who trapped Pausanias, raped him and then handed him over to his slaves, who gang-raped him. Argead court life was not for the fainthearted. Olympias was more than capable of suborning an assassin. Philip had already decided that Alexander would remain at home as regent, missing out on the Asian adventure – for Alexander the last straw. The Bodyguards caught and crucified Pausanias before he could speak.

Alexander was led out of the theatre by his father's general Antipater and proclaimed king, whereupon he ordered the murder of rival princes – and of Attalos. Then Olympias murdered Philip's baby daughter, and her teenaged mother Cleopatra committed suicide. Philip was cremated on a pyre, his bones then washed in wine and placed in the gold larnax box in the family's Aegae tomb. Hearing of this in Susa or Pasargadae, Darius III must have reflected that Philip had ruled Greece for scarcely five years before Macedonia dissolved in blood-spattered chaos.

Alexander III, short, compact and fair, maybe redheaded like his father, was a man of action, destroying a Theban rebellion by razing the city, slaughtering 6,000 Thebans and enslaving 30,000. He was idealized thanks to his extraordinary career, but he was both exceptional and typical of a Macedonian king. He was a born killer, living in a state of ferocious, energetic vigilance, hand on sword: killing was at once a necessity, an inclination and a profession, essential for survival and success. He ruled amid an informal macho entourage of interrelated nobles, aware that their connecting threads were woven around him. These men had called Alexander's father 'Philip son of Amyntas' and regarded 'Alexander son of Philip' as first among equals – a view that later become dangerous. Alexander's friends served as the Bodyguards, led by his soulmate and lover Hephaistion, a capable royal page who had studied under Aristotle with him and his trusted henchman Ptolemy.

As a Greek, Alexander existed in a world illuminated by Aristotle's philosophy but also bestridden by gods, spirits and humans descended from divinity. He believed like all his contemporaries that gods, often close at hand in their human guise, decided everything. As a king he presided over the sacrifices and regularly asked his diviners to read the livers of the slaughtered animals. He saw himself too in terms of the Homeric and mythical heroes. As a boy one of his slaves nicknamed him Achilles – and he believed it.

In spring 334, accompanied by 48,000 infantry and 6,100 cavalry, he crossed to Asia on an adventure in the footsteps of gods. He jumped off the boat and threw his javelin into the sand, then sacrificed to Zeus, Athena and his ancestor Hercules. Then he proceeded to Achilles' shrine at Troy. By identifying with Achilles, Alexander drew attention to his own semi-divine brilliance as warrior, his leadership of a band of Companions, his friendship with Hephaistion (his own Patroclus) and perhaps his expectation of a short heroic life. If the gods blessed him, he would conquer.

When his soldiers advanced into Anatolia, they encountered first the armies of Darius' satraps led by the Greek mercenary Memnon of Rhodes, brother of Mentor who had fought so well for Artaxerxes III and husband of the beautiful Persian girl Barsine, who had met Alexander when they were young. On the River Granicus near Troy, two Persian satraps charged at Alexander, riding at the forefront of his cavalry on his favourite horse Bucephalas, and struck his helmet, but he was rescued at the last minute by his old nurse's son Cleitus. He won – and marched on.

Darius was overconfident: he should have rushed to destroy Alexander as soon as he could. He left his queens and daughters at Damascus then marched his huge army of over 100,000 to Issus, south-east Türkiye, where the king of kings in his golden chariot, surrounded by 10,000 Immortals, faced Alexander's 40,000. Aiming to demoralize the enemy and transform numerical disadvantage into kinetic aggression, Alexander charged straight at Darius, hacking his way through Immortal flesh, ignoring a stab in the thigh, hoping to knock out the king himself, until they must have locked eyes. The Persians lost their nerve. As his troops fell back, Darius raced away on his grey horse, leaving 20,000 dead, and returned to Babylon, his priority being empire, not reckless courage.

Afterwards in Darius' tent, Alexander mused, 'Let's cleanse ourselves in Darius' bath.'

'No, Alexander's bath,' replied his aide. His paladin Parmenion galloped south to secure Darius' family. When the diminutive Alexander entered the imperial tent with the strapping Hephaistion, the queens – Darius' mother Sisygambis and his sister-wife Stateira with her daughters – fell to their knees before the taller man. Hephaistion was embarrassed. Alexander touchingly corrected them by saying, 'He's Alexander too,' and raised them to their feet, content to treat them as queens. Here too he met an old acquaintance – Barsine, half-Persian, half-Greek widow of both her uncles Mentor and Memnon. Alexander lost his virginity to her – late for a Macedonian.

For his family Darius offered a regal ransom – Syria, Ionia and Ana-tolia – and marriage to his daughter. Parmenion advised acceptance.

'If I was Parmenion,' replied Alexander, 'I'd accept too, but I am Alexander.' He then wrote to Darius: 'I've already defeated you and your satraps in battle and now, since the gods give all to me, I control you and your country. Do not write to me again as an equal . . . Think of me as the master of everything you have.'

ALEXANDER, ROXANE AND CHANDRAGUPTA:
WORLD KING, AFGHAN QUEEN, INDIAN KING

Alexander swung southwards, with Hephaistion in command of his fleet shadowing and provisioning him from the coast. Marching towards Egypt, which fascinated him, he took Sidon, but Tyre, aided by its sister city Carthage, defied him. When Tyre fell, Alexander let his troops run amok, massacring 8,000 Tyrians and crucifying 2,000. He planned vengeance against Carthage. On the way into Egypt, he massacred every person in Gaza.

At Memphis he had himself crowned pharaoh, son of Amun-Ra, and descended the Nile by royal barge to visit Amun's home, the Temple of Luxor, where he ordered the engravings that still show him as Lord of Both Lands. Back at the Nilotic delta, he founded a city named Alexan-dria.

Now that Alexander had become a god, his retinue questioned why he was dallying in the land of mummies while Darius was mustering in Babylon. But the god-king was keen to visit the famous Oracle at Siwah, an oasis in the Libyan desert, to confirm his apotheosis. After an exciting pilgrimage across the Sahara, accompanied by Ptolemy and Hephaistion, he was told by the oracle that he was indeed the son of Amun, Horus. He asked if the murder of Philip had been avenged, maybe to lift suspicion from his mother or himself, though he never revealed the answer. But Parmenion's son Philotas mocked the idea that Alexander's father was Zeus–Amun: Philip was his father.

Darius moved towards Nineveh (Mosul) and waited on the plain at Gaugamela. As Alexander marched into Iraq, he learned that Darius' wife Stateira had died in childbirth: the baby was almost certainly Alex-ander's. The possession of her body was the possession of Persia. Was she seduced by Alexander? Raped?

At dawn on 1 October 331, Parmenion found Alexander over-sleeping, a sign of his preternatural calm and confidence. Darius presided over the centre of his army. Alexander, at the head of his cavalry, suddenly charged obliquely across the field into the Persian left, cleaving their line. Darius then led a chariot charge, ordering his archers to fire at the king, outstanding in his golden breastplate and purple cloak, while a corps of cavalry was to liberate his mother and wives. But Alexander wheeled round the rear and headed for Darius, who galloped off the battlefield, heading across the Zagros to Ecbatana (Iran).

Alexander now assumed a new title, king of Asia, but his Companions remained dubious: Philotas mockingly said that he felt sorry for the Persians since they were fighting a demi-god. An officer offered to assassinate Alexander for Philotas. Philotas discouraged him but reported nothing. Alexander next took Babylon, where he honoured the god Marduk, whom he regarded as another Zeus. He pursued Darius, first taking Susa where he admired the inscription of Hammurabi's law code from ancient times, then Parsa where he avenged the Persian burning of the temples of Athens. Legend recounts a drunken party at which the *hetaira* Thaïs encouraged Alexander to pillage the royal city, legend thus typically blaming a woman for the mayhem. No doubt there was much carousing, but he needed no encouragement. Parmenion warned against the destruction, but Alexander had promised his army 'the most hated city in Asia'. The Macedonians ransacked the palaces, raping, killing, torturing, enslaving, smashing over 600 vessels of alabaster, lapis, marble, even decapitating a Greek statue – and Alexander systemically burned the palaces.

Alexander chased Darius towards Rhagae (Teheran), where in July 330 the king's cousin Bessus, satrap of Bactria, murdered him and declared himself king. Darius' body was still warm when Alexander arrived. Alexander wept and had the last of the House of Cyrus buried in the family tombs.*

The Companions may have hoped the pursuit was now over, but Alexander reorganized his entourage and set off on a year-long, 1,000-mile manhunt for Bessus, first into Helmand in Afghanistan, where he started to wear a Persian tunic and the royal tiara. In his spare moments, he cavorted with a beautiful young Persian eunuch who sang like an angel. When one of the pages informed the general Philotas of a plot to assassinate Alexander, he again did not report it, so the page went to Alexander directly. Even though Philotas had not conspired himself,

* Darius' pragmatic mother, Sisygambis, did not mourn him, never having forgiven him for abandoning her at Issus. 'I have one son,' she said, 'and he is King of Persia.' She meant Alexander.

Alexander launched a purge, holding a series of show trials accusing Philotas and his father Parmenion of high treason. The soldiers stoned Philotas to death, while Alexander sent hitmen to kill Parmenion. As his army marched further into Afghanistan – where Alexander founded a second Alexandria near Bagram, and another that became Kandahar (Iskandera) – he appointed Hephaistion and Cleitus as his deputies with the new title chiliarch.*

When the snows melted, they climbed up through the Hindu Kush – Killer of Hindus – like Hercules, and chased Bessus into Bactria and Sogdiana, where he was captured by Ptolemy before being publicly executed by being tied to two bent trees and then torn apart. The Afghans resisted; Alexander slaughtered thousands, burned towns, destroyed temples and desecrated the *Avesta* – earning himself the title the Accursed. Though he was wounded again in skirmishes, Alexander's amazing constitution ensured that he rapidly healed and he established tense winter quarters in Markanda (Samarkand), where his Companions demanded a return to Macedonia.

At a drunken *symposium*, his general Cleitus the Black, who had once saved his life, mocked his divine despotism and his lesser talents compared to his father Philip, ending by reminding him, 'This is the hand that saved your life.' Alexander tossed aside his goblet, threw an apple at Cleitus, then jumped up from his couch, grabbed a spear from a Bodyguard and ran at him, only to be restrained by Ptolemy and a general called Perdiccas who begged him to forgive a man who was almost family. Alexander stormed out, seized another spear from the guards and waited. When Cleitus staggered out, Alexander speared him to death. He repented for days, then returned to war.

Alexander advanced into Sogdiana (Tajikistan/Afghanistan), where a local warlord Huxshiartas defied him from his impregnable fortress, the Rock. Alexander sent his Macedonians to scale the eyrie. After its fall, Huxshiartas offered his daughter Roxane – Rauxshana, Bright Star – who became Alexander's wife in a Persian marriage, a new affront to his Macedonian officers. He demanded they make the *proskynesis*, prostration, owed to a Persian king. This was a long way from the matey informality of Macedonian companionship. Outraged officers and even the court historian Callisthenes, great-nephew of Aristotle, refused to prostrate themselves, and a group of pages conspired to kill Alexander in his sleep and put his elder brother Arrhidaios on the throne. But

---

* Commander of a Thousand, a Greek version of the Persian rank *hazahrapatish* – Master of the Thousand – that denoted field marshal and chief minister of the Great King.

the king stayed out all night on a drinking spree and the culprits were arrested then stoned to death.

Now in 327, Bactria and Sogdiana secured, Alexander emulated Hercules by invading 'India' through the Khyber Pass, bursting into the Punjab , recruiting Indian princelings as allies and receiving dissidents from local kingdoms who may have included a young Indian exile named Chandragupta.

His two-year Indian campaign only penetrated what is now Pakistan and appears in no Indian sources because he never threatened the Nanda or Gangaridai kingdoms of northern and eastern India, but the Macedonians also encountered city states resembling Greek *poleis*. Alexander defeated the army of the raja of the Pauravas, the seven-foot Puru who fought from the back of one of his war elephants. Alexander may have sent Chandragupta to negotiate an alliance with Puru; he was certainly eager for further conquests. Nearing Amritsar, the army was now close to mutiny. At a council, the older generals advised a return to the Mediterranean, promising to join Alexander against Carthage: even his friends Hephaistion and Ptolemy said nothing. After an Achillean sulk in his tent, Alexander agreed to leave India, but in his own adventurous fashion, solving the mystery of the South Ocean by descending the Indus to the Gulf of Arabia and thence to Babylon. On the way, still infuriated by the reluctance of his troops to storm a hostile city, he scaled the ladders first and then jumped down almost alone into the fray. An arrow hit him in the side, puncturing his lung, and he collapsed, only just rescued by his frenzied troops who slaughtered the defenders in revenge. Air bubbled bloodily out of the wound – yet Alexander recovered.*

After just surviving a desert crossing, Alexander made it back to Susa, where the royal Persian women awaited him. There, ever practical, he decided to merge the elites of his new empire, Macedonians and Persians, in a mass multicultural wedding. The Macedonians hated this forced splicing. Such relationships between conquered and conqueror were a way of founding enduring empires through children with a familial stake in a hybrid realm. During a three-day fiesta, a hundred couples were married on a hundred couches, with wedding presents, silver and purple robes, silverplate and jewels, and a Persian bridal

---

* Back in Athens, as Alexander, believing himself a god, hacked his way to India, his tutor Aristotle, himself a disciple of Plato, was teaching his Lyceum students about his experiments with natural organisms that established scientific enquiry by experimentation, later the foundation of science, and his philosophy that humans should 'strive to live according to the finest thing that is within us' – reason.

tent for each. At its heart was the ultimate royal marriage: Alexander married Darius' daughter, young Stateira, and Parysatis, daughter of Artaxerxes III. Kings, distrusting their own families, have to make their own: Hephaistion married Darius' other daughter Drypetis. Alexander was crafting an Argead–Haxamanishiya world dynasty.

DEATH IN BABYLON: THE KILLING COMMENCES

Instead of administering his empire from his capital Babylon, Alexander could not resist more expeditions, sailing down the Tigris towards the Gulf and back up to Opis, where his army mutinied. Alexander ordered Seleukos,* commander of the Silvershield guards, to execute the rebels and then, after addressing the troops on the achievements of his father and himself, he was reconciled with his army. Paranoid about the loyalty of his satraps in an atmosphere of rising menace and megalomania, he purged his entourage, killing four of his satraps, sacking four (four more died or were executed), and recalled his longstanding Macedonian viceroy, Antipater.

Suddenly he lost the man he most trusted: Hephaistion died after a drinking bout. Alexander was poleaxed, murdered Hephaistion's doctor, cut the manes off his horses, extinguished the sacred fires of Persia, the signal for the death of a king, and ordered the carving of a lion sculpture that still stands in Hamadan.

Back in Babylon, where he lived in Nebuchadnezzar's palace with wives, mistresses, eunuchs and Companions Ptolemy and Seleukos, Alexander – in between wild drinking bouts, gambling parties and boating trips, sometimes dressing up with horns as the god Amun-Ra – received ambassadors, threatened the Carthaginians with conquest, planned a new expedition into Arabia and proposed the building of an Egyptian pyramid bigger than Giza. He was unsentimental about love but he needed an heir and now he conceived a child with Queen Roxane.

Four days before he was due to invade Arabia, he fell ill with a fever. With his courtiers panicking and conspiring, his soldiers filed past his bed, as doctors bled and purged him. He requested he should buried divinely and pharaonically – at Siwah in the Libyan desert – then gave his ring to his long-serving Bodyguard Perdiccas, chiliarch since Hisphaiston's death, to enable him to conduct business while he was ill. He

---

* Starting as one of King Philip's pages, Seleukos was one of the few paladins satisfied with his Persian marriage: he wed Apama, daughter of a Bactrian warlord Spitamana – a happy union that founded one of the great dynasties of the ancient world.

joked weakly but with characteristic realism that he left everything 'to the strongest' or 'the best'. His successors would have to compete like contestants at a funeral games. Then he sank into a coma, dying, whether of booze, poison, typhoid or old wounds reinfected, at thirty-two.

The killing started at once. Family rivalry and cold politics were entwined: the pregnant Roxane, convinced she was carrying a boy, heard that Stateira was pregnant – any child of hers would be certain to succeed. Forging a royal order in the chaos, she invited the Persian queens to Babylon and poisoned both Stateira and Parysatis, daughters of Darius III and Artaxerxes III, while Sisygambis starved herself to death – thereby ending the dynasty.

Perdiccas, chiliarch, claimed the regency and murdered an officer who challenged him. The meetings of the grandees were tense. Perdiccas assigned jobs and provinces: Seleukos became chiliarch; Ptolemy asked for and received Egypt. While Egyptian sacred taxidermists embalmed Pharaoh Alexander's body, the paladins debated who should succeed him, considering his five-year-old son Hercules by his Persian lover Barsine, but Alexander's brother Arrhidaios was present. He was not capable of ruling but they chose him as Philip III – to share the throne with Roxane's unborn foetus. Weeks later she gave birth triumphantly to the joint king Alexander IV. Far away in Greece, Olympias, Alexander's mother, offered Alexander's sister Cleopatra to Perdiccas who, in possession of one dead king and two live ones as well as the main army and backed by his able chiliarch Seleukos, was poised to rule the empire until the baby Alexander IV grew up. As the king had predicted on his deathbed, the swaggering paladins who had conquered the world – 'men whose greed recognizes no limits set by sea, mountain or desert and whose desires overleap even the boundaries that define Europe and Asia', in the words of the historian Plutarch – were unlikely to be confined to any small province, and all of them, infected with the World Game of Alexander, rushed to seize whatever they could.

The shrewdest, Ptolemy, boyhood friend of Alexander, Bodyguard and Companion, now departed to take possession of Egypt.

In 321, as Perdiccas tried to win control of Anatolia, Philip III, baby Alexander IV and Queen Roxane escorted Alexander's colossal and sumptuous hearse. Gold-embossed, myrrh-scented, sculpted with Ionic columns, figurines of Nike at each corner and busts of Ammon's sacred horned ibex, friezes of elephants and lions, the vast hearse containing Alexander's Egyptian human-shaped coffin and embalmed mummy, pulled by sixty-four bejewelled mules, and a guard of honour of elephants and guardsmen, wended its slow glorious way towards Aegae.

As it hove into view, it must have presented a fabulous spectacle, but it was even more welcome to Ptolemy.

Somewhere in Syria, Ptolemy kidnapped the sarcophagus – history's ultimate corpse-napping – and escorted it back to display in Memphis. Although the kings arrived safely in Greece, Perdiccas, outraged, marched down to Egypt to steal back the world-conquering mummy, but Ptolemy defeated him, whereupon Seleukos assassinated Regent Perdiccas. In the carve-up of empire that followed, Ptolemy kept Egypt, Seleukos was given Babylon and the long-serving general One-Eyed Antigonus controlled central Anatolia. In the ensuing wars, Seleukos lost Iraq, returning to serve Ptolemy in Egypt, and Antigonus emerged as a surprise winner.

The fighting between the paladins was complex, vicious and ever changing. Each time one gained ascendancy, the others banded together to stop him. Olympias, now fifty-five, was the homicidal equal of the men. In 317, the queen seized Macedonia to support baby Alexander IV and his mother Roxane, opposed by her stepson Philip III. Olympias won and at once murdered Philip, but within months another general had seized and tried her. When the soldiers refused to shed Alexander's blood, they instead stoned her to death. King Alexander IV and Roxane were imprisoned; meanwhile Hercules and his mother Barsine lived quietly in Anatolia. But no one had forgotten them. Alexander's family was dwindling in a cut-throat competition to liquidate all rivals.

The Mauryans and the Qin

SELEUKOS IN INDIA:
THE RISE OF CHANDRAGUPTA

Thanks to his general Seleukos, Ptolemy seized not only Libya but also Cyprus, Judaea (the Graeco-Roman name for Judah), Coele-Syria and much of the Aegean. As a thank-you, in 312 BC Ptolemy lent Seleukos a tiny corps of 800 infantry and 200 cavalry with which he managed to reconquer not just Babylon, where he had been a popular governor, but then, in an astonishing performance of almost Alexandrian proportions, the rest of Syria, Iraq, Iran, Afghanistan and Pakistan.

Foxy, pointy-faced and fearless, Seleukos had the gift of winning over different nationalities to work with his Macedonians. In the last year of Alexander's life he had joined the king's inner circle, present at the final drinking parties before his death, and unlike henchmen of longer standing he had not at first requested a satrapy. Alone among the Companions, he had stayed with his Bactrian wife Atama, a decision that was to pay off when he retook the east. But the biggest threat to Alexander's heir was his own blood: in 310, Alexander IV and Roxane were murdered, followed soon afterwards by Hercules. Finally Ptolemy decided to marry Alexander's sister Cleopatra, but she too was murdered before the ceremony could take place. After 300 years of rule by one family, the House of Alexander had vanished.

In 306, Ptolemy and Seleukos declared themselves to be kings, founding two Alexandrian dynasties that would rule for centuries, setting new lows for depravity down to their last great ruler, Cleopatra. Egypt was Ptolemy's heartland; while he created a Greek-speaking bureaucracy there, fortified by a Macedonian army, he backed the Egyptian priests and embellished their temples. In return, they hailed him as pharaoh.* Towards the end of the reign, he settled himself

---

* Ptolemy's Egyptian adviser, the priest Manetho, was the great historian who divided the Egyptian pharaohs into the dynasties that we still use today.

and Alexander the mummy in his expanded Alexandria.*

In 287, now in his eighties, Ptolemy chose a younger son, the twenty-two-year-old Ptolemy, intellectual and thoughtful, to succeed him instead of his elder son, Thunderbolt, then aged thirty-two. It was a sensible decision: Thunderbolt was a psychopathic wrecking-ball. When Ptolemy died in 283, the only one of Alexander's successors to die in his bed, he was smoothly succeeded by Ptolemy II, while Thunderbolt escaped to seek his fortune elsewhere.

After a murderous rampage around the Mediterranean, Thunderbolt fled to Seleukos and invited him to seize the west. Seleukos, now seventy-five and the last of the successors, was up for the challenge. His eldest son Antiochos, who accompanied him on his campaigns, was half-Persian, which helped as they established a Greek empire from Syria to Pakistan, earning Seleukos the epithet Nicator – Victor. Like Alexander, the Victor was an avid founder of cities, building two capitals – an eastern one, Seleucia (near Baghdad), and a western one, Antioch (Antakya, Türkiye). When, as part of an alliance, he took a new young wife, Stratonice, his son Antiochos fell ill. Consulting his doctor, the old king discovered that the boy was in love with her. Seleukos fixed his own succession and his son's sickness by giving the boy both the crown and the girl, announcing their marriage and then crowning them king and queen of Asia, progenitors of the Seleucid dynasty.

Before he returned to the west, Seleukos had marched into the Punjab, where he discovered his limits. In 305, he clashed with a new dynasty there led by an Indian king who may have met Alexander.

Twenty years earlier, Chandragupta Maurya, who may have advised Alexander on Indian affairs, led a rebellion against the unpopular Nanda kings of Pataliputra (Patna). Chandragupta may have been an illegitimate relative of the Nandas, hidden by his mother and brought up far from court. It was said that a courtier, Chanakya,† invited the

---

* It was Ptolemy who planned his own royal district around the *Soma* – Tomb of Alexander – adding the 400-foot Pharos lighthouse, one of the wonders of the ancient world; the *Museion*, sanctuary of the Muses (the first museum), an academy for Aristotelian study including the Library for which all the works of the world were to be translated into Greek. He welcomed intellectuals from all over the Greek world.

† Chandragupta was guided by the semi-mythic Chanakya. It was long believed that Chanakya wrote at least some of the *Arthashastra* (Science of Politics), a guide to staying in power: 'You can lose a war as easily as you win. War is unpredictable. Avoid war.' Chanakya understood the essence of politics, 'The root of right governance is victorious inner restraint,' and used the ancient Indian image of the wheel to describe the *rajamandala*, the circle of kingdoms, the tributaries around a powerful empire. The *Arthashastra* identifies Kautilya as its author; this was presumed to be another name for Chanakya, but it is now believed that Chanakya was not the author.

boy to his philosophical school at Takshashila (Taxila). Little is known about Chandragupta, but he may have served King Dhana Nanda until he became jealous of the young general and ordered his killing. Chandragupta finally took Pataliputra and, when the Macedonian rule in Punjab collapsed, he expanded there too.

In 305, Seleukos arrived to retake these Indian provinces but, after failing to defeat Chandragupta, he met the Indian monarch on the Indus and ceded territories, agreed a marriage alliance and exchanged ambassadors. Ambassador Megasthenes wrote a (mostly vanished) book *Indica*, describing the heavily guarded monarch, his orderly empire and his capital Pataliputra, one of the world's biggest cities. Chandragupta sent Seleukos a useful gift for an ageing warlord: Indian aphrodisiacs. Even more useful, he gave Seleukos the equivalent of a twentieth-century panzer division – 500 war elephants, which he would use to conquer the west.

ASHOKA – WHEEL-TURNING KING

Seleukos, now aged seventy-five, accompanied by his twenty-two-year-old son Antiochos and his corps of Indian elephants and Scythian chariots, marched all the way from Pakistan to the Aegean, defeating all contenders. In 281 BC, they crossed the Hellespont but, as Seleukos – the last of Alexander's Companions and, with Ptolemy, the most gifted – stopped to admire an ancient shrine, the psychopathic Thunderbolt, who had invited him into Greece, stabbed the old Victor. Then, seizing control of the army, he marched into Macedon and claimed the throne. It was an astonishing turn of events, but it did not last. Thunderbolt was himself killed in battle, the end of the wars of Alexander's successors. Seleukos' family kept Syria, Iraq and Iran; the Ptolemies ruled Egypt, Israel and Lebanon.

The great Ptolemy's daughter Arsinoe was left high and dry in Greece: twice married to warring kings, twice widowed, she wanted her share of power and headed to Alexandria to join her brother Ptolemy II. Arsinoe framed his wife for planning to kill the pharaoh, had her killed and then married Ptolemy II. The incest pleased the Egyptians but disgusted the Greeks. 'You're pushing your cock into an unholy hole,' wrote a lampoonist named Sotades. Ptolemy had Sotades sealed in a lead coffin and dropped into the Nile. Ptolemy II called himself and his wife Philadelphoi – Sibling-lovers, a divine pharaonic couple.

Philadelphos did everything with extravagance – what the Greeks called *tryphe** – making his father's library the greatest collection in the world and inviting all peoples to settle in Alexandria, which was soon home to a million people, Greek, Egyptian and Jewish. When he commissioned Greek-speaking Jews to translate their Torah into Greek, he made the Bible available to non-Jews, a move which later had world-changing consequences.

In 275, Arsinoe and Philadelphos held a sacred festival combined with military parade and trade fair to celebrate their power: 80,000 troops marched through Alexandria with floats and statues of Zeus, Alexander and the Sibling-lovers themselves, elephants, leopards, giraffes and rhinoceroses, and delegations of Nubians and Indians in national dress. The Nubians advertised Ptolemy's trade with Arkamani, *qore* (ruler) of Kush, who operating from his capital at Meroe, where he built many pyramids that still stand, sold war elephants to Philadelphos. As for the Indians, the festival's theme was Dionysios returning from India – and Philadelphos had founded new Red Sea ports on the Egyptian and Arabian coasts to trade with the emperor of India, Ashoka, who boasted of his Greek links, naming Philadelphos in his inscriptions.

Born around the time that his grandfather Chandragupta was giving Seleukos those elephants, Ashoka was just one of the possible heirs of an expanding empire. Around 297, Chandragupta abdicated from the throne to devote himself to Jain asceticism, handing over to his son Bindusara, who maintained his father's friendly relations with the Seleucids, asking Antiochos to send figs, wine and a Greek philosopher. Bindusara appointed Ashoka as governor in the north-west at Taxila and Ujjain, where he fell in love with a merchant's daughter, Devi – Vidisha-Mahadevi – whom Buddhists later claimed was related to Buddha.

In 272 BC, as Bindusara lay dying, Ashoka, reported by one tradition as unattractive and suffering from a fainting condition, possibly epilepsy, fought and killed his brothers. Calling himself Beloved of the Gods (Devānampiya) and the Kindly (Piyadasi), Ashoka expanded down the east coast, vital for Mauryan links to eastern Asia: 'King Piyadasi conquered Kalinga, 150,000 people were deported, 100,000 were killed and many times that number perished,' and 'Kalinga was annexed.' Leading an army of 700 elephants, 1,000 cavalry and 80,000 infantry and protected by a bodyguard that included female archers, he may have

---

* Philadelphos supposedly kept nine paramours, of whom the star was a badass chariot-racing Greek beauty Belistiche, who – despite rules against female participation – somehow won the Olympics and moved to Alexandria as Philadelphos' lover: they had a son together. This pleasure-loving daredevil sportswoman was so celebrated that when she died Philadelphos had her deified and buried in the temple of Sarapis.

conquered lands from Afghanistan to Bangladesh and south to Deccan – probably the largest raj until the British. When he had the luxury of security, he did what he thought was right, encouraged by his Buddhist lover Devi. 'Now that Kalinga was annexed, the Beloved of the Gods felt remorse,' he declared in one of the thirty-three remarkable inscriptions he raised around his empire.* The killing 'is extremely grievous to the Beloved of the Gods and weighs heavily on this mind', and he even mentioned the suffering of slaves.

Rebranding himself as *chakravartin*, wheel-turning monarch, and *dharmaraja*, he 'very earnestly practised *dharma*, desired *dharma* and taught *dharma*', which was the universal law of righteousness, one of the essential teachings of Buddha. He preached tolerance and peace – 'the essential advancement of all sects . . . One should honour each sect by the other.' According to Buddhist sources, he opened up seven of the original eight stupas that contained the Buddha's relics, and built 84,000 stupas – clearly an exaggeration – to redistribute the relics. He also oversaw the Third Buddhist Council and sent missionaries, led by his son Mahendra and daughter Sanghamitra, to spread the teachings south to Sri Lanka, but also westwards to five Greek kings – just as a Greek satrap, Diodotos I, seized parts of Afghanistan and Tajikistan to found his own Hellenic-Bactrian kingdom.

Ashoka's Buddhism had to be enforced by special officers , *dharma-mahamattas*: 'This *dharma* edict is engraved so it may long endure . . . as long as my sons and grandson live . . .' Buddhist sources claim his beliefs were resisted by Brahmins among his own family. Meanwhile to the east a conqueror was uniting China for the first time.

HEART OF TIGER AND WOLF: ENTER THE QIN

In 247 BC, the militaristic kingdom of Qin – pronounced Chin – was disastrously inherited by a thirteen-year-old boy, Ying Zheng, who was humiliatingly dominated by his mother, said to be addicted to her prodigiously well-endowed lover. From this ill-starred beginning, this homicidal, brilliant and half-mad visionary would create China.

Ying was the scion of a family who had started in the 860s as horse breeders for the Zhou kings. For centuries, the family had governed a

---

* There is very little known about Ashoka except through his inscriptions – clearly inspired by those of the Persian Great Kings – on which these claims are based. Probably they are exaggerated. This account also uses the obscure and contradictory myths of Ashoka from the point of view of Sri Lankan and Indian Buddhist and Brahmanical sources.

small remote north-western fiefdom that was on the edge of civilization, regarded by the Zhou as barbarians. At a time when ideas of morality later known as 'Confucian' were embraced by a small number of followers, the Qin forged their kingdom into a brutal and efficient force that thrived in the Warring States period – that is, during the perpetual wars over several centuries between the seven or so contending kingdoms who ruled what would become China. A century earlier, the Qin had appointed a minister, Shang Yang, who enforced a system that placed the clan above the individual, dividing people into units of families which were responsible for the actions of all its members collectively: 'Whoever didn't denounce a culprit would be cut in two; whoever denounced a culprit would receive the same reward as he who decapitated an enemy.' Before his own execution, Shang started the aggressive expansion of Qin.

Now after a succession of feckless dukes, Ying found himself ruler. His father Zhuangxiang had not expected to rule but, while held as a hostage abroad, he met a merchant, Lu Buwei, who had a beautiful concubine, Lady Zhao. The prince fell in love with her and Lu presented her to him as a present. When Zhuangxiang became king, he appointed Lu as his chancellor, while Lady Zhao gave birth to the boy Ying Zheng, whose enemies would naturally claim that the merchant rather than the king was his real father.

In 246, the king died, and the thirteen-year-old Ying bided his time as he was guided by Lu and his mother, who became lovers again. Thinking better of this, Lu distracted the queen mother by introducing her to 'a man named Lao Ai who had an unusually large penis'. To make sure she heard about his equipment, Lu had Lao dance to sensual music and supposedly 'stick his penis through the centre of a wheel . . . so as to excite her interest'. This artful presentation worked. The queen was hooked. Lao Ai, now promoted to marquess, secretly had two sons with her, convinced he could outwit the young king and enthrone one of these babies. Women in east Asian kingdoms were often politically active – and the denunciation of female potentates for their sexual voracity would be a way of denigrating their rule throughout history. On the other hand, private and political lives were intertwined in personal monarchies; spatial and emotional closeness to the ruler was essential to win the trust of vigilant rulers; and women were neither more nor less likely to be influenced by sex or friendship than their male equivalents. Whatever the proportions of his penis, Lao was no match for the young king's 'heart of tiger and wolf'. Ying Zheng was terrifying, with a 'waspish nose, eyes like slits, a chickenish chest and a voice like a jackal', according to a visitor, and 'he's merciless' . . . but he could also be charming, lavishing 'clothes, food, drink' on his visitors.

In 239, the king, at the age of twenty, advised by the Councillor, a minister named Li Si, provoked Lao Ai to seize power. Ying defeated Lao's army, slaughtered his entire clan and had him torn into pieces by five horses, then exiled his mother. A master of human manipulation, the king could be kind – or predatory. 'When in difficulties he humbles himself; when successful he swallows men up without a scruple,' wrote a visitor. 'Should he succeed in conquering the world, we will all be his captives.'

In swift campaigns, devised with the Councillor, Ying Zheng conquered three of the contending kingdoms. In 227, the king of Yan sent two assassins who were to present a map and the head of a traitor to Ying and then kill him. Receiving them in an audience hall (recently discovered by archaeologists) at his capital Xianyang (near modern Xi'an), Ying so terrified the assassins that they dropped the head. One of the hitmen drew a dagger and slashed at Ying, who drew his sword and staged a fighting retreat, managing to cripple both his would-be assassins. Ying soon conquered Yan and the rest of the kingdoms, taking the last one, Qi, in 221, uniting China for the first time – at a cost of around a million lives: 'Insignificant as I am, I have raised troops to punish rebellious princes and thanks to the sacred power of our ancestors all six kings have been chastised so at last the empire is pacified.'

Now thirty-eight, the king declared himself Shi Huang-di – the First August Thearch, a sacred and cosmological title, emperor of China – boasting that 'he was the first to achieve a single great peace'. The First Emperor had invented China as a political entity, ruling through forty commanderies, collecting all weapons which were melted down and cast into colossal statues set up in the palace, and adding that new throne hall at Xianyang and a huge pleasure park, the Supreme Forest, containing more palaces. He built the 500-mile Straight Road highway, just one of 4,200 miles of roads, along with a network of canals. The fighting was not over in the north, where a nomadic federation based in Mongolia, the Xiongnu, raided the empire: Ying Zheng started the Great Wall to expand into the grasslands that were crucial to the Xiongnu's seasonal migrations. Sections of his roads and the Wall survive.

The only obstacle to his ruling forever was the mortality he shared with all people: determined to achieve immortality, he consulted magicians, who advised pursuing immortality through pilgrimages to sacred mountains or over the sea to find the Island of Immortals: fleets were dispatched to look for it.

The First Emperor's movements were secret, a sensible policy in the wake of two more assassination attempts. When he realized that the Councillor always knew where he was, he had his entire retinue executed. And when his magicians started to call him 'violent, cruel, power-greedy' he launched a campaign of terror, executing 460 scribes. Father of scores of children, the First Emperor favoured his eldest son Fusu as heir, but the boy criticized him too, and was sent to serve at the frontier.

Many must have witnessed the emperor as he travelled and inspected his projects: one day, a minor official from Henan, named Liu Bang, born a peasant, escorted some prisoners to work on the emperor's building projects and was lucky enough to see him in person. Strangely though no one would have believed it at that moment, the future belonged to this young provincial.

Ying Zheng forced 700,000 enslaved labourers to build a colossal tomb at Mount Li, thirty miles east of the capital, a four-sided pyramid within a man-made mountain 400 feet high, which displayed the strange grandeur of its creator – the emperor's unique and sacred cosmic role. His tomb exceeded anything built anywhere else except the Great Pyramid. It was one of the paramount building projects in world history.*

There was certainly contact between Qin China and northern India. It was probably Ashoka and his courtiers who first used the name Qin not just for a dynasty but for that vast country, China. The Chinese themselves called it The Central Country. Yet, as Qin united China, Ashoka was losing India.

Ashoka's decline is mired in legends, some Buddhist, some Hindu, but he may have fallen in love with one of his wife's maids, Tishyaraksha, a singer-dancer, who turned against Buddhism and flirted dangerously with his favourite son Kunala. In the ensuing showdown, both the latter were blinded. Young wives and aged kings do not go well together. As

---

* The emperor's concept was to create an afterlife version of his empire. Beneath vaulted roofs depicting the heavens and stars flowed bronze-lined rivers of mercury, symbolizing the Yangtze and Yellow, while 7,500 terracotta soldiers guarded the entrances to the tomb, reinforced by crossbow boobytraps. The statues were unlike any previous Chinese statues, realistic in their physique and faces. Some had moustaches, some had hairbuns, some paunches; many had different eyes; all were fully fitted out with armour and weaponry. Most were built from a limited number of modular parts, but the generals were probably sculpted from life. These were probably inspired by smaller figures found in Warring States tombs, but it is just possible they were influenced by Greek sculpture, brought eastwards by Seleukos and his fellow Greeks. The first century BC historian Sima Qian is the source for the outrageous tales of Ying's madness and cruelties but they may in fact be indirect descriptions of his master, Han emperor Wu.

another son, Samprati, took control, the ailing Ashoka found himself powerless.* Indian and probably Chinese goods were starting to reach the Red Sea ports of the Ptolemies, who sold them into the Mediterranean. In 236, the marriage of Ptolemy III Euergetes took place amid a murderous–incestuous imbroglio peculiar to the Ptolemy family.

---

* Ashoka's death led to a vicious fight for the succession not just between different princes but between Brahmins, Buddhists, Jains and Ajivikas that was temporarily won by in 232 by a grandson, son of Kunala, Dasaratha Maurya, but ultimately his favoured son Samprati, a Jain not a Buddhist, seized the crown. The empire started to break up.

The Barcas and the Scipios:
The Houses of Carthage and Rome

LOVE AMONG THE PTOLEMIES

King Philadelphos planned to bring Cyrene (Libya), ruled for fifty years by Ptolemy I's stepson King Magas and his wife Apama, under Egyptian rule. He arranged the marriage of their daughter Berenice to his son Euergetes. But Apama, a Seleucid princess, wanted to keep Cyrene as a Seleucid base and, after Magas had died of gluttony, she tried to foil the plan by inviting the son of the Macedonian king, Demetros the Pretty, to marry her daughter instead. Berenice wanted to marry her cousin in Egypt, but she reluctantly married the popinjay Demetros, who was then seduced by her mother.

Berenice solved the problem in family style. Bursting into the maternal boudoir with a posse of killers, she surprised her husband and her mother in bed. Berenice killed her husband, spared her mother and then proceeded triumphantly to Alexandria to marry Euergetes.

Egypt gained Cyrene; and Euergetes and Berenice had six children during their first seven years of marriage, a rare oasis of wholesomeness in this murderous family. The Ptolemies were committed to winning Mediterranean hegemony, which in the east meant competing with their cousins and rivals, the Seleukos family that still ruled from Syria to Iran. Once he was king, Euergetes, energetic and charismatic, saw an opportunity: his sister was married to King Antiochos II, but his sudden death put both of them in danger from his rapacious brothers. Euergetes sailed up to Antioch, the Seleucid capital, rushing into the palace moments too late. His sister and her child had just been murdered, but he managed to secure the Mediterranean seaboard from Thrace to Libya. At his zenith, Euergetes received a request for help from a city state that was his neighbour in Africa: Carthage asked for a loan to fund a war against an Italian city state.

The two seemed evenly matched, but Carthage, capital of a Mediterranean trading empire, would surely win. Its forces were commanded by a young general, Hamilcar Barca, whose family would dominate Carthage for the next fifty years. Hamilcar was already the father of three daughters, but before he left Carthage for the front, his eldest son was born: Hannibal.

AFRICAN LIGHTNING AND HUMAN SACRIFICE: BARCA OF CARTHAGE

The Barcas had their origins in the mother city Tyre (Lebanon): Hamilcar's family called themselves the 'Tyrian house of the ancient Barcas', though Barca also meant Lightning. Established, according to its foundation myth, in 814 BC by Dido, a Phoenician princess driven out of Tyre by her brother Pygmalion, Carthage – Qart-Hadasht (New City) – was a city of temples and palaces with two harbours, all guarded by huge walls, with a population of 700,000 and several million subjects in its Tunisian hinterland.

These Phoenician settlers – they called themselves 'Canani', Canaanites – initially paid tribute to the rulers of Numidia, a kingdom of Berbers, a name derived from the Greek word barbarian, though they called themselves Mazigh-en. Berbers and Phoenicians initially intermarried. But ultimately the Carthaginians forced the Berbers to pay tribute, hired their superb horsemen – they rode without bit, saddle or stirrups – and enslaved those who resisted.

Carthage had grown into the metropolis of a trading empire: its shekels were the favoured Mediterranean currency. Its shipbuilders and their Greek rivals developed the trireme and larger quinquereme warships – rowed by three and five banks of oars – that dominated the Mediterranean. As sailors they were sophisticated enough to voyage into the Atlantic, sailing down to west Africa where they captured three African women who were flayed, their skins displayed long afterwards in the Temple of Tanit. In Africa, they encountered huge apes that they called 'gorillas', a Carthaginian word.

Carthaginians worshipped Baal Hammon and his wife Tanit in temples where, like their Tyrian cousins, they made animal and, in times of crisis, human sacrifices at the special altar, the *tophet*, where human bones, usually of children, have been discovered. As they challenged, and traded with, their Greek rivals, they syncretized their god Melqart, legendary first king of Tyre, with Hercules, son of Zeus and a human mother, bridging the human and divine. Speaking Phoenician (which had much in common with Hebrew and Arabic), along with Greek and Numidian, they did not eat pork, circumcised their children and dressed in robes and sported earrings. Carthage was a semi-democratic republic controlled by a balance of aristocratic families and a popular assembly of all male citizens.* Deploying African elephants, Numidian cavalry,

---

* The assembly annually elected two suffetes – leaders who ruled in peace – and a

Spanish, Celtic, Greek and Italian infantry and fleets of quinqueremes, all officered by aristocrats, the Carthaginians, funded by their productive slave-powered farms and mines and by trading, had expanded into Spain, Malta, Sardinia and Sicily.

On his deathbed, Alexander the Great was planning to destroy Carthage, which then formed an alliance against his successors with a city state, Rome, that was consuming the Italian peninsula. It was an alliance that did not last. The Romans expanded into Sicily, which the Carthaginians regarded as their own. In 264 BC, what started as a minor proxy war escalated into a war between the Italian and African republics.

The Romans possessed plentiful manpower but no fleet; the Carthaginians depended on mercenaries but had the best fleet in the Great Sea. Yet technology never remains a monopoly for long. Copying a captured Carthaginian ship, Rome built its first fleet. Both sides were frequently defeated on land and sea as the action moved from Sicily to Africa and back to Sicily where Hamilcar harassed Roman positions and raided Italy, confident in victory. Then a Roman fleet defeated the Carthaginians at sea. Carthage was astonished.

The unbeaten Hamilcar was ordered to negotiate peace and was obliged to agree to the unthinkable: the loss of Sicily and payment of an indemnity. Resigning his command, Hamilcar sailed home, accusing a rival faction of a stab in the back. His unpaid Celtic mercenaries mutinied and threatened to destroy the city: he took command of a small army, backed by African cavalry under a Numidian prince to whom he married his daughter, and over three years of gruesome warfare (in which the besieged mutineers were forced to cannibalize their slaves) saved Carthage. But Hamilcar, glamorous war hero, aristocratic adventurer, popular favourite, was in danger.

The aristocrats criticized him, but he appealed to the people of Carthage, who were now asserting themselves. While they were fighting for survival, the Romans had broken the treaty by grabbing Sardinia as well. Playing the demagogue before the assembly, Hamilcar proposed a solution – a small expedition to raise cash by looting and conquering Spain, where the Carthaginians had a colony at Cadiz: its silver mines would fund the Roman war. While his ally Handsome Hasdrubal won backing among the elite, Hamilcar won over the people.

---

commander-in-chief or a committee of generals, and a Council of 104 to judge and punish them. Generals were given political autonomy, but if they failed they were crucified. The suffetes were members of the Council of the Mighty – the Adirim, 300 grandees – who had special influence. When suffetes and generals and even the Mighty could not decide, the People were consulted.

In 237, Hamilcar sacrificed a cow's head to his god Melqart–Hercules and when the entrails were auspicious he turned to his nine-year-old son Hannibal and asked if he would like to join the adventure. The boy eagerly agreed, at which the father made him promise 'never to show goodwill to the Romans'. Then with a small army, including his Numidian son-in-law with his cavalry and African elephants, he marched around Africa towards the Straits while Handsome, now also his son-in-law, led the fleet along the coast and ferried the Barcas to Cadiz.

Hamilcar conquered most of Spain, securing the silver mines and sending back cash to Carthage. Hannibal was tutored in history and Greek by a Spartan philosopher, but learned war in the field with his father. When Numidian tribes rebelled in Africa, Hamilcar sent Handsome Hasdrubal home to suppress them. But in 228, campaigning near Toledo accompanied by sons Hannibal and Hasdrubal, Hamilcar was betrayed by a tribal ally. As his sons galloped away, their father, at the age of forty-seven, drowned in a river.

The army elected Handsome, Barca's son-in-law, as commander with Hannibal, now eighteen, as cavalry general. Handsome founded New Carthage (Cartagena) and it was he who had the idea of attacking Rome in Italy itself. But before they could depart, he was assassinated and Hannibal inherited the command. Before long Hannibal had captured a Spanish city allied to Rome; Rome seized Malta, consolidated Sardinia, planned a raid on Africa and sent an army to take Spain. Although Hannibal was attacked in the Council of the Mighty by rivals who believed Carthage was flourishing without a new war, he argued that Rome would never respect Carthage. The people backed House Barca. It was war.

Sending home a Spanish corps to defend Carthage, Hannibal imported 12,600 Berbers and thirty-seven elephants. He sacrificed at the island temple of Melqart–Hercules at Gades, then marched 120,000 men across the Rhône towards the Alps, just as the Roman consul, Publius Cornelius Scipio, was sailing from Pisa to attack Hannibal in Spain.

No family would equal the laurels of the Scipiones in the fight against the Barcas – and no family so represented the martial aristocracy of the Roman Republic that in many ways resembled Carthage.

In 753 BC, sixty-one years after Carthage, Rome was founded – though archaeology proves there were already settlements on the site.* Ruled

---

* The myth of Rome's foundation revolved around two brothers abandoned in infancy and raised by a she-wolf, an image of nurture and ferocity that Rome adopted as its symbol. One brother, Romulus, had killed the other, Remus, in a feud over the borders of the city and became the first king of his eponymous city – a timeless homily on the tragedy of family power.

initially by kings, by war-band chieftains and then by colonels, probably patrician oligarchs, Rome, like Carthage, developed around 420 BC into a democratic republic, dominated by aristocratic clans of whom the Scipiones were typical.* Rich and ancient landowners, enthused with the martial spirit of Rome, the Scipiones would provide sixteen of Rome's ruling consuls, some serving more than once. Starting as one of many Italian city states, surrounded by rivals, the Sabines and Etruscans who had provided some of its early kings, Rome conquered all of its Italian neighbours. But its rise was neither smooth nor inevitable: it was on several occasions threatened by invasions of Gauls who, in 387, actually sacked the city – and in 280, King Pyrrhus of Epirus, cousin of Alexander the Great and aspiring empire-builder, invaded Italy and won a series of costly (Pyrrhic) victories.

The Scipiones personified the machismo, aggression and discipline of Rome, prizing *pietas* (piety), *dignitas* (prestige) and, above all, *virtus*, what we call virtue. The very concept of virtue derived from *vir* (man), god-fearing virile decency was male: men ruled the *familia*, the household. Noble fathers organized their daughters' marriages to other grandees; it was easy for men to divorce and they did so often.† Women were *sub manu* – under the hand: they could technically be executed by their fathers and husbands and were expected to display *pudicitia*,

---

* All Rome's major offices, consuls, praetors, tribunes, were elected: office holders were elected by various assemblies of citizens, either the Centuriate, Tribal or Plebian assemblies, often meeting at the Comitum of the Forum. By the time much of Italy had been conquered, the electorate contained as many as 900,000 voters, but many fewer – 30-50,000 – actually voted; bribery was rife; factional violence endemic. These citizens – the males, not women and not slaves – elected two consuls annually who served as political and military leaders. Consuls were virtually always patricians (noblemen), while its Senate, filled with 600 patricians (resembling the Carthaginian Council of the Mighty), instructed the consuls and in times of crisis appointed dictators to rule for short periods. These patricians wore the national dress, the toga, a white garment with a purple border for office holders (hence the word candidate, from *candidatus*, meaning a man who wore the white toga of election campaigns). There was a growing tension between the patrician oligarchs and the people, the plebeians, whose elected tribunes could intervene and veto laws.

† In order to divorce his wife a man just said, 'Take your things for yourself.' Noble marriage was often political, but not always. There were cases where happily married couples were forced to divorce and make political marriages. Babies were born at home, and many women died in childbirth. Where Caesarean section was undertaken, the mother always died, even if (as with Scipio) the baby was saved. Imperfect babies were rejected and exposed. Most noble women had their babies breastfed by enslaved wetnurses. In the aristocracy, both girls and boys were educated, but the status of girls was shown by the fact that they were often given the family name – Cornelia in the case of Scipiones – with a number. A relationship between a man and a woman without marriage was called *concubinatus*. Concubine came to mean a non-married woman, a junior wife or, more often, an enslaved girl in the harem of a potentate.

chastity and fidelity, to ensure the bloodline of their children, while running the home and keeping out of politics – though of course they exerted power behind the scenes. Once the childbearing was done, it is clear they enjoyed affairs with other nobles and even sex with slaves – provided they did not flaunt their pleasures. The *familia* included the family's slaves, who were expected to be loyal to the *dominus* (master) and his household even more so than to the state. Domestic slavery, male and female, always involved sexual predations by masters – and mistresses. The killing of slaves by masters was entirely legal. In a slave-owning society, with as many as 40 per cent of the population enslaved, family and slavery were entwined. But slaves were often educated, sometimes revered and loved by their masters. They were frequently freed and freedmen could become citizens, later even potentates.

Rome's success was, its people believed, owing to the favour of chief god, Jupiter Optimus Maximus. Roman religion was not one of doctrine, improvement or salvation but one of ritual and lifestyle, based on sacrifices to a pantheon to ensure success and prosperity. Only later did Romans believe that Jupiter had offered them 'empire without limit'. Rome's growth was marked by monumental building – starting with the gigantic Temple of Jupiter Optimus Maximus on the Capitoline Hill – as well as its Senate-house and later amphitheatres and theatres. Baths came later: austere Scipiones had small baths in their villas, but 'they smelt of camp, farm and heroism,' claimed the philosopher Seneca later. With empire came cleanliness.

At the beginning of the century, Lucius Scipio Barbatus (Beardy) helped defeat a coalition of Italian rivals, but more importantly he was the first definitely known consul, a man of a new, free republic who, dying in 280, boasted on his grandiose tomb of victories and *virtus*. His two sons, both of them consuls, fought the Carthaginians, but Gnaeus was captured and thereafter nicknamed She-Ass.

Now Beardy's grandsons Publius Cornelius Scipio and his brother Gnaeus arrived in Spain to find they had been outmanoeuvred by Hannibal in a duel between two republics – but also between two families.

SCIPIO, HANNIBAL AND MASINISSA

In spring 218 BC, Hannibal marched his elephants and 46,000 troops over the Alps and into Italy. Most of the elephants perished, but along the way he picked up new allies, the Gauls of southern France. Leaving some troops in Spain commanded by Gnaeus, Publius Cornelius Scipio, the consul, ferried his army back to Italy to meet Hannibal. Accompanied by his twenty-year-old son, another Publius, the future Africanus, he tried to stop Hannibal at Ticinus, where he was severely wounded, and again on the Trebbia River where the other consul was killed in a rout. In spring 217, Hannibal crossed the Apennines, losing an eye to infection, and tore into central Italy.

Chastened, the Romans elected Fabius Maximus Verrucosus (Warty) as dictator on a programme of attrition and harassment rather than pitched battles. But when the Romans mocked the dictator's courage, calling him Cunctator – Delayer – the consuls massed an army of 80,000 to confront Hannibal. At Cannae, the Carthaginians surrounded and slaughtered as many as 70,000 legionaries at a rate of a hundred a minute. The younger Scipio, now elected tribune, was in the thick of the fighting and helped save the last 10,000 survivors, but it remains the greatest Roman defeat. The aristocratic consul Lucius Aemilius Paullus was killed; afterwards Scipio married the dead consul's daughter, Aemilia, the very definition of an ideal Roman girl.

Hannibal collected the signet rings of the dead *equites* or knights and sent his brother Mago to Carthage where he dramatically cast them on to the floor of the Council. But when Maharba, his Berber cavalry commander, urged him to storm Rome, Hannibal refused. 'You know how to conquer, Hannibal,' said Maharba, 'but not how to clinch victory.' Instead Hannibal sent reasonable peace terms to the Senate, implying that his expedition was to force Rome to acknowledge Carthaginian Spain and probably return Sicily, not to conquer Italy.

Back in Rome, panic beset the city. Four traitors, Gauls and Greeks, were buried alive on the Forum, a human sacrifice to save the republic, which had lost 200,000 men. Its Italian and foreign allies, including Macedonia, defected to Hannibal. Fabius Warty Delayer restored order, purifying the city with religious rituals. When the tribunes of the army discussed abandoning Italy, young Scipio plunged in and drew his sword, making them swear 'with all the passion in my heart that I will never desert our homeland. If I wilfully break my oath may Jupiter, Greatest and Best, bring me and my *familia* a shameful death! Swear the same oath!' They did. The Romans held their nerve.

The two older Scipios had been sent back to Spain where they won victories against Hannibal's brother Hasdrubal Barca, but now in 211 BC they were both killed. Eager to avenge his father, the younger Scipio, aged twenty-five, requested the command and, since no one else offered themselves, he and his army landed in Spain, where in 209 he defeated Hasdrubal, who was about to leave with reinforcements for Hannibal. Scipio combined dynamic energy with measured diplomacy: as he was notorious as a womanizer, his men hoped to please him by presenting him with a prisoner – the most beautiful woman in Spain – but he returned her to her fiancé, a Spanish chieftain who gratefully joined the Roman side.

Hasdrubal Barca set off with reinforcements for his brother, managing to cross the Alps with another corps of elephants and break into Italy, but on the Metauro River he was killed in a clash with a Roman army commanded by Gaius Claudius Nero, scion of a great patrician clan and ancestor of the Julio-Claudian dynasty of emperors, who had Hasdrubal's head tossed over the fence into Hannibal's camp.

Two Barca brothers were left alive: Hannibal had now been in Italy for almost fifteen years; he was undefeated, but Rome was undefeatable. He could not deliver the killer blow. The Romans' losses were punishing, but they an advantage over the Carthaginians – 500,000 potential soldiers of whom somewhere between 10 and 25 per cent served annually while Hannibal depended on mercenaries, and the bad news kept coming. Scipio defeated Mago and conquered Spain; the Numidians rebelled; and Hannibal's enemies criticized him in Carthage just as Scipio was persuading the Senate to let him attack Africa. Warty Delayer opposed him, but in 204 Scipio, consul at thirty-one, commanding 35,000 men, landed in Africa.

Scipio persuaded the African prince Masinissa, son of a longstanding Carthaginian ally, to change sides. Masinissa – 'the best man of all the kings of our time', a shrewd and resourceful Numidian cavalryman who fathered forty-four children – could now counter Hannibal's cavalry. When his siege of Utica was broken by the Carthaginians, Scipio ambushed their camp, slaughtering 40,000 of their troops, a fiasco from which the city never recovered. Scipio recognized Masinissa as the Berber ruler, setting up his kingdom of Numidia as a Roman ally. Hannibal was recalled, at the age of forty-six: it was twenty-five years since he had last been in Carthage; Mago perished on the journey home. Now in Africa, Hannibal and Scipio faced one another in person. Hannibal mustered 40,000 men and eighty elephants, Scipio had fewer men but more cavalry thanks to King Masinissa.

On 19 October 202, at Zama, Scipio narrowly defeated Hannibal, whose elephants went berserk and charged into the soldiers on their own side. The war had cost the Scipios and Barcas many lives. Hannibal remained in Carthage, where he was elected suffete, organizing the payment of an indemnity and backing democratic reforms, having the

Council elected for a year instead of being inducted for life. Masinissa, whose agricultural ingenuity later made his kingdom an essential source of grain for Rome, founded a dynasty that ruled for two centuries.

Now possessing unrivalled *auctoritas* – sacred authority – Scipio was awarded a triumph,* then offered the consulship for life and dictatorship; but, criticized for his luxury and grandeur, he accepted only the victory *agnomen* Africanus.† He then retired.

Anxious lest Carthage recover under Hannibal's rule, Rome sent envoys to arrest or extradite him. Hannibal fled eastwards to the court of Antiochos III, scion of Seleukos, who was performing astonishing military feats in the east.

DEMETRIOS, KING OF THE INDIANS

Antiochos the Great, tense, lean, frenetic, was as ambitious as the founder of his house, conquering much of Türkiye, Iraq and Iran, even campaigning into Arabia and India. In Bactria, his satrap Euthydemos had declared independence and held out in Balkh. Unable to defeat him, Antiochos married his daughter to the satrap's dashing sixteen-year-old son, Demetrios. One of the most extraordinary figures of his time, Demetrios, who succeeded his father as Greek king of Bactria, then invaded India in 186 BC, where the kingdom of Ashoka had collapsed. Launching two centuries of hybrid Greek–Indian rule (longer than the British Raj lasted), Demetrios – known to the Indians as Dharmamita and to the Greeks as Aniketos (Invincible) – ruled from Taxila (Pakistan). This Yavana (Graeco-Indian) king fused Indian and Greek pantheons: on his coins, he wears elephant tusks and python crowns, linking Hercules, Buddha and possibly the Brahminist goddess Lakshmi.‡

---

* A triumph was the victory parade in which, after waiting outside the boundaries of Rome with his army, the *triumphator*, his face painted with red lead to resemble Jupiter and accompanied by a slave whispering 'Memento mori' (Remember you're mortal), led his troops (singing bawdy songs about their general), wagons of booty and manacled prisoners on a procession through a celebratory Rome, culminating in sacrifices and then, in an underground dungeon, the strangling of VIP prisoners.

† Only the grandest Roman families like the Scipios had *tri nomina*: Publius the first name or *praenomen*, Cornelius the clan *nomen* and Scipio the *cognomen*. Most Romans just had two names; slaves had one. An *agnomen* was a nickname, often humorous, or a senatorial reward. The *agnomen* Africanus was awarded by the Senate as a victory name that became hereditary.

‡ One of Demetrios' successors, Menander (Milinda), ruled north-west India and Pakistan, presenting himself as a Greek basileos and Indian maharaja: 'learned, eloquent, wise and able', he followed Buddha, who was not yet presented in statues, but these Greek monarchs may have influenced his presentation as a human. When Menander died, his widow Agathokleia became queen in her own right – a first for the Hellenistic and Indian worlds.

Antiochos the Great accepted a division of elephants from Demetrios and rode westwards, where he seized Greece. But he accepted Hannibal as an adviser – which made him an enemy of Rome: the Romans were keen to settle scores, realizing they had to control Greece, a natural staging post against them. They sent in the Scipios, Africanus and his brother Lucius, who defeated Hannibal at sea and then Antiochos himself on land. Lucius thereby won the *agnomen* Asiaticus, but both Scipios were accused of accepting bribes from Antiochos and letting Hannibal escape. Africanus smashed the incriminating tablets and advocated mercy for Hannibal, but the Romans were determined to hunt him down. Surrounded, the paladin took poison, dying in the same year as Scipio. The latter, embittered by Roman ingratitude, ordered his own burial at his villa at Liternum, not Rome, with the epitaph: 'Ungrateful fatherland, you shan't even have my bones.' Scipio Africanus too may have been poisoned.

Chastened by his Roman defeat, Antiochos gave up on Europe, promised to relinquish his elephant army and his fleet and send his younger son as a hostage to Rome, but he kept Iran and Iraq and seized all of Syria and Judaea, treating the Jews well and granting them semi-independence and freedom of worship in their Jerusalem Temple. It looked as if House Seleukos would destroy their cousins the Ptolemies, take Egypt and reassemble Alexander's conquests. Meanwhile in China, Qin had created a vast new empire.

Yet there were signs that all was not well: the First Emperor sailed up and down the coast, shooting whales with a giant crossbow while seeking the Island of Immortality.

ROTTING FISH OF QING: THE RISE OF LITTLE RASCAL

The emperor, forty-nine years old, was travelling with Prince Huhai, aged twenty-one, his eighteenth and favourite son, when he died, possibly poisoned by his own mercury-infused immortality elixirs. His chancellor, the seventy-year-old Councillor, concealed the death: the dead emperor was served meals while his eunuchs pretended to transmit reports to 'the slumbering chariot', but the body soon stank so pungently that the Councillor procured a cart of rotten fish to mask the royal putrefaction. The Councillor and the young prince's eunuch chamberlain Zhao Gao decided to give the throne to Huhai, which meant they would remain in control.

When he reached the capital Xianyang, the Second Emperor was enthroned while his father was buried in his mausoleum with a human sacrifice in which ninety-nine concubines who had not delivered sons were buried with him. Their young female skeletons have been found, revealing violent deaths – and one girl still wearing her pearls. As the workmen who had created the complex were killed and thrown into a mass grave, royal princes were dismembered in the main square.

The rebellions started. In August 209 BC, in Henan, two hired labourers were in charge of delivering a chain gang of 900 convicts, but a rainstorm delayed their arrival. Knowing that in Qin lateness was punished by death, as was escape, they decided that 'flight means death, plotting means death' so 'death for establishing a state is preferable'. After all, said one, 'Are kings and nobles given their high status by birth?' At the same time, a local sheriff named Liu Bang, the peasant from central China who had once seen the First Emperor in person, was leading another chain gang to Mount Li to work on the First Emperor's tomb. A few prisoners escaped, which meant that Liu and his charges would be executed, so he liberated them all. More men joined his band when he killed the local magistrate.

As a boy in his village, Liu had been nicknamed Little Rascal by his father for his mischievous laziness, yet he was also genial, cheerful and loyal. A late starter, serving as companion to a local lord and enrolling as a village policeman, he rose slowly, impressing those he met including a local gentleman who was so taken with his physiognomy, which he took to indicate a glorious future, that he married him to his daughter Lu Zhi. Now forty-seven, he joined a multifaceted civil war in which warlords set up their own kingdoms.

The Second Emperor floundered: in August 208, his eunuch, Zhao Gao, framed the Councillor, who was sentenced to the gruesome Five Punishments, a horror probably developed by the First Emperor that would endure for centuries: the victim was tattooed on the face, then the nose was cut off, the limbs dislocated then amputated, the genitals sliced off and the body cut in half at the waist.* Zhao Gao staged a rebel attack on the palace, manipulating the Second Emperor into committing suicide, then appointing a biddable prince as king. But it was too late.

In July 207, Liu Bang – Little Rascal – attacked the capital, captured the last of the Qin and, to secure the loyalty of recently conquered populations, announced a reduction in the dynasty's punishments. After five years fighting rival warlords, in February 202 Liu Bang routed his rivals

---

* Zhao Gao, now chancellor, tricked the emperor by forcing a loyalty test on courtiers: he presented a deer but insisted it be called a horse. 'Is the chancellor perhaps mistaken calling a deer a horse?' asked the emperor, but his courtiers backed the eunuch. It is a story that every leader should bear in mind – and the first historical case of gaslighting.

and accepted the title Huang-di, emperor, known posthumously as Gaozu – High Progenitor – of his new Han dynasty. Emperor Gao divided the empire into kingdoms which he granted to members of his own family and, not far from the ruined Xianyang, he built a new capital Chang'an. While he took many concubines, his partner was still his original wife Lu, mother of a son and daughter, but he worried that the son was 'too weak'. Instead he favoured a younger concubine Qi and her son Liu Ruyi, whom he promised to promote. This unleashed a vicious rivalry between the two mothers that would be a feature of many Chinese courts.

Gaodi, born a peasant, was a rough, unpretentious, hard-drinking soldier. Once, the emperor stopped by at his peasant homestead where, playing a zither, he sang about his unlikely rise:

Now my power rules all Within the Seas,
I've returned to my old village.
Where else would I find braves
To guard the four corners of my land?

Within the Seas was the description that the Han gave to China itself; the challenge was guarding its Four Corners, particularly from the horsemen of the north who formed a confederation that preyed on Chinese cities, and at times in future centuries would conquer the whole of China. These Xiongnu were led by Modun, who as *shanyu* – king – had united these horse-riding tribes into a federation that, reacting against Chinese expansion, extended across Manchuria, eastern Siberia and central Asia: the first of the three great steppe empires. In 200, the emperor attacked Modun, but the shanyu soon surrounded him. Desperate to escape, Emperor Gao recognized Modun, paid him tribute and gave him a Han princess as wife, the start of *heqin* – Harmonious Kinship – in which Chinese princesses were married to these rather sophisticated barbarians, who were also bribed with thousands of bales of silk. Modun got both.

Liu never stopped fighting. At a minor siege, he was hit by an arrow, dying slowly from the wound in the company of his old henchmen, reminiscing about their astonishing rise. His soft-hearted eldest son succeeded to the throne. But he was controlled by the Dowager Empress Lu, who was as terrifying as she was competent.

MONSTRESS: MEET THE HUMAN SWINE

Emperor Hui, upon his accession, was just fifteen years of age, and naturally his mother made all the policy decisions, including the decision to marry him to his cousin, but they were childless. When he fathered two sons by a concubine, Lady Qi, Empress Lu had the imperial couple adopt them as their own and plotted to have the real mother killed.

Determined to torpedo the ambitions of Lady Qi, she first tried to entrap the emperor's son Liu Ruyi, prince of Zhao, who was only twelve. The emperor repeatedly intervened to keep the boy out of his mother's clutches, but when he was away hunting she poisoned him. With the son gone, the mother was exposed. The empress seized Lady Qi: her hands and legs were cut off, her eyes were gouged out and then, paralysed with poison, she was thrown into a cesspit to die. There she was shown to the emperor and others with the words: 'Meet the human swine.' The emperor hardly dared contradict his mother, leaving the politics to her. She was good at it, keeping many of her husband's henchmen in position while crushing dissent. The inner court of palace women, eunuchs and affines was often portrayed by the bureaucrats who compiled the histories as decadent and rotten. Yet often, throughout this history, these trusted relationships formed the emperor's essential base against the bureaucracy of the outer court. In China, as in most other monarchies, family and gender – so often presented in terms of vicious sex-mad women and weak-willed men – were forces in the eternal competition for power and legitimacy.

By the time Empress Lu finally died in 180 BC, her own family were planning to supplant the Han, but the old ministers had other ideas, massacring the entire Lu family and enthroning the Progenitor's son, Wen, who consolidated the dynasty that would rule east Asia, almost in parallel with Rome.

Yet between Rome and China, another power, Antiochos the Great, descendant of Alexander's general Seleukos, still dominated west Asia.

MIHRDAD AND JUDAH: JEWISH HAMMER; PARTHIAN SHOT

Yet the power of Antiochos the Great depended on his own peripatetic energy: in 187 BC he was killed raiding a temple in Iran. His son, Antiochos IV Epiphanes, even more manic and frantic that his father, had spent his youth in Rome. Inspired by Rome's semi-democracy, the flashy king liked to greet and chat with his subjects on walkabouts and hold spectacular parties into which he was carried dressed as a mummy before bursting out of his bandages to the applause of the crowds. But he also thought he was a god manifest – a bad combination. Keen to complete his father's dream of an empire from India to Libya, he invaded Egypt. But Rome now protected the Ptolemies. A Roman envoy intercepted him and drew a 'line in the sand' at his feet: if he advanced one step further, Rome would intervene. Antiochos retreated to Judaea. There the Jews, connected to Egypt where members of the priestly family served as generals, conspired against him. Antiochos slaughtered Jews, banned their faith and founded a shrine to himself in their Temple in sacred Jerusalem, sparking a rebellion by Judah the Maccabee (the Hammer) that ultimately led to the creation of a new Jewish kingdom.* Antiochos' Iranian provinces were also under attack. Galloping east to save them, he was unlucky enough to confront a warlord named Mihrdad who would create an empire powerful enough to hold Rome at bay for four centuries.

Mihrdad was the great-nephew of Arsak, probably an Afghan chieftain who fled to Parthia (Turkmenistan), becoming sacred ruler of a semi-nomadic tribe of horsemen who worshipped the Zoroastrian pantheon but were influenced by their Hellenic neighbours. Their power derived from their combination of armoured and light cavalry, who could fire their crossbows from the saddle: what the Romans called 'the Parthian shot'. In 164, Antiochos arrived to defend Iran, but Mihrdad killed the last great Seleucid king and then took Persia and Babylon, where he was crowned king of kings, parading statues of Marduk and Ishtar, before moving to Seleucia where he and his successors built a new capital, Ctesiphon, fusing Greek and Persian kingship. Mihrdad's heirs were prone to succession bloodbaths, but their cavalry was formidable, their treasure bountiful, thanks to a tax on the silk, perfumes and spices traded between China and the Mediterranean now dominated by Rome.

AFRICANUS THE YOUNGER AND THE KING OF NUMIDIA: THE DEATH OF GREAT CITIES

When Carthage recovered from its defeats, the Romans turned to the Scipios to destroy the great city once and for all. After Greece and Hispania – as the Romans called Spain – had been conquered, the ambitious generals and legions of the Carthaginian wars had to be used: new victories meant new loot, new temples, new slaves for Rome. Carthage was no longer a threat, but when a curmudgeonly ex-consul, Cato, visited, he was horrified to see that it was flourishing. In the Senate, he

---

* This is the story told today in the Jewish festival of Hanukkah. The Maccabean kings ruled Judaea – encompassing most of today's Israel, Jordan and Lebanon – for over a century.

brandished a fresh Carthaginian fig to demonstrate that the city was just a short voyage away. 'Carthage,' he declared, 'must be destroyed.' It was the only time in history that a fruit served as a *casus belli*.

It was Rome's African ally King Masinissa who provoked the Carthaginians into breaking their treaty. That meant war, and the Romans turned to a young Scipio, rich, cultivated, grand, a superb orator and patron of a circle of Greek intellectuals, a man who prided himself on exercising both a mind admired for wit and a body for its buffness. In 149 BC, the twenty-six-year-old Scipio Aemilianus* led the Roman army to Africa, accompanied by his old Greek tutor Polybius, who was fascinated by expanding Roman power and the new connections between east and west. Elected consul, still only twenty-eight, Scipio, aided by Masinissa, defeated the Carthaginians and then cut off the city from the sea. After Roman prisoners had been skinned and dismembered on the walls, he stormed the city. Carthaginians burned themselves to death in their temples. The Romans slaughtered thousands, the troops flinging bodies off buildings which they set on fire – a dystopia confirmed by archaeology. As they watched, Polybius wept. 'All cities, nations and powers,' he said, 'must like men meet their doom.' The fall of a great city has a special poignancy. It is like the death of a piece of ourselves.

'This is glorious,' agreed Scipio, 'but I have a foreboding that one day the same doom will be pronounced upon my own country.' He razed the city, selling 80,000 of its citizens into slavery and returned as Rome's reigning hero. Polybius, going home to Greece to write a world history, saw the opening of a new act – the age of *symploki* or interconnectedness: 'In earliest times, history was a series of unrelated episodes but from now on history becomes an organic whole,' he wrote. 'Europe and Africa with Asia, and Asia with Africa and Europe.' And the greatest Afro-eurasian continental powers would be built by two families.

---

* A statue known as *The Greek Prince* shows a ripped Roman patrician who may well be this Scipio. Roman intermarriage between patrician clans was complex, made worse by adoption that meant a grandee would adopt someone else's son as his own, complicating already tangled relationships. Publius Cornelius Scipio Africanus Aemilianus had been adopted by Africanus' son because his own father Lucius Aemelianus Paullus, conqueror of Macedonia, had so many other sons. While in Greece, his father encountered the future historian Polybius, who, forced to live in Rome as a hostage, became the boy's tutor. The great Africanus had married his teenaged daughter Cornelia Africana, famed for her virtue and intelligence, to an elder senator Gracchus: their daughter Sempronia, a paragon of Roman *pudicitia*, was married to Scipio Aemilianus.

ACT THREE
120 MILLION

The Han and the Caesars

KING FATSO, HIS SON AND THE CLEOPATRAS

As if to demonstrate this new interconnectedness, Rome now turned to Egypt, Mediterranean breadbasket and gateway to Asia. After destroying Carthage and fighting in Hispania, Scipio Aemilianus – loathed by the popular faction in Rome for his aristocratic grandeur – was dispatched to talk sense to the most atrocious of Egyptian pharaohs, depraved even by the standards of the degenerate Ptolemies.

Fatso (Physcon) – as Ptolemy VIII was called by the Alexandrians – was effete, obese and sadistic, thriving in a period of mob violence and factional intrigue. Marrying his sister Cleopatra II and fathering a son Memphites, Fatso then fell in love with her daughter, child of his sister-wife and late brother – his niece and stepdaughter Cleopatra III – and married her too, further poisoning the family since the mother and daughter became jealous rivals. Cleopatra II was shocked at the betrayal by husband and daughter, sparking a loathing that led to a revolution. Fatso and his younger wife fled to Cyprus, while Cleopatra II ruled Egypt as sole queen. But Fatso had not given up. Realizing that their son Memphites might replace him, he kidnapped the fourteen-year-old, who trusted his father. Then Fatso had him strangled in front of him before cutting off his head, legs and hands, which he then sent to the boy's mother, his sister-wife, the night before her birthday. Heartbroken, she displayed the body parts to Alexandrians. Fatso then outplayed her and invaded, taking a terrible vengeance on his enemies, who were burned alive. Rome cared little about Ptolemaic atrocities and much about Roman influence and trade: Fatso, who had visited Rome, carefully cultivated the Scipio family, even proposing to marry a Scipio daughter. Around 139 BC, Scipio was sent to Alexandria to overawe the egregious Fatso, now so fat he could scarcely walk. The Alexandrians watched the royal blancmange bulging out of his silken gowns, moistly panting to keep up with the craggy Roman. 'The Alexandrians owe me one thing,' joked Scipio. 'They've actually seen their king *walk*.'

Family politics bolstered the rule of women. Cleopatra II survived the murder of her son. After Fatso's death in 116, she and her daughter Cleopatra III ruled with a son who adored houmous, nicknamed King Chickpeas by Alexandrians. When a king is named after his favourite dish, a dynasty is in trouble.

Yet Scipio – and his historian Polybius – would have appreciated Fatso's only positive achievement: his sailors discovered the Indian monsoon, which meant they could sail to Parthia or India in summer and return in winter. In 118, he sent the sailor Eudoxos of Cyzicus directly to India.

HARMONIOUS KINSHIP, BLOOD-SPATTERED MARRIAGE: A PRINCESS WITH THE NOMADS

The Chinese were probing from the opposite direction. In Chang'an, a remarkable young Han emperor would rule for fifty-four years and establish a short-lived empire that extended from Korea in the east to Uzbekistan in the west. Emperor Wu was initially curious, cultivated and bold, sending an ambassador westwards to contact other great powers – the start of China's western path.

Wudi was made by women and almost destroyed by women: in 141 BC, aged fifteen, he was placed on the throne by his aunt and mother-in-law, Princess Guantao, and immediately started to restore imperial power. Yet his grandmother, Empress Dowager Dou, who held the Tiger Tally* essential for giving orders to the military, crushed his proposals. Using his failure to produce an heir with his empress Chen, she planned his removal. Wudi pretended to devote himself to partying, showing no interest in politics as he secretly gathered a brains trust of henchmen. When the chance arose to expand southwards, he dared to bypass his grandmother's Tiger Tally and annexed parts of today's south China, seizing Minyue (Fujian). At home he fathered a child with a favourite concubine. Both moves outmanoeuvred his grandmother, who died soon afterwards. Wudi promoted promising candidates for office if they could draft documents in his favoured antique rhetorical style, but while a few Confucian scholars tutored imperial princes, he did not develop a coherent set of

---

* The Tiger Tally, Hu-Fu, was the proof of imperial authority, a golden tiger divided into halves, one held by the ruler, one by the general. It was the second-century BC equivalent of the nuclear codes.

Confucian doctrines. He did have an artistic and intellectual streak himself,* enlarging the old Qin emperors' Music Bureau which handled court spectaculars and cultural matters. But at heart he was an empire builder. Enriched by tax revenues, he launched offensives on all fronts. To build an alliance against the Xiongnu, Wudi, using Harmonious Kinship, sent a princess, Jieyou, impoverished granddaughter of a fallen prince, to marry the chieftain of the Wusun tribe (in today's Xinjiang).

Accompanied by a lady-in-waiting Feng Liao, Jieyou married three times: first she wed the chieftain, then when he died his brother and heir, whom she loved and with whom she had five children, and then finally his nephew too. In the process, this remarkable woman sent Feng Liao to negotiate alliances and appeal to the court in Chang'an with such success that she briefed the emperor and was appointed an ambassador.†

Simultaneously, Wudi dispatched an intrepid soldier-courtier on a trading mission to the west. In ten years of adventure, Zhang Qian was captured, enslaved, imprisoned, escaped, married, enslaved again and finally in 122 BC returned to report to the emperor. He described the Parthians and the Indo-Greeks, spoke of his discovery of a Sichuan berry sauce already on sale in the area we now call northern India and recommended a breed of horses in Fergana (Uzbekistan), known for 'bloodsweating' – most likely because they were victims of parasites that caused them to bleed. Wudi was impressed – he wanted those 'heavenly horses' and these reports encouraged trade with Parthia. Persian luxuries now appear in Chinese tombs, and, starting in 110, Parthia sent delegations to Chang'an.

As China encountered Parthia, so did Rome: while the Han were perfecting dynastic monarchy, the Romans spent the next fifty years in civil

---

* When a beloved concubine died, Wudi lamented:
  The whisper of her silk skirt has gone.
  Dust gathers on the marble pavement.
  Her empty room is cold and still.
  Fallen leaves are piled against the doors.
  How can my aching heart rest?
† Whatever her success, Feng Liao missed home in her 'strange land on the other side of heaven'; instead, as she wrote in a beautiful poem that speaks for so many princesses married to uncouth strangers, they sent her:
  To live far away in the alien land of the Asvin king,
  A yurt is my dwelling, of felt are my walls,
  For food I have meat, with kumis to drink
  I'm always homesick and inside my heart aches
    I wish I were a yellow-beaked swan winging myself back home.
After fifty years, she finally winged herself home to Chang'an.

wars, out of which their own monarchy emerged. The first one-man ruler of Rome since the kings, Lucius Cornelius Sulla was the precursor of Caesar – and the first to take Rome into Asia.

THE KING WHO COULDN'T BE POISONED, THE MONORCHISTIC DICTATOR AND THE TEENAGED BUTCHER

Sulla was a new type of Roman. He spent his youth partying with actors and courtesans, a patrician so poor he lived in an apartment in a city block, not a villa. Athletic, blue-eyed, with bright red-blond hair and freckled skin, Sulla was both breezy and terrifying: rumoured to have one testicle, he cheerfully let his soldiers sing songs about his monorchistic anatomy yet punished any indiscipline with instant crucifixion. His motto was 'No better friend, no worse enemy'.

Sulla, leader of the optimates – the 'Best' elite – rose in the shadow of Gaius Marius, an older leader of the *populares* people's faction. In 107, when Marius fought Jugurtha of Numidia, Masinissa's grandson, Sulla, serving as his deputy, captured the Berber king and made his name. In 102, Marius saved Rome from the greatest threat since Hannibal: the Germanic-Celtic tribes of the Cimbri and Teutons, starting in Denmark and migrating southwards, had routed a Roman army – a crisis so grave that the Romans conducted their last human sacrifices to appease the gods. Marius destroyed their invaders. Together Marius and Sulla then crushed the revolt of the Socii, the allied Italian cities in the so-called Social War. In 96 BC, Sulla was dispatched eastwards to rule as governor of Rome's first Asian province, Cilicia, where he observed the meteoric rise of a talented, indefatigable monarch, Mithridates, king of Pontus, descended from Darius and Seleukos, who was conquering an empire that encompassed much of Asia Minor and the Black Sea. Said to be able to speak all the twenty-five languages of his subjects, Mithridates had hardened himself by living in the wild and made himself immune to poison by daily imbibing small doses, created by his Scythian hierophants. In 88, the Poison King orchestrated a massacre of Romans in Asia, before moving into Greece.

Sulla exploited a growing unease that Marius, who served as consul seven times, was too powerful. Their rivalry undermined the republic. In 88 BC, when the Senate planned Mithridates' expulsion from Greece, Sulla won the command but Marius tried to procure it for himself. Outrageously breaking republican norms, Sulla marched his legion into

Rome and outlawed Marius.* Then he departed for Greece, where he expelled the Poison King.

In his absence, Marius seized back power, promoting a young man – his nephew, Gaius Julius Caesar. He was one of the patrician Julians who claimed descent from Aeneas and Venus, but his father, a governor of Asia, had died young. This cold, lithe, irrepressible life force with his avian, balding head, depilated body and dandyish style was close to his shrewd mother Aurelia. He was not rich and he suffered fits, possibly epilepsy, but did not let anything hold him back: Marius helped nominate him as a priest of Jupiter. But in 82 BC, after Marius' death, Sulla returned, marched on Rome, routed his opponents and was elected dictator (the first since Hannibal's invasion) – awarded the *agnomen* Felix (Lucky). He issued a *proscriptio*, a notice of condemnation that became a euphemism for a kill list. He was vindictive. 'No friend ever served me, and no enemy ever wronged me, whom I have not fully repaid' were the words Sulla had engraved on his tomb.

Caesar was the one of three young meteors particularly affected by Sulla's bloody rise. Gnaeus Pompey, son of a rich potentate, raised his own legion and backed Sulla, murdering his enemies so efficiently he was nicknamed Adulescentulus Carnifex – Teenaged Butcher. Marcus Crassus – for whom the word crass should have been invented – was a homicidal speculator who added landowners to the death lists then grabbed their properties, making him very rich. As a Marian, Caesar was vulnerable. Sulla ordered Caesar, just eighteen, to divorce his wife Cornelia, daughter of a political enemy, but Caesar dared refuse: he was sacked as priest, his money confiscated, and added to the kill list. Only his mother Aurelia saved him by appealing to Sulla. Caesar fled to Asia where, serving with the Roman governor, he flirted with the king of Bithynia, a subordinate liaison he never lived down.†

In 79, once his enemies were dead, Sulla, singular in so many things, retired from his dictatorship and returned to his earlier life of debauchery: he had shown what could be done in Rome. 'If Sulla did it,' reflected Pompey, 'why not me?' Caesar would emulate the dictator while noting that 'Sulla was a political illiterate to resign the dictatorship.'

---

* When one of his enemies, the tribune, was betrayed by one of his slaves, Sulla killed him. He freed the slave for his service and then had him thrown from the Tarpeian Rock – the eighty-foot cliff close to the Capitol used for killing egregious traitors and rebel slaves – for betraying his master. Romans were very nervous about slave revolts.

† The implication was that Caesar had taken the inferior sexual position to King Nicomedes. Much later, even during his first Triumph, his soldiers sang, 'Caesar laid the Gauls low; Nicomedes bent him over.'

As Sulla was killing his enemies in Rome, Emperor Wu was losing control of himself and his family in Chang'an.

THE CASTRATED HISTORIAN AND EMPEROR WU

Wudi enjoyed a spree of successes: in 112 BC, he took Guandong in the south and more of Vietnam; in 109, he invaded Korea; in 108, he attacked the Xiongnu, then seized much of Xanjiang and expanded through Kazakhstan to Fergana in Uzbekistan; in 104, he demanded the special horses of Dayan (Kokand), sending his general Li Gungli to fight the War of the Heavenly Horses, thus securing 3,000 of these blood-sweating steeds.

Yet at court things were turning sour. When Wudi's sister introduced him to a lowly born singer-dancer, Wei, he fell for her and their sons provided the essential heirs. But Empress Chen's attempt to curse Wei with witchcraft was denounced and exposed, and she was destroyed. The new empress Wei Zifu brought him luck – for a while.

Capricious and increasingly murderous, Wudi became ever more improvident. He built vast new palaces, embarked on expensive tours, executing grandees who failed to feed his vast entourage, and staged elaborate sacrifice rituals on the sacred Mount Tai to confirm the Mandate of Heaven.* Empress Wei came to be overshadowed by his beloved Consort Li, whose brother won laurels in central Asia, winning fame as the Flying General. But the Xiongnu hit back, defeating a Han army. In 99, when the Flying General's grandson Li Leng defected to the nomads, his friend the court historian Sima Qian went to intercede with the emperor – with atrocious consequences.

Wudi believed that history was as important as war: it legitimized the dynasty. But it had to be the right history. Wudi commissioned his grand scribe – part historian, part astrologer – Sima Tian to write the first full Chinese history, known today as the *Shiji, Records of the Grand Historian*. When Sima Tian died in 110, he passed his quill to his thirty-five-year-old son Sima Qian, who recalled him 'grasping my hands with tearful eyes' and saying, 'Don't forget what I intended to write down.'

---

* Han tombs, even those of minor princes and kings, reveal the culture and splendour of the court, not least the jade suit (for example, of a king of Zhongshan), constructed from around fourteen pieces, that covered the entire body like a suit of armour, including gloves and helmet, stitched together with gold thread. In the tomb of a government minister, the marquess of Dai, were painted silk banners, inventories on bamboo slips, cooking recipes and a sex manual.

Sima Qian, an attendant of the emperor, who had served in the army against the Xiongnu, set to work. Scribes like Sima used a writing brush, ink slab, knife and seal to write on narrow wooden strips, silk being used only for important documents. Like Polybius, his contemporary in Rome, he believed in world history 'to examine all that concerns heaven and man, to penetrate the changes of past and present'. But the history of the past is always about the present: when he criticized 'expedient' royal advisers and denounced the First Emperor's cruelties, he offended his own paranoid emperor.

In 99 BC, Sima Qian interceded with the emperor for Li Leng – 'to widen His Majesty's view' – at which the emperor accused him of Grand Insult and sentenced him to death by suicide, a sentence that could be commuted on payment of a fine or castration. Sima did not have the money and refused to kill himself, so he was forced to choose 'the punishment of rottenness'. He dreamed of his book being read in 'villages and great cities' but 'since I regretted that I had not finished [the book], I submitted to the extreme penalty without bitterness' – the shame of castration, performed in the silkworm chamber, where mutilated men were kept like silkworms in a warm, airless room, believed to help prevent infection. He survived, was promoted to court archivist/ astrologer and palace secretary and finished his classic history. But his involvement in intrigues was not quite over.

In 96 BC, after a dream about an assassin and killer puppets, Wudi was convinced by his chief of security that his illnesses were the treasonous work of black magic. In a spiralling vortex of denunciations and witch-hunting, he ordered foreign shamans to excavate the palaces to find magical dolls and unleashed witchcraft trials against his own ministers, executing no less than six of his chancellors, butchering entire clans, tens of thousands of innocent people. Even Wudi's own daughters were sucked into the vortex and executed. Killing sons was sometimes necessary for monarchs – but not daughters.

Wudi's eldest son Ju with Empress Wei was the heir apparent, but at sixty-two the emperor fathered a son with a younger concubine, Lady Gouyi. Wudi's security chief framed Prince Ju for witchcraft and for wishing his father dead – probably no more than the truth since the emperor had been on the throne for so long. As tension rose, Ju – realizing he was being framed – forged an order from Wudi and killed the security chief, before rushing to explain himself to his father. So, backed by his mother the empress, he tried to seize power.

After five days of fighting in the streets of Chang'an, the emperor restored order, Empress Wei committed suicide, her clan was eliminated and Ju hanged himself. All the emperor's sons – and anyone who had shown any hesitation in backing him – were killed except the baby. Yet the witch-frenzy changed China forever, liquidating the old clans and creating a vacuum that was filled by officials of obscure birth.

Finally, the emperor realized that his henchmen had framed his son. Grieving and blaming himself, he issued his public Repenting Edict of Luntai, but now punished the family of his Consort Li who had managed to destroy most of the Wei family. The Li were killed to the ninth degree.

The only heir left alive was the boy, now aged nine, born to Lady Gouyi. In 88 BC, the emperor appointed him as his heir but, fearing the mother would become too powerful after his death, he summoned the young woman and ordered her arrest: she kowtowed in amazement, at which he ordered, 'Out, quickly! You can't be saved!' He had her killed.

When Wudi died in 87, buried, no doubt in a jade suit, in the Maoling tomb, his concubines may have been sacrificed, though this might be an echo of the First Emperor. Among the beautiful artefacts buried with him was the Golden Horse, a two-foot-high statue of the one of Wudi's 'heavenly horses'. Even more than the First Emperor, Wudi was the creator of Chinese empire: he had doubled its size, yet his killings, witch-hunts and extravagance had unleashed court feuds and '100 peasant revolts'.

In 73, the slaves of Rome rebelled – and the city's potentates, Pompey and Crassus, competed to crush them.

BALD FORNICATOR AND EGYPTIAN QUEEN:
CAESAR AND CLEOPATRA

It started in the gladiator school at Capua where seventy gladiators – all of whom were slaves – escaped and elected a Thracian, Spartacus, as leader. Establishing his headquarters near Mount Etna, he repeatedly defeated Roman units, assisted by his partner, a Dionysian priestess. Rome was run on slave labour, boosted by captives from its wars, and Romans were terrified of revolt: 40 per cent of its Italian population were enslaved, and this was the third slave revolt in forty years. Spartacus' rebels, recruited from the rural slaves who laboured in mines and plantations, could not decide whether to escape across the Alps or go looting in Italy, but they had no programme to liberate all slaves. Within a year, 40,000 ex-slaves and their families had joined Spartacus, who had seized a swathe of southern Italy before marching north. Since

Pompey was conquering Hispania, and other legions were confronting the Poison King in Asia, Rome was vulnerable. The property speculator Crassus raised forces and defeated the slaves, crucifying 6,000; Pompey mopped up. Both claimed credit.

In 67 BC, Pompey was sent east to crush the resurgent Mithridates of Pontus. First, he defeated the Poison King, whom he pursued into the Caucasus where Mithridates committed suicide, then he annexed much of Asia Minor and Syria. He deposed the Seleucids, and brought under Roman sway the kingdoms of Arab Nabataea and Jewish Judaea. When a Judaean prince of the Maccabean family defied him, he stormed Jerusalem, violating the Temple by entering the Holy of Holies, and left a rump Judaea under Jewish rule. The Egyptian king Piper (Ptolemy XII Auletes) courted Pompey, winning his support with eyewatering bribes. It is possible that Pompey met Piper's six-year-old daughter, Cleopatra, who would later be adept at negotiating with Roman potentates. Suddenly Rome was a tricontinental empire: only in Parthia had Pompey met his match. Pompey invaded Georgia and Armenia, but Farhad II of Parthia seized back Armenia. Pompey and Farhad negotiated as equals.

Back in Rome, democracy was being destroyed by fights for the prizes of its growing empire. A conspiracy to overthrow it in a bloody massacre was only defeated thanks to the eloquence of consul, brilliant orator and sublime writer Marcus Tullius Cicero. Arriving home in Rome, flaunting Alexander the Great's cloak (captured from Mithradates), Pompey, richer and more powerful than any Roman had ever been, was awarded an unprecedented third triumph for victories on a third continent and granted the *agnomen* Magnus – Great. The *tri-triumphator* launched a spectacular building programme. There was something of the modern politician about this man, described as 'honest of face, shameless of heart', but even self-righteous Cicero was dazzled by his 'incredible godlike *virtus*'. Pompey dominated the fragile Roman democracy but did not seize total power. Instead the senators, wary of this bumptious meteor, procrastinated in confirming his Asian arrangements. Crassus tried to undermine him by backing Caesar, who lagged behind the other two.

Caesar had only returned to Rome when he learned that Sulla was dead. The journey home revealed much about him: on his way he was captured by pirates. He warned them that, if freed, he would kill them all. Once freed, he hired a flotilla, hunted them down and crucified them. Back in Rome, he married Sulla's granddaughter Pompeia (after his first wife had died), borrowed heavily and ran for office. As he told his mother, his debts were so big, it was either 'election or prison'. In the end, Crassus paid his debts. Embracing the *populares* faction, Caesar was elected as chief priest – *pontifex maximus* – in preference to two venerable aristocrats, before distinguishing himself fighting in Spain. On his return, elected consul, Caesar proposed a populist programme in informal alliance with Pompey and Crassus. Yet they struggled to control factional violence; democracy was disintegrating; at one point, elections were delayed and Pompey served as sole consul. Pompey and Caesar crowned their alliance with marriages: Pompey divorced his wife and married Caesar's only child, his daughter Julia.* The two were now family. Caesar and Crassus both dreamed of emulating Pompey's conquests: Caesar became proconsul of Gaul; Crassus got Syria.

In 57 BC, the triumvirs received Egyptian visitors: King Piper and his daughter Cleopatra, now twelve. After impoverishing Egypt to bribe Pompey, Piper had just been deposed and replaced with his own eldest daughter Berenice IV. Escaping from Egypt, Piper came to rally Roman help, winning over Caesar and Crassus, who dispatched Roman troops from Syria – including a swaggering cousin of Caesar, Mark Antony. Restored to his crown, Piper murdered one daughter, Berenice, and replaced her as queen with another, Cleopatra. Back in Alexandria, she met Antony, who was impressed by the teenaged queen. At eighteen, Cleopatra inherited Egypt and married her brother, Ptolemy XIII.

As Pompey remained in Rome, in 53 BC Crassus sailed for Syria, hoping to out-Pompey Pompey and throw back the Parthian House of Arsak.

CRASSUS' HEAD AND THE MILLION DEAD GAULS

Crassus and 40,000 legionaries crossed the Euphrates and followed it southwards towards Seleucia. The Parthian king, Urad II, offered to

---

* In 62 BC, Caesar's second wife Pompeia, granddaughter of Sulla, had embarrassed Caesar. The notorious adulterer and *pontifex maximus* was himself being cuckolded by his pretty young wife. When Pompeia hosted the women-only festival of the Bona Dea ('Good Goddess'), the celebration was crashed by her secret lover, Clodius, an outrageous young patrician who, disguised as a woman, hoped to enjoy an assignation. Instead his gender was literally exposed; he was later tried and acquitted. But Caesar divorced Pompeia anyway, saying, 'Caesar's wife must be above suspicion.' Clodius became a murderous populist demagogue until killed in factional fighting. Caesar was a compulsive and successful lover of women: he had slept with the wives of both his fellow triumvirs Pompey and Crassus and his legionaries nicknamed him the Bald Fornicator. His favourite and most enduring lover was a married patrician, Servilia, whose first husband Marcus Brutus had been executed by Pompey. Now Caesar remarried a teenaged aristocrat, Calpurnia.

negotiate. Crassus refused. Opening his hand, Urad warned, 'Hair will grow here before you see Seleucia.' Crassus was advised to avoid the plains, ideal terrain for the Parthian cavalry; he ignored the advice.

At Carrhae, exhausted legionaries were confronted by the Parthians on a hill above them. Initially camouflaged by animal skins, they threw them aside in unison to reveal 1,000 cataphracts, armoured cavalry, and 17,000 light horsemen, helmets agleam. As the Romans assumed their classic *testudo* formation, the Parthians launched a devastating barrage of Parthian shots. Crassus retreated. When he parleyed with the Parthians, he was unhorsed and beheaded. The Parthians poured gold into his throat to mock his crassness, then sent the head to Urad, a philhellene married to a Greek princess, who was watching Euripides' tragedy *The Bacchae*. The play's director commandeered the head as a stage prop: an actor appeared on stage holding it and singing the words, 'We bring from the mountain / A tendril fresh-cut to the palace / A wonderful prey.'

Far to the west Caesar was conquering Gaul. Caesar was already forty-one and still heavily indebted when he launched his campaigns, only now displaying his homicidal ambition, adventurous spirit (at one point scouting out enemy territory in Gallic disguise) and indefatigable energy. He ensured that Romans read all about his exploits – he claimed to have killed a million Gauls, whom Romans regarded as savages – by sending home reports (narrated in the third person). Despite two crowd-pleasing raids on the benighted, barbaric island of Britannia, Caesar's *imperium* was about to run out and his aristocratic enemies, backed by Pompey, challenged him. Pompey's wife, Caesar's daughter Julia, had died in childbirth, loosening their uneasy ties. Pompey, who had most to lose, was reluctant to fight, yet he left Caesar little choice.

'Let the dice roll!' said Caesar as, channelling Sulla, he crossed the Rubicon into Italy. Pompey supported the democratic republic against a potential tyrant but was unprepared, and was forced to abandon Italy and muster forces in Greece. Caesar followed him. At Pharsalos, he defeated Pompey, who sailed to Egypt, where he had just recognized the twelve-year-old Ptolemy XIII as pharaoh with his sister-wife Arsinoe, after they had fallen out with their masterful elder sister Cleopatra. She was now fighting for her life.

The Ptolemies needed to back Roman winners: as Pompey was rowed ashore, he was beheaded. Elected dictator, Caesar left Antony, *magister equitum* – master of horse (the traditional deputy of a dictator) – to govern Rome while he sailed for Alexandria with a mere 4,000 troops, chasing Pompey. On arrival the Egyptians presented Pompey's head. Caesar wept and mourned his former son-in-law, then took up residence at the palace, demanding that the rival siblings, Ptolemy and Cleopatra, present themselves. Cleopatra refused to be judged, arranging to be delivered to Caesar in a laundry bag carried by a strapping factotum. Even if Caesar was not already the sort of man to be delighted with her haughty charisma, he was dazzled by this sexy *coup de théâtre*. He was fifty-two, she was twenty-two.

WHO I SCREW: CLEOPATRA, CAESAR AND ANTONY

Yet they were well matched. Both were political animals, theatrical maestros and born survivors and killers. Caesar was a perennial practitioner of the adventurous style of politics; she was the heiress of the world's grandest dynasty, proprietress of the body of the great Alexander, which Caesar visited. The queen was educated, intelligent, possibly a virgin, and polyglot, speaking Greek, Latin, 'Ethiopian', Egyptian (the first Ptolemy to do so; her mother may have been Egyptian) and the language Caesar most respected: power. If she lost her struggle with her brother, she would be killed. She needed Caesar.

Caesar was ill prepared for street fighting but he backed Cleopatra. Ptolemy rallied the mob while his troops besieged Caesar and Cleopatra in the palace. The fighting was vicious; Caesar was risking the world for a girl he barely knew. His small force retreated: the museum caught fire. Finding himself trapped, Caesar dived into the harbour and swam to one of his ships – quite an exploit at his age. With reinforcements, who included Jews sent from the high priest of Jerusalem and Arabs sent from the Nabataean king, Caesar routed Ptolemy, who was drowned, and secured Alexandria.

Caesar and Cleopatra celebrated on a Nilotic cruise – his first rest in ten years. Leaving a pregnant Cleopatra as pharaoh with a younger brother, Caesar hastened to crush Mithridates' son, Pharnaces, who had seized Pontus and ordered the castration of Roman citizens. Caesar defeated him so easily he boasted, 'I came, I saw, I conquered.' When he had finished mopping-up operations in Asia, Hispania and Africa, where typically he had an affair with the Berber queen, Eunoe of Mauritania, he celebrated a unique quadruple triumph* and was

* During this extravaganza – to mark victories in Gaul, Pontus, Egypt and Africa – the *triumphator*'s devoted legionaries jovially sang about his exploits and even his gay affair with the King of Bithynia, their songs culminating in the lines: 'Citizens, lock up your

appointed the first ever *dictator perpetuus*; he was further honoured by having his face put on the coinage and his name added to the calendar as the month of July. Caesar did not liquidate his opponents but instead boasted of his mercy. Cleopatra was visiting Rome with their son Little Caesar – Ptolemy Caesarion. But Caesar grew bored in Rome and planned to emulate Alexander and avenge Crassus by striking Dacia (Romania), before attacking Parthia and going on to conquer Scythia (Ukraine). Knowing that Caesar might never return, Cleopatra tried to get the three-year-old Caesarion recognized as his heir. But while she lived in one of his villas, Caesar only discussed his Egyptian family with intimate friends. Romans were fascinated by her and the baby: Cicero was received by her, and grumbled about her arrogance. When Caesar made his will, he did not mention Cleopatra's baby, instead naming a great-nephew Octavian, aged nineteen, who had joined him in Spain, as his heir.

The Perpetual Dictator thrice turned down the diadem of kingship offered by Antony but his enemies, led by Brutus, son of his lover Servilia, loathing his near-monarchy, planned to kill him before he departed. A prophetess warned Caesar about the Ides of March; Antony and Calpurnia warned of plots; but Caesar dismissed his Spanish bodyguards and walked to the senatorial meeting at Pompey's Theatre where, in the portico, Brutus and a cadre of familiar faces approached. One asked for a signature and then all drew daggers and stabbed him. Such was the frenzy that the assassins also stabbed each other. Caesar defended himself with his stylus, a sharp writing tool, but when he saw Brutus, Servilia's son whom he had pardoned, he just said, 'You too, my child,' falling to the ground and covering his head with his toga. He was stabbed twenty-three times (though the second strike to the chest was said to be fatal).

The assassins wanted to restore the republic but had no plans. Antony, now consul, outmanoeuvred them: at Caesar's funeral in the Forum, he hailed Caesar's divinity and greatness and displayed his bloodied toga, so inflaming the crowd that they drove the assassins out of Rome. (They set up headquarters in Greece). Sturdy and curly-haired, violent and virile, a cold-blooded politician, mediocre general and impulsive showman, the forty-two-year-old Antony was no understudy to Caesar: he

wives; we bring home the bald fornicator! All the gold you lent him went to pay his Gallic tarts.' The defeated Gaulish king Vercingetorix and the deposed Egyptian queen Arsinoe IV, who had fought Caesar, were paraded – watched by Arsinoe's sister Cleopatra. Vercingetorix was garrotted, the traditional climax of a triumph. Arsinoe was spared. For now.

craved power for himself. A playboy who studied philosophy in Athens, he was an enthusiast for seductions and banquets, often half soused. He sometimes dressed in Herculean lionskins and drove round Rome in a convoy of Britannic chariots, bearing his mistress, the courtesan Cytheris – and his mother. Now he abandoned Cytheris to marry Fulvia, a fierce political arbiter, once married to the demagogic agitator Clodius – a move much mocked by Cicero. Disdaining Caesar's callow heir Octavian, now officially named 'Caesar' himself, Antony finally allied with him, launching a hit list – a proscription – through which Antony took revenge on Cicero for his witticisms. 'There's nothing proper about what you are doing, soldier,' Cicero told the hitman, 'but do try to kill me properly.' Antony nailed his victim's hands and head to the rostrum in the Forum, while Fulvia cut out his tongue and pierced it with her hatpin – an ugly display even by Roman standards.

Now that Rome was secured, Antony and Octavian pursued the assassins to Greece, where they were defeated and driven to suicide. Then they divided the empire, Antony taking the east, Octavian the west.

Antony had inherited Caesar's Parthian expedition. As he mustered forces in Tarsus (Syria), Cleopatra, now twenty-eight, came to secure his support, arriving in her royal barge as a royal Isis–Aphrodite. Like Caesar, he had a taste for eastern monarchs, having just had an affair with the ex-courtesan queen of Cappadocia, Glaphyra.*

On their first night together, Antony fell for Cleopatra. She celebrated in Ptolemaic style – with Bacchic banquets and sibling murder: she had Antony kill her sister Arsinoe. During his wild stay in Alexandria, she gave birth to twins. But soon afterwards, in 40 BC, Antony negotiated a new partnership with Octavian and jilted Cleopatra to marry Octavian's sister Octavia. The two leaders now focused on retaking Judaea and Syria from the Parthians, appointing a young Jewish ally, Herod, as king of an enlarged Judaea.

In 38, Antony went east to attack Parthia – and returned to Cleopatra, giving her new territories in Lebanon, Israel and Cyprus, while together they had another son. But his army was obliterated in what is today Azerbaijan and he barely made it back to Syria. Cleopatra sailed

---

* Back in Italy, Antony's wife, Fulvia, and brother Lucius had challenged Octavian who, besieging them in Perusia, had written a bawdy poem that reveals another side of the young warlord:

Because Antony fucks Glaphyra, Fulvia has arranged this punishment for me: that I
fuck her too.
That I fuck Fulvia? . . .
'Either fuck or fight,' she says. Doesn't she know
My prick is dearer to me than life itself? Let the trumpets blare!

up the coast with supplies. Her support, along with her tantrums and their shared children, convinced him that his destiny lay with her, so he abandoned Octavia in Athens.

Antony and the queen paraded through Alexandria as Dionysios and Sarapis, then married. She was enthroned as queen of kings, Caesarion as king of kings, acclaimed as son of Caesar, and their three children received kingdoms. Octavian criticized this unvirile eastern debauchery, to which Antony replied: 'Do you object to me screwing Cleopatra? But we are married and it's not as if it's anything new.' Indeed Octavian was a hypocrite, being an avid adulterer himself. Octavian, whose wife Scribonia was then pregnant, had recently fallen in love with Livia, the clever and beautiful twenty-year-old pregnant wife of Tiberius Claudius Nero, one of the Claudian clan and an Antony supporter, who agreed to divorce her. Octavian divorced Scribonia on the day his daughter Julia was born and married Livia, three days after she gave birth, at a sumptuous ceremony embellished with *deliciae* – half-naked boy slaves – and attended by her compliant ex-husband. 'And what about you? Are you faithful to Livia?' Antony naively asked Octavian. 'What does it really matter where or with whom one gets it up?'

It did matter, politically. Octavian revealed Antony's will, which acclaimed Caesarion as Caesar's son and left everything to Cleopatra, with whom he wished to be buried, presumably embalmed pharaonically in Alexandria. Octavian denounced Cleopatra as a *fatale monstrum*, and the Senate declared war on her. Antony and Cleopatra mustered impressive resources – 250 galleys and 20,000 troops.[*] If Octavian won, his empire would speak Latin and be based in Rome; if Antony, it would be Greek-speaking, ruled from Alexandria – and today we would all speak Greek rather than Latin languages. They fought for the Mediterranean world.

CLEOPATRA'S SNAKE, ALEXANDER'S NOSE

On 2 September 31 BC, the two fleets clashed. When the armies massed in Greece, Antony was outmanoeuvred by Octavian's general Marcus Agrippa, who blockaded the Antonian army and fleet at Actium. Antony's fleet featured multi-rower ships, quinqueremes, *octeres* and even giant *deceres*, but he was less good on the detail. At their war council, Cleopatra, commanding her fleet of 200, voted to break out of Actium,

---

[*] Antony's Semitic clients, the Jewish king Herod and the Arab king Malik, delayed sending troops – both aggrieved by gifts of valuable territory to Cleopatra.

but in battle their coordination was disastrous. Cleopatra fled back to Alexandria with sixty ships, planning to use her Red Sea fleet to escape to her trading posts in Arabia if not India, only for the Arab king Malik to burn her ships. When Antony sailed after her, Octavian marched through Syria, negotiating secretly with Cleopatra, who offered to abdicate providing her children, especially Caesarion, kept their crowns. It is not clear if she really welcomed the defeated Antony.

She negotiated with Octavian, setting up headquarters in her mausoleum within the palace. Antony was possibly betrayed by Cleopatra, who misinformed him that she was dead, clearly a signal to commit suicide. After stabbing himself with his sword, he was borne to her tomb where he died in her arms aged fifty-two. Allowing her to reside in the palace, Octavian took her three Antonian children into custody. When they met, she learned there was no third act: Octavian would display her in his triumph. 'I will not be triumphed over,' she told him – she had seen her sister Arsinoe paraded through Rome – but concealed her plans. After feasting in style, her devoted attendants Eiras and Charmian arranged for a peasant to bring a basket of figs, containing a snake or at least a poison which all three of them somehow imbibed. She sent a sealed letter to Octavian asking to be buried with Antony, at which his guards rushed to stop her – too late. Cleopatra, at the age of thirty-nine, laid out in her glory wearing her diadem, was dead, along with her ladies-in-waiting. One was still just alive when Octavian's troops burst in and saw Cleopatra in her final magnificence: 'What a majestic scene!'

'Extremely,' the girl murmured, 'as becomes the descendant of so many kings.'

Cleopatra had hoped that Caesarion would rule Egypt. 'Too many Caesars,' warned Octavian's advisers, 'is not good.'

Cleopatra had sent King Caesarion, seventeen years old, with his tutor down to the Red Sea port of Berenice to escape to India, but Octavian tricked the tutor into bringing him back, hinting that the boy could rule Egypt – and then had him strangled.*

Octavian visited the tomb of Alexander, but when he touched the mummy, he knocked off its nose – a moment that marked the end of

---

* The three children of Cleopatra and Antony were raised by Octavia in Rome. Two died young, but the third, Cleopatra Selene, was married to Juba II, king of Mauritania. This was the Berber prince Juba's reward for fighting for Octavian at Actium, along with a newfangled kingdom named Mauritania in today's Algeria. Together they built a Grecian–Roman capital of cultural sophistication, while Juba sent trading expeditions that reached the Canary Islands. Cleopatra Selene died in AD 6. Their son Ptolemy, a mixture of Euro-African, Berber, Roman and Greek, Antonian and Ptolemaic, succeeded his father in AD 23.

the Alexandrian age, the fall of the Roman Republic and the launch of an imperial monarchy.

AUGUSTUS, JULIA AND THE ONE-EYED QUEEN OF KUSH

Master of the empire, the young warlord Octavian behaved as he wished, seducing the wives of his henchmen whom he would take into another room at a dinner, returning them to their husbands with their ears red, hair tousled. While they were on their own, he cross-examined them on their husbands' politics, finding out who was conspiring against him.

Octavian was a master of political dosage, understanding, after years of war and murder, that abrupt measures offend while respectful adaptation can mask dramatic change. While purportedly respecting the republic, he was now the most powerful Roman ever, adopting a new title, *princeps* – meaning 'the first' – and a new name; he was offered Romulus but finally settled on Augustus, meaning Awesome. Yet he remained modest, staying in his comfortable villa on the Palatine Hill.*
But the humility was contrived. His household was enormous, with freedmen doing the secretarial work while the graves of Livia's staff show she was served by a thousand slaves, including entertainers and dwarves. Nor was his reign as easy-going as he liked to pretend. Vicious when necessary, merciful when possible, he used informers to report any dissidence; conspirators were eliminated fast; when his secretary took money to reveal the contents of one of his letters, Augustus personally broke his legs.† Yet he was not a humourless megalomaniac either; his letters to intimates are bantering and affectionate. An enthusiastic gambler, he was highly social, regularly dined with friends and toyed with writing a tragedy while, through his wealthy advisor, Maecenas, promoted and befriended his court poets, Virgil and Horace. He praised Horace's athletic love life, nicknaming him 'Perfect Penis', but did not threaten the poet when he failed to praise the *princeps*. He just teased him.

Caesar Augustus projected Rome as a divine world empire that, behind the republican façade, was already a dynasty: married thrice but

---

* *Princeps* was the origin of our word prince, much as the Palatine was the origin of palace. Augustus avoided the title *dictator*, abolished after Caesar's assassination. From now on, *dictator* became an insult, not an office.

† Yet he disliked cruelty for its own sake: one of his earlier supporters, Vedius Pollio, was a rich but a notorious sadist who fed slaves who angered him to his carnivorous lampreys in the pond at his villa. When Augustus was there for dinner, a slave dropped a valuable cup and Vedius ordered him thrown to the lampreys, at which Augustus ordered his retainers to smash the rest of the cups until the slave was released and spared.

without sons, his ambitions rested on his daughter Julia. After marrying her to a nephew who died young, Augustus married her to his partner in power Agrippa, then aged forty, who was granted the same powers as the *princeps* himself. 'Agrippa is so great,' Augustus' minister Maecenas had warned, 'he must either be killed or become a son-in-law.' The marriage delivered two sons, Gaius and Lucius, who became the heirs. But Julia found her destiny a tedious burden, as was being continually pregnant by a much older husband. But pregnancy had its benefits.

While Augustus championed his family values and enforced a new conservative morality policy including anti-adultery legislation, Julia pursued a string of love affairs, having sex with her husband only when she was pregnant: 'I take on a passenger only when the ship's hold is full.' As her sons grew up adored by Augustus, her promiscuity became a problem.

The empire was now so big that Augustus sent Agrippa to rule the eastern half: first they signed a treaty with the young *kandake* (queen) of Kush. But the queen, Amanirenas, 'a masculine sort of woman', wrote the geographer-historian Strabo, 'fierce and one-eyed' – one of a succession of female warrior-rulers – and her husband King Teriteqas were dissatisfied with the Roman vassaldom. Her opportunity came when Augustus ordered his Egyptian prefect, Aulus Gallus, to invade Arabia Felix (Fertile Arabia – Yemen). Spices, medicines, perfumes, jewels arrived by sea from India at Egyptian or Arabian ports on the Red Sea and overland in caravans from Marib in Sheba (Yemen/Ethiopia) through Nabataea (Jordan). Augustus wished to control these trades.

Ten thousand legionaries crossed the Red Sea from Berenice, landing not far from Jeddah, marching down through Medina to take Aden, but they got lost in the desert, failed to take Marib and, their fleet destroyed, perished.

In Meroe, Teriteqas and Amanirenas learned that Augustus' Egyptian garrison had departed for Arabia and invaded Egypt. When Teriteqas died, Amanirenas succeeded him, leading their army up the Nile, an exploit she celebrated on a stela and by burying a huge head of Augustus in front of a temple. Egypt was Rome's essential breadbasket: Augustus attacked Kush, Amanirenas counter-attacked, then they agreed to negotiate. Augustus lifted taxes imposed upon the Kushites; Amanirenas ceded a strip of Lower Nubia, but she had successfully defied Rome's greatest emperor.

Augustus made a deal with Malik of Nabataea, enabling him to beautify his red-rose capital Petra as well as Mada'in Salih, while the emperor backed his Jewish ally Herod – despite his massacres and his killing of his own belovèd if traitorous wife and three of his many sons. Shrewd, charming, visionary and psychotic, Herod ruled for forty years, remodelling Jerusalem, where he built a gigantic and magnificent Jewish Temple.*

Soon 120 Roman boats were sailing annually from Red Sea ports to India. Around 20 BC, a delegation from an Indian ruler arrived to see Augustus with a gift of tigers. Roman traders, usually Arab or Egyptian rather than Italian, traded amphorae of wine, mirrors, statues and lamps in return for ivory, spices, topaz and slaves. And a new luxury was starting to arrive from China, via Parthia and Eudaemon (Aden): silk.

FLYING SWALLOW AND THE PASSION OF THE CUT SLEEVE

Her name was Flying Swallow and she was dancing at the palace of Princess Yamma when the emperor came to watch. Flying Swallow – Zhao Feiyen – was a dancing girl who came from a family so poor that they had exposed her as a baby until, overcome with regret, they returned to find her still alive. Emperor Cheng saw the slender, graceful Flying Swallow, then just fifteen, dancing with her sister – and fell in love.

Coming to the throne in 33 BC just as Augustus was confronting Antony, the eighteen-year-old Cheng had a wife, Empress Xu, and an adored consort, Ban, but neither had provided him with an heir. Cheng was a cheerful playboy, almost disinherited by his father for his hedonism, who loved sensual music and liked to plunge incognito into the stews of Chang'an for whoring and cockfighting. Flying Swallow was right up his street. As for politics, he left that to his mother, the Dowager Empress Wang, whose brother Wang Feng and others of the family ran the empire as marshals of the state. Now, brought back to the palace and enrolled with her sister Zhao Hede as a concubine, Flying Swallow brought new levels of murderous envy to the already charged court. Within a year of arriving, the two girls had framed the empress and Consort Ban for using black magic, getting Cheng to declare Flying Swallow empress in 16 BC. While Flying Swallow failed to deliver children, Cheng fathered sons by two concubines. Persuaded by Flying Swallow or Zhao Hede (who did the dirty work), the emperor or the empress killed the babies themselves to protect the two sisters; one of

---

* Herod was a brilliant player of Roman politics, switching from Antony to Augustus, then becoming almost a foreign member of the Caesar dynasty. Much of his monumental building work survives today. Of his Temple, only the outer walls survive: its western wall is the Kotel, the Western Wall, today's most sacred shrine for Jews.

the mothers was forced to commit suicide to keep the secret. The sisters fell out when the emperor favoured Zhao Hede, then colluded to poison any other girls who got pregnant.

In 7 BC, Cheng died suddenly, possibly after an over-generous dose of aphrodisiac administered by Zhao Hede. Frightened as the ensuing investigations into murdered babies and aphrodisiac overdosing closed in, she committed suicide as Cheng's nephew became emperor Ai. He excited great expectations, but illness prevented him governing and he did not like 'music or girls'. Instead he fell in love with a teenaged male courtier Dong Zian: such was his devotion that the emperor preferred to cut off the sleeve of his gown rather than wake his sleeping lover. Many emperors had male lovers, openly listed among their favourites, but 'the passion of the cut sleeve' went much further: Aidi overpromoted the twenty-two-year-old Dong to the role of commander of the army, and when Aidi was dying he left the throne to his boyfriend. Instead, granny intervened: Dowager Empress Wang orchestrated the suicide of Dong and promoted her own nephew to regent. Aged eighty-three, the dowager alone preserved Han stability, but when she died in 13 her nephew tried to found his own dynasty – a lesson in how not to manage an empire – just as, at the other end of the Silk Road, another emperor, aided by a capable female potentate, demonstrated how it should be done.

THE REPTILE OF CAPRI

Augustus, now seventy-five, was dying at his villa in his home town, Nola, south of Rome, with his wife Livia, also in her seventies, and her capable but morose son Tiberius beside him. His own direct family would not succeed him, but instead he had woven a tangled web of marriages to bind together his blood with that of Livia.

His hopes to leave a dynastic coterie of heirs had long been based on Gaius and Lucius, teenaged sons of his daughter Julia and her husband Agrippa. Julia had been pregnant when in 12 BC Agrippa died, and she gave birth to a son, Postumus, who grew up to be irresponsible if not unbalanced. But they also had a daughter, Agrippina.

Now Augustus ordered Julia to marry Tiberius, with whom he had shared the tribunicial power since 6 BC. Julia was happy with the choice. Tiberius was not. But, intelligent and exuberant, Julia was both sexually adventurous and politically dissident, bridling at her father's control. Augustus was distracted by the rise of her sons, as Gaius and Lucius were elected consul. He adored the boys, nicknaming Gaius his 'most beloved little donkey' and looking forward to a time when they would 'succeed to my position'. But then in quick succession both of them died – just as Augustus discovered their mother's antics.

Dressing in the showiest dresses, Julia flaunted affairs with a string of senators and generals, including a Scipio and Antony's son Iullus Antonius, a dangerous choice. If she had been a man, such exploits would have been regarded as virile peccadillos, but she was heiress to an empire, perilously popular, and her libertinism undermined Augustus' conservative crackdown on immorality. In AD 3, he banished her for life – but, just as he feared, she became a symbol of resistance, attracting the support of popular protests against him. Iullus Antonius was executed.

Augustus was forced to turn to his wife Livia's sons Tiberius and Drusus. Tiberius found politics a strain. Repulsed by Julia's promiscuity and resenting his mother's orders, sated with war, he retired to Rhodes. Nor was this the end of it: Julia's daughter, also called Julia, had brazen love affairs with among others the erotic poet Ovid. But this was about much more than poetry and sex: Julia's husband Aemilius Paullus was planning Augustus' assassination. In AD 8, Paullus was executed, young Julia exiled.*

Augustus brokered the marriages that ultimately produced the emperors Caligula, Claudius and Nero. Livia's younger son Drusus, married to Antonia, daughter of Octavia and Antony, delivered two sons, the handsome, charismatic Germanicus and the stammering, limping Claudius. Claudius was lucky not to be exposed as a baby – his mother reviled him as 'the monster' – but he married four times and had children. Their father Drusus died young, but Augustus promoted Germanicus, who won laurels in the wars against the Germans. Augustus married Germanicus to Agrippina, daughter of Agrippa and Julia, who produced six children, three girls and three boys. Agrippina insisted on serving in camp with her husband, giving orders in battle when necessary and turning her youngest son, Gaius, into a military mascot, dressed in a mini-legionary's uniform, hence his nickname Caligula – Little Boots. Augustus merged these plans by naming Tiberius as his heir but ordering him to adopt Germanicus as his son.

As he lay dying, Augustus talked about his one big fiasco: in AD 9, three legions had been wiped out by German tribesmen in the

---

* Ovid was the outrageous chronicler of just the sort of delicious love affairs with other people's wives that were now out of favour under Augustus. Admitting not just a 'poem and a mistake' but also a 'crime worse than murder', Ovid was lucky to be alive, exiled to the faraway town of Tomis (Romania). He never returned.

Teutoburg Forest. Archaeologists have found Roman armour there. Augustus spent his last years murmuring, 'Give me back my legions.' 'If I played my part well,' said Augustus before he died, with Livia beside him,* 'then give me applause.' He had and they did, deifying him like Caesar as he was cremated and buried in his magnificent mausoleum, which still stands in Rome.

As soon as Tiberius took power, advised by his mother Livia – her female *auctoritas* recognized in the *cognomen* Augusta – he ordered the killing of Augustus' last grandson, Postumus. Tiberius retired to Capri, where this reptilian *princeps* petted his tame iguana and enjoyed swimming while, according to lurid historians, being probed by the tongues of a troop of boys whom he nicknamed his 'minnows'. (Then as now, an orgy in a swimming pool was shorthand for depravity).

In Rome, he delegated his power to a henchman, Sejanus, prefect of the Praetorian Guards,† whom he used to purge his enemies. His heir was his son Drusus, married to Germanicus' sister, Livilla. Livilla, however, started an affair with Sejanus, who aspired to rule and may have poisoned Drusus. Finally, in 31, Antony's daughter Antonia visited Capri to reveal Sejanus' treason. The *princeps* appeared in Rome and had him executed. Livilla's fate was to be starved to death by her steely mother.

An empire is only as good as its governors. Tiberius' focus was drawn to the east, to where he dispatched his adopted son Germanicus as viceroy. The old iguana was jealous of this princeling. When Germanicus, at the age of thirty-three, fell fatally ill in Antioch, he accused Tiberius of poisoning him – and died watched by his wife and sons, who included the seven-year-old Caligula. Later Tiberius drove his widow to starve herself and then arrested, and quietly killed, Germanicus' elder sons.

Further south, Tiberius' prefect Pontius Pilate struggled to control

---

* Livia was said to have poisoned Augustus with figs. She was also rumoured to have poisoned all his earlier prospective successors. There is no proof of any of this and much of it was pure chauvinism, as poison was supposedly feminine – secret, insidious, concealed in food consumed trustingly. In an era when many died of scarcely understood infections, poison or necromancy could explain the sudden deaths of healthy people. Yet, as we have seen, poison was the ideal weapon for family murders: it preserved the image of a smooth succession. In an age when auguries, spells and omens were believed by everyone, poison was part of the political arsenal and all potentates had access to experts on necromancy and poisons. 'Livia, remember our married life,' said Augustus as he died, 'and farewell.'

† Traditionally the praetorians were the guards of a Roman general on campaign: they slept across the doorway of his tent. Since the legions were not allowed inside the *pomerium*, the city limits (except when a Sulla or Caesar broke the rules), Augustus had created his own praetorians who along with a guard of Germans protected the emperor.

the turbulent Jews, who were wary of Roman idolatry and despotism.*
Pilate's violent suppression of Jewish protests in Jerusalem and Samaria had exacerbated tensions. Now in AD 33, Pilate confronted a Jewish
prophet, Jesus, one of many such preachers. Jesus – Joshua in Hebrew –
was a scion of the Davidic dynasty who had been brought up in Galilee,
which was ruled by one of Herod's sons. Like all Jews, he had been circumcised in the Temple in Jerusalem, and regularly travelled to the city
for Passover and other Jewish festivals. The first decades of his life are
unknown. When he emerged as a preacher, he did not claim to be the
Messiah, though he performed acts of healing and the magical delivery
of provisions. Instead, criticizing the Temple grandees and supporting
the downtrodden, he preached moral conduct in this life in preparation
for an imminent End of Days, prophesied in the Jewish Torah. It struck
a chord with the human need for a moral mission that offered meaning
in life and redemption in death. Faced with disorders during the Jewish
festival of Passover when Jerusalem was packed with pilgrims, Pilate
crucified Jesus on a hill outside the city. When the body disappeared
from his tomb, his followers believed he was the Messiah – son of God
– risen from the dead to bear the sins of mankind.

Tiberius would not have spent long on this minor incident among
the crazy Jews, but, hearing of Pilate's bungling, he recalled him. On
the succession, he selected the last of Germanicus' sons as the Caesar to
deliver calm and continuity: Caligula.

IF ONLY ROME HAD ONE NECK: CALIGULA AND SISTERS

No *princeps* ever came to power with such popular enthusiasm as Little
Boots. He was raised by stern women – first by his great-grandmother
Livia (whom he called 'Odysseus in a dress'), then by Antonia, daughter
of Antony – in a vortex of murder and ambition. No wonder he was
damaged and insecure.

In AD 36, Tiberius invited Caligula to live with him in Capri, 'rearing
a viper for the Roman people'. Yet he appointed joint heirs, Caligula
and his own grandson, the eighteen-year-old Tiberius Gemellus, but the
boy was suspected of being Sejanus' son. When Tiberius died, Caligula,
a twenty-five-year-old epileptic, gangly, pointy-faced and balding, was
hailed by the people as 'our chick' in an orgy of celebration as he promised

---

* After Herod's death, the ineptitude of his sons and a rash of Jewish messiahs – sacred
kings – had convinced Tiberius to annex Judaea, which was governed by a mix of Roman
prefects, Jewish high priests and Herodian princes.

to end treason trials and restore elections. The Senate appointed Caligula as sole heir, but while his predecessors were experienced commanders, he himself had no laurels. After a short illness, he ordered the execution of his cousin Gemellus, an act that so horrified their joint grandmother Antonia that she starved herself to death. Attracted by the Egyptian tradition of sister-marriage, he gathered around him his sisters Agrippina (the Younger), Julia Livilla and Drusilla and may have slept with them, or just claimed that he did. Agrippina, married to the aristocrat Gnaeus Domitius Ahenobarbus, had just had a son, Lucius – the future Nero. When Drusilla died, Caligula deified her, the first Caesar woman to be so elevated. It implied that Caligula too was a god.

Starting with public gifts of cash and public construction projects, he also orchestrated spectacular shows, and rode his horse Incitatus across a bridge of boats on the Gulf of Naples, wearing the breastplate of Alexander the Great. Caligula could not resist boasting of his power; as he told his grandmother Antonia, 'Remember that I have the right to do anything to anyone.' He had a hangman's wit. When killing his victims, he ordered the executioner to 'strike so he feels he is dying'. As he began to sense his unpopularity, he quoted a Greek play, 'Let them hate so long as they fear,' adding, 'If only Rome had one neck.' At dinners, he demanded the right to seduce the wives of his guests and then rated them afterwards. He must have heard that Augustus had done something similar, but somehow Augustus befriended his victims while Caligula repelled them. At one of his dinner parties, he burst out laughing: 'At a single nod from me,' he told the consuls, 'both of you would have your throats cut on the spot.' And whenever his kissed his wives, he would sigh, 'Off comes this beautiful head whenever I give the word.' To torment the Senate, he threatened to make his horse a senator. Jealous of the brilliant speeches of Seneca, a forty-four-year-old senator, son of a historian from Hispania, he ordered his execution for conspiracy – but, hearing that he was mortally ill, he laughed that he would die soon anyway and just exiled him. Seneca understood that 'all cruelty springs from weakness.'

Caligula had affairs with the beautiful actor Mnester and Drusilla's husband Marcus Aemilius Lepidus, a great-great-grandson of Augustus, a taste totally acceptable in the Roman male provided he was married, feared the gods and took the active position in sex. But later, fearing Lepidus' pedigree, he had him executed. His trusted praetorian prefect Cassius Chaerea tortured women for sport, often joined by Caligula. The emperor exiled his two surviving sisters. Rightly suspicious of all members of his family, he was indulgent towards his lame uncle

Claudius, who had spent his life writing a history of the Etruscans. Caligula promoted him to consul as a joke and, in a clear sign that he did not regard him as a threat, he married him to their teenage cousin Valeria Messalina, also descended from Octavia and Antony. Meanwhile, anxious for a successor, he tried to father a son, finally marrying for the fourth time his mistress Milonia Caesonia, with whom he had a daughter.

In pursuit of military success, he travelled up to Gaul where he supposedly ordered his troops to collect seashells to dedicate to Neptune, the sea god. More likely they built military huts (mistranslated as seashells) while Caligula received the allegiance of that tempting target – Britannia.

Such was the competence of the administration – overseen by Caligula's secretary, the Greek freedman Callistus – that the empire continued to run even under the rule of a demented freak. Keen to secure the east, the emperor sent his friend the Jewish prince Herod Agrippa to remove the untrustworthy prefect of Egypt, then promoted him to king like his grandfather Herod the Great. He next ordered the Jews to worship a statue of himself in the Temple in Jerusalem. The Jews seethed. Herod Agrippa persuaded him to cancel the order.[*]

Caligula was spoiled, damaged and clueless, making enemies on all sides. A basic rule of power is: mock anyone, but never your bodyguards. Caligula teased Chaerea, giving insulting passwords like 'phallus' and 'girlie'. Chaerea started a conspiracy with two others, chief secretary Callistus and probably his uncle Claudius. Caligula had encouraged a slave of Claudius' to denounce him, an act guaranteed to alienate any Roman. In AD 40, Caligula declared himself a god and was about to leave Rome and move the capital to Alexandria. There was no time to lose. On 24 January 41, Caligula, still only twenty-nine, left the theatre where he was presiding over a show celebrating the Divine Augustus on the Palatine Hill and took the covered passageway, the *cryptoporticus*, through the imperial complex back to take a bath in the palace. His limping uncle Claudius asked permission to be excused. As Caligula stopped to watch a performance of singers, three of his most trusted praetorians surrounded him and drew their swords.

---

[*] At the same time, Caligula summoned his African cousin King Ptolemy of Mauritania, only grandchild of Cleopatra and Antony, and had him executed, annexing the kingdom, possibly because his royal Ptolemaic descent could have interfered with his plans in Egypt.

Trajans and First Step Sharks: Romans and the Maya

'So be it!' shouted Chaerea. He drew his sword and swung it against Caligula's neck, but it only shattered his jawbone. Another slash almost sliced off an arm. One forgets the sheer messiness of assassinations. Caligula twitched on the ground. 'I am still alive!' he cried, begging to be finished off.

'Hit him again!' shouted the praetorians, who stabbed Caligula thirty times, including in the genitals. When his German guards learned what had happened, they went berserk in the theatre, nearly slaughtering the entire crowd. Chaerea planned to liquidate the whole family, sending guards to kill Caesonia and her baby daughter, but she had rushed out and lay sobbing next to the deserted body of Caligula. They killed her there, then dashed the baby's head against a wall.

Excited senators debated who to appoint *princeps*, but some praetorians found Claudius hiding behind a tapestry. Aided by his longstanding friend the Jewish king Herod Agrippa, Claudius negotiated with the praetorians and the Senate.

While he purported to be uninterested in power, and even privately hoped to restore the late republic, this was all designed to stay alive and contrast him with Caligula. Ambition was bred into the Julio-Claudians. Claudius embraced the crown and proved almost as vicious and capricious as Caligula.

Claudius started his reign with surprising rigour, bribing the praetorians, forgiving Caligula's assassins (though executing Chaerea) and promising the Senate to respect its privileges. Abroad, he granted his friend Herod Agrippa an enlarged Jewish kingdom encompassing much of Israel, Jordan and Lebanon. Then he ordered a prestigious little war: the conquest of Britannia. The empire was run by three efficient freedmen, led by his trusted Narcissus, who became so powerful that before the British invasion, when some legions became restless, he addressed them himself in the emperor's name.

At the centre of his court was his wife Messalina. Claudius was fifty-three; Messalina, aged twenty-three, was born into the imperial family. She had already delivered a daughter, and now, just as Claudius conquered Britannia, she delivered a son, Britannicus.

Once southern Britannia had been pacified, Claudius travelled to accept the surrender of eleven Britannic kings and parade through his new colony, in the town of Camulodunum, riding an elephant (quite a sight for Colchester high street then and now), but this left Messalina in Rome. Encouraged by Claudius' freedmen, she started to sell governorships and toy with power.

The young empress embraced what we might today called a swinging lifestyle, yet this was not just about her capacity for pleasure; her thrill-seeking was also an expression of power gone to a young person's head. Experiencing wild crushes on her fancies, she was in a position to enforce her wishes. But she also regarded anyone who did not support her as an enemy – and she was a dangerous enemy to have. One of her favourites was the actor Mnester, sometime lover of Caligula. When he resisted her, she supposedly got Claudius to tell him innocently to obey *all* her orders – and he became her lover, delighting her so much she had a bronze cast made of him. When the crowds in the theatre called out that Mnester was with Messalina in the palace, Claudius naively waved them away. She saved the life of one of Caligula's German bodyguards, condemned to die in the gladiatorial ring, because he had slept with her. She was said to have won a sexual endurance competition by having twenty-five men in twenty-four hours, her exploits protected by a ring of silence. But the *omertà* was unlikely to last.

Claudius' crown was recent and vulnerable. 'This man, fellow senators, who looks to you as if he couldn't hurt a fly,' Seneca wrote, 'used to kill people as easily as a dog shits.' The fuddled *princeps* killed thirty-five senators.

Messalina meanwhile was threatened by Caligula's sisters. She exposed Julia Livilla for having an affair with Seneca, and both of them were exiled. Claudius later had the recently returned Julia Livilla and her sister Julia Livia killed for plotting, supposedly on Messalina's advice. Messalina also feared Agrippina, the last of Caligula's sisters, and her son Lucius Domitius Ahenobarbus – the future emperor Nero – who was becoming popular. It was said that when she went to suffocate baby Nero, a snake slithered out from under the pillow. She later tried to have Agrippina exiled and the boy killed, but Nero was cheered more at the Games than her own son Britannicus.

Around AD 47, Messalina, now thirty, started to overreach herself.

When she framed the powerful freedman Callistus, his colleagues Narcissus and Pallas realized they were in danger themselves, just as Messalina was moving from shameless sex to political conspiracy. Her favourite lover, Gaius Silius, was a dashing senator: she felt so invulnerable she started to plan an actual seizure of power, hoping to retire (more likely kill) Claudius and rule with Silius on behalf of Britannicus.

Knowing that Messalina could easily discredit him, Claudius' loyal exslave Narcissus persuaded his master's favourite prostitutes, Cleopatra and Calpurnia, to tell him the truth – unusual receptacles of integrity. While Claudius was inspecting his new port at Ostia, Messalina was celebrating a Dionysian wedding to Silius, which was the start of a coup backed by the city militia. When the prostitutes told the emperor, Narcissus confirmed their tales. Claudius panicked, but the praetorians were still loyal and Narcissus arrested the conspirators. Messalina hitched a lift in a rubbish cart and begged for her life by presenting her two children to Claudius, who was rushing back to Rome. He was rendered speechless, but Narcissus had the children taken home. Arresting Messalina, Claudius and Narcissus proceeded to Silius' house, which was filled with treasures purloined from the palace. Claudius, enraged, had Silius, Mnester and other conspirators killed. Then, as he dithered, Narcissus had Messalina beheaded. Claudius said nothing and asked for another flask of wine.

Claudius now looked weak, and he must have doubted that Britannicus was really his son. That opened the door for Agrippina – and her son: Nero.

RULE OF THE FREEDMEN: AGRIPPINA'S MARRIAGE

Agrippina made a show of consulting her uncle on all matters and as a direct descendant of Augustus she would consolidate his principate. Narcissus promoted one of Claudius' earlier wives, but Pallas, now secretly sleeping with Agrippina, backed her. In AD 50, Claudius married Agrippina, who was promoted to Augusta, and adopted her son Lucius, who assumed the Claudian name Nero. Agrippina appointed Seneca to tutor Nero, while accusing Narcissus of corruption. Nero was married to Claudius' daughter, Claudia – and appointed joint heir with Britannicus.

Claudius, sixty-three and drunk most of the time, started to worry about the boy's safety. He grew closer to Messalina's mother Domitia, grandmother of his children, and reflected aloud that his fate was to marry women then punish them. Agrippina feared that Claudius would dispose of her and marry Domitia. She and Nero testified to Domitia's disloyalty; Claudius acquiesced in her execution.

Then in October 54, sending Narcissus away to treat his gout, Agrippina procured the skills of a poisoner named Locusta, already in prison for murder, and – suborning Claudius' trusted server-taster and doctor – she poisoned Claudius' mushrooms. The *princeps* was sick, but survived, so she then had the doctor poison him, this time successfully.

Agrippina sent the seventeen-year-old Nero to promise the praetorians a bonus and executed Narcissus, while her lover Pallas remained secretary for financial affairs.

On Nero's first day as *princeps* he gave the praetorians the cloying password 'best of mothers', but swiftly his surging adolescent ambition clashed with Agrippina's *auctoritas*. Nero, preeningly overconfident, blond, bullnecked and fleshy, had achieved power far too easily to appreciate it. Instead, regarding himself as too talented for politics, he flaunted his skills as actor and charioteer, a surprisingly modern politician for whom politics was an extension of showbusiness.

Agrippina tried to refresh her fading maternal influence by becoming Nero's lover. But he had fallen in love with the beautiful wife of his friend Otho, Sabina Poppaea. When Nero wanted to divorce his wife Claudia, Agrippina advised against it. Poppaea mocked his inability to overrule his mummy.

Poppaea dressed gorgeously in the material that was suddenly fashionable: women started wearing Chinese silk with nothing underneath. 'I see clothes of silk,' grumbled Seneca, 'if materials that don't hide the body nor even one's decency can be called clothes. Wretched flocks of maids labour so that the adulteress may be visible through her thin dress – and her husband has not more acquaintance with his wife's body than any stranger . . .' The fashion required the shaving of pubic hair, which appalled the well-connected naturalist Pliny the Elder. The Senate several times banned the immoral wearing of silk – but fashion was stronger. As was money.[*]

In the Central Country, the source of this silk, a brilliant family of Chinese writers and soldiers was experiencing the opportunities and perils of serving the other great dynasty of world power, the Han.

---

[*] Pliny estimated that, thanks to its 25 per cent tax on Indian Ocean trade in luxuries such as silk from China, and nard and ivory from Muziris, the port of the Chera rulers of south-western India, Rome earned 100 million sesterces a year, perhaps a third of imperial revenue. There is evidence, including a statue of Buddha found at Berenice, to confirm that a community of Indians, probably merchants, lived in the ports on the Red Sea. This trade – by many routes, land and sea – was in 1877 dubbed the Silk Road – *Seidenstraße* – by a German traveller, Baron Ferdinand von Richthofen, uncle of the First World War pilot the Red Baron.

MOTHERS, BROTHERS AND SISTERS:
NERO, AGRIPPINA AND THE BANS

In AD 54, Ban Biao, who had started to write a private history of the imperial family, perished, leaving his masterwork *Hanshu* – the *Book of Han* – unfinished. The brutality and avarice of court feuding had almost destroyed the Han, but after a bloody civil war a masterly Han cousin, Emperor Guangwu, had restored the dynasty and appointed Ban to write its history. When Ban died, he left three children: two sons, a dreamy poet, Ban Gu, then aged twenty-two, a tough soldier, Ban Chao, twenty-one, and a daughter, Ban Zhao, nine, who would be the most remarkable of a talented family. All three would change history in different ways that extended from the imperial court all the way across the Silk Road towards the west. Each became famous, one as a historian, one as a conqueror and one as a writer, courtier and female advocate – one of the first women to achieve such prominence.

Ban Gu started to work in private on his father's book. His ruffian brother Ban Chao had no interest in such delicate activity: he had joined the court, serving the emperor as a clerk of the Orchid Terrace, but its slow pace bored him. He craved adventure.

When the old emperor died, he was succeeded by his son, the thirty-year-old Ming, who heard that Ban Gu was 'privately revising the national history' – a euphemism for failing to extol the virtues of the dynasty. Ban was arrested, his library impounded. Fortunately his brother, Ban Chao, appealed to Ming on his behalf. Mingdi released him, summoned him to court and appointed him official Han historian while his brother Chao preferred rougher pursuits: 'Throw away your writing-brush,' he advised the delicate historian, 'and join the army!' Chao joined General Dou Gu on a campaign against the barbarians, in which his bloody exploits, cultural curiosity and political gifts made him the greatest Chinese conquistador, expanding the Western Region (Central Asia). The Bans were flourishing, but the Han court was as dangerous as that of the Caesars.

Nero was squeezed between his mother and his mistress. Agrippina, still in her early forties, got Nero drunk and seduced him, but then threatened to enthrone Claudius' son Britannicus. Nero had abused Britannicus, even raping him. When he ordered the younger prince to perform a poem at the theatre, Britannicus recounted in verse how he had been passed over, speaking with such dignity that the crowd cheered. The fact that Britannicus was a better actor so infuriated the omnipotent narcissist that he ordered the poisoner Locusta to provide two poisons, one fast, one slow, to be served to Britannicus at family dinner. When her slow poison failed, Nero tricked Britannicus into taking the fast one. He looked on as Britannicus went into convulsions.

Nero's mother Agrippina and his wife Claudia (Britannicus' sister) realized that the emperor was out of control. Nero moved Agrippina out of the palace, and discussed how to destroy her. The praetorians would never kill a daughter of Germanicus, and poisons often failed, so he was delighted when a sleazy freedman called Anicetus came up with a plan.

In 59, attending a festival on the Bay of Naples, Agrippina was taken out for a cruise on a specially sabotaged murder boat. When she survived the lead roof of a canopy falling on her, the boat itself came apart, but she managed to swim to shore. Nero feared her vengeance and dispatched the freedman back to her villa. As she was held down and butchered, she pointed to her belly and cried, 'Strike here, Anicetus, for this womb bore Nero.'

Helped by his minister Seneca, Nero squared his matricide with the Senate by framing Agrippina for treason. Now he was liberated.

In 62, he had Pallas killed, harvesting his fortune. Finally, Nero could marry Poppaea – except that he was still married to Empress Claudia, whom he loathed. When there were rumours that he would divorce her for infertility, the people protested and Nero panicked. Once again Anicetus proved useful, testifying to adultery with the empress. She was exiled to the island of Pandateria, where, still just twenty-two, she was tied down and her veins opened. The head was presented to Poppaea as a marriage gift. In 63, Nero and his new empress had a daughter together.

The next year, while Nero was at his villa at Antium (Anzio), fire broke out in Rome, spreading fast among the closely packed multi-storey wooden buildings. The inferno was one of history's super-propellants – pandemics and disasters – that implacably test leaders and systems in what we might call the Nero Test. He did all the right things, offering his private gardens as refuge, reducing the grain price, erecting shelters, inviting refugees to live in his palaces, but in his self-absorbed need to dramatize his own importance at all times he put on a show about the fire in which he sang with his lyre. Its charm deteriorated even more as the Roman fire flared up again. Nero's oblivious decision to take advantage of the space cleared by the fire to build a new palace, the Golden House, added to the impression that he had ignited it. In its vestibule, he erected a colossus of himself as a ninety-nine-foot naked god holding a rudder on a globe to express his world power.* The truth matters less

---

* The Golden House was so magnificent it embarrassed the more austere Emperor Vespasian, Nero's ultimate successor. Gradually dismantled, it was replaced by the Baths of Titus

than the impression: Nero had failed the Nero Test.

Poppaea was raised to Augusta after the birth of their short-lived daughter and, chatelaine of the hundred-acre palace, was powerful enough to appoint her own inept protégé to govern Judaea.

Untrammelled by any sensible advisers, Nero sought scapegoats for the fire and other inauspicious events, focusing on a newly popular Jewish sect named Christians who followed Jesus, the prophet executed by the Romans during Tiberius' reign. They were an object of special suspicion because they rejected the essential Roman rite of sacrificing to the gods – and the *princeps*. This behaviour was just acceptable among Jews, whose beliefs were ancient, but not among the new-fangled Christians, whose egalitarian beliefs seemed to challenge the entire order of society – a *superstitio* that championed the slaves, always a very touchy subject. Nero had Christians slaughtered in the arena, and one of Jesus' surviving apostles, Peter, crucified upside down.*

In the Golden House, Nero's relationship with the pregnant Poppaea was deteriorating: during a row, Nero supposedly kicked her in the belly, killing her. Single again, he tried to marry Claudius' last daughter by an earlier marriage, but when she refused she too was murdered. He set off for Greece to race chariots and perform as an actor, and there fell in love with a young eunuch and freed slave saucily named Sporus (Seed), who looked strangely like Poppaea. Nero encouraged him to transition into Poppaea – and married him.

Conspiracies intensified; rebellions multiplied. Seneca liked to say, 'Poison is drunk from gold,' but even the philosopher had amassed such riches that he started lending money at high interest rates – to the British chieftains among others. It may have been his aggressive debt collecting that accelerated a rebellion in Britannia, led by Queen Boadicea. A legion was destroyed before the rebels were crushed. Seneca, by now sixty, had already retired to his villa to write outrageous satires on emperors he had known when he was tenuously linked to a conspiracy. Nero ordered him to kill himself. 'We're always complaining our days are few, and acting as though there would be no end of them,' Seneca reflected. Now there was an end: Seneca, taking poison and cutting his wrists, died in his bath, surrounded by friends.

and other buildings until only its lower rooms survived. When discovered in the fifteenth century, they were initially thought to be caves or grottoes, so their decadent frescoes which so inspired the artists Raphael and Michelangelo were described as 'grotesques' – hence the modern word.

* His secret burial place became a Christian shrine – it was beneath what is now St Peter's Basilica.

In 66, Judaea exploded. The rebels, provoked by egregious Roman venality, eliminated a legion and founded a Jewish state based in the magnificent near-impregnable Temple city of Jerusalem, a development that threatened the eastern empire and sparked a rash of revolts. The Gallic and Hispanic legions rebelled; as they marched on Rome, senators and praetorians at last turned against Nero, who tried to flee to Ostia and then to Parthia – a hare-brained scheme. Returning to the palace in Rome he awoke the next morning to find himself abandoned and exclaimed, 'Have I neither friend nor foe!' On the run with a tiny retinue, including his beautiful Poppaean eunuch Sporus dressed as a girl, he tried and failed to kill himself, by drowning in the Tiber and by the sword, all the time declaiming theatrical lines loudly: 'Is it so terrible a thing to die?' Finally cornered, the arch-exhibitionist paced up and down crying, 'What an artist the world is losing in me,' before persuading his secretary to cut his throat. Just then an emissary of the Senate rushed in, but Nero, bleeding out, murmured, 'Too late! That's loyalty!'

The Caesars had destroyed themselves. In the years 68–9, there were three emperors before a fourth, Vespasian – an unpretentious old general nicknamed the Muleteer, who had helped conquer Britannia and whom the historian Suetonius described as looking 'like a man always straining to have a shit' – was hailed as emperor. At the time, he was crushing the Jewish rebels. In 70, his son Titus stormed Jerusalem and destroyed the Temple, leaving just the supporting walls of Herod's magnificent edifice.*

In 97, the triumphant Chinese paladin, Ban Chao, brother of the court historian, sent an envoy to visit Rome via Parthia. This pungently energetic general had taken his troops as far west as the shores of the Caspian Sea. While his brother Ban Gu wrote his history at court, and their talented sister Zhao married in their home province, Ban Chao always wanted to fight barbarians on the frontiers, telling his writer brother, 'A brave man has no other plan but to ... do something and become somebody in a foreign land.' His mission was to seize the trade to Parthia and Rome – and break the Xiongnu. 'If you don't venture into the tiger's lair,' said Ban Chao. 'You never catch its cubs.'

---

* This triumph yielded vast riches – including the candelabra from the Holy of Holies – and tens of thousands of Jewish slaves. Titus embellished Rome, building an arch and a huge new amphitheatre. Adapting Nero's Colossus, he and Vespasian added sunrays to dedicate the statue to Sol Invictus (Invincible Sun) and placed it outside the amphitheatre – hence its name, Colosseum. While that still stands, the Colossus itself, a sight in Rome for four centuries, vanished some time around the fall of the western empire.

AUTHORESS AND THE PROTECTOR-GENERAL IN THE TIGER'S LAIR: BAN CHAO AND THE WISE ONE

In 75, the new Emperor Zhang, discouraged by the endless costs incurred in putting down the tribes in central Asia, recalled Ban Chao, who decided to disobey orders, having realized that to abandon the Western Region now would lose it for ever. Instead he advised Emperor Zhang that his new empire – like so many others – could be held with very few troops backed by local auxiliaries and by ostentatious displays of ferocity. While negotiating with a local chieftain, he heard that Xiongnu ambassadors had arrived to undermine his mission. He slaughtered the envoys and, brandishing their heads, he successfully concluded his negotiation with the now cooperative potentate. During another negotiation, when he saw that the chieftain was distracted by the unhelpful advice of his sorcerer, Ban Chao beheaded the sorcerer mid-conversation and then, unabashed, continued. Eventually he defeated the Xiongnu, and took the kingdoms of Kashgar and Khotan.

Ban encountered one people, the Yuezhi (Guishuang), who, defeated by the Xiongnu, rode southwards and built their own kingdom: these nomadic horsemen the Kushan – who practised skull deformation then – conquered Bactria and burst into northern India.* Ban Chao defeated a Kushan army, but ultimately he made peace with these new players.

The Bans flourished as protégés of Zhang's Empress Dou, who skilfully played the game of power, using accusations of witchcraft to destroy the crown prince, then, adopting the son of another concubine, forcing his mother to kill herself.† The heir grew up believing that Empress Dou was his mother.

---

* The vast Kushan empire, founded by the warlord Kujula Kadphises and ruled from Pataliputra, endured for three centuries, a people bearded and moustachioed with long hair, sporting long coats, trousers and boots, brandishing lance and sword. The founder's great-grandson Kanishka helped expand Indic culture and religion into central Asia and China and central Asian culture into India. He revered Greek, Indian and Persian pantheons – Shiva, Buddha, Hercules and Ahura-Mazda in a unique hybridity – and called himself king of kings. He also transported Chinese silk to the Indian Ocean and thence to the Mediterranean

† The female household of the Han was carefully regulated. Selections were made every eighth month of the year when virgins of flawless families would be inspected by a three-man committee – a palace counsellor, a eunuch and a physiognomist who graded the girls from 1 to 9. The lucky one would then be brought to the capital Luoyang for intimate examination: 'Skin white and fine . . . belly round, hips square, body like congealed lard and carved jade, breasts bulging and navel deep enough to take a half-inch pearl,' read one report. 'No haemorrhoids, no blemishes, no moles, no sores nor defects in the mouth, the nose, armpits, private parts or feet.' Concubines were ranked as either Honourable, Beautiful or Chosen Ladies. One of the Honourable Ladies was usually made empress.

In 88, aged nine the boy succeeded his father as Emperor He. Dowager Empress Dou stayed in control, her brother Dou Xian ruling as general-in-chief or regent. But his arrogance offended everyone – even the boy emperor. Dou Xian won victories against the Xiongnu, which he celebrated with a ceremony at Yanran where an inscription written by Ban Gu was dedicated. Ban Gu was promoted to the regent's secretary with the title marshal of the Black Warrior Gate, and was joined at court by his sister Zhao, now a widow. Refusing to marry again, she became a royal tutor in the imperial library.

In 92, the thirteen-year-old boy emperor was 'capped' – the ceremony to celebrate his majority – and, backed by a trusted eunuch Zheng Zhong, he turned on the Dous: the regent was eliminated, the empress retired and their pet historian Ban Gu, now sixty-one, arrested. Ban's sister, who knew the young emperor, appealed, but Gu was executed. History writing again proved a perilous pursuit. Emperor He rewarded eunuch Zheng with the titles of marquess and director of the royal palace, the first eunuch to rise so high. One of the Dou's trusted eunuchs, Cai Lun, keeper of tools and weapons, survived the downfall of the regent to continue his development of a new material on which to write. The court wrote on heavy bamboo and expensive silk, but now, after watching how paper wasps mixed tree bark with saliva, Cai invented paper, for which the emperor promoted him. But Ban Gu was dead: who would finish the *Book of Han*?

The coup that killed one sibling made the others. The emperor promoted Ban Chao to protector-general of the Western Region – and wanted the *Hanshu* finished: he ordered the scholarly sister Ban Zhao to complete the book. Still only about forty-five, she taught the Han princesses mathematics, history, morality and feminine comportment, becoming close to Empress Deng Sui, who elevated her to lady-in-waiting. Starting like other girls as a concubine, she had been chosen as consort at fifteen, ultimately replacing the ruler's wife and becoming empress herself. Intelligent and competent, she encouraged the use of the new invention, paper, probably advised by Ban Zhao, who presided over the transferral of the imperial library from bamboo to the new medium. Her *Hanshu* was one of the first history books written on paper and her *Lessons for Women* was written as a guide to female survival at court. Nicknamed the Wise One, Ban Zhao gave advice on all matters including Taoist sexual techniques while serving as court poet, writing verses for special occasions and memoranda on politics. Long after the death of the meek Emperor He, Dowager Empress Deng ruled China, advised by this remarkable woman.

While she was teaching empresses about astronomy and marriage, her brother Ban Chao, protector-general, had heard of the Roman empire, which the Chinese complimented by giving it the name Da Qin – Big China. Ban Chao would have seen the goods and coins of the Romans, so the old general sent an envoy called Gan Ying to report. His sister recorded in her history how Gan Ying made it to the Western Sea, maybe the Persian Gulf, where the Parthians discouraged his enterprise, as he explained: 'The Romans trade with Parthia and India by sea. Their king always wanted to send envoys to Han, but Parthia, wishing to control the trade in multicoloured Chinese silks, blocked the way.' Here was a global Eurasian world. There is nothing modern about trade wars. As for the Roman emperors, Gan Ying explained, 'Their kings are not permanent. They select and appoint the most worthy man. If there are unexpected calamities in the kingdom, such as frequent extraordinary winds or rains, he is unceremoniously replaced but the dismissed one is not angry . . .'*

If Gan Ying had a rose-tinted view of Roman successions, he was right up to date: that year of 97, the Romans rejected dynasty and instead chose 'the most worthy man': their finest soldier, the contemporary and equivalent of Ban Chao, was named Trajan. And Trajan planned to emulate Alexander the Great by invading Persia and India.

STAR WARS, PIERCED PENISES, SEX SLAVES AND STEAM BATHS

Trajan looked the part of the bluff, old-fashioned Roman soldier – tough, clean-shaven, severe grey hair worn in a classic Caesar and usually portrayed wearing a gleaming engraved breastplate – and played it well.

Trajan was never happier than when sharing the rations and camps with 'my excellent and most loyal fellow soldiers'. His only indulgences were wine and boys, actors and dancers mainly. Trajan was plainspoken and sociable: when he travelled in a carriage, he always invited three friends to chat along the way and he had the rare confidence to have talented men around him. 'I like what I hear,' he gruffly told a philosopher,

---

* In 102, Wise One, Ban Zhao, petitioned Empress Deng to let her brother Protector-General Ban Chao retire. Deng agreed and he returned to Luoyang where she debriefed him on his adventures in the west before he died at seventy, leaving his son to run his territories. Ban Zhao's influence continued: when the authoress finally died in 115, she was mourned by the royal family. She was the first famous female author: Empress Deng had her works collected in three volumes after her death.

'but I don't understand a word of what you're talking about.' Yet he had an instinct for power.

Born in Italica, Spain, the emperor had no sons with his wife Pompeia Plotina, but he lived at the centre of a female household consisting of her sister, niece and two great-nieces, who all now moved to Rome. When Empress Pompeia arrived at the palace, she told the spectators, 'I enter here as the same kind of woman I'll be when I depart.'

Trajan liked to tease his entourage about the succession, once asking them to name the ten best candidates for emperor: it is a strange feature of successful epochs that there are many men gifted enough to rule while in meagre times there appears to be almost none. Hadrian was always the frontrunner. Like Trajan, he hailed from Hispania: Trajan had been Hadrian's guardian when the boy's father died young and he curated his protégé's rise, but there was something about Hadrian that irritated Trajan. Hadrian had charmed Trajan's wife and sister-in-law, who orchestrated his marriage to Sabina, the emperor's beloved great-niece, positioning him perfectly. But it is always dangerous to be the prime candidate: maybe Trajan's wife protected him by not over-promoting him. But at one point Trajan disapproved of his extravagant partying, and then Hadrian was caught hitting on Trajan's male lovers. Older autocrats are likely be touchy on such matters. 'Everything depended,' wrote Trajan's scholarly friend Pliny the Younger, 'on the whims of a single man,' but the emperor's decisions were usually sensible.*

No epoch realizes at the time quite how lucky it is until it is gone. But the spirit of this epoch was a lucky one of clement weather, lush harvests and plentiful revenues from an imperial population of between fifty and seventy million. Trajan possessed the three essentials of greatness – acumen, vision and resources. Between wars to annihilate the Dacians (Romania), he embarked on a massive building programme in Rome, boasting of his grandeur and victories with new temples, his triumphal column and the new stadium called Circus Maximus.

The rich, served by droves of slaves, enjoyed luxury and ease – 'Red Sea pearls and polished Indian ivory', in the words of the poet Martial

---

* When Pliny, governor of Bithynia, encountered the growing sect of Christians, he executed those who refused to sacrifice to the gods in honour of the emperor and in the spirit of enquiry he tortured two Christian slaves yet 'discovered nothing else but depraved, excessive superstition'. So he consulted Trajan. 'You observed proper procedure, my dear Pliny,' replied Trajan. 'They're not to be sought out; if denounced and proved guilty, they're to be punished, with this reservation, that whoever denies that he's a Christian and really proves it – by worshipping our gods – shall be pardoned . . . Anonymous denunciations have no place . . . They're out of keeping with the spirit of our age.'

– but the realities of urban life, imperial power and Roman society remained gritty and messy, corrupt and brutal.

Rome was now a seething mega-city of a million people, with the emperors enjoying vast palaces, the rich in sumptuous villas and the poor piled high in *insulae*, ten-storey blocks of flats. 'I live in a little cell, with a window that won't even close,' wrote Martial, 'in which Boreas [god of dark winter] himself wouldn't want to live.' Martial, another well-born Spaniard doing well in Rome, had been in and out of imperial favour but chronicled the hypocritical lubricity of high and low with irrepressible mischief. 'With your giant nose and cock /', he wrote, 'I bet you can with ease / When you get excited / Check the end for cheese.' He hated the cruelty of sadistic slave masters: 'You say that the hare isn't cooked, and ask for the whip; / Rufus, you prefer to carve up your cook than your hare.' Yet he had a heart too. His most touching poem was in praise of a beloved enslaved female who died young: 'A child with a voice as sweet as the fabled swan's.'*

Yet even the poor could enjoy what Juvenal called 'bread and circuses' – the bloody spectacles at the Colosseum and the Circus with 50,000 and 200,000 seats† – and the baths. Trajan was just the latest potentate to build his own *thermae*. Sixty thousand Romans could bathe at any one time – ideal for what Ovid had called 'furtive sport'. Nothing so defined urbane luxury as the baths that became the mark of Romanness: 'To bathe is to live,' a Roman scrawled on a wall, while the gravestone of a jolly *bon vivant* declared, 'Baths, sex and wine ruin our bodies but make life worth living.' A timeless truth. Yet it is ironic that the baths define Roman civilisation since they also probably spread the waterborne diseases that killed so many. In the baths, Martial chronicled naked Rome: he noticed that men tried to cover circumcised penises (the mark of Jewish slaves and therefore very unfashionable) and recorded the hilarity

---

* Martial revelled in the sexual freedoms of well-off Roman women such as his wanton friend Caelia, who was spoiled for choice by the diversity of the slaves that flooded into Rome with each victory: 'you grant your favours to Parthians . . . Germans . . . Dacians, and for you from his Egyptian city comes the gallant of Memphis, and the black Indian from the Red Sea; nor do you shun the lecheries of circumcised Jews.' His contemporary the poet Juvenal agreed that an honest wife was a 'rare bird' in a world where the slaves who were meant to guard her virtue could so easily collude in her pleasures. 'Who guards the guardians?' he asked in an often misunderstood line. 'Who now keep silent the sins of the promiscuous girl when paid in the same coin?'

† Champion charioteers became rich – even though they were slaves. Most famous was Scorpus who won 2,048 races until he was killed, probably in a chariot crash. Martial wrote his epitaph: 'Here I lie, Scorpus, pride of the noisy circus, darling of Rome. Spiteful fate snatched me aged twenty-six. She must have counted my victories, not my years, and decided I was old.'

as thousands of bathers applauded when a spectacularly well-endowed man disrobed. He mocked the virtuous wife who was so excited by mixed bathing that she eloped with a youth, and the macho man who went to ogle young penises. A graffito from this time reads: 'Apelles and Dexter had lunch here most pleasantly and fucked at the same time,' adding, 'We Apelles the Mouse and his brother Dexter lovingly fucked two women twice.' The Roman city was replicated across the empire from Mauritania to Britannia: the word civilisation derives from *civis*, town, and civilisation comes from *urbis*, city. But cities were flourishing not only in Europe, Africa and Asia.

Across the Atlantic, in a world cut off from Afro-Eurasia for millennia, Trajan's Mesoamerican contemporary First Step Shark – Yax Ehb Xook – the *ajaw* or lord of a thriving city state Tikal (Guatemala), one of many Mayan-speaking cities, was founding one of the great dynasties that would rule for eight centuries. Founded around 300 BC, Tikal – known by the Maya as Yax Mutal – had 100,000 inhabitants, much smaller than Rome, Luoyang, Chang'an and Seleucia, the biggest cities of Eurasia, each with a million. But Tikal was just one of many Mesoamerican city states that boasted sophisticated urban life. They developed glyphic writing (using logograms to represent words), charted the stars and created a calendar, celebrating their festivals according to their knowledge of the heavens. They lived on maize, tomatoes, beans, and drank chocolate. In their workshops, they crafted obsidian, volcanic glass, into weapons, tools, jewels and mirrors, and they spun cotton, which they traded, along with slaves, to their neighbours. They were skilled dentists, inserting turquoise and quartz into their front teeth so firmly that they remain in Maya skeletons. They knew of the wheel, but they did not use it for travel, only for children's toys, yet they built straight, raised roads, known as white roads, to reflect the Milky Way. In their monumental pyramidal temples, they worshipped an array of gods who demanded blood: their rulers had to draw stingray spines through their penises, a painful ritual that demonstrated the need for divine approval to rule. At the temples, they made human sacrifices, by beheading, scalping, skinning, disembowelling their offerings, cutting out their hearts and burying them with wild animals. The best victims were high-born prisoners. The cities featured ballcourts where the Maya played sacred games with rubber balls, which had even higher prizes than our football. Their gods were said to have clashed with mortals on the ballcourts; some gods were top ballplayers and mortals became gods by beating them. Their rulers played to demonstrate their power. Sometimes they used balls containing human heads.

The games represented the wars fought against rival cities in which they deployed blow darts and obsidian spears. Major conflicts they called 'star wars', represented by a glyph of a star scattering the earth. The Maya traded their jewels, obsidian crafts and slaves with other American peoples,* including the biggest city on the continent, Teotihuacan in the Valley of Mexico, City of the Sun. Teotihuacan's apogee coincided with Trajan's reign. It had a multi-ethnic population of 150,000 – Maya and others, and a hinterland containing a million people – and boasted a central avenue, the Avenue of the Dead, lined with monumental pyramids and temples. The Pyramid of the Sun, site of mass sacrifices, was the third highest edifice on earth.

Teotihuacan was the centre of obsidian craftsmanship, its people mining the glass from an old volcano, and many of them worked in obsidian laboratories, making weapons, mirrors and jewellery. Yet the city was built with no wheeled vehicles, no animal power and, unlike the many Maya cities, few inscriptions and no ballcourt. Lacking portraits or tombs, it may have been a sort of republic. After a revolution around 200, the Teotihuacans stopped building temples and palaces and started building comfortable apartment buildings decorated with colourful psychedelic murals, their inhabitants praying at communal altars where the heads of sacrificed victims were displayed. This was perhaps the first social housing and urban-renewal scheme.†

Back in Rome, Trajan, granted the *agnomen* Optimus Princeps – Best Emperor – decided to conquer Parthia, which had been weakened by the feuds of House Arsak. Rome was gradually swallowing up the kingdoms that controlled Eurasian trade. In 106, when the Nabataean king died, Trajan annexed Arabia, giving Rome another border with Parthia and control of most trade routes except the Parthian ports on the Persian Gulf. The Best Emperor could not fail . . .

---

* The Maya were in contact with the Caribbean where invaders and traders from the mainland were slowly conquering the islands. New DNA analysis shows that for millennia the Caribbean had been home to archaic foraging peoples, but now invaders in canoes from America, makers of ceramic goods, were occupying the islands, wiping out the existing peoples, who vanish in most places, through either intermarriage or killing. These occupiers were the ancestors of the Taíno, who inhabited the islands until the Spanish conquest.
† Teotihuacan's connections extended not only to the south: there is evidence of links to north America too. This was the time of a system of settlements around Hopewell in Ohio where after 100 BC people built burial mounds and large earthworks based on complex astronomical measurements, created beautiful artefacts – ranging from copper breastplates to pipes adorned with animal carvings that evoked shamanic rituals – and buried their dead with ritual costumes made up of ornaments that originated from Mexico to the Great Lakes. This culture broke up around AD 500.

HADRIAN IN LOVE: DEATH ON THE NILE

Trajan's Iraq war started well. As Hadrian covered his rear in Syria, Trajan, deploying a cosmopolitan army, which was only about 2 per cent Italian and included Arab cameleteers from Palmyra, Balearic slingers and African horsemen under a Berber general Lucius Quietus, found the Parthians in disarray. After swooping on the capital Ctesiphon, he sailed down the Tigris to the Gulf, where he gazed at the ships: 'I should certainly have crossed to India too if I were still young.' But the Parthians regrouped, while their allies – the Jews in Alexandria, Cyprus and Judaea – rebelled. Facing an Iraqi insurgency, the sixty-three-year-old Trajan had to fight desperately, 'his majestic grey head' attracting enemy fire. Retreating to Antioch, he ordered Quietus to cull the Jews, who were slaughtered and enslaved in huge numbers. The Best Emperor suffered a stroke – though he was convinced he was being poisoned. At his bedside, Empress Pompeia and her niece Matidia forged or coaxed Trajan's adoption of Hadrian. Anyone who knew too much paid the price. Two days after Trajan's death, in August 117, his wine taster died aged twenty-eight, as noted on his gravestone – surely more than a coincidence and a hint of dark deeds around the deathbed.

Emperor Hadrian abandoned Trajan's conquests in Parthia, a sensible decision given that Jewish rebellions were still being suppressed. But he did not trust Quietus, so he had him killed. Then, arriving in Rome, he pre-empted any opposition by executing four ex-consuls.

Hadrian was nicknamed the Greekling, a fan of Hellenistic culture, fashion and love, wearing his full head of hair curled and a well-tended beard, Greek-style. He liked to be an expert on everything: he was certainly one of the most talented of emperors. He wrote witty poetry, possessed the gift of the gab and worked hard. His expeditions from Syria to Britannia make him the best-travelled of monarchs until the age of steam. He was jealous of experts, yet he promoted talented people, enjoying cheeky repartee with poets. When a woman gave him a petition and he said he might not have time to read it, she retorted, 'Don't be emperor then.' He praised her and gave her an audience. But this highly strung and restless emperor was also as lethal as he was subtle, liquidating enemies fast and deploying spies, the *frumentari*, commissaries, who gave him reports on the personal lives of his subordinates, always useful knowledge. He could be pompous, pedantic and touchy, never forgiving Trajan's architect, who told him, 'Be off, and draw your gourds' – Hadrian was designing domes – 'you don't understand these things.' Hadrian later had him killed.* And he once stabbed a slave secretary in the eye, blinding him.

While he adored his mother-in-law Matidia, whom he deified on her death (not always the attitude of sons-in-law), his marriage with her daughter Sabina deteriorated, but he insisted on her travelling with him. In 119–21, on a trip to Germania and Britannia, where he built his wall across the north, the relationship hit a crisis. His chief secretary, Suetonius, now forty, born in Africa, a friend of Pliny, was Trajan's ex-archivist who had sifted the imperial papers to compile his *Lives of the Caesars*. He was accused of having an affair with Sabina, then in her thirties. Pliny said he was 'quiet and studious', but judging by his eye for outrageous material (he was also the author of a vanished masterpiece, *Lives of Famous Whores*), he was playful company. The historian was sacked – and then vanished. Did Hadrian quietly kill him?

Sabina continued to accompany Hadrian on his travels: in Bithynia, he fell in love with a beautiful Greek boy, the fourteen-year-old Antinous, who became his permanent companion. Travelling in 129 through Judaea and visiting the ruins of Jerusalem, a reminder of the ongoing rebellions by the Jews, he decided to build a shrine to Jupiter on the site of the Temple and a Roman city on the site of the holy city that he renamed Aelia Capitolina (after his own family Aelus and Jupiter's temple on the Capitoline Hill). Moving on to Egypt, he was celebrating the festival of Osiris – which marks the death of the Egyptian god and his rebirth as the Nilotic waters – when somehow Antinous, now twenty, drowned, whether by accident, suicide, a ritual gone wrong or a sacrifice in return for Hadrian's life. Poleaxed, Hadrian founded a new city, Antinouspolis, around his lover's tomb, then established a cult across the empire that celebrated the life-giving death of divine youth. The cult became popular, evidence that a sacred young man offering salvation through his own death and resurrection was a persuasive narrative. But Hadrian's luck changed in those Nilotic waters.

---

* Hadrian's buildings were spectacular: his palace at Tivoli – where remains are still being discovered – was nothing less than an imperial theme park designed to show his power. In Rome, his tomb, known today as the Castel Sant'Angelo, is magnificently bold, and the beauty of his Pantheon, with its open-eyed dome representing the world itself, boasting the widest vault of any building until 1436, still takes one's breath away.

Severans and Zenobians: Arab Dynasties

THE EUNUCHS, THE IMPERIAL PHILOSOPHER
AND THE PANDEMIC

While Hadrian was visiting Greece, revelling in the rituals of Greek culture and projecting himself as a new Pericles, he was also channelling another hero, Antiochos Epiphanes. Back in Jerusalem, the building of Aelia on the site of the Jewish Temple sparked a new revolt led by a self-declared prince of Israel, Simon Bar Kochba, who annihilated one Roman legion and threatened the security of the entire east. Rushing back to Judaea and summoning his best general from Britannia, Hadrian supervised the start of the harsh campaign, regaining control by 136 only by killing 580,000 Jews and enslaving 97,000, so many that they caused a slump in slave prices. But Hadrian persisted in building Aelia, banning Jews from Judaea, which he pointedly renamed Palestina – after the Philistines. The Jews cursed Hadrian, but after this third catastrophe, following the destructions of Jerusalem in 586 BC and AD 70, the Jews – settling in large numbers in Alexandria and Hispania – survived as both a religion and a people, never losing their link to, and reverence for, Jerusalem and Judaea.

When he returned to his Tivoli villa, the sixty-year-old Hadrian fell ill with arteriosclerosis and fretted about the succession. His great-nephew Pedanius Fruscus, backed by his distinguished nonagenarian grandfather Servanius, expected to be named, but instead Hadrian chose a playful aristocrat, Ceionius. When Pedanius and Servanius grumbled or perhaps even plotted, Hadrian had the boy executed and forced the old man to kill himself, which he did with the curse that the emperor should 'long for death but be unable to die'. And so it happened.

Suffering bitterly, Hadrian drew a circle around his nipple as a bullseye and begged a slave to kill him, but he could not do it. The emperor had not completely lost his wit, writing brilliantly about death.[*]

---

[*] Little soul, little wanderer, little charmer,
   Body's guest and companion,

In 138, Ceionius died young, at which Hadrian created around himself a new adoptive family to rule into the future. First he adopted as his son Antoninus, already fifty-two, a decent and efficient proconsul who was required to adopt in turn Lucius, the son of the late Ceionius, and the sixteen-year-old Marcus Annius Verus.

Hadrian had been close to the Verus family since his Spanish childhood. Marcus' grandfather, another respected proconsul, was one of Hadrian's trusted friends, a subtle political veteran who is acclaimed on his marble inscription for his skill in 'juggling the glass ball' – a perfect definition of politics then and now. 'From my grandfather Verus,' wrote Marcus later, 'I learned a kindly disposition and sweetness of temper.' Something about the grandson Marcus Verus had struck Hadrian: he nicknamed the boy Verissimus, Most Truthful, a play on his name. Antoninus was also Marcus' great-uncle. It was an intricate but well-judged web he spun.

In 138, Hadrian – denouncing the murderous ineptitude of medicine: 'Many doctors have killed the king' – finally died. Emperor Antoninus Pius moved the two Caesars into the palace and had them tutored by the best teachers. While Lucius was a playboy, Marcus was a philosopher, who used the Greek ideas of Stoicism as a guide to living as trainee emperor. Expected to die like most Romans in his fifties, Antoninus actually ruled for twenty-three stable years. In most previous reigns, the long apprenticeship of Marcus would have been untenable: either emperor or heir would have had to kill the other, but Marcus was neither ambitious nor entitled. Living in Tiberius' old palace on the Palatine, he warned himself, 'Don't be Caesarofied! Don't be dipped in the purple – for that can happen!'

In 145, Antoninus married his daughter Faustina to Marcus, who was unusually innocent for a young prince surrounded by available slaves: 'I preserved the flower of manhood, didn't seek proof of my virility, even deferred the time.' Faustina became the Augusta, outranking Marcus, who was the Caesar. The cleverness of Hadrian's web was that it allowed Antoninus to leave the empire to his own daughter.

In 161, the guards asked the dying emperor for his password. 'Equanimity,' he said, and died. Equanimity would indeed be Marcus' ideal. Marcus made Lucius his junior co-emperor – even though he was an inept jackanapes who toured the empire with a circus of actors and clowns. This ancient fratboy even built a tavern inside his villa so he

To what places will you set out for now?
To darkling, cold and gloomy ones –
And you won't make your usual jokes.

could wassail day and night.

Faustina had spent most of the previous decade pregnant, bearing fourteen children, of whom six died in infancy. Childhood mortality was high: only 50 per cent of Roman females lived to twelve, only 50 per cent of boys lived to seven; smallpox, which probably evolved from a rodent virus in prehistorical Africa, killed many, as did waterborne diseases. Marcus adored his children, describing one daughter as 'a cloudless sky, a holiday, hope close at hand, a total joy, an excellent and flawless source of pride'. When one of those children died, he attempted a Stoical response: 'One man prays: "How I may not lose my little child," but you must pray: "How I may not be afraid to lose him."' On death he reflected, 'Loss is nothing but change.' In the year of their accession, Faustina gave birth to twin boys. One died at four but the other, Commodus, grew up to be golden-haired, blue-eyed and energetic, the first son born to a ruling *princeps* since Britannicus. To protect little Commodus, Marcus married one daughter to his co-emperor Lucius and the rest to husbands who would not threaten the succession.

Having survived so much dangerous childbearing, Faustina, passionate and outspoken, grew more distant from the cerebral Marcus and threw herself into affairs with gladiators and actors. Marcus even caught her in flagrante with one, but he was tolerant, though Faustina's affairs were even mentioned on stage in Rome. When his aides advised him to exile her, he joked, 'If we send her away, we must also send away her dowry' – the empire. But Faustina's intrigues would almost cost Marcus his head.

No Roman emperor so deserved a serene reign of philosophical contemplation, but Marcus was confronted by war on all fronts. From the north-east Germanic tribes galloped south and broke into Italy; in the east the Parthians attacked Syria. Lucius was dispatched to oversee a counter-attack that culminated in the burning of Ctesiphon. At the same time, keen to take advantage of Parthian defeat, Marcus sent an embassy to China.

In 166, envoys of An-dun (Marcus Aurelius Antoninus), king of Da Qin (Rome), probably Romanized Greek or Arab merchants from a Red Sea port, arrived in the capital Luoyang to meet the Han emperor – the first direct contact. There had been several moments in the previous century when Romans and Han were close: when Trajan was in Ctesiphon he was only a few hundred miles from the garrisons of Ban Yao, son of Protector-General Ban Chao. Roman coins have been found in China and Vietnam but especially in India, suggesting that most of the trade took place there. Bearing presents of ivory, rhino and tortoiseshell and an essay on astronomy, Marcus' envoys were probably supposed to discuss direct silk trade, cutting out the Parthians. But they arrived just in time for high drama in Luoyang: Emperor Huan, thirty-four years old, took control of his kingdom from overmighty courtiers – with the help of trusted eunuchs.

In China, candidates for the knife were sometimes castrated by their families to prepare them for service at court, but others presented themselves outside the court. Having been asked thrice, 'Will you regret it or not?', they were anaesthetized with opium and held down for the operation – in China they were not just castrated but emasculated, losing not only testicles but penises. The wound took a hundred days to heal. Survival rates are just guesswork, but somewhere between 90 per cent and two-thirds died from an infection. If they survived as 'un-men', they applied to the Inner Court. For their services in helping emperors crush overmighty ministers, they were given titles and allowed to adopt heirs to whom they could leave riches and honours. Yet un-men were hated for their differentness – they often remained tiny, their voices were high, and they were partly incontinent, urinating through quills they kept in their hair – hence their nickname Urine-Sacks.

Huandi failed to control his powerful eunuchs, who framed his empress and had her and her entire clan executed for witchcraft. When Huandi died in 168, the eighteen-year-old Dowager Empress Dou appointed her father Dou Wu as regent. The dowager decided to kill the late emperor's nine favourite concubines, but the eunuchs let her kill only one of them. The throne was vacant until the regent found a Han princeling in the provinces who was enthroned in the capital at the age of eleven as Emperor Ling. But the chief tutor, head of the civil service, Chen Fan, persuaded the regent to purge the eunuchs. Seventeen un-men gathered in secret and 'smeared blood on their mouths' in a pact praying to August Heaven to help them annihilate the Dou family. The eunuchs seized the dowager empress and surrounded the regent. Dou killed himself, his family was annihilated, the chief tutor was trampled to death by irate un-men. The castrated potentates, the ten so-called central regular attendants, now ruled China – but an anti-eunuch backlash was coming.

Marcus Aurelius' envoys were probably in Luoyang for the triumph of the eunuchs, but it is not known if they made it home. Lucius' successes against Parthia must have yielded a bounty of prizes, but that was not all he brought back.

A pandemic had hit China in waves between 151 and 161. The world was much more global than one might expect; the disease was reported among Roman soldiers at Lucius' siege of Ctesiphon and it returned with them. Lucius and Marcus celebrated Parthian triumphs, but soon afterwards a plague ripped through the empire. Marcus understood in a very modern way that the cure and the panic of plague could be 'far more corrupting' than the sickness itself. The pandemic, probably a strain of smallpox – incessant killer throughout history – was observed by Marcus' doctor Galen, a Greek philosopher from Pergamum who had studied medicine in Alexandria. A doctor for gladiators, he became expert at dressing the wounds inflicted on soft flesh by cold steel, understood that the brain was the seat of the soul and realized that blood circulated. Yet he was hopelessly wrong about most things: he believed that health was the result of four humours (blood, phlegm, black bile and yellow bile) and that there were two different circulatory systems: his remained the dominant medical theory for over a thousand years, and doctors were an iatrogenic menace to their patients until the late nineteenth century. Over the next two millennia, whenever you read the words 'doctors were called', prepare for death.

Now accompanying Marcus and Lucius as they travelled north towards the German war, Galen watched the army being annihilated by the plague, noting its symptoms. In this period, and during its second surge a few years later, its mortality rate was 25 per cent and it killed 2,000 a day in Rome, 250,000 in total. Rome never recovered, and Europe knew no more million-strong cities until 1800. Villages all over the empire were left empty, with as much as 10 per cent of the population killed, and the army was ravaged too, all of which created a labour shortage that may have affected the Roman ability to find troops to hold the German and Danube frontiers. The plague hit the Germanic tribes as well, but they did not live in cities and could move camp easily. Its effect in weakening the empire was as important as it is incalculable: pandemics are invisible and inexplicable, but they have brought down more empires than any number of demented emperors and fierce battles.

Marcus kept away from Rome, while Galen prescribed a special tonic of theriac, myrrh, snake flesh and, perhaps most usefully, opium poppy juice. On the way back home Lucius, just thirty-nine, contracted the plague and perished. Now Marcus concentrated on protecting his eight-year-old son Commodus, who was cared for by Galen.

In 169, Marcus launched his war against Germanic tribes, who resisted strongly, defeating at least one of his armies and invading both Italy and Greece. But the emperor, learning the military craft on the job, persisted, aided by miracles such as a lightning bolt that destroyed German siege engines and a freak rainstorm that rescued a beleaguered legion. At last defeating the Germans in battle, in 175 he negotiated a peace, allowing many Germans to settle within the empire and serve in the Roman army, including the horsewomen whose skeletons were found near Hadrian's Wall in northern Britannia.

Marcus spent several years at the front, contemplating the meaning of existence.* But absence from Rome was dangerous. A rumour spread that he was dead, reaching Faustina, whose priority was to safeguard the succession for Commodus. This false news was the first in a series of misunderstandings: Faustina wrote to Avidius Cassius, *rector orientis*, eastern viceroy, to get his backing if Marcus really was dead. Whether deliberately or not, Faustina had betrayed her husband.

THE PHILOSOPHER'S MONSTER: COMMODUS

A vicious martinet who claimed descent from Seleukos, Augustus and Herod – an ominous combination – Avidius declared himself emperor. But in the west Marcus was popular – and very much alive. A centurion beheaded Avidius and sent the head to Marcus, who just had it buried, refusing to take vengeance ('May it never happen,' he told senators, 'that any of you should be killed either by my vote or by yours'), and he burned Avidius' correspondence with his wife without reading it.

Somehow Marcus and Faustina reconciled, but soon afterwards, travelling with Marcus, Faustina died, aged forty-five. Marcus grieved for her – 'such a fine woman, so obedient, so loving, so simple' – but on his return from his eastern travels he promoted Commodus, just fifteen, to co-emperor and consul, the youngest ever. As Marcus returned to fight the Germans, Commodus was his companion, but the smirking hellion came to loathe his fastidious father. Marcus knew that Commodus was flawed, but fortunately parents are programmed to be deluded about their children. Many teenagers are spoiled, but imperial heirs were superlatively spoiled. 'If you can, convert him by teaching; if not

---

* At the front he wrote his *Meditations*, a unique work for a ruling autocrat in its quest for self-knowledge and reconciliation with the cruel truths of life and death: 'A river of all events, a violent current, that is what Eternity is,' he wrote, channelling Heraklitos. 'No sooner has each thing happened than it has passed; another comes along and it too will pass away . . . Substance is like a river in perpetual flux.' As for himself, 'I have a city and a fatherland. As Antoninus I am a Roman, as a man, I am a citizen of the Universe.' But he was also pragmatic: 'Each hour, decide firmly like a Roman and a man to do what is at hand.' Many leaders have read it; few managed to live by it; and Marcus himself struggled to do so.

remember that kindliness was given to you for this very thing,' Marcus suggested. 'Kindliness is invincible,' so he would say, 'No, child, you are harming yourself, child.' But he was faced with a simple but terrible dilemma understood only by autocrats: either he chose Commodus as heir and ensured a smooth succession, or he named someone else and had to kill his own son or condemn him to rebellion and death.

In 179, Marcus captured 40,000 Germans and celebrated with an equestrian statue and a column boasting of his victories, both of which still stand in Rome. But soon afterwards, at Vindobona (Vienna), he caught the plague. Knowing the symptoms well, he called in his courtiers, rebuked them for weeping, then summoned Commodus, telling his friends, 'Here's my son, whom you brought up and who's just reached adolescence and stands in need of guides through the storms of life . . . You must be fathers to him in place of me alone . . . In this way you will provide yourselves and everyone else with an excellent emperor . . .' The courtiers must have quaked at the prospect of Commodus. Marcus had won real affection and respect by learning war with the men. He was a student of deathbeds, those strange theatres of bodily disintegration and political transference. Marcus noticed Commodus 'standing by his deathbed welcoming the evil happening to him' and muttering, 'We'll breathe more easily now this schoolmaster is gone.' When a tribune asked for the watchword, Marcus, now fifty-eight, retorted, 'Go to the rising sun. I am already setting.'

SLAUGHTER OF EUNUCHS AND THE MEGALOMANIA OF EXSUPERATORIUS

Commodus was 'most attractive to look at, because of his well-proportioned body and manly beauty, his hair natural, blond and curly. When he walked in sunlight, it shone like fire (some thought he sprinkled it with gold dust before going out) . . . and the first down was beginning to appear on his cheeks.' If strangers admired him, those who knew him best hated him most: the first conspiracy was led by his own sister Lucilla, but the assassin, their cousin Quadratus, bungled the hit and was killed. Lucilla was murdered. A second plot gave Commodus the pretext to execute his father's ministers and then his own wife. One of the plotters along with his sister was a Christian freedman's daughter named Marcia, who had been the mistress of Quadratus. Somehow Marcia not only avoided denunciation but became the emperor's mistress and adviser.

Yet Commodus possessed a cunning instinct for weakness and a gift for manipulation, bribing the army with money and peace and entertaining the people with thrilling spectacles. Revelling in his taboo-breaking antics, this vicious buffoon charged a million sesterces for his performances as a gladiator, traditionally the job of a murderous slave and therefore a way of projecting a popular touch. Commodus performed as a *secutor*, the elite gladiator who wore a full-face helmet with slits for the eyes, a loincloth, a leather belt, a thong on one arm, a greave on one leg, shield and sword, to fight the *retiarius*, a light gladiator who brandished trident and net. He always won, but when his opponents surrendered, he spared them. He killed a hundred lions, three elephants and a giraffe.

Practical jokes are always the resort of the witless; his were mirthless and cruel. Relishing his entourage of giants and dwarves, a wrestling hulk named Narcissus and a man with a penis larger than any animal except an elephant, Commodus' practical jokes involved blinding and dissecting people. Spectators did not know whether to giggle at his absurdity or bite their lip in terror.

By 189, he was presenting himself as Jupiter and Hercules, sporting lionskin and a club, and adopting the extravagant *agnomen* Exsuperatorius (a delicious word meaning Supersuperlative). When he called himself Amazonius, he renamed Marcia Amazonia. She was an unlikely Christian but managed to protect the bishop of Rome, Victor, and free Christians from the mines. Unlike his predecessors, who regarded Christianity as a dangerous *superstitio*, Commodus saw it as just another eastern cult; perhaps Marcia encouraged his idea of himself as a reincarnated god. His misrule sparked more conspiracies that fed his paranoia. The plague returned with a vengeance; thousands were dying while Commodus' killings became frenzied. His hitmen used infected needles dipped into pox sores so that the murdered would die of supposed natural causes – perhaps the first biological warfare. Now the emperor planned a reckoning with his enemies just as the slaughter of the eunuchs began in China.

On 22 September 189, the generals and bureaucrats decided to deal with the omnipotent Ten Eunuchs once and for all. It was the culmination of a decade of peasant rebellions, outrageous corruption and eunuch misrule. The Ten Eunuchs had repeatedly manipulated the weak emperors and used brazen brutality to liquidate all challengers. When they enthroned a child emperor and slaughtered their enemies, the generals decided to slaughter all the un-men. To that end they surrounded the Northern Palace and lit a fire at the gate to smoke out the eunuchs. Three days later, they stormed the palace and systematically killed every eunuch they could find – 2,000 of them. Anyone they came across without male genitalia (except women) was beheaded, so boys and adolescents had to prove their wholeness by dropping their trousers and revealing their penises. The all-powerful eunuch Zhang managed to seize the boy emperor Shao and flee towards the Yellow River, but they were hunted down and cornered. 'We're going to be destroyed and chaos will break out in the empire,' said the eunuch. 'Your Majesty, please take care of yourself!' and he threw himself into the river.

The power of the Han had vanished with their eunuchs. When the general Dong Zhuo found the emperor and his little brother, they were riding in a peasant's cart lost, almost alone, by the Yellow River. An entire cosmic system, headed by the Han emperors, was shattered by peasant rebellions. 'The deer was running loose' – the vivid Chinese expression for mayhem – and it would be four centuries before anyone caught it and a family united China again.*

In December 192, in Rome, Commodus, still just twenty-nine, mustered a posse of gladiators to kill both consuls and terrorize Rome. But he had gone too far.

ELAGABALUS IN TRANSITION:
THE AFRICAN EMPEROR AND THREE ARAB EMPRESSES

Languishing in his bath, Commodus wrote out his hit list and gave it to his beloved slave Philcommodus (Lovecommodus). His megalomania was raging, his administration in disorder, as he ruled through his lover Marcia, his manservant turned chamberlain Eclectus and a thuggish praetorian, Laetus.

In 191, he declared himself Pacifier of the World, renamed all the months after himself and rededicated Rome as Colonia Commodiana. When he planned a slaughter on 1 January 192, Marcia advised caution.

Lovecommodus showed the hit list to Marcia, and she saw that her name was at the top. 'Well done, Commodus,' she said, activating her conspiracy with her lover Eclectus. 'What repayment for the kindness I've lavished on you and for the drunken insults endured all these years. A drunkard can't outplay a sober woman.'

---

* It was now that the Chinese court had the first recorded contact with Japan: the islands were not yet united, no concept of Japan existed, but the Chinese called the people 'dwarves'. Little is known of its politics but in 190, a female shaman-queen named Himiko, aged twenty, succeeded to the throne of the small realm of Yamatai that controlled a federation of rice-farming chieftainships. Later she sent slaves as a gift to the Chinese emperor.

Marcia decided to poison Commodus and acclaim the city prefect Pertinax as emperor. Meanwhile Commodus held games at which he cut off an ostrich's head. He then, recalled a witness, 'came up to where we were sitting holding the head in his left hand and raising the bloody sword in his right.' Saying nothing, he grinned, eyes gleaming eerily.

On 31 December, Marcia brought the bathing Commodus a poisoned glass of wine. Exsuperatorius started to vomit, at which Marcia sent in Narcissus the personal trainer, who strangled him with the cord of his dressing gown. Pertinax was hailed as emperor and Marcia married Eclectus. But all three were killed in the civil wars that followed, out of which emerged a dynasty, led by an African emperor and an Arab empress.

His beard thick and curled Greek-style, Septimius Severus, African-born son of a Berber-Carthaginian family, had risen fast under Marcus thanks to the pandemic. In his forties serving in Syria, he married an Arab girl, Julia Domna, a princess of Emesa (Homs),* and they had twins sons. From 193, when Septimius was acclaimed emperor, he campaigned east and west, and expanded the empire to its greatest extent, always accompanied by Domna.

In 208, he invaded Caledonia (Scotland), where he fought to the northernmost point but only managed to hold the centre. He promoted his tough elder son, Caracalla (who earned his nickname by wearing a rough Caledonian hoodie), to co-emperor, followed by his brother Geta. But the two boys hated each other. Withdrawing to Eboracum (York), frustrated by the Caledonians, Septimius planned genocide: 'Let no one escape total destruction . . . not even the male baby in the womb.' Domna publicly criticized the promiscuity of the Scottish women. 'We satisfy the call of nature much better than you Roman women,' replied the wife of the Scottish chieftain, 'for we openly take the best men, whereas you're debauched in secret by the worst.' In York, the emperor sickened and died, advising his sons: 'Be harmonious, pay the soldiers, scorn everyone else.'

Their mother worked on family unity, but back in Rome, Caracalla ordered Geta's murder. When Domna tried to defend him, he was killed

---

* Julia Domna's father, descended from kings appointed by Pompey, was high priest of the Arab sun deity Allah-Gabal – God of Mankind, Elagab in Latin – worshipped in the form of a black meteorite, probably just one of many across the Arab world. There was no evidence that Mecca existed at this point, but a similar black meteorite – the Kaaba – would be worshipped there. Julia's name Domna – black in Arabic – referred to the divine stone of Emesa.

in her arms. Caracalla granted citizenship to all free men in the empire, regardless of class or race, displaying the tolerance that helped make Rome so successful. Racially inclusive empires last longer than those that are not. But Caracalla's motive was to maximize tax revenues, to fund his giant baths and his invasion of Parthia. Leaving his mother in Syria to govern, he marched into Parthia but was assassinated by a disgruntled officer. Domna, at the age of fifty-seven, was suffering agonizing breast cancer and committed suicide, but her sister Julia Maesa assumed family leadership, and then appointed her fourteen-year-old grandson, Elagabalus, priest of the family shrine, as emperor, claiming he was Caracalla's son by her daughter.

Augusta Maesa ruled with her daughter, both sitting in the Senate, while Elagabalus explored his sexual and religious identities. Marrying five times, he shocked Romans with his Syrian gods, sacred dancing and eccentric sexuality, falling in love with his charioteer Hierocles – 'I'm delighted,' he said, 'to be the mistress, wife, queen of Hierocles' – and with a well-hung wrestler called Aurelius Zoticus, to whom he said, 'Don't call me lord, I am a lady,' before asking his doctors to surgically craft him a vagina. It is possible he was merely being circumcised, a practice favoured by Jews and Arabs. Much of this was merely anti-eastern propaganda. Whether he was really the first transsexual or just a Syrian boy in love with a buff charioteer, his eastern religion offended many Romans.

When Elagabalus, now eighteen, turned against his heir, his more conventional first cousin Alexander Severus, the praetorians demanded his killing. In 222, his septuagenarian grandmother Maesa acquiesced in the killing of her daughter and grandson, and both were beheaded, their nude torsos hurled into the Tiber. Raised to the purple, Alexander Severus, pinheaded and beardless, was first dominated by his murderous granny and after her death by his mother Mamaea, the third female potentate of the family, who accompanied the emperor even to war. Mamaea was attracted to Christianity, studying with the Alexandrian scholar Origen, who had more than proved his ascetic credentials by castrating himself. But Mamaea and Alexander struggled to withstand German and Parthian attacks. In 235, on the German front, facing an army mutiny, mother and son – clinging to each other in their tent – were killed together, throwing the state into its greatest crisis since Hannibal, an eclipse that benefited a new Persian potentate, Ardashir.

No one knows his real origins, but the integrity of his new dynasty was bizarrely proven by the gift of a pair of testicles.

THE SHAH, THE STUFFED EMPEROR AND THE
SALTED TESTICLES

Grandson of a Zoroastrian priest-prince named Sasan, Ardashir was a master of war and peace, first taking control of old Persia, then restoring the Zoroastrian faith and identifying himself as the choice of the god Ahura-Mazda. In 220, Ardashir killed the Parthian king and married one of his daughters, offering the Parthian grandees the chance to join his Iranshahr – Empire of Iranians. In the turbulence of his early wars, his pregnant wife Mirdad was guarded by his henchman Abarsam, who was accused of fathering the baby. Hoping to prove the integrity of the royal line, Abarsam had himself castrated and sent his testicles to the king in a box of salt – surely an example of protesting too much.

Promising loot and glory in war against the beleaguered Romans, Ardashir, accompanied by his teenaged son Shapur, raided Syria, perfecting the force that would be the Sasanian contribution to warfare: the armoured knights of his heavy cavalry known as cataphracts that could break Roman infantry. Now he took the fortresses Nisibis and Hatra and secured the trading entrepôt of Charax on the Persian Gulf, seizing control of the caravan and sea routes to India. Then he rode eastwards to finish off the Kushans. When his father died in 240, Shapur ravaged the Roman east.

Two of the shah's retainers would be especially important: Kirder, a militant Zoroastrian magus, and Mani, an aristocratic prophet of Jewish-Christian background who founded a new religion, around a struggle between good and evil inspired by the visions of a sacred voice known as the Twin. Manichaeanism spread not just through Persia but to China and Rome too – a religion that could, instead of Christianity, have become one of the great world religions. Mani converted the king's brother Peroz and many others, and Shapur allowed him to preach his faith freely. Kirder urged a purge of these heretics, but the shah concentrated on breaking Rome.

Three Roman emperors perished fighting Shapur, and at least one had to submit to the king of kings. The cruellest cut came in 260, when Shapur defeated and then captured Emperor Valerian 'with his own hands', he claimed, before going on to take the eastern Roman capital, Antioch. Valerian was used as Shapur's mounting block, then flayed alive, the skin painted red and stuffed with straw and exhibited in a temple.

As Rome descended into civil war, it looked as if Persia would replace Rome in the east – until a Arab conqueress changed the World Game.

ZENOBIA AND CONSTANTINE

Just as Shapur was returning laden with loot, Odeinath, ruler of Palmyra, declared himself king, and attacked Shapur, defeating him near Samosata. Bearded with curled hair and Greek diadem, Odeinath (Odaenathus in his Roman identity), forty years old, was an Arab merchant prince, *ras* (*rais*) – chief in Arabic – and exarch of Palmyra, a desert trading city of 200,000 Arabs, Aramaeans, Greeks and Romans, grown rich from the caravans of the eastern trade, its ruins still magnificent even today. Odeinath was married to an Arab-Greek girl, Zenobia, who was descended from the Ptolemies, related to Cleopatra – though her achievements would make the Egyptian queen seem footling.

'Her face was dark and swarthy,' wrote a Roman historian, 'her eyes were black and powerful, her spirit divinely great, and her beauty incredible. So white were her teeth that many thought that she had pearls in place of teeth.' Marrying the exarch when she was around fourteen, she hired a Greek-Syrian tutor named Longinus to teach her Greek philosophy.

Now Odeinath recaptured Edessa and Emesa for Rome, then in 262, mustering a large army of Palmyrene archers, cataphracts and Arab cavalry, invaded Persia, besieging Ctesiphon. Odeinath was hailed by Palmyrenes as a god and rewarded by the latest, weak emperor as *Corrector Totius Orientis*, eastern viceroy, granted the *agnomen* Persicus Maximus, but instead he declared himself king of kings, portraying himself as the divine hunter killing two tigers – Rome and Persia. In 267, when a horde of nomads, Goths – making their first appearance – raided Syria/Iraq, Odeinath repelled them, but was then assassinated by a disgruntled nephew who had been humiliated on a royal hunt and now seized the crown – for one day. Zenobia, now twenty-five, was with him. She rallied the army, killed the nephew and seized the throne, crowning her baby son Vaballathus (Wah-ballāt, or Gift of Allat, an Arab goddess). During an astonishing three years, she seized Antioch, where she set up court, advised by Longinus her philosopher, and, commanding an army of 70,000, directed the conquest of today's Lebanon, Syria, Türkiye, Israel, Arabia and Egypt – just as Shapur, vanquisher of so many emperors, died, leaving Zenobia unchallenged, and Persia paralysed by religious schism.*

In 272, Zenobia declared herself Augusta – empress – and her son Augustus, but to the west, a dynamic Roman general, Aurelian, first expelled rampaging barbarians from Italy then marched eastwards to regain Egypt, then Syria, defeating Zenobia at Emesa (after seeing a vision of Sol Invictus, Invincible Sun god, promising him victory). Trying to escape on a camel, Zenobia was captured.† Serving in Aurelian's army when it took Palmyra was a young Roman officer named Constantius Chlorus, whose son would radically change the world.

Born of humble family in Roman Dacia (Serbia) in 250, Constantius won the attention of the emperor, who made him one of his bodyguards. At a tavern in the east, Constantius met a Greek girl from Bithynia named Helena, whom he married, and while he was governing Dalmatia she gave birth to a son, Constantine. It is likely that Helena was already a follower of the Christian sect. Bold-faced, big-jawed and pointy-chinned with a Caesar haircut – a proper Roman general – Constantius was not a Christian. Instead he revered Sol Invictus, the god who had helped Aurelian defeat Zenobia.

After the assassination of Aurelian, Constantius backed a new claimant to the throne, Diocletian, a Dalmatian general who struggled to repel or absorb waves of tribes migrating from the eastern steppes. Goths, Saxons, Samaritians, Franks and Alemanni probed his frontiers in a stampede migration: each fearsome invasion was also a terrified migration fleeing a more fearsome attack. Behind Goths and Franks came the Huns, who now raided eastern Persia.

In 285, Diocletian, realizing that his job was too much for one man, raised a general Maximian to co-Augustus. While Diocletian ruled the east from Nicomedia (near the Bosphoros), Maximian, based at Mediolanum (Milan), promoted Constantius to govern Gaul.‡ Constantius

---

* Shapur's successor Bahram II backed the fanatical Zoroastrian priest Kirder, who restored the Persian religion, turning on the prophet Mani, who was arrested, beheaded, flayed and stuffed. His death, a martyrdom like that of Jesus, encouraged the spread of his religion: the Uighurs in central Asia converted en masse to Manichaeanism.

† Palmyra was sacked, with thousands of Palmyrenes enslaved, and Zenobia was paraded in Aurelian's Roman triumph. She was not executed but married to a Roman senator, living out her life in suburban obscurity after founding the first Arab empire in one of the most extraordinary female careers before modern times.

‡ The coasts of Gaul and Menapia (Netherlands) were cursed by the depredations of Frankish and Saxon pirates, so Maximian appointed one of his officers, Mausaeus Carausius, to build a fleet and destroy them. Instead Carausius first colluded with the pirates, then declared himself emperor of northern Gaul and Britannia, backed by Roman, British and Frankish troops. He even cast his own coins emblazoned with the world-beating slogans *Restitutor Britanniae* (Restorer of Britain) and *Genius Britanniae* (Spirit of Britain) – literally the first British empire.

married Maximian's daughter, without ever rejecting Helena and her son Constantine. But the connection paid off when the two Augusti appointed Caesars – Constantius in the west, Galerius in the east, creating a tetrarchy – the rule of four.

Constantius attacked the Franks and other German tribes first, then invaded Britannia, liquidating Carausius. His twenty-year-old son Constantine accompanied Emperor Diocletian as far as Egypt and Babylon. Craggy Constantine impressed Diocletian, who married him to his niece; she delivered his first son, Crispus.

Why was Rome in crisis? Diocletian believed that the gods were displeased by the neglect of the old religion and the spread of new superstitions. In Antioch he and Caesar Galerius ordered the haruspices (observers of entrails) to sacrifice animals and read the auguries. But something was wrong, and Diocletian believed there were too many Christians. He ordered everyone to sacrifice to the gods and emperors. When Christians refused, the killing started. Christians and Manichaeans were flayed, burned and decapitated. When Diocletian's palace in Nicomedia caught fire, the terror intensified. Constantius, with his Christian wife Helena, and his own leaning towards Sol Invictus, kept quiet while in Diocletian's retinue their son Constantine silently regretted the 'bloody edicts' against the 'worshippers of God'. He was about to experience a momentous conversion.

ACT FOUR
200 MILLION

Houses of Constantine,
Sasan and Spearthrower Owl

In 304, Diocletian fainted in public and decided to retire, the first emperor ever to do so; he withdrew to grow cabbages at his palace in Split (Croatia).* Forcing Maximian to do the same, Diocletian promoted Constantius and Galerius to be Augustus of west and east. Sensing danger from Galerius, Constantine galloped westwards. After he had met up with his father in Gaul, they crossed to Britannia to fight the Picts, but in 306, in York, Constantius died. A German king acclaimed Constantine as Augustus. Taking control of Britannia, Hispania and Gaul, Constantine, thirty-four years old, repelled a Frankish raid and captured their kings, whom he fed to the lions in the amphitheatre of his capital Triers. Muscular and hefty with a thrusting jaw, blunt nose and cleft chin, Constantine led his troops from the front and killed anyone who stood in his way, but he was also a thoughtful and cautious man.

Maximian backed his son Maxentius to become emperor and offered his pretty teenaged daughter Fausta to Constantine, whose first wife had died. The couple went on to have three sons, but the alliance with Fausta's family had become fraught. After his father-in-law had tried to have him assassinated, Constantine outmanoeuvred the old emperor, forcing his suicide. Fausta was now stuck with a husband who had effectively killed her father – while her brother Maxentius still ruled Italy.

Constantine issued edicts of religious tolerance, suggesting sympathy for the Christianity embraced by his mother Helena. In 312, while he was close to a temple of Sol Invictus, Constantine saw a ring around the sun. Christians insisted that Jesus Christ was the 'light of the world' – the sun – and Constantine concluded he had received a sign from

---

* They were very special cabbages: 'If you could show the cabbage that I planted with my own hands to your emperor,' Diocletian replied to an envoy who asked him to return to politics, 'he definitely wouldn't dare suggest that I replace this calm and happiness with the storms of insatiable ambition.' Much of his palace survives in Split.

Christ. As he marched into Italy, he ordered his troops to inscribe the *Ch-Rho* – the first two Greek letters of the word Christ – on their banners.

As Constantine advanced on Rome, Maxentius lacked confidence, hiding his regalia, including an exquisite sceptre with a blue orb for the world, on the Palatine Hill. At Milvian Bridge, Constantine routed Maxentius, who fell off his horse into the Tiber; his head was later paraded round Rome atop a lance.

Now Constantine revealed himself as a Christian sympathizer. Even though the sect's absolute moral certainties ruled out compromise with the Roman pantheon, Constantine moved slowly, building new churches on the site of the tomb of St Peter and a splendid, still-standing basilica at the Lateran. Yet his triumphal arch featured Sol Invictus, Companion of Unconquered Constantine. But victory is always the most persuasive religious argument: Constantine believed Christ had won his battles for him.

Constantine ruled only the western empire; his colleague as Augustus, Licinius, ruled the east. In 313, the two Augusti met and Constantine married his half-sister Constantia to Licinius. But the empire was too small for two Augusti. When the showdown came in 324, Constantine, lightly wounded, smashed Licinius near the old Greek town of Byzantion. His sister Constantia, mother of his nephew, negotiated Licinius' surrender – but Constantine quietly killed husband and child. He was no saint.

Constantine now emerged as a Christian emperor, promoting the hierarchy of the Church in parallel with that of the state, and enforcing a new morality: he abolished crucifixion in honour of Jesus, banned murderous games, fortified marriage, discouraged adultery, made Sun-day the Christian sabbath, fixed the dates of Christmas (already celebrated as the winter solstice) and Easter and persecuted the Jews, whom he called 'murderers of the Lord'.*

Accustomed to being a divine ruler, Constantine ranked himself high on the hierarchy between God and man, seeing himself as the thirteenth apostle. But now he had to deal with the fissiparous debates about the relationship between God, Christ and the Holy Spirit that were already

---

* Slavery was inimical to Christian ideals; many early Christians had been slaves or freedmen, indeed it was in some senses an egalitarian slaves' religion. Now it was no longer acceptable to enslave Christians nor to have sex with slaves: a master had to free an enslaved woman then marry her in order to have sex. Of course these rules were unenforceable: slavery – usually the enslavement of non-Christians – thrived in Christendom for another two millennia.

leading to murderous feuds. How divine was Jesus? Many Christians regarded all three as divine, but Arius, an Alexandrian priest, believed Jesus was a divine-touched human subordinate to God. Salvation was a matter of life and death; factions fought the Christological debates in the streets of Alexandria. Constantine ordered the burning of Arius' writings, and at Nicaea he dictated a compromise formula that became the orthodoxy. A religion that believed in one absolute truth and one unwavering route to salvation could not compromise.

Constantine discovered that the Christians were more difficult to regulate than anything else.* Except his family.

In 326, Constantine arrested his eldest son, Caesar Crispus, and ordered his killing by poison. Somehow his wife Fausta – mother of three of the emperor's sons and two daughters – was implicated. Either Crispus had conspired with his glamorous stepmother or he had had an affair with her. She seems to have denounced him to Constantine. She had given birth to a child just three years earlier, so her marriage to Constantine was at least active. But Constantine had killed her father and brother, a record that might cast a shadow over any marriage.

A year after Crispus' execution, he ordered Fausta's arrest. Constantine's mother Helena (now aged seventy-five) made a sinister intervention: she criticized his killing of Crispus and convinced him the boy had been seduced then framed by Fausta. As a result Fausta was boiled to death in the steam baths. It is ironic that this murderous mother-in-law would become a Christian saint. Helena, promoted to Augusta, was dispatched on an imperial mission to rediscover relics of Jesus in Aelia Capitolina, once known as Jerusalem.

The most successful archaeologist of all time, Helena swiftly identified the location of Jesus' crucifixion and tomb, beneath Hadrian's Temple of Venus, then uncovered pieces of the True Cross itself, and finally commissioned the transformation of Aelia into the Christianized Holy City, centrepiece of a new Christian Holy Land in which splendid churches marked the vital events of Jesus' life, grafted on top of its

---

* As for Arius himself, he returned from exile to Constantinople where his theological incontinence led to a faecal explosion: while walking in the Forum, 'a terror arising from the remorse of conscience seized Arius', expressed in 'a violent relaxation of the bowels'. Rushing behind the Forum, 'a faintness came over him, and together with the evacuations his bowels protruded, followed by a copious haemorrhage, and the descent of the smaller intestines: portions of spleen and liver gushed out in effusions of blood, so that he almost immediately died'. Heresy was a messy business: the churchman Socrates Scholasticus noted that tourists still pointed to the spot decades later. But Arius' homoiousian views on the humanity of Jesus appealed to many of the Germanic tribes that converted to Christianity during the 360s.

discredited Jewish sanctity.* Helena brandished a letter from her son
– one of the many through which we can hear his emphatic, magniloquent voice: 'I have no greater care than how I may best adorn with
a splendid structure that sacred spot, which, under Divine direction,
I have disencumbered of the heavy weight of foul idol worship.' The
Temple of Venus was demolished, replaced by a basilica to mark the
Holy Sepulchre and Golgotha, with another church on the site of Jesus'
birth in Bethlehem. Afterwards, Helena delivered her splinters of the
True Cross and the nails of the crucifixion to Constantine: she set the
nails in his helmet and bridle.

As she died in Constantine's arms, he had already decided to found
a new capital in the east. After reviewing and rejecting Troy, Chalcedon
and Thessalonica, in May 330 he dedicated a new city on the European
side of the Bosphoros at Byzantion, with its superb harbour and defensible peninsula – just across from the site of his victory over Licinius.
Declaring that God had told him to name it after himself – Constantinople – he planned a New Rome, with its own senate, but also an
imperial–Christian capital. His palace stood on its acropolis. Hulking
Christian basilicas vied with a huge hippodrome and a forum featuring
a porphyry pillar with the pagan-style naked emperor, himself, on top,
radiating sunrays.

His conversion made Christianity as attractive and powerful as the
Roman empire itself: power is always the lodestar of faith. Three centuries after Jesus' obscure death, Christ now became the central moral
figure of western civilization: millions converted. In 319, Constantine's
neighbour Iberia (Georgia) followed suit,† while in Africa, Ezana, king
of Aksum in Eritrea and Ethiopia, who had finished off Kush and
expanded into Yemen, had long interacted with merchants and missionaries from Alexandria. Around 350, he converted too. But Constantine's
conversion led to new tension with Persia, where the Sasanians were
coalescing around the belly of a pregnant queen.

THE CROWNED EMBRYO AND THE PAGAN EMPEROR

* Already viciously persecuted, Jews were banned from Jerusalem for the next three centuries, though many risked death to worship there covertly and secretly visit the Temple
Mount and its walls to pray.
† Georgia was not the first. In 301, Tiridates III, the king of Armenia, the buffer state
between Rome and Persia, had converted after a Christian saint cured his mental illness
– though this was done partly to assert his independence from the stridently Zoroastrian
Persians.

In 309, Persian grandees murdered their king, then crowned the unborn foetus – the embryo king – within the belly of the queen without knowing if the baby would turn out to be male.

They got lucky: the baby was Shapur II, who by the time Constantine had founded Constantinople, had emerged as a forceful autocrat. Shapur spent his first years chastising the Lakhm Arab tribes of Iraq, whom he recruited as allies under Amr, the self-styled king of all the Arabs,* and then, still barely out of his teens, managed to fight off the Huns. Constantine's Christianity made Shapur question the loyalty of his many Christians. Armenia, itself Christianized, appealed for Constantine's help and he prepared for war. He had already named his three sons by Fausta as Caesars, along with his half-brother's sons, while a nephew Hannibalianus became king of kings, prospective ruler of Persia. But as he moved east Constantine, now sixty-five, fell ill, so he sent Constantius, his middle, favourite son, ahead to repel Shapur. When Constantius, still in his teens, heard that his father was dying, he rushed back. Constantine was baptized on his deathbed, as Constantius organized a family massacre of the late emperor's half-brothers and six nephews.

The three sons met to divide up the empire: Constantine II the eldest, now twenty-one, who regarded himself as the main heir, got Britannia, Hispania and Gaul; Constans Italy and Africa, Constantius the east, where he soon halted Shapur. However, the brothers quickly fell out and two were killed, leaving Constantius as sole emperor. But he was thinly stretched.

Only two male Constantinians had survived his family hecatomb – his cousins Gallus and Julian, who lived quietly on a Cappadocian estate, lucky to be alive. Gallus was ambitious; Julian eschewed politics and studied philosophy. Constantius appointed Gallus as Caesar, who then unwisely presided over the games in Constantinople, prerogative of Augusti. Constantius had Gallus beheaded, and wondered whether to kill Julian too. The emperor's wife Eusebia, a cultivated, kindly Macedonian, now brought Julian to the emperor. Constantius agreed to let him study philosophy in Athens, where he rejected Christianity and embraced the worship of the sun god.

---

* Empires throughout history favour the appointment of one ruler – a king – as intermediary to control their unruly subjects, in this case their Arab allies. The Assyrians too had appointed kings of the Arabs. This was the start of a long relationship between the Sasan shahs and the Lahkm Arab kings, but strangely the tomb of Amr was found in Roman Syria, suggesting that he later defected from Iran to Rome, the first of many such switches by Arab leaders between superpower patrons. Soon the Romans would find their own Arab protégés.

Constantius needed a partner in the west even though he was 'suspicious' of Julian's popularity. But, encouraged by Eusebia, he raised Julian to Caesar and sent him to Lutetia Parisiorum (Paris).

Julian surprised everyone (especially himself) by defeating the Alemanni, but in 360 Shapur attacked in the east backed by an army of Hunnish auxiliaries. Already both the Roman and Persian armies deployed large corps of 'barbarians'. Constantius ordered Julian to send half of his legions eastwards. Julian had just lost his sole ally, Eusebia having overdosed on fertility drugs. In Paris, he was declared Augustus. Constantius rushed back to destroy him, but died of fever on the way.

Now sole emperor, Julian tilted the empire back towards paganism, attacking Christianity and restoring pagan temples, even giving Jerusalem back to the Jews so that they could rebuild the Temple. One man, his uncle, had imposed Christianity; the nephew could have overturned it – if he had been lucky. But his most urgent business was Persia, where he planned to take Ctesiphon, rowing his army of 65,000 down the Euphrates and along a canal into the Tigris. When he disembarked, he showed his confidence by burning his flotilla but failed to destroy the Sasan army. Ctesiphon did not fall and Julian retreated, harassed by Sasan cavalry. On 26 June 363 near Samara, he rushed towards the fighting, forgetting to pull on his mail. A javelin struck him in the side. His Greek doctor tried to sew up the torn intestine, but Julian died – and the Romans, desperate to get home, gave Shapur everything he demanded.

In the chaos after Julian's death, which ended the Constantinian dynasty, an irascible general Valentinian was chosen as Augustus, appointing his brother Valens as eastern emperor, but both were forced to firefight invasions of barbarians. When Valentinian died of a stroke when enraged in 375,* Valens faced the armed migration of Germanic Goths, known as the Thervingi, cousins of peoples who lived in Ukraine and Russia.† Valens had hired them as *foederati* or allies and granted them lands, only for Roman officials to steal those lands: the furious Goths went to war. In 378, at Adrianople (Edirne), a Gothic horse archer got a bullseye, hitting Valens in the face.

In 378, as Valens fell, so, far to the west, did the ruler of Tikal in

---

* Apart from the ill temper that killed him, Valentinian cultivated a brutish image, travelling the empire accompanied by a cage containing two bears, named Innocence and Goldflake, to whom he fed unfortunate dissidents. In a heart-warming landmark for wildlife conservation, Innocence was returned to the wild for having loyally eaten Valentinian's victims.
† Later the Thervingi became known as the Visigoths (western Goths) and moved westwards, soon followed by their eastern brethren, the Ostrogoths.

Mesoamerica when Spearthrower Owl, a warlord from Teotihuacan, the magnificent city in the Mexican valley, ordered Tikal's conquest.

FIRST CROCODILE AND RUGILA THE HUN

Spearthrower's general Siyah Kak (Fire-Is-Born) marched six hundred miles southwards to defeat Tikal's *ajaw*, Great Jaguar Paw, who was defeated, captured and most likely sacrificed. While some scholars doubt that a leader could have arrived from Teotihuacan, people certainly moved between the two cities – and it would not be the last dynasty founded by a stranger steeped in the mystery of faraway places. Much of this narrative remains mysterious but probably Fire-Is-Born became regent – Lord of the West – while Spearthrower Owl appointed his young son, First Crocodile, as *ajaw* of Tikal. Spearthrower Owl ruled for many years, but this was not the end of the dynasty of First Step Shark: Spearthrower married his son First Crocodile to Lady Kinich, daughter of Great Jaguar Paw, uniting the two families. First Crocodile ruled for many decades and when he died he was entombed with a headless crocodile and nine young sacrificed humans, the youngest being a boy of six, along with a censer statue of an old god sitting on a stool of human bones. This conquest marked the apogee of Teotihuacan.[*]

The body of Valens was never found. The Goths marauded through the Balkans while Burgundians, Saxons, Franks and Vandals penetrated the Roman borders. The fall of the Roman empire was more of a fragmentation, less an event than a transformation. The barbarians were already not so much at the gates as in the kitchen and bedroom: the empire's borders were porous, its peoples and especially the army already a hybrid honeycomb of Romanized Christian barbarians. If the Romans were scared of the Goths, the Goths were even more terrified by what lay behind them.

Out on the steppes of Eurasia, a people called Huns were galloping westwards, and among them was the family of Attila. Originating far to the east on the vast grasslands, precisely where is unknown, they were not a single people but a federation of ferocious raiders and pastoral nomads. Their language is unknown too, but it was probably Turkic in origin. Their migration may have been connected to the splintering of

---

[*] The world's biggest cities were Constantinople, Ctesiphon/Seleucia, Pataliputra (Patna), Rome, Nanjing, Antioch, Alexandria and Teotihuacan.

the Xiongnu. Now living east of the Black Sea, the Huns were drawn westwards by meteorological changes, dynamic leadership, the need for new pastures and news of rich plunder. Remarkably symbiotic with their horses which they were first tied on to at the age of three, they had honed the horse archery of the steppes into a conquering machine that could fight in any season and cover vast distances. Each warrior travelled with two or three remounts, armed with their composite bows and iron-headed arrows, guarding families who travelled in big wagons, stopping to camp and cook around cauldrons, served by enslaved prisoners. In war, they advanced in units of a thousand or more, their recurve bows firing arrows at 125 miles per hour. 'In five seconds 1,000 arrows could hit 200 of the enemy,' writes John Man, 'another 1,000 in the next five . . . a rate of 12,000 shots per minute, equivalent to ten machine-guns.' Once their enemies were wounded, they lassooed them and dragged them off their feet or from their horses. Until the spread of gunpowder a thousand years later, such mounted archers were a deadly threat to sedentary societies.

They worshipped the sky god, Tengri, their shamans divining the future, but their kings also revered a numinous sword of war that enabled its bearer to rule the world. Their faces were scarred by grieving rituals, while Hunnish skeletons show that the skulls of some of their children, boys and girls, had been bound in order to create loaf-shaped crania – all of which horrified the Romans. A warlord named Rugila, along with his brothers Octar and Mundzuk, unified the Huns and others into a confederacy, conquering and co-opting the Ostrogoths and many other peoples, which suddenly galloped towards the Roman empire, which was at the time divided between the sons of Emperor Theodosius, one in Ravenna, the other in Constantinople.

Two extraordinary characters, one male, one female, were at the centre of this clash: one was a Hun, Rugila's nephew, who became engaged to a Roman princess, and other was a Roman emperor's daughter who married a barbarian king.

ATTILA AND EMPRESS PLACIDIA

Galla Placidia was the daughter of Emperor Theodosius, who had held the empire together for twenty stormy years. When he died, he left his two sons, his daughter and the empire in the care of a half-Vandal paladin named Stilicho. While the empire was divided between his sons, Stilicho fought barbarians on all fronts, among them a former Roman ally, Alaric, king of the Visigoths, whose ancestors had killed Emperor Valens and now invaded Italy. But in 408 the weak young emperor Honorius, jealous of Stilicho's supremacy, had him executed – with disastrous consequences.

In 410, Alaric besieged Rome, forcing its citizens to starve and eat each other, then he sacked the city, smashing the urns of Augustus and Hadrian in their mausoleums – and leaving with a special prisoner, the emperor's twenty-year-old sister Princess Placidia, whom he married to his son Ataulf. Placidia found herself queen of the barbarians who had destroyed Rome.

Yet the marriage was short. Ataulf was assassinated, and his successor humiliated Placidia, who was forced to walk through mocking crowds for ten miles before she was returned to her brother. Yet her life was an exercise in strength and survival. Now that she was safely back at court in Ravenna, Honorius married her in 417 to a general with whom she had two children, a daughter Honoria, as irrepressible as her mother, and a son. When Honorius died, she fled the ensuing chaos to join her nephew Theodosius II in Constantinople, negotiated military assistance for her cause, then presided over the expedition that restored her and her son, Valentinian III, to power in the west.

Ruling as Augusta and regent, educated and haughty, she built her own palace and chapel in Ravenna while she played off barbarian kings and her own half-barbarian generals. Her chief commander was a half-Goth called Flavius Aetius who had spent his youth as a hostage at the Hunnish court, where he had befriended the Hunnish warlord Rugila. When Aetius threatened her, she dismissed him. Aetius fled to Rugila, who lent him an army which he used as leverage against Empress Placidia. In 432, she appointed him her military supremo, *magister utriusque militiae*. Placidia and Aetius managed the transformation of the empire, settling their allies the Franks and Goths in the west, but losing Africa to the Vandals.

To the east, Aetius' friend Rugila was expanding into central Europe and menacing Theodosius in Constantinople, who paid him with 350 pounds of gold and prayed for his death. In 435, Rugila was struck by a thunderbolt, more likely smallpox, leaving the confederacy to his nephews, Bleda and Attila. The brothers forced Theodosius to double his tribute to 700 pounds of gold, open markets with the Huns and return two cousins who had defected. When the latter were handed over, Attila immediately had them impaled as the Romans watched.

Although Attila and Bleda blackmailed Theodosius, they helped Empress Placidia and Aetius defeat an invasion of another Germanic tribe, the Burgundians. But they wanted more gold. In 440, they crossed the Danube to plunder Roman cities, stopping only when paid yet more. Bleda was then killed by Attila, who, wielding the sacred sword of world rulership, united 'Scythia and Germania' from the Caspian to the Danube. He held court at his capital of wooden houses built around a huge wooden palace with all the Roman comforts – wine, carpets, couches and a bathhouse. An African jester named Zercon* performed for the frequent Roman envoys, who were offered 'attractive women for intercourse, a mark of honour among the Huns', recalled the Roman diplomat Priscus, before adding primly, 'We plied the women with foods but refused intercourse.' He was fascinated by Attila, remarking that he was 'short of stature, broad-chested with a large head, small eyes, thin beard flecked with grey, snub nose', and that he moved with 'haughty gait, eyes darting, his power and pride apparent'. Attila was illiterate, so his Roman secretary Orestes handled his correspondence. While a 'lover of war, he knew restraint, excellent in council, sympathetic to supplicants, gracious to those under his protection'. But he was lethal too – 'I'll have you impaled and fed to the birds,' he would say – and Attila's capital usually featured a 'spy' or two impaled on stakes.

Theodosius II, after completing new walls that would make Constantinople near impregnable for almost a thousand years, stopped paying Attila – and ordered his assassination, suborning a Skirian ally, Edika, to do the job. But the plot was exposed, and Attila relished the revelation of Roman duplicity. 'Theodosius's father was royal; I'm Attila son of Mundzuk,' said Attila. 'I've preserved *my* nobility, Theodosius has not. Now who's the barbarian; who's civilized?' But Constantinople was unconquerable and Attila needed loot for his voracious chieftains: should he conquer Persia or go west? As the Vandals settled in Africa, with Goths, Franks and Burgundians in Spain, France and the Low Countries, Attila received a surprising invitation:† a royal proposal of marriage.

---

* During their Roman negotiations, Attila and Bleda received a human gift – Zercon, a lame noseless dwarf from Mauritania, who had been captured in Africa. He survived as a jester at the court of the Huns performing in a mixture of Latin and Hunnish, to the delight of King Bleda, who dressed him in a suit of armour and screamed with laughter at his skits. Zercon hated it and escaped. Bleda sent cavalry to bring him back at all costs and asked him why he had fled. Zercon replied that it was because he had no wife, at which Bleda, roaring with laughter, gave him a daughter of one of his wives' maids, presiding over the marriage. Now he was inherited by Attila.

† Aetius and Attila remained friendly. Aetius sent him two Roman scribes to serve as secretaries. Attila sent him Zercon the African dwarf, whom he had never liked and whom Aetius passed on to his original owner, Aspar, the half-barbarian general who had found him in Africa. After that, Zercon vanishes from history.

ATTILA'S BLOODY WEDDING — AND JUSTINIAN'S BRIDE

In Ravenna, the sexagenarian Empress Placidia was retired; her son Valentinian III ruled, but her reckless, restless daughter Honoria, aged around thirty, bored by the dreary existence of an Augusta, craved adventure and started an affair with her chamberlain Eugenius. When it was discovered by her mother and brother, they had the paramour executed and betrothed her to an antique senator, at which the Augusta wrote a letter to Attila. A fragrantly named eunuch, Hyacinthus, secretly carried it with her ring to the Hun.

Attila accepted her indecent proposal, suggesting she deliver half the western empire as dowry. Placidia was outraged. Valentinian beheaded Hyacinthus and ordered Honoria's execution, but their mother interceded. Honoria was swiftly married to the old senator. 'Honoria shouldn't be wronged,' wrote Attila when he heard that his fiancée was under arrest. If she didn't receive the sceptre of sovereignty, he continued, he would avenge her. Perhaps the longueurs of marriage killed Honoria; perhaps the drama killed Placidia; but both died as Attila and his horde of Huns, Goths, Burgundians, Gepids, Alans and Lombards crossed the Rhine and ravaged Gaul, while Aetius mustered his equally barbarian coalition of Romans, Franks, Burgundians and Visigoths. At Troyes, Attila was confronted by its bishop, who demanded mercy as a man of God.

'I am Attila,' laughed Attila grimly. 'Scourge of God. What mortal could stand against God's scourge?' He spared Troyes. In battle, near Châlons, Aetius halted Attila, the Roman-Visigoth troops trapping the Hun in a circle of wagons. Attila, refusing to be taken alive, prepared for the traditional nomad's self-immolation on a bonfire of wooden saddles. But the Huns got lucky, killing the Visigoth king, who was burned right there on his own saddle-pyre. Aetius did not wish to destroy the Huns, for that would leave him at the mercy of the Goths.

At dawn, Attila was amazed to find the Romans had gone – and he led his horde back to Hungary.

In 452, he invaded Italy, successfully taking Milan, but disease ravaged the Hun forces, which withdrew, consoled with Roman gold. The following spring, the polygamous Attila married a new bride, Ildico. After a hard-drinking wedding banquet, he staggered to bed where he haemorrhaged and drowned in his own blood.* Ildico awoke to find her-

---

* Most likely Attila's haemorrhage was a symptom of oesophageal varices, bleeding veins suffering by alcoholics. He was buried in a coffin, sealed with gold, silver and iron, at a secret site, after the sacrifice of gravediggers and servants. Three sons vied for power:

self covered in blood and Attila dead beside her. The next day, 'when a great part of the morning was spent, the royal attendants suspected foul play and, after a great uproar, broke down the doors', wherein, wrote Priscus, they found the king with no wounds, blood everywhere and the beautiful girl 'with downcast face weeping beneath her veil'. Ildico had unknowingly saved Europe, but she is never mentioned again: she may have been sacrificed and buried with Attila.

Soon after Attila's death, a young Thracian swineherd of Scupi (Skopje) named Justin escaped from raiding barbarians to set off for Constantinople, where he arrived with nothing more than the rags he wore and some bread but managed to get a job among the Excubitors – the security unit that guarded the Sacrum Cubiculum, the octagonal bedchamber of the emperor.

Constantinople was now one of the biggest cities in the world, ruled by its emperors from the Mega Palation – Great Palace – linked by secret passageways to the hippodrome and forum. Enriched by the agricultural wealth and tax income of Egypt, Syria, Greece and the Balkans, administered by a sophisticated court and civil service, often directed by the castrated chief chamberlain, the Great City had an increasingly Greek-speaking population of 500,000* whose twin obsessions were soteriology – the quest for salvation – and sport. Their Christianity was viciously divided between Christological sects, while the prizes of the hippodrome, where contests could be watched by 100,000, were ruthlessly competed for by five chariot-racing teams, each sporting a different colour, that, in modern terms, were a mix of sports fanatics, soccer hooligans, mafiosi and paramilitary. The emperors called themselves the vicegerents of God, and, apart from their plenitude and panoply of monarchy, the only real tests of God's approval were domestic order, the absence of natural disaster and victory in war, particularly against nomads in the Balkans and the Shah of Persia.

Justin, the Illyrian peasant boy, distinguished himself against the Persians before returning to the palace as *Comes Excubitorum*, count of the bodyguards. He had summoned his sister Vigilantia and her son

Dengizich was killed by the eastern Romans, his head paraded through Constantinople, then displayed at the hippodrome where 'the whole city turned out to look at it'. But none of the sons possessed Attila's prestige, and the confederacy disintegrated, liberating his former allies, the Ostrogoths, who would ultimately conquer Italy itself.

* The people of the eastern Roman empire called themselves Romaioi – Romans; Arabs and Turks called the empire Rum – Rome; medieval western Europeans called them Greeks. Byzantine is an exonym invented by western scholars in the seventeenth century and popularized by nineteenth-century British historians to describe the particular Greek Orthodox culture after AD 500.

Peter Sabbatos from Skopje to join him and his wife, who adopted the boy, giving him a new name: Justinian.

At this point, the emperor was Anastasius, a sexagenarian courtier who struggled to cope with the latest Christological controversy and his own succession. In July 518, as Anastasius, now aged eighty-seven, sank, Justin and his nephew Justinian were at the centre of the court intrigues. Sacred emperors were meant to be above grubby ambition since only someone who did not covet the purple could deserve it. But Justin had Justinian, now in his thirties, do the dirty work. Amantius, eunuch provost of the bedchamber, gave Justin a bounty to bribe the guards to back his candidate, but instead Justinian diverted it to win support for his uncle. When the emperor died, Justin was given the task of announcing his death to the hippodrome, where Justinian rallied the crowd to demand a general. But there were two; fighting broke out between the supporters of Justin and his rival. Justinian was almost killed but finessed his uncle's acclamation. In the imperial box, the eunuchs handed over the regalia of an emperor to Justin, who then addressed the crowd. This was how emperors were made in Constantinople.

Emperor Justin, around sixty years old, was experienced but uneducated; Justinian, aged thirty-six, was 'short with a good chest, a good nose, fair-skinned, curly-haired, handsome', wrote a contemporary, John Malalas, 'round-faced with receding hair, florid complexion with greying hair and beard'. He was the obvious heir, but all leaders loathe their own mortality, and the idea that anyone is qualified to succeed them. Justinian almost fell into disfavour – for the sake of love.

His paramour was Theodora, a blonde actress twenty years younger, daughter of a bear trainer in the hippodrome, who had performed in live sex shows on stage with penetration of all orifices by multiple partners and geese eating grain off her private parts – according to the embittered courtier Procopius, whose satire was only funny because it was partly true.* Eschewing bear pits and sex shows, she embraced religion with humourless solemnity, but it was the meeting with Justinian that truly changed her life.

---

* Procopius, legal official and obsequious court historian, knew both Justinian and Theodora, but in secret he wrote *Anekdota*, a semi-satirical cross between the *Daily Mail* and *Saturday Night Live* in which he accused the emperor of being an avaricious war-crazed demon and Theodora of being a vicious nymphomaniacal vamp. He would have been executed for treason had his authorship been revealed.

QUSAY AND JUSTINIAN: FROM CONSTANTINOPLE TO MECCA

Justinian was determined to marry Theodora, but the law banned noble-actress marriages and Empress Euphemia disapproved. Finally, in 521, Justin legalized the *mésalliance* but also allowed an investigation into Justinian's schemings. Justinian worked his way back into favour with a plan to show that God favoured the Justin dynasty: war against Persia.

Both empires were fighting proxy wars using Arab allies from Syria to Yemen. The Sasanian shah backed the Lakhm Arabs of Iraq and Justin, advised by his nephew, recognized the sheikh of the Ghassan tribes, headquartered on the Golan Heights, as king, patrician and phylarch. The Arab potentates fought so viciously that their imperial masters struggled to restrain them. In southern Arabia, the Romans vied with the Persians. Himyari (Yemen) had been conquered by the Christian kings of Axum (Ethiopia). But then a Himyari king, Abu-Kariba, expelled the Africans, defied Axum, Constantinople and Persia: he converted to Judaism and conquered Arabia as far north as Yatrib (Medina). When the Jewish king Yusuf persecuted his Christians, King Kaleb of Axum got Justin's backing to retake Yemen. The African army crossed to Asia and overthrew Yusuf, who rode his steed into the sea. The Christians won – for now.

Between the three Arabian kingdoms were the small towns of Arabia that contained Christians, Jews and pagans, stops on the caravan routes that ran from the Red Sea and the Arabian Gulf to Egypt and Syria. One of them was Mecca, which was both trading centre and numinous shrine, governed by the family of a sheikh named Qusay, who had come up from Himyari and become the guardian of its Kaaba, a black mete-orite surrounded by a pantheon of statues.* After Qusay's death around 480, his sons and grandsons ruled Mecca, the founders of the most powerful family in world history.

Back in Constantinople, Justinian succeeded his uncle and proceed-ed to demonstrate his high-mind Christian legitimacy, persecuting Jews and Manichaeans, building new churches with a new design feature, the dome, codifying the laws and fighting Persia. Yet rolling the iron dice of war is always a gamble. The shah unleashed his Arab ally, King al-Mundhir, who raided Roman Palestina, Egypt and even the outskirts of Antioch, where he captured two Roman generals (whom

---

* There were said to be 365 gods, but the chief ones were the gold-handed god Hubal, who offered divinations, the goddesses Al-Lat, Manat and al-Uzza, for whom humans were burned as sacrifices, a couple Isaf and Nailah who had been petrified for copulating there, and Jesus and Mary, all of them under the aegis of the chief god, Allah.

he ransomed) and 400 nuns (whom he burned alive as sacrifices to al-Uzza).

Justinian promoted a Thracian general who had started in Justin's bodyguard. Belisarius, whose strapping figure and good looks were in stark contrast to the meagre, gingery Justinian, was married to Antonina, daughter of a chariot racer and best friends with Theodora from their racy youth. Belisarius, whose staff included Procopius the pornographic historian, was an innovator who, starting with his own regiment, devised a new army of multipurpose heavy cavalry and light mounted archers. Justinian and Belisarius formed a winning partnership, though the emperor, arch-manipulator, never forgot that a triumphing general was a threat. Now Belisarius won victories against the Persians but was let down by his unruly Arabs, and the shah was soon advancing into Syria. Just when it seemed things could not get any worse, they did.

JUSTINIAN: SOLOMON, I HAVE SURPASSED YOU

In January 532, Justinian ordered the hanging of some chariot-racing hooligans of the Greens and Blues, but the ropes broke and the thugs escaped. At the hippodrome, the crowd shouted at Justinian to pardon the escapees. When he refused, the factions, united and shouting the war cry 'Nika!' – Victory! – stormed the prison, and then went berserk as fire raged. Besieged in the Mega Palation as a new emperor was acclaimed in the hippodrome, Justinian wavered, ready to escape by boat. But Theodora declared that she preferred to die as an empress. 'Purple,' she said, 'makes the best burial shroud.'

The couple had a surprise up their sleeve: Belisarius – leading his vanguard of *bucellarii* (biscuit eaters) and Balkan *foederatii* – arrived from the front and burst into the hippodrome slaughtering 30,000 people, an astonishing 5 per cent of the city's population. Justinian was there to stay.

Reeling from this fiasco, Justinian had to make an Eternal Peace with the new shah, Khusrau, at the cost of 11,000 pounds of gold. Humiliated, Justinian learned that his ally, the king of Vandal Africa, based in Carthage and also ruling Sicily, had been overthrown in a coup by a nobleman Gelimer. In 533, Justinian dispatched Belisarius and 92 warships, 30,000 sailors and 15,500 troops. The general discovered that Gelimer was away in Sardinia and, after resupplying in Sicily, sailed for Africa. In March 534, he took Carthage, first deporting and annihilating the Vandal ruling class, then returning to Constantinople for his triumph which ended with the *triumphator* wisely kissing Justinian's feet before 100,000 spectators in the hippodrome.

Next Justinian used the killing of his ally, the Goth queen of Italy, as a pretext to retake Rome. In 535, Belisarius and a small army captured Sicily, Rome and Ravenna, before going on to take southern Spain.

Justinian celebrated these triumphs by embellishing Constantinople to reflect his vision of Christian empire: he raised a 230-foot column topped by an equestrian statue of himself in armour, and built thirty-three new churches and, most dramatic of all, a monumental church, Hagia Sophia (Holy Wisdom).* 'Solomon,' he mused, looking up at Hagia Sophia, 'I have surpassed you!' But invincibility is always temporary.

In 540, the Persian shah invaded Syria in response to the raids of Justinian's Arab king al-Harith, who had attacked the Persian ally al-Mundhir. The proxy war spun out of control: al-Mundhir hit back, captured al-Harith's son and sacrificed him to the sun goddess, al-Uzza. The feud did not end until al-Harith killed al-Mundhir in battle, but behind this sideshow was a Sasan shah who was Justinian's match as conqueror, builder and lawgiver. Khusrau Anushirvan – Immortal Soul – had spent the years of peace liquidating any family rivals and crushing a new religion founded by a Zoroastrian priest called Mazdak, who had fused the dual cosmology of Ahura-Mazda and Manichaeanism with revolutionary ideas of equality and charity that had much in common with Christianity, together with a strain of feminist hedonism. Mazdak taught that wives were not owned by men, and his critics denounced Mazdakites as socialistic swingers. Seeing a threat to Zoroastrianism, Khusrau buried many of these Mazdakites alive with just their feet showing, telling Mazdak to admire his 'human garden' before using him for archery practice. Despite his human garden, Khusrau was more tolerant and eclectic than Justinian, inviting Indian, Christian

---

* No longer based around the chunky Roman basilica, this was a new conception of sacred space: a gigantic brick square with its knave 260 feet long, crowned with a sixteen-sided 115-foot dome, still one of the most gloriously successful buildings ever raised. 'Its interior is not so much illuminated from without by the sun but the radiance comes into being from within,' wrote Procopius; its dome 'somehow flies in the air . . . overlaid with gold'. At its launch, much of the city participated in the procession led by the emperor and his ever more meticulously calibrated courtiers – marking the sacralization of the emperor, the vicegerent of God himself, who now insisted on being approached with elaborate ceremony, ushered by eunuchs, before being greeted with a full prostration like a Persian monarch. It also heralded a new, more popular Christianity in which people participated in a calendar of saintly festivals. All across his empire, monumental sacred spaces were created, in Jerusalem, Bethlehem, Sinai and Ravenna, where, in mosaics that still exist, we can see Justinian and Theodora as they saw themselves, he decisive, russet-haired and rosy-cheeked, she skinny, intense, pale, sanctimonious, imperious.

and Jewish sages to his court, men who were soon joined by the pagan Greek philosophers expelled by Justinian. 'We studied the customs and conduct of Romans and Indians and accepted those that seemed reasonable and praiseworthy,' Khusrau explained. 'We haven't rejected any because they belonged to a different religion or people.'

It was no coincidence that he championed the Indian game of chess: now the Immortal advanced into Roman Syria, and avoiding time-wasting sieges, stormed the eastern capital, Antioch. Khusrau enslaved thousands, who were sent on a death march eastwards to populate a new city named Veh-Antioch-Khusrau (Khusrau's-better-Antioch).*

Justinian recalled Belisarius from Italy and sent him to Syria, but then fell desperately ill – infected by a catastrophic pandemic that Procopius called 'a pestilence, by which the whole human race came near to being annihilated'.

JUSTINIAN'S PANDEMIC – AND THE
KILLER BIRDS OF MECCA

The pandemic forced Khusrau to retreat, but by summer 541 it was hitting Constantinople with lethal randomness, killing 10,000 a day at its height. Between 20 and 40 per cent of the city perished. This was the bubonic plague, carried by fleas bearing the bacterium *Yersinia pestis* that nested in the fur of marmots in the Tian Shan mountains of central Asia, and probably transmitted by the migrations of Huns and other steppe nomads, then spreading via rats in cities and on ships, travelled southwards into India, on to Persia and Egypt, then westwards to Constantinople.†

The conditions were set for disaster: in 536, a volcanic eruption had spurted dust into the atmosphere, and 'the sun,' recalled Procopius, 'gave forth its light without brightness'; temperatures fell, harvests failed, people weakened.‡ The disease started innocently but killed quickly:

---

* At Ctesiphon, he celebrated with a vast new palace, funded by Justinian's gold, where the throne hall boasted an archway 121 feet high, 85 feet across, 164 feet long – for centuries the world's largest.
† In 1894, Alexandre Yersin, a French scientist from the Pasteur Institute investigating an outbreak of the plague in Hong Kong, discovered the bacillus, named *Yersinia* after him, and the fact that it was present in both the rats and the humans infected with the disease, proving the means of transmission. New palaeogenetic research shows that the Justinian plague probably hit Britain, Spain and Germany too.
‡ Far away, either in Iceland or in east Asia, these massive volcanic eruptions were spurting clouds of dust into the sky, generating what today's scientists call a 'dust-veil event' that may have created the conditions for a rising world crisis: it changed the weather in ways

they had a sudden fever of such a languid sort from its commencement and up till evening . . . Not one of those who had contracted the disease expected to die. But not many days later, a bubonic swelling developed; and this took place not only in the particular part of the body which is called *bubon*, that is, 'below the abdomen', but also in the armpit, beside the ears, on the thighs. There ensued with some a deep coma, with others a violent delirium [wrote Procopius]. Those who were seized with delirium suffered from insomnia and distorted imagination; for they suspected that men were coming to destroy them, and they would become excited and flee, screaming loudly . . . The bubonic swelling became mortified [as gangrene set in] and the sufferer, no longer able to endure the pain, died. Death came immediately, in others after many days; and with some, the body broke out with black pustules about as large as a lentil [the rash later called Black Death] and those did not survive even one day, but died immediately.

In March 542, Justinian issued laws to prop up the economy, referring to the 'encircling presence of death' that had 'spread to every region'. When he fell sick he had to at least preserve order in this charnel house, but the city was veering out of control: 'Initially each man attended to the burial of the dead of his own house; but afterwards confusion and disorder everywhere became complete.'

Conspiracy theorists spread panic in a way that sounds very familiar. 'They love to conjure up causes which are absolutely incomprehensible to man,' observed Procopius, 'and to fabricate outlandish theories of natural philosophy. But for this calamity it is quite impossible either to express in words or to conceive in thought any explanation, except indeed to refer it to God.' That at least let the politicians off the hook: no one expected Justinian or Khusrau to be able to deliver safety as modern leaders are; only God could wreak or end such havoc. 'A chastening sent by God's goodness', wrote Justinian, that should have made workers better people 'but instead I hear they are turning to avarice'. In Constantinople, Procopius saw how 'the bodies even of grandees were left unburied'. Finally Justinian 'deployed soldiers from the palace and distributed money . . . Tombs were filled with the dead, then they dug graves around the city.' The 'evil stink' was unbearable. When even the mass graves were full, 'they mounted the towers of the fortifications, and tearing off the roofs threw the bodies there in complete disorder,

that may have forced nomadic peoples to leave the steppes and ride westwards to attack the Roman and Persian empires – and that may have brought rats closer to humans, perfect conditions for a pandemic.

piling them up until all the towers were filled with corpses and they put the roofs back.'

When news spread that Justinian was infected – 'for he too had a swelling of the groin' – the hierarchy was shaken: 'it wasn't possible to see a single man clad in the *chlamys* [cloak of an officeholder]'. A lockdown ruled: 'in a city which held dominion over the whole Roman empire, everyone dressed befitting private station and remained quietly at home'. Khusrau too was infected. But both emperors recovered. 'Where the swelling rose to an unusual size,' wrote Procopius, 'it discharged pus and they survived.'

After four months, the plague receded, only to rebound again in waves. The pandemic proved a super-propellant, one of those catastrophes that propelled tectonic changes. As many as 25 per cent of Europeans and many Persians died; agriculture suffered; revenues fell. The two empires were weakened.

In 548, Theodora died of cancer at the age of fifty-one. Justinian sobbed as she was buried in the Church of the Holy Apostles. He lived for another twenty years, struggling to hold on to Italy and Africa which, as in so many wars, were easier to conquer than to hold. His wars were expensive in an empire desolated and haunted by the plague, ruled obstinately by this pedantic, righteous and geriatric megalomaniac. Berber tribes rebelled in Africa; Rome was repeatedly won and lost as Belisarius and his generals fought a Gothic insurgency before Germanic peoples from the north, the Lombards, moved south to challenge the Romans, turning Justinian's glorious adventure into an interminable quagmire. Yet Constantinople kept southern Italy for centuries.

In 562 Justinian finally made peace with Khusrau, paying further gold subsidies. The treasury was bare, though taxes were still collected from plague-scourged agricultural heartlands. Justinian's less eminent successors must share responsibility for the sequel.

Justinian, soi-disant 'conqueror of many nations', lived on, gripping the sceptre with sclerotic fingers, and refusing to name a successor. But Theodora had arranged the marriage of her niece Sophia to Justinian's nephew, Justin, now serving as his *kouropalates*, palace director. By November 565, when Justinian died aged eighty-three,* Justin II already controlled the Mega Palation, announcing that Sophia would rule with him as Augusta. At the lying-in-state of the embalmed old

---

* Belisarius had died the year before in the wake of a last heroic command when he defeated a nomad army approaching Constantinople. Not long afterwards he faced a trial for conspiracy against Justinian, judged by a city prefect, Procopius, probably the historian and his former secretary. Justinian pardoned him. It is not known when Procopius died.

maestro, Justin kissed him saying, 'You, my venerable father, are joyful in the ranks of the angels . . . You see God.' Already forty-five, Justin II was determined to prove he was God's choice. So, in denial about his overstretched resources, he prepared to confront Iran where Khusrau the Immortal, flush with Roman gold, was keen to expand into Arabia.

Khusrau's Arab ally, King Amr the Burner (who often incinerated his captives as human sacrifices), clashed with the African king of Himyari, a Christian from Axum called Abrahah (an ex-slave of a Roman merchant), who now marched on Mecca with a corps of elephants.

The Meccans, now led by Abdul Muttalib, nicknamed Whitestreak because of his hair, guardian of the Kaaba, sheikh of the Quraysh clan, leader of regular caravans to Palestine, in 570 repelled the Ethiopian and his pachyderms using a targeted assassination: Abrahah was strafed by a killer flock of sacred birds which dive-bombed him with rocks. The elephants were defeated, the African king dismembered. This semi-mythical victory – the Year of the Elephant – took place the very year that a child named Muhammad* was born in Mecca.

---

* 'Have you not seen how your Lord dealt with the owners of the Elephant?' recounted Abdul Muttalib's grandson, Muhammad, in the Quran. 'Did He not make their treacherous plan go astray? And He sent against them birds in flocks, striking them with stones.'

ACT FIVE
300 MILLION

The Muhammad Dynasty

FAMILY FEUD

The boy's father Abdullah died before he was born, his mother Amina died when he was young, so Muhammad bin Abdullah was brought up by his legendary elephant-vanquishing grandfather, Abdul Muttalib. Whitestreak and his sons al-Abbas and Abu Talib led caravans of spices and perfumes from Yemen and on to Gaza and Damascus. Before his death at eighty-one, Whitestreak ordered his son Abu Talib to raise Muhammad, who was nurtured by an Ethiopian nurse and a retinue of slaves. Abu Talib took young Muhammad on caravans to Syria.

Yet the family was divided into the two branches, descended from conjoined twins Umayya and Hashem, who had supposedly been cut apart with a sword. Hashem was Abdul Muttalib's father, Muhammad's great-grandfather. With Whitestreak gone, the Umayya clan pushed out Muhammad's Hashemites. The two lineages fell out over the Kaaba shrine and caravan revenues, but later it became a battle for power, a family feud that still divides the Arab world today.

As Muhammad grew up in Mecca, Arabia was changing radically and the African kings of Yemen had reason to regret their attack on Mecca. Khusrau, informed by King Amr the Burner, his Arab ally, of an appeal by the Yemenites for help against the Ethiopians, sent a force down to Yemen that expelled these African Christians and annexed the kingdom. Here was a pretext for war if Emperor Justin needed one.

While Khusrau and Justin were still fighting their bipolar war, another people who would change the world were galloping across the steppes to their north. The Turks were nomadic horse archers from the borderlands of Mongolia/Manchuria, who, displaced by the turmoil in China, gradually moved westwards, sparking a stampede migration. Justin dispatched delegations to encourage the Turks to attack Khusrau, and he ceased his Persian payments. The Turks would open a northern front. But when the war started, Khusrau the Immortal, vigorous at sixty, took the Roman fortress of Dara, while the Turks never showed up. The humiliation drove Justin mad.

THE EMPEROR WHO CROWED LIKE A COCK AND BARKED LIKE A DOG: THE MADNESS OF JUSTIN

Justin tried to throw himself out of windows. Then he thought he was a shopkeeper hawking his wares around the Mega Palation: 'Who'll buy my pans?' Next he started biting his eunuchs. Finally he just 'barked like a dog, bleated like a goat, mewed like a cat and crowed like a cock'. The only things that quietened him were being wheeled fast by breathless eunuchs on a mini-wagon conveying his throne while listening to organ music – or hearing the threat that the Arab king 'Al-Harith is coming.' Empress Sophia took over, saying, 'The kingdom came through me, and has come back to me' – a true niece of Theodora. But the madness undermined the family. Sophia planned to give the throne to a Justinian cousin but, faced with raids by nomadic Avars in the Balkans and Persian advances in the east, Justin adopted a general, Tiberius. As commander-in-chief, Tiberius II, emperor from 578, selected an ex-clerk and his count of the Excubitors, Maurice, who, despite having no military experience, managed to hold off the Avars and halt the Persians. But Maurice struggled to control his flamboyant Arab ally al-Mundhir: in 581, the two of them just failed to take Ctesiphon. Maurice had the Arab king arrested. Their fallout would play a role in destabilizing the bipolar Roman-Persian world. In 582, on his deathbed, Tiberius married his daughter to Maurice, who started his own reign as emperor with a stroke of luck.

Shah Khusrau II arrived in Roman territory. The grandson of the Immortal, he was just twenty when a coup against his inept father brought him to the throne, but he had already shown his mettle running Iranian Armenia. His father was blinded then strangled by his voracious uncles, but as generals bid for power, young Khusrau escaped, accompanied by Shirin, his 'extremely beautiful' Christian queen,* and aided by her fellow Christian, the Arab king al-Numan. Once in Roman territory, the boy shah proclaimed himself supplicant of Maurice, who adopted him as a son and, in return for western Armenia, lent him an army: in 591, Khusrau retook Ctesiphon.

---

* Khusrau fell in in love with Shirin when he saw her bathing – an echo of King David and Bathsheba. Their romance later inspired two classics of Iranian literature, *Shahnameh* and *Khusrau and Shirin*.

Maurice and Khusrau both now terminated their unreliable Arab allies. Al-Mundhir's Arabs, infuriated by Maurice's arrest of their king, looted Palestine. Maurice ended their subsidies. Khusrau wanted to marry the daughter of his Arab ally al-Numan III, who refused this 'vile abomination'. Arab and Iranian mutual disdain is ancient. 'Aren't the cattle of The Darkness [females of Iran] enough for him,' replied al-Numan, 'or does he have to have Arab women as well?' Khusrau had al-Numan trampled to death by elephants. The defiant Arabs fought the shah in the War of the Camel's Udder. On both sides of the desert, the monarchs had cut the Arabs loose. Amid a strange atmosphere of apocalyptic expectation, the World Game started to spin in unpredictable ways.

Khusrau remained loyal to his 'father' Maurice until 602, when the emperor, who had driven his troops too hard, was overthrown by a mutiny led by Phocas, a centurion. Phocas made Maurice watch the beheading of his six sons before he was killed himself – later followed by his wife and three daughters – an atrocity that shocked the bishops of Rome in a west that still revered the Roman emperors.

It was now in a benighted Rome, neglected by its distant ruler Phocas, ruined by Justinian's wars, decimated by the plague, repelled by Constantinopolitan murders, that a bishop started almost by default to assume a sacred importance. The bishops of Rome – not yet called popes – were chosen informally by other bishops, Roman magnates and the emperors of Constantinople. Now a pious, charismatic aristocrat, Gregory, by then aged fifty, who as prefect (mayor) of Rome had made his name by feeding the poor, became the bishop who laid the foundations of the papacy, and of western family values. The west was dominated by Frankish and Lombard kings who were Christian but openly practised polygyny, keeping many concubines as well as a main wife, while marrying cousins and nieces to keep property and power within their clans. Gregory called this incest and banned it, the start of the Church's obsessive multi-century campaign to promote a new vision of marriage. Simultaneously, he launched a mission to convert northern pagans.

In 597 Gregory sent an envoy called Augustine to Kent. Britannia had already been converted to Christianity once – by Constantine – but in 410, when Roman troops left, Roman luxury and Christianity vanished in some places, endured in others. The loss of running water, hot baths and villas with glass windows was dramatic, but in some towns mosaic floors were still being laid in villas decades after the Romans had gone. The Christianity of the Britanno-Romans was frayed if not erased by pagan invaders, Angles and Saxons, who arrived from Germany. They slaughtered, raped and looted, their depredations recorded by the monkish historian Bede. Yet DNA reveals that the invaders also by force or affection had families with the Britanno-Romans and settled. While north-western Britannia remained defiantly Celtic under the kings of Strathclyde and others, the east – known as Anglia – was colonized by Angles, the south by Saxons, who founded their own kingdoms. The Saxon king of Kent, Aethelberht, was married to queen Bertha, daughter of the Frankish king of Paris, who had brought her own bishop with her. Gregory ordered Augustine to assert papal control.

Aethelberht acquiesced, and Augustine became the first bishop of Canterbury. Although it was much less dramatic than advertised, Gregory trumpeted the 'conversion of Britannia'. The rise of the papacy was further boosted by what happened next in Constantinople.

When Khusrau learned of the assassination of his adoptive father Emperor Maurice, he went to war. The shah had much to prove: everything had to be gigantic. He would sit enthroned in the colossal *iwan* – throne room – of his grandfather in glittery jewel-infested robes on a 1,000-square-foot carpet called the Shah's Spring depicting his gardens. Sporting gold-trimmed armour, he would ride a towering black stallion named Midnight at the head of an army of cataphracts, knights and horses, while his tiger-skin banner, 130 feet long, fluttered overhead. But he wanted more than pomp. He wanted the world.

Khusrau planned a multifront offensive, unleashing Khoream, a Parthian princeling married to the shah's sister who revelled in the title Shahbaraz or Royal Boar, against Armenia, then against Syria. Phocas was out of his depth, his legions breaking before Royal Boar's cataphracts. But the Romans turned to a competent young nobleman, Heraclius, son of the exarch of Africa, who was ready to step up. Heraclius sailed for Constantinople, killed Phocas, seized the throne and tried to stop Royal Boar. But the empire was collapsing.

RECITE! I CANNOT RECITE! RECITE!
THE REVELATION OF MUHAMMAD

The Persians swept west. Royal Boar took Damascus and Jerusalem, sparking apocalyptic fervour among the Jews, whom he delivered from centuries of Christian persecution. In Antioch his soldiers castrated the Christian patriarch and threw his genitals in his face. Khusrau restored

Jerusalem to the Jews, who ruled there for a few years – the last time before 1967 – while Royal Boar tortured that city's patriarch until he handed over the relic of the True Cross, which was then sent to Queen Shirin.

Emperor Heraclius was chastened. The fall of Jerusalem seemed to herald the End of Days – not just to Christians but to pagan Arabs too: in Mecca, the merchant Muhammad, now in his forties, heard of these astonishing Roman defeats which signalled a new era, a new revelation. 'Rome has been vanquished in a land nearby,' he reflected. Admired for his decency, geniality and serenity, he was nicknamed al-Amin – the Reliable. He had travelled into Roman lands, first visiting Syria with his uncle, then being sent there by an older female merchant, Khadija, when he was twenty-five. She was wealthy, the personification of female independence. Muhammad's conduct on this trip earned him another nickname, al-Sadiq – the Truthful – and afterwards, he married Khadija, who was still young enough to have six children. The boys died young, but Fatima and three other daughters survived. Along with their own children, Muhammad's cousin Ali (son of his guardian Abu Taleb) was brought up in the household, together with a boy named Zayed who had been kidnapped and enslaved before being freed and adopted by Muhammad. Muhammad lived happily with Khadija for twenty-five years.

At forty, he was meditating in a cave at Hira when he felt strange, feverish and limp. Engulfed in humming sounds, sweat pouring from him, he believed he was visited by the Archangel Gabriel, who told him he was God's Messenger and Prophet. 'Recite!' ordered Gabriel.

At first Muhammad told no one except his wife Khadija, then he disclosed the visitation to a small coterie led by a friend, Abu Bakr. His message, incanted in mesmeric rhyming Arab poetry that dazzled its listeners, was universal and lucid, yet often expressed in the obscure language expected of sacred texts. Muhammad knew the Bible, partly from his travels in Palestine and Syria, partly from the many Jews and Christians in Arabia. His teachings co-opted and commandeered the prophecies and prophets of the Jews and Christians that bestowed ancient, sacred legitimacy on a new message. At its heart was a creed of pure monotheism, shorn of Jewish ritual and exclusivity and the Christian worship of a man and his image with its tangled concept of the Trinity. 'There is no god but God,' recited Muhammad, in the earliest version of the *shahada*, and this God had no son. The only path was submission – Islam – living according to the rules of worship in a religion that welcomed everyone, regardless of class, gender or nation, offering moral universality, the incentive of afterlife, and easily understood

rituals and rules. Unlike Christianity Islam allowed polygamous marriage, permitting up to four wives and multiple concubines.

Anyone could join Islam. One of his first followers was an enslaved
African, Bilal ibn Rabah known as al-Habashi – the Abyssinian. All the
People of the Book – Jews and Christians – were welcomed: Muhammad
called them 'the Believers'. He would form a community, the *ummah*,
of faithful believers to spread his message: the apocalypse – the Hour –
was imminent. That could take place only in Jerusalem; he had dreamed
that he visited the city in what is known as the Night Journey. When he
prayed, he turned towards the Holy City, an orientation later called the
qibla. But God had withdrawn his blessing from Jews and Christians:
the Jews had lost their Temple, Rome was falling before the Persians.
The revelation of Islam was the third and last of the revelations.

Muhammad started to criticize the Kaaba, which made him unpopular among his cousins in the Quraysh, led by the wealthy sheikh Abu
Sufyan, who ordered his assassination. In 622, taking his followers with
him, Muhammad escaped to the oasis of Yatrib further north, where he
gathered his Meccans and his devotees, including Jews, in his *ummah*.
He 'could not write well', according to Abu Bakr, but his followers wrote
down his words, which they called the Recitation – the Quran; other
sayings were later compiled in the Hadith.

Yatrib, renamed Medinat un-Nabi – Prophet's Town, Medina – became
a small theocratic state led by Muhammad, who, unlike Jesus, was a
political and military leader as well as a religious visionary. Muhammad
promoted the manumitted African Bilal to become the first muezzin –
caller to prayer – thanks to his resonant voice. But some Jewish tribes in
Medina rejected Islam, so Muhammad changed the *qibla* from Jerusalem to Mecca and, as Allah told him, preferred to 'overlook their faults
with gracious forgiveness'. But power was essential, war fundamental,
to the success of every revelation.

At Badr, in 624, Muhammad ambushed a Meccan caravan led by Abu
Sufyan. The sheikh counter-attacked. At the battle of the Trench, his
ferocious wife, Hind, chanted encouragement to her men:

Our necks are hung with pearls,
And musk is in our hair,
If you advance we'll hug you,
Or if you flee we'll shun you.

When Abu Sufyan won, Hind gleefully ate the liver of Muhammad's
uncle Hamza and crafted necklaces from the ears of Muslim dead.
It was all the more vicious for its intimacy: another of the Prophet's

uncles, Abbas – who would be important later – fought for the pagan Meccans. In 627, Muhammad punished one tribe of Jews who had colluded with the Meccans: 'he struck off their heads as they were brought out in batches' and enslaved the women and children.

His words fell on fertile ground in Arabia not just because he was charismatic but because the world seemed atilt. Empires were rising and falling in astonishing twists of fate; the Arabs had been cut adrift from their patrons; trade was shattered and times were desperate. 'Nobody was more destitute than us, our religion was: kill one another and raid,' recalled one of Muhammad's soldiers. Monotheism, with its consolations of eternal salvation, was more persuasive than al-Uzza with her hunger for human sacrifice. Muhammad was just one of many holy leaders preaching in Arabia – Musaylima, Tuhayla, Aswad, the prophetess Sajah. Muhammad himself, observing the surreal tottering of eastern Rome, felt himself much closer to Christians than to Zoroastrians. 'After their defeat,' he predicted, 'they shall be victorious again.'

Tang and Sasan

DEADLY HUNTER, LION OF THE EAST: KHUSRAU'S MEGALOMANIA

Oblivious to revelations in Arabian oases, ultimate victory did not seem inevitable to the Romans. Royal Boar seized Egypt. In 619 Khusrau's general Shahin advanced through Anatolia as far as Chalcedon, across the Bosphoros from Constantinople. Heraclius considered moving the capital to Carthage, then, meeting Shahin in person, offered to recognize Khusrau as supreme emperor with the ability to appoint Roman rulers. It looked as if Khusrau had won the 600-year World Game between Persia and Rome. In the north-east, the Turks had been defeated by another of his generals, the Armenian prince Smbat Bagration, but they would have their revenge. Khusrau called himself Parviz – the Victorious; world domination was in his grasp. Iranian aristocrats recommended Heraclius's offer. Khusrau turned it down.

The challenge was how to take Constantinople, its walls almost impregnable. Khusrau negotiated with the Avar khagan, who was rampaging through the Balkans. But in 622 Heraclius envisaged a bold counter-attack. Leaving the Great City well defended, he transported 20,000 men along the Black Sea coast and landed behind Persian lines in eastern Anatolia, where he received a letter from the shah calling himself 'the deadly hunter, Lion of the East' and 'Noblest of the Gods, King and Master of the Whole World' and mocking Heraclius as a 'vile and foolish slave of Khusrau'. The words were magniloquent enough to be authentically composed by Khusrau, encamped with his army in Azerbaijan. 'You say you trust in God. Why then has He delivered to me Caesarea, Jerusalem, Alexandria?' He suggested Heraclius retire to grow vines in Ctesiphon.

Heraclius turned the disaster of Jerusalem into the first holy war, literally a crusade to regain the True Cross. 'Our danger,' he declared, 'is the harbinger of everlasting life ... Let's sacrifice ourselves to God ... Let's win the crown of the martyrs.' He marched fast towards Khusrau, surprising him and driving him into an ignominious retreat, then burning the great Zoroastrian shrine of Adur-Gushnasp, vengeance for Jerusalem. Early in 625, Heraclius contacted the Turkish khan, Sipi, nephew of their supreme khagan Tong, to propose an alliance. He manoeuvred brilliantly against the overconfident Persians, ambushing Royal Boar, who fled naked on horseback, leaving behind his gold shield and even his bejewelled sandals.

To the west, Khusrau the Victor now ordered the last battle to conquer the Great City, an endgame of the End of Days. As he had warned Heraclius, 'Could I not destroy Constantinople?' Royal Boar advanced to Chalcedon; the Avars and another tribe from the east, the Slavs, arrived on the European side, rowing into the harbour, wheeling up siege engines to the Theodosian Walls. The situation looked desperate. Yet the Romans managed to foil any transfer of Iranians to the European side. As the Persians watched across the Bosphoros, the Avars attacked the walls, but, aided by the Virgin Mary patrolling the ramparts, the Romans repelled them and they withdrew.*

Far away in Iraq, Heraclius, now in alliance with 40,000 Turks under Sipi, outmanoeuvred three Iranian armies, killing Shahin. Khusrau now feared Royal Boar, ordering his deputy to kill him, but Heraclius intercepted the letter and sent it to the general himself. A secret understanding was reached and Royal Boar set up court in Alexandria. In 627, Heraclius met Sipi at a summit outside Tbilisi and promised the shamanist khan his daughter. Leaving Sipi to besiege Tbilisi, Heraclius galloped towards Ctesiphon.

Panic struck the Persian capital. The shah was blamed. 'How long shall we fear and tremble before this bloody king? Didn't many of our brothers perish on countless occasions in thousands by all manner of tortures, some even by drowning, at his command?' Khusrau ordered all his prisoners to be murdered – the last straw. The Victor had ridden Iranshahr into the dust. His elder son Kavad II betrayed 'that evil man' his father, who escaped in disguise but was hunted down. The grandees spat on him; sixteen of his sons were murdered in front of him, then he was shot with arrows. His widow Shirin refused to marry her stepson Kavad and was murdered too. The plague flared again, killing Kavad II – just as Royal Boar arrived to make himself shah. He restored the

---

* Around 650, the greatest city in the Americas, Teotihuacan, was systematically burned in a revolution of the ordinary people. It was not a foreign invasion: invaders usually destroy homes and the infrastructure of ordinary people but keep the monuments. Here it was the opposite: palaces and temples were burned. In the resulting vacuum, the much smaller city of Tula, capital of the Toltecs, and the Maya cities in Yucatán continued to thrive.

True Cross to Heraclius, who betrothed his son to Royal Boar's daughter – a couple who could one day rule the world. But his usurpation was resisted: Royal Boar was assassinated. Two daughters of Khusrau were enthroned, but one was strangled, the other poisoned. In Medina, the Muslims observed the downfall of Persia, 'where women now rule', and appreciated the apocalyptic significance as Heraclius celebrated the success of his holy war by bearing the True Cross into Jerusalem. In Ctesiphon, a Sasan prince, grandson of Khusrau and Shirin, the eight-year-old Yazdgard, was installed on the throne in 632 just as the Turks swooped in to destroy Persia.

Yet suddenly the Turks vanished. At the other end of the Eurasian steppe, as Heraclius was joining forces with the Turks and Muhammad was adapting his own concept of holy war, the new emperor of the Tang dynasty was making his own Turkish deal.

The rise of the Tang started with a dangerous rhyme.

TAIZONG AND THE KING OF TIBET

In 614, a poem circulated in China declaring that someone called Li would kill the emperor, who therefore executed thirty-three Li – and, unsurprisingly, one of the few who were not killed considered his position. In 617, Li Yuan, the partly Turkic duke of Yuan, and his second son, the future Taizong (born Li Shimin), decided to rebel not just out of self-preservation but also to fulfil that prophecy of 'Heaven's conferment'. 'If we don't take what is conferred,' said the father, 'calamity will befall us.'

Peasant risings had destroyed the Han but during their rule they had resettled many steppe nomads within the empire, fostering a multi-ethnic empire, while the Indian religion of Buddhism had become popular, coexisting with traditional Chinese beliefs.*

In 618, Li Yuan, later Gaozu – High Progenitor – of the Tang dynasty, made a deal with the khagan of the Gokturks (Celestial Turks) to give him the cover to seize China. After a decade of wars, he and Taizong had unified the empire. Yet quickly all of this was placed in peril by the fratricidal rivalry of the heir apparent and his brother – both of them opposed to the dynamic Taizong. When the brothers tried to poison him, Taizong accused them of having sex with the emperor's concubines, knowing that they would be summoned to explain themselves. On their

---

* The first evidence of the fusion of Indic and Chinese culture, mixed with Persian Zoroastrianism, is found in the beautiful and colourful frescoes of the Kizil Caves at Turfan in Xinjiang, dated between 300 and 400.

arrival, he shot one brother with his crossbow and beheaded the other. Gaozu, who was fishing, was shocked to be informed that he was now retired and Taizong in charge. China did not practise primogeniture: since emperors were meant to be sages, dynasty was balanced by the selection – by choice or force – of the ablest prince to succeed.

Taizong, aged twenty-six, was both killer and humanitarian, scholar and soldier, brusque, energetic and fiercely intelligent, ice-cold and yet emotional. He had not been raised as heir so he had seen the grit of ordinary life – 'When I was eighteen,' he later wrote to his son, 'I was still living among the people and I knew everything true and false' – but he was the son of a well-connected, part-Turkic general, educated in Confucian ideals and Taoist ritual, and trained in Turkic archery. He was one of those who defy pigeonholing – a poet and calligrapher who killed his own brother with his own bow. At fifteen he volunteered to fight against the Turks and at eighteen he helped Gaozu plan their coup. Taizong was a conqueror who ruled for twenty-three years, pushing Chinese power as far west as the Han. But it was also he who found the most extraordinary woman of Chinese history, Empress Wu. Between them they would dominate the century.

Taizong was immediately challenged by the Goturk khagan who had forced his father to make embarrassing concessions. Starting in 629, Taizong deployed generous diplomacy, such as exchanging bales of silk for myriads of horses, cunning manipulation, such as 'using barbarians to control barbarians', and savage violence. After the Goturk khagan tried to assassinate him, he fought the khaganates of the eastern and western Turks,* forcing them to recognize him as Tengri Khagan, Heavenly Khan of the Turks, and propelling Tang power back into central Asia. Taizong personified his multi-ethnic 'empire open to all', in which Turkic fashions and dances were popular, where elites spoke Turkic as well as Chinese and embraced Turkic equestrian style, women riding horses and men playing polo, where caravans of Bactrian camels bearing Indian pepper, Malay patchouli, aromatic woods from Java and figs from Persia joined Uighurs, Persians and Indians in the markets of his million-strong capitals Chang'an and Luoyang.

Yet each move has its unpredictable consequence. In this case the

---

* In the Tarim Basin, today's Xinjiang, Taizong conquered the Tocharian peoples, who had partly intermarried with the Uighurs, but live for us vividly because of the love poems they left behind. 'A thousand years, you will tell our story,' reads one. 'There was no human dearer to me than you and likewise hereafter there'll be no one dearer to you than me. Your love, your affection, my jubilant song rises up. I will live with one love for the whole of my life . . .'

breaking of the Goturks presented an opportunity for the Tibetans, under a young king called Songtsen Gampo, to extend their mountain kingdom southwards into northern India and eastwards into Szechuan province, an expansion that would one day cost the Tang dear. The son of a murdered chieftain, Songtsen united much of Tibet, sending his minister to India to learn about government, Buddhism and language, and devising a Tibetan script. He married Bhrikuti, believed to be an Indian princess, an incarnation of Tara, a Hindu and Buddhist goddess. When he campaigned against barbarian Tanguts on the Chinese border, he won the attention of the Chinese emperor.

Songtsen requested the greatest recognition an Asian king could receive: a Tang princess. Taizong grandly refused. The Tibetan raided Tang provinces in Szechuan and, once pushed back, Songtsen again sent an envoy. The emperor was not going to give a daughter to such a barbarian. Instead in 640 he found a cousin, created her Princess Wencheng and sent her to marry Songtsen. Later Taizong lent troops to back a Tibetan raid into India – the first Indo-Chinese clash.

Taizong now became fascinated by Buddhism and studied its spread in China. In his *Emperor's Preface to the Sacred Teachings*, he tried to reconcile Indian Buddhism and Chinese Tao. When a Buddhist monk named Xuanzang asked permission to embark on a pilgrimage to India, Taizong refused, but in 629 Xuanzang ignored orders and set off on an astonishing journey, almost dying several times, to reach Samarkand and then Afghanistan, where at Bamiyan he admired the giant statues of Buddha before trekking through the Khyber Pass to make a pilgrimage to study and pray at Peshawar and Nalanda. Xuanzang was witnessing an extraordinary conquest of the east, not by armies but by a culture. 'People of distant places with diverse customs,' he noticed, 'generally designate the land they admire as India.'

XUANZANG'S TRAVELS: THE OPENING OF THE INDOSPHERE

Xuanzang was right. An Indic florescence had spread Sanskrit language, Indian art and Brahmin and Buddhist religions right across east Asia from as early as the Bactrian Greek kings, with their Shiva and Krishna coins. The spread of this Indosphere had intensified under the influence of a Hindu dynasty in northern India, the Guptas,* but their glory

* The dynasty had been founded by Gupta, maharaja of a sliver of Uttar Pradesh. His grandson Chandragupta I – ruling at the same time as Constantine the Great – conquered enough territory in north-eastern India, by marriage and war, to call himself

was short-lived. It was their downfall, smashed by invading Huns in the 480s, that dispersed their court of priests, missionaries, merchants and artists not just within India but also west to Afghanistan, east to the islands and mainland of south-east Asia and north to Tibet, China and Japan. Now it was Taizong's contemporary and member of the Pallava family, Narasimhavarman, nicknamed Mahamalla or Great Wrestler, who conquered much of southern India and Sri Lanka. He also built a port at Mahabalipuram, from which merchants and missionaries spread Indic culture through east Asia. His capital at Kanchipuram was visited by Xuanzang.

The Indic culture flowed east and west. In Afghanistan, the Bamiyan Buddhas, seen by Xuanzang, had just been completed. To the east, Khmers and Malays learned Sanskrit as the language of power and sanctity; kings titled themselves in Sanskrit and Tamil. Buddhism arrived first with merchants, and Hinduism followed. The first Sanskrit inscription, found at Vo Canh (Vietnam), was the work of an Indic king from around 250; in 400, parts of Borneo were ruled by a Brahmin raja, Rajendra Mulwarman, who erected pillars inscribed in Sanskrit and boasted of the arrival of Shaivite Brahmins from India. An Indian prince, Kaundinya, was said to have married a Cambodian queen called Soma to found an Indianized kingdom of Funan that ruled much of the south-eastern mainland during the Tang era. Around 717, a Javanese prince named Sanjaya, a Shaivite Brahmin, founded the Mataram raj in Java, based around a *devaraja* – the cult of the king-god in which the *chakravartin* was the embodiment of Lord Shiva or Vishnu. Mataram dominated Java for centuries; the Sailendra dynasty embraced Buddhism, and their temples around Yogyakarta, far from India, are among the greatest Indic monuments.

Buddhism now reached Japan. In 552, Korean envoys arrived in Japan bearing a statue of Buddha. A powerful kingdom was developing there, encouraged by contacts with Tang China. The ruling Yamato family claimed descent from the sun goddess Amaterasu in unbroken succession since 660 BC, but this was entirely dynastic myth. The real as opposed to legendary dynasty emerged now in the sixth century AD as the ruling clan in central Japan mediating between the people and the gods: their title *tenno* literally meant Heaven-Descended, translated as

Maharajadhiraja – great king of kings. His grandson Chandragupta II, a contemporary of Julian, conquered much of northern India, from Afghanistan to Bengal and the Himalayas, ruling in splendour from Pataliputra, the personification of the ideal Brahmin emperor alias Vikramaditya (Sun of Courage). He oversaw a golden age of writers – the Navaratnas (Nine Jewels), led by the playwright Kalidasa. He promoted the god Vishnu as the supreme deity, along with his avatars, but he also built Buddhist shrines.

emperor. Heavily inspired by Taizong and Tang, the emperors created a system of court ranks for the aristocracy and an academy to train civil servants, who spoke Chinese, wore Chinese robes and read Chinese poetry. In 587, a semi-mythical emperor's son, Prince Shotoku, merged Buddhism with the Japanese pantheon.

When Xuanzang returned to Chang'an leading a caravan bearing 500 trunks full of treasures (though an elephant, gift of an Indian ruler, had fallen off a cliff), Taizong said, 'Welcome back after seventeen years, Xuanzang, but you never asked permission to go.' Taizong forgave the insubordination and invited him to be his minister. Xuanzang declined. 'It would be like taking a boat out of water,' he replied, 'not only ceasing to be useful but it would just rot away . . .' Instead the emperor made the traveller his blood brother and rewarded him with his own monastery (which still stands in Xi'an – the Great Pagoda of the Wild Goose). Buddhist monasteries became wealthy, though Taizong limited their riches. Ideas flowed both ways: in 635, a Christian monk, Rabban Olopun, arrived from Constantinople and was welcomed by Taizong, who explained, 'Right principles have no invariable location,' and ordered the building of the first church in China.

Yet Taizong remained a soldier, even into his last years, leading his troops into battle and ordering that his beloved steeds be sculpted for his tomb. He spent his last years trying to subdue the three Korean kingdoms in the east and the western Turks in central Asia. His Turkish wars had saved the new shah Yazdgard from the Turks, little realizing that to the south another nomadic army was gathering.

THE FAMILY OF MUHAMMAD

In 630, Muhammad, Prophet of the Believers of Medina, led his army south against Mecca, where he negotiated with his relatives. The cannibalistic Hind was not impressed, tormenting her husband by crying, 'Kill this fat greasy bladder of lard.' Instead Abu Sufyan negotiated a peaceful handover of Mecca.

Muhammad kissed the Kaaba but smashed the idols around it. Abu Sufyan was a pragmatist and later converted. Muhammad needed him: he married his daughter Ramla and hired his son Muawiya as secretary.

Muhammad still ruled from Medina. When delegations arrived to offer submission, he sat on the ground in his mosque with the steadiness and conviction that won so many followers, never claiming to be anything more than the Messenger of God. His humour was dry: once an old woman asked if Allah allowed old women into Paradise. No, he replied. She started to weep, at which he added, 'He changes them first into nubile virgins.'

Born into a world of family feuds, he knew the strength but also the danger of dynasty. 'Genealogy is lies,' he said, but he took immense trouble with an increasingly complex court. The family is important: its fissures still exist in Islam today.

When Khadija died, Muhammad married around thirteen more wives, many of them political alliances. First he married his follower Abu Bakr's daughter, Aisha: he was in his fifties, she a teenager, but he adored her, his favourite. Two younger wives, widows of fighters killed in battle, joined the household along with a Jewish girl, Rayhana, who had been enslaved after the crushing of her tribe. He had married his beautiful first cousin Zaynab to his adopted son, the ex-slave Zayed; they were unhappy, but Muhammad admired her. When she heard that 'The Messenger of God is at the door,' she dressed up and 'excited the admiration of the Messenger'. His son offered her to him and he finally agreed to marry her. Zaynab was jealous of Aisha. 'Zaynab was my equal in beauty,' admitted Aisha, 'and in the Prophet's love for her.'

Along with the wives, Muhammad's daughter Fatima cared for him: married to his cousin Ali, she was the mother of his grandchildren Hussein and Hassan. Moving between their separate houses, the Prophet liked to sit with his wives and joke and discuss life, sometimes remembering Khadija. He loved to play with his grandsons, letting them ride on his back, saying, 'Oh, what a fine camel you have.'

Yet already there was tension at his court. During the wars against Mecca, Aisha, looking for a lost necklace, became separated from her husband in the desert until rescued by a young man who returned her to the Prophet. She was accused of adultery. The loudest accuser was Muhammad's son-in-law Ali. Aisha was supported by her rival Zaynab and Muhammad ultimately believed Aisha, but this was just the beginning of the feud that still divides the Islamic world.

Heraclius' concept of holy war had reached Muhammad – Abu Sufyan had actually seen the emperor parade through Jerusalem – and he commandeered it as his jihad. Muhammad offered peace – 'Invite all to the way of your Lord with wisdom and beautiful preaching,' he said – but he also advocated war: 'Kill the idolaters wherever you find them.' He wrote letters demanding conversion even to the emperor, who sent back a fur coat as a gift; and the Roman governor of Egypt sent back a Coptic girl, Maria, whom he married. Later, in 630, Muhammad sent two columns to raid Syria. One reached Aqaba (Jordan); the other was intercepted by Roman troops and defeated. But they brought back interesting intelligence: Rome was rotten. The spoils of the empires, Persia and Rome, weakened by plague and war, were irresistible. But everything depended on one man, and there was no plan for the succession: who can succeed God's last prophet? There was only one Messenger of God.

PRUNE THE FORESKINNED ONES WITH YOUR SWORDS! CONQUESTS OF THE MUHAMMAD FAMILY

In 632, Muhammad, by then aged sixty-two, caught a fever. Realizing he was dying, his followers asked where he wanted to be. 'Aisha,' he said, so they took him to her and he died in her arms, leaving the elders to choose his veteran companion Abu Bakr as Amr al-Mu'min, Commander of the Believers, later known as khalifa – caliph. But Ali and the family disagreed. The Meccan aristocrats were sceptical, while much of Arabia now broke away under their other prophets. Abu Bakr sent forces under his top paladin, Khalid bin Walid – Sword of Islam – to retake these backsliding provinces. Khalid killed one prince who had converted to Islam so he could marry his beautiful wife. It caused a scandal in Mecca, but in 634 Abu Bakr dispatched Khalid, his other general Amr al-As and Abu Sufyan's two sons, Yazid and Muawiya, into Syria with 20,000 troops.

To contemporaries – and historians – the Arab invasions seemed astonishing in their speed and span, but only recently the Arab armies of Ghassan and Lakhm had galloped through Palestine and Syria; now it is likely those warriors served a new cause. Plague had culled Roman and Persian cities but had barely touched the desert. The Arabs were fielding armies of 12,000 or more at a time when Heraclius could muster only 5,000. They travelled fast on camels, leading their horses. Then for battle they transferred to horseback.

Heraclius, exhausted by two decades of warfare, took command behind the lines as the Arabs besieged Roman Damascus, negotiating its surrender just as the caliph died and was replaced by Omar. Hulking and indomitable, a wrestler in his youth, Omar, who wore plain robes and brandished a whip, started to compile the Quran and Hadith of the Prophet. An austere and prudish man, he devised restrictions on women never mentioned by Muhammad, and had his own son thrashed to death for corruption. He loathed the freebooting swagger of Khalid, whom he recalled to Mecca. 'Take your booty out of your arsehole!' he growled. Khalid surrendered his treasure and was dispatched back to Syria.

Heraclius ordered his brother Theodoros to stop the Arabs. At Yarmuk, south of Golan, the two evenly matched armies faced each other. The cannibal poetess of Arabia, Hind, was there to encourage her two sons, crying, 'Go on! Prune the Foreskinned Ones with your swords!'

Khalid told his men, 'This is one of God's battles!' His cavalry trapped the Romans between rocks and rivers, then cut them up, aided by the defection of their Christian Arab allies. Theodoros was killed.

Amid the booty, the Arabs received another gift from the Romans: plague. Yazid, first governor of Syria, died of it, handing over Damascus to his brother Muawiya. The cities of Homs, Tyre and Caesarea negotiated their surrender in return for promises of freedom of Christian worship and payment of *jizyah*, the tax for People of the Book.

Omar sent Khalid raiding into Persia where Shah Yazdgard struggled to resist as the Arabs galloped right up to the wall of Ctesiphon–Seleucia, that complex of canals and palaces, the fruit of centuries of civilization, that the raiders called the Cities. When Yazdgard mobilized his army with its colossal tiger banner, his armoured steeds and elephants, he drove off one Arab army, but in 636, at Qadisiyya and then Jalula, his forces were defeated. The Arabs besieged Yazdgard in the Cities until their fall was imminent, whereupon he fled eastwards, leaving the Bedouin to enjoy their astonishing good fortune. They prayed in the splendid *iwan* of Khusrau amid statues of Sassanian monarchs. Unlike the Persians with their gold-trimmed armour and caparisoned horses, the Arabs were rough riders who wore robes of camel blanket belted with reeds, bandannas made of a camel's girth rope, hair sticking up like 'goat horns'. They rode stumpy horses and bore a shield 'like a thick round loaf of bread' together with bows and lances, but their one indulgence was their *saif*, not the curved scimitars of legend but straight, polished and much-loved weapons about which they wrote poems and sang songs. The poet Amir ibn al-Tufayl had spoken of 'swords that reap the necks, keen and sharp of edge, kept carefully in sheaths until the time of need'. Even more exciting were the spoils. The Arabs were so bewildered by Khusrau's carpet, the Shah's Spring, that they snipped it into pieces; used expensive camphor scent as cooking salt; and harvested a bounty of loot – cash, treasures and hundreds of thousands of slaves. A small campaign in Sistan by itself yielded 40,000 slaves. At first the Arabs were not keen on converting the conquered peoples for then they would have to be freed, but gradually the slaves did convert, becoming the *mawla*, freedmen of their Arab patrons.

In 638, Arab armies converged on Jerusalem with its special eschatological aura that Muhammad had often cited: 'The Hour has drawn nigh!' and it would take place in Jerusalem. The patriarch of the Holy City refused to surrender to anyone but the Commander, so Omar rode up on a mule and negotiated the covenant, witnessed by Muawiya, that protected Christian worship. Then Omar entered the city, walking up to the Temple Mount where, shown the location of the Jewish Temple by a Jewish Believer, he prayed, setting up an open-air mosque. But after hearing that Khalid had enjoyed a wine-soaked bathhouse orgy where poets had sung of his exploits, he sacked the Sword of Islam.

When Omar returned to Mecca, he left Muhammad's brother-in-law and secretary Muawiya in charge of Syria, where the population was overwhelmingly Christian.

Christian Arabs fought for the Muslims, as did Jews; and even Persian Zoroastrians were accepted in the form of a corps of cataphract cavalry. In Jerusalem, Jews were allowed to pray with Muslims at the mosque on the Temple Mount for many decades, while in Damascus Christians and Muslims prayed together in the Church of St John (today's Umayyad Mosque). Monophysite and Nestorian Christians persecuted by Heraclius probably regarded the Arabs as uncouth ruffians but fellow monotheists.

In 640, Omar ordered Amr al-As to invade Egypt. When Alexandria fell, it marked the end of nine centuries of Graeco-Roman culture and three of Christianity. The Arabs then rode on westwards across north Africa. Some 150,000 Arabs had conquered much of west Asia, fanning out across the world.[*]

Even though there were already lethal divisions in the Muhammad family, soon to break out into war, Commander Omar was not finished. Heraclius died in 641, and it could only be a matter of time before Constantinople too fell, but first Omar sent more troops to catch Shah Yazdgard, who was chased, now alone and abandoned, to a remote mill near Merv (Turkmenistan), where he spent the night in a heap of straw until the mill owner returned and killed him, tossing him into the pond. But the last of the Sassanian shahs had a final idea that could change everything: he dispatched his son Peroz to call in the Chinese.[†]

---

[*] Muhammad's uncle al-Abbas was born in Mecca but his five sons died in places as far-flung as Medina, Syria, Tunisia and Samarkand, where Qutham ibn al-Abbas became a mystical saint known as the Living King, his tomb the centre of a sacred complex that became the location for the tomb of the conqueror Tamerlane and is still revered.

[†] In Chang'an, the emperor refused to intervene against the Arabs, but he gave asylum to

The next half-century of Chinese power belonged to women.

In 637, as Arab armies swept into eastern Persia and northern Africa, Emperor Taizong lost his beloved wife. To cheer up the emperor, the Inner Palace eunuchs recruited new concubines. Taizong noticed the 'enticing beauty' of a fourteen-year-old girl, who was the well-educated daughter of a Tang official and merchant, related through her mother to the recent emperors. Nicknaming her the 'enchanting Miss Wu', Taizong enrolled her as a concubine of the sixth rank, a talent.* When Wu's mother burst into tears, the precocious daughter replied, 'How could looking upon the Son of Heaven be anything but a blessing! Why weep like a child?' Sexual magnetism, fearless intelligence, cultured wit and a sense of adventure may have made her unusual in the Inner Court, where a strict hierarchy could be overturned by a beguiling glance. There, Wu was educated by eunuchs and learned the arts of cosmetics – eyebrows were plucked and embellished with 'moth antennae', cinnabar gloss applied to lips, faced whitened with lead oxide.

The emperor rarely visited, but one day when she was attending him, Wu cleverly engaged him on his favourite subject. 'Emperor Taizong had a horse named Lion Stallion,' she remembered later, 'who was so big and powerful that no one could mount him.' She offered to break in Lion Stallion. 'I only need three things to break him,' she said. 'An iron whip, an iron hammer and a sharp dagger. I will whip him with the whip. If he doesn't submit, I'll hit his head with the hammer. If he still doesn't submit, I'll cut his throat with the dagger.'

'Do you really believe,' replied Taizong suggestively, praising her boldness, 'that you're qualified to stain my dagger?' This was probably when the emperor had sex with her, but by the early 640s he was struggling with bad health and insubordinate sons. The crown prince turned out to be mad, two more princes planned to assassinate him; as heir Taizong chose his reticent ninth son, Li Zhi, the future Gaozong.

the Sassanians, appointing Peroz, the last shah, as head of a Persian Area Command which he controlled for a decade until the Muslim advance led him to retreat to the Chinese capital, where Emperor Gaozong gave him the title Awe-Inspiring General of the Left Guards. Peroz died in 680.

* At the top was the empress, then four consorts, nine concubines and beneath them nine ladies of handsome fairness, nine beauties and nine talents, including Miss Wu. Beneath her were the ladies of the precious bevy, secondary concubines and selected ladies, 27 of each – 122 in total. No men apart from the emperor and his eunuchs, who grew rich selling luxuries such as Boreal camphor and Malayan patchouli to the girls, enjoyed access. The Confucian scholar-bureaucrats who wrote the histories of China were misogynists who presented female potentates as sex-crazed megalomaniacs, a chauvinism that must be taken into account; equally, sexual attraction was one way that women won political power in dynastic monarchies.

Seeking diversion in a disastrous campaign to conquer Korea, Taizong found power draining away. His hair turning white with the strain, Gaozong sat by Taizong's bed while Wu waited on the crown prince, four years her junior, who was increasingly attracted to her. But it was a sensitive situation since technically she was a stepmother and any liaison incestuous. Nonetheless they started an affair.

ENCHANTING WU: THE EMPRESS KILLED MY BABY

In 649, Taizong died at the age of fifty-one. Young Emperor Gaozong sent all his father's girls to the Buddhist convent for 'purification', their heads shaven and wearing sackcloth, before they would emerge for marriage and normal life. After a year Gaozong visited them to honour his father and saw Wu. The chemistry was reactivated, and both of them started to weep. He allowed her to grow her hair while she wrote a sensuous poem that encouraged his frequent visits:

> I look upon your disc of jade and my thoughts scatter in disarray
> As haggard from grief sundered and separate I so keenly miss my Sovereign.
> If you don't believe this endless litany of tears
> Then open my chest and examine my tear-stained pomegranate red dress.

Gaozong was married to Empress Wang, who made the mistake of encouraging his passion to distract him from another mistress, Consort Xiao. But, as so often, the cure was lethal. Moving back into the Inner Palace, Wu dazzled the emperor and charmed the maids, eunuchs and concubines who became her devoted agents, while the anxious Empress Wang, who was childless, adopted another girl's son to appoint as crown prince, hoping to stop the rise of this gorgeous upstart. After a son, Wu had a daughter whom the empress liked to dandle on her knee. In 654, the empress played with the baby; when she left, Wu suffocated her own daughter and then, when the emperor visited, she revealed in an agony of grief the blue-faced child, blaming Empress Wang. Gaozong questioned the staff, all of whom replied that 'the Empress' was responsible. Gaozong cried, 'The Empress has murdered my baby!' Wu's career was recorded after her death by hostile historians, but even if she did not murder her own daughter, she used the death to destroy Gaozong's relationship with his wife, whose barrenness was a tragedy in a dynastic court when her rival would deliver six children.

Empress Wang resorted to magic to get pregnant, which allowed Wu, informed by her spies, to accuse the wife of illegal witchcraft. Gaozong proposed to divorce Wang and marry Wu, a move that was opposed by veteran ministers who cited her intimacy with the dead emperor. But in 655 Empress Wang and Consort Xiao were both found guilty of sorcery and imprisoned in a turret. Wu, now thirty-one, became empress consort and her eldest son Li Hong was appointed crown prince. But one day, passing the tower where his ex-wife and ex-consort were imprisoned, Gaozong was touched by their cries. This provoked Wu to have them flogged, dismembered alive then drowned in a flagon of wine with the words, 'Now you crones can get drunk to your marrow!'

Gaozong was devoted to Wu, who gave birth to a last daughter, the Taiping Princess, at the age of forty. While always protecting her power with ingenious energy and seeking to destroy her enemies, never forgetting a slight, she ruled in partnership with the emperor, who appreciated her acumen. Wu's power reflected the way forms of family shaped east and central Asia: women among nomadic peoples enjoyed more freedom and authority than those in sedentary states. Yet no emperor, especially not Gaozong, could fill the gap left by Taizong and the couple struggled to hold the empire together.

Gaozong suffered a stroke early in his long reign, but he recovered and Wu shared much of the work with him – they were nicknamed the Two Sages. She refused to promote her own family, helping to organize a campaign against Korea, another to defeat the Turks, initiating the use of meritocratic examinations for the civil service, fostering a bureaucracy controlled by the monarch rather than a hereditary elite and arranging the complex ritual spectacular of the Feng and Shan sacrifices at Mount Tai. They celebrated their double act by adopting the Taoist titles of Celestial Emperor and Empress. Wu revered Buddhism and Taoism, though she was, like everyone at that time, extremely superstitious. Her patronage of a magician was denounced to the emperor by a eunuch. Gaozong consulted his veteran chancellor Shangguan Yi, who advised, 'The empress has no control of herself, and the entire empire is dissatisfied with her. Please depose her.' Gaozong was about to sign this edict when the empress's spies informed her and she arrived just in time. The emperor blamed Shangguan Yi, who, accused by the empress of planning to assassinate Gaozong, was then executed together with his son. Yet much later the chancellor's granddaughter would play a special role with Wu.

Wu understood her husband's sexual appetites. She first imported her widowed sister as mistress (the emperor nicknamed her Beauty of State and she bore him a son); then on her death, the sister's daughter,

Wu's niece the Lady of Wei became imperial paramour – too successfully. Ever vigilant, Wu had her niece poisoned.

After the crown prince died of tuberculosis (some historians claim Wu killed him too), Gaozong promoted their son, Li Xian. But here there was a problem. As the emperor weakened, Li Xian planned to remove his mother from power. The coldness between them became icier. The boy had discovered a secret. He was not really her son at all but her late sister's bastard, born in secret then adopted by her. The emperor did not improve matters when he announced that his wife and son would be joint heirs. The couple consulted a mystic who warned that Xian was unsuitable. Xian heard this and had the mystic murdered. He was duly exiled and his brother Li Zhe became crown prince in his stead. With famines, earthquakes and epidemics suggesting that the Mandate of Heaven was in doubt, Gaozong deteriorated, dying in 683. As Wu laid her plans, they received reports from Syria of a new monarch named Mo-yi: the opening of the age of Arab dynasties.

ACT SIX
207 MILLION

Houses of Muhammad and Charlemagne

ARAB CAESAR AND YAZID OF WHORING,
YAZID OF MONKEYS

Mo-yi was Muawiya. By the time Gaozong and Wu heard his name, Muawiya had seized the throne of a new empire in a vicious family war. It is a hard thing to run an empire: Caliph Omar travelled the provinces on his mule with a single servant, leaving Muawiya to govern Syria. Muawiya wanted to build a fleet to confront the Romans, but Omar refused. Suspicious of Muawiya's worldliness, he nicknamed him Arab Caesar.

In 644, Omar was assassinated by a disgruntled slave and the elders again overlooked Ali, Muhammad's son-in-law, and chose the genial Othman, also married in turn to two elder daughters of the Prophet. He favoured his clan, House Umayya, confirming Muawiya as governor of Syria. So far the caliphate's subjects were overwhelmingly Christian and Zoroastrian. Inheriting the Roman tax system, Muawiya used Roman officials led by Sergios – Sarjun ibn Mansur in Arabic – to run the bureaucracy. His doctor and court poet were Christian, his first governor of Jerusalem was supposedly Jewish and his favourite wife Maysun was a Christian princess. Amr al-As teased him for being bossed around by his wife. 'The wives of noble men dominate them,' replied Muawiya. 'Low men lord it over their women.'

He prided himself on his sexual virility, but as he got older and fatter he laughed at himself. He slept with a Khorasani slave whom he asked, 'What is a lion in Persian?'

'*Kaftar,*' she replied.

'I am a *kaftar,*' he boasted as she left, but when he asked a courtier what it meant he replied, 'A lame hyena.'

'Well done,' Muawiya told the girl.

In 655 Muawiya's new Arab fleet defeated Emperor Constans II (Heraclius' grandson), marking a new era. But a year later mutineers from Egypt and Iraq assassinated Muawiya's cousin, Othman the caliph in

Medina. Ali, now in his fifties, was chosen as his successor, appointing some of the assassins to his retinue. Muhammed had ordered his wives to keep out of politics after his death, but his favourite surviving wife Aisha (daughter of the first caliph) and respected as Umm al-Mu'minin – Mother of Believers – denounced Ali and the assassins of Othman. She led an army against Ali, pursuing him into Iraq. On the battlefield, she harangued the troops, commanding them from the armoured canopy of a red camel. But Ali won; her famous camel was killed and she was captured.*

Muawiya, firmly in control of the centre, demanded that Othman's killers be punished, a challenge that Ali could not satisfy. Channelling Antony's theatrics with Caesar's bloodied toga, Muawiya displayed the relics of the caliphal assassination, the sanguine robes of Othman and the severed fingers of his wife Naila.

The two armies met at Siffin near Raqqa (Syria) where, with the intense savagery of fraternal hatreds, 70,000 were killed in hand-to-hand fighting. Finally Muawiya's troops stuck pages of the Quran on their lances, shaming the other side into stopping. Ali agreed to negotiate. Muawiya's envoy Amr al-As outmanoeuvred Ali, whom Muhammad had never given an important job. 'The Messenger of God appointed only capable men,' said Muawiya, 'not men strained beyond their capabilities.' Ali's army disintegrated. In 660, Muawiya held a conclave on the Temple Mount of Jerusalem where he was acclaimed as Commander, channelling the sanctity of the Holy City.†

Soon afterwards Ali was assassinated in Iraq, leaving his two sons Hassan and Hussein as his heirs. But while Muawiya and the Umayya dynasty had triumphed, the Party (Shia) of Ali, who believed the succession should descend through Ali, would be a sempiternal schism at the heart of Islam.

In 674, Muawiya, having routed the Roman fleet, attacked Constantinople. The siege, commanded by his son Yazid, lasted four years. The Arabs thought the city would fall, a view probably shared by Emperor

---

* Ali reprimanded her but spared her – and she lived on in Medina for forty years.

† Muawiya's philosophy was the perfect expression of statesmanship: 'If there is but a single thread between me and my subjects I will never let it go slack without tugging on it and I never let them pull it tight without loosening it.' He added, 'I don't use my tongue where money will suffice; I don't use my whip where my tongue will suffice; I don't use my sword where my whip will suffice. But when there's no choice I will use my sword.' He was the personification of *hilm*, the measured cunning of the traditional Arab sheikh. He was even tolerant of criticism: 'I don't insert myself between the people and their tongue so long as they don't insert themselves between us and our kingship.'

Constans, who moved to Sicily where he was murdered in his bath by a slave with a soap dish. But the walls of the Great City and the restored Roman fleet, along with the first use of a new secret weapon, Greek Fire, an early flamethrower that squirted burning naphtha oil through a tube, finally forced Muawiya to recall his fleet.

Caliphs had always been chosen by the elders. Muawiya created a family monarchy, controversially nominating Yazid, son of his Christian wife, a playboy who enjoyed wine and girls and walked around Damascus with a pet monkey. As for any rival, 'If you seize him,' advised Muawiya, 'chop him limb from limb.' But when Muawiya died aged eighty, Yazid's debauchery shocked the Medinese, who called him 'Yazid of the liquors, Yazid of whoring, Yazid of monkeys'. Muhammad's grandson Hussein declared himself caliph in Iraq but was killed at Karbala, playing into the Shia narrative of martyrdom, still expressed in the lamenting and whipping of the holy day of Ashura. Hussein's head was sent on tour and Yazid stuck his sceptre in its mouth. When Yazid died unexpectedly, probably of the plague, contenders in Kufa (Iraq) and Medina claimed the throne.

Far to the east, the Arabs were approaching Chinese territory – just as Emperor Gaozung's extraordinary widow seized control.

POLITICAL JISM: THE TEETH AND CLAWS OF EMPRESS WU

Wu, dowager empress and regent, was sixty. The late emperor's will specified that 'great matters of state shall be determined by the Celestial Empress', but their son Li Zhe – under the influence of his young empress Wei – planned to give power to his wife's father. When confronted about appointing his father-in-law Wei Xuanzhen as minister, the young emperor shouted, 'If I wish to give the empire to Wei, what is there to stop me?' But there *was* something to stop him: Wu. She rallied the ministers and generals. Facing Turkish and Tibetan advances,* famines and rebellions, they appreciated her experience and nerve. The boy was deposed. He asked what his crime was.

'You wished to hand over the empire to Wei,' snapped Wu. 'How's

---

* To control the Tibetans, she turned to the Indian Pallava raja, Narasimhavarman II, known as Rajasimha, whom the Chinese granted the title General of South China. But Rajasimha's greatest influence was cultural – he was both a playwright and builder of temples that still stand, the Kailasanatha at his capital Kanchipuram and the Shore Temple at his port Mahabalipuram, whence Pallava influence, Brahminism and Sanskrit were exported to the Indosphere of south-east Asia.

that not a crime?' While he was sent into well-supervised obscurity,* Wu appointed her youngest son Li Dan, aged twenty-one, as emperor. Unsurprisingly he was terrified of her, particularly after she forced another of her sons, the exiled Li Xian, to commit suicide.

When her gambits provoked a rebellion by Tang princes, she orchestrated a terror led by a trio of sadistic secret policemen – her 'teeth and claws' – led by Lai Junchen, a psychotic former cake salesman who used denunciations to frame princes and officials, even compiling a *Manual of Entrapment*. Thousands were killed in Wu's newly opened prison where Lai tortured his victims, devising ingenious atrocities.† Eighty per cent of Wu's ministers were removed, many killed. Lai requested promotion to censor. 'But you can't read,' teased Wu. She promoted him anyway, but preferred to consult her capable daughter, the Taiping Princess.

Wu was also a master of public presentation, regularly 'rectifying names' – changing regal names both to bring luck and for rebranding – to relaunch her reign, publicizing her views on good government in her *Regulations for Ministers* and ordering that family members should betray treason committed by their relatives – loyalty to the state was everything.

Wu was recommended a lover by Princess Qianjin, a fifty-something daughter of the founding emperor Gaozu – an example of the uninhibited earthiness of Tang women. The candidate was a strapping and much younger snake-oil salesman from a poor family called Xue Huaiyi whose sexual athleticism and gigantic member had first impressed a maid of the princess, who in turn enjoyed his gifts before raving about them to the empress.

When his regular visits led her ministers to suggest archly that he should be castrated, she ordered instead that Master Xue should be tonsured as a Buddhist monk and promoted him to abbot of the White Horse Monastery.

Brusque, colourful and arrogant, the Master soon wielded immense power, escorted by ten eunuchs and a posse of heavies. Wu's image as a power-mad ageing nymphomaniac was unfair, given the hundreds

---

* Living in exile with his wife ex-Empress Wei, he feared every messenger from the capital would bring terrible punishments, and was always ready to commit suicide. But his wife always restrained him: 'There is no set pattern to bad and good fortune. Since we will die one day, why hasten it?'

† The tortures enjoyed picturesque names: 'Dying Swine's Melancholy', 'Piercing a Hundred Veins' and 'Begging for the Slaughter of my Entire Family'. In 'Phoenix Suns his Wings', the victim was lashed to a wheel in the sun; in 'Uprooting a Stubborn Foal', the prisoner was collared; and in 'Offering Fruit to the Immortals', tiles were piled on the victim's back. In one episode, more than 300 dissidents were massacred.

of young concubines enjoyed by male emperors, and her well-hung youth did perform a mystical seminal rite: Taoists believed that the life essence – semen – of a young man rejuvenated his older lover. Yet the Master had other talents too, as organizer and architect. He advised Wu on religion, and together they endorsed Buddhism, its otherworldliness and emotional equanimity complementing the dutiful ethics of Confucius and the mystical rites of Tao. She built pagodas, welcomed Buddhist sages and ordered the compilation of sacred text, *Great Cloud Sutra*, assuming the titles *chakravartin* (wheel-turning monarch) and *bodhisattva* (compassionate being close to nirvana). After she had made the Master her commissioner of works, he deployed 30,000 workers to build an exquisite Buddhist Heavenly Hall in the centre of her capital Luoyang: 300 feet up, nine dragons bore a canopy bearing a colossal gilded phoenix.

She sponsored talent wherever she found it, once jokingly upbraiding her ministers for persecuting a critic who had dared to attack her: 'How could you waste such a gifted person?' The most surprising of her advisers – and probably the most talented – was her young, beautiful female secretary, Shangguan Wan'er, whose father and grandfather had been executed by Wu for trying to get the empress consort dismissed; the child was then enslaved. But she was a brilliant poet; Wu saw the poems and hired her. Shangguan Wan'er thereafter wrote her decrees, but when she was caught disobeying an order, the empress had her face tattooed. The enslaved, manumitted, branded amanuensis became a potentate in this unusually feminine regime.

In 690, Wu secretly orchestrated popular demonstrations and auspicious omens demanding she become empress regnant. Finally she agreed and forced her son Li Dan to retire and, assuming the dynasty name of Zhou, she became the first empress regnant, donning the yellow robes of a Huang-di (emperor) – but this made her even more ferociously vigilant. When two ministers made the mistake of visiting the ex-emperor Dan, she had them sliced in half. In 693, she murdered Dan's wife and consort.* When he met his mother, Dan carefully pretended nothing had happened.

In 694, Wu wearied of the Master, taking her doctor as a new lover. The spurned Master burned down the Heavenly Hall, his jealousy flattering her. She promoted him to duke and had him rebuild it, but there is nothing as dead as dead love and his tantrums angered her. So he was

---

* All the family must have been thoroughly traumatized. Li Dan tried to live obscurely far from the capital with his sons including Li Longji, the future Emperor Xuanzong, avoiding politics, yet being carefully watched and often persecuted.

beaten to death and incinerated, the ashes stirred into mud.

By now, she had successfully repelled and outmanoeuvred Tibet-ans, Koreans and Turks, adding a million non-Chinese to her empire, receiving tribute-bearing embassies from Japan, India and central Asia, victories that justified her Mandate of Heaven. She felt confident enough to reduce the terror. Her hated torturer Lai, enriched by bribes and insatiable for sexual favours from terrified families, overreached by denouncing Wu's daughter the Taiping Princess. As he was about to be publicly sliced, the mob went berserk, tearing out his heart and trampling him to pulp.

Wu was now in her seventies, maintaining her beauty with cosmetics. She also resorted to Taoist charlatans, appointing as chancellor one who claimed to be 400 years old, though she soon forced him to commit suicide.

In 697, the Taiping Princess, who resembled Wu herself, recom-mended a new lover for her mother. Beautiful, young and a fine singer, Zhang Changzong was one of five ambitious brothers. The empress was enraptured by him, and he introduced his brother Zhang Yizhi as even more adept in bed. Flashy, effeminate and arrogant, 'the Boys' – as she called them – wore vermilion robes and held outrageous parties at court. Wu was dazzled by them, creating for them a literary power base known as the Reigning Storks Institution – storks being the tra-ditional conveyance for Taoist fairies – reflecting her new belief that Zhang Changzong was a stork-riding Taoist immortal and she herself Queen Mother of the West who hoped that the Boys' semen, male yang essence, would rejuvenate her.

With the Boys on the loose, her court was exuberant. Her festivals celebrated her own agelessness or triumph over age including her claim that her teeth were growing back, her eyebrows had realigned in an aus-picious 8-shape – leading her in 699 to stage an 'Anthem of the Sage's Longevity' with 900 dancers. Mortality is always a galling liability for any tyrant whose boundless power can only be curtailed by the terminal inconvenience of death. She gorged on Taoist elixirs, as her alchemists developed an ancient mix of heated saltpetre and sulphur – a stage in the long process that would lead to gunpowder.

When she was around eighty, Wu felt she had to consider the suc-cession. She had advanced her own Wu family and renamed the Li princes Wu as well, but the Boys, fearing what would happen after Wu's death, persuaded her to recall Li Zhe, the deposed emperor, as crown prince. But she was not softening. When the Boys snitched that her granddaughter and husband had criticized their antics, she had them beaten to death and the Boys raised to dukes. But their peculation was so brazen that ministers accused them of theft. She confronted the Boys before her court.

'Your minister has accumulated merit in state service,' insisted Zhang Changzong. 'My offence should not result in dismissal.'

'What meritorious service', asked Wu, 'has Changzong performed?'

'Changzong', replied the Boys' most sycophantic courtier, 'concocted a divine elixir and when Your Saintliness drank it, the draught proved most efficacious.' This was surely the only court in history at which corruption was excused by the drinking of semen.

THE FLY KILLER OF DAMASCUS AND THE
EMPRESSES OF TANG

Wu forgave Zhang. In late 704, she fell ill in the Longevity Basilica as her children feuded and opposition to the Zhangs whirled around the sickbed. Crown Prince Li Zhe and the Taiping Princess, realizing that the Boys were threatening the succession, recruited the guards. In February 705, Li Zhe and 500 guards broke into the Palace of Welcoming the Immortals, located the Zhang Boys and beheaded them on the spot. Then they burst into the empress's bedroom, where they encircled her bed.

'Who's the cause of this ruckus?' she demanded.

'The brothers plotted rebellion,' explained one of the accompanying ministers. 'The crown prince ordered us to execute them.'

She spotted her anxious forty-eight-year-old son: 'And you? Now the Boys have been executed, you may return to the Eastern Palace.'

Li Zhe was about to obey when a minister intervened: 'We humbly desire Your Majesty transfer the throne to the crown prince.'

Casting a terrifying glance around the chamber, reminding the rebels of how she had promoted them, she sneered, 'So this is your idea of payback is it?'

Three days later, as the five heads of the Boys were displayed near Heaven's Ford Bridge, Li Zhe again became emperor, the Tang dynasty restored. On 16 December 705, Wu, honoured but under house arrest, seeming to have aged centuries without her cosmetics, died, buried in the same tomb as her husband.

Yet the age of female power was not over. The emperor's wife, Wei, had survived Wu's terror. 'If we see the light of day again,' her husband had promised, 'I won't stop you from doing anything.' Wei took power, assisted by her lover Wu Sansi (Empress Wu's nephew), who was also the lover of the old empress's face-branded, formerly enslaved secretary Shangguan Wan'er, now in her forties. When this polyamorous foursome sat at a table in the Inner Court to play cards, the empress's legs would become entangled with Wu Sansi's under the table. So strong seemed feminine power that the empress persuaded her husband to declare their twenty-one-year-old daughter Princess Anle as crown princess. When the emperor resisted, Anle retorted, 'If that Wu woman could become the emperor, why can't the daughter of the emperor become an emperor?'

When the emperor tried to stop his wife's abuses, Wei poisoned him with his favourite cakes, but she kept his death secret until she had appointed a teenage emperor whom she could dominate. The Taiping Princess now discovered that Wei planned to kill her, her brother (the ex-emperor) Li Dan and his sons. She had to act, recruiting her impressive nephew Li Longji, aged twenty-five, who one night in June 710 visited the Palace Gate, won over the guards and then, entering the palace, hacked down Empress Wei as she ran, stabbed Princess Anle as she put on make-up in the mirror and beheaded the great survivor, the tattooed Shangguan. Li Longji emerged from the showdown as Emperor Xuanzong. The Taiping Princess, very much Wu's daughter, tried to poison him and launched a coup attempt which ended in the beheading of her sons and her own forced suicide.

Emperor Xuanzong, the soldier, calligrapher and poet who had cut down four powerful women to seize the crown, would deliver the apogee of Tang success – attaining power just as the Tang and the Arab empires came into contact for the first time.

In 689, the Commander of the Believers, Abd al-Malik, had fixed a silver collar around the neck of a captured rebel and led him through the Damascus streets on a leash before straddling his chest and hacking off his head, which he then tossed to the crowd.

Abd al-Malik had long hair, gold teeth, a cleft lip and such vile breath that he was nicknamed the Fly Killer (though this might just be Shiite propaganda), but he was also the monarch who created an Islamic state out of the personal empire of Muawiya – and constructed the most beautiful religious building of his century. His coins show him as a warrior in a brocaded robe drawing a big bejewelled sword and holding a whip, with the inscription Commander of the Believers and Servant of God. 'The only way I'll cure this community is with the sword,' he preached. 'I won't be the kind of caliph who'll be duped or thought weak.'

In the meltdown after Yazid's death, his family summoned his aged but experienced cousin Marwan to Damascus, where he ensured the succession of his able son, Abd al-Malik. Marrying Atika, widow of Yazid, one of many wives, the new Commander faced rebellions in Iraq and Arabia where Mecca was ruled by a rival caliph. The loss of Mecca was embarrassing. As a young man in that city, Abd al-Malik had been a 'mosque dove', learning to recite the entire Quran. But now he possessed the Syrian army, invincible confidence and the ability to choose gifted henchmen: his hatchetman was a schoolmaster turned warlord called al-Hajjaj who spouted exquisitely murderous poetry at Friday prayers in Kufa, Iraq – 'I see hungry stares and straining necks; I see ripened heads ready to be picked; I am their master . . . By God, I'll grind you down to dust' – before slaughtering its mutinous people. The Commander encouraged Believers to take the pilgrimage to Jerusalem where, over the Foundation Stone of the Jewish Temple, he built the sublime Dome of the Rock, a shrine designed to emulate the Temples of Solomon and Herod but also to rival Mecca and outshine Hagia Sophia. It was completed in 691, Jews and Christians initially joining Muslims to pray on the Temple Mount. It took seven years to subdue his rivals and by the time the Dome was finished, he had retaken Mecca.

After making the *hajj* – the pilgrimage to Mecca – Abd al-Malik recast the caliphate in terms of faith and family: Islam would be central. He was the first to be widely called caliph instead of the more military commander, and his later coins eschewed the human imagery previously employed, a prohibition that came to be part of Islamic tradition. Arabic became the language of government, a decision that changed the world, imposing the language from Morocco to Iraq, and he relaunched Muawiya's jihad against Constantinople.

His sons dominated the caliphate – four of them ruled after him and then a nephew, Walid, who converted St John's of Damascus into today's Ummayad Mosque and built the al-Aqsa Mosque of Jerusalem. Then he restarted the world conquest on three fronts. He inherited as eastern viceroy the killer pedagogue al-Hajjaj, who encouraged the eastward march, and he offered the governorship of China to anyone who could conquer it.

In 1712, his armies took Samarkand. In 715 and 717, small Arab armies were defeated by Chinese and Turkish troops. Not all the Arab generals were brilliant. One whom the poets mocked was known as the Flirt: 'You advanced on the enemy at night as if you were playing with your girl; your cock was drawn & your sword sheathed.' To the west, Walid relaunched the jihad against the Romans, encouraged by the mayhem in Constantinople. In 695 Heraclius' vindictive great-great-grandson

Justinian II was overthrown and mutilated by having his nose sliced off, but he seized back the throne, wearing a golden proboscis and now nicknamed Slitnose. The vengeance he took on his enemies was savage but counter-productive, as it led to his assassination. In 716, Walid sent an army of 120,000 and 1,800 ships against Constantinople, commanded by his half-brother Maslama. The siege seemed perfectly timed as civil strife paralysed the Romans. Maslama negotiated with the *strategos* of the Anatolian Theme or district, an Isaurian general named Leo who promised to aid him. Instead Leo III seized power himself, rallied resistance and hired pagan auxiliaries from a new arrival in the Balkans, Tervel, khan of the horde of Bulgars, who was rewarded with the coveted title Caesar.

The Arabs did not take the city. The new caliph Umar ordered Maslama to retreat. Natural disasters now dovetailed with existential threats: the volcano beneath the Aegean island of Thera exploded, pumping jets of smoke and launching tsunamis. Just as modern rulers consult scientists, medieval potentates turned to theologians. In Constantinople, the people wondered if their revered religious images – icons – were graven images banned in the Ten Commandments. The caliph had just banned such imagery, and though Constantinople had survived, he was victorious on many fronts. Emperor Leo and many others concluded that their own idolatry explained their disasters. The emperor's campaign to destroy icons launched ninety years of *eikonomachia* – a self-destructive battle between iconoclasts and iconophiles, each keen to win salvation after death, that cost thousands of lives and consumed Constantinopolitan politics.

Far to the west, Arab forces advanced along the coast of north Africa, converting Berber tribes, until they reached Tangier (Morocco), whence they could see the coast of Europe.

In 711, Tariq bin Ziyad, a *mawla* of the governor of Ifriqiya, Musa bin Nusayr, was invited into Spain by a noble dissident, whose daughter had supposedly been raped by Rodrigo, king of the Visigoths who had ruled there since Roman times. Sailing across with 7,000 Berbers, he landed at the rock later named after him – Jibral Tariq, Gibraltar – and then killed Rodrigo and took the capital Toledo. Tariq's superior Musa arrived to assert official control over the new province, al-Andalus. But the conquistadors were recalled to Damascus by Caliph Walid, suspicious of overmighty freelancers, and both died in prison. The Arabs seized much of Spain, though they never reached the less lush north, which remained under Christian warlords.

Al-Andalus was the ideal launchpad for raids across the Pyrenees into Francia. In 719, the Arabs conquered Septimania (Narbonne); in 721 and 725, they attacked Toulouse.

In 732, the governor of al-Andalus pursued a Berber rebel into western Francia and then galloped northwards towards Paris. But while Spain had fallen easily into their hands, here the Arabs encountered a different breed of enemy, the Franks under their *dux*, Charles, who was about to win his nickname: the Hammer.

THE HAMMER AND THE PLAYBOY CALIPH:
CUNTS ON A LION'S BROW

Charles had something to prove. He was the son of his father Pepin's concubine, not his chief wife, and they did not choose him as heir.

In the last years of the Roman empire, a Germanic war-band chieftain, Clovis, based in northern Gaul – Neustria – had declared himself king of the Franks, conquering much of Roman France and Germany, naming his Merovingian dynasty after his grandfather Merovec. Roman order gradually vanished: some cities almost emptied; coins were less used; slavery declined; epidemics raged; bishops and lords, ruling from their manors, amassed the best land and controlled the peasantry, who became *servi* – serfs. Yet the Merovingians – who marked their sanctity by growing their hair very long, a dynasty of Frankish Samsons – feuded among themselves, splintering into smaller realms. In the 620s, a nobleman named Pepin, who owned estates in Brabant, became mayor of the palace for the king of Austrasia – northern Germany and the Low Countries – founding his own dynasty but it was a dangerous game: his son and son-in-law were executed by Merovingians. In 687, his grandson, also Pepin, united the kingdoms with himself as *dux et princeps Francorum* under the nominal king.

Pepin had sons by Plectrudis, chief wife, but he also had a son by his concubine Alpaida named Charles. But when his legitimate sons died, Plectrudis persuaded Pepin to leave the throne to their grandson. In 714, Pepin died and Plectrudis promoted his grandson and imprisoned Charles – but he managed to escape. By 719 having defeated all contenders he emerged as duke-prince himself, and for the rest of his life he fought a war every summer and never lost one.

In late 732 al-Ghafiqi, the Arab governor of al-Andalus, led 15,000 Arabs into Francia, defeating Odo, duke of Aquitaine, before heading north. But Odo warned Charles, who, mustering around 15,000 Franks, rode out to stop the Arab invaders. For seven days, near Tours, they faced each other. When the fighting started, al-Ghafiqi's light cavalry disintegrated against the armour of the Frankish knights. When Charles made a feint to threaten their booty, the Arabs broke and al-Ghafiqi was killed. The Arabs withdrew overnight. The encounter was far from decisive – it was just a raid. The Arabs still held Septimania and they were back raiding soon afterwards. But Charles saw himself as Martel, the slayer of the infidels, a latter-day Maccabee – the Hammer – and champion of Christ.

Soon after Charles's death, the family had a stroke of luck. In 751, Pope Zacharias requested help from Martel's son Pepin the Short against the Lombard kings who ruled northern Italy. Popes were at the mercy of voracious Lombards and Roman magnates. Pepin had his price: a crown. As a result, the last Merovingian, Childeric III, was tonsured, losing his regal locks. Pepin favoured a new look – short hair and long moustaches – as king of the Franks. In 753, when a new pope, Stephen, travelled north to court King Pepin, he was greeted by his six-year-old son Charles – later known as Charlemagne. Stephen anointed Pepin, Charlemagne and his brother Carloman as kings and patricians of the Romans.

Pepin the Short intervened in Italy, granting Pope Stephen bountiful estates and ordering the payment across Europe of tithes to fund the papacy, gifts that made the popes players for the first time. Then he expelled the Arabs from Septimania. When he was thirteen, Charlemagne accompanied his father to war; when he was fifteen, Pepin gave him his first concubine, Himiltrud, with whom he had a child. Looking out across the world, Pepin and Charlemagne knew nothing of life across the Atlantic; to the north, they enjoyed good relations with the main British kingdom, Mercia; to the east, they clashed with the pagan Saxons of central Europe; further away, the Greek world of Constantinople was strange and distant; and beyond them were the Islamic caliphs whose lands were so vast that they circled round the Mediterranean to Spain in the west. Now, an Islamic rebel, al-Mansur, sent an envoy, probably a Jewish trader, to ask for Pepin's assistance against the decadent caliphs of Damascus.

In 743, when Abd al-Malik's grandson Walid II became caliph, his extravagant debauchery seemed to confirm the anti-Islamic rot of the Umayya dynasty. The seed didn't fall far from the tree: it was the age of the *jarya*, enslaved singers who were bought for massive sums. Walid's father, Yazid II, had fallen in love with the enslaved singer Hababah, whom he saw as a youngster in Mecca but could not afford until he became caliph in 720, when he paid 4,000 gold pieces. In Damascus, Hababah starred in spectacular productions with fifty other singers which the caliph found so enrapturing that he thought he was in paradise: 'I want to fly away.' After she choked to death on a pomegranate seed, he could not bear to part with her body for three very unMuslim days. When Yazid II died in 724, Walid, then a teenager, was passed over for his uncle Hisham. While Hisham spent twenty years enjoying his harem, Crown Prince Walid, poet, lover, gambler and hunter, flaunted his outrageous pleasure-seeking – 'in love with love' – in poetry:

> I would that all wine were a dinar a glass
> And all cunts on a lion's brow
> Then only the libertine would drink
> And only the brave make love.

His paramour was an enslaved singer, Nawar, nicknamed Salma, whom he compared to a lush harvest and whose features he eulogized: 'Salma my love, an antelope I adore for the dark eyes and flawless neck and throat.' But Salma was unfaithful, and Walid revelled in this tormented passion.*

Walid's rock-star behaviour was so debauched that Hisham decided to disinherit him in favour of his own son Muawiya, but he died – and the playboy inherited the empire. When Walid was too drunk to leave his orgies, he did the unthinkable: Salma, the *jarya*, dressed up in caliphal vestments and led Friday prayers. Or so his enemies claimed.

Walid partied in his new pleasure palaces in the desert,† wallowing soused in bathhouses decorated with mosaics that were more Persian and Roman than Islamic. At Qusr al-Amra, he commissioned frescoes that show him lording it over the conquered monarchs of Constantinople, Persia, China, Ethiopia and Spain, while its bathhouse features naked girls, smoking, dancing and banqueting. When a poet visited Walid, he fell dead drunk and then shouted after him, 'Son of a whore, if so much as a whisper passes your lips, I'll have your head off.'

'Wake up, Umayya!' warned a dissident. 'Search for the caliph of God among the tambourines and lutes!' As Walid partied, rumours and

---

* They told me on a Friday Salma had gone to prayers.
  Just then upon a branch a pretty bird sat preening.
  I said, 'Who here knows Salma?'
  'Ha!' said he; then flew away.
  I said, 'Come back, birdy,
  Have you seen Salma?'
  'Ha!' said he; and struck a secret wound in my heart . . .
† The Umayya caliphs ruled from their palace complex in Damascus, spending summers in pleasure castles in Golan, the Bekaa valley and the Jordanian desert. Many of these 'castles' survive.

revelations swarmed; rebels besieged him in 744 and the caliph, now thirty-eight, was beheaded. Meanwhile not far from his party house, something strange was happening.

THE BLOODSHEDDER AND THE GIANT BABY:
RISE OF ABBAS, FALL OF TANG

In a rustic hamlet named Humayma (Jordan) lived a well-connected but obscure squire with his sons. Muhammad ibn Ali was unexceptional, except that he was a great-grandson of Muhammad's uncle Abbas, and he was disgusted by the effeminate caliphs 'whose only ambition', remarked his son Mansur, 'was the satisfaction of pleasures forbidden by God'. As the Umayya faltered, a perfume seller arrived at the farm on a secret mission from Iraq, where support was growing for a furious revolution far to the east in Khorasan. In June 747, a sacred warrior, a manumitted slave who called himself Ibn Muslim, emerged from nowhere to launch a rebellion of Khorasanis, excluded by the Arab Umayyas, that quickly gathered a militant alliance of black-bannered warriors – Persians and Afghans, dissidents and adventurers, followers of the Ali lineage of Muhammad's family and sectarians named Kharijites – who took an oath of allegiance to 'An Acceptable Member of the House of the Prophet'. Knowing that the Ali family offended many in Syria, Ibn Muslim backed Abbas's descendants and sent the trusted cosmetics salesman with an invitation to destiny.

Muhammad ibn Ali agreed to support the revolution, a cause inherited by his sons, only for the Umayya to hear the rumours and kill the eldest. A younger son, Abbas, went underground as Ibn Muslim galloped out of Khorasan into Iraq. There the two met, united in disgust and outrage at the decline of the House of Islam. Proclaiming himself caliph of House Abbasiya of the Muhammad dynasty, Abbas warned, 'Hold yourselves ready for I am the pitiless bloodshedder and destroying avenger.' His regal name was al-Saffah – the Bloodshedder.

At the River Zab in February 750, Ibn Muslim and al-Saffah defeated the army of Marwan II, who was hunted down in Egypt and killed – the last Umayya caliph.* In April, al-Saffah, his brother al-Mansur and his

---

* Marwan's sons fled southwards to Makuria (Sudan), which had converted to Coptic Christianity in the time of Justinian. During the Arab conquest, Makuria faced Arab attacks until its kings signed a mercantile treaty in which their chief export, slaves, were traded for Egyptian grain and cloth. In 747, exploiting the Arab civil war, King Kyriakos of Makuria raided Egypt. But when he saw the Abbasiya were winning, he won favour by killing

troops took Damascus. Bloodshedder personally beheaded Umayya princes, dead caliphs were disinterred, 'scourged with whips then crucified', skulls smashed. Bloodshedder announced an amnesty for the Umayya family, who were invited to a reconciliatory dinner near Jaffa. But it was a trick: as Bloodshedder watched gleefully, the guests were slaughtered. 'Never have I eaten a meal', he said, 'that did me such good or tasted so delicious.'

Only one prince escaped, but he would eventually found a new paradise kingdom in the west. Prince Abd al-Rahman, grandson of the poetry-lover Hisham and son of his heir Muawiya who had died young, fled from Damascus with his brother and Badr, a Greek slave. Hunted by Bloodshedder's henchmen, they were trapped at the Euphrates, where the brother was beheaded. But Abd al-Rahman swam for his life, the start of a five-year adventure across Syria and Africa, towards the last place where his family still had friends: Spain.

Bloodshedder moved the capital to Kufa, closer to the Persian homelands of the revolutionaries, Damascus being tainted with Umayya filthiness, and his success was capped by advances towards the borders of China's Western Region. Arabs, Chinese, Tibetans and Turks fought in ever-changing alliances. The Chinese, backed by Turkic allies, repelled Bloodshedder's armies until a clash at Talas where the Turks switched sides. The Arabs won, but this was a minor encounter compared with the catastrophe that was enveloping the Tang.

Emperor Xuanzong had ruled conscientiously for decades, but now, beguiled by Taoist alchemy and depressed by traitorous sons, he lost focus. He liquidated three of his sons, leaving power to a minister named Li Linfu who recruited a professional army that included Sogdians from central Asia. Among them was an ostentatious, illiterate and Brobdingnagian soldier, An Lushan. As a boy An Lushan had been arrested for stealing, as a general almost executed for insubordination, yet he proved a master manipulator of his patronizing Tang masters, who fatally underestimated him as he played the fat, coarse, devoted bumpkin. When Emperor Xuanzong asked what was in his belly, he replied, 'Other than a faithful heart, there is nothing else,' and at other times he pretended not to know what a crown prince was, insisting, 'I'm

the Umayya princes. Speaking Coptic, Greek and Arabic, Makurian kings ruled from a Constantinopolitan gold-encrusted palace in Dongola, a city where wealthy homes boasted ceramic lavatories, which did not appear in Europe for centuries. Their cathedral at Faris featured exquisite frescoes. When the Abbasiya caliphs demanded arrears of 5,000 slaves, King Zakarios sent his son Georgios to Baghdad to negotiate. The kingdom flourished until the thirteenth century.

a barbarian! I don't understand formal ceremony.' But he had a nose for weakness and understood that the essential person was not the emperor but a certain concubine.

At fourteen Yang Guifei was married to one of the emperor's sons but spotting her beauty as she bathed at Huaqing springs – 'the hot water running down her glistening jade-like body', as a poet put it – the sixty-nine-year-old emperor ordered her enrolment as a Taoist nun so that she could remain in the palace; meanwhile he foisted another wife on his son. Yang had a porcelain complexion and a curvaceous figure which she displayed in a bodice she had designed herself.

Yang was also irrepressible, quick to joy, fast to fury. The rows she and Xuanzong had were tumultuous. Finally the offended emperor sent her away. 'My offence deserves death, and it is fortunate that His Imperial Majesty did not kill me,' she wrote to him. 'I will forever leave the palace. My gold, jade and treasures were all given me by His Imperial Majesty, and it would be inappropriate for me to offer them back to him. Only what my parents gave me I would dare give.' Typically she was keeping the jewels.

When she cut off some tresses and sent them to the emperor, he could not resist her scent and ordered his eunuch Gao Lishi to summon her back. Of course she returned. Wherever she was, Xuanzong ensured that her beloved lychees were delivered by relays of horses and that Gao served her every wish. He also promoted her cousin to chief minister. This paladin, An Lushan, was so sycophantic that she proposed to adopt him as her son, leading to a comical scene in which Consort Yang dressed the gargantuan, bewhiskered old ruffian in baby clothes and bathed him as he gurgled, a favour which he repaid by always bowing first to her: 'Barbarians bow to mothers first before fathers.' Xuanzong found all this charming, and raised An to prince.

Yet as the empire was rocked by floods and rebellions, the emperor failed to control a feud between the chief minister and General An Lushan. In December 755, mustering his army, he rebelled and quickly defeated the Tang armies. The brittle regime collapsed at once. An Lushan took Luoyang, where he declared himself emperor. Emperor Xuanzong, Consort Yang, her cousin the minister and eunuch Gao, guarded by cavalry, fled Chang'an towards Sichuan. The soldiers killed the minister, then seized the emperor, demanding the end of the Yangs and the execution of his mistress. The emperor could not bear the thought, but Gao persuaded him to go ahead. Yang asked to die by silk rather than beheading, so that her looks would remain perfect for the afterlife. Eunuch Gao strangled her and buried her with a sachet of perfumes.

An Lushan occupied the other capital, Chang'an, amid apocalyptic scenes. 'I remember when we first fled the rebels, / Hurrying north over dangerous roads,' wrote an eyewitness, Du Fu, a government official and China's greatest poet, who witnessed and experienced the suffering of millions of refugees:

> Night deepened on Pengya Road,
> The moon shone over Whitewater Hills.
> A whole family endlessly trudging,
> Begging without shame from the people we met.

Just months after capturing the two biggest cities on earth, An Lushan, holding court in Luoyang, was going blind, probably from diabetes, and was now so obese that he supposedly crushed a horse to death and it took a team of eunuchs to pull him out of bed. His sons plotted. He executed one of them.

In December 757, another son murdered An and seized the throne. But the Tang generals, now under the former crown prince, Emperor Suzong,* moved against the An family. Unable to muster large armies to retake Chang'an, Suzong turned to the khagan of the Uighurs, Bayan-chur Khan, who had hacked a new empire out of the ruins of the Goturk confederacy, based in his Mongolian capital, Ordu-Baliq, and was ruling eastern Siberia, Mongolia and most of central Asia. Bayanchur's Uighur troops joined the Tang armies and took Chang'an and Luoyang, which they were allowed to loot for three days. Suzong gave them 20,000 bales of silk and married his own daughter, Princess Xiaoguo, to Bayanchur, the only emperor's daughter ever married to a barbarian. But Suzong and his son Daizong still struggled to control the empire as the Tibetans, who had already conquered Nepal and Assam as far the Bay of Bengal, seized most of central Asia.

In 763, the Tibetan emperor Trisong Detsen dispatched 200,000 troops into China, storming Chang'an. The Tang soon pushed the Tibetans back with Uighur help. Tang gratitude was short-lived: the Uighurs were massacred and driven out, though their khagans ruled their vast empire into the ninth century.† The Tang had been fatally damaged: the rebellion and its sequels were among the most catastrophic wars

---

* Xuanzong had agreed to hand power to his son Suzong. As retired emperor, he sent Gao to retrieve Consort Yang's body, but it had decayed: the eunuch just brought back the bag of scents.

† In 779, meeting some Manichaean priests as he looted the Chinese capital, the Uighur khagan Bogu converted his empire to Manichaeanism. Though he was then murdered by his Tengrist chief minister, the Uighurs remained Manichaean until they later converted first to Buddhism and then to Islam.

in human history, with thirty-six million killed or displaced. 'Weeping in the wilderness, how many families know of war and loss,' wrote Du Fu. 'All word of events in the human world lost in those vast silent spaces.'*

At the height of his crisis, Emperor Suzong, bearing no grudge after the modest Arab victory at Talas, asked al-Mansur for help, and the caliph may have sent a small Arab contingent to China. It is said that enslaved Chinese prisoners brought the Chinese invention of paper to the Arab world, whence it ultimately reached Europe.

Without al-Mansur, the Abbasiya caliphate might have been a passing moment; instead he became founder of the most powerful state in the world, ruled by the Muhammad family for the next two centuries. It was when Caliph Bloodshedder died of smallpox at the age of thirty-two that his remarkable elder brother took the title al-Mansur – the Victorious.

Tall, thin, leathery-skinned, yellow-bearded, saffron-dyed, al-Mansur sensed that the greatest threat to him came from his enforcer, Ibn Muslim. Inviting Ibn Muslim to visit him in his tent, even while his soldiers were in the camp, al-Mansur clapped his hands, the sign for his bodyguard to slit the Khorasani's throat. The body was wrapped in a carpet and left in a corner of the tent. When al-Mansur's adviser asked where the warlord was, the caliph replied, 'Rolled up over there.' The remains were dumped in the Tigris. When Muhammad the Pure Soul, leader of the Ali family, senior line of House Muhammad, rebelled, al-Mansur had him killed and displayed his head on a silver platter.

After moving between Kufa and armed camps, al-Mansur decided to build his own capital and, rising at dawn every day, he supervised every detail, earning himself the nickname Abul Dawanik, Father of Pennies. Choosing a location on the Tigris, surrounded by fertile land, twenty miles north of Ctesiphon–Seleucia, whose bricks he purloined for its walls, he built a round city Medinat al-Mansur, soon known as Baghdad, setting up court in a vast Palace of the Golden Gate on the west bank of the river topped with a 130-foot gold dome. He himself often lived in a small tent. Then he moved into 'a tiny apartment of one room' with 'a felt mat and nothing else except his quilt, pillow and blanket'.

---

* The Tang ruled a rump empire until 879, when they finally fell in an apocalyptic dystopia as armies of starving peasants harvested 1,000 humans a day for food at a time when 'human flesh was more plentiful than dogmeat'. Chang'an was destroyed; after a thousand years, a world vanished.

Pious and austere, tempered by his obscure beginnings and violent rise, al-Mansur did not drink or party. He also respected his wife Arwa, descended from Yemenite kings, but he did prize a Christian concubine with the evocative name Restless Butterfly.

The wealth of the caliphate was based on an efficient tax system and on trade not just between east and west but also with east Africa. Arab merchants were starting to trade with the African coast, conveying to Iraq not just ivory and spices but humans: thousands of black slaves, the *zanj*, were sold to work the plantations of Iraq – the start of the east African slave trade.

Al-Mansur controlled the government through a *wazir* or vizier, premier of the empire, but it was a dangerous job. After eight years, al-Mansur's first vizier and his family were executed, but by the mid-760s al-Mansur had found a sophisticated minister. This was Khalid, aristocratic Persian son of Barmak, a Buddhist priest from Balkh (Afghanistan) who had been respected as a doctor, treating Abd al-Malik's sons Maslama and Hisham, before converting to Islam and joining the bureaucracy. Now as vizier Khalid became a munificent patron – the second family of the empire. Al-Mansur kept a wizened eye on his courtiers, once suddenly demanding a payment from Khalid al-Barmaki, who managed to pay it by borrowing from all the grandees that he had helped.

In 758, al-Mansur sent his crown prince al-Mahdi to govern Khorasan, where the boy was joined by Khalid's son Yahya. When al-Mahdi's favourite concubine, Khayzuran, gave birth to a son, Haroun, Yahya's wife was given the honour of breastfeeding the baby prince while Khayzuran did the same for the Barmaki baby, Fadl. These milk-sharing arrangements gave the Barmaki a special intimacy.

Holding court in his *iwan*, with a mace by his side, al-Mansur was guarded by 4,000 mace-wielding palace guards, who doubled as executioners, and was attended by 700 courtiers in black, standing in ranks. He created a network of spies around the *barid*, the imperial mail. 'I always need four people at my door,' he said, 'the judge, the police chief and the tax collector – and the chief of the *barid* to give me reliable intelligence on the first three.' Al-Mansur relished the liquidation of his enemies, and was said to keep a secret cellar where he stored the heads of the Ali family, each meticulously labelled.

Only one enemy had escaped him: the boy prince of the Umayya, Abd al-Rahman.

THE FALCON OF AL-ANDALUS AND THE CROWNED DOVES OF AIX: ABD AL-RAHMAN AND CHARLEMAGNE

Chased by al-Mansur's hitmen, Abd al-Rahman with his Greek slave Badr moved westwards in a series of escapades. On one occasion he had to hide under the fragrant skirts of a beautiful female cousin, an experience that he happily remembered in old age: 'I recall your earthy aroma to this day!' Finally he reached Morocco and, after sending his freedman to test support, he arrived in Gibraltar in 755, winning his nickname the Arriver (al-Dakhil), gathering followers: in 756, he declared himself amir of al-Andalus. Al-Mansur sent an army to crush him but the Arriver routed it, pickling the heads of the generals and despatched them in giftboxes all the way to the caliph who was on *hajj* in Mecca. 'God be praised for placing a sea between us and this devil!' al-Mansur exclaimed. 'Who deserves the title Falcon of Quraysh?'

'You, O Caliph,' replied his courtiers.

He shook his head. 'The Falcon is Abd al-Rahman.'

Abd al-Rahman, then aged twenty-six, spent his life fighting to keep the title, but he also started to beautify his capital Cordoba, crafting a mosque out of a Visigothic church that would become a wonder of the west with its forest of columns borrowed from Roman ruins across Spain and perhaps designed to recall the palm trees of Syria. He never ceased to miss Syria, comparing himself to a palm tree who was also 'a stranger in the west / Far from your oriental home, like me unblessed . . . / You would weep if you had tears to pour / For my companions on Euphrates' shore'. Yet the Falcon could not rest on his laurels. His enemies invited Charlemagne, king of Francia, to cross the Pyrenees and destroy him.

Bathing in his pool at the hot springs of Aix (Aachen), at the centre of his court of paladins, scholars, concubines and sons, Charlemagne, suffering gout and aching after weeks in the saddle, would swim a few lengths then question his Anglo-Saxon scribe – 'Master Alcuin, allow me to ask you a few questions' – on the planets or Pliny, while his mischievous daughters flirted with his courtiers.

From the moment he ascended the throne in 768 at the age of twenty, Charlemagne, blond, giant and irrepressibly energetic, galloped, broadsword in hand, from one end of Europe to the other, dominating the continent more than anyone else until Napoleon and Hitler, with the difference that he ruled for forty years – and virtually every monarch in Europe down to 1918 was descended from him. He outmanoeuvred his brother, along with anyone else who threatened his power, conquered Aquitaine and married Princess Desiderata, daughter of the Lombard king of Italy, Desiderius, who almost immediately moved to take over Rome. Pope Hadrian appealed to Charlemagne, who switched sides, routed Desiderius and seized the crown of Italy, in the process rejecting his Lombard wife and marrying a German princess, Hildegard.

Charlemagne loved women, marrying five times. Hildegard bore him nine children before dying at twenty-six, but he had many more – eighteen in all – with a host of concubines. This royal brood naturally revolved around the strapping king, six foot five, usually clad in simple Frankish garb, with silk-trimmed tunic, fur coats, linen trousers and gold-hilted sword, but his extraordinary confidence and ambition were not effortless: he often suffered insomnia, getting up five times a night and then holding court in bed the next day.

He initially considered marrying his seven daughters to foreign princes, but he could not bear to be parted from them – and there are hints of incestuous liaisons.* Notorious for their games, teasing and sexual adventures, the girls were like 'little crowned doves', wrote the Anglo-Saxon courtier Alcuin, that 'flit around the chambers of the palace, come to your windows' and then 'like wild horses, break in at the door of your chamber'. The 'crowned doves' were hard to restrain, being young, alluring and fearless, each of them made pregnant out of wedlock by young courtiers, one by an abbot. So brutal at war, Charlemagne's court was cultured† and easy-going, tolerating this erotic atmosphere while also supporting the papal campaign to promote single sacred marriages, discouraging annulments, concubinage and cousin marriages.‡ At the same time the popes encouraged the inheritance of property only by legitimate sons. The Church claimed the right to inherit lands that lacked legitimate heirs, and by 900 it owned a third of western farmland. Charlemagne, who linked his own power to that of the papacy, backed this European version of marriage, fixated on legitimacy and sex (not having much) that was peculiarly Christian. European families developed differently from those of Asia and Africa,

---

* Charlemagne planned to marry his son Charles to Aelfflaed, the daughter of King Offa of Mercia, but when the Anglo-Saxon demanded Charlemagne's daughter Bertha, he cancelled the marriage. The minor Britannic king had overreached.

† Charlemagne educated his daughters as well as his sons. He believed it was his mission to halt the decline in education during recent centuries and to preside over a restoration of faith, order and culture. Inviting scholars to his capital at Aix, he sponsored the *scriptoria* of monasteries which produced around 10,000 exquisite illuminated manuscripts: the Dagulf Psalter was produced for Pope Hadrian, others for wider distribution. Aristotle and Plato were translated into Latin. Ovid, Pliny and other Latin masters were copied on to vellum.

‡ Marriages to sisters-in-law and mothers-in-law were banned as incestuous – hence these phrases, which are still in use.

where people still remain loyal to wider clans. Increasingly Europeans married once, loyal to their nuclear families; they married later and had fewer children; some women never married since they could no longer become junior wives; property was inherited by legitimate eldest sons; and moralistic people could signal their virtue by living according to Church rules. Sex for procreation was God's work, for pleasure a delicious taboo. This changed Europe, but it didn't change Charlemagne, who enjoyed concubines unabashed. It did affect his sons, however, as they jostled for power.

Yet Charlemagne lived for war, sacred war. Every summer he went to war on one of eight different fronts where his heavy cavalry on towering destrier warhorses seemed to give his armies a superiority over all other forces. He granted property and titles to his magnates in return for the supply of cavalry, a feudal relationship between king and vassal that came to militarize and shape society in hierarchies that were regarded as natural and sacred. 'It's our role', he told Pope Leo III, 'to defend by force of arms the Holy Church of Christ everywhere from the attacks of pagans and the devastations of infidels.' He was preparing for the imminent End of Days, his respect for the Church a means of promoting eternal life as well as his own dynasty – partners in power and salvation. To the west were the Muslims, and it is easy to forget that at this time eastern and northern Europe – eastern Germany, Poland, Scandinavia, Baltics, Russia – were pagan. Charlemagne's mission in life was to convert these monsters – or kill them all.

KILLING THE DEMONS: THE SWORD OF CHARLEMAGNE

'Baptism or death!' was Charlemagne's offer. Mass killing was the solution. In 772, Charlemagne attacked the Saxons, who worshipped the gods Thor, Wotan and Saxnot, and burned down their sacred World Tree, the shrine of the Irminsul, believed to support the sky. It was the start of a thirty-year mission to eliminate the 'cult of demons'. In 782, Charlemagne slaughtered 4,500 Saxons to make the point: they must embrace Christianity or be 'entirely eliminated'.

In 778, an Arab rebel from Zaragoza arrived at this court and invited Charlemagne to attack the Falcon, Abd al-Rahman. The king crossed the Pyrenees and took Girona, north of Barcelona, but Zaragoza closed its gates, and after a terrifying retreat across the Pyrenees, retold in the chivalric *Song of Roland*, Charlemagne just made it back to Aquitaine.

Undaunted, he switched eastwards to swallow Bavaria, a move which brought him into contact with the Avars, once nomadic pagans who ruled Pannonia (Hungary/Romania), which now also fell to Charlemagne. He started to see himself as a Christian Augustus, a project made possible by some shocking atrocities in Constantinople, seat of the only real Roman emperor. But now a murderous filicidal woman was on the throne.

CHARLEMAGNE'S CORONATION, HAROUN'S WEDDING

Irene of Athens, now fifty years old, an emperor's widow who was guiding Constantinople out of its frenzy of icon smashing, was keen to appease Charlemagne, who could threaten her southern Italian holdings. In 781, Irene as regent negotiated marriage between her young son, Emperor Constantine VI, and Charlemagne's daughter Rotrude, but both Irene and Charlemagne delayed the wedding. Constantine was both inept and vicious: he was defeated in battle by the Muslims, and when an uncle rebelled he not only blinded him but tore out the tongues of his other four uncles. His mother was convinced she would do better. In 797, she deposed her twenty-seven-year-old son and blinded him. This demonstration of female misrule convinced Charlemagne and the Franks that the Roman throne was vacant. It helped that Pope Leo III was so terrorized by the grandees fighting for control of central Italy that he would agree to anything to win Charlemagne's protection. Indeed, as he was negotiating the Frank's new title, assassins attacked Leo and tried to blind him. In Rome on Christmas Day 800, Charlemagne and his sons donned Roman togas as the pope crowned him 'Emperor of the Romans'. Charlemagne's first act was to try and execute 300 of the conspirators who had just tried to assassinate Leo.

His new title would need Constantinople's recognition. Irene considered marrying Charlemagne herself, but she was then deposed and exiled to spin wool on Lesbos. Charlemagne extended the hand of friendship to the caliph, Haroun al-Rashid. This was a way of putting pressure on Constantinople, which had just blundered into a war with Baghdad. Charlemagne sent gifts of Frisian cloaks, Spanish horses and hunting dogs to the caliph in Baghdad. The caliph sent him an array of gifts – an ivory chess set, a caliphal tent, an elephant named Abul-Abbas (walked all the way from Baghdad to Aix by his Jewish envoy) and an astonishing work of Arab sophistication, a water clock in which knights

appeared out of little doors every hour.* Charlemagne could not help but
be impressed by the splendours of Haroun al-Rashid.

In 1782, Haroun's wedding to his double first cousin Zubaida was
said to have been the greatest party of all time. Held at the Eternity
Palace in Baghdad, the wedding was hosted by the groom's father Caliph
al-Mahdi and his mother Khayzuran, and every guest received 'goody-
bags' of jewels, scents and handfuls of gold dinars. The groom was
eighteen, the young bride was presented with the bejewelled sleeveless
badana, seized from the Umayya and handed down through the family.
Both were grandchildren of Caliph al-Mansur. It was he who had given
the bride the nickname Butterpat – Zubaida.

Haroun's mother was his champion. The slim and beautiful Khayzuran had been kidnapped and sold into slavery, until spotted by Crown
Prince al-Mahdi, who fell in love with her and then freed and married
her, giving her the name Reed – Khayzuran. Refusing to remain in the
harem, she revelled in her prominence.

The diffident and shy Haroun was not the heir, but like so many royal
scions dreamed of retiring with his lovely Zubaida to an estate away
from what he called the 'boiler room' of Baghdad. Yet he had already
shown his acumen: he had led an army that raided all the way to the
Bosphoros before Empress Irene bought off the caliphate with golden
tribute; the caliph then awarded him the title al-Rashid – the Righteous.

Haroun's elder brother al-Hadi succeeded as caliph, but, beset by
rebellions, abandoned Baghdad and clashed with their mother Khayzuran, whom he tried to kill. In September 786, al-Hadi, lying sick,
was suffocated by the girls of the harem and Khayzuran took control,
advised by Yahya the Barmaki. Granting the troops a bonus, they organized Haroun's acclamation. Caliph Haroun then appointed his mentor,
Yahya the Barmaki, as vizier: 'I've invested you with the rule of my flock.
Govern as you think is right.' The Barmaki were almost family. Haroun
had been brought up with Yahya's playboy son Jafar, and his first mistress was probably one of Yahya's concubines, Hailana, who begged the
prince to rescue her from the old minister. When Haroun voiced his
desires, Yahya gave him Hailana.

---

* Haroun allowed the Patriarch of Jerusalem to send Charlemagne a key to the Holy Sepulchre, the start of a new west European interest in the Holy City, where Christians enjoyed
tolerance – for the moment. Charlemagne's relations with Haroun in Baghdad worked in
both east and west. To the east, Constantinople was defeated by the caliph, encouraging
the emperors to appease the Franks; Charlemagne got Rome and Ravenna; Constantinople got Venice, Dalmatia and southern Italy. In the west, Haroun was also the enemy of
the Umayya of al-Andalus. In 797, Hisham, Abd al-Rahman's son, ordered a successful
invasion of Aquitaine (sixty years after the supposedly decisive victory of Charles Martel).

Haroun, often wearing disguise, partied with Jafar, as portrayed in *The Thousand and One Nights*. In 'The Porter and the Three Ladies of Baghdad', a girl shops sensuously for delicious foods and scents – Omani peaches, Egyptian cucumbers, Damascene nenuphars (water lilies), ambergris and musk – before returning to a party house where a procuress warned them that discretion was essential. They were then joined by Haroun and Jafar for an orgy in the world's greatest metropolis, obsessed with music and poetry, food and sex.[*]

THE THOUSAND AND ONE NIGHTS:
THE CALIPH AND THE SINGER-STARS OF BAGHDAD

Star poets and enslaved singers, trained in Medina, were bid for by the caliph or the Barmaki for vast sums 'like football transfers', writes Hugh Kennedy. 'Girls would be traded up gaining in value in each transaction.' These enslaved superstars, part courtesan, part artiste, played men off against each other, wrote poetry and often enjoyed the sex in ways that would be unthinkable in today's Islamic world.[†]

Haroun was devoted to his mother Khayzuran and happy with his wife Zubaida, who behaved and dressed like an empress, wearing bejewelled boots and slippers, travelling with an escort of eunuchs and concubines. Khayzuran ruled the *hurram* – the sanctuary or harem – where Haroun kept his wives, 2,000 female slaves and his children.

Boredom must have played a large part in the life within the harem, boredom vying with desire: there are tales of Haroun's girls keen to party even if they were risking their lives, and there are hints of lesbian consolations in the niches of the *hurram*: during the reign of Haroun's brother al-Hadi, one of his courtiers recalled how a eunuch carried in a tray covered in a cloth.

'Lift the cover!' said Caliph al-Hadi.

---

[*] Baghdad's luxuries arrived in huge dhows eastwards from Egypt and Africa and westwards from China on round trips of 12,600 miles. Around 828, a ship, built in Persia out of African mahogany and Indian teak, held together by Malay twine, sailed from Guangzhou with silks, spices and 60,000 tiles, 18 silver ingots, gold ornaments, 55,000 glazed bowls from Changsha, 763 inkpots (for the poets of Baghdad), 915 spice jars and 1,635 ewers decorated with lotuses for Buddhist customers in Indo-China and geometric designs for Muslims, along with jars and utensils from Vietnam and Thailand. It sank near the island of Belitung, off Java, and the wreck was not discovered until 1998.

[†] In rare cases, these showgirls could become free and rich: Arib, later the favourite poet-singer of Haroun's son al-Mamun, was a superstar who sang for five caliphs. When she died at ninety-six, she was a wealthy landowner.

And there were the heads of two slaves. And by God I have never seen more beautiful faces or lovelier hair. Jewels were entwined and the air was fragrant with their perfumes.

'Do you know what they had done?' asked the caliph. 'They fell in love with each other, meeting for immoral purposes. I sent a eunuch to watch them. He told me they were together. I caught them under a quilt making love and killed them.' Then he said, 'Take away the heads, boy,' and carried on the conversation as if nothing had happened.

Zubaida, the definition of virtuous Arab beauty, was sometimes alarmed by Haroun's love affairs, once giving him ten new girls to distract him. Haroun and Zubaida had one son together, al-Amin, who was thus a double member of House Abbas. He had other children by twenty-four of the girls. When the concubine Marajil died young, Zubaida adopted her son, the future caliph al-Mamun.

Haroun had to have the best slave singers, paying a colossal 70,000 dirhams for 'the Girl with the Mole'. But he then insisted on her telling him if she had slept with her former master. When she admitted 'just once', he gave her away to a governor. Sometimes even he could not get every singer he wanted. The star of the day was the gifted Inan. Haroun sent his African eunuch Musr to pay 100,000 gold dinars for her, but the owner would not sell, driving the caliph to such distraction that his mother intervened. He claimed he only wanted Inan for her poetry, in which case, it was pointed out to him, why not sleep with a male poet? Haroun laughed.

Haroun wasn't the only one in love with Inan. Abu Nuwas (Son of the Dangling Locks) was an outrageous bisexual literary rock star who craved Inan: 'Find pity for a man yearning for just a small drop from you?' Inan replied:

Is it *you* that you mean by this?
Be off with you! Go and masturbate!

And he answered:

If I do that, I fear,
You'll be jealous of my hand.

Abu Nuwas celebrated the seduction of girls and boys with verses depicting sexual antics and impotent failures. The wantonness of Baghdad women intimidated him. 'I found myself in the middle of large sea,' he wrote, unable to cope with this lubricious enthusiasm. 'I cried out to a young man "Save me." If he hadn't thrown me a rope, I'd have fallen to the bottom of that sea. After this I swore . . . I'd only travel on back-sides.' He was happier with male lovers: 'He prized open the boy's arse with the edge of his sword . . . Show pity and compassion only where fitting. Squeeze his balls gently.' He relished male beauty: 'How lucky is the one who can land a kiss on him, and garner what his trousers hold!' He recounted nights of drinking and gay sex, favouring court eunuchs and Christian monks:

> Auspicious stars had risen on the night
> When drunkard assaulted drunkard
> We passed the time kowtowing to the Devil
> Until monks sounded the bells at dawn
> And the youth left, donning delightful robes
> Stained with my iniquitous behaviour.

He loved the company of showgirls, recalling four of them discussing sex: 'My vagina is like a split pomegranate,' said one, 'and smells of ground amber. Lucky the one who gets me when I'm shaven.'

Haroun refused to be the poet's patron. Instead Abu Nuwas became the lover of al-Amin, the heir, who was less interested in concubines than in boy eunuchs, leading his mother Zubaida to dress her young servant girls in turban, male tunics and sashes with hair done up in bangs and sidecurls. This sparked a fashion for gamine page girls known as *ghulamiyyat*.

Yet pleasure had its limits. Haroun made the *hajj* ten times; Zabaida's palace resembled a 'beehive' with so many girls reciting the Quran; and in 803 the caliph managed both a *hajj* and a successful jihad, defeating the Roman emperor, who had ended payment of Irene's tribute. Haroun was less playful than his reputation implied. When he turned, he was deadly.

BRING ME THE HEAD OF JAFAR, MOTHERFUCKER

One night in early 803, Haroun partied into the night as usual with Jafar al-Barmaki. But when they went their separate ways the caliph established himself on a boat in the Euphrates and ordered his African eunuch Musr to take his trusted guards and bring back the head of Jafar.

The Barmaki, vizier Yahya and son Jafar, had overreached. Jafar sometimes entered Haroun's rooms without being announced. Haroun had executed the head of House Ali, yet may have discovered that the Barmaki were in contact with the rival dynasty. Their taxes had provoked

revolts; their grandeur alienated the army. Distrusting many of his courtiers Haroun prepared their destruction.

Jafar tried to play for time. 'He only ordered this while drunk,' he
told Musr. 'Don't do anything till morning, or at least discuss it with
him again.' Musr double-checked the order. Haroun's reply? 'Bring me
Jafar's head, motherfucker!'

Simultaneously he summoned Sindi, a devoted freedman, who was
sent with guards to arrest all the other Barmaki. Yahya died in prison.
Jafar's head was brought to Haroun, who spat at it and sent it to Sindi:
the head was then displayed on the bridges of Baghdad. The Barmakis'
downfall astonished everyone.

In February 808, Haroun left Baghdad with his favourite son al-
Mamun to put down unrest in Khorasan where the boy was governor.
Haroun agonized over the succession. 'If I choose Amin, my people will
be unhappy, if Mamun, my family will be.' The caliph compromised:
al-Amin, son of Zubaida, was to be senior monarch while al-Mamun
would rule the east. In March Haroun, then forty-seven, suddenly died;
al-Amin succeeded, supported by Zubaida. Al-Mamun respected the
arrangement, basing himself in Merv (Turkmenistan).

One of the few who were happy with this was Abu Nuwas, al-Amin's
lover, though even the poet was careful what he wrote about this friend:
'I am in love but can't say with whom; I fear him who fears no one; I feel
for my head and wonder if it is still attached to my body!' Yet al-Amin's
feckless incompetence and homosexual preferences destroyed him.*

By 810, the caliphal brothers were estranged; both raised armies. Al-
Mamun's Khorasani army defeated al-Amin and laid siege to Baghdad,
where a tragedy began to unfold. Street youths known as Naked Ones
fought the invaders in the streets; mangonels (stone-throwing artillery)
bombarded the city: 'Here lies a stranger far from home; headless in
the midst of the road; caught in the middle of the fighting; and no one
knows which side he was on.'

Al-Amin tried to escape, but his boat capsized and he was captured:
'Zubaida's brat' was thrown into prison, where he found himself with
a former courtier. 'Come closer and hold me tight in your arms,'
said al-Amin shaking. 'What will my brother do? Kill me or forgive
me?'

---

* 'The caliph's sodomy is amazing,' went a satirical poem of the time. 'While the vizier's
passive homosexuality is even more so. One of them buggers and the other is buggered;
that's the only difference between them. If only the two managed to use each other . . . but
Amin plunged into the eunuch Kawthar; while being fucked by donkeys didn't satisfy the
other . . .'

After midnight, armed Persians erupted into the cell. Al-Amin stood up: 'We are from God and to Him we return.' The Persians beheaded him and sent the head to al-Mamun, who wept, then told his advisers: 'What's done is done. So start thinking how to explain it.' Facing Shiite revolts, al-Mamun appeased the House of Ali, promising to make Ali al-Rida his heir. But once the danger had passed, he ordered the poisoning of Imam Ali (known later as Ali Reza, a saint of Shiite Iran). In 819 he arrived in devastated Baghdad and started to restore the city.

Good-looking, talented and curious, al-Mamun was an original. He was kind to al-Amin's mother Zubaida, calling her the 'best of mothers' – and she forgave him. The court was different, more Persian than Arab, but al-Mamun commissioned translations of Greek and Indian works, which were stored in his House of Wisdom, an old institution – library-cum-academy – dating from the Sasanians.* Meanwhile he oversaw a flowering of science, medicine, astronomy and geography, all of which fascinated the poetry-writing caliph: 'If I flew up to the starry vault; / And joined heaven's westward flow,' he wrote, 'I'd learn as I traversed the sky, / The fate of all things below.'†

Mumun was the ultimate patron of *adab*, refined and urbane literature. The author al-Tahiri celebrated food and sex in his books *Adultery and its Enjoyment*, *Stories about Slave Boys* and, bracingly, *Masturbation*. Writers could even celebrate female sexual pleasure in a way that sounds very modern. Al-Jahiz (the Bug-Eyed), born in Basra and descended from an enslaved *zanj* African, won al-Mamun's patronage with essays on the Quran, translations of Aristotle and worthy polemics but preferred to write about the superiority of black men over white (a subject close to his heart). His *Pleasures of Girls and Boys Compared* was a compendium of interviews with both sexes about sexual pleasure.‡

* Arab society was highly sophisticated but the House of Wisdom did not singlehandedly rescue Greek learning for benighted, primitive, medieval Europe. Its importance was exaggerated by western historians after 9/11 to demonstrate US–European ignorance of Arab culture. Those accounts have somehow forgotten the existence of Constantinople: all Greek literature was available in Constantinople for another 500 years. Charlemagne's scholars were also translating Greek works into Latin, and other works were translated at the Umayya court in Cordoba.

† Al-Mamun commissioned the Banu Musa brothers to calculate the world's circumference and the Persian polymath al-Khwarizmi to write his mathematical treatise *Al-Jabr* (the origin of algebra) that helped introduce modern figures and decimal points, importing the zero from India. His name also inspired a constant of modern life – the algorithm. For those of us who do not understand mathematics, Abu Musa Jabir ibn Hayyan – known as Geber in Europe – inspired another word: gibberish.

‡ Jahiz quotes a grand dame of Medina who was asked by young girls if sex was enjoyable. She recalled a pilgrimage with Caliph Othman: 'On the way back, my husband looked at

Al-Mamun hired Jahiz as tutor to his sons, but they were frightened by the writer's bulging eyes.*

As ruler and imam, sympathetic to the Shia approach and suspicious of literal-minded following of the Hadith, al-Mamun insisted that the Quran was created from God's word, not literally written by God, and forced his scholars to agree. Jihad was a duty, security a necessity: in 830, al-Mamun, along with his much younger brother al-Mutasim, attacked the Romans. Al-Mutasim persuaded the caliph to buy Turkish slaves – *ghilman*, tough horse archers with Asiatic faces. In 836, as caliph, al-Mutasim moved from Baghdad to a new capital at Samara where he hoped to be protected by his Turkic praetorians. Instead they took over. In 861, the *ghilman* murdered a caliph. Discontent among enslaved *zanj* on the sugar-cane plantations and irrigation works of southern Iraq exploded in 869 into a rebellion of Marsh Arabs and free and enslaved Africans that lasted for fourteen years. It led to the fall of Basra, and the slaughter of all its inhabitants; in 879 the rebels even came close to Baghdad. Some 500,000 people, even a million, were killed in the mayhem, which discouraged Arab rulers in the future from using African slave labour. The revolt fatally weakened the caliphate, just as its Spanish rival was thriving.

THE BLACKBIRD OF CORDOBA

The grandson of the Falcon, Abd al-Rahman II, personified the new ideal of Andalusian machismo and cultured *adab*, writing poetry and promoting new fashions while fighting Charlemagne's son Charles the Pious, one of the three who inherited the empire.

While Charlemagne's heirs – known after his Latin name Carolus as the Carolingians – fought each other, Abd al-Rahman II held court in Cordoba, which now outstripped Baghdad in its sophistication, a culture personified by a person of colour who called himself the Blackbird and was patronized by the amir. Ziryab, child of *zanj* sold to Baghdad, was a connoisseur of civilized living who was invited to Cordoba by a Jewish musician. Ziryab not only introduced Persian and Iraqi cuisine, poetry

---

me and I looked at him. He fancied me and I fancied him, and he leaped on me just as Othman's camels were passing. I cried out loud as there came to me what comes to the daughters of Adam. And all five hundred camels scattered. It took two hours to collect them all.'

* After a long career in Baghdad, Jahiz's patrons were executed and he retired to Basra. There, literary to the last, he was crushed and killed by a heap of books, the ideal death of any bibliophile. Abu Nawus had died soon after his patron Caliph al-Amin.

and wit to al-Andalus but also developed the guitar when he added strings to his *oud*, and founded a music school for girls as well as boys. He invented the concept of the meal that started with soup or salad, moved on to savouries and finished with sweets, served on different plates; fostered the idea of different fashions for the seasons; devised early versions of toothpaste and deodorant (litharge, a lead monoxide compound) and a new hairstyle, a Mohican mullet, with bangs at the front, long at the back and short at the sides, favoured by *zanj* in Baghdad.

Yet the amir, not just an aficionado of fashionistas and singing girls, was constantly fighting northern Christians and internal challengers, aided by his enslaved corps of *ghilman*, and a vizier, Nasr, a Christian nobleman captured and castrated by the Muslims. When the amir fell ill, the eunuch tried to fix the succession by bribing a doctor to finish him off with poison. The doctor's wife informed the amir, who waited until Nasr brought his 'medicine' then made him drink it himself.

Then in 844 the era of refined *adab* was interrupted by a terrifying visitation: a fleet of fifty-four longships appeared out of nowhere bearing a race of shaggy axe-wielding pagans who attacked Seville while another fleet stormed al-Ushbana (Lisbon) and Cadiz. The Vikings had arrived.

Rurikovichi and the House of Basil

THE MAGIC: RURIK AND THE VIKINGS — BERSERK WAR, GROUP SEX AND HUMAN SACRIFICE

Abd al-Rahman II built a fleet to repel the Vikings, using Greek Fire, but al-Andalus was not the only region suffering. The Vikings attacked north Africa too, yet the most intense raids were already hitting the Frankish and British coasts.

In 793, a flotilla attacked the monastery at Lindisfarne, ravaging Northumbria and the sacred island of Iona, before returning to assault Scotland and Ireland. Charlemagne himself witnessed the first raids on his shores, and was able to strike back. Now, in 845, a fleet of 120 long-ships carrying 5,000 Vikings sailed up the Seine and attacked Paris. The invaders sacrificed Frankish prisoners to their god Odin and departed only when the king of West Francia, later emperor, Charles the Bald, Charlemagne's grandson, paid them Danegeld of 7,000 livres of silver and gold.

The war bands, led by lords and kings, had originally sought slaves and loot, but now they started to settle, founding kingdoms in Dublin, the isles of western Scotland, and York, the start of an advance into England that threatened the existence of the Anglo-Saxon kingdoms. The king of Wessex, Alfred, was driven by them into the Somerset marshes, but in 878 he defeated a Viking army, becoming strong enough to divide the island with the Danes, whose leader Guthrum he helped convert to Christianity. In 886, after merging Wessex with Mercia, Alfred called himself King of the Anglo-Saxons,* but the Vikings now ruled much of Britain and Ireland, and were soon attacking Francia again.

Who were they? They were Scandinavians who shared a worldview and cosmology based around their gods led by the one-eyed god of war

---

* The sole British king to be known as the Great, Alfred ruled only the south-west. Wales was divided between the Celtic kingdoms of Deheubarth, Powys and Gwynedd; Scotland was divided between the Celtic realms of Strathclyde and Alba and the Viking kingdom of Man in the western isles; the rest was ruled by the Vikings.

Odin, who appeared as a warrior adventurer, and by Thor, god of farming. Theirs was a cult of war and heroism,* whose followers worshipped at annual festivals where horses and humans were sacrificed, the latter hung from trees – which had a special place in their beliefs – or torn apart by bending a tree back and releasing it. Their heroes and exploits were celebrated in epic stories and engraved runestones, their dead burned in or buried alongside their superb longships.

Arabs called them al-Madjus, fire worshippers, because they burned their dead; Europeans called them Norsemen; and they may have called themselves Vikings or *Vikingr*, the 'men of *vik*' – that is, of the inlets or fjords. They were raiders but also traders, specializing in slavery, and they were remarkable navigators, visiting America centuries before Columbus.

No one knows why these Scandinavians embarked on their adventures at this moment: a rising population maybe created competition for land; civil strife made life difficult; their ritual exposure of female babies may have created a shortage of women that required bride stealing. They initially took a delight in killing priests and raiding churches, revenge perhaps for Frankish atrocities, but the original motive was treasure, and then slaves – the grandees of Baghdad, Constantinople and Cordoba craved their furs and slaves. But perhaps the chief reason for launching their raids was that they could. Their improved shallow-draught, full-sailed ships, guided by lodestones, meant they could travel across oceans and up rivers. They were led by warrior kings yet they were partly governed by *things* – quasi-democratic assemblies, led by elected lawspeakers – and their elites were literate readers of sagas and runestones.

How they really lived is mysterious enough that modern historians can project just about anything – including wild drug taking and transvestism – with the clues that have been left us. In battle they fought with a frenzy that may or may not have been stimulated by a hallucinogen – sticky nightshade. They were polygynous; some women may have been warriors, given that a very few female tombs contain broadswords – though it may be that everyone was buried with swords. Christians and Muslims were certainly amazed by their lack of sexual inhibitions.

In 862, a Viking chieftain named Rurik, the founder of a family that would rule Russia until 1598, led a war band southwards from Scandinavia down the Dnieper into an ever-changing riverine borderland

* Their conception of the human self was singular: they believed each person was divided into a hamr (the physical body), the hugr (the essence), the hamingja (the personification of luck) and the fylgja (a female spirit that was within even the most virile man).

where Turkic and Slavic pagans, dominated by a rising Turkic khanate, the Khazars, vied for the rich prizes of trade with Constantinople and Baghdad. At this time, Arab writers mention a grouping called al-Rusiyya – the Rus, probably derived from the Old Norse *roa* (to row) – connected to the Scandinavian raiders and traders who starting from their trading station Staraia Ladoga in the north had long been plying the great rivers, the Volga and Dnieper. It is likely Rurik was one of these Rus.

As they rowed south, Rurik's men first had to deal with the Khazars, who since the break-up of the western Turks around 650 had ruled from central Asia to Ukraine, fighting the Arabs for fifty years while enjoying good relations with Constantinople's emperors, two of whom married Khazar princesses. Ruled by two kings, a khagan and an *isa*, from a palace on the Volga island, Atil, the Khazars worshipped Tengri, the sky god of the steppes. But holding the line between Christian Constantinople and Islamic Baghdad, their khagan Bulan converted to Judaism, confirmed by coins dated 837–8 and inscribed *Mûsâ rasûl Allâh* ('Moses is the messenger of God', echoing the Islamic *shahada*). Bulan's son Obadiah built synagogues, but not all Khazars practised Judaism.

These Jewish khagans controlled the riverine trade. Rurik and his federation of Slav, Viking and Turkic peoples traded furs, amber, wax, honey, walrus tusks and slaves, for which they received payment from Khazars, Romans and Arabs in silver dirhams, the dollars of the day, which allow us to imagine trade routes that extended from India to Britain. Hoards of the caliph's coins – 100,000 so far – have been discovered in Sweden, as has a small bronze Buddha cast in Kashmir, while in Britain Mercian kings adapted dirhams, still marked in Arabic, for local use. But the chief Viking merchandise was human: Slavs were sold so widely through the Black Sea and the Mediterranean that the very word for slave was named after them.

Both Baghdad and Constantinople bid for the support of the Khazars and other tribes in these turbulent borderlands, dispatching brave envoys to treat with these terrifying barbarians. Meeting the Rus, Ibn Fadlan, a caliphal envoy, was as excited as he was disgusted: 'I've never seen more perfect physical specimens, tall as date palms, blond and ruddy,' he wrote. Their chieftain sat on his throne surrounded by 400 warriors and forty slaves 'destined for his bed'.*

---

* The Rus were traders, as one told the Arab envoy: 'O my Lord, I have come from a far land and have with me such and such a number of girls and such and such a number of sables.' Their hygiene shocked the envoy: 'They're the filthiest of God's creatures – no modesty in defecation and urination, nor do they wash after orgasm, nor wash their hands after eating – like wild asses.' Then there was the group sex: 'Each man sits on a couch. With

Ibn Fadlan witnessed the group sex and human sacrifice of a young intoxicated enslaved girl at a chieftain's funeral supervised by a female shaman, the Angel of Death, 'a strapping old woman, fat and louring'. Ibn Fadlan was surely relieved to make it back to Baghdad.

Rurik, a semi-mythic hero of whom we know little, ruled a fiefdom from Gorodische, or the Town, a trading settlement, later refounded as New Town, Novgorod. His successors expanded southwards. His descendant Igor was brought to the Slav town Kyiv on the Dnieper, founded around the sixth century, later making this the headquarters for trading furs and slaves to Constantinople where Rus – known to the Romaioi as Varangians – often served as elite guards.

The Great City was a tempting prize: Igor launched two raids during which his longboats were torched by Greek Fire. Later, he was captured by a Slav tribe who tied him to two branches which were then released, tearing him in half. Yet his widow Olga defeated his Slavic enemies, then travelled to Constantinople, where she was baptized after meeting the emperor. The empire was resurgent thanks to a remarkable Armenian peasant whose career was made by his buff physique, grim charms and skill with horses.

CONSTANTINOPLE AND ROME: BASIL THE UNIBROW HORSE WHISPERER AND MAROZIA THE SENATRIX

Basil's rise started when, as a young servant, he encountered the richest woman in the empire, Danielis, a widow who owned 3,000 slaves and eighty estates and became his patroness – and surely his lover. It may be that he spent many years with her before she introduced him to the courtier who brought him to the notice of young Emperor Michael III, an expert on horseflesh, who hired him as a groom, then as a bodyguard, then as a chamberlain. Michael restored Roman rule in Greece and, guided by his mother, ended the iconoclastic agony, but he was infatuated, probably sexually, by the heft of the muscled Basil, thirty years older than him. Born in Thrace, known as the Macedonian but probably an Armenian, Basil was the 'most outstanding in bodily form and heavy set; his eyebrows grew together, he had large eyes, a broad chest' and a morose expression. The emperor enjoyed watching him

them are pretty slaves for sale to merchants: a man has sexual intercourse with his slave while his companion looks on. Sometimes whole groups come together in this fashion in the presence of others. A merchant who arrives to buy a slave from them may have to wait and look on while a Rus completes the act of intercourse with his slave . . .'

in wrestling bouts with Bulgarian champions. When Michael resented his influential uncle, Basil executed him, leaving the unibrowed horse whisperer as his omnipresent *parakoimomenos* – He Who Sleeps Beside (the imperial chamber). While his marriage was childless, Michael had a son by his mistress, Eudokia Ingerina, whom he soon shared with Basil (Basil seems to have been irresistible to men and women). To legitimize this son, Leo, he ordered Basil to marry Eudokia and crowned him co-emperor, giving him his own sister Thekla as mistress. When Michael, boozing hard, widely nicknamed the Drunk, had second thoughts and plotted his favourite's murder, Basil got in first, assembling a family hit squad (including his father and brother) that broke into the imperial bedchamber, stabbed the inebriated emperor and sliced off his hands – possibly vengeance for the unchristian homosexual side of their relationship.

It was an unlikely rise, but the uneducated Basil turned out to be a serious and intelligent *basileus*,* fighting the Arabs, codifying the laws and striking the Bulgars. He was never quite sure whether Leo was his or Michael's and disliked the nerdy boy. Basil died in 886 at the age of seventy-five after a hunting accident which saw him dragged for miles, his clothes having been snagged in a stag's antlers: his groom was executed for cutting the emperor's belt to free him from the antlers (it was illegal to bare a blade in front of the emperor). When he died, Emperor Leo too was unsure who his father was, but he honoured the giblets of Michael, which he buried in the Church of the Apostles along with Basil.

Talented, scholarly but tormented, Leo the Wise held back the Arabs in the east but lost his last strongholds in Sicily to Arab invaders, who then landed in southern Italy and threatened not just his last territories but Rome itself.

In 846, Arab raiders had landed at Ostia and then struck Rome, looting St Peter's. Now that they were advancing again, Pope John VIII, who had seen the Arabs assault Rome, alternately begged Emperor Leo and the Carolingian kings to send help. Constantinople had traditionally selected and menaced popes, and Justinian had kidnapped one. Now the popes were on their own: the chaos in Italy, the loss of papal incomes to the Arabs, the fall in prestige and the rise of voracious Italian barons undermined John VIII, who was poisoned then bludgeoned to death

---

* Basil not only welcomed his patroness, Danielis, to court, he raised her to the title of Emperor's Mother (*basileometor*) which says much about their relationship. The Greek-speaking Romaioi now called the empire *Basileia Romaion* – Roman monarchy and their emperor *basileus* – king.

by his own clergymen. Thus opened a bloody new era, dominated by a single extraordinary woman: Marozia. If Cleopatra can be regarded as a feminist heroine, so should Marozia, ruler of Rome, and mother, grandmother, great-grandmother, lover and murderess of a succession of popes and princes.

The turmoil that had started with the killing of John VIII culminated in the trial of a dead pope. In January 897, the corpse of Pope Formosus, who had been dead for over a year, was exhumed, dressed in its papal robes, enthroned and then placed on trial for perjury and violation of canon law before a synod in Rome, chaired by his successor Stephen VI, with a deacon representing the cadaver as its lawyer. Found guilty, Formosus was stripped naked, the three fingers he used for papal blessing were cut off and his body was flung into the Tiber. The motive for this necrospectacle was to undermine the legitimacy of a predecessor and so enhance the legality of the new pope. But it did not work: Stephen was strangled, and three popes were then elected by different factions. But one, Sergius III, managed to win the backing of Teofilatto, Marozia's father, and they murdered the other two.

Elected consul for the year 915, Teofilatto ruled Rome alongside his wife Theodora, appointing their nominees to the papacy. Teofilatto – Theofylactus – was one of the rising warlords who treated the papacy as just one of the urban offices through which they could control a Rome already divided into armed camps, the ancient monuments such as the Colosseum or Hadrian's mausoleum now serving as fortified strongholds. If the reality resembled gang warfare, the titles were still dazzling: Eminentissimus, Magnificus, consul and of course pope.

When the Arabs seized Minturno, a town eighty miles south of Rome, Christians panicked. Yet Teofilatto could not control Rome alone: the papacy was spiritual leader of western Christendom; Italy was strategically vital, with the Arabs and Romaioi in the south and, in the north, ever since Charlemagne, the kings of East Francia (Germany) had a big stake.

Teofilatto consolidated his power by marrying off his daughters. His wife Theodora was a 'shameless whore who exercised power over the Roman citizenry like a man', wrote Liutprand, bishop of Cremona, a retainer of the family's chief enemy, Otto of Germany: his claims are often German propaganda and male chauvinism.

In 909, Teofilatto married Marozia to a rival warlord, Alberic, margrave of Spoleto, with whom she had several sons. She may have become the mistress of Pope Sergius and have had a son with him too. Her sister was also married off. But unusually Marozia started to exert her own political power in a way that alarmed Liutprand, who called the pair 'the sister whores' dominating the papacy in a 'pornocracy' – rule of prostitutes. Actually they were potentates and women were more powerful in Rome than anywhere else at the time.

In 915, Alberic, Marozia's husband, now elected as patrician – *Patricius Romanorum*, one of many titles borrowed from ancient times – joined forces with Teofilatto and the pope to expel the Arabs from Minturno. In 924, when her husband was assassinated and her father died, Marozia, in her mid-thirties, assumed leadership of the faction as *domina*, *senatrix* and *patricia*, ruler of Rome. After an affair with Pope John X, who then tried to assert his own control, Marozia married Guido, margrave of Tuscany, great-grandson of Charlemagne, who fell in love with her beauty as much as with her power.

In 928, the couple attacked and arrested John X; imprisoned in Hadrian's mausoleum, now fortified as Castel Sant'Angelo, the pope was later suffocated. Guido himself died soon afterwards. Meanwhile Marozia placed her son by Alberic (if not by Pope Sergius) on the papal throne as Pope John XI, aged only twenty. Her other son, Alberic II of Spoleto, now believed he should succeed his father as ruler of Rome. Marozia resisted, but a woman of power needed male help: she negotiated a marriage with Hugh of Provence, a Charlemagne scion, king of Italy, who duly arrived in Rome.

Many sons have loathed their mothers' new husbands but few have stormed the wedding reception. Marozia's son Alberic II launched a wedding coup and besieged the wedding party in Castel Sant'Angelo; the bridegroom abandoned the bride by shinning down a rope; Marozia herself was arrested and imprisoned in Castel Sant'Angelo, where she later died. Alberic II ruled Rome as *princeps* for the next twenty years, marrying his new stepsister, the daughter of King Hugh and portentously naming their son Octavian. On his deathbed in 954, Alberic persuaded his magnates to appoint Octavian as *princeps* and then as Pope John XII. This overpromoted teen popinjay became tyrant of Rome. His sins, even listed by the panting Liutprand, sound unremarkable except for the surprising absence of sodomy: 'He had fornicated with the widow of Rainier, with Stephana his father's concubine, with the widow Anna, and with his own niece, and he made the sacred palace into a whorehouse. They said that he had gone hunting publicly; that he had blinded his confessor Benedict, and thereafter Benedict had died; that he had killed John, cardinal subdeacon, after castrating him' and 'he toasted the devil with wine.' But struggling to defend Rome, in 962, John XII called in the East Francian king Otto I, who marched south, accompanied by

Bishop Liutprand, to protect him in return for his own coronation as Roman emperor. Unsurprisingly John fell out with the Germans but perished – characteristically – during a bout of adulterous sex.

Otto and his imperial sons regularly stormed down to Rome but were unable to gain control of the papacy for long. In 974, Crescentius, Marozia's great-nephew, seized Rome for the Marozians and overthrew the German-backed popes, strangling several inconvenient pontiffs. The family appointed popes until 996, when Emperor Otto III, who was just sixteen, famed for his classical intellect, swooped on Rome and deposed Crescentius. Otto then had him beheaded, his wife gang-raped and his pope, the Marozian cousin John XVI, blinded, with his nose, ears and tongue cut off. Otto, assuming the titles Emperor of the World and Consul of the Romans, planned to rule his German empire from his new Roman palace, only to die at just twenty-one.

The Crescentians still dominated the old Rome when in the eastern New Rome, Leo the Wise's illegitimate son Constantine VII, born in the porphyry chamber of the Great Palace where empresses gave birth, asserted his legitimacy with the title *Porphyrogennetos*. A scholar and writer, he focused on the conversion of the Slavs to Christianity. In 957 it was Constantine who welcomed Olga of Rus on the first Russian state visit: she was baptized with Porphyrogennetos as her godfather. The Slavs claimed he fell in love – an unlikely event for the fastidious Porphyrogennetos – but he encouraged her Christian tendencies and granted trading rights.

The Rus now challenged the Khazars. In 971, Prince Svyatoslav attacked and burned their capital Atil and then, blessed by Constantinople, he attacked the Bulgars with 60,000 troops, routing them and seizing their capital and so much of Bulgaria that the Roman emperor was alarmed and orchestrated his assassination. In the ensuing chaos, Svyatoslav's youngest son by a concubine, Valdemar, who had been driven out of Novgorod, was given troops by his cousin, the king of Norway. He then defeated all his brothers to seize Kyiv.

Valdemar kept a harem of 800 girls, took seven wives, several bearing him children, and worshipped the pagan gods Dazhbog, Stribog and Mokosh, celebrating his victories by sacrificing two children. But his envoys were overwhelmed by the Christian magnificence of the Great City and its Hagia Sophia – 'We no longer knew whether we were in heaven or on earth' – and when Valdemar himself realized the benefits of conversion, his timing was excellent. The latest of the Macedonian dynasty, Basil II, faced a rebellion and needed help.

The thirty-year-old Basil was a force of nature: 'From the day that the

King of Heaven called upon me to become the Emperor, overlord of the world,' he wrote for his own epitaph, 'no one saw my spear lie idle.' In a city of berobed luxury, scented eunuchs and Byzantine intrigue, he was a compact, plainspoken swordsman, a pious ascetic uninterested in women and probably homosexual.

Valdemar sent the new emperor a unit of Varangians as a present with the warning, 'Don't keep them in your city or they'll cause you harm – and don't allow a single one to return this way.' The Kyivan next demanded marriage to a sister of the emperor. This was an impertinence, but Basil, recognizing Kyivan power, agreed, provided the grand prince of Kyiv converted and helped retake his Crimean colony, Chersonese. Valdemar played his part, but when Basil delayed sending his sister, Valdemar kept Chersonese; Basil immediately dispatched his sister. In 988, Valdemar, taking the name Vladimir or Volodymyr, was baptized according to the rites favoured in Constantinople, a decisive moment in world history which, together with the Bulgar conversion, ensured Russia and eastern Europe would develop their own distinctive rituals and doctrine – later known as Orthodox.* The emperor's sister Anna Porphyrogenita dreaded her marriage to an oafish barbarian, but Basil begged her: 'God turns the land of Rus to repentance through your agency and you'll save Greece from the danger of grievous war.' God's work was hard to refuse.

PAGAN CONVERTS: VLADIMIR AND ROLLO

Poor Anna sailed for Crimea to wed Vladimir, who returned Chersonese to Basil II as 'a bridal gift'. Vladimir converted his Rus Land with characteristic energy – concubines were retired, pagan statues beaten with rods, and churches founded. Kyivans were ordered to attend a mass baptism on the banks of the Dnieper: 'Whoever doesn't turn up, rich, poor or slave, shall be my enemy.' His new conquests and his Roman connection helped make him a European potentate, and three of his daughters married monarchs.† After his death in 1015, his

---

* The early work of two missionaries, Cyril and Methodius, who had translated the Greek Bible into Slavic script, later developing into Cyrillic, meant these newly Christian people could understand the new services.

† Little is really known of Vladimir, beyond a priestly chronicle, *Tale of Bygone Years*, written three hundred years later. Most of the story is a myth but Ivan the Terrible in the sixteenth century used it to justify his wars to 'regather' western lands. Peter the Great adapted the word 'Rus' to create the name of his new empire, Russia. Russian nineteenth-century Slavophiles and twenty-first-century believers in 'the Russian World' – such as President

son Yaroslav the Wise presided over Rus at its height, ruling from a Kyiv filled with churches. But its apogee was short. After Yaroslav, Rus fragmented into smaller principalities, always ruled by Rurikovichi,* one of whom would built a small fortress beside the River Moskva – Moscow. Having won Kyiv for Christ, Basil rushed southwards to stop a new Arab advance in Syria, fighting from the Caucasus to the Balkans, a warrior emperor, who shared rations with his men and several times was almost killed in battle, always saved by his 6,000 Varangian guards.

As many a Viking headed southwards to serve Basil, other compatriots raided Francia where Charlemagne's heirs – whose epithets, the Fat, the Simple, the Stammerer, reveal their weaknesses – made at least thirteen Danegeld payments. Emperor Charles the Fat had managed to reunite the entire empire of his great-grandfather – from Italy to East and West Francia – but he lacked the killer instinct to keep it. In 885, a Viking fleet under several chieftains sailed up the Seine and besieged Paris. One of the Vikings was a young warlord named Rollo. The small city – just 20,000 inhabitants – was held by the emperor's young barons Odo, count of Paris, and his brother Robert, sons of a self-made warlord, Robert the Strong, who begged for his help. Instead Fat Charles paid 700 pounds of silver to the Vikings, an appeasement so brazen that Odo was elected king of West Francia. His reign was short but he founded a new dynasty and a kingdom that evolved into France. Odo's was not the only family hacking out a new realm.

As for the Norse raider Rollo, the battle of Paris made him too. In its aftermath, he stole a Frankish count's bride, Poppa of Bayeux, with whom he founded a dynasty that in some ways still endures. So hulking that no horse would hold him, Rollo the Walker, now captured Rouen, then in 911 attacked Paris again. The Carolingian king of West Francia, Charles the Simple, bought him off with a deal to keep his lands provided he converted to Christianity, and repelled Viking raiders and overmighty barons. Rollo agreed: he and his Norsemen became known as Normans, his duchy as Normandy; his descendants conquered England, and today's British monarchs are descended from him. In 922, after deposing Simple Charles and fighting Rollo, Odo's brother Robert

---

Vladimir Putin – used it to promote the myth of a Russian nation, encompassing the peoples of Russia and Ukraine. For Ukrainians, the story of Volodmyr is the founding myth of their nation.

* Two of Vladimir's sons, Boris and Gleb, were killed in the struggles after their father's death and became the first saints of the new church, seen as sacrifices for this new sacred land, Holy Rus, and launching the sacralization of the rulers of Russia.

was elected king: his descendants, would be kings of France as Capets, Valois and Bourbons (with a few interludes) until 1848 – almost a millennium.

Yet the Normans did not give up raiding: Rouen was famed for its slave market and they needed Islamic slaves to sell. They were still raiding al-Andalus during the 950s but encountered the great monarch of the west who now had his own fleets that he used to raid the shores of Francia and Africa.

CALIPH OF CORDOBA

Seethingly vigilant and ferociously martial, Abd al-Rahman III was muscular with short legs, blond, fair-skinned and blue-eyed, his grandmother being a Christian princess, Onneca Fortúnez, daughter of the king of Pamplona; his mother was an enslaved Slav, one of thousands traded by the Vikings from Russia. The Umayya court was a bearpit – his father murdered by his uncle, and his uncle by his grandfather – but he was trained for power by his tough aunt Sayyida.

In 912, within a week of inheriting at the age of twenty-one a kingdom beset with rebellions and challenges, Abd al-Rahman III was displaying the head of the chief rebel to the people of Cordoba. But it took twenty years to restore Umayya power, striking north at the Christian kingdoms and south into Morocco. In 929, Abd al-Rahman assumed the caliphate, a celebration of military success and disdain for the frayed caliphs of Baghdad. He liked to receive Christian visitors seated in plain robes on a linen mat with just a Quran, a sword and a flame before him, offering them either the Quran or the sword followed by the fire.

Yet he was a European titan, receiving ambassadors from the two Christian emperors, a humanistic patron of the arts with the greatest library outside Constantinople. Cordoba was now the biggest city in Europe along with Constantinople: its emperors sent gifts, marble fountains and Greek classics which the caliph had translated into Arabic. He built a new palace complex, Medina al-Zahra, probably named after a slave girl and modelled on the Umayya palace in Damascus, six miles outside Cordoba, with a colossal throne room built around a huge mercury pool, a menagerie of lions (a gift from his African allies) and one of Europe's first flushing bathrooms at a time when London and Paris were tiny towns with open sewers. His court was cosmopolitan: his guards and concubines were Slavs, his viziers often Jewish or Christian. His Jewish doctor Hasdai ibn Shaprut served as ambassador and treasurer, corresponding with popes and with German and eastern emperors, as well as with the Jewish khagans of Khazaria.

Yet neither caliphal grandeur nor *adab* diminished Abd al-Rahman's sybaritic ferocity. He presided over a harem of 6,750 females and 3,750 male slaves. A female slave who betrayed him was fed to the lions; a Christian boy – later St Pelagius – who rejected his advances was dismembered. These may be stock anti-Muslim stories, but he certainly relished his lack of ruth. His executioner, always ready with sword and leather mat, grew rich. Once, while he was beheading a concubine, her jewellery fell out of her hair and the caliph let him keep it. When one of his sons conspired against him, he publicly executed the boy himself.

He launched annual invasions of the north, always leading his own armies, until he was almost killed in battle. When the Vikings attacked al-Andalus, Abd al-Rahman repelled them with his fleet, while he expanded along the European and African coasts, establishing a Côte d'Azur pirates' nest at Fréjus and campaigning in Morocco, where his general was a Slavic eunuch nicknamed the Castrated Cockerell. His capture of Ceuta and Tangier gave him access to the trans-Saharan caravans, but just as he hoped to control the trans-Saharan trade, the caliph was foiled by a messianic dynasty that arose in an oasis halfway between Morocco and west Africa. The caliph* would scarcely have believed that this obscure desert uprising would tilt the balance of Afro-Asia, challenge Constantinople, Cordoba and Baghdad and lead to the founding of the greatest Arab city of all: Cairo.

---

* 'I've now reigned over fifty years in victory or peace,' Abd al-Rahman mused on his deathbed in 969, 'beloved by my subjects, dreaded by my enemies and respected by my allies. I have diligently numbered the days of pure and genuine happiness which have fallen to my lot: they amount to fourteen. O man, don't place confidence in this present world!'

The *Ghanas* and the Fatimiyya

It started deep in the desert. In 905, when Abd al-Rahman III was a boy, Said bin Husain, at the age of thirty-five, proclaimed himself the Mahdi – the chosen one, God's representative on earth, in the remote Moroccan oasis of Sijilmasa where recently converted Berber tribes had already been convinced of his sanctity by secret missionaries. They were part of a clandestine Shiite network of Dawa – the Calling – who from Yemen to the Atlantic preached the restoration of the dynasty of Ali and Fatima, Muhammad's daughter. Said claimed this descent and his family called themselves the House al-Fatimiyya. Said's family had been hunted and killed by the caliphs of Baghdad, but he himself, disguised as a merchant, had escaped with his son. Though pursued by assassins, he reached Morocco, where he adopted the title al-Mahdi Billah and launched his jihad, aiming to march all the way to Iraq and destroy the heretical caliphate.[*]

It seemed unlikely that this would ever happen when al-Mahdi took command of a tiny posse of Berbers in Sijilmasa, gateway to the most powerful African kingdom, Wagadu, ruled by the Soninke *ghanas* – kings – who commanded an army of 200,000. In their capital Koumbi Saleh in Mauritania, 'the *ghana* sits in audience . . . in a domed pavilion around which stand ten horses covered with gold-embroidered materials,' wrote an Arab visitor, al-Bakri, a little later. 'Behind the king

---

[*] The split between Sunni and Shia was the schism within the House of Muhammad. Ever since the assassination of Ali, the faction – Shia – of Islam had regarded the Umayya and Abbasiya caliphs as impostors, revering the descent of the People of the House of Muhammad as sacred imams. Different Shiite sects followed the descent of different imams, but the Fatimiyya claimed descent from the mysterious seventh Imam Ismaili – hence known as Ismailis – who had occulted or vanished around 762 and now they awaited the Mahdi – Messiah – a member of the family. The Mahdi would restore the unity of Islam before the End of Days, the apocalypse that thanks to chaos of the Baghdad caliphate was believed to be imminent. Al-Mahdi Billal claimed to be the eleventh imam.

stand ten pages holding shields and swords decorated with gold, and on his right are the sons of the kings of his country wearing splendid garments, their hair plaited with gold.' Gold was everywhere: even the *ghana*'s guard dogs had 'collars of gold and silver studded with a number of balls of the same metals'. When *ghanas* died they were buried with treasures and sacrificed servants; such tombs were found in the Niger River area. Western and eastern Africa were not unknown before the Europeans arrived. In fact Afro-Asia was a single world linked by tenuous but ancient caravan and shipping routes across the desert and seas to the Maghreb, Spain, Egypt and the Indian Ocean. Across the Sahara, the *ghanas* traded ivory, copper, bronze and gold from Barmaka (today's Ghana) and bronze from Igbo-Ukwu (Nigeria), where craftsmen produced bronzes of snakes, birds and vessels set with beads imported from afar: the *ghanas*' treasure house contained 100,000 glass and carnelian beads from Egypt and India. Wagadu was just the biggest of the west African realms – Gao, Timbuktu and Kanem-Bornu – that traded with the north. Two-thirds of European gold came from west Africa, and so probably did the lions in Abd al-Rahman's menagerie.

The caravans were manned by Berber cameleteers who were often Muslim, so that Islam flowed like the salt from the north into the land of gold. Islam had reached Wagadu: Koumbi Saleh was divided into two towns, one mainly Muslim, the other following Soninke pagan religions, and the *ghanas* practised a hybrid of both. Al-Bakri witnessed human sacrifices of servants, intoxicated with 'fermented drinks', to accompany dead kings.

To the east, on the coast of the Indian Ocean, Arab traders in ivory, spices and slaves already traded in Zanj – east Africa – and they too brought Islam with them. The link between Arabia and Africa was as ancient as Solomon and Sheba. The Arabs traded with the Bantu-speaking Africans, gradually developing a new hybrid language, Swahili, from the Arabic *al-Sahel* – the Coast. In Sudan (from the Arabic Bilad al-Sudan – Land of the Blacks) and Ethiopia (which the Arabs called al-Habasha – Abyssinia), the old Christian kingdom of Axum was disintegrating.*

---

* Muslim, Jewish and Christian potentates vied for power. Both Jews and Christians in Ethiopia claimed mythical descent from Solomon and Sheba, but there were ancient links between Arabia and Ethiopia and it is likely these Jews were connected to the interactions between the kingdom of Axum and the Jewish kingdom of Himyar (Yemen). Himyar was Jewish from around the fourth century to its conquest by Axum in the sixth. A significant Jewish community remained in Ethiopia known as the Beta (House of) Israel. At some point, the kings of Axum tried to convert the Jews of the kingdom of Simien situated in north Ethiopia. A Jewish king, Gideon IV, was killed in the fighting, but just around this time, 960, his daughter Queen Gudit (Judith) hit back, destroying Axum and establishing

Wars and raids produced prisoners who were traded to the Swahili coast where Gulf traders – the sons of Omanis and Persians married to local African women – founded a port, Kilwa, the first of the Swahili trading cities. Voyages went both ways across the Indian Ocean: bananas that originated in south-east Asia arrived in these ships and were planted in Africa to become a quintessentially African crop, spread by the Bantu as they moved southwards. Kilwan sailors crisscrossed the Indian Ocean. The first outsiders to reach Australia were not Europeans (the Dutch landed there in 1606), but African sailors from Kilwa, as evidenced by the discovery of copper Kilwan coins, inscribed in Arabic with the name of an amir of Kilwa, dug up on Marchinbar Island, Northern Territory. Asians had travelled east and west much earlier: Javanese and Malays had probably reached Australia, as suggested by two Javanese inscriptions.

Indians, Javanese, Malays and Polynesians frequently sailed to Africa. Around 400, Malay sailors started colonizing Madagascar, the last major landmass, other than Iceland and New Zealand, to be settled.* In 945, according to an Arab history, a Javanese–Malay fleet from Mataram/Srivijaya landed on the Swahili coast to seize ivory, furs and black slaves, but failed to seize whichever city they coveted.

The Arab slave traders, based in the Swahili cities from Mogadishu (Somalia) and Zanzibar (Tanzania) to Sofala (Mozambique), ruled by African-Arab merchant dynasties, bought slaves from Africans in the hinterland and traded them with the Indic and Arab worlds as far as Mataram. Medieval slavery was based on religion: Islam technically banned the enslavement of Muslims, but most east and central Africans were pagan, ripe for enslavement. That did not mean the Arabs who were now penetrating Africa were not racist: their guides to slavery shows their enjoyment of racist stereotyping.† The tales of Buzurg in

a Jewish kingdom that endured for several centuries alongside Muslim and Christian realms. Historians debate all this; much of it is based on Beta Israel tradition; but it is likely that these Gideonites were the ancestors of today's Beta Israel (Falashas). Makuria continued to thrive after repelling the Arab armies in 652, enduring until around 1000 when it merged with Christian Dotawo, a regional power until the sixteenth century.

* Madagascar became a uniquely Afro-Polynesian society, where the Merina, a Malay elite, crushed earlier settlers, the Vazimba, hunted to extinction the giant animals (including lemurs the size of gorillas) and imported African slaves to work for them there in a singular caste system that lasted into the late nineteenth century.

† A Christian Arab doctor, Ibn Butlan of Baghdad, wrote a guide to slaves in the 1050s. He flaunted racial stereotypes, but colour was not the ideological basis for slavery. Like most medieval people he regarded race 'not in binary terms', writes Hannah Barker, 'but as a profusion of human diversity signifying the endlessly fertile creativity of God'. The best slaves he claimed were from India and Afghanistan. Those from Syria and Maghreb were inferior; Rus and Slavs were strong. 'Were a Zanj (east African) slave to fall from

the Persian Gulf recount how the African king of Sofala traded 'man-eating Zanj' slaves (average price 20–30 dinars) with Omani traders, until he was captured himself and traded to Oman, then Cairo, before converting to Islam and returning to retake his throne. We have no idea of the numbers, but it is likely many millions of Africans were enslaved.*

Back in north-west Africa, in Sijilmasa, the Mahdi's jihad had almost ended before it started. In 910, the local sheikh arrested him, but his agents stormed the jail. On his liberation, riding on a wave of religious fervour, flourishing the white banners of House al-Fatimiyya, he and his Berbers galloped eastwards to seize Qairawan (Tunisia), founded a new capital, al-Mahdiya, and then advanced on Egypt. Soon declared caliph, his flotillas, commanded by his son al-Qaim, captured Sicily and raided Calabria, even Genoa. Al-Qaim reached Alexandria, but was beaten back by the ruler of independent Egypt, a talented Nubian eunuch.

AL-MISK'S PERFUMES, JAWAR'S FISH AND THE JEWISH VIZIER: THE HOUSE OF FATIMIYYA

Abd al-Misk Kafur, known as the Master, had been captured somewhere in east Africa, enslaved and castrated, then sold to a Turkic general, the Ikhshid (viceroy), who had ruled Egypt as an autonomous realm when the caliphs in Baghdad lost control of their empire. The Ikhshid noticed that while the other slaves rushed to stare at wild animals that arrived from inner Africa, Kafur never took his eyes off his master. Said to be ugly and deformed but sensitive and intelligent, he was such a connoisseur of perfume that he was named after two of them: black musk and white camphor. On his deathbed, the Ikhshid advised his son to employ Kafur as vizier, and ultimately he became the ruler in his own right: the Master.

Kafur was a talented general and artistic patron, but he fell out with the poet al-Mutanabbi (who mocked him when Kafur did not appoint

sky to earth, the one quality he'd possess would be rhythm.' The doctor warned against the customs in Bagawi (Sudan/Ethiopia) where 'they practice excision. Using a razor they completely remove external skin on top of the vulva.' His conclusion: 'Armenian slaves are the worst of the whites; Zanj worst of the blacks.'

* A fifth of slaves may have died on the nightmarish journeys across the desert, where their bones were a well-known sight. Between 700 and the abolition of slavery, it is likely that as many slaves were traded from east Africa as in the Atlantic trade. Ralph A. Austen estimates 11.75 million were traded – but the numbers are educated guesses.

him minister).* Kafur protected Christians and Jews, including his
treasurer Yakub ibn Killis, a Jew who converted to Islam. But when Ibn
Killis lost out in a court intrigue, he fled to the Fatimiyya, joining the
talented, cosmopolitan entourage of Caliph al-Muizz. Al-Muizz ordered
his paladin, Jawar the Slav, a blond freedman enslaved in eastern Europe
who had been given to al-Muizz's father, to crush all resistance as far as
the Atlantic. Jawar sent a tank of fish to al-Muizz to demonstrate the job
was done. As long as Kafur lived, Egypt would not fall, but on his death
it lay open. In 969, Jawar stormed into Egypt, where he and al-Muizz[†]
founded a new city that they called the Conqueror, al-Qahirah – Cairo.

Egypt was just a step towards the liquidation of the godless usurpers
of Baghdad and the infidels of Constantinople. Jawar advanced into
Syria, but was thrown back. Ibn Killis, the Jewish vizier, was reappointed
by al-Muizz's son al-Aziz, 'tall, with red hair and blue eyes' – his mother
was al-Muizz's favourite slave singer Durzan, nicknamed the Tweeter.
Al-Aziz's partnership with Ibn Killis, whom he called Yakub, was almost
familial; there were rows, and Ibn Killis was fined and fired but always
reappointed. Ibn Killis was so rich that he had his own guards of 4,000
male slaves, a harem of 5,000 and built a mosque and university named
al-Azhar (the Shiites called Fatima al-Zahra – the Luminous).

The dynasty ruled magnificently, creating a court designed to impress,
projected by resplendent dress and spectacular processions. Cairo, initially just a few palaces and the al-Azhar mosque and university, only
gradually became the capital, while Fustat and Alexandria thrived on
the trade between the Mediterranean and the Indian Ocean. Ibn Killis
was the first of a line of Jewish converts who served as viziers. Egyptian
Jews were a powerful and numerous community, led by the family of
Rais al-Yahud – chief of the Jews, appointed by the caliphs – who served
as royal doctors as well as advisers. Families of Jewish merchants of
Fustat traded across a tricontinental Afro-Eurasian span from Egypt to
Seville, Sijilmasa to Samarkand to Constantinople, al-Mahdiya to Kyiv,
India and China. Some 400,000 documents, found in the Genizah[‡] of
Fustat's Ben Ezra Synagogue, reveal a web of Jewish family businesses

---

* As he fled Egypt, Mutanabbi, the whole white man, flung this at the black eunuch:
    A well-hung, well-heeled white man's sense of gratitude soon palls;
    What thanks can be expected from a black man with no balls?
† Al-Muizz was also the inventor or commissioner of the fountain pen, telling his scribe:
'We wish to construct a pen which can be used for writing without dipping it in an inkbot-
tle, whose ink will be contained inside it . . . and it will not stain nor will any drop of ink
leak out of it.'
‡ The Genizah was an accidental archive since it was the rubbish dump of the Jews there
who believed that God's words in Hebrew should never be burned, only buried.

at the centre of an almost global market. Jewish as well as Coptic merchants became vastly rich.

Loathing the Sunni Abbasiya even more than the Christians, al-Muizz and Ibn Killis invaded Syria, capturing Jerusalem and Damascus, bringing them to the Roman border. But here Ibn Killis encountered the ferocious energy of Basil the Bulgar Slayer. The Shiites so hated the Sunnis that in 987 the vizier signed a truce with Roman Emperor Basil II to allow him to destroy Baghdad. The Round City temporarily fell to the Shia, but not for long.

When Ibn Killis was ailing, al-Aziz cried, 'O Yakub! If you'd recover, I'd sacrifice my son.' In 991, Ibn Killis died and al-Aziz turned his jihad against Constantinople's ally Aleppo. In April 995, Basil halted his advance. In 996, al-Aziz, now forty, collapsed near the front and summoned his eleven-year-old son al-Hakim. The boy recalled, 'I kissed him, and he pressed me to his bosom, exclaiming: "How I grieve for you ... beloved of my heart. Go and play; I'm fine."' Al-Hakim was climbing a sycamore when he heard his father's *wasita* (minister), a eunuch called Barjawan, shouting, 'Come down, my boy.'

'When I descended,' recalled al-Hakim, 'he [Barjawan] placed on my head the turban adorned with jewels, kissed the ground before me, and said: "Hail to the Commander of the Believers." The people kissed the ground before me.' As he followed his father's cortège Hakim's inheritance of sacred omnipotence in a time of feverish millenarian expectation was enough to go to a sensitive boy's head.

THE CALIGULA OF CAIRO, THE LADY OF POWER AND THE BULGAR BLINDER

Al-Hakim was handsome, strapping and blond, with blue gold-flecked eyes, the son of a Christian concubine. While the boy caliph pursued his studies and adventures in the stews of Cairo, Barjawan, a dandyish connoisseur who owned 1,000 pairs of ornate trousers and cummerbunds, restored order in the empire. They pursued their Syrian war, but in 999 Emperor Basil himself hit back furiously as far as Baalbek (Lebanon), causing a crisis in Cairo. Turkic and Berber troops clashed in the streets in an atmosphere of apocalyptic turbulence, intensified by the approach of the 400th anniversary of Muhammad's journey to Medina and the resurgence of Christian power in the person of Basil, who was fortunately diverted to Georgia. Al-Hakim negotiated a truce with Basil, who was finally free to strike north. A new Bulgar Caesar,

Samuel, had exploited Basil's Arab wars to re-establish a kingdom from the Black Sea to the Adriatic. Now in 1000, Basil stormed into Bulgaria, the start of fourteen atrocious years that culminated in 1014 with victory at Kleidion, where the emperor blinded ninety-nine out of every hundred of his 15,000 prisoners, with each unit led home by their solitary one-eyed guide – a sight that so horrified Samuel that he died of a stroke. There is no reason to doubt the atrocity. Basil had demolished the Bulgar state, re-establishing his empire as an Eurasian power. After a reign of forty-nine years – the longest of any Roman emperor east or west – the titanic but terrifying Bulgar Slayer, died aged sixty-six, hand on sword, planning to reconquer Italy.

Basil's focus on the Balkans allowed the fourteen-year-old Caliph al-Hakim to concentrate on his own power and salvation. He had promoted Barjawan to vizier, but the eunuch gave him orders and, he heard, nicknamed him the Lizard. Al-Hakim ordered another eunuch to stab Barjawan to death, appeasing the alarmed crowds by claiming that he was a traitor. But Barjawan's death unleashed more skirmishes between Berber and Turkic troops in Cairo, while the caliph of Baghdad mocked al-Hakim as half-Christian and the Fatimiyya as semi-Jews unrelated to Muhammad.

Al-Hakim was wildly inconsistent, founding a Dar al-Ilm – House of Knowledge – similar to al-Mamun's House of Wisdom – where not only Ismaili theology but astronomy and philosophy were taught in sessions that he himself often attended. But once Barjawan was gone al-Hakim seems to have believed that tolerance had displeased God. In 1004, noticing rich Christian caravans setting off for Jerusalem, he started executing Christians and converting churches into mosques. On hearing of the frenzied Christian rite of the Holy Fire that took place every Easter in the Church of the Holy Sepulchre, he banned Christmas, Epiphany and Easter, and wine drinking as well. Then he ordered that Jews and Christians wear distinguishing clothing, a Jew a wooden cow-yoke (and in the baths a cowbell) and Christians a cross. Jews and Christians were ordered to convert or die; many pretended to convert.

Next, in 1009, al-Hakim ordered the Jerusalem basilica of Jesus' Sepulchre, built by Constantine the Great, to be demolished 'stone by stone' – to the horror of Christendom, which began to take a new interest in the Holy City. In Rome, where Pope Sergius IV (nicknamed the Pig's Mouth either for his good looks or for his greed) and his master John Crescentius proposed an expedition to save Jerusalem. Nothing came of it, but it was the first flicker of a movement that would change the world.

In 1027, Pope John XIX, descendant of Marozia,* crowned a new German king, Conrad II, as Roman emperor, a coronation attended by King Canute of Denmark and England. The Vikings were no longer just traders and raiders: in Kyiv and Normandy, and now England, Iceland and America, they were settlers and empire builders too.

THE BLUETOOTHS TAKE ENGLAND: UNREADY, IRONSIDE, FORKBEARD AND HAREFOOT

In 1013, Canute's father Sweyn Forkbeard intensified his raids on a prosperous England, almost united by the family of Alfred the Great. Alfred's grandson Aethelstan had seized York and Northumbria. In 927 he received the submission of the Scottish and Welsh monarchs of Alba, Strathclyde and Deheubarth, declaring himself King of All Britain, *basileus* and *imperator* – the invention of English independence.[†]

Needing money to pay off Danish raiders and build ships to repel them, Aethelstan and his family were among the first in Europe to collect an efficient tax on agriculture. But now that the Danes were back in force, King Aethelred the Unready[‡] was forced to pay Danegeld to new raiders: the Bluetooth family, founded a century earlier by a warlord, Old Gorm, who ruled Jelling in Denmark, a realm expanded by his son Harold Bluetooth (probably named after the pagan fashion for colouring teeth).[§] Bluetooth announced his conversion to Christianity in runic inscriptions on the Jelling Stones, but struggled over thirty years to control Jutland and southern Norway. In 986, his son Sweyn Forkbeard deposed Bluetooth, seized Denmark and Norway and started raiding Britain.

On St Brice's Day 1002 after four years of Forkbeardish raids, Aethelred ordered that 'All the Danes who had sprung up in this island,

---

* John Crescentius was the last of the Crescentii but the other Marozian line, the counts of Tusculum, controlled the papacy until 1049. Nor was this the end of the family: the Colonna princes, potentates for centuries to come, were and are descended from the Tusculum counts.

† Yet the Anglo-Saxons were already a hybrid of English and Viking. DNA shows that Vikings may have started with murder and rape but ultimately settled and intermarried with Celts and Anglo-Saxons.

‡ It was the age of eponyms that defined men by their looks and actions instead of their birth. Aethelred's was a (rather bad) joke. His name meant Well Advised. Unready meant Badly Advised. So he was Well Advised the Badly Advised.

§ In 1997, a computer engineer in California, a Viking-history buff, chose the name Bluetooth for short-duration communications as a tribute to the king's uniting of Scandinavian peoples.

sprouting like cockle amid the wheat, were to be destroyed by a most just extermination,' as he put it a royal charter. In a day of the long knives, Anglo-Saxons murdered Danes, burning many in an Oxford church where thirty-four skeletons, charred and butchered, have been unearthed. Among them was Forkbeard's own sister Gunhilde, married to a Danish lord at Aethelred's court. Forkbeard planned revenge, though he had rivals for the English prize: a Danish warlord Thorkel raided on his own account and after a massive tribute payment joined Aethelred.

In 1013 Forkbeard invaded in force and defeated Aethelred, who accompanied by his son Edward fled to Normandy. There he was given asylum by Rollo's descendant Duke Robert. But it all depended on Forkbeard. When he suddenly died, it all fell apart.

His younger son, the twenty-year-old Canute, 'exceptionally tall and strong, handsomest of men, all except for his nose, thin and rather hooked', took control of Norway, then raised a coalition of Scandinavians and Poles, lent by his cousin Bolesław, duke of Poland, which landed at Sandwich in Kent. He devastated England. Canute was joined by an English warlord, Godwin, who became his hatchet man, rewarded with the earldom of Wessex. Canute agreed to divide England with Aethelred's son Edmund Ironside of Wessex until his death, an occurrence that the Dane surely accelerated: Ironside was murdered defecating in his privy – always a vulnerable moment.

In 1017, Canute was crowned king of England, marrying Aethelred's widow Emma, daughter of a duke of Normandy. Playing both sides, Emma's brother protected her sons by Aethelred. Canute killed the one that fell into his hands, while he and Emma had their own son, Harthacnut. Confident of himself as 'king of all England and Denmark and the Norwegians and of some of the Swedes', Canute travelled to Rome for the imperial coronation and European summit, where he boasted that 'I spoke with the Emperor himself and the Lord Pope.'* But, as with Forkbeard, Canute's sudden death in 1035 unleashed chaos: Harthacnut was in Scandinavia, so his son by his concubine Aelfgifu, Harold Harefoot, seized England. When Aethelred's son, Aethling (heir) Alfred, returned,

---

* Canute negotiated free trade and free movement with European leaders, announcing, with echoes of today's Brexit negotiations, he had ensured that 'a juster law and securer peace might be granted to them on the road to Rome and that they should not be straitened by so many barriers along the road, and harassed by unjust tolls'. Canute's noble humility and ecological sensitivity was illustrated by his placing his throne on the beach saying, 'Let all see how empty is the power of kings.' This story was later recast to illustrate the exact opposite of the original, that Canute's humiliation by the defiant waves symbolized the arrogance of kings.

Godwin of Wessex blinded him, then scalped his troops. On Harefoot's death by elf-shot (a lovely euphemism for natural causes), Harthacnut claimed England* but was forced to recognize his half-brother Edward as Aethling. A fatal mistake.

The return of House Alfred was backed by Richard III, duke of Normandy, where Rollo's Vikings were now thoroughly Christian and Frankified. But the Vikings were still raiding and venturing. Now they reached a continent that had been separated from Afro-Eurasia for many millennia: America.

THE AMERICANS: FREYDIS AND FEATHERED SERPENT

Around 960, Thorvald Asvaldsson was exiled from Norway for murder and sent to settle in a new Viking colony far to the north: Iceland. The island, which had only been settled in the 870s by Naddod, a Viking from the Faroes, became a refuge for killers and dissidents. DNA reveals that many of the settlers hailed from Ireland or the Isles, victims of slaving raids. The 10,000 Icelanders founded a 'domain of our law' controlled by an *althing*, an assembly, run by a lawspeaker elected for three years.

A cousin of Naddod, Thorvald arrived with his equally lethal family: his son Eric had murdered someone in Norway and soon killed several more in Iceland. Some time late in the century, unwilling to return to Norway and outlawed in Iceland, Eric the Red (known either for his hair or for his homicidal incontinence) sailed westwards and landed in what, in an early example of branding, he called Greenland because 'people would be much more tempted to go there if it had an attractive name'. Returning there with fourteen ships he built two settlements that were run by an assembly. His wife Thjodhild was a Christian whose piety 'irritated him greatly'. She built a chapel (where a small cemetery contains bodies probably of the family), but punished him for his paganism by withholding sex, a serious punishment in such a remote place. But perhaps he converted, because they did produce four children.

---

* Scotland shook off Bluetooth empire. In 1031, Canute had invaded Scotland and forced High King Malcolm II and a kinglet, Mac Bethad of Moray, to submit. In 1039, Scottish king Donnchad the Sick, grandson of Malcolm II, ineptly raided England, a disaster that led to a rebellion by his magnate the *dux* and mormaer of Moray, Mac Bethad, who killed him in battle and ruled as king for seventeen years with his queen Gruoch. Gruoch's first husband had been burned to death, probably by Mac Bethad, whom she then married. In 1057 Donnchad's son Malcolm III invaded and killed Mac Bethad with English help. In 1606 Shakespeare premiered a play about these characters. Mac Bethad became Macbeth – though Shakespeare missed a trick in not using the name Gruoch.

Their houses were built with turf dung and stone with animals living closely for warmth, while household items were carved from reindeer antler, bone and wood. Greenland was not empty: Inuit tribesmen whom the Vikings called Skraellings lived there in sunken huts, hunting walruses and seals and even whales with harpoons, travelling by kayak. Eric and his family lived by hunting, and it is probable Viking hunters crossed Davis Strait into north America, settling at Kimmirut on Baffin Island (Canada), where whetstones and rat droppings been found. Since rats were not native to America, it is likely they accompanied the Vikings, who soon realized there was another land further west.

Eric's son Leif the Lucky, a Christian, was encouraged by the king of Norway to convert the Greenland Vikings. Now he joined an expedition to America. Eric wanted to come too but, having fallen off his horse, had shown himself to be too old. Sailing down the coast of Canada, the voyagers (including one of Leif's brothers, Thorvald) first stopped at Baffin Island, then sailed on to Newfoundland (Markland), where Nordic houses for around 100 have been found and dated to this moment – the arrival of the first Europeans to settle in America. The brothers then sailed on to found a second settlement, at L'Anse aux Meadows, where wooden objects had been carbon-dated by geoscientists to prove that the Vikings were there in 1021. It is unclear if this is the place they called Vinland, where they found vines growing. When they discovered three strangers sleeping under a boat, they encountered Skraellings – native Americans of the Boethuk and Mikmaq tribes – and killed two of them. The tribes hit back, shooting Thorvald with an arrow.

More Vikings arrived, including one, Porfinn, who fell in love with Thorvald's widow Gudred. Their child together was the first European colonist born in America. Leif's half-sister Freydis seems to have assumed power. Arguing with another group of settlers, she attacked them, ordering the men to be killed, but when her henchmen refused to kill the women, Freydis took an axe and butchered five women herself – 'a monstrous deed'. She was forgiven when they were attacked by Skraellings: she rallied the defence by slapping her sword against her breast. L'Anse aux Meadows looks like a halfway point to somewhere else – but where?

Some historians have claimed that the Vikings made contact with other Skraellings. Far to the south, in Mexico, the Maya city at Chichen Itza, built around a pyramid 100 feet high, was now home to 40,000 – larger than London. In a 200-columned temple to war, paintings show prisoners with fair hair, light eyes and pale skin being killed. 'The timing coincides perfectly with the Norse voyages,' speculates Valerie

Hansen; ' . . . the Vikings could have arrived in the Yucatán.' If so, the adventure was disastrous – and left no other trace.

The Maya did not trade directly with north American peoples but there was indirect movement in goods and ideas: in the Mississippi Valley, the cultivation of maize and beans fuelled the building of small feuding towns, the largest of which was Cahokia in Illinois, whose population around 1050 seems to have expanded from 10,000 to 40,000, nourished by maize growing. A hundred mounds, still to be seen today, the remains of earthen pyramids that held ritual sweat lodges, charnel houses and temples, were centred around the original 100-foot mound and a giant plaza used for rituals. Cahokia was ruled by a family in which succession may have descended through the female line. Its elite played a game, chunkey, employing stones and linked to war and mythology. The losers were sometimes killed. Top men and women were buried together with beaded capes and shells, alongside hundreds of sacrificed victims, beheaded, dismembered or buried alive. Four mass graves contain fifty sacrificed young women.*

The Viking colonies in America did not endure. Leif returned to Greenland, where his son Thorkell succeeded him as chieftain; Gudred made the pilgrimage to Jerusalem and ended as a nun on Iceland, where her American son became the forefather of many Icelanders. Their American adventure did not change the world – the colonists were too few and the European prizes were too rich. Yet, as a newly discovered Milanese document reveals, knowledge of the continent's existence was passed down by Nordic sailors.†

A Danish king Harthacnut still ruled England, recognizing as his heir the Aethling Edward, son of Aethelred, later celebrated for saintly piety as the Confessor. But on 8 June 1042 Harthacnut, attending a wedding in London, raised a toast to the bride and 'suddenly fell to the earth with an awful convulsion'. The saintly Edward probably poisoned

---

* The Cahokians were in contact with the north, where turquoise was acquired from Utah, and with the south, bringing jade and obsidian from Mexico. They filed their front teeth and ate chocolate as Maya did, using Mesoamerican cacao. One of the technologies they sent south was the bow and arrow, which had spread southwards from the Arctic peoples, reaching the south-west around 500 and then on to Mexico. In New Mexico, at Chaco Canyon, other peoples, known as Pueblans, built villages with houses (one complex had 800 rooms), underground storage rooms and squares, along with a road system that had mysterious ritual purposes. They too drank chocolate, lived off domesticated turkeys and wore turquoise and macaw feathers from the south.

† Iceland stayed inhabited, and was visited by English seamen, but the ancient Norse settlements in Greenland did not last, suffering as they did from falling temperatures, Inuit attacks and starvation. Bones discovered record their malnourishment, while Icelandic sagas recount that 'the old and helpless were killed and thrown over cliffs'.

him. Edward was supported by the prince blinder, mass-scalper and kingmaker Godwin of Wessex, who, married to Canute's sister-in-law, had helped destroy his father and killed at least one brother. But now they soothed these crimes with marriage: Edward married Godwin's daughter Edith and raised his son Harold to earl. When Godwin died, Harold, half Anglo-Saxon, half Dane, succeeded as the first potentate of the kingdom, earl of Wessex. Since Edward had no children, who would inherit England?

The island was on the edge of Europe, but Canute's Roman trip showed how this Scando-Britannic empire was now linked by Mediterranean trade routes to Asia. Two coins from a resurgent China have been found in Edward's England, while in Egypt the Mad Caliph, al-Hakim, had gone much further, contacting the new Chinese emperor.

But in Cairo this Arab Caligula turned on his entourage. Once, passing a butcher's shop, he just took a cleaver and killed one of his courtiers without even stopping. Then he cancelled his anti-Jewish, anti-Christian decrees and enforced a new puritanism on the Cairenes. All women had to wear veils and alcohol was banned – a sign of how lax society had become in Cairo. He beheaded many of his own concubines, banned all singing and dancing, then forbade women from going out at all, even to shop. When they ignored his orders, they were killed. When they protested that they had to go out shopping, al-Hakim told them to order deliveries to the home – a caliphal version of Amazon. Other strange measures followed: his *wasita* (chief minister) and generals were frequently executed; cats and dogs were destroyed; eating watercress, grapes and fish without scales was banned.

Touched by the sanctity of the imamate and the young caliph's wild charisma, some Ismaili sectarians believed that al-Hakim 'personified God within him' and hailed him as divine, an idea that appealed to the caliph, who now wandered Cairo streets in drug-fuelled trances. But the grandees were worried.

Al-Hakim was close to his sister Sitt al-Mulk – a title that meant Lady of Power. She was fearless, fortyish, as blonde and blue-eyed as the caliph. But he now became paranoid about her intrigues. Some of his suspicions were correct. Sitt al-Mulk lived in splendour in her own palace where she dared to hide potential victims of her brother's insanity. Al-Hakim accused her of 'fornication' with generals and viziers, executing one who may have been her lover. Sitt al-Mulk realized she was in peril and made her plans.

When al-Hakim nominated a cousin, not his young son al-Zahir, as heir, Sitt al-Mulk protected the child and wrote to a general called Ibn

Daws to tell him that the caliph accused the two of them of having an affair. It was either kill or be killed.

In 1021, al-Hakim, now thirty-six, rode out of Cairo to meditate and never came back. His body was never found, just bloodied rags.

Yet his influence has endured to this day.* Al-Hakim, whose ports in Arabia and the Red Sea regularly traded with India and China, learned from these seafarers that something had changed in China. In 1008, he sent a sea captain, Domiyat, to China to deliver gifts and letters to Zhenzong, emperor of a new dynasty – the Song – that had opened a new act and made the Central Country the most dynamic, prosperous, sophisticated and technologically innovative empire on earth. As if inventing gunpowder, printing and the compass was not enough, its founder may have invented football.

---

* This occulted vanishing only added to al-Hakim's mystique among his disciples, who were massacred on his sister's orders. Some of them escaped: today two million Druze in Israel, Lebanon and Syria still revere his divinity. Sitt al-Mulk covered her own traces, executed Ibn Daws and ruled the Fatimiyya empire as princess-aunt, reversing al-Hakim's bans: wine drinking and music playing were restored, women were allowed to dress as they wished and to shop; Jews and Christians could return to their faiths and stop wearing distinguishing clothes; Easter and Christmas were back.

ACT SEVEN
226 MILLION

Song, Fujiwara and Chola

DREAM POOL ESSAYS: GUNPOWDER, PAPER MONEY, POETRY — THE SOPHISTICATES OF SONG

Emperor Zhenzong welcomed contact with Egypt along with other trading partners in India and Malaysia, as his China – its population having doubled to 120 million – was becoming the most refined state in the world. But the Song dynasty's founder, his uncle, Zhao Kuangyin, was a roughhewn horse archer who was so tough that once, riding without stirrups, he was thrown by his horse and concussed but still chased it, caught it and rode on. Rising to the top during fighting between warlords, in 960 he declared himself Emperor Taizu – the Great Forefather. He had fought savagely to defeat multiple contenders but was always innovative. In one battle, he used explosive 'fire arrows' to bomb war elephants; in another case his generals ate 'fat captives' in front of other, thinner prisoners, who were then released to spread word of Song ferocity. It worked.

An avid martial artist who supposedly invented the Taizu Long Fist technique, he promoted a game called *cuju* which he was painted playing: football. But once in power this semi-literate conqueror proved constructive and creative. He persuaded his paladins to retire, reassured by marriage into the family, and insisted that 'my chief counsellors should be men who read books'. He also restored the civil service examinations, founded academies and tried to avoid capricious terror: 'Officials and scholars must not be executed.' Choosing his brother Taizong rather than his sons for a smooth succession, he called his reign 'Nation Restored'. So it was.

Now his nephew Zhenzong ruled from Bianjing (Kaifeng), the biggest city in the world with a million people, on the banks of the Bian River. It was filled with shops, restaurants, tea houses, taverns, palaces, teeming with merchants, shopkeepers, palm readers, hustlers, hucksters, psychics and designers. As Michael Wood writes, this was the 'first great restaurant culture of the world complete with cookbooks and dining etiquette guides' – which recommended a variety of meats from quail and venison to badgers and pangolins – for 'the best-fed people who had lived so far in history'.

Fielding an army of over a million, Taizu and his successors deliberately encouraged technical learning and rewarded inventors, measures that 'brought about a great number of cases of people presenting technology and techniques'. Taizu's fire arrows were shot out of the tubes propelled by the Chinese invention, gunpowder, an accidental by-product of the Organic Fire Medicines, immortality elixirs, that had poisoned so many emperors. Now his engineers added extra saltpetre to produce a more powerful gunpowder, and later Song engineers created Thundercrash Bombs fired by trebuchets, and shoulder-fired Sky Erupters, an early firearm.*

The Song's standing navy, China's first, perhaps the world's first, would be equipped with these weapons while navigating with magnetized compasses, their battleships and paddleboats made safe by watertight compartments not used in the west until the nineteenth century. Their goods were moved along the Grand Canal network improved by the Song, who used pound locks so that boats could travel from Kaifeng all the way to their southern port, Hangzhou; meanwhile a postal service improved communication. Rich aristocrats and merchants lived in exquisite palaces, using paper money to buy books written by male scholars and female poets, whose works were printed on paper using movable type. These works were read by a huge literate fanbase. The dynasty's silk and porcelain were manufactured in state factories; its foundries produced so much iron – 100,000 tons annually, increasingly using coal in its furnaces – that Britain did not equal that output until the eighteenth century. Its scientists dissected cadavers for cause of death; astronomers mapped the heavens; its ministers created public clinics, welfare systems, paupers' graveyards and aid for peasantry. The Song illustrate how rulers could deliver economic prosperity and technological advances by centralizing the rule of their vast market and encouraging ingenuity, both of which boosted foreign trade. Wealth and freedom were encouraged, providing they never challenged Song power. But the hierarchy was strict: men wore ornate robes according to their court ranks. The risk was that ultimately political control would crush the ingenuity that had created the Song miracle in the first place.

It was made possible by a succession of capable rulers who appointed

---

* In 1044, a printed technical guide the *Wujing Zongyao* specified formulae for manufacturing appropriate gunpowder for different bombs.

some of the most refined statesmen to rule any country. At the time of al-Hakim and Canute, the real ruler of China was Empress Liu. She had started as an orphaned dancing girl married off to an impoverished silversmith who actually sold her to the future emperor. She and her new husband were childless, but she adopted the son of a concubine who was brought up as her own. After Zhenzong's death in 1022 when she was fifty-two, she effectively made herself emperor, ruling for her supposed son Renzong. Coarse and fierce, she was a competent decision maker while the long-reigning Renzong was cultivated and self-deprecating: 'I've never used the word "death" to threaten others, how dare I abuse the death penalty?' But he made a fatal decision. The Song ruled only a quarter of today's China; the north was dominated by a nomadic kingdom, the Khitan, which ruled Manchuria and Mongolia. To avoid constant war, he negotiated a truce by which he conceded vast tribute payments that ultimately destroyed Song from within while empowering deadly nomadic enemies without.

Of Song's refined statesmen, Shen Gua, the polymathic courtier who served Renzong's son Emperor Yingzong, was one of the most extraordinary. He rose to be chief of the emperor's Bureau of Astronomy, a reforming Assistant Minister of Imperial Hospitality and ambassador to the Khitans, and as a general he led Song forces against the Tanguts.* All the while he experimented with the magnetic compass needle and the concept of true north, researched the orbit of planets, designed a water clock, analysed geological history using marine fossils and climate change, improved the designs of drydocks for ships and pound locks for canals, analysed pharmacology, refined iron forging, dissected corpses of executed bandits to study the throat and conceived a pinhole camera. But his luck ran out at court and he was framed for a defeat by the Tanguts. He finally retired to his country estate Dream Pool, where he wrote his collection *Dream Pool Essays* – enjoying his 'nine guests'.†

He was one of many luminaries. At the southern end of the Great Canal, the port of Linan (Hangzhou), briefly administered by a famous poet, Su Shi, was the world's supreme entrepôt, its canals, restaurants and streets crowded with Persians, Jews and Indians, its ships bearing

---

* A people from Tibetan-Burman marches who had moved into north-western China.
† The nine guests of Chinese culture were good wine, poetry, zither music, calligraphy, the boardgame weiqi (Go), Buddhist meditation, tea, alchemy and talking with close friends. As a man devoted to scientific enquiry Shen Gua observed that there were phenomena that could not be easily defined: 'Most people can only judge of things by the experiences of ordinary life, but phenomena outside the scope of this are really quite numerous. How insecure it is to investigate natural principles using only the light of common knowledge . . .'

silk, velvet, porcelain, iron and swords to western Asia and Europe, via Egypt and the Gulf, eastwards to Japan and southwards to Sumatra and India.

In 1033, a delegation arrived in Hangzhou from a Song trading partner, Rajendra Chola, the *chakravartin* (world emperor) of a Tamil empire who had conquered the eastern coast of India up to Bengal as well as the Maldives and Sri Lanka. Champion of Hinduism, builder of the majestic Brihadishvara temple and his capital Gangaikonda Cholapuram, Rajendra created a powerful Indian navy, based at Nagapattinam, supposedly with 500 enormous ships, some bearing 1,000 sailors and boasting the latest Chinese technology – compartmentalized hulls, compasses and flamethrowers. He also backed the Ainnurruvar – 'the five hundred [lords] from the four countries and the thousand directions' – and other piratical Tamil trading guilds whose fleets were precursors of European armed trading corporations. Rajendra's two embassies to China reflected his frustration that Indian trade had to be mediated through a seafaring kingdom, Srivijaya in Sumatra, that was closer to Huanzong.

Srivijaya was an Indic thalassocracy ruled by a raja who sent traders across a wide *mandala* – sacred circle – of power, selling spices, camphor (from Borneo), cloves, sandalwood and brazilwood to the Chinese court in return for porcelain and silk and recognition of its rajas as kings. Its people paid tribute to the Chinese but thought in Sanskrit. This mercantile confederacy enjoyed close relations with another Indic power, the Sailendra family, who ruled the Mataram raj, building magnificent temples in Java and presiding over a *mandala* extending as far as the Philippines and Thailand. Later its Buddhist and Shaivite branches split and fought, a schism in the Indosphere with political consequences: Mataram and Srivijaya separated. Yet both thrived as trading empires: a shipwreck, found in Srivijayan waters, carrying an estimated 70,000 pieces of ceramic shows the scale of this trade to China and Iraq. Riches attract enemies, and the Srivijayan confederacy sanctioned pirates who preyed on Arab, Indian and Chinese convoys, pushing up the prices for Arab horses for the Chola armies.

Rajendra got his pretext in 1025 when the most powerful king in south-east Asia,* Suryavarman, ruler of the Khmer empire and a fellow

---

* In the 780s, King Indra, the Sailendra maharaja of both Mataram and Srivijaya, a Buddhist who may have planned the great Javan temple of Borobudur, ruled much of mainland south-east Asia as well as Indonesia. A Cambodian prince may have served as Indra's general, having perhaps started as a hostage or prisoner. Either set up by Indra or having escaped from his clutches, the prince established himself as ruler of Kambujadesa (Cambodia) around 781 – just as Haroun was dominating western Asia and Charlemagne was conquering Europe. In 802, on a sacred hill, and now styling himself Jayavarman II,

Shaivite Hindu, requested Rajendra's help against the Buddhist Srivi-jayans. Rajendra sailed with his fleet, sacked their capital, captured their raja. There, much of the Chinese trade was taken over by his Tamil trading companies, which gloried in names such as the Merchants of the Three Worlds (Arab, Indian and Chinese). But Song influence also extended eastwards to Japan, where a female writer was inventing the novel.

'No matter how amorous or passionate you may be, as long as you are straightforward and refrain from causing others embarrassment, no one will mind,' wrote Lady Murasaki, a widow aged around thirty, in her diary in 1010 as the all-powerful regent Fujiwara Michinaga, fifty-five years old, flirted with her at the court of the emperor of Japan.

TWO FEMALE WRITERS – MURASAKI AND THE POETESS

A few days after Lady Murasaki's diary entry, Michinaga – whom Mura-saki always calls His Excellency – was visiting his daughter, the empress Shoshi, when he noticed that she was reading a chapter of Murasaki's novel *The Tale of Genji*, the story through which she invented the novel. These circulated chapters were parts of a narrative in prose that explore human experience through imagined characters in a new way pioneered by Murasaki. 'Out came the usual comments,' wrote Murasaki, mean-ing flirtatious admiration, 'and then on a piece of paper that held some plums' the regent scribbled this poem:

> She is known for her tartness
> So I am sure no one seeing her
> Could pass without a taste.

'I am shocked,' she said, in response to his pun on tastiness, a prop-osition in front of his daughter to her literary mentor. But Murasaki was capable of teasing him back, noting in a poem of her own, 'You have neither read my book nor won my love.' Learning that every writer

---

he crowned himself *chakravartin*. A devout Shaivite, he threw off the yoke of the Buddhist Sailendras, but channelled their cult of the god-king – *devaraja* – around himself as Shiva. Ruling from the capitals Hariharalaya and Mahendraparvata, he embarked on a series of campaigns to unite the Cambodian principalities and so conquered a Khmer empire that extended from 'China, Champa [Vietnam] and the land of cardamoms and mangoes [Thai-land?]'. The Khmers, ruling from ever more elaborate and massive cities, would be the dominant power for the next five centuries. The *chakravartins* had already started building royal palaces and temples at Angkor: now Suryavarman I built the three-terraced pyramid at Phimeanakas within the Angkor Thom palace.

expects their lovers to have read their books, the regent crept into her room and stole a new chapter – and kept chasing her: 'One night as I lay asleep, there came the sound of someone tapping at the door. I was so frightened that I kept quiet for the rest of the night.' It is hard to tell if this was the harassment of an ageing sex pest or the flattering attention of a charismatic potentate.

She never admitted to becoming Michinaga's lover, but it is possible she did. Murasaki,* lady-in-waiting, novelist and poet, found herself at the very centre of the court in Heian-kyo – Kyoto – during the time of her older suitor, Fujiwara Michinaga, ruler of Japan for thirty years. She too was a Fujiwara, a distant poor cousin grateful for the favour of her relative. Yet her words are still read today.

Murasaki had married late but happily and had a daughter, but her husband died in an epidemic and she did not remarry. From the earliest age, her intelligence and learning had impressed her father, who exclaimed, 'What a pity she wasn't born a man!'

Hearing of her talents, Michinaga hired her as an attendant to discuss literature with his daughter Empress Shoshi. In 794, some 200 years earlier, Emperor Kanmu had consolidated a confident state, Nihon – meaning Root of the Sun – based at Heian-kyo. Arriving from Korea, Buddhism had fused with the Japanese system of deities – *kami* – later known as Shinto. Japan was much influenced by China, but a newly confident Japanese culture now developed.

The Fujiwara were already the leading clan when in 729 one of their daughters became the first non-royal to receive the title empress. In 850, Fujiwara Yoshifusa managed to arrange the imperial succession of Montoku his nephew. After that, the Fujiwara ruled as 'regents' for young emperors and 'spokesmen' for older ones. Their paramountcy was based on their vast wealth and constant marriage into the royal family, from whom they frequently chose child emperors. Michinaga's father married three of his daughters to emperors. Michinaga himself introduced his daughter Shoshi into Emperor Ichijo's harem. There was usually only one empress and many concubines, and Ichijo already had an empress, Teishi, who had delivered a son. But Michinaga demanded that Shoshi also became empress – and he got his way.

The best way to understand their world is through the writings of Michinaga's protégée, Murasaki. It was male-dominated, calibrated

---

* Female names were not preserved in Japan. Lady Murasaki was a descriptive nickname, based on the character in her novel, but her real name may have been Fujiwara no Kaoruko, one of the ladies-in-waiting mentioned in Michinaga's diary.

strictly by rank and centred around the Great Imperial Palace compound in a grid-system capital that was similar to the Tang capital Chang'an. Life in the compound was divided between the emperor's palace and the Court of Government where Michinaga governed. His daughter Shoshi, the empress, lived in the rear palace with her ladies-in-waiting, and lesser consorts, perhaps a thousand women altogether.

Men had more than one wife, while women could have only one husband. In *The Tale of Genji*, the wives all lived around the courtyard of the husband's mansion, though more often different wives lived in different houses. Women whitened their faces, rouged their cheeks, painted their eyebrows, scented their hair and blackened their teeth, and they dressed in multilayered robes of silk, damask and brocade, dyed and changed according to the occasion. They shared in the property of their parents. Women had considerable freedom even for sexual trysts, as recounted by Murasaki: 'All these ladies-in-waiting must have been approached by senior courtiers at one time or another. If anyone is careless there is no hiding the fact but somehow, by taking precautions, they do seem to keep their affairs secret.' When Michinaga learned Murasaki was sharing a room with another girl, he asked (hopefully), 'What happens when you entertain someone the other doesn't know?'

'A tasteless remark,' Murasaki notes.

When Empress Shoshi, Murasaki's patroness, became pregnant at the age of twenty-one, Michinaga moved the empress into his own Tsuchimikado mansion where, soothed by readings from the Buddhist *Lotus Sutra*, she awaited the birth with Murasaki. The chaotic birth was every woman's nightmare. Shoshi lay on a raised dais in the suffocatingly hot upper gallery surrounded by curtains; courtiers peered into the chamber; rice was thrown to expel evil spirits; Michinaga shouted orders; priests and exorcists competed and jostled to chant 'loud spells cast to transfer evil influences'. A preceptor 'was thrown to the ground in spasms by the spirits'. Murasaki notes wryly, 'You can imagine every Buddha in the universe flying down to respond.' When the poor empress went into labour, she 'was in great distress'. Childbirth was dangerous – Shoshi's rival empress had just died that way – and child mortality high.

Then, suddenly, the baby arrived. 'Our delight knew no bounds,' wrote Murasaki, and when the baby was seen to be a boy, they were 'ecstatic'. It was the triumph of Michinaga's policy of marrying his daughters to emperors. In 1017, after the birth of another prince, he celebrated his power: 'No waning in the glory of the full moon – this world is indeed my world.'

Michinaga possibly asked Murasaki to keep her diary to celebrate the birth. Many women were keeping diaries; everyone wrote poetry, men in Chinese, women in Japanese, in this refined and literary world where 'sensitivity', notes Murasaki, 'is a precious gift'.

Murasaki divided her capacious novel *The Tale of Genji* into chapters that were read around the court like serializations. At its heart is the character of Genji, an emperor's son (possibly based on Michinaga), and his relationships with women, not just romantic but also familial. While he philanders with younger women, his second wife, Lady Murasaki – Wisteria – provides real friendship. 'Coming from the presence of younger women,' she writes, 'Genji always expected Murasaki would appear a little bit jaded . . . He had lived with her so long . . . yet it was just these younger women who failed to provide any element of surprise whereas Murasaki was continually astounding him, her person more radiant this year than last year.'

Murasaki described herself as a melancholic 'old fossil'. 'No one liked her,' she writes about herself. 'They all said she was pretentious, awkward, difficult to approach, prickly, too fond of her tales, haughty . . . but when you meet her, she is strangely meek.' No wonder the other girls were jealous. No one knows when Murasaki died, but in 1019 her patron Michinaga retired to a Buddhist monastery, handing over the regency to his son and arranging the succession of his grandsons as emperors, ensuring Fujiwara rule for two more generations. As Fujiwara power started to wane, the Song emperors were facing a catastrophe that was narrated by the other great writer of the time, who was also a woman.

Born in 1084 in Shandong, Li Qingzhao was the clever daughter of a scholar-official who had studied under the poet Su Shi: at a young age, she started to write poetry of 'delicate restraint'. At seventeen, she married Zhao Mingcheng, a well-connected connoisseur of epigraphy, literature and antiques with whom she collected books and period pieces, co-wrote essays, ate at restaurants and played board games, living in Shandong – a life of provincial Song refinement.

As parents could afford to pay higher dowries, the status of Song women increased, perhaps aided by the competent rule of Empress Liu. Women could own and inherit property, but now they were so highly educated that they published poetry and often tutored sons. Shen Gua was taught military strategy by his mother, something unimaginable anywhere else for many centuries.*

Li was enjoying the zenith of Song prosperity: 'we lived happy together' – though she could not have children. Instead she worked on her art. 'Concentration leads to refined skill,' she writes, which means 'everything you do can reach a level of real excellence'. But the course of her marriage mirrored the trajectory of the Song. Her husband fell for a concubine with whom he had children. The marriage deteriorated:

> A cold window, broken table and no books.
> How pitiful to be brought to this . . .
> Writing poetry I turn down all invitations, shutting my door for now.
> In my isolation I have found perfect friends:
> Mr Nobody and Sir Emptiness.

Then came the invasion.

Emperor Huizong had neglected the frontiers and the armies, admitting, 'I inherited a great flourishing empire but I myself was a mediocre person not up to the job.' In 1125, after a twenty-year war, Jurchen semi-nomads from Manchuria destroyed and replaced the Khitan as the rulers of northern China, declared their own Jin empire and invaded Song. The unthinkable happened quickly: the barbarians, using Song military technology learned from prisoners, besieged the capital Kaifeng. In 1127, they stormed the city, rounding up princesses, concubines and actor-singers of the court, mass-raping women and then forcing Emperor Huizong, 14,000 courtiers and women on a snowy death march northwards. The emperor's consort was raped and miscarried, then was forced to sing before the Jurchen commander. 'Once I lived in heaven above in pearl palaces and jade towers,' she wrote. 'Now I live among grass and brambles, my blue robe soaked in tears.' But she refused to perform. She had nothing left to lose. The empress committed suicide; princesses were sold for ten ounces of gold.

As the Jurchen advanced, the poetess Li and her husband loaded fifteen carts of antiques and books and headed southwards. But the Jurchens burned much of their collection. As they trudged among crowds of refugees, her husband Zhao, in an unconscious statement of Song delicacy, told her to 'discard furniture, then clothes, then books, then

---

* Yet everything revolved around male power; men had several wives and concubines. As Li's experience shows, it was a struggle to be an independent woman – and even that freedom did not last as later women less lucky than Li became confined to the house, their movement agonizingly confined by a new practice designed to emphasize female delicacy: foot-binding.

antiques' but to 'carry the most treasured items with you' so 'you can live or die with them'. But he died of dysentery while writing a poem and still holding his writing brush.

The emperor also died; a world was dying, but one of the emperor's sons escaped to the south. Gaozong re-established the Mandate of Heaven. He had lost of much of China but crossed the Yangtse and established the Song at a new capital, Linan (Hangzhou), where many of the poets and polymaths of Kaifeng now settled. The poetess Li joined them. Aged forty-eight, she remarried disastrously. Her new husband was a mendacious mountebank and their union lasted just a hundred days. 'At my advanced age, I'd married a worthless shyster,' who beat her. She won a divorce (not because of his violence but because of his social lies). Finally liberated, she wrote disdainfully of the useless politicians of her time:

> Our high-ranking ministers still run away in all directions;
> Images of the great steeds of the old heroes fill my eyes.
> In these dangerous times where can we find real horses like them?

As the Song developed new paddle-powered battleships that used the latest bomb-throwing trebuchets and specially trained marines, they defeated the Jurchens. Guangzhou (Canton) and their southern ports sent huge dhows filled with luxuries to Egypt and to Iraq, where an upstart family of Turks was taking over the caliphate.

Seljuks, Komnenoi and Hautevilles

ARSLAN RAMPANT LION AND THE AGELESS ZOË

'God created them in the shape of lions,' wrote a courtier of the Seljuk Turks, 'with broad faces and flat noses, muscles strong, fists enormous.' A Turkmen warlord named Seljuk had fought for the Jewish Khazar khagans in his youth. The names of his sons – Israel, Yusuf and Musa – suggest the family may have converted to Judaism, but in the 990s Seljuk switched to Islam, embracing jihad as his mission, and gathered a federation of tribes in Transoxiana, assisted by warlike sons. 'They ascend great mountains, ride in face of danger, raid and go deep into unknown lands.' Seljuk and son were just one of the Turkic warrior clans carving up the Arab empire.*

After Seljuk's death in 1009, his grandson Tugril defeated the Ghazni sultans before moving on to the big prize. In 1055, his troops galloped into Baghdad, rescuing Caliph al-Qaim from the Shiites. While fighting the Fatimiyya and the Romans and conquering an empire, Sultan Tugril, like many a Turkish warlord, aspired to the Persianate culture of Baghdad. His nephew Alp Arslan – Heroic Lion – was the greatest potentate of his time, ruling from Pakistan to Türkiye. He promoted a Persian vizier, Abu Ali Hasan, granted the title Nizam al-Mulk – Order of the Realm – who embellished the Seljuk capitals Isfahan (Iran) and Merv (Turkmenistan) with mosques, libraries and observatories.

As the Seljuks attacked the Roman marches, the heiress to the glories

---

* To the east, a warlord named Mahmud hacked out a new realm, based in Ghazni (Afghanistan), which he expanded from Persia to Pakistan, repeatedly raiding northern India. The Ghaznavis fought like Turks but embraced refined Persianate culture. Mahmud patronized a Persian poet, a Khorasani landowner's son called Ferdowsi (Paradisiacal, his nom de plume), who for thirty years had been writing the *Shahnameh* – the Story of Kings – an epic poem of gods and heroes starring a strapping Prince Rustam and promoting the Persian over the Arab, fusing pre-Islamic and Islamic Persian culture. Mahmud promised Ferdowsi a gold piece for every couplet but took so long to pay up, the money arrived as the poet's funeral cortège left. While the caliph remained nominal overlord, he granted the Ghaznavis a new title of secular authority: sultan, the power.

of the Basil Bulgar Slayer was his niece Zoë. After a disappointing trip to Italy to marry a German emperor who died before her arrival, Zoë spent the rest of her life with her two sisters in the *gynaeceum* (women's quarters) of the Great Palace. Basil had prevented the spinsters from marrying aristocrats who could threaten his crown. Theodora Porphyrogenita was known for her piety, Zoë Porphyrogenita for her blonde beauty and her lovers.

On the day he died, her father Constantine VIII married Zoë, now fifty, to a sexagenarian aristocrat, Romanos Argyros, who at once became emperor. 'Every part of her,' wrote historian Michael Psellos in his *Chronographia*, 'was firm and in good condition.' Zoë devoted much attention to cosmetics, installing a *myrepseion* (laboratory) in her apartments.* The effort paid off: her mosaic portrait in Hagia Sophia, created when she was in her sixties, shows a handsome woman. Doctors and charlatans were consulted to help her conceive, but she quickly turned against her husband. Joannes the Eunuch, a Paphlagonian peasant's son who had been Basil II's secretary, and was now *parakoimomenos* (chief minister), introduced Zoë to his younger brother, Michael, an epileptic former money changer, who charmed the empress.

In April 1034, when Zoë was fifty-six and Michael twenty-five, they strangled Romanos in his bath and married the next day. As his passion for Zoë cooled, Michael IV became anxious that she would turn against him. When Michael was incapacitated, Zoë and Joannes the Eunuch promoted his nephew to Caesar. This was Michael the Caulker. The Eunuch became a monk and retired, ostensibly just serving as *orphanotrophos*, curator of Constantinople's largest orphanage. But the omnipotent Eunuch was now hated. The Caulker exiled his uncle, castrated all his cousins and then in 1042 moved against Zoë. He accused her of treason, tonsuring and then imprisoning her on an island from which she was unlikely to return.

But the Basil family was still loved. In the hippodrome, Michael was bombarded with fruit, then besieged in the palace by the women of Constantinople, united in female solidarity. Zoë, now sixty-four, returned to power; the Caulker was blinded and castrated. Zoë and her nunnish sister Theodora were enthroned. Two months later, Zoë married (an old lover) Constantine Monomachos, who as emperor moved his mistress into a ménage à trois. The Romans feared that their beloved old sisters

---

* Blondeness and pallor were much prized: myrrh, lime, saffron, sandarach and thapsia were used for hair dye; chalk and lead powder for face make-up. Her ingredients were imported from Egypt and India.

were in danger, and they were pacified only by the appearance of Zoë and Theodora in the hippodrome. Just as Zoë planned to reconquer Italy, five sword-swinging Norman brothers changed everything.

IRON-ARM WILLIAM, WILY ROBERT AND AMAZONIAN SICHELGAITA

In 1035, William Iron-Arm, the first of the Hauteville boys, arrived in southern Italy to back a Lombard nobleman against Zoë's forces. Sicily remained Muslim, while Naples and Apulia belonged to Zoë – and Rome was ruled by the Marozian pope Benedict IX, son of Alberic of Tusculum. Benedict, elected at twenty, became notorious for 'his rapes, murders and other unspeakable acts of violence and sodomy', according to a later pope. 'His life as a pope was so vile, so foul, so execrable, that I shudder to think of it.' But Benedict's conduct was typical of a priesthood that was denounced by the reforming priest Damian in his aptly titled *Book of Gomorrah* for rampant simony, venality, concubinage, sodomy, paedophilia and mutual masturbation. In 1045, priests rebelled and invited the German emperor king Heinrich III to rescue them from the Marozian pornocrats. Heinrich took Rome and destroyed the Marozians once and for all. But all this volatility was irresistible to a gifted family of swaggering blond giants.

Tancred de Hauteville, a minor Norman baron descended from a Viking named Hiallt, had twelve sons, so most of them had to seek their fortunes abroad.

The two eldest brothers, Drogo and William, arrived in Italy where they fought for all sides. In 1036, one of the Arab amirs of Sicily appealed to Empress Zoë, who raised an army that included Viking mercenaries led by a Norwegian prince Harold Hardrada and the Hauteville brothers. Zoë's Sicilian expedition was a disaster; the imperious Romaioi disrespected the Hautevilles, who thereafter hated Constantinople. The brothers changed sides, joined the army of Heinrich, defeated Zoë's forces and seized Apulia. Heinrich (now emperor) recognized Iron-Arm William as count of Apulia. In 1042, they were joined by Humphrey and Robert. The latter was known as Guiscard, meaning Wily, and was best described by Anna Komnene, emperor's daughter and the finest (female) historian of the era: 'His stature was so lofty that he surpassed even the tallest, his complexion was ruddy, his hair flaxen, his shoulders were broad, his eyes all but emitted sparks of fire – he was neatly and gracefully formed from tip to toe.' Robert arrived alone, too poor to afford a

servant, but his brother Iron-Arm died soon afterwards and Count Drogo
fobbed him off. Robert earned his nickname with his trick of taking castles by pretending to be dead, being borne into the castles inside a coffin
by his solemn warriors – only to kick the lid off and spring out, sword
in hand.

In 1053, the rise of the Hautevilles was suddenly challenged from a
surprising direction. A new pope, Leo IX, a German priest backed by
Heinrich, launched a resurgence of the papacy, banning simony and
ordering celibacy for priests, a concept unique to the Catholic Church.
And terrified of the 'wicked race' of Hautevilles, he led an army southwards to destroy them. Instead Wily Robert and his brother Humphrey
defeated and captured Leo, an experience that convinced the Holy
Father that he needed closer relations with Constantinople, where – Zoë
having died – her widower Monomachos now ruled. But in Constantinople Leo's delegates achieved the opposite, aggressively confronting the
Greeks about their differences in doctrine.* Behind this lurked a rising
confidence as western Europe became richer and more populous, combined with a seething jealousy of Constantinople, metropolis of sacred
Autokrators, venomous conspiracies and incomprehensible Greek. The
papal envoys stormed into Hagia Sophia and excommunicated the patriarch – creating a schism that has never healed, a theological divergence
that remains today.

The Hautevilles released Leo only when he recognized their territories. After the death of Humphrey, Robert became the count, now joined
by the eighth brother, Roger, 'a youth of the greatest beauty, of lofty stature, of graceful shape, eloquent in speech, cool in action, pleasant and
merry, furious in battle'. Wily Robert already had a son Bohemond, but
the foundation of a royal house was now within his reach so he rejected
the first wife as a concubine and married a Lombard princess whose
flaxen locks and Amazonian swagger equalled his own. This Sichelgaita
fought in battle brandishing an axe. 'When dressed in armour,' writes
Anna Komnene, 'this woman was a fearsome sight.'

The schism with Constantinople left Pope Nicholas II no choice but
to turn to the Hautevilles, whom he commissioned to conquer Sicily
from the Arabs in a holy war. In 1060, they landed on the island.

North and south, the descendants of the Vikings were changing
Europe. In Sicily, 1066 was another of year of stalemate for the

---

* Some of these differences were minor, others significant. The easterners rejected the
western reforms – priestly celibacy and new wording in the Credo that the Holy Spirit
derived not just from the Father but also from the son (*filioque*). The westerners in turn
rejected the Roman emperor's title, Equal of the Apostles.

Normans, but not in northern Europe. That year William the Bastard, duke of Normandy, descendant of Rollo the Viking, invaded England.

William, illegitimate son of Duke Robert by an embalmer's daughter, was seven when he succeeded to the duchy. The Bastard grew up in a rough school – one of his guardians was actually murdered in his bedroom right in front of him – and from an early age he had to fight nobles, family and invasions by King Henri I of France, who ruled only the Île-de-France around Paris and coveted Normandy. The Bastard had inherited a forward policy towards England where the Alfred and Canute families were intermarried with his own. In 1051, Edward the Confessor, last of the Alfred dynasty, promised the throne of England to his first cousin William. When Harold, earl of Wessex, son of Godwin, was shipwrecked in Normandy, the Bastard squeezed an oath of loyalty out of him before sending him home. Harold had no real claim to the throne, except that his sister was married to the king. When Edward died, Harold hurriedly had himself crowned as enemies across the sea raised their armies.

The Bastard commissioned a fleet to invade. Yet he had competition from the Hard Ruler: Harold Hardrada had as a boy lost his kingdom to King Canute, escaping abroad to serve Yaroslav the Wise in Kyiv, then joining the Varangian Guard of Constantinople and fighting beside the Hauteville brothers, before in 1046 reclaiming Norway. Now he invaded England with 10,000 troops and Harold's dissident brother Tostig. Landing in Tyneside, Hardrada defeated the northern earls, as Harold galloped north. If one had to back anyone in this tournament, one would have backed Hardrada – but a lucky thrust or arrow changed all. Harold killed Hardrada at Stamford Bridge – just as the Bastard landed at Hastings. Harold headed south with an exhausted army. At Hastings, an arrow struck him in the eye. The surprise results of two small battles directed England towards Normandy instead of Scandinavia. The Bastard became the Conqueror.*

In 1071, while William crushed English resistance, Palermo, the great Arab capital of Sicily, finally fell to Roger de Hauteville, great count of Sicily, who instead of massacring its Arabs and Jews embraced their

---

* This was not just about England and Normandy. All of these princes were players in a complex eastern world. Hardrada was married to Elisiv, the daughter of Yaroslav of Kyiv. On the English defeat, many Anglo-Saxon exiles went to serve in Constantinople and were granted a colony called New England, probably in Crimea. Harold and his wife Edith Swanneck had four sons, who each invaded England to expel the Bastard – three were killed in the attempt. Their daughter Gytha was married to Vladimir Monomakh, prince of Kyiv, and it was their son, Harold's grandson, Yuri Dolgoruky, who was the founder of Moscow and progenitor of all the tsars down to Ivan the Terrible.

culture and made Arabic an official language. Wily Robert meanwhile waged war against Constantinople, taking its last Italian outpost, Bari. Then a disaster in the east encouraged him to seize the big prize: Constantinople itself.

PENIS IN A PALM TREE: THE POET-PRINCESS AND THE VAIN LION

As William scoured England and Roger besieged Palermo, Emperor Romanos IV was marching out to fight Alp Arslan, the Seljuk sultan, who was making advances into today's Anatolia, the beginning of its transformation into a Turkish heartland. But Arslan's chief war was against the Fatimiyya caliphs, so he renewed an earlier treaty with Romanos, then headed southwards into Syria. But, provoked by Seljuk raids, the emperor advanced with a disorganized army of Varangians, Pechenegs and Anglo-Saxons. Arslan headed north but offered a generous peace which Romanos impulsively rejected. At Manzikert, on 26 August 1071, unwisely dividing his army and feuding with his generals, Romanos was routed.* Arslan made him bow low, resting his boot on the imperial neck, but then he raised him to his feet, asking, 'What would you do if I were brought before you as a prisoner?'

'Perhaps I'd kill you,' replied Romanos, 'or exhibit you in the streets of Constantinople.'

'My punishment is far heavier,' said Arslan. 'I forgive you, and set you free.'

If the battle was small and not particularly bloody, 'the fortunes of the Roman empire had sunk to their lowest ebb'. Back in Constantinople, Romanos was clumsily blinded, and died from an infection.

Arslan marched eastwards to crush a rebel, whom he captured and was just sentencing to death when the desperado lunged at him. Proud of his archery, the sultan coolly waved aside his bodyguards and raised his crossbow, but his foot slipped and the assassin stabbed him. 'Alas, I was surrounded by great warriors, who guarded me day and night . . . yet here I lie dying in agony,' he told his paladins. 'Remember this lesson learned: never allow vanity to overcome good sense.' Buried in Merv beside his father, the forty-two-year-old Arslan surely dictated his

---

* Manzikert is still celebrated by Turks every year. Western Europeans understood that the weakening of the eastern empire was a catastrophe. In 1074, after Manzikert, Pope Gregory VII had proposed a war to support Constantinople – the first step towards the Crusades twenty-five years later.

tomb's inscription: 'O those who pass behold the sky-high grandeur of Alp Arslan! He is under black soil now.'

His son Malikshah, then only fifteen, and his veteran vizier Nizam al-Mulk* were with him, struggling to hold Arslan's realms together. A cousin set up a sultanate of Rum (Rome) in the formerly Roman provinces of Anatolia, and their campaigns against Constantinople brought the Romans to the negotiating table.

In Merv, Nizam introduced Malikshah to the Persian polymath Omar Khayyam, deviser of algebraic formulae, observer of stars, poet of wine-sipping girls and transient life. Khayyam worked in the Seljuks' observatories, the jewel of their court, at a time when Merv itself became Mother of the World, home to 500,000, endowed with a library and observatory, the world's biggest city outside China.

The sultan adored Nizam, calling him 'father', and with his assistance stabilized his vast empire, reflecting on the paradox of earthly supremacy: 'I can cope with hunger,' Malikshah used to say, 'but save me from the curse of abundance.' Yet as his confidence grew he came to resent Nizam, who lectured him: 'Remind the sultan, I'm his partner. Doesn't he remember when his father was killed, and I crushed the rebels? If ever I close this vizieral inkstand, the sultanate will topple.' The indispensable are soon dispensed with. Nizam moved against the Assassins, Shiite sectarians,† who had just set up a little theocracy at Alamut in the Iranian mountains and had started a terrorist campaign against Sunnis. Nizam besieged Alamut, but failed to take it. The Assassins ordered Nizam's assassination, but there were rumours that Malikshah had encouraged them.

In October 1092, the vizier, seventy-four years old, was stabbed to death in his litter, but a month later Malikshah was poisoned by the

---

* Nizam wrote a guide to politics for Malikshah, reflecting amid much sage advice on the danger of family. 'One obedient slave is better than 300 sons,' he wrote, 'for the latter desire their father's death, the former their master's glory.'

† In 1090, the fissiparous schisms of the Fatimiyya caliphate produced the Assassins. Like Shia itself, it started with a family split when the caliph handed the succession to his son al-Mustali over the claims of the eldest al-Nizari, who in 1095 rebelled and was killed by immurement (entombed while alive). Nizari's backers, led by a mystic-scholar named Hassan i-Sabbah, believing that the immured prince was occulted and would return as the Mahdi, fled Egypt and seized the castle of Alamut in the mountains of northern Persia, founding a principality that lasted two centuries. Its early leaders called themselves the Dai – the Missionary – but later they claimed descent from Nizari, ruling as sacred imams. The Nizaris compensated for their small size by fanaticism, assassination (and, some claimed, drugs, hence the nickname Hashishim – Assassins). Their hitmen killed thousands of Sunnis, including two Abbasiya caliphs. Later: Saladin twice survived their attacks; a hit squad disguised as monks assassinated a Crusader king of Jerusalem; another wounded the English prince who survived to become Edward I.

caliph – and the Seljuks shattered into baronial fiefdoms, leaving the House of Islam in the east as vulnerable as it was in the west.

In 1091, in Cordoba, a libertine Arab poet-princess died as a new force of Berber invaders from Morocco galloped into the city. The story of this caliph's daughter shows how the richest kingdom in the Europe, the caliphate of Abd al-Rahman, fell to an African invasion.

She was Wallada, a caliph's daughter. The caliphs had lost power to a brilliant warlord who had ravaged the Christian north but hollowed out the caliphate. In 1025, her father Muhammad III was poisoned, and al-Andalus broke up into little kingdoms ruled by warring kinglets – the *taifas*.

Blonde and blue-eyed with 'flowing hair and white shoulders', Wallada enjoyed a rare life for an Islamic woman in Corboda, now ruled by noble clans. No longer secluded in the Umayya harem, independently wealthy, she appeared in public, wearing silks that showed off her beauty and her figure, recited her poetry in public, competing against men in poetry contests, and set up a school for female poets. She flaunted her lovers. When the religious authorities grumbled, she had lines of poems defiantly written on her dresses: 'I allow my lover to touch my cheek and bestow my kiss on him who craves it.' Around 1031, she fell in love with an aristocratic vizier, Ibn Zaydun, who naturally proposed in poetry:

> Between you and me (if you wished) there could exist
> What cannot be lost: a secret undivulged.

She relished her sensuality – 'When night falls, anticipate me visiting you; / For I believe night is the best keeper of secrets' – but she was tormented by jealousy, particularly when Ibn Zaydun slept with one of her black slaves:

> You know that I am the clear, shining moon of the heavens,
> But to my sorrow, you chose, instead, a dark and shadowy planet.

Ibn Zaydun claimed, 'You compelled me to commit the sin ... You were right, but pardon me, O sinner!' She paid him back with her most talented female protégée, the poetess Muhja bint al-Tayyani, and a male vizier. Ibn Zaydun turned nasty, writing to Wallada, 'You were for me nothing but a sweetmeat that I took a bite of and then tossed away the crust, leaving it to be gnawed on by a rat.' Wallada got her revenge by exposing his affairs with slave boys:

Because of his love for rods in trousers, Ibn Zaydun,
In spite of his excellence,
If he would see a penis in a palm tree,
He would turn into a woodpecker.*

Exiled to Seville, Ibn Zaydun regretted losing Wallada: 'I remember you with passion ... Delicious were those days we spent while Fate slept. There was peace, I mean, and we were thieves of pleasure.' As for Wallada, this proto-feminist leaves history in her own words – of course: 'Respected I am, by God of the highest, and proudly I walk with head held high.'

The sybaritic life of the small Muslim kingdom was short-lived. In 1091, on the day Wallada, last of the Umayya, died at the age of ninety-one, blue-veiled Berber horsemen of the Atlas mountains rode with their elephants and camels into Cordoba – masters of a new Euro-African empire that stretched from the Senegal River to the Pyrenees mountains.

The conflicts between Islamic and Christian kings looked like a holy war, but religion was just one element; greed, ambition and family were just as important. Often there were Muslims, Christians and Jews, not to speak of Berbers and Normans, on both sides at each battle. Samuel ibn Naghrillah was a Jew born among the palace elite in Cordoba who escaped the turbulence there to set up a sweetshop in Granada. There he was invited to write letters for the local king, and ended up becoming his secretary and then vizier. Holding court in his palace the Alhambra, for thirty years he ruled Granada, won battles against Christians and Muslims and wrote erotic poetry to boys and girls, while naturally assuming the leadership of the Sephardim, Spanish Jews, to whom he was haNagid – the prince. After his death in 1056, his young son Joseph succeeded him for a decade until this Jewish vizier was accused of planning a coup, whereupon the Granadans stormed the Alhambra and crucified Joseph – not only as a reprisal against Jewish presumption but as the traditional punishment for treason.

While the Jewish prince was ruling Granada, a Castilian knight named Rodrigo Díaz was serving the kings of Castile, the largest of the Christian kingdoms in northern Spain. When he was exiled in a court intrigue, he changed sides and fought for the Islamic kings. Never losing

---

* The trope of penises and palm trees refers to the Arab story that Mary shook a date tree while giving birth to Jesus, leading to much ribaldry among these female poets. In Muhja's shocking verses, she compares Wallada's mysterious pregnancies to that of the Virgin Mary: 'Wallada has become fertile by another man; the secret-keeper revealed it. To us, she resembled Mary, but this palm tree is an erect penis.'

a battle, Díaz won the nickname El Campeador – Champion – among the Spaniards and El Sayyid – the Lord – among the Arabs, Hispanicized into El Cid. In 1085, his former master, Alfonso VI el Bravo, who had united the kingdoms of Castile and León, took Toledo from the Muslims. But instead of expelling Muslim subjects, Alfonso declared himself Emperor of the Two Faiths, a vision reflected in his own love life: in addition to five wives, he also kept Muslim concubines.

The Islamic collapse so alarmed the poetry-spouting king of Seville, al-Mutamid, that he appealed to a horde of fundamentalist tribesmen, the rising power of north Africa. He was playing with fire. 'I've no desire to be the man who delivered al-Andalus to the infidels,' he said. 'I'd rather be a camel driver in Africa than a swineherd in Castile.'

An African army prepared to invade Europe.

ROGER'S FART, ZAYNAB'S MAGIC AND EL CID'S SWORD

An extraordinary quartet – two brothers, a nephew and the wife of two of them – had radically changed west Africa before they even reached Spain. In the deserts of Mauritania, on the borders of the kingdom of Wagadu, a Berber convert named Abdullah ibn Yasin launched a jihad among recently converted Berber tribes who called themselves al-Murabitin. Wearing their blue tagelmust veil below the eyes, the Murabits – now led by Abdullah – quickly conquered the vital trading towns Sijilmasa and Awdaghost, before turning north and defeating the Maghrebi kings.* After Abdullah was killed in battle, his brother Abu Bakr besieged the Maghrebi capital Aghmat, defended by its governor Luqut. When it fell in 1058, Abu Bakr married Luqut's widow Zaynab an-Nafzawiyya, daughter of a Berber merchant from Tunisia, beautiful, intelligent and rich in gold, experience and supernatural powers. Nicknamed the Magician, she refused to entertain offers of marriage until Abu Bakr had conquered much of the country, at which she blindfolded him and took him to a treasure-filled cave, where she unveiled him: all now belonged to him. That was a legend, but she negotiated with existing elites on Abu Bakr's behalf. The Berbers, like the pre-Islamic Arabs, had a tradition of female leaders, including the queens who had resisted Arab conquest.

While fighting to the south, Abu Bakr appointed his nephew Yusuf

---

* The name al-Murabitin (possibly meaning people of the *ribat* after their fortress-monasteries) was translated as Almoravid in English.

ibn Tashfin as his co-ruler, giving him his wife Zaynab, who became his co-ruler. Yusuf gradually conquered much of the Maghreb, but finding the capital Aghmat too suffocating, he created a new one – Marrakesh, the city that gave Morocco its name.

In 1076, Abu Bakr, now calling himself Amir al-Muslim – Commander of the Muslims – pushed southwards along the caravan route into west Africa, where he broke the Wagadu kingdom of the *ghanas*. Taking a Fulu girl as one of his wives, Abu Bakr fathered a boy (who later founded a Jolof kingdom) before he was killed by an arrow fired – in an example of very bad luck – by a blind Soninke warrior. Inheriting this new empire that extended from Algeria and Morocco to Mali and Senegal, Yusuf now received al-Mutamid's invitation from Spain.

King Alfonso warned Yusuf against invading. 'Wait and see what happens!' replied Yusuf. In 1086, some 15,000 men including 6,000 shock cavalry from Senegal crossed to Gibraltar on rafts, with elephants and camels. Yusuf's blue-veiled warriors defeated Alfonso, who just managed to hold on to Toledo and appealed to the pope for a holy war. When Yusuf sailed back to Africa, El Cid helped Alfonso restore his power over his Islamic allies before striking out for Valencia, which he captured, declaring himself the prince – an independent ruler at last. But Yusuf was not finished: in 1090, he crossed the straits again, exiling or killing the decadent Islamic kinglets.*

While the Veiled Ones besieged Valencia, its prince, El Cid, died and his wife Jimena held out for three years until Alfonso evacuated her. She then rode into Burgos with the body of the Champion. Yusuf had conquered a new Islamic empire in Spain. Christendom was in crisis.

Only in Sicily had Islam been overcome by the Hauteville brothers. In 1081 Wily Robert, sensing Constantinople's weakness, attacked the *Basileia Romaion*, sending a vanguard under his eldest son, the twenty-seven-year-old Bohemond, across the Adriatic into the Balkans. Son of Wily's first wife, Bohemond, even more colossal and flaxen-haired than his father, was nicknamed after the mythical giant Buamundus

---

* The poet-king al-Mutamid was exiled to Morocco. When Cordoba fell to the invaders, his daughter-in-law Princess Zaida fled to Alfonso, who made her his concubine before converting her to Christianity and marrying her as Queen Isabella. In 2018 newspapers claimed that the British queen Elizabeth II was descended from the Prophet Muhammad, citing Zaida as her ancestor. Zaida had two daughters; one, Elvira, married Roger, the Hauteville count of Sicily; the other, Sancha, is the progenitor of a line of royalty, via Richard earl of Cambridge and Mary queen of Scots, to George I. It is a link between Islam and Christendom from a more cosmopolitan time. Al-Mutamid was descended from the Arab kings, the Lakhm of Iraq – royalty older than the Prophet but not related to him – and al-Mutamid was Zaida's father-in-law, not her father. There is no evidence Zaida, let alone Elizabeth II, was descended from Muhammad.

Gigas. Robert and his duchess Sichelgaita marched east. In Constantinople, an aristocratic general named Alexios Komnenos, who was
lucky, tireless and talented, seized the throne, facing enemy advances
on all fronts – Normans in the Balkans, Pechenegs and Cumans in
Ukraine, Seljuks in Anatolia – but backed by his Varangian Guard
(which now included Anglo-Saxon axemen) and by the fleet of Constantinople's client city Venice, he marched into the Balkans to stop the
Hautevilles.

Sichelgaita rode into battle with her husband and stepson. When
the Hauteville troops almost broke, Sichelgaita rode after them with
a spear, a sight so fearsome to her fleeing soldiers that they turned,
rejoined the battle and won. But Alexios, aided by the plague, broke the
Hauteville forces, and Robert was recalled by the pope. Alexios switched
to repel Pechenegs and Cumans of Ukraine and then pushed back the
Seljuks – a remarkable performance that saved the *Basileia Romaion*.
No wonder his daughter Anna adored Alexios, who reminded her of 'a
fiery whirlwind . . . His dark eyebrows were curved, the gaze of his eyes
both terrible and kind . . . his broad shoulders, muscular arms and deep
chest were of heroic mould' – and he would be the hero of her history,
The Alexiad.

Afterwards, Alexios rewarded Venice, founded in 421 by refugees
from Roman Aquileia and Ravenna escaping from barbarians, by
granting it special trading rights in the empire and bestowing on its
elected ruler the titles '*dux* of Venice'. Isolated on its lagoon, Venice
had developed from a Constantinopolitan colony into an aggressive
seafaring state, ruled by a *dux* who became the doge of the *Serenissima
Respublica* which expanded into Dalmatia and took up the trading of
spices and slaves before starting to seize its own colonies. It was not
the only sea state thriving on trade with the east: Genoa and Pisa, both
similar Christian oligarchies, were its rivals.

Alexios enjoyed another stroke of luck. In 1085, Wily Robert died of
the plague aged sixty-nine, succeeded by his brother Great Count Roger
of Sicily, who was now invited by Genoa and Pisa to attack Islamic Tunis,
an early crusade. Roger was more interested in selling Sicilian wheat
to Tunisia than in massacring Muslims. His response was pungent:
'Roger lifted his foot and made a great fart, saying "Here's better counsel!"' But the Hauteville fart was not enough to still the winds of holy
war. A new pope was about to rearm Christendom with a new mission:
Crusade.

CRUSADERS: THE GIANT AND THE EMPEROR'S DAUGHTER

Emperor Alexios appealed to the new pope Urban II for aid in fighting the Seljuks. All popes had to balance the power of the German emperors against the Hautevilles. Urban's election had been opposed by the German emperor, who had set up a counter-pope. Already eager to reinvigorate the Church, to buttress Alexios and probably also to divert Germanic baronial aggression, Urban learned of a new Turkic massacre of Christian pilgrims to Jerusalem. He convened a council at Clermont, where on 27 November 1095 he incited an assembly of princes, clerics and people 'to destroy that vile race' of infidel Turks and 'enter upon the road to the Holy Sepulchre; wrest that land from the wicked race, and subject it to yourselves . . . for the remission of your sins, with the assurance of the imperishable glory of the Kingdom of Heaven'.

His audience chanted *'Deus vult!'* – God wills it! – a militant mantra that resounded through Europe. Bohemond de Hauteville was besieging Amalfi when he heard it. Then, 'inspired by the Holy Ghost', the Giant ordered 'the most valuable cloak to be cut up immediately into crosses and most of the knights at the siege began to join him'. It was the same with his nephew, the twenty-year-old Tancred, whose crusading zeal was compared to 'the vitality of a previously sleeping man'.

Princes and peasants alike awoke to this frenzy, rushing to take the Cross – the promise to undertake the 'pilgrimage' to conquer Jerusalem. The word crusade was not used until later. The numbers were astonishing. In the first wave, led by a barefoot preacher known as Peter the Hermit, 80,000 peasants, princes and priests surged across Europe towards Constantinople, where they hoped with all the vagueness of fanatical believers that they would somehow reach Jerusalem. Princes mustered armies of knights and soldiers, led naturally by the Normans. William the Conqueror's eldest son Robert, demeaningly known as Curthose – Shortpants – who had inherited Normandy (while his brother William II Rufus received England), immediately joined a movement that was inspired by a mix of faith, ambition and adventure, stimulated by the energy released by economic and population growth. There was no need to choose between motives: zealotry, plunder, travel, opportunism dovetailed precisely with religious salvation and violent adventure.

Roger's fart notwithstanding, Bohemond, prince of Taranto, son of Wily Robert, now forty years old, had seven Hautevilles in his retinue including his nephew Tancred, whose 'powers were roused, boldness set in motion, eyes opened'. Like so many thousand others, 'His soul was at a crossroads. Which of the two paths to follow? The Gospels or the world?' Now he could have both.

It must have seemed doubtful the pilgrims would ever reach Jerusalem and kill 'the accursed race' of Muslims, so they turned on the infidels in their midst: the Jews. One of the crusading princes, Godfrey of Bouillon, the Franco-German count of lower Lorraine, who was accompanied by his two brothers, announced he was 'avenging the blood of the crucified one by completely eradicating any trace of those bearing the name "Jew"'. In May 1096, Jews were massacred in Trier, Mainz and Speyer, the first spasm of anti-Jewish racism that would become a bacterium within European culture.

'The whole of the west living between the Adriatic and Gibraltar migrated in a body to Asia, marching from one end of Europe to the other,' recalled Anna Komnene, then awaiting the pilgrims in Constantinople. After a decade of war against rebels, Alexios had stabilized the empire. But Anna hoped to succeed him.

Alexios had left his mother in charge when he was fighting the Hautevilles, and he had initially planned to leave the empire to his eldest daughter Anna, who had been born into the purple with both parents present: 'This signified even in the womb the love I was destined to have for my parents.' As a child betrothed to her father's early co-emperor, then almost married to a Seljuk sultan's son, she grew up believing she would rightfully rule, and when she was later married to an aristocrat she and her mother believed the couple would succeed. Instead Alexios crowned his son Joannes as co-emperor. Anna was disappointed.

Alexios was alarmed by the pope's populist war: all wars led by Roman emperors were holy by definition and his experiences with the Hautevilles had taught him that the Franks – as he called all westerners – were brutes of 'uncontrollable passion, erratic character, unpredictability and avarice'.

When the ragged mob of Frankish pilgrims arrived outside Constantinople, Alexios fed them and hurried them on their way into the sultanate of Rum. Then Bohemond de Hauteville and the princely armies arrived. Receiving them in the Great Palace, Alexios did not rise to greet them, confident of his Roman superiority. He was friendly even to his old enemy Bohemond, though the Giant suspected his food might be poisoned. Anna called him 'a born perjurer', but couldn't lift her gaze from this brutish blond, 'a marvel for the eyes . . . so perfectly proportioned'. And he was no dumb blond: 'His wit was manifold and crafty . . . he was well informed.' Bohemond, who had so much to gain and nothing to lose, was persuaded by the princes to take the oath of friendship to Alexios, meaning that he would be their lord, a humiliation eased by roomfuls of gold.

Dealing with these armies, the emperor 'used every means possible, physical and psychological, to hurry them across the Straits' to Asia. Once across, the peasant rabble encountered the horse archers of the sultan of Rum, Kilij Arslan (Sword Lion), who massacred 17,000 of them. Few survived. The princely armies were next. Sword Lion confronted the Crusaders at Dorylaeum, but his horse archers failed to break heavily armoured knights.* In October 1097, they arrived at Antioch, where they discovered the miraculous ripeness of their timing. The House of Islam was shattered, ruled by feuding Turkic atabegs – barons – while the Fatimiyya caliphs struggled to control their own generals and the Cairene crowd; and they still hated the Sunnis more than the Christians, and signed a non-aggression pact with the Crusaders.

Bohemond besieged Antioch, aided by supplies delivered by Genoese ships to St Simeon, the nearest port. The Crusades were made possible by the Italian trading cities, led by Genoa,† followed by Pisa – a massive commercial opportunity which the shrewd Italians did not miss. Venice took the Cross as a city and built a special crusading fleet.

At Antioch, where the Crusaders were growing desperate, Bohemond cultivated an Armenian Christian in command of one of the towers. When he was ready, the Giant persuaded the princes that whoever took Antioch should keep it as their own. As the atabeg of Mosul galloped to save the city, Bohemond's agent opened the gates; Hauteville forces poured in, killing every Muslim. But then the Turks arrived. Now it was the Crusaders' turn to be besieged, obliged to eat horses, dogs and rats, and experiencing trances of hunger. One pilgrim was inspired by a vision to unearth the Holy Lance that had stabbed Jesus' side on the Cross, discovered beneath a church floor. It certainly raised morale: as priests brandished the Lance in sacred procession, the Giant led out his starving army, routed the Turks and claimed the city as his own principality.‡

Godfrey and other princes led the army southwards, finally arriving

---

* Kilij Arslan was killed fighting rival Turkic lords; in 2020, his tomb was discovered at Sivlan, Türkiye.

† Genoa had initiated the Crusades with raids on Mahdia and Tunisia (in 1016 and again in 1087, the one rejected by Roger I's fart). It was a republic, known as *La Superba*, ruled by consuls chosen by a cartel of mercantile families – led by the Doria, Grimaldi (today princes of Monaco) and Embriaco. The Genoese traded silver from Sardinia and wool, but above all gold and slaves, black and white, from Africa and Russia, trading between Nile and Atlantic, building up colonies from Ceuta in Morocco to their slave market in Kaffa (Feodosia, Crimea). But they spent much of their energy fighting their hated rivals, Pisa and later Venice.

‡ It was the second Crusader state. Baldwin of Boulogne, brother of the Jew-hating Godfrey of Bouillon, had already galloped off and seized Edessa (Urfa, south-eastern Türkiye) as his own county.

outside Jerusalem. The astonishing beauty of the Dome of the Rock and al-Aqsa Mosque crowned Mount Moriah where the Jewish Temple had once stood, its surviving golden walls still revered by its Jews. But it was the Holy Sepulchre that was the object of the Crusade. Sacred to three Abrahamic religions, Jerusalem was a small fortified town of 20,000 Muslims and Jews, its walls defended by several thousand Egyptian troops, including Nubian cavalry.

As the Crusaders, now reduced to a mere 10,000, besieged the Holy City in the blistering heat of the Judaean wilderness, they were again rescued by the Genoese, who arrived at Jaffa on the Mediterranean and, dismantling their ships, brought the wood with which to build mangonels and siege engines.

On 15 July 1099, as the mangonel stones and the arrows flew on both sides, as battering rams smashed against the gates, the thirty-eight-year-old Godfrey accompanied the first troops from his siege engine on to the north-east walls while others broke in from the south. Opening the gates from within, the Crusaders, who had only just survived their 3,000-mile journey, slaughtered everyone they encountered, men, women and children, Muslims and Jews. While the Egyptian general and his troops negotiated their escape, everyone else was killed. Desperate Jerusalemites crowded on the Haram al-Sharif (as the Muslims called the Temple Mount), clambering on to the roof of the Dome of the Rock and praying to be delivered. Tancred de Hauteville, penniless and ambitious but at least more humane than his comrades, tried to negotiate a safe conduct in return for ransom, but 'Some of the pagans were mercifully beheaded, others pierced by arrows plunged from towers and yet others, tortured for a long time, were burned to death,' wrote one of the Crusaders. 'Piles of heads, hands and feet lay in streets and houses,' trampled as 'men and knights were running to and fro over the corpses'. Babies were brained against the walls. The Jews were burned alive in their synagogue. Tancred supervised the looting of gold and treasure from the Dome and al-Aqsa. The princes rode horses with gore up to their bridles and then proceeded, their tunics, faces and hands besmeared with blood, to pray at the Sepulchre, tearfully praising God. While the bodies were burned in bonfires, the princes and soldiers raced to grab the best houses. Godfrey was elected king, but, insisting that Jesus was the only king of Jerusalem, he chose the title Advocate of the Holy Sepulchre and converted al-Asqa, believing that it had once been Solomon's Palace, into the royal residence. Although a few connected Muslims and Jews were kept alive and ransomed to the Egyptians, virtually every Jerusalemite was killed.

At Christmas, when the city still stank of human putrefaction and many knights headed back to Europe, Bohemond and Godfrey's brother, Baldwin, arrived for their first pilgrimage. The new patriarch of Jerusalem, Daimbert of Pisa, blessed Baldwin as count of Edessa and Bohemond as prince of Antioch.* When Godfrey died in 1100, his brother Baldwin was chosen as king of Jerusalem, founding a French dynasty there, while Bohemond, basing himself in Antioch, expanded his principality – until he was captured that year by a Turkic warlord and held for ransom.† His nephew Tancred, glorying in the title prince of Galilee, served as regent of Antioch until the Giant's return. Bohemond's Antiochene principality, to which the family later added Tripoli (Lebanon), lasted more than twice as long as the kingdom of Jerusalem – an eastern branch of the Hautevilles.

Infuriated by 'that thorough rogue', Emperor Alexios tried to buy the Giant, but Bohemond instead persuaded King Baldwin to pay his ransom. Needing more cash and knights, Bohemond sailed for Europe where, revelling in his new status, he married the king of France's daughter Constance, who delivered the required son. Back in Antioch, the Giant set off to attack Alexios, but was defeated and in 1108 forced to submit to the emperor. He died not long afterwards.

By 1118, Alexios too was dying, determined to leave the throne to his son Joannes, known for his dark looks as the Moor and for his measured personality as the Beautiful. His wife still championed her daughter Anna. The night before his father's death, Joannes pre-empted mother and sister by taking his father's signet ring and seizing the Great Palace. Anna tried to raise troops and planned a hit on Joannes, who did not attend Alexios' funeral for fear of assassination. The Beautiful kept the throne, soon uncovering another conspiracy by Anna, who was thereafter confined to a convent.‡ Joannes and his son Manuel were as capable as their father, doing their best to destroy the Hautevilles, who were meanwhile planning to seize Jerusalem.

---

* Genoese ships commanded by the merchant prince Gugliemo 'Hammerhead' Embriaco were essential not just for the conquest of Jerusalem but also of Caesarea, Acre (where they received a third of the income) and (in today's Lebanon) Tripoli, Tyre and Gibelet (Byblos) which became a family fiefdom of the Embriaco family. The Venetians, arriving later, clashed with their Pisan rivals and afterwards stormed Haifa, where the mainly Jewish population was slaughtered.

† The Crusader paladins were not all male: in 1101, a small German crusade was partly led by Ida, margravine of Austria, who aged around forty-five was ambushed by Sword Lion, the Seljuk sultan of Rum, and killed in battle.

‡ While her brother turned out to be the greatest of the late emperors, Anna survived for decades, writing her history to exorcise her bitterness: 'I died a thousand deaths,' yet 'after my misfortunes, I am still alive – to experience yet more'. Her loss was history's gain. Just as Ban Zhao was the first female historian in China, Anna was the first in the west.

From the very start the Hautevilles of Sicily had ruled differently, promoting Arabs and Greeks. When the great count Roger, brother of the Wily and uncle of the Giant, died in 1101, his widow Adelaide ruled on behalf of his sons Simon (briefly) and Roger II. Baldwin of Jerusalem needed cash; Adelaide wanted Jerusalem. Ridding himself of his first wife after a childless marriage, Baldwin wed the thirty-seven-year-old Adelaide, on the understanding that if they had a son he would inherit Jerusalem and, if they did not, Roger II would become king. In Jerusalem, Adelaide was bilked by Baldwin I, then dispatched humiliatingly back to Sicily. Her son Roger was incensed. He claimed Jerusalem, and Antioch on behalf of his younger cousins, a plan foiled by the Antiochene barons who married their heiress Constance (Bohemond's granddaughter) to a French prince, Raymond of Poitiers.*

The Crusades inspired the stirrings of coordinated Islamic resistance. In 1144, Edessa fell to Zengi, the atabeg of Mosul and Aleppo, which served as the catalyst for the second Crusade, led by the pious young Louis VII of France (accompanied by his wife Eleanor of Aquitaine) and the king of Germany, Conrad III. Crusader strategists recognized that for the Crusader states – known as Outremer, Across-the-Sea – to survive, they had to win either Syria or Egypt. They chose Syria. Travelling down to Antioch, the monkish Louis was cuckolded by his feisty wife Eleanor, heiress to Aquitaine, who had an affair with her urbane uncle, Raymond. After a rendezvous with the Jerusalemites led by Baldwin III, the three kings bungled their siege of Damascus. Their failure played into the hands of Joannes' heir Emperor Manuel, who was now able to force the Hautevilles to acknowledge his overlordship.†

---

* When Bohemond died at fifty-six, Antioch was inherited by his son, Bohemond II, who was brought up by his mother in Europe until he was of age. In 1126 he arrived to build his own realm, allying himself with Baldwin II of Jerusalem, cousin of the first, who married him to his daughter Alice, thereby linking the largest of the fragile Crusader states. But being a Crusader monarch was a risky enterprise. Bohemond II, 'forceful' like his father but less lucky, fought Frankish rivals and Islamic foes before invading Syria with his father-in-law Baldwin II. There he was killed four years later – his head sent to the caliph of Baghdad – leaving Antioch to his baby daughter, Constance. Raymond of Poitiers was the son of William IX the Troubadour, duke of Aquitaine, who had campaigned against the Muslims in Spain, bringing back from al-Andalus the knightly poets and enslaved dancer-singers who helped promote a fashion for courtly love, sung in French by singer-songwriter-knights – the troubadours. William personified the cult of love, devoting himself to his beautiful mistress, the wondrously named Dangereuse de l'Isle Bouchard, who was the grandmother of Eleanor of Aquitaine.

† After Raymond was killed in battle, his widow Constance, liberated from political marriage, fell in love with a reckless, penniless adventurer, Reynald de Châtillon, whom she married and raised to titular prince – while her stammering son Bohemond III succeeded to the throne. Constance had to recognize Manuel, to whom she married her daughter Maria, thereby joining the Hautevilles to their enemies, the Komnenoi.

Not all the Hautevilles had to compromise. Swarthy and Italianate, taking after his mother rather than the flaxen Hautevilles, Roger II may have been foiled in Outremer but in Sicily and southern Italy he built Europe's greatest kingdom, a source of much jealousy on the part of German emperors who had been accustomed since the days of Charlemagne and Otto to dominating Italy, and of Roman popes who feared Norman power.

Embracing the multi-ethnic nature of Sicily, Roger II created a unique court that combined Norman, Greek, Arab and Jewish culture. Married to the half-Arab daughter of Alfonso of Castile, he ruled through George of Antioch, a Greek corsair who had formerly served Arab rulers in Tunisia and gloried in the title *amir amiratus* – amir of amirs (the origin of the word admiral). George took Tripoli in 1146 and a swathe of north Africa, then Corfu, and he next attacked Constantinople, firing arrows right into the Great Palace. Manuel was defended by his Venetian allies, to whom in gratitude he granted a bespoke trading quarter in Constantinople. But when he asked them to attack Sicily, they refused. Outraged, he awarded special status to the Genoese.

At home, Roger commissioned the breathtaking Palatine Chapel with its Byzantine domes and mosaics and Fatimiyya *muqarna* – stalactite vaulting – and the only contemporary portrait of Roger himself, presented as a sacred ruler. Escorted by Arab bodyguards, he favoured Arab and Jewish scholars. In 1138, the geographer Muhammad al-Idrisi created the *Tabula Rogeriana*, a world map or planisphere, engraved on silver, incorporating the best knowledge available until the voyages of Columbus, and wrote *The Avocation of a Man Desirous of Full Knowledge of the Different Countries of the World* – which described the journeys by Arab sailors to the Saragossa Sea off Bermuda – and a description of China.* But it did not show Mongolia, where during the 1120s, as Roger built his Sicilian empire, a chieftain of the Mongols was conquering his own.

---

* When Roger II died in 1154, his third wife was pregnant. A girl, another Constance, was born posthumously. Given the number of sons and male relatives, it seemed unlikely that she would be politically significant.

ACT EIGHT
360 MILLION

Genghis: A Conquering Family

Khabul Khan, chieftain of the Borjigin clan, was successfully uniting the nomadic peoples who had long lived around their sacred mountain, Burkhan Khaldun, and now acclaimed him as khagan of a mysterious federation, Khamag Mongol – the Whole Mongol.* His great-grandson, raised in a family totally destroyed by fate, would revere his memory and avenge his downfall.

Khabul benefited from the division of China into warring kingdoms – the sophisticated Song in the south vying against the Jurchen-led Jin dynasty in the north, the Xi Xia realm of Tangut peoples, in the west dominating Xinjiang and, in Central Asia, the Qara Khitai Liao empire. When he was invited to pay tribute to the Jurchen emperor in Zhongdu – Central Capital (later Beijing) – Khabul behaved like the most 'uncooked' barbarian, gorging and quaffing with unrestrained oafishness, then jovially tugging the beard of the emperor. Courtiers ordered Khabul's assassination, but he escaped and defeated the Jurchen, winning their recognition.

His Mongol tribe were just one of the many that existed in a constant struggle for power, an ever-mutating kaleidoscope of alliances sometimes coalescing into confederacy. Usually an aristocracy of *baghaturs* (paladins), who treasured their genealogy, ruled these pastoral keepers of yaks, horses, sheep and cattle, huntsmen and fishermen, spread between forest and steppe. Conflicts were ferocious, feuds nursed, and when the time came, 'Vengeance is taken – blessed by Tengri [chief deity], we empty their chests, break off a slice of their liver, end the male line and rape all the women that survive' – as Khabul's great-grandson, Genghis Khan, put it.

Mongol warriors wore fur hats with earmuffs, a tunic covered in fur for winter, felt stockings and boots, with a leather helmet reaching over

---

* Khabul was not the first of the family to create a kingdom: around 900, his great-grandfather Butunchar Munkhag had ruled the Mongols.

the neck and a breastplate of lacquered leather. In summer they wore silks from China. 'The men shave a little square on the top of their heads and what is left of their hair they braid into plaits which hang down either side as far as their ears,' noted a western visitor much later. They were 'astounding men, alien in face, customs, full bodied, bold, strong, handsome with small narrow dark eyes, thick black hair, flat-browed, noses set so low that their cheeks stood out, completely without facial hair'.

Calling themselves the Peoples Who Dwelt in Felt Tents, their homes were the *gers*, tents mounted on hulking carriages pulled by oxen that could be placed together like a wheeled town. Their horsemen – 'the peasantry in military dress' – could gallop sixty miles a day at top speed and survive long periods in the saddle, living on milk, dried marmot meat or the blood of their horses, and they also dried milk that could be mixed with water to make a nutritious drink. Each carried two composite bows, a curved sword, an axe, a mace, a lance and a lasso. They trained for war in the *nerge* or hunt, pursuing antelope and martens often with the aid of a falcon. Marmots – groundhogs – were a staple, used for fresh food that could be dried for winter and as a source of fur. But these animals, or rather the fleas that lived in their fur, would play a special role in world history. All these delicacies were drunk with lashings of *kumis*.* Alcohol was the Mongols' Achilles heel: they were boozers, and three of Genghis's sons would die of alcoholism.

Eclectic in their beliefs, they revered Tengri (meaning Blue Heaven), worshipped on sacred mountains and in river springs, and relied on shamans to interpret auspices. But the steppe peoples respected other gods: around 1000, a rival tribe, the Keraits, converted to Nestorian Christianity.†

In 1146, after ruling for fifteen years, Khabul died, succeeded by his son Ambagai Khan. In 1161, Ambagai was captured by a rival tribe, the Tatars, who handed him over to the Jurchen. 'Avenge me' was the message Ambagai sent to his brother Kutula, a man whose 'voice resounded like thunder, with hands like bear paws that could snap a man in two like an arrow', and who on 'winter nights slept naked by a fire'. But Kutula too was captured and the Jurchen placed the two khans on to a

---

* *Kumis* is an alcoholic drink of fermented mare's milk drunk by all the steppe peoples from the Scythians onwards and, in recognition of the sanctity of horses, offered as sacred offerings. It remains a national drink of Kazakhstan today.
† Nestorius was the Byzantine archbishop who had argued that Christ had two simultaneous natures, divine and human. He was deposed and exiled in 431, but his views became popular in the east.

gruesome torture machine called a wooden donkey. There ended the short Mongol khanate.

*

THE FALL OF TEMUJIN

The family fell on such desperate times that Yesugei, grandson of Khabul, was no longer a khan, just a *baghatur*. Riding across the steppe, he encountered a carriage pulled by yaks, the equipage of an Olqunnut girl called Hoelun, newly married to a Merkit, whom he kidnapped and married in turn, having four children with her. The first, born in 1162 just after the downfall, was Temujin (Ironsmith) – 'born holding in his right hand a clot of blood the size of a knuckle'.*

When Temujin was about nine, his father selected a wife, Börte, for him and by tradition left him at her father's camp. Riding home, Yesugei accepted hospitality from old enemies, members of the Tatar tribe, who poisoned him. Yesugei died three days later after telling the son of a family ally, Munglig, to get Temujin back – to defend a family that was still in catastrophic freefall.

Their herds were stolen, the children almost starving. 'We have no friends other than our shadows,' they said. Temujin argued with Bekter, a half-brother, about a stolen fish; then, together with his brother Qasar, shot him with their bows. Their mother raged at them, 'You destroyers, like a wild dog eating its own afterbirth!' A rival chieftain decided to liquidate Temujin; he was captured, locked into a cangue – neck fetter – and destined for slavery, but he escaped and went into hiding. He became *anda* – blood brothers – with Jamuqa, another ambitious boy, but both were masterful characters and they soon argued. Soon afterwards, thieves stole the family's horses, and Temujin, aided by a boy named Boorchu, later one of his companions, got them back. Later he met another family who offered their son Jelme as his sidekick.

There was something about Temujin: 'He has fire in his eyes, light in his face.' He never forgot a friend but nor did he forget a slight, repeating like a mantra his determination in 'avenging the avengement;

* The main eastern sources of the life of Genghis and his family are the works of three remarkable historians. The most important is the so-called *Secret History of the Mongols*, original title unknown, commissioned by Genghis's son Ogodei not long after his death and, some believe, written by his adopted son and chief judge, Shigi. The other two historians – the Persian treasurer Ata-Malek Juvayni, writing twenty years later, and the grand vizier Rashid al-Din a hundred years later (but using another official family history which was afterwards lost) – were both high-ranking ministers of Genghis's descendants who were thus able to learn much family history at first hand.

requiting the requital'. Now he arrived at the *ordu* – court, (origin of the word horde) – of Toghril, khan of the Christian Keraits, once his father's *anda*. Accepting the gift of a black sable coat, Toghril appointed Temujin chieftain of his Borjigin clan. Afterwards, Temujin's wife Börte was kidnapped by the Merkit tribe in revenge for the stealing of his mother Hoelun twenty years earlier.

Temujin sent Boorchu and Jelme to track the Merkits while he retreated to Burkhan Khaldun, where he meditatively recalled, 'When my life was worth no more than a louse, I escaped. Spared only my life and a horse, walking the paths of elk, making a home with a tent of willow.' Temujin sacrificed to Tengri and 'hung the belt over his shoulder and, kneeling nine times towards the sun, offered a sprinkling of *kumis* and prayer'. Telling his family, 'I was protected,' he believed he had been spared and chosen by Tengri. Yet his ambitions must have seemed delusional. It seemed unlikely the world would ever hear of Temujin again.

TAMARA, CHAMPION OF THE MESSIAH

Far to the west, in 1159, Emperor Manuel rode through the streets of Antioch with its prince Reynald and King Baldwin III of Jerusalem walking behind him. Manuel negotiated marriages to celebrate Roman resurgence – his own to Maria of Antioch, his niece Theodora to Bohemond III, and his great-niece to Amaury of Jerusalem. In 1169, Manuel and King Amaury attacked Egypt, an ill-coordinated plan that failed to take the rich port of Damietta and had lethal blowback. They so weakened the Cairene regime that, after the death of Caliph al-Adid, his vizier, a talented Kurdish amir named Saladin, terminated the Fatimiyya caliphate and united Egypt and Syria into a single Sunni sultanate, a strategic nightmare for the wilting kingdom of Jerusalem, which was now surrounded.

Nor was this the only catastrophe looming for Christendom. In 1172, to the west, a new Berber dynasty had destroyed the Murabits, conquered north Africa all the way to Libya and then crossed to Europe to take much of Spain.*

---

* This time the charismatic preacher-warrior was Ibn Tumert, who fulminated against the decadence of the Murabits in favour of a mysticism mixed with puritanical fundamentalism that promoted a return to the Quran. His followers called themselves al-Muwahhidun – people of unity (Almohads). In 1121, Tumert declared himself Mahdi. In 1147 his successor Abd al-Muamin declared himself caliph and captured Marrakesh, before conquering the Maghreb and then in 1172 crossing to Spain, where he based himself in Seville and launched a vicious persecution of Jews and Christians. The great Jewish philosopher

Saladin was fortunate that Manuel the Great was overstretched. In 1176, the emperor, by now fifty-eight, was ambushed by the Seljuk sultan of Rum, a setback that exposed the fragility of Outremer. Jerusalem and the Christian states were crippled by a shortage of manpower. The original Franks had intermarried with eastern Christians and Armenians but also with Arabs: their mixed-race children, mocked by westerners as *pulains* (poultry), often served as turcopole (sons of Turks) cavalry in multi-ethnic armies, fortified by celibate special forces, starting with the military-religious Order of Solomon's Temple based in the Dome of the Rock – the Templars. But after Amaury, Outremer's luck ran out.* The teenaged king of Jerusalem, Baldwin IV, suffered from leprosy, yet bravely managed in 1177 to defeat Saladin's army with just 500 knights and Templars. But his terrible death, his face decaying behind a mask, was an inescapable metaphor for the body politic itself.

In July 1187, at Hattin, Saladin surrounded and routed a feckless, underqualified king of Jerusalem, Guy of Lusignan, beheading the ex-prince of Antioch, Reynald, the 200 crack Templars and all the mixed-race turcopoles, who were especially despised. Then on 2 October he took the Holy City for Islam, showing remarkable mercy in contrast to the butchery of the Crusaders eighty-eight years earlier.

Christendom was shocked. In Ethiopia, King Gebre Mesqel Lalibela built a complex of rock-cut churches to create an African Jerusalem. In Europe, three impressive monarchs – Emperor Frederick Barbarossa, Richard the Lionheart of England and Aquitaine and Philippe Auguste of France – raised armies. The failure of the Crusades unleashed anti-Jewish attacks: in York the entire community was burned alive as the kings set off for the east. Barbarossa died on the way, drowning in a river.† The other royal divas bickered with one another, but at Acre

---

Moses Maimonides escaped their repression and arrived in Cairo, where he became doctor and adviser to Saladin and his sons. These Berber caliphs were avid minaret builders: after his father's death in 1163, the second caliph Abu Yaqub Yusuf built the Giralda Tower as a minaret to his mosque in Seville, as well as the palace that became the Alcazar. The third caliph, al-Mansur, who in 1195 massacred a Castilian army, built the Hassan Tower in Rabat. There was no reason to suppose that Spain would ever be fully Christian again.

* The competence of the first five monarchs was formidable: Baldwin I and II were gifted, indefatigable warrior-kings, while Queen Melisende (the latter's daughter with his Armenian queen Morphia) was every bit their equal as a potentate – though she required a husband, Fulk, to lead her armies. It was she who built the Church of the Holy Sepulchre and the market that we see today in Jerusalem. Her son Baldwin III deposed her, but inherited the family gifts, as did his obese brother Amaury.

† Barbarossa's death spawned the legend of a sleeping emperor who would rise again at the End of Days, his mystical prestige inspiring a later German ruler, Adolf Hitler, who named his invasion of Russia in his honour. Richard inherited the bountiful accumulations of his father Henry II, duke of Normandy, count of Anjou, and his mother Eleanor, duchess of

fought Saladin to a stalemate: Acre survived as capital of a rump Outremer, of which it was the main port; Saladin ruled from Egypt to Iraq;
and Jerusalem remained under Islamic rule until 1917.

The eclipse of Manuel and the fall of Jerusalem benefited a remarkable queen, Tamara of Georgia. The southern Caucasus was a natural
buffer between empires: there the ancient kingdoms of Georgia and
Armenia, the first to convert to Christianity, nonetheless oscillated between Arab and Roman alliances.*

In 1178, the eighteen-year-old Tamara was crowned co-ruler alongside
her embattled father Giorgi III, who married his other daughter Rusudan to a Komnenos prince. In the Latin west, most women in power
were swiftly deposed by magnates, but influenced by the Constantinopolitan tradition of empresses, Tamara at least had a template. Queen at
twenty-four on the death of her father, Tamara manoeuvred carefully to
appease rebellious potentates who resented feminine power, but in 1185
she was forced to marry a Russian prince descended from Rurik, Yuri
of Vladimir-Suzdal. The heyday of Rus was long gone. The Rurikovichi
feuded constantly as they struggled to rule the most powerful principalities. Yuri got lucky, becoming king of Georgia, but Tamara was king
of kings. She loathed the oafish Yuri, who, 'when drunk, showed his
Scythian habits; utterly debauched and depraved, he even embraced
sodomitic behaviour'. In 1187, she accused him of unnatural vices, divorced him and exiled him to Constantinople.

Liberated from the patriarchy of clergymen and barons, she now
married – unusually, for love – her attractive, intelligent cousin David
Soslam, an Ossetian prince whom she had known all her life. Faced
with Islamic resurgence, she formed an alliance with Saladin, then

Aquitaine: all of England and the western half of France. Persecutor of the Jews, whom he
expelled then allowed to return, Philippe later won the epithet Augustus for dramatically
expanding France, reducing the English holdings, aided by the spectacular and vicious
incompetence of Richard's brother John. But the English kept Gascony for three centuries.
* In 806, Ashot the Carnivorous (a meat-chomping enthusiast even at Lent) was appointed by Haroun al-Rashid as prince of Armenia, founding the Bagration dynasty
that ruled in the Caucasus for the next thousand years, until 1810. In 885, Ashot the
Great was recognized by both caliph and Roman emperor as the first king of Armenia,
and three years later another of the family, Adarnase IV, was installed as king of Tao, in
south-western Georgia, by Emperor Basil the Bulgar Slayer. In 1122, King David IV the
Builder took advantage of Islamic distraction during the Crusades to take Tbilisi, unite
an expanded Georgia and wage holy war against the Seljuks so ferociously that, after
one battle, blood supposedly poured out of his belt when he took it off. Fusing Persian,
Turkic and Frankish troubadour cultures, marrying one Christian and one Turk, splicing one daughter to a Seljuk and another to a Komnenos, David travelled with sword
and library, reading the Quran and Persian poetry and, like his biblical namesake,
writing hymns.

unleashed her husband David against the Turkic rulers of eastern Türkiye and western Iran. When she was challenged by a Seljuk prince, she told him, 'You rely on gold and numerous warriors, I on God's power.' Her coins, in Arabic and Georgian, just read: 'Champion of the Messiah'.*

As her Ossetian prince won his victories for 'the goddess whom David the sun serves', Tamara now ruled an empire that stretched from the Black Sea to the Caspian. Meanwhile the marriage of Tamara's sister Rusudan into the Komnenoi could hardly have been more ill-starred.

The *Basileia Romaion* was about to fall apart. but the real change would come from the east where the rising Mongol chieftain Temujin faced an unbearable prospect. 'My wife', lamented the future Genghis, 'has been raped.' And she was pregnant.

TEMUJIN BOUNCES BACK

Temujin learned that Börte had been given as war spoils to a Merkit prince. He appealed to his patron Toghril (his 'father-khan') and blood brother, Jamuqa, who attacked the Merkits at night. The Merkits, warned of the ambush, fled helter-skelter into the steppe. The rescue, told in Genghis's family history, reveals a rare side of Temujin. 'As pillage and rape went on, Temujin galloped through the fleeing Merkits, crying out "Börte! Börte!" Recognizing his voice, she got off her cart and ran towards him, grabbing his reins. It was moonlight; he recognized Lady Börte, and they fell into each other's arms.'

Yet she was eight months pregnant. Temujin did not reject her, and she gave birth to Jöchi, whom Temujin treated as a son. But together they had three more sons, Chagatai, Ögodei and Tolui, and five daughters. When Tolui was five, a Tatar tried to kidnap him from the family camp, but he was saved by his sister Altani who held the kidnapper until the bodyguards killed him. The guards claimed credit but Temujin promoted the girl to *baghatur*.

---

* The queen's treasurer, Shota Rustaveli, was also a poet, author of the Georgian epic *Knight in the Panther Skin*, in which the beauteous princess and her suitor are tributes to Tamara and David. Rustaveli celebrated the rare partnership of the king of kings and her king consort: 'She who strikes terror from the East to the West, wherever she fights: / Those who are traitors, she destroys; those who are loyal, she delights.' As with Melisende in Jerusalem, the partnership showed that a woman could remain in charge in Crusader times even when married to a warrior-consort – precedents later relevant to Queen Elizabeth I of England, who feared this was not possible in her time.

Gradually Temujin's exceptional character was recognized – he was 'tall, vigorous, sturdy, with cats' eyes, possessed of a focused energy'. He had black hair and a steely constitution, with the rare ability to listen, and the superabundant vigour and invincible confidence, fortified by sacred mission, essential for transcendent leadership. He was a spotter of talent and a winner of loyalty. Three cousins from the House of Khabul declared that 'Blue Heaven has ordained that Temujin be our khan,' promising to bring 'beautiful virgins, palatial tents, fine-rumped geldings', and in return he praised his early henchmen, telling them, 'When I had no companions other than my shadow, you were my shadow. I'll promote you.' Followers began to call him Genghis (Fierce) Khan.

When the Jurchen emperor of northern China asked them to attack the ferocious Tatars who were raiding across Chinese borders, Toghril and Genghis killed the Tatar chieftain – vengeance at last for Genghis's father. The emperor made Toghril *wang-khan* (king-khan) and Genghis keeper of the frontier: both still recognized Jin authority. Genghis promised loyalty to Toghril: 'Like a falcon I flew upon the mountain, for you I caught the blue-footed cranes.'

Massacring many Tatars, Genghis took two girls as concubines and captured a privileged, literate boy called Shigi, wearing a gold nose-ring and silken sash, whom he gave to his mother to bring up and who later became his chief judge. When the tribes elected Jamuqa as Gur (Universal) Khan to lead them against Toghril and Genghis, it became likely either Genghis or Jamuqa, boyhood pals, would end up as ruler of the steppe. In 1201, Jamuqa and his coalition of tribes attacked Temujin, who was backed by old Toghril. The Battle of the Thirteen Sides was so closely fought that their armies slept almost propping each other up. Genghis's horse was shot, then he himself was hit in the neck by a poisoned arrow. Jelme rescued him, sucked out the poison, then crept across the battlefield to steal bean curd and water for him from the enemy camp. At dawn, Genghis recovered – 'my eyes feel bright again' – and recognized that Jelme had 'saved my life thrice'.

After the victory was won, the archer who had shot his horse was brought before him, admitting what he had done. Remorseless yet empathetic, Genghis forgave him, granting him the name Arrow – Jebe – and adding, 'I'll use him as *my* arrow.' Jebe would soon be one of his paladins.

Now the relationship between the old khan Toghril and young Genghis soured: when Genghis proposed marrying his son Jöchi to Toghril's daughter, the king-khan refused, perhaps because Jöchi was not really Genghis's son.

In 1203, Toghril joined forces with Jamuqa: 'Let's seize Temujin and kill him,' they agreed, and hunted him down. Genghis only just escaped, but he noticed his son Ögodei was missing. When the boy was brought in, wounded by an arrow in the neck and hanging over his saddle bag, the khan wept. Vanishing into Transbaikal (Siberia), Genghis recovered, then re-emerged. At the Battle of the Burning Sands, he defeated the ailing Toghril, who fled and was beheaded.

Conquered tribes sent girls for him and his sons: girls were treated as trophies, and rape was a vicious rite of Mongol conquest. Yet some of the women showed defiant agency in the face of male cruelty, and a few rose to become the most powerful women in the world – and to tell their own stories.

After breaking the Tatars, Genghis chose the chieftain's daughter Yesugen as his concubine. As they were having sex, she suggested, 'If it pleases the khan, he will take care of me, regarding me as a human being and a person worth keeping. But my elder sister, who is called Yesui, is superior to me: she is indeed fit for a ruler.' Genghis kidnapped the other sister, and both girls became senior wives. Now that he was in love with Yesugen, she accompanied him on future expeditions. When he defeated the Merkits, he captured another girl, Khulan, who was kept by one of his generals for himself – a dangerous impertinence. As Genghis interrogated the officer, Khulan herself frankly challenged the khan to inspect her virginity and have sex with her himself. He gave Töregene, the wife of the Merkit khan, to Ögodei.

When Toghril's two Keraite nieces were delivered to him, Genghis kept one for himself and gave the other, Sorqaqtani, to his youngest son Tolui. She would be the mother of two monarchs and, for thirty years, the most powerful woman in Eurasia.

Finally, Genghis captured his blood brother turned nemesis Jamuqa, who begged to be executed, saying, 'The sun rose with my name and now sets with it.' Genghis generously delivered a bloodless royal death: Jamuqa's back was broken.

Like his great-grandfather Khabul, Genghis was ruler of the People Who Dwelt in Felt Tents – but it was unlikely that anyone outside the barbarian marches would ever hear of him.

The fall of Constantinople, Queen of Cities, seemed more important: the rot started when the Komnenoi, who had produced three outstanding emperors, delivered history's most toxic playboy.

THE SEDUCER AND THE AVENGER: THE TEETH OF
ANDRONIKOS AND THE EYES OF THE DOGE

Andronikos, grandson of Emperor Alexios and cousin of Manuel, was a vainglorious, incompetent and overpromoted buffoon whose rise to the top seemed an impossible joke – until the process of momentous inevitability made it imminent. His ambitions were vaulting, his seductions priapic, his succession catastrophic. After first marrying a sister of King Giorgi III of Georgia (Tamara's aunt), he started by seducing his cousin Eudokia Komnene, then he bolted, pursued by her furious brothers, and settled in Antioch, where he had an affair with Empress Maria's sister, the Hauteville princess Philippa. After bolting again, to Jerusalem, Andronikos (now fifty-six, antique in medieval times) seduced Queen Theodora Komnene, the beautiful widow of Baldwin III, who was three decades younger. Together they eloped to the court of the atabeg of Mosul and leader of the jihad against the Crusaders, Nur al-Din.

Andronikos had retired to the provinces as an international joke when a rare set of circumstances removed his rivals and closed alternative roads: Manuel the Great died of a fever; his widow Maria of Antioch, an unpopular Hauteville, became regent for a child, Alexios II, and a wave of xenophobia made Italians hated for their trading privileges. In 1183, Andronikos rode the wave, marched on Constantinople and massacred Pisans and Genoans. Then he had Maria drowned and the fourteen-year-old Alexios strangled, before marrying the boy's fiancée Agnes of France. She was twelve, he sixty-five – though proudly flaunting his lustrous hair and all his teeth. As plots multiplied, Andronikos slaughtered his opponents, but both ancestral enemies launched incursions – Seljuks from the east, Hautevilles from the west. In Venice, Andronikos' depredations provoked outrage. Enrico Dandalo, merchant nephew of the Venetian patriarch, blind since a blow to the head twenty years earlier, possibly in Constantinople, led a fleet that was struck by the plague and achieved nothing. But Andronikos, abandoned by everyone, was forced to negotiate with Dandalo, releasing Venetian prisoners and returning their quarter to them.

In 1185 a popular rebellion, led by the aristocrat Isaac Angelos, overthrew Andronikos, subjecting him to three days of torture. After he had been hung upside down in the hippodrome, his eyes were gouged out, his genitals amputated, his teeth extracted, his face burned, all designed to destroy the features with which this cruel peacock of contumacious narcissism had beguiled not just many women but also the people of Constantinople.

Then he was stabbed and quartered. Soon thereafter one of his sons was killed; another, brother-in-law of Tamara of Georgia, was blinded and sent to Tbilisi.

In 1192, Venice elected a new doge, Dandalo, who received a delegation of French Crusaders seeking a loan to fund their Crusade against Egypt.* When they could not raise the lucre, Dandalo commandeered the entire operation, took the Cross and declared that, although he was 'old and weak, no one knows how to govern and direct you like me, and I will go and die' on 'the greatest enterprise anyone has ever undertaken'. Sailing across the Adriatic to Venetian Croatia, with 12,000 Venetians and Frenchmen, he attacked a rebel city Zara, where he was joined by a Romaioi prince, Alexios IV Angelos, who asked for his help in overthrowing his uncle, the emperor of Constantinople. Dandalo, enthusiastically backed by most of the Crusaders, sailed to the Bosphoros, expecting the citizens of the Great City to welcome Alexios, but they did not. Exasperated, he ordered the storming of Constantinople. Listening to the sounds of battle from the deck of the vermilion galley, he suddenly ordered his ship to be beached as he stood defiantly in the prow – a sight that inspired his troops and possibly the Constantinopolitans for they overthrew their emperor and welcomed the Venetian candidate. He paid some of the gold owed to Dandalo – not enough for Venice – but too much for his subjects: he was assassinated.

On 12 April 1204, Dandalo, infuriated, stormed the city, using merchant vessels lashed together as platforms for siege engines, while Venetian and French troops scaled the walls. This was possible only because the demoralized city was thinly defended. But, once inside, the Latins, disgusted by the effete, traitorous, icon-loving Greeks, sacked the city, raping nuns, killing children and desecrating the silver iconostasis of Hagia Sophia, where they enthroned an ancient prostitute. The doge organized the looting of the porphyry sculptures of the tetrarchs of Rome and the bronze horses that had stood above the starting line of the hippodrome (they still stand within and – in replica – outside St Mark's

* Saladin and his brother Safadin, who ruled Egypt, most of Israel and Lebanon, Syria, half Iraq and Yemen, had also conquered Mecca where they installed Qatada, a Hashemite descendant of Muhammad, as amir, controlling the revenues of the *hajj* pilgrimage. Using an army of Nubian slaves, navigating between Saladin's successors and the Baghdad caliphs, Qatada took control of both holy places, founding the Hashemite family that, with short intervals, ruled Mecca until the 1920s and provided the kings of Hejaz, Syria, Jordan, Jerusalem and Iraq. They still rule Jordan. In 1221, an ailing Qatada was strangled by his son Hassan.

in Venice). From the territories of the Romaioi, Dandalo created a new empire called Romania. Dandalo himself, now ninety-seven, was offered the throne but refused. A Frenchman was chosen instead, but Dandalo won for Venice three-eighths of the *Partitio Romaniae*. After accepting the resonant titles Despot of Romania and Lord of Three-Eighths of the Roman Empire, he died – the only person ever buried in Hagia Sophia. Constantinople never recovered; Venice seized Crete, Cyprus and southern Greece for its own mercantile empire. But Dandalo's very success provoked war with Genoa, in which the doge's only son was killed.

Queen Tamara of Georgia had watched all of this with horror: her blinded brother-in-law Manuel Komnenos lived in Tbilisi with his son Alexios. Now Tamara sent Georgian troops to take Trebizond, and there Alexios Komnenos declared himself emperor, founding a Trapezuntine client state of Georgia.* As for Tamara, her beloved king David died and she suffered from a 'feminine infirmity', possibly uterine cancer, which prompted her to crown their son, Giorgi IV the Resplendent, as co-ruler. Hearing that there was a new crusade, Resplendent Giorgi took the Cross to liberate Jerusalem, encouraged by (fake) news that a Christian king, Prester John, was advancing from the east. Some of the news was correct, however: there *was* a new king in the east, and he *was* coming.

GENGHIS – MY GOLDEN LIFE – AND THE BLACK DEATH

In 1206, Genghis summoned a *qurultai* – the assembly that confirmed leadership of the steppes not by voting but by attendance – to celebrate his accession as khagan. Blessed after sacred consultation with Blue Heaven by his court shaman Kokochu, who had been with him since his youth, he officially became the khagan of All the Tribes Who Live in Felt Tents – Keraits, Naimans, Merkits, Tatars – at the head of a new nobility of trusted commanders, united under his white standard of nine yak tails. Genghis praised his retainers, telling stories from his past, and dubbing Jebe, the brothers Jelme and Subotai, and Kublai 'the Four Hounds'.

His code of laws, the *Yasa*, was read out, cases to be judged by his adopted son Shigi, enforced by his son Chagatai. Although he was

---

* After they had recognized the Greek emperors who retook Constantinople from the Latins, the emperors of Trebizond used the title Emperor and Autocrat of all the East, and survived by trading with Venice and Genoa and with Islamic rulers who were offered prestigious Trepuzuntine princesses. This kingdom lasted until 1461.

illiterate, Genghis hired a Uighur scribe to be his keeper of the seal, using Uighur script for business. A mounted courier service, the Yam, would communicate between armies and provinces. This was the enterprise of a divinely blessed dynasty now called the Golden Family: only the Golden Family would rule the world, only the Golden Family would select the khan at the *qurultai* and no Golden blood could ever be spilt. Genghis's four daughters were entrusted with considerable power; all were married to potentates and given kingdoms to rule in their own right. The eldest daughter, Alakahi, ruled the Ongud tribes and later much of northern China, becoming chief horse supplier to her father, who called her Princess Who Rules.

At his supreme moment, his shaman Kokochu accused Genghis's brother Qasar of treason: 'The Spirit has revealed to me – Temujin will rule first, then Qasar. Unless you remove Qasar, you'll be in danger.' Kokochu had inviolable status – as the son of the khagan's oldest adviser Munglik who was married to his mother Hoelun, he was Genghis's stepbrother. Genghis arrested Qasar, but his mother harnessed a white camel, drove her carriage through the night and arrived to appeal to her son, baring her breasts and crying, 'These are the breasts that suckled you both!' But his wife Börte warned him that Kokochu could threaten their own sons. Releasing Qasar, Genghis ordered his brother Temüge to kill Kokochu by breaking his back. 'He was no longer loved by Heaven,' said Genghis, warning Kokochu's family, 'You were beginning to think you are my equals.' He appointed another shaman. 'Heaven has ordered me to rule over all men,' said Genghis. 'The protection and promotion of Blue Heaven has enabled me to destroy my enemies and achieve this elevated dignity.'

The exceptional talents of Genghis combined with the blessings of good harvests and equable climate, the large human and equine population of the steppe and the division of China meant that the khagan now deployed 80,000 horse archers who regarded victory, adventure and loot as the essential prizes of loyalty and proof of sacred leadership. The prizes were the three kingdoms of the Song, the Tanguts and the Jurchens.

In 1209, Genghis defeated the Buddhist Tangut empire of Xi Xia in north-western China,[*] but, unable to take their walled capital, he accepted their emperor's submission. Next he turned to the Jurchen empire of

---

[*] Genghis distilled his tactics into three manoeuvres: first, the Thorny Sarayana Shrub, the march in which troops massed in close order; then the Lake, in which troops flowed over a wide area; and finally the Chisel, in which the horsemen were concentrated with devastating force.

Jin that ruled forty million people in north-eastern China, sneering to their envoy, 'I thought the emperor was appointed by Heaven.' This, he said, was revenge for the killing of his forefathers Kutula and Ambagai. Reaching the walls of Zhongdu (Beijing), he found he lacked siege machines, so he raided the south. In 1214, Genghis reassembled his armies north of Zhongdu, but they were now suffering from an epidemic of unknown pathology. The Jurchen emperor made peace, sending a daughter as the khagan's bride, plus 500 boys and girls, 3,000 horses and 10,000 bolts of silk – but the Jin dynasty was falling apart. Genghis hired Chinese engineers to build his siege engines, shoot firebombs and rockets, originally developed by the Song, and employed a Chinese prince to advise on strategy. In 1215, he took Zhongdu, sacking it, killing thousands, their corpses rotting in heaps. Then Genghis turned west, leaving his general Muqali with a smaller force of around 23,000 Mongols to reduce the shattered empire.

In 1218, switching eastwards, Genghis swallowed the Kara-Khitai (Kazakhstan) khanate, where he captured the famously svelte Empress Juerbiesu. She mocked the stink of Mongols, an affront which was reported to Genghis. He cross-examined her but, dazzled by her looks, kept her for the night. She became his third-ranking wife.

These movements in remote lands would reverberate across Eurasia, unleashing a new pathogen that would become the Black Death. Tiny but mysterious changes in global climate and human nourishment can lead to outbreaks of diseases that have been present but dormant for centuries. The plague has been discovered in an ancient Swedish tomb from 3000 BC, suggesting it may have originated in Europe long before it appeared in the east. The bubonic plague had for a long time been enzootic, commonly carried by the fleas in the fur of marmots, in camels and in the rats that thrived wherever humans left the detritus of their daily life. Marmots were a staple of Mongol life, given that the tribesmen wore marmot fur and leather, and ate their meat. The plague did not flare up in the west for another century, but new research proves that it began much earlier.

Somewhere on the slopes of the Tian Shan mountains, the fatal transfer between humans and animals took place – with a Mongol eating the flesh of an infected marmot or being bitten by a flea from one of the rodents. Infected with the pathogen *Yersinia pestis*, the flea fed on the blood of a human or defecated into a skin abrasion, spewing bacilli into the bloodstream. Once infected, humans transferred the disease directly by coughing or indirectly via their ever-present companions, flea-ridden rats. The flare-ups were scarcely recorded. If nomads were hit by the plague, they could move camp. But cities could not just move. Mongol armies unknowingly bore the pathogen into China and then westwards.

GENGHIS AND SONS:
WHAT IS THE GREATEST JOY FOR A MAN?

The conquest brought Genghis to the borders of Khwarizm, a new Islamic kingdom encompassing Uzbekistan, eastern Iran and Afghanistan, conquered by a cruel jackanapes, Shah Muhammad, who had heard eyewitness accounts of the sacking of Zhongdu. The shah was convinced of his own superiority over the coarse Mongols and by his own success. But the conqueror was about to be out-conquered, the classic case of jaguar–crocodile predation. When Genghis dispatched Mongol envoys and around 400 Muslim merchants, the Khwarizmians executed them, sending the heads to Genghis.

'Avenging the avengement; requiting the requital', Genghis planned the invasion of this new theatre. His favourite wife Yesui warned, 'When your body falls like a great tree, to whom will you leave your peoples? Which of the four sons?'

'Even if she's a woman,' mused Genghis, 'she's righter than right.' All the sons had distinguished themselves as commanders but all were flawed: Jöchi had an uncontrolled temper; Chagatai was meticulous but harsh; Tolui was the best general; Ögodei, the favourite, was big, cheerful and conciliatory. All were raging alcoholics. Chagatai hated Jöchi.

'Do we have to be governed by this Merkit bastard?' cried Chagatai.

'Our father never said I was different, how come you do?' replied Jöchi. The princes fought but were pulled apart.

'Ögodei is merciful,' proposed Genghis's generals. 'Let's have Ögodei.'

'Jöchi, what do you say? Speak!' cried Genghis.

'Let's say Ögodei,' agreed Jöchi.

'Ögodei, speak!' said Genghis.

'How can I say, I can't do this? ' replied Ögodei, displaying the required but also characteristic modesty. 'I will do my best.' The princes approved.

'That will do,' said Genghis.

In 1219 Genghis invaded Khwarizm, sending Jebe and Subotai as the vanguard, followed by Prince Jöchi* with one column, while he led the other with Prince Tolui towards Bukhara (Uzbekistan), a cultured Persianate city with 300,000 inhabitants and a famed library. Genghis used the great mosque as stables – 'There's no fodder in the countryside; fill my horses' bellies!' Then he addressed the elite: 'You've committed great sins. What proof? I am God's punishment.' Then the citadel was stormed, the people enslaved, the library burned, before he moved on to Samarkand, where he was joined by his other sons. They were dispatched to take the Khwarizmi capital Gurganj (Urgench, Turkmenistan). When the city fell, 50,000 Mongol soldiers were ordered to kill twenty-four Gurganj citizens each, which would mean 1.2 million people. This may have been the largest single massacre in history.

The shah fled, pursued by Jebe the Arrow and Subotai, in a hot chase that ended with Muhammad's lonely death on a Caspian island. His more able sons did not give up: they sought an alliance against Genghis with the sultans of Delhi in India but were ultimately destroyed.

Genghis mopped up Afghanistan and northern Iran, slaughtering the entire populations of Balkh and Herat. Tolui took the resplendent former Seljuk capital Merv,† where Genghis sat on a golden throne and ordered the burning of Nizam al-Mulk's library. Next, declaring, 'These people resisted us,' they separated hundreds of thousands of men, women and children into herds and then slaughtered most of them like sheep. 'Genghis Khan ordered the counting of the dead,' wrote the Arab historian al-Athir, who interviewed survivors, 'and there were around 700,000 corpses' – an exaggeration, but again one of the most atrocious days in all history. Those kept alive as slaves were driven ahead of the Mongols as human shields, a practice already used in China. During the siege of Nishapur (Iran), Toquchar, married to Genghis's daughter Checheikhen, was killed by an arrow. When the city fell, his widow took command, orchestrating the killing of everyone, the heads of men, women and children collected in different unisex head towers. Perhaps it was Genghis's daughter who devised these dread towers, which became architectural statements of Mongol ferocity. Genghis's favourite grandson Mutugen, son of Chagatai, was killed at the siege of Bamian (Afghanistan). At dinner, Genghis informed the father, banned

---

* Genghis's eldest son by a Merkit rapist, Jöchi, was treated as a Golden prince, receiving a vast appanage, but he was not considered for the succession. He may have fallen out with Genghis, but the son died first, his territories inherited by his able son, Batu.

† A Turkish Oghuz clan who had lived in Merv escaped the Mongols to seek refuge in the Seljuk sultanate of Rum where they were granted lands. They were led by a chieftain named Osman, the founder of the Osmanlik or Ottoman family who would rule a Eurasian empire until 1918.

grieving and then ordered the destruction of Bamian: there would be no plundering, just fire and death. Even dogs and cats were killed. These cities never recovered.

In 1220, Genghis was fifty-eight but had not lost the exhilaration of conquest. Once, feasting with his marshals, he asked: 'What's the greatest joy for a man?' The generals chose different pleasures – drinking, hunting, feasting – until Genghis said, 'The greatest pleasure for a man is to crush a rebel and defeat an enemy, destroy him, taking everything he possesses, seize his married women and make them weep, ride his fine beautiful horses and fornicate with his beautiful wives and daughters – and possess them completely.' This 'possession' was literal: nomads regarded their conquests as total – treasures, cities, livestock, humans were now theirs to share or kill. Sexual warfare was regarded as a right of conquest and a pleasure of life. DNA evidence shows that millions of people are descended from a single ancestor who travelled across Asia at this time. It is most likely that this was Genghis Khan himself, who, after centuries in which his descendants have multiplied, is literally the father of Asia.

While in Afghanistan, Genghis summoned a revered Taoist philosopher Qiu Chuji, recommended to him in China: 'Master, have you brought me an elixir of immortality?'

'I can protect life but no elixir will extend it,' replied the Master, who recommended the curbing of appetites for girls, hunting, fighting and boozing.

'Heaven sent this Holy Immortal to teach us these things,' the khagan told his courtiers. 'Engrave them on your hearts,' though 'unfortunately we Mongols are raised to shoot arrows and ride – habits hard to give up'. But by his orders Taoism was encouraged across China, and Buddhism fell out of favour.

Success had not spoiled Genghis, who like all autocrats enjoyed talking about himself: 'Heaven disapproves of the luxury of China,' he reflected. 'I cleave to the simplicity of the steppe. I wear the same clothes, eat the same food, as cowherds and grooms do, and I treat soldiers as my brothers; in a hundred battles I was at the forefront of the fray. In seven years, I've performed great deeds; in six directions, everything is subject to a single rule.'

As Genghis held court, he was in contact via his pony mail with the *noyan* (marshal) Jebe and the one-eyed *baghatur* Subotai, whom he had sent on the greatest raid in history. Setting off with 20,000 men on a 4,500-mile adventure across Iran, they galloped into Georgia. In February 1221, they obliterated the knights of Tamara's son. Giorgi the Resplendent died of wounds, succeeded by his sister Rusudan, as beautiful as her mother Tamara but less shrewd and less lucky. 'A savage people, the Tatars,' she wrote, the first European to encounter the Mongols, 'hellish of aspect, as voracious as wolves, have invaded my country.'

The Arrow and Subotai rode north into Russia and Ukraine, where they defeated a coalition of steppe peoples. Now they faced the Russians ruled by House Rurik. The Mongols were outnumbered: 30,000 Russians led by Prince Mstislav Mstislavich the Daring of Galich and the princes of Kyiv, Chernigov, and Smolensk met them at Kalka close to the Sea of Azov. The Mongols routed them. Mstislav Romanovich, grand prince of Kyiv, submitted – providing there was no bloodshed. Jebe and Subotai slyly honoured the promise, feasting on a wooden platform that gradually crushed the Russian princes.

The Rurikovichi had not lost their biggest army, that of Grand Duke Yuri of Vladimir-Suzdal. As Jebe and Subotai swerved homewards, summoned by Genghis, the Europeans now learned about the Mongols.

If Genghis was the khagan of the east, the khagan of the west was the most extraordinary of the Hautevilles. Emperor Frederick II, who gloried in the nickname Stupor Mundi – Wonder of the World – prepared to defend Christendom.

Khmers, Hohenstaufen and Polos

Many children would have been overwhelmed by Frederick's inheritance. He was the grandson of Roger II of Sicily and Frederick Barbarossa, half Hauteville, half Staufen – the Germanic rulers of Swabia, descended from Charlemagne. Frederick was singular first in his lineage then in his character. His mother Constance, intelligent, resilient and red-blonde, was the posthumously born daughter of Roger II, kept sequestered in the Hauteville court in Palermo until it became clear that she was the heiress to Sicily, whereupon in 1186 her nephew William the Good negotiated a peace crowned with the marriage of Constance, thirty, to Heinrich, son of Frederick Barbarossa. When her nephew died young, she and her husband, who was now German emperor Heinrich VI, had to fight for the kingdom.

Then came unlikely news: Constance was pregnant at forty. Their healthy son, named Frederick Roger after his two storied grandfathers, would be the key player in Europe for the fifty years that saw the rise of Genghis. After the death of her husband, Queen/Empress Constance devoted herself to protecting Sicily for her baby, whom she placed under the protection of the pope. Crowned king of Sicily at the age of three, he was educated by Islamic, Jewish and Greek tutors, guarded by Saracen bodyguards and liberated by a Sicilian informality that allowed him to play with his friends in the streets.

After the death of his mother, and now elected Roman emperor and king of Italy, Frederick, red-haired and green-eyed, grew up fluent in six languages including Arabic. He regarded himself as the universal emperor of Christendom, and he was flamboyant, talented and curious, with the acumen to rule his complex inheritance and fight for it. He wrote a guide to falconry and founded Naples university, but, irritated by Catholic piety, he enjoyed baiting popes and priests, making risqué jokes about Christ, keeping a harem of concubines and writing love poetry to many mistresses. He also relished debating with Arabic and

Jewish astronomers and English magicians, and created an Arab town on the mainland where he settled Muslim rebels from Sicily.

Frederick was alarmed by the Mongols' raid, but their mysterious vanishing allowed him to focus on crusading. Pope Innocent III, having called for crusades in Spain* and Outremer, ordered Frederick to take the Cross, which would distract him from building power in Italy. Frederick prepared to capture Jerusalem on battlefield and in bed: he recruited a German military-religious order, the Teutonic Knights (in return for his assistance in the other crusade against the pagans of Lithuania and Prussia); and he married Yolande, aged thirteen, nominal queen of Jerusalem, which allowed him to call himself king, though Saladin's grandson actually ruled the city, the Christians just Acre and a strip of coast. Although the queen of Jerusalem died just two years later while giving birth to a son, Frederick prevaricated about leaving for Outremer, outraging Pope Gregory IX, who called him 'Precursor of the Anti-Christ' and excommunicated him. In 1228, when he and his Teutonic Knights at last sailed for Acre, the Mongols were again riding westward.

After seven years at war in the east, Genghis headed home, his ambitions still boundless. India was unconquered, as was Song China. Probing Punjab, where the fugitive prince of Khwarizm was lurking, Genghis sent a warning to the paramount ruler in northern India, a former Turkic slave called Iltutmish, who sensibly appeased the Mongol. Islam had dominated northern India since 1192 when a Muslim Afghan warlord had invaded and defeated the Hindu Rajputs, establishing a sultanate based in Delhi. From then until 1857, Muslim kings ruled; until 1947, India was dominated by foreign conquerors.

Recognized as sultan by the caliph of Baghdad, Iltutmish and his Turks pillaged the 'idolatrous' Hindu temples and Buddhist stupas. Religions flourish when they are backed by earthly powers: Islam had a champion in the sultans; Buddhism, already undermined in India by the popularity of Tantric Hinduism, never recovered. The Hindu Chola family had dominated southern India and south-east Asia, and as their

* In 1212, Innocent encouraged the three Christian potentates, Alfonso VIII of Castile, Sancho VII of Navarre and Pedro II of Aragon, to unite to fight the Berber rulers of al-Andalus. At Las Navas de Tolosa, the Christians routed them, trapping Caliph al-Nasir, who ran for his life but fell into a trench. Ferried back to Marrakesh, he died of his wounds. The Berbers' victorious aura was broken: Yusuf II was gored while playing with one of his pet cows – not a death fit for a caliph. Several Islamic cities fell to Alfonso, who boasted that at Ubeda he had killed 60,000 Muslims, men, women and children, a crime worse than Jerusalem in 1099. His grandson Fernando III mopped up Cordoba and Seville. By the time of his death, Granada was the last Islamic kingdom in Spain.

last great emperor faced disaster, their Indic influence lived on in the crowning glory of the Indosphere. Now a dynamic Buddhist sovereign was building a Khmer empire across south-east Asia that was based at the resplendent capital, Angkor. Jayavarman VII, a contemporary of Genghis, defeated the Hindu Cham kingdom in southern Vietnam and expanded Angkorian influence as far as Myanmar, Malaya and Yunnan (China).

In 1113, an exuberant warrior god-king, Suryavarman II, had seized the Khmer throne by slaughtering much of his family and then routing all contenders, aided by his ally the Chola emperor of India and appeasing the Chinese emperor, to whom he sent delegations. This contemporary of the Crusader kings was a visionary determined to make Angkor a timeless monument to his greatness by adding an array of astonishing monuments, culminating in the five-towered, multiple-courted temple Angkor Wat dedicated to Vishnu.* After his death, the Chams raided up the Mekong and sacked Angkor. As a young prince, Jayavarman VII struck back and in a thirty-seven-year reign established an empire from coast to coast. Embracing Buddhism, adapting the existing Hindu temples of Angkor, he made it into one of the world's biggest and most beautiful cities, its royal-sacred precinct covering almost 500 acres. Greater Angkor with a population of over a million people stretched over 400 square miles of suburbs, lakes and villages, sustained by sophisticated hydraulic systems of canals and *barays* (reservoirs) that irrigated rice and palm plantations. When Jayavarman, remarkable in many things, died in 1218 aged ninety-five, he was succeeded by a son, Indravarman II, who rededicated many of his father's temples to celebrate Shiva.

As Indic culture flourished in Angkor, and Iltutmish was promoting Islam in northern India, Genghis galloped home.

GENGHIS AND FREDERICK: SHOWDOWN AT THE DEATHBED

Genghis travelled back to Mongolia with his grandsons, the fifteen-year-old Möngke and the ten-year-old Kublai. He hunted antelope with

---

* By some calculations, it is the largest religious building in world history and is certainly the biggest Hindu temple ever built. Five-towered (in honour of the five peaks of the mythical Mount Meru), built around courtyards, it remains a wonder to behold, decorated with over a thousand bare-breasted dancing girls, goblins and yogis, lions and elephants, its friezes depicting Suryavarman himself along with war elephants and his court of Brahmins and courtiers bearing palanquins and parasols.

them and performed the rite of smearing fat and blood as a coming of age. Both these sons of Tolui would rule as khagans. Genghis worried that 'After us, our race will wear golden garments, eat sweet food, ride splendid horses, kiss the loveliest women – and forget they owe these things to us!'

There was still much to do. The full conquest of China was not possible without the territory of the Tanguts, who had refused to send troops on the Khwarizmian campaign. 'While we eat,' Genghis told his courtiers, 'let's talk of how we made them die and destroyed them. That was the end, they are no more.' Genghis devastated their cities. Yet he saved some rare manuscripts and special medicinal drugs, sometimes holding back on his massacres.

'Are you going to weep for the people again?' Ögodei teased his father. A general advised Genghis to exterminate the Chinese and rusticate the Central Country as pasture, but his Chinese advisers explained the potential tax revenues. 'An empire that can be conquered on horseback,' he mused, 'can't be ruled from it.' Whether or not he really said that, Genghis now commissioned a system of taxation.

As the Tangut emperor was on his way to submit, Genghis, out riding, fell from his horse and that night he was sick. 'Princes and generals,' said Khatun Yesui (a khatun was the wife of a khan, or empress), 'consult each other; last night the khan was feverish.' The generals proposed a withdrawal.

'The Tangut will say our hearts are failing,' Genghis replied, dictating specific orders: Khatun Yesui was to receive Tangut territory; he was to be buried close to his sacred mountain of Burkhan Khaldun. 'Don't let my death be known. Don't weep or lament but when the Tangut ruler and his people leave the city, *kill everyone!*'

Genghis was secretly dying as the Tangut ruler arrived at the Golden *ordu* in August 1227. He presented his gifts – giant golden Buddhas, boys and girls, camels and horses, all in sets of sacred nine – but he was then seized and strangled, his entourage slaughtered. Informed of this, Genghis said, 'We've taken our vengeance. They have vanished.' Now he could die, leaving an empire four times as big as Alexander's, twice the size of the Roman imperium – but only half as expansive as it would soon be. The body was borne northwards to be buried secretly on the sacred mountain, accompanied by sacrificed horses and slaves, on a site never yet found. Then the Golden princes led by Tolui, Genghis's daughters and his generals assembled at a *qurultai* where, as agreed with their father, Chagatai proposed Ögodei as khagan. Ögodei consulted his brothers and took the decision to resume world conquest, taking command of the campaign to finish off the Jurchen – otherwise 'People will ask by what ability I've succeeded my father.' In 1231, Ögodei, accompanied by Tolui, took the Jurchen capital of Kaifeng, but fell ill from cirrhosis, caused by alcoholism. Tolui was also addicted, drinking so much *kumis* that he sometimes just wept publicly, leaving politics to his wife, Sorqaqtani Beki. Ögodei recovered; Tolui died of alcoholism, leaving Sorqaqtani to rule his appanage across northern China. Ögodei respected her, first asking her to marry him, then suggesting his useless son Güyük. But she refused graciously, saying her own four sons were her priority. She was right: she and they were the future. Instead she became Ögodei's adviser. 'No turban-wearer [male] could have dealt with these matters with similar brilliance,' wrote the Persian historian Juvaini. 'In any business which Ögodei undertook, whether concerning empire or army, he consulted her, changing arrangements according to her recommendations.'

Often soused, Ögodei founded a more permanent capital at Karakorum (Mongolia) and commissioned a family history. Although he sometimes pardoned those sentenced to death, he also ordered the rape of thousands of girls of the conquered Oirat tribe after their ruler, his sister Checheikhen, died. His addictions were so out of control that Chagatai forced him to allow a 'supervisor' to limit the number of his drinks, which he got around by quaffing from larger goblets of wine.

As Ögodei declined, his wife Khatun Töregene ran more of the government, appointing Muslim officials, Turks and Persians, to raise Chinese taxes. In 1236 the khagan dispatched an army of 150,000, under his nephews Batu (son of Jochi) and Möngke (son of Tolui) plus his own son Güyük, all commanded by the marshal Subotai, to conquer Europe.

The Wonder of the World, Frederick II, was unprepared. Soon after Genghis's death, he had arrived in the Holy Land where he negotiated a peace plan with Saladin's nephew Sultan al-Kamil. Saladin's heirs had demolished the walls of Jerusalem to avoid it being used by family rivals or Crusaders. Now Frederick and al-Kamil agreed that each religion would control its own shrines, the Muslims the Haram al-Sharif, the Christians the Sepulchre. In Jerusalem, a triumphant Frederick wore his crown as king of the sacred city while also writing love poetry to his 'Syrian' mistress: was she Frankish or Arab? By now he was balding and short-sighted. An Arab writer who spotted him in Jerusalem joked, 'The emperor, covered with red hair, was bald and myopic. Had he been a slave, he wouldn't have fetched 200 dirhams at market.' Yet Frederick's visionary compromise was hated by the diehard Crusaders. Back in Acre, butchers pelted him with entrails.

He rushed home to deal with his enemies, first Pope Gregory,* who sent an army to seize Sicily, then the obstreperous German princes, who were encouraged by his high-handed son Heinrich, king of the Romans. Frederick fought a long war to retake his territories.† Italy was divided between his own supporters and the pope's, the two sides having factions in each city, Ghibellines supporting the emperor, Guelphs the pope, in a conflict that lasted for a century. In Germany, Frederick disinherited and imprisoned Heinrich, who died of leprosy in prison, and won back German supporters. One of these was his godson, an aggressive young knight named Rudolf who was expanding his estates around his Swiss castle, Hawk Mountain: Habsburg. Rudolf specialized in switching sides to win concessions, manoeuvres that now laid the foundations for the Habsburg dynasty that would conquer a new continent and rule swathes of Europe until 1918.

Calling himself the count of Habsburg, he proved his martial credentials by leading his own contingent in the northern crusades against the pagans – where, starting in 1237, the emperor was backing his ally, Hermann von Salza, master of the Teutonic Knights, against the pagan Lithuanians, Prussians, Sambians and Semigalians who still ruled much of today's Germany, Poland, Belarus and the Baltics. It was a chance to kill infidels but also to carve out new territories.

Just as Frederick was winning these wars, Subotai, the one-eyed Mongol marshal, accompanied by Genghis's grandson Batu Khan, burst into Europe. In 1237, they crossed the Volga, rapidly overrunning what is today Russia, Ukraine and Belarus. In 1239, when they took Vladimir, its prince Yuri II, pre-eminent Rurikovich, was killed and his wife burned to death in church. In 1240, Prince Möngke destroyed Kyiv.

---

* Gregory IX created the Papal Inquisition to prevent local rulers or mobs taking on supposed heretics without papal supervision. He burned copies of the Jewish Talmud and ordered that all Jews should be regarded as *perpetuam servitus judaeorum* – in servitude until Judgement Day.

† Frederick's third wife was Isabella, daughter of the late King John of England. As part of an alliance with her young brother Henry III against France, Frederick married her in 1235. The emperor was often away fighting for years on end, leaving Isabella sometimes pregnant and always guarded by African eunuchs. She corresponded with Henry III while Frederick continued to enjoy his big love affair with his Sicilian mistress Bianca Lancia, with whom he had children, and his Arab harem. The English empress of Germany, queen of Sicily and Jerusalem, died in childbirth like his second wife, aged only twenty-five. Frederick later married Bianca on her deathbed. In this period, German sovereigns were elected as king of Germany but only enjoyed the title Emperor of the Holy Roman Empire of the German Nation or Caesar (*kaiser* in German) if they were crowned by the pope. Their heir was entitled king of the Romans.

On 9 April, at Legnica, after burning Lublin and Kraków, a Mongol army routed Poles, Bohemians and Saxons, killing the Polish duke whose naked headless body was recognized by his wife only because he had six toes on one foot. Another army under Batu and Subotai rode into Hungary. 'You dwell in houses and have fixed towns and fortresses,' Batu said menacingly to Bela IV of Hungary, 'so how will you escape me?' A Hungarian-speaking Englishman arrived from Batu to demand submission: Bela refused.

The day after Legnica, Subotai and Batu fought Bela at Mohi, where they killed 65,000 men: they may have deployed gunpowder and naphtha bombs brought from China – if so, the first use of gunpowder in Europe. But Batu was criticized for incompetence by his first cousin Güyük, son of Great Khan Ögodei, who demanded a retreat. Subotai refused and advanced to take and burn Pest on the Danube. Their detachments rode west into Austria where the locals captured eight of their number. One of these turned out to be the Englishman who had offered terms to Bela.*

Batu Khan crossed the borders into Frederick's empire. Now thirty-five, the senior grandson of Genghis menaced the grandees of Europe. 'I am coming to usurp your throne,' he told Frederick, advising him to abdicate and become a falconer in Karakorum. Frederick, a connoisseur of falconry, laughed that he was well qualified for the job. Even faced with the Mongols, Europe was incapable of unity: emperor and pope declared a crusade but hated each other.

Batu and Subotai were poised to take Europe when dramatic news arrived: Ögodei had died in December 1241, without naming his son Güyük as successor. To elect the new khagan, the princes had to return for the *qurultai* in Karakorum – where it was the women who dominated for the next decade.

WHEN WOMEN RULED THE WORLD: SORQAQTANI AND RAZIA

After the death of Ögodei, his widow Khatun Töregene ran the empire. Widows ruled until a new khagan was elected. But the senior prince, Batu Khan, known as Agha – Big Brother – refused to come to Karakorum,

---

* Probably named Robert, it is plausible that the Englishman was the chaplain of the barons who in 1215 had rebelled against King John and who forced him to concede a charter of noble privileges, Magna Carta. Taking service on the continent he had been captured by Batu Khan, whom he served for twenty years – one of those characters whose bizarre trajectory illustrates the surprising flows of history.

fearing for his safety, and Töregene was not strong enough to crown her eldest son Güyük. Instead she governed through a most unlikely channel, a female Persian prisoner of war called Fatima who became 'the sharer of intimate confidences and depository of hidden secrets', overruling officials, 'free to issue her own commands' and earning herself the sarcastic nickname of Khatun. As her rival Sorqaqtani conspired against her, Töregene trusted Fatima totally, but she distrusted Ögedei's officials, executing one by having stones forced down his throat. But she feared Genghis's daughters, killing the youngest, Ilalti, ruler of the Uighurs, by framing her for the poisoning of her brother Ögodei.

At Karakorum, Töregene received Seljuks of Rum, Bagrations of Georgia, Rurikovichi princes of Russia and western envoys seeking Mongol backing. An intrepid sexagenarian priest, Giovanni da Pian del Carpine, arrived as the legate of Innocent IV. Some princes were feasted and promoted, others feasted and murdered.

Töregene was not the only female potentate. In Delhi, Sultan Iltutmish favoured his eldest daughter Razia: 'My sons are incapable,' he said, 'and for that reason I've decided my daughter should reign.' Instead, on his death, his amirs enthroned his son Ruknuddin Firuz, a playboy who rode drunk on elephants accompanied by a retinue of eunuchs and overpromoted mahouts while his mother, Shahturkhan, ruled, settling scores by blinding and killing one of Iltutmish's sons. She saw that her stepdaughter Razia was a threat and ordered her assassination. Instead, at Friday prayers Razia appealed to the people, inciting them to storm the palace. When they had done so, she arrested and killed Shahturkhan and Firuz before becoming sultan in her own right. The amirs who backed her had presumed she would be a figurehead; initially she respected Islamic modesty, watching councils from behind a screen, escorted by female bodyguards, but then she started to rule publicly and unveiled, cutting her hair, sporting dashing male gear – breastplates, sword and boots – and riding her own elephant through Delhi.

Her chief adviser was an enslaved Habashi (from Abyssinia) who had risen to general, named Jamaluddin Yaqut, and whom she appointed master of horse, thereby offending her Turkic generals. When she was dismounting from a horse, the courtiers noticed that Yakut slipped his hands under her armpits, a sign of shocking intimacy: they were clearly lovers. The combination of a woman and an African man, her gender, his race, was too much for them.

Razia promoted Yakut to *amir al-amira* – commander-in-chief. Their enemies conspired against them, assassinating him and then arresting Razia in order to place another half-brother on the throne. When he turned out to be obstreperous, one of the warlords, Altunia, who was Razia's jailer, fell in love with her and offered marriage in return for a partnership. She agreed, but they were defeated and he was killed. Dressed as a man she sought refuge in a peasant cottage, but when she was asleep her host noticed the jewels under her coat and killed her, burying her in the garden. He was caught trying to sell her gems and revealed his secret. Her domed tomb, Delhi's Turkman Gate, was long a place of pilgrimage.

In Karakorum, Töregene ruled for five years until in 1246 Baku Khan agreed to send envoys to vote for the unimpressive Güyük, who left most of the decisions to his mother. Güyük, 'astute and very grave, hardly ever seen to laugh or make merry', was determined to enforce Genghis's discipline after the easy-going Ögodei. Now he resented his mother's power and loathed her factotum, Fatima, finally sending guards to arrest her. Töregene refused to surrender her. Güyük and his khatun Oghul Qaimish publicly tried and tortured Fatima, who, naked, was burned and then had her orifices sewn up before being tossed into a river.

After eighteen months, Güyük marched east to attack Iraq and destroy Batu, who probably poisoned him. His widow took over as regent, negotiating with the French envoy André de Longjumeau, whom she told, 'Peace is good' but 'you can't have peace until you have peace with *us*!' If not, 'we shall destroy you'. But she united her enemies by fatally alienating Sorqaqtani.

Tolui's widow was 'extremely intelligent and able . . . the most intelligent woman in the world', according to the historian Rashid al-Din. Carefully bringing up her four able sons, teaching them key languages – Kublai learned Chinese – this Christian, born into royalty, was open-minded, building churches but also a madrasa. Now she sent her shrewd son Möngke to see the Big Brother in Russia. Batu welcomed him warmly, reuniting the winning team that had invaded Hungary. Calling a *qurultai* far from Karakorum, Batu invited the widows of Genghis and of Ögodei and Sorqaqtani herself, who finessed the deal. In July 1251, Batu was offered the khaganate but refused, proposing the forty-three-year-old Möngke, who was chosen and, after graciously refusing twice, accepted on the third offer. Then they marched on Karakorum. Möngke loathed Oghul Qaimish – 'more contemptible than a bitch' – having her tortured just as she had tortured Fatima, naked, her orifices sewn together, then drowned in a sack. Sorqaqtani and Möngke purged the family and ended the reign of the khatuns: no women were to have power again, ordered Möngke, or 'we shall see what we shall see' – a euphemism for death. When the purge was at its height, Sorqaqtani fell ill, believing that her Christian God was punishing her for the killings, which she now tried to stop before her own death.

Genghis's Tengri-blessed mission to conquer the world was far from over.

ALEXANDER NEVSKY AND MÖNGKE KHAN: WORLD CONQUEST RESTORED

Möngke, who had fought in Hungary and Poland, had the acumen to direct a Eurasian world conquest and govern it – commissioning a tax census in territories from Korea to Ukraine. At the centre, Karakorum, he held court in a basic palace, hung with gold cloth, warmed by a brazier burning wormwood roots and cattle dung. He would be 'seated on a little bed dressed in a rich furred robe which glistened like the skin of a seal' while showing off his gyrfalcons.

Still obsessed with the loss of Jerusalem, and the fantasy of Prester John, European potentates sent envoys to Karakorum: Willem van Ruysbroeck, Flemish envoy of Louis IX of France, arrived to convert Möngke to Christianity or at least to negotiate an alliance between the Mongols and the Crusaders against Islam.

Möngke was the son of a Christian married to a Christian wife whom he sometimes accompanied to chapel, reclining during the service on a golden bed. 'We Mongols believe in one God,' he told Willem. 'Just as God gave different fingers to my hand, he's given different ways to men.' But when it came to sacred power he was as severe as his grandfather: 'If, when you hear the decree of the eternal God, you're unwilling to pay attention and send an army against us, we know what we can do.' The world was now about to see what he meant.

Möngke ruled in partnership with Big Brother Batu, whose khanate, known as the Golden Horde and based at Sarai on the Volga, covered much of European Russia and Ukraine. Batu was 'genial and good-natured' but 'cruel in war'. He used the Rurikovichi as enforcers. The ablest of his Mongol vassals was the twenty-five-year-old Alexander, son of the prince of Vladimir, who understood the benefits of appeasement. His father Yaroslav II had been poisoned in Karakorum by Khatun Töregene, after which Alexander travelled there, bent the knee to his father's murderers and was granted Kyiv. Now Batu was in charge, he often visited Big Brother and his son Sartuq at Sarai to bend the knee. Strapping and shrewd with a voice like a trumpet, Alexander impressed

Sartuq so much that they became blood brothers. He needed the Mongols: Novgorod, a mercantile republic,* was under attack from the west. A new rising power, the pagan duchy of Lithuania, was expanding into Poland, Belarus and Ukraine. Sweden threatened Novgorod, which invited Alexander to defend it. In 1240 he defeated the Swedes on the Neva River (much later earning the sobriquet Nevsky). Then he faced the Teutonic Knights and other Germanic crusaders who had taken Prussia, Livonia and Semigalia before turning on the Orthodox Russians. In 1242, Alexander's cavalry charging across the ice of Lake Peipus defeated the Livonian Brothers of the Sword.

In 1252, threatened by his rebellious brothers, Alexander won Batu's backing to defeat his own blood and was appointed paramount prince of Vladimir; in return he enforced Mongol control and collected the khagan's taxes. When in 1258 Novgorod and other Russian cities rebelled, Alexander gouged out the eyes and cut off the noses of the rebels, riding into the city accompanied by Mongols: his status as patriotic Russian hero is thus dubious. For reasons unknown, the khans became displeased. In 1263, Nevsky, still only forty-three, died while under arrest in Sarai, probably poisoned. His brothers and sons bid for the succession, the start of almost two centuries of submission to the Golden Horde.

Daniel, Alexander's youngest and weakest son, was left the most meagre portion – Moscow† – but it was from him and the princes of Muscovy that the tsars and Russia would descend.

As Batu secured Russia, Möngke ordered his brothers to continue their world conquest – Kublai to take Song China, and Hulagu to suppress Persia, then conquer Iraq, Israel and Egypt. Kublai, viceroy of northern China, was already at war. A frontal assault on the Song was perilous, so Möngke ordered him to encircle the empire by conquering the independent kingdom to its south, Dali. As Kublai prepared a multipronged assault on the Song, Möngke, learning that an Assassin hit squad was on its way to kill him, ordered Hulagu to destroy the Assassins and then the caliphate of Baghdad: 'Establish the laws of Genghis

---

* Novgorod, founded by the Rurikovichi or other Nordic trader-raiders, had developed into an oligarchical republic, not dissimilar to Venice and Genoa. Ruling from the Baltic to the Urals, its exact constitution is unclear but there was an assembly – the *Veche* – that elected a leader known as the *posadnik* who ruled somehow with a council of grandees and the archbishop, who in turn often chose a Rurikovich prince to lead the republic when it was in peril. It proves there were traditions in medieval Russia other than autocracy.

† In 1156 Prince Yuri 'Long-Arm' Dolgoruky, whose mother was Gytha of Wessex, daughter of King Harold, built a stronghold on a hill overlooking the Moskva River. At times he was grand prince of Kyiv, then of Vladimir-Suzdal. It was the Mongol invasions that ultimately made this fortress, Moscow, the pre-eminent principality of the Rurikovichi and future fulcrum of Russian empire.

Khan from the banks of the Amu Darya [central Asia] to Egypt. Those who submit, treat gently; those who resist, exterminate.'

HULAGU AND SAADI: ENTERTAINING AN ELEPHANT, SLAUGHTERING A CITY

Hulagu marched west with 100,000 men (each with two slaves, five horses and thirty sheep), a corps of Chinese siege engineers with 1,000 mangonels, possibly gunpowder bombardiers with thundercrash bombs – and new allies, Christian princes and knights from Antioch, Georgia and Armenia, eager to destroy the caliphate. This horde of men was accompanied by a horde of pathogens. Hulagu brought his own food supplies – huge quantities of grain, escorted by rats, and dried meats, including cured marmot. New research suggests that this was the moment the Black Death transferred from the east, a century earlier than the previously accepted date.

The khan crushed Transoxiana, then besieged the Assassins in their eyrie of Alamut. In November 1256, the Assassin imam, Rukn ad-Din, surrendered. One of Hulagu's Persian aides, Ata-Malik Juvaini, whose father had served the Khwarizmian shah and then Genghis, encouraged the burning of the library, but the Persian polymath Nasir al-Din al-Tusi explained that Assassin theology did not depend on books. Hulagu spared the library. As for Rukn, he was wrapped in a carpet, then hoof-stomped to pulp. Hulagu concluded by ordering the assassination of 12,000 Assassins.[*]

On 22 January 1258, Hulagu encircled Baghdad, having warned the caliph that 'Humiliation by the grace of Tengri has overtaken the dynasties of Khwarizm, Seljuk, Daylam [Assassins], yet the gates of Baghdad were never closed to them. How then should entry be closed to us who possess such power? Once I lead my forces to Baghdad in righteous anger . . . I will bring you crashing down from the summit of the sky. I won't leave a single person alive.'

'Young man,' retorted the Abbasiya caliph al-Musta'sim (who was forty-five to Hulagu's thirty-eight, 'you who have barely started your

---

[*] But the Assassins still controlled castles in Syria and Lebanon. In 1271, they attempted to assassinate Prince Edward of England who was on Crusade in Acre: the future Edward I survived to hammer the Scots. After the destruction of the last Assassin castles, the Nizaris split once again, with one branch continuing the sacred succession. In the nineteenth century, their imam was appointed governor of Qom by the Persian shah who granted him the title Aga Khan before he moved to British India, flourishing as a British client. In the twenty-first century, the Aga Khans are still imams of fifteen million Nizaris.

career and are drunk on a ten-day success, believing yourself ruler of the world, don't you know that from the east to the Maghreb all worshippers of Allah are slaves to *my* court?' Hulagu ordered his paladin, Kitbuqa, a Christian, to rain rocks, bombs and naphtha on to Baghdad, which was soon blazing, while they destroyed the dykes, flooding the countryside. When the city fell, Hulagu's Christian wife Doquz, cousin of his mother Sorqaqtani, persuaded him to spare Christians, but his allies the Georgians took special pleasure in killing Muslims.

On 10 February 1258, the caliph arrived at Hulagu's *ordu* to surrender. Hulagu drove out all Baghdad's inhabitants. Outside the wall, Baghdadis were slaughtered – some sources claim 800,000 were killed; Hulagu himself boasted of 200,000 – and the Mongols looted Baghdad 'like hungry falcons attacking a flight of doves or raging wolves attacking sheep, with loose reins and shameless faces, cutting with knives any cushions and beds of gold encrusted with jewels, dragging veiled girls from the harem through the streets to become their playthings', burning mosques and hospitals, shattering the Abbasiya tombs, though much of al-Mamun's library was saved by the bibliophile hero Nasir al-Din al-Tusi. Hulagu held court in the Octagon Palace where at a victory banquet he menaced the broken caliph: 'You're the host, we're your guests. Bring us whatever you have.' Al-Musta'sim opened his treasure chests. 'Now tell my servants,' ordered Hulagu 'where your *hidden* treasures are.' Al-Musta'sim revealed gold hidden in an ornamental pool. Then the caliph and his sons were rolled up in carpets and stomped to death by horses.* It was not only Hulagu killing people. His camp in Baghdad was now hit by a mysterious epidemic, scarcely recorded amid the murderous mayhem, but it flared up too at his other sieges.

Leaving his Iranian epigone Juvaini to rebuild Baghdad, Hulagu galloped into Syria, meeting his Hauteville ally Bohemond VI le Beau, the twenty-one-year-old prince of Antioch, and his father-in-law King Hethum of Cilician Armenia, a small Christian kingdom, who joined his horde and helped capture Aleppo and Homs. Inspired by his Frankish friends, Hulagu punished a Turkish warlord who had crucified a Christian: the man was bisected while being forced to eat his own body.

It is hard to grasp the tragedy of Hulagu's depredations, but a witness, a Persian poet called Saadi, talked to Arab soldiers and recorded in his masterpiece *Bustan* what it was like to fight the khan: 'From the raining of arrows descending like hail, the storm of death arose on all sides,'

---

* A cousin of the last caliph escaped to Cairo where he was set up as honorary caliph, a lineage maintained by the Mamluk sultans there until 1517, when the Ottomans took the last of the family to Istanbul and, after almost a thousand years of greatness, into obscurity.

unleashed by the attacking Mongols, who resembled 'a pack of leopards, as strong as elephants. The heads of the warriors were encased in iron, so were the horses' hoofs.'*

In March 1260, Mongol marshal Kitbuqa rode into Damascus, accompanied by Beau Bohemond and King Hethum, who joyously held mass in the former St John's, now Great Mosque. As Hulagu's cavalry took Nablus and reached Gaza, the fulfilment of the Crusader dream of Christian Jerusalem and the Mongol conquest of Egypt seemed inevitable.

I WISH I WERE DUST:
THE SLAVE KING AND THE LAST HAUTEVILLE

Hulagu demanded that Egypt surrender, but on 11 August 1259, far away to the east, Möngke, who was accompanying Kublai in the war against Song China, died of dysentery. Hulagu moved back into Iran, leaving Kitbuqa in charge. Franks clashed with the Mongols, who favoured the Orthodox or Nestorians instead of the Catholics, while the Egyptians beheaded Hulagu's envoys. Kitbuqa could not ignore such a slight. The Egyptians marched to stop him.

The new Egyptian rulers were tough soldiers who had started as slaves – Mamluks. They were Russians and Turks, Georgians and Circassians, blue-eyed blonds being specially prized, stolen or bought from their villages, sold in the Genoan slave markets of Crimea and bought by Saladin and his family. Converted to Islam, trained as soldiers and then manumitted, they became ferocious paladins, united by Islamic fervour and esprit de corps, who dominated then destroyed the Saladin dynasty.

Their rise was accelerated by a new crusade. In 1249, Louis IX of France landed with an army that nearly conquered a chaotic Egypt, which was saved only by a blond Turkish Mamluk of Pantagruelian

---

* When Genghis took Persia, Saadi became a Sufi pilgrim – Sufism being Islamic mysticism. Saadi studied in Baghdad and Cairo, visited Mecca and Jerusalem until he was captured and enslaved by the Crusaders in Acre for seven years and then ransomed by the Egyptians. After fifty years of wandering, Saadi went home and wrote his masterpieces. The wars inspired his love of humanity: 'All human beings are members of one frame, / Since all, at first, from the same essence came,' he wrote in *Bani Adam*. 'If you feel not for others' misery, / A human being is no name for you.' But his aphorisms are sharp: 'Don't make friends with an elephant keeper if you have no room to entertain an elephant.' On war, he advised: 'Before drawing your weapons for battle take care / That the pathway to peace is discreetly cleared.' He lived into his nineties.

proportions with one blue eye, one totally white, named Baibars. A junta of Mamluk amirs murdered the young sultan and replaced the Saladin family* as Baibars advanced against the thinly spread Mongols. At Ain Julut (Goliath's Spring) near Nablus, Baibars's 15,000 Mamluks, on bigger warhorses than the Mongols, ambushed Kitbuqa's forces, who fought to the last man. 'It's here that I must die,' the marshal said. 'Some soldier will reach the khan and tell him Kitbuqa refused to retreat. Happy life to the khan!' When finally his horse was brought down, he was taken before the Mamluks.

'After overthrowing so many dynasties,' teased the Mamluks, 'look at you now!'

'Don't be intoxicated by a moment's success,' replied Kitbuqa, the conqueror of Iran and Iraq unexpectedly defeated by ex-slaves. 'When the news of my death reaches the khan, Egypt will be crushed beneath Mongol hooves.' As the sword swung, he ended with 'I was the khan's slave. I am not – like you – the murderer of my master.'

Baibars – who called himself the Panther, leaving his insignia all over the region – made himself sultan. Gleefully bloodthirsty and demonically energetic, he campaigned for seventeen years, holding the Mongols at bay, darting down the Nile against the Nubian kingdom of Makuria, then launching an onslaught against all Christians, taking Caesarea and Jaffa, then in 1268 storming Antioch, seat of the Hautevilles. He wrote to Bohemond le Beau, 'You'd have seen your knights prostrate beneath horses' hooves, your houses stormed by pillagers, your wealth weighted by the quintal, your girls sold four at a time and bought for a dinar of your own money!' In 1277, while poisoning an enemy, Baibars absent-mindedly swallowed the wrong glass, an occupational hazard for those who become blasé about murdering guests. He was succeeded by a veteran amir, Qalawun, who with his sons and grandsons conquered Israel and Syria† while the Mongols were busy in China.

When Möngke died, Kublai, laying siege to Wuchow, raced northwards to his summer palace Xanadu (Shangdu) and proclaimed himself khagan, brushing off the challenge of his youngest brother, Ariq-boga.

---

* The sultan was replaced by his widow, Shajar al-Durr, a former slave who now ruled as sultan, like Razia in Delhi – a rare thing in Islamic history, a woman ruling in her own right as Malikat al-Muslimin (Queen of the Muslims). But when her rule was challenged she was forced to marry a Mamluk general. She later had him murdered in his bath, a deed that infuriated the guards and led to her, naked except for a diamond-encrusted shawl, being beaten to death by the shoes of her palace-slaves: death by stiletto.

† After losing Antioch in 1268, Bohemond VI kept the Lebanese port of Tripoli, which was inherited by his sister Lucia. Sultan Qalawun took the port in 1289. Lucia, countess of Tripoli, the last Hauteville, may have perished in the ruins.

Kublai abandoned Karakorum to found a new winter capital known as Dadu in Chinese (Great Capital) or Khanbalic in Mongolian (Khan's City; later Beijing), which he had designed by an Arab architect, Iktiyar al-Din. Its only surviving building, the White Pagoda, was the work of Arniko, a Nepalese. Dadu was thus a carefully created Chinese city built for a Mongol by an Arab and a Nepalese.

Encouraged by his influential favourite wife, Chabi,* the Buddhist Kublai tolerated all. 'I'm interested not in the stones that make the bridge,' he said, 'but in the arch that supports it.' He protected Buddhists. Speaking Chinese, he was keen to advertise his Mandate of Heaven and raise Chinese taxes, recruiting a Golden Lotus Advisory Group – a think tank of Chinese advisers.

He was still a Mongol, often reclining in a *ger* next to his palaces or leading hunts accompanied by 14,000 huntsmen, 2,000 hounds with their dog handlers, 10,000 falconers, trained Siberian tigers and African cheetahs, eagles and thousands of troops who helpfully trapped hundreds of animals that were shot by the portly, gout-ridden khagan from a mega-howdah atop four elephants lashed together.

In 1264, Kublai would receive Niccolò and Maffeo Polo, two young Venetian merchants specializing in Constantinopolitan trade. Their expertise was jewellery and their biggest client would be Kublai.

KUBLAI AND THE POLO BROTHERS

In 1259, leaving Niccolò's pregnant wife behind in Venice, the Polos arrived in Constantinople, which had been dominated by Venice ever since Dandalo's conquest but would not be so for much longer. They left just as it was about to fall.[†]

The Polos invested in jewels then crossed the Black Sea, going straight to Sarai, capital of Berke, khan of the Golden Horde, brother of Batu, to whom they 'gave freely of all their jewels'. The Polos always thought big and went to the top: Berke 'directed that they should receive double the value of the jewels'. The Polos must have been charmers, for wherever

---

* In addition to his four wives, each with a court of several hundred, Kublai's favourite concubines, were 'very beautiful fair-skinned girls' from Afghanistan. All his concubines were were trained by experienced Mongol women.

† The Great City was retaken by the Greek prince Michael VIII Palaiologos, whose family would rule the restored *Basileia Romaion* for the next two centuries. The Romaioi celebrated by burning Venetian ships, blinding Venetian merchants and promoting the Genoese, who received their own quarter, Galata, where they built the Tower of Christ, the watchtower that still stands there.

they went grizzled khans welcomed them. Berke even appointed them as his fixers.

In 1252 Berke converted to Islam – the first of the family to do so – and was disgusted by cousin Hulagu's butchery at Baghdad: 'He must pay for killing the caliph.' The Golden clan was turning on itself. Three of his family were killed by Hulagu – 'Mongols killed by Mongol swords'. They clashed in the Caucasus; yet, even when the khans fought, a Mongolsphere – every bit as influential and pervasive as the power of the Angloworld of the last two centuries – extended from Korea to Novgorod for 200 years. In 1262, Berke allied with Hulagu's chief enemy Baibars, not without reflecting that 'If we'd been united, we'd have conquered the whole world.'

If there ever was a Pax Mongolica, it was sporadic, as the Polos found. 'The roads being rendered unsafe, the brothers couldn't return' to Venice, and were stranded for three years in Bukhara, learning Mongolian, before charming an envoy of Hulagu on his way to Kublai – who, he explained, was fascinated by Europe and Christianity. After all, his mother was Christian. The Polos joined the caravan.

The Keitas of Mali and the Habsburgs of Austria

RAPACIOUS RUDOLF AND MARCO MILLION

At Dadu, around 1271, Kublai received the Polos, interrogating them genially about the two Christian emperors, then ordering them to take a letter to Pope Clement IV requesting 100 scholars to teach Mongols as well as some oil from the lamp of the Holy Sepulchre in Jerusalem. The Polos were dazzled by Kublai's eight palaces, their 'rooftops of green, azure peacock-blue, bright as crystal', and a banqueting hall that seated 6,000.

Armed with an imperial pass,* the Polos set off back to Venice, but when they arrived Niccolò 'discovered his wife was dead, and that she had left behind her a son of fifteen years of age, whose name was Marco' – as Marco himself put it. The Polos found a Europe in chaos – Clement was dead, the heirs of Frederick had been murdered,† Ghibellines and Guelphs fought for Italian power. But one family thrived: the Habsburgs.

No one could agree who should be emperor of Germany, but Rudolf of Habsburg aspired to the crown as the godson of Frederick and grandson of a Staufen princess. Tall, swaggering, greedy, vicious and long-nosed, he was in his own words 'an insatiable warrior', burning monasteries, razing villages, hanging bandits and slaughtering Baltic pagans. But in 1273, now old (fifty-five), he was elected king of Germany.‡ He began by

---

* This was a *paiza*, a golden tablet a foot long and three inches wide, reading: 'By the power of Eternal Heaven, by order of the Khagan: whoever does not show respect to the bearer will be guilty of an offence punishable by death.'
† Frederick II's son Conrad by the queen of Jerusalem had been elected king of the Romans in his father's lifetime and had then inherited Sicily too, but he died in 1254 of malaria. The succession of his half-brother Manfredi, son of the emperor's *favorita* Bianca, was shattered by Pope Urban IV's granting of Sicily to a challenger, Charles of Anjou, brother of the French king, who in 1266 killed Manfredi and then had Conrad's sixteen-year-old son Conradin, 'as beautiful as Absalom', beheaded. But Manfredi's daughter Constance married King Pedro III of Aragon and retook Sicily. As for Charles, he kept Naples. When his family married into the royal houses of Mitteleuropa, his descendants for a while ruled Hungary, Croatia, Bosnia, Poland and Romania.
‡ The German princes who elected the kings of Germany were known as the electors. The

announcing sanctimoniously that 'Today I forgive all those wrongs done to me and I promise to be a defender of peace just as I was formerly a rapacious man of war.'

His rival was the flashy Czech king of Bohemia, Ottokar the Golden, whose silver mines made him Europe's richest sovereign with the bling-iest court.* Ottokar and Rudolf knew each other well, having crusaded together against the Lithuanian pagans: Königsberg (King's City, today Kaliningrad) was founded in Ottokar's honour. But they loathed each other. When the rightful duke of Austria died, the auric Czech king married his sister Margaret who was thirty years older, grabbed Vienna and then claimed the imperial throne, mocking Rudolf Habsburg for his dour 'grey mantle'.

Kaiser Rudolf won over five princes by marrying daughters to them: marriage not war would make the Habsburgs. Then, granting Austria to himself, he attacked Ottokar, who effulgent in his golden glamour pros-trated himself. Rudolf deliberately sat low on a stool. 'He mocked my grey mantle,' he growled. 'Let him mock it now.' When Ottokar, craving revenge and Austria, broke his word, Rudolf defeated him at Dürnkrut near Vienna. The Golden was stripped naked, then his genitals were sliced off and stuffed in his mouth. Rudolf eviscerated him, displaying him gutless and memberless in Vienna, and made his son Albert 'One-Eye' the duke of Austria.†

On Rudolf's death, the electors, fearing Habsburg power, elected an-other prince as king of Germany. One-Eye finessed his own election and cut his rival's throat. His 'looks that made you sick' were not improved by the empty eye socket caused by his doctors trying to cure a case of poisoning by hanging him upside down too long. Right up until the middle of the eighteenth century, doctors were so destructive that it is likely that aristocrats with access to expensive medics lived *less* long than peasants with none. Ultimately One-Eye was undone by his own avarice, failing to share his father's inheritance with a nephew who suffered under the nickname John NoLand. After rejecting a disdainful bouquet from One-Eye, NoLand and his henchmen ambushed the king, cleaving his skull with a mace. Habsburgian revenge was atrocious: Albert's children Leopold, duke of Austria, and Agnes, queen of Hungary, sat on

kings were crowned in Aachen, Charlemagne's old capital.
* Ottokar was the greatest so far of the Czech Přemyslovci family, who had started as Slavic chieftains around Prague and created a Bohemian kingdom.
† But it was not the end of the Přemyslovci: his son Wenceslas II became king of Poland and Bohemia and procured Hungary for his son, ruling a Mitteleuropean empire that fell apart after his death.

a dais as sixty-nine innocent retainers of John's hitmen were beheaded one by one, their headless bodies laid out in rows. As blood spurted, Agnes supposedly sighed, 'I am bathed in May dew.'

The Habsburgs were now the House of Austria – and the Polos were on their way back to Kublai Khan, now joined by Niccolò's teenaged son Marco. The Venetians travelled via the Crusader capital Acre, where they enjoyed a stroke of luck: a friend was elected pope and they headed for China bearing papal letters and the sacred Jerusalem oil – though it seems they forgot the hundred scholars.

After an exciting journey, during which Marco was fascinated by the sexual libertinism of Tangut girls, whom he found 'beautiful, vivacious and always ready to oblige',* the Polos arrived in Dadu, prostrated themselves before Kublai and presented Marco: 'Sire,' said Niccolò, 'my son and your man, the dearest thing in the world brought with great peril.' Kublai was charmed by the dashing Italian teenager, enjoying his lively stories and 'noble aspect'. As Marco boasted, 'This noble youth seemed to have divine rather than human understanding.' Mongol courtiers could scarcely conceal their 'great vexation' at this popinjay, later nicknamed Marco Million for his bumptious grandiloquence.

As papal envoys, the Polos tried to convert Kublai to Catholicism, but his heterodoxy was impregnable.† Yet Marco was delighted by Kublai's jovial grandeur. While the older Polos traded, Kublai sent Marco on international missions, though he exaggerated his importance. The truth was extraordinary enough: no westerner ever got so close to Kublai. Polo claimed he was appointed a governor; more likely he operated as a tax collector, among many other exploits during his seventeen years serving Kublai. If the khagan was curious about the Polos' stories and jewels, he was now most interested in the conquest of Song China. Marco claimed that his father and uncle advised on developing his cannon to breach the walls of Song cities. The Mongols had brought Chinese gunpowder

---

* Marco praised the town of Kamul (Hami, Xinjiang) where 'If a stranger comes to his house, a man receives him with great joy', ordering 'daughters, sisters and others to do all that the stranger wishes', even leaving the house while 'the stranger stays with his wife, does as he likes and lies in bed with her, continuing in great enjoyment. All the men are thus cuckolded by their wives and not the least ashamed of it . . . All the women were very fair, exuberant and very wanton, greatly enjoying this custom.'
† Kublai did not just tolerate but celebrated the festivals of 'the Saracens, Jews and idolaters (Buddhists).' On being asked the reason, Kublai replied, 'There are four prophets. The Christians had Jesus, the Saracens Muhammad, the Jews Moses and the idolaters Buddha, who was the first. I reverence all four.' When the Polos asked him to be baptized, he jovially replied that his shaman, astrologers and sorcerers were much more powerful than Christians: 'My lords and other believers would demand "What miracles have you seen of Jesus?"'

weaponry to Europe, but no technology spreads so fast, nor is improvised faster, than the technology of killing. Europeans were already improving Chinese designs. It is likely that Kublai was manufacturing the first iron cannon,* and this was the first full gunpowder war.

Kublai sent his generals Bayan (nicknamed Hundred Eyes) and Achu (grandson of Subotai) with huge Chinese and Mongol armies to take the great cities of the Song heartland. After Achu had failed to advance, Kublai asked his cousins in Iraq to send him Arab engineers to build trebuchets, copied from Frankish designs, that he combined with Chinese thundercrash bombs; the Song fired back. The fighting was slow and ferocious, on land, in sieges and by river. In 1275, Hundred Eyes slaughtered all the 250,000 inhabitants of Changzhou; the next year the entire population of Changsha committed suicide; finally, after fifty years of war, the capital Linan (Hangzhou) surrendered. It was the first time a nomadic invader had conquered all China and the first time, since the downfall of the Tang, that all of China was united under one ruler. Now Kublai, khagan of all the Golden realms,† and founder of the Yuan dynasty of China, ruled the greatest empire in span and population, the largest that would ever exist. Seeing himself as Universal Emperor, it was just a matter of conquering the last independent powers of Asia.

KUBLAI'S INVASION OF JAPAN

'We think all countries belong to our family,' Kublai told the Japanese regent menacingly. 'No one would want to resort to war.' Tibet‡ and Korea had been subjugated, leading Kublai to reach fifty miles across the sea to Japan, still ruled from Kyoto by nominal emperors directed by hereditary regents. The regent rejected his demand for submission.

In 1274, Kublai sent 150 ships to conquer Japan, landing in Hakata, where they were to their surprise repelled by a tiny Japanese army. But this was just one of Kublai's multi-front wars. In the south, he turned

---

* The Song manufactured iron bombshells, fire arrows and fire lances, but in 1257 an official who inspected the arsenals concluded that their supplies were totally inadequate 'in the event of an attack by the barbarians. What chilling indifference!' The earliest iron cannon that actually exists comes from Kublai Khan's summer palace in Xanadu, which is dated to 1298.

† Kublai appointed his brother Hulagu the Il-Khan of Persia-Iraq: when he died in 1265, he was buried with the human sacrifice of his favourite slaves. The Golden Horde (Russia) remained the khanate of Batu's family, now Muslims.

‡ Kublai invited the young Tibetan lama Phags-pa to join his debates on religion and also to create a new writing based on the Tibetan alphabet. Phags-pa helped him add Tibet to his empire, ruling there as his 'master of the realm'.

to the kingdoms of the Indosphere, sending Marco Polo on delegations to Burma and Vietnam. His son Toghon invaded Annam then Champa (northern and southern Vietnam), but the Vietnamese, using guerrilla warfare, defeated him and, thus humiliated, he found himself rejected by his father: Mongols don't lose. Angkor, further inland, avoided submission, but Burma, based in its red-pagodaed capital Pagan, and the two Thai kingdoms, Chiangmai and Sukhothai, were obliged to yield. With south-east Asia secured, Kublai's fleet landed 30,000 men in Java and smashed the Indianized trading empire of Singhasari with the help of a Javanese ally, Raden Wijaya, who then double-crossed and expelled the Mongols.*

The failure in Japan rankled. In 1281, the sixty-five-year-old Kublai commissioned two armadas at breakneck speed and sent 45,000 Mongols and 120,000 Chinese-Koreans, accompanied by thousands of horses and armed with firebombs, to invade Japan. The fleets failed to meet as planned. But in August 1281 Kublai's southern fleet landed at Kyushu, where Japanese nobles used small fireships to create havoc among the gargantuan Mongol vessels and defeated the invaders, aided by the Sacred Wind (kamikaze) of a fortuitous typhoon. Shipwrecked Mongol vessels, discovered by naufragiologists, were enormous – one was 230 feet long with watertight compartments and colossal anchors – but their shoddy workmanship explains their failure. The loss of life was eyewatering, perhaps the most lethal day of naval warfare ever.

As the obese Kublai, in his mid-seventies, deteriorated, gorging on immortality elixirs and food, his heir died of the family disease – booze – and even old Hundred Eyes who sat with him reminiscing about their triumphs could not cheer him up. The three Polos were still at court, twenty-five years older and considerably richer, but Kublai refused to let them go home – the problem with befriending capricious autocrats. They begged to leave.

'Why do you wish to die on the road?' asked Kublai. 'Tell me. If you need gold, I'll give you more.'

Niccolò Polo fell to his knees. 'I have a wife at home and I can't forsake her in our Christian faith.'

---

* Raden Wijaya's Hindu Majapahit kingdom was expanded by his remarkable daughter, Princess Gitarja, who as Rana Tribhuwana – often portrayed as Parvati, goddess of beauty, love and courage – after the murder of her brother the raja in 1328 sometimes commanded her own forces to conquer an empire that extended across Indonesia from Borneo to the Philippines and southern Thailand before her death around the age of forty. The empire controlled the spice trade between China and the Indian Ocean for three centuries.

'On *no* condition can you leave.' They feared they would never see Serenissima again.

THE POLOS ESCAPE AND THE IL-KHANS' HISTORIAN

In 1291, Kublai was sending a young Golden bride, Kököchin (Blue Like Heaven), to marry his great-nephew, Arghun, Il-Khan of Persia. Kököchin needed an experienced traveller as her guardian and her retainers suggested the thirty-eight-year-old Marco Million. After a touching goodbye in which they received jewels and agreed 'one day' to return, Kublai ordered the Polos to accompany her, giving them letters to all the kings of Christendom. The bride, aged seventeen, was 'very pretty and amiable', wearing a bejewelled *bochta* headdress as they made the journey by sea in fifteen ships with 600 courtiers. After a hellish voyage in which everyone died – probably of the plague – except eighteen who included Kököchin, the three Polos and their Mongol slave Peter, they landed at Hormuz.

Arghun, grandson of Hulagu, was negotiating with the pope to lead a crusade against the Mamluks of Egypt, an enterprise just agreed when he started to sicken. Arghun sent a Genoese envoy westwards to offer Jerusalem to Edward I of England and Philippe of France in return for Frankish help.* But they were too late. In apocalyptic scenes, Acre fell to the Mamluks.

Arghun, already an alcoholic addicted to immortality elixirs, was about

---

* The failure of the Crusades intensified anti-Jewish persecutions in Europe. Banned from owning land or joining trading companies, forced to wear special clothing, Jews were often involved in moneylending, supposedly taboo for Christians. Kings borrowed money from them, and so protected them, but whenever society was strained, by recession or plague, they were attacked. In 1144, after a boy was murdered in Norwich, England, Jews were accused of killing Christian children to make Passover matzoh, unleashing the 'blood libel' which in various forms – but always featuring a conspiracy of Jews to harm non-Jews – reverberates down to the twenty-first century. It spread: in 1171, it hit Blois, France, where thirty-three Jews (seventeen women) were burned alive. In the failed state of England, where Henry III struggled to maintain royal power in the face of endemic noble revolt, both king and rebels borrowed from a wealthy banker, David of Oxford. After David's death, his widow Licoricia of Winchester, the richest non-noble in England, lent to both sides, partly funding the building of Westminster Abbey. But her murder in 1277 showed the perils of being a prominent Jew. In 1290, Henry's son Edward I expelled the Jews from England. Yet in 1264 Bolesław, duke of Poland, had granted the Statute of Kalisz which gave Jews the right to trade and worship freely and banned the blood libel, legislating against Christian conspiracy theories and denunciations: 'Accusing Jews of drinking Christian blood is expressly prohibited,' declared the Statute. 'If, despite this, a Jew should be accused of murdering a Christian child, such charge must be sustained by testimony of three Christians and three Jews.' Poland would be a Jewish sanctuary for many centuries.

to marry Kököchin when he overdosed. Most Il-Khans died so young of booze and drugs that no royal death was complete without accusations of a poisoning. The Polos were detained. Kököchin did not want Marco to leave, but fortunately Arghun's son, Il-Khan Ghazan, married her instead. She too died young – either by poison or the plague.

Diminutive and 'uglier than the ugliest trooper in his army', Ghazan, secretive, cunning and cultured, speaking Arabic, Persian, Hindi, Tibetan, Frankish and Chinese, was an authority on Mongol history, a ferocious commander and a maestro of bloody intrigues. Raised in a mixture of Christianity, Buddhism and Tengrism, he converted to Islam to link the dynasty to his people. He was soon therefore persecuting Buddhists, Christians and Jews, but he continued to seek a joint offensive with Christian powers against the Mamluks. In 1300, his cavalry and his Armenian allies took Damascus and Israel, galloping through the unwalled Jerusalem to reach Gaza. The outstanding personality of the Il-Khanate was Ghazan's vizier, his Persian-Jewish doctor Rashid el-Din, son of Arghun's apothecary, who, after converting to Islam, ruled for almost twenty years. Ghazan commissioned him to write his *Universal History*, collecting many of the family stories from a lost work, *The Golden Book*, and from the Il-Khan himself. When Ghazan died at the height of the khanate, his brother Öljaitü reappointed Rashid. While Öljaitü could not sustain Ghazan's conquests he shared his cultural tolerance and ambitions, and started a new sacred metropolis, Soltaniyeh.* But in 1316 the death of Öljaitü from booze destroyed Rashid, who was accused of poisoning him. 'Here's the head of the Jew!' his enemies cried, parading his detached head. 'God curse him!'

After nine months in Tabriz, the Il-Khan capital, the three Polos finally escaped. As they approached Venice, they heard that their patron Kublai had died. The Polos fascinated Venetians with their stories, their Mongol slave Peter, their Chinese inventions – paper money, eyeglasses and a fortune that paid for their palazzo. At a dinner, the three sported

---

* Öljaitü's mosque complex and tomb with its stunning turquoise double-shell dome still stand. Although textbooks still frame the 'Renaissance' as an Italian phenomenon, this Persian-Mongol masterpiece probably inspired Brunelleschi's Duomo in Florence, which it anticipated by a century. The Il-Khans were allied with the Palaiologoi emperors of Constantinople. To cope with marauding Turkic amirs, led by a warlike family, the Ottomans, operating between their empires, the desperate emperor, Andronikos II, sent a daughter, Eirene, to the khanate; she married first Ghazan and then Öljaitü. These imperial Greek wives were always known as Despina Khatun – *despoina* being the female for *despotes*, usually the title of the emperor's son-in-law. This mixing was now normal: Andronikos gave another daughter Despina Khatun – Maria – to the khan of the Golden Horde.

their shabby Mongol fur coats, then suddenly cut open the lining, out of which flowed hidden jewels.

SUNDIATA THE LION KING: THE *MANSAS* OF MALI AND THE MEXICA OF THE ISLAND CITY

Marco now became embroiled in the bloody rivalry of Genoa and Venice as they fought for the prizes of trade in spices and slaves from Black Sea to Atlantic shores. The maritime cities also traded wool from England, which was often treated and finished by an inland city, Florence, that was thriving as a leather-manufacturing, textile-processing and banking centre, propelled by its own gold currency the florin and its pioneering use of bills of exchange and joint-stock companies.

Both Genoa and Venice became rich by trading slaves. The belea-guered emperor of the Romaioi, Michael VIII Palaiologos, granted the two cities and the Mamluks rights to the Black Sea slave trade. The Ge-noese entrepôt Kaffa was the capital of its territory Gazaria in Crimea, governed from 1281 by a Genoese consul and later by special govern-ment offices – the greatest slave market in Europe. The Venetians used Tana, a Mongol port in Crimea. Italians bought mainly female slaves for service, personal and sexual; as we will see, the Medici owned both white and black female slaves. The identity of the slaves depended on the wars being fought at any given time: the Mongol wars generated incalculable numbers of slaves, as every Mongol soldier was expected to own two as part of his equipage. Enslaved Turks, Russians, Circassians and Georgians poured into Europe and Egypt. The greatest demand for male slaves came from the military commandos of Egypt: Sultan Qalawun, himself formerly enslaved, promised Italian traders to pay over the market price, and his household contained as many as 12,000 Mamluks. Later sultans owned 25,000, but they were ultimately manu-mitted and could rise to be generals if not monarchs.

The Genoese were more adventurous than the Venetians, paying for their Asian goods in bullion, which originated in western Africa at a time when Genoese and Catalan sailors began to venture down the Moroccan coast. In 1291, two Genoese brothers, the Vivaldis, tried to find a route 'by the Ocean Sea' to India, sailing down the Moroccan coast and then out in the unknown, whence they never returned. Later, another Genoese, Lancelotto Malocello, set off to find the Vivaldis. The Venetians meanwhile concentrated on their Mediterranean empire and the Egyptian trade.

The gold that lubricated all this trade was now in the hands of a powerful African dynasty. Just at the time of Marco's return, a mysterious
African potentate named Sakura emerged out of the Sahara and arrived
in Cairo on his way to make the *hajj*. Sakura was *mansa* – emperor – of
a rich new realm built on military conquests and gold trading on the
ruins of Wagadu.

Its founder, Sundiata Keita,* was the outcast son of a Mandinke
farma or king, Naré Maghann Konaté, who was told in a vision that he
would marry an ugly woman who would deliver a great king. Instead
this junior wife, Sogolon, gave birth to a cripple, Sundiata; mother and
son were mocked by the king's senior wife, Sassouma Bereté, and the
crown prince, Dankaran. Sundiata did not walk until he was seven.
When Naré died, Dankaran ordered Sundiata's killing. Mother and
son fled to the court of the Sosso king Soumaoro Kanté, encouraging
him to expel the vicious Dankaran, but the Sosso instead occupied the
kingdom. The Mandinke elders then invited Sundiata to return. Around
1235, he raised an army and at Kirina defeated the Sosso, after which the
Gbara assembly, made up of grandees, sorcerers and Islamic holy men
(marabouts), chose him as *mansa* in return for his recognition of an
oral law code† and agreed that *mansas* would be chosen from the Keita
family – which ruled until 1610.

Basing himself at a new capital Niani (Mali), Sundiata – known as the
Lion King – expanded to Senegal and Gambia on the Atlantic and along
the Niger River to northern Nigeria, co-opting conquered princes. The
mansa controlled the supply of gold from the Bamaka and Bure mines
worked by Akan people (Ghana), the ultimate source of their wealth,
but as the Lion King's descendant Musa explained, they did not own
the mines; instead they procured the gold by trade or tribute: 'If we
conquer them and take it, it won't yield anything.' But the gold was
all-important. Indeed, one of Sundiata's titles was Lord of the Mines of
Wangara.

Islam had been brought across the desert by Berbers and Arab

---

* The history of Mali is told partly through the observations of Arab scholars – Ibn Battuta,
Ibn Khaldun, al-Kathir (author of the world history *The Beginning and the End*), the Egyptian al-Umari (who visited Cairo twelve years later), al-Sadi (scholar of Timbuktu) – and
partly through the traditional storytelling of the griot troubadours, the *Epic of Sundiata*,
the research into the stories by French anthropologists in late colonial times, and lastly
through the architecture of the Keitas in Timbuktu.
† The Kouroukan Fouga's approach to women reflected the Mandinke's matriarchal traditions: 'Never offend women, our mothers'; 'Always consult women in government'; 'Never
beat a married woman until her husband has tried to solve the problem.' Divorce was permitted if the man was impotent or incapable of protecting or if either spouse was insane.

traders. Sundiata claimed descent from the Abyssinian freedman Bilal, Muhammad's first muezzin, but he was also described as a Mandinke magician. This empire was fuelled not just by gold but by textiles and slaves, the latter usually pagans captured in Sundiata's endless wars who served as labourers, servants and concubines.*

Around 1255, Sundiata somehow drowned in the Sankarani River – at a place still called Sundiatadun (Sundiata's Depths) – but his son, Uli (Yérélinkon), continued the expansion, making the first mansal pilgrimage to Mecca. But when two Keita brothers fought for the throne, Sakura, a freedman general, seized power, rebuilt the realm and set off to Mecca, only to be killed on the way home, at which the Keitas were restored.

The Genoans were not the only ones lured by the Atlantic: Mansa Abubakr II, grandson of Sundiata, 'didn't believe it was impossible to discover the furthest limits of the Atlantic Ocean and wished vehemently to do so', explained his successor, Musa, 'so he equipped 300 ships filled with men, gold, water, provisions to last years' and dispatched them. Only one ship returned, so the *mansa* 'got ready 2,000 ships – 1,000 for himself and his men, 1,000 for water and provisions – and left me to deputize for him' as he embarked on the Atlantic. The fleet is be exaggerated, but why should not African kings crave exploration any less than Genoese: did the *mansa* sail for America?

The American south-west was in turmoil. Just around this time, something terrible happened to Cahokia and the other Mississippi kingdoms. Drought, disease or war broke these settlements, which were then abandoned. Mass graves of dismembered, sometimes cannibalized, bodies suggest a violent cleansing, and a stampede migration. Out of this mayhem, in ways we may never understand, came a realignment of the peoples of north America and the migration southwards of the people who would found the Mexica empire. The Cahokians were pressured by migrations of other tribes, which the survivors probably joined; some may have continued to grow maize but most lived as both hunter-foragers and planters of maize and beans. After the downfall of the Mississippian kings, these tribes were probably governed by assemblies in which respected elders debated decisions with the entire tribe including women, choosing leaders for wars or special hunts. But their world was not peaceful. They constantly fought each other; no tribe was dominant; power politics among the peoples of the

---

* On slavery the *Kouroukan Fouga* specified, 'Do not ill-treat slaves. We are the master of the slave but not of the bag he carries. You should allow them to rest one day per week and to end their working day at a reasonable time.'

vastness of North America were for the next two centuries in constant flux.

The advancing tribes who may have pressured Cahokia or exploited the chaos were peoples speaking Uto-Nahuatl or Uto-Aztecan languages moving eastwards from California. Some stayed in the north – later they became the Comanche and Shoshane peoples – but many others, gradually over centuries, were drawn to the rich cities and fecund land of the Valley of Mexico and migrated south. They all came from a semi-mythical land they called Aztlan – origin of the word Aztec. In around 1300, one of the poorest and latest to arrive were the Mexica (pronounced me-*sheek*-a), who were treated as outcasts and driven on to the least desirable land.

The Mexica arrived in a land of powerful cities, Texcoco and Azcapotzalco, where peoples lived on maize and beans, cooking tamales and tortillas, drinking alcoholic *pulque* made from the agave cactus (much weaker than tequila and fermented rather than distilled). Women spun cotton textiles; men farmed and fought – they deployed neither metal nor the wheel but their children's toys had wheels; they used rubber mixed with the sap of morning glory (a process not discovered in the west until the nineteenth century) to make balls for their games. In the absence of metal, they crafted obsidian volcanic glass for their weapons.*

The Mexica were inspired not only by the existing cities but also by the astonishing ruins of the mysterious city that they called Teotihuacan – Home of the Gods – and Tula – Place of Reeds. In 1325, the supreme god of the Mexica chose a marshy island site by killing his nephew Copil, throwing the heart into Lake Texcoco and telling the Mexica to build their city where they found an eagle eating a snake. They built Tenochtitlan there because no one else wanted this swampy place, but, like Venice, once the drainage was solved, it would become a defensible, almost impregnable city linked to the mainland by a causeway.

At first the Mexica served as soldiers for the nearby city state of Azcapotzalco, home of the Tepanecs, fellow Nahuatl-speakers from north America, ruled by a family descended from the Toltec kings, but they established relationships with many of the local cities. Around this time

---

* The Mexica had no domesticated pack animals; porters were their only transport. Their most valued material was jade, followed by gold or silver. They traded goods and enslaved people at huge markets where hair was cut, food was served, gold and silver exchanged, using cacao beans and cotton as currency (a fresh avocado was worth three beans, a turkey 100). People were enslaved by virtue of war, debt and punishment, but slavery was not hereditary. Enslaved people worked as servants, the unlucky were sacrificed, the lucky freed.

they decided to choose a monarch – *tlatoani*, which means Speaker – marrying their leader Acamapichtli to a Tepanec princess. Chosen from the family by a council of grandees, the new Speaker stood naked before their patron god, then led a military expedition to capture prisoners for sacrifice before the installation ceremony of pageantry, dancing and human sacrifice. His son Huitzilihuitl (Hummingbird Feather) expanded city and territory while building alliances through marriages to princesses from kingdoms outside the Valley. He backed the victorious Tepanecs, who allowed the Mexica to build their own relationship with nearby Texcoco. Formally just the first among equals in an oligarchy of aristocrats, the Speaker technically owned all land, which he assigned to his nobles, an elite served by slaves. When a ruler died, his slaves were killed with him. The Mexica were established at their island city – but it would take a conqueror to win them an empire.

THE WORLD'S RICHEST MAN – MUSA IN CAIRO

Abubakr, *mansa* of Mali, probably never reached America.* 'That was the last we saw of him,' said his nephew Musa, 'and so I became king in my own right.' The twenty-five-year-old Musa, great-nephew of Sundiata, now *mansa*, may have assassinated his uncle; but, whatever happened, he started to expand, conquering 'twenty-four towns'. As a devout Muslim the enslavement of fellow Muslims was banned. Instead the *mansa* 'wages a permanent holy war against the pagans of Sudan who are his neighbours', capturing numerous prisoners who were promptly enslaved. There were hints that Musa may have killed his own mother, perhaps an accident which encouraged him to make a *hajj*: he asked his lawyers what he could do to earn Allah's forgiveness. Musa planned a grandiose pilgrimage to Mecca via the greatest city of Islam, Cairo, setting off with an entourage of 20,000 courtiers (some sources claim 60,000), numerous soldiers, 14,000 female slaves and 500 male slaves. 'Each of the slaves,' wrote al-Sadi of Timbuktu, 'bore in his hand a staff fashioned from 500 mithqals of gold [five pounds].' Camels carried '100 loads of gold'. While north Africa was in chaos, the Mamluk

---

* Most historians believe that it is impossible that Africans crossed the Atlantic because they lacked the shipbuilding technology. But of course they could have copied Genoese ships that were shipwrecked down the African coast. A Spanish friar who interviewed Yucatán Maya in 1588 was told that 'in ancient times seventy Moros [black people] reached the coast in a vessel that must have been through a great storm' led by a 'xeque' – a sheikh: all, he claimed, were killed.

sultan, al-Nasir Muhammad, son of Qalawun, was at the height of his prestige, ruler of Egypt, Israel, Syria, Mecca and Medina, yet even the Cairenes were dazzled by the splendours of Musa – and could not wait to relieve him of as much gold as possible. As he approached, Musa sent 50,000 dinars of gold as a present to al-Nasir, who then received him in his palace in Saladin's Citadel where the *mansa* 'refused to kiss the ground'.

'I don't prostrate myself before anyone but God,' Musa said, at which al-Nasir 'excused him' and they sat together as equals – the greatest of sultans and the greatest of *mansas*, the former the son of a slave, the latter a descendant of kings.

Spending a year in Cairo, Musa 'and his followers bought all kinds of things, they thought their money was inexhaustible'. But the Egyptians systematically bilked the Malians. Musa spent such quantities that the gold market collapsed. During conversations with Egyptian luminaries, he discussed the strange oceanic death of his predecessor and the source of his family's incredible wealth. After making the *hajj*, Musa had to borrow to maintain his style on the way home. Most of his slaves died en route, so he bought Turkic, Slavic and Ethiopian replacements, 12,000 of them, whom he took back to west Africa.

Back home, Musa annexed the ancient trading cities of Jenne, Gao and Timbuktu. In the latter city he used his new Andalusian architect al-Sahali to build the Djinguereber Mosque (made of earth) and the Sankoré madrasa (both still stand), as well as the *mansa*'s palace. Musa and his successors held court in a domed pavilion, guarded by 300 archers and lancers, announced by trumpets and drums. All of this was observed by the sharp eye of a pilgrim from Morocco who made his *hajj*, passing through Cairo around the same time as Musa: Ibn Battuta then embarked on an incredible journey that saw him meeting the khan of the Golden Horde, serving a psychopathic sultan of Delhi* and bumping into Moroccan friends in Mongol China. After narrowly surviving robberies, tragedies and assassinations, he helped rule the Maldives, where he got married. Everywhere in Asia and Africa, he encountered slavery and enjoyed its benefits

---

* The despot of Delhi, Muhammad bin Tughluq, who in 1325 inherited a powerful sultanate of northern India from his Turkish father Ibn Tughluq, expanded southwards, persecuting Hindus. He ordered the evacuation of Delhi and moved his capital to Devagiri in Deccan, executing those who resisted. When Ibn Battuta visited, the sultan appointed him a *qadi*, Islamic judge, but the traveller noticed pieces of executed men dangling over the streets. Ultimately Muhammad's eccentricities led to revolts by his generals in the north, while two Hindu brothers – Harihari and Bukka Ray – established a new kingdom, Vijayanagara, in the south. Ibn Battuta was lucky to get away alive.

– collecting and jettisoning slaves, wives, lovers, their qualities lovingly chronicled.*

When he visited Mali under the Keita dynasty, he was impressed by the magnificence of the *mansas*, yet ready to lecture the Malians on their relaxed approach to female freedom: women sat chatting freely without confinement to any harem or face covering, while their slave girls and daughters 'appear naked before them, exposing their genitals'.

On his return, the king of Fez ordered him to write his memoirs. Perhaps the greatest travel book, *A Gift to Those Who Contemplate the Wonders of Cities and the Marvels of Travelling* is an account of the 117,000 miles he had travelled. Marco Polo had managed only 12,000 but he was about to write the other great travel book of its time.

Marco Million had never fought, but Venice and Genoa were now at war. Marco fitted out his own galley and joined the fleet commanded by Andrea Dandola, the doge's son and descendant of the blind con- queror of Constantinople. But in September 1298 it was routed off Dalmatia; Venice lost eighty-three of ninety-five ships and over 5,000 sailors (many of them galley slaves), Dandolo dashed out his brains against a mast, and Marco was captured. Imprisoned in Genoa, Marco was soon recounting his exploits to captivated jailers and prisoners including a writer of Arthurian romances, Rustichello, who decided to write Marco's over-egged but delicious *Travels*, which were now read by everyone and introduced China, India and Persia to people who had never left their home towns. When he was released, Marco finally married, but he had developed into a rich, mean-spirited and litigious oligarch. In the streets, children called out, 'Tell us another lie, Marco!' but he always kept a copy of the *Travels* in his pocket to read out. As he was dying in 1324, the contents of his will – manumitting his Mongol slave Peter and leaving Kököchin's headdress and Kub- lai's *paiza* to his daughters – revealed that Xanadu was always on his mind.

Polo and Ibn Battuta were unicorns of adventure. Although most people stayed in their towns and villages, more were travelling or connecting to different worlds and much of this was due to the Mongol- sphere of the Golden Family, whose armies and connections had linked east and west more than ever before. But that could be a mixed blessing:

---

* On the Mahratta girls of India, Ibn Battuta decides that 'They have in intercourse a deli- ciousness and a knowledge of erotic movements beyond that of other women.' It was not just about sex but also about joyfulness: of one of his wives in the Maldives he wrote, 'She was one of the best girls and so affectionate that when I married her she used to anoint me with perfume and incense my garments, laughing all the while.'

the plague would accelerate their downfall as it mutated into a much more contagious pneumatic strain.

In 1347, the swollen and decaying bodies of dead soldiers started to rain down on the besieged Genoese slave-trading merchants of Kaffa.

THE DESTRUCTIVE DEATH:
FOUR WRITERS IN THE GREAT MORTALITY

Janibeg, the khan of the Golden Horde, ruler of Russia, ordered plague-ridden bodies to be catapulted into Kaffa to accelerate its surrender. Often cited as the moment when the plague transferred from the Mongolian empire to western Europe, it is more likely the pathogens were already over the walls.

Just as the plague had travelled west, it had simultaneously travelled east, starting in the centre: Nestorian gravestones near Issyk-Kul in Kyrgyzstan mention the plague in 1338–9. As Kublai's feckless descendants fought for power, natural disasters – flood and famines – combined with a wave of peasant rebellions to spread the disease through China and undermined the dynasty. China's population of 120 million may have halved. It also travelled west along the Mongol trade routes to the Il-Khanate, now ruled by the young Abu Said, described by Ibn Battuta as 'the most beautiful of God's creatures'. But the Il-Khan was at war with his cousin, Özbeg, khan of the Golden Horde, who in 1335 invaded the Caucasus. Abu Said, thirty years old, rushed to repel Özbeg, but died of the plague with six of his sons. The sudden deaths led to the disintegration of the Il-Khanate, the second Golden kingdom to be ravaged.

Somewhere during their clashes, the pathogen was transferred to the third khanate. Özbeg had expanded into Europe, attacking Thrace and forcing Emperor Andronikos III to give him a daughter as a wife. In Russia, he murdered at least four Rurikovichi and promoted as chief Mongol enforcer Yuri of Moscow, to whom he married his sister. Moscow became so rich that Yuri's son was nicknamed Ivan Moneybags.[*] In Crimea, Özbeg confirmed Kaffa as Genoese and Tana as Venetian, but in 1343, after his death, it was the Genoese killing of a Muslim that provoked his son Janibeg to besiege Kaffa. In 1346, as Janibeg returned

---

[*] The Golden khans deployed the Muscovites not only to police and tax Russia but also to repel the rising power in the north, the pagan dukes of Lithuania. When he died in 1377, Europe's last great pagan monarch, Algirdas, was cremated on a pyre with human and equine sacrifices.

with forces including his Muscovite allies, the plague struck his camp; ultimately 25 per cent of the population of the Golden Horde would die – and whether or not he fired infected bodies into Kaffa, the Genoese caught the disease.

Janibeg broke camp, his troops thus spreading the disease through Russia and Scandinavia. A Genoese slave ship sailing from Crimea to Alexandria was struck so badly that, of 300 passengers, only forty-five were alive when it docked, and they all died too. In October 1347, twelve Genoese ships docked at Messina in Sicily with a gruesome cargo: dead and dying people, covered in black, blood-filled, egg-sized, pus-seeping swellings. As we have seen, the fleas of marmots, delicacy of nomadic horsemen, then of rats, lurking in the fetid camps of armies, the alleyways of docks and the holds of ships, proved relentlessly efficient vectors of death. Europe was already weakened by a great famine: malnutrition diminishes resistance to illness. The best way to grasp the course of the pandemic – the Great Mortality – is through four of the most refined men of their age, writers in different worlds who, faced with the utterly unbearable and unthinkable, did what writers do: write.

In Aleppo, ruled by the Mamluk sultans, al-Wardi, a world historian and author of the geographical treatise *The Uniqueness of Strange Things*, was one of the first to understand the strangeness of a global pandemic. 'The Plague began,' he declared, 'in the land of darkness.' Even in the face of horror, al-Wardi wrote with dark wit:

> Ah, woe to him on whom it calls!
> It found the chink in China's walls –
> they had no chance against its advance.
> It sashayed into Cathay, made hay in Hind
> and sundered souls in Sind.
> It put the Golden Horde to the sword, transfixed Transoxiana and pierced Persia.
> Crimea cringed and crumpled.

But now it was getting closer: 'It destroyed mankind in Cairo . . . stilled all movement in Alexandria, attacked Gaza, trapped Sidon, and Beirut; fired its arrows into Damascus. There, the plague sat like a lion on a throne and swayed with power, killing daily one thousand or more.' Finally it arrived in Aleppo.

At the same moment, down the African coast in Tunis, the capital of a Maghreb kingdom, a seventeen-year-old named Ibn Khaldun and his brother Yaha were studying philosophy, mathematics and history with famous scholars. Their family were Andalusian aristocrats who had escaped Spain. But now the plague hit Tunis.

Across the Mediterranean in Italy, a Florentine poet, Francesco Petracco – which he latinized to Petrarca – was at the height of his fame. Petrarch's poetry-loving Italy was beset with wars, the arena for conflict between German emperors and French kings, who established their own papacy in Avignon. Florentine politics was typically vicious: Petrarch's father, a politician, was exiled from Florence, as was another Florentine, Dante Alighieri, who in the 1320s finished the epic poem *Commedia*, which deeply influenced Petrarch. The boy trained as a cleric and notary, serving as secretary to a cardinal in Avignon, but sought illumination in the classical world, studying Cicero's letters, and he wished only to be a poet. He also did a peculiar thing that would become part of European civilization: communing with nature and walking up a mountain just for the fun of it.

His epic *Africa* – about Scipio – made his name as a young man. In 1327, when he was twenty-three, his life changed when he saw a married woman in church. 'I struggled constantly with an overwhelming but pure love affair,' he wrote, 'my only one.' But it inspired his *Songbook* of love sonnets that made him famous.

As a priest he was not allowed to marry or have lovers, but he had a son and a daughter with a paramour. In 1341, his poetry won him the honour of being crowned poet laureate in Rome. Now, he was in Verona, his career was at its height, when he witnessed the arrival of the 'death-dealing scythe'. His brother, a Carthusian monk, saw thirty-four of his fellow monks perish. 'Oh my brother!' lamented Petrarch. But worse was to come. He lost two of his dearest – his son and his mysterious muse:

> Laura, illustrious by her virtues, and long celebrated in my songs, first greeted my eyes in the days of my youth ... but in the year 1348 withdrew from life, while I was at Verona, unconscious of my loss ... Her chaste and lovely body was interred the same day: her soul, as I believe, returned to heaven, whence it came. To write these lines in bitter memory of this event, and in the place where they will most often meet my eyes, has in it something of a cruel sweetness ...

In Aleppo, al-Wardi observed the desperate measures being taken against the Mortality: 'Oh, if you could see the nobles of Aleppo studying their books of medicine. They follow its remedies by eating dried and sour foods. The buboes which disturb men's lives are smeared with Armenian clay.' But still it came. In Verona, Petrarch watched his loved ones die – 'Where are now our sweet friends, where their beloved faces, their soothing words, their mild and pleasing company?' – while he corresponded with a new, younger fan, Giovanni Boccaccio. His fellow Florentine, whose father worked for the banking Bardis, disliked banking. Dispatched by his father to the louche Neapolitan court, young Boccaccio fell in love with a muse, whom he called Fiammetta, and it was she who inspired his own early poetry.* When Boccaccio tried the law, he loathed that too. Dreaming of literature, he longed to meet Petrarch.

As 100,000 Florentines died in three months, Boccaccio fled to the countryside. He was able to witness how 'At the start, certain swellings, either on the groin or under the armpits, grew to the size of a common apple, others to the size of an egg, some more, some less, and these the vulgar named plague-boils.'† No one understood how it spread, but they sensed it was through a 'miasma'. Their suspicions were not completely wrong for the pneumonic mutation passed in breath, in furs, in food. 'Some said: the air's corruption kills. I said: the love of corruption kills,' wrote al-Wardi, laughing at the way 'they perfumed their homes with camphor, flowers and sandalwood, wore ruby-rings, ate onions, vinegar and sardines'. Boccaccio noted that 'The mere touching of the clothes appeared by itself to communicate the malady to the toucher.' Many believed it had a divine origin: 'Oh God, it is acting by Your command,' as Al-Wardi put it. 'Deliver us from this . . . We ask God's forgiveness for our bad souls . . .'

Then the plague killed its witty chronicler al-Wardi. In Tunis, Ibn Khaldun watched his mother and father die of the Mortality along with many of his teachers; he and his brother survived and watched as 'Cities

---

* The real Fiammetta was Maria d'Aquino, King Robert of Naples's illegitimate daughter. Petrarch also visited Naples as a papal envoy. Both he and Boccaccio wrote about the lurid court where a young girl, Joanna, succeeded her grandfather Robert. Naples had been ruled by the French princes of Anjou, whose descendant Louis the Great now ruled Hungary and much of eastern Europe, later adding Poland. Louis's brother Andrew was married to Joanna to bring Naples back into the family. Joanna and many of her court resisted the Anjous. In 1345, Joanna acquiesced in the murder of her husband, aged only seventeen, who was half strangled then tossed screaming out of a window with a rope tied around his genitals. Fiammetta too was said to be party to the conspiracy. In 1347, Louis the Great invaded and seized Naples, but spasms of the plague drove him out of Italy. Joanna was restored, but her lover, Louis of Taranto, whom she married, ruled until his death by plague in 1362. When her cousin Charles of Durozza overthrew her, he had her strangled, and then beheaded Fiammetta for her role in the killing of Andrew. Fortunately Boccaccio did not live to see Fiammetta's end.

† The bacilli travelled to the lymph glands, which swelled up into buboes – hence the name bubonic – that oozed blood and pus as other organs were infected. Internal haemorrhaging filled bags of skin with blackened blood: the Black Death. Victims experienced fever, blood-vomiting and agony, often going to bed well and dying by morning.

and buildings were laid waste, roads obliterated, mansions emptied, dynasties and tribes weakened. The entire inhabited world changed.'

Feelings of impotence, fear, loathing and suspicion ran wild. In Germany and Austria, Jews, the outsiders within, were accused of poisoning wells and burned alive. Flagellants travelled from town to town whipping themselves in displays of repentance. 'Fear and fanciful notions' spread while 'ignorant men and women set themselves up as doctors', wrote Boccaccio. No treatments worked; lancing the buboes just spread the pathogen; burning spices covered the stench of putrefaction; bleeding, cupping and placing half-dead pigeons on the buboes saved no one.

At dawn bodies were dumped outside the houses, before being tossed on to corpse-heaped carts: 'A dead man was of no more account than a dead goat.' Gravediggers got rich and arrogant, supervising mass graves where 'Bodies were stowed like bales in the hold of a ship.' Most of the population fled to the countryside, hoping the cleaner air and greater space would alleviate the Mortality, but stories of villages filled with dead and bodies lying beside the roads proved that rusticity was no refuge. Recent research shows it was not the density of people but the density of rats that decided the death rate. Besides, chicken, cows and pigs were also carriers. 'Some lived in small communities'; others 'ate and drank immoderately, going from tavern to tavern, satisfying every appetite'. Noblewomen showed their bodies to the servants and slept with them. Then inexplicably the first wave of the Death ebbed.

In October 1350, Florence commissioned Boccaccio to welcome a famous returning son, Petrarch, who stayed in his house. Petrarch was nine years older but the two became friends. Boccaccio called him 'Master' and together they watched the Mortality return: 'We have mourned the year 1348. But now we realize it was only the beginning of mourning and this strange force of evil, unheard of through the ages, has not ceased since then, ready to strike on all sides, to the right and left like a most skilled fighter. So after sweeping across the whole world several times, now that no part is left unharmed, it has struck some regions twice, thrice and four times . . .'

The death rates were astonishing – 50 per cent of England's six million people; 75 per cent of Venice's population; 98 per cent of parts of Egypt – ultimately killing a third to a half of Eurasia and north Africa. Out of seventy-five million Europeans, twenty-five million died. The virus also reached west and central Africa, where villages have been found abandoned. Worldwide, the total number of deaths was somewhere between 75 and 200 million. And nor was this the end: pandemics always return, and the plague struck repeatedly over the next centuries.

Finally in Ragusa (Dubrovnik), the Venetian authorities ordered sailors to stay on their ships for thirty days (*trentino*), later raised to forty (*quarantino*) – a system that started to work. But, for most, it was too late. The ultimate super-propellent, the Great Mortality changed everything.

ACT NINE
350 MILLION

The Tamerlanians, the Ming and the *Obas* of Benin

All these acute observers wondered at the horror that had, wrote Ibn Khaldun, 'swallowed many of the good things of civilization and wiped them out'. Petrarch asked, 'How will posterity believe that there has been a time when ... well nigh the whole globe remained without inhabitants? Houses vacant, cities deserted, countryside neglected and a fearful and universal solitude over the whole earth? ... Oh happy people of the future, who haven't known these miseries and perchance will class our testimony with the fables.'

The Destructive Death inspired a new sense of God's higher power, but also an appreciation of the value of humanity itself, God's greatest creation. Petrarch, looking back at the light of classical culture, called the intervening centuries 'the Dark Ages'. He was heralding a new lightness – the celebration of learning and beauty, including that of the human body, that became the Renaissance. While praying to God, Petrarch's later works placed man at the centre of the world. Boccaccio too celebrated the vivacious genius of humanity in the face of catastrophe, imagining seven women and three young men escaping the Mortality to shelter in a rustic villa outside Florence where they tell a hundred stories of love, sex and absurdity over a period of ten days – *The Decameron* – which would reveal the 'human comedy'. (It was Boccaccio who called Dante's masterpiece the *Divine Comedy*.)

The Mortality changed society and power 'like a pristine repeated creation', wrote Ibn Khaldun, 'a world brought into existence anew'. Boccaccio noticed the survivors' exhilaration in 'the looser morals of the women who survived'. Women became more independent and more pleasure-seeking, which Boccaccio celebrated with the first biographical work on the lives of 106 women, many of them mythical: *De mulieribus claris* – 'Of Famous Women'. Even though deaths were lower among the rich who lived more spaciously and moved residence more easily, the plague reduced their control, creating a shortage of manpower that raised the status of ordinary people. The wool-processing workshops of Italy and Flanders, England and France were short of workers. The rise in wages and the fall in inequality led to higher spending power which doubled per capita investment, leading in turn to higher production in textiles and other consumer goods. Fewer mouths to feed meant better diets. Female wages – once half those of men – were now the same. Workers formed guilds. The new confidence felt by ordinary people empowered them to launch a spate of peasant revolts. The shortage of labour necessitated new sources of power – hydraulics were harnessed to drive watermills and smelting furnaces – and new unpaid workers were obtained from a new source altogether: African slavery. Demand for silk, sugar, spices and slaves inspired European men, bound by a new esprit de corps, to voyage abroad, to destroy their rivals, in the east and in Europe itself, so that they could supply these appetites. The competition intensified improvements in firearms, cannon, gunpowder and galleons. The paradox of the Great Mortality was not only that it elevated the respect for humanity, it also degraded it; it not only decimated Europe, it became a factor in Europe's rise.

And of course pandemics change families: ever since Pope Gregory I at the end of the sixth century, the Church had tried to impose its own peculiar anti-kinship marriage policy. Now the Mortality helped it. Young workers, including women, worked for longer and saved more before they married later at around twenty, so that they could afford to live in their own homes, little production units, where they made homespun cloth to sell. In grander families, this concentrated the ownership of land in the eldest legitimate sons. The institution of the nuclear family thrived peculiarly in Europe.

No one expected kings and queens to solve the crisis. While in modern times pandemics empowered governments, then, initially, 'It overwhelmed the dynasties at the time of their senility,' wrote Ibn Khaldun, 'and weakened their authority.' The Mortality killed rulers from Semyon, grand prince of Moscow, to the khans of Asia.

In France, where the kings had seized most of the territories inherited by the English monarchs, half the population perished; order broke down. Insular England held together better: at seventeen, Edward III – one of the few English kings who might deserve the epithet 'Great' – had seized power from his mother and her lover in a nocturnal coup that he led personally with a posse of friends. Now he was in the middle of a successful but expensive campaign to seize the French throne, to which he had an excellent claim. Just before the Mortality hit, he defeated the

French at Crécy, then captured Calais, threatening to swallow all of France aided by a network of European alliances.

As the plague struck, in 1348, he was dispatching his fourteen-year-old daughter Princess Joan to marry Prince Pedro of Castile, son of Alfonso XI the Avenger. When she landed at Bordeaux, however, the Mortality killed her and most of her retinue. While her body still lay in the castle, the plague raced through the port, killing so many that the mayor burned it down, cremating the body too. 'See, with what intense bitterness of heart we have to tell you this,' wrote Edward to Alfonso, 'the Destructive Death (who seizes young and old alike, sparing no one and reducing rich and poor to the same level) has lamentably snatched from both of us our dearest daughter.'* As the Destructive Death killed a third of the English population, pushing up wages, Edward tried to limit wages for labourers. Yet England recovered so fast that by 1356 he was again fielding a small army of 6,000 to attack France. At Poitiers, his son the Black Prince routed the French and captured their king, who died in British captivity.

Petrarch lost his son to the Mortality, but after working as a diplomat for a decade he retired with his daughter to Padua. He and Boccaccio, who also served as a diplomat, remained close friends and correspondents. When Petrarch died, he left fifty florins to Boccaccio 'to buy a warm winter dressing gown'. Ibn Khaldun served kings from Granada to Cairo, but it was the experience of the Mortality that inspired his great project: a world history. In his extraordinary career, he personally witnessed how the fall of dynasties and the Destructive Death opened the World Game for two new Turkic contenders.

Two castles and a wedding marked the arrival of a new power in Europe. The wedding, held in 1346, just as the Mortality was about to hit Constantinople, was between Theodora, the sixteen-year-old daughter of imperial claimant Joannes VI Kantakouzenos, and a Turkish bey – war-band leader – named Orhan, aged sixty-five, whose family

---

* The marriage was part of Edward's policy of marrying into the Castilian family. But, had the Mortality not been such a cruel death, one might have thought Joan lucky to avoid her husband, Pedro the Cruel, who had his first wife, Blanche de Bourbon, murdered, supposedly by two Jewish assassins, and abandoned his second after two nights of marriage. Edward III did not give up his Castilian policy, marrying his younger son John of Gaunt (Ghent) to Pedro's daughter. John launched a long, failed campaign to win the Castilian throne. Notorious for his indulgence towards the Jewish community and his Jewish treasurer Samuel Ha-Levi, Pedro finally tortured his Jewish minister to death and, despite English backing, managed to unite Castile against himself. He lost the throne to his bastard half-brother Enrique (the Brother Killer) of Trastámara, who personally slaughtered him with his ballock knife (as in 'bollocks' – named for the two testicular shapes at the guard) and founded a new dynasty.

would one day dominate south-eastern Europe and western Asia until 1918.

Orhan was the descendant of a warlord, Ertuğrul, granted lands by the Seljuks in north-western Türkiye. Ertuğrul's son Osman – or Othman, hence the family name Ottoman – had carved out a principality near the Bosphoros by exploiting the civil wars in Constantinople, which was also fatally weakened by the Mortality; the Ottomans were less affected. In 1329, Osman's son Orhan, a tireless warlord who ruled for almost forty years, defeated Andronikos III, annexed Nicaea and Nicomedia and forced Roman emperors to accompany him, a mere Turkish bey, on campaign. In return for backing a claimant to the throne of Justinian, he won this Roman imperial marriage.

Then, in 1354, the Ottomans made their European debut. The Mortality had scarcely restrained the outbreak of a new war between the rapacious Italian cities Genoa and Venice, fought out in Constantinople. Orhan backed the Genoese and crossed into Europe, where he occupied a fortress, Gallipoli, its walls shattered by a fortuitous earthquake.

It was the beginning. Orhan sent his son Murad, son of a Greek concubine, to take command in Europe, where he later seized Bulgaria, attacked Wallachia (Romania) and invaded Albania, Bosnia and Serbia. Emperor Joannes V appealed to the nearest Christian kings of Serbia and Hungary for aid against the Ottomans. In 1371, Murad smashed the Serbians on the Maritsa River. The Ottomans had taken much of the Christian Orthodox Balkans although they only ruled a small territory in Asia – and this shaped the nascent state. Recruiting his infantry from among these Christian Slavs, Murad annually bought or kidnapped a quota of Christian boys, aged eight to twelve, a practice known as the *devshirme*, to serve as courtiers and soldiers in his *Jeni Ceri* – new army – the Janissary corps; the cavalry was still drawn from Turkish levies under Anatolian beys. Those enslaved would number uncountable millions. His harem was simultaneously drawn from girls stolen from Slavic villages or Greek islands, often sold via Mongol khans and Italian slave traders. While Ottomans were Turks from Turkmenistan, Murad's system meant that the Ottomans were often the sons of Slavic concubines, and viziers were often Slavs too. Declaring himself sultan and appointing the first grand vizier to run the Ottoman state, Murad conquered the Balkans, oblivious to the rise of a ferocious force to the east who would challenge the Ottomans and terrorize the known world from China to Syria.

A master of spectacular violence and connoisseur of exquisite art, he was a collector of writers and female slaves, cities and kingdoms who built both towers of human heads and minarets of surpassing beauty. Borrowing the game of chess from India, and typically developing his own rules, this harsh predator was lame and mutilated – but far from crippled.

THE HEAD TOWERS: TAMERLANE AND THE POET HAFIZ

As a teenager in the 1350s, Timur, son of the chieftain of the Barlas tribe of Turko-Mongols, born at Kesh (Shahrisabz near Samarkand), was raiding a neighbour's village when a shepherd shot him with arrows that pierced his leg and hand. He lost two fingers, his arm was damaged and his limp must have been marked, yet these injuries neither inhibited his riding or marksmanship nor dampened his astonishing confidence. At forty, tall with a huge head, reddish hair and barrel chest, his encompassing charisma had allowed him to master the chaotic rivalries of the Golden khanates and build a coalition of Mongols, Turks and Persians that would soon dominate western Asia. His contemporaries called him Timur the Lame: Tamerlane.

Only the Golden Family of Genghis could rule as khan, so while he crowned himself amir of Transoxiana, making Samarkand his capital, Tamerlane set up a puppet khan and married a khan's widow, Saray Mulk Khanum. She was around thirty years old, 'surpassingly beautiful' and directly descended from Genghis, allowing Tamerlane to adopt the title *gürkan* – imperial son-in-law. Constantly at war expanding his territories, he was an emperor in all but name. He had forty-three favoured concubines, but Saray alone was his adviser, serving as his regent in Samarkand when he was away fighting, the chief of his wives. Only four of his many sons made it to adulthood, and his favourite was Jahangir, whom he married to a Golden heiress, Khanzada, granddaughter of Janibeg Khan of the Golden Horde. When Tamerlane had marched against her father in 1374, the latter sent his beautiful daughter out to meet the conqueror at the head of a procession of gifts. Tamerlane made peace immediately and married Khanzada to Jahangir, only for his son to die of illness two years later. The steely Tamerlane was heartbroken, burying the youth in a splendid tomb (still standing) in his home town of Kesh where he planned to be buried himself. 'Everything then became melancholy to him, his cheeks were almost always bathed in tears.' As he promoted his sons and family to command the growing empire, he paid special attention to Jahangir's widow Khanzada and their sons.

Tamerlane was the child of the ferocity of the steppe and of the

refinement of urban Persian culture, projecting himself as both connoisseur and butcher. Adoring Persian poetry, the conqueror welcomed
the Persian poet Hafiz, a wise, playful chronicler of love, sex, wine and
mysticism, who had written a famous *ghazal* – a poem of love and longing – for a girl:

> If that beauty of Shiraz would take my heart in hand,
> For the black mole on her cheek
> I would give the cities of Samarkand and Bukhara.

Now Tamerlane teased him: 'By my sword, I've conquered the greater
part of the world to beautify Samarkand and Bukhara – and you'd exchange them for a girl from Shiraz?'

'O Sovereign of the world,' replied Hafiz, 'it is by such generosity
that I have been reduced, as you see, to my present state of poverty.'
Tamerlane laughed and rewarded him. Hafiz's real view of politicians
and paladins was:

> Darius, Alexander, their great hullabaloo
> Can be summed up simply in a line or two.*

Tamerlane's coalition of Mongols, Turks, Persians and Uzbeks, was held
together by constant victory and the delivery of endless plunder to distract
and reward his voracious amirs. But the only way to sustain his power
was by interminable war, fuelled by ambition so colossal that it exhausted even his paladins, who – like those of Alexander – begged him to rest
and let them enjoy their prizes. Embarking on twenty years of inexorable
fighting, sacking cities from Bursa and Baghdad to Damascus and Delhi,

---

* Hafiz was the other great Iranian poet to come from Shiraz – after Saadi the Master.
He became a poet when he fell in love with a girl, pining for her until a vision converted
his romantic fervour into Sufist passion for God. His nom de plume meant Reciter of the
Quran, but his delicious poems about the relationship between love and God were mystical
and sensual:

> Ah foolish heart! The pleasure of today.
> Although abandoned, will tomorrow stand
> A surety for the gold you threw away.

He embraced old age like this:

> The time is drawing near for me to find
> Some quiet tavern; unmaligned
> With no companion but my cup and book . . .

His *Diwan* is as widely read in Iran as the Quran. It is traditional in times of crisis to open
the book at random to find the solution to any dilemma.

often having to retake rebellious Khorasan, Tamerlane claimed all the lands of the Golden and Seljuk dynasties, using terror on a Mongol scale, gleefully stacking towers of heads to advertise his ferocity. At Sebzewar in Iran he piled 2,000 living prisoners on top of one another and had them plastered into living towers. At Isfahan, his towers contained by his own boast 70,000 heads. No one knows the numbers of his victims, but one estimate claims he killed 17 million – 5 per cent of the world population.

In the early 1380s, he welcomed as an ally an ambitious Golden khan named Toqtamish. Russian princes led by Dmitri Donskoi of Moscow had just defeated the Horde, but two years later Khan Toqtamish restored Golden power, burning Moscow, and slaughtered half the Muscovites.* Then Toqtamish challenged Tamerlane himself.

Starting in 1385, in a campaign that lasted for ten years, he gradually defeated Toqtamish in a series of battles – one of which he 'regarded as his greatest victory' – sweeping northwards across Russia towards Moscow: headless, handless, footless skeletons tell of his passing. In Crimea, he enslaved Genoese and Venetians at Kaffa and Tana.

As Tamerlane galloped across Russia, the Ottoman sultan Murad and his son 'Thunderbolt' Bayezid led a 30,000-strong Ottoman army into Kosovo to face 15,000 Serbs. On 15 June 1389, at the Field of Blackbirds near Pristina, the sixty-three-year-old Murad, commanding the centre amid 'a circle of chained camels' while his sons Thunderbolt and Yakub took the right and left, withstood a charge by Christian heavy cavalry. Twelve Serbian knights led by Prince Lazar tried to hack their way to the sultan. One of them, Miloš Obelic´, surrendered but as he prostrated himself before the victor he plunged a hidden dagger into the sultanic belly. Lazar was brought in and beheaded. His father's body still warm, Thunderbolt, twenty-nine years old, invited his brother Yakub into the grisly sultanic tent and had him strangled – that very inverted compliment of the steppe peoples who never shed royal blood. It was the first Ottoman fratricide, the start of a gruesome institution. After marrying Prince Lazar's daughter Olivera and defeating the king of Hungary's crusade to stop him,† Thunderbolt believed it was time to take Constantinople. He besieged the much diminished Great City, building a castle

* In September 1380, Dmitri's victory at Kulikovo on the Don River was the first time a Rurikovich prince defeated a Mongol army. It earned the prince his nickname, Donskoi, and later it became the legendary battle that broke the invincible Golden Horde. But only in hindsight. Moscow remained a Mongol vassal until 1502.

† After the battle, Christian prisoners, including a fourteen-year-old Bavarian squire named Johann Schiltberger, knelt piteously for beheading before Thunderbolt, who, as heads rolled, spared the boy, making him a slave – the start of an extraordinary life.

on the Asian side, Güzelce Hisar, that still stands. With the west secure, Thunderbolt switched eastwards where he encountered a triumphant Tamerlane, ruler now of all the Golden khanates of central Asia, Persia, Iraq, Afghanistan and Georgia, to which he had added a new prize: India.

TAMERLANE TAKES DELHI; THUNDERBOLT IN A CAGE

On 17 December 1398, as Tamerlane approached the great city of Delhi, its sultan confronted him with a huge army of armoured elephants. Tamerlane's cavalry started to panic at the smell of the pachyderms, but Tamerlane loaded his camels with hay and wood, set their loads alight and drove them towards the Indian lines. The camels, maddened by the fire, shrieking in pain, charged the elephants, which, terrified, stampeded into the Indian army. The Indian sultan – whose northern Indian kingdom had been undermined by the psychotic predations of his grandfather* – was a fellow Muslim, but Tamerlane claimed that this was a holy war because the Indian rulers were appeasing Hindu idolatry. The sultan fled, leaving tens of thousands of prisoners whom Tamerlane executed en masse. On seizing Delhi, Tamerlane spared the people but looted the city so aggressively that the Indians rebelled. At this his troops went berserk, massacring thousands. Enthroned in Delhi, Tamerlane took the salute from 120 elephants while he slaughtered Hindus and destroyed their temples.

Taking Indian artists to embellish Samarkand and elephants to fortify his army, Tamerlane returned to his capital, knowing that it was time to settle the succession. He chose as heir his eldest grandson Muhammad Shah, son of Jahangir and Khanzada: vigorous and capable, the young man had the blood of Genghis Khan and Tamerlane in his veins. But Tamerlane had a family problem in the form of his youngest son Miranshah. Married to Khanzada, Jahangir's widow, Miranshah was a chubby wife-beating alcoholic who dared to say his father was old and should let the sons rule. Khanzada went to her father-in-law, showed him her blouse bloody from Miranshah's beatings and reported his treasonable tendencies. Tamerlane, who had wept at Jahangir's death, now wept again. Miranshah begged for mercy with a rope around his neck and was forgiven, but he was never promoted again. Khanzada joined Tamerlane's household.

---

* The sultan, Nasir-ud-Din Mahmud Shah Tughluq, was the grandson of Muhammad bin Tughluq, who had been visited by Ibn Battuta.

Tamerlane could never rest for long. Thunderbolt was expanding eastwards, adopting the title sultan of Rum which Tamerlane himself claimed. 'You are but an ant,' Tamerlane told Thunderbolt; 'don't seek to fight the elephants for they'll crush you under their feet. How can a princelet like you contend with us? But your boastful prattlings aren't extraordinary: Turks always talk gibberish.'

'We'll chase you all the way to Tabriz,' replied Thunderbolt, who formed an alliance with the Mamluks of Egypt. Tamerlane's exhausted generals asked for a rest, warning that war against two powerful kingdoms was unwise, but the conqueror, though he was now in his sixties, overruled them. In 1401, he crushed rebellious Baghdad, where each soldier was ordered to deliver two heads to the tower builders, then he advanced towards Thunderbolt. But the Mamluk sultans threatened his flank, so he swerved into Syria.

The Mamluk sultan, a boy of fourteen, headed north accompanied by his long-suffering tutor, Ibn Khaldun, the seventy-year-old celebrity historian.* Tamerlane made short work of the boy sultan, who fled back to Cairo, leaving Ibn Khaldun to negotiate the surrender of Damascus.

The old historian was lowered from the Damascene walls in a basket and summoned into Tamerlane's magnificent tent. 'I found him reclining on his elbow, while platters of food were offered,' recalled Ibn Khaldun. 'I bowed. He raised his head and stretched out his hand for me to kiss which I did.' Then Tamerlane asked him his life story, and the historian recounted his adventures. 'That isn't enough,' said Tamerlane. 'I want you to write down a detailed description of the Maghreb in such a way that I can see it with my own eyes.'

'I've been wanting to meet you for thirty years,' said the historian.

'Why's that?'

'You're the supreme sovereign of the universe. No one's comparable – not Caesar, Khusrau, Alexander, Nebuchadnezzar . . . Sultan Timur's invincible.'

Tamerlane shrugged modestly. 'Me? I'm just an emperor's deputy.

---

* Ibn Khaldun had seen a lot since the Mortality: he served the kings of Fez, Tunis and Granada as vizier, was imprisoned in palace conspiracies and was attacked and robbed by thieves before joining the Mamluk court in Cairo. He understood the importance and perils of history: his brother Yahya, a fellow historian, was assassinated on orders of a rival historian (a cautionary tale of the perils of literary rivalry!). But he had finished his world history. He was fascinated by dynasties, arguing that family power initially fortified the essential *asabiyya* – social cohesion – that held together any society, but 'the term of life of a dynasty does not normally exceed three generations' because the *asabiyya* was lost. His analysis of slavery reveals the Arab attitude to race: 'The only people who accept slavery are the blacks owing to their low degree of humanity and proximity to the animal stage.'

There's the sovereign!' he said, pointing to a gawky Golden princeling, his stepson. Negotiating the surrender of Damascus and inviting the historian to join his council, Tamerlane discussed Babylonian history until an amir whispered that his forces were ready to storm the Damascene citadel that was still holding out.

The conqueror 'was borne away, because of his bad knee, and mounted on his horse, sat upright and rode towards Damascus, bands playing in a triumphant frenzy'. Then, accompanied by Ibn Khaldun, he unleashed ballista catapults and naphtha flame launchers at the citadel. When it had fallen, Tamerlane ordered the sacking of the city, then the slaughter and burning alive of 30,000 people, their heads immured in the inevitable towers. Ibn Khaldun, chatting genially about history and life with the diabolic conqueror, knew he had to speak carefully to stay alive.

'Ask for anything,' Tamerlane said, as the city burned. 'I'll do it for you.'

'My exile has made me forgetful,' said Ibn Khaldun, an expert at appeasing lethal monarchs. 'Perhaps <u>you</u> can tell me what I desire.'

'Stay with me,' said Tamerlane.

'Is there any generosity left beyond that which you've already shown me? You've heaped favours upon me . . .'

Tamerlane understood. 'You wish to return to Cairo?'

'My only desire is to serve you. If my return to Cairo serves you, I'll go. If not, I've no wish to go.'

'I'll fulfil your wish,' said Tamerlane and sent Ibn Khaldun back to Cairo. He then swivelled towards the Ottomans. Thunderbolt now broke off the siege of Constantinople. At Ankara, Tamerlane's 150,000 men with thirty-two elephants, their mahouts armed with flamethrowers, faced Thunderbolt's 100,000.* Thunderbolt was surrounded and his horse was shot from under him, before being captured by Tamerlane's grandson Muhammad Shah (son of Jahangir and Khanzada), who was wounded and later died. Constantinople submitted to Tamerlane, who advanced to the Aegean, storming Smyrna (İzmir). Tamerlane treated Thunderbolt decently, but after he tried to escape he was confined in a barred carriage and died three months later. (His young Bavarian slave, Schiltberger, was inherited by Tamerlane.)

The Ottoman moment was surely finished.

---

* The size of these armies put the tiny scale of the Anglo-French war in perspective. At the battles of Poitiers and Agincourt, fifteen years later, the English armies of the Black Prince and Henry V numbered around 6,000.

WORLD EMPEROR: TAMERLANE IN SAMARKAND

The world was at Tamerlane's feet. In Samarkand, he contemplated his next conquests while he supervised his Indian and Arab architects and artists and received an envoy from faraway Spain.*

'Samarkand was the most wonderful city in the world,' reported that Castilian Clavijo who found the grizzled Tamerlane holding court in a paradisiacal garden. He was reclining under a canopy on an embroidered dais, wearing a plain silk coat and a white bejewelled hat, 'so old and infirm that his eyelids barely stayed open'. The conqueror lived in domed, crimson tents while his wives resided in palaces. Tamerlane, 'in excellent humour, drank much wine, making all his guests do the same', as lambs (and criminals) were slaughtered. Every morning he inspected his building sites, 'spending most of the day there'.

His most important visitors were from China. In 1403, Chinese envoys announced the accession of a new emperor and requested tribute. Tamerlane arrested them. A new emperor had had the impertinence to expel the Golden Family from China. Tamerlane claimed to be their heir and declared jihad against China.

Tamerlane was right to see China as a threat. Its emperor was at that moment preparing an astonishing enterprise – sending a vast fleet to advance Chinese power as far as Persia, right into the conqueror's sphere. And the new dynasty had been founded by the humblest man who ever created a dynasty, the only emperor who literally started life as a beggar.

BEGGAR EMPEROR: DEATH BY A THOUSAND CUTS AND EXTERMINATION TO THE NINTH DEGREE

His staring eyes, pointed jutting jaw, bulging forehead, lumpy pock-marked face, brawny build and unusual height did not condemn Zhu Yuanzhang – the future Hongwu Emperor – but instead, in a strange time of millenarian portents and mystical rebellions, his startling ugliness augured a remarkable future for the man of unrestrained violence and boundless vision. In any other era he might have been a village official, but in times of extreme opportunity, extreme characters thrive.

* In a huge square, the Registan, Tamerlane was constructing the three-domed Bibi Khanum Mosque in honour of his empress Khanum Saray, as well as palaces and a gorgeously simple turquoise-domed tomb, the Gur Amir, for his favourite grandson Muhammad Shah. Perhaps he built the mosque too fast; parts of it collapsed in an earthquake, but some of it still stands.

As the Mongol dynasty of Kublai Khan deteriorated, weakened by the plague, Zhu Yuanzhang was born (at almost the same time as Tamerlane) into an itinerant family so poor that his siblings were sold by his parents. At sixteen, his parents and his last brother perished of the plague. No one could afford to bury them nor feed him and he was given to a Buddhist monastery, whose monks sent him out to beg. As China was torn apart by the millenarian rebellions of the Red Turbans (who awaited the coming of Maitreya, the Future Buddha, King of Light), the begging novice joined an insurgent warlord, who promoted him and married him to his daughter.

In 1356, Zhu, now warlord of his own army, crossed the Yangtze and took Nanjing, making it his capital. He started to recruit distinguished literary scribes as his advisers, learning about history and ritual and modelling himself on the founder of the Han dynasty. Next, fighting his way across China, he waged war on a massive scale, using cannon and gunpowder. In 1363, deploying a flotilla of colossal tower ships, bigger than anything even imagined in the west, and an army of around 300,000, he defeated his enemies – 200,000 strong – on Lake Poyang in a battle that is still the biggest marine engagement in history. Some 60,000 enemy sailors were killed.

'We are the ruler of the Central Country ... we stem from the common people of Anhui,' admitted the ex-beggar in 1368, explaining how the Mandate of Heaven had passed from the family of Kublai Khan to him. 'Bearing the Mandate of Heaven and the spirits of the ancestors, we took advantage of the "autumn of chasing the deer" [chaos] ... Today the great civil and military officers and the masses join in urging our accession.' Just as Tamerlane emerged as ruler of Central Asia, Zhu declared himself Hongwu (Vastly Military) Emperor of a new Ming (Radiant) dynasty.

Hongwu, ruling from Nanjing, was as remarkable as he looked. After capturing Dadu (Beijing), he restored imperial power and the Confucian civil service exams, and prosecuted corrupt officials, who were flayed alive. But he was increasingly paranoid and murderous, turning on his own friends who had advised him during his rise and unleashing his secret police, the Embroidered Uniform Guard, which had its own torture chambers. He enforced the collective punishment of Nine Familial Exterminations, meaning that the victim's families were killed to the ninth degree – in effect all relatives. Leaders climbed with their clans and fell with them too; women faced slavery or death. The principals suffered death by a thousand cuts, the ancient *lingchi*, dismemberment and slicing into four sections while alive, which could be made less painful by opium. Courtiers and ministers were beaten in Hongwu's presence, sometimes killed. In 1380, he executed his chief adviser and 15,000 members of his family (by his own count); a minister was killed with 30,000 of his clan. Only the mystic signal of a lightning strike on his palace stopped the terror.

'Countless numbers of people' were killed, he admitted in his edict of instruction, the *Great Warnings*, excusing his purges and taking control of the government himself. As denunciations aroused him into homicidal frenzies, he reflected, 'If I am lenient people say I'm muddle-headed . . . If harsh, they call me tyrant.' Sometimes he felt all the killing was futile: 'The empire was pacified, people were wicked, officials corrupt. Even if ten were executed in the morning, a hundred would be at it again that night.'

His sons, appointed to govern regions, were terrified. When he urgently summoned a son and daughter-in-law, they both committed suicide. Another son overdosed on Taoist elixirs. He appointed his eldest grandson Zhu Yunwen as heir, imposing a rule of primogeniture to avoid the chaos of Mongol successions, but that gravely disappointed his fourth son, the ferociously able Zhu Di (prince of Yan) who had expected the throne.

Zhu Di was appointed guardian of the hottest military sector, the north, where the war against the Genghis family and the Mongols continued. In the south his father campaigned in Yunnan, where among the prisoners taken was a Muslim orphan, Zheng He, who was castrated and given as a present to Prince Zhu Di.

In 1398, as Tamerlane advanced in the west, the old monster Hongwu finally died, buried with thirty-eight sacrificed concubines. His twenty-year-old grandson Zhu Yunwen, gentle and intellectual, became the Jianwen (Establishing Civility) Emperor, cancelling his grandfather's brutal edicts. He diminished his overmighty uncles, but the strongest – Zhu Di, aged thirty-eight – resisted.

Visionary, flamboyant and arrogant, an energetic warrior as bloodthirsty as his father yet a student of Confucian classics, Zhu Di was a dangerous enemy. Before the emperor could move against him, he marched south with his army. In July 1402, he burst into the Southern Capital – Nanjing. When the palace caught fire, the emperor vanished, but his charred body and those of his empress and eldest son were conveniently found in the ashes and displayed (while a surviving son was imprisoned for fifty-four years). All this, despite romantic tales suggesting that the kind young emperor had escaped, allowed Zhu Di to succeed as the Yongle (Perpetual Happiness) Emperor.

He dealt with the resistance sustained by his nephew's supporters by dismembering thousands, using his father's Embroidered Uniform Guard but also creating a secret police of eunuchs, the Eastern Depot. When his nephew's tutor, Fang Xiaoru, was sentenced to extermination to the ninth degree, he shouted, 'Never mind nine! Make it ten!' Yongle agreed. As Fang was bisected at the waist, with 872 relatives waiting to be dismembered, he drew the word usurper in his own blood.

Yongle regarded the Central Country as the world's paramount power, declaring that his father 'had received the Mandate of Heaven and became the master of the world'. But one man stood in his way: Tamerlane.

FOLLOW THE CHINESE WAY:
THE EUNUCH ADMIRAL AND TAMERLANE'S TOMB

Straight after his accession in 1403, Yongle ordered the thirty-three-year-old Zheng He, his director of palace servants with the rank 4A – the highest rank a eunuch could hold, wearing a red instead of blue robe – to build a massive fleet to project Chinese power into the Indian Ocean, a region familiar to Chinese sailors. There is no record of Yongle's conversations with Zheng He, but the coming clash with Tamerlane surely played a role. Zheng's project was not a voyage of exploration or trade or conquest – 'The four seas are too broad to be governed by one person,' said Yongle. The armada was designed to overawe local rulers into recognizing Chinese paramountcy and paying tribute, though it could also, if necessary, eliminate pirates and crush resistance.

Given Tamerlane's jihad, the choice of Zheng He was ironic: he was the great-grandson of Omar of Bukhara, Kublai's Muslim governor of Yunnan, a descendant of Muhammad, who had converted many in his province to Islam. The boy's father and grandfather had both made the *hajj*, but his father had been killed in the Ming invasion after being castrated. Joining Yongle's entourage, the hulking six-foot-five soldier – 'cheeks and forehead high, a small nose, glaring eyes, voice loud as a gong' – won battles in the civil war.

As the fleet was being built, in early 1405 news reached Yongle that Tamerlane was approaching with a vast army. Tamerlane 'was already weak in health', Clavijo noted. 'He could no longer stand for long on his feet, or mount his horse, having always to be carried in a litter.' But Tamerlane had never lost a war. Frontier defences were tightened and Zheng He's fleet was almost ready to sail. Yet just after joining the army, Tamerlane, around sixty-eight, died, unleashing war among his sons and grandsons, from which his youngest son Shahrukh emerged as the successor.* Ruling from Herat (Afghanistan), Shahrukh made peace with Yongle, who in July ordered Zheng to sail, with his fleet of 255 ships each with twenty-four cannon, bearing 27,500 men. The sixty-two nine-masted 'treasure ships' were gigantic, 400 feet long and 170 broad.†

'Palace Official Zheng He and others,' reported the Court Chronicle, 'were sent bearing imperial letters to the countries of the Western Ocean with gifts to their kings of gold, brocade, patterned silks and silk gauze.' Zheng sailed to Champa, which recognized Chinese overlordship, then to Malaya and Java and on to Sri Lanka and Calicut (India); on the same voyage he defeated a pirate fleet, killing 5,000 pirates. He left inscriptions at various stops, invoking Buddha, Allah, the sea goddess Tianfei and Hindu gods too, combining political mastery with poetical respect for the seas: 'We have crossed 100,000 li of vast ocean and beheld great ocean waves, rising as high as the sky ... Whether in dense fog and drizzling rain or wind-driven waves rising like mountains ... we spread our cloudlike sails aloft and sailed.'

Arriving back in Nanjing in 1407, accompanied by a pirate king ready to be beheaded and tribute-bearing envoys from south-east Asia and India, Zheng was commissioned to set off on two more expeditions. On the third, a Sri Lankan king challenged him. Zheng He attacked his capital and captured the king, replacing him with a Chinese nominee. States in Luzon and Sulu (Philippines), Sumatra and Brunei‡ exchanged

* Tamerlane had planned to be buried with Jahangir in his home town of Kesh, but instead he rested in the Persian-style octahedral Gur Amir with its azure dome in Samarkand beside his grandson Muhammad Shah. Legend claimed that if Tamerlane's grave was disturbed, a more terrible conqueror would arise. In 19 June 1941, on Stalin's orders, the Soviet archaeologist Mikhail Gerasimov opened the grave – identifying the leg fracture of Tamerlane and using the skull to recreate his face, thus enabling us to see what he looked like. Three days later Hitler invaded Russia.
† If correct, the fleet was comparable in numbers to the Spanish Armada or the combined British, French and Spanish fleets at Trafalgar. But in vessel size these were 'the largest wooden ships ever seen in the world', writes Edward L. Dreyer, dwarfing anything in the west, not least Columbus' tiny vessels ninety years later. It is possible there was exaggeration in both numbers and size of the ships. Zheng He's voyages were not Yongle's only expeditions: he also sent another trusted eunuch Yishiha to sail down the Amur River, establishing Ming power in today's Siberia (Russia).
‡ The Hindu spice empire of Majapahit was breaking up. On Borneo, three brothers created the spice-trading city state of Brunei, where they welcomed an Arab adventurer, Sharif Ali, a Hashemite from Mecca, who married into the family and succeeded to the throne, building a thalassocratic empire that, survives today as an oil-rich monarchy, still ruled by his dynasty. The raja of Singapore, also a convert to Islam, founded his Malacca sultanate that now took over the spice trade. This was the world that would be encountered by the

envoys and sent tribute to the Yongle Emperor. 'From the edge of the sky to the ends of the earth,' Zheng boasted, 'there are no peoples who have not become subjects and slaves.' His mission was most clearly stated in his inscription in Malacca, which declared that 'its righteous king, paying his respects to imperial suzerainty, wishes his country to be treated as one of our imperial domains and follow the Chinese way'. On 19 December 1416, Yongle celebrated Zheng's return by receiving eighteen ambassadors of south Asian monarchs who recognized his power. The emperor then commissioned a fifth voyage, to take these envoys home to their kings, and to go much further than before: to Arabia and Africa.

Yongle was tireless, fighting six Mongol and one Vietnamese wars, restoring the Grand Canal and building a new city, Beijing – meaning Northern Capital – where a million labourers, many enslaved, toiled (and many perished) in the construction of vast palaces in the 180 acres of his inner sanctuary, the Forbidden City. Privately Confucian scholar-officials regarded the voyages and palaces as megalomaniacally extravagant. Yongle became addicted to Taoist elixirs containing arsenic, lead and mercury that were slowly poisoning him.

Just as he unveiled his new capital, he was undermined by a humiliating sex scandal that raised an awkward question: Could the greatest warrior emperor on earth be cuckolded by a man without testicles?

MASSACRE OF THE CONCUBINES

Not all eunuchs had suffered amputation of their penises as well as their testicles: sexual liaisons – known as vegetable relationships – with concubines were possible but forbidden. The girls belonged to the emperor. Many concubines enjoyed emotional attachments to eunuchs, some of which led to discreet romances. But courtiers were spied on by the eunuchs of the Eastern Depot secret police.

In 1421, after Yongle had moved into the Forbidden City, a concubine committed suicide after an affair with a eunuch. Yongle, humiliated by being cuckolded by a half-man, ordered the instant slaughter by slicing of 2,800 girls, some as young as twelve, and their eunuchs. The girls were 'rent, split, ripped and torn to shreds'. A young Korean-born concubine, Lady Cui, survived because she was recovering from illness in Nanjing, and wrote an account that was preserved. She returned to find

Europeans when they arrived in the east.

that her world had been liquidated. 'There was such deep sorrow in the palace that thunder shook the three great halls,' she recalled. 'Lightning struck them and, after all those years of toil, they all burned to the ground.' The fire chastened the declining emperor.

In 1424, the sixty-four-year-old Yongle dispatched Zheng on a small expedition and then proceeded to the Mongolian front. There he had a stroke caused by overdosing on his immortality elixirs.

Lady Cui, only thirty, and fifteen of his other girls were strangled by white silk nooses then buried with Yongle in his tomb. Yongle's ultimate successor, his grandson Xuande, diverted his admiral to other tasks, appointing him to run Nanjing and to the post of Grand Director of the Buddhist Three Treasures – though he allowed him a seventh and final voyage. The last voyages connected many worlds – none more different than that of the Ming of Beijing and the Swahili sultans of east Africa.

THE LEOPARD KING AND JOÃO THE BASTARD

In January 1419, Zheng He, the eunuch admiral, after receiving the submission of Hormuz (Iran), landed in Aden (Arabia) where the local sultans, keen to avoid the power of the Mamluks of Cairo, submitted to Yongle and exchanged gifts before the Chinese fleet sailed on to Malindi in Africa, collecting a menagerie of leopards, lions, camels, rhinos and giraffes for the emperor. The sensation created in Beijing by these beasts encouraged further voyages to Africa.

China and Africa had long been connected: Chinese, Malay and Arab merchants traded porcelain and silk for ivory, ebony and gold; thousands of Chinese coins and much porcelain have been found on Zanzibar. On Zheng's sixth voyage, which sailed in November 1421, the treasure fleet visited Barawa and Mogadishu, ports of the Somalian kingdom of Ajura that stretched as far as the Ogaden on the borders with Ethiopia.*

Zheng's fleet sailed down to Kilwa, founded by African converts to

---

* In Ethiopia, a Christian emperor Yeshaq (Isaac) was fighting Islamic and Jewish warlords. His ancestor Yekuno Amlak had seized the throne in 1270, claiming descent from King Solomon and the Queen of Sheba, and more plausibly from the last kings of Axum. The Solomonic grandeur lent much needed biblical glamour to a dynasty that ruled parts of Ethiopia, occasionally united under one ruler, until 1974. These Christian emperors – *negus negust* (king of kings) – now found themselves under aggressive attack by Islamic rulers backed by the Mamluks of Cairo. In the north, a Jewish kingdom, known as the Gideonites as their kings were often named Gidewon, ruled the Simien Mountains, the highest in the Horn of Africa, and the vicinity. The Gideonites defied Emperor Yeshaq, who was killed fighting the sultan of Adal.

Islam who invented a mythical descent from a Persian aristocrat from Shiraz. These princes, now intermarried with Africans and Arabs, maybe Omanis, controlled a littoral empire from Mombasa (Kenya) to Sofala (Mozambique), with colonies on the Island of the Moon (Madagascar). When the sultan of Kilwa crossed him, Zheng stormed the city and later sailed down to Sofala. The Swahili monarchs then recognized the emperor of China. After collecting frankincense, ambergris, ivory, more animals (including elephants and 'camel-birds' – ostriches), Zheng, now on his seventh voyage, probably died at sea on the way home. Emperor Xuande and his bureaucrats rejected Yongle's improvidence and docked the superfleets, burning Zheng's records, confident that Chinese superiority required no connection with the outside world. China would not project global power like this again nor return in force to Africa until the Belt and Road Initiative of 2013.

The Chinese recorded that the Swahilis traded in enslaved 'savages' from the African interior as well as in ebony, ivory and gold. Elephants and men were hunted throughout what is today Kenya and Tanzania, but the gold and copper that arrived in Sofala for export across the Indian Ocean came from a kingdom inland: its capital, Zimbabwe,* was a stone city, the oldest one south of the Sahara, founded around 900, its towered and walled Great Enclosure built during the 1200s. Its Bantu-speaking Shona princes were gold traders, cattle herders and pottery manufacturers. They were also owners of golden artefacts and sculpted eagles found there, along with porcelain from China and Persia. By the time Zheng visited Sofala, Zimbabwe was falling apart, its ruler Mukwati undermined by a younger prince, Nyatsimba Mutota, who challenged its trade in salt and gold, breaking away to become *mwene* (king) of a new realm, Mutapa. Encompassing Tanzania, Zambia and Zimbabwe, Mutapa was expanded further by Mutota's son, Nyanhewe Matope. The *mwene*, residing at Zvongombe on the southern Zambezi and wielding a ceremonial axe and golden spear, governed through nine ministers known as the King Wives, some of them actually his queens and sisters, others male advisers. But Zimbabwe lost its importance, and later it was abandoned.

The very different worlds of east and west Africa were connected by Saharan trade routes that led to Egypt and the Maghreb, but movement between them was blocked by the intervening vastness of the jungle and savannah. Yet the politics of western Africa was just as dynamic and

---

* The real name of the kingdom is unknown. Zimbabwe simply means 'stone buildings'; the area has other smaller zimbabwes – one survives at Bambusi.

complex: a few powerful kingdoms and a multitude of smaller entities fought for territory, for control of gold from the Akan goldfields, and for slaves captured in war. Gold and slaves were traded across the Sahara via Arab caravans, probably over six million slaves between the eleventh and seventeenth centuries. The Bantu-speaking kingdoms, many of them new, were founded, like their European equivalents, by gifted warlords using personal charisma, bloody conquest and shrewd marriage. Around 1375, when Tamerlane and Hongwu were rising warlords, the biggest of these kingdoms, Kongo, was created by a marriage between two royal families. The king of Mpemba Kasi, Nima a Nzima, married Luqueni Luansanze, the daughter or sister of the king of Mbata, Nsaku Lau. Their sons merged the kingdoms and then, ruling until 1415, conquered much of Angola and Congo (Brazzaville) republic and built a capital, Mbanza, that was soon home to tens of thousands. Chosen always from this lineage, the *manikongo* (king) held court wearing gold and feathers, on a covered throne, and could be approached only by making prostration. No one was allowed to watch him eat.

Around Mbanza, slaves worked farms – 'Collecting slaves gave the Kongo kings great power.' Slavery was an ancient part of African society, 'widespread because slaves were the only form of private revenue-producing property recognized in African law', writes John Thornton; in fact slaves were the 'main form of wealth in central Africa'. But this was not the chattel slavery – the ownership and trading of people and their children – of later European empires. Kongo was founded on expert artisanship with a speciality in blacksmithery. The first king was said to have designed a special forge, but the *manikongos* traded ivory, furs, cloth, pottery and slaves, constantly replenished in slave raids and wars of expansion.

To the north, a dynamic *oba* (king), Ewuare the Great, was expanding a small Yoruba kingdom named Ibini – Benin (Nigeria). Descended from the Ogiso – Sky Kings – of a medieval Edo kingdom Igodomigodo,* his real name was Ogun, an *oba*'s son driven out by his brother who, in exile, learned confidence and magic, partly by pulling a thorn from the paw of a lion which then granted him supernatural powers. Assassinating his brother and renaming himself Ewuare (Strife-is-Over), he simplified the succession rules, reducing the elective influence of the *umaza* (chiefs), before embarking on a spree of conquests and embellishing

---

* The same family also founded another kingdom, Oyo, that was closely connected to Benin by familial intimacy and vicious rivalry that endured into the nineteenth century. Oyo was now the leading power; Benin's expansion took longer. Still nominally ruled by branches of the family, their dynasties still reign in republican Nigeria.

Ibini's palaces. Calling himself the Leopard King, Ewuare centred all life around himself and his family, promoting the queen mother to special rank. His Benin City became the biggest city in sub-Saharan Africa, soon to be described by a European visitor as 'larger than Lisbon; all the streets run straight and as far as the eye can see. The houses are large, especially that of the king which is richly decorated and has fine columns.' Ewuare commissioned naturalistic sculptures and carvings, made of coral, wood, terracotta, stone, iron and bronze, which portrayed earlier *obas* – who were worshipped as divine or as possessing supernatural powers – or himself and his pantherine avatars; his artisans also produced pillars, altars, doors and masks. All were used in a calendar of festivals to celebrate and restore the power of the *oba* and purge evil spirits that might threaten the kingdom.*

The city contained many slaves captured in Ewuare's wars, used as servants, as labourers and as currency to exchange for gold, ivory and copper. The free were distinguished from the enslaved by scarification rituals. Human sacrifice, attended by dancing rituals, honoured the *oba* and appeased the god-king of death. On the death of an *oba*, his guards were sacrificed, his wives committed suicide and all were buried with him.

Ewuare, already known as the Great, was just starting out – unaware that another family at the northmost corner of the continent were taking their first steps into Africa.

On 21 August 1415, while the Chinese visited the east coast of Africa, a fleet of 200 Portuguese ships, bearing 45,000 troops led by King João and his sons, invaded the north-west, landing at Ceuta (Morocco) on a minor crusading adventure that would gradually bring Iberian adventurers all the way around Africa to India.†

---

* The Yoruba worshipped a large pantheon of gods and spirits (*orishas*), but their cosmology placed art at the centre of life itself. They believed that their chief god, Olodumare, source of *ase*, the life force of the universe, ordered the god Obatala to fashion the first Yorubas, who lived at the holy city of Ile-Ife under a king – the *Ooni* – descended from a god-king. Ile-Ife, settled as early as 400 BC, had thrived since around AD 700 as the sacred city of west Africa. Even when political power moved to the Oyo and Benin kingdoms, Ile-Ife enjoyed an artistic golden age, and royal heads from the other kingdoms were still sent there for burial. At just this time, the king of Ile-Ife, Obalufon, was commissioning artists there to create sculptures featuring himself.

† A week earlier, on 13 August, a small English army under the twenty-seven-year-old king Henry V had landed in France to restart the conquest of France, successfully begun by the vigorous Edward III then lost by his psychopathic grandson Richard II. Richard had been overthrown and murdered by his cousin, Henry, duke of Lancaster, who became Henry IV. The most extraordinary thing about Henry V was that he was alive at all. When he was sixteen, fighting with his father against a rebel nobleman, he was hit in the face by an arrow that entered below his eye and lodged in the back of the neck – without touching

Portugal was tiny, just 900,000 people, culled by the Great Mortality. On the edge of Iberia, a hinge between the Mediterranean and the Atlantic, Europe and Africa, it was ideally located to trade north to England and south along the African coast.

Portugal had become an independent kingdom under a family of Burgundian adventurers in the 1140s, but its relationship with its larger rival Castile was intimate and suspicious, wars alternating with marriages for centuries. In consequence their royal families were densely interrelated to the extent that a Castilian takeover of Portugal or vice versa was never far away, while an English bid for the Castilian throne meant repeated interventions from London. The three Christian kingdoms, Portugal, Castile and Aragon, had all played heroic roles in the *Reconquista*, a crusade against the Muslims, that left Granada as the last Islamic kingdom in Spain. Portugal's tough but poor noblemen, the *fidalgos*, were keen for new spoils – and their new king, the Bastard, had something to prove.

João had never expected to rule, but he had thrived in a murderous, louche court, ruled by his erratic and concupiscent father.[*] As a late son by a mistress, the Bastard, promoted to the office of master of the crusading Order of Aviz, was more popular than his legitimate half-brother who succeeded to the throne. When that brother died, the legitimate line – through the king's daughter married to the king of Castile – would have led to Castilian annexation. Instead the nobility backed João as the

his brain. Usually this would have led to death from infection and most physicians would simply have pulled the arrow out through the face, tearing the flesh inside. An initial team of doctors – later described as 'lewd chattering leeches' – bungled this, breaking off the arrow. But the royal doctor, John Bradmore, a brilliant man, was also a metalworker and gemestre (jeweller). He disinfected the wounds with honey, washed them with alcohol and devised an instrument to grip the arrow head within a cylinder and pull it through the skull and out the other side. Astonishingly this operation worked and the wound did not become infected; Bradmore was richly rewarded. Henry, tall and powerful, must have been heavily scarred. On succeeding to the throne, he gathered his fleet in Southampton, before swiftly killing his best friend and two other barons who were caught in a conspiracy. In France, he took the port of Harfleur, then fought a French army double the size of his own at Agincourt, massacring most of the French prisoners, the first of several such atrocities. After his victories, the French king agreed to marry his daughter Catherine to Henry. Their only son was a baby when Henry died at thirty-six from dysentery. After his death Catherine married a Welsh steward, Owen Tudor, from whom the Tudors were descended.

[*] João's father Pedro, erratic and lascivious, had married a Castilian princess, Constanza. But she arrived with a lady-in-waiting, Inês de Castro. Pedro had a son with his wife but fell in love with Inês. After Constanza's death, he started to advance Inês's family: in a showdown with the hostile court, Inês was beheaded in front of her children. When Pedro became king, he hunted down her killers and personally tore out their hearts in revenge. It was said he exhumed Inês, dressed her in crown and jewels and had the court pay tribute. He certainly built her a tomb, facing his own, engraved with the words 'until the end of the world'.

popular Portuguese option. Foiling Castilian attempts to seize the kingdom, he saved Portuguese independence. His marriage to an English
princess, Philippa, delivered a line of five impressive infantes, who were
now excited to embark on a Moor-killing invasion of Africa: war was
God's work, and vengeance for the many Moroccan invasions of Spain.
João's third son, Henry, later known by foreigners as the Navigator, was
the most enthusiastic.

João's timing was good. Morocco was hopelessly divided while the
adventure satisfied his restless *fidalgos*.

As João landed at Ceuta, the surprised Moroccans sortied out, but
they were too late. After vicious fighting, João's *fidalgos* rushed the gates,
racing into the thriving city. Prince Henry displayed insane courage in
the attack, becoming cut off among hacking Moroccan warriors, and
had to be rescued by a knight who gave his life for the infante. Henry
himself suffered only light wounds. João unleashed three days of looting, killing Muslims with crusading glee and torturing rich Arabs to
death. They plundered not only Arab but also Genoese merchants, already in Morocco. The Genoese were the vanguard of African venturers:
they had already tried to seize Ceuta and helped Castile make the first
Atlantic conquest, the Canary Islands.* João converted the mosque to
a church and knighted the three infantes, Duarte, Pedro and Henry.
Such was the meagreness of Portuguese comforts that their soldiers
were dazzled by the luxurious houses in Ceuta.

It happened that the Portuguese had developed new naval technology:
their light vessels – *barcas* and *bergantinas*, then *caravelas*, all tiny, less
than eighty feet, were hardy and manoeuvrable. Henry's sailors had
begun to understand the *volta do mar* (literally, return from the sea), a
navigational technique which exploited the Atlantic's circular wind and
sea currents, allowing a swing out into the unknown that would lead
to new shores. These caravels were ideal for ocean-going voyages; later
when the Portuguese crammed them with new weaponry, *bombarda* –
cannon – this mix of gunpowder and lightness proved formidable. The

---

* The Canary Islands had been inhabited since around the birth of Christ by the Guanche,
Berber Canary islanders, enjoying occasional contact with Europe or Africa and maintaining a Stone Age civilization without boats or metal. The discovery of their mummified
ancestors reveals a sophisticated alternative way to embalm, leaving brains and intestines
intact by smoking the bodies in bonfires then wrapping them in goatskins. In 1312, the
Genoese banker-adventurer Lancelotto Malocello had tried to find what happened to the
Vivaldi brothers, who had landed on the islands; he gave his name to Lanzarote (Lancelotto) and founded a fortress there, but was eventually expelled in a Guanche rebellion.
Now, in 1402, a French Crusader colonized the islands and declared himself king – but,
facing revolts by the indigenous peoples, he ceded the islands to Castile. The islanders were
rapidly enslaved, killed and decimated by disease.

Navigator was not an explorer or scientist (there is no evidence that he founded navigational schools or scientific academics) but, appointed by his father as administrator of the crusading Order of Christ, he saw no contradiction between God's work, the grandeur of Portugal and the exploitation of Africa. This was the start of a process that created the world today; later came empire, and alongside it came the settlement – 'the reproduction of one's own society through long-range migration', says James Belich – started now by the Portuguese, followed by the Spanish, English, French and Dutch, that, ultimately, by killing and destroying, building and procreating, created often unique hybrid societies and later modern states on four distant continents.

João decided to keep Ceuta, the start of a new age of imperial seafaring in which a European power family, the Aviz, used their new ships, *bombarda* and ferocious crusading-mercantile ambition to blast their way into Africa and Asia.

ACT TEN
350 MILLION

Medici and Mexica, Ottomans and Aviz

HENRY THE NAVIGATOR: SLAVES, SUGAR AND GOLD

In 1425, Infante Henry, duke of Viseu, ordered the planting of a new crop on one of his new territories. It was a crop that would change the world: sugar cane. The location was the formerly uninhabited Atlantic island of Madeira, claimed by two of Henry's knights, and developed for him by a merchant from Piacenza, Bartolomeu Perestrello.

Sugar originated in the South Seas, probably in Papua New Guinea, reaching India around AD 350 and then the Arab caliphate. *Al-sukkar* was a labour-intensive crop, worked by *zanj*, African slaves, in their Iraq plantations, later transplanted by the Arabs to Sicily and al-Andalus. As the resurgence of the Ottomans was blocking sugar supplies from the east, Henry, backed by the Genoese, brought sugar saplings from Sicily and planted them on Madeira. There Perestrello, *capitão donatário* and Lord of Porto Santo, one of the islands of the archipelago, used Italian and Portuguese workers, soon joined by 2,000 slaves, probably Berbers from Morocco. Later his daughter married a young Genoese sailor: Columbus.

Next, Henry developed the Azores, tried to steal the Canaries from Castile and then in 1434 commissioned his men to sail further south. Three years later, realizing that Saharan caravans were avoiding Ceuta and arriving at Tangier, he persuaded his brother King Duarte to back a Tangerine assault, which was a disaster.* Henry's sailors started to sail around the coast of west Africa.

In 1444, one of Henry's henchmen arrived at Lagos on the Algarve with caravels filled with 225 slaves, some Berbers, some black Africans:

---

* Their brother Fernando was captured. Henry negotiated through a Jewish doctor to swap him for Ceuta, but just as the king was about to approve the deal, he died of the Destructive Death – and their brother died in confinement after six years of humiliation. Infante Fernando was eviscerated and embalmed, his fellow Christian prisoners hiding his heart and viscera in pots under the jail floor while the prince's naked body was hung for years from the battlements of Fez.

'some white enough, fair to look upon ... others ... less white like mulattoes; others again were as black as Ethiops, and so ugly'. Henry exhibited them on the river front. 'It's not their religion but their humanity that makes me weep in pity for their sufferings,' wrote a witness, Gomes Eanes de Zurara, royal archivist and Henry's biographer. 'To increase their sufferings still more they now began to separate one from another in order to make the shares equal. It now became necessary to separate fathers from sons, wives from husbands, brothers from brothers ...' Much of the slave trade had originally been driven by demand for domestic slaves who joined family households. Now at the birth of Atlantic slavery, slave traders captured entire families and then tore them apart. Slavery was an anti-familial institution. This small scene, filled with cruelty, hypocrisy and avarice, was the beginning of an industry that would sweeten European palates and poison society for five centuries.*

After 1445, Henry's captains travelled past the Senegal River and started to negotiate with African potentates who had their own complex interests, experienced as they were in trading pepper, ivory, gold and slaves with Arab or Berber merchants across the Sahara.† Portuguese venturers exchanged horses or paid in local currencies, iron bars, cloth or, most commonly, cowrie shells, receiving in return slaves, usually prisoners from wars against neighbouring enemies, pepper, gold and ivory. These traders divided the region known as Guinea (based on a Berber word for black people) into product sections – Gold Coast, Pepper Coast, Ivory Coast and Slave Coast – like a continental hypermarket.

On the coasts of west Africa, palm tappers were drinking palm wine and playing *akonting* music beside the beach when suddenly, lit by lights on the sea, 'cannibal ghosts' landed and seized them, never to be seen again. These handed-down memories, recalled by Daniel Jatta, a Gambian musician-historian, mark a pivotal moment: the 'cannibal

---

* Zurara himself, who so admired Henry – 'Our prince' – sensed the ominous implications in this invocation to cruel Fate: 'O powerful fortune, that with your wheels makes and unmakes, encompassing the matters of this world as pleases you, do you at last put before the eyes of that miserable race some understanding of matters to come; that they may receive some consolation in the midst of their great sorrow? And you who are so busy in making that division of the captives, look with pity upon so much misery; and see how they cling one to the other, so that you can hardly separate them.'

† Conquest was inconceivable: Europeans, checked by the power of African rulers and their armies, daunted by the inhospitable vastness of Africa, decimated by malaria, did not conquer the continent for another four centuries. They lacked military supremacy and the physical endurance until the development of steam, machine guns and quinine in the late nineteenth century.

ghosts' were Henry's Portuguese; the palm tappers were among the first to be seized from African beaches and enslaved – probably taken to work on Perestrello's Madeiran plantations. As the Aviz probed Africa, in Lisbon Henry sent a gift to Pope Martin V, who was already interested in Africa and slavery. In 1418, soon after his election, Martin recognized the Portuguese campaign in Morocco as a crusade, but African slavery was not yet an issue. Mediterranean slaves were still usually Turks, Slavs and Georgians traded by Genoa, Venice and Egypt via Crimea to the Islamic and Christian markets. In 1425, Martin banned the sale of Christians to Muslims, but not to Christians because wealthy Italians often owned Slavic (Orthodox) slaves, usually girls for domestic work and sexual exploitation. But now Henry sent the pope ten African slaves.

Martin was engaged in a world-changing project – the re-establishment of a single, Roman papacy after a century of multiple simultaneous popes and anti-popes, backed by German and French potentates, and brought with him a family that defined a new mercantile world and a new sort of dynasty: the Medici.

COSIMO AND THE PIRATE POPE:
IN THE NAME OF GOD AND GOOD BUSINESS

In 1417, when he was elected, Pope Martin was living in Florence where a banker named Giovanni de' Medici was immediately keen to win his favour. Already rich from papal business, Medici personified the rising prosperity of Florence, a landlocked Tuscan city state, a republic ruled by the *Signoria*, a nine-man committee, and several other councils, all elected by its trading guilds and dominated by its mercantile dynasties who competed for power. These oligarchs juggled their urge to flaunt their magnificence in clothes, palazzos and churches with the populist austerity and Christian philanthropy expected of a prosperous Florentine. The Medici, descended from apothecaries who inspired their name and insignia – the *palle* or red balls that represented pills – had served as *gonfaloniere* (commander) several times but now seemed to be in decline.

Giovanni changed that. Florentines were experts in refining, dyeing and exporting wool shipped to them from England, Flanders and Burgundy, a trade aided by their capture of Pisa and its port, Livorno. Medici was the owner of two wool workshops, but then he expanded into the other Florentine expertise, banking,* which was aided by the widespread use through Europe of the city's gold coins, florins. In 1401 Giovanni had played a role in commissioning the new doors of the Baptistery, a thanksgiving for Florentine emergence from a spasm of the plague, to be decided by a competition. It was jointly won by Lorenzo Ghiberti and Filippo Brunelleschi, and Giovanni then commissioned the latter to build a Medici family basilica, the San Lorenzo. Afterwards Brunelleschi created the 138-foot-diameter dome of the city cathedral, Il Duomo, which was consecrated by the pope.

Medici had become rich through his friendship with the most unlikely pope since Marozia. A Neapolitan pirate, Baldassare Cossa, had flourished in the chaos of multiple popes, murdering his predecessor, winning election as John XXIII, his papacy and wars funded by 'my very great friend' Medici. Often accompanied by Giovanni's son, Cosimo, Cossa hoped to end the schism of popes but in 1414 he was deposed, accused of sodomy, piracy, murder, incest and the seduction of 200 girls. Cossa escaped but was captured and imprisoned. Medici ransomed his piratical patron, but he now backed a rising cardinal, Oddone Colonna, a Florentine monk and descendant of Marozia. Ecclesiastical potentates then elected Colonna as Martin V in order to reunite the Church. In September 1420, Martin formally processed from Florence to Rome, where he appointed Medici as papal banker assisted by his son Cosimo.

Already experienced in trading in Rome and Flanders, Cosimo, now thirty, had been educated by Florence's humanist scholars. As the Medici became richer, their rivals in the *Signoria* became jealous. 'Don't appear to give advice, but put your views forward discreetly in conversation,' Giovanni advised Cosimo on his deathbed. 'Don't make the government house your workshop, but wait until you are called to it . . . and always keep out of the public eye.'

Just after his father's death, an anti-Medici party on the *Signoria* had Cosimo charged with treason and he was lucky to be banished: 'Should you send me to live among the Arabs, I'd go most willingly.' Politics is often simply the art of waiting. In 1434, he was invited back. He ruled while contriving to appear a private citizen, rarely serving as *gonfaloniere* but becoming 'king in all but name', according to one of the popes, for the next thirty years. He poured money into the embellishment of Florence and continued his father's patronage of the artists, which he regarded as a bet against the upheavals of politics. 'I know the moods

---

* The word banking derives from *banco*, the marketplace stall from which these early financiers did their business.

of the city,' he said. 'Before fifty years have passed, we shall be expelled, but my buildings will remain.'

When his Tuscan friend and fellow bibliophile Tommaso Parentucelli was elected Pope Nicholas V, Cosimo helped fund an astonishing project: the new Rome. He opened banks all over Europe, with the slogan 'In the Name of God and Good Business', trading wool, spices, brocades. But much was based on the trade in alum, a mineral necessary for dyes, glassmaking and tanning. As the Ottoman advance cut off eastern supplies, alum mines were developed in the papal lands. Medici was appointed papal alum agent and alum became the windfall that funded the start of a two-century enterprise of urban regeneration: a Christian sacred city grafted on to the pagan splendour.

Rome was a ruin. Its monuments – the Colosseum, the tombs of Augustus and Hadrian – were now fortified as the headquarters of gangsterish feuding clans, Colonnas and Orsinis. In the nine years of his reign, the pope, flush with money channelled from wars in Italy, tithes from Europe, alum, and a cult of pilgrimage, started to restore Rome, a project that would be one of the engines of a new intellectual radiance. This was the florescence heralded by Petrarch in the darkest days of the plague that had broken Europe but also cracked the mould of its structures and ideas – just as the competition of European states encouraged new technologies of war, new media of information and new conceptions of humanity and beauty. At its heart was a gradual shift from belief in total divine agency to the idea that humanity itself was sacred and beautiful, worthy of expression and improvement.* All of this engendered an invincible sense of possibility that, while expressed as a return to classical knowledge, was actually all new, bracingly brutal and brash, shiny and shameless, based on new technologies – ships, guns, voyages and an invention that allowed ordinary people to read all about it: the printing press.†

Nicholas V and Cosimo de' Medici were uninhibited by contradictions between Christian glory and pagan grandeur: all was to be mobilized

---

* The word Renaissance was not used by contemporaries. It was the polymath Leon Battista Alberti who, advising Pope Nicholas V on the rebuilding of Rome and designing the Vatican, sensed the possibilities of *Uomo Universale* – 'A man can do all things if he will.' Giorgio Vasari, biographer of Michelangelo, used the word *rinascita* (rebirth) in his *Lives of the Artists*, but Renaissance was really coined by English historians in the 1830s.

† A German goldsmith, Johannes Gutenberg of Mainz, was the first to use movable print, modelled on a wine press, to publish 180 copies of the Bible. The spread of reading, like the internet in the twenty-first century, did not only enlighten people's minds, it also darkened them: the hysteria of witch trials and witch burning was at least partly intensified by the popularity of books such as one of the first bestsellers, Henricus Institor's 1487 *Malleus Maleficarum* or *The Hammer of Witches which destroyeth Witches and their heresy as with a two-edged sword*.

for the greater glory of God and God's pontiff and God's banker. Nicholas converted Hadrian's mausoleum into his papal fortress, Castel Sant'Angelo, restored the Leonine walls plus forty old churches and Roman viaducts and moved his residence from the Lateran Palace to the Vatican. An innovator, he survived Roman conspiracies to assassinate him, but he was also a European player, eliminating the last anti-pope, appeasing France and, in March 1452, anointing the new German king, Frederick III, the first Habsburg actually crowned emperor by the pope.

The thirty-seven-year-old Frederick was a dull, somnolent and soon obese plodder who would ironically be the architect of the rise of the Habsburgs, but his slim, beautiful Portuguese bride Eleanor, who would find his Viennese court tedious and philistine and loved dancing and gambling, no doubt helped her brother, King Afonso V, procure papal backing for new African expeditions – in return for help in a more urgent crisis in the east.

In April 1453, Mehmed II, the twenty-one-year-old Ottoman sultan, surrounded Constantinople with an army of 160,000, including thousands of elite arquebusiers, a flotilla of 110 ships and 70 cannon, including one so huge it took sixty oxen to pull it. The age of the cannon and firearm had truly arrived.

THE THROAT-CUTTER AND THE CONQUEROR:
THE FALL OF CONSTANTINOPLE

Emperor Constantine XI Palaiologos appealed for European help. Pope Nicholas V dispatched a flotilla, partly funded by the Portuguese, under Isidore, metropolitan of Kyiv, and 2,000 Genoese volunteers rushed to aid Constantinople. The city, home now to just 50,000 Romaioi, had long been the coveted prize of the Ottomans.

Tamerlane had almost destroyed the sultanate, but Mehmed's father Murad II, energetic, able but inconsistent, unstable and distracted, had exhausted himself fighting: in the Turkish marches, where the beys seized independence, backed by Tamerlane's son Shahrukh;* in the Bal-

---

* A refined, merciful Persianate padishah (emperor), Tamerlane's son Shahrukh ruled the core empire for forty years while his son Ulanbeg governed Samarkand. Ulanbeg's interests were astronomy and science, building his observatory – parts of which survive in Samarkand – to aid his calculations; his catalogue of the stars and measurements of the earth's tilt and sidereal years were highly accurate. But perhaps astronomy distracted him from politics: he was assassinated and the empire disintegrated. Shahrukh and Ulanbeg joined Tamerlane in the Gur Amir, which later inspired the domed Persianate style of Tamerlane's Mughal descendants.

kans, where Hungary, Venice and Serbia rebelled. On the Aegean coast, Gjergj Kastrioti, a Christian princeling coverted to Islam, brought up at the Ottoman court – where he was known as Iskender Beg – had served as a governor. Now he rebelled, recoverted to Christianity, declared himself Lord of Albania and defied Murad for twenty-five years, calling himself Scanderbeg. But the sultan improved his forces, commissioning cannon and something new: handheld, shoulder-fired firearms, successors to the Chinese fire-javelins, later known as arquebuses. These were the earliest muskets, first used by Murad's Janissaries and soon adopted by their Christian opponents.

In 1444, at Varna, after ostentatiously kneeling to pray in the midst of battle, Murad defeated the Hungarians and killed their king. But then the forty-year-old sultan suffered a personal crisis. He called his son Mehmed, aged only twelve, to the capital Edirne (Adrianople) and abdicated. Mehmed was girded with the sword of Osman. But in 1448 the Hungarians, Poles and Wallachians advanced, and Mehmed, exasperated by his father's midlife crisis, told him, 'If *you're* the sultan, lead *your* armies. If *I'm* sultan, I hereby *order* you to come and lead *my* armies.' Murad returned and together they defeated the Christians. The sultanate was restored – but amid its European and Asian territories stood the much-diminished Great City: Constantinople.

Mehmed had planned to take Constantinople but was foiled by his patronizing Turkic grand vizier Çandarlı Halil Pasha, who received bribes from Constantine IX. When his father died in 1451, Mehmed had his brother strangled, a fratricide that he made policy,* and then turned on Constantinople. Çandarlı preferred to keep Constantinople as a client state but when the Romaioi intrigued against Mehmed, the vizier warned them, 'You stupid Greeks. All you will do is lose the little you have.'

Mehmed was a cosmopolitan visionary. Educated by Turkish and Italian tutors, he read the *Iliad* and Arrian's *Life of Alexander the Great*, spoke seven languages and wrote Turkish and Persian poetry. He grew up among Christian princelings, not least Radu the Beautiful, one of the Dracula brothers.† They became lovers, Mehmed penning erotic poems – 'His lips gave life anew to one whom his glances kill' – in a culture

---

* 'Whichever of my sons inherits the sultan's throne it behoves him to kill his brothers in the interest of world order,' decreed Mehmed. 'Most of the jurists have approved this. Let action be taken accordingly.' Altogether around eighty Ottoman princes were strangled by the bowstring so as not to shed royal blood in the only family in which filicide and fratricide were not just occasional and accidental but religious and political policy.

† They were the sons of the *voivode* (prince) of Wallachia, Vlad II, known as Dracul after his membership of the Order of the Dragon.

that regarded sexuality as a question of power rather than identity: the penetrator, virile, the penetrated, submissive. Aspiring to the Roman legacy and international prestige of Constantinople, which the Turks called the Red Apple on account of its desirability, Mehmed realized that its defences were manned by scarcely 5,000 men, and that gunpowder had diminished the impregnability of its walls. Approached by Orbán, a Hungarian cannoneer, he commissioned a full gun park ranging from a monstrous showpiece to smaller, manoeuvrable cannon.

Mehmed built a castle, Rumelihisarı, on the European side of the Bosphoros that he called the Throat-cutter, designed to blockade the city. When a Venetian captain tried to run the blockade, Mehmed's guns sank the ship, and he had the captain anally impaled on the Bosphoran shore as a living scarecrow.

On 5 April 1453, Mehmed arrived to oversee the encompassment of the city with an army that included Christian detachments of Serbians and Wallachians under his favourite, Radu the Beautiful. But full encirclement from the water was prevented by a huge chain boom stretched across the Golden Horn estuary, so he created a pathway of greased logs across Galata and had the entire fleet dragged over it then floated on the Golden Horn. The Romaioi tried unsuccessfully to burn the fleet by using fireships. Forty captured Italians were impaled on the sultan's orders, at which the Christians slaughtered Ottoman prisoners on the walls. Ottoman attackers were fried in spurts of Greek Fire.

Mehmed mined the walls; a Romaioi expert, John the German, who was supposedly Scottish, countermined under Ottoman positions. Mehmed's cannon repeatedly damaged the fortifications (though Orbán was blown to smithereens by one of his own creations). After midnight on 29 May, the sultan ordered the assault. His troops broke in through the damaged north-western section of wall as the last emperor tore off his purple regalia and threw himself into the fighting. His body was never discovered. In scenes of apocalyptic havoc, Venetians and Genoese jumped off the walls, heads bobbed in the Bosphoros like 'melons in a canal' and the Turkish conquerors ran amok, pillaging the Red Apple for three days – as Mehmed waited outside.

The pope was so depressed, he wished he was still a librarian. As Europe recoiled in horror, the pope's flotilla, funded by the Portuguese king Afonso, arrived after the city had fallen. But in return Nicholas V recognized the Portuguese conquests in Africa as a crusade permitted 'to invade, search out, capture, vanquish, and subdue all Saracens, and other enemies of Christ . . . and to reduce their persons to perpetual slavery', a right expanded to include 'Guineans and other negroes captured by force or bought with legitimate contracts'. Afonso expanded his Moroccan territories – winning the epithet O Africano – and backed his uncle Henry the Navigator.

In 1456, two of Henry's captains, one Venetian, one Genoese, settled Cape Verde, an uninhabited island off Senegal that became the Portuguese slaving headquarters and the first tropical colony. The settling of islands in the Atlantic naturally encouraged the idea that there could be other, larger islands. Around 1139 – a century and a half before Columbus – a Milanese monk, Galvano Fiamma, wrote in the newly revealed *Cronica Universalis* about 'another land, further westwards, named Marckalada' – Markland, the Norse name for the coast of the USA–Canada – which he said had been described by 'sailors who frequent the seas of Denmark and Norway'. English sailors had visited mysterious islands, probably Newfoundland, and Perestrello, the colonizer of Madeira, also possessed papers about a mysterious land there. Bodies said to have washed up in Ireland with Mongol faces were surely the corpses of Native Americans somehow lost at sea.

ITZCOATL'S MEXICA: THOSE WHO DIE FOR THE GOD

Just as Afonso the African was advancing across Morocco and down the African coast, another empire builder, no less ambitious and self-righteous, was aggressively expanding his Mexica empire, ruled from his island capital of Tenochtitlan. Motecuhzoma I was forty-two when he succeeded to the throne of the Mexica empire in 1440.

It was a civilization of sophisticated organization, of storytelling that was recorded in illustrations painted on to deerskin and accordion-folded books made of maguey-plant fibres, of constant war against rival cities and of voracious gods. Worshipped at monumental temples, these deities demanded human sacrifices, offered by having their still-beating hearts pulled out of their chests, their skins often donned by dancing priests. But Tenochtitlan was just one of many city states within the empire, that existed alongside a variety of polities, some autocracies, some theocracies and some semi-democracies.

As a young prince, Motecuhzoma was one of the trio that had created the Mexica empire. Around 1427, over twenty years after the death of Tamerlane, the council of Tenochtitlan had chosen the dynamic Itzcoatl – Obsidian Serpent – as ruler or *tlatoani*, the Speaker – who created the empire, aided by his nephew Motecuhzoma, son of an earlier monarch.

The Mexica had been restless vassals of the dominant Tapenec city state Azcapotzalco whose Speaker Tezozomoc had in a long reign conquered much of the Valley of Mexico. His death loosened the city state's hold over the Mexica: in 1427, Itzcoatl led a coup, asserted independence, killed his pro-Azcapotzalco relatives and formed an alliance with two fellow rulers in nearby city states, Texcoco and Tlacopan. Together they defeated Azcapotzalco and secured the Valley, then they expanded outside it, fighting constant wars on the south shores of Lakes Xochimilco and Chalco. When they crushed other states, Itzcoatl burned their histories, recorded in a pictorial writing system written on codices of bark or leather, because it was 'not wise that all the people should know the paintings'. Instead he promoted the official history of Mexica's national god of war and sun, Huitzilopochtli, who demanded the blood of human victims. In his honour, Itzcoatl started to build the centrepiece of the city's sacred precinct, the Great God's House (Great Temple) dedicated to Huitzilopochtli and to Tlaloc, god of rain, each with their own shrines atop a massive stepped pyramid.

At the base of the stairway stood the round carved figure of Coyolxauhqui between two huge serpent heads, engraved with depictions of the dismemberment of the goddess which was re-enacted in sacrificial rituals annually.

The sacrifices were carried out by the priests, mainly men but also women, who blackened their faces and bodies, scarring their ears, genitals, arms and chest in autosacrificial rituals, wearing their hair long and matted with human blood that also stained their mouths and faces. The victims, slaves or prisoners, were transformed into God Impersonators, first spoiled with feasts, sex and cleansing before being led up the steps of the Great Temple by the fire priests who laid them on the sacrificial stone. 'Four men stretched [the victim] out, grasping arms and legs'; the fire priest raised the knife 'and then when he had split open the chest, he at once seized the heart. And he whose chest was open was still alive. And the priest dedicated the heart to the sun.' The victims, Those Who Have Died for the God, 'were sent rolling down the steps bathed in blood', whereupon a priest beheaded them and mounted the skull on a rack which held hundreds of thousands of others.*

---

* At other times of the year, the priests celebrated the Flaying of Men in honour of the skin-hungry god Xipe Totec, when the Speaker watched gladiatorial fights and wore the flayed skin of victims. Such sacrifices were emphasized by the Spanish to justify their conquest, but the Mexica's sophisticated and literate culture was much more complex than that: it is likely that in these earlier decades the rate of sacrifice was less frenzied than it later became.

On Itzcoatl's death in 1440, his successor and nephew Motecuhzoma Ilhuicamina completed both the Great Temple and the empire, taking Chalco. Together they further expanded around the Sky Sea (Gulf of Mexico), calling themselves Neighbours of the Sea of the Sky.

Yet the Mexica's elected autocracy were not the only Mesoamerican system: their rival Tlaxcala was a semi-democratic republic, ruled by around 100 elected *teuctli* – councillors – who had to demonstrate a civil ethos of humility, including fasting, bloodletting and moral preparation, before taking office, for which showy eloquence was required. There were no royal ballcourts or palaces in Tlaxcala. Democracy, far from being exported to the Americas by Enlightened Europeans and Founding Fathers, was already there. These elected republicans were the opposite of the monarchical Mexica, against whom their warriors and *otomi* fighters held out, preserving their independence and loathing the arrogant Mexica imperialists.

Motecuhzoma promoted himself to *Huehuetlatoani*, Supreme Speaker, translated as emperor. The Mexica differentiated themselves from their allies, believing that as the chosen people of the gods and successors to Teotihuacan, they were destined to rule the world. Their Speakers were surrogates of the gods, hailed at their accession: 'You are their flute . . . they make you their fangs, claws, you are their wild beast, their eater-of-people, their judge.' They also created a new nobility with military-religious orders of *quauhpili* knights who enjoyed privileges – only nobles being allowed to wear lip plugs, cotton cloaks, golden armbands.* Noblemen owned hundreds of concubines, including slaves captured in war, but within the royal family women were powerful.†

Yet as the empire expanded and tension rose with its allies, the bloodletting at the Great Temple‡ became ever more frantic. Their allies and vassals bitterly resented them. Given a chance, they would rise and destroy them.

---

* Noble children were educated in special schools linked to temples. Children and adults played *patolli*, a rubber-ball game, on special courts, that had been since the Maya kingdoms part of royal ritual. The monarchs often played the game; spectators sometimes bet so heavily on the results that they had to sell themselves into slavery; and losers were often killed – a sort of real Squid Game.

† The ultimate grand dame, Atotoztli, daughter of Motecuhzoma I, married Tezozomoc, son of Itzcoatl, and was the mother and often regent of the next three rulers, starting in 1478 with Axayacatl, grandson of both Motecuhzoma I and Itzcoactl (and father of the last of them Motecuhzoma II).

‡ The capital Tenochtitlan, built on a grid system and approached across the water by a causeway or in a barge or canoe, was now a wonder of the world with 250,000 inhabitants, much larger than Seville with 45,000.

Incas, Trastamaras and Rurikovichi

THE EARTHSHAKER AND THE IMPOTENT

Just as Motecuhzoma was consolidating his empire, far to the south-west, unbeknown to him, another empire builder, Inca Yupanqui, was creating the *Tawantinsuyu*, the Four Parts Together, the largest empire of the Americas.

Born in the small kingdom of Cusco in Peru, Prince Yupanqui (Honoured) seized the throne from his father and brother. The family believed they were descended from a sacred and wandering stranger-king. Yupanqui's father Inca Viracocha named another son as heir, but the two of them abandoned the capital during an enemy invasion. Yupanqui refused to go, rallied the people and defeated the invaders, taking the spoils to his father, who refused to recognize him as senior to the chosen heir and ordered his killing. Rebranding himself as Pachacuti – Earthshaker – Yupanqui seized the throne, humiliating the father and embarking on almost forty years of conquests that subdued most of Peru. He beautified Cusco, building the monumental Golden Temple of the Sun at its centre and the Saqsawaman fortress complex with its zigzag walls above the city, and in the mountains he erected the mysterious but astounding terraced palace of Machu Picchu with its royal quarters and Sun Temple.

When he was too old to fight, his son Tupac Inca Yupanqui expanded along the Andes into Ecuador, building a second capital Quito and embarking on an expedition into the Pacific.

These two charismatic Sapa Incas almost completed the empire in just fifty years. The Sapa Inca – Unique Inca – was the title of the divine monarch whose mission from the Sun was to rule the world, but he was also the Son of the Sun and the Lover and Benefactor of the Poor, though he would eat off gold and silver. Wearing a braided turquoise diadem, with a tassel on his forehead, and pendulous earspools, and bearing a feathered staff and a golden mace, he was guarded by 5,000 Long-Ears in red and white tunics. The coronations of Sapa Incas were celebrated by the strangling of 200 children aged four to ten, whose death rites, designed by Pachacuti, saw the burning of mourning clothes and the slitting of the throats of 2,000 llamas, while 'A thousand boys and girls will be brought and buried for me in places where I slept or enjoyed myself.'

Pachacuti was the ninth Sapa Inca, a god-king who never died. After death, Inca royalty was mummified and revered alongside a golden statue, a surrogate, sitting in their palaces where attendants served them drinks and dressed them in gold decorations; sometimes they attended important events on their thrones. These long-dead ancestors, kings and queens, advised the Sapa Incas. The Incas deployed armies of around 35,000 soldiers and even, on rare occasions, of 100,000, all wearing multicoloured plumes and gold, silver or copper plates, wielding maces, clubs and bows, and singing songs such as 'We will drink from the skull of the traitor, we will adorn ourselves with a necklace of his teeth, we will play the melody of the *pinkullu* with flutes made from his bones, we will beat the drum made from his skin and thus we will dance!' War and trade were facilitated by pack animals, llamas and alpacas; the empire, 2,500 miles long, was linked by 25,000 miles of roads. Agriculture was aided by sprinkling a natural fertilizer, guano – bird faeces – on the fields that grew maize, potatoes, sweet potatoes and tomatoes.

The Incas had 2,000 concubines – quotas of 'conquered women' were dedicated as Brides of the Sun. The *coya* or queen, a sister or cousin of the Inca, was powerful. The Incas were polygynous; noble descent passed through both men and women; and children could inherit from either parent. There was no word for virgin, and premarital sex was not condemned. It was thought unhealthy to repress sexual urges. Only noble children were expected to do so, and then only until marriage. Speaking Quechua, the Incas had no writing but communicated by a system of knots. They sacrificed humans to their pantheon but not on a scale comparable to the Mexica.

Tupac expanded into Colombia, Argentina, Bolivia and Ecuador, an aggressive, covetous empire, like that of his contemporaries the Mexica and the Aziz-Trastámara family of Iberia, led by warrior monarchs and martial aristocracies, and inspired by religious cults of conquest, loot and redemption. Their conquests seemed unstoppable – but it was the Iberians who first fell apart in a vicious and farcical family feud.

The masturbation of King Enrique IV of Castile by his doctors led to ejaculation, but the royal Trastámara sperm was 'watery and sterile'. The physicians and courtiers despaired – so the frottage went on. The sperm was collected in a golden tube and given to Enrique's queen, another

Portuguese princess, Juana, to inject into her vagina in a desperate attempt to inseminate an heir. Their Jewish doctor Samaya supervised proceedings 'to see if she could receive semen – but she could not'.

Blue-eyed and athletic with his English red hair, elongated jaw, bulging forehead and flat, broken nose, Enrique resembled either a lion or a monkey but, shy, gentle and unpretentious, he lacked the extrovert dynamism necessary to control the warriors of Castile.

His father Juan II was a cheerful, hunt-obsessed half-English poet fancier who married Enrique to Bianca of Navarre, but the groom failed to consummate and, embarrassingly, the bloodied wedding sheets were not displayed. While courtiers gossiped about the shape and alignment of the royal penis and possible homosexuality, his father sent priests to interview Enrique's lovers, prostitutes who testified that 'his virile member was firm and produced manly seed' in fecund profusion. Enrique himself believed it was 'reciprocal impotence due to malign influences' – bewitchment – and poor Bianca was sent home to her father. In 1451, King Juan, remarried to a Portuguese princess, had another legitimate child – the infanta Isabella, twenty-six years younger than Enrique.

Worried about Portuguese interference, Juan married Enrique to his Portuguese first cousin Juana: interbreeding was already a problem in the Iberian royal family. But as Enrique was again unable to perform, after seven years the independent-minded Juana made her own arrangements, embarking on an affair – the first of many – with her husband's *mayordomo*, Beltrán de la Cueva, leading to the birth of a daughter. Europe's potentates discussed the Trastámara in gynaecological detail. 'The queen was impregnated without losing her virginity,' Pope Pius II was informed by his secretary; 'the sperm [that was] poured into the entrance had penetrated the most hidden places inside her'. But 'others believed a man other than Enrique was the father'. The daughter was nicknamed La Beltraneja after her natural father.

This was all the more galling because Enrique's half-sister Isabella possessed all the qualities of a king except masculinity. It was the need to stop her succession that made Enrique's sperm so important. Isabella's youth was spent either in impoverished seclusion with her insane mother or resisting her brother's shameless attempts to marry her off to inappropriate husbands. Surviving in a dangerous and unstable court, keeping her own counsel, she proved intelligent, secretive and fearless, fortified by fanatical Catholic piety and Trastámara grandeur.

As Enrique struggled to impose himself, and the Portuguese king intervened in the hope of taking the kingdom himself, Isabella secretly started to arrange her own marriage – the marriage that would create an empire. But Enrique's impotence had empowered the Berber kings of Granada, the last Islamic power in Iberia, which now refused to pay its tribute. Enrique tried to prove his martial machismo by leading attacks on Granada, a kingdom so prosperous that its eponymous capital city was, with 165,000 people, by far the biggest city in Iberia and one of the biggest in Europe. Islam was resurgent: Granada easily fought off the Christian attacks, while at the other end of Europe the Ottoman conqueror was mopping up the last outposts of Christendom.

THE SECOND AND THIRD ROME:
CAESAR MEHMED AND SOPHIA OF MOSCOW

As Mehmed waited outside Constantinople, his troops raped women and boys, killed and enslaved thousands. 'Every tent was heaven,' boasted an Ottoman soldier, 'filled with boys and girls, sexual servants of paradise, each a stately beauty offering a juicy peach.' At the end of the third day, the sultan ended the pillage and entered on horseback, dazzled by the Queen of Cities. In the old Boukoleon Palace – its ruins still stand – he reflected on the transience of empires by quoting Saadi:

> The spider is curtain bearer in the palace of Khusrau,
> The owl sounds the relief in the castle of Afrasiyab.

Visiting Hagia Sophia, he caught a soldier looting treasures and clobbered him with the flat of his sword.

Mehmed was now master of a ruined, half-empty Constantinople. Acclaiming himself *Kayser-i-Rum*, Caesar of Rome, he converted Hagia Sophia into a mosque and built his own palace on the Forum and a second New (Topkapı) Palace on the site of the Mega Palation, which he demolished.* As for Halil, his grand vizier, who had foiled all his schemes since 1444, he was beheaded, the first of many viziers to be

---

* Constantinople's population may have been just 30,000, but Mehmed ordered his magnates to sponsor new neighbourhoods, protected Greeks and invited in Jews, who were being persecuted in western Europe. Within twenty-five years, its population was 80,000, of which 60 per cent were Muslim, 20 per cent Christian, 10 per cent Jewish. Mehmed demolished the Church of the Apostles (tomb of Constantine and emperors), built his own mosque complex on top and constructed the Ayyub Ansari Mosque (on the 'discovered' site of a Companion of Muhammad who died during the siege of 668), as well as the fortress-arsenal of Seven Towers. Although still called Constantinople by the Turks, it was also known as Istanbul, derived from an old Greek nickname 'eis ten polin' ('to the City'), adapted to Istambol. It remained the Ottoman/Turkish capital until 1923, and its name was officially changed to Istanbul in 1930.

killed. Henceforth most viziers were not Turks but formerly enslaved Slavs or Greeks, all converted to Islam. At least one of the Palaiologos nephews of the last emperor converted to Islam and rose to grand vizier. Ottoman tolerance has been exaggerated by historians. 'Tolerance is not the same as celebrating diversity,' writes Marc David Baer, but 'a state of inequality'. Jews and Christians existed at the mercy of the ruler, providing they offered total submission, often having to wear special badges and costumes to mark their inferiority to Muslims and suffering bursts of persecution. There were always exceptions: Caesar-sultans do not have friends, but Mehmed's closest courtier was his physician, an Italian Jew named Giacomo of Gaeta who converted to become Hekim Yakub (Dr Jacob) Pasha, later chief vizier.

The pope called for a crusade to restore the Second Rome, but to the north Mehmed's conquests contributed to the rise of Russia, transforming the princes of Moscow from recent Mongol enforcers to haughty Orthodox Caesars.

Scarcely resting after taking Constantinople, Mehmed looked to exploit the ruin of the Golden Horde, forming an alliance with Haji Giray, descendant of Genghis and Jochi. Giray founded his own family kingdom, the Tatar khanate of the Crimea, which remained a formidable European power for 300 years, fielding armies of 50,000 cavalry that at various times took Moscow and almost Vienna.

Mehmed and Giray attacked the Italian cities of the Crimea and took over their slave markets. Giray then started raiding Christian Poland, Muscovy and Lithuania to capture fair-skinned slaves. Mehmed galloped around the Black Sea into Wallachia (Romania) where, backed by Radu the Beautiful, he attacked the prince's defiant brother Vlad, who hated the Ottomans. Vlad made up for his meagre resources by intrepid tactics and eyewatering cruelty, killing Mehmed's envoys by driving nails into their turbans. In between Ottoman invasions and during three reigns as voivode, Vlad purged enemies, Saxons and Turks, by rectally impaling them in forests of stakes – a practice which shocked even the sultan and earned him the epithet the Impaler, inspiration for Dracula – before he was driven out and replaced by Radu.*

In 1460, Mehmed mopped up the offshoots of Constantinople; he captured Trebizond and advanced into Greece, which remained Ottoman until the 1820s. There he expelled the last emperor's brother,

---

* While the Impaler died fighting, Radu and the Dracula dynasty ruled on as Ottoman clients. For 250 years, the sultans appointed trusted Greek princes, some of them descended from emperors, from the Phanariot district of Constantinople to rule Moldavia and Wallachia, later combined to form Romania.

Thomas Palaiologos, Despot of Morea, who escaped with his baby daughter Zoë. The girl was adopted by the pope. In a demonstration of how female power could connect and transform, this gifted princess would have a special role in the creation of Russia: in 1472, when she was twenty-three, the pope married her by proxy in St Peter's to the thirty-two-year-old grand prince of Muscovy, Ivan III. Adopting the Orthodox name Sophia, this Greek-Roman sophisticate arrived in rough, cold Moscow to meet her fearsome husband for the first time.

Ivan had been raised in the toughest school. Moscow's rise was far from assured. For a long time it looked as if Lithuania, not Muscovy, would unite a Slavic empire. The dukes of Lithuania were the last pagan potentates in Europe until in 1385 the pagan potentate Jagiełło, thirty-three years old, converted to Catholicism to win the crown of Poland by marrying Jadwiga, its heiress.* While the two monarchies remained formally separate, Jagiełło called himself grand duke of the Lithuanians, king of Poland and lord of Rus, creating a singular Lithuanian–Polish union that became the biggest state in Europe. Jagiełło, who took the name Władysław II, defeated the Teutonic Knights in the north, later swallowing Prussia before expanding southwards, gobbling up the lands of old Rus.

Moscow was eclipsed: its prince Vasili II lost control of his kingdom and family, was captured by the Mongol khan of Kazan and then blinded by a cousin. His son Ivan, aged six at the time, witnessed the blinding. But Vasili the Blind won the family war just by waiting, and his return to Moscow was marked by a savage showdown, aided by Ivan, whom he proclaimed co-ruler. Vasili had emphasized his Constantinople link – his sister was the penultimate empress. Now he and Ivan claimed leadership of the Orthodox by *translatio imperii*, the transfer of power from Constantinople to Muscovy – later hailed as the Third Rome – aided by his family link, and then Ivan's marriage to Sophia.

Nicknamed Grozny – Terrible – Ivan was lean, tall, with terrifying eyes, a heavy boozer capable of showy vision and quicksilver action, conquering swathes of the territory of old rivals, Novgorod and Tver. Sophia supposedly encouraged him to stop paying Mongol tribute. Golden

---

* Queen Jadwiga was one of the two daughters of Louis the Great, the Anjou king of Hungary and Poland whose widow Elisabeth of Bosnia tried to preserve the kingdoms for the two girls. Maria became queen of Hungary, but her mother Elisabeth overplayed her hand, murdering the male claimant, which led to her arrest and strangling in front of her daughter. Faced with marriage to a pagan, Jadwiga prayed and finally agreed, provided he converted. Jadwiga and Jagiełło were a successful partnership, she dying in childbirth, he ruling the joint kingdoms until 1434, establishing a dynasty that ruled for over a century and provided kings to Hungary and Bohemia.

Khan Ahmed, taking advantage of fraternal fighting among the Muscovites, attacked with the encouragement of Poland–Lithuania. Moscow
was in peril, but Ivan secured the backing of Ahmed's rivals, the Girays
of the Crimea. In October 1480, he faced the Mongols at the River Ugra,
a standoff that ended when Ahmed withdrew, marking the eclipse – but
not the end – of Mongol power* and a setback for Poland–Lithuania,
which temporarily divided in the 1490s.

Ivan had doubled Muscovy and his own magnificence, now calling
himself Autocrat of All the Russias and, for the first time, Caesar – tsar.
The Muscovites used the title for both the Mongol khan and the Roman
basileus. As a vassal and later successor state to the khans, Ivan and
his heirs commandeered the Mongol belief in absolute power of the
sacred tsar, his holy mission to conquer, total ownership of the land
and control of over all their 'slaves' – as all subjects, even nobles, were
known. The imperial splendour and Orthodox mission of Constantinople were vital too, but it was the Mongol tradition that is probably key to
understanding Russia right into the twenty-first century.

Sophia, princess of Constantinople, could have been a colourless
cipher, but not only was the marriage surprisingly successful – she
produced eleven children, five sons and six daughters – theirs became a
remarkable partnership.

A HIT GONE WRONG: MAGNIFICO AND MICHELANGELO

Although women in Moscow resided in separate quarters, the *terem*,
Sophia – this 'cunning woman' – chaired her own council and freely received envoys; moreover 'The prince acted very often on her suggestions.'
She supervised the commissioning of Italian architects to embellish
the Kremlin. Ivan and Sophia looked towards Italy and its arbiters of
taste, the Medici. Yet those Florentines had just survived a terrifying
assault.

On a Sunday morning in April 1478, the two Medici brothers, Lorenzo and Giuliano, rulers of Florence, accompanied a visiting cardinal,

---

* Ahmed, khan of the Golden Horde, had been a Eurasian potentate, a Golden prince, married to a Tamerlanian princess. After the debacle on the Ugra, Ahmed was assassinated by
his cousin Ibak Khan of Sibir, his wife returned to Herat and the Golden Horde shattered
for ever into several kingdoms. In the east, the khanate of Sibir, one of the lesser-known
successor states of the Mongol empire, had been founded by Taibuga, a descendant of
Jochi, who ruled from a town near today's Tyumen. On the Volga and on the Caspian,
a Golden khan ruled Kazan and Astrakhan. In Crimea, the Girays ruled a buffer state
between Ottomans, Poles and Muscovites.

the city's archbishop and a fellow banking heir to the cathedral. Unbeknown to the Medici, the young cardinal and the men around them were all assassins. Seven hitmen, including two priests, lurking behind the high altar, pretended to be waiting for the service to begin. At the ringing of the sacristy bell, they drew their daggers and fell upon the Medici brothers.

Dark-eyed with his black hair parted in the middle, Lorenzo de' Medici, not yet thirty, brought up by humanists and scholars, was already celebrated for his 'joyful nature', his kindness to friends, his saucy poetry, his patronage of artists, the pleasure he took in singing, hunting and playing *calcio*, a football-like game. He was no less admired for his adroit management of Florence amid the perpetual tournament of power between the many city states and larger kingdoms that made up Italy. When his father, Piero, died, the *Signoria* invited Lorenzo, then just twenty, 'to take on myself the care of the state as my father and grandfather did'. He hesitated, he said, 'considering that the burden and danger were great'. Then: 'I consented unwillingly.'

In 1471, Francesco della Rovere, an energetic, uncouth, toothless fisherman's son, was elected Pope Sixtus IV and immediately reappointed Lorenzo de' Medici as his banker. Sixtus enhanced Rome, building the first bridge across the Tiber since antiquity, established the Vatican Library and commissioned a small chapel, named Sistine after himself, inviting Ghirlandaio and Sandro Botticelli to paint its frescoes. Sixtus was an enthusiastic 'lover of boys and sodomites' who took his own nephews as lovers. Since priests could no longer marry, popes promoted their nephews as territorial magnates during their short reigns – hence the word nepotism. Sixtus raised six nephews to cardinal. But when he asked the Medici to lend the 60,000 ducats to buy the town of Imola for one of them, Girolamo Riario, Lorenzo refused, hoping to buy it for Florence.

Sixtus was infuriated, borrowed the money from another Florentine family, the Pazzi, and decided to destroy Lorenzo the Magnificent. He encouraged his seventeen-year-old nephew Cardinal Raffaele Riario, along with the young banker Francesco Pazzi and the embittered archbishop of Pisa, Francesco Salviati, to murder the Medici and seize Florence. Sixtus tried to cover himself: if Lorenzo were to be killed, Girolamo Riario asked, 'will Your Holiness pardon who did it?'

'You're a beast,' replied Sixtus. 'I don't want anyone killed, just regime change,' adding, 'Lorenzo's a villain.' The Riarios decided that a visit by the youngest cardinal would lure the Medici to their deaths.

As the sacristy bell rang, a priestly hitman stabbed Lorenzo in the neck but the fit Medici jerked free, swung his sword at the assassins and vaulted the altar rail just as another assassin, shouting, 'Take that traitor,' raised his dagger and shattered the skull of Lorenzo's brother Giuliano. The assassins stabbed him nineteen times, so frenziedly that Francesco Pazzi cut himself.

Lorenzo, escorted by his retainers, ran back to the Medici Palace. 'Giuliano? Is he safe?' asked Lorenzo as his friends sucked his wound clean, in case the dagger was poisoned. At the Palazzo della Signoria nearby, Archbishop Salviati stormed the seat of government with a posse of Perugian mercenaries, but as the Vacco bell tolled, Medici henchmen ran in and slaughtered them, parading their heads on lances as they hunted for the assassins. Francesco Pazzi's uncle Jacopo was caught, tortured and hanged, then propped up at the door of the Pazzi Palace where his head was used as a doorknob, while the two murderous priests were castrated. A rope was tied around the neck of the archbishop, who was stripped naked, then tossed out the window where he hung beside the naked Pazzi. As they wriggled and struggled to survive, the nude archbishop sank his teeth into Pazzi's thigh. A young artist, living at the Medici palace, was fascinated by this: Leonardo da Vinci sketched one of these bodies.

The coup made Lorenzo even more powerful. Sixtus excommunicated him and invited the sinister King Ferrante of Naples, who liked to mummify his enemies and keep them fully dressed in a macabre museum, to overthrow the Medici, but Lorenzo set off for Naples. There was a risk he would end up in Ferrante's museum. 'My desire is that by my life or my death, my misfortune or my prosperity, I may contribute to the wealth of our city.' He returned, hailed as the Magnificent, having delivered peace.

'If Florence was to have a tyrant, she could never have found a better or more delightful one,' a Florentine writer later commented. Neglecting his bank – it had lent far too much to the English king Edward IV, who was mired in a civil war between different lines of royal family – Il Magnifico devoted himself to politics. Married to a Roman Orsini,* he adored his children, writing plays for them to perform, but he was realistic about their talents. 'I have three sons,' he said, 'one good, one shrewd, one fool.' The fool was the eldest Piero, clumsy and tactless, lined up to succeed to his role in Florence. The good one was the second

---

* Like his father, Lorenzo bought slaves with whom he had illegitimate children: these slaves were not from Africa but from Circassia in the Caucasus, probably traded through Genoese and Ottoman traders.

son Giuliano, but the shrewd one was Giovanni, fat, genial, sybaritic. Sensing that the key to Florence was Rome, Lorenzo married his daughter to a natural son of Pope Innocent VIII, whom he persuaded to make Giovanni a cardinal. 'You're the youngest cardinal not only today but at any time in the past,' he wrote to the boy. 'Show your gratitude by a holy, exemplary and chaste life in Rome, which is a sink of iniquity.' The son of his murdered brother, Giuliano, joined the household, also destined for Rome.

Lorenzo founded a neo-Platonic school in the San Marco gardens next to the Medici Palace where young artists lived in an atmosphere of artistic freedom and erotic exploration. One such young protégé was an illegitimate artisan from the Tuscan village of Vinci. Leonardo da Vinci, son of a notary, had been arrested in 1476 for sodomy but then released. 'Police records,' writes Catherine Fletcher, 'show the majority of men in later fifteenth-century Florence had or were accused of having sex with other men on at least one occasion.' Lorenzo admired a silver lyre in the shape of a horse's head that Leonardo had made. When in 1482 the duke of Milan asked for a sculptor, Lorenzo sent him Leonardo, who advertised himself as a military engineer, adding that he could also sculpt. Italy was a battlefield of northern dynasties – the French Valois, the German Habsburgs – and local warlords, who enhanced their power with war and art. War came first. Without victory there was nothing for the artists to celebrate and no spoils to pay them with. These warlords were innovators in military technology, improving the velocity and facility of arquebuses and artillery, and fortifications designed to withstand their bombardment.* Leonardo got the job in Milan – just one of Medici's protégés.

In 1489, Lorenzo invited Ghirlandaio to send gifted pupils from among his apprentices. Ghirlandaio sent a boy of thirteen whose talents in sculpture were so striking that he exclaimed, 'Why, this boy knows more than I do.' Raised in a small Tuscan town, son of an official appointed by the Medici but descended from impoverished nobility, Michelangelo di Buonarroti bristled with family pride yet was attracted to the rough workmanship of marble: 'Along with the milk of my nurse I received the knack of handling chisel and hammer, with which I make

---

* In 1482, when Leonarda da Vinci offered his services to the duke of Milan, he boasted of his expertise in '1. "burning and destroying" enemy bridges; 2; "I make infinite numbers of bridges, mantlets and scaling ladders" for sieges. 3. "I have also types of cannons" 4. "Mines and secret passages" 5. "I will make cannon mortar and light ordinance . . . that are quite out of the ordinary"' and only in point 6 does he add: 'Also I can execute sculpture in marble bronze and clay.' He did not mention he could also do some painting.

my figures.' He was an irrepressible, obstreperous youth, short-fused and often impossible, yet also passionate and witty; his shoulders and chest were muscular from the physical labour of sculpture, his body sinewy and strong, 'his eyes brown the colour of horn but changeable and flecked with yellow and blue'. In Lorenzo's school, he was involved in homosexual love affairs with older men, an ephebophilic relationship being a rite of passage in Italy at that time. These sometimes led to fights, one of which saw him getting his nose broken. But he focused on his art, and enjoyed choosing his marble from the quarries. When he crafted a faun's head in classical style, Il Magnifico was dazzled, asking the boy's father if the boy could stay. Invited to dine with the Medici family daily, Michelangelo grew up knowing the children, particularly the future pope Giovanni. He was also encouraged to show 'the results of his labours to Il Magnifico each day'.

The magnificence of Lorenzo impressed Europe, even the Muscovites. When Ivan the Great wished to create a fitting citadel for the newest power in Europe, he and Sophia, raised in Italy, turned to the Medici.

SOPHIA'S KREMLIN; SCANDERBEG'S ALBANIA; BELLINI'S PORTRAIT

The tsars hired one of Lorenzo de' Medici's architects, Aristotele Fioravanti, who travelled to Moscow and started the Dormition Cathedral, while also serving as an artillery engineer for Ivan's sieges. When Fioravanti wanted to go home, Ivan arrested him and he perished in prison. But all tsars down to Nicholas II were crowned in the Dormition Cathedral.*

As befitting a Byzantine, Sophia proved adept at Kremlin intrigue. Her eldest son, Vasili, was half Rurikovich, half Palaiologos, but in 1497 Ivan crowned his grandson Dmitri as grand prince, which drove Vasili, backed by Sophia, to attempt a coup. When it failed, Sophia and son fell from favour, but they somehow destroyed their rivals and Vasili returned to power, crowned as co-ruler, while Dmitri and his mother were arrested. Dynasties have always set women against women and

---

* Next, Ivan and Sophia invited Marco Ruffo and Pietro Solario, who built the Palace of Facets and the red crenellations of the Kremlin walls, including Ivan's Belltower – all of which now appear distinctively Russian but derived from a clever merging of Byzantine and Italian styles. While Ivan's army was traditionally Mongol-style cavalry with bows and arrows, the Italians brought cannon and firearms.

pitted mothers against mothers. Here, Sophia was triumphant. Elena was probably poisoned; Dmitri died in prison. 'I'll give the principality to whoever I like,' said the dying Ivan handing over to Vasili III,* who would be the father of Ivan the Terrible.

Across the Balkans, Mehmed enforced Ottoman control, incorporating Serbia and Bosnia; only the Lord of Albania, indomitable mountain warrior Scanderbeg held out, backed by Venice until his death when Albania too was subjugated. Mehmed then built a Mediterranean navy to confront Venice, which faced the prospect of losing its empire. When the Venetians made peace, they sent Mehmed a special present in the form of Gentile Bellini, official artist of the doge who, with his brother Giovanni, were Venice's most famous. Artists, like everything else, existed in dynasties: their father Jacopo had trained the boys alongside the Paduan artist Andrea Mantegna, who then married their sister Nicolosia. Once in Constantinople, Bellini painted the sultan, catching his alert, foxy intelligence – an intelligence crudely demonstrated when Mehmed was said to have won a debate with the artist on the anatomical perspective of his *Head of St John the Baptist* by beheading a slave.

Having taken the Second Rome, Mehmed turned to attack the first, in 1480 dispatching his fleet from Albania to take Otranto, causing panic in Italy and encouraging a new holy war against Islam that was to earn its first success in Spain.† There Queen Isabella of Castile created an Inquisition to investigate and purge secret Jews poisoning the purity of Christians and launched a war to eliminate the Muslim kingdom of Granada.

---

* It was during Vasili's reign that Muscovite clergymen started to push the idea of Moscow as the Third Rome in succession to Constantinople.
† Just after taking Otranto in 1481, Mehmed the Conqueror died at the age of forty-nine. In the ensuing showdown, possibly overseen by his son Bayezid II, his grand vizier, the Jewish doctor Hekim Yakub, was accused by the Janissaries of being a Venetian agent: he had just negotiated a peace treaty with Venice. The Janissaries murdered Hekim and looted his palace. Ottoman tolerance had its limits: thereafter there were many more Slavic-born viziers but no more Jews.

Manikongos, Borgias and Columbuses

Red-haired, blue-eyed, pale-skinned, pious and acute, Isabella was the antithesis of her thin-spermed half-brother Enrique, who harassed her to marry a rash of unsuitable husbands – including a hunchbacked Englishman (the duke of York, future Richard III). Isabella defied him and, as the family feud went against Enrique, he recognized her as heir.

Isabella meanwhile secretly negotiated her own marriage. She had known her candidate since childhood: Ferdinand of Aragon was playful, handsome and cunning but he was a double cousin: his father, Juan, king of the maritime Aragonese empire of Catalonia, Sicily and Sardinia, was a Trastámaran and his mother was Castilian; and their marriage would unite two kingdoms. It was a lot to arrange: Isabella also had to fix papal dispensation for consanguinity. Just eighteen years old, she enjoyed the drama, signing cryptic messages as The Princess. She was both an excited teenager planning an elopement and a hard-headed politician designing her future reign, in both of which she would perform God's work.

When Enrique ordered 'that I be captured and deprived of my freedom', Isabella sent a note to Ferdinand redolent with romantic conspiracy, 'Order me and I'll do it.' Ferdinand replied with a gold necklace adorned with 'seven fat rubies'. 'To run the same risks she is running', the seventeen-year-old Ferdinand, king of Sicily, wearing disguise, galloped by night to Valladolid to fulfil their assignation, accompanied by five horsemen.

On the road, they met an urbane Spanish cardinal who had rushed from Rome with the bull permitting the marriage. The deliverer was Rodrigo Borgia, whose libertinism and vulgarity horrified Isabella. The Borgias, minor Aragonese nobles, had already flourished in Rome: Rodrigo's uncle, Calixtus III, had promoted him to cardinal. Borgia proved a masterful Vatican player. When Paul II suffered a coronary (according to his enemies, while being sodomized), Borgia delivered the tiara to Sixtus IV, who backed Isabella. She was informed of Borgia's 'uncontrollable passions' and his 'depraved games' featuring naked mudwrestling 'courtesans, Jews and donkeys' – but he was her cardinal.

In October 1469, she spotted Ferdinand riding into Valladolid – 'That's him! That's him!' – where they swiftly married. 'Last night in the service of God, we consummated the marriage,' announced Ferdinand. Isabella added, 'This subject is embarrassing and hateful to noblewomen,' but 'our actions are the evidence we must present'. The bloody sheets were displayed.

Ferdinand 'loved [her] greatly although he also gave himself to other women'. Suffering regular pangs of jealousy, Isabella tolerated his mistresses and bastards. Four infantas arrived fast. Keen to conceive a son, they consulted their Jewish doctor Lorenzo Badoc before the birth of Infante Juan. They kept the kingdoms separate but agreed never to overrule each other. Ferdinand was a lover of 'all kinds of games' whose 'special gift [was] that whoever spoke to him wanted to love and serve him because he talked in such a friendly way'. He was happy to take Isabella's advice because, wrote a courtier, 'he knew she was so very capable'.

On Enrique's death, the couple created a new entity, Spain, but they had to fight for it. Afonso the African and his Portuguese troops invaded, joining their other enemies. 'You can freely kill them without any punishment. I'm just a weak woman,' Isabella announced, rallying her knights, but 'If there's danger, it would be better to take it like medicine and for it to be over in an hour than to suffer a prolonged illness,' adding, 'If you tell me women shouldn't talk about this, I answer: I don't see who's risking more than me!' At sea the Portuguese routed her Castilians at the battle of Guinea, winning the gold and slave trades, the first European clash for Africa; but on land Isabella expelled Afonso. Spain was home to many Muslims and 150,000 Jews. The latter had been there since Roman times, though many more had converted to Catholicism; these *conversos* were now the subject of suspicion as alien subverters of Christendom.

Isabella's itinerant court, moving between Seville, Toledo and Valladolid, was pious and prim yet not joyless – she enjoyed dancing, music, singing and dressing up, sporting dresses of scarlet brocade and gold. She knew the Jewish leaders well: the octogenarian Abraham Seneor was a veteran adviser, and her doctor was Jewish. But in 1478 she asked Pope Sixtus for her own Holy Office of the Inquisition, appointing her childhood confessor, the ascetic Tomás da Torquemada, as grand inquisitor. The couple sought denunciations of secret 'Judaizers' who were tortured on the rack and by waterboarding, their property seized. Then if they were declared to be 'relapsed', these *relapsos* – not practising Jews but Christians found to have secretly practised Judaism – were dressed in coned *sanbenito* caps and gowns at public ceremonies known as *autos-da-fé* – acts of faith, ritualistic penitential sessions. From 1481, these were witnessed by the monarchs and nobility. If guilty of relapsing, recalcitrant heretics were 'relaxed to the justice of the secular arm' and incinerated naked and alive outside the city. If they confessed, they were garrotted before burning.*

Enriched by the estates of the dead and the elimination of 'this heretical crime', Isabella, confirmed in her belief that Castile was riddled with Judaizing heretics, was enthusiastic. The Seville Inquisition dealt with 16,000 cases, and 2,000 were executed in the first ten years. Isabella then turned to the Muslims.

In 1481, a posse of Islamic Granadan horsemen captured a Castilian town, an embarrassment that accelerated Isabella's crusade to eliminate the rich but chaotic amirate of Granada. Ferdinand commanded in the field, while Isabella arranged the supplies, financed by her Jewish advisers Samuel Abulafia and Isaac Abravanel.

On horseback, power-dressed to maximum effect, Isabella delivered provisions to the military camps while overseeing the negotiations that encouraged civil war among the Granadans. In this she was aided by the capture of Amir Muhammad XII who, leaving his son El Infantico Ahmed as a hostage, became their vassal. The Muslims won some skirmishes – 'I heard what happened with the Moors,' she wrote. 'I am greatly displeased' – and in 1487, while the monarchs were besieging Málaga, a Muslim tried to assassinate them. After he had been killed by Isabella's guards, the man's body was catapulted into Málaga. When the city fell, Isabella enslaved everyone, distributing as many as 11,000 slaves. As the war dragged on, the queen in 1489 visited the siege of Baza, where her entourage was joined by a rumpled Genoese sailor who had just arrived in Castile.

Son of a Genoese weaver, taverner and cheesemonger, Cristóbal Colón – Columbus – had sailed with Genoese traders to England, Iceland and Guinea. A compiler of apocalyptic prophecies and travel books – particularly those of the Bible and Marco Polo respectively – he was

---

* Practising Jews were not burned by the Inquisition: Jews and Muslims were outside its jurisdiction, which only covered self-identifying Christians who were accused of judaizing, secretly indulging in Jewish rituals. In the half-century after 1480, perhaps 2,000 such *conversos* were executed. Jews and Muslims could be punished only by the king.

visionary, loquacious, insecure, mendacious and shamelessly pushy, but also a tough and enterprising sailor, obsessed like so many, then and now, with the coming end of the world. Columbus was married to Felipa Perestrello, daughter of the late Madeiran potentate, who had shown him family papers suggesting the possibility of western access to the Indies – and given him an entrée to the Portuguese court.

Columbus presented the vigorous new king, João II, Isabella's cousin, with his vision of a world-changing voyage.

THE *MANIKONGO* OF KONGO AND EL HOMBRE OF PORTUGAL

João was a good fit for Columbus: as great-nephew of the Navigator, he had accompanied his father Afonso the African on his conquests. Inheriting an overextended crown aged twenty-six, betrayed by over-mighty grandees, he beheaded one cousin, the duke of Braganza, and invited another, the duke of Viseu, to his chamber for 'an act of private justice': there he personally gutted Viseu before killing all his associates. No wonder Isabella always called him El Hombre; for the Portuguese he was O Príncipe Perfeito.

In 1482, he built a castle on the Gold Coast, São Jorge da Mina (The Mine, still standing), as a base for the gold trade which now provided a quarter of royal revenue.* Around 8,000 ounces of gold a year were sent to Lisbon, rising to 25,000. The Portuguese inserted themselves into the local slave trade, buying around 500 slaves a year from Oba Ewuare's Benin. Some were sold through Elmina or Cape Verde to Akan kings of Denkyira, who used them as porters and labourers; others were sold to Europeans to work on São Tomé, Madeira and Canaria.

While Isabella fought Granada, El Hombre dispatched a courtier, Diogo Cão, to push further south, where he penetrated the Congo River and heard of the powerful Kongo kingdom inland. Cão started to nego-tiate with the *manikongo* Nzinga a Nkuwu, who saw the Portuguese as useful allies. In 1491, Nzinga gave João II's delegation a magnificent welcome – 3,000 warriors with bows and parrot-feathered headdresses, dancing to drums and ivory trumpets, who escorted them to his capital

---

* It was far from a conquest: the Portuguese started building on territory controlled by feuding Akan warlords. João negotiated with an Akan *omahene* (king), Kwamena Ansa, a vassal of the small kingdom of Egyafo, who impressed the Portuguese with the amount of gold he was wearing in bracelets and necklaces. But when Kwamena saw the Portuguese building on a sacred cliff, his archers and swordsmen wearing crocodile helmets forced them to retreat and build on land he specified.

Mbanza. There, holding court, he agreed to an alliance with Lisbon in return for his own baptism, taking the Christian name João I of Kongo, while his son Nzinza a Mbemba became Afonso. Their vision of Catholicism was a syncretic merging with their own religious customs, a royal cult linked to the sacred power of the *manikongo*, suffused in baKongo spirituality. When Portuguese priests demanded he dismiss his harem, João changed his mind, but his son Afonso, a regional governor in his thirties, went on to study Catholicism. On his father's death in 1505, aided by his mother, Afonso bid for the throne and defeated his anti-Christian brother in a battle in which he was aided by a vision of St James. Creating a Portuguese-style nobility with titles, family crests and Christian religious-military orders, he learned to read, built schools for biblical studies and founded a capital of stone palaces and churches. Using Portuguese muskets and horses, he expanded his kingdom, keeping some of his captured slaves to work on his own plantations, giving hundreds to the king in Lisbon while selling thousands to Portuguese merchants.

But this was not the only choice for African kings. Oba Esigie of Benin traded captives and pepper with the Portuguese, but devised a wiser relationship, strictly maintaining his independence.*

In 1488 El Hombre sent a squire, Bartolomeu Dias, to sail round Africa's southern tip, which he named Cape of Storms (later Cape of Good Hope), opening a route to the spicy riches of the Indian Ocean – just at the moment when Columbus may have proposed his own voyage in the opposite direction – though there is no evidence he spoke to João. But the Iberian courts were one big vicious family. João had just married his son to Isabella's eldest daughter – so Columbus moved on to the Trastámarans. Around 1482, he had arrived in Seville to find a place to educate his son, visiting the Franciscan convent La Rábida, where he met the brilliant, well-connected friar Antonio de Marchena, who encouraged the idea of sailing to India across the Ocean Sea (Atlantic) – enabling a Last World Emperor to conquer Jerusalem. This was Ferdinand, who as king of Aragon had a claim to Jerusalem (a fief of Naples). Marchena introduced him to the aristocrats who launched him at court.

Columbus dispatched his brother to propose the plan to the new

---

* In 1504, when Esigie's father Oba Ozolua died, two of his sons fought for the throne; the neighbouring Igala rebelled and invaded. But Prince Esigie was advised by his mother, Idia, who served as his consigliera and priestess in his campaign to destroy the brother and the invaders, for which he rewarded her with a new title of *Iyoba*, queen mother. The *Iyoba* received her own capital, regiments and court, but she was forbidden to see her son again. Perhaps the beautiful bronze bust of Idia's face – now in a Berlin museum – was not only for religious purposes. Perhaps Esigie missed his mother.

English king, Henry Tudor. Insecurely established and notoriously miserly, Henry demurred, thus missing an opportunity to create an earlier English empire. Columbus therefore trailed after the Spanish monarchs. Just after the birth of her youngest daughter Catalina, Isabella listened to the fascinating and frequently preposterous Genoan. Often she and Ferdinand burst out laughing at his performances, moments he mentioned proudly in his letters.

Just as the monarchs called an end to their crusade, leaving Muhammad XII with Granada as a tributary city state, he defied his Christian patrons. They moved in for the kill. As they besieged the city, Isabella resided in an almost caliphal tent in camp. When she went to view the battlements, Arab knights sortied out; she watched as 600 were killed. Granadans were now eating 'horses, dogs, cats'. Finally the amir negotiated peace with the monarchs' general, Gonzalo Fernández de Córdoba, who spoke fluent Arabic.

On 2 January 1492, Isabella, dressed theatrically in Arab *morisca* style in *al-juba* (an all-embracing cloak), knee-length skirt, long sleeves, brocaded silk, accompanied by Ferdinand and their son Juan, themselves in Arab gear, together with their retinue, including the white-haired Columbus, watched Muhammad XII ride out towards them. The amir doffed his hat, unstirrupped one foot and leaned forward to kiss the queen's hand, until she magnanimously waved this aside and handed over his son El Infantico Ahmed, receiving in return 400 Christian slaves and the city keys. After taking his leave, Muhammad paused at the top of the hill – the Moor's Last Sigh – to look back on 700 years of al-Andalus as the Catholics celebrated mass. While the Granadan nobility sailed for Morocco, the Trastámarans now had around 400,000 Muslims to add to their 150,000 Jews.[*]

Appreciating the feverish millenarian exhilaration of this moment, Columbus requested an audience. Finally he had timed it perfectly.

ANACAONA, THE ADMIRAL AND THE QUEEN

In the Santa Fé camp, awaiting their entrance into Granada, the monarchs listened to Columbus' magical vision of an oceanic empire, and Ferdinand as the Last World Emperor and King of Jerusalem. While the Portuguese were coining gold in Guinea, Isabella had only the Canaries.

[*] The Granadan aristocracy included a courtier, Moulay Ali al-Rashid, his wife, the former Spanish slave Zohra Fernandez, and their daughter Aisha, who would become the pirate queen of the Mediterranean.

The monarchs were minded to back Columbus, but the expulsion of the Moors encouraged a radical solution to the Jewish problem, which may have been Ferdinand's idea. They asked Torquemada to draft an order of expulsion for all Jews. The spirit was not entirely new: the Crusades had launched a spree of Jewish massacres. English, French and Austrian Jews had already been expelled. The plague had unleashed a spasm of anti-Jewish violence, and there had been a Castilian massacre in 1391. But Spain was home to the world's biggest Jewish community.

'Why do you act in this way against your subjects?' asked their Jewish courtier Abravanel. 'Impose strong taxes on us!'

'Do you believe this comes from me?' protested Isabella. 'It is the Lord who put this idea into the king's heart.' The Jewish leaders tried again with Ferdinand, who blamed God and wife. 'We worked hard without success,' recalled Abravanel. 'It was the queen who stood behind him and hardened his resolve.' He offered 30,000 ducats in return for withdrawing the expulsion decree.

'Judas once sold the son of God for thirty pieces of silver,' cried Torquemada, laying a crucifix before the monarchs. 'Your majesties think of selling him for a second time for 30,000! Well, here he is, sell him!'

On 31 March 1492, just after the monarchs had taken up residence in Granada's Alhambra Palace, they issued their decree 'send[ing] all Jews out of our kingdoms' and ordering that they should 'never return'. Either they must convert or they must leave, without exception, in four months' time. Confronted by the most traumatic experience in Jewish history between the fall of the Jerusalem Temple and the Holocaust, many Jews including their leader Seneor chose to convert. But tens of thousands (including the family of this author) refused to betray their faith, first losing all their property – either it was stolen or they were forced to sell – then leaving el-Sefarad, their homeland for over a thousand years. Some, suffering the predations of people smugglers who prey on migrants, embarked on voyages to Islamic Morocco or to the mercantile cities of Italy and Flanders. But they found the greatest safety in two eastern kingdoms: in Poland–Lithuania, which, due to its own spirit of idiosyncratic tolerance, starting with the Statute of Kalisz back in 1264, was now the freest country in Europe, and in the Ottoman sultanate, Mehmed having already invited Jews to settle in Constantinople. His son welcomed the Sephardi Jews. 'You call Ferdinand a wise ruler,' observed Bayezid II, 'but he's impoverished his own country and enriched mine.' Thousands settled in Constantinople and Thessalonica. But initially many Jews, including this author's ancestors, tramped across the border to Lisbon, paying a tax to João.

Exhilarated by this stringent anti-Jewish action, on 17 April the monarchs recalled Columbus, who after praising them for expelling 'the Jews from all of your kingdoms' and unleashing the Inquisition, again proposed his voyage. Finally he was commissioned to sail, receiving 10 per cent of revenues in perpetuity and the titles admiral of the Ocean Sea, viceroy and governor of any lands he might discover, all hereditary because he hoped to found a dynasty. After the death of his wife, he brought up his son Diego, but his new teen girlfriend Beatriz Enríquez also delivered a son, whom they named Fernando after the king.

On 3 August, Columbus set sail in three little ships with ninety sailors of many races, including Pedro Alonso Niño, a free African, an experienced pilot. On 12 October, they struck land in the Bahamas, then sailed on to Cuba and Haiti, where Columbus encountered local peoples: friendly and peaceful ones whom the Spanish called Taínos, and hostile and martial ones whom they called Caribs. The admiral was convinced this was the Indies and so called all the inhabitants *los Indos*.*

Isabella ruled that her Christian free subjects could not be enslaved. Columbus initially applied this principle to the peaceful Taínos, who were instead forced to work as indentured labourers while the cannibalistic Caribs were enslaved. Returning home to report to the monarchs with gold artefacts and a group of Taínos, he stopped off at Lisbon and boasted of his finds to a jealous King João, who considered having him liquidated. Back in Spain, he presented his treasures and prisoners to the monarchs, who were excited: 'We have recently brought about the discovery of some islands and mainland in the Ocean Sea that's part of the Indies.' Appointing the two Columbus boys as pages to the heir Don Juan, Isabella sent the admiral back with seventeen ships, funded by money taken from the Jews, filled with colonists and soldiers to found a colony. On his four voyages, Columbus landed at Jamaica, Costa Rica and Panama, but Hispaniola (Haiti/Dominican Republic) was his headquarters, where he appointed his brother Bartolomeu as *adelantado* – military governor – and where they founded a town, Santo Domingo. But first Hispaniola, divided into chieftainships, had to be conquered; in response, the *kasike* of Maguana, Caonabo, tried to destroy the Spanish.

---

* This was an ancient world of connected islands settled first in the seventh millennium BC. Around 500 BC, as new DNA research shows, they were invaded by conquerors from the mainland who massacred them: the Taínos of Haiti, Cuba and Jamaica, ruled by chieftains (*kasike* in Taíno, *cacique* in Spanish), were their descendants. The islands were known vaguely to the Mexica. While the Spanish believed there were millions of Taínos, it is likely they were far fewer, perhaps no more than tens of thousands. The Caribs gave their name to the sea and to the word cannibal, given their taste for eating enemies. Bahama, Cuba, Haiti, Jamaica were Columbus' version of their Taíno names.

Quickly the Columbuses exploited rivalries to recruit Taíno auxiliaries, while Spanish men seized local women as sex slaves or partners. The Columbuses led 200 Spanish troops and Taíno auxiliaries with war dogs against Caonabo, who was captured but died on the voyage to Spain. His widow, Anacaona (Golden Flower), fled back to the court of her brother Bohechío, *kasike* of the western Xaragua. Together they made peace with Bartolomeu Columbus and recognized Isabella. When her brother died, Anacaona ruled as *kasike*.

Columbus was determined to make a fortune. Nicknamed Pharaoh by his underlings, he turned out to be a thin-skinned, narcissistic tyrant. He sent 4,000 enslaved Caribs for sale in Spain, explaining that the settlements could be 'paid for in slaves taken from these cannibals; we think they'll be finer than other slaves once freed from their inhumanity'. Isabella disapproved, fearing that enslavement would undermine evangelization, but already Columbus' depredations were provoking native resistance and Castilian resentment. Taíno rebellions were repressed. Rushing back to justify himself to Isabella, he mixed Christian mysticism with auric promises and whining insecurity, denouncing her courtiers who 'criticize and belittle the enterprise'. The monarchs backed Columbus: 'Your Highnesses' reply was to laugh and say I shouldn't worry about anything.' Columbus returned to Hispaniola. But his misrule now provoked Castilian mutinies.

Finally Isabella sent a courtier, Francisco de Bobadilla, to find out what was going on and to help Columbus. Bobadilla arrived to find a heart of darkness – hanged bodies swinging from gibbets, the Columbuses hunting Spanish rebels, lording it over estates of Taíno slaves, cutting off tongues, ears and noses. The tropical colonies became a sexual playground for Spaniards: Columbus admitted their paedophilic depravity – 'A woman can be had for a hundred castellanos . . . and there are plenty of merchants on the lookout for girls of nine or ten years old, currently the most expensive group.' Columbus was arrested and sent back to Spain. His slaving offended against Isabella's morality. 'What power does my admiral have to give any of my vassals away?' she asked, though she allowed the sale of more slaves while ordering, 'You will ensure that the Indians are well treated as vassals.' Instead these 'vassals' were installed as forced labour on plantations – *encomienda* – for Columbus and his henchmen. Yet Bobadilla proved no better. In 1502, Isabella sent Nicolás de Ovando, who arrived with thirty ships carrying 2,500 settlers. Among these were two settlers who would play major roles in the Americas: a young friar, Bartolomé de las Casas, and an ambitious youngster from Extremadura, Francisco Pizarro. The latter's cousin, Hernán Cortés, missed the trip because he was caught in bed with a married woman and managed to fall out of the window – but he soon joined them. Ovando planted sugar cane; the Taínos were set to work on estates, treated as sex slaves and killed, often for little reason.

In 1503, Ovando and 300 solders approached the realm of Anacaona, *kasike* of the Xaragua, who welcomed them in style, but something went wrong. Fifty Spaniards were killed in the fighting. Anacaona was hanged, her people slaughtered. Ovando's massacres showed his subordinates Pizarro and Cortés how to handle local rulers, but they appalled his priest, de las Casas.

The Taínos were hit by smallpox and other pathogens brought by the Spanish, to which they had no resistance. They perished fast, ceasing to exist as a separate race, though DNA analysis of today's inhabitants reveals they interbred with the Spanish. Only their words – canoe, hammock, hurricane and tobacco – survived. The Spanish were infected with syphilis, which they brought back to Europe where it raced through the population.*

When she learned that Columbus had been arrested, Isabella released him and reimbursed him, but he was bitter. 'I have established the sovereignty of the king and queen over a new world,' he wrote in one of the first uses of the phrase 'new world', 'so that Spain once reputed to be a poor kingdom is now among the richest.' This was not true. While Portugal was booming, little gold had been found in the Caribbean. So many Taínos died that Ovando imported the first black slaves from Spain.

Back in Castile, Isabella remained grateful to Columbus, dispatching him again with his brother Bartolomeu and son Fernando on a final expedition, though he was banned from returning to Hispaniola. He made it to Honduras. On the voyage, the admiral sent Bartolomeu to capture a Maya trading canoe from Yucatán, looting it then sending it back, allowing its survivors to carry news of the arrival of pasty, red-bearded giants that would reach the ears of the Supreme Speaker of the Mexica at that empire's zenith.

---

* The disease – passed by sexual contact and manifesting in three states, starting with genital sores and culminating many years later in facial swellings and decay along with degeneration of the nervous system leading to insanity – was first recorded during the French invasion of Naples two or three years later. The Neapolitans called it the French disease, the French called it the Italian disease. One of the few diseases named after a fictional character, the name was coined by the Veronese physician Girolamo Fracastoro for his syphilitic shepherd boy in his poem *Syphilis sive morbus gallicus* (Syphilis or The French Disease). It raged for the next four centuries, cured only by the invention of antibiotics. On the islands, Columbus saw 'men and women with a half-burned weed in their hands, being herbs they're accustomed to smoke'. His sailors were the first Europeans to sample tobacco.

After being stranded in Jamaica for a year, Columbus returned to Castile in November 1504 in exhausted despair. 'Today,' he told Isabella, 'I don't even own a rooftile in Castile. If I want to eat or sleep, I must go to a tavern . . . I've been treated as a foreigner. I was in your court seven years and everyone I talked to about this enterprise treated it as a joke. Now even tailors are asking to make discoveries. I came to serve you when I was twenty-eight and now I don't have a single hair that isn't white. I'm sick.' He was right: even tailors were becoming 'discoverers', including his Florentine friend Amerigo Vespucci, a Medici protégé, who in 1502, after two voyages, realized that the Indies should 'properly be called a New World since our ancestors had absolutely no knowledge of it'.[*]

Isabella's empire was challenged by João el Hombre, who claimed it was rightfully Portuguese, but the queen was backed by her ally, Rodrigo Borgia, the Valencian cardinal who, thanks in part to her backing, got lucky. 'I am pope! I am pope!' Rodrigo cried when he won the election in 1492. As Alexander VI, he was determined to make the Borgias into European potentates – and to have fun in the process.

BONFIRE OF THE VANITIES:
POPE ALEXANDER AND THE BORGIAS' CHESTNUT ORGY

Alexander VI was 'handsome, with a very cheerful countenance and genial bearing, gifted with the quality of being a smooth talker. Beautiful women were attracted to him and excited by him in quite a remarkable way, more strongly than "iron is drawn to a magnet".' Even as a young cardinal, he had been reprimanded by Pius II for taking part in an 'orgy' in a Sienese garden with 'several women wholly given over to worldly vanities . . . We've heard the dance was indulged in all wantonness.' As vice-chancellor to five pontiffs he was an expert in the dark arts of Roman power and pleasure: he had four children by his long-time paramour Vannozza dei Cattanei (a Mantuan girl who later owned a Roman tavern named The Cow).

---

[*] Vespucci's grandfather, also Amerigo, was chancellor of Florence under Lorenzo de' Medici the Magnificent and he himself had worked for Lorenzo di Pierfrancesco de' Medici, who sent him to run his Seville office. There he first helped to finance Columbus' voyages, then became a sailor himself on voyages recorded in his published letters to the Medici, before King Ferdinand appointed him to run the House of Contracts in Seville. In 1507 a German cartographer, Martin Waldseemüller, named the continent after him, a honour he may never have known about. The oddity is that Waldseemüller used Vespucci's first name: why did he not call the new continent Vespuccia? It is just as resonant as America.

Alexander did not have long to wheedle and carve out a family fiefdom, quickly promoting his eldest son Giovanni to *gonfaloniere* of the papal armies and procuring a dukedom for him from the Catholic monarchs while raising his eighteen-year-old son Cesare to cardinal scarlet. He cut expenses and lived austerely, existing on that Catalan delicacy the sardine, but he loved women. At the age of sixty-two, the pope fell in love with Giuliana Farnese, then eighteen, *La Bella Giulia*, who, nicknamed the 'bride of Christ', moved into a palace with the pope's daughter Lucrezia. At the Palazzo Apostolico, Borgia parties usually featured lascivious cardinals (some ancient, but many of them teenagers) and young prostitutes playing ingenious games designed to show off the latter to the former. When Cesare organized a party at the Vatican, fifty girls danced naked, then chestnuts were scattered which the courtesans, illuminated by strategically placed candelabra, 'picked up, creeping on hands and knees, while the Pope, Cesare and his sister Lucrezia watched'. This was according to the papal master of ceremonies Johann Burchard, who, though keen to blacken the Borgias, was describing a scene that might seem believable at a frat-house party but not at a Renaissance court. The games ended with a papal gang bang. 'Prizes were announced for those who could perform the act most often with the courtesans.'

The pope tried to keep his Spanish patrons happy, yet when Isabella demanded he persecute and expel the Jews in Rome, Alexander refused. Ferdinand and Isabella were determined to hold on to southern Italy, but to the north a young French king was equally determined to reclaim Naples, an ambition encouraged by the Borgias' enemy, Cardinal Giulio della Rovere, the nephew of the late Pope Sixtus. Stuck in the middle, the Borgias chose what seemed to them the only possible option: duplicity.

Alexander's position had been complicated by the death at the age of forty-three of Lorenzo the Magnificent, who on his deathbed received a Dominican priest, Girolamo Savonarola, prior of San Marco, who listened to El Magnifico confess his sins. The forty-year-old Savonarola, tiny, cadaverous, bald, hook-nosed with droopy lips, bushy eyebrows and green eyes that 'sometimes gave forth red flashes', was already the author of *On Contempt for the World* and the deliverer of sex-obsessed sermons that warned against the evils of sodomy and adultery. Savonarola prophesied the Sword of the Lord loomed over Florence and warned that armies would cross the Alps like 'barbers armed with gigantic razors'.

Sure enough, in autumn 1494 the French army hoved into view

under the youthful King Charles VIII, who ruled a kingdom that, after a hundred years of conflict with England, had emerged as a single state, the most populous in Europe (15 million people, against England's 3.7). Charles was 'hideous and small, his ill-made mouth hanging open and hands twitching with spasmodic movements', but the French indulged his womanizing, calling him *L'Affable*.

Pietro de' Medici, twenty-two years old, Lorenzo's eldest – and stupidest – appeased King Charles by surrendering Pisa and Livorno, which so outraged the *Signoria* and the people that the Medicis were driven out of Florence. When the French arrived, Savonarola hailed Charles as 'Chosen of God'. Crying, 'Repent, O Florence, while there is still time,' Savonarola asked God's advice: 'The Lord has driven my ship into open waters. The wind drives me forward. I spoke last night to the Lord: "I will speak – but why need I meddle with the government?"'

'If you make Florence a holy city,' answered God, 'you must give her a government which favours virtue.'

To rapt and terrified congregations, Savonarola fulminated: 'Behold the Sword has descended; the scourge has fallen. It is coming. It has come!' His high-pitched screech of a voice was so terrifying that Michelangelo said he could still hear it forty years later. 'It's not I who preach,' claimed the Dominican, 'but God who speaks through me!' The Messenger of God warned Florentines to show virtue, desist from gambling, carnivals, scent, cosmetics and sex, reject the Medicis and the Borgias – and the pagans Plato and Aristotle. In a frenzy of apocalyptic commands, he and his followers, the Wailers, presided over a terror of virtue. His reign demonstrates how a small but determined clique of self-righteous, self-selected extremists can dominate a society, rewarding their supporters with spoils and destroying those deemed unvirtuous – a template for authoritarian ideologies ever since. They can always be foiled by the will of the majority, but they flourish when others fail to organize or lose their courage. Savonarola's 'blessed bands' – posses of righteous children and teenagers – forced Florentines to kneel, pray and fast and to sing hymns aloud, then shaved their own heads as virtuous signals. Attractive women were denounced as prostitutes – 'pieces of meat with eyes', said Savonarola – and were whipped in public; fashionable women retired to convents. Wailers smashed mirrors, fans, rouge pots and cosmetics. Books and paintings were burned in 'bonfires of the vanities' on a pyramidal scaffold.

Leaving Savonarola as sacred dictator of Florence, Charles, dubbing himself *Le Victeur*, marched southwards, occupying Rome, where Cardinal della Rovere urged him to depose Alexander. Instead Borgia held his nerve, encouraging Charles to take Naples, which proved a victory too far. Alexander negotiated support from the Habsburgs and Trastámarans. *Le Victeur* had overreached. Charles fled back to France, leaving among his splendid belongings a pornographic 'book in which were painted nude images of the king's mistresses'.

Now Alexander was ready to deal with Savonarola, whose hold on Florence was wavering. Alexander excommunicated him. Savonarola threatened his critics: 'Seats are prepared in Hell. Tell them the rod has come!' Challenged to prove his relationship with God by walking through fire, he was saved by a rainstorm, but the people then arrested him. He was tortured with the *strappado*, found guilty of heresy, then hanged in chains and burned; his 'legs and arms gradually dropped off' until only ashes remained. The Medicis longed to return but a rival, Piero Soderini, opposed to their regal style, reasserted republican power, his policies devised by the twenty-nine-year-old Niccolò Machiavelli, playful writer and cynical diplomat.

Alexander planned a kingdom for his eldest son Giovanni, duke of Gandía – until the young man was found in the Tiber with his throat slit and nine stab wounds. It revealed something about the family that among the endless list of suspects were two of the duke's own brothers, Joffre, incensed at fraternal cuckolding, and Cesare, who was jealous of the paternal favourite and also sleeping with his wife. Alexander was broken: 'We loved the duke of Gandía more than anyone else in the world; we'd have given seven tiaras to recall him to life.'

Cesare stepped forward, renouncing the scarlet and soaring like a vicious star. Appointed *gonfaloniere* and duke of Romagna, he was exceptional – flashy, indefatigable, murderous, priapic, fathering at least eleven children. His ambition was boundless, his motto 'Caesar or nothing'. Behind all this lurked the stiletto and the garrotte: as Machiavelli put it, Cesare believed it was 'better to be feared than loved'.* Even his proud father took the view that 'The duke is a good-hearted man but he can't bear an insult.' When Alexander told him to tolerate animadversion, Cesare replied, 'The Romans can publish slanders but I'll teach them to repent.' Murder was his tool: 'Every night four or five men are discovered assassinated , bishops and others, so that all Rome trembles for fear of being murdered by the Duke.' When his brother-in-law Alfonso, duke of Bisceglie, cousin of Ferdinand and Isabella, crossed the family – who no longer needed a Spanish ally now they

---

* Later, in retirement, Machiavelli used his experience of Cesare Borgia and Ferdinand of Spain to write *The Prince*, his guide to the practice of power. It was not published until after his death.

were allied to France – his Spanish hitman Don Micheletto strangled him in the Vatican.

Cesar conquered his principality of Romagna, moving so fast that 'he arrives in one place before it's known he has left another'. Micheletto strangled some captured commanders and bisected others: 'Ramiro this morning was found in two pieces on the public square,' wrote Machiavelli. 'It has pleased the Prince who shows he can make and unmake men as he likes.'*

Yet Borgia success was shallow, dependent on the ageing Alexander, who in May 1499 orchestrated a further French invasion by the new king Louis XII in return for arranging Cesare's marriage to Charlotte of Navarre. Louis made Cesare duc de Valentinois, nicknamed Valentino for his love affairs, but the king disdained his preening as 'vainglory and foolish bombast'. On his wedding night, Cesare boasted he gave himself 'eight marks for his virility', though actually the young syphilitic required aphrodisiacs – which were secretly replaced by laxatives, an *escamotage* that led to a very different sort of ejaculation. The syphilis started to rot Cesare's face, eating his nose until he was forced to wear a leather mask to conceal the decay.

Queen Isabella lectured Alexander with 'great love' on her 'displeasure and disgust' at his outrageous 'parties', but he delivered on the things that mattered, so favouring Castile over Portugal in his bull *Inter caetera* that the two had to negotiate a more realistic carve-up of the world in the treaty of Tordesillas. Now the Catholic Monarchs had bigger plans.

Isabella was negotiating a double marriage with the Habsburgs that would create the first world empire.

---

* Cesare appointed Leonardo da Vinci as architect and chief engineer. While devising new fortresses and military vehicles that resembled tanks and helicopters, Leonardo also sketched Cesare himself.

Habsburgs and Ottomans

ARCH-SLEEPYHEAD OF THE ROMAN EMPIRE – AND JUANA THE MAD

In August 1496, Isabella escorted her sixteen-year-old daughter Juana on to a carrack at the northern port of Laredo and then watched her sail away to Flanders to marry Philip the Handsome, duke of Burgundy. Almost simultaneously her only son Juan would wed Philip's sister Margaret.*

The two foreign spouses were the children of Kaiser Maximilian, 'the German Hercules', strapping, blond, blue-eyed, his beard concealing a prominent jaw. He was a late developer, not speaking until he was nine and growing up in a family in crisis.

His father, Frederick III the Fat, the same kaiser married and crowned in Rome forty years earlier, had endured decades of catastrophe, surviving with impressive serenity a desperate siege of Vienna, which he eventually lost. 'Happiness,' he said, 'is to forget what cannot be recovered.' Nicknamed Arch-Sleepyhead of the Roman Empire, he ate prodigiously, prognosticated endlessly, collected mouse droppings and tended flowers, boring his vivacious Portuguese wife. But his motto – 'Hold the measure and look to the end' – was abundantly justified. Outlasting all his enemies, Arch-Sleepyhead reclaimed his territories, promoting the House of Austria with the acrostic AEIOU (*Alles Erdreich Ist Österreich Untertan* – The Whole World is Subject to Austria) – a dream that Maximilian brought to fruition.†

Nothing like Arch-Sleepyhead, Maximilian grew up into an athletic gallant with a taste for what he called 'being naked with women',

---

* The queen's eldest daughter, also Isabella, was married to Manuel of Portugal, while her youngest Catalina would marry Arthur, Prince of Wales, son of that cadaverous miser Henry VII. Arthur died within five months and she married his younger brother, Henry VIII. She was known to the English as Catherine of Aragon.

† When Frederick was seventy-seven, arteriosclerosis led to gangrene in his leg; his doctor performed a successful amputation, regarded as a medical triumph – though he died two months later. The leg was buried with him in his magnificent tomb in St Stephen's, Vienna.

adding, 'I have danced, tilted lances, paid court to ladies. Mostly I have laughed heartily.' This tireless extrovert galloped across Europe to claim the hand of the greatest heiress of the day, Marie the Rich, duchess of Burgundy that encompassed the Low Countries.

Maximilian's marriage made the Habsburgs, producing the essential son, Philip. Mary loved hunting even when pregnant, but she was fatally thrown. Maximilian was bereft, yet his vision of a universal Christian emperor and *Hausmachtpolitik* – family power – was irrepressible. 'After serving God,' he said, 'I place the advancement of my dynasty above all things.' Among his many schemes of family promotion, he decided after the death of his wife that he should be pope and started to bribe cardinals, promising his daughter Margaret that he would 'never again pursue naked women' and signing off, 'Maxi, your good father, future pope'. It was not to be, but this multifaceted empire demanded perennial wars, with the German Hercules fearlessly modelling his exquisite gold-trimmed armour.* The struggle between Habsburgs and Valois, Germany and France, for the strategic Burgundian borderlands would extend into the twentieth century, but it began now. Maximilian fought France, he fought in Italy and in Germany – seventeen campaigns altogether. But war requires money, not just courage. There were many soldiers but only one Fugger the Rich.

Always broke, the kaiser depended on Jacob Fugger, a dour red-headed banker from Augsburg, who started in textiles but then persuaded the king of Hungary to leverage his silver mines: Fugger paid a sum to market the silver. Focusing on the Habsburgs, he gave loans to Arch-Sleepyhead during his dark days and then helped Maximilian pay off more loans using his copper mines. Fugger's handling of Maximilian made him probably the richest commoner in Europe, the first millionaire. Yet Hercules' greatest success was a double splicing of his children Philip and Margaret to Isabella's Juana and Juan. Such marriages sacrificed royal children – this was especially true for daughters, who were sent abroad to marry foreign strangers, never to see their parents again and most likely to perish in childbirth – for the sake of power that was also a biological gamble.

If Philip had failed to produce children and Juan had succeeded, the Spaniards could claim Austria. Instead the Infante Juan, Isabella's 'Angel', was said to be so attracted to Margaret that he exhausted himself

---

* The suit was crafted by the famous dynasty of armourers, the Helmschmieds of Augsburg. Maximilian eccentrically gave Henry VIII of England a helmet with a face, modelled on himself, with his long nose and spectacles, and topped off with a pair of ram's horns. Yet armour was already an obsolete fashion: in battle, bullets could penetrate it.

sexually, dying after six months, supposedly of excessive fornication but more likely of smallpox.* Isabella was poleaxed by the loss of Angel.

His sister's marriage was almost too successful, but in a different way. Juana, well-educated, red-haired like her mother, was obsessional and free-thinking. As a girl, she challenged Catholicism. Her mother 'treated' her refusal to take confession with torture, prescribing *la cuerda*, being suspended with weights hanging off her legs and arms. It did not work. Now living in Bruges, Juana watched Philip strut from 'from banquet to banquet, lady to lady', and was outraged by his promiscuity. He in turn was infuriated by her criticism. Juana clung pathetically to her four female African slaves, who shared her bed.† When she gave birth to a girl, Philip snapped, 'As this one is a girl, put her in the archduchess's accounts; when God gives us a son, put him in mine.' More pregnancies followed. For the birth of the heir, Charles, Juana was at a ball when her waters broke and the baby was born in a Ghent latrine, though brought up in Burgundy; a second son, Ferdinand, was raised in Spain.

Juana and Philip were now heirs to Spain as well as to Austria and Burgundy. A trip to Spain was overdue, but when the young couple arrived Isabella's attempts to force Philip to follow her anti-French policy angered him. Fearing that her mother wanted to break up her marriage, Juana collapsed under the stress. 'She sleeps poorly, eats little, she is sad and very thin,' warned the doctors, as the infanta camped outside on the ramparts, refusing to come in. The destructive clash of state and family was being driven, not by cold-hearted statesmen, but by a woman: Isabella. Philip returned to Burgundy, but when Juana joined him she was so jealous she scratched one of his girlfriends with scissors. Now she only trusted her slaves.

'I'm not happy with the slaves,' he ordered. 'Expel them.'

Juana exploded, threatening to kill his messenger and refusing to eat. Philip locked himself in his rooms. She banged on the doors.

'If you don't do what I say,' warned Philip, 'I'll leave you.'

'I'll let myself die', she cried, 'rather than do anything you ask.'

'Then do whatever you want!' he shouted, convinced she was insane.

---

* The monarchs in Europe used this story as a warning against excessive sex. In this macho environment, ejaculatory bombast was part of royal promotion: when Louis XII married Mary Tudor, eighteen-year-old sister of Henry VIII, he 'boasted of having ejaculated five times in their first encounter', at which a contemporary noted, 'One must assume he has just dug five graves with his hoe.' He did die after three months. Most of these sex deaths were actually of smallpox.

† There were now many enslaved Africans serving in the Portuguese and Spanish courts: each of Isabella's children had Africans in their entourages. Juana's sister Catherine arrived in London with John Blancke, who served Henry VIII as a trumpeter at the Tudor court.

Hearing of this, Isabella and Ferdinand both fell ill with fever; he re-covered but she died at fifty-three. Juana now became queen of Castile. She and Philip sailed to claim the kingdom. They were shipwrecked in England, staying with the old king Henry VII and Juana's sister Catherine, widow of Prince Arthur. Henry watched Juana carefully. 'She seemed fine, restrained and gracious,' he noted, 'although her husband [Philip] and those with him made her out to be mad.'

When they reached Spain, her father and husband decided Juana was indeed insane, agreeing that if 'the said most serene Queen, either from her own choice or from being persuaded by other persons, should attempt to meddle in the government, both would prevent it'. It is now impossible to gauge how much her confinement was a male conspiracy, how much manic depression. She was ill-treated: when she refused to eat, Ferdinand ordered her whipped, then, entrusting Spain to Philip, he sailed for Naples.

Despite her 'insanity', the couple were still sleeping together. In September 1506, after hard partying, Philip died either of typhoid, sun-stroke or alcohol: Ferdinand returned to rule Castile. While Philip was being embalmed, Juana, who was pregnant with a sixth child, seized the body and took it with her to Tordesillas Palace, refusing to bury him and travelling with the body. But, however mad Queen Juana was, the biological gamble of Maximilian's marriage alliances paid off for both families in ways they could not yet imagine.

Ferdinand ruled the expanding empire alone. America now attracted shiploads of aspiring conquistadors, often energetic and talented, if voracious and ruthless, who went to the Indies to 'serve God and the King and get rich', objectives in which, like the Crusaders, they saw no contradiction. In 1504, trained as a notary, Cortés settled in Santo Domingo, earning an *encomienda* of forced native labourers, then attaching himself to Diego Velázquez, henchman of the Columbuses. Appealing to Ferdinand, Diego Columbus won back the hereditary viceroyalty. In 1511, Velázquez, governor of Cuba, embarked on that island's conquest, assisted by Cortés. Taíno resistance was led by a Haitian *kasike* named Hatuey who had fled with his men by canoe to Cuba. Brandishing gold, Hatuey warned the Cuban Taínos, 'Here's the God the Spaniards wor-ship. For these they kill . . . they speak to us of an immortal soul and of their eternal rewards and punishments, yet they steal our belongings, seduce our women, rape our daughters.' In the course of a three-year war, Velázquez crushed Hatuey, eventually burning him alive, and, in one atrocity among many, slaughtered 2,000 Taínos who had merely gathered to gawp at the Spanish and their horses.

The chaplain on these killing sprees was the angular, bald, intense Dominican friar Bartolomé de las Casas, who had received his own estate on Hispaniola, but now he declared, 'I saw here cruelty on a scale no living being has ever seen or expects to see.' He went on to denounce the cruelty to King Ferdinand, who recalled Diego Columbus. It was not enough: de las Casas himself sailed for home to see the king. Yet the conquest had now reached the mainland.

Pizarro joined one of these expeditions led by Vasco Núñez de Balboa, who founded the future Cartagena (Colombia), then crossed the Isthmus of Panama where, falling to his knees in wonder, he was the first European to see the ocean he called the South Sea. Balboa, *adelantado* of the South Sea, fought the natives, converting some to Christianity, but clashed with his ferocious superior, Pedrarias Dávila, known at court as the Jouster, who, arriving in America, had fallen ill and been buried alive in a coffin, only rescued by a servant who heard shuffling within. Now Dávila, who always travelled with the coffin, suborned Pizarro and ordered him to arrest Balboa, whom he then had beheaded. Pizarro now had a patron. When Dávila founded Panama City, Pizarro was its first mayor – and he started to hear of a vastly rich kingdom to the south.

In Italy too, Ferdinand was triumphant, recovering Naples and Sicily. He no longer needed the duplicitous Borgias. It was they who needed him.

'I had foreseen my father's death and made every preparation for it,' Cesare Borgia confided to Machiavelli, 'but I hadn't anticipated that I'd myself be wrestling with death.' In August 1503, Alexander VI and Cesare both fell ill. When Alexander died, his corpse – 'its face changed to the colour of mulberry, covered with blue-black spots, nose swollen, mouth stretched by a double-sized tongue' – was, according to the gleeful Burchard, 'rolled up in a carpet and pummelled' into a narrow coffin. Lucrezia had adored her father: the poet Pietro Bembo saw her after her father's death 'in that dark room, in your black gown, lying weeping'. And Cesare was too ill to prevent the enthronement of his deadliest enemy.

THE BIGGEST BALLS: TWO *TERRIBILES* – JULIUS AND MICHELANGELO

Pugnacious and vindictive, Giuliano della Rovere, nephew of Sextus, chose the name Julius II after Caesar, determined to reconquer papal power, play what he called 'the World Game'* and beautify Rome for the glory of God and the della Roveres. Autocratic and short-tempered, nicknamed *Il Terribile*, he regularly beat his courtiers with his cane. As a cardinal he had fathered a daughter – the shrewd Felice, to whom he entrusted diplomatic negotiations – though his enemies claimed he was 'a great sodomite', and later he was so riddled with syphilis that courtiers had to stop visitors kissing his decaying feet.

First, he outplayed Cesare Borgia, who fled to Spain. 'I won't live in the same rooms that the Borgias lived in,' said Julius, relishing his triumph, 'and I forbid under the pain of excommunication anyone to speak or think of Borgia again – their name must be erased.' But really there was little difference between the Borgias and the della Roveres.

Julius was eager to go to war. 'Expel the barbarians,' he roared. The chief barbarians were the French, who controlled northern Italy, but he also hated the Venetians and coveted Bologna. Creating a crack army of Swiss Guards, funded by Fugger the Rich, he donned papal armour, forcing the hedonist Giovanni de' Medici to march north in his entourage. Julius threatened captured enemies, 'Do it again and I'll hang you.' When he attacked the French in Mirandola, he said, 'Let's see who has the bigger balls, the king of France or I!' before scaling a ladder. In 1506, he took Bologna, returning to Rome as both Caesarian *triumphator* and Christian pontiff. He ordered the destruction of the old St Peter's and its total reconstruction, funded by Fugger. It was designed by Donato Bramante, who devised a five-domed Constantinopolitan scheme very different from the one that was finally built. But Bramante also advised Julius to summon a young artist from Urbino, Raffaello Sanzio.

Urbane and sociable, Raphael, in his late twenties, was the son of the duke of Urbino's artist. Orphaned at eleven, he studied in Florence, where he was inspired by the much older Leonardo da Vinci. In 1508, Julius commissioned him to decorate his Borgia-free apartments on the third floor of the Vatican, starting with the papal library, the Stanza della Segnatura, where his *School of Athens* features Julius as well as Giovanni de' Medici. At the same time, he hired Michelangelo, who had made his

* One of Julius' first decisions was to allow the English prince, Henry, to marry his brother's widow, Catherine of Aragon. The eighteen-year-old Catherine, princess of Wales, had been in limbo since the death of Prince Arthur in 1502. Ferdinand did not want to pay any more dowry; Henry VII, now in his late forties, did not want to repay it, so he decided to marry her himself, but finally both sides agreed another solution. This had its own problems. The Church banned marriage of sister-in-law and brother-in-law as part of its anti-incest, anti-kinship policy. Catherine could marry Henry only if the marriage with Arthur was unconsummated. Once this was agreed, the marriage could go ahead. In 1509, when Henry VII died, Henry VIII married her.

name with his statue of *David* for the republican regime in Florence.

Julius supervised his artists fiercely, managing 'the humours of men of genius', driving them hard, often withholding promised funds. Raphael was genial, Michelangelo irascible. Julius and Michelangelo, both nicknamed *Il Terribile*, sparked off each other. 'It kills you trying to negotiate with this man, who refuses to listen,' grumbled Michelangelo, 'and loads you with the worst insults ever.' Michelangelo demanded total freedom 'to do as I liked'. When Julius was high-handed, Michelangelo, who had received an offer from Sultan Bayezid, threatened to accept and stormed off to Florence, chased by papal guards on horseback. Julius demanded that Florence surrender the artist.

Not risking a war, the Florentines sent him to Bologna. 'You were supposed to come to us,' said Julius. 'You've waited for us to come to you.' The artist knelt for forgiveness. Artists had hitherto been regarded as artisans-cum-engineers. The disadvantage was they were treated like brilliant servants; the advantage was that they were totally uninhibited by the limitations of professional specialization. But Michelangelo demanded that the pontiff treat him with respect – the first artist to win such treatment. Keeping him in Bologna, Julius visited his studios, commissioning a sculpture of himself. Michelangelo asked how to present him.

'Give me a sword,' growled *Papa Terribile*, 'not a pen.'

Julius first commissioned him to build his tomb – a grandiose project that took decades and was never finished – but then he ordered Michelangelo to paint the ceiling of the Sistine Chapel, built by his uncle Sixtus. 'Painting is not my art,' replied Michelangelo, still most at home as sculptor, but Julius bullied and coaxed him into becoming a painter. Michelangelo regarded all his work as an expression of divinity. 'If my rough hammer shapes human aspects,' he wrote, 'out of hard rock, now this one, now that, it is held and guided by Divine Fiat, lending it motion, moving as He chooses.'

In the chapel, Michelangelo built himself wooden scaffolding and lay upside down 140 feet above the floor, painting on to wet plaster nine scenes starting with the beginning of time, dominated by his portrait of God and his divine energy. It took four years, hanging upside down. 'I lead a miserable existence,' he told his father. 'My stomach's squashed under my chin, my beard's pointing at heaven, my chest twists like a harpy. My brush above me all the time dribbles . . .' For all his gifts, he had moments of doubt: 'My painting is dead . . . I'm not a painter.' Julius inspected the work, clambering up the ladders.

Julius' artists watched each other jealously: Michelangelo, now thirty, rough and brawny, tormented, infuriated, homosexual; Raphael debonair, courtly, slim, handsome, lover of his model Margherita Luti known as *La Fornarina*, 'the baker's daughter'. While Raphael lived and dressed in style, Michelangelo looked like a peasant, despite earning huge sums that he spent to build up his family's aristocratic holdings. Leonardo's fame and Raphael's rise exasperated the obstreperous and paranoid Michelangelo, who disdained both, particularly the smooth Raphael nine years his junior: 'All the discords between Pope Julius and me were owing to the envy of Bramante and Raphael.' When Bramante showed Raphael the Sistine Chapel, Michelangelo sneered, 'Raphael had good reason to be envious since what he knew of art, he learned from *me*.'

They tried to avoid each other but met once, Michelangelo brooding alone, Raphael with an entourage. Michelangelo cattily asked if this was the chief of police with his posse, at which Raphael wondered if he had encountered an executioner, cast out from society. Yet Michelangelo's image as a loner is misleading: he lived amid his *brigata* – the brood – a household of assistants and artists whom he helped train and loved as family. He had a gift for friendship with women, his letters to them witty and loving; and when he fell in love with men, his love letters were vulnerable and passionate.

Julius' wars started to go wrong. He lost Bologna and grew a beard to grieve – the one depicted by Raphael. In April 1512, he was defeated by Louis XII of France at Ravenna, where his friend Cardinal de' Medici was captured and almost killed before escaping. Julius sent his daughter Felice – also painted by Raphael – to negotiate with the French, while Medici asked him to use their Spanish allies to retake Florence. Julius agreed. The Spanish stormed the city; Soderini and Machiavelli were overthrown. Cardinal de' Medici and his brother Giuliano returned as the crowds shouted, 'Balls! Balls! *Palle! Palle!*', referring to the family's heraldic emblem. The Medici were back.

The balls were spinning. When Julius died of syphilis, Giovanni de Medici was elected pope as Leo X and the cardinals burst out of the Sistine Chapel shouting 'Balls! Balls!'

LUTHER AND LEO:
THE DEVIL'S FAECES AND THE POPE'S ELEPHANT

'God's given us the papacy,' said Leo. 'Let's enjoy it.' And he did, presiding over feasts of ape meat, monkey brains and parrot tongues with sixty starters, naked boys jumping out of pies and a jester who gulped down forty eggs or twenty chickens. He was obese, short-sighted, red-faced and, though often tormented by an anal fistula, cheerful and playful. Yet he was careless with others: when huntsmen were killed on his hunting expeditions, he scarcely noticed: 'What a day!'

He had known Michelangelo since they were boys in Lorenzo the Magnificent's palazzo – 'brothers, nurtured together', he said – and commissioned him to design the Medici Chapel of Florence's San Lorenzo. 'He's terrible,' he complained of the artist. 'One can't deal with him.' He preferred Raphael, now painting the Stanze di Raffaello and, after the death of Bramante, in charge of St Peter's.

Leo, gleaming with jewels, wafting the scents of expensive spices and anal putrefaction, emulated the Borgias and della Roveres in promoting family, choosing his good-natured nephew, Lorenzo, son of Piero, to be ruler of Florence. For Lorenzo, Leo arranged a semi-royal marriage to a cousin of the French king, Madeleine de La Tour d'Auvergne, with whom he had a daughter, Catherine – future queen of France. Days after she was born, Lorenzo died, at which Leo appointed his cousin, Giulio, bastard son of the Giuliano killed by the Pazzi, as cardinal and lord of Florence. While living in Rome, Giulio had fathered a son, Alessandro, with a girl of colour, Simonetta, probably the daughter of African slaves. Medicis owned both white and black slaves.

Leo's intrigues destabilized the *Curia*, the papal court. One of his first appointments as cardinal was his young lover, Alfonso Petrucci, who came to resent his patron bitterly, putting together a conspiracy in which Leo's doctor would treat his anal fistula by injecting poison into his fundament. When the plot was revealed, Petrucci, under torture, implicated other cardinals, who were pardoned in return for their fortunes. But Leo had his ex-lover strangled with a scarlet ligature by a Moorish executioner. His new lover was the half-Ottoman singer Solimando.

To pay for St Peter's, Leo needed more cash, raised from loans from Fugger the Rich, from payments for cardinals' hats and from the sales of indulgences (whereby a sinner could be delivered from purgatory in return for payments to the Church). Indulgences were just the latest outrageous papal abuse of sanctity that particularly disgusted a German monk from Wittenberg in Saxony. His real name was Martin Luder but he changed it to Eleutherius – Freed – which he Germanized into Luther.

When he was almost struck by lightning, he experienced a Damascene revelation, gave up his legal studies and became a monk. But a visit to Rome horrified him. 'That filthy stinking puddle full of the wickedest wretches in the world' was, he wrote with typical ferocity, awash with 'filthy nonsense. If there is a hell, Rome is built on it.' Rome was indeed a modern Babylon in which, as Leo's obscene poet Pietro Aretino put it, visitors 'usually wanted to visit not only the antiquities but also the modernities, that is the ladies'.

Luther, that pungent firebrand, theatrical and righteous, was even more disgusted by Leo's hucksterism: 'Why does the pope, whose wealth today is greater than the wealth of the richest Crassus, build the basilica of St Peter with the money of poor believers rather than with his own money?' In October 1517, Luther wrote an attack on the pope, his *Ninety-Five Theses*, which he nailed alongside other notices on the door of Wittenberg's Schlosskirche. But he didn't depend on the church doors: he deployed the new medium of printing. Ultimately, 3.1 million copies were published. He had himself repeatedly painted by his friend Lucas Cranach, making his pugnacious mug one of the most famous in Germany.

A vicious and visceral polemicist, he was fixated on faeces and sex, later denouncing the pope as a transsexual sodomite, his orders 'sealed with the Devil's own faeces, written with the anus-pope farts'. He unleashed savage diatribes against the Jews: 'We're wrong if we don't kill them', those 'devil's people', 'poisonous worms' full of the 'devil's faeces . . . which they wallow in like swine', their synagogue 'an incorrigible whore, an evil slut'.

Luther's fury gave a voice not just to resentment of papal corruption but also to a dawning scepticism. Sanctity, he argued, was based not on the titles, payments and magical rituals of the Catholic Church but on the direct relationship between man and God (without priestly intermediaries), guided by the scriptures – *sola scriptura* – which would soon be translated from Latin into German and so could be read by anyone. All people needed to enter the kingdom of heaven was literacy, which Luther now promoted.

As his teachings spread, twenty-seven nuns in a nearby Cistercian monastery wanted to join his movement. Luther, now forty-one, arranged for them to be smuggled out in herring barrels and, presumably once they had been cleaned of fishiness, found himself attracted to one of them, the twenty-six-year-old Katharina. He had never considered marriage – 'not that I'm insensible to my flesh or sex (for I'm neither wood nor stone) but because I daily expect the death of a heretic'. Now 'suddenly I was occupied with far different thoughts. The Lord has plunged me into marriage.' He argued that 'A woman has no control of herself. God has made her body to be with man, to bear children,' so she was welcome to enjoy sex – and they were blessed with six children. But Luther must have been exhausting. 'Dear husband, you're too rude,' Katharina said once. Yet the nun in the fish barrel was decisive: Luther decreed that Protestant priests could marry.

This Protestant spirit spread quickly through northern and central Europe from princes to peasants, based on the fundamentals – the Word of the Bible. The more personal religiosity of Protestantism encouraged a new independent spirit in business, art and daily life. Protestant nations – much of Germany, then the Low Countries, Britain and Scandinavia – became more literate than Catholic ones. Literacy changed the psychology (even the formation of the brain), but also surely increased self-confidence and knowledge, just as it increased self-discipline, self-motivation, analytical thinking and sociability, contributing to what later made northern Europe so successful. Protestantism was not the only factor in this European spirit of 'hard work, patience and diligence', but it was, as Joseph Henrich writes, 'a booster shot . . . both a consequence and a cause of people's changing psychology'.

Hoping to ignore Luther, Leo scoffed at this 'monkish squabble'. He now received an amazing gift from India: a white elephant named Hanno who in his size and joviality almost seemed a metaphor for Leo himself. 'In my brutish breast,' Leo wrote in elephantine voice, 'they perceived human feelings.' Kept in a bespoke elephant house between St Peter's and the Lateran, Hanno was sketched by Raphael, and when the Pope wished to mock a pretentious poet he arranged for him to ride Hanno to the Capitol with blaring trumpets until the pachyderm, alarmed by the noise, refused to go further. But Hanno's foolish keepers mistakenly poisoned him with a gold-laced laxative. On his death, Raphael designed the memorial ('That which Nature has stolen away, Raphael of Urbino with his art has restored'), Leo penned the epitaph to his 'mighty beast', while Aretino wrote a pornographic *Last Will and Testament of the Elephant Hanno* in which the pachyderm's penis was left to the priapic Cardinal di Grassi 'so that he can become more active in the incarnation of bastards with the help of Madama Adriana'.* Leo

---

* Aretino was a cobbler's son whose scathing verses made him a 'scourge of princes'. During the reign of the next Medici pope Clement, Aretino intervened to rescue his friend Marcantonio Raimondi, who had produced the first printed book of erotica, engravings based on drawings by Giulio Romano entitled *I Modi* (*The Ways*, also known as the *Sixteen Positions*), which celebrated not only the Church-blessed missionary position but also the woman on top, each dedicated to a specific Medici courtesan and her sexual speciality. The pope banned *Sixteen Positions* until Aretino appealed to him, and once the ban was lifted 'I tossed off the verses seen beneath the figures. With all due respect to hypocrites, I dedicate these lustful pieces to you, heedless of fake prudishness and asinine prejudices that forbid

forgave Aretino's impertinence; but he understood his own link with Hanno, writing on his grave: 'But I wish, oh gods, that the time which Nature would have assigned to me, and Destiny stole away, / You will add to the life of the great Leo.' The elephantine Leo did not long outlive Hanno, but in his epitaph the frivolous pontiff touched on something much more important:

> Mighty elephant which the King Manuel
> Having conquered the Orient
> Sent as captive to Pope Leo X.

This 'conqueror' was Manuel I, the Portuguese king who masterminded a messianic world conquest from Brazil and Kongo to India and Indonesia by the aggressive crusading sailors of his tiny kingdom.

MANUEL'S EASTERN MARAUDERS:
DA GAMA AND ALBUQUERQUE

As a young prince in 1493, when summoned by his cousin João II, Manuel feared the king would gut him like his brother. Instead he was appointed heir. His luck in surviving João's purge added to his belief in his destiny as a Latin King David who would retake Jerusalem, raze Mecca and destroy Islam. Aged twenty-six when he succeeded, with a round face and long, apish arms, he was influenced by his cousins Ferdinand and Isabella, and married their eldest daughter; when she died in childbirth, he wed her sister.* But the eldest Spanish infanta had refused to marry him unless he expelled all Portuguese Jews.

Manuel had protected Portuguese Jews, who owned a fifth of the country's movable wealth, their numbers boosted by refugees from Isabella's Expulsion, but Spain and God were more important. In October 1497, he forced a mass conversion of Jews.

---

the eyes to gaze at the things they most delight to see.' These are his *Sonetti lussuriosi* (Lust Sonnets). The Church reformer Bishop Gian Giberti who had denounced the book was a victim of his verses and tried to have Aretino assassinated. The poet escaped to Milan. Self-described as a 'sodomite', a friend of Titian who painted him, he was said to have been hired by both Charles V and François I to write verse about the other.

* Manuel's first wife, Isabella, princess of Asturias, had formerly been married to the Portuguese heir who was killed in a riding accident. She went home to her parents until Manuel requested her hand, her second Portuguese marriage. For a while she was heir to the Castilian throne. Manuel's second wife Maria had ten children, inevitably dying in childbirth, after which he married Leonor, the eldest child of Juana and Philip and favourite sister of Charles V, who afterwards married François I of France. If this sounds tangled, it is: all three were highly consanguineous.

The wealthiest Jewish family in Portugal had pretended to convert: the malagueta-pepper merchant Francisco Mendes married the heiress Beatriz de Luna, who became known as Gracia Mendes, in a Catholic ceremony in Lisbon cathedral. But when expelled they returned to their Judaism and escaped to the Netherlands – the start of a journey that culminated in them becoming Ottoman potentates and Jewish royalty. But for now even being a New Christian was dangerous. In 1506, Dominican friars led a pogrom that burned several thousand Jews and New Christians alive in a bonfire in Lisbon's main square.

Manuel spent the money from the Jews on four ships, packed with cannon and led by a *fidalgo* in his retinue, Vasco da Gama, member of the crusading Order of Santiago whose late father had originally been appointed to lead the voyage. Their mission was to follow the route of Bartolomeu Dias and then seize control of the Indian Ocean spice trade, aiming to scourge the Muslims and compensating for their small numbers with cannonades and ferocity.

Sailing round southern Africa, da Gama raided up the Swahili coast, attacking Arab shipping off Malindi, where he found allies, recruited an Arab pilot in Mombasa and then sailed across to Calicut (Kozhikode) on India's Malabar coast, the pre-eminent among a constellation of city states trading pepper, cinnamon, cardamom, ginger, cloves, jewels, ebony, amber and tamarind. India was fragmented, the north ruled by a weakened Muslim Delhi sultanate, the south divided between a Hindu raj of Vijayanagara and the Islamic sultanate of Bijapur.

In cosmopolitan Calicut, da Gama met Arab and Indian traders as well as an Italian-speaking Polish Jew, born in Alexandria and an envoy of the sultan of Bijapur. Da Gama first tortured, then baptized him as Gaspar da Gama and used him as interpreter and negotiator. The Portuguese mistook the Hindu temples with their statues for Christian churches, but the *samoothiri* (*zamorin*), Lord of the Sea, Hindu ruler of a partly Islamic city, was unimpressed by Vasco's meagre gifts. These Indian merchant-princes were accustomed to dealing with foreigners – Chinese, Malays and Arabs in contact with the Mamluk sultans of Egypt. But Portuguese methods were an unpleasant surprise.

After barely surviving the return journey on which two-thirds of his men perished, da Gama was raised to the nobility, granted the title Admiral of the Seas of Arabia, Persia, India and All the Orient and sent back by Manuel, who boasted of his exploits and now called himself Lord of the Conquest, Navigation and Commerce of Ethiopia, Arabia, Persia and India.

Inspired by his divine destiny, Manuel dispatched a series of fleets eastwards, eighty-one ships in five years, many of them funded by Fugger the Rich. In March 1500, the king saw off Pedro Álvares Cabral, a favourite courtier, and thirteen ships with Bartolomeu Dias and the converted Polish Jew Gaspar da Gama on board. Looping out into the Atlantic, Cabral landed on a new 'island' that he claimed for Manuel as Ilha de Vera Cruz (later known as Brazil), before heading round Africa (where Dias was lost in a storm) via Sofala and Malindi and onwards to India. When the *samoothiri* turned hostile, killing fifty of his men, Cabral bombarded Calicut, killing 600, then joined forces with the raja of Cochin, who resented his subordinate position to Calicut. Seven of the thirteen ships returned filled with spices that were sold profitably.

Manuel, sensing the opportunity of the 'island' (Brazil), sent more ships to investigate, including one under Amerigo Vespucci, who realized that it was not an island but a continent. Gathering information in his office of colonial affairs, the India House, Manuel resolved to challenge not just the Egyptian and Arab traders of the Indian Ocean but also his European rivals, Venice and Genoa. His vision was extraordinary – to dominate a vast territory controlled by Swahili, Arab and Indian traders – with tiny flotillas of Portuguese sailors, commanded by his top courtiers, using carracks, overwhelming artillery force and spectacular acts of murderous terror. His monopolistic rapacity made him the first truly entrepreneurial monarch: the French king, envious of his wealth, nicknamed him *Le Roi Épicier*, the Spice King.

Manuel created a Revenge Fleet to make the Indians pay for their impertinence to Cabral, who was appointed to command it. But the contest between allies of Cabral and those of da Gama was won by the latter. Now the killing started. Admiral da Gama, fitted out in satin crimson and blessed by the king, raided Kilwa (Tanzania), then, crossing the Indian Ocean, burned alive an entire ship of pilgrims on their way home from Mecca, then bombarded Calicut while hanging Indians from his masts and fighting off an Arab fleet of privateers. His cruelty was spectacular: victims were dismembered and decapitated, heaps of body parts sent to the rulers; he cut off the lips and ears of the *samoothiri*'s ambassador, then sent him back to Calicut with a dog's ears sewn on to his head.

Manuel kept up the pressure, challenging the overlord of the Indian Ocean: al-Ghaury, sultan of Egypt. Manuel sent two further fleets, now packed with cannon, under Dom Francisco de Almeida, veteran of the Spanish conquest of Granada, as first governor and viceroy of the Portuguese State of India, whose crew included a young nobleman, Fernão de Magalhães – Magellan. But then he sent after him an irrepressible courtier-soldier, Afonso da Albuquerque, a white-bearded veteran who had helped take Tangier and defeat Mehmed II's Otranto incursion.

Almeida bombarded Kilwa, aided by his rival, the sultan of Mombasa, then crossed to India and built Fort Manuel at Cochin and other forts that now formed the State of India. Albuquerque's first mission was to take the island of Socotra off the coast of Yemen and the port of Muscat. He planned to land at Jeddah, raid inland and steal the Prophet's body. The amir of Mecca, Sharif Barakat II, appealed to Sultan al-Ghaury as did the sultan of Gujarat. Al-Ghaury ordered Venetian shipwrights to build a fleet which under his Kurdish admiral, Hussein al-Kurdi, who rendezvoused with a Calicut–Gujarati flotilla commanded by a Georgian ex-slave, Malik Ayyaz, and confronted Almeida. An Egyptian–Indian fleet built by Venetians, manned by Russian galley slaves and Ethiopian bowmen and commanded by a Kurd and a Georgian, fought a Portuguese force at Chaul, where Almeida's son was killed. It was a draw that was avenged a few months later at Diu where the Portuguese slaughtered the Mamluks and killed their prisoners by dissection, by firing from cannon and by hanging.

Once Manuel realized Albuquerque's commanding acumen, he promoted him. Albuquerque read the Indian Ocean world quickly and understood that, to establish a permanent presence, the Portuguese needed a few strategically placed fortresses. He planned to attack Egypt in the Red Sea, but his new Indian ally Timoji, a corsair who had served the Vijayanagarans, prompted him to seize Goa from the sultan of Bijapur as Manuel's Indian capital, and together they stormed the city, killing 6,000 defenders.

In 1511, Albuquerque, newly minted duke of Goa, sailed for the centre of the spice trade, the sultanate of Malacca (Malaysia), which he took on the second attempt, killing every Muslim, though sparing Malays and Indians; he then sent three ships to seize the Molucca (Spice) Islands, source of cloves, mace and nutmegs, but they were shipwrecked. Albuquerque filled ships with nutmegs and cloves, then sailed for Hormuz in the Persian Gulf, building a fortress to master the Straits.

Celebrating his global project, Manuel held parades in which elephants and rhinoceroses, adorned with gold, processed through the city followed by Arabian horses and a jaguar. In 1514, Albuquerque received a gift from the sultan of Cambay, Hanno the elephant, that he sent with a rhinoceros back to Manuel in Lisbon. The king arranged for the two beautiful animals to fight, but the elephant sensibly refused to take on the rhinoceros and Manuel sent him to Pope Leo.

In Lisbon, Manuel built his massive Ribeira (Riverside) Palace, containing his Houses of India, Slaves and Guinea and his Arsenal. The city was one of Europe's principal markets for spices, sugar and increasingly slaves: by 1500, around 15 per cent of the population were African slaves. The trade intensified: 10,000 were traded between 1500 and 1535. Gold and sugar required cheap labour. The sweet tooth of Europe was gratified by the vampiric fangs of the slave traders. The sugar plantations on São Tomé, Madeira and Cape Verde were profitable but labour intensive. Akan rulers bought 10,000 slaves from Portuguese middlemen between 1510 and 1540. But now slave traders expanded from the Bight of Benin – the Slavery Coast – 600 miles south to Kongo. The slave trade would become a gargantuan atrocity and a murderous business, the greatest forced migration in history, but only 3 per cent of it took place between 1450 and 1600: the hellish trade was just starting.

Both race and faith mattered to the Portuguese. In India and Africa, the empire builders displayed the same racism and appetite for coercion of other nations, but they quickly settled with Indian and African women. In Goa, Albuquerque consciously built a new Portuguese city, but he encouraged Portuguese settlers to marry Indian women. It is easy to exaggerate the scale of the Portuguese empire: it was shallow and thinly spread; only a few towns were conquered.*

As Albuquerque was arriving in south-western India, another foreign warlord – whose family would conquer much of the subcontinent – was invading the north.

---

* European histories traditionally now claim that Portuguese imperialists dominated the Indian–Malay spice trade. Though they certainly heralded European power in the east, that is to exaggerate their power and neglect the local powers. Portuguese numbers were small, their strongholds few, the trade complex, and southern India was dominated by the all-conquering warrior king Krishnadevaraya, maharaja-dhiraja of the Hindu empire Vijayanagara, who himself defeated many of the Islamic sultanates; eastern India was ruled by the Gajapati kingdom; and the Ottomans were about to replace the Egyptians as masters of Arabia and Yemen. Malacca, which had only been Muslim for thirty years, had been a Chinese vassal ever since Zheng's treasure fleets: the Ming emperor was furious.

ACT ELEVEN
425 MILLION

Tamerlanians and Mexica, Ottomans and Safavis

BABUR TAKES DELHI

In January 1505, Babur, twenty-two years old, raided India for the first time. Since he was just a minor prince struggling for his very existence, his raid was tiny compared to the invasion of his great-great-grandfather Tamerlane, who had sacked Delhi. Babur – Tiger – was an irrepressible, exuberant and playful extrovert with an awesome lineage – his mother was descended from Genghis Khan, his father from Tamerlane. But in the half-century since 1447 when Tamerlane's son Shahrukh had died, the descendants of the conqueror had failed to control his former empire. Like any mirza,* Babur longed to sit on the conqueror's throne in Samarkand. But many mirzas were no longer warriors; rather they were playboys, who were 'fine as companions, in conversations and at parties, but strangers to war'.

Babur, contemporary of Manuel and Michelangelo, was twelve when his father, womanizer, poet, swashbuckling warrior and pigeon fancier, 'fat, brave, eloquent', was killed – he was visiting his doves and his dovecote fell down a ravine. 'Umar Sheikh Mirza,' wrote Babur, 'flew with his pigeons and their house and became a falcon.' Inheriting the Fergana Valley, the mirza depended on his grandmother, Ësan Dawlat Begum, 'for tactics and strategy, an intelligent and good planner'. Babur was a Chagatai Turk, adept with the crossbow, sword, six-flanged mace and axe of the steppe horseman, and thanks to his flamboyant memoir *Baburnama*, written in Turkish, he is one of the first statesmen we can know personally.

As a teenager, Babur married for the first time, to Aisha, but his first love was a boy: 'I discovered in myself a strange inclination for a boy in the camp bazaar, his very name Baburi suited me well.' Sometimes, 'Baburi came to me but I was so bashful I couldn't look him in the face,' and when Babur bumped into him, 'I went to pieces . . . I'm so

---

* The descendants of Tamerlane were entitled amir-mirza; the descendants of Genghis were entitled khan.

embarrassed every time I see my beloved.' Tortured by his infatuation, 'that frothing up of desire and passion, and the stress of youthful folly, I used to wander bareheaded and barefoot through street, orchard and vineyard. I took no notice of myself or anyone else.' Afterwards he married his beautiful, intelligent cousin Maham, whom he trusted implicitly, saying, 'Treat Maham's words like a law,' especially after she gave birth his beloved son Humayoun.

In 1496, Babur seized Samarkand, but lost it after 100 days. 'I cried involuntarily,' he admitted. 'Is there any pang, any grief, my wounded heart has missed?' In 1500 when he was nineteen, 'I took Samarkand' again; 'I had 240 men.' A year later, humiliated in battle, he fled, so desperate that he and his posse ate their horses. 'When one has pretensions to rule and a desire for conquest, one can't sit back and just watch when events don't go right once or twice.' But he also knew that power is solitude: 'Other than my own heart, I never found a confidant.'

Then, just as he planned to flee to China, his fortune turned: he seized Kabul, famed for its gardens and its poverty, with 200 ruffians whom he had to discipline: 'I had four or five shot, one or two dismembered.' Starting with this shambolic warband, he would go on to conquer the richest land on earth. 'My desire for Hindustan [India] was constant,' wrote Babur, raiding through the Khyber Pass, where he saw the wealth of India: 'Every year, twenty thousand animals bring slaves, textiles, sugar, spices.' Even better, the Delhi sultanate, ruled for fifty years by the Lodi dynasty of Afghan descent, was weak.

In between raids into India, Babur enjoyed booze and drugs. 'There was much disgusting uproar,' he reminisced. Once, 'We rode off, we got on a boat and drank spirits, left the boat roaring drunk and mounting our horses let the horse gallop free-reined. I must have been really drunk.' He was the only psychedelic conqueror: 'How strange the fields of flowers appeared under its influence,' he raved about narcotics. 'Nothing but purple flowers, sometimes yellow and purple together with gold flecks.'

In November 1525, he led 20,000 men including 4,000 arquebusiers and artillery sent by the Ottoman sultan into the Punjab (Pakistan), then swooped on Delhi. At Panipat, on 21 April 1526, just north of Delhi, Sultan Ibrahim's 100,000 men and 100 elephants challenged Babur's small force. The invaders' musketeers and cannon probably won the day. Ibrahim's head was taken to Babur. At the age of forty-three, he had conquered northern India. 'I ordered [my eldest son] Humayoun Mirza to occupy the capital, Agra. But after he had given away his spoils, his troops wanted to return to Kabul; he wanted to stay.

It was not that he liked India – 'A country of few charms, its people have no good looks ... no good horses, no good dogs, no grapes, no musk melons or first-rate fruits, no ice or cold water, no good bread or cooked food in bazaars, no hot baths,' and there was 'remarkable dislike between its people and mine'. But it had been prize enough for Tamerlane – and glory was what he wanted: 'Give me but fame and if I die, I am content.' Babur summoned Mongol and Turkic grandees. 'God's given us sovereignty in Hindustan,' he declared, sounding very like those other predators – the Portuguese and Spanish – granted empire by God.*

Babur decided to try Indian food, keeping the cooks of the late sultan, which almost proved a fatal mistake. The mother of the late sultan suborned the cooks to poison Babur's food. 'I vomited a lot,' he wrote to his son Humayoun. 'I never vomit after meals, not even after drinking. A cloud of suspicion came over my mind.' Four cooks were tortured and confessed. 'I ordered the taster to be hacked to pieces, the cook to be skinned alive; one of the women I had thrown under elephants' feet and another I had shot.' The sultan's mother was killed quietly, while Babur understood that 'He who reaches the point of death appreciates life.'

Babur was challenged by Rana Sanga, a Rajput,† whose 200,000 men marched on Agra, keen to expel House Tamerlane. Babur temporarily renounced booze, pouring out carafes of wine in front of the army. 'Noblemen and soldiers,' he said, 'whosoever sits down to the feast of life must before it's over drink the cup of death, but how much better to die with honour than live with infamy!' As they joined battle at Khanua, the soldiers gripped their Qurans. 'The plan was perfect, it worked admirably,' noted Babur, whose Ottoman artillery 'broke the ranks of pagans with matchlock and cannon' as the soldiers 'fought with delight'. He celebrated by building towers of skulls like Tamerlane before carving up India with his Turk, Mongol and Afghan henchmen in return for military service. Then he wrote his memoirs, built gardens, smoked opium, quaffed wine (quoting the verse 'I am drunk, officer. Punish me when I am sober') and caroused with two Georgian slaves sent by the shah of Persia – 'dancers with rosy cheeks'. As Babur declined, Humayoun who ruled Kabul fell ill. Babur was heartbroken.

'You're a king and have other sons, I sorrow because I have only

* Once in power, he promoted himself from mirza to padishah – emperor in Persian – styling his first wife Maham and his sister Khanzada as begum-padishahs or lady empresses. Babur and his successors called his dynasty the Gurkanis, after Tamerlane's title gürkan meaning imperial son-in-law, or House of Timur. Their enemies denigrated them as Mongols. The British, attracted to the dynasty in which they saw parallels to their own empire, called them the Mughals.

† The Rajputs were Hindu princely dynasties descended from kshatriya warlords.

this one,' his empress Maham admonished him from the prince's bedside.

'Maham,' he replied, 'although I have other sons, I love none as I love your Humayoun.' Babur offered his own life in exchange for his son's. In December 1530, the twenty-three-year-old Humayoun recovered – as Babur sickened. Babur's last advice was: 'Do nothing against your brothers even if they deserve it.'*

Humayoun was 'brave in battle, ingenious and lively, full of wit', but he 'contracted bad habits, such as the excessive use of opium', and preferred to spend his time in chatter and pleasure, lacking killer grit: his worst insult was just to say 'You stupid!' Immediately, he was challenged in all directions, by his brothers, by the Gujaratis, by the Portuguese and more seriously by one of his father's Afghan generals, who advanced on Agra. In 1541, Humayoun fled westwards into Sind (Pakistan).

On the way he met a half-Persian teenaged girl called Hamida who resisted his courtship, possibly because his prospects were so disastrous, but finally he married her and then with forty retainers they escaped across the blistering Thar Desert. At Umarkot, Hamida gave birth to Humayoun's first son, who was born on a camel. Humayoun was forced to leave the baby in Kandahar with his aunt Khanzada. She thought the baby looked just like Babur: he would grow up to be Akbar the Great. Humayoun fled to Persia. It looked as if the rule of this conquest dynasty would be no more than a flash in the pan of his arquebusiers. Indeed their victories had been had won thanks to their artillery, a present from the Ottoman sultan, Selim the Grim, who now changed the entire balance of Eurasia.

SELIM – SUNKEN DEEP IN BLOOD

In March 1517, Selim galloped into Cairo, having destroyed the Mamluk sultanate and conquered the entire Arab world, increasing his empire by 70 per cent and giving it, for the first time, an Islamic majority. Grandson of Mehmed the Conqueror, third son of Sultan Bayezid, Selim was lithe, lean and cadaverous, clear-sighted and paranoid, impatient and implacable. His success was founded on his arquebusiers, who could be trained in two weeks; it took a lifetime to master bow and horse. Arquebuses, fired from the shoulder using a crossbow stock, lit

---

* Babur was buried in his beloved gardens in Kabul where his tomb still stands, originally inscribed: 'If there's paradise on earth, it is this, it is this!'

by a matchlock and detonated with a new invention, the trigger, were becoming muskets.

Frustrated by his father's vacillations and his own isolation as prince-governor of Trebizond, where he complained he was 'weak and helpless', Selim marched on Constantinople and overthrew his father, whom he probably poisoned. Then one by one he strangled his three brothers and seven nephews. Once on the throne, most of his own sons vanished, probably strangled too, to make way for his chosen successor, Suleiman. Always accompanied by his executioners, the Tongueless,[*] the padishah – emperor – killed three of his six viziers, kicking around one of their heads: 'the man-eating king of beasts', one of his officials called him. When one was rash enough to request a warning if he was to be executed, Selim replied he might consider it but at the moment lacked a replacement. He prided himself as a killer: 'Drowned in a sea of blood', he described himself in one of his poems, written under the name Selimi, 'sunken deep in blood'. As soon as he was secure, Selim renewed treaties with Venice and Poland, signalling to Europe his desire for peace as he faced a mounting challenge from the east: the god-king of Persia.

THE ALEXANDER–JESUS OF PERSIA BIDS FOR WORLD CONQUEST

In 1501, Ismail, aged thirteen, declared that he was the Mahdi, the messiah. Poet, hunter, lover of boys and girls and heroic drinker, Ismail – 'fair, handsome and very pleasing; not very tall, but of a light and well-framed figure with broad shoulders and reddish hair' – declared his divinity, advertising in his poetry his aspirations to divine and military leadership. In the 1320s, his Kurdish grandfather Safi al-Din (founder of the Safavis) had undergone a Damascene revelation and converted from Sunni to Twelver Shiism.[†] After his grandfather, father and his eldest

---

[*] The special executioners were the Tongueless or *Dilsiz* (known as deaf-mutes by European visitors) who served as pages, couriers and executioners. The Tongueless were part of a secretive unit, the *Enduran* – interior service – within the harem who, wearing blue robes and trousers, and red boots, ensured privacy and were regarded as special, sometimes mentally challenged outsiders devoted to the ruler. First hired by Mehmed the Conqueror, they became the padishah's special killers for strangling princes and viziers with the bowstring. Executions were also conducted by the *Bostandji Bachi*, once Chief Gardener, who became the pasha of 3,000 red-hatted, yellow-robed bodyguards who protected the sultanic palaces.

[†] Safi al-Din's fanatical followers – Twelver Shiites – believed that, after the first ten imams, the eleventh had been murdered by the Sunni caliph in 874 and his son the twelfth imam

brother had all been killed, Ismail was raised and trained in secret. Then, hailed by an army of Turkmen believers, the Redhats (named after their twelve-folded scarlet bonnets), as the Perfect Guide and occulted imam, he launched a conquest of Persia and Iraq.

Ismail ordered the killing of all Sunnis: he slaughtered 20,000 in Tabriz and destroyed Sunni shrines. This young shah, part Jesus, part Alexander, prepared to destroy the Ottomans. He turned the head of one Sunni khan into his drinking cup, fed the body to the Redhats and sent the skin to Selim.

The Ottoman denounced Ismail's divine delusions – 'You have incited your abominable Shiites to unsanctified sexual intercourse and shedding of innocent blood' – and prepared a pre-emptive strike. The two competed as poets: shah sent sultan a box of opium, joshing that his egregious poetry must be the work of a junkie.

In summer 1514, Selim massacred 40,000 Redhats before invading Iraq, fighting Ismail at Çaldıran, where his 60,000 men, armed with muskets and 200 cannon, routed 75,000 Turkman horse archers who did not possess a single gun.

The shah was wounded, his favourite wife captured, his invincible divinity shattered. He rebuilt his kingdom, swearing never again to lead his armies in battle. Sponsoring beautiful miniaturist painting and working as an apprentice in his own royal workshop, he assisted in the creation of a gorgeous illustrated *Shahnameh* – before sinking into boozing and depression, dying at just thirty-seven. But he left Iran as the Twelve Shiite nation that endures today.

It was in order to back an eastern rival to Ismail that Selim lent his artillery to Babur and Humayoun which enabled them to seize India, but when Selim demanded support from Egypt, the Mamluks refused to help.

In 1516, Selim marched east again. Ismail feared the worst, but it was a feint. Selim swerved into Mamluk Syria where the Egyptians were defeated, their sultan killed: muskets trounced crossbows. Heading south, visiting Jerusalem on the way, Selim hanged the last Mamluk sultan from the gates of Cairo. Now ruler of Mecca and Jerusalem, and

vanished, occulted or hidden, poised to re-emerge as the Mahdi at the day of judgement. Ismail went even further. 'My name is Shah Ismail,' the boy told his followers. 'I am God's mystery. I am the leader of all the ghazis [warriors]. My mother is Fatima, my father is Ali; I am the sacred master of the Twelve Imams ... I am the living Khidr [heroic saint of Islamic theology] and Jesus, son of Mary. I am the Alexander of my contemporaries.' Ismail's blondness reflected his descent from the Komnenoi dynasty of Constantinople: in 1439, Emperor John IV of Trebizond married his daughter Theodora to Ismail's other grandfather Uzun Hasa, khan of the Ak Koyunlu.

the riches of Egypt, Selim celebrated himself as the messianic Master of the Auspicious Conjunction and Alexandrine World Conqueror.*

Meanwhile in his tent outside Cairo his sea captain Piri Reis presented a map of the world inscribed in colour on gazelle hide. Its details had been given to the Ottomans by a Spanish nobleman, captured by Piri's uncle Kemal Reis off Valencia in 1501 and enslaved.† The Ottomans did not reach the Americas only because they never conquered Morocco, which controlled access to the Atlantic. But to the east Selim built fleets in the Red Sea and supplied artillery to allies in Ethiopia, India and Indonesia.

Christendom was alarmed by Selim. Pope Leo and Emperor Maximilian called for a crusade. The emperors of east and west – Selim and Maximilian – died almost at the same time, succeeded by young sons who inherited territories so vast they seemed beyond the abilities of any individual.

ROXELANA AND SULEIMAN:
THE JOYFUL AND THE MAGNIFICENT

Maximilian prepared for death, exhausted by the strain of defending his lands, suffering from an encyclopaedia of diseases from colitis to syphilis. He travelled with a coffin but planned for the future, negotiating one more double-marriage gambit: forging a Habsburg connection to the Jagiełło family that ruled Bohemia and Hungary. He married his grandson Ferdinand to the Hungarian princess Anne and his granddaughter Mary to Ludwig, king of Hungary. This could have led to a Jagiełło takeover of Austria but a tragedy meant that this union paid off too. Maximilian was the winner in the marital gambling stakes. In 1519, outraged that local tradesmen had refused him credit, he suffered a stroke, after which on his own penitent specifications, his body was

---

* Arab potentates rushed to pay court: Selim received Abu Numeiri, the young amir of Mecca, who offered the keys of Mecca and Medina on behalf of his father Barakat, the Hashemite sharif descended from Qatada. Selim reappointed them amirs of Mecca. Selim himself commandeered the titles Shadow of God, Messiah of the Last Age and Renewer of the Religion.

† Still in the Ottoman archives, the map's eastern half including China is missing; the western half shows not just the Mediterranean but the discoveries of 'Colon-bo' – Colombus. America was labelled 'Vilayet Antilia': Antilia was the legendary island of the Atlantic; *vilayet* was an Ottoman province, so its name suggested it could be next for Ottoman conquest. Selim supposedly rejected the idea of an Atlantic conquest by tearing the map in two, keeping the eastern half and returning the American section. Actually no one knows what happened to the map.

whipped and teeth hammered out. His nineteen-year-old grandson Charles of Ghent inherited an empire that extended from Panama to Vienna, from Bruges to Palermo.

Soon afterwards, Selim, riding through Bulgaria, died either of skin cancer or of the plague. Having strangled so many members of his family, he was succeeded by the only Ottoman left alive, his son Suleiman, aged twenty-five, inheriting lands from Mecca to Hungary.

Charles and Suleiman believed they were universal monarchs of universal faiths; both faced militant heresies; both fought simultaneously on multiple fronts, land and sea. They looked immensely powerful but both had to navigate between competing interests. Suleiman could execute his viziers at will yet had to watch the Janissaries, the clergy, his local governors, his sons. Limited by the same laws and traditions that had delivered such extensive lands, Charles's monarchy was woven into a tapestry of rights and institutions – assemblies, guilds, towns and republics with their own constitutions and customs, granted by earlier monarchs. They were frustrating for Charles but they made Europe peculiarly creative and dynamic. These sovereigns, rivals for almost half a century, both craved conquest, the mark of worldly greatness and divine favour.

Just after his accession, Suleiman, 'tall but wiry, thin-faced, his nose aquiline, with a shadow of a moustache and a small beard', reticent and inscrutable, stern and vigilant, met a Slavic female slave whom he named Hürrem – Joyful – for her looks and exuberance, though Christian envoys called her Roxelana – the Ruthenian: she would become the most powerful Ukrainian in history. That year, this priest's daughter aged thirteen had been kidnapped from her village in a slave raid by the Crimean khan. Mongol horsemen seized good-looking children and enslaved them. Coffles of enchained slaves were marched across the steppe to Crimea where the slave market of Kaffa, seized from Genoa, provided the biggest component of Ottoman income – an empire funded by slavery. So important was it that Suleiman's first assignment was to govern Kaffa, accompanied by his mother Hafsa, who herself had been seized on a slave raid. The first slave raid by the Girays in 1468 captured 18,000, but the raids kept getting bigger – one in 1498 was said to have taken 100,000. The number captured in this way is incalculable: one historian guesses ten million between 1450 and 1650, others suggest six and a half million between the eleventh and nineteenth centuries. More obscure than its Atlantic equivalent – and not based on race – this slave trade was also vast, cruel and deadly for its victims.

Its slave markets were desperate places. 'A man who has not seen this has not seen anything,' as a Turkish traveller later noted. 'There a mother is severed from her son and daughter, a son from father and brother, sold among lamentations, cries of help, weeping and sorrow' – a scene similar to the tragedies of the African slave markets. Yet there were big differences. If they survived the journey across the steppe, there was a route out of slavery. An enslaved boy, converted to Islam and manumitted, could rise to grand vizier, while a girl, as Roxelana would now demonstrate, could end as empress.

Some time in his first weeks, Suleiman, who was 'very lustful' and frequently visited 'the palace of the women', was given a present of Roxelana. It was said that his intimate friend Ibrahim, a Greek fisherman's son, was the giver. The enslaved Ibrahim, who spoke Greek, Turkish and Italian, had been fortunate to be presented to the young Suleiman, who promoted him fast to chamberlain and then, at the age of about thirty, to grand vizier. Jealously nicknamed Frenk (the Westerner) and Makbul (the Favourite), he would be architect of Suleiman's expansion on three continents. His power would be enhanced if Suleiman's favoured concubine was his protégée – provided he could maintain control of her. But no one could control Roxelana.

In Constantinople, Roxelana was received into the female world of the Old Palace, the first built by Mehmed in the city centre, which was run by the sultan's mother, the *valide sultan*, managed by eunuchs and inhabited by unmarried royal daughters, royal children, retired concubines and fresh young captives like Roxelana who were trained in needlework, the Quran, the Turkish language and sexual virtuosity. A girl started often as an *odalık* or servant and might never meet the sultan, spending her life until retirement serving the *valide* in this special world, ringing with voices in Russian, Albanian, Turkish, Italian. But Roxelana would have learned instantly that the power rested not in the female realm of the Old Palace but up on the acropolis in the male-dominated New Palace. Sophisticated, cosy, sensual, polyglot and obsessed with politics and its intimate avatar, gossip, the harem was a family sanctuary and power house as well as crèche, maternity ward, university and bordello. The hundreds of Russian-Ukranian, Greek and Italian girls were there to sexually serve the padishah whose duty was to father sons, from among whom the next ruler had to be chosen. Every girl wanted to be *gözde* – in the eye of the sultan; every *odalık* wanted to become a sultanic paramour, but their dream was to be *umm al-walad* – mother of an Ottoman son – with special status and the promise of manumission on the death of her master.

Roxelana had 'beautiful hair' – red-gold – which Suleiman praised.

He moved her, travelling in a closed carriage guarded by uniformed eunuchs, into his Hall of Maidens, a micro-harem in the New Palace. After Suleiman had left to attack Serbia, Roxelana delivered a son Mehmed. He already had three sons by different odalisques: there was a rule that after the birth of a son the sultan did not return to the same odalisque, so that each prince would be supported by one mother. But when Suleiman returned after capturing Belgrade, Roxelana was recalled to the New Palace, where she was showered with jewels made personally by the sultan, who had learned the craft from Greek artisans in Trebizond. In between his military expeditions, they conceived a daughter, Mihrimah, and then three more boys.

Roxelana's fertility and physical strength were remarkable, as was the survival of most of her children while epidemics killed two of Suleiman's sons by other women. As Suleiman's contemporary Henry VIII would soon learn, child mortality was high, and many women died in childbirth. Within five years, Roxelana was so powerful that when the sultan's mother gave him 'two beautiful Russian maidens' she 'flung herself to the ground weeping' and made such a protest that Hafsa took the girls back. The sultan was committed to 'my one and only love'.

As Suleiman was often at war, the two wrote constantly to each other. 'My sultan,' she wrote, 'there's no limit to the burning anguish of separation.'

When he teased her for not reading his letters, or 'you would have written more of your longing to see me', she replied, reminding him of their children: 'Now, my sultan, that's enough, my soul is too touched. When your letters are read, your servant and son Mir Mehmed and your slave and daughter Mihrimah weep and wail from missing you.' But she does not conceal her playful impatience: 'Their weeping has driven me crazy.' His poems – written as by Muhibi (The Lover, perhaps her nickname for him) – hint at how she appeared to him: 'My girl of the beautiful hair, my love of the slanted brow, my love with eyes full of mischief.'

'I am happy,' said this ruler of Olympian detachment, calling her 'my most sincere friend, my confidante'. In the midst of interminable stress, he granted her the biggest compliment: she was 'the only one who does not distress me in this world'. The padishah compared her not only to provinces he owned but to those he hoped to conquer – 'My Istanbul, my Caraman, the earth of my Anatolia; / My Badakhshan, my Baghdad and Khorasan'. She may have been enslaved, but he called her 'my sultan': she was ungovernable. He signed off: 'I'm your Lover, You bring me Joy.'

Both young monarchs surely needed such companionship to survive. Charles too would find consolation for the stress of his inheritance in a loving relationship.

CHARLES AND THE *MANIKONGO*

Charles, who combined German, Spanish, Burgundian and Portuguese blood, grew up in Bruges and, speaking first French, then Flemish and German, and later Spanish, was known as Carlos in Spain, Karl in Germany, Charles in Brussels. His face was like a hereditary cartoon of his complex domains: 'he is tall and splendidly built, with a long face, beautiful light-blue eyes, his mouth and chin not as beautiful as his other features, a lopsided mouth with a drooping lower lip'. The elongated jaw and prominent lip – pathologic mandibular prognathism – was a feature of his Trastámara as well as his Habsburg ancestry, his mouth gaping open from elongated adenoids, 'his tongue short and thick which means he speaks with great difficulty'. Yet he was irrepressibly ambitious with a vision of universal Christian monarchy and expansive empire, choosing the motto *Plus Ultra* – Further Beyond. He was energetic and dutiful, measured and capable of taking decisions on many fronts despite perpetual stress and constant travelling: 'nine times to Germany, six times to Spain, seven to Italy, to Flanders ten times, four times to France, twice to England, twice to Africa, eight voyages in the Mediterranean, three in the seas of Spain', he later recalled. Hunting, partying and womanizing – fathering illegitimate children along the way – were his relaxations, his favourite treats iced beer and oysters, but it was not surprising that he, like Suleiman, tended to melancholy. Given that his mother and grandmother were insane and that he himself suffered depression, it took an impressive constitution and personality just to survive. But he did better.

First he rushed to Spain to claim his kingdom. There he was received by his manic mother, whom he had not seen for twelve years. The sixteen-year-old knelt before Juana, who 'asked the king three times if he was really her son he had grown so tall' but confirmed his right to rule in her name. While in Castile, Charles had an affair with his step-grandmother, Germaine de Foix, the twenty-nine-year-old widow of King Ferdinand. Yet arrogant Flemish officials sparked a rebellion of Spanish *comuneros*. It was suppressed, its leader, a bishop, tortured on Charles's orders, then garrotted.

This political funambulist was also negotiating election as emperor and coping with a seething religious crisis. His rivals François I of France and Henry VIII of England also fancied Charlemagne's crown. 'If you aspire to this throne,' his grandfather Maximilian had advised, 'you mustn't hold back any resource.' Charles borrowed from Fugger the Rich, paid 1.5 million florins to the electors and emerged as Emperor Charles V,* whose first problem was Martin Luther. Charles summoned the faecal fulminator for trial by the princes. In April 1521, at the diet (imperial assembly) of Worms, Charles confronted Luther with his heretical diatribes.

'I don't trust in the pope,' retorted the incorrigible Luther. 'I'm bound by the Scriptures and my conscience is captive to the Word of God. I can't and won't recant anything,' and he made a knightly salute. Charles – sympathetic to Lutheran sentiments but convinced that papal authority and ritual were essential – ordered Luther's killing or burning: 'We want him apprehended and punished as a notorious heretic.'

'Burn him! Burn him!' shouted the Spanish, but Luther was secretly protected by his patron, Frederick III, bewhiskered elector of Saxony, whose retainers carried Luther triumphantly out. Charles let him escape and Frederick arranged his 'kidnap' by 'armed robbers' who hid him in a Saxon castle as Protestantism spread fast. One of the first princes to convert was the grand master of Teutonic Knights, Albert, who converted his Order's Prussian lands into his own fiefdom. This younger son of the minor German family of Hohenzollern became duke of Prussia.

Charles's chief rival was François of France, alarmed by having to face the Habsburgs on both borders; but, thanks to Luther, Charles had to fight popular Protestantism in a series of wars and peasant revolts – the start of 150 years of sectarian conflict, equivalent to the schism of Sunni–Shia in Islam. Yet he could not rule all his lands on his own, so he appointed his brother Ferdinand to be Austrian archduke in Vienna. Ferdinand, who was as pragmatic and able as Charles, had been brought up in Spain, speaking Spanish. The brothers were strangers. When they met after ten years, they spoke different languages. Yet, despite many crises, God and dynasty always came first.

'Anyone who believes the empire of the entire world falls to anyone by virtue of men or riches is wrong,' Charles told the Castilian assembly in 1520. 'Empire comes from God alone.' He added, 'I'd have been content with the Spanish empire,' which included 'the gold-bearing world' – America.

---

* When Fugger's own interests were at stake, he was not shy in reminding Charles V: 'It's known that your imperial majesty could not have claimed the Roman crown without my help.'

There, he only ruled over Panama, Cuba, Jamaica and Hispaniola, inhabited by 5,000 Spaniards, the benighted Taíno peoples and a few enslaved Africans – and encompassing limited gold. Charles supported Bartolemeu de las Casas, the friar horrified by the killings of Taínos, as Protector of the Indians. Yet the friar devised an atrocious solution: save the Taínos by importing African slaves. In August 1518, Charles licensed a Flemish courtier to export 4,000 slaves from Africa to protect the Taínos: many of these first American slaves were Muslim Wolofs from Senegambia.

In 1520, Charles reappointed Diego Columbus as viceroy. Columbus, duke of Veragua (Panama) and marquess of Jamaica, and now married into the aristocracy, arrived in Santo Domingo in style, holding court at a new palace, Alcázar de Colón (still partly standing). Columbus pioneered the sugar industry in Jamaica – which he owned entirely – but treated his Wolof slaves so appallingly that in December 1522 they launched the first slave rebellion, some escaping to form a community of enslaved rebels, known as Maroons from the Spanish for wild cattle, *cimarrón.**

Yet the Portuguese were far ahead of the Spanish, with their distant outposts in Goa, Cochin (both in India), Hormuz (Iran), Malacca (Malaysia), Sri Lanka and Africa, where they found that Kongo was ideal for sourcing slaves. The demand was rising; they had realized they now possessed a vast, scarcely settled coastline with unknown lands to the interior, Brazil, which became the most important market for slaves. These were overwhelmingly taken from Kongo, where the Portuguese now used African mercenaries and allies from the neighbouring kingdom of Ngola to seize the slaves, and their own mixed-race enforcers to deliver them.† Their ally Manikongo Afonso acquired thousands of slaves during his military campaigns. The *manikongo* swiftly lost control, unable to restrict the slave trade to his war captives. 'Each day the traders are kidnapping our people,' he wrote to João III, the successor of Manuel, in 1521, 'children of this country, sons of our nobles, even

* Columbus' other son Fernando followed the opposite path: he retired to a Seville mansion, wrote his father's biography and collected 15,000 manuscripts and printed books. When Diego Columbus died in 1526, his son Luis Columbus de Toledo inherited the titles admiral of the Indies, duke of Veragua and marquess of Jamaica. Jamaica, its Taínos almost extinct, now populated by African slaves, remained a vast personal estate – the last one – of the Columbus family, until 1655, when it was captured by the English. Today's duke of Veragua is named Cristóbal Colón.

† The Portuguese had seized, raped or married African women, creating a new caste of mixed-raced Luso-Africans, who, until 1976, essentially ran their empire as enforcers and slave traders. African kings and traders brought them ivory, ebony and slaves, who were then marched back to the coast, often cruelly supervised by higher-status enslaved guards.

people of our own family,' adding in another letter that 'Many of our own subjects eagerly covet Portuguese merchandise,' for which 'they seize many of our black free subjects'. Priests were now shameless slave traders too, inflamed with 'the lusts of the world and lure of wealth just as the Jews crucified the Son of God because of covetousness'. Ten of his own nephews, dispatched to Portugal to be educated, were enslaved and sold to Brazil: 'We don't know so far if they are alive or dead.' But João III needed the trade. 'The Portuguese there on the contrary tell me how vast Kongo is,' he replied, 'and how it's so thickly populated it seems as if no slave has ever left.' The Pious King brought da Gama out of retirement for one last voyage.[*]

In 1518, Charles received the thirty-nine-year-old Magellan, veteran of Albuquerque's wars whose misconceived plans had been turned down by João. In proposing to sail westwards to reach the Spice Islands, on the assumption that America was close to China and the Moluccas, Magellan did not plan to circumnavigate the world. But when he hinted that the Portuguese did not know of this route, Charles backed him.

Soon after Magellan had sailed with five ships and 260 sailors (including Germans, Frenchmen, Italians, Africans, an Englishman and his Malay manservant known as Henrique, possibly the first person to circumnavigate the globe), the governor of Cuba, Diego Velázquez, asked permission to send an expedition to Yucatán in central America. Charles agreed. Velázquez fitted out an expedition under his secretary, Hernán Cortés, part of the first wave of adventurous Spaniards who followed Columbus. Founding a new town on the Gulf coast, Cortés learned of a gold-infested kingdom inland and immediately planned to defy Velázquez's control.

In June 1519, Cortés sent Charles a letter promising 'as much gold as Solomon accumulated for the Temple' along with a golden moon six feet wide and six Caribbean slaves, and requesting 'the offices of conquistador, captain-general and chief justice' of his town. Simultaneously Velázquez requested the execution of Cortés for insubordination. The glint of gold convinced Charles.

Cortés set off into the interior of the Mexica empire, accompanied by 500 Spaniards, Juan Garrido (Handsome John), born in Kongo,

---

[*] Da Gama died in India. Like the Columbuses, the da Gamas became a colonial dynasty: his three sons governed Gold Coast in Africa, Malacca and the State of India in Asia while in 1540, one of them, Estauvo, fought Ottoman fleets and aided the Christian emperor of Ethiopia, raiding up the Red Sea to Sinai, at the height of Portuguese empire. Vasco's grandson Joao da Gama was captain of Macau and then, in 1588, sailed across the entire Pacific exploring the north American coast before arriving at Acapulco to be arrested by the Spanish.

captured by the Portuguese and later manumitted, a woman named María de Estrada (who fought in all the battles and was the sister of one of the conquistadors), several Jewish *conversos*, and an unknown number of Taíno and African slaves.

CORTÉS, MALINCHE AND MOTECUHZOMA

On the way up the coast in his eleven ships, Cortés landed in the Maya kingdom of Putunchan and, using his cannon and eleven horses, subdued any resistance. He was given thirty enslaved women, including a young Nahua noblewoman, Malinche, 'the prettiest, the most lively', reduced to slavery by the Maya. She was bilingual in Mayan and Nahuatl and quickly learned Spanish. The girls were distributed among Cortés's henchmen and converted to Christianity. Cortés gave Malinche to the most aristocratic of his Spaniards.

Motecuhzoma sent envoys with gold and feathers. The Spaniards 'seized upon the gold like monkeys', but no one spoke Nahuatl until Malinche offered to interpret. Realizing her talent not just for translation but for diplomacy, Cortés took her back, promising her rewards if she got him to see Motecuhzoma. Later he said that, after God, he owed the conquest to Malinche – known to the Spanish as Doña Marina. Cortés showed off his cannon and arquebuses; the envoys returned to report to the Supreme Speaker. 'It especially made Motecuhzoma faint when he heard how the guns went off at the Spaniards' command,' recalled one of the Mexica, 'sounding like thunder, fire showering and spitting out. It turned a tree to dust. Their war gear was all iron, their armour, swords, bows, lances, iron.' America had no horses. 'Their deer [horses] were as tall as the roofs; their war dogs huge creatures,' with 'great dragging jowls and fiery yellow eyes'. Steel, horses and gunpowder gave the Spanish a commanding technical superiority.

Yet Motecuhzoma was also certain the Mexica were destined by the gods to rule the world and, after a lifetime of martial success and political glory, he vacillated. As Cortés negotiated with the local rulers, interpreted by Malinche, he learned that the Totonacs and many other peoples were discontented with the exacting Mexica empire. It was here that Malinche's gifts were essential. The offer of the chance to join the Spanish overthrow of the evil empire of Motecuhzoma was irresistible. Next, Cortés and Malinche encountered the powerful and unconquered republic of Tlaxcala which, Cortés was amazed to discover, had 'no supreme ruler' but was run by councils of chiefs who 'all gather together and, thus assembled, they decide' like 'Venice or Genoa'. After clashing with the Tlaxcalteca, he recruited them as allies, and 10,000 Tlaxcalteca joined his army. Cortés was a gifted leader, but his conquest was made possible by tens of thousands of local allies. He led this Hispano-Tlaxcalteca army to conquer the holy city of Cholula, a theocracy with rotating officials, dominated by its Temple of Quetzalcoatl, taller even than the Great Temple of Tenochtitlan.

Cortés was welcomed into the city, but remained vigilant in its crowded streets. His Tlaxcalteca allies hated the Choluteca and influenced his next move, but it was Malinche who warned him of a plot to kill the Spaniards. Cortés slaughtered thousands of Choluteca and looted their gold, predations in which the Tlaxcalteca joined enthusiastically before sacrificing many of the survivors.

Boosted by thousands of local troops, in November 1519 Cortés approached the resplendent imperial city of Tenochtitlan, where Motecuhzoma debated how to react. His brother Cuitláhuac argued for war; Motecuhzoma decided on temporary peace. Borne in his litter among 200 courtiers, a confident monarch in his forties, his hair long, his manner cheerful, wearing the turquoise diadem and golden sandals under a canopy of quetzal feathers, he met Cortés on his warhorse: two men convinced of the righteous destiny of their sacred empires. But Motecuhzoma had everything to lose, Cortés everything to gain. They each saw the other in the terms of their own worlds. Both dismounted, Cortés tying a necklace around the Speaker's neck, but when he tried to embrace him the courtiers stopped him. They then led the Spaniards into the unforgettable city of gleaming temples, multicoloured houses, canals and squares, watched by crowds from rooftops and canoes. Some Spaniards thought they were dreaming, others that it resembled Venice.

Cortés was settled in a royal palace, where Motecuhzoma visited him. The Spaniards in turn visited the Supreme Speaker's palace, where they were dazzled by its facilities including baths (the Mexica, unlike the grubby Spaniards, washed daily and changed clothes regularly), sated by the dishes – roast turkey and quail, tortillas – and impressed by a cocoa drink and a new intoxicant, tobacco, which Motecuhzoma smoked. All of these novelties would later catch on in Europe. But the Spaniards were horrified by the temples, where the priests, hair clotted with fresh human blood and earlobes bleeding from ritualistic piercings, showed them the staircase where sacrificed people were tossed, dripping with blood, and the top of the pyramid where a humanoid statue gripped a stone receptacle for human hearts. They also saw the *techcatl*, the spattered green execution stone, and braziers holding warm human hearts from the sacrifices that day. Their righteous horror should have been qualified by the knowledge that European cities were decorated with the heads of the executed, while they had regularly seen heretics burned alive.

Then Cortés discovered that Motecuhzoma's troops on the coast had clashed with Spanish forces. He punished the Mexica commanders by having them mauled by his war dogs – mastiffs and wolfhounds trained to kill – and then burned alive, which shocked the Mexica.

As fear spread across the city, Cortés agonized over what to do and decided to arrest the monarch, afraid that he was about to be double-crossed. When he heard that Velázquez had sent a force to arrest him, he rushed back to the coast and succeeded in winning over the Span-iards. Meanwhile his henchmen in Tenochtitlan tried to stop a sacrifice, thus sparking a massacre followed by an uprising. Motecuhzoma was hit by stones thrown by outraged Mexica and then arrested. His bro-ther Cuitláhuac, married to Motecuhzoma's eleven-year-old daughter Tecuichpoch Ixcaxochitzin, was chosen as Supreme Speaker just as Motecuhzoma died, either of his wounds or on Cortés's orders. Cortés hurried back to save his comrades.

In June 1520, besieged in the palace and lacking the forces to defeat the raging Mexica, Cortés broke out under ferocious attack, losing much gold and 600 men, a Night of Sorrows, escaping across the causeway. Facing defeat, he now proved his acumen, telling his men, 'Onwards, for we lack nothing!' Regathering his strength, he reported to Charles, 'It seems to me the best name for this country is New Spain,' of which he could call himself emperor 'with no less title than of Germany'. But most significantly he sent gold regalia. 'The gold-bearing world' im-pressed the emperor.

Cortés rebuilt his army. The Mexica mystique had been shattered and the subjugated peoples were now keen to join the Spaniards in attack-ing the empire, now being devoured by an even more voracious hunter – a case of jaguar–crocodile predation. The second city of the Triple Alliance, Texcoco, now joined Cortés, who had left a worse weapon in Tenochtitlan: pathogens of smallpox. 'A great plague broke out, lasting for seventy days, killing a vast number of our people,' a victim later told Spanish priests. 'Sores erupted on our faces, our breasts, our bellies, we were covered in agonizing sores from head to foot. The illness was so dreadful that no one could walk or move. A great many died from this plague, and many others . . . starved to death in their beds.' Cuitláhuac perished, succeeded by a young nephew Cuauhtémoc, a respected warrior who also married Motecuhzoma's daughter Tecuichpoch Ixcaxochitzin.

As soon as he was chosen, Cuauhtémoc killed Motecuhzoma's sons. Cortés struck back with terror, now deploying 700 Spaniards and 70,000 local troops, a hybrid army of warriors, Spaniards, Tlaxcalteca and Texcoca, the former in armour with arquebuses and Toledo swords shouting 'Castile!', Mesoamericans in feather headdresses and carrying *machuahitl* maces edged with obsidian shouting 'Tlaxcala!' First they attacked one of Tenochtitlan's allies, Tepeaca, killing 20,000, tearing some to pieces with war dogs, eating others in cannibalistic feasts, then enslaving women and children, branded G for *guerra* – war. Cortés was guided by his Tlaxcalteca and Texcoca allies, eager for vengeance against their own enemies. 'Clearly Cortés had to mould his plans to the objects of his indigenous allies,' writes Fernando Cervantes. They believed they were using the Spanish – and vice versa.

On 22 May 1521, Cortés surrounded Tenochtitlan, cutting off food supplies.

ISABEL MONTEZUMA: THE LAST EMPRESS AND THE FALL OF THE MEXICA

In late July, with 900 Spaniards and as many as 150,000 Tlaxcalteca and Texcoca, supported by brigantines on the lake, Cortés assaulted the city. Trained since childhood, hardened by cutting themselves with thorns and hallucinating on peyote, the Mexica fought wildly, sinking a brigantine and almost capturing Cortés himself, sacrificing prisoners and stringing up fifty-three heads. But in the end, wrote Cortés, they 'could no longer find any arrows, javelins or stones' and 'our allies were armed with swords and breastplates and slaughtered so many of them on land and in the water that more than 40,000 were killed'. He freely admitted that his Tlaxcalteca auxiliaries 'dined well' on prisoners, 'for they carried off all those killed, sliced them into pieces and ate them'. He did not give his allies credit for their help in battle, but conceded that 'We had more trouble in preventing our allies from killing with such cruelty than we had in fighting the enemy. For no race, however savage, has ever practised such fierce and unnatural cruelty as the natives of these parts.' Far from being a victory over four million people by 900 Spaniards, it was the triumph of overwhelming numerical and technical superiority, aided by the most punishing epidemic ever seen in the Americas. On 13 August, Cuauhtémoc was finally captured.

'Strike me dead immediately,' he told Cortés, asking him to spare his young wife Tecuichpoch. 'So loud was the wailing of women and children,' wrote Cortés, 'that there was not one man among us whose heart did not bleed.' It took a lot to make his heart bleed: 'We could not prevent more than fifteen thousand being killed and sacrificed that day.' The triumphant Spaniards and Tlaxcalteca soldiers looted and raped. The Mexica lamented their downfall in this threnody:

> Broken spears lie in the roads
> We've torn our hair with grief
> The houses are roofless now
> And their walls red with blood.

Cortés dismantled Tenochtitlan and built instead Mexico City, the Great Temple replaced by a great church. When the gold discovered proved inadequate, he had Cuauhtémoc tortured with fire to make him reveal more, while he rewarded his henchmen with *encomiendas* and sent treasures and a jaguar back to Charles. But at first no one paid much attention in Europe. His first treasure trove was captured by a French pirate, and the jaguar escaped, killing two sailors and then jumping into the Atlantic.

Shortly before Cortés laid siege to Tenochtitlan, Magellan was killed fighting locals in the Philippines who refused to convert to Christianity. Just as Cortés's treasures reached Spain, one ship of desperate, cadaverous survivors arrived there from Magellan's voyage. On a catastrophically bungled odyssey around the tip of south America into a 'peaceful' ocean that he named the Pacific, Magellan had lost men and ships to storms, mutinous fighting and fatal scurvy, before reaching Guam and then Brunei, the Moluccas and the Philippines,* where the explorer himself was smote. But one captain, Juan Sebastián Elcano, filled his ship with spices and with eighteen survivors sailed back around Africa to Spain. Charles, boasting that they had gone 'where neither Portugal nor any other nation has been', granted Elcano a coat of arms featuring a globe and the words *Primus circumdedisti me* – You encircled me first. The emperor along with the Fugger bankers backed a return voyage, during which Elcano starved to death, lost in the Pacific.

These Iberian adventurers had scarcely touched the vastness of the Pacific and its island realms. Some of these islands had been settled by Polynesians only recently: the last wave of Polynesian settlers had occupied the two islands of Aotearoa (New Zealand) only around 1300.

---

* In the Philippines they were intrigued by the tattoo-covered indigenous men who pierced their penises with studs which, they explained, initially discomfited their female partners but ultimately delivered a remarkable intensity of 'lustful pleasure'.

The Maori remained in Aotearoa and for reasons unknown lost the will
and technology to sail long distances. On Rapa Nui (Easter Island), settled since the third century, the islanders had built massive statues and
temple platforms to honour ancestors and observe the stars.

In the middle of the Pacific, the four main islands of Hawaii were
ruled by dynasties of intermarried chiefs descended from a founding
goddess, Papa. The exact sequence is still unknown but around 700
Hawaii may have been settled by Polynesians from Tahiti, while it was
a few centuries since new conquerors from Nuku Hiva (named the
Marquesas by the Spanish) had arrived on the islands.

While starry-eyed European travellers later idealized Hawaii as a
free-loving, easy-going paradise, this was a hierarchical, polyamorous
society of warriors dominated by *kapu*, the Polynesian religion, with
rituals, foods and lands specified for each class. The chieftains earned
mana, divine charisma, by inheritance and war, which granted them the
right to sacrifice humans to the gods. Subjects bowed to the floor before
chiefs. The struggles for power were as ferocious as those in Europe;
noble babies were killed if they cried when they were laid on the sacred
Naha Stone; victories were celebrated by human sacrifices. The losing
chieftain was personally sacrificed – usually strangled – by the victor.

Their entire concept of family was more flexible than that prevailing
in Europe: women, high and low, enjoyed a degree of independence
unthinkable in China or Europe and were allowed lovers; children often
treated two men as fathers and were usually raised by cousins rather
than parents. Older men took teenage boys as *aikane* – lovers. But genealogy was chronicled and treasured. Around this time, the main island
was governed by a semi-mythical *alii nui* or queen called Kaikilani, the
ancestress of the kings who would encounter the Europeans.

Cortés knew little of the Pacific, but he understood there were lands
there to conquer. At forty-nine, he had lost none of his ambition or
energy. Before permitting more expeditions, Emperor Charles ordered
that indigenous peoples 'must be allowed to live in liberty', but Cortés
was already forcing them to work to death in *encomiendas*, while spasms
of epidemic – measles, smallpox, mumps, haemorrhagic fevers, – were
killing large numbers of them: by 1580, some 88 per cent of the people
of the Valley of Mexico had died.

As other conquistadors competed with Cortés to 'explore' (seize) the
lands around the Valley, he felt forced to pre-empt them, orchestrating
expeditions up the Pacific coast, starting with his own to the Sea of
Cortés followed by that of a henchman who sailed up the coast as far as

San Francisco, mapping the coast of a new territory named California.*

Cortés's allies remained independent, with many kingdoms untouched by Spanish control for over a century. In 1523, Cortés sent his sidekick Pedro de Alvarado to conquer the Maya kingdoms of Kiche and Kaqchikel in Guatemala and Salvador, but failed. Ultimately it took massive assistance from Nahua peoples to crush the Kaqchikel; to the north, Zapotecs helped Cortés take the lush Oaxaca Valley. The second largest kingdom, that of the Purépecha, was conquered in 1530, but the last independent Maya kingdom did not fall until 1697.

North America was even more challenging. In 1528, an expedition led by Pánfilo de Narváez tried to found a colony in La Florida, the vast lands between Alabama and modern Florida, but it was a disaster. Trudging 2,000 miles, starving and eating each other, the Spaniards were enslaved by Coahuiltecan Indians: four survivors made it to Mexico City.†

On his own expedition to Honduras, Cortés took with him Cuauhtémoc, the Supreme Speaker, afraid to leave the last ruler in Mexico City. But when he discovered a plot to rebel, he had him beheaded and impaled.

Back in Mexico City, Cortés was joined by his long-time wife, Catalina Suárez, but she died mysteriously, probably murdered by her husband. Malinche, his Maya interpreter and in some ways the architect of the decisive alliance with the Mesoamerican allies, became his mistress – whether by force or choice we cannot know – giving birth to his first son Martín known as El Mestizo (the Mixed Race). Cortés took the boy away, had him legitimized by the pope and raised in Spain. As for Malinche herself, Cortés gave her an *encomienda* and married her to another Spaniard, with whom she had a daughter. Still only around twenty-three, this remarkable woman had endured fourteen years a slave; now she was a landowner and the wife of a Spanish gentleman. But she died soon afterwards, perhaps in one of the epidemics.

Amid the killing of Mexica, Cortés presided over a strange melding of Spanish conquistador and Mexica royalty, Motecuhzoma's bloodline being especially revered. Cortés regarded Motecuhzoma's daughter Tecuichpoch, now twenty-five, this widow of three Supreme Speakers, as

* This was said to resemble the island kingdom of Calafia, queen of the black Amazons of California in the popular chivalrous novel *Las sergas de Esplandián* (Adventures of Esplandián) by Garci Rodríguez de Montalvo. California is the only territory named after a fictional character. The Sea of Cortés is now the Gulf of California.

† Among them was Cabeza de Vaca, who wrote a chronicle of his adventures, and Mustafa, known as Estevanico, an enslaved African Muslim with a gift for languages – 'the negro who talked to them', in Vaca's words. Mustafa, African explorer of the American west, was later killed in New Mexico acting as a guide for a return expedition.

an important symbol of the new order. He converted her to Christianity with the name Isabel Montezuma, marrying her to a henchman (who soon died) and granting her an *encomienda*, worked by local and African slaves. Described as 'very beautiful', she became a devout Christian, but she too was unable to avoid becoming Cortés's mistress.[*]

Cortés was now super-rich, but denunciations by his enemies, led by Diego Columbus, flooded in to Charles V, though he gladly received the first 60,000 gold pesos from his 'gold-bearing lands'. The emperor took control, chairing a Council of the Indies in the Alhambra Palace, Granada, and confiscating some of Cortés's sultanic holdings. In 1528, Cortés, fulminating against 'powerful rivals and enemies' who have 'obscured the eyes of Your Majesty', sailed home to face the emperor.

Although Charles disliked the coarse conquistador who had so enriched his empire, he created him captain-general of the South Sea and marquess of the Valley of Oaxaca, granted him 23,000 vassals and pardoned his insubordination. Cortés celebrated by marrying a noblewoman with whom he had a legitimate son, Don Martín. Cortés returned to New Spain, living in splendour at his palace (the first Spanish building on the mainland that still stands at Cuernavaca).

As Charles took control of New Spain, he received Cortés's cousin Francisco Pizarro, who asked the emperor's support for an expedition to conquer another fabulous auric kingdom – Piru. As long-serving mayor of Panama City, Pizarro had been exploring down the Pacific coast, gathering intelligence. Charles agreed. When his men grumbled about the hardships, Pizarro shouted, 'There lies Piru with its riches; here, Panama and its poverty. Choose, each man, what best becomes a brave Castilian. For my part, I go to the south.'

As ever Charles was desperate for cash, personally exhausted, mentally stressed and politically overextended – and he needed a companion if not a wife.

---

[*] Pregnant, Isabel was quickly married to another Spaniard (she married six times in all), and then gave birth to a daughter, Leonor Cortés Montezuma. Altogether she had seven children by her two Spanish husbands and Cortés. Part pawn, part symbol, she became strong-minded, liberating her slaves during her lifetime and in her will: 'I want, and I order, that all my slaves, Indian men and women, born from this land, shall be free of all servitude and captivity, and as free people they shall do as they will; so if they are [slaves] I will and command for them to be free.' One son, Juan de Montezuma Cano, married the Castilian aristocrat Elvira de Toledo, building the Toledo-Montezuma Palace, still standing in Cáceres with its murals of Mexica Speakers and Spanish grandees; another son was progenitor of the counts of Miravalle, while the descendants of her brother Pedro (de) Montezuma Tlacahuepan, who accompanied Cortés back to Spain, became dukes of Montezuma.

Incas, Pizarros, Habsburgs and Medici

The emperor faced challenges on all fronts. In the east, Suleiman advanced; in the west, François of France, the personification of macho, lascivious yet cultured Renaissance monarch, known as *Le Grand Nez* (Big Nose) and *Grand Colas* (Big Cock), hated Charles as much as he resented Habsburg encirclement. The hatred was mutual. Charles challenged François to personal combat. François tried to seize Milan in Italy, where outside Pavia on 24 February 1525, Charles's arquebusiers scythed down François's charging cavalry* and captured *Le Grand Nez*, who was transported back to Spain. 'Nothing remains to me,' François told his mother, 'except honour and life.' After he had tried to escape disguised as an African slave, wearing blackface, he capitulated to Charles, whom he refused to meet, winning his freedom, though he had to leave his sons as hostages. Galloping exuberantly into Paris, he shouted, 'I'm king again,' reneged on the deal and signed an alliance with England.

The twenty-six-year-old Charles celebrated victory as he celebrated marriage to a girl he came to adore. After an engagement to Mary, the six-year-old daughter of Henry VIII and his aunt Catherine, designed to undermine the Franco-English entente, he switched to marrying Infanta Isabella, aged twenty-three, the pale, red-haired daughter of Manuel of Portugal who offered a Croesan dowry. Isabella was well educated

---

* Charles fielded an army of Swiss and German *Landsknechte* and Spanish *tercios*, experts in the use of pike and arquebus. Their pike squares allowed them to reload and fire in unison. François also employed *Landsknechte* but fewer of them. Arquebuses were constantly improved, with Italy as the laboratory of technical innovation. Imperial troops started to use heavier arquebuses, supported on a rest, that penetrated armour: they became known as *moschetti* – muskets – and they quickly made armour obsolete, ending the era of heavily armoured knights that had started with cataphracts in Persia a millennium earlier. The most famous gunmaker was naturally an Italian. Da Vinci experimented with musket designs. In 1526, an Italian artisan, Bartolomeo Beretta, founded a foundry in northern Italy that manufactured muskets. In the 1530s, Beretta was experimenting with a new, smaller firearm: pistols – from the Czech *pistole* – became an aristocratic fashion item, bespoke and intricately ornamented. As for the Beretta, the factory is still producing guns today.

and, confidently wearing a medallion inscribed *Aut Caesar aut nihil*, determined to marry only a great monarch. She got her Caesar, while her brother João III married Charles's sister, Catarina. The first cousins met for the first time at their Seville wedding, but she was extremely pretty. They fell in love, honeymooning happily at the arabesque Alhambra in Granada, where he built a new palace and imported carnations to plant in her honour.

The young empress 'sleeps every night in her husband's arms; they stay in bed until 10 or 11', observed a Portuguese diplomat, 'always talking and laughing together'. Charles boasted that his hands were shaking from erotic exhaustion – 'I can't write with my own hand' – as he was 'still a new bridegroom', and Isabella conceived at once, surviving an agonizing labour with regal grit. She requested a veil, and when a midwife advised her to scream if necessary, she replied, 'I'd rather die. Don't talk to me like that: I may die but I will *not* cry out.'* The baby was named Philip. Although Charles selfishly treated her as a breeding machine – she endured seven pregnancies – and left her for four years at a time as he defended his empire, he loved her, praising her 'great beauty'. He trusted her too, appointing her regent; he praised her decisions as 'very prudent and well conceived'.

In May 1529, it was Isabella who permitted that coarse conquistador Pizarro to set off for somewhere called Piru. 'We order that Captain Pizarro be entrusted with governing it for the rest of his life,' she wrote. 'We give permission for him to take 250 men with him.'

In December 1530, Pizarro sailed from Panama, arriving fortuitously just as the Empire of the Four Parts Together reeled from a war of succession. Conqueror and father of fifty sons, Inca Wayna Capac, who had ruled for thirty years, had expanded Four Parts to its greatest extent, from the Peruvian heartland to the Andean mountains and Amazonian swamps, pushing into today's Bolivia, Argentina, Chile, Ecuador

---

* Childbirth, conducted at home, was still lethal; women made wills before going into labour. The pain was scarcely eased by doses of myrrh, valerian root and 'Turkish poppy' – opium. Statistics are guesswork but over many centuries, child mortality before the age of five varied from 20 per cent to 50; as many as 20 per cent of births ended in death for the mother. Midwives, often operating in families who passed on their knowledge, dilated mothers with unsterile fingers and, if a baby could not be delivered, Caesarian section killed the mothers; doing nothing killed both; and generally midwives used a hook, a crochet, to save the mother and remove the baby. Even in successful births, tearing could lead to fatal puerperal sepsis. Often the infection of the open wound left by the placenta developed into puerperal fever; mothers often died of peritonitis. So far doctors – all men – were uninvolved. When doctors started to get involved and in the next century maternity hospitals were founded, the mortality rates soared. For a long time, home births were considerably safer.

– victories celebrated by flaying vanquished lords, impaling their heads on stakes and stretching their skins on to drums. The Sapa Inca knew about the European arrival even before Cortés's conquests, but in 1524, while fighting in south-western Colombia, he contracted smallpox brought by the Spanish, dying in an epidemic along with his chosen heir. The Four Parts was divided between two sons, Huáscar Inca who was to rule from his new city of Quito, and the favourite Atahualpa as autonomous king of Cuzco in the south – an arrangement that soon proved disastrous. Huáscar seduced the wives of his nobles and seized the fiefdoms of former Incas, leading to tension with his brother whom he arrested. When Atahualpa escaped, the brothers, backed by feuding royal clans, fought one another with armies of 50,000 apiece until Huáscar was captured.

Just as Pizarro was about to arrive, Atahualpa laid on a sadistic show, forcing his half-brother to watch as all his wives and children were tortured then killed. He was leading an army of 40,000 towards the capital Cuzco when he encountered Captain-General Pizarro and his 106 infantrymen and 62 cavalrymen, a family affair that included three Pizarro brothers. The Spaniards agreed to greet Atahualpa, who was resting in a nearby spa in Cajamarca. In the city square there, the Castilian artfully concealed artillery in surrounding buildings. When Atahualpa was borne by his retainers into the square, Pizarro's friar offered a breviary. The Inca threw it to the ground, and the conquistador 'gave a signal to the gunner that he should fire shots into the midst of the Incas'.

THE INCA AND THE CONQUISTADOR

Pizarro's few warhorses charged into the Incas, who did not fight back. Seven thousand were slaughtered. Atahualpa was arrested. Pizarro demanded a vast ransom of gold. Offering a military alliance to the victor, Atahualpa gave his fifteen-year-old half-sister Quispe Sisa to Pizarro. She was first baptized as Inés Yupanqui and then seduced by the grizzled Pizarro, who nicknamed her Pispita after a beautiful Spanish bird. While in custody Atahualpa, still fighting his civil war, ordered his brother's murder – 'How shall my brother get so much gold and silver for himself? I would give twice as much as he can, if they would kill him and leave me as lord.' He ordered gold from Cuzco for Pizarro. Six tons of gold and five of silver were melted down, but as the Inca's generals raised new armies to attack the Spanish, Pizarro panicked and decided to kill the monarch, accusing him of idolatry and murdering his brother. He then sentenced him to burn, an unbearable fate for an Inca. Pizarro's friar offered Atahualpa strangulation if he converted, so he took the name Francisco after his killer and was then garrotted.

Now a young Inca, Manco Yupanqui, another son of Huáscar who had survived Atahualpa's massacre of the family, offered Pizarro an alliance, believing he could re-establish the Four Parts with Spanish help. In Cuzco, the Pizarro brothers installed Manco as Inca, watched by his regal mummified ancestors.

The capital was dazzling. 'This city is the greatest and the finest ever seen in this country or anywhere in the Indies,' Pizarro wrote to Charles. 'We can assure your Majesty that it is so beautiful and has such fine buildings that it would be remarkable even in Spain.' Pizarro presided over the looting of the Coricancha, Temple of the Sun, its gold and silver walls, its garden of golden plants, sacrificial altar and image of the sun and the many golden statues of early Inca rulers, all of it melted down. Pizarro sent his brother Hernando homewards with the emperor's first share.

Charles dominated Italy. In Rome, Leo X excommunicated Luther, who fulminated about 'how openly and shamelessly the pope . . . practises sodomy'. After Leo's death and a short-lived successor, Charles backed the election of another Medici, Giulio, who became Clement VII. Genial and cultivated, Clement commissioned Michelangelo, whom he had known since they were young, to finish the family chapel in Florence, telling him, 'Think only of work' and 'Spare no expense.' Michelangelo celebrated. 'Medici is pope. Which will cheer the whole world,' he told his quarryman. 'With regards to art, many things will be accomplished.' Instead Rome was to be sacked in an orgy of violence and rapine.

THE BLACK DUKE, MICHELANGELO AND THE SACK OF ROME

Pope Clement betrayed Charles and allied with François. Charles was incensed: 'You must know the part we played in your election.' His army, unpaid and roiling, marched on Rome. Clement prepared to fight, but he had grossly miscalculated. In early May, the imperialists stormed Rome, slaughtering Clement's Swiss Guards on the steps of St Peter's. Clement fled to the Castel Sant'Angelo, where he melted down jewellery to plan his escape. Outside the Hadrianic fortress, Charles's *Landsknechte* – many of them Protestants – went wild, raping nuns, defacing

Raphael's paintings in the Vatican with the graffito 'luther' and killing 10,000 Romans – until the plague culled the *Landsknechte* themselves. The catastrophe that befell Clement led to a revolution against the Medici in Florence. These apocalyptic scenes helped inspire Michelangelo's vision of hell in the *Last Judgment* and intensified Catholic–Protestant hatred. 'Christ reigns in such a way that the emperor who persecutes Luther for the pope,' gloated Luther, 'is forced to destroy the pope for Luther.'

On 6 June, Clement, terrified of Charles, surrendered, promising a ransom. He escaped to the countryside, where he received English envoys seeking permission for Henry VIII to annul his marriage to Catherine of Aragon, Charles's aunt, and marry a feisty paramour, Anne Boleyn. At any other time, such a request would have been fixable, but politics, like love, is all about timing: Clement could not risk offending Charles. Henry, who started as a slim, genial, gingery charmer and developed into a vicious, narcissistic, semi-impotent bloviator, desperate to produce a son for his parvenu dynasty and in love with Boleyn, was a religious conservative. But his talented Protestant minister Thomas Cromwell was a religious radical who orchestrated divorce from Catherine, marriage to Boleyn, schism with Rome and a step towards a Reformist England. Clement's decision to refuse justified Henry's move against European interference that both formed and reflected England's autonomous instincts.

In 1530, Charles arrived in Bologna to receive his reward from Clement: a papal coronation, which proved to be the last. In return Clement asked for the Medici to be restored in Florence, where Michelangelo, despite his relationship with the family, backed the republic, serving as anti-Medici governor-general of fortifications. But his battlements were of no avail: Charles restored the Medici.

Clement, like Henry, had no legitimate heirs. Only two young bastards were left, but one of them was probably his own son by a black slave. The illegitimate Alessandro Medici had grown up in obscurity, his mother described as a 'slave', 'Moorish' and 'half-Negro'. But now family necessity trumped racial prejudice. Alessandro enjoyed an astonishing reversal of fortune, first tutored and trained, then unveiled as duke of Florence and betrothed to Charles's illegitimate daughter Margarita. Nicknamed *Il Moro* – the Black – Alessandro, the first and only European ruler of colour, proved adept at murderous Florentine politics, poisoning his cousin Cardinal Ippolito Medici and possibly having his own African mother murdered to avoid social embarrassment. Spending extravagantly on his superb clothes and exquisitely engraved pistols, the

Black Duke was now an Italian magnifico. If Charles was impressed, Michelangelo was not: when he refused to design a fortress for Alessandro, the duke ordered his assassination. Fortunately, 'someone spoke in my ear that I shouldn't stay there any longer if I wanted to save my life' and the artist escaped to Rome, where Clement* forgave him.

Yet Clement was still playing Habsburgs against Valois, marrying the other Medici heiress, the fourteen-year-old Catherine, nicknamed *Duchessina*, to François's second son Henri. While it seemed unlikely Henri would ever be king, Catherine would dominate France for forty years.

MICHELANGELO'S *LAST JUDGMENT* AND THE FALL OF THE BLACK DUKE

As Clement was dying, he commissioned Michelangelo to paint the back wall of the Sistine Chapel. Yet the death of Michelangelo's generous patron led to the election of an even better one. Paul III, the former Alessandro Farnesse,† urbane, astute and sometimes murderous, summoned Michelangelo, aged sixty, who insisted he was too tired and overstretched to accept more work. 'I've nursed this ambition for thirty years and now I'm pope I won't be dissatisfied. I'm determined to have you in my service,' insisted Paul.

Michelangelo duly painted *The Last Judgment*, a fresco of the dead awakening at Judgement Day and the second coming of Christ. Then Paul commissioned him to design a piazza on the Capitoline Hill, the Campidoglio, where he placed Marcus Aurelius' statue, then appointed him overseer of St Peter's. Paul and Michelangelo became friends.

The artist now thrived in Rome, sending money to his feckless family to relaunch them as nobility while presiding over his brood of protégés and enjoying friendships high and low. He sent love letters and drawings to a young nobleman, Tommaso dei Cavalieri, but it was to his dear friend Princess Vittoria Colonna that he wrote most intimately about

---

* Clement was an open-minded humanist, who protected the Jews of Rome against the Inquisition and was interested in the theories of a well-connected, Italian-educated Polish priest, Nicolaus Copernicus, who argued that the earth revolved around the sun. Clement saw no threat to the Church from heliocentricity. Ironically the radical Luther rejected Copernicus as 'that fellow who wishes to turn the whole of astronomy upside down'.

† A throwback to the Borgias, Farnese was known as the Petticoat Cardinal, raised to the scarlet because he was the teenaged brother of Pope Alexander's mistress. Paul also hired Titian, who painted revealing portraits of the aged pope and his shifty nephews. Titian balanced papal with imperial patronage, playing the Farnese against the Habsburgs. But Paul never paid for the paintings. Finally in 1548, Titian left for Augsburg to become the Habsburgs' top painter.

art: 'For a reliable guide in my vocation, beauty was set before me as a birthright, a mirror and a lamp for art.' He tempered his curmudgeonliness with laughter and wit, mocking his ageing bladder: 'Urine! How well I know it – drippy duct, compelling me to awake too early, when dawn plays at peekaboo, then yonder – yuk!' He was getting older, and at one point he fell off the scaffold in the Sistine.*

In Florence, Alessandro Medici had only just married Charles V's daughter, the fourteen-year-old Margarita of Austria, but his cut-throat swagger and enthusiastic seductions attracted bitter envy, particularly in his penniless cousin and companion Lorenzaccio. So often in politics the greatest peril lies within not without, and nothing surpasses the intimate loathings of family.

Lorenzaccio decided to kill the Black Duke. In 1536, he offered the duke every womanizer's dream: the seduction of a wholesome wife. Luring him to the assignation, he burst in on the sleeping Alessandro with a hitman. As Lorenzaccio stabbed him in the stomach, Alessandro fought back, almost biting off the killer's finger until the hitman slashed his throat.†

Charles was the universal emperor of Christendom, his armour engraved 'Charles the Divine'. But his enemy Suleiman regarded himself not just as sultan, khan and padishah but as the *real* Caesar. Disdaining Charles as mere 'king of Spain', he advanced on Vienna.

SULEIMAN'S FAVOURITES: ROXELANA AND IBRAHIM

'The king of Spain,' Suleiman told a French envoy, 'has proclaimed he wants to act against the Turks and now I am advancing against him. If the man has balls and courage, let him come.'

His favourite, Ibrahim Pasha, commissioned Venetian jewellers to

---

* In 1549, Pope Paul III died with Michelangelo at his bedside. Michelangelo was close to those who flirted with Protestantism, but now he had to be very careful. In 1555, the zealous Giampietro Carafa was elected Paul IV and launched a crackdown on dissent, deploying the Inquisition and ordering some of the nudes in *The Last Judgment* to be painted over. Michelangelo died aged eighty-eight in 1563.

† As Lorenzaccio escaped, the Medici invited a cousin, Cosimo de' Medici of Urbino, to become duke. Cosimo turned out to have the right stuff. He was as murderous and cultivated as a Medici should be, killing enemies, hunting down Lorenzaccio and personally stabbing to death his own disloyal valet. His descendants ruled Tuscany for two centuries. As for the Black Duke's widow, Margarita, Charles married her to another papal popinjay, Paul III's grandson Ottavio Farnese, duke of Parma. Free-spirited and intelligent, she refused to consummate the marriage for several years and then only on the condition that she kept her own court. Later she was a competent and tolerant governor of the Netherlands. Her son would be the duke of Parma who in 1588 failed to rendezvous with the Armada.

craft a four-crowned imperial tiara. The vizier ruled supreme, based in a new palace on the hippodrome (still standing) where he presided over spectacular shows of imperial power. Grand viziers had the right to display five horsetails on their banners, but Ibrahim was allowed six, just one fewer than the sultan. Only Ukrainian Hürrem, nicknamed Roxelana – mother of five sultanic children – had the power to challenge him.

The sultan's teenaged son, Mustafa, was jealous of Ibrahim. The system played teams of mother and son against mother and son. Unable to undermine Hürrem, Mustafa's mother, Mahidevran, attacked her, scratching her face and tearing her hair. Summoned by Suleiman, Hürrem refused to come, saying her looks had been destroyed. Mahidevran was exiled.

Suleiman's life seemed stable with Ibrahim and Roxelana. While his mother Hafsa ruled his family world, Suleiman did not change Roxelana's status. But when the *valide sultan* died, he first manumitted Roxelana, still in her twenties, then married her.[*]

After several sons, only one of whom could succeed, Suleiman and Hürrem stopped having children, aware that losers in the power tournament would be strangled. Hürrem probably used intravaginal suppositories, with oil from cabbage leaves, pepper, juice of peppermint, leaves of pennyroyal and dill. She inherited control of the Old Palace and the harem, emerging out of the shadows, corresponding with the queens of Poland and Hungary while endowing her own charitable foundations in Istanbul and Jerusalem. 'You know I'm never content with the least thing,' she admitted to Suleiman.

Suleiman and Ibrahim were planning wars, treaties and construction on a vast scale. In the east, Suleiman fought the Shiite Persians; in the west, in 1524, he defeated the Hungarians and killed young King Ludwig of Hungary, triggering one of the Habsburg marriage deals made by Emperor Maximilian: Charles's younger brother Ferdinand, archduke of Austria, was married to Ludwig's sister. So Ferdinand now claimed Hungary, Bohemia and Croatia, which would remain Habsburg kingdoms until 1918. Then in 1529 Suleiman and Ibrahim invaded Austria, 120,000 Ottomans besieging Vienna, which was saved only by the heavy rains that forced them to leave behind their heavy guns. Three

---

[*] Roxelana now officially became Hürrem Sultan with the title of Royal Consort *Ḥaseki Sultan*. *Valide* and *haseki sultans* were traditionally served by a Jewish lady-in-waiting – known as the *kira* – mediating with the male and Christian worlds, often acting as a diplomat with foreign monarchs. Hafsa's *kira* Strongila was inherited by Hürrem and later converted to Islam.

years later, they attacked again; this time Charles counter-attacked into Ottoman Hungary.

Charles and Suleiman did not just conduct their duel on land. In 1528, facing Ottoman advances on land and slave-hunting Islamic pirates by sea, Charles hired the best Christian admiral, Andrea Doria, ruler of Genoa as Perpetual Censor, heir to a dynasty of seafaring oligarchs. When Suleiman was distracted by war against Iran, Doria raided Ottoman Greece. Suleiman in turn summoned the greatest corsair of his time: Barbarossa.

Tamerlanians and Rurikovichi, Ottomans and the House of Mendes

In 1533, Barbarossa sailed into the Bosphoros and past the Topkapı Palace with forty vessels, banners aflutter, before presenting Suleiman with camel-loads of gold, jewels and textiles escorted by lions and a procession of Christian enslaved girls, each bearing a gift of treasure. Suleiman appointed Barbarossa, red-bearded, burly, bushy-browed, as *Kapudan-ı Derya* – Captain of the Sea – while ordering Ibrahim to create shipyards and build a fleet.

Barbarossa was born on Lesbos, son of an Albanian Christian cavalryman turned potter and a Greek priest's widow, converts to Islam. Two of his brothers, Oruç and Ilyas, had started as traders until they were captured by the crusading Knights of St John. They killed Ilyas and enslaved Oruç in their galleys until Khidr, the future Barbarossa, freed his brother. When Isabella and Ferdinand started to persecute their Muslim subjects, the brothers launched a rescue mission, ferrying some of the refugees to safety in Morocco.

Many ex-Spanish Muslims became Barbarossa's associates, led by the noble girl Aisha, whom we saw leaving Granada in 1492 with the last amir. When the noble refugees arrived in Morocco, now beset with factional war, her father married her to the potentate of the port of Tétouan. When the husband died, Aisha took over Tétouan as Lady of Power, Sayyida al-Hurra, fortifying the town and creating a fleet that raided Christian shipping – known to Christians as the Pirate Queen. Basing themselves on the island of Djerba, the brothers raided Italy and Spain, seizing Christian children and girls to sell in the slave markets. Raids often enslaved as many as 6,000. The brothers captured African ports, first Oran then Algiers and Bougie, where Oruç lost his arm. When he replaced it with a silver prosthetic, Turks called him Silver Arm. Offering Algiers to Selim the Grim, who accepted it as a *sanjak* (province), Silver Arm infuriated Charles, who ordered attacks on Oran and Tlemcen during which Silver Arm was killed. The last brother Khidr, red-bearded Barbarossa, took command. Sending ships to aid the new sultan Suleiman's attack on Rhodes, Barbarossa again raided Italy and Spain; his captains hit northern France, Cornwall and the Isle of Wight, while he made Algiers into a luxurious slaving boomtown – the start of what Christians called the Barbary Coast.

When Barbarossa, chief admiral and governor of north Africa and Rhodes, left Istanbul, he pursued Doria, landing at Ostia, the port of Rome, and capturing Capri (he built Castello Barbarossa there, whose ruins still stand). Thanks to her intelligence network operated through her Jewish *femme d'affaires* Strongila, it was Hürrem who informed Suleiman of Barbarossa's first victories.

Faced with a Habsburg counter-offensive, Ibrahim pulled off a treaty with France against Charles, partly negotiated by Barbarossa, who visited Toulon with his fleet. Charles V dispatched an envoy to offer Barbarossa the lordship of Africa or assassinate him. Barbarossa beheaded the hitman.

In 1535, Charles struck back, seizing Tunis while Suleiman and Ibrahim were leading an offensive against the Safavi shah of Iran, Tahmasp, capturing Baghdad. But Ibrahim, after ten years of viceregal power, had grown too comfortable with Suleiman, and too cosmopolitan, even for the easy-going Ottomans. The longer a minister is in office, the more enemies are made. Ibrahim was not shy of his magnificence. 'Though I am the sultan's slave, whatsoever I say is done. I can at a stroke make a pasha out of a stableboy, I can give kingdoms and provinces to whomsoever I choose,' he told foreign envoys. Outside his palace on the hippodrome, Ibrahim erected the statues of Hercules, Diana and Apollo captured in Hungary, which shocked the iconoclast Muslims. 'Two Abrahams came into the world,' joked the poet Figani, 'one a destroyer of idols, the other an idol worshipper.' Ibrahim had Figani strangled. Although Ibrahim had a male Italian lover, he had long loved the sultan's sister Hatice, sending her poems – without Suleiman's permission. On campaign he let his flunkies call him 'sultan'. He had executed a rival vizier – and he had clashed with Hürrem. 'An explanation has been requested for why I am angry with the pasha,' she had written to Suleiman in 1526. 'It will be heard. For now, send greetings to the pasha if he'll accept them.' Suleiman let Ibrahim marry his sister, with a fiesta in the hippodrome. But the vizier was close to the sultan's eldest son Mustafa, whose likely succession would be a death threat to Hürrem's sons.

On the Ides of March, 1536, the padishah and vizier broke the Ramadan fast together. Then Ibrahim went to bed in the inner Topkapı.

Some time in the night, Suleiman sent his killers, the Tongueless, into Ibrahim's apartments where they garrotted his childhood friend. The *Makbul* (favourite), wits said, had become *Maktul* (killed), buried in an unmarked grave. Hürrem's position was enhanced: Suleiman appointed Rüstem, their son-in-law, as grand vizier. His wife, their favourite daughter Mihrimah (Son of Moons), would become an Ottoman potentate in her own right.

As a young slave Rüstem, a Croatian pig farmer's son, had riskily jumped out of a window to grab a trinket Suleiman had dropped. Hürrem had favoured a more handsome man for Mihrimah, but Rüstem paid the sultan's Jewish doctor to declare that the man had syphilis. His enemy counterclaimed that Rüstem had leprosy, which was disproved by the presence in his robes of a louse – lice were believed to avoid lepers. In 1539, Rüstem, nicknamed Lucky Louse given his rise to power, and by now in his mid-forties, married the seventeen-year-old Mihrimah, becoming a *damad*, imperial son-in-law. Amassing great wealth, he would ultimately own 1,700 slaves. But Ottoman princesses had special power: they could divorce their husbands, amass wealth themselves and discreetly deploy power. Like her mother, Mihrimah was beautiful, blonde, forceful and intelligent, later negotiating for her father and brother with the Polish monarchs.

Suleiman was directing a global war, long neglected by European historians. In 1538 he sent eighty vessels and 40,000 men through the Red Sea to the Indian Ocean – probably the largest to ply those seas since the Ming treasure fleets. The Admiral of the Indian Ocean was an enslaved Hungarian eunuch and future grand vizier, Hadım Suleiman Pasha, now sixty-nine, who sailed from Jeddah, seized Aden (Yemen) from the Portuguese and then rendezvoused with the sultan's Gujarati ally in an unsuccessful attack on Portuguese Diu (western India). In the Horn of Africa, Suleiman invaded Habesh (Eritrea) and captured Massawa, which remained Ottoman into the nineteenth century. He also sent troops and cannon to his allies, the sultans of Adal in Ethiopia and Ajura, in Somalia, to help their attack on local Christian enemies. These conquests brought a new intoxicant, derived from beans, long favoured by Yemenite sufis, to Cairo then to Constantinople: coffee. Coffee became a global commodity, with coffee houses contributing to the new sociability in cities. Barbarossa was the one of the first to add a coffee house to his mansion.

In the Mediterranean, Barbarossa seized Otranto as Suleiman threatened northern Italy; the admiral captured many of the last Venetian islands and strongholds, driving the republic to join the Holy League arranged by Pope Paul III against the Ottomans. In September 1538, near Preveza (Greece), Charles's admiral Doria led 112 galleys and 50,000 troops against Barbarossa's fleet of 122 as the latter's Jewish-born admiral Sinan landed troops on the coast, covering the Ottoman rear. Barbarossa destroyed thirteen ships and captured thirty-six along with 3,000 prisoners, winning domination of the Mediterranean.

Charles was distracted by the decline of Isabella. Pregnant for the seventh time and possibly consumptive, she was 'the greatest pity in the world, so thin as not to resemble a person'. In May 1539, she gave birth to a stillborn son, then died of postnatal fever at thirty-five. Charles collapsed – 'Nothing can console me,' he told his sister Maria – sending their son Philip to oversee her burial in Granada and commissioning Titian to paint her from existing portraits, thereafter always travelling with her image. He soon returned to his womanizing ways, secretly fathering a son, Geronimo, by a teenaged German servant girl. The boy was taken away from her and raised by courtiers – to emerge later.

Recovering from these blows, Charles planned a powerful attack on Algiers, but as usual he was impoverished – until the arrival from America of a dazzling fleet of treasure, dispatched by captain Pizarro, whose brother Hernando presented Charles with his first tranche of Peruvian gold and news of its conquest.

THE HABSBURG BROTHERS AND THEIR CONQUISTADORS

The emperor disapproved of Pizarro's murders – 'The death of Atahualpa displeased me because he was a sovereign' – but added, 'Since it seemed to you necessary, we approve it for now.' Later he granted him the grandiloquent title marquess of the Conquest while agreeing 'permanent allocations of indigenous inhabitations' as effective slave labour.

The conquistadors were fortunate in their timing: Xauxa and Wanka tribes, who resented the Incas, served as Spanish auxiliaries, as did the anti-Atahualpa Incas. Without these allies, Pizarro's coup would have been impossible.

The Pizarros relished and abused their domination of the Inca princesses but also upgraded their middling family by breeding with Inca royalty, not to speak of getting their hands on their property. Many of these girls were very young. The Spaniards used a sickening Cape Test to see if they were old enough for intercourse: if, struck from behind by a cape, they fell over, they were too young; if they remained standing, they

were ready. It was a fiesta of rape for the Spaniards, though some of the
Inca women were proud to attract the omnipotent strangers. Pizarro,
who never married, came to love Atahualpa's sister Quispe Sisa (Inés),
who gave birth to their daughter, Francesca. She was legitimized by
Charles and became the greatest heiress of the New World. But Pizarro
could not resist taking another of Atahualpa's sisters, Azarpay, whom he
also installed in his palace, much to Inés's fury.

Pizarro returned to the coast to found a City of Kings (Lima), but his
brothers Gonzalo, Juan and Hernando, back from Spain, humiliated the
young Inca, Manco, who had consolidated power by killing any family
contenders. Now these brothers raped his princesses and extorted
more gold. Gonzalo seized Manco's *coya* (queen) and sister, Cura Ocllo.
The Incas criticized him. 'Who told you to talk to the king's *corregidor*
[judge]? Don't you know what kind of men we Spaniards are?' snarled
Gonzalo. 'I swear if you don't shut up, I'll slit you open alive and make
little pieces of you!' Gonzalo raped Cura Ocllo and imprisoned Manco,
who was chained, tortured, burned and urinated on by the brothers.
Manco escaped and gathered an army of 200,000, laying siege to the
ninety Spaniards in Cuzco and to Francisco Pizarro in Lima. The governor felt he could no longer trust his harem: his loyal Pispita, Inés,
denounced her half-sister Azarpay, 'so without further consideration,
he ordered that she [Azarpay] be garrotted', along with other mistresses.
Inés's mother sent troops to help Pizarro hold Lima.

Manco made his headquarters in the sacred citadel of Sacsayhuamán, looming over Cuzco, but took time to gather his forces. Besieged
in Cuzco, the Pizarro brothers just held out. Francisco's expeditions
were beaten back. Juan Pizarro was killed attacking Sacsayhuamán. The
brothers were rescued only by their rival Diego de Almagro, who retook
Cuzco but then clashed with and imprisoned the Pizarros. Francisco
Pizarro hit back, capturing and garrotting Almagro – an act that would
rebound on him. Manco, now deploying the arquebuses and swords
that had given the Spanish their advantage, retreated to found a new
kingdom in the jungles of Vilcabamba.

Francisco Pizarro took vengeance, burning many of the Incas alive.
When he captured Manco's queen, Cura Ocllo, already raped by his
brother, he and his secretary gang-raped her and then had her stripped,
tortured, shot full of arrows and floated in a bucket downriver to Manco,
who 'wept and made great mourning for he loved her much'.*

---

* Manco's brother Paullu enthusiastically embraced Spanish rule and the Christian faith,
wearing Spanish clothes, receiving lands and palaces from the Crown and fostering a
Hispanicized Inca aristocracy that would form the foundation of a new Peruvian society. In

Now that the Manco revolt was over, Pizarro sent more gold back to Charles to 'aid His Majesty in the war against the Turks'.

'Send me the most unusual gold and silver work,' ordered the emperor. 'You can coin the rest.' His conquistadors were on his mind. In 1535, Charles appointed a viceroy of New Spain, Antonio de Mendoza, to manage the bumptious Cortés. Mendoza boasted of the way he continued the conquest, killing the locals 'by firing at them with artillery until they were cut to pieces, setting the dogs on them or giving them to African slaves to kill – to punish those who are most guilty and make the rest more fearful'. When he had served in the conquest of Granada, he added, 'we used to beat and stone many Muslims'; the rest 'were treated as slaves and divided up'. Mendoza's arrogance made Cortés seethe.

In 1540, the marquess of the Valley of Oaxaca returned to Spain, rich but embittered and keen to be recognized. Charles avoided him until Cortés pushed past the outriders and jumped on to his carriage. 'Who are you?' asked the alarmed kaiser.

'I'm a man,' answered Cortés, 'who gave you more provinces than your ancestors left you cities.' Charles let him and his son Martín, *El Mestizo*, join his entourage for his crusade to seize Algiers – just as in Lima the other conquistador, marquess of the Conquest Pizarro, finally enjoyed his success. But not for long. The half-Inca son of Almagro known as *El Mozo* (the Lad) sought revenge on Pizarro. In June 1541, he and a hit squad attacked the Lima palace. Pizarro fought back with a halberd, killing two assassins, before collapsing, stabbed in the neck, and begging for mercy from Christ.

'Confess in hell,' cried the Lad, smashing an urn into his face as his hitmen stabbed Pizarro another twenty times and then beheaded him. But this was not quite the end of the Pizarros nor of the Incas.*

In October 1541, Charles embarked from Palma with a fleet of 500

1538, Pizarro granted Inés her own estates and married her to his ex-page in church while he himself took a new Inca mistress, Atahualpa's queen, Cuxirimay Ocllo, baptized as Angelina Yupanqui. She had been raped as a child by Pizarro's interpreter but had won his favour by leading him to a priceless gold statue. Together they had two sons. Both women lived long afterwards: Inés had three children with her husband Francisco de Ampuero, whom she hated and tried to poison, only to be caught and forgiven by him. In 1547 she sued him for mismanaging her dowry and won. Her descendants included Bolivian and Dominican presidents. Cuxirimay, granted estates by Pizarro, later married Juan de Betanzos, who wrote a history of the Incas.

* The Lad was later hunted down and killed by assassins who then sought refuge with Manco Inca in his jungle kingdom. Manco trusted them but, hoping to win a pardon from Spain, they then assassinated him. He was succeeded as Inca by his son; their kingdom survived for another thirty years before the Spanish finally stormed it and ended the rule of the Incas.

ships and 30,000 troops – and the Cortés father and son. But a storm destroyed the fleet; the Algerines counter-attacked, nearly capturing the emperor himself. Cortés and Martín almost drowned, losing all their jewels, but they survived.

Cortés's presence focused the emperor's mind on Spanish abuses. In 1542, Charles signed the New Laws, setting up the Council of the Indies, limiting the *encomiendas* and protecting the Indians, outraging the last Pizarro brother left in America. Gonzalo Pizarro galloped into Lima, clad in bejewelled black velvet and feathers, encouraged by his followers to declare himself king of Peru and marry Francisco's eleven-year-old Inca heiress, Francesca, fusing Inca and Pizarro blood. The rebels defeated and killed the viceroy, but in April 1448 Charles's new legate rallied imperial forces then captured and beheaded Gonzalo.*

Yet the protection of the indigenous people, as suggested by *El Protector de los Indios*, Bartolomeu de las Casas, accelerated the import of African slaves. Juan Garrido, who had accompanied Cortés, was probably the first African to settle in the Americas.† Three skeletons found in a mass grave at the Hospital Real de San José de los Naturales in Mexico City dating from the 1520s may have been the first slaves – they originated in Africa and show the broken bones and wear of physical labour; one had been shot dead with a copper bullet. Since the kings of Portugal held the rights to Africa, the Spanish slave trade was initially handled by Portuguese and *pombeiro* merchants.‡ It became very

---

* That left just one of the Pizarro brothers, Hernando, 'a tall coarse man'. When he had returned to Spain in 1539, Charles had him imprisoned for killing Almagro, though he lived in luxury, eating off gold plate, gambling with friends, even receiving visits from mistresses. When his niece, Francisca Inca Pizarro, seventeen and beautiful, arrived in Spain in 1550, Hernando, thirty-three years older, cultured, harsh and mean, married her. She moved into his prison, where she gave birth to five children. Finally released, Hernando and Francisca returned to Trujillo where they built the splendid Palace of Conquest which still stands, owned by the family who succeeded as marquesses of the Conquest. After Hernando's death in 1575, Francisca married a younger man in 1581 and lived until 1598.

† After the conquest, Handsome John settled in Mexico City where he claimed to be the first to plant wheat in the Americas: 'I, Juan Garrido, black in colour, resident of this city [Mexico],' he wrote to Charles in 1538, 'appear before Your Mercy and state that I am in need of providing evidence to the perpetuity of the king, a report on how I served Your Majesty in the conquest and pacification of this New Spain, from the time when the Marqués del Valle [Cortés] entered it; and in his company I was present at all the invasions and conquests and pacifications which were carried out, always with the said Marqués, all of which I did at my own expense without being given either salary or allotment of Indians or anything else . . . And also because I was the first to have the inspiration to sow wheat here in New Spain and to see if it took.'

‡ Slave traders gradually became known as *pombeiros* after a *feira* – fortified slave market – at Pumbe, on the border between today's republics of Congo and Brazzaville Congo.

profitable. As the Amerindians perished, the price of African slaves rose exponentially from four or five pesos in 1527 to fifty in 1536 to 200 in 1550. During Charles's reign, 30,000 enslaved Africans arrived in Habsburg America.

America swiftly affected the world: its gold and silver funded the Habsburgs but ultimately flowed eastwards to India and China to pay for their luxuries. The decaying faces of popes and princes revealed that syphilis was ravaging Europe almost as fast as smallpox had decimated America.* Foods from the New World conquered the old like culinary conquistadors: the Andean potato, easily cultivated, became an instant staple everywhere, particularly in Russia and Ireland. The sweet potato, transplanted by European traders, became popular in Africa and especially in China, where it helped propel Chinese population growth. Corn (maize), imported by European traders, changed farming in Asia, while in west Africa its resistance to drought and ease of storage helped concentrate power for local kings of Oyo and Benin. But it also helped slave traders to feed the enslaved on the crossings of the Sahara and the Atlantic. Chilis, vanilla, turkeys, tomatoes, pineapples and pumpkins followed in their wake. Tobacco became a global addiction, chocolate a popular drink (long before an English chocolatier made solid chocolate in 1847). Intellectually, the revelation of other civilizations with their own values and knowledge challenged European thought and ultimately inspired a new curiosity and openness.

The 'twin' monarchs – Habsburg and Ottoman – were now both exhausted by their duties, coarsened by power. Charles was fortunate in having a healthy and able son, Philip, who possessed the steely control and intense focus that he himself often lacked. After Philip had promised to remain a virgin until marriage, Charles arranged the boy's consanguineous marriage to Maria Manuela, daughter of João II of Portugal and Charles's sister, niece of the groom's mother. Charles gave Philip sensible advice on politics: 'Never do anything in anger' and, best

---

* It is unknown how many people lived in Mexico when Cortés arrived. It is often claimed there were thirty million people, but this is probably too high. They were certainly hit hard by European diseases. Western history writing often describes these epidemics as if they were episodes of deliberate European biological warfare. This was not the case. But the indigenous peoples were culled by different epidemics at different times, some of which killed over 25 per cent of the population. The smallpox epidemic of 1519–20 killed five to eight million people. But it was the later epidemics in 1545 and 1576 that were most catastrophic, killing around seventeen million people. New research using Spanish accounts of the symptoms suggests that these were cases not of smallpox but of haemorrhagic fever, more like ebola, with bleeding from ears, nose and bowel, spread by rats who flourished massively during wet years after droughts caused by climate change. If so, this may not have been brought by the Spanish; it may have been an indigenous disease.

of all, 'Trust no one; listen to everyone; decide alone.' But his advice was less good on sex.

While Charles continued to seduce girls and father children, he tried to control his son: 'You'll soon be married; it is important you restrain your desires' which 'can be dangerous both for the body's growth and its strength. It even causes death as it did with Prince Juan which is how I came to inherit these kingdoms . . . I require and request that once you've consummated the marriage, you plead some illness and keep away from your wife.' On the wedding night, a courtier dashed into the bedchamber after two and half hours and removed the bridegroom. When he heard that Maria was pregnant, Charles congratulated Philip: 'I thought it would take you longer.' Philip was not the grim fanatic of legend: he enjoyed dancing and flirting, and was now enjoying an affair with a beautiful lady-in-waiting (even though she had a rabbi among her ancestors). His wife gave birth to a son, but died of infection, at seventeen. The baby Carlos was born with physical and mental handicaps – the result of intermarriage and perhaps oxygen starvation – that ultimately threatened his father and the monarchy itself. Philip, filled with 'anguish and regret', retired to a monastery for a month.

In 1543, when Charles left Spain, Philip started to rule in that kingdom. 'Don't fail to send me soldiers,' his father demanded. Philip resisted, reminding his father 'of the exhaustion of your kingdoms'. Demands for soldiers and cash, and nagging, soured their relationship. At the same time, Charles beat François in a race to win over the ageing and obese Henry VIII, conveniently overlooking his oafish treatment of his aunt Catherine.* In 1544, Henry landed in Calais and both monarchs

---

* This was easier since the Protestant Thomas Cromwell was no longer on the scene. Cromwell was not the first self-made man to rise to power in England, but the Church was the traditional route – his patron Cardinal Wolsey was a butcher's son from Ipswich. But Cromwell, who resembled an indefatigably efficient but implacable badger, was a new sort of minister. Son of a middle-class brewer, who as a youngster had fought for the French in Italy against the armies of Ferdinand of Spain, he looted the wealth of Catholic monasteries which Henry distributed to loyal courtiers, providing the fortunes of many aristocratic families. Amid the murderous paranoia of Henry's court, the new queen Anne floundered after delivering a daughter – Elizabeth. As her sultriness turned to desperation, Henry fell out of love and into hate. Cromwell, playing on her mockery of Henry's virility, framed her for treason and incest. Boleyn was beheaded and Henry married her demure lady-in-waiting Jane Seymour, while Cromwell, secretary, lord privy seal, vicegerent in spirituals and earl of Essex, married his own son to the new queen's sister. Queen Jane delivered a son but died in childbirth. Cromwell's arrangement of a fourth, Protestant marriage to a German princess led to Henry's sexual humiliation and Cromwell's own beheading. Henry afterwards regretted Cromwell's killing. Even a further humiliation from his fifth marriage to a saucy, unfaithful teenager did not douse Henry's uxoriousness: he married one more time. Henry was an inscrutable showman who consolidated his dynasty and eliminated any threats, but his reputation rests on the fact that his capricious break with Rome reflected a deeper

attacked France, forcing François to sue for peace.

Charles had promised his brother Ferdinand that he and his son would succeed him as emperor but then suddenly announced he would nominate his own son Philip. The brothers almost fell out. 'We have to decide who is emperor, you or me,' Charles told Ferdinand. This could have caused the fracturing of the Habsburgs, but instead Charles backed down. In a Family Compact that would last for the next 150 years, the two branches of the family would help each other. Philip would inherit Spain, which he was already ruling, the Netherlands, Italy and the Americas; Ferdinand would rule Austria and the empire.

In 1547, Charles defeated the Protestant princes at Mühlberg,* a Catholic triumph – the culmination of his life's work. Yet in 1552 the Protestant princes, fortified by France, bounced back, routing Charles, whom they almost killed or captured, forcing him to flee, semi-conscious in a litter, tormented by debts, haemorrhoids and gout – the nadir of his reign – while the Ottoman admirals retook Tunis. 'I can't be everywhere and do everything,' he wrote forlornly to Ferdinand. Bankrupt and broken, he complained, 'I can't find a penny, or anyone who wants to lend me one or a man in Germany ready to declare support for me.' He even distrusted his brother: 'I begin to wonder whether Ferdinand might have some secret understanding with the authors of this conspiracy.'

In 1556, Charles finally allowed Ferdinand to negotiate a German peace that allowed German princes to choose their sect: *cuius regio, eius religio* (whose realm, his religion). It is rare for any family to produce two able statesmen simultaneously, but Charles V's brother, the cautious, wise, conciliatory Archduke Ferdinand, had created a Habsburg realm in Mitteleuropa encompassing Austria, Bohemia, Hungary and Croatia, had rebuilt the Hofburg Palace of Vienna as his headquarters, had achieved a happy marriage with his heiress wife that produced thirteen surviving children, had trained a moderate heir, Maximilian, whom he married to Charles's daughter Maria of Spain, and had fought off four invasions by Suleiman. The sultan, now sixty, was now dealing with his own family crisis the Ottoman way – with the bowstring.

English instinct for both political independence and religious reform. The Cromwell family would produce two rulers of England and almost became a royal dynasty of their own: Cromwell's nephew Richard Williams-Cromwell was the great-grandfather of Oliver Cromwell.

* Charles was joined by Titian, fifteen years after first sitting for him. The artist's equestrian portrait of the kaiser in triumph after the battle of Mühlberg throbs with martial power, echoing the equestrian statue of Marcus Aurelius that both had seen in Rome, but it also reveals the gruelling existence of an emperor. 'My whole life was a journey,' Charles said, and indeed he looks exhausted, frazzled, haggard.

THE OTTOMAN EMPRESS, THE LUCKY LOUSE AND
DOÑA GRACIA

Hürrem, the Ukrainian-born ex-slave who was now his empress, remained Suleiman's companion, constantly corresponding with him on his campaigns and acting as his eyes in Constantinople. 'Sometimes you treat me with kindness, sometimes you torment me,' he wrote. 'My love, whatever your mood, I will always adapt to it.' When his first son with Roxelana died, he wept desperately, refusing initially to let the body be buried, then prayed for forty days. But he was ice-cold in politics.

Wizened, watchful, world-weary, Suleiman monitored his sons carefully. He was close to Mustafa, his eldest, who had become dangerously popular with the Janissaries, the elite musketeers feared by the sultan.

On campaign against the Persians in 1548, taking Tabriz and much of the Caucasus, Suleiman, now thin and gouty, was feeling his age.* 'You said your noble foot was aching,' wrote Hürrem. 'God knows, my sultan, I was so upset I cried.' In 1553, Shah Tahmasp counter-attacked and Suleiman dispatched the Lucky Louse, married to his daughter Mihrimah and grand vizier for nine years, to repel him. The padishah was informed by the Louse that Mustafa was discussing Suleiman's 'retirement'. The prince may have believed that the Louse – backed by his wife Mihrimah and mother-in-law Hürrem – wanted to kill him.

'God forbid,' retorted Suleiman, 'my Mustafa Khan should dare such insolence.' But wearily he led his own army to join the Louse, travelling with his youngest son, the hunchbacked Cihangir, who suggested to his father that his hunchback would prevent him being killed by his brothers. 'My son,' replied Suleiman, 'Mustafa will become sultan and kill you all.'

At Ereğli, Suleiman summoned Mustafa, whose mother begged him not to go. Leaving his bodyguards, Mustafa entered his father's tent where, watched by the padishah, the Tongueless jumped on him with their bowstrings. He fought back but when he tried to escape he tripped on his robe and was strangled, his body tossed outside the sultanic tent. The army mourned him and demanded the head of the Louse. Suleiman agreed to dismiss the vizier. From Constantinople, Hürrem

---

* Suleiman was increasingly pious: after rebuilding the walls of Jerusalem (demolished by Saladin's family three centuries earlier) and embellishing Mecca, in 1550 he ordered his court architect Sinan to design his own Suleimaniye Mosque in Constantinople. Sinan, one of the greatest architects in world history, designer also of the Selimiye Mosque in Edirne and creator of as many as 300 projects, was born a Christian, probably Armenian or Greek, named Joseph, who was enslaved and converted to Islam, later distinguishing himself as a military engineer on Suleiman's campaigns from the Tigris to the Danube.

warned him to send good news to calm the city and pleaded for the life of the Louse, signing off, 'And that's that. Your lowly slave.'

The Lucky Louse was lucky again: although his wife Mihrimah was unhappy in her marriage, she continued to promote her husband. Two years later, Suleiman had his vizier strangled and reappointed the Louse. Hürrem had won: only her two sons were left, Selim and Bayezid. But one would succeed – and one would have to die.

Selim was plump, genial and hedonistic, a bibulous poetaster whose favoured concubine Nurbanu was a Greek noblewoman enslaved by Barbarossa. He was unpopular with the army who called him the Ox; in Constantinople, he was called the Blond. Bayezid was martial and ambitious.

While Hürrem promoted Selim, Bayezid toyed with rebelling. Hürrem brokered his pardon. But in 1558 she died in the Old Palace, buried in the tomb of the Suleimaniye Mosque that the padishah had prepared for them both. After her mother's death, Mihrimah moved into the Old Palace and became her father's companion and adviser, building charitable foundations and mosques (including commissioning Sinan – who was said to be in love with her – to design the exquisitely blue Rüstem Pasha Mosque in honour of her late husband). A painting shows her haughty good looks: she had become a Euro-Asian potentate, trying to keep peace between her brothers.

Yet Bayezid still planned to seize power. Here was a power family that talked about death and treason in poetry. Suleiman warned the boy, who wrote back:

> Forgive Bayezid's offence, spare the life of this slave.
> I'm innocent, God knows, my fortune-favoured sultan, my father.

Suleiman replied:

> My Bayezid, I'll forgive you your offence if you mend your ways.
> But for once don't say 'I'm innocent'. Show repentance, my dear son.

It was now that Europe's wealthiest private family arrived in Constantinople. They were Iberian Jews, the Mendes, led by Doña Gracia and her nephew Joseph Nasi, married to her daughter Reyna. They had already lived an extraordinary life: Doña Gracia, the heiress to the banking house of Mendes/Benveniste, had been expelled from Spain to Portugal whence she had escaped to Antwerp. When Charles V tried to steal her fortune, she and Joseph fled through France to Venice before negotiating their arrival in Istanbul. With a background of fake conversions and secret Jewish observance, they were born survivors who enjoyed a portfolio of different names.* The Venetians imprisoned Gracia, at which her nephew Joseph wrote to Suleiman's Jewish doctor. Suleiman ordered the *Signoria* to release *La Signora*. She and her daughter arrived in style, sailing in a splendid flotilla into the Bosphoros, followed by Joseph. She did business with emperors, popes and kings, holding her own, a remarkable achievement for a woman and a Jew. When the pope burned Jews at the stake, Doña Gracia organized a boycott of papal ports. Joseph advised and financed Selim during his struggle with his brother.

In 1559, Bayezid mustered troops. Suleiman sent Selim to defeat the rebel, who fled with his four sons to Persia where he was granted asylum by Shah Tahmasp.

The shah was a master at playing family politics with his neighbours. To the west, he won a fortress and 1.2 million florins from Suleiman. In return he allowed Selim and a team of Tongueless to slip into Persia and strangle Bayezid and his four sons.† To the east, he was playing a different game, helping the fallen emperor of India, Humayoun, son of Babur, scion of House Tamerlane, to get back his Indian realm – in the hope that he would convert to Shiism and make India a grateful client state. Instead he helped restore the greatest ruler of India since Ashoka.

THE PRUDENT KING AND THREE ENGLISH QUEENS

Humayoun's son Akbar had been brought up in Kabul by Babur's sister, but when the shah lent Humayoun a regiment of cavalry to help retake India, the boy joined his father as they galloped towards Delhi. The invasion force of 5,000 Persians and Afghans, led by a tough Afghan paladin, Bairam Shah, was a tiny army to take on a sub-continent. In exile, Humayoun had imbibed the Persianate culture that was to be such an intrinsic part of the Mughal style. An opium-sampling bibliophile like many of the family, he fell from his library ladder and met a book lover's death. Emperor Akbar appointed Bairam as his *vakil* – premier – until retiring him in 1562. Increasingly, he consulted his former wet nurse, the loyal and capable Maham Anga, to guide him, overpromoting her teenaged son Adham Khan, who had grown up with Akbar. When his foster brother Adham dared to cross him, Akbar unleashed his inner

---

* Joseph was João Miques, Dom João Migas Mendes, Giuseppe Nasi and Yasef Nassi; she was Doña Gracia, Hannah, Beatrice de Luna and La Señora.
† A painting of Blond Selim shows him signalling to one of the Tongueless whose sign language he partly understood.

Tamerlane: in front of his court, he smashed him in the face, shouting 'You sonofabitch,' then flung him off a balcony. Adham survived, so Akbar ordered him to be carried upstairs and defenestrated him again, breaking his neck. 'You did well,' Adham's mother said, though the 'colour had left her face'.

Akbar had taken power with Persian horse archers, but he built the empire with Ottoman muskets and cannon, soon manufacturing his own. Akbar and the House of Tamerlane were now conquerors of India. Akbar's building of towers of Indian heads was a sign of predatory conquest if ever there was one: a Rajput maharana named Pratap typically called him a 'vile Turk' invader. Akbar was at war for twenty years, first approaching enemies in massive hunts, accompanied by a thousand cheetahs and escorted by his armies – 'hunting another kind of wild elephant' as his minister put it, a ritual that often brought submission. If that did not work, he deployed his Mongol horse archers, war elephants and the latest artillery. He himself was a crack shot with his favourite gun called Sangram (guns and swords were named). Using his cannon, in 1556 Akbar first retook Delhi and Agra, then Lahore and Punjab and, after 1558, Rajputana, one by one breaking the Rajput grandees, led by the maharana of Mewar, Udai Singh, builder of the exquisite lacustrine city Udaipur. In February 1568, when Udai's fortress Chittorgarh fell, Akbar slaughtered 30,000 people, displaying heads on the battlements. Most Rajputs submitted: he befriended Man Singh, raja of Amber, appointing him a *mansabdar* of 7,000,* calling him *farzand* (son) and marrying his sister. His Rajput marriages led to a fusion of Tamerlanian and Rajput lineages with Sanskritic and Persian cultures. Thanks to his mastery of imperial powerplays, the conquest dynasty became rooted in India.

Then Akbar swung south-west to seize Gujarat – the coastal sultanate which, via its entrepôt Surat, linked India to European trade – and Ottoman military supplies. He granted the Portuguese, who had arrived in India before Babur, rights to Goa. In 1573, when he stormed the capital Ahmedabad, Akbar celebrated by building more towers of heads. Gujarat trade made the dynasty a global mercantile power. Then the padishah swerved eastwards and northwards, taking Bengal and Kashmir.

Clean-shaven, except for side whiskers, lean, tall, athletic with long eyelashes, Akbar looked like a Mongol, and his black radiant eyes were said to 'hurt you with their brightness'. He was secretive – he 'guards

---

* Akbar organized his nobles strictly by the numerical *mansab* (rank) of 1,000, 5,000, 7,000 or 10,000 soldiers.

over his motives and watches over his emotions' and 'never wastes time', using a water clock to 'cherish time', convinced that 'Idleness is the root of evil.' He loved to test his fate by riding elephants in *musth* (their season of heightened aggression), 'intentionally riding murderous elephants so that if I've done something displeasing to God, may that elephant finish us'. He lived dangerously, playing nocturnal polo with specially designed luminous balls and hunting riskily: he was gored in the testicles by an antelope. He was also wounded in the groin fighting in Gujarat, giving him a slight Tamerlanian limp. In 1564, an assassin shot him in the shoulder with an arrow. Security was paramount. Akbar was a consummate deployer of poison, either smeared on the cuffs of a robe presented by the emperor or else offered personally by his own hand in a folded betel leaf.

Although he was illiterate, possibly dyslexic, he patronized intellectuals, led by his *vakil* and ideologist Abul-Fazl and his brother the poet Faizi, luminaries of his Nine Jewels.

Akbar believed he was a sacred emperor, and incorporated not only Islamic and Persianate traditions but also their Turkic and Rajput counterparts. He appeased Hindus, abolishing the *jizyah* tax and the slaughter of cows, questioned Islam itself and envisioned an eclectic religious hybrid *Din-i Ilahi*, Divine Faith, that encompassed Islam, Hinduism and Zoroastrianism. As the Islamic millennium got closer, he called himself the Mahdi or Renewer of the Second Millennium. In 1585, he minted coins that read '*Allahu akbar jalla jalaluhu*', which would usually mean 'God is great' but could also mean 'Akbar is God', as he toyed with substituting himself for Muhammad. He pulled back from his own apotheosis, but projected the sanctity of Mughal monarchy, promoting himself as Tamerlanian padishah, Islamic saintly ruler and Hindu *chakravartin*. He adopted the Hindu tradition of appearing daily at sunrise on the balcony of the Agra Fort: this *jharokha darshan*, watched by crowds, became an essential rite of Mughal kingship.

As energetic sexually as in all things, he insisted on having the wives of his amirs if he fancied them, and his demands for new girls were 'a great terror ... in the city'. Like all the steppe monarchs, however, he consulted wise women in the family, particularly his senior wife and first cousin, Ruqaiya.

Amid all this success lurked stress: Akbar suffered 'melancholy'. 'My heart is oppressed by this outward pomp,' he said. 'I experienced an internal bitterness, my soul was seized with exceeding sorrow.' In 1573, when he was thirty-one, drunkenly discussing the courage of Rajput heroes who rushed at spears until pierced through, he suddenly fixed his blade to the wall and rushed at it, only stopped when he was tackled by his Rajput brother-in-law Man Singh.

Like Genghis's khans, the Tamerlanians were prone to alcoholism: two sons died of drink; his heir Salim (later Emperor Jahangir) was addicted to opium, wine and arrak. Understandably the girls in the *zenana* were avid consumers of these intoxicants and became so addicted that Akbar had visitors searched. Sometimes Akbar fell asleep during discussions with the Jesuits while drinking *post*, opium water. Later, he enjoyed tobacco, brought by Portuguese visitors. Nicotine was not the only American commodity pouring into India: American gold and silver enriched Akbar's kingdom. He promoted trade: as Abul-Fazl put it, 'By wise regulations, revenue is preserved.' Thanks to growing cities, good harvests, rising wages and the success of home workshops specializing in weaving (powered by female artisans who could combine raising families with their skilled work), India – with a population of 150 million, of whom Akbar ruled 110 million – produced a quarter of the world's textiles, as well as pepper, coffee, opium, tea, spices, ivory and saltpetre. Akbar encouraged Portuguese and later English traders because they paid in gold and silver, which made Tamerlanian India rival Ming China as the richest kingdom on earth.

Yet all these steppe monarchies had a fatal flaw: family. The tournament of sons designed to select the most able also ensured murderous bouts of family contention that could bring down an empire. As Akbar tried to manage his sons, the exhausted Christian padishah, Charles V, the source of all that gold and silver, delivered a masterclass on how to handle a succession.

Charles was having a breakdown: he 'occupies himself day and night adjusting and synchronizing his clocks; he often wakes his valets to help him dismantle and reassemble them'. Craving order amid chaos, he wanted them to tick together.

Yet in the midst of his breakdown, Charles fixed Philip's next marriage. Henry VIII had died, leaving a puny son, Edward VI, who, despite his youth, was a masterful Protestant. Dying at fifteen of TB, it was he personally who diverted the succession from his Catholic half-sister Mary to his first cousin once removed Jane Grey, Protestant daughter of the duke of Suffolk and great-granddaughter of Henry VII. Queen Jane, sixteen years old, became England's first queen regnant: after thirteen days, she was overwhelmed by support for Mary, daughter of a formidable king and a popular Spanish queen. Mary executed Edward's minister, swung England back towards Rome and was delighted with the prospect of marrying the dashing Philip, now king of Naples and

Sicily.* The Catholic marriage – designed to echo Ferdinand and Isabella's in 1469 – was popular in England. But Mary and her ministers used
an anti-Catholic plot as a pretext to behead her rival, ex-queen Jane.

Philip sailed for England and married the unprepossessing Mary,
by then aged thirty-seven, in Winchester Cathedral, becoming king of
England and Ireland. 'Once you've celebrated and consummated your
marriage with the queen,' ordered Charles, 'leave her after six or eight
days.' Philip was uninspired by Mary's looks – 'It will take a great God to
drink this cup,' sighed his best friend – but he manfully consummated
the marriage to the extent that a delighted queen required four days in
bed recovering. Then, to Mary's dismay, Philip escaped to Brussels to
attend his father's abdication.

Departure is one of the tests of political acumen; few know when
or how to do it. Succession is the great test of a system; few manage it
well. Paternal acceptance of filial independence is a test of any family's
solidarity. Charles succeeded in all three. In October 1555, Charles, leaning on the shoulder of his Dutch favourite, William the Silent, prince
of Orange, addressed his grandees. 'I had great hopes – only a few have
been fulfilled,' he said, 'and only a few remain to me: and at the cost
of what effort! It ultimately made me tired and sick . . .' Few leaders
ever have the courage to confess: 'I know I made many mistakes, big
mistakes, first because of my youth, then because of human error and
because of my passions, and finally because of tiredness. But I did no
deliberate wrong to anyone, whoever it was.' He then handed over the
Spanish realm to Philip. Accompanied by his beloved sister Eleanor and
his Titian paintings, especially the portrait of the long-dead Isabella, and
his clocks, Charles retired to a monastery at Yuste in Spain where he
prayed and tinkered with timepieces, dying at fifty-eight.

Mary persecuted Protestant heretics, burning 283 at the stake, and
placed her Protestant half-sister Elizabeth under house arrest. But
she was ailing; Philip enjoyed being king of England and Ireland but
dreaded his marital duties. The poor queen so craved a child that in
September 1554 her stomach swelled, she was sick every morning and
her periods stopped. But Philip doubted her and gradually her courtiers
realized it was a false pregnancy.

Philip was pale, fair-haired, slight with ice-cold blue eyes, his
slight Habsburg jaw concealed in a fair beard. He was intelligent and

---

* Titian helped with the courtship: his gorgeous full-length painting of Philip II, handsome,
slim, arrogant and sporting intricately gold-trimmed armour, was sent to Mary Tudor
during their marriage negotiations. In London and Winchester, Philip was accompanied
by among others Martin 'El Mestizo' Cortés.

meticulous, with the acumen to make decisions across a global empire, an excellent memory, the stamina to put in hours of work and the sangfroid necessary to order wars and killings. The young king could be charming, he liked dancing and women, appreciated art and had a sense of humour, enjoying pushing his pet elephant into the cells of po-faced monks; later he proved a loving husband and indulgent father to his daughters. Yet he shared his father's messianic mission without his winning humility and, as a courtier recalled, 'He had a smile cut with a sword.'

Philip desperately needed a family – and a healthy heir. At the heart of his court lurked the problem of his son, who from early on was torturing animals, blinding horses and whipping servant girls. Don Carlos, prince of Asturias, whose Portuguese mother had died four days after his birth, may have been damaged by lack of oxygen; he was hunchbacked, lame and violent. An only child, he was certainly emotionally neglected, his father absent for years at a time; but his major problem was his deficient gene pool.* Inbreeding had gathered a world empire, but the very policy designed to strengthen it had weakened it fatally.

Philip, ruling fifty million people in four continents, from Asia to America and Europe, was, like his father, perpetually at war – against France, the pope, the Ottomans – and that was before he faced heretical challenges on every side.

This messianic imperialist believed God would perform miracles for him; anything seemed possible. 'The world is not enough' was his motto. The flow of paperwork was endless, but he acted as his own secretary – 'They're killing me with work by day which means I'm worn out by night.' One evening he wrote, 'It's 10 p.m., I feel shattered and I'm dying of hunger.' His single-mindedness led to mistakes and delusions. The predicament of prodigious power is that it exceeds a single human's ability to wield it. 'His Majesty has been working even more than usual,' wrote an aide, 'reading and writing papers until they come out of his backside (may your lordship forgive me) because on Saturday morning at 3 a.m. he had terrible diarrhoea.' He decided everything. Autocracy grants the consistency that democracy lacks but replaces it with rigidity petrified by delusion and drowned in detail.

---

* Consanguinity is best measured by an inbreeding coefficient. The breeding of parent and child or brother and sister is 0.25. Inbreeding was already high thanks to the repeated intermarriage between the Trastámara and the Aviz even before it became Habsburg policy. Carlos was great-grandson of Juana the Mad whose own grandmother had died as a crazed prisoner; his grandfather Charles and his father Philip had both married double cousins, raising his inbreeding coefficient to 0.211, close to pure incest. The Habsburg jaw was its least damaging symptom.

Philip was already at war with France for control of Burgundy and Italy, a conflict that had lasted almost a century. He ordered an advance from the Netherlands into France. On 10 August – St Lawrence's Day – 1557, at Saint-Quentin, his *tercios* defeated the French, a victory he celebrated by building the colossal palace-monastery-mausoleum of St Lawrence of Victory of El Escorial near Madrid that would reflect his grandiose messianic vision of sacred monarchy.

All victories were attributed to divine favour: 'God did this.' Philip collected a saintly reliquary of 12 bodies, 144 heads and 306 limbs, labelled by hand and regularly used to treat his family's ailments. His mission in life was to fight the heresy of Protestantism while championing the Catholic counter-attack led by the papacy. He often told his ministers that being engaged in his service and in that of God 'is the same thing', a conviction that justified anything. All over Europe the clash between the two denominations intensified. Philip insisted, 'Rather than suffer the least injury to religion and the service of God, I would lose all my states and a hundred lives if I had them for I don't intend to rule over heretics.' He attended many *autos-da-fé*. When one victim shouted at him, he answered, 'I would carry the wood to burn my own son if he was as wicked as you.' At a time when there was no division between secular and religious, Philip believed heresy and impurity by Protestants and crypto-Jewish Christians infiltrating God's kingdom must be prosecuted, but there were no more executions than in most other European kingdoms. The hunt for crypto-Jews was linked to a certificate of racial purity – *limpieza de sangre* – that was usually easy to procure, and essential to hold any office, but it could be used against dubious *conversos*. Philip overlooked impurity when it suited him. He asserted royal power in the Americas, crushing the insubordinate Cortés family and encouraging young Spaniards to settle there.*

---

* In 1562, the three sons of the conquistador returned to Mexico bearing the body of their father. There they became embroiled in a conspiracy of Spanish *encomienderos* and Mexica nobility to hail Marques Martín Cortés as king of New Spain. The brothers were arrested; El Mestizo was waterboarded. Amid many executions, the Cortés were spared.

Philip encouraged *conversos* with impure (Jewish) blood to govern the Americas but also exported the Inquisition to Peru and New Spain. In 1579, he appointed a *converso*, Luis Carvajal, born in Portugal but returning to Spanish service, as captain-general of New Leon, with the mission to 'discover, pacify and settle' north-west Mexico and Texas. Carvajal's rivals denounced him and his family to the Inquisition as relapsed Jews. Luis died in prison. On 8 December 1596, Luis's sister and her teenaged daughters and son courageously declared their Judaism and were burned alive in the main square of Mexico City. But some of the family escaped to Italy where, settling at the Florentine port of Livorno – Medici territory – a Carvajal boy adopted the name of a Tuscan village, Montefiore – the ancestors of this author.

A typical recruit was a young Basque, Simón Bolívar, who thrived in Caracas, developing plantations, copper mines and a port, importing enslaved Africans and then founding schools and seminaries. He also served as Philip's procurator. Around 5,000 Spaniards now ruled 10,000 Africans and 350,000 Amerindians. Bolívar personified the white *mantuanos* elite who revelled in their racial separation while actually interbreeding with Amerindians and Africans, to create a new world of mixed-raced peoples.*

In 1557, after Philip, king of England, visited Mary, now forty-one, she again thought herself pregnant, but tragically both her false pregnancies were probably early symptoms of the uterine cancer that killed her in November of the following year. She was succeeded by her Protestant half-sister, Elizabeth, daughter of the executed Boleyn.

Philip mourned Mary 'as you might well understand', and missed his English kingdom. He proposed marriage to Elizabeth. The intellectual, masterful and single-minded queen rejected him and restored Protestantism to her realm. Philip and Elizabeth both saw religion as essential to their mission. His crown was forged by holy war; she had to be more pragmatic to survive – she had 'no desire to make windows into men's souls'. She once provocatively said, 'There's only one faith; all else is a dispute over trifles,' but both monarchs were willing to kill for those trifles. Elizabeth executed almost 200 Catholics in her small kingdom. Yet, tempered by her dangerous trajectory from princess to bastard to prisoner and sovereign, she was a master of political theatre, of opacity and trimming. But now she defied Philip so successfully that he decided on more drastic action.

As Philip took the helm, a young Rurikovich was imposing himself on Muscovy. They were opposites: one was a definition of control, the other of frenzy. Philip called himself *El Prudente*; Ivan became *Grozny*: the Terrible.

HOYDA! BLOODTHIRSTY WILD BEAST

On 2 October 1552, the twenty-two-year-old Ivan IV knelt in prayer as his army – traditional horse archers and his new *streltsy* musketeers and

---

* The *limpieza de sangre* was required by the elite in South America but was hard to maintain. Even elite creoles who prided themselves on their whiteness were usually mixed-race, a fact that only encouraged a fixation with racial and racist categories from *mestizo* (Spanish-Amerindian), *mulatto* (African-European), *sambo* (African-Amerindian), *pardo* (triracial) and *cuarterón* (quadroon, with one African grandparent).

150 cannon – stormed Kazan on the Volga, the capital of a khanate, and slaughtered its Muslim inhabitants, liberating thousands of Christian slaves. On his way back from Kazan, his beloved wife Anastasia gave birth to the first of three sons.

The Christian conqueror celebrated in Moscow, building the garish nine-domed St Basil's in Red Square. In just a few years this energetic young autocrat had expanded his kingdom, modernized the army, promulgated a new legal code and guaranteed the dynasty. But a sickness and then a death would destabilize him, unleashing his peculiar mix of sacred charisma, keening energy and demented sadism.

Grandson of the fearsome Ivan the Great and his Palaiologos wife Sophia, the boy had been grand prince since he was three when his father Vasili III died, leaving his mother Elena Glinskaia as regent. Her death left Ivan with only his deaf and dumb brother for company. 'My brother Yuri, of blessed memory, and me, they brought up like vagrants. What have I suffered for want of garments and food.' His claims are hard to believe, but he was a murderous melodramatist and hysterical fabulist, haunted by biblical purgatory. He grew up to be tall, as lithe 'as a leopard' with an aquiline nose, sensual mouth and flashing eyes.* Already torturing animals which he threw from the Kremlin towers, he spent his adolescence running wild with a gang of ruffians, committing acts of brigandage, and as soon as he got power he executed some of these friends by having them impaled. He had heard of the cruelties of Vlad the Impaler and his remarkable grandfather Ivan, whom he greatly resembled.

In January 1547, Ivan was crowned in the Dormition Cathedral as Autocrat of all the Russias – and for the first time – Tsar. He was crowned with the 'cap' of Constantine Monomachos, which was probably a Mongol gift, while his patriarch now merged Mongol-Roman ideology to declare the tsar, the embodiment of God and personification of the state.

Ivan then presided over a bride-show – a beauty contest of part-Byzantine, part-Mongol origins, in which orders were sent out to the kingdom stating, 'Those of you who have daughters who are maidens proceed without delay to our lieutenants for inspection . . . Anyone who conceals a maiden daughter will be punished.' Ivan chose Anastasia Romanovna Iureva-Zakharina – the first of the Romanovs – who gave birth to the required sons and whom he came to love or at least depend upon as an emotional support.

---

* This is according to the reconstruction by Gerasimov who, on Stalin's orders, opened Ivan's tomb in 1953 and based on the tsar's skull crafted an artistic version of his face.

Ivan lived inside the Kremlin, a red-walled fortress of palaces and churches, amid a pious court that was dominated by a web of inter-married boyars (aristocrats) and an influx of Mongol princes known as *tsarevichi* – sons of the Golden khans. Ivan favoured these *tsarevichi*, who were no political threat; it is likely he spoke Tatar, and though he was fanatically pious, his court also had a strong Mongol flavour: even his nobles called themselves 'your slaves', in Mongol fashion.

Revelling in sprees of partying and fornication interspersed with prayer and fasting, Ivan was influenced by a white-bearded priest called Silvester who regarded even mirrors and music as satanic manifesta-tions. Young Ivan was clean-shaven until Silvester persuaded him that shaving was for sodomites, prompting him to enforce the growing of beards.

Shortly after his coronation, fire destroyed much of Moscow, killing thousands. Ivan was rushed out of the city, and a mob, inspired by public hysteria and court conspiracy, demanded the life of his Glinsky grand-mother, accused of being a witch, and lit more fires. Ivan refused to give up his grandmother; then, rallying his forces, seized and impaled the ringleaders. Court life was inherently stressful, but the frequent fires that swept through Moscow and repeated spasms of the plague added to his sense of a world forever on the edge of an apocalyptic inferno.

In March 1553, Ivan fell ill. He was determined that his baby son, Dmitri, should succeed him, but there was no rule of succession; cour-tiers wished to avoid another regency and to stop Anastasia's family from gaining power. Many turned to Ivan's first cousin, the seventeen-year-old Prince Vladimir, a better prospect than a baby. For twelve days, Ivan, passing in and out of consciousness, tried to force the boyars to swear allegiance to his baby. Vladimir was forced to do so. Then Ivan recovered, and began accusing the boyars of wanting 'to raise Vladimir to the throne and like Herod destroy his God-given son'. He went on pil-grimage to a distant monastery, demanding the presence of Anastasia and the baby Tsarevich Dmitri, but the journey was perilous. When the baby's nurse was getting off their boat, she dropped the baby into the river. (The fate of the nurse is not recorded.) Ivan had lost his only heir.

Fortunately Anastasia gave birth soon afterwards to a strong new son, Ivan. In twelve years she bore six children, including another son Fyodor, who was probably born with Down's Syndrome. The strain took its toll. Ivan was needily uxorious, demanding Anastasia's constant presence even on unsuitably dangerous trips, yet he remained highly sexed and unrestrained.

In 1556, Ivan followed up his capture of Kazan by attacking Xacitarxan

– Astrakhan – the chief slave market of the Volga, storming and razing it. The fall of these khanates was the start of Russia's rise as a Eurasian empire. He backed a family of Russian conquistadors as important to Russia as Cortés to Spain. A tough old merchant, Anikei Stroganov, aged sixty-seven, and his three fissiparous but able sons, were rich from their fur-trapping east of the Volga and from salterns around Solvychegodsk in the north. When an English merchant, Richard Chancellor, sailed northwards to reach China and ended up where Archangel was later built, Ivan controlled it personally, hoping for benefits from England. He commissioned the Stroganovs to probe across the Urals into the khanate of Sibir, controlled by Kuchum Khan, a descendant of Genghis and populated by Mongols and indigenous tribes. Ivan gave the Stroganovs lands in the Urals and Sibir, where they built fortresses, settled peasants, developed mines and salterns, traded timber and furs, purveying saltpetre and sable to Ivan, and ran their own army, a posse – *druzhina* – of freebooting frontiersmen named Cossacks.* But Ivan's next target was the Baltic, where he hoped to secure a port in Livonia (Estonia/Latvia) and gain access to European trade.

In 1558, when the old crusading order of Livonia, officially called Terra Mariana, tried to join Poland–Lithuania, Ivan attacked, initially taking Narva, but then sparking a complex conflict that embroiled Poland, Sweden, Denmark and the Crimean khanate. Ivan played this game ingeniously and won early victories, but ultimately the twenty-year war almost destroyed Muscovy – and drove Ivan mad.

In September 1559, Ivan dragged Anastasia on pilgrimage to Mozhaisk just as the war lurched into crisis, but she fell ill, wearied by her husband, weakened by her grief at losing four children and exhausted by childbirth. Ivan rushed her back to Moscow: 'How shall I recall the merciless journey to our ruling city with our ailing Tsarina?' In August 1560, the twenty-nine-year-old Anastasia was dying, just as many courtiers were encouraging Ivan to make peace, as fires burst out in Moscow and as Devlet Giray, the Crimean khan, raided the south,

---

* The word Cossack derived from the Turkic *kozak*, meaning a freebooter. These ferocious frontiersmen thrived in the borderlands between Muscovy and the Mongol khanates and Poland–Lithuania, adopting by land the cavalry tactics of Mongol fighters, by sea the raiding tactics of Viking forefathers. Composed of runaway Ukrainian peasants, Muscovite deserters and Mongol renegades, their twenty or so communities developed an idiosyncratic Orthodox and meritocratic culture, each *voysko* (warband), translated into English as 'host', elected their own headmen – *ataman* or *hetman*. They were not yet cavalry but infantry who often used longboats, known as *chaiki* (seagulls) for their raids – even, in 1614, attacking Constantinople. The Hosts maintained independence, fighting sometimes for the tsars, at other times for the kings of Poland, their leaders trying to win nobility. Only in the eighteenth century did the Russian tsars transform them into cavalry units.

seizing thousands of slaves. Ivan was convinced she had been bewitched and poisoned. Analysis of her remains reveal 0.8 milligrams of arsenic per 100 grams of bone and 0.13 of mercury, but similar amounts were found in other royal bones, symptoms of iatrogenic quackery, not of murder.

Ivan broke down, oscillating between bouts of killing and bouts of sex while his advisers begged him to remarry – one of his sons was too sick to rule; dynasty demanded an heir – but his catalogue of marriages would make Henry VIII look like a wholesome husband. After trying to wed the heiress of Poland, Katarzyna Jagiellonka, and then a Swedish princess, he did something extraordinary: in August 1561 he married into the Genghis family and House of Islam, falling for Princess Kucheny, pretty daughter of Temriuk, khan of Kabarda, an alliance that strengthened Ivan's position in the Caucasus. She converted to become Tsarina Maria (while her brother Salmuk was baptized as Prince Mikhail Cherkassky, thus founding one of the aristocratic families of imperial Russia). But Ivan had changed: boozing and cavorting, attended by a circus of *skomorokhi*, clowns and minstrels, he started an affair with a beautiful young courtier, Fyodor Basmanov, who became his 'catamite'. When a magnate, Prince Dmitri Obolensky Ovchinin, sneered at Basmanov, 'We serve the tsar in useful ways, you in your filthy sodomitical dealings,' Ivan scalded him with boiling water, then stabbed him.

As more aristocrats fled to Poland, Ivan with his commander Shahghali, Muslim ex-khan of Kazan, seized Polotsk (Belarus), drowning its entire Jewish population in the Dvina. On his return, critics of his war, Tatar marriage and homosexual affair plotted to make Vladimir tsar. Ferocious vigilance was – and is – the only way to survive in the Kremlin, but Ivan went much further, beating and strangling boyars, having them sewn into bearskins and thrown to the hunting dogs, or cooked alive in burning stoves. Ivan, inspired by the image of hell in the Bible, believed it was his right and mission to scourge his kingdom, his victims bearing the guilt of the tsar just as the tsar bore the guilt of the kingdom. To the peasants, this was the behaviour expected of their 'Little-Father-Tsar' – *tsar-batiushka*.

His courtier Prince Andrei Kurbsky was horrified to see his tsar and his retainers become 'raging bloodthirsty wild beasts' who used 'unheard of tortures and death'. When Kurbsky learned that he was to be arrested for murdering Anastasia, he defected to Poland, leaving his wife and son whom Ivan immediately murdered. Kurbsky denounced Ivan's 'intolerable wrath, bitter hatred and burning stoves'.

In December 1564, Ivan denounced the boyars as 'traitors' – 'They

want to devour me,' he said – and offered to 'give his realm to the traitors, though a time might come when he would demand it back and
would take it'. Accompanied by Maria's and Anastasia's sons, and by
Maria herself, Ivan left Moscow and sledged to a hunting lodge, Alexandrovskaia Sloboda. Muscovites begged Ivan to return, asking, 'How
can we live without a lord?' and offering to butcher 'evildoers named by
the tsar'.

That same month, Ivan divided his kingdom into two: his *oprichnina*
contained the best and richest lands, while leaving the rest of the land,
the *zemshchina*, to be run by the boyars. To guard his sacred person, he
formed a corps of killers, the *oprichniki*, led by a group of boyars, adventurers, foreigners and Tatar tsareviches including his wife's brother,
who wore black over their sumptuous clothes, rode with the head of a
dog on their bridle and a brush on their whip handles and took an oath:
'I swear to be true to the Lord Grand Prince . . . and not to maintain
silence about any evil I may know that is being contemplated against
the Tsar . . .' Often accompanying and micromanaging their predatory
sprees, shouting 'Hoyda!', a Mongol war cry, Ivan killed magnates and
their children, who were beheaded, impaled and pushed under ice, an
apostate's death sending them to hell.

At Alexandrovskaia Sloboda, Ivan, coenobite and sybarite, oversaw
a diabolical monastery where he and his monkish murderers rose at 4
a.m. for matins and heartily sang hymns of repentance before joining
homosexual sex parties and torture sessions until bedtime at 9 p.m.
Three blind old men then told stories to the insomniac tsar. Ivan was
joined by a German astrologer-physician, Eliseus Bomelius, who had
fallen out with Queen Elizabeth of England and now became his magus
and poisoner.

In 1567, Ivan uncovered a conspiracy to enthrone his cousin Vladimir
of Staritsa. Vladimir, afraid of a trap, himself revealed it to Ivan, who
pounced first on a long-trusted boyar, Ivan Fyodorov. The tsar, accompanied by a terrifying new henchman, Malyuta Skuratov, imprisoned
Fyodorov's retainers in a chamber full of gunpowder which he then
ignited, whooping as body parts flew into the air. Then 'He and his children of darkness, verily like a madman surrounded by raving madmen,
galloped at full rein to gaze upon the mangled corpses.' Ivan stabbed
Fyodorov, who was then gutted by Skuratov. A total of 150 boyars – and
most of their households and families – were killed by the *oprichniki*,
but the war was deteriorating along with Ivan's mental health, possibly
exacerbated by mercury prescribed for back pain. On 6 January 1569,
as boyars defected to the Poles, Ivan, accompanied by his son and

musketeers and *oprichniki*, stormed the cities of Tver and Novgorod, a secondary residence of Prince Vladimir, where the people, heirs to a republican and mercantile tradition, were weary of the war that interfered with their trade with Sweden. Thousands were killed by grilling them alive, roping them together and pushing them under the ice. In October, Ivan seized his cousin. Vladimir, his wife and nine-year-old daughter were forced to drink poison.* Then he turned on his lover Basmanov, who was made to kill his own father before being killed himself; and then on his ministers, led by keeper of his seal Ivan Viskovaty, for whom he devised a gruesome spectacular.

On 25 July 1570, Ivan, black-clad and brandishing axe and crossbow, arrived at a Poganaia Meadow outside Moscow, accompanied by his son Ivan, now sixteen, and 1,500 mounted musketeers, to find twenty stakes hammered into the ground and linked by beams, along with cauldrons of boiling and cold water. As he watched with diplomats and the public, the *oprichniki* brought forward Viskovaty and 300 noblemen – most of the Muscovite government – who, after atrocious tortures, could barely walk.

'I intend to destroy you so completely,' Ivan told them, 'that no memory of you will survive,' and riding on horseback he asked the crowd to 'come closer to witness the spectacle'.

Viskovaty, who had handled negotiations with Poles, Swedes and Ottomans, was accused of treason and strung up on the beams. Ivan ordered him to confess.

'Go ahead and drink your fill of an innocent's blood,' cried Viskovaty. 'I curse you bloodsuckers and your tsar—' His words were cut off as Malyuta Skuratov sliced off his nose, ears and genitals, which killed him fast, infuriating Ivan who suspected that this was an act of mercy.

One boyar after another, some with their wives and children, were beheaded, boiled to death, flayed alive or, in a favourite new method, hanged by their ribs – 116 victims in total. But Ivan's self-inflicted disasters were just starting: now a new Ottoman padishah invaded.

BLOND SULTAN, JEWISH DUKE, SERBIAN VIZIER

That summer, Selim the Blond, aware of the mayhem Ivan was creating, dispatched his tough grand vizier, Mehmed Sokollu (a Serb, born

---

* The bones of the daughter and mother, tested in the 1960s, reveal arsenic levels of 12.9 for the mother, 8.1 for the child: lethal doses.

Sokolović, a former grand admiral) to invade Muscovy, seize Astrakhan and build a Volga–Don canal to link the Caspian and Black Seas, but Ivan's garrison held out and the campaign failed. With the Ottomans already fighting from Sumatra to the Mediterranean, it was just one adventure among many at the zenith of their empire. Selim had inherited his father Suleiman's worldly ambitions, if not his glacial hauteur and the serene acumen, to run wars on three continents.

Four years earlier, the seventy-year-old Suleiman had reluctantly joined Sokollu, Prince Selim and the army in a thrust into Hungary. During a battle, Suleiman died in his tent. Sokollu won the battle, sent the news to Selim, who was now in Serbia, executed any witnesses of the sultan's death and, propping up the cadaver in his carriage, kept the news secret for forty-eight days – quite a performance.

Selim reappointed Sokollu as grand vizier and granted his Jewish adviser, Joseph Nasi, monopolies on wine and beeswax as well as appointing him duke of Naxos and the Seven Isles (the only Jewish prince since the Khazars).* The two grandees loathed each other, but Selim regarded both as indispensible.

Selim, guided by Joseph and Sokollu, directed a world war against the Spanish and Portuguese. He had just dispatched a fleet to Sumatra to aid the sultan of Aceh against the Portuguese and another flotilla to back the sultan of Gujarat. Joseph, who after his aunt's death lived in the sumptuous Istanbul palace of Belvedere, negotiated with the Habsburg emperor, the kings of France and Poland and the *Signoria* of Venice. Receiving letters from the emperor and a clutch of kings, running his own espionage network, Joseph was a unique figure, known as the Great Jew, negotiating peace with Poland and guiding its royal election, mediating with the princes of Moldavia and Wallachia, sustaining the alliance with France and, when the French refused to repay a debt to him, seizing their ships in Constantinople and selling the contents. Finally he encouraged William the Silent and the Dutch to rebel against Philip.

Selim was keen to expand his father's mastery of the Mediterranean. When Joseph heard that the Venetian arsenal had blown up, he advised Selim to conquer Cyprus, launching an expedition that finally took the island. This was a challenge that the Habsburgs could not ignore but first Philip needed peace in the north – and a new wife.

---

* Joseph won Selim's support for Jews to return to Israel, a Jewish dream since AD 70. As Ottomans protected the holy cities including Jerusalem, Joseph restored the mystical town of Safed (Galilee) and when Pope Pius V expelled Jews from his states, Joseph settled them there.

In 1559, he got both when he negotiated the peace of Cateau-Cambrésis with the French, marking the end of the Habsburg–Valois war for Italy, won by the Habsburgs. Philip's new wife was French, Isabel, the fourteen-year-old daughter of Henri II and his Italian wife, Catherine de' Medici, who escorted her to the frontier. The marriage was part of the Catholic counter-attack against Protestantism, but when Philip saw her he was delighted: Isabel was chic, extravagant, addicted to gambling and full of Gallic fun.* Philip fell in love, visiting her in the middle of the night. Isabel was surprised by his passion; her mother advised her to be grateful. Soon, the birth of their two daughters softened Philip, who finally experienced the joys of family life.

But Isabel tried to influence Philip in the French interest, trained by Catherine de' Medici, the outstanding female politician of her time, and one so hated she was nicknamed the Maggot from Italy's Tomb.

---

* A lady-in-waiting who accompanied her to Madrid was one of the first signed female painters, Sofonisba Anguissola.

Valois and Saadis, Habsburgs and Rurikovichi

LA SERPENTE: A MEDICI QUEEN IN FRANCE

On 10 July 1559, celebrating their daughter's wedding on the Place des Vosges, Catherine watched her husband Henri II, son of *Le Grand Nez*, seated on his horse Unhappy and wearing the colours of his long-time mistress Diane de Poitiers, snap his vizor shut and lower his lance. Catherine asked him not to continue but he shouted back, 'It's precisely for you that I fight.' The two riders, wearing full armour, galloped towards each other.

Jousting was built into their marriage: the erotomane King François was said to have monitored their wedding night. 'Both,' he adjudicated, 'showed valour in the joust.' But the death of her uncle, Pope Clement, cancelled the dowry. Worthless to France, regarded as a scheming Italian from a family of traders, Catherine, 'her mouth too large and eyes too prominent and colourless for beauty but a very distinguished woman with a shapely figure', watched her husband fall in love with Diane de Poitiers, nineteen years older than her; Medici called her the Old Lady. Henri talked of repudiating Catherine when no pregnancy ensued, though Diane encouraged Henri to visit his wife. Catherine drank mule's urine to guard against sterility, painted her 'source of life' with poultices of ground stags' antlers and cow dung embellished with crushed periwinkle and mares' milk – hardly the perfumes to encourage lovemaking.

Finally a sensible doctor examined the couple and discovered slight abnormalities of their sexes that he managed to correct. Catherine became pregnant, surviving nine births. Six children lived to adulthood, four sons and two daughters, including Isabel, high-spirited queen of Spain. Three sons became kings, all sickly and unbalanced, perhaps from inherited Medici syphilis, but their births gave Catherine prestige. When Henri succeeded his father, Catherine had to please his mistress Diane, remembering later, 'It was the king I was really entertaining, acting sorely against the grain, for never did a woman who loved her husband succeed in loving his whore.' But she tolerated it because 'I loved him so much.'

The jousters clashed with the horrendous crack of splintered lance. Catherine screamed; the crowd gasped; Henri tottered; his vizor gaped open, blood gushing from splinters sticking out of his eye and from his temple. Wife, mistress and son all fainted. Philip's doctor Vesalius* was summoned; Henri howled as doctors tried to remove the splinters. It was a dangerous moment for a divided France: 10 per cent of the population were Huguenots – as French Protestants were known – led by Queen Jeanne of Navarre and Admiral Coligny of the Montmorency family, and Henri was determined to exterminate the 'Protestant vermin'.

Catherine rushed to her weakling son, François. 'My God, how can I live,' he sobbed, 'if my father dies?' Septicaemia set in. The new king, François II, was married to the sixteen-year-old Mary, the diminutive, impulsive, half-French Scottish queen, descended from Henry VIII's sister, and handed power to her ultra-Catholic uncles, the Guise brothers, who were determined to destroy the Huguenots.

When after sixteen months François himself died of an ear infection, Catherine took power as *gouvernante de France* for another meagre son, Charles IX, aged ten, nicknamed the Brat. If Catherine's orphaned youth personified the plight of women in power families, her adulthood demonstrated the opportunities for exercising power.[†]

'I was not loved by the king your father as I wished to be,' Catherine confided in her daughter Isabel, 'and God . . . has left me with three little children and a divided kingdom where there is not one man I

---

* Andreas Vesalius practised what to do with Henri by sticking shards into the heads of recently executed criminals, their bodies often snatched still warm from the gallows. In this era, surgery was limited by anatomical knowledge, the inability to stop bleeding, the absence of anaesthetic and antiseptics. Only two internal operations were possible: trepanning the skull and 'cutting for the stone'. In the latter procedure, known as a lithotomy, a patient was trussed and held down by strong men without anaesthetic while the surgeon inserted a tube through the penis to hold the bladder stones in place, then cut the perineum and used a scoop extractor to drag out the stones; the wound was not sewn up but left to heal itself. Many patients died. Vesalius experimented with both procedures.

He was born into a dynasty of Flemish physicians: his grandfather was Emperor Maximilian's doctor, his father was Charles V's apothecary and valet de chambre, while the son became his doctor and the greatest of the pioneering anatomists: dissecting humans and macaques, he discovered some of the essentials of circulation and the skeleton, disproving many of the claims of Galen believed for over a millennium. Fighting off accusations of heresy by the Inquisition, he had become Philip II's physician.

† Catherine was an innovator, said to have made forks and cutlery fashionable; until this time, even kings ate with their fingers, cutting up meat with a knife and eating with a spoon. Ordinary folk travelled with wooden spoons; grandees used silver. Catherine was also said to have introduced underwear, a fashion that became a French speciality – and she smoked American tobacco that was known as *la herbe de reine*.

trust.' Catherine believed she must compromise with the Protestants to preserve France for her sons,* but the Guises traduced her to Philip, claiming that she was compromising with heretics. He called her *Madame la Serpente*. 'Therefore, my daughter, my friend, don't let your husband the king [Philip] believe an untruth,' Catherine beseeched Isabel. 'I don't mean to change my life or my religion.'

In January 1562, Catherine appeased the Huguenots with her tolerant Edict of Saint-Germain, which disgusted Philip. That March, in a clash at Vassy, seventy-four Protestants were killed by François, duc de Guise, leading to full-scale civil war and then to the assassination of Guise. When Catherine proposed a summit with Philip, he refused to see *La Serpente*, sending Isabel, who defended him against her mother.† Catherine proposed marrying her daughter Margot to Philip's bizarre son, Don Carlos. But Philip had a new family member to promote instead of his demented son. He summoned a boy of twelve named Geronimo.

'I was delighted to learn that he is my brother,' Philip wrote. He was the emperor's illegitimate son by a German serving girl, raised in obscurity. Philip asked him if he knew who his father was. 'No,' said Geronimo. Philip kissed him, granted him his own court and renamed him Don Juan of Austria. Don Juan was brought up with his cousin Carlos, who was exactly the same age.

But they were very different. Don Juan grew up into a competent and flashy paladin; Carlos was deteriorating into a murderous maniac. But both craved power.

---

* Catherine started to negotiate the marriage of her sons, Charles, Henri or Hercule-François, to Elizabeth of England. The rival queens were tough politicians who approached family differently. Elizabeth, a Protestant queen regnant, treated as illegitimate, possibly molested by her guardian, harassed by her half-sister, regarded family – and marriage – as perilous. A Catholic mother and wife, Catherine, far from her Italian roots, based everything on her sons, whose marriage to Elizabeth could avoid civil war in France, balance Spain and win England: Catherine's son François had been married to Mary, Queen of Scots, the Catholic claimant to the English throne. Now Catherine played the aspiring mother, Elizabeth the prospective daughter. The candidate was first Charles, who was seventeen years younger than Elizabeth; then Henri, eighteen years younger, who disdained Elizabeth as '*putain publique*'; then, much later, in 1559, when the machinations also involved the leadership of a new Dutch state, Elizabeth, now forty-six, hosted and flirted with Hercule-François, duc d'Alençon, twenty-four, and at least pretended to be engaged.

† On the way, Catherine met Nostradamus, Michel de Nostredame, astrologer, necromancer and physician, born of a family of Jewish converts, paying him 200 écus for his horoscopes of her sons. But he noticed instead one of her pages, Henri of Navarre. The hierophant 'read' the moles on his torso. He was sixth in line to the throne, unlikely to be relevant. Yet Nostradamus predicted that he would be king.

PHILIP'S MURDEROUS FLAGELLATING SON AND
SWASHBUCKLING BROTHER: VICTORY AND HEARTBREAK

In 1562, when chasing a serving girl whom he liked to flagellate, Don Carlos fell head first downstairs. His head swelled, he lost his sight and he feverishly asked for the fragrant body of a revered Franciscan (who was later canonized as St Didacus), which was put into his bed. Carlos slept, but his head had become infected. The physician Vesalius trepanned the skull, drained the fluid off Carlos's brain, removing a piece of skull, and saved his life – though Philip gave the credit to the shrivelled saint's 'odour of sanctity'.

Philip promised Carlos the governorship of the Netherlands but gradually realized that 'Although my son is nineteen and although other children develop late, God wishes that mine lags behind all.' Don Juan asked permission to fight the Ottomans in the Mediterranean. Philip refused, but the dashing bastard disobeyed the king and served at sea. When he returned, Philip was impressed by his glamorous energy. But Carlos was envious; his behaviour was becoming more alarming: though he studied German and the empire, and was happy that he was now engaged to his double cousin Anne, he stormed out of a meeting of the Castilian Cortes (parliament), threw a page out of a window, set fire to a house, tried to murder several courtiers and avidly flagellated more servants.

Philip was now facing a crisis in his Seventeen Provinces (Netherlands and Belgium) which gave his mad son a chance to meddle in dangerous matters. In 1566, Philip's aggressive enforcement of Habsburg power in the form of taxation and Catholicism provoked rebellion in the independent-minded, sophisticated and often Protestant cities of his richest territories. While kings swaggered front of stage, in most places their powers were always limited to some extent by assemblies, cities and guilds but nowhere more so than in the pluralistic Seventeen Provinces where their rights and privileges had been confirmed by the dukes of Burgundy. Philip's governor, his half-sister Margarita of Austria, widow of the Black Medici, was conciliatory. Philip disagreed.

'In matters of religion, don't temporize,' he ordered. 'Punish with the utmost severity.' In 1567, he dispatched his drear paladin Fernando de Toledo, duke of Alba, veteran of Tunis and Mühlberg, to crush the rebellion. When Philip used Margarita to lure rebel nobles and arrest them, she resigned and Alba (whom the Dutch called the Iron Duke, the Spanish the Great one) launched a conventional war and campaign of repression to defeat the rebels, beheading two noble leaders. He boasted that he went on to execute 18,600 people and killed many thousands when seizing Dutch towns. He summoned the provinces' pre-eminent Protestant, William the Silent, prince of Orange, a protégé of Charles V, whom Philip had appointed as *stadtholder* (lieutenant) of Holland and Zeeland. Discreetly encouraged by Elizabeth of England and, via the Jewish duke Joseph Nasi, by Sultan Selim, William escaped to Germany, where he and his brothers assumed the Protestant leadership, appealing to the French Huguenots, signing letters of marque to Protestant privateers, the *Watergeuzen* (Sea Beggars), who soon defeated Spanish warships, and led an army into Holland.* For the rest of Philip's reign, the Seventeen Provinces, where he had to deploy as many as 80,000 troops, became a quagmire – out of which much of what we think of as the modern world would emerge.

His son, Don Carlos, made secret contact with the Dutch rebels and proposed to Don Juan, his trusted uncle of the same age, that he procure him a galley to escape, to seize power in the Netherlands. In return Carlos offered him the crown of Naples. Don Juan reported this treason to Philip. Worse was to come. When Carlos later received Don Juan, he tried to shoot him with his arquebus, but his servants had uncocked it. He drew a dagger and threw himself at his uncle, who disarmed him, tossed the diminutive, hunchbacked prince aside and drew a sword: 'Don't come one step closer, Your Highness!' Carlos decided to kill his father.

At midnight one night in 1568, Philip donned helmet and breastplate, gathered a posse, then led them through the corridors of the Madrid Alcázar and burst into the bedroom of Don Carlos, who awoke to find his bed surrounded by his father and several courtiers, swords drawn. 'My aim,' wrote Philip, 'was to find a permanent remedy. Time is unlikely to find a cure.'

Carlos was imprisoned in the Alcázar, where he starved himself and tried to commit suicide by swallowing a diamond. He died six months later. That death was a relief for Philip. But in October 1568, his adored Isabel, aged twenty-three, died of infection after a miscarriage. Heartbroken, Philip did not want to remarry, but his niece Anna, twenty-one-year-old daughter of his cousin Emperor Maximilian II, betrothed to Carlos, was now available. Even the pope warned against inbreeding, but he needed a son more than ever.

---

* The name Sea Beggars originated when a Dutch delegation called on Margarita. 'Fear not, madam,' said an adviser, 'they're only beggars.' The Beggars adopted the beggar's pouch as a rebel symbol. Within four years, there were eighty-five privateers in action, precursors of the armed trading corporations.

To ensure that his Austrian cousins supported his anti-Protestant crusade, Philip invited their son, Rudolf, brother of his new wife and now his own heir apparent, to Spain. 'May no one deter you from your faith,' he told Rudolf, 'which is the only true one!' Rudolf was trained in Spanish ceremonial, ever after sporting its 'Spaniolated' ruff and black hose, but he was horrified by Philip's dogmatism. It was the art of the Escorial – where Titian was painting *The Last Supper* – that impressed him. Rudolf the Mad would be the most unbuttoned and eccentric of all the Habsburgs.

As Philip settled into a happy fourth marriage, his half-brother Don Juan won glory.

In January 1567, Philip banned the faith, customs, language and costumes of the 400,000 Moriscos – Muslims forcibly converted to Catholicism in 1501 – who, encouraged by Joseph Nasi from Constantinople, reacted by launching a rebellion in the mountainous Alpujarras under a mysterious leader, El Habaquí, boosted by jihadis from Africa and Ottoman Janissaries sent by Selim. Philip appointed Don Juan to crush the Muslims, the start of a dirty war in which Morisco villages were exterminated and Muslim rebels tortured Catholics. Don Juan was wounded in the fighting. 'You must preserve yourself,' Philip told his brother. 'I must keep you for great things.' Philip ordered mass deportations. 'The saddest sight in the world,' wrote Juan. 'There was so much rain, wind and snow the poor people clung together lamenting. One cannot deny the spectacle of depopulation of a kingdom is most pitiful.' Some 90,000 died; Philip planned to expel the remaining Moriscos – a tragic solution carried out by his son, Philip III.

Soon afterwards the news arrived that Selim had taken Cyprus from Venice. Pius V invited Philip, whose commitments were eased by a truce with the Dutch, to join a Holy League against the Ottomans. Philip nominated the twenty-five-year-old Don Juan as commander of 208 galleys, 6 galliasses, 24 other warships and 60,000 men (including Miguel de Cervantes, future novelist) to fight an Ottoman fleet of 300 ships and around 100,000 men. The Ottoman galleys were more manoeuvrable; the Christians had better artillery. Overlooking Philip's instructions to avoid military impetuosity as much as sexual incontinence, Juan was determined to fight, asking advice of experienced admirals in the fleet and repeatedly practising manoeuvres.

Dressed in gleaming armour, Juan toured the fleet in a frigate, addressing the sailors in different languages: 'My children, we're here to conquer or die!' He ordered his galley slaves, mostly Muslims, to be double-shackled, while the Ottoman Capitan-Pasha Ali promised his Christian slaves, 'If I win the battle, I promise you liberty.'

At Lepanto off the Greek coast, the Ottomans tried to wrap their crescent formation around the Holy Leaguers. The fighting was savage as Ottoman galleys were blasted out of the water by Don Juan's cannonades; Don Juan, commanding at the prow of his *El Real*, ordered the storming of *Sultana*, flagship of the capitan-pasha, whose head was taken to Don Juan, then mounted on a pike, destroying Ottoman morale. Seagulls feasted on eviscerated bodies floating in a crimson Mediterranean. Altogether 35,000 Turks were killed, 130 Ottoman ships captured, while 8,000 Christians were killed, 20,000 wounded. Thousands of Christian slaves, chained to their ships, went to the bottom, but 12,000 were liberated. The victory made Don Juan the pre-eminent hero of Christendom and convinced Philip of his own messianic destiny. Don Juan wanted to sail on to Istanbul, but Philip restrained him. Instead Don Juan seized Tunis. Now he wanted a kingdom of his own.

Philip, triumphant over Islam, now encouraged the death knell of heresy in France that was linked to his Dutch problems. In August 1572, Catherine de' Medici was planning a magnificent Parisian wedding – and the slaughter of half her guests.

RED WEDDING: BRAT KING, CROCODILE QUEEN AND PSYCHOTIC TSAR

Once sceptical about Philip's repression in Holland, Catherine now planned to destroy her own Protestants, who were recklessly supporting the Dutch against Spain.

She was negotiating the marriage between her daughter Margot and the Protestant prince Henri, eighteen-year-old son of Queen Jeanne of the little Pyrenean kingdom of Navarre and Antoine de Bourbon, duc de Vendôme, a cousin of the king by a junior branch of the Capet family. The marriage was designed to reunite the family across the religious divide. But when the Huguenots planned to kidnap Catherine herself, she started to consider combining the marriage with an extreme solution.

Margot, a dazzling brunette whose 'lovely face shone with faultless white skin', resisted the marriage. As they grew up, Catherine struggled to control her vicious children: Charles was spineless, devious and tubercular; Henri, duc d'Anjou, was artful and depraved, his looks spoiled by a seeping fistula between eye and nose. Anjou favoured wild transvestite orgies. Catherine tried to divert him by giving a party where the serving girls were naked, but, in between bouts of self-flagellation, prayer and fasting, Anjou preferred his male lover sieur de Lignerolles. Catherine had Lignerolles stabbed in an alleyway, and that was just the beginning.

The boys were locked in a sinister dance with their mother. 'I'm not one of those mothers who love their children only for themselves,' Catherine told Henri. 'I love you because I see you foremost in greatness and reputation.' They were attracted to their sister Margot. Now the brothers seduced or raped her: 'It was you who first put my foot in the stirrup,' she later told Anjou, trembling with secret excitement when he embraced her.

Margot was already in love with a non-royal cousin. When her mother and brother Charles discovered her flirtation, they awoke her in the night and punched her viciously, tearing her nightdress to shreds. She agreed to obey her mother: 'I had no will nor choice but hers.'

As the guests arrived in Paris, Catherine met with her son Anjou. King Charles the Brat had a close, almost filial friendship with the Protestant leader, Gaspar de Coligny, so the mother and Anjou decided that since 'the admiral [Coligny] had inspired His Majesty [Charles] with a bad and sinister opinion of the queen', in Anjou's account, 'my mother and myself, we resolved to rid ourselves of him'.

In August 1572, broiling and tense, Paris filled with sumptuously dressed guests. The Protestant bridegroom, Henri of Navarre, dark, aquiline, muscular, had arrived with 800 black-clad, heavily armed horsemen. Margot dazzled the courtiers: 'Besides the beauty of her face and her well-turned body, she was superbly dressed . . . her hair was dressed with big white pearls and rare diamonds – [like] a brilliant night sky full of stars.'

On 18 August, in Notre-Dame, Margot, wearing an ermine-rimmed crown, a jewel-spangled dress, stood beside Henri, who was accompanied by Admiral Coligny, to take her vows. It was claimed that when twice asked by the cardinal for her assent Margot said nothing, so Charles reached out and pushed her head down in a nod. This might be later Bourbon propaganda, but the ceremony was laden with menace. During the next four days Catherine prepared her strike. Not for nothing did she collect embalmed crocodiles: seven hung from the ceiling of her study.

On the 22nd Catherine and Anjou ordered a hitman to shoot Coligny, but he only wounded the admiral's hand. The king was furious when Coligny whispered that his power had been usurped by his mother and brother. Catherine and Anjou were made to pay their respects to the bedridden Coligny, surrounded by Huguenots eager for revenge.

Within the Louvre, Catherine and Anjou agreed 'to finish the admiral by whatever means. It was necessary to bring the king round. We decided to go to him in his study after dinner . . .'

The crocodile queen decided to massacre not just Coligny but the Huguenot nobility. When he was told of Coligny's plan to attack him and his mother, Charles shouted, 'Lies! The admiral loves me as though I were his own son.' Catherine argued that Coligny was tricking him. Suddenly the unbalanced king was convinced. 'Then kill them all!' Brat shrieked. 'Kill them all!'

In the early hours of St Bartholomew's Day, the hit squad of Anjou's Swiss Guards stormed Coligny's house and erupted into the bedchamber. 'Are you the Admiral?' they asked.

'I am. I should at least be killed by a gentleman and not this boor,' but the boor drove his sword through Coligny's chest, then threw him out of the window, the signal for the hecatomb to begin. At the Louvre, where her new husband Henri and his retainers were lodging, Margot was suspected by both sides, 'so that no one told me anything, until that evening'. She finally confronted her mother. 'God willing, my mother replied, I'd come to no harm but in any case I must go, for fear of awakening their suspicions.' After praying for her life, Margot joined Henri in his bed, surrounded by forty Huguenot guards. Margot fell asleep. Henri later wandered out of his room, but he was detained and safely locked up as the royal guardsmen went from room to room, killing the guests. When Huguenots escaped into the courtyard, archers shot them.

'Navarre!' Margot was awoken by banging on the door. When a servant opened the door, a Huguenot covered in blood staggered in, pursued by five royal hitmen, and clung on to Margot, covering her in blood. Laughing, the captain of guards 'gave me the life of that man clinging to me'.

'They're killing them all,' the Spanish ambassador wrote to Philip, 'stripping them naked, dragging them through the streets, sparing not even children. Blessed be God!' Philip 'experienced one of the greatest pleasures I've had in all my life'.

King Charles panicked, crying, 'What bloodshed! God, forgive me . . . I'm lost,' then blamed it all on his mother: 'God's blood, you're the cause of it all!' Henri of Navarre converted to Catholicism. Bodies were heaped around the Louvre. Coligny was castrated and gibbeted, his head delivered to Catherine, who forwarded it to the pope. Three thousand were killed in Paris, 20,000 nationally.

The French, said a foreign monarch, were barbarians. That monarch,

Ivan the Terrible, was himself no humanitarian* and now his capital was lost thanks to his own atrocities. In May 1571, the Crimean khan Devlet Giray galloped north and stormed Moscow, enslaving tens of thousands and leaving the city a smoking ruin. 'They burned Moscow, and didn't dare tell me for ten days,' he grumbled. 'That's treason' – and traitors had to be killed, some poisoned by Dr Bomelius.

Deciding he needed to marry again, Ivan held a bride-show at which the German doctor helped him select the final twelve girls. His role was to 'inspect their urine in a glass and define and explain its nature', after which the tsar chose one for himself, but she died soon after the wedding. He married for a fifth time just before Khan Devlet raided northwards again. On this occasion Ivan's generals used his artillery, manned by German mercenaries, to hold off the Tatars. Ivan now re-united the kingdom, terminating the division between *oprichnina* and *zemshchina*. Dismissing or killing his fifth wife, Ivan wanted a sixth royal wife from England or Poland. Dr Bomelius proposed Elizabeth of England, who had already agreed to grant Ivan asylum if he lost his throne. Ivan criticized Elizabeth for not being 'sovereign-born' and for remaining single. Now Poland offered an opportunity.

In July 1572, its king died, leaving his sister Anna, half Italian, well educated and unmarried at forty, as heir. But the Polish nobles – the *szlachta* – rejected a female queen and their *Sejm* (parliament) gathered to select a new king who would marry Anna. Ivan, supported by some Lithuanians, proposed, as did a Habsburg, but a surprising outsider proved irresistibly flexible. Henri of Anjou, Catherine de' Medici's effete, vicious son who had failed to become king of England or Holland and was keen for his own crown, charmed Anna, whom he promised to marry, and agreed to terms that created the most free and democratic state in Europe.† Henri won the election, but when he arrived, amazing the Poles with his heavy make-up and flamboyant entourage, he de-layed marrying Anna and then suddenly received news that his brother Charles was dead. Henri was king of France *and* Poland. Abandoning

---

* But his moniker – Terrible – only became current in the seventeenth century, when it meant 'awesome' rather than the modern meaning of 'atrocious', and his atrocities were not so different in cruelty from those of Catherine de Medici or Henry VIII or Cesare Borgia. In many ways, he was a man of his time.

† This colossal state of Poland–Lithuania – forgotten because it has no modern equivalent – became a Serene Republic under the presidency of a king elected by the *Sejm* of the nobility. The nobility formed around 15 per cent of the population, so there was an elec-torate of over 500,000, larger than anything in England or France until the 1830s. It most resembled the oligarchy of Venice, dominated by magnates, but religious tolerance, even for Jews and other minorities, was guaranteed. *This Złota Wolność* – Golden Liberty – lasted for the next two centuries.

Anna, infanta of Poland, who now sought a husband to fight on against Muscovy, Henri flounced away in the night like a scented, rouged thief, pursued by outraged Polish horsemen, to re-emerge in Paris as Henri III. 'France and you,' he told his mother, 'are worth more than Poland.'

MURDER OF THE SONS: KING OF THE HERMAPHRODITES AND TSAR OF SIBERIA

Dressed in coral bracelets, earrings, doublets pleated and slashed in scarlet, and violet ribbons, his hair scented and curled, King Henri was nicknamed King of the Isle of Hermaphrodites or King of Sodom, but he was unable to stop the religious war, again banning Protestantism. Margot's marriage to Navarre, sanctified amid the red wedding, was cursed: she had so many love affairs that the king had her arrested for promiscuity. Incensed, Margot remembered how he and his brother Charles had seduced her. Their mother Catherine hinted to her son-in-law Navarre that they should perhaps liquidate Margot.*

Henri III recognized that Navarre, who had returned to Protestantism, was his heir but he was determined to be master. Forming his own hit squad, the Forty-Five, he had his Catholic rivals, the surviving Guise brothers, assassinated: one was killed in front of him as he sneered 'King of Paris, eh? Not so big now' – and the other was diced and cooked in a fireplace like an aristocratic kebab. Furious Parisians drove Henri out of Paris. Catherine was horrified: 'Wretched man, what's he done? Pray for him. He's headed towards ruin.' In August 1589, just after his mother died at sixty-nine, Henri received a visitor, a friar, while sitting on his commode. The friar drew a dagger and stabbed the defecating king. 'Ah my God,' cried Henri, holding his guts in, 'the wretch!' Before dying, he gave Navarre some final advice: 'You'll experience many calamities until you change your religion.' With the passing of the last of the Valois branch, Navarre, now Henri IV, first of the Bourbons, fought for his kingdom – 'I rule with my arse in the saddle and my gun in my fist' – until he realized that his predecessor was right. Henri converted for the fifth and last time to Catholicism with the sentiment if not the words: 'Paris is worth a mass.'†

* Amazingly the St Bartholemew's Massacre did not end Catherine's marriage negotiations with Elizabeth who in 1579, now over forty, entertained the youngest Valois, the duc d'Alençon whom she flirtatiously called 'my frog'. But Alençon died soon after this futile trip.
† Henri IV the Great settled the religious wars by granting toleration to the Protestants, laying the foundations of modern France. He divorced Margot and married Marie de' Medici, the plump, plain but masterful and tumultuous daughter of the grand duke of Tuscany, a marriage that paid off his debts. Henri's mistress called her 'the fat banker'. Henri

Henri's second marriage did not bring him close to the record of Europe's most uxorious monarch. In Muscovy, Ivan now married a seventh and eighth time, his last wife producing a son. In autumn 1575, Dr Bomelius cast a horoscope that predicted danger for the tsar. Ivan abdicated as grand prince of Russia and appointed in his place a scion of Genghis and nephew of Tsarina Marina, Simeon Bekbulatovich, who 'reigned' for a year before Ivan took back the crown. But in 1579 the war turned decisively: the Poles retook Polotsk and invaded Muscovy. Ivan blamed his disasters on Dr Bomelius, who tried to escape, jewels sewn into his clothes. He was caught and roasted on a spit.

It was not easy to be Ivan the Terrible's son and heir. Ivan Ivanovich was in his prime, while his father was crippled by arthritis, barely able to move, according to an examination of his skeleton: there is nothing more dangerous than a lame tiger. His father had twice chosen wives for him, then dismissed them. Finally, young Ivan married a third for love. In November 1782, the older Ivan, hobbling on his sharp metal tsar's staff, saw his pregnant daughter-in-law wearing only one robe instead of the traditional three and slapped her.

'You thrust my first wife into a nunnery,' shouted his son, 'then my second. Now you hit my third.' The tsar stabbed him in the head with his staff. The tsarevich died soon afterwards. The daughter-in-law miscarried. Ivan grieved madly, scratching the walls. 'Alas for me a sinner,' he wrote in a typical lucubration, 'I, a stinking hound . . . always wallowing in drunkenness, fornication, adultery, filth, murders, rapine, despoliation, hatred and all sorts of evildoing.' He listed his victims killed unshriven, ordering prayers for their souls. Ivan had lost a war and a son – just as he gained a new empire.

In September 1582, his conquistadors, the Stroganovs, harassed by Kuchum, khan of Sibir, hired a Cossack captain Yermak to attack the khanate. Yermak and 840 freebooters and slaves, armed with muskets and a couple of cannon, crossed the Urals, allied with some of the indigenous animist Khanty peoples who resented the Tatar Muslims, and defeated Kuchum, seizing Qashliq, the Mongol capital. Accepting the title offered by Yermak, tsar of Siberia, Ivan was exultant, ordering bells rung and sending gifts to Yermak plus a unit of musketeers.

In March 1584, Ivan, fifty-four but ailing, told the English ambassador, 'I'm poisoned with disease.' He was playing with turquoise stones. 'You see? The change of pure colour into pall heralds my death.'

and Marie de' Medici fathered the future Louis XIII and Henrietta Maria, wife of Charles I of England. As for Margot, irrepressible and sensual, she took ever-younger lovers into her fifties, dying in 1615.

It was said that the colour of turquoises changed in the presence of poison.

THE BATTLE OF THREE DEAD KINGS:
SEBASTIAN THE ASLEEP AND MANSUR THE GOLDEN

That afternoon, the Terrible bathed and sang hymns loudly, and then, while playing chess, was felled by a stroke.

As Ivan died, Yermak was in desperate straits in Qashliq, besieged by Tatars and Ostiaks, whom he managed to repel, but he was isolated and almost out of gunpowder. On 5 August 1585, the conquistador was ambushed by Kuchum, his men slaughtered, and he himself, escaping by river, drowned under the weight of the Terrible's armour.

Yermak's Cossacks panicked and abandoned Qashliq. But in 1598 they encountered reinforcements and returned, founding the first European city in Siberia, Tobolsk. The conquest and settlement of Siberia, much neglected by historians, was similar to that of north America two centuries later: the colonizers crushed indigenous resistance by Tungus and Buriat peoples, burning villages, raping and enslaving women and bringing catastrophic diseases, particularly smallpox; some indigenous tribes killed themselves en masse.*

It would take the Russians just forty years to reach the Pacific Ocean, where the Spanish had seized the Philippines, originally named for Philip II who then ordered its conquest.† Anything now seemed pos-

---

* Ivan was succeeded by his son, Fyodor, known as the Bell-ringer for his simple piety. The Bell-ringer died without children, the throne seized by the Terrible's last favourite, Boris Godunov, who was married to his sister. Boris was accused of the murder of Dmitri, last son of Ivan the Terrible. Once in power, he promoted the colonization of Siberia and contributed to the tightening of controls over Russian peasants. But Boris failed to win the glory or enjoy the longevity necessary to found a dynasty, his death unleashing a decade of war and invasion by Poles, Swedes and Tatars, exacerbated by three impostors, the False Dmitris – who claimed to be the Terrible's murdered son – that almost destroyed Muscovy. The Poles captured Moscow, a trauma that engendered a fear of a resurgent Poland that lasts to this day. Out of this mire, a sickly teenager, stammering and lame, Michael Romanov, the great-nephew of the Terrible's first beloved wife, Anastasia, and first cousin of Tsar Fyodor, reluctantly emerged as the tsar of a new Romanov dynasty. His survival looked unlikely, but his commanders drove the invaders back. But the wars had impoverished the peasantry, who often escaped to the borderlands: Michael's son Alexei enforced stability by allowing the nobility total control of their peasants, who became serfs, no longer allowed to leave their estates. Serfdom was similar but not the same as chattel slavery: serfs owed service to their masters and could be punished, raped and killed, but they also farmed for themselves, paid taxes and often served in the army. Later they could be sold like slaves and were often transferred with their estates.
† A fleet of five galleons and 500 soldiers, more than half of them Inca and Mexica, had

sible to El Prudente, who ordered the conquest of China, a plan diverted by challenges closer to home.

While enjoying this streak of successes, Philip struggled to control his flamboyant half-brother Don Juan, whom he decided to send to Holland as governor-general to negotiate a permanent peace. He dangled an amazing prize: Don Juan was also to command the 'Enterprise of England', destroy Elizabeth, marry Mary of Scots and become king. Abetted by two of Philip's secretaries, Juan disobeyed Philip and bungled the Dutch negotiations. Philip probably had Juan's secretary assassinated in the back streets of Madrid.

Philip was simultaneously trying to restrain his Portuguese nephew King Sebastian, another strange child of consanguinity, sometimes hyperactive, sometimes becalmed, but always enraptured by a messianic crusading mission.

Sebastian's very existence was regarded as miraculous: his family had almost died out when in 1554 the king's only son died of consumption, leaving a pregnant wife Juana, daughter of Charles V. But eighteen days later she gave birth to Sebastian O Desejado – the Desired. Sebastian, relishing the company of young monks and avoiding female company, presided over further imperial expansion: off China, Macau was secured, while in south-east Africa, he founded the fortress of São Sebastião (Mozambique) and, in the west, built a new slaving port, Luanda (Angola), and expanded into the kingdom of Ndongo – making the Portuguese so far the only Europeans to build a territorial, rather than coastal, empire in Africa. Nearer home, Sebastian aspired to become 'emperor of Morocco', exploiting a fissure in the ruling Saadi dynasty, backing a pretender against his pro-Ottoman uncle, the sultan.

Philip advised Sebastian against his plan, but in 1577 the Desired landed at Tangier with the cream of Portuguese nobility, 17,000 men and many volunteers,* who marched in full armour into the interior.

---

crossed the Pacific, under Miguel López de Legazpi. The Philippines were the outer rim of the Indic world, Polynesian peoples ruled by Hindu rajas as well as Islamic amirs under the loose rule of Brunei, whose sultan Bolkiah had conquered an empire in the 1490s that was now ended by the Spanish. In 1570, Legazpi, now capitán-general, defeated Ache, raja of the Maynila kingdom on Luzon, and built his capital Manila, seat of the Spanish rulers until 1898. Philip's treasure fleets now sailed across the Pacific to China, usually manned by Spanish officers and often Mexica or Amerindian troops.

* The most pre-eminent was Sir Thomas 'Lusty' Stuckley, sixty years old, son of a Devon knight, who commanded the Portuguese centre. Stuckley had fought all over Europe: he served Mary I but as a recusant Catholic he defied Elizabeth, about whom he boasted he 'didn't give a fart' and whom he impertinently told he would found his own kingdom before escaping to serve Philip and Don Juan of Austria in plots to invade England and Ireland. The Mediterranean was a small world: Stuckley had fought for Don Juan at Lepanto while

The heat was so intense that Sebastian had cold water poured into his armour, but he was unprepared when, on 4 August 1578, at Ksar el-Kebir, he encountered 60,000 Moroccan troops. Sultan Abd al-Malik was dying but his brother Ahmed encircled the Portuguese. Sebastian had three horses shot from under him. Then he charged and was cut off; his Moroccan pretender was drowned (later flayed and stuffed) and the victor Abd al-Malik expired – three kings dead during one battle. Eight thousand Portuguese were killed, 15,000 – many of them female camp followers – were enslaved. Sebastian's body was never found: he became the Sleeping King, expected to awaken and rule in the End of Days. But two monarchs benefited from his folly.

Abd al-Malik's brother, Ahmed – now Sultan al-Mansur, the Victor, later known as the Golden – was ferociously capable, making Morocco a pivotal power and allying himself with Elizabeth of England, with whom he hoped to reconquer Spain. Al-Mansur also hoped to colonize America with Moroccan settlers, blessed by a transatlantic advent of the Mahdi, which did not come to pass. To the south, he envied the wealth of the Songhai kingdom that replaced Mali, demanding revenues from their salt and gold. The *askia* (king) arrogantly sent two metal shoes as an insult. Twelve years after Ksar el-Kebir, Mansur dispatched a small army armed with cannon across the Sahara under a blue-eyed Spanish renegade, Judar Pasha, enslaved and castrated as a boy. The eunuch took Timbuktu and returned with thirty camel-loads of gold. For a decade, al-Mansur ruled a slaving, salt and gold empire in west Africa.[*]

Philip was the other beneficiary. The Aviz were almost extinct and he was the heir: he seized Portugal and united the first two world empires. His flashy brother Don Juan died ingloriously of typhoid, but his death undermined negotiations with the Dutch, who went back to war – and this time Philip appointed his talented Italian nephew, the duke of Parma, who captured Antwerp and the southern provinces. The division was decisive: at Utrecht in 1579, the seven northern provinces – Holland, Zeeland and others – formed a military defence union, directed by their States-General, with help from William and the Orange family. Two years later, the United Provinces declared independence, while the south (Belgium) swore allegiance to the Habsburgs. The union had just 1.5 million people and its forces under William and his brother were

the Moroccan sultanic brothers Abd al-Malik and Ahmed had fought for the Ottomans at the same battle.
[*] In Marrakesh, he built a fantastical palace, al-Badi – the Marvellous – embellished with marble columns from Italy; some of it still stands. The labourers were white slaves, Portuguese prisoners, treated abysmally.

defeated by Parma. Elizabeth helped with a meagre army that Parma trounced. Yet the United Provinces, forged by religious war, rising patriotism and international voyaging and well served by their many walled cities and watery terrain, proved resilient; the union was also powered by a pluralistic society that welcome talented immigrants, by a sophisticated economy and financial markets, and by an early welfare system for poor relief. As the Sea Beggars harassed Habsburg shipping, Elizabeth unleashed her own privateers – the 'seadogs' led by Jack Hawkins and Francis Drake – for a spree of English raiding. The war against the Habsburgs became a fight to the death.

KING BAYANO, DRAKE AND DIEGO

On 26 September 1580, a grizzled Devonian sea captain, Francis Drake, sailed into Plymouth with the most profitable cargo ever for an English raid on Habsburg treasure. But he arrived back with just one of the five ships in his flotilla and only fifty-six of that ship's original crew of eighty. Elizabeth was delighted: her profit is estimated at 4,700 per cent.

Drake was the scion of a cousinhood of Devon seafaring families – Hawkins, Gilberts, Raleighs – that would form the spearhead of English expansion and of involvement in the slave trade. At its centre were Drake's kinsmen, the Hawkinses, to whom he owed his rise. The Hawkinses had long traded English wool with the Italian cities, and in 1530 William Hawkins started trading ivory in Guinea. As a boy, his son Jack had met and served Philip of Spain ('my old master') when he landed to marry Queen Mary, but he embraced the opportunities of the rising tension with the paramount Catholic power. In 1562, he raised funds from London merchants to raid the African coast and trade slaves, setting off with his twenty-year-old cousin Drake to attack Portuguese traders, taking 'into his possession, partly by the sword and partly other means, to the number of three hundred Negroes'. He then sailed to Hispaniola, where in exchange for the slaves 'he received such quantities of hides, gingers, sugars, pearls' that he filled five ships. He sold 500 slaves on his second voyage; on his third he was contacted by two African kings asking for his help against their rival, for which his payment was to take 'as many Negroes as by warres might be obtained'.

Blunt, gritty and dour with acute porcine eyes, Hawkins was the pioneer of the English slave trade that was to become a financial juggernaut of profit and cruelty, though at this point the trade was still dominated by the Portuguese. In the first half of the century, 120,000 slaves were traded across the Atlantic; in the second half, the figure had doubled to 210,000. The gold from Colombia and the silver from Peru were even more valuable: two fifty-galleon treasure fleets sailed back and forth between Europe and the Caribbean, while another sailed across the Pacific to China. By 1590, Philip's fleets delivered eleven million pesos a year. Elizabeth appointed Hawkins controller of the navy, for which he helped design light, fast ships that could circumnavigate the globe and outfight the majestic Spanish galleons, but he also led more raids on Africa and America.

Philip was infuriated by the English 'pirates'. Yet the Spanish bought their slaves until in 1568, at San Juan (Mexico), they routed a Hawkins flotilla: the Devonian cousins barely escaped with their lives. But Drake had identified the weakest link in the sea transfer of silver from Peru, by land across Panama then by sea to Cadiz, and found allies to assist his heists.

In 1572, he negotiated with King Bayano of the Maroons in Panama. The slaves on Spanish plantations in Jamaica and Panama regularly rebelled and soon founded their own rebel Maroon communities ruled by elected kings, who were often kidnapped African royalty. In the gold mines of Venezuela, a slave from the Bay of Biafra named Miguel killed his cruel foreman and escaped, founding a community that he structured like the Spanish monarchy, with himself as king, his wife Guiomar as queen, crowned by their own bishop, before King Miguel was killed and his queen re-enslaved. Now, raiding Panama, Drake encountered King Bayano. A Panama Maroon named Diego negotiated an alliance and became Drake's companion on future voyages. In March 1573, Drake succeeded in capturing an entire convoy of Spanish silver.

Elizabeth and her retainers invested in his transcontinental anti-Habsburg raids. 'We'd gladly be revenged on the king of Spain,' Elizabeth told Drake, 'for divers injuries that we've received.' In December 1577, five ships set off from Plymouth. Drake, accompanied by Diego and possibly other ex-slaves, argued with his co-captain during the journey: Drake accused the captain of witchcraft and betrayal and had him beheaded. Sailing into the Pacific, losing his other ships, he captured Spanish treasure ships, sailed up the Californian coast and across the Pacific to the Moluccas (where Diego died of wounds), before limping back to Plymouth in his *Golden Hind* to deliver such bounty that the queen's half-share, £160,000, was greater than her annual revenues.

Drake was knighted, but his ascendancy as naval adventurer was challenged by another tough son of the west country. Walter Raleigh was also a member of the Plymouth cousinhood, but younger, smoother and romantically literary, an irresistible combination of killer, lover and poet.

His half-brother Humphrey Gilbert, nephew of Drake through his wife, had fought with the Dutch Sea Beggars and then helped organize a ferocious reconquest of Ireland which had never been fully subjugated by England. The Plantation, a cleansing operation in which Catholic Anglo-Norman-Irish earls who had traditionally run the island were replaced by Protestant, English lords and settlers, was led by the same west country men who were driving the war against Spain. Gilbert, joined by Raleigh and Drake, treated Ireland like a conquistador, decorating his camp with rows of Irish heads. It was almost a rehearsal for later conquests: when they captured Spanish troops, sent by Philip to aid the Catholic Irish, Raleigh personally helped behead over 200 of them. The cousins were granted 50,000 acres in Ireland. When Drake was there he joined the slaughter of 600 retainers of the Irish chieftain Sorley Boy MacDonnell.

Gilbert and Raleigh were friendly with Elizabeth's magus and astrologer, John Dee, who was so influential that he had cast the stars to choose her coronation date. In 1577, Dee wrote his *Perfect Arte of Navigation* proposing what he called a British empire in north America, inspiring Gilbert in 1582 to claim Newfoundland (Canada) as the first English colony. When Gilbert died on the way home, Elizabeth authorized Raleigh to colonize 'remote, heathen and barbarous lands . . . not actually possessed of any Christian Prince or inhabited by Christian People' in return for a fifth of all gold discovered there. In 1587 Raleigh sponsored an English colony, Roanoke (North Carolina), but his settlers vanished, dying as a result of starvation, epidemic or attacks by Native Americans. Yet Raleigh's abortive colony had, as Dee predicted, founded a new enterprise: the empire.*

Raleigh himself was appointed captain of Elizabeth's bodyguard just as Philip ordered her assassination. His threats were not to be taken lightly. He had offered a bounty for anyone who killed his other Protestant enemy, William of Orange.† Philip hoped to enthrone Mary, the

---

* The French had been ahead of the English but no more fortunate: in 1534, François I had dispatched his own conquistador Jacques Cartier to north America where he founded various settlements in Quebec, the start of New France. But the settlements were wiped out by disease and Native American attacks.

† In 1584, William was the first national leader to be assassinated using a handgun, but his killing changed nothing: his son Maurice replaced him as stadtholder. His assassin did not collect the prize, being captured and subjected to one of the most gruesome executions: the right hand that had pulled the trigger was burned off, his flesh cut and torn from his bones in six places; he was then burned with bacon fat, dismembered then disembowelled alive, before his heart was cut out of his chest and tossed in his face before his head was cut off. But Philip did ennoble his family and give them estates.

Scottish queen, a calamitous bungler of impulsive stupidity and unwise passion. In 1567, after the death of her French husband François II, she returned to rule an increasingly Protestant Scotland inspired by the firebrand John Knox who, authoring *The First Blast of the Trumpet against the Monstruous Regiment of Women*, openly attacked Mary in person until she exiled him. Her second marriage to a dashing Catholic cousin, the eighteen-year-old Henry Stuart, earl of Darnley, six foot tall and known as the Long Lad, successfully delivered a son, James, but provoked Protestant rebellion. Long Lad murdered her Italian confidant, at which Mary most likely acquiesced in his own assassination, organized by a ruffian earl who then kidnapped and married her. Their homicidal alliance sparked such outrage that the Protestants enthroned the baby James and Mary fled to England, where Elizabeth granted her asylum, which she repaid by plotting with Philip. 'Alas the poor fool will never cease until she loses her head,' commented Charles IX of France. 'They'll put her to death. It's her own fault and folly.'

Now in February 1587, when Mary's plots were exposed, Elizabeth had her beheaded, provoking Philip to invade England on a scale only a world empire could muster.

TWO ARMADAS: PHILIP AND HIDEYOSHI

Philip's strategy was correct: it was impossible to defend every port of his world empire; only a focused offensive against the base of his enemy could succeed. This was not the deluded folly of a Catholic fanatic. Plenty of seaborne invasions of England – from Forkbeard to Henry Tudor – had succeeded but God is in the detail: a simple plan and clement weather were essential.

Yet Philip knew better than the experts: his 'masterplan' envisaged a fleet sailing from Cadiz, fighting off English attacks, rendezvousing off Flanders with an army under his nephew Parma that had to board the fleet and then invade England – a welter of precise timings afloat on a tide of unpredictable contingencies. While shipyards built his fleet to carry 55,000 infantry and 1,600 cavalry, Philip, now sixty, chose as the Armada's commander a grandee, Alonso de Guzmán, duke of Medina Sidonia, who had neither combat experience nor imposing personality. As Drake raided Cadiz, destroying many ships, and Philip became sick with stress, both Medina Sidonia and Parma criticized the plan. 'I've dedicated this enterprise to God,' Philip told Medina Sidonia. 'Pull yourself together and do your part.'

In July 1588, the duke sailed with 130 ships manned by 8,000 sailors and carrying 18,000 soldiers as Philip prayed in the Escorial chapel. Surviving English attacks in the Channel commanded by vice-admirals Drake and Hawkins, hardly the victories portrayed in English histories, the duke and his intact fleet waited off Calais for Parma's army of 30,000. When these troops tardily discovered that the fleet had arrived, they marched towards their ships. But the English sent in fireships that drove the Armada out into a storm, scattering it. Some ships were wrecked, others embarked on a 3,000-mile voyage around Scotland and Ireland. Fifteen thousand sailors perished.

At the same time, across the world, another megalomaniacal visionary, this time a self-made peasant's son, Hideyoshi, the Japanese imperial regent, was launching his own fleet for an invasion that Philip had himself considered: China.

In May 1592, Toyotomi Hideyoshi ordered 158,800 men on 700 troopships accompanied by 300 warships to land in Korea and invade China, the culmination of an extraordinary career. He planned to go on and conquer India. Japan had been nominally ruled for over a millennium by an emperor or *tenno* of the divine Sun family, but real power had been wielded by a regent, most gloriously under Fujiwara Michinaga, as described by Lady Murasaki. But recently the regents had lost power to regional *daimyo*, somewhat akin to feudal lords.

During the 1560s, the *daimyo* Oda Nobunaga, head of a powerful clan, started to impose himself on the other warlords, spurred by the slogan 'Rule the Realm by Force'. Oda was so eccentric he was known as the Idiot until he succeeded his father and started winning battles. He celebrated victory at a feast where platters held the lacquered, gilded heads of his enemies.

At the start of this rise, he had recruited a poor boy, Hideyoshi, who began as his sandal-bearer and rose to become his general. In 1581, Oda reviewed his troops in Kyoto with the emperor, but when he was assassinated his avenger and successor was the indefatigable, flamboyant and manic Hideyoshi, who went on to complete the unification of Japan.

In this he was aided by a remarkable rival and ally, Tokugawa Ieyasu, a *daimyo* who shared his acumen but not his impatience. Once Ieyasu backed someone, he never betrayed them but he regarded patience, not strength, as the essential quality for success. Early in his life, he had been a hostage and almost lost his family's power, but he rarely lost a battle and showed his mettle when his wife and son were denounced for disloyalty: he had his wife Lady Tsukiyama beheaded and forced his eldest son to commit suicide by *seppuku*, slicing open the belly. He was already devoted to a twice-married girl whom he chose for her looks and political wisdom: Lady Saigō. A contributor to his rise, she died young at thirty-seven, leaving two healthy sons who became his heirs.

Hideyoshi, appointed regent, now regarded himself as the Sun Child, his mother having been impregnated by a ray of the sun, the World Emperor, pivoting towards China. The Ming emperors received nominal tribute from Japan and recognized the regents as kings of Japan. But now the Sun Child called Japan 'Land of the Gods': 'To take by force this virgin of a country Ming will be as easy as for a mountain to crush an egg!' The plan was to 'slash his way' through Korea, but its king refused to allow Japanese passage. While Ieyasu cleverly kept his troops at home, Hideyoshi dispatched his armada, which enjoyed instant success. Three weeks after the first landing, the Japanese defeated the Korean army, took the capital Seoul and invaded Manchuria. But the Japanese soon faced a Korean insurgency. All Korean officials captured were executed along with their wives and children. So many noses and ears were salted, packed in crates and sent back to Hideyoshi that he built the *Mimizuka* – Mound of Ears. One detachment recorded 18,350 noses and was rewarded accordingly. Another 60,000 Koreans were enslaved by Japanese merchants: 'Having tied these people together with ropes around the neck, they drive them along. The sight of the fiends and man-devouring demons who torment sinners in hell must be like this.' Then the invasion went wrong.

In February 1593, the Celestial Army of the Ming, 400,000 strong, burst into Korea, routing Hideyoshi's army and slaughtering more Koreans. Hideyoshi opened negotiations, demanding Korean territory. Instead Beijing offered the traditional recognition of Hideyoshi as its vassal king. Hideyoshi sent another army of 100,000 while he messily tried to manage his own family: he had dreamed of founding his own dynasty, appointing his arrogant nephew Hidetsugu as regent while he took the title of *taiko*, retired regent. The arrangement was already strained when Hideyoshi's concubine Lady Chacha gave birth to another son, Hideyori, whom he named as his successor. Hideyoshi then decided to exterminate his nephew and his entire family. Hidetsugu was made to commit suicide and his thirty-nine concubines and children were all beheaded. Meanwhile the *daimyos* led by Ieyasu swore allegiance to the baby, signed in blood.

Hideyoshi was weakened by his Korean quagmire, which had killed nearly a million people, 750,000 Koreans and 100,000 Japanese, but it also fractured the Ming of China, opening the gates for a 'barbarian',

Nurhaci, khan of the northern horsemen the Jurchens,* who offered to help the Chinese. Within twenty years, Nurhaci united the Jurchen and Mongol tribes. It was just the start: his Manchu dynasty would destroy the Ming and rule China until the twentieth century.

In 1597, the ailing Hideyoshi turned on Japanese Christians, provoked by a Spanish captain who had revealed how Spain used priests as the vanguard of its colonial conquests. Portuguese Jesuits and Spanish Franciscans had converted 300,000 Japanese and secured Nagasaki as a base. Hideyoshi had copied Portuguese designs for his ships and musketry, but now he declared, 'My states are filled with traitors . . . serpents I cherished in my bosom.' In Nagasaki, he crucified twenty-six Catholics.

When this news reached Madrid, Philip was horrified. He had already faced a much greater fiasco in his English war. The failure of the Armada 'hurts so much', he wrote. 'And if God doesn't send us a miracle (which is what I hope from Him) I hope to die and go to Him.' But he did not, micromanaging his empire from his relic-infested apartments in the vast Escorial as his Protestant enemies, English and Dutch, were shaped and energized by his enmity and enriched by his treasure. As Philip mustered his second armada, he anxiously watched the libertine antics of his nephew Emperor Rudolf who was shocking Europe.

THE MAD EMPEROR OF PRAGUE

The corridors of Prague Castle were stalked by Rudolf's bizarre cast of necromancers, magi, scientists, artists and rabbis, along with a gold-nosed Danish astrologer, a swinging English hierophant, an earless Irish devil-worshipper, an Italian mistress, a converted Jewish lover, a psychotic son named Julius Caesar – and uncaged pet lions.

Rudolf was the strangest Habsburg, turning Prague into a laboratory for original thinkers and new ideas while fighting the Ottomans and attempting to manage the religious wars.

---

* Born in 1559, Nurhaci started as a soldier in the armies of the Ming, learning Chinese by reading *The Water Margin*, but by the age of twenty-one both his father and grandfather had been killed by a rival chieftain. His life story has many parallels with that of Genghis. Asserting his supremacy by killing his elder brother and nephews, he organized the Jurchens into an elite corps, divided into Banners, then launched an attack on Ming China, conquering a northern region. He changed the name of the Jurchens to Manchu and called his family the Aisin (Golden) Gioro. In 1626, now in his sixties, he discovered his crown prince in a relationship with his young wife. He imprisoned and murdered the son, with whom he buried his unfaithful wife. On his death, his younger son declared himself emperor of the new Qing dynasty.

Long-jawed, bulbous-eyed and fair-haired, Rudolf was a late starter, barely speaking for several years. While his father Maximilian II was sympathetic to Protestants, his mother, Philip's sister, was a terrifying fanatic who, on his accession, tried to bully the shy, fragile young emperor into marrying Philip's daughter. He wanted to get out of it. 'You fear losing your states and peoples?' sneered the mother. 'What figure will you make before God and the world if you repay his kindness with an insult and put your mother in an intolerable situation?'

Refusing to conform, ambiguous about his Catholicism, avoiding any marriage, Rudolf left his mother in the dreary Hofburg Palace in Vienna to create his own secret world at Prague Castle. The city was cosmopolitan and Protestant with a rich community of 10,000 Jews and many artists and astrologers already patronized by his father. Cancelling restrictions on Jews, Rudolf was determined to learn all the secrets of the cosmos. He curated a chamber of curiosities, collecting two-headed babies and unicorn horns. In his laboratories, he investigated the obsessions of the age: alchemy, a widely believed 'science' aiming to transmute base metals into gold; and Hermetic occultism, the belief that spirits and mathematical formulae allowed man to access divine power. He dabbled in Kabbalism with Rabbi Loew who was said to be able to create a *Golem* – mystic monster – from mud. In 1583, he hired the white-bearded English magus John Dee, the imperialist visionary, who arrived with a sinister sidekick, Edward Kelley, an Irish charlatan whose ears had been clipped for forging coins.

In 1588, Rudolf recruited a freethinking Neapolitan, a former priest called Giordano Bruno, who questioned Catholic dogma and expanded on Copernicus, arguing that there were 'innumerable celestial bodies', that the stars were other suns, that the universe was infinite and that souls might migrate to other bodies after death. Bruno was excommunicated by Protestants and Catholics but rewarded by Rudolf.* In 1599, Rudolf attracted a Danish nobleman, Tycho Brahe, who had lost his nose in a duel with a cousin over a mathematical debate and sported a gold prosthetic. He amassed data on the stars in the Rudolfine Tables, labelling new stars as novas. While he half accepted Copernicus' heliocentricity, he argued that the earth orbited the moon. His assistant, Johannes Kepler, a Lutheran mathematics teacher, disagreed cordially.

* Such views were not new: Copernicus had presented his heliocentricity to Clement VII but what was regarded as fascinating eccentricity in 1533 was dangerous during the Catholic revival of 1600. Bruno foolishly returned to Venice whence he was extradited to Rome, where Pope Clement VIII supervised his trial, accused of contradicting Catholic dogma. He refused to renounce the plurality of worlds. Sentenced to death in 1600, he supposedly replied, 'Maybe you give this sentence with more fear than I receive it.' With his tongue 'imprisoned for his evil words', he was hung upside down naked and burned alive.

Rudolf, so impressed by his uncle Philip's Titians at the Escorial, was also an avid collector, buying his own Titians and backing his father's court painter, Giuseppe Arcimboldo, who painted faces using natural objects: in his *Seasons*, Rudolf, appearing as the Roman god of abundance Vertumnus, is constructed out of fruit.

But Rudolph's world was darkening: the lions ate his courtiers, and his account books record his compensation payments for their maulings. He even singed his beard in conducting his explosive experiments. 'Imperial girls' and young men were procured. Falling in love with his artist Strado's daughter Katarina, he had five children including Don Julius Caesar of Austria, a diabolic freak who would soon do terrible things. The magi fell out; after the two had experimented with wife-swapping, Dee fled for his life, while earless Kelley, arrested for fraud and devil worship, poisoned himself.

Though he was no soldier, living for art and sex, Rudolf was the defender of Christendom. A young padishah, Mehmed III, grandson of Blond Selim,* was keen to lead his army, defeating the Habsburgs at Keresztes, forcing Emperor Rudolf to strike back. As he fought a long war that stretched his resources and sanity, Rudolf struggled to balance Catholics and Protestants.

His ailing uncle Philip, criticizing Rudolf from the Escorial, made a decision that would affect millions. In 1595, keen to maintain supplies of the enslaved from Africa, he started to award licences – *asiento de negros* (agreement of black people) – to Portuguese and Genoese traders to deliver 3,000–5,000 Africans each. As he died of cancer, the only balm for his agony was his daughter placing relics against his body. Yet even now he was directing the war against the Dutch and English. Elizabeth intensified her counter-attacks. But the Spanish repelled Drake at Coruña, where he lost 10,000 men and twenty ships, then in 1595 they

---

* On his accession, Mehmed ordered the strangling of nineteen of his young brothers – they kissed his hand, were circumcised and then snuffed out with one saying pluckily, 'Let me eat my chestnuts and strangle me afterwards.' Crowds wept as they watched the tiny coffins wend their way to Hagia Sophia, where their miniature tombs remain poignant. Mehmed was directed by his Bosnian-born mother Safiye, who relied on her Italian-Jewish *kira*, Esperanza Malchi. Her Jewishness proved a lightning rod for discontent. In 1600, unpaid troops rioted, demanding her head. Mehmed and Safiye sacrificed her: Esperanza was led on a packhorse to the hippodrome where the mob 'cut off the accursed one's hand and cut out her vulva, nailing them to the doors of conceited ones who obtained their posts by bribing that woman'. Her 'shameful part' was then paraded through Constantinople. 'If her execution was necessary, why like this?' the *valide sultan* asked the sultan. 'She could have been thrown into the sea. Such an execution of a woman so closely connected is damaging to imperial authority.' From now on, Jews no longer held high office and were forced to wear caps and insignia to mark their inferiority.

routed him and Hawkins at San Juan (Puerto Rico). The two Devonians died of dysentery and both were buried at sea, Drake in full armour.

The next year Elizabeth hit back, sending a small fleet under the erratic leadership of two favourites, an overpromoted young popinjay, the earl of Essex, and Raleigh, to seize Cadiz. In June 1596, they sacked the city. But Philip was not finished with God's work. In October, while Essex was away raiding, the Prudent King sent his second armada – 130 ships and 20,000 *tercios* – to take England. As Elizabeth and her paladins panicked, a storm scattered the fleet. But, dying as he was, Philip was still not finished: in 1597, he sent the third armada – 140 ships and 10,000 men. Elizabeth was furious that Essex had not returned, but again Philip's God did not deliver. Two galleons exploded and a storm intervened, although one ship landed 700 *tercios* in Cornwall. Finding they were alone and surrounded by English militia, they re-embarked two days later and sailed away. Elizabeth – now old, bald, toothless and caked in white lead and vinegar make-up – had survived. But the greater threat was of her own creation: Essex.

On 13 September 1598, Philip died, succeeded by his only surviving son, Philip III, who continued his works, sending a fourth invasion of Britain to land in Ireland and expelling all the Muslims in Spain. Back in Prague, his cousin Rudolf, confronted by madness and treason among his own family, was convinced that the Church must strike back against the Protestants, using all the weapons at its disposal – war, politics and art. As Protestants dominated the Habsburg lands, Rudolf persecuted them in Hungary and Austria but tolerated them in Prague, inconsistent in all matters. Yet though the popes had led a Catholic counter-attack, it still looked as if the Protestants were winning. In alliance with the pope, Rudolf's brothers, led by Matthias, believing Rudolf was a threat to monarchy and Church, started to encourage opposition and enforce conversion to Catholicism. Rudolf was stuck between the two sides. In 1605, the Hungarians and Transylvanians rebelled; Austrian Protestants recoiled from aggressive Catholic persecution. The strife was watched closely in London by a monarch who shared Rudolf's ambivalence. They were not only the ones who feared an imminent religious conflict was about to embroil Europe.

On St Stephen's Day, 26 December 1606, in a London where a wave of plague was killing many, leading to a lockdown of theatres and alehouses, and a conspiracy of Catholic terrorism had shaken the kingdom, James I, veteran king of Scotland, new king of England, was joined in the Grand Chamber of Whitehall by 300 of his courtiers to watch a new play by an actor-writer named William Shakespeare.

ACT TWELVE
545 MILLION

Dahomeans, Stuarts and Villiers, Tamerlanians and Ottomans

The play the court was watching was *King Lear*, a dark drama of senescent power, paternal folly, political division and filial ingratitude, ending in mayhem and tragedy. But it scarcely seemed out of place in the unstable and unsettling new union of England and Scotland, where the last six years had seen abortive coups against the old Queen Elizabeth and the new James, as well as a Catholic conspiracy to murder the entire royal family and ruling class.

James had been a king since he was one year old; both his parents died violently and he was raised within a court of murderous grandees and religious zealots in a kingdom dominated by a Protestant sect, the Presbyterians, who rejected priests and bishops. The king was a boozy and blowsy pedant who moistly lectured courtiers on witchcraft and theology from sap-dripping lips: some English observers claimed he had an oversized tongue, but this was just a slur on his thick Scottish accent. Brought up as a Presbyterian, he emerged intelligent and curious, but unsurprisingly hungry for love – and a believer in the maleficent power of witches.

The need to explain the streak of disasters – religious wars, pandemics and bad harvests – along with a fear of unconventional women and the popularity of printed works on witchcraft, had unleashed a spate of witchcraft trials. At Trier in the 1580s an archbishop orchestrated attacks on Protestants, Jews and witches that led to the burning of 386 people. In 1589, at the height of this lurid hysteria, James married Anne of Denmark by proxy, but her voyage to Scotland was abandoned due to storms. James set off to collect her – a rare moment of heterosexual romance – but he was sure the storms were the work of witches and on his return encouraged a case in North Berwick that led to many being tortured and burned. James would be Britain's only intellectual monarch: he wrote first on witchcraft, *Daemonologie*, then a tract extolling the divine right of kings.

As Elizabeth aged, James had secretly negotiated with her courtiers: Essex was in a rush to accelerate James's succession. But Elizabeth had lost patience with Essex's tantrums. In February 1601, the narcissistic jackanapes launched a coup, hiring Shakespeare's theatrical company to perform his play *Richard II* as a signal to destroy the tyrant and deliver England to James. 'I am Richard II,' said Elizabeth ruefully afterwards. Essex was beheaded. Shakespeare was probably interrogated; it was a close call, but he survived. On her death in 1603, Elizabeth's trusted minister Robert Cecil facilitated the succession of the king of Scots.*

In one of his first decisions, James appointed the lord chamberlain's troupe of actors, part-owned by Shakespeare, as the King's Players, performing for the king ten times a season. James's two sons, the attractive Henry and the meagre, shy Charles, promised stability, and in London Anne survived three more pregnancies, the babies delivered by a French doctor with secret equipment that enabled safer births.† Yet the atmosphere was tense as a new wave of the bubonic plague hit London, deaths rising from twenty a week to a thousand, prompting James to order a lockdown of theatre and bear-baiting. The king started to negotiate peace with Spain, but he did not cancel restrictions on Catholics, sparking the conspiracy of Robert Catesby to blow up the State Opening of Parliament. The plot is now regarded as a jape, but this terrorist spectacular would have killed not just most of the royal family but the entire elite, thousands of people. On 4 November 1605, an anonymous letter tipped off Cecil, and thirty-six barrels of gunpowder were discovered under Parliament. The conspirators were hunted down.

The paranoia and equivocation, plagues and lockdowns, the twists of power and the importance of character inspired Shakespeare, who had himself come close to destruction. As England watched the trial of the terrorists and celebrated the survival of their Scottish king and his

---

* Yet as James processed southwards, a conspiracy of noblemen, in correspondence with Madrid, planned to acclaim his cousin Arbella, great-great-granddaughter of Henry VII. This 'main plot' was mainly talk, but it implicated Walter Raleigh, whom James sentenced to death. He later pardoned Raleigh but kept him in the Tower. James recognized Arbella as fourth in line to the throne, but when in 1610 she tried to marry another royal cousin he imprisoned her for the rest of her life. Dying in the Tower aged thirty-nine, unmarried and childless, she was another female victim of a power family.

† Peter Chamberlen was a surgeon and *accoucheur*, a Parisian Huguenot, who arrived in England in 1596 around the time he invented a new instrument that revolutionized childbirth – an obstetrical forceps that gripped the skull of babies. Peter was the first of four generations of the family, who delivered most of the Stuart babies while disgracefully keeping their device secret, arriving at births with the simple contraption in a large gilded box, insisting that midwives were blindfolded. Untold numbers of women died because they did not share their invention: the Chamberlens became rich, buying a country house where centuries later their device was found hidden under floorboards.

young sons, Shakespeare wrote a Scottish story, *Macbeth*, based vaguely on history, about the unholy crime of killing a king and the fascinations of witchcraft. Now forty-two, Shakespeare, balding with a small moustache and beard, was the son of an impecunious glovemaker from Warwickshire born in the year Michelangelo died. He may have started as a schoolmaster, and switched to acting in the 1580s. Shakespeare made his name with two epic poems, a series of sonnets and, even though waves of plague led to periodic closures of theatres, a mix of comic and historical plays. But he made his fortune as actor-manager, part-owner of the Lord Chamberlain's Men that enabled him to buy the largest house in his home town of Stratford-upon-Avon. There he had married young, having two daughters and a son Hamnet, who aged eleven had died ten years earlier. When he was in London, he moved between the raffish taverns of Southwark, where he stayed in lodgings, and the rotten gleam of court, where he was a groom of the chamber. Discreet and private, his passionate sonnets of love and betrayal, describing affairs with women and men in a London of bawdy houses and venereal diseases, suggest worldly experience: 'When my love swears that she is made of truth, / I do believe her though I know she lies.'

On 5 January 1606, James attended an entertainment at the Banqueting House in Whitehall to celebrate the marriage of the earl of Essex, fourteen-year-old son of the executed favourite, to Frances Howard, daughter of one of the grandees who had destroyed the groom's father. This marriage, devised by James as an act of reconciliation, would become a murderous scandal. But, for now, Shakespeare watched the young noblewomen dancing in scarlet costumes in a show written by his rival playwright Ben Jonson, a rambunctious Catholic sympathizer who had killed two men in duels yet made it from bricklayer and murderer to national poet. The joyful extravagance of the show inspired Shakespeare to write *Antony and Cleopatra*, in which the Egyptian queen's arrival on a resplendent barge would demand a similarly spectacular mise en scène – very different from the unbearable anguish of his other work in progress, *King Lear*.

In the days after the show, James secretly observed the trial of the Catholic conspirators. On 30 January, eight of them were dragged backwards in wicker baskets to the gallows where they were half hanged, their genitals cut off and burned, their bowels and hearts cut out, before they were decapitated, a process designed to put them 'halfway between heaven and earth as unworthy of both'.

Soon after he had attended *King Lear*, James watched a jousting match where a young Scottish courtier, Robert Carr, was unhorsed and broke his leg. James fell in love with him on the spot, nursed, educated and knighted him. Carr started to dominate the court, and was soon raised to earl of Somerset. Queen Anne loathed him, and Parliament despised James's generous gifts to this upstart Caledonian. Fortunately, Carr's rise was balanced by the charisma of Henry, prince of Wales, who was fascinated by the opening up of the world.

London in 1606 was unexpectedly cosmopolitan. The voyages of English slavers had brought a few hundred Africans to London, where Africa was on people's minds. Elizabeth had ordered their deportation, but it had never been enforced. Londoners had been fascinated by the visit of a Moroccan ambassador. Shakespeare had written love sonnets to a 'dark lady': she may simply have been a brunette, but she may well have been African,* while his play *Othello*, premiered in 1604, starred a Moorish general. On Twelfth Night the next year, Anne presided over Jonson's *Masque of Blackness* in which the queen and her ladies, wearing blackface and costumes by Inigo Jones, played the daughters of the god Niger who wished to have their skins whitened by the god Oceanus.

Self-confident, scholarly and a jouster, tennis player and early golfer, Prince Henry asked his father to let him study with the imprisoned Raleigh. The swashbuckler, locked in the Tower, was happy to receive Henry, for whom he probably started writing his *History of the World*. Henry was so inspired by Raleigh's tales of a gold-rich kingdom in South America, Eldorado, that he funded his own adventurer, Thomas Roe, on an expedition to Guiana. Raleigh was the authority since it was his Roanoke colony in America and his capture in 1592 of a majestic Portuguese carrack, stacked with east Asian delicacies – gold, amber-gris, cloves, cinnamon and cochineal – that inspired the founding of two companies: an East India Company (EIC), set up in 1600 to trade Asian spices and backed by James, who knighted the captain of its first voyage, and a Virginia Company, chartered in 1606 to found a colony on the American coast.† The latter company's expedition hit land which they named Cape Henry and founded a settlement, Jamestown. Even

---

* 'My mistress's eyes are nothing like the sun; / Coral is far more red than her lips' red; / If snow be white why then her breasts are dun, / If hairs be wires, black wires grow on her head / . . . And yet by heaven I think my love as rare, / As any she belied with false compare.'

† Raleigh was said to have brought the first tobacco to England. James grumbled that tobacco was 'hateful to the nose, harmful to the braine, dangerous to the lungs and in the black stinking fume thereof, nearest resembling the horrible Stigian smoke of the pit that is bottomless'. Later, when the Stigian stinking fume became the only profitable crop grown in Virginia and increasingly popular in England, James granted himself the lucrative tobacco monopoly.

though the Native American peoples around the site, the Powhatan confederacy, were initially friendly, the settlers died in droves of disease and starvation. These disastrous voyages inspired Shakespeare's last single-authored play, *The Tempest*.

As for the EIC, it dispatched only three ships annually in its first decade. The real dynamos were the Dutch, way ahead of the English. When Philip II closed his ports to Dutch seamen in 1598, he unconsciously opened the world to Dutch ambition. Between 1595 and 1602, the Dutch sent fifty ships to attack Habsburg shipping. In 1602, the Heeren XVII – the Seventeen Gentlemen, many of them members of the interrelated merchant dynasties of Bickers and de Graeffs that dominated Dutch politics – founded their own East India Company (VOC), chartered by the ruling States-General with military and government powers to conquer and maintain trading posts in Asia. The Amsterdam stock exchange – the first – was founded to trade in its stocks. The VOC fitted easily into the pluralistic structure of the Netherlands with its seven provinces, powerful cities and guilds, but it became the first multinational company, the first publicly owned, the first war corporation. Its ruling families reflected the changes in society, fostering modern organization, industrious values and artistic patronage, as well as technical innovation and vicious competition.

The VOC based its trading on violence. 'We can't conduct trade without war,' Jan Pieterszoon Coen, the VOC director-general, told the Seventeen, 'nor war without trade.' The profits were bounteous, the rivalries with Portuguese, English and Chinese merchants brutally pursued.* In 1607, Coen joined an expedition to the Banda Islands – richest of the Moluccas – where the local Indonesians massacred most of the Dutch. Coen, a severe conquistador and fanatical Calvinist, deployed eyewatering violence to establish VOC factories (trading posts), playing local rulers against one another and striking at Portuguese and English rivals. Convinced he was doing God's work, his style – 'Don't despair, don't spare your enemies, God is with us!' – was harsh even with his

---

* These quasi-governmental war companies were invented by the Dutch. They were not totally new, reviving the armed commercialism of the military-religious orders of the Crusades and the Reconquista and of the semi-state companies like Genoa's Bank of St George that ran its colonies in Crimea. Nor were they particularly European: the Chola rajas had allied with the Ainnutruvar and other privateering guilds, while networks of Chinese privateers ruled parts of China and Japan, most prominently the Shuangyu syndicate. The new version was forged in the wars against Spain as trade and conflict fused at a time when European sovereigns and states were too weak to compete in foreign adventures. Instead Protestant leaders Elizabeth and William the Silent invested in the expeditions of Drake and the Sea Beggars. The companies were a compromise that enabled the monarchs, as shareholders, to participate but spread the risk and cost.

own men. When he found a Dutch officer in bed with a girl, he had him beheaded. The VOC competed with the English, Spanish–Portuguese and Chinese to control the Moluccas, seizing Ambon from the Portuguese. One of its earliest successes was penetrating Japan.

Tokugawa Ieyasu, that master of patient force, had no problem dealing with these traders. In 1598, the would-be conqueror of China, Hideyoshi, died of fever at forty-seven, leaving a council of regents led by Ieyasu to govern for his five-year-old son. Ieyasu soon slaughtered Hideyoshi's faction, emerging as shogun of a new government at Edo that later became Tokyo and founding a dynasty that ruled Japan until 1868. The Spanish–Portuguese were already trading through Nagasaki; now the Protestants arrived too. The Dutch and English were initially welcomed by the shogun. In 1600 an adventurous Kentish sailor named Will Adams, a veteran of Drake's raids, was one of the few survivors of the first VOC flotilla to the east. While the Spanish–Portuguese demanded his execution as a pirate, Adams was taken to Osaka Castle. After winning the favour of Ieyasu himself in an all-night interview, Adams joined his court, learned Japanese, trained as a samurai and advised the shogun on European technology, building him his first European warship. Adams worked against the Spanish and Dutch while advancing the interests of the EIC. The Dutch and English were allowed to keep a trading presence, but in 1628 Ieyasu's son Hidetada, now shogun, turned against Christianity, expelling Catholic priests and burning fifty-five Catholics. For two centuries, under the Tokugawa shoguns, European access to Japan was limited.

Elsewhere, the VOC campaigns continued with maximum force. In 1618, Coen secured Jakarta (renamed Batavia) on Java, rewarded by the Seventeen with the governor-generalship. The Seventeen demanded the seizure of the spice-rich Banda Islands. 'To adequately deal with this matter,' wrote Coen, 'it's necessary to once again subjugate Banda, and populate it with other people.' Over 10,000 indigenous people were killed and others were deported, as the VOC secured a monopoly of cloves and nutmeg. They were equally cut-throat with European competitors, waterboarding and beheading twenty-one English merchants at Ambon.

Wherever the Portuguese had a presence, the VOC attacked these Habsburg outposts: in Taiwan, its troops stormed a Portuguese fort in order to develop its China trade. At the same time, it turned to India. In 1608, the VOC attacked the Portuguese in Coromandel, seized Pulicat and negotiated a concession with the maharajas of Vijayanagara, before approaching the greatest monarch of the east, the new Mughal emperor,

Jahangir. Here too they were swiftly followed by the English.*

When the VOC and the EIC approached Jahangir, scion of Tamerlane and Babur, they were courting the ruler of the greatest power on earth. Jahangir, then known as Salim, was the opium-addicted son of Akbar the Great: his father at one point locked him up and made him go cold turkey in a bid to cure the addiction. While Salim remained an addict all his life, it did not restrain his ambitions. In the Tamerlane family, sons and grandsons competed for the crown, and those who lost died: 'Throne or tomb!' As Akbar aged, the prince had bid for power, assassinating the vizier Abul-Fazl. Akbar struck back by threatening to leave the empire to Jahangir's own son, Khusrau.

On 3 November 1605, when the great padishah died (the week of the Catholic plot to blow up Parliament in London), Salim took the name World Seizer – Jahangir – as his son Khusrau rebelled and seized Punjab. Jahangir crushed his son, telling his general, 'Do whatever you must. Kings don't have families.'† Khusrau was paraded on an elephant down an avenue of pikes; his supporters were forced to make obeisance before being anally impaled, 'the most excruciating punishment', noted Jahangir. Amazingly, after this the boy plotted again and was blinded.

Jahangir displayed flashes of the Tamerlanian temperament, in both expanding the empire and possessing a streak of cruelty, once killing a waiter for dropping a plate and a huntsman for interrupting his aim. But he was fascinated by art, science and architecture, was influenced

---

* Not everything went well. In June 1629, one of the VOC's first voyages to Australia, on board the ship *Batavia*, went spectacularly wrong when, after a shipwreck on the Abrolhos Islands, off Australia, its deputy captain Jeronimus Cornelisz mutinied and launched a demented terror against his crew out of personal megalomanic and Calvinist righteousness, killing 120 people in a orgy of stabbing, bludgeoning, drowning, hanging while the seven surviving girls were turned into sex slaves – until his reign was ended by the arrival of another VOC ship: Cornelisz had his hands amputated by a chisel then was beheaded. A little later, another tough VOC Dutchman, Abel Tasman, reached islands off Australia, first a small one which he named Van Deiman's Land after the governor-general in Jakarta, who planned the conquest of Great Southland – Tasmania – and then a larger one that he called Staten-Landt after the States-General back in Holland – Aotearoa, today's New Zealand – where Maori warriors in canoes killed several of his men.
† One of Prince Khusrau's supporters, Guru Arjun, was the leader of the Sikh religion in Punjab, founded in the 1530s by the poet-saint Guru Nanak, who created a movement independent of Islam and Hinduism. Sikh just means learner in Sanskrit. Nanak preached against Brahmin exploitation and Muslim oppression in favour of one God, one community, abolishing caste – a sect that blossomed under his successors, the nine gurus, who developed a sacred city, Amritsar, a shrine (the Golden Temple) and a scripture (the *Adi Granth*). But their independence clashed with Mughal authority. Now Jahangir tortured then executed Arjun, whose son Guru Hargobind responded by fostering Sikh martial culture: his wearing of two swords symbolized *miri piri* – the union of spiritual and temporal power. Savagely repressed by the Mughals, the Sikhs thrived in adversity.

by European Renaissance art which he regarded as a scientific instrument – a means to study the world. His painter Abu al-Hasan perfected the flamboyant, exquisite Mughal style for an imperial drug addict who increasingly depended on his wife, Nurjahan.

THE EMPRESSES OF AGRA AND CONSTANTINOPLE: LIGHT OF THE PALACE AND BEAUTIFUL MOON

Nurjahan was born Mihr al-Nisa, daughter of one of Akbar's ministers, an Iranian who had taken service in India. Jahangir had first met her when she was still married to a reckless paladin who had saved Jahangir from a charging tiger. He gave him the name Sher Afgan – Tiger Tosser. Years later, after Tiger Tosser was dead, Jahangir saw her again.

At court in Agra, the *meena bazaar* for the Nowruz festival was the ideal occasion for flirtations. Mihr al-Nisa was thirty-four, a widow with a daughter; Jahangir was already fifty-one with fifteen wives and a packed harem, but 'I didn't think anyone was fonder of me.' This astute Persian, raised in Kandahar, was not only tempestuous, lithe and beautiful, fluent in Persian and Arabic, but also fun. She loved to paint with a drink in her hand, and she was a crack markswoman who once shot four tigers from an elephant, using only six bullets, without a miss. 'Such shooting had never been seen,' wrote Jahangir; 'the four tigers never got a chance to spring.' An English merchant once saw the couple riding gaily into a hunting camp together on a cart, alone, with the emperor driving.

In 1612, after their wedding – at which he gave her the name Nurmahal, Light of the Palace, later promoted to Nurjahan, Light of the World – they arranged the match of his disciplined, abstemious third son Khurram (later Emperor Shahjahan) to her niece Arjumand Banu, who was as erudite and charming as her aunt. Khurram had been the favourite grandson of Akbar, who named him Joyful then took him from his Rajput mother and had him raised by his childless senior wife Ruqaiya, who 'always promoted him', and told Jahangir 'there was no comparison between him and my other children'. Akbar 'regarded him as his real child', while Ruqaiya loved him 'a thousand times more than if he'd been her own'. Raised by these two titans, Khurram was unimpressed by the feckless Jahangir but he fell in love with his new wife at once, renaming her Mumtaz Mahal (Exalted of the Palace). But Nurjahan then married her own daughter to another of Jahangir's sons, the footling youngest Shahryar, sparking Khurram's suspicion that she was planning to destroy him.

It was now that the Dutch and English companies arrived in Agra to request trading concessions. Jahangir's empire was the richest power on earth, approaching the height of its economic power: it is estimated that its share of world GDP was climbing fast, from 22.7 per cent in 1600 to 24.4 per cent in 1700, bigger than China's. Its population – 110 million – was larger than all Europe combined. Its textiles, manufactured in thousands of small cottage-scale craft shops, were exported to Europe, where they were becoming fashionable, along with jewels, ivory and spices supplied by Portuguese and Arab traders. But in 1616, Jahangir granted the Dutch trading factories first in Surat, then in Bengal. At the same time, the EIC sent their flashy plenipotentiary, Thomas Roe, veteran of the hunt for the Guyanese Eldorado, to charm Jahangir. The two boozed together and Jahangir granted Roe a factory at Surat. But these Europeans were very small fry for the World Seizer.[*]

Jahangir ruled northern India but not the south. Keen to expand, he ordered Khurram to advance southwards into Deccan (from *Dakhin* meaning south), earning his father's promotion to the highest *mansab* (the rank system created by Akbar) and the title Shahjahan – World King. 'With an impulse of unabashed paternal affection I took him in my arms,' wrote Jahangir. 'The more he expressed his reverence for me, the more my tenderness increased.'

Yet their southern advance was blocked by the sultanate of Ahmadnagar, ruled at the time by a gifted African paladin, Malik Ambar, one of the Habashi, usually pagans from the African interior who were captured by Christians or Arabs then sold to Gujaratis to serve as soldiers for the sultans of east and south India.[†] Sold by his parents, converted to Islam by his first master in Baghdad, Ambar was eventually manumitted. 'A black kafir [an Arabic word for infidel which became a European racist epithet for Africans] with a stern Roman face,' according to a Dutch

---

[*] The negotiations reveal the real power matrix between Europeans and the Asian empires. It is easy to exaggerate the span and power of the EIC and its Dutch rival, the VOC: they could defeat local potentates; they could hold fortresses; but the European companies were not strong enough to conquer broad territories or challenge great monarchies. In 1623, when the VOC seized the Penghu islands, its troops were defeated by a Chinese fleet and not for the last time. In Japan, Tokugawa and sons banned Europeans. The Dutch and English had to negotiate cringingly with Ming or Mughals, Vijayanagarans or Safavis. It was only later when these kingdoms disintegrated that the VOC and EIC shapeshifted into empire-building company states.

[†] The Habashi play a major but often neglected part in Indian history. They were often freed after a few years of service, but even when they were enslaved, many were promoted as courtiers and generals – and sometimes they seized power for themselves. In Bengal in 1487, Barbak Shahzad, chief of the black palace guards, had assassinated the Bengali sultan and ruled until he was killed by another Abyssinian.

merchant, he commanded 10,000 Habashi, taking over Ahmadnagar as *peshwa* (chief minister), marrying its sultan to his daughter. Repeatedly defeating Jahangir, Ambar was almost eighty by the time Shahjahan humbled him, a triumph celebrated by Jahangir in a painting of him shooting a bow at Ambar, an allegory of wish fulfilment, showing how powerful the Habashi had become. Only after Ambar's death did the Mughals swallow Ahmadnagar.

Yet relations between father and son were frosty. The warmer Jahangir was, the colder was Shahjahan. Even in this bout of familial love, there was bloodletting too: Shahjahan asked for the custody of his blinded brother Khusrau, whom he then killed. His affection was reserved for Mumtaz Mahal. 'Don't father children on any other woman,' she told him, 'lest hers and mine fight for the succession.' He ordered other women to abort their pregnancies. Now he observed his father's decline.

'Nurjahan Begum, whose skill and experience are greater than those of the physicians, tried to diminish the number of my cups and carry out remedies,' recalled Jahangir. 'Gradually she reduced my wine.' Nurjahan's power depended on the life of one Tamerlanian junkie, but her contemporary in Constantinople was an even more remarkable woman who would dominate the Ottoman empire for forty years.

When the Ottoman sultan, Ahmed, first saw her, she was Anastasia, a newly enslaved Greek odalisque in the harem. Both of them were thirteen and he renamed her Mahpeyker – Beautiful Moon. But when he fell in love with her, he renamed her Kösem – Leader. 'Beautiful and shrewd,' noted the Venetian envoy, 'with many talents, she sings beautifully, is extremely well loved by the king,' who even 'listened to her in some matters'. Together they had nine children, of whom five were sons, one of brilliant gifts, one of homicidal insanity. Kösem faced competition: Ahmed's eldest son, Osman, was by another odalisque, yet she became close to him, though her priority would always be her own children.

Sultan Ahmed, prompted supposedly by Kösem, ended the tradition of strangling royal brothers: he preserved his own brother in the 'golden cage' of the harem. The padishahs now spent less time commanding armies, which empowered their palace staff: their African eunuchs now ranked equal to grand viziers.*

---

* Traditionally eunuchs had been white slaves from Russia/Ukraine and the Caucasus who, following Byzantine practice, lost only their testicles, but now African children, captured in Ethiopia and Darfur by Arab slavers, were traded to Coptic priests who subjected them to Mamluk castration, chaining them to a table and cutting off their penises as well as their

Playful, cultured and athletic, a poet and fencer, Ahmed, who always wanted Kösem beside him, worked hard on his Blue Mosque, designed with Mehmed Agha, who had been trained by the great Sinan. With its breathtaking five domes, eight smaller domes and six minarets, and its aquamarine tiles, a cascade of Byzantine–Ottoman styles, it remains one of the joys of Istanbul. The Ottomans had recently won victories in Hungary and had seized the Caucasus from Persia which led Ahmed to take his eyes off his main duty: war. Suddenly in 1605, he was attacked by a terrifying new shah.

Great-grandson of the messianic boy-king Ismail, Abbas had been formed by the murderous purges of the Safavi shahs and the over-mighty swagger of their Turkman generals, who had blinded his father and sliced up his mother. When he was seventeen, one of the generals deposed his father and crowned him.

Stocky, agile and swarthy with green eyes and droopy moustaches, Abbas was pleasure-loving but with a will to power, focused and un-predictable, always wearing a sword, frequently beheading prisoners in front of the court. In battle he was strong enough to wrestle an Ottoman assassin to death. Once in a towering rage at the clumsy blunder of troops in a mock battle, he ran among them slicing four men in half. Yet he was informal, cooking his own food and exercising his horse in the square at Isfahan, chatting to passers-by. He checked food prices by wearing disguise in the bazaar: when tradesmen tricked him, he had a baker baked in his oven, a butcher roasted alive.

Abbas was an enthusiast for girls and boys, both usually enslaved Georgians. In the harem, the girls sometimes 'swept him off his feet, whirled around the rooms, threw him down on the carpet as he called out, "You strumpets, ah you crazy things!"' As in Constantinople it was run by African and Georgian eunuchs. Abbas sometimes performed the orchiectomies himself with such precision that fewer died than usual. His new army was mainly manned by *ghilman* slaves from the Caucasus. In 1605 he attacked the Ottomans and retook Tabriz and the Caucasus where he enslaved 160,000 people.

After his initial successes against the Ottomans, Rudolf sent an envoy to Abbas, who welcomed him cheerfully while examining two swords before choosing one and beheading an Ottoman prisoner, with

testicles. Given fragrant names such as Hyacinth, in adulthood they were either very fat or very thin, suffered osteoporosis, skeletal abnormalities including elongated fingers, and premature wrinkling. The chief eunuch – *kizlar aga* – was always an African, and was now steward of the harem whose power was often based on his relationship with the sultan's favourite or his mother.

the advice that the emperor should treat the Turks the same way. But the real world was now catching up with the emperor of fantasy.

HIGHFALL: PRINCE OF DARKNESS AND THE COPROPHAGIAN JULIUS CAESAR

'They say you're an alchemist, astrologer and given to necromancy,' Rudolf's brother Albrecht wrote to him. 'If this be true and Your Majesty has fallen into the habits of using the services of the dead, pity the House of Austria.' The pope, Clement VIII, was now leading a militant Catholic revival, a reaction to the passion of Protestantism, and planned regime change in Prague, spying on Rudolf and encouraging his brothers, led by Archduke Matthias, to depose him. 'It is generally agreed among Catholics in Prague,' reported Clement's envoy, 'that the emperor has been bewitched and is in league with the devil. I've been shown the chair in which His Majesty sits holding conversations with the Prince of Darkness . . . and the little bell HM uses to summon spirits of the departed.'

In 1606, the Habsburg brothers and their nephew Ferdinand of Styria met secretly in Vienna. 'His Majesty has now reached the stage of abandoning God entirely,' said Matthias, and was devoting himself to 'wizards, alchemists, Kabbalists'. Matthias forced Rudolf to make peace with the Ottomans. In Prague, Rudolf, distrusting everyone and convinced his brothers wanted to kill him, stabbed his chamberlain in the middle of the night, then attempted suicide. In search of a loyal servant, he promoted a Tyrolean converted Jew, Philip Lang, to chamberlain – they may also have been lovers – allowing him control of the government, while this epigone sold paintings and betrayed him to his brothers. 'I know I am dead and damned,' Rudolf told Lang, 'possessed by the devil.'*

Both brothers were now bidding for Protestant support. In July 1609, Rudolf signed a Letter of Majesty that promised religious tolerance for

---

* Rudolf's collapse was exacerbated by the crimes of his eldest son, Don Julius Caesar. That year, Rudolf bought him Castle Krumlov, where the diabolic boy, twenty-one years old, hunted girls in the villages until he found a barber's daughter, Markéta Pichlerová. He became obsessed with her and took to torturing her, until finally he stabbed her and threw her out of a window. But she landed on a rubbish heap and survived. Julius Caesar begged the parents to send her back to him. They resisted until he threatened to kill the family and then arrested the father. The Bluebeardian monstrum finally had Markéta back in his clutches. He tortured her for days. He was found naked and covered in excrement embracing her headless, dismembered body, ears cut off, eyes gouged out. A month later, the horrified emperor imprisoned the monstrum.

the Protestants, but when they threatened his power he brought in a detachment of mercenaries who alienated all sides. Matthias's troops advanced into Bohemia, forcing him to cede Hungary and Austria. In March 1611, as Rudolf ranted in the castle corridors, 'He's snatched my crowns one by one,' Matthias marched on Prague, which welcomed him. 'Prague, Prague,' Rudolf cursed, 'I made you famous but now you drive me out . . . Vengeance upon you!'

Matthias let Rudolf keep the castle. When Rudolf's favourite lion died, he knew it was the end. Now emperor, Matthias confirmed Rudolf's promise of tolerance, but the Protestants claimed the right to build new churches on Catholic land. As Matthias lay dying, his successor Ferdinand II promised a Catholic crackdown, aided by Catholic officials Jaroslav Bořita and Vilém Slavata. Bohemian nobles raided the castle, telling the officials, 'You're enemies of us and our religion,' before they hurled the two of them and their secretary Philip Fabricius out of the window, defenestration being something of a tradition in Prague: a messy death. But all three survived the seventy-foot drop, with Catholics claiming that their fall had been eased by the Virgin Mary, and Protestants citing a heap of garbage. Fabricius galloped to inform Vienna, where he was ennobled by Emperor Ferdinand with the epithet von Hohenfall (Highfall). Ferdinand cracked down on the Bohemian rebels, who then deposed the Habsburgs and elected the Protestant prince, Frederick, elector Palatine, married to James I's daughter, Elizabeth.

James was under pressure to support his son-in-law, but he was much diminished by the death of his beloved son, Henry, in 1612, leaving as heir the unglamorous Charles, not yet twelve. James paid more attention to his favourite, the earl of Somerset.

Then on 14 September 1613, a courtier, Sir Thomas Overbury, died in the Tower of London after an injection into his rectum.

MURDER BY ENEMA: THE FAVOURITES OF JAMES

James was now shocked to learn that Overbury had been murdered on the orders of his darling Somerset and his new wife. Overbury had been Somerset's political adviser, until the earl fell in love with the married Frances, countess of Essex, whose wedding theatricals had been attended by Shakespeare. Overbury did not approve, warning his patron of her 'injury and iniquity', penning an entire poem *The Wife* against her. Instead her powerful pro-Spanish family, the Howards, framed Overbury and persuaded James, jealous of Overbury's relationship with

Somerset, to imprison him in the Tower – and allow her marriage to
Somerset on the basis that her husband Essex was impotent. The couple
decided to eliminate Overbury, first sacking the Tower governor and
replacing him with a corrupt placeman, then inserting a thuggish jailer.
They recruited a witchy whoremonger, Anne Turner, to procure poison
from a pharmacist's wife. The poison was delivered by Overbury's suborned doctor, who fed him cakes painted with arsenic. Overbury fell ill
but did not die, so the Somersets ordered the doctor to deliver a glister
(enema) of mercury chloride into Sir Thomas's rectum. Overbury died
in agony just before Somerset married Frances Howard. Somerset was
constantly promoted by James, who was nonetheless becoming weary of
his greed and grandiosity. Just then the king spotted a gorgeous young
man at a hunt: George Villiers became the means to overthrow Somerset, whose enemies raised money to buy the Adonis a new bejewelled
suit. Villiers was then dangled before the king, lithely dancing in court
masques, his famous legs on show. Now that Somerset was no longer
invulnerable, the governor of the Tower denounced him for killing
Overbury.

   The murderers were arrested and under torture confirmed that their
patrons were indeed the Somersets, who were imprisoned in the Tower.
In November 1615 Anne Turner, described at her trial as 'whore, bawd,
sorcerer, witch, papist, felon and murderer', was hanged with three
others. James was distraught, begging Somerset not to lay 'an aspersion
upon me of being, in some sort, accessory to his crime'. At the most
famous trial of the reign, watched nervously by the king, the Somersets were found guilty and sentenced to hang. The forty-eight-year-old
James pardoned them, consoled by George Villiers, aged twenty-one,
described by a slavering bishop as 'the handsomest-bodied man in all of
England': James fell in love with him, installing him as master of horse,
then elevating him to the rare title of marquess of Buckingham. He
called him 'my sweet wife', while Buckingham later remembered how
the king loved him 'at the time which I shall never forget at Farnham,
where the bed's head could not be found between the master and his
dog'. Buckingham called him 'dere Dad and Gossope'.

   As this jewel arrived at court, another vanished. After staging his last
(and lost) play, *Cardenio*, Shakespeare, either ill or tainted in some scandal, retired to Stratford. On a rare visit to London, the playwright had
a 'merry meeting' with his friend and rival Ben Jonson, and 'it seems
drank too much' for on his return home, on 23 April 1616, he 'died of a
fever there contracted'.

   In Europe, James's dream of conciliating the two sects was drowned in blood. On 8 November 1620, at White Mountain, Kaiser Ferdinand routed the Bohemians. James's son-in-law and daughter fled, losing Bohemia and the Palatinate. Appointing Buckingham as lord high admiral to direct policy, James negotiated with the Spanish, hoping to save his daughter's lands in return for marrying Charles to Infanta María of Spain.

Charles was delighted. Tiny, elegant, tortuously polite, a devout High Anglican with an obsessive belief in the sacred nature of kingship, he was obsessed with the Habsburg princess he had seen only in a portrait. His romance was encouraged by Buckingham, eight years his senior, who taught the awkward prince to dance. Craving his father's approval, he revered Buckingham, who seemed able to deliver it.

The Protestants in Parliament disliked this Catholic appeasement. In early 1623, as Parliament attacked his ministers. James confronted the growing popularity of an ever more devout Protestant sect which looked to the Word of the Bible, a more ascetic lifestyle and an immediate, intimate engagement with God and Christ, bringing a grace that made its believers regard themselves as the Elect and the Saints. 'I'll harry them out of the kingdom,' warned James. But the religiosity was infectious, its intensity increased by its opposite. The more militant the Catholic resurgence, the more fanatical became the black-clad, Bible-spouting and censorious Saints – jokingly called puritans – a breed mocked by Shakespeare through his character Malvolio. They were increasingly powerful in the opposition of ascetic and self-righteous lords and gentlemen that challenged James and his messy, splashy court as the Spanish negotiations became sticky. But Charles was sure he could break the impasse, planning the most bizarre exploit ever attempted by an English prince.

In June 1622, in Prague, Ferdinand celebrated his victory with his 'theatre of blood', killing forty-eight Bohemian Protestants; some were hanged; those who blasphemed had their tongues cut out or nailed to the gallows; all were quartered. The Habsburgs had won.* For now.

The peace with the Ottomans had allowed the Catholic kaiser to break Protestant power. Now an energetic padishah tried to redress the balance – an intervention that helped bring the remarkable female politician Kösem to power.

---

* After the death of Brahe, Rudolf's astronomer Kepler finished the Rudolfine Tables and charted planetary motion, but placed God at the centre of the universe. Three emperors, Rudolf, his brother Matthias and later Ferdinand, consulted the Protestant Kepler's readings: astronomy and astrology were seen as scientific studies. Kepler also invented a new genre, science fiction, writing an autobiographical story *Somnium* (The Dream), predicting space travel. He lived until 1630, leaving this epitaph: 'I measured the skies, now the shadows I measure; / Skybound was the mind, earthbound the body rests.'

ASSASSINATION BY TESTICULAR COMPRESSION:
KÖSEM AND HER BOYS

Family power allowed women to play very different roles. In monarchies, the powerless daughter sent to marry a distant potentate was less valued than the peasant's wife or daughter who were essential to running a smallholding. But Kösem – and women like her – were the protectors of sons and often regent of kings, allowing them to become potentates themselves. In 1617, on the death of her husband Ahmed, Kösem negotiated the succession of his brother Mustafa. But Mustafa was too simple: his hobby was throwing coins to the fish in the Bosphoros. Kösem could no longer delay the accession of Ahmed's eldest son, the fourteen-year-old Osman II, but she ensured that he did not immediately kill his half-brothers – her sons.

The headstrong young padishah planned to force Poland–Lithuania to back the underdog Protestants against the all-conquering Habsburgs, and to centralize power in Istanbul. Osman was friendly with Kösem but lacked a *valide sultan* of his own to manage the Topkapı Palace. He ceded Georgia to Shah Abbas, and then (after having his brother strangled) led his army into Poland. But across Eurasia a change in climate, dubbed the little ice age, destabilized societies, contributing to turbulence from Constantinople to China, from Ukraine to Paris: it was so cold that the Bosphoros froze, people starved, Janissaries grumbled and, at the front, Osman's huge army was halted by the Poles.

On his return to Istanbul in May 1622, just as Ferdinand devised his Theatre of Blood in Prague, Osman's plan to demote the Janissaries and create an army similar to that of Abbas sparked a coup in which Janissaries descended from the palace roof on ropes and arrested the sultan. Imprisoned in the Yedikule Fortress, Osman was too forceful to accept dethronement. He resisted strangling so energetically that a strapping wrestler killed him by compression of the testicles – a respectful method in that it did not shed royal blood, but it certainly signalled the anger Osman inspired. It was the first Ottoman regicide, soon to be followed by an English version, marking a retreat from boundless monarchy.

Out of the chaos, Kösem finessed the accession of her boisterous eleven-year-old son, Murad IV. Now in close alliance with the grand vizier and the *kizlar aga*, she returned to power, seeking to protect Murad and her two surviving sons. In her frank letters to the grand vizier, Kösem – admired by the crowds as *Valide-i Muazzama*, the Magnificent Mother – was a master of business. 'How are you getting along with salary payments? Is there much left?', tolerating no nonsense and giving firm orders: 'You can say attention should be paid to provisions for the war. If it were up to me it would have been taken care of earlier, it's no fault of me or my son.' She had a sense of humour too: 'You really give me a headache, but I give you an awful headache too. How many times have I asked myself, "I wonder if he's getting sick of me," but what can else can I do?'

Growing up amid Janissary conspiracies and mob lynchings of his ministers, Murad would emerge as the greatest padishah since Suleiman. But, for now, a child sultan was too good a chance for Shah Abbas to miss. When Baghdad rebelled against the Ottomans, Abbas broke the peace and seized Iraq. That was not all: he also grabbed Bahrain from the Habsburgs and coveted their fortress at Hormuz that dominated the Persian Gulf. He lacked ships, but the English EIC was trying to negotiate trading concessions with Persia, so in 1622 he borrowed a flotilla of four – and stormed Hormuz.

The new king of Spain and Portugal, Philip IV, eighteen-year-old grandson of the Prudent King, was concerned less with Persia and more with two mysterious Englishmen named Smith who had unexpectedly arrived in Madrid.

THE SMITHS, THE PLANET KING AND TWO ARTISTS

On 7 March 1623, Philip was amazed to learn that Thomas and John Smith were in fact Charles, prince of Wales, aged twenty-three, and the thirty-one-year-old marquess of Buckingham, who had enjoyed a thrilling trip across Europe. James bemoaned the antics of 'my babies' but called them his 'venturesome knights' and promoted Buckingham to duke to help with the negotiations.

James was pursuing a Spanish match with the Infanta María, Philip's sister, to keep England out of the war, to win back his son-in-law's Palatinate and to obtain a useful dowry payment.* Charles had convinced

---

* James's Spanish detente had already cost Walter Raleigh his life. In 1616, he persuaded James to release him and send him to find Eldorado in Guiana, provided that he did not attack Spanish interests. But Raleigh lost control of his officers, attacked the Spanish – his son was killed in the fighting – and found no gold. On his return, the Spanish ambassador demanded Raleigh's head as the price for the treaty. James agreed. Raleigh gave a virtuoso performance on the gallows, inspecting the axe, 'This is a sharp medicine, but a physician for all diseases and miseries,' then telling the executioner, 'What dost thou fear? Strike, man, strike!' The execution was widely regarded as a disgrace – and Raleigh never finished his world history.

himself that he was in love with María. Buckingham, keen to deliver the alliance to James but also to bind himself to the heir, encouraged a risky plan that appealed to the prince's sense of romance. The duke should have known better. Ignoring the complexity of religion, the pair galloped for Paris where they admired the green-eyed Habsburg queen of France, Anne of Austria, Philip IV's sister, whom Charles called the 'handsomest'; he scarcely noticed her sister-in-law Henrietta Maria.

The Smiths galloped on towards Madrid. Their arrival embarrassed and fascinated Philip, who welcomed the 'Smiths' to the Alcázar Palace. A child of first cousins, his mother being Emperor Ferdinand's sister, Philip had inherited the Spanish–Portuguese empires stretching across five continents but also the Habsburg jaw and the sacred formality of Spanish kingship. He was the centrepiece of the court's 'theatre of grandeur', hailed as *El Rey Planeta* – the Planet King (the sun was then regarded as the fourth of the planetary hierarchy) – who at meals was served by courtiers on their knees. Philip moved slowly and unsmilingly like a ghostly human galleon; it was joked that he only laughed thrice in his long reign.

Yet in private the planetary one was insecure, pious, playful and amorous, directed by a masterful *valido* (premier), the count-duke of Olivares, a sturdy and florid extrovert with a nose like a red hammer, who promoted himself in martial magnificence. The *valido* had won favour by a mix of old-fashioned sycophancy – bearing the brimming royal chamber pot and arranging royal assignations with actresses – and magnetic confidence: he had a plan to invigorate Spain, tarnished by financial crisis and military overstretch, and it was already working. Red-haired with flying moustaches, Philip was no fool but admitted to being overwhelmed by a 'sea of confusions and ocean of difficulties', which is why he needed Olivares. The king 'is endowed with all the gifts', wrote the artist Peter Paul Rubens, who knew him well, but 'mistrusts himself, and defers to others too much'.

It was just at this time that another artist, the twenty-three-year-old Diego Velázquez, a notary's son from Seville, arrived to meet the king – just before Charles and Buckingham. Olivares had invited him for a royal audition. Now he had to wait while Philip and Olivares dealt with the clumsy Englishmen. The English marriage could not happen without the liberating of English Catholics and Charles's conversion to Catholicism. Had Buckingham come to offer Charles's conversion? If not, the visit was going to be very awkward. Philip allowed Charles to glimpse his veiled sister, but she refused to marry a heretic. Meanwhile, the two macho showboats Olivares and Buckingham argued and almost came to blows.

The one thing Philip and Charles shared was a love of art, the only winner in the whole debacle. Charles was given two Titians by the exceedingly polite Philip. Both men sat for Velázquez. Philip loved Velázquez's style, showing the Habsburg as both flawed man and planetary majesty. After painting Olivares in all his bloated self-importance and sensitively portraying Philip and his jaw, Velázquez was appointed usher of the privy chamber.

Charles now realized that unless he signed a face-saving agreement Olivares would not let him return to London. He signed. Determined to avenge themselves on the Habsburgs, he and Buckingham returned home, where the public were delighted that they were not accompanied by an infanta. But all factions now wanted war against Spain – and a French alliance. Charles and Buckingham unwisely allowed the impeachment by Parliament of their own treasurer in return for war subsidies. In March 1625, James died with Buckingham holding his hand – shortly before Charles married the fifteen-year-old French princess, Henrietta Maria, whose dark eyes revealed her Medici blood.

Travelling to Paris to collect the bride, Buckingham flaunted his glamour in twenty-five diamond-encrusted suits and at a garden party shamelessly flirted with Louis XIII's wife, Anne of Austria. At court, he met one of the most fascinating figures in Europe, the Flemish diplomat-artist Rubens, whose extraordinary energy and ambition owed something to the notorious downfall of his father.* Rubens's extravagant, glitzy, colourful, sensuous art was the aesthetic wing of the Catholic resurgence, designed to outshine as well as outfight dour Protestantism

---

* The artist was the son of Jan Rubens, a leading Antwerp lawyer during the golden age of the city as capital of the Habsburgs' Seventeen Provinces and mercantile hub. Its prosperity was ruined by the Dutch revolt, after which it was replaced by Amsterdam. Jan had become legal adviser and then lover of William the Silent's widow Anne of Saxony, fathering a child with her. He was arrested and likely to be executed; his wife (the artist's mother) may have saved her unfaithful husband's life by having an affair with the prince's brother. Either way, young Rubens received unusual benefits for the son of a scandalous attorney. He was brought up in ignorance of the scandal but when he learned of it he changed, pursuing his career with discipline and self-control. He studied art in Italy (he signed paintings as Pietro Paolo) and then enjoyed an astonishing career of art combined with diplomacy. He became the court painter for the Habsburg governors of the Netherlands, Albert and Isabella, who used him as a diplomat and spy, promoting him to secretary of their privy council. Living in luxury in Antwerp, he trained the young Anthony van Dyck, who would soon set off for London. In Paris, Louis XIII's mother and widow of Henri IV, Marie de' Medici, had hired him to paint a series for her Luxembourg Palace while he negotiated with France and Spain.

and to display Habsburg magnificence.* But he was unimpressed by the diamond-spangled Buckingham, who hired him to decorate his London palace.

When Charles met Henrietta Maria he could not believe how small she was. They matched, but she was irked by the restrictions at court. 'I'm the most afflicted person on earth,' she wrote. Brought up in Paris, daughter of a great king, the assassinated Henri IV, she was devoutly Catholic and very extravagant, her entourage numbering 200, including her favourite dwarf, Jeffrey Hudson. The latter was presented to her by Buckingham, jumping out of a pie in a suit of armour and becoming her inseparable Lord Minimus. Hudson would have a life almost as dramatic as those of his royal masters. But Charles's marriage was dominated by Buckingham, while their policies floundered in the escalating European war.

Charles and Buckingham went to war against Spain and sent an expedition to restore Frederick of the Palatinate, yet they also supported the French Protestants, who were being crushed by Louis XIII, Henrietta Maria's brother. They ended up at war with both Spain and France – a perfect muddle, as well as placing Charles's marriage under strain. Buckingham took command but his expeditions were all disastrous. He spent £10,000 on his own clothes for the expedition to save Protestants at La Rochelle (including £367 for a silver perfuming pan) but then did not pay his soldiers. He grew to be hated. Even Rubens, painting the duke, remarked, 'When I consider the caprice and arrogance of Buckingham, I pity the young king,' and predicted that the duke was 'heading for the precipice'. Parliament insisted that 'until this great person be removed from intermeddling with the great affairs of state, we are out of hope of any good success'. But Charles instead dismissed Parliament and the wars went on.

On 23 August 1628, Buckingham, still only thirty-five, headquartered at the Greyhound Pub in Plymouth to organize his Spanish expedition, was stabbed in the chest by an embittered soldier. 'Villain,' shouted Buckingham, then collapsed. His pregnant wife rushed downstairs to find him dead on the breakfast table. While crowds celebrated, Charles 'threw himself upon his bed, lamenting with much passion and with abundance of tears', and stayed in his room for two days. Later, disgusted by parliamentary delight in the murder, he heaped praise on Buckingham and effectively adopted his two sons, who were brought up

---

* In the next century, this movement became known as baroque, possibly from the Portuguese *barrocco*, meaning a flawed pearl, but there are many other possible explanations.

with his own children. But the assassination ended Charles's Spanish war, the peace negotiated by Rubens, and saved his marriage.* Without Buckingham around, the chilly Charles thawed, and came to love Henrietta Maria. 'Dear Heart,' he wrote later, 'thou canst not but be confident that there is no danger which I will not hazard, or pains that I will not undergo, to enjoy the happiness of thy company.' In 1630, Henrietta Maria gave birth, aided by Peter Chamberlen and his secret forceps, to a prince of Wales, Charles, followed by a duke of York, James, and five other children.

Warm in private, Charles was obstinate and haughty in politics. He believed in divine kingship, even though English successions had long been confirmed by Parliament, made up of a House of Lords, hereditary and appointed, and a House of Commons of gentlemen, elected by around 5 per cent of the population – though women did not have the vote. Charles now dispensed with parliaments, funding himself through aggressive taxes. He was far from tyrannical: no one was executed, but his innovative taxes, levied without parliamentary consent, inspired loathing. Disapproving of the puritans in parliament, Charles adopted a High Church Protestantism that beautified churches and supported royal authority. Unlike continental rulers, English kings deployed fleets but not standing armies – and that meant they lacked the force to overrule their parliaments. Vicious religious strife became the sparkwheel that, combined with an ambitious but underfunded monarch, a divided nobility, an increasingly confident Parliament and a sense of millenarian catastrophe exacerbated by European war and economic hardship, cast England into sixty years of crisis. England was not alone, however: Germany, France, Spain, Poland, China and the Ottomans experienced their own devastating crises.

In this apocalyptic atmosphere, two men from opposite sides – a Catholic lord and a provincial puritan – looked not to England but to the New World. Jamestown had almost withered away: 3,000 out of the 3,600 settlers sent out between 1619 and 1622 had perished. But now Englishmen of different stamps sought a new life in America, not so much freedom for all as freedom for themselves from others.

---

* Charles I and Philip IV both knighted Rubens. In Madrid, Philip commissioned over eighty paintings from him, and loved watching him paint. The artist was rich enough to buy an estate outside Antwerp. Fifty-three when his first wife died, he then married her sixteen-year-old niece, Hélène Fourment, whose sister he had also had an affair with. One of Rubens's friends called her 'Helen of Antwerp, who far surpasses Helen of Troy'. Hélène modelled naked for him – rare in a woman of her status. In *The Pelt*, she glows in just a fur. Her red-blonde tresses, white skin and voluptuous figure appear in so many of his paintings that she inspired the adjective Rubenesque. She had five children with Rubens.

SAINTS OF AMERICA: CROMWELL, WARWICK AND WINTHROP

A Huntingdonshire gentleman, elected to Charles's last Parliament, was so disgusted by the king's religious tyranny that he started to consider emigration to America. Oliver Cromwell would be the second remarkable statesman from his family.

Descended from the sister of Henry VIII's enforcer Thomas Cromwell, his family were rich from the distribution of monastic loot that had survived the beheading of the vicegerent in spirituals; his rich uncle, Sir Oliver Cromwell, knighted by Queen Elizabeth held court at a great mansion, Hinchingbrook, that often hosted James I and Prince Charles, both of whom young Cromwell would have seen, but he inherited little from his father. Ten years earlier he had married Elizabeth Boucher, uncouth daughter of a well-connected puritan merchant who gave birth to nine children. Following fitful legal studies, he found himself in the midst of a cascade of crises: after being elected MP for Huntingdon, he argued with the gentry, left the town and suffered *valde melancholicus*, a nervous breakdown. His only expertise was in horseflesh, an invaluable gift when he took command of cavalry. Redemption came with a Damascene conversion through which this 'chief among sinners' believed himself 'among the congregation of the first born', chosen by God to be one of the Saints predestined for heaven. He wrote endlessly about God and providence, yet he was surprisingly loving and tolerant of his children, even though as a believer he worried that his fun-loving favourite daughter Bettie 'seeks her own vanity and carnal mind'. While Cromwell always presented himself as a plainspoken everyman raised by God – a portrait repeated by most historians – he was not quite what he seemed: gruff, mercurial and confrontational, he tended towards the cyclothymic, swinging between elation and despair.

As Charles seemed to have triumphed over Parliament and puritans, Cromwell was typical of those who dreamed of a 'pilgrimage' to a new Promised Land and he was probably distantly acquainted with the greatest advocate of colonization with whom he would be intimately linked: Robert Rich, earl of Warwick. Splendidly rich, gorgeously attired, supremely well connected, an early investor in both the East India and Virginia companies and admiral of his own anti-Spanish privateering flotilla, Warwick was a puritan sympathizer and innovative colonial entrepreneur. Intense, foxy, wearing a spur-shaped beard on the end of his chin, he was a man 'of courage for the greatest enterprises', playing the key role in two great events – the foundation of America and the fall of Charles I.

While the first colonists are often portrayed as humble hymn-singing puritans, the creation of America was always a joint venture of grand-ees and people: after the starvation of Jamestown, it was a series of aristocrats who rescued Virginia and confronted the Powhatan peoples, who struck back with a series of massacres. But it was the planting of a new crop, tobacco, originally from south America and now re-exported from Europe, that gave the colonists their livelihood – and their biggest landowner was Warwick, proprietor of the Richneck tobacco plantation.

At just this time, 1630, seventeen ships bearing a thousand settlers led by an affluent puritan leader called John Winthrop, who had been sacked from office by Charles, arrived in New England to found the commonwealth of Massachusetts, envisioning a theocracy inspired by the Jerusalem of the biblical Israelites – 'a city on a hill'. Warwick and his 'godly friends' had invested in the Massachusetts Bay Company. In March 1628, Charles granted Warwick land for a new company, the New England Company, and the earl now backed others, Saybrook in Connecticut, and Providence in Honduras/Nicaragua.

New England had been founded by accident. In 1620, two ships of ultra-puritan Pilgrims, the *Mayflower* and the *Fortune*, sailed for Virginia but instead arrived in New England where they founded a settlement, Plymouth. The settlers tried to create a sacred community while falling out among themselves about what that meant. During the 1630s, a further 21,000 settlers followed. Yet it was not only puritans who found America.

In 1632, Charles authorized a Catholic politician, George Calvert, Baron Baltimore – like Warwick an early investor in the Virginia and East India companies – to found a colony originally to be called Carola after the king. Charles renamed it Maryland after his wife.[*] Exhausted by his voyages, Baltimore died in 1632, his son Cecil succeeding him as First Lord Proprietary, Earl Palatine of the Provinces of Maryland and Avalon in America, and sending out two ships, the *Ark* and *Dove*, with two Jesuits and 200 settlers, followed by his younger brother as governor.

These colonies were immediately different from their mother country. Very early on, it was clear that the proprietors and founding companies could not control the colonists. Enjoying abundant land, but also afflicted by a shortage of labour and rising friction with the Pow-hatan, the first Virginians founded an elected assembly in July 1619.

---

[*] Baltimore could not have been further politically from the likes of Warwick and Cromwell: he had been James's secretary of state who had championed the Spanish Match, losing his job after Charles's escapade, and had then converted to Catholicism.

Elections were annual, and electorates were wider (over 70 per cent of white males), far ahead of the motherland. But the settlers needed a solution to the labour crisis. Settlers received headrights – the grant of fifty acres per settler – which encouraged the affluent to bring indentured servants to accumulate more land. The indentured labourers, often boys, who formed 70–85 per cent of settlers, worked for around seven years before being freed. But tobacco plantations, owned by Warwick and other planters, required even cheaper labour – and it was the puritan earl who showed the way.

In 1619, a Portuguese slave ship *San Juan Bautista* bearing 350 enslaved Mbundu left Luanda. During the hellish crossing, 143 perished. On reaching the Caribbean, twenty-four children were sold in Jamaica, ruled still by the Columbus dynasty, but twenty adults were captured by one of Warwick's ships, which conveyed them to Virginia where they were set to work at Richneck. There were probably already a few Africans in the colonies, but these were the first to be traded to north America. In 1625, further south, in the Caribbean, English settlers claimed a former Spanish island, Barbados. During the next eighty years, 21,000 enslaved Africans were brought to north America,* but it was a century before slavery became essential to colonial life.

As England was founding these colonies, Spain claimed territory from Texas to California; the French had founded Quebec in 1608 and were exploring the Great Lakes and the Mississippi River. In 1624 the Dutch bought Manhattan off a Native American ruler and founded New Amsterdam.† They did not arrive in an empty continent. Whatever European maps might show, the continent would remain the realm of the many indigenous nations for centuries to come. But it was thinly populated, perhaps two to seven million people, divided into a plethora

---

* In 1640, two white indentured servants, a Dutchman and a Scotsman, and an African, John Punch, escaped from an English proprietor's estate, only to be recaptured and sentenced to thirty lashes. The whites were returned to servitude 'and the third being a negro named John Punch', ruled the judge, was enslaved 'for the time of his natural life here'. The judgment hinted at what was to come: a legal and ideological system so founded on human bondage, and so afraid of rebellion by enslaved Africans, that slave masters were discouraged from ever manumitting their own slaves. DNA suggests that Punch was the progenitor of many Americans, white and black, including the white mother, Ann Dunham, of the first black president, Barack Obama.

† It is hard to find any region of the world that has not been created by migrants, but in modern times it was America, North and South, that was most shaped by settlement, conquest and intermarriage. Between 1492 and 1820, around 2.6 million Europeans, half of them English, 40 per cent Spanish and Portuguese, migrated to the Americas, while around 8.8 million Africans were enslaved and forced to work there. Between 1492 and 1640, 87 per cent of these 446,000 migrants were Iberians. The Atlantic world was dominated by Spanish and Portuguese, not the Anglos. But that was about to change.

of warring tribes – Massachusetts, Abenaki, Mohawks – who lived with minimal property, no central government and no formal law. Instead they discussed policies at assemblies in eloquent debates, electing leaders only for wartime. They lived by both horticulture and hunting, moving between seasonal hunting grounds. All were weakened by the pathogens brought by the Europeans, but their lack of any formal command structure put them at a disadvantage anyway. Often at war with one another, keen to obtain European musketry, their leaders allied with the Europeans to win an advantage against their rival tribes.

Had they united against the colonists, the American story might have been very different. But, for the moment, the Europeans clung to tiny, splintered European settlements, farming and praying, their muskets at their side in their fortified palisades. They were able in a series of small-scale but atrocious wars against mutating federations of tribes to hold their own. From the start, the settlers fought Native American ferocity with their own savagery, paying bounties for scalps.*

Cromwell was now tempted to join the puritans of Warwick's Connecticut. Instead his life stabilized when he inherited property in England from a cousin. But a wider instability was developing. In 1637, King Charles's religious innovations ignited a Scottish revolution when he imposed his new prayer book. The Scots signed a Covenant to resist. The king tried to repress them by force. An aesthete whom Rubens called 'the greatest student of art', Charles was no soldier, and his forces were defeated by the Scots whose success, coinciding with raging religious war in Europe, inspired opposition to his taxes in England. Warwick and his coterie of other lords and MPs were now convinced that Charles was an ungodly tyrant in cahoots with his Catholic wife. Warwick personally reprimanded Charles for his taxes. To pay for the Scottish war Charles now had to call Parliament, but he also appointed a dynamic enforcer, his lord lieutenant of Ireland, the earl of Strafford. The accelerating spiral of fear and hatred spun both sides towards violence. Warwick and his allies were encouraging a Scottish invasion, Strafford planning to import an Irish army. If Parliament did not destroy Strafford, he would destroy Parliament: in April 1641, MPs passed a bill of attainder, effectively convicting him of treason. In May, a righteous killing and a Protestant wedding showed

---

* It was not just the men who were tough. Later in the century, in 1697, Hannah Duston, aged forty, a farmer's wife and mother of nine, was captured with her baby in an Abenaki attack during which twenty-seven colonists, mainly children, were slaughtered. After the Abenaki had killed her baby, Hannah rebelled with two other captives, scalped ten Indians (including six children) and then escaped with the scalps to claim the scalp bounty, that ironically could only be paid to her husband.

the way things were going: meagre crowds celebrated the marriage of Charles's nine-year-old daughter Mary to the Dutch prince of Orange, aged twelve, but thousands enjoyed the beheading of Strafford. In October 1641, the already heightened tension was redoubled by a Catholic rebellion in Ireland in which English Protestants were murdered. The parliamentarians believed Charles had fomented the rebellion and dared not give him an army to suppress the Irish lest he use it on them. Irish strife poisoned London politics: both sides now feared that this was a struggle for survival in which one side would destroy the other.

In December, the opposition successfully proposed a Grand Remonstrance against Charles calling for the reform of Church and state. In the House, Cromwell, now forty-one, whispered to his neighbour that had it failed to pass, he would have gone to America: 'I'd have sold all I had the next morning and never seen England more.' The committees of Parliament now seized much of government. On 4 January 1642, Charles and his guards entered the Commons and tried to arrest five MPs,* but they had fled and he was jostled by hostile crowds. A week later he left London and at Nottingham he raised his standard: it was war.

As England became a failed state, Shahjahan was taking Mughal India to its zenith.

Nurjahan had weaned Jahangir off the opium but it was too late: the padishah had lost control, humiliatingly taken prisoner by a mutinous general, though he was almost liberated by Nurjahan leading a rescue mission on an elephant. On Jahangir's death,† Emperor Shahjahan ordered his vizier Asafkhan, Nurjahan's brother and Mumtaz's father, to kill his brother, two nephews and two cousins. As the son succeeded the father as padishah, the niece succeeded her aunt as empress.

Shahjahan was passionately in love with Mumtaz, whom he entitled Malika-i-Jahan – Queen of the World. 'His entire delight,' wrote his court historian, 'was centred on this illustrious lady to the extent that he didn't feel for his others one-thousandth of the love he had for her.' She spent most of their nineteen-year marriage pregnant, bearing a child every sixteen months. Four boys and three girls survived.

---

* Henrietta Maria, the target of so much anti-Catholic hate, was wise enough to advise Charles to negotiate with Parliament, even offering: 'Leave me to do it, for the good of your affairs in this country.' But Charles was unsuited to compromise, and refused. Once it was war, she backed him, delivering arms and even commanding troops, and was nicknamed the *Generalissima*.

† Jahangir died travelling from Kashmir to Lahore, where he was buried in the resplendently Persianate–Mughal Shahdara Bagh tomb. Shahjahan retired his stepmother Nurjahan to Lahore, where she lived quietly for eighteen years. When she died at sixty-eight, she was buried with Jahangir.

It should have been a recipe for respect and loyalty. Instead power beat family: all seven, even the girls, would throw themselves into a gory tournament of power. Their first daughter, Jahanara, was the father's favourite; the eldest boy, Darashikoh, was the heir, but the third, Aurangzeb, showed the necessary killer instinct: when he was charged by an elephant as a teenager, during an elephant fight, he coolly held his horse steady and waited, spear at the ready.

No one could play the emperor like Shahjahan, brought up not by his Rajput mother but by Akbar and Ruqaiya. While Akbar was portrayed in court art taking part in athletic hunts and Jahangir as a sensitive prince, Shahjahan cast himself as quasi-divine, messiah-like, the 'second Lord of the Conjunction of Jupiter and Venus', alongside Tamerlane the first Lord.

Mumtaz was his partner in all this, granted an unprecedented million-rupee allowance and given the imperial seal to enable her to check all documents. She always accompanied him, whether in war or peace.

In June 1631, the emperor and Mumtaz, aged thirty-eight, pregnant for the fourteenth time, travelled southwards to campaign in Deccan. At Burhanpur, she endured a thirty-hour labour before giving birth to a daughter, Gohara, and then haemorrhaging. Her eldest daughter Jahanara ran out to pray and distribute alms to the crowds, while a 'paralysed' Shahjahan sobbed desperately. But the bleeding would not stop.

TAJ MAHAL: MUMTAZ'S DAUGHTER AND
KÖSEM'S MAD SON

When Mumtaz died, Shahjahan howled for a week, his hair turning white. Jahanara thought he might die. After a year of recovery, he re-emerged, backed by Jahanara, who acted as his empress in the place of Mumtaz. Shahjahan conceived a white marble tomb for Mumtaz and himself that would express his love for her, the Crown of the Palace (Taj Mahal) – the statement of the ruler of the greatest state in the world at that time who recognized few limits.* Nonetheless Shahjahan did not

---

* The Taj Mahal was built in a Persianate design that owed something to the simplicity of Tamerlane's tomb in Samarkand and Humayoun's in Delhi but was vast in scale and blazing pristine whiteness. It took sixteen years to build. But it was only a part of his dedication to sacred monarchy; he also moved the capital from Agra to Shahjahanabad at Delhi built around a new palace, the Red Fort, itself centred around the emperor's *diwan-i-khas* (audience hall) where he held court on a Peacock Throne and appeared daily on the marble balcony for his *jharokha darshan* – the rituals that defined House Tamerlane. The Mughals

neglect the first job of House Tamerlane: conquest.

It is not cheap maintaining an empire: the greater the power, the greater the aspirations, the higher the costs. It is a rule of imperial power and human nature that every state will expand its ambitions beyond its resources, by at least one degree. The second Lord of the Conjunction aspired to rule the rest of India, expelling impertinent Portuguese from Port Hooghly in Bengal, advancing southwards into Deccan and westwards into Afghanistan. The decline of his aggressive Persian neighbour, Abbas the Great, offered western opportunities: Abbas destroyed his own achievements by liquidating or mutilating all three of his sons. In 1629, he died, leaving the throne to a vicious, illiterate, opium-addicted grandson, Safi, spawn of his murdered crown prince, who killed most of the family. Shahjahan later seized Kandahar, while further west the Ottomans – led by a predatory but talented young padishah – joined the carve-up.

Kösem's irrepressible son, Murad IV, was a muscular taurine giant who lived for hunting, drinking and wrestling. As he grew up, the Magnificent Mother ran the empire as regent – *naib-i-sultanat* – but she could not control him. Murad did as he wished: for example, he would gallop around the hippodrome. 'Make them stop javelin-throwing in the hippodrome,' his mother asked grand vizier Halil Pasha. 'My son loves it, I lose my mind over it. Caution him but not right away.' Kösem guided Halil – a female potentate in a male world running a tricontinental empire.*

The Magnificent Mother was loved because of her authority and beauty, not to speak of her charity: during the month of good works, Rajab, she dressed incognito to pay the debts of jailed debtors. But Murad resented her. 'What can I do? My words are bitter to him,' she wrote, sounding like any mother coping with a defiant teenager. 'Just let him stay alive,' she wrote to Halil, 'he's vital to us all.'

In 1628, when he was sixteen, Murad took power, launching a wave of terror, executing corrupt viziers with his own sword, banning drinking and coffee-housing, while patrolling Istanbul in disguise, executing

---

had become gradually Indian thanks to their Rajput wives, who brought their culture to the central Asian harem. Shahjahan, whose mother was a daughter of the raja of Jodhpur, was three-quarters Indian, only a quarter Tamerlanian, but their style was Persianate; his vizier and queen Mumtaz were Persian; and he preferred Persian to the Turkish of Tamerlane and Babur.

* 'My son leaves in the morning and comes back at night. I never see him. I'm distraught . . . He won't stay out of the cold and he'll get sick again. I tell you, this worrying is destroying me. Talk to him.' Kösem trusted the vizier, offering, as was the tradition, one of her daughters as wife: 'Whenever you're ready let me know . . . We'll take care of you immediately. I have a princess ready.' The Armenian-born Halil married one of the daughters, becoming a *damad* – imperial son-in-law – quite a rise from enslavement.

any fraudsters. But he particularly watched Shah Safi's declining Persia – and coveted Iraq. He took personal command of the armies. After defeating the Poles, in 1634, he stormed into the Caucasus to retake Yerevan, a feat celebrated in a Romanesque triumph in Istanbul (and the strangling of two half-brothers).

While he was away, Kösem was his ears and eyes. When she heard that the mufti (Islamic jurist) was conspiring, she had him strangled.

At home, Murad held court, showing off his wrestling skills, often challenging his courtiers to bouts that ended with him holding them above his head, as recounted by his friend the Sufi poet, adventurer and outrageous raconteur Evliya Çelebi, who was writing the world's greatest travel book. Murad enjoyed the satirical verses of the poet Nefi but warned the wit against mocking the grand vizier and ordered a black eunuch to draft his apology. When a drop of black ink spattered the eunuch's letter, Nefi could not resist a racist joke: 'Your blessed sweat dripped.' Hearing this, Murad ordered him strangled. The padishah was becoming a Neronian sadist: he would sit in a kiosk on the Bosphoros boozing and firing his crossbow at boatmen who came too close. In 1638, he invaded Iraq and routed the Iranians. Shah Safi died after a drinking contest and Murad secured Baghdad. Iraq remained Ottoman until 1918.

Murad held another Roman triumph in Constantinople, his mother Kösem parading in a golden carriage. He was only twenty-nine but, falling sick with cirrhosis, he lashed out, killing first his grand vizier and then his younger brother – and would have executed his last brother, the lunatic Ibrahim, had Kösem not begged for his life. When he died in 1640, the only Ottoman prince left alive was Mad Ibrahim, a murderous erotomaniac whose outrages forced Kösem to make an unbearable decision for a mother.

The Ottomans were not the only dynasty in crisis: the Stuarts in England and Bourbons in France were mired in civil war as the Habsburgs fought for their position in Germany. The European crisis now escalated into a world conflict as the Dutch attacked the Habsburgs in Africa and America.

In 1641, Garcia II, *manikongo* of Kongo, was determined to expel the Portuguese, 'who, instead of wanting gold or silver, now trade slaves, who aren't made of gold or cloth, but are creatures', and so he invited the Dutch in – a decision that would unleash a war from Brazil to Angola, destroy his own kingdom and intensify the European competition to control sugar and slavery. Ultimately it would open up the Atlantic not to the Dutch, but to a new player: England.

MANIKONGO GARCIA, QUEEN NZINGA AND AHOSU
HOUEGBADJA: THREE AFRICAN KINGS

Manikongo Garcia was a hybrid Kongo and Portuguese monarch, 'dressed in finery, with golden brocade sewn with pearls . . . on his head the royal crown embossed with the thickest pearls and jewels, his throne of crimson velvet'. He held court amid Flemish tapestries, wearing Indian linens, eating with cutlery of American silver in the company of titled Kongo nobles and bishops in red sashes, while secretaries took dictation. Ruling the region around the Congo River from his capital São Salvador (Mbanza Kongo), Garcia – also named Nkanga a Lukeni a Nzenze a Ntumba – was literate in Portuguese, having been educated by Jesuits, and practised in his private chapel a Catholicism infused with Kongo religion. He was not exactly a victim of Portuguese slave trading: after murdering the king and his own brother, he became notorious for the profits he made from slavery.

Just as the *manikongos* adopted European trappings, so the Portuguese were becoming increasingly Africanized in a way that was different from other Europeans. Many *lançados* – outcasts, the original settlers – had settled with African women and had Luso-African children who often adopted African traditions, even scarification, while practising a hybrid of Catholicism and Vodun (voodoo). *Lançados* married into African dynasties: Tomás Robredo married the daughter of Manikongo Álvaro V. Many Luso-Africans became aggressive slave traders, *pombeiros*.

Originally the Kongo dynasties were close to Portugal, but the expansion of Luanda and intensification of the slave trade had broken the relationship when the *manikongos* invited the Dutch to intervene. Now Kongo was being torn apart, not just by the Portuguese but also by incursions by African raiders of uncertain origin, the Jaga, and the Imbangala, a war band with a killing cult, which trained child soldiers initiated with gruesome rites – grinding babies into a grain mill, and cannibalism. Both would thrive in the coming mayhem.

Garcia had a further problem with his southern neighbour, Ndongo, and its remarkable queen. To supply slaves, the Portuguese had first encouraged Ndongo to raid Kongo. Then they tried and failed to conquer Ndongo, which was ruled by a *ngola* (king) named Mbandi who defeated the Portuguese forces. When Ngola Mbandi was poisoned, his sister, Nzinga Mbande, then in her twenties, seized the throne, keeping her brother's remains in a reliquary so that he could be consulted. The queen had been baptized and educated by Jesuits, speaking and writing Portuguese. Now she defeated all claimants and seized a neighbouring kingdom, Matamba, hiring her own Imbangala auxiliaries, led by a war-lord who called himself Nzinga Mona (Nzinga's Son). Nzinga constantly facing male challenges, presented herself as a male king, sporting male garb, daggers and spears, enjoying male concubines and proving every bit as good a commander as her male rivals, European or African.

The Portuguese were the only Europeans who really penetrated the African interior: in west Africa, 50 per cent of Europeans died within a year of arriving, whether from malaria, yellow fever or dysentery, making deeper conquest impossible. Since European involvement barely ex-tended beyond the ports, other rulers could handle things differently. The *obas* of Benin (southern Nigeria) rejected foreign interference; as a Dutch trader noted, 'When it comes to trade, they are very strict and will not suffer the slightest infringement of their customs, not even an iota can be changed,' and after the 1520s started to limit direct involvement in slaving – though they appointed the slave-trading *obas* of Lagos on the Slave Coast, Benini vassals who paid them tribute.

Simultaneously the conquests of a new potentate, Ahosu Houegbad-ja, a Fon warlord, generated thousands of new slaves that he sold to the Europeans.

His kingdom, Dahomey (today's Benin) was founded by three broth-ers who around 1600 carved their own realms. Now Houegbadja, third *ahosu* (king) of the Alladaxonou family, united many of the Fon people, building a capital Abomey, where twelve palaces stood decorated with bas-reliefs recording the history of the kingdom and depicting sacred ancestors. Houegbadja presided over a complex court, always sheltered by a slave bearing a parasol, and escorted by a guard of female warriors who later became the vanguard of Dahomean armies. Every year, he held a festival that included military parades, the receiving of tribute and the ceremonies of *xwetanu* at which 500 and sometimes as many as 4,000 slaves were decapitated, often by female bodyguards, as offerings to the king's ancestors. The kings were sacred but were elected by a council of princes and a family of priests; on their deaths, thousands of slaves were sacrificed.

Houegbadja received muskets for slaves, an incentive for African kings to capture more prisoners, but this implies a lack of agency on their part: the rivalry of these kingdoms, still barely understood by Europeans, led to wars just as such rivalries did in Europe and Asia. African wars, like those in Asia, yielded slaves. What was unique was the demand for chattel slavery in the Americas. African rulers sacrificed some of their slaves – though most others were later freed – but now a new European version of this servitude – chattel slavery – was being formalized. It is unlikely African leaders who sold enslaved captives to the Europeans initially understood that they were selling them into a new crueller bondage, designed to supply the tobacco and later sugar plantations of the Americas, though later they would surely have known the details. Most Africans believed that Europeans were cannibals and that slaves were destined to be eaten.

It was Portugal's sugar empire of Brazil that was the voracious furnace of chattel slavery, its appetite and profits being the catalysts for this new global conflict. In 1530, the Portuguese exported a new plant to Brazil – sugar cane – but they were slow to develop their vast colony. By 1548, some 3,000 Amerindians were slaving in six sugar mills, but the Amerindians were being wiped out by disease, slave labour and suicide until in 1570 the king, prompted by the Jesuits, forbade the enslavement of the indigenous peoples unless they were captured in a 'righteous war'. Mixed-race warlords known as *bandeirantes*, most famously António Raposo Tavares, launched *saltos* (raids) into the interior killing and enslaving thousands. The Amerindians struck back and launched messianic revolts, the *sandidades*, that justified yet more *saltos*. By the end of the century, around 50,000 slaves had been worked to death, creating shortages that were filled by Africans.

Sugar changed the world. It was not just a product, it was a destroyer and maker of worlds on both sides of the Atlantic. The trade now expanded into a vast diabolic enterprise. Portuguese planters migrated to Brazil, where they were enriched by the sugar and slave industries. By 1600, this involved 30,000 Portuguese with 15,000 African slaves; by 1620, there were 50,000 Portuguese ruling the same number of African and Amerindian slaves. After that, African slaves started to outnumber Amerindians and the trade became frenzied: by 1650, a total of 250,000 had been brought to Brazil and in many areas 75 per cent of the populations were slaves.

Luanda was the gateway of the new trade; the kingdoms between today's Angola and Congo were its hunting grounds: between 1502 and 1867, around 2.8 million Africans were traded through Luanda. North America never challenged the scale of Brazil: of the estimated eleven million transported across the Atlantic, 4.9 million were delivered to Brazil. The slaves were seized in raids by African rulers. Those of lesser value, the old and sometimes children too young or too sick to work, were often killed.

At Pombe and other slave markets, they were sold to *pombeiros* who marched them, guarded by other slaves, in coffles across Africa. Out of slaves captured in Angola, it was estimated that 10 per cent died during capture, 22 per cent on the way to the coast. At the coast, those who had survived the journey were confined within hulking slave castles along the coast from Luanda in the south-west, to Elmina in west Africa. In the crowded dungeon barracks – barracoons – they were systematically broken, chained and branded, men whipped, females raped, as part of their 'seasoning'. Killings and rapes took place only yards from luxurious European dining rooms and chapels. The slaves were depersonalized, known as *peças* (pieces) or *cabeças* (heads) or 'Guinea ebony'. Ten per cent of those enslaved died in the castles.

Survivors were marched through the 'doors of no return' into the *tumbeiros* (undertakers), slave ships, which had often arrived from Brazil full of *cachaça*, rum, and *fumo*, coarse Brazilian tobacco treated with molasses. The traders bought grain from local rulers to feed (meagrely) their human property.

While the traders had every interest in not killing or damaging their merchandise, they also wanted to make as much money as possible, packing them into holds and feeding them just corn, olive oil and water. The journeys were hellish, marked by unbearable suffering: an estimated 6–10 per cent, sometimes 20 per cent, died during the voyages – fifty days to Rio – mostly from gastroenteritis, but there were also many suicides, the bodies tossed to a ravening escort of sharks. 'That ship with its intolerable stink, the lack of space, the continual cries and infinite woes of so many wretched people,' recalled Friar Sorrento, an Italian Capuchin on such a voyage with 900 slaves in 1649, 'appeared to be hell itself.' This hell was intensified because Africans generally believed that to join their ancestors after death they had to die among their own, but death on a slave ship, thrown into the sea, meant their spirits could never rest, their souls lost.

On arrival, they were washed and oiled and given ginger and tobacco to overcome their sadness; they were then auctioned, with the rule that if they became ill within a fortnight, they could be returned. A further 3 per cent died at this stage. As few as 50 per cent of those attacked in that African raid started work.

Sugar plantations were labour-intensive, the work brutally hard, the loss of life demanding ever more slaves. It was often easier to work slaves to death and import more than to let them have families. Known like cattle as 'self-moving goods', enslaved Africans started work at eight years old. After eight hours in the fields, they toiled in the mills. Average life expectancy was twenty-five. One plantation manager recorded that 6 per cent of his slaves needed to be replaced annually. The women were constantly raped by prowling masters, sexual abuse being endemic, even essential, to the psychology and practice of slavery. Slave masters propagated the myth that slaves were promiscuous, but actually slaves often abstained by choice so as not to bring children into this life. Suicides were frequent, often by eating earth. Slave masters feared tribal solidarity would lead to rebellions, so they suppressed tribal and family connections, separating clans and renaming slaves as if they had not existed before.* Every enslaved person dreamed of liberation, if not revolt. Submission required the constant threat of violence. Planters deployed an array of punishments: the whip, the iron collar, the slow death by iron mask. Slavery could not be sustained without violence, and ultimately both the violence and profitability could not be justified to white planters without a sense of natural racial superiority that later became a pervasive ideology.

Back in a Europe benighted by the spreading religious war, the Habsburgs, led by Emperor Ferdinand, performed well, conquering northern Germany thanks to an irrepressible, mercurial and mysterious Czech warlord, Albrecht von Wallenstein. But the Habsburg victory destroyed the balance of power, while the meteoric Wallenstein threatened to overwhelm the uncharismatic Ferdinand, who cautiously dismissed him.

In 1628, the Swedish king Gustavus Adolphus, Lion of the North, who had already taken Livonia (thus excluding Muscovy from the Baltic for a century), stormed into northern Germany with a small but superb army and turned the tide back towards the Protestants. Heralding the Swedish empire – *Stormaktstiden* – Gustavus advanced into southern Germany. Ferdinand quickly recalled Wallenstein, who had some early success against Gustavus. Then during the drawn battle of Lützen against Wallenstein, the Lion was twice wounded, then assassinated with a shot to the temple as he lay on the ground.† The bankrupt and exhausted Habsburgs nonetheless needed help.‡ The Planet King sent

---

* The slaves embraced a secret culture of their own, publicly worshipping Catholicism but cultivating music, dancing and religions, *vodun* (Fon people), *santería* and *candomblé*, brought by Yorubas, which fused African gods, *orishas*, with Catholic saints. *Vodun* became voodoo.

† One of Gustavus' favourite commanders at Lützen was Alexander Leslie, an illegitimate Scottish nobleman, promoted to field marshal in 1636, who would later, as earl of Leven, command troops at the battle of Marston Moor against Charles I.

‡ Victory had almost bankrupted Ferdinand, who turned for troops and money to Wallenstein, imperial generalissimo and admiral of the North and Baltic Seas, granting him a personal kingdom of the dukedoms of Friedland, Sagan and Mecklenburg. Wallenstein now planned to negotiate a European peace, betraying the Habsburgs. Ferdinand, fearing that Wallenstein aspired to seize the empire, ordered his assassination. In February 1634, in Cheb, Bohemia, three Irish and Scottish officers slaughtered his retinue then, awakening him in his bedroom, speared him to death – the definition of Icaran downfall.

a Spanish army under his brother, Cardinal-Infante Fernando, who at Nördlingen in September 1634 overruled cautious generals and defeated the Protestants. In Madrid, Philip and Olivares celebrated by building the colossal Buen Retiro Palace, decorated with portraits by Velázquez who painted both monarch and *valido* as armoured paladins on muscle-ripped horses. Faced with Habsburg victory, Louis XIII, now guided by the consummate Cardinal Richelieu, declared war.

It was now that Garcia of Kongo appealed to the Dutch who, allied with France, put into action their *Groot Desseyn* – grand plan – to destroy the Habsburg empire and steal the sugar and slave trades.

Zumbas and Oranges, Cromwells and Villiers

On 7 September 1628, a Dutch admiral, the fifty-year-old Piet Heyn,[*]
attacked a Habsburg treasure fleet off Cuba and grabbed the greatest
prize in the history of naval pillage: sixteen galleons worth so much –
eleven million guilders – that the silver market crashed, throwing the
Habsburgs into a financial crisis. The silver paid for a Dutch offensive:
the *Groot Desseyn*.

In 1621, at the start of the war, the States-General had awarded a western monopoly to the Nineteen Gentlemen who floated the new West
India Company (GWC) to dominate the Atlantic sugar world. Sugar
meant slaves. The Dutch were not new to the slave trade: since Charles
V, Flemish and Dutch merchants had supplied slaves. Now in 1624 the
Dutch tried to seize Luanda and Elmina, but failed; in 1627 they grabbed
Gorée (Dakar, Senegal). Nor were they the only Europeans interested in
sugar: in 1627, English merchants were planting sugar cane on their
newly secured Caribbean island, Barbados; in 1635 the French planted
Martinique. But the Dutch were playing on a different scale.

The success of the tiny, resourceful and sophisticated Netherlands
reflected the singular development of European societies, where perpetual warfare inspired extreme competition, technical innovation and
loyalty to states and faiths. Passionate Protestantism encouraged the
family values, mutual trust and sombre industriousness personified by
Jacob de Graeff, the most pre-eminent of the *regenten*, the oligarchs, rich
on sugar, spices, slaves, who dominated Dutch politics for thirty years.
His de Graeff and Bicker cousinhood masterminded the rise of Holland
in uneasy cohabitation with the princes of Orange, whom they regarded
as dangerously monarchical. The Netherlands pioneered the rule of law

---

[*] As a young man, Heyn had been captured by the Spanish and enslaved to work the
galleys for four years, making him a rare opponent of slavery.

that was essential to trade and competition with their rivals, and founded universities that trained students in law, while the need for expertise encouraged others to concentrate on professions. Traders no longer just sold to people they knew at nearby markets but also did business with strangers, which meant they had to cultivate fairness, politeness and trust, alongside the ruthless avarice necessary to make profits: the conundrum of capitalism. Amsterdam, where Jacob de Graeff and his sons Cornelis and Andries were mayor one after the other, was at the forefront of urbanization: between 1500 and 1800, twenty million moved to cities mainly in northern Europe. Cities were unhealthy: many died – 1 per cent of city dwellers annually – but they were replaced by others. The bigger the cities, the more artisans, the greater the skills and comforts on offer. The grandee Andries de Graeff stands ruddy and gingery, proudly clad in Calvinist black with a white collar, in a painting that he commissioned from one of the most favoured artists of this Dutch golden age: Rembrandt.

In 1637, the GWC seized much of Brazil, whence it sent flotillas in further attempts to grab Elmina and other African slaving castles. In 1641, invited by Manikongo Garcia, they stormed Luanda. The Dutch were the first northern Europeans to enter the slave market on a vast scale. Queen Nzinga joined Garcia and the Dutch in a ferocious war that ruined Angola. In 1647, Nzinga defeated the Portuguese. Garcia's gamble and the Dutch *Groot Desseyn* had paid off: suddenly the militarized corporations of the small hybrid republic of the United Provinces spanned the world.

On the way to the east, the Dutch stopped for provisioning at the Cape where Dutch frontiersmen founded Cape Town, then started to move inland and claim farms, suppressing, annihilating and mixing with the first people they encountered, the Khoikhoi, pastoral nomads who were rapidly broken by musket and pathogen. Across the Atlantic, in the New Netherlands, the GWC expanded their town on the island of Manhattan, New Amsterdam, where in the early 1640s an adventurous settler, Claes Martenszen van Rosenvelt, progenitor of the Roosevelts, arrived as a teenager to start a new life, buying a small farm in what would later be midtown.

A less typical founder but also progenitor of a New York dynasty was Anthony Janszoon van Salee, the strapping son of a renegade Dutch pirate Murad Reis, president of the Salé pirate republic in Morocco, and his Moorish wife, who arrived in 1630 with some of his father's ill-gotten treasure. Van Salee, a Muslim described as a 'Turk', and 'mulatto', protected free Africans and read the Quran. Even by the standards of this rough port, the son of an African head of state and his saucy German wife, Grietse Reyniers, ex-barmaid, scandalized the Dutch Reformed Church. Grietse was accused of flashing at sailors, measuring penises of patrons in her tavern with a broom and being the governor's mistress, of which she joked, 'I've long been the whore of the nobility; now I'll be the whore of the rabble.' The Church tried to expel the couple for impiety, but they stayed, had four children and died rich, the biggest landowners on Manhattan. Cornelius Vanderbilt, robber baron of the Golden Age, was descended from their daughter Annica. The Dutch traded furs and bought land from the Algonquin, who were then driven out by the Iroquois. The newcomers called the seafaring Dutch the Saltwaterers.

The scale of these Dutch triumphs was possible because the other Protestant sea power – England – had disintegrated.

SAINTS AND CAVALIERS: CHARLES, HENRIETTA MARIA AND CROMWELL

It was late afternoon on 2 July 1644, amid ferocious fighting on Marston Moor, near York, when Lieutenant-General Oliver Cromwell and the 5,000 cavalry under his command charged. It was the largest battle ever fought on British soil – 28,000 parliamentary and Scottish soldiers under the Scottish general Leven, opposed 18,000 Cavaliers under Prince Rupert of the Rhine, King Charles's nephew. No one knew it then but it would be the decisive battle of the war, and the making of Cromwell.

It had been two years since Parliament and king had resorted to war. Neither side had yet landed a decisive blow or found a brilliant paladin. Charles had the advantage at first; the trained bands of Parliament were undisciplined enthusiasts. But one of the first to raise a troop of cavalry was the former Huntingdonshire farmer Cromwell.

Prince Rupert, still only twenty-five, was six foot tall, given to wearing the high boots, silk and velvet suits and broad hats of a cavalier, keen to enjoy mistresses and gambling and never seen without his lucky dog Boye; he possessed elan but lacked discipline. Cromwell was proud in his plainness: ruddy, balding with reddish hair, high cheekbones, 'his voice sharpe and untunable, and his eloquence full of fervour', his clothes rough and dark. As Rupert's dashing cavalry had dominated the early battles, Cromwell noticed that 'their troopers are gentlemen's sons' while parliamentary horsemen were 'old decayed serving men and tapsters'. He decided to recruit believers instead: 'You must get men of spirit.' Some complained that these Cromwellians were 'proud, self-conceited hot-headed sectaries' who 'call themselves godly' and see 'visions and revelations'. Cromwell called them his Lovely Company. Promoted quickly to colonel, he built around himself a 'family' of like-minded officers, led by Henry Ireton, who married his daughter Bridget. The parliamentary press called him Old Ironside; his godly horsemen became the Ironsides.

Until that day in Yorkshire, the two sides had been stalemated in a war where the early courtliness had now deteriorated into a ferocious sectarian scrimmage. But when the Scots, signing a Solemn League and Covenant that agreed to follow 'the word of God' and seek 'the extirpation of popery', joined the war, sending 22,000 men to form the Army of the Two Kingdoms, they tipped the balance towards Parliament.

The anxious king said goodbye to Henrietta Maria. When the war started, the queen, whose Catholicism attracted violent parliamentary hostility, was in Holland. She only just made it back, being nearly ship-wrecked. Reunited with the king, she became pregnant again, but was forced to move from town to town, hunted by parliamentarians. She duly gave birth to a daughter, but their two younger children were already parliamentary prisoners. Just before Marston Moor, Charles sent her to France to raise funds. 'Adieu, my dear heart,' she wrote. 'If I die, believe you lose a person who has never been other than entirely yours.' They never met again. 'I ought never to have left the king,' she later told her son. Warwick, Parliament's lord high admiral, pursued her, hoping to kill the papist queen, but she made it to France, accompanied by her court and Lord Minimus.*

As the Anglo-Scottish army threatened to take York, Rupert prepared to fight at Marston Moor, already afraid of Cromwell's Ironsides.

On an early summer's evening, Rupert could hear the puritans singing hymns as Cromwell led his 4,000 Eastern Association cavalry plus 1,000 Scots in the charge, breaking one division of royal cavalry. Cromwell was a zealot but far from dour: instead he was impassioned, often giddy, charging into battle transfigured by a manic righteous glee, laughing aloud. 'I could not, riding about my business, but smile out to

---

* Jeffrey Hudson no longer enjoyed the mockery of her courtiers. When her master of the horse bullied him, he challenged him to a duel. The courtier arrived armed with a marrow, but Hudson was armed with a pistol and shot him in the forehead. Still only twenty-five, he was sentenced to death, but the queen pardoned him. She sent him back to England but somehow his ship was captured by Barbary pirates who enslaved him for over twenty years, during which he endured rape and servitude, and he only returned to England in 1669.

God in praises, in assurance of victory,' he wrote. The Ironsides charged with the shouts 'God and our Strength' and 'The Lord of Hosts!'

Then Rupert charged. 'Cromwell's own division had a hard pull of it,' observed a parliamentarian, 'charged by Rupert's bravest . . . they stood at the sword's point a pretty while, hacking one another.' Cromwell was wounded in the neck. 'But at last (it so pleased God) he brake through them, scattering them before him like a little dust.' Cromwell (and English historians) conveniently forgot that Marston Moor was really a Scottish victory: the Scottish paladin Leven occupied northern England for the next two years.

After the battle, the moderate Parliamentarians, the Presbyterian faction, wanted to negotiate but Cromwell, leader of the Independents, insisted on total victory. 'Why did we take up arms at first?' he asked. The power had moved from Warwick and his God-fearing magnates to the new hard men. Arguing for 'vigorous and effectual prosecution of the war', Cromwell urged, 'Let us apply ourselves!' While he advertised his God-fearing humility, he was the ultimate humble bragger, advertising his prowess in pamphlets, claiming as his own the exploits of others and undermining his superiors, whom he subverted and displaced one by one. The ruling Committee of Both Kingdoms commissioned a New Model Army under the dashing commander Sir Thomas 'Black Tom' Fairfax, a Yorkshire grandee, who became lord general with his deputy, Cromwell, promoted to lieutenant-general of horse. The duo worked well together: at Naseby, on 14 June 1645, the two finally won decisively with Cromwell leading the charge.

Charles surrendered to the Scottish marshal Leven, hoping to turn him against Parliament. Instead the Scots traded him to his enemies. In June 1647, the king twice negotiated with the parliamentary commanders, including Cromwell, who allowed him to meet his two imprisoned children, Elizabeth and Henry, duke of Gloucester: 'the tenderest sight that ever eyes beheld', in Cromwell's view. Little Gloucester, not yet seven, did not recognize the king. 'I am your father, child,' Charles said.

Parliament was now dominated by diehard puritans who that June abolished all theatre, as well as Christmas and Easter, but moderate Presbyterians still hoped for a negotiated peace. In August, the army put an end to any talk of compromise. Fairfax rode into London at the head of the New Model Army with Cromwell commanding the rearguard. Their army was growing increasingly radical: some officers proposed a written constitution, universal rights, the abolition of the House of Lords and full male suffrage. Cromwell, socially conservative and monarchical by instinct, was appalled by this, but probably approved the military purge of Parliament that followed. While Fairfax was still lord general, the more political Cromwell became a master of inscrutable withdrawals and ever more ostentatious self-deprecation, yet always emerged with greater power. At times of tension, debates in Parliament or the army council, he would burst into manic laughter or start pillow fights. From now, he and his coterie of generals were the potentates. But what to do with the king?

The English meltdown was a tiny skirmish compared to the bedlam that was destroying the world's largest kingdom. Charles was a desperate prisoner, but far to the east the Ming emperor, facing peasant revolts, famines and the invasion of the ferocious Manchu cavalry, found a uniquely extreme solution.

KILLING KINGS: BADGERS AND HETMANS, SUGAR CUBES AND BOWSTRINGS

On 25 April 1644, the Chongzhen Emperor, just thirty-three years old, after summoning his wife and daughter, killed both with his sword and then walked alone out to Jingshan Park in Beijing where he hanged himself on a tree, leaving a note that read: 'I die ashamed, unable to face my ancestors.'* As Beijing was ravaged by rebels, he had lost control of much of China and faced the advance of the Manchus from the north. Beijing descended into chaos until six weeks later, on 5 June, a Manchu warrior, wearing armour, his hair with the front shaven and a queue behind, rode up with a small escort of horse archers, dismounted and announced to the crowds simply, 'I am the prince regent, Dorgan. The crown prince will arrive presently. Will you allow me to be the ruler?'

'Yes,' replied the citizens. Dorgon (whose name meant the Badger) was soon joined by a horde of horse archers; a boy, Shunzhi, Dorgon's six-year-old nephew and grandson of the family founder Nurhaci, was now emperor of a new Qing dynasty. The talented Badger, formally styled Uncle and Prince Regent, conquered the rest of China, slaughtering entire cities. Then he forged a new order: he settled the elite corps – the Eight Banners – in Beijing, yet reinstated the civil service exams and promoted Han Chinese scholars, asking, 'How can the Manchu and Han be united?' Nonetheless Dorgon murdered all the Ming princes

---

* The tree famously still stands, though it may be a more recent replacement.

and ordered that all Chinese men wear their hair shaved at the front with a queue at the back or be put to death.*

The boy emperor resented his uncle, whom he had assassinated during a hunt, but Dorgon had by then won a new Mandate of Heaven; the family would now restore the Central Country as the greatest empire on earth – just as the Habsburg world empire was falling apart.

Philip IV's war had almost shattered both Habsburg Monarchies. France defeated the Austrians, then invaded Spain. The Portuguese had lost much of their empire to the Dutch and blamed the Habsburgs; in 1640, an assembly declared the duke of Braganza, great-grandson of Manuel the Fortunate, as João IV. The Swedes took Prague. The Planet King consulted a charismatic nun who, mystically transported to the Jumanos indigenous people of Texas, advised him to rule in his own right. He sacked Olivares and prepared to negotiate.

All sides were stalemated and exhausted. In October 1648 at Westphalia, Philip and his Austrian cousin Kaiser Frederick III agreed a compromise end to what became known as the Thirty Years War that recognized the right of Germans to worship as they wished. Germany was by then ruined: in thirty years of war, the horses of the apocalypse had killed around ten million people. Westphalia established the sovereignty of states in a multipolar Europe, ensuring creative freedom – and destructive competition – for centuries to come. There were many losers but three winners: Sweden ruled the Baltic and a slice of Germany, Pomerania; the Dutch won independence; and an obscure old Swabian family.

The House of Hohenzollern, led by Elector Frederick William, had converted its impoverished sandpit of fiefdoms, built around Brandenburg and Prussia, into a north German power. The Great Elector saw his lands destroyed in the war – Berlin had just 6,000 inhabitants by 1648. Nonetheless, convinced that 'Alliances are good but one's own forces are better,' he forged his Junker nobility into a warrior class, exploiting the war to break the representative Estates and impose the autocracy that would last until 1918.†

The Elector was duke of Prussia, which was part of the huge Commonwealth Poland–Lithuania: in its southern provinces, Cossacks, free people, often petty nobles, burghers and escaped peasants and soldiers,

---

* The Chinese hated this submissive hairstyle and rebelled rather than wear it. The Manchu enforced it. While Manchu women, like those of the Tang and the Mongols, were liberated and rode horses, Han Chinese women increasingly were confined to the home, binding their feet as a sign of submission and delicacy.

† In 1678, when he fell out with his Swedish allies, the Great Elector commandeered peasant sleighs to transport his troops. In 1929, the Great Sleigh Drive inspired a German officer, Heinz Guderian, to devise panzer warfare.

founded a republic, ruled by elected hetmans, on the Sech islands beyond the Dnieper rapids. They and the peasants, who spoke Ukrainian, suffered the dominance of Polish Catholic lords. A series of Orthodox Cossack rebellions against the Catholic Polish kings had sought recognition for their noble status. In the spring of 1648, the year the Muscovites reached the Pacific, a nobleman and Cossack officer, Bohdan Khmelnytsky, who had long served the king against the Ottomans and been captured and enslaved for two years, feuded with a Polish grandee over land and the Pole's beautiful Cossack wife – known as Helen of the Steppes. Khmelnytsky, elected hetman of the Cossacks, launched a rebellion that spread across Ukraine. In May, his Cossacks, in alliance with the Nogai cavalry sent by the Crimean Giray khans, defeated the Poles, and in Kyiv that December he declared himself hetman, prince of Ruthenia and the Sole Autocrat of Rus. His Cossack armies, joined by some rebel burgers and Ukrainian-speaking peasants, slaughtered Polish nobles and priests, and, in 1648 alone, 60,000 Jews who had lived safely there for centuries but were trapped between Catholic masters and Orthodox Cossacks.

Khmelnytsky's independent hetmanate scarcely lasted five years: Khmelnytsky needed a patron to protect his realm. Betrayed by the Crimean khan, he offered submission to the Ottoman sultan, who abandoned the hetman to the Tatars, forcing him to turn to Moscow.

In January 1654, the hetman swore allegiance to the Muscovite tsar Alexei, who along with his successors into modern times regarded Ukraine as a province – Little Russia – forever united with its fraternal Great Russia.* The Ottomans were not interested, because Constantinople was embroiled in its own crisis. There, the mad sultan's Magnificent Mother, Kösem, was facing a dilemma.

Could a mother kill her own son?

At first, Crazy Ibrahim, now thirty-three, was content to let his mother rule for him. Initially uninterested in women, possibly impotent, he turned to a charlatan spiritualist, Cinci Hoca, who prescribed

---

* The prize of adding the heart of Rus to his tsardom helped the second Romanov consolidate his weak new dynasty, and for future rulers, right up into the twenty-first century, Ukraine became essential – as historic realm and breadbasket – to a certain vision of Russia. Ukrainian nationalists later regarded the Cossack hetmanate as the first modern Ukrainian state though it was dominated by Cossack nobles. The crisis drew Tsar Alexei into Poland–Lithuania, which was shaken by what Poles called 'the Deluge' and never recovered its power. Khmelnytsky died and so did the story of the hetmanate. In 1667, Romanov tsar and Polish king divided Ukraine. Alexei got Kyiv and the lands on the left bank of the Dnieper, while the Cossacks remained autonomous under their hetmans; the south was ruled by the Crimean khan with key fortresses held by his Ottoman masters. There would not be another independent Ukraine until 1917.

aphrodisiacs and pornography. Ibrahim became priapic. When his mother was presented with an enslaved Russian girl called Turhan, Kösem gave her to the sultan, who quickly made her pregnant. But his depravities were expanding as the empire shrivelled: he favoured gigantic women and furs, preferably at the same time. He could only perform in a room full of sable, but he was so priapic that he tried to confine himself to one new girl a week on Fridays. Orders were sent out around the empire to find the biggest women. Then in 1644 the padishah started to assert himself, promoting to positions of power Cinci Hoca and his covin of bunglers, as well as a harem manageress.

He dispatched the cast of a cow's udders and vagina around the provinces in order to find a woman who matched. A sixteen-year-old Armenian girl, Maria, whom he nicknamed Sugar Cube, was extremely fat. In addition to the Russian-born Turhan, he now appointed another seven *hasekis* (consorts), including Sugar Cube, whom he renamed Sivekar Sultan, granting them the revenues of his richest provinces, Damascus and Egypt – a grave error.

Sugar Cube supposedly told Ibrahim that one of the concubines had been unfaithful. On hearing this he had 280 odalisques sewn into sacks and drowned in the Bosphoros; for this, Kösem invited Sugar Cube to dinner and secretly poisoned her.

The padishah's next error was catastrophic. Infuriated by Maltese pirates who had attacked a boat carrying Muslim pilgrims, Ibrahim ordered the navy to seize Crete, a Venetian province. The Venetians declared war, raided Ottoman Greece and blockaded the Bosphoros, causing food shortages and riots in Constantinople. The grand vizier and Kösem discussed deposing Ibrahim, who struck back, executing the vizier and banning his mother and his sisters from the harem. He was planning her murder, Nero-style.

On 8 August 1648, the Janissaries and the mob were so outraged by Ibrahim's ineptitude that they lynched the new vizier, who was kebabbed and sold in the streets – he was known ever after as Thousand Pieces. Ibrahim, now rightly paranoid, had Mehmed, his little son with Turhan, thrown into a cistern. His selfishness was risking the very dynasty. Kösem rescued the boy.

The viziers approached Kösem, remarkably calling her Umm al-Muminin – Mother of Muslims, the title of Muhammad's favourite wife – and hinting at the caliphal authority of the dynasty. 'You're not only the mother of the sultan; you're the mother of all true believers. Put an end to this chaos.' Eventually she agreed: 'Ultimately he'll kill you and me. We'll lose control of the government. I'll bring my grandson, Mehmed.'

She insisted that Ibrahim should not killed. The pashas arrested Ibrahim and girded Mehmed with the sword of Osman. Then they asked the Magnificent Mother to execute her son. Only a ruling by the empire's religious authority – the *sheikh ul-Islam* – could permit a mother to kill her son. The sheikh signed a *fatwa*: 'If there are two caliphs, kill one of them.' Kösem acquiesced.

As the pashas and concubines watched from the windows of the Topkapı, the Tongueless came silently for Ibrahim.

'Is there no one who's eaten my bread who'll take pity on me?' cried Ibrahim. 'These cruel men have come to kill me. Mercy!' The bowstrings tightened.

As the Ottomans were executing a king so were the English.

In London, Oliver Cromwell, in his crablike way, was debating what to do with his captive, King Charles. If anyone had suggested trying the king, he claimed, he would have called him 'the greatest traitor in the world'. The lord general Fairfax was uncomfortable with the idea, but the godly radicals in the army and probably his American chaplain, Hugh Peters, were proposing a trial. Cromwell looked to heaven: 'Since providence and necessity hath cast them upon it, he should pray God to bless their councils.' In other words, he believed it was time to try Charles. 'I cannot but submit to providence.'

INCORRUPTIBLE CROWN AND THE MAGNIFICENT MOTHER

In January 1649, Cromwell got what he wanted: the rump of the Parliament voted to exclude the Lords from government, to declare a 'Commonwealth and Free-State' and to try Charles. The heavily guarded king, diminutive and elegant in black silk, was brought to Westminster Hall and accused of 'a wicked design' – treason. Lord Fairfax was chosen to head the court, but then absented himself. 'I would know by what power I am called hither,' Charles demanded. 'Remember I am your king, your lawful king, think well upon it.' He refused to cooperate, but Cromwell had no more doubts. 'I tell you,' he said, 'we'll cut off his head with the crown upon it.' As the sixty-eight commissioners of the High Court of Justice sat, Hugh Peter orchestrated a chant, 'Execution! Justice!', though there were also shouts of 'God save the king.' When Fairfax was mentioned, his wife Anne shouted from the gallery, 'He had more wit than to be here,' and when the judges claimed to act for 'all the good people of England', she declared, 'No, nor the hundredth part of them,' and was removed. The commissioners voted that the 'tyrant, traitor, murderer, and public enemy to the good people of the nation' should be 'put to death by the severing of his head'.

'I'll have you hear a word, sir!' said Charles.

'No, sir!' replied the judge. 'Guard, withdraw your prisoner.'

When Cromwell became an advocate of his execution, his guidance was nothing less than divine: 'we have not been without our share of re-markable providences and appearances of the Lord. His presence hath been amongst us.' Without consulting them beforehand, 135 'commis-sioners' were named to try the king; forty-seven never turned up. At the end of the four-day trial, sixty-seven found him guilty but some resisted signing the death warrant. Cromwell signed third, then menaced the others: 'These that are gone in shall set their hands; I will have their hands *now*.' In one of his manic interludes, he roared with laughter as he and one of the commissioners splattered ink on each other's faces. Fifty-nine ultimately signed.

In St James's Palace, Charles realized he would never again see his eldest son, the prince of Wales, nor his second James, who had escaped parliamentary captivity in female dress. 'I'd rather you be Charles le Bon than Charles de Grand,' he wrote to the prince. 'Farewell, till we meet, if not on earth, yet in heaven.' But he asked to see his children, the thirteen-year-old Elizabeth and eight-year-old Henry. Their adieu was heartbreaking. As Elizabeth sobbed, Charles asked her 'not to grieve and torment yourself . . . for it should be a glorious death'; he suggested she console herself in reading, and sent his love to Henrietta Maria. 'His thoughts never strayed from her, his love should be the same to the last.' Then he hugged the girl: 'Sweetheart, you'll forget this.'

'I'll never forget this,' she replied, 'while I live.'

Then he invited Henry on to his knee. 'Sweetheart . . . they'll cut off my head and perhaps make you a king,' he said. 'But you must not be a king while your brothers Charles and James do live.'

'I'll be torn in half first,' replied the boy. Charles kissed both, crying with 'joy and love'. As they were led away, Charles, watching from the window, ran after them and kissed them again, then fell on his bed.

On 30 January 1649, a freezing afternoon, as Cromwell worshipped at a prayer meeting, Charles, aged forty-eight, hair and beard now white, donned two shirts, so that he would not be seen to shiver in the freezing temperatures, and a garter band with 412 diamonds, divided up his belongings for his children (and a gold watch for the daughter of his never-forgotten friend, Buckingham).

'Come, let us go,' he said, before walking through St James's Park, surrounded by troops, drums a-beating, into the rambling Whitehall

Palace and then out through the Banqueting House, with its ceilings by his friend Rubens, on to the scaffold. There waited 'Young Gregory' Brandon, hereditary headman, and his assistant, both in wigs, sailors' garb and fishnet masks, with the axe. As Charles addressed the crowd, a soldier twice knocked against the axe. 'Hurt not the axe that may hurt me,' Charles said, before concluding: 'I go from a corruptible crown to an incorruptible crown where no disturbance can be. It's a good exchange.' Then he laid his head on the block and stretched out his hands to show he was ready. Brandon cut clean. The assistant raised the head: 'Behold the head of a traitor!' The soldiers cheered and clapped; others stood in respectful silence. The assistant – who may have been the American preacher Peter – dropped the head, bruising the face. Soldiers and spectators jostled to cut locks of royal hair, dip kerchiefs in the blue blood and chisel the scaffold for keepsakes.* Days later the news reached his family. At the Louvre in Paris, where the queen was dining, she sat 'without words' for a long time, while in The Hague their son Charles realized his father was dead when he was addressed as 'Your Majesty'. He sobbed.

In Constantinople, Kösem ruled for her seven-year-old grandson, Mehmed IV. Presiding over the councils from behind a screen, in the presence of the boy padishah, the Magnificent Mother tore a strip off male viziers. 'Have I made you vizier to spend your time in gardens and vineyards?' came the voice from behind the curtain. 'Devote yourself to the affairs of the empire and let me hear no more of your cavortings.' But the sultan had his own mother Turhan, who had been trained by Kösem and then presented to Ibrahim. She aspired to be regent and plotted against Kösem, who in turn planned to depose the boy and enthrone another grandson with a less ambitious mother. But fatally Kösem had a spy in her own retinue, who informed Turhan of her mistress's plan. Now it was a race to see which woman would kill the other first.

'Thanks to God, I've lived through four reigns and I have governed for a long time,' Kösem told the council. 'The world will neither be improved nor destroyed by my death.' Turhan moved first. On 2 September 1651, the sixty-three-year-old Kösem was hunted down through the palace as a loyal slave tried to save her by crying, 'I am the *valide*.'

Kösem hid in a cupboard, but her dress was spotted. As she was

---

* Among those watching the execution and celebrating it was a St Paul's schoolboy, Samuel Pepys, who later served Charles's son. 'Thus it was my chance to see the King beheaded at Whitehall,' he wrote eleven years later. At the time, he supported the execution, an attitude he came to regret: 'I was a great Roundhead when I was a boy.'

strangled by a curtain, she fought so desperately that blood came out of her ears and nose. When the news got out, the people shut down Constantinople for three days to mourn the Magnificent Mother.

A new family were taking control in London – and they were not royal. The body of Charles I, its head sewn on to the neck, lay embalmed in St James's Palace where it was shown to paying viewers. Cromwell was said to have gazed upon it, murmuring, 'If he had not been king, he'd have lived longer.'

THE BOWELS OF CHRIST:
PROTECTOR OLIVER AND PRINCE DICK

The new republic was embattled. The army under Cromwell and his conservative officers clearly dominated – but its ranks seethed with dangerously radical ideals of democracy. In Ireland, Catholic rebels attacked Protestant settlers. The parliamentarians had been terrified of a royal Irish army crushing England, but English colonizers had long treated the Irish as semi-barbarian, outside the usual rules of warfare. The fact that they were also Catholic placed them beyond redemption. Cromwell crossed to Ireland. In a frenzy of self-righteous hatred, he stormed Drogheda, burning soldiers sheltering in a church; priests had their heads shattered after surrendering; captured units were decimated; 3,000 were killed. 'This is a righteous judgement of God upon these barbarous wretches,' Cromwell explained, 'who have imbrued their hands in so much innocent blood.'

Charles II, aged twenty, now landed in Scotland where the Scots under Leven, alarmed by Cromwell, switched sides. Fairfax finally resigned as commander-in-chief, and Cromwell was appointed captain-general. Warning, 'I beseech you, in the bowels of Christ, think it possible you may be mistaken,' Cromwell smashed the Scots at Dunbar, whereupon Charles marched south with another army. Cromwell gave chase, defeating the boy at Worcester in 'a crowning mercy' that fortified his invincible prestige as what his Latin secretary, a half-blind poet named John Milton, called 'our chief of men'. Cromwell ordered Parliament to agree on a new British state, but when they resisted his management he barged into the chamber in a fit of fury, ranting like a madman at 'whoremasters': 'I'll put an end to your prating. You are no parliament.' He then summoned soldiers: 'Call them in!' Seeing the Speaker in his chair, he snarled, 'Fetch him down!', and seized the ceremonial mace. 'What shall we do with this bauble? Here, take it away!' Next, addressing the amazed parliamentarians, he declared, 'It's you who forced me to do this for I have sought the Lord night and day.' Cromwell disdained Parliament: 'There wasn't so much as the barking of a dog!'

As one radical general proposed a theocracy that he called the Sanhedrin of Saints – an optimistic name for any group of politicians – the gifted general John Lambert crafted a mixed monarchy under Cromwell, a council of state and an elected parliament. At Westminster Hall, on 16 December 1653, wearing black, escorted by his old ally Warwick and other peers, he was sworn in as 'His Highness Lord Protector'. He was granted royal apartments in Hampton Court and Whitehall, he was to be greeted with a raised hat like a king, his wife was to be addressed as 'Your Highness', his sons and daughters were to be princes and princesses, his decrees were to be signed 'Oliver P' – and he could name his own successor. Oliver's court lacked Stuart splendour, nor would there be a whisper of Jacobean scandal, but it was not completely joyless either: Oliver enjoyed the company of his bevy of cheerful daughters and the glamorous countess of Dysart. He ruled through a coterie of generals and relatives; one daughter married two top generals; two married Cromwellian peers; and the fourth married into the greatest puritan–colonial dynasty – that of the earl of Warwick.* Both his sons, Richard, known as Dick, and Henry, joined the council of state, but the future depended on Dick, chinless, long-faced and extravagant, drowning in debt – very different from His Highness Oliver, who tried to groom him, advising, 'Seek the Lord and His face continually.' He preferred the capable Henry, but Dick was the eldest, so Dick must succeed.

Oliver, like many dictators, sought power yet pitied himself for attaining it: 'You see how I am employed. I need pity. I know what I feel. Great place and business in the world is not worth the looking after; I should have no comfort but my hope is in the Lord's presence. I have not sought these things; I have been called to them by the Lord.' Oliver was just God's 'poor worm and weak servant'.

The 'worm' was now almost king of a new Israel: 'You're as like the forming of God as ever people were,' he told his new Parliament. 'You're at the edge of promises and prophecies.' This Second Coming could happen only when biblical prophecies were honoured, the Jews returned

* The secretary of the new council of state was John Milton; one of the council's clerks was a young republican: Samuel Pepys, who owed his job to his patron, Edward Montagu, a genial but competent Huntingdon grandee whose mother was a Pepys. Montagu, who now owned Hinchingbrook, the grand pile of Sir Oliver Cromwell, the protector's grandfather, was an old friend of Cromwell with whom he had fought at Naseby but retired to his estates for the second bout of civil war, recalled by Cromwell to join his house of peers and council of state and command his fleet.

to Zion and then either converted or destroyed in the End of Days. It was this role in cosmic providence that endeared the Jews, long banned from England, to Cromwell, who met the Dutch rabbi Menasseh ben Israel and began the process that allowed them to return.

While he acted to seize control of the American colonies,* Oliver envisioned a sacred offensive against the Catholic Habsburgs to establish an English empire. This was inspired by Thomas Gage, a Catholic monk turned Protestant avenger who proposed a 'Western Design' – the conquest of the Spanish Caribbean and south America.

'God has brought us where we are,' said Oliver, 'to consider the work we may do in the world as well as at home' – and providence had never denied him a victory. Over 25,000 white settlers had already flocked to the colony of Barbados with its new, lucrative sugar plantations, which were worked by white indentured workers (many of them deported Irish Catholics, others impoverished children), but they were now replaced by African slaves. The English planters were soon outnumbered and now confronted a fear of slave rebellions, along with the problem that slavery did not exist under English law. Their answer was the Act for Better Ordering and Governing of Negroes, which would be the cruel basis for all American and Caribbean slave legislation, stating that 'being brutish slaves', they had no rights; punishment for disobedience would be whipping for a first offence, nose-slitting, whipping and branding for a second; and if 'any Negro under punishment by his master unfortunately shall suffer in life or member, no person shall be liable to any fine therefore'.

As he planned his Western Design, Oliver found himself at war with his Catholic enemies, the Spanish, but also with his traditional Protestant allies, the Dutch, over trade and the support for the Stuarts from Charles II's brother-in-law William, prince of Orange. Keen to make peace with these fellow Protestants, he proposed a political union with the United Provinces, then, forming an alliance with Cardinal Mazanin of France, he unleashed his fleet against the Spanish. Now he dispatched his 'Invincible Armada' under the joint command of an irascible republican, Robert Venables, and a vigorous young gentleman, William Penn. The timing was good: the Habsburgs were struggling as English troops landed on the rich sugar isle Hispaniola.

* Among those driven out of the Anglican Church during Cromwell's reign was Lawrence Washington, a minister sacked from his parish, accused of being a 'frequenter of alehouses', who now left for America. In 1656, his son John Washington traded tobacco and, after being shipwrecked in Virginia, voraciously gathered land, importing indentured servants to capitalize on the law that gave each fifty acres, as well as slaves, was elected to the House of Burgesses and commanded the militia, fighting Native Americans. George Washington's great-grandfather left 8,500 acres.

GANGA ZUMBA – KING OF PALMARES

The invasion was a fiasco. The soldiers fought 'in a most sad and miserable manner', admitted General Venables, 'tormented with heat, hunger and thirst'. Instead in May 1655 they seized Santiago (Jamaica), which was still owned by the Columbuses. As the Spanish resisted and the local Maroons supported the English, the first governor invited the Brethren of the Sea, English pirates, to base themselves in Jamaica and raid Spanish ports. Led by a Welsh adventurer, Henry Morgan, they turned their headquarters, Cagway (soon Port Royal), into the world's sleaziest, gaudiest, deadliest stew.

The English now started to accelerate the import of African slaves for their Jamaican and Barbadian plantations.* But at home the failure of the godly empire stunned Oliver: God had withdrawn his blessing from this nation of sinners. Cromwell sought to correct the moral venality of his people, ruling through his major-generals, who closed taverns and banned ungodly dancing, cockfighting, football, bear-baiting. Christmas remained cancelled. But England was about to receive an opportunity thanks to the modest new king of Portugal, João IV, who struck back against the Dutch. Their *Groot Desseyn* had won them an Atlantic nexus from Elmina and Luanda to Manhattan and Brazil, where the brutal efficiency of the Calvinist Dutch slave masters had alienated white nobles and mixed-race Amerindians, Catholic slave masters and slave hunters who led an insurrection in Pernambuco. The war, fought in Brazil and Angola, was viciously multi-ethnic: both sides recruited Amerindians and Afro-Lusitanian auxiliaries; the Portuguese recruited slaves, who were promised freedom in return for service.

In February 1649, João's multiracial army, led by an Afro-Brazilian called Henrique Dias, a freed son of slaves, entitled Governor of all Creoles, Blacks and Mulattoes, and a Potiguaran Amerindian, Felipe 'Poti' Camarão,† defeated the Dutch at Guararapes. Then the Afro-Brazilians sailed across the Atlantic to restore Portuguese rule in Africa under an Afro-Lusitanian commander, Salvador Correia de Sá. During fifteen years of war, the Dutch, their Kongo ally Garcia and Queen Nzinga of

---

* Peter Beckford, who arrived in Jamaica aged twenty, became the richest English slave owner, leaving twenty Jamaican estates, 1,500 slaves and £1,500,000 earned by exporting sugar.

† Poti hinted at the complexity of the Atlantic world: 'Why do I make war against people of my own blood,' he warned a rival Amerindian fighting for the Dutch. 'Come to me and I will forgive you. I will make you one with your ancient culture again. Those that stay there will be destroyed.' The king ennobled the Amerindian Poti but may have resisted promoting the black Dias.

Ndongo fought back, both sides fielding cannibal Imbangala militias. The Portuguese retook Luanda; retreating into the interior, Garcia of Kongo and Nzinga of Ndongo survived, both dying peacefully, while the Imbangala under a *jaga* (king) named Kasanje formed their own kingdom which lasted for two centuries. But now came a settling of scores.

In 1665, at Mbwila, Garcia's son, Manikongo António, backed by the Dutch, fought the Portuguese. Among his commanders was a royal princess, Aqualtune, two of her sons, Ganga Zumba and Ganga Zona, and her daughter Sabina. The Bakongo were routed, António killed, the princess and family enslaved and sent to Brazil. But that was not the end of the story, for they would become the rulers of America's biggest rebel slave kingdom.

Slaves had resisted from the start, but revolts were crushed ferociously. The other choice was to 'head to the bush', but they needed somewhere to go. Slave catchers – *capitães do mato* – were dismal manhunters, righteously protected by St Anthony, paid by masters to retrieve or kill escaped slaves, travelling with their leather bags in which they stowed the slave's head to be presented for payment. But since early in the century runaway Brazilian Maroons had created *quilombos* – rebel slave communities – named after the Imbangala war camps of Angola. In these *macombos* – hideaways – ex-slaves built villages, lived on palms, beans and chickens, and became expert guerrillas, using guns and *capoeira*, a discipline that is both dance and martial art. Early in the century, forty slaves from one estate had fled and formed a *quilombo* near Recife at the eastern extremity of Brazil that they named Palmares after the palms they ate. Known as Little Angola since so many Palmarians were Bakongo, its elected leaders were often princes from Africa whose prestige continued into their slave lives. When the Dutch were defeated, the Portuguese tried to crush Palmares, launching over twenty attacks, all of which failed. 'It is harder,' reflected a Portuguese governor, 'to defeat a *quilombo* than the Dutch.'

When Princess Aqualtune and her sons Ganga Zumba and Ganga Zona were enslaved, they were placed on a sugar plantation, Santa Rita, in Pernambuco, north-eastern Brazil, not far from Palmares where their sister Sabina, enslaved earlier, was already living. Soon after their arrival, Ganga Zumba and his family escaped to Palmares where this grandson of a *manikongo*, aged around thirty-five, an experienced fighter, was chosen as king. His name is unknown – Ganga Zumba is a title based on the Kikongo for great lord – but he placed his brothers and his mother Aqualtune in charge of the different villages as he repeatedly defeated Portuguese attacks, attracting more rebel slaves until he was ruling 30,000 people (Rio had 7,000 citizens) and a territory the size of Portugal. He held court in a small palace with three wives (two black and one mixed-race), guards and courtiers, advised as in Africa by older females, his mother and a matriarch named Acotirene.

The king was greeted with kneeling and clapping as in Kongo. Each town, fortified with palisades and traps, had a chapel with a priest, yet this was a hybrid creole Catholicism which tolerated polygamy and Bakongo rites. Ganga Zumba promoted his nephew Zumbi. While the dates and relationships between the family are uncertain, Zumbi, born in Palmares in 1655 before his uncles arrived, had been captured on a raid by the Portuguese and raised by a priest António de Melo. Baptized as Francisco and taught Portuguese and Latin, he impressed his teacher with 'a skill which I never imagined in the black race, and which I have very rarely seen among whites'. At fifteen, he escaped back to the *quilombo* where he took the name of Zumbi, linked to the immortal nocturnal spirits in the Bakongo cult of ancestors. Now his uncle appointed him commander of the Palmarian army.

By the late 1670s, Zumba's Palmares kingdom was famed throughout the Americas, encouraging other rebellions. In 1677, Ganga Zumba was wounded in an assault, in which some of his family were captured. The next year, the Pernambuco governor Pedro Almeida, offered a peace deal in which those born in Palmares would remain free if they recognized the crown, while recent runaways would be returned to their masters.

Exhausted by fifteen years of war and twenty campaigns, Ganga Zumba decided to negotiate, but his nephew Zumbi opposed the return of any runaways. When Zumba signed the agreement, Zumbi, advised by his wife Dandara, poisoned his uncle and was elected king.

THE WORLD SEIZERS: SHIVAJI, AURANGZEB AND THE POETESS

Zumbi repeatedly repelled Portuguese attacks, almost one a year, yet he had not forgotten his priest teacher, secretly visiting him three times at great personal risk. Even Almeida admired Zumbi, a 'black man of singular valour, great spirit and rare constancy, the overseer of the rest, because his industry, judgement and strength to our people serve as an obstacle; to his, an example'.

In September 1657, as the Ganga dynasty ruled Palmares,* the world's

---

* Zumbi ruled for around twenty years. But in 1694 around 9,000 Portuguese musketeers and Amerindians led by the harshest *bandeirante*, Domingos Jorge Velho, bombarded and stormed Palmares. Dandara was captured but committed suicide; Zumbi led a breakout

greatest potentate Shahjahan did not appear at the balcony for the *jharokha* at the Red Fort: he was ill.

After Mumtaz's death, Shahjahan had consoled himself in a priapic spree, powered by aphrodisiacs, ranging through his harem but also seducing wives of his courtiers, often picked up at palace bazaars that he patrolled, accompanied by two Tatar concubines who noted his choices. Later his beautiful Mumtazesque daughter Jahanara arranged his assignations, an intimacy that led to gossip that she also became his lover. Of his four sons, he favoured the first, Darashukoh, who was diffident, naive and innovative, challenging religious orthodoxy as Akbar had done. But this offended strict Muslims – such as the third son. Aurangzeb, fierce, morose, abstemious, who now served as his father's roving paladin. Starting in 1636, aged only seventeen, he tried to expand from their Afghan base of Kabul and, failing there, he turned to Deccan.

Aurangzeb was married to an Iranian princess, Dilras Banu Begum, with whom he had five children.* Then in 1653 the prim ascetic noticed Hira Bai Zainabadi, a singer-dancer in his aunt's household, climbing a tree to pick a juicy mango, 'a heart-robbing movement'. Aurangzeb 'obtained her possession from his indulgent aunt and . . . he gave her his heart'. He poured her wine but refused to drink himself, until one day she 'put a glass in his hand and urged him to drink. Though he begged and prayed, she had no pity and the prince was about to drink when the sly girl drank it.'

'It was to test your love,' she laughingly told the mortified Aurangzeb.

When just a year later Hira Bai died, Aurangzeb was heartbroken, but, he reflected, 'God had been gracious to him by putting an end to that dancing girl's life.' He emerged from the affair ice-cold.

Now that Shahjahan was ill, Darashukoh claimed the regency, sparking a ferocious family war. Aurangzeb watched and waited while the other two brothers, Shahshuja and Murad, declared themselves padishah. Shahjahan wanted to leave his sickbed to persuade his sons to return to their provinces, but the overconfident Darashukoh refused.

---

and vanished, adding to his reputation for immortality. Betrayed in 1695, Zumbi was mutilated, his head packed in salt and then displayed in Recife to prove his night spirit was really dead.

* Dilras Banu Begum was so intelligent and haughty that even he admired her 'imperiousness, but to the end of her life I always loved her'. Together they had three girls and two sons; the eldest was a talented princess, Zebunnissa, who wrote poetry under the pseudonym Makhfi (Secret); their son Azzam became heir apparent. Dilras died just before Aurangzeb became emperor, inspiring his most sumptuous monument, the Bibi Ka Maqbara in Aurangabad, designed by the son of the architect of the Taj Mahal. He also built the Pearl Mosque in the Red Fort of Shahjahanabad.

Their sister Jahanara tried to mediate, until Aurangzeb discovered his father was colluding with Darashukoh. In June 1658, Aurangzeb besieged Shahjahan in the Agra fort, cutting off the water and reducing the old emperor to pathetic poetry:

My son my hero . . . yesterday I had an army of 900,000,
Today I'm in need of a pitcher of water.

'As we reap, we sow,' wrote Aurangzeb on his father's letter. 'You did not love me,' he later told his father. Shahjahan surrendered. Aurangzeb invited Murad to a boozy feast. Sleeping it off, Murad was arrested then later murdered. While Darashukoh fled, Shahshuja was defeated and escaped to Burma, where he perished.

'Darashukoh must be exterminated,' said Aurangzeb. In August 1659, Darashukoh was betrayed and then beheaded, his son Sulaymanshukoh forced to drink opium until he overdosed. Aurangzeb had Darashukoh's headless body paraded on an elephant. When the head was delivered to him, Aurangzeb refused to look – 'As I didn't wish to see this infidel's head in his lifetime, I don't now' – but it is possible he sent it to their father, who resided at the Agra fort with Jahanara. Aurangzeb insisted that he only assumed 'the perilous burden of crown out of necessity and not free will'. He lectured his father: 'When you fell ill, Darashukoh usurped power to promote Hinduism and destroy Islam,' while he himself had won because 'I've always been a faithful defender of the Quran.' His brothers had to die, 'due to the demands of justice'.

Emperor at forty, Aurangzeb became Alamgir – World Seizer. Under him, House Tamerlane reached its Indian zenith. Alamgir at first enjoyed music and patronized musicians. He fell for an enslaved teenaged Georgian concubine-dancer, Udaipuri, whom he had inherited from his murdered brother Darashukoh. His favourite daughter, the poetess Zebunnissa, on his succession was permitted considerable freedom, but she became too independent. 'Oh Makhfi, it is the path of love and alone you must go,' she wrote. She was also having a public affair with a young nobleman and communicating with her mutinous brothers. Alamgir imprisoned her for twenty years.

This micromanaging puritan tried to limit sensuality, banning women from wearing tight trousers and in Kashmir ordering people to wear drawers instead of nothing. As his court became more rigorous and orderly, he lectured his son Azzam, 'Fear the sighs of the oppressed,' and warned his vizier, 'Oppression will cause darkness on Judgement Day.' Alamgir was probably the hardest-working ruler in

Indian history, barely sleeping, poring over his paperwork: 'I was sent into the world by providence to live and labour, not for myself but for others.' Often reflecting on power, he was a Machiavellian – 'One can't rule without deception' – and violence.* 'The greatest conquerors,' he claimed, 'aren't the greatest kings,' but this scion of Tamerlane lived for conquest: 'When you have an enemy to destroy, spare nothing, anything is permissible . . . that can deliver success.'

For all his talk of justice, Alamgir restored dominion over Punjab by executing the Sikh guru Tegh Bahadur, crushed Afghan resistance, then devoted his reign to conquest of the south, where his ambitions collided with those of a charismatic Hindu warrior.

In 1660, Alamgir sent an army to destroy a descendant of one of Ambar's generals, a Hindu warlord named Shivaji, who based at Pune rebelled against the sultan of Bijapur and started to craft a kingdom in the Deccan. In 1659, at a meeting with a Bijapuri general, Shivaji used a tiger claw in his sleeve to eviscerate his opponent, then smashed his army. He stressed that the Mughals were Turkish foreigners. Instead he aspired to create a *Hindavi swarajya* – a Hindu Indian kingdom. When he routed Alamgir's armies, the emperor invited him to court, hoping to co-opt him and his son Sambhaji with the traditional blandishments, only to humiliate then imprison the proud Marathas. While he debated whether to kill Shivaji or appoint him governor of Kabul, the Tiger of Deccan was daily sending out baskets of sweets for the poor. One day he and his son escaped in their sweet baskets and returned to Deccan to conquer their own empire.

Soon after Alamgir seized the world, the century's greatest English ruler fell ill.

QUEEN DICK

In September 1658, Oliver Cromwell, now fifty-nine and poleaxed by the agonizing death from cancer of his favourite daughter Betty, took to

---

* Alamgir is now notorious among Hindu nationalists in India as an Islamic enforcer and persecutor of Hindus. Indeed he saw himself as an Islamic warrior, but also as the all-Indian padishah, promoting more Hindu officers (31.6 per cent) than his father (22.4 per cent) and refusing to sack non-Muslims: 'What connection have earthly affairs with religion?' He corresponded with Rajputs and patronized Hindu temples – but if the temples were used by rebels, he destroyed them. His predations were conducted for political and not religious purposes. But against his sister Jahanara's advice, he reintroduced the *jizyah* tax for non-Muslims, a measure to raise revenue but one clearly aimed at Hindus. His repression of any Hindu or other resistance was merciless.

his bed suffering blood poisoning from a kidney infection. His generals planned the succession around his deathbed.

In March 1657, the Speaker of the House had again offered Oliver the crown. His eldest son Dick, who would succeeded to the crown, was uncertain. But the younger son Henry, lord lieutenant of Ireland, good-looking and competent, regarded it as 'a gaudy feather in the hat of authority'. Cromwell chain-smoked as he mulled over the idea, which he too called 'this feather in a cap'. He decided to accept it – until he took a walk in St James's Park and encountered three of his republican generals who told him they would resign if he did. 'I can't undertake this government with that title of king,' Oliver told Parliament. 'God hath blasted this title.' Instead, in June, he was invested with a quasi-royal panoply, a procession with the sword of state, borne by Warwick, and a sceptre, riding through London with his eldest son Dick by his side. When he fell ill, he prevaricated about naming his successor.*

'Tell me, is it possible to fall from grace?' he asked those around him, adding the certainty: 'Faith is the covenant, the only support.' As he sank into a coma, the generals asked him to name his successor: Dick? 'Yes,' he whispered, rallying in the morning to tell his children, 'Go on cheerfully,' before meeting his maker.

Dick, thirty-one years old, was at the bedside along with the Protector's son-in-law General Charles Fleetwood and brother-in-law John Desborough, who represented the army. Henry Cromwell held Ireland. That evening the council visited Dick and appointed him head of state. Dick genially accepted. 'The Most Serene and Renowned Oliver, late Lord Protector, having in his lifetime declared and appointed the most noble and illustrious Lord Richard, eldest son of his said late Highness, to succeed him in the government of this nation,' the Cromwellians on 9 September 1658 declared him the rightful Protector. Charles II, watching from Holland, despaired that he would ever return. But Dick, unvarnished by charisma, unguided by experience, unblessed by providence, lacked authority.

While the Cromwellians supported Dick's protectorate, many of the

---

* It was now that George Villiers, the young duke of Buckingham, son of James I's favourite, returned to England, earning a living as a masked busker, performing skits and songs as an actor-singer, on the streets and on stage at Charing Cross, demonstrating that Cromwellian London was not totally grim – but it was a unique role for a duke. Politician, lover, playwright, actor and murderer, his career would be almost as extraordinary as his father's. Next, he headed north on his real mission – to court and marry Mary Fairfax, daughter and heiress of the parliamentary general Fairfax, who had been granted all the Buckingham estates. Buckingham married Mary, but Cromwell ordered his arrest. Fairfax got him released, just in time to enjoy his estates in the Restoration.

generals, diehard puritan republicans, wanted a saintly republic. Dick raised army pay but, short of cash, he launched a coup to seize control of the army, dissolved the council of officers and summoned a new Parliament, but it failed. In the event he could control neither the assembly nor the generals, who forced its dismissal and recalled the remains of the Parliament that had been elected in 1640. His French allies offered to invade and back him, but crushed between generals and Cromwellians, republicans and monarchists, with zealots on both sides, 'Richard P' – now nicknamed Queen Dick – floundered, musing that he would never spill blood to hold power 'which is a burden to me'. His debts were so great that Parliament had to grant him immunity from arrest and agree his pension. There is only one thing more contemptible than a competent dictatorship and that is an incompetent one. On 25 May 1659, after eight months in office, Dick was deposed and a junta, the Committee of Safety, took power. As General Lambert, popular with the army, hoped to rule himself, the Cromwellian commander in Scotland, George Monck, aided by Black Tom Fairfax, defeated the radical general and marched south, secretly advising Charles II to declare reconciliation and then return.

Tumbledown Dick, lingering in Whitehall and besieged by debtors, appealed for Monck's help: 'as I can't but think myself unworthy of great things so you will not think me worthy of utter destruction'. As Oliver's secretary Milton wrote *Paradise Lost* about the Fall in the Garden of Eden, many Cromwellians, including the clerk Samuel Pepys, negotiated pardons and rewards. Oliver's naval commander and friend Edward Montagu changed sides with the fleet, and with his young cousin Pepys onboard sailed to collect Charles II from Holland. Monck protected Dick, who wrote sadly that 'out of town' was 'the most proper place for persons that are out of employment' and fled to the continent.* By then, in May 1660, Charles II, Dick's junior by four years, had disembarked at Dover. England celebrated Restoration.

The Planet King must have envied England its jovial young prince. Philip IV's need of sons would lead to the incestuous marriage that would spawn the most freakish tragedy of the dynasty.

---

* Leaving his wife with the children in England, Dick travelled for twenty years, using the alias John Clarke, 'drawing landscapes' and avoiding assassination, until he was able to return in 1680, unmolested by Charles II. Almost outliving the Stuart dynasty, Dick died in 1712 aged eighty-five, England's longest-lived head of state until Elizabeth II.

Manchus and Shivajis, Bourbons, Stuarts and Villiers

VELÁZQUEZ, BERNINI AND ARTEMISIA

Long married to a French princess, Philip saw seven of their eight children die, followed by their mother. The monarchy had no heir. In 1649, Philip, now forty-four, married his pious fourteen-year-old niece, Mariana, who was only four years older than her stepdaughter María Teresa and heroically spent the next decade giving birth to babies who died. Yet the grinding mission to procreate went on as Velázquez recorded the development of the family.

Philip often spent hours in Velázquez's studio watching him paint. Velázquez was fascinated by his baroque peers: Rubens befriended him and the two visited the Titians at the Escorial. But Velázquez longed to make an aesthetic pilgrimage to Rome, drawn there by the other baroque titan.

'You are made for Rome,' Pope Urban VIII told a young sculptor's son, Gian-Lorenzo Bernini, 'and Rome is made for you.' Urban had been introduced to Bernini when he was still a cardinal. 'This child,' Paul V told him, 'will be the Michelangelo of his age.' Now Urban appointed him to reinvigorate Rome. 'It's a great fortune for you, O Cavaliere, to see Cardinal Maffeo Barberini made pope,' said Urban, 'but our fortune's even greater to have Cavaliere Bernini alive in our pontificate.' Bernini agreed.

As papal curator and chief architect of St Peter's, Bernini delivered the flashy gigantism of the basilica's colonnade and the auric gaudiness of the baldachin inside – and, for later popes, the fountain of the four rivers on his Piazza Navona. His faith was embellished with creamy sexuality: his St Teresa was sculpted writhing in ecstasy, but the swagger of his Rome concealed a sexual brutality. Bernini had an affair with a married woman, Costanza Bonucelli, whom he adored and sculpted, but he was so outraged when she slept with his wild brother Luigi (a monster who later anally raped a young studio assistant) that he ordered a servant to slash her face with a razor blade. The furious pope forced

Bernini to marry a young Roman woman at once and the razor-slashing servant was imprisoned – but so was Costanza, the victim, for adultery.

Bernini's crime was forgiven. His contemporary, Artemisia Gentileschi, also an artist's child recognized as a prodigy, was another victim treated as a criminal. Her father Orazio was son and brother of painters who had painted for Henrietta Maria in London and many other royal clients. In 1611, Artemisia, seventeen years old and a virgin with curly auburn hair, full lips and a wide face, was painting with the artist Agostino Tassi, twenty years older, when he and a male helper raped her, aided by a female tenant.* Tassi, who had been tried for incest and would later be tried for trying to kill a pregnant courtesan, promised marriage but then changed his mind, at which her father brought charges. Gentileschi had to relive the agony by giving testimony. Tassi, devious and violent, tried to suborn witnesses and taint her as a whore. Astonishingly, she was then taken to visit Tassi in prison and tortured with a thumbscrew to test her veracity. '*È vero, è vero, è vero*,' she repeated. 'It's true!'

'You're lying in your throat,' Tassi shouted. He was found guilty, though his sentence was later overturned.

Artemisia – passionate, independent, inconsistent – rebuilt her life. Soon after her ordeal, she painted *Susanna and the Elders*, showing a half-naked girl disdaining the ogling elder men; her later works *Judith and Holofernes* and *Salomé with the Head of John the Baptist* depict women decapitating men. They were typical subjects for their time, but all gleam with the glee of redemptive vengeance. Moving to Florence, where the Medici and the poet Michelangelo Buonarroti (the artist's great-nephew) became her patrons, Gentileschi married a Florentine painter with whom she had children – but he also managed her business and colluded in her romance with the aristocratic Francesco Maringhi. Both lover and patron, Maringhi was the love of her life. Now in her fifties, this *donna forte* grew in confidence: 'I will show Your Illustrious Lordship,' she wrote to her Neapolitan patron Antonio Ruffo, 'what a woman can do,' adding, 'You will find the spirit of Caesar in the soul of a woman.' In 1649, when Philip allowed Velázquez to go to Italy for a second visit, to buy and study art, both Bernini and Gentileschi were in their prime – and he met and painted the new pope, Innocent

---

* 'He threw me on to the edge of the bed,' she recalled, 'pushing me with a hand on my breast, and he put a knee between my thighs to prevent me from closing them. Lifting my clothes, he placed a hand with a handkerchief on my mouth to keep me from screaming. I scratched his face and pulled his hair and, before he penetrated me again, I grasped his penis so tight that I even removed a piece of flesh.' Afterwards she grabbed a knife and shouted, 'I want to kill you because you have shamed me!' 'Here I am,' sneered Tassi. She threw the knife but it missed.

X.* Velázquez imbibed the sensuality of Italy, leaving a child behind. In Italy or soon afterwards, the Habsburg courtier painted *Venus and Cupid*, his back view of a lushly beautiful woman who admires herself in a mirror that reflects her face but should reflect the view between her legs.

Velázquez returned to a crestfallen Philip IV, who promoted him to director of palace spectacles, in which role he redesigned the pantheon of Habsburg coffins at El Escorial† while still painting the now sad, saggy face of the Planet King until he banned more portraits. When Queen Mariana delivered a daughter, Margarita, Velázquez recorded the development of this very Habsburgian child whom Philip called 'my joy'. Philip gave him the Main Room of his dead heir's apartments in the Alcázar, where he spent much time and which inspired his *Las Meninas* – the Ladies-in-Waiting – painted around 1656. At its centre is the flaxen-haired, cheerful Margarita herself, joined by two *meninas*, three courtiers, her dog, two female dwarves, a self-portrait of the artist – and Philip and Mariana watching: the realities and deceptions of court alongside universal themes of family.

Now Velázquez, finally knighted by the king, produced a different sort of masterpiece. On 7 June 1660, at the Isle of Pheasants on the French border, he stage-managed a marriage – the handover of Philip's daughter María Teresa to the young French king who would dominate Europe for the next fifty years.

ANNE AND MAZARIN

Louis XIV, aged twenty, could not wait to consummate his marriage,‡ but he had not wanted to marry at all. He had been tutored in statesmanship and intrigue by his glamorous Habsburg mother Anne and Julio Mazarini, an Italian priest transformed into a professional Frenchman as Cardinal Jules Mazarin.

It was Mazarin who had negotiated the Habsburg marriage. He had

---

* Velázquez was accompanied by a slave, Juan de Pareja, son of an African mother and Spanish father, his studio assistant, who himself showed talent and became a painter in his own right (his *Calling of St Matthew* is in the Prado). In Italy, Velázquez manumitted Juan and painted him.

† During the works, Philip enjoyed a macabre audience with the family. 'I saw the body of Emperor Charles V,' he wrote, 'and although he died 96 years ago, his body was whole. In this it can be seen that Our Lord has repaid all that he did in defence of religion.'

‡ The ailing Philip IV, lacking a male heir, returned to Madrid with Velázquez, who soon after sickened with fever and died. 'I am crushed,' said Philip.

been selected and trained by Louis XIII's minister Cardinal Richelieu, whose far-sighted finesse he shared, to which he added an Italianate flamboyance and shameless venality all his own. On his deathbed Louis XIII had appointed Anne his son's regent, Mazarin his godfather.

They were the most important people in Louis's life, and they were almost certainly lovers. In their surviving letters, peppered with secret signs and codes that semaphored love and sex, Mazarin reflects, 'Never has there been a friendship approaching what I have for you,' and 'I am till the last breath ***,' while the queen, admitting she could not put much in writing, proclaimed, 'I will always be as I ought to be, whatever happens . . . a million times till the last breath.' Their codename for the little king was the Confidant. Unusually for a royal family, Louis was extremely close to his mother, and to her lover, whom he adored like a father. Royalty can never trust their own families; they have to make their own.

Yet as the war against the Habsburgs bled the state, France was hit by five years of turbulence – La Fronde, named after the slings used by the mobs to smash the windows of their enemies – as bad harvests, exorbitant taxes and royal corruption unleashed Bourbon princes, overmighty grandees, Parisian mobs, unpaid soldiers and parlements (the ancient law courts which also registered royal edicts). At its worst, mobs terrified the boy-king who along with his mother and Mazarin was forced to flee Paris. That the Fronde coincided with the execution of Charles I and the enthronement of Cromwell only heightened that terror. The humiliations never left Louis. After Mazarin had fled into temporary exile (accompanied by his most trusted henchman, d'Artagnan), mother and son returned. But when the danger had passed and peace had been signed with Spain, the threesome were reunited.

Louis's first loves were Mazarin's nieces (known as the Mazarinettes), Olympe and Marie Mancini, but this rapidly became a problem. His libido was as powerful as his appetite for *la gloire*: in his late teens, his bouts of frottage with Marie Mancini so chafed his genitals that 'essence of ant' had to be applied.

When Anne and Mazarin started to negotiate his Spanish marriage,* Louis refused to contemplate it, determined to marry Marie Mancini. 'Remember I beg you what I had the honour to tell you several times

---

* Mazarin was a master of realpolitik – before the word was coined. Still fighting the Habsburgs, he allied with the republican regicide Cromwell against the Spanish, whom they defeated at the battle of the Dunes. And when Oliver died, it was Mazarin who offered to invade England to support Protector Dick. In the twentieth century, Mazarin was the hero of President François Mitterrand, who named his illegitimate daughter Mazarine.

when you asked what you needed to be a great king,' wrote Mazarin to Louis. 'It was this: not to be dominated by any passion.' When Louis sent Marie a puppy with a collar engraved 'I belong to Marie Mancini', Mazarin was beside himself. Finally Louis gave her up. 'You are king,' she said: 'you cry and I leave.' Nine months after his marriage to his cousin María Teresa, a son, the dauphin, was born – but their consanguinity explains why, of their six children, only the first survived beyond the age of fifteen.

In March 1661, Mazarin, fifty-eight, was dying. Louis was at the bedside, tearfully bringing water and medicines. He sobbed so loudly he was asked to leave the chamber. The cardinal left France as the greatest state in Europe – an absolutist monarchy of nineteen million people (with England an unstable mixed monarchy of four million), but his death was, Louis wrote to Philip IV, 'one of the greatest afflictions I could feel'. Soon afterwards, Louis's mother fell ill with gangrene, abscesses and ulcers. Louis slept at the foot of her bed, and, as he watched her dying, murmured, 'Look how beautiful she is, I've never seen her look so beautiful.'

'Do what I told you,' Anne whispered as she died.

'What I've suffered in losing the queen, madame my mother,' confided Louis, 'surpasses anything you can imagine.'

Now Louis declared, 'I am determined henceforth to govern the state by myself,'* with a mission to win France world dominion in place of his Habsburg cousins. While he enjoyed a string of love affairs (ignored by Queen María Theresa, who just said, 'I'm not a dupe as they imagine, but I'm prudent, I see things clearly'), Louis devised a new French court. He improved the Louvre (advised by Bernini, who arrived from Rome but hated Paris), but then in 1665 commissioned a new palace at Versailles, where he staged elaborate rituals around his own sacred person to distract his nobles from power and Paris.†

---

* Louis first had to solve a problem inherited from Mazarin: his superintendant, Nicolas Fouquet, who bought the title 'Viceroy of the Americas' as he planned the French takeover of the New World, lived so regally that he overshadowed the king. Louis learned from spies that Fouquet planned to rule, 'making himself sovereign arbiter of state'. Louis decided to destroy him. Moving fast and secretly, he turned to a trusted retainer – d'Artagnan. As a young man, Charles de Batz, later comte d'Artagnan, had joined the Mousquetaires du Roi – the royal bodyguard – and served Mazarin as bodyguard and spy. Louis always knew he could trust d'Artagnan. Now he ordered the fifty-year-old d'Artagnan to arrest Fouquet. Fouquet, sentenced to solitary confinement for thirteen years, was joined by a man in an iron mask whose identity was never revealed but was most likely Eustache d'Auger, the valet of Mazarin's treasurer who knew the details of the cardinal's colossal corruption. The story contains the germ of two Alexandre Dumas novels.

† His daily *lever* and *coucher* were minutely choreographed. His awakening, attended by

Louis knew he was giving 'an infinite value' to something in itself worth nothing. The court was a multipurpose institution, family hive, power brokerage, job centre, escort agency, marriage market, art bazaar and theatre, served by 10,000 servants. 'Sit down when you can; piss when you can,' joked courtiers, 'ask for any job you can!' A lack of latrines meant courtiers urinated in the stairwells. When a treasurer was dying, Louis complained, 'The man's not dead and sixteen people have asked for his job.' His usual answer was '*Je verrai*' – I'll see.

He had a sense of humour, joking to his ailing artist Le Brun, 'Don't die, Le Brun, just to raise the prices of your pictures.' He understood the theatre of royalty: 'Kings should satisfy the public.' Until he was thirty he himself acted and danced on stage – he loved dancing; and it was Jean-Baptiste Poquelin, a well-off courtier known to his family as *Le Nez* for his proboscis and to his audiences as Molière, who wrote many of the plays, his mission being 'to bring laughter to the monarch who makes all Europe tremble'. But behind the pleasure and gossip was a dark struggle for one man's favour.

SEX, POISON AND WAR AT THE COURT OF THE SUN KING

Louis was a promiscuous serial monogamist, turning the position of *maîtresse en titre* into a semi-official job. The first was the ambitious, voracious, blue-eyed, blonde and witty Françoise-Athénaïs de Rochechouart, born into the grandest nobility and married to the marquis de Montespan. When both the queen and Louis's existing mistress were pregnant, they unwisely asked Montespan to entertain the highly sexed king, who fell in love with her. For a while he kept both mistresses in adjoining apartments, even as he regularly seduced just about any girls who crossed his path, including servants of all three women. Montespan ruled the court and produced seven royal children. But she was grasping and petulant: her nickname was Quanto – how much? When she herself was supplanted by the most unlikely rival, she lost all perspective.

over a hundred people, started with valets shaving and dressing him, then came the *grandes entrées* of the *premiers gentilshommes*. As he washed his hands and prayed, his favourites and illegitimate children entered. His shirt and jacket were presented to him by the *premiers gentilshommes*, and the third level, the *entrées de la chambre*, the bishops, marshals and ambassadors, were allowed in. Finally, wig in place, he ate a quick breakfast; then, gloves and cane in hand, he started his day. At 10 p.m., he feasted in public *au grand couvert*, after which his undressing took an hour and a half, with the top honour going to those who handed him his candle and accompanied him to the commode where special favourites – the *brevets d'affaires* – chatted to a king in motion on his throne.

Montespan chose a safe option as governess for her children: the thirty-nine-year-old Françoise d'Aubigné. Dark-eyed, pious, intelligent, childless, she was the daughter of a murderer, widow of a drunken poet. But to everyone's surprise, after a run of younger girls, Louis started to fall in love with her, raising her to marquise de Maintenon; and later, in 1683, after the death of the queen, he married her. Maintenon spoke to him plainly, loathed court, believed the minds of men and women were equal and was sceptical of patriarchy. 'Men are unbearable when you see them at close quarters,' she said. Instead she ran a school where girls were taught history and mathematics, and soon she herself was powerful, though she claimed she was 'nothing'. Louis adored her: 'I always cherish you and respect you to an extent I can't express,' he wrote, 'and indeed whatever affection you have for me, I have even more for you, being totally yours with all my heart.' Although she was *seconde dame d'atours* to the dauphine, she now dominated the court.

Her rise was unbearable for the now obese Madame de Montespan, who consulted denizens of the twilight zone where high society and underworld overlap: La Voisin, sorceress, abortionist and purveyor of poisons and love potions, and La Bosse, who used the blood of killed or stillborn babies in black rituals. These harridans were regularly employed by courtiers and fallen mistresses. Montespan's maid Claude des Oeillets, whom Louis had slept with, consulted La Voisin, while another ex-mistress, Mazarin's niece Olympe de Soissons, had resorted to Voisin when Louis moved on. Voisin was said to have jinxed Louis's food by sprinkling it with baby's blood. The hex came to light during the murder trial of an aristocrat. When the king was informed, he ordered an investigation that, exploited by politicians and garnished with denunciations, exposed witchcraft,* poisoning and infanticide: 194 people were arrested and tortured. Voisin and thirty-five others were burned at the stake, tortured to death or broken on the wheel. But, as the police chief put it, the real culprits were too important to fall: 'The enormity of their crimes proved their safeguard.' Louis called a halt, and Montespan retired to a convent.

The other way to distract the nobility was war and empire. Louis regarded *la gloire* as the pastime and duty of kings, his huge population allowing him for fifty years to field and fit out bigger armies than anyone else. He drilled his troops for hours while encouraging his nobles to dress up as if battle was a party. His splendidly attired killer dandies

---

* L'Affaire des Poisons took place twelve years before the Salem witch hysteria in Massachusetts.

were copied by aristocrats across Europe, though the bright coats worn
by officers and soldiers helped identify them in battlefields obscured
by the smoke of black gunpowder. Louis systematically embarked on
expansion: in 1667, he invaded and seized Spain's Netherlands and
Franche-Comté, then swallowed Luxembourg. But in 1672 he came up
against the 'ingratitude, ignorance and insupportable vanity' of the tiny
Dutch republic – its population just 1.5 million to Louis's twenty – now
directed by the most brilliant of the dynasts. This was Johan de Witt,
imperial mastermind and mathematical scholar – he used survival rates
from the first studies of the causes of death to calculate life insurance
rates and also devised the financial annuity – who had ruled, informally,
for twenty successful years.

Slim, dark, handsome and intense, de Witt was the protégé of Cornelis
de Graeff, long-serving regent of Amsterdam and president of the VOC,
whose niece Wendela Bicker he married, placing him at the fulcrum of
the patrician dynasties that had, through the East and West Indies companies, promoted the global Dutch offensive. In 1650 William, prince
of Orange, died young – a son, the William who would rule England,
only being born eight days after his death. De Graeff and de Witt, then
aged twenty-four, saw the chance to dispense with Orange stadtholders,
declaring the prince a Child of State (a ward of the government), his
education vigilantly managed by the *regenten*.

Three years later, de Graeff helped raise de Witt to *raadpensionaris*
– grand pensionary of Holland, effectively premier. De Witt waged war
against England so implacably that it drove its new king Charles II into
the arms of Louis, with catastrophic consequences.

THE MERRIE BROTHERS AND THE AFRICA COMPANY

On 14 May 1660, when the admiral Montagu arrived in The Hague
with the tranche of cash granted by Parliament for Charles II, the king,
dressed shabbily, was so excited at the sight of money he called in his
brother, James, duke of York, just to gaze at it in amazement. The brothers were determined to enjoy the throne and, by any means possible in
an England bedevilled by religious rancour and political instability, to
preserve the monarchy for which their father had died.

Conveyed in Montagu's flagship, Charles arrived in Dover accompanied by a mix of royalists – led by James, ex-Cromwellians* and a

---

* Pepys started his famous diary on 1 January 1660 in time to recount the Restoration – he

waspish clergyman, Gilbert Burnet, who noted that the king 'has a very ill opinion of men and women, and so is infinitely distrustful; he thinks the world is governed wholly by [self-]interest'. But he admired his 'strange command of himself: he can pass from business to pleasure, and from pleasure to business, in so easy a manner that all things seem alike to him'.

In exile, pleasure-seeking had been the Stuarts' consolation, in power their revenge. In twelve penurious years, Charles had indulged in just two recorded mistresses, complaining that the 'blind harpers [gossips] have done me too much honour assigning me so many fair ladies as if I were able to satisfy the half'. He had fallen in love with Lucy Walter, who had given birth to a son he doted on: the duke of Monmouth. Now he would make up for those dark years.

There was no purge and many prizes, but the dizzy merriness of Charles's court glossed over a precarious and darkling tension: this England was paranoic, fissiparous and vicious. Regicides were hanged and quartered; the great Oliver was exhumed, his head displayed.

Tall, swarthy, playful, insouciant and Italianate (via his Medici grandmother) in looks and temperament, Charles was a maestro of secret manoeuvrings, but no orator – 'he speaks the worst ever I heard a man', noted Pepys. 'All I observed is the silliness of the king, playing with his dog or his codpiece.' As flawed as he was debonair, Charles avoided decisions whenever possible – not always a bad habit in politics. 'The king,' wrote Pepys, 'do mind nothing but pleasures and hates the very sight or thoughts of business.' Charles made no apology. 'Appetites are free,' he said, 'and Almighty God will never damn a man for allowing himself a little pleasure.' In fact his appetites were far from free, and he still depended on Parliament for money.

An heir was essential: a Portuguese princess, Catherine of Braganza, brought the dowry of Bombay and Tangier, but she was unable to have children, awkward when her husband could not stop fathering them. His heir remained his brother, James, duke of York, which soon became a problem that encapsulated and exacerbated the English crisis.

The 'Merrie brothers' were very different: Charles, a wavering Protestant, was courageous but supple, subtle and patient; James, who

---

sailed back to England with the king – with an irrepressible *joie de vivre* that at least partly derived from his survival of a lithotomy procedure or 'cutting for the stone'. He celebrated the date annually with a feast for the rest of his life. The Cromwellians who delivered the army and navy, Monck and Montagu, were made duke of Albermarle and earl of Sandwich, becoming two of the king's top courtiers: young Pepys rose with them. The king appointed him clerk of the acts at the Navy Board.

converted to Catholicism in 1669, was darkly sturdy, brainlessly brave and obstinate. He shared the king's sexual enthusiasm but not his taste: Charles laughed that James's 'ugly wenches' were so plain they must be a penance ordered by his confessor.* While they were in exile, James had seduced Anne, daughter of his brother's adviser, Edward Hyde, later earl of Clarendon and Lord Chancellor, promising her marriage if she succumbed. Honouring his word, he married her and, after six of their children had died, she gave birth to two daughters, Mary and Anne, both raised as Protestants, both future queens. James was lord high admiral and so worked closely with Pepys, who praised his modesty and industry, and observed how affectionate he was with his daughters – 'like an ordinary private father' – though he was also a lothario who 'did eye my wife mightily'.

The brothers immediately unleashed England's mercantile spirit to compete globally with the paramount trading power, de Witt's Holland. Charles followed Oliver in passing Navigation Acts designed to promote trade in African slaves and Indian luxuries. Hearing about Gambia's 'mountain of gold', Charles and James founded the Company of Royal Adventurers, rechartered as the Royal Africa Company (RAC) in 1672, which traded 16,000 Africans in seven years, founded forts along the coast and seized the Dutch slave castle Cape Coast, built by the Swedes. James was its governor, its shareholders ranging from Charles and Prince Rupert to the philosopher John Locke (whose ancestor John Lok had been a west African pioneer), Pepys and a merchant from Bristol named Edward Colston, later its deputy governor. In Africa, nine out of ten of its English representatives died of disease, and the RAC like other European slave traders were never powerful enough to defeat the African leaders who often challenged them. Nonetheless, the British share in the trade rose in the first ten years from 33 per cent to 74. Between 1662 and 1731, the Company transported approximately 212,000 slaves, of whom 44,000 died en route during over 500 voyages. Most were sold to the Caribbean.

Clashes with the Dutch outraged the 'mad for war' public. 'All the world rides us,' said James to Pepys, 'and I think we shall never ride anybody.' Actually England's time was coming. In 1665, the two

---

* James's favourite, the acute Catherine Sedley, was under no illusions about the duke's stupidity nor her own looks. 'It can't be my beauty for he must see I have none,' she joked. 'And it can't be my wit, for he has not enough to know that I have any.' Her wit remained sharp. Years later, at the court of George I, she bumped into the mistresses of Charles II (duchess of Portsmouth) and William III (Elizabeth Villiers, countess of Orkney). 'God!' she laughed. 'Who would have thought that we three whores should meet here?'

Protestant powers went to war with James commanding the fleet, fitted out by Pepys. Off Lowestoft, James defeated the Dutch, though he was spattered with brains when the head of a nearby officer was pulped; and the English took Trinidad and New Amsterdam, which Charles renamed New York, completing the contiguous coastline of English colonies from New England to another newly created estate, the Carolinas, named after Charles himself.*

De Witt and the Dutch believed that God would punish English depravity. Sure enough, in 1665, a wave of plague sent the country into a lockdown: thousands left London; universities closed. Even as 7,000 Londoners died a week, Pepys was on a professional and sexual roll – 'I've never lived so merrily' – while one Oxford student who had no interest in girls or parties benefited from being locked down for two years at his parents' Lincolnshire home: Isaac Newton experimented on himself. 'I took a bodkin [needle] and put it betwixt my eye and bone as near to the backside of my eye as I could,' he wrote, drawing his eyeball. It was a revelatory moment: Newton, experimenting in gravity and mathematics, was one of the new European polymaths who believed above all else that science demanded proof – even if it meant a bodkin alongside his own eyeball.

The epidemic was followed by a fire that demolished much of London; it was Pepys who rushed to warn the king at Whitehall and advised him to blow up houses to stop its spread.† Then de Witt orchestrated

---

* Charles carved out territory for William Penn, the Quaker son of that pragmatic Admiral Penn who had commanded the Caribbean expedition for Cromwell and had then managed to accompany Charles II back to London, lending him much-needed funds. Rather than pay them back, Charles granted Penn a vast stretch of north America, enabling Penn to found Pennsylvania as his 'Holy Experiment' where he drafted a tolerant constitution and initially negotiated gentle relations with the Lenape Native Americans. But the unclear borders brought him into conflict with the royalist Catholic family of the second Lord Baltimore, proprietor of Maryland. Both families remained the proprietors until the American revolution. But their border tensions led to years of antagonism and even to a short Baltimore–Penn war. Starting in 1730 in the Conejohela Valley with the forward actions of Colonel Thomas Cresap, an Indian-killing agent of the fifth Lord Baltimore, against Quaker settlers loyal to the Penns, Cresap's War culminated in a mobilization of Maryland and Pennsylvanian militias. It was ended by the mediation of George II, who ordered Baltimore and John Penn, son of the founder, to negotiate a new border, confirmed in 1767 as the Mason–Dixon Line, which became the border between the slave-owning south and the north. At the same time John Penn tricked the Lenapes into ceding a territory that could be walked in a day and a half, then hiring fast runners to inflate its span – the so-called Walking Purchase.
† The plague had killed 30,000 people in the first years of James I's reign, and 40,000 in 1625. This wave first killed 50,000 in Amsterdam, then killed 100,000 Britons out of a population of 5.2 million in the summer of 1665. A quarantine imposed on plague-ridden houses – marked with a red cross and the words 'Lord have mercy on us' – and the Great Fire may have halted its spread. In 1720, the plague's last European wave killed 90,000 out of 150,000 people in Marseilles. It was far from finished in the east.

a killer blow. He visited the Dutch fleet and hanged three captains as encouragement, then, placing his brother Cornelis de Witt on board, he unleashed his plan. On 19 June 1667, the Dutch broke into the Medway and raided the naval base at Chatham, burning or capturing fourteen ships-of-the-line as London descended into panic. 'The whole kingdom is undone,' thought Pepys, who now found himself missing Cromwell: 'strange how . . . everybody doth nowadays reflect upon Oliver and commend him'. Charles mocked 'those pure angelical times', sacrificed his chancellor Clarendon and sued for peace, marrying James's daughter Mary to the young William of Orange.

Charles turned to his best friend in the world to deliver vengeance against the Dutch and money to stave off Parliament: his twenty-six-year-old sister, Henrietta.

MINETTE, BARBARA AND THE EATING OF DE WITT

The princess, whom Charles called Minette, was married to Louis XIV's vicious brother, Philippe d'Orléans, known as Monsieur. Clever, cultured and passionate, she had charmed Louis and endured the bullying of Monsieur and his envious male lovers. Charles adored Minette and missed her a great deal: 'I'm sure I'll be very impatient till I have the happiness to see my chere Minette againe.' And nothing pleased her like pleasing Charles. 'Everyone has his private fancy, and mine is to be very much alive to all that concerns you!' she wrote, adding, 'There's no one who loves you as well as I do.' Now she proved it by shuttling between the kings, negotiating a secret treaty under which Louis XIV promised payments that offered Charles independence from Parliament in return for Charles's secret promise to convert to Catholicism – none of which was contained in the associated public treaty. Minette's performance showed how dynasty could empower women. But on her return to France she died in agony of a punctured ulcer. 'Monsieur's a villain!' shouted a heartbroken Charles, sure Minette had been poisoned.

Now committed to a Catholic alliance, backed by a 'cabal' of ministers* led by George, duke of Buckingham, slippery, graceful and vicious,

---

* 'The Duke of Buckingham doth rule all now,' wrote Pepys. The word cabal derives from the ministry led by Buckingham (an acronym from the names Clifford, Arlington, Buckingham, Ashley and Lauderdale). The Restoration was less merry than thuggish, rapacious and venal, with 'a lazy prince, no council, no money, no reputation'. What Pepys called 'the viciousness of the court' was personified by Buckingham. Although he wrote plays, performed his own sketches and studied science at the Royal Society, the duke openly brawled with rakes at the theatre and court and in 1666 fell in love with Anna Maria, countess of

who had negotiated the public treaty with Louis, Charles was already in bed with the Catholics.

Charles's favourite for over a decade was the exuberant Barbara Villiers, great-niece of the first Buckingham, a curvaceous, tempestuous libertine, promoted to countess of Castlemaine* and giving birth to five children, all ennobled. But she was brazenly Catholic.

While the king encouraged tolerance of Catholics, Parliament banned Catholics from office. Buckingham lost power when Charles's secret treaty was in part exposed. It suited Charles, who had moved on to younger mistresses, telling Barbara he 'cared not whom she loved'. She took new lovers, from acrobats to a young Guardsman called John Churchill, whose father was Winston Churchill, a royalist officer, and whose mother was another great-niece of Buckingham. Churchill's 'figure was beautiful, his manner irresistible, either by man or woman'; the phrase 'as slender as Churchill' became a court saying. His sister Arabella fell off her horse while out hunting with the duke of York, revealing her fine legs and more. She became James's mistress.

Barbara Villiers used Churchill to discredit a rival royal mistress; he claimed he had had to jump out of the window without his trousers when the king arrived. Charles confined him to barracks, and Barbara compensated him with an annuity. Such was the start of the career of the future duke of Marlborough. Soon afterwards, Churchill married the beautiful, masterful Sarah Jennings. At court he became friends with the courtier Sidney Godolphin, whom the king praised as 'never in the way, and never out of the way'; Sarah befriended the duke of York's daughter, Princess Anne. The quartet who would one day rule Britain became inseparable.

In 1672, Louis and Charles went to war against de Witt's Holland. French armies swept into Holland and the Dutch collapsed, only rescuing their country by flooding it. The Dutch rightly called this *Rampjaar*

Shrewsbury. The affair led to a duel in which he killed her husband and his second, while she ordered the ambushing and stabbing of an ex-lover who had mocked the pair. 'This will make the world think the king hath good councillors,' wrote Pepys in disgust, 'when the duke, the greatest man about him, is a fellow of no more sobriety than to fight about a whore.' Buckingham then moved Anna Maria into his household with his wife, who naturally complained. Buckingham sent her back to her father and lived with a 'widow of his own creation' at their new and grandiose lovepad, Cliveden House.

* Her first title was Baroness Nonsuch – Charles actually gave her the royal palace of Nonsuch – and she was later promoted to duchess of Cleveland. Pepys was excited by her, noticing in the Privy Garden that she wore 'the finest smocks and linen petticoats, laced with rich lace at the bottom, that ever I saw, and did me good to look upon them'. He ogled her madly at the theatre – 'I glutted myself with looking at her' and 'filled my eyes with her', though 'I know well enough she's a whore.'

– their disaster year – and never recovered their global pre-eminence.

The Orangeists furiously blamed de Witt, who was wounded in an assassination attempt and then forced to resign. All eyes turned to the prince of Orange, the twenty-two-year-old William, who was appointed stadtholder and captain-general and desperately tried to hold back the French. 'My country's indeed in danger,' he said, 'but there's one way to never see it lost and that's to die in the last ditch.' Flinty, angular and tough, William had known little love, his father dead before he was born, his mother tormented by the killing of her father Charles I, and his frosty relationship with de Witt scarcely alleviated by games of tennis. He saw his chance. Orangeite militiamen, organized by or on behalf of William, seized and shot de Witt and his brother before handing them over to a mob that eviscerated and skinned them, hung them naked, selling ears, fingers and other 'scraps' in the streets and then cooking and eating their livers – an astonishing cannibalistic feast in Europe's most sophisticated city. Yet the gruesome ritual had a logic: Witt had 'disembodied' the Dutch state; now the Dutch disembodied him.

Louis seemed unstoppable, next annexing Strasburg and Alsace. Hailed as the Sun King, spoiled by fortune, touched with the self-righteous narcissism that is the fate of those eternally in power, he believed he was master of Europe. French glamour concealed cold ambition. He had the iron constitution necessary for interminable war, ceremony and intrigue: when later he endured an excruciating six-hour operation to cut out an anal fistula without anaesthetic, he never cried out except to say '*Mon Dieu*' twice.* But now he was going to need his nerve: as the Oranges and Habsburgs plotted against him, he was laying the foundations for a worldwide French empire to challenge England in America and India.

---

* The operation's success was responsible for the improved status of surgeons. The king's barber-surgeon Charles-François Félix, who had succeeded his father as *premier chirurgien du roi*, had practised the procedure for six months on seventy-five humbler anuses, mainly belonging to 'fistulous' criminals, and had developed new instruments, a scythe-like scalpel and a retractor. There were no antiseptic measures. The king loathed bathing, the fistula seeped and a Russian ambassador reported that Louis 'stunk like a wild animal'. At 7 a.m. on 18 November 1686, Félix operated on the royal anus in the presence of the king's mistress, Madame de Maintenon, the dauphin, his confessor and his minister of state who held his hand. The king was back on horseback within three months; since everything the king did was fashionable, courtiers wore celebratory bandages around their bottoms. Most importantly, Félix was awarded nobility, estates and money, and was succeeded as first surgeon by his son, who served Louis XV.

HIGH QING, GREAT MUGHAL AND *CHHATRAPATI*

In 1664, Louis founded matching *Compagnies Françaises des Indes Occidentales* and *Orientales* to promote, by trade and sword, French empire – though he was far behind his Portuguese, Dutch and English rivals. In 1682, in 'our territory of New France', his explorer sieur de La Salle, aided by Native American allies, built forts around the Great Lakes, adding to France's earlier settlements in Quebec, and claimed the entire Mississippi valley which he called Louisiana. Yet the French colonists were few. Starting in 1663, Louis sent out over 800 women – *les filles du roi* – to marry settlers.

Louis's conquistadors were fascinated by the strange liberty of Native Americans, who disdained the Europeans as cruel, money-crazed, status-obsessed slaves to kings and aristocrats. 'They imagine,' wrote a French Jesuit, 'they ought by right of birth to enjoy the liberty of wild-ass colts rendering homage to no one.' Another observed, 'There's no people on earth freer than them,' noting, 'Fathers here have no control over their children.' Ruled by assemblies in which women as well as men could speak and argue, a sort of democracy with elements of matriarchy, they elected rulers only to command wars or special hunts.

In 1691, an ambassador of the Wendat confederacy (Ontario, Canada) was received by Louis, but was unimpressed by the Sun King. The envoy's identity is still debated but he was probably Kandiaronk, elected 'speaker' of the Wendat council, an eloquent and gifted Thuron soldier-politician who had expertly played the French against the rival Iroquois. Debating the merits of French versus Iroquois society with one of Louis's officers, Louis-Armand, baron de Lahontan, Kandiaronk mocked 'the faults and disorders they observed in our towns as caused by money'. The natives 'laugh at the difference of ranks . . . they brand us slaves . . . alleging we degrade ourselves subjecting ourselves to one man . . . They say the name of savages which we call them would fit ourselves better.' The Native American was touching on the essence of western freedom: much of it was – and is – theoretical since most people were actually bound by their place in society. In Kandiaronk's society, people often defied their lords and left to join another tribe. He wondered why anyone would allow those with money to establish authority over them and regarded the Jesus story ('the life and death of the son of the Great Spirit') as preposterous – though he pragmatically converted later. 'To imagine one can live in a country of money,' he said, 'and preserve one's soul is like imagining one could preserve one's life at the bottom of a lake.' In 1703, when Lahontan published his conversation with Kandiaronk, entitled *Curious Dialogues with a Savage of Good Sense Who has Travelled*, it inspired a new generation to question European authority and the origins of civilization.

In the Caribbean, Louis competed in sugar and slaves with the Spanish and English: he took over Saint-Domingue, Martinique and Guadeloupe where, along with Louisiana, the sugar plantations were worked by 2,000 new slaves supplied annually by his *Compagnie de Guinée et du Sénégale* (in which the French king was a shareholder) from Africa.* By the time of Louis's death there were 77,000 slaves in French America. But he also followed the English and Dutch eastwards, pursuing the conversion and annexation of Ayutthaya – Thailand† – and backing his *Compagnie des Indes Orientales* that claimed Isle de France (Mauritius) and Île Bourbon (Reunion), where new sugar plantations were now worked by slaves transported from east Africa. In 1674, Louis's envoys approached Emperor Alamgir for Indian concessions to compete against the English, just as his Hindu nemesis – Shivaji – created his own kingdom.

In June 1674, at his mountain fortress Raigad, the great Shivaji was crowned *chhatrapati* of Maratha Swaraj, a hugely symbolic act that sent shockwaves across India – the creation of a new language of Hindu sovereignty that made no mention of the Muslim Mughals. This outraged

---

* In 1685, Louis signed a *Code Noir* to manage '*les Esclaves Nègres de l'Amérique*'. The Code stipulated that slaves had no legal rights, could not marry, inherited the servitude of their parents and could be whipped and chained but not mutilated or tortured by masters. But runaways could be branded and their ears cut off after one escape attempt; after two misdemeanours, their hamstrings would be cut; after three: execution. For striking a master, they could be executed; a master who killed a slave would merely be fined. The Code banned the break-up of enslaved families but only while the children were prepubescent; it prohibited masters from having sex with slaves (the fine for fathering a child by a slave: 2,000 pounds of sugar). All of this was ignored by governors and slave masters. In 1684, the French physician François Bernier, who had served Alamgir in India, devised a theory of racial superiority that would later be used to justify slavery: 'A New Division of the Earth According to the Different Species or Races of Men Who Inhabit It'. Yet French law specified that slavery could not exist in mainland France: in 1691, Louis freed two slaves who had escaped in Martinique and arrived as stowaways in France, 'their liberty being acquired by the laws of the kingdom concerning slaves as soon as they touch the soil'.

† In Ayutthaya, a Greek adventurer called Constantine Phaulkon, who had fought for the Dutch and the English, had become the top aide to King Narai, hinting to Louis that he could convert the kingdom to Catholicism if Louis sent French troops to guard against the English EIC. Narai and Louis exchanged embassies, and 1,300 French soldiers arrived in Thailand. But Phaulkon's domination provoked a coup in 1688 by Phetracha, royal cousin and elephant corps commander, who overthrew the king, murdered his sons, executed Phaulkon and, marrying Narai's daughter, usurped the throne – thus defying French imperialism and ending Louis's dream. One of Narai's ambassadors to Louis, Kosa Pan, was the great-grandfather of Rama I, the king who in 1788 would found the dynasty that still rules Thailand today.

Alamgir, who denounced the 'mountain rat'.* But he failed to defeat the *chhatrapati*. In 1680, when Shivaji died of dysentery, his eldest wife committed sati on his funeral pyre and his son Sambhaji emerged as *chhatrapati*. Sambhaji knew the Mughals well, helping Alamgir's son Akbar in a rebellion that ended with the prince's death. Alamgir planned a terrible death for the Hindu who had meddled with his family.

In 1684, Alamgir himself tried to take the Maratha capital, Raigad Fort, but failed as Sambhaji ranged up the west coast, attacking Alamgir's Portuguese allies in Goa. But finally he overreached: in February 1689, Alamgir captured Sambhaji himself. His revenge was terrible: at Bahadurgad, Sambhaji was brought before Alamgir and forced to run the gauntlet through Mughal soldiers, before being ordered to embrace Islam. When he refused, his tongue was sliced and he was asked again. 'Not even if the emperor pimped me his daughter!' he wrote. Alamgir was outraged. Sambhaji was tortured for two weeks with metal claws that gouged out his eyes, cut out his tongue, pulled out his nails, then flayed him alive and then quartered him with the claws in mouth and fundament, the body parts fed to dogs. Raigad fell to Alamgir, who relentlessly pursued Rajaram, the new *chhatrapati* – but he could not quite destroy the dynasty.

Alamgir granted the French a factory in Surat, followed by Pondicherry on the east coast; the latter became the French headquarters (and remained French until 1954). But Louis was most fascinated with the new Qing emperor of China, to whom in 1687 he sent two delegations of Jesuit scholars. In 1669, at the height of Louis's successes, the Kangxi Emperor started his personal rule: the two had much in common.

At seven, the Kangxi Emperor, great-grandson of the Manchu conqueror Nurhaci, was chosen by his grandmother, Xiaozhuang, widow of the first Manchu emperor, who loved him and whom he loved back. After seven years dominated by the regent Oboi, the grandmother and grandson together plotted his arrest and downfall.

Athletic, pitted with smallpox,† his eyes bright and intelligent,

---

* Shivaji had conquered much of southern-central India from coast to coast, setting up his *ashta pradhan*, a modern council of ministers led by a *peshwa*, chief minister, who organized the building of hundreds of forts and the commissioning of a navy from the Portuguese, manned by Malabar pirates and commanded by a Portuguese renegade. All this was funded by tribute and conquest, and by lucrative raids on English and Dutch factories in Surat and Bombay that interfered with Mughal profits. Ruling as much of southern India as had great medieval kings like the Cholas, Shivaji aspired to the crown, but his Bhonsale family had been mere village chiefs; the Brahmins regarded him as a member of the *shudra* (farmer) caste; only a *kshatriya* could be a king. So Shivaji persuaded a respected pandit to invent his *kshatriya* genealogy and took the title *chhatrapati* – Lord of the Parasol – equivalent to emperor.

† Scarring was an advantage: smallpox was so deadly that it became usual to choose

Kangxi embraced absolute power, possessing the three necessities of politics – the acumen, the vision and the resources. As a Manchu, he had been trained from childhood in archery and riding, and he spent three months a year hunting. 'When Manchus go hunting in the north,' he said, 'the riders mass like storm clouds, the horse archers are as one with horses, they fly together!' But as a Chinese prince he was also trained in Confucian ethics. The role of an emperor, he said, was simply 'giving life to people and killing people'.

Ruler of over 150 million, Kangxi was a workaholic, rising at dawn to pore over reports, 16,000 of which survive, all marked in his red ink. He studied cases carefully. 'Errors are inexcusable in matters of life and death,' he reflected. 'I got into the habit of reading the lists, checking name and registration of each man sentenced to death ... then I'd go through the list with the Grand Secretaries and decide who to spare.'* Kangxi waged war on a continental scale, first against overmighty Manchu generals, then against Oirats (western Mongols) in today's Mongolia and Tibet, but he regarded independent Taiwan, ruled by the pirate king Koxinga, as a special insult to Chinese grandeur.† Koxinga's son and grandson defeated a joint Dutch–Manchu fleet and thrived,

emperors who had already survived a bout of the disease.

* Few rulers have mastered all the facets of power so well and thought about them so deeply. 'Be kind from afar and keep able ones near,' he advised his successor, 'nourish the people, think of the profit of all as being the real profit; be considerate to officials and act as father to the people and maintain the balance between principle and expedience,' adding with dry humour: 'That's *all* there is to it.' Kangxi carefully supervised the history of the dynasty. History remained a dangerous pursuit in China. 'It's the emperor in whose reign the history is written who is finally responsible and will be blamed by posterity if there are distortions and errors.' When the historian Dai Mingshi criticized Manchu rule, Kangxi ordered his execution – 'the only scholar I executed' – though 'The Board of Punishment recommended Dai be put to lingering death and all his male relations over sixteen be executed, females and children enslaved, but I was merciful and lowered it to beheading.'

† When the Manchus had taken northern China from the Ming, an extraordinary polyglot pirate, Zheng Zhilong, had backed a Ming emperor in the south. Zheng started as a translator for the Dutch VOC, which he helped seize Taiwan from the Portuguese, and then moved on to building a fleet of 400 warships and his own army. Protected by a bodyguard of enslaved Africans escaped from the Portuguese, he led the piratical cartel *Shibazhi* of 800 ships, which was not dissimilar to the Dutch or English trading companies, and which then defeated the Dutch, whereupon he enrolled as admiral for the southern Ming. In 1645 the Manchus persuaded him to defect but his dementedly ferocious son Zheng Sen, half Japanese and trained as a samurai, took over the command, with the title Koxinga (Lord of the Imperial Name), of the southern coast, fighting the Manchus for fifteen years. Then in 1661, just as Louis XIV started his rule, Fujian, on the south-western coast, fell to the Manchus and Koxinga expelled the Dutch from Taiwan. Many of the Dutch wives were enslaved as Chinese concubines. Syphilitic, unstable yet capable, Koxinga killed a Dutch missionary and took his daughter as concubine. Advised by a renegade Italian friar, he established his own kingdom which blocked the expansion of Kangxi's China. In the twenty-first century, China, again defied by an independent Taiwan, promotes the example of Kangxi.

but finally off Penghu, in 1683, Kangxi defeated the Koxingan fleet and stormed Taiwan.

Kangxi upgraded the Grand Canal and improved communications, all the more important given that the population was surging thanks to new strains of rice combined with American crops – sweet potatoes and maize – leading to bigger cities. Chinese merchants exported tea, porcelain and silk and were paid in American silver: Kangxi's income soared – but he was careful to limit the wealth of merchants and the access of foreigners. Kangxi's revenues were so large that he was able to cut some taxes, but his multi-fronted wars absorbed much of his income.

His sense of Manchu superiority was tempered by his curiosity about European innovation: he took lessons from Louis's Jesuit priests on science, mathematics, astronomy and music, and studied the harpsichord. Yet, while Louis was delighted to help a non-Christian potentate, when the Ottomans menaced the heart of Christendom, he refused to help his Habsburg rivals.

Vienna was about to fall.

Afsharis and Manchus, Hohenzollerns and Habsburgs

HOGMOUTH LEOPOLD, GUNPOWDER SOBIESKI AND QUEEN CLEOPATRA: THE LAST GREAT CHARGE

On 14 July 1683, around 170,000 Ottoman troops, led by the grand vizier, Merzifonlu Kara Mustafa, surrounded the city they called the Red Apple. After the murder of the great Kösem, her female nemesis Turhan, now *valide sultan*, ruled for her young son Mehmed IV, solving a crisis of confidence by appointing as vizier a septuagenarian of murderous vigour: Köprülü Mehmed Pasha. Born an Albanian Christian, enslaved and enrolled as a scullion, Köprülü killed anyone who resisted, writing to a childhood friend, 'It's true we were both raised in the harem and both protégés of Murad IV; nevertheless be informed if the accursed Cossacks pillage any of your villages and towns, I swear I will ignore your righteous character and cut you into pieces as a warning to the world.' It worked. Köprülü and his son added Transylvania and Crete to the empire, while Mehmed was diverted by his obsession with hunting: 'The father [Ibrahim] was mad for cunt; the son's mad for the hunt.'

After Mustafa, Köprülü's son-in-law, won a limited victory against the Poles, he convinced Mehmed to Hunter that the overstretched, inter-bred Habsburgs were ripe for conquest.

The jaw of Emperor Leopold was so elongated he was nicknamed Hogmouth. 'God made his skull in the shape of a gourd or a water bottle,' noticed the Ottoman writer Evliya Çelebi, 'eyes round as an owl's; face long as that of mister fox, ears as large as a child's slippers, nose as shrivelled as a grape, three fingers could fit inside each nostril from which black hairs like a bravo's beard mix in confusion with his moustache; lips like a camel, and whenever he speaks, saliva pours from his camel lips.' Hogmouth was married to his niece, Margarita, the blue-dressed, blonde infanta in Velázquez's *Las Meninas*, daughter of Philip IV of Spain. He called her Gretl, she called him Uncle, and their marriage was happy, though unsurprisingly three of their four children died. Her fun-loving spirit inspired their baroque court. Hogmouth was a talented flautist and composer, and impresario of astonishing shows in which fireworks lit up the sky and carriages and horses seemed to fly through the air. Yet his empress also brought her Spanish antisemitism. Horrified to find Jews thriving within Vienna, she encouraged him to expel and plunder them.*

Hogmouth had bigger problems. In the west, his cousin Louis had invaded the Habsburg Netherlands, and now in the east the Ottomans were coming. Hogmouth turned to the most gallant paladin of the east: the king of a Poland–Lithuania weakened by Cossack revolt and Muscovite expansion. Jan III Sobieski was a sophisticated Polish bravo, fluent in French, Turkish and Tatar, who had toured the west, married a French aristocrat Marysieńka, (with whom he fathered twelve children) and fought with and against the Turks, Tatars and Swedes, personifying the Serene Republic at its best. His daily letters to Marysieńka were filled with gossip and politics, but suffused with their love: he called her Cleopatra; she called him Gunpowder. Realizing that Poland would be next if Vienna fell, Sobieski, now fifty-four and fat, agreed to help Hogmouth, who abandoned the city along with 60,000 Viennese. He left a veteran, Count Ernst von Starhemberg, to hold the capital with just 15,000 men. But he had 370 cannon, while the overconfident Mustafa, accompanied by 1,500 concubines supervised by 700 black eunuchs, and with his own private zoo, had neglected his artillery, fielding just 130 cannon. The fighting was desperate, with mining and countermining of the walls. When the vizier started his bombardment, it looked as if Vienna would fall, but Sobieski took command of a papal Holy Alliance. Leading 70,000 men, starring his Ukrainian Cossacks of the Dnieper and Polish winged Hussars – who sported ostrich feathers on the back of their armour – Sobieski galloped to the rescue.

Mustafa had not covered his back, instead depending on the 40,000 horsemen of the Crimean khan who were more interested in plundering Austria. Vienna was close to catastrophe when on 9/11 1683[†] Sobieski appeared behind Mustafa.

'This man is badly encamped,' Sobieski noted, 'he knows nothing of war.' At 6 p.m. on 9/11, he and 18,000 Polish winged Hussars flew (almost) down Kahlenberg Mountain through Ottoman lines and into

---

* When the Jews were expelled from their suburb across the Danube, Im Werd, the Austrians celebrated by renaming it Leopoldstadt, but later this neighbourhood again became popular with Viennese Jews, their lives celebrated in Tom Stoppard's play, Leopoldstadt.
† Four centuries later, in 2001, an Islamic terrorist regarded 9/11 as the moment the righteous mission of Islam had been halted by Christendom: Osama bin Laden chose the date for his own attack on the leading Christian power, America.

Mustafa's encampment. Mustafa ordered his favourite ostrich to be beheaded as he fled with his harem. 'God and our blessed Lord forever granted us victory,' Gunpowder told Cleopatra. 'The tents and wagons have fallen into my hands, *et mille autres galanteries fort jolies et fort riches.*'*

The Polish king rode into Vienna, not waiting for Kaiser Hogmouth to return. 'All the common people kissed my hands, my feet, my clothes,' he boasted, sending Marysieńka one of Mustafa's golden stirrups. 'Others only touched me, saying: "Ah, let us kiss so valiant a hand!"' Hogmouth rushed back, resentful of Sobieski, and their meeting was frosty – there was nothing as cold as Habsburg ingratitude. Hogmouth presented himself as victor; the Ottoman cannon was melted down to cast new bells for St Stephen's. Poland had saved Christendom, but Sobieski was its last great king.

In Belgrade, Mehmed sent the Tongueless to the vizier with their bowstrings. 'Am I to die?' Mustafa asked the Tongueless, then bowed his neck. 'If God wishes.' But the sultan was himself deposed and the Ottomans never regained the initiative. Hogmouth ordered his best general, Prince Eugen of Savoy, a young French officer who had fallen out with Louis XIV, to counter-attack, seizing Buda and Belgrade and so almost doubling Habsburg territory. But in the west Louis was close to dominating Europe, an achievement he celebrated by cancelling toleration of Protestants, granted by Henri IV, his grandfather.

Only William of Orange could stop 'my mortal enemy' Louis from seizing Universal Kingship, and to accomplish this he pulled off an extraordinary coup: on 5 November 1688, the thirty-six-year-old stadtholder of Holland and husband of Princess Mary of England invaded England.

THE CHANGELING, THE KING'S UNDERWEAR AND THE ORANGES

It was in one sense a bitter family feud, whirling around the two brothers, Charles II and James, and their first cousin William. Charles, who had fourteen illegitimate children and was nicknamed Old Rowley after a famous stallion, had no legitimate heir except his unpopular Catholic brother, James. The Protestant Parliament objected to his succession,

---

* This included sacks of what the Poles initially thought were camel feed: coffee. Coffee houses were already popular in London – Pepys wrote, 'Thence I to the coffee house where much good discourse' – but Vienna did not yet have any. A legend claims that Sobieski gave the sacks to a Ukrainian soldier-spy Jerzy Franciszek Kulczycki, who founded the first Viennese café. The crescent shape and name of croissants was said to originate in this victory.

thereby launching a deadly crisis – part of fifty years of religious and political strife.

It started in 1673, when James married a 'tall and admirably shaped' Italian princess, Maria of Modena, who was only a little older than his daughters Mary and Anne. 'I've brought you a new play-fellow' was how he tactlessly introduced his wife to his daughters. His 'Popish bride' and the possibility of a Catholic heir inspired a malicious conspiracy-theorist, Titus Oates, who had already falsely denounced a schoolmaster for abusing his pupils and now claimed that there was a Popish Plot by Maria's doctor to kill the king (via poison or a golden bullet) and enthrone James. His allegations became the sparkwheel of hysteria and terror.* Charles interrogated Oates – this 'wicked man' – but was forced to approve the execution of twenty-two innocents. Pepys, now an MP and recently promoted to Admiralty secretary, decried 'such a state of distraction and fear' but was denounced because he was a protégé of James. But he was cleared of being a Catholic agent and reappointed.

Parliament tried to exclude James and make Charles's eldest illegiti-mate son, Monmouth, the heir. Charles, whose sex life always reflected his politics, tacked towards two Protestant actresses, Moll Davis and Nell Gwynne. He had Nell painted naked, keeping the painting behind another painting and unveiling it to ogling friends. Pepys did not think much of Nell's acting – 'a serious part, which she do most basely' – but she had the gift of the gab, telling a crowd that stopped her carriage and accused her of being one of Charles's Catholic paramours: 'Good people, you're mistaken; I'm the *Protestant* whore.'

Yet Charles believed exclusion would lead to the end of his vision of monarchy. 'I'll never yield and won't let myself be intimidated,' he said. 'Men become ordinarily more timid as they grow old; as for me, I shall be bolder.' In any witch-hunt, it takes time, but 'good men will be with me'. He was right. Emerging near absolute, he ruled through young ministers – nicknamed the Chits – who included Godolphin, a favourite courtier. Charles and the Chits decided to dismantle Tangier, part of the queen's dowry, which was under pressure from a new Moroccan sultan.

---

* The fantasist's lies were initially exploited by the king's own chief minister, Thomas Osbourne, earl of Danby, who hoped to purge the court of pro-Catholics, then by the ex-Cromwellian Antony Ashley, earl of Shaftesbury, who became a shameless inquisitor. Buckingham at times joined in. In 1774, the young Lord Shrewsbury, whose father had been killed by the duke, led an attack on Buckingham in Parliament that prompted his downfall and enforced separation from Anna Maria. Embittered, Buckingham joined the attacks on Charles II, who imprisoned him. The rake finally retired to his Yorkshire estates. After the government had orchestrated a case of sodomy against him, he went into a decline, reflecting, 'O! what a prodigal I've been of that most valuable of all possessions – Time!'

Pepys was sent out to supervise. Soon afterwards, it was captured by Ismail ibn Sharif, the Warrior, Moroccan empire builder, whose Alawi family, descended from the Prophet, started in Sijilmassa before uniting the country and conquering southwards to Timbuktu and the Senegal River. Ismail, son of an enslaved African mother, had seized the throne in 1672. The greatest slave trader of his time, Ismail enslaved 220,000 Africans – some of them forming crack regiments – who were joined by thousands of Europeans, enslaved by his corsairs based in Salé. All of them were treated abysmally: he used the Africans to police the whites.*

On his deathbed, Charles converted to Catholicism and did not forget his girlfriends, telling James not to 'let poor Nelly starve'. James became king. 'He would have been a very good king,' said Sarah Churchill, a courtier of the queen, 'if it hadn't been for Popery.' James signed a Declaration of Indulgence for non-Protestants, using it to liberate Catholics while he built up his army and arrested dissidents. Opposition seethed around the dashing but callow Monmouth, who fled to Holland. When Monmouth invaded England with just eighty-five followers, William warned James, whose general, John Churchill, easily crushed the invasion. James then beheaded his nephew; yet his heir remained his Protestant daughter Mary, married to William of Orange.

Charming the Dutch but unable to warm up William, the genial, pretty Mary suffered miscarriages and the death of a baby, the result of their consanguineous marriage. James tried to divide husband and wife by warning his daughter about William's affair with her courtier Elizabeth Villiers. Mary ambushed William coming out of his mistress's bedroom, but he promised to give her up – hardly a concession since the stadtholder preferred the companionship of a handsome officer, Hans Bentinck, who had nursed him when he was ill with smallpox.

Seven dissident English grandees approached William just as Queen Maria took the waters at Bath and fell pregnant. In June 1688, to Catholic jubilation and Protestant disbelief, the queen, attended by Hugh

---

* Said to wear green when genial, white when murderous, Ismail was always escorted by eighty African bodyguards, 'his long face more black than white, a mulatto', according to the French envoy. 'One of his normal entertainments,' reported a European, 'was to draw his sword as he mounted his horse and decapitate the slave who held the stirrup.' His chief wives were Zaydana, an enslaved African and 'Mrs Shaw', an enslaved Englishwoman whose respective sons, Zaydan and Muhammad, fought for the succession. Ismail had Zaydan's hand and foot amputated as punishment and later had him murdered by his own concubines. There was no shortage of heirs: Ismail was the most prolific father in history. By now, in 1703, he had 868 children; by his death in 1727, the figure was 1,171 – so much of today's Morocco is descended from him. He negotiated with Louis, demanding an illegitimate daughter as wife. When he died at eighty-one, he was planning an invasion of Spain. His family still rules Morocco today.

Chamberlen with his secret forceps,* gave birth to a son, a Catholic heir. James had not allowed his daughter Anne or his Protestant courtiers to attend, sparking a birther conspiracy theory that a changeling had been smuggled into St James's Palace. Mary turned decisively against her father to 'save Church and State', and the seven noblemen signed a coded letter to William inviting him to invade. William mustered his fleet.

James, foolish as ever, turned down Louis's offer of military support. As Mary waited in The Hague, William sailed with 250 ships and 35,000 men, including '200 Blacks brought from the Plantations of the Netherlands in America', and landed at Torbay, Devon.

William advanced slowly. Lord Churchill, James's commander, defected (later rewarded by William with the earldom of Marlborough), followed by Princess Anne, who was intimate friends with Churchill's wife Sarah. James, heartbroken that both his daughters had betrayed him, panicked, throwing the Great Seal into the sea so that his enemies could not call Parliament. But he was captured by fishermen who roughly searched his underwear. William warned his uncle James that he could not guarantee the king's safety. Pepys, navy secretary, arranged the ship that conveyed Queen Maria and her son to Europe.† As William entered London, he let James escape to France where he set up a rival court, his followers known as Jacobites. While the *mobile vulgus* – Latin for fickle crowd, henceforth shortened to the mob – rioted and celebrated the Orange invasion by waving oranges, the dour Dutchman summoned Mary from Holland. Filled with 'secret joy' that was 'soon checked with the consideration of my father's misfortunes', she agreed that William was in charge: 'she would be no more but his wife; that she would do all that lay in her power to make him King for life'. When the assembled convention – not Parliament since only a sovereign could call one – challenged this, William threatened to return to Holland unless he

---

* Hugh was the great-nephew of the first Peter Chamberlen who had delivered James I's children. The last of the dynasty, Hugh's son (also Hugh) junior had no heirs, and allowed the forceps to become public knowledge; the device saved millions of lives.

† After handing over his naval papers to William, Pepys retired. He was an indefatigable state servant and incorrigible lover of life – 'I think I may reckon myself as happy a man as any is in the world' – but he was also a master storyteller, witness to the plague, the Fire, Medway and the Merry Monarch. His diary is a masterpiece, recording his marriage and rise at the Admiralty, his experiences of court politics and 'towsing' his girlfriends. Yet it covered only nine years of his successful career from election to Parliament and to presidency of the Royal Society. His zenith was his 1782 appointment by Charles as admiralty secretary, a post he held until 1688. During the insecure early months of William's reign, one of those arrested as a suspected Jacobite was Pepys. He was released but, content with his well-born mistress, he retired to Clapham, dying in 1703.

was made king. The convention agreed. The royal couple's heir, Mary's sister Anne, had betrayed her father for the sake of Protestantism and regarded Mary as first in line, but then resented yielding the succession to William, whom she called 'the Dutch Abortive'.

In return, William III approved a Bill of Rights that solved the lethal conundrum that had paralysed England during fifty years of state failure. It agreed a balance of power between a powerful Parliament, the noble oligarchs and the monarch, who kept control of the executive.*

No one knew how this new arrangement would work. Kings remained the chief rulers of England for another century, able to appoint governments and wage war – and might have remained so if more of them had been masterful warlords like William.

The Dutchman delivered the stability, the rule of law and the creative energy needed to forge a world power. He oversaw the creation of the Bank of England and, realizing that the English coinage was dangerously debased, launched the Great Recoinage, which was managed by an English luminary, Isaac Newton. Now fifty-three, Newton had been given a sinecure wardenship of the Royal Mint, but its management was so incompetent that he agreed to run the vital recoinage himself as master, a highly lucrative position, earning a percentage of every coin produced.

One of the first members of Charles II's Royal Society for scientists, he was a touchy loner, awkward friend and vindictive feuder, who never married and was probably asexual. His passionate friendship with a Swiss scientist Nicolas Fatio could have been a typical male affinity of the time – or his only love affair; its end sparked an emotional breakdown. He fell out badly with his friend John Locke, who 'endeavoured to embroil me with women'. His new job was just his latest service to a new spirit of rational scientific inquiry. 'I do not feign hypotheses,' he wrote in his *Principia Mathematica*:† knowledge must be based on the

---

* Combining the best parts of Oliver's republic and Charles II's monarchy, it delivered. Frequent parliaments, in which MPs could freely criticize government, would oversee royal finances. Sovereigns became paid presidents of the state but with enormous power, provided they had parliamentary majorities. This was not democracy, just the launch of a new oligarchy that endured for a century in which the monarchs ruled in a fluctuating partnership with a tiny coterie of landed magnates, squires and City merchants. These were divided into two factions: the supporters of the new settlement, known as Whigs, and its enemies, known as Tories. Its Toleration Act was the first of its kind in Europe, yet it was not particularly tolerant: Jews could neither vote nor own property nor enjoy office; Dissenters and Catholics were also excluded from office.

† *Principia* explored calculus and gravity and demonstrated that all matter is attracted to other particles, explaining the motion of the planets and tides. This rational analysis did not rule out his belief in a unitarian God nor in alchemy: like most clever people of his

need for evidence, not on superstition – a conviction shared by a constellation of thinkers across Europe at this time who were increasingly in contact with each other – the start of an intellectual candescence that would illuminate the next century.

Leaving Cambridge, Newton moved to London to mastermind the modern currency and prosecute counterfeiters, a capital crime. He hunted down counterfeiters with all the relish and ingenuity of a detective and prosecuted twenty-eight coiners, many of them hanged, drawn and quartered – though there is no evidence that Newton penetrated the underworld in disguise. Now rich from the Mint, he increased his wealth by shrewd investments.

William commandeered England in his tireless campaign against the Sun King. James, backed by Louis, tried to have William assassinated, incited a Scottish revolt which was defeated at Dunkeld, sparking a massacre of Jacobite clans at Glencoe, then invaded Ireland. William routed his father-in-law at the Boyne and Aughrim, then fought Louis to a standstill – the start of England's 127-year war to prevent French dominion in Europe. But both were focused on the imminent death of the Habsburg king of Spain, *El Hechizado* – Carlos the Hexed.*

Everyone had been amazed that the ensorcelled Carlos, brother-in-law of Louis, was still alive. Son of the long-dead Planet King and his niece Mariana, he had been implacably visited by the curse of Habsburg intermarriage – born with a brain swelling, one kidney, one testicle and a jaw so deformed he could barely chew yet a throat so wide he could swallow chunks of meat. He was never fully literate, he limped and he suffered a multimorbidity of diseases, including measles, smallpox, rubella. Carlos had, writes Martyn Rady, 'an intersexual state with ambiguous genitalia': his urethra drained from the underside of an undeveloped penis, a detail on which peace in Europe was founded: could he father a child? If not, who would inherit his empire?

His mother had married him to a pretty French princess with whom he fell in love, but understandably their sex life, which must have caused them unbearable stress, failed. After years of cosy marriage, the confused girl mused that she 'was really not a virgin any longer, but that as far as she could work things out, she believed she would never

---

time, he thought such secret knowledge did not contradict the laws of nature.

* After Mary's death in 1694, William's heir was Mary's sister Anne and her son the duke of Gloucester, but in 1701, when the child died, William and Parliament agreed an Act of Settlement, organizing the succession through the nearest Protestant heir, Sophia, electress of Hanover, granddaughter of James I, and her son George, bypassing the rightful but Catholic family of James II. The Act arranged the succession into the twenty-first century.

have children', confiding to Louis's ambassador that 'despite too much vivacity' on his part, 'the coction, as the doctors call it, was not perfect'. Those doctors prescribed an unhelpful aphrodisiac: sleeping with the embalmed body of his father would help Carlos achieve an erection. When Carlos's first wife died, he married a German princess who pilfered from his palaces and forced him to undergo exorcisms against witchcraft. His mother had *El Hechizado* borne on a chair to save his energy; he was sane enough to reject making her all-powerful regent, pious enough to sit through an auto-da-fé for fourteen hours, strong enough to hunt and clever enough to invite his court painter Giordano to view Velázquez's *Las Meninas*. 'What do you think of it?' asked Carlos.

'Sire,' replied Giordano, 'this is the theology of painting.'

As Carlos declined, he visited the pantheon at Escorial to gaze upon the bodies of his family. Meanwhile the Habsburgs of Austria and the Bourbons of France bid for the succession.

Four deathbeds – those universal setpieces of family life, those lethal transfers of power that could destroy an empire – now destabilized Europe and Asia. 'In a twinkle, in a minute, in a breath,' said the greatest monarch of his time, Alamgir, 'the condition of the world changes.'

TITANIC DEATHBEDS: CARLOS, ALAMGIR, LOUIS, KANGXI

In late October 1700, in Madrid, Carlos suffered explosive dysentery with '250 motions in nineteen days', enduring Spanish fly painted on his feet as a blistering agent, dead pigeons on his head and draughts of milk of pearls. At last, on 1 November, he murmured, 'Now I am nothing,' and left the monarchy to Louis's grandson, Philippe.*

Louis could not resist accepting, but his Spanish gambit, vigorously resisted by the Austrian Habsburgs and England, launched a fifteen-year war that would bring his dreams to the edge of catastrophe. Far to the east, the crabbed old emperor Alamgir continued his twenty-year war to destroy the Shivaji kingdom.

Like Louis's, Alamgir's conquests in his own continent were unprecedented: he ruled more of India than anyone else in Indian history except the British in later centuries – but pride and empire have no end. Neither of them could stop. When Alamgir's vizier suggested they return to Delhi, World Seizer snarled, 'I wonder how an omniscient

---

* Carlos was thirty-eight. His post-mortem revealed that 'His heart was the size of a peppercorn; his lungs corroded; his intestines rotten and gangrenous; he had a single testicle, black as coal, and his head was full of water.'

hereditary servant like you could request this.' All the while, the family of Shivaji still held out in Deccan, now led by Rajaram's remarkable widow Taibai, just twenty-five years old, warrior queen daughter of Shivaji's commander-in-chief. 'So long as a breath of this mortal life remains, there's no release from toil,' said Alamgir. One of his weary officers complained, 'Such was his longing for taking all the forts, he personally runs about, panting for any heap of stones.' Yet his war was a gigantic enterprise: in 1695, his camp was thirty miles in circumference, with 60,000 cavalry, 100,000 infantry, 50,000 camels, 3,000 elephants and 250 bazaars ranged around his imperial red tent, where he held court with his sons and his Georgian dancer-paramour, Udaipuri.

Only the biggest economy in the world could fund war on such a scale: 24 per cent of global GDP was Indian and Alamgir's annual revenue was ten times that of Louis. While Europeans had traditionally clothed themselves in wool or linen, now their access to Indian cotton launched such a 'calico craze' for Indian textiles – *chintz, pyjamas, khaki, taffeta* and *bandanna* entering the language – that by 1684 the EIC alone was importing 1.76 million pieces a year or 83 per cent of its trade. In Africa, slaves were now being bought with Indian cotton.

Alamgir treated the Europeans in India as lucrative and useful intermediaries, buying ships and cannon from the Portuguese, but there was no doubt who was in charge. In 1686, the EIC, alarmed by French growth in India, demanded more trading rights. In 1688, Alamgir conquered Golconda, focusing his attention on the English Fort St George, Madras (Chennai). The EIC and Alamgir were expanding into the new areas at the same time, but when the clash came, Alamgir won easily.

Alamgir demanded higher taxes; the English resisted, at which Alamgir attacked Bombay and Surat: the English submitted humiliatingly, prostrating themselves before the emperor and paying a huge indemnity to get back their factories. Then in September 1695 a slave-trading English pirate, Long Ben (aka Henry Every), pulled off a remarkable heist, attacking Alamgir's annual twenty-five-ship flotilla to Mecca and capturing the gold-packed dhow the *Ganj-i-Sawai* (Excessive Treasure). The pirates tortured the Indian officers to make them hand over the gold and gang-raped the girls on board – many committed suicide – but Long Ben bagged the unprecedented swag of £600,000, supposedly the largest prize in history but certainly an incalculable sum, indeed so vast that it almost derailed the English presence in India.* Demanding

* As Long Ben divided up the swag, the English launched a worldwide manhunt to catch him. He escaped to the Caribbean, bribing his way. Six of his pirates were tried and hanged for the outrage, but Long Ben himself and the treasure vanished, fate unknown.

Long Ben's head, Alamgir's navy stormed Bombay and seized all EIC factories.

London sent out a veteran India merchant as the new president of Madras to negotiate. Thomas Pitt was the classic poacher turned gamekeeper. Thirty years earlier, this vicar's son from Dorset had started trading as a non-EIC trader (an 'interloper'), earning a fine and a fortune that enabled him to return home and buy a country estate and a seat in Parliament. Now hired by the EIC, Pitt was sent out to appease Alamgir, who was besieging Fort St George. Pitt folded and went on to negotiate a gigantic fine of 150,000 rupees before Bombay was restored and a new factory founded at Calcutta (Kolkata), while in Madras, he fortified the growing town. Taking advantage of the many Indian soldiers fighting in the Deccan, he started to hire Indian mercenaries, known as sepoys.

Pitt hated the English humiliation, complained that the 'native governors have the knack of tramping upon us and extorting what they please' – something they would never stop doing 'until we have made them sensible of our power'. That was impossible while Alamgir ruled.

Pitt had depleted his first fortune, but now, about to retire, he acquired a 426-carat diamond, mined at Kollur and smuggled out by a slave who concealed it within a wound in his body. It was then stolen by a Englishman who murdered the slave and sold it to an Indian merchant. In 1701, for around £20,000, the merchant sold it to Pitt, who sent it home to England in the heel of his son Robert's shoe and later sold it in Paris for the gargantuan sum of £135,000.* England's rise in India and elsewhere would be directed by the Pitts.

Now aged eighty-nine, Alamgir, wizened, morose and ailing, finally collapsed at Ahmadnagar – 'my journey's end' – tended by his daughter Zinatunnisa. 'I don't know who I am and what I've been doing,' he confessed to his son Azzam. 'I entirely lacked statesmanship.' In his will he advised his successors, 'never trust your sons, nor treat them intimately . . .' Signing off to Azzam – 'goodbye, goodbye, goodbye' – on 3 March 1707, he died as 'a whirlwind arose so fierce that it blew down all the tents standing in the encampment. Many persons and animals were killed . . . Villages were destroyed.' This time, the war between his sons, won by Muazzam (Bahadurshah), who killed Azzam, broke the empire. 'After me,' he had warned, 'chaos!'

'Après moi, le déluge,' agreed his contemporary Louis XIV, who would

---

* It took a few years to cut and sell: the buyer was the regent, Philippe, duc d'Orléans, who had it set into the crown of Louis XV.

similarly realize the futility of his intermediate war against England – and William of Orange.

In March 1702, William III was riding close to his home, Kensington Palace, when his horse tripped on a molehill and threw him. He died as Jacobites toasted 'the little gentleman in the black velvet waistcoat' – but the war against Louis went on and the new Queen Anne promoted John Churchill, earl of Marlborough, to captain-general and co-leader of a ministry with his dearest friend Sidney Godolphin, lord treasurer. Sarah Churchill tried to direct the insecure and ailing queen, tormented by twelve failed pregnancies. The two women were intimate friends, using the codenames Mrs Freeman (Sarah) and Mrs Morley (Anne), but there were two others in the partnership: Mr Freeman (Marlborough) and Mr Montgomery (Godolphin). 'Every day,' wrote Anne to Sarah, 'makes me more and more sensible of the great blessing God Almighty has given me in three such friends as your dear self, Mr Freeman and Mr Montgomery.'

Small, dark, reticent and incorruptible, Godolphin, who had served in the treasury under Charles, James and William, became the first real prime minister, a magisterial administrator of Parliament and finance, whose protégé Robert Walpole praised his 'good management, prudence and dexterity'.* No minister before had ever had to raise such vast sums as Godolphin did to fund a European war, but he also negotiated a union between England and Scotland, persuading the Scottish parliamentarians to merge with the London Parliament† and so becoming in 1707 the first lord treasurer of Great Britain. His fellow duumvir Marlborough was now fifty and untried, yet he proved the greatest of British generals. 'I long to be with you,' Marlborough wrote to Godolphin, whose letters were 'one of the greatest pleasures I have'. While the general was away, Sarah closely advised Godolphin. The duumvirs arranged marriages between their children.

Sailing for Europe, Marlborough directed the coalition of the Dutch and the Habsburgs, but he also won the battles, his finest hour being

---

* There is a tendency to backdate the rise of democracy. As we will see, Walpole is traditionally named as 'the first prime minister', but there was little difference in style from his patron Godolphin. Both were appointed by sovereigns, not chosen by Parliament, and both were expert managers of finance and Parliament. But Godolphin was the first to fund a European war; Walpole never had to. Godolphin trained Walpole, who adored and respected him, even resigning to protect his patron. It would be eighty years before Parliament could force a monarch to appoint a minister and before prime ministers became the leader of their cabinet in the modern sense.

† Scotland's population was one-ninth of England's, its wealth a fortieth of England's: by population, the Scots would receive eighty-five MPs at Westminster; by wealth thirteen. It was agreed that Scotland should receive forty-five MPs in the Commons and sixteen lords.

a forced march 250 miles southwards in summer 1704 to save Vienna from a French army. He rendezvoused with the Habsburg commander, Prince Eugen of Savoy, and together they routed the French–Bavarian army at Blenheim. 'Give my duty to the Queen,' wrote Marlborough to Sarah, 'and let her know her army has had a glorious victory.' Eugen – angular, ugly, slovenly, peppered with snuff but brilliant – was no less remarkable* and they formed a rare double act. 'Prince Eugen and I never differ about our share of the laurels,' said Marlborough. 'I not only esteem but I really love the prince.' Leading charges in battles, sometimes unhorsed as equerries were beheaded beside him, Marlborough won a spree of victories and as ambassador-general held the coalition together. In April 1707, he set off on an important mission, to visit the ascetic warrior king of Sweden, Charles XII, in Saxony.

The Muscovite tsar Peter I and his ally Augustus the Strong, king of Poland and elector of Saxony, had attacked Sweden, hoping to carve up its Baltic lands. But Charles stormed across the Baltic, defeated Peter and deposed Augustus, before occupying Poland. Still only twenty-five, he was debating whether to join France against the Habsburgs or attack Muscovy. Marlborough, keen to ensure that he attacked Peter,† flattered Charles, who anyway saw Muscovy as the bigger threat. On 1 January 1708 the Swedish king invaded Muscovy, the first of three modern invaders to underestimate the span of Russia. Charles swerved south into Ukraine.

Peter, a twitching giant of six foot seven, was a soldier-reformer, obsessed with technical novelties in ships and cannon, determined to transform and rearm his kingdom. He was gifted with the three essentials that every politician requires to achieve anything: VAR – vision, acumen and resources – as well an invincible constitution and a taste for wild wassailing that involved lethal alcoholic consumption, dwarves jumping out of cakes and naked girls, and fistfights. Yet he had visited the Netherlands and London to procure military technology. After enforcing his power, massacring and personally torturing rivals, this terrifying and capable autocrat reformed his nobility, making them

---

* Eugen was the son of a Savoy prince and Olympe, niece of Mazarin, mistress of Louis. But Olympe was implicated in the Affair of the Poisons, which cast a shadow over Eugen. Part of a coterie of homosexual aristocrats, the unprepossessing Eugen was despised by Louis, who told him to become a priest. Driven out of Versailles, he served the Austrian Habsburgs, seizing much of the Ottoman Balkans. As a general he was mobile, fluid and clear-sighted, reflecting on discipline: 'You should only be harsh when, as often happens, kindness proves useless.'

† Peter offered Marlborough the exotic titles prince of Kyiv or prince of Siberia if he could persuade Charles to attack the Habsburgs.

wear German clothes and shave their beards. He founded a new capital, St Petersburg, on captured Swedish territory, but also modernized his army, funded with peasant taxes, and created a Baltic navy. His conscription of peasants to serve for life in his army alongside the enforced service of nobles militarized society to create a huge standing army of 300,000. Its scale allowed the tsars to use its men as cannon fodder to compensate for Russian backwardness.

On 8 July 1709, at Poltava (Ukraine), Peter routed Charles, making Poland a Russian satellite and mopping up the Swedish lands of the southern Baltic.* The Romanov tsar became Peter the Great, first *imperator* (emperor) of Russia (*Rossiiya*, a Hellenization of Rus), a new European power and Eurasian empire, forged with European technology, embellished with European art, manners and luxuries. But the very state itself was an empire inspired by an exceptional national and religious mission of rapacious expansion and ruled by an autocrat who personified the state without the restraint of representative assemblies, noble rights or civil institutions found in other European kingdoms.

Mission accomplished in the east, Marlborough faced a challenge at home. He had earned himself a dukedom, a principality of the Holy Roman Empire, a palace, Blenheim near Oxford, and a fortune, but, less steady than Godolphin, he was highly strung and mercurial, swinging between elated energy and cyclothymic collapses at times of crisis. 'I really am so weary of the business of the world,' he told Godolphin. 'I've no pleasure but the expectation I have of being with you and Lady Marlborough.'

Yet Anne and Sarah's relationship soured. Anne, overweight, blotchy and sickly, worshipped the beautiful Sarah, but her royal grandeur and emotional neediness were matched by Sarah's termagant unkindness. 'I am very sorry to find Mrs Morley and Mrs Freeman can't yet bring things quite right,' wrote Mr Montgomery to Mr Freeman. 'I'm sure they will at last.' But they did not. The jealousy and suspicion of Marlborough's opponents engendered the fear that the paladin could become a Cromwell: they used Anne's Stuart pride and Sarah's malice to promote a more affectionate royal friend, Abigail Masham, who,

---

* Peter crushed the Ukrainian Cossacks under Hetman Ivan Mazeppa, who, after being his ally, had switched sides to support the Swedes and bid for independence. Charles and Mazeppa escaped to Benderi in Ottoman territory. Charles later made it back to Sweden, an eclipsed force. Mazeppa died, succeeded as hetman by Ivan Skoropadsky, a Russian client. A semi-independent hetmanate, closely allied to Russia, survived until 1775. Peter's attempt to expand into Ottoman Ukraine, Moldova and Wallachia (Romania) ended in disaster in July 1711 when he was defeated and almost captured by the grand vizier at Stănilești. In 1722–3, the voracious empire builder attacked Persia, seizing parts of Azerbaijan.

prompted by their rival Robert Harley, turned the queen against her three friends.

In 1708, Harley persuaded Anne to dismiss Godolphin, but Marlborough's threat to resign forced his reinstatement, now backed by a young protégé, a coarse, ruddy-cheeked Norfolk MP, Robert Walpole, secretary at war. By now, Anne and Sarah were having altercations of blistering malice. Sensing Anne's dislike, Marlborough requested the captain-generalship for life, alarming the Stuart monarch who feared a Cromwellian dictatorship. 'I have reason to be convinced', Marlborough told Sarah in one of their coded letters, that '42 [Anne] has been jealous of the power of 39 [himself]'.

Anne unsurprisingly had come to hate Sarah: 'I don't love complaining but it's impossible to help saying nobody was ever so used by a friend as I have been by her ever since my coming to the Crown,' she told Marlborough. 'I desire nothing but that she should leave off teasing and tormenting me.' Few monarchs have ever written such a letter, but Sarah was now 'saying many shocking things' – even accusing Anne of lesbianism. Marlborough and Godolphin must have despaired, while Walpole called Sarah the 'Damned Bitch'. Marlborough's peace negotiations with Louis XIV collapsed and Anne finally dismissed Godolphin, his character now blackened as the insinuating Volpone (in Ben Jonson's play), and appointed Harley, who went on to win a parliamentary majority. Marlborough was dismissed, and Godolphin died the following year. Harley, now earl of Oxford and prime minister, orchestrated the impeachment of Marlborough, who was devotedly defended by Walpole but nonetheless forced into exile. The queen, realizing she had been manipulated and regretting her treatment of the duumvirs, sacked Oxford just before she died in 1714.

The oligarchs of 1688 ensured a Protestant succession, ushering in the new king, George I, the fifty-four-year-old elector of Hanover,* who, since many Tories favoured a Stuart restoration, sensibly promoted the Whigs and reappointed Marlborough as captain-general. Backed by Louis, James Stuart, James II's heir, landed in Scotland, holding court in Edinburgh, but Marlborough's last service was to coordinate the defeat of the rebellion.

---

* George I arrived with his German mistresses, one so cadaverous she was nicknamed the Scarecrow, the other obese. Londoners nicknamed them Elephant and Castle after a famous London pub, itself named after the west African trade. George was even less attractive than he looked: in 1694, the elector had discovered that his wife was having an affair with a young Swede, Count Philipp von Königsmarck, whom he had murdered and probably dissected and buried under the Hanover palace; his wife was imprisoned for thirty years and never allowed to see her children again.

Marlborough's victories had marked the rise of Britain, increasingly a global force, as a European power for the first time since the loss of its French territories in 1453. The peace of Utrecht was a stroke of luck for the ageing Louis XIV, whose grandson Philippe remained king of Spain while the Habsburgs were compensated by Naples, Milan and Belgium; Britain only got Gibraltar – and the *asiento de negros*, the Spanish licence to supply slaves which was vested in the specially founded South Sea Company. Investors – from the king and his mistresses to Walpole and Newton – traded the shares, which went up and up.

The peace was some consolation to Louis, but 'France had expanded too far and perhaps unjustly,' wrote Louis's wife, Maintenon. 'Our court is still very sad. We talk only of wheat, oats, barley and straw. He's very occupied with the relief of the people.' In April 1711, smallpox killed Louis's eldest son – and then *his* eldest son too, followed by *his* eldest son.* Louis was heartbroken. 'I've never,' noted Maintenon, 'seen such sorrow . . . at court.'

On 1 September 1715, after the longest reign in European history, seventy-two years, Louis, riddled with gangrene, his left leg completely blackened, managed his deathbed with faultless style. 'My dear child,' he told his five-year-old great-grandson, soon to be Louis XV, 'you're going to be the greatest king in the world,' but 'Don't imitate me in my wars.' Then he addressed his ministers: '*Adieu, messieurs* . . . I'm leaving but the state will always remain.' Lastly he turned to Maintenon: 'What will become of you, madame?'

'I'm nothing,' she replied. 'Think only of God.' The servants wept loudly.

'Why are you crying?' asked Louis. 'Did you think I was immortal?'

---

* Smallpox killed 400,000 Europeans annually during the eighteenth century. Yet variolation – the introduction of the antigen – from a smallpox scab, long practised from Africa to China, was about to change this. In 1706, an Akan slave given to an American Protestant minister, Cotton Mather, who named him Onesimus, explained the procedure to him. 'Enquiring of my Negro-man Onesimus, who is a pretty Intelligent Fellow,' Mather told the Royal Society of London, 'whether he ever had the Small-Pox; he answered, both, Yes, and No; and then told me, that he had undergone an Operation, which had given him something of the Small-Pox, and would forever preserve him from it, adding that it was often used among the Guramantese . . . and showed me in his Arm the Scar.' Despite resistance by those who did not believe Africans could be more advanced than Europeans, Mather used variolation to mitigate a smallpox epidemic in Boston. In 1715, the British duke's daughter and wife of the British ambassador to Istanbul, Lady Mary Wortley Montagu, her beauty spoiled by smallpox, returned to London with an Ottoman version. Her variolation of her own children persuaded Princess Caroline, wife of the future George II, to inoculate her children. It is worth pointing out that it was not doctors who recognized the possibilities of inoculation but intelligent amateurs. Among those inoculated in childhood was Edward Jenner, who later improved this method.

Reciting a prayer, he passed 'like a candle going out'.

In China, the other titan of the age, Kangxi, faced his own agony of succession.

'If I can die without there being an outbreak of trouble,' he wrote in his late sixties, 'my desires will be fulfilled.' His son Yinreng, whose mother had died in 1674 giving birth to him, grew into a vicious paedophile who bought children for sexual abuse and tried to overthrow his father – he may have been insane. As his own decline encouraged conspiracy among his twenty-four sons, Kangxi ordered Yinreng's perpetual imprisonment for 'inhumanity and devilry'. The emperor started to show favour to his eleventh son, Yinzhen, who introduced him to his own son, the eleven-year-old Hongli, whom Kiangxi soon doted on. When the old emperor met the boy's mother he called her a 'lucky woman' for bearing a child who would bring her 'great honour' – an unmissable hint.

Dying on 20 December 1722, he left the throne to Yinzhen, who became the Yongzheng Emperor. France was in recovery; Mughal India was dissolving into chaos; but Kiangxi left China as the greatest power on earth: his grandson Hongli became the Qianlong Emperor, who ruled into another age.

The resurgent Habsburgs on the other hand were haunted by an issue of gender. In Vienna, Karl VI, son of Hogmouth, had failed to take Spain but had been consoled by his succession as emperor-archduke. Yet his young daughter was his heir – and a predator stalked the empire.

COCK ROBIN, PRUSSIAN MONSTER, POLISH HERCULES

Karl had married a German princess, Elizabeth, blonde, delicate and spirited: he called her White Liezl. In 1716, Liezl gave birth to a daughter Maria Theresa, but to help her conceive a son doctors had prescribed a calorific diet lubricated with liquor that so bloated her she ultimately had to be conveyed in a mechanical chair.

Maria Theresa, blonde, blue-eyed, devout and intelligent, was educated by Jesuits, sang in family operas and enjoyed riding. At nineteen she married a genial prince, Franz Stefan, duke of Lorraine, whom she adored, giving birth to sixteen children in twenty years. She showed no special talents, but they were not looked for in her either. Only extreme jeopardy would reveal them. Karl frittered away his resources, just as a second-rank power, Prussia, was saving every pfennig and collecting giants.

Its Hohenzollern sovereign, Frederick William, whose father had negotiated an upgrade to king, was a half-demented martinet but also a frugal, shrewd visionary who turned Prussia into the Sparta of Europe. Inheriting the throne at twenty-five, he purged the kingdom of his father's Frenchified frippery and instead focused on attracting industrious settlers to his territories, advancing trade and creating a disproportionately large army, featuring infantry that fired 'like a walking battery whose speed in reloading tripled its firepower' (in the words of his son) – and a regiment of 'Potsdam giants'. He hired colossi from all over Europe, dispatching giant-nappers to capture them. 'The most beautiful girl or woman in the world would be a matter of indifference to me,' he said, 'but tall soldiers – *they* are my weakness.'

He loved his queen Sophia Dorothea of Hanover but she loathed his violent abuse, 'horrible avarice' and oafish philistinism. He considered divorcing her, but he could not risk offending the family: her father had become George I of Britain.

London was in the grip of a speculative frenzy, ignited by shares of the slave-trading South Sea Company, which was structured to pay off government debt. Fortunes were made trading in and out of the shares. The elderly Isaac Newton made so much selling shares that he could not resist rebuying them. But few realized that the company was badly run. When it crashed, it wiped out many investors. Newton, who in old age lived with his niece (her husband had succeeded him at the Mint), was abashed to lose half his fortune – though he remained very rich. A furious backlash blamed corrupt politicians, Elephant and Castle, and the German king. George turned to Robert Walpole, Godolphin's protégé, who first acted as 'the Skreen', protecting those at fault, then turned to solving the crisis. Known as Cock Robin, unflappable, cynical and earthy, jovially munching apples in the House of Commons, Walpole boasted he always opened his gamekeeper's letters first, and described himself as 'no saint, no spartan, no reformer', but he had remained so loyal to Godolphin and Marlborough that he had been imprisoned by Harley. He had traded in South Sea stocks and had made losses (not the 1,000 per cent profit of legend), but he was compensated by massive profits in another slave-trading stock, Royal African. Now he turned the crash into a success by dividing the South Sea Company into two, a slave-trading company that profitably sold human beings for decades more and a bank that issued government bonds. Walpole converted decades of random debt into a single easily traded bond, creating the first modern bond market which gave Britain unique access to the capital that was crucial in making a world power.

Walpole mocked public virtue, which he called 'schoolboy flights', teasing youngsters, 'Well, are you to be an old Roman, a patriot? You'll soon come off of that and grow wiser.' He was, recalled a friend, 'good-natured, cheerful, social, inelegant in his manners, loose in his morals' with 'a coarse wit' but 'the ablest manager of a parliament I believe ever lived'. Accumulating a fortune and art collection for his palatial Hought-on Hall in Norfolk, Walpole was married to Catherine, a merchant's daughter, both of them sensual enthusiasts who when their marriage cooled took a bevy of lovers. After her death, Robin married his witty, glamorous mistress, Maria Skerritt, twenty-five years younger, but three months later she died in childbirth, leaving him bereft.

Robin was a master at managing his royal masters, first the sausagey George I then his son George II.* 'All men,' he often said, 'have their price.' When a rival tried to cultivate George II's mistress, Walpole countered by befriending his vivacious wife Queen Caroline; he earthily joked that his rival 'took the wrong sow by the ear, I the right'. Gos-sips claimed that he had pimped his wife to George II (when prince of Wales) and slept with the queen. His twenty-year rule confirmed the supremacy of the House of Commons, and his Whig oligarchy – the 'Robinocracy' – ruled Britain for the next forty years.

The Hanoverians feuded with their sons – but this was nothing com-pared to family atrocities of Hohenzollerns and Romanovs.† Frederick William and Sophia, George II's sister, had fifteen children; she was devoted to the eldest, Frederick, whom she hoped to marry into the British dynasty. The king ruined the negotiations and then when she got pregnant unexpectedly tried to kill her for adultery. He bullied and beat Frederick, punishing him for small infractions such as wearing gloves or being thrown by a horse. Sophia supported the children. 'Whatev-er my father ordered my brother to do,' remembered Frederick, 'my mother commanded him to do the very reverse.'

---

* Walpole never called himself prime minister. The top office was lord treasurer, last held by the Duke of Shrewsbury, who lived an extraordinary life. In 1668, he was the child whose father was killed by his mother's lover, Buckingham, whom he in turn later destroyed. Twice he was the helmsman who steered Britain in dynastic crisis: in 1688, he invited William III to invade; rewarded with a dukedom and regarded as the noblest patrician of his time, even William called him 'king of hearts'; in 1714, he ruled as all-powerful lord treasurer when the last Stuart, Queen Anne, died, ensuring the Hanoverian succession. Since 1715, the treasury has been 'in commission' under the first lord of the treasury, in-creasingly known as prime minister. In 1732, George II gave a townhouse to Walpole, who accepted it as a residence for the first lord: Ten Downing Street.
† Before his death in 1725, Peter had tortured his own son, Alexei, to death for fleeing to Austria. He left the throne to his wife, Catherine, a former Lithuanian laundress and camp follower – a rise unique in European history and the first of a line of female Russian autocrats.

Just five foot three, the king terrorized his soldiers and courtiers, his furies aggravated by the agonies of porphyria – mania, gout, pus-filled sores, fevers and cramps. 'I wish to suffer everything patiently,' he said, taking up painting to ease his 'torments'. The queen encouraged Frederick, now sixteen, to follow his artistic inclinations, practising the flute in between military drills, secretly amassing a French library. His monstrous father now suspected him of lacking 'truly manly inclinations'.

In 1728, father and son set off to visit the ruler of Prussia's traditional rival, Saxony. A strapping athlete, Augustus the Strong, who supposedly fathered 365 children, was also king of Poland and he was everything Frederick William loathed: depraved, extravagant, godless – he had become Catholic to clinch the Polish throne – and powerless. His ally Peter the Great had reduced Poland to a Russian client state. Augustus, a champion fox-tosser (once presiding over a gruesome festival at which 647 foxes, 533 hares and 34 badgers were tossed), promoted himself with pageants, operas and Meissen china (kidnapping its creator to develop the technology) to make Dresden the 'most dazzling court in Europe'.

Augustus' legion of mistresses was led by the talented, spirited Aurora von Königsmarck* and his Turkish slave Fatima, but it was also said to include his own beautiful, hard-smoking, cross-dressing daughter Anna, Countess Orzelska, aged twenty, who immediately dazzled the visiting Frederick, still only sixteen. Frederick remembered her as 'this little miracle of nature who possessed every possible charm, together with good taste and delicacy', and according to his elder sister Wilhelmine he 'promised everything to gain possession of this beauty, his first lover'.

Hoping to divert him from his daughter-mistress, Augustus shocked the Prussians by opening a curtain to reveal a naked opera singer in a niche. Frederick William hurried his son out of the room, but by then Frederick was in love with Orzelska and suffered depression when he got back to grim Berlin. Shocked by what he had seen on the visit, his father boasted, 'I am pure as when I left home.' But on their return king and prince were on collision course thanks to what the father called Frederick's 'effeminate, lascivious occupations'.

The king beat Frederick with his cane, punched him in the face and threw him to the ground, forcing him to kiss his feet. When his daughter Wilhelmine supported her brother, he smashed her in the face, knocking her unconscious. But now Frederick fell in love with a boy.

---

* Aurora was the daughter of a Swedish-German general; it was her brother Philipp who was murdered by George I of Britain for adultery with his wife.

THE PHILOSOPHER PRINCE, THE *PHILOSOPHE*
AND THE MARQUISE

After an intimate relationship with a Scottish officer,* Frederick was sent away to repent. Instead the eighteen-year-old prince of Prussia established an affinity with Hans von Katte, an aesthetic officer who was eight years older; together they planned the prince's escape to England, an act of treason.

In August 1730, when Frederick was caught, his father interrogated him, asking, 'Did you seduce Katte or Katte seduce you?' He then ordered that Katte be beheaded – 'better that Katte came to death than the justice out of the world' – in front of the boy, who was brought out and forced to watch, clearly to purge him of unnatural desires.

'Please forgive me, my dear Katte, in God's name, forgive me,' cried Frederick.

'There's nothing to forgive,' replied Katte. 'I die for you with joy in my heart!' Frederick fainted. Frederick William decided to execute Frederick, telling his queen he was already dead. 'What!' she screamed. 'Have you murdered your son?'

'He wasn't my son. Just a miserable deserter!'

'*Mon Dieu, mon fils!*' The queen and her daughter Wilhelmine shrieked. The king beat the girl and had to be pulled off before he killed her. The Habsburgs' Kaiser Karl was present and interceded to save Frederick's life – a mercy that must later have been regretted by his daughter Maria Theresa.

Frederick never forgave his father – 'what a terrible man' – but over the next ten years he grew to appreciate that Frederick William 'knew the best interests of his country better than any minister or general. It was through his efforts, through his tireless labour, that I have been able to accomplish everything that I've done since.'

Frederick planned a delicious revenge on his father, hungrily consuming the literature of a new movement that was sweeping Europe – the Enlightenment – represented by his hero Voltaire, with whom the prince now started to correspond.

On 28 March 1727, Voltaire, already at thirty-three a notorious playwright, sometime royal favourite, sometime dissident, now exiled in London, attended the funeral of Isaac Newton. It was a seminal moment. Already convinced that Britain's mixed constitution was

---

* Scottish and Irish officers – usually Jacobite exiles after 1688 – now filled the armies of the Hohenzollerns, Habsburgs, Bourbons and Romanovs. They were known as the Wild Geese.

superior to French absolutism and an admirer of Newtonian science, Voltaire interviewed Newton's doctors, fascinated to discover that the scientist had died a virgin but also to hear from his niece that his theory of gravity originated in a falling apple. It was a passing of the baton: Voltaire saw himself as Newton's heir.

Born François-Marie Arouet, the son of a lawyer, nicknamed Zozo in the family, Voltaire refused to study law and wrote poetry instead. When his father sent him to work for the French ambassador to Holland, his affair with a teenage girl known as Pimpette got him sacked just as his poem on the French regent's incest with his daughter got him imprisoned in the Bastille. Later his cheek to an aristocrat got him beaten up and imprisoned again. Returning from England, he joined a consortium that bought up the state lottery, making a fortune. Next he fell in love with a talented, beautiful, younger writer, Émilie, marquise du Châtelet, and settled (with her husband's permission) at her chateau where they wrote philosophy, history, fiction and science* – she translated Newton, he popularized Newton; and she was the first woman to have a paper published by the French Academy. Later they each took other lovers – he fell in lust with his niece – but remained partners until she died in childbirth.

In 1734, his *Lettres philosophiques*, arguing for religious and political tolerance, won European fame, but it was just the start of his campaign against superstition that he later expressed in a slogan: '*Écrasez l'infâme*'. It was the unjust torture and execution of a wrongly convicted Protestant, Jean Calas, much later in 1762 that inspired his most famous campaign. He believed in human progress, but not too much: Voltaire mocked foolish optimism with his character Pangloss in *Candide*. He criticized all religions – Christians, Jews and Muslims – mocking priests who 'rise from an incestuous bed, manufacture a hundred versions of God, then eat and drink God, then piss and shit God'. But he joked, 'There's no God, but don't tell that to my servant lest he murder me at night.'

Voltaire was the first of the *philosophes*, who advocated a new, sceptical, rational, scientific, tolerant state of mind that sought the greatest happiness for mankind and challenged blind faith and sacred monarchy. If we choose to worship God, argued Immanuel Kant, the German *philosophe* of Königsberg later in the century, 'we finite creatures can never understand the infinite nature of reality'. Kant summed up the

---

* Even if they did not yet understand the practicality of their discoveries, Daniel Fahrenheit invented the thermometer in 1714, Antoine-Laurent Lavoisier discovered the nature of oxygen and its role in burning, while Alessandro Volta invented the electric battery, though electricity was seen as entertainment rather than useful.

Enlightened spirit in two words: *Sapere aude!* – Dare to use your own intellect!

Voltaire, who was richer and more famous than his cohorts, being an adept financier in addition to all his other talents, played the role of protector: when a young, poor writer got into trouble, Voltaire intervened. Denis Diderot, son of a provincial cutler who cut him off when he refused to enter the priesthood, was a messy, mischievous, manic force, curious about everything from hermaphroditism to acoustics, pouring out works that challenged royal and Catholic rule, love letters to his many paramours, novels and pornography: his *Indiscreet Jewels*, an erotic fantasia recounted by the vaginas of odalisques talking about a voyeuristic sultan, written to show how women enjoyed sex as much as men, got him arrested. Voltaire ensured Diderot's release, after which he launched the work that came to define the new thinking, the *Encyclopédie*, featuring articles on every subject illuminated by this new Enlightenment.

Yet it was not the end of the old thought: there were still plenty of religious fanatics; some *philosophes* opposed slavery; some did not; few were even democrats. 'Democracy,' wrote Kant, 'is a despotism because it establishes an executive power in which "all" decide for or against the "one" who does not.' Most believed in mixed monarchies with reform from above but Voltaire wrote a biography of Peter the Great and encouraged 'philosopher-kings'.

The vaunted Enlightenment was actually the intellectual movement of a feverishly interconnected European elite close to a nervous breakdown and identity crisis, still honeycombed with snobbery, bigotry, conspiracy theories and magical hucksterism. It was an era of disguise and reinvention, a time of sociability, travel, individuality and sexual freedom personified by a writer named Giacomo Casanova. After a famous escape from a Venetian prison, Casanova travelled through Europe, habitually cursed with indebtedness, religious persecution and venereal disease, studying science and alchemy, seeking aristocratic patronage, proposing financial schemes, adopting false names and titles, losing money in *faro* games and meeting emperors and *philosophes*. All the while he was relishing sexual encounters with women high and low, young and old, some romantic, some adventurous (a threesome with nuns) and others predatory, rapey and even paedophilic.

When he retired to be the librarian of a Bohemian count, he recounted it all in memoirs that were the expression of the new sensibility of self amid a new consciousness of community. 'I pride myself,' wrote Diderot, 'on being a citizen of that great city, the world.' The spirit was expressed in letter writing: educated people from Massachusetts to

Moscow stayed up late by candlelight manically writing letters that they often expected their friends to copy and share with cognoscenti around the world.

In 1736, one of the best letter writers, Prince Frederick, wrote a letter to another virtuoso epistolarian, Voltaire, who recognized his correspondent's rare character but also like all writers lost his mind as soon as he was flattered by a leader. Frederick was secretly rebelling against his father, growing his hair long, dressing in scarlet brocaded dressing gowns. He despised Christianity, Germanic philistinism and martial machismo; he worshipped everything French, sending Voltaire his poetry and philosophical writings. But at the same time he mulled over the Habsburg succession: he considered marrying Maria Theresa until his father forced him to marry a German princess who his sister said smelled so foul that 'she must have a dozen anal fistulas'. 'Thank God that's over,' Frederick told his sister after the wedding night, callously ignoring his wife for the rest of their marriage. During this time, his father let him accompany the ageing Prince Eugen on campaign, enabling Frederick to study the brilliant old man – waspish, cultured, homosexual: 'If I understand anything of my trade I owe it to Prince Eugen.' Although attracted to the Enlightenment, writing an attack on Machiavelli, Frederick planned a Machiavellian gambit that would shock Europe.

As Frederick dreamed of a bold conquest, another upstart prince, another exceptional ruler, Iran's Nader Shah, planned his own invasion. The target was India. In 1738, Nader seized Kandahar and Kabul, then Lahore. Then the greatest conqueror of the century and the last of the tribal marauders emulated his heroes Genghis and Tamerlane and advanced on Delhi.

On 24 February 1739, the Mughal emperor Muhammad Shah, great-grandson of Alamgir, who wrote poetry as Sada Rangila (Eternal Playboy), made his stand at Karnal. Rangila was a connoisseur of the music of Sadarang, the painting of Nidha Mal and the singing of the *tawaifs*, courtesans, led by Nur Bai, gap-toothed singer-poetess, 'bulbul-voiced and houri-like in beauty', who was richly paid by the line of the *ghazals* she sang. A regular paramour of Rangila, Nur Bai enjoyed tormenting his official wife, Qudsia Begum, herself an ex-singer, but she was more interested in a colossal diamond he kept in his turban. While the elephants of potentates queued up outside her mansion, Nur Bai herself paraded around Delhi on her own bejewelled elephant. After the atrocious murders of his predecessors, it was no wonder Rangila devoted himself to love and music. Playboy's court artists portrayed him penetrating dancing girls with an invincible phallus, but this was no use against Nader.

After Alamgir's death, the Mughals had lost control of their magnates and *subahdars* (governors). The young Rangila had turned to one
of Alamgir's protégés, Chin Qilich Khan (Lord Boy Swordsman), son
of a Turkic paladin from Bukhara, now viceroy of Deccan with the title
Nizam al-Mulk (Regulator of the Realm). Yet Nizam was infuriated
by Emperor Playboy's 'jesters and harlots', who mocked him as 'the
Deccan Dancing Monkey'. The Nizam retired to carve out his own kingdom, founding a dynasty that would rule Hyderabad until 1947. But
he was not the only one. Across India, *subahdars* seized revenues and
territories, setting themselves up as princes – nawabs. The Tamerlane
family had arrived as Turkic conquerors, becoming Indianized through
their marriages with Hindu princesses, but the dynasty and a tiny clique
of courtiers had squeezed the empire to pay for their wars and luxuries.
A total of 655 grandees, suggests one estimate, out of 150 million Indians, owned a quarter of GNP. Shahjahan's failed attempt to conquer
Samarkand and his vanity projects – the Taj Mahal – followed by Alamgir's interminable wars contributed to the collapse of the Mughals. 'I
failed,' Alamgir admitted on his deathbed, 'to protect the people.' Now
this predatory rent-seeking system, dependent on strong emperors
and weak competition, had fallen apart, 'undermined from within and
below,' writes Richard M. Eaton, 'in the way termites silently hollow out
the base of a wooden structure'. In the east, Bengal was privatized by its
subahdar; in the west, a Sikh chieftain, Banda Bahadur, seized Punjab.

In the centre, Shivaji's grandson, Shahu, had appointed a fierce,
capable Maratha general called Baji Rao as *peshwa* (minister). Baji had
expanded aggressively into Mughal territory and hacked out a Maratha
empire, training his son Balaji Rao as successor: this cavalry maestro
had defeated the Nizam of Hyderabad and other princes, finally turning
to the decaying House of Tamerlane: 'Let's hack at the trunk of the
withering tree and the branches will fall off themselves.' In 1737, Baji
galloped north to Delhi, defeated the Mughals and the branches started
to fall off. But he himself was exhausted, dying before his fortieth birthday. The House of Tamerlane ruled no further than Delhi, but it took a
foreign predator to break the Mughals.

THE ORGASM, THE CONQUEROR, THE DIAMOND AND THE COURTESAN: NADER, RANGILA AND FREDERICK

'I haven't come to leave the country in peace but to turn everything
upside down,' declared Nader, an athletic, weather-beaten, rugged, six

foot lifeforce. 'I'm not a human, I am God's wrath.' His rise was made possible only by the degeneration of the Safavi shahs, whose early deaths from alcoholism, syphilis and opium had so weakened Persia that an Afghan warlord with a tiny army managed to conquer the empire. It was a catastrophe that empowered Nader.

In 1709, the Pashtun Ghilzai tribes, Sunnis who hated the Shiite Safavis, led by a respected chieftain, Mirwais Hotak, rebelled against their Persian rulers. The Safavis, who also ruled the Caucasus in the west, promoted Bagrationi kings – descendants of Queen Tamara – to high offices and recruited armies of Georgian soldier-slaves: Shah Hosain defeated a rebellious Georgian king Giorgi XI, a tough paladin, then restored him to his throne, appointing him commander-in-chief and governor of Kandahar. Giorgi, who converted to Islam under the name Gurgin Khan, marched east with his Georgian army and retook Afghanistan, letting Hotak massacre his fellow Pashtun rivals, the Abdalis. These rivalries would soon explode out of Afghanistan in the shape of two Afghan empires.

King Giorgi sent Mirwais Hotak to Isfahan, where he warned the shah against the overmighty kinglet who governed Afghanistan and Georgia. Mirwais Baba – Granpa Mirwais – was sent back to watch Giorgi, who demanded the Afghan's daughter as concubine. Hotak sent another girl disguised as his daughter, then orchestrated the slaughter of Giorgi and his Georgians at a banquet. He united Afghan chieftains, asking, 'if there are any among you who lack the courage to enjoy this precious gift of heaven-sent freedom'. On his deathbed, Mirwais Baba ordered his eighteen-year-old son, Mahmud, to 'take Isfahan itself'.

In May 1722, Mahmud Hotak and 15,000 Afghans, armed with a Pashtun innovation, light cannon mounted on camels – *zamburaks* (wasplets) – invaded Iran. At Gulnabad, 50,000 splendid Persian troops blocked the way. 'If you win, the treasure of Isfahan is your prize,' Hotak told his Pashtuns. 'If you fail, you've no retreat and will face death, embittered by disgrace.' Thanks to their 100 *zamburaks*, they routed the Iranians, then laid siege to Isfahan, where 80,000 died of starvation. Taking the city, Mahmud declared himself shah, but he struggled to control Persia. Maddened by paranoia and projectile dysentery, he killed first most of the Safavis, then his own family. 'His bowels were so disordered that he defecated excrement from his mouth,' until he was strangled by his own nephew Ashraf. Persia disintegrated.

Only one Safavi prince, Tahmasp, survived, but his prospects were dire until he was rescued by an obscure warlord: Nader. Born in 1698, Nader, son of an Afshari Turkman goatherd, started as a brigand with feral charisma but soon commanded his own army: he knew the name of every officer and many troopers, who called him Baba Bazorg – Big Daddy. He now offered his 2,000 men to the beleaguered shah, but he had a rival, the khan of the Qajars, a Turkman clan from Caspian shores, Fath-Ali Khan. In 1726 Nader had him murdered, though later the Qajars would rule Iran. Now Nader retook ruined Isfahan. As Ashraf Hotak fled back to Afghanistan, Big Daddy restored Tahmasp, a drunken jackanapes. Then, deploying a semi-tribal, semi-regular army of horse archers, *zamburaks* and *jacayerchi* (musketeers), Iranians, Kurds, Turkmen, Afghans, Uzbeks, Nader seized back swathes of Iraq and the Caucasus. Tahmasp awarded him the title Tahmasp-Qoli – Tahmasp's Slave – then regent. But Nader wanted more.

In 1731, Tahmasp lost Nader's Caucasian gains. In Isfahan, Nader boozed with the fuddled shah until he collapsed then invited in the magnates to observe the stupefied shah whom he replaced with a baby, Abbas III. It was unthinkable for a ragged Turkman to replace the sacred Safavis, but by a process of momentous inevitability Nader was increasingly regarded as a contender for the throne. In four years, he defeated foreigners east and west, took the Gulf, Muscat and Bahrain, then convened 20,000 notables who proposed that he assume the crown. He graciously accepted. When the chief mullah privately asserted loyalty to the Safavis, Nader had him strangled, demanding total loyalty to himself and, radically, abandoning Shiism.

Proud of his base origins, he and his eldest son Reza Qoli married sisters of the shah – his Afghans merging with Safavis. Big Daddy's pastime was drinking parties with his concubines, which could be dangerous for any loose-lipped companions: one who made a pun on Nader's name was strangled on the spot. But his real pleasure was war.

In 1729, Nader crushed the Abdalis of Herat and recruited 12,000 of them as special forces. Just as the Persians had used Georgians to crush Afghans, now Nader used Afghans to crush Georgia. Nine years later, he swung eastwards into Afghanistan, expelling the Hotaks from Kandahar, which he gave to the Abdalis. He chose as his bodyguard their chieftain's sixteen-year-old son Ahmad, later known as Durrani (Pearl), handsome, tough, genial.

When his Afghan enemies fled to Rangila, the Mughul emperor, Nader demanded their return. Rangila refused – and Nader had his pretext to attack India first, taking Lahore. In January 1739, he marched on Delhi, ready to channel Tamerlane against his descendants. Rangila summoned his veteran adviser, the Nizam, as Nader and 100,000 troops – including a Georgian unit commanded by a teenaged Georgian king, Hercules II, and his Afghans under Durrani – advanced towards his 300,000 men and 2,000 elephants. Nader's *zamburaks* and *jacayer-chi* scythed down the Mughals. The Nizam did not make it into battle at all, sipping coffee in his howdah atop his elephant, until afterwards he arranged the emperor's submission.

Riding into Delhi – Shahjahanabad – with its 400,000 inhabitants, Nader, guarded by 20,000 cavalry, was received by Rangila, seated on the bejewelled Peacock Throne in the colossal Audience Chamber commissioned by Shahjahan with its inscription: 'If there is paradise on earth, it is this, it is this!' Nader banned looting, but as Iranians celebrated Nowruz, rumours spread that Nader had been assassinated and crowds began to attack his troops. Galloping to the Roshan ud-Daula Mosque, he climbed on to the roof. At 9 a.m. a shot was fired and Nader drew his sword, unleashing slaughter. By 3 p.m. some 25,000 lay dead. Rangila sent the old Nizam to Nader: He quoted Hafiz:

> Oh king, you've killed so many
> If you wish to kill more, bring them back to life.

'I pardon you for your grey beard,' replied Nader, stopping the cull. Then, leaving the bodies in the streets, he started to gather his spoils, both humans and gems. A great-granddaughter of Alamgir was married to his son Nasrullah, joining upstart Afsharis to Tamerlanians. When courtiers charted the traditional seven generations of the groom's genealogy, Nader just replied, 'Tell them he is the son of Nader Shah, son of the sword, grandson of the sword and so on for seventy generations.'

The Nizam noticed Nader's bodyguard, the Afghan Durrani. 'He will be a king,' he said. Nader called in Durrani, drew his dagger and clipped his ears.

'When you're a king,' he said, 'this will remind you of me.' Later he called Durrani forward. 'Come near. Remember you'll be a king one day.'

'Execute me if you wish, Majesty. There's no truth in these words.'

'Treat the descendants of Nader kindly,' said Nader.

Enjoying the blood-spattered calm, Nader invited the courtesan Nur Bai to perform a *ghazal*. 'What have you left of my heart,' she sang – she told him about a mega-diamond hidden in Playboy's turban. Nader decided to seduce the famous *tawaif* and take her home. She pretended to fall ill and vanished: sleeping with Nader, she said, 'I'd feel as if my body itself was guilty of a massacre.'

Nader recrowned Emperor Rangila, with the *jiqe*, the imperial ai-grette attached to the royal turban, restoring power to 'the illustrious family of Gurkan' (one of Tamerlane's titles), and added, 'Don't forget, I'm not far away.' Nader loaded 30,000 camels and 20,000 mules with plunder, including the Peacock Throne, which became the symbol of Iranian royalty, and Rangila handed over the 105.6-carat diamond that the shah compared to a 'mountain of light' (Koh-i-Noor). The journey of this bauble would chart the trajectory of south Asian power, passing through the treasure houses of Iranian, Afghan and Sikh monarchs to end up in the British crown. Nader had shattered the fragile prestige of the Mughals: their delicate, delicious symbol, Nur Bai, suspected of collaboration, died in poverty; voracious Mughal governors and Rajput rajas vied for the prizes, now joined by equally voracious foreigners. Nader planned to send back his son Nasrullah, married into the Tamerlane family, to rule India.

Watching the predations of Nader from Petersburg, the new empress of Russia, Elizaveta (Peter's daughter), compared him with horror to Europe's own version, Frederick the Great.

In May 1740, an attack of porphyria killed the ogre Frederick William, liberating his twenty-eight-year-old son Frederick, brilliant, reckless, neurotic. He came out in glorious fashion, creating a homoerotic court that would have driven his father crazy. His greatest love was a bisexual Venetian aesthete, Francesco Algarotti, and the new king celebrated their *coup de foudre* with a poem 'The Orgasm', sent to Voltaire and addressed to 'Algarotti, Swan of Padua'. It reveals a very different Frederick.*

Now he could put Voltaire's ideas into practice, calling himself 'the first servant of the state': 'My principal occupation is to combat ignorance and prejudice, enlighten minds and make people happy.' Voltaire hailed him as a 'philosopher-king'. Frederick invited him to visit Berlin.

Yet Frederick was also his father's son – a micromanaging dictator whose malice, not just about his rivals but about his siblings and ordinary people, was ferocious. He bullied his brothers, sneered at everyone and hated most women, once shouting at ladies-in-waiting, 'You can smell these horrible cows ten miles away.' The only woman he loved was his sister Wilhelmine. While parading philosophical virtues, he was cynical: 'If anything is to be gained by honesty, then we'll be honest; if deceit is called for, let's be knaves.' He dismissed his father's Giants,

---

* 'During this night, satisfying his fierce desires, / Algarotti swam in a sea of pleasure . . . / Our happy lovers, in their extreme delirium, / In the fury of their love, they know only each other; / Fucking [*baiser*], climaxing, feeling, sighing and expiring, / Resuming fucking, rushing back for more pleasure.' Algarotti had scandalized London by enjoying a ménage à trois with Lady Mary Wortley Montagu and Lord Hervey, then accompanied Lord Baltimore, proprietor of Maryland in America, on his yacht to attend a Russian wedding, stopping off in Germany where he met Frederick.

but, encouraged by his 80,000 troops and full treasury, he saw an opportunity: France, now under the self-indulgent Louis XV and his shrewd mistress Madame de Pompadour ('a wretched whore', said Frederick), struggled to defend its pre-eminence; Russia was often paralysed by murderous Romanov intrigues; and Britain tried to avoid European entanglements. Then in October the Habsburg Karl VI died after what Voltaire called 'a pot of mushrooms that changed the course of history'. Maria Theresa, aged twenty-three, found herself archduchess of Austria, queen of Hungary and Bohemia, but she could not become empress. Frederick was ready to exploit the felicitous conjunction, writing, 'I am the luckiest child of nature.'

STOP MAKING THE QUEEN WRETCHED: MARIA THERESA – MOTHER, EMPRESS, WARLADY

On 16 December 1740, Frederick invaded the rich Habsburg province of Silesia, still writing to Algarotti but now grimly focused on advancing Prussia at any cost, even his own death in battle. Beleaguered in Vienna, Maria Theresa reflected, 'I found myself without money, without credit, without army, without experience and knowledge of my own.' Her generals were placemen. 'As for the state in which I found the army, I can't begin to describe it,' she said. 'History hardly knows of a crowned head who started under circumstances more grievous.'

Maria Theresa faced the demolition of the dynasty, yet she rose to the challenge with brisk acumen, frequent rages, romantic theatricality and a light touch. She was also pregnant, giving birth in March 1741 to a son, Joseph, a male Habsburg at last. But her ministers were craven antiques: 'Each one of them at first wanted to wait and see how things would develop.' Faced with the resignation of one of these relics, she replied, 'You'd much better stay and try to do what good you can,' adding, 'I shall see to it you do no harm.' To another, she snapped, 'Dear me, what mutterings and ugly faces ... Stop making the Queen wretched and help her instead!' Dealing with a baby, a war, a failed monarchy, she had to boost her needy husband Franz: 'Dear sweetheart ... I was uneasy like a little dog about you. Love me and forgive me that I don't write more ... Adieu, Little Mouse ... I am your happy bride.' Yet she loved being pregnant. 'I wish I was in the sixth month of a new pregnancy,' she said just after giving birth to Joseph.

Frederick erupted into Silesia, unleashing twenty years of war. At his first battle Mollwitz, he fled from the battlefield only to find he had won. But, as the greatest general between Eugen and Napoleon, he quickly learned the art of command, routing Maria Theresa's ponderous generals. The war swiftly expanded as Louis XV, keen to demolish his Habsburg rivals, joined in the carve-up of the Habsburg monarchy. The elector of Bavaria, chief of house Wittelsbach, rival of the Habsburgs, won election as emperor and seized Prague. Hungary toyed with independence.

Maria Theresa held her nerve. She rushed to Budapest, dressed in mourning black, to declare that 'The very existence of the kingdom of Hungary, of our own person, of our children and our crown are now at stake. Betrayed by all, we place our sole resource in the loyalty, arms and ancient valour of the Hungarians.' They promised 40,000 troops and more taxes, promises she rewarded theatrically by brandishing her baby, introducing them to their future king Joseph. Through it all, she ruled her massive court with its mixture of rigid bewigged Spanish ceremonial and family informality, deploying her characteristic gaiety, loving the 'carousels' in which she and her ladies, dressed to the nines, rode through Vienna side-saddle firing pistols in the air, before dancing all afternoon then holding a masque ball dressed as a peasant girl.

After eight years, she realized that Frederick could not be destroyed by war. While never giving up on the reconquest of Silesia, she negotiated peace and won the election of her husband as emperor, then focused on reforming the monarchy.

Her marriage to Little Mouse was happy except for her jealousy of his actresses. Their rows over mistresses and his other demands ended with 'our usual refuge, caresses and tears . . . I got into another temper', and Franz walked out. 'If he really leaves,' she wrote, 'I'll either follow him or shut myself in a convent.' She was usually pregnant during the Silesian wars, raising her sixteen children, between the Hofburg and her new summer palace, Schönbrunn: 'I had to write this in four instalments,' she wrote to a minister, 'six children in the room with me and the emperor too: it reads like it.' She micromanaged the children, writing long orders to their tutors: 'I insist on their eating everything with no fault-finding, no picking and choosing.' She treated her daughters as dynastic assets, bred just for marriage: 'They must not be allowed to talk to doorkeepers and stokers, or give orders; they are born to obey . . .' The children's virtues were witheringly analysed: 'Joana is pig-headed though clever enough; Joseph a good child but not so capable.' Her favourite was the pretty and intelligent Mimi – Maria Christina – who remembered how 'mixed with love was always a dose of mistrust and palpable coldness'. Power is a cruel mother.

Her penultimate child, born when she was thirty-nine, was Maria Antonia – later Marie Antoinette – who grew up impulsive and frivolous.

The heir, Joseph, was fiercely intelligent but lacked empathy and tact – 'My son was brought up from the cradle with the greatest tenderness and love, but it must be admitted that his desires and requests have been deferred to in many ways, flattering him and allowing him to develop a premature conception of his exalted station.' He admired the *philosophes*, but his hero was his mother's nemesis, Frederick. The empress worried about the future.

Little Mouse's infidelities intensified her priggish piety: nude paintings were covered, and her Chastity Commission spied on love affairs, expelled saucy actresses and packed prostitutes into barges to be settled further down the Danube – earning her the mockery of enlightened Europe. Although she was suspicious of the *philosophes*, her reforms worked. 'These are no longer the same Austrians,' noted Frederick, who now complained of this 'ambitious vindictive enemy, who was the more dangerous because she was a woman'. She had survived, yet Frederick kept Silesia. Voltaire hailed him as the Great, but he had a sneaking suspicion of warlords. 'It's forbidden to kill,' wrote Voltaire. 'Therefore all murderers are punished unless they kill in large numbers and to the sound of trumpets.' Their meeting was disappointing. The two greatest men in Europe expected to be the master – and they clashed bitchily, each roiling the other. They were better apart – and the war was not over.

The Frederick of Asia, Nader, similarly could not rest on his laurels. He returned from Delhi as the most successful shah in a millennium. Yet success is never final. Brilliance is never far from madness.

WHAT'S A FATHER, WHAT'S A SON?
THE MADNESS OF BIG DADDY

Now calling himself Shahanshah – king of kings and Lord of the Conjunction – Nader returned to find that his beloved eldest son Reza Qoli, a successful general whom he had left as viceroy, had conspired to take the throne if anything happened to Nader, murdering the ex-shah Tahmasp and his young sons. Reza's wife, Tahmasp's daughter, had committed suicide, while the prince griped, 'My father wants to conquer even the ends of the earth and oppresses us all.' Reza's behaviour was recounted by Nader's favourite, Taqi Khan, who entertained the shah during his drinking bouts. Nader loved him so much he even promised he would never execute him whatever he did. Yet there was a touchiness in their relationship. Nader was suspicious of Taqi, who in turn felt undervalued by Nader.

Reza arrived to greet his triumphant father with his own retinue of 12,000 musketeers. Nader was gripped by paranoia, favouring a younger son and his nephew Ali Qoli. He demoted Reza and gave the prettiest of the Mughal princesses to Ali Qoli. In 1741, as Nader was out riding, an assassin fired at him, and when Reza rode up to console him the shah accused him of complicity. He then found the assassin, who confessed all under torture. Nader threatened to take out Reza's eyes.

'Cut them out and shove them up your wife's cunt,' shouted Reza.

'What's a father,' sobbed Nader when the boy's eyes were brought to him, 'what's a son?' Nader hugged Reza and howled.

'You should know,' Reza said finally. 'By taking my eyes, you have blinded yourself and destroyed your own life.'

Nader campaigned against the Ottomans, but withdrew from Mosul, ailing and looking much older than his years, faced with a spate of rebellions.

In Shiraz, his intimate Taqi rebelled. Nader crushed Shiraz in a frenzy, building towers of heads. Having sworn never to execute his friend, he devised an ingenious torment in which he was not to be killed. Taqi was castrated, one eye torn out, the other left intact so he could watch as his sons and brothers were executed, before his beloved wives were gang-raped by soldiers. When the one-eyed, castrated Taqi was brought before Nader, he managed to crack a joke that saved his life, and he was sent to govern Kabul. But the tyrant was alienating many of his retainers. When he ordered the arrest of his nephew Ali Qoli, the prince started to plot.

In 1747, Nader summoned his children and favourite grandson Shahrokh (son of the blinded Reza and his Safavi wife), staring at them strangely for a long time then begging them to take the throne. All feared a trick. In June, fighting Kurdish rebels, Big Daddy camped at Fathabad, where, alone and paranoid, he suspected his Afshari bodyguards of plotting with Ali Qoli. So he ordered Durrani and his Afghans to execute his Iranian praetorians, but somehow the guards heard of the plan. Nader was sleeping with his favourite concubine, Chuki, when the assassins burst into the tent. Chuki awoke him; Nader jumped up but tripped as one of the guards swung his sword, lopping off his arm. As he begged for mercy, they beheaded him.

Durrani and the Afghans tried to rescue him, weeping when they found his headless corpse. They then looted the tent, seizing the Koh-i-Noor diamond off Nader's arm and wrenching off his signet ring.

Then they galloped back to Kandahar.

Durranis and Saids, Hemingses and Toussaints

Nader's head was sent to Ali Qoli, who declared himself Shah Adil and then hunted down his uncle's sons and grandsons, not only killing them all, even two-year-olds, but also eviscerating Nader's pregnant concubines. When the Qajar tribe bid for power, Adil killed their chieftain but castrated his four-year-old son, Agha Muhammad Khan, who decades later would avenge himself on all, restore Iran and become that rare thing, a eunuch who founded a dynasty. The atrocious Adil was himself assassinated and Shahrukh, Nader's surviving grandson, was blinded, launching decades of turmoil – though out of the flames his bodyguard Durrani thrived while his Arabian allies shook off Iranian power.

The Afghan, riding home, stopped and held a *jirga* (assembly) which elected him shah, Durr-i-Durran, Pearl of Pearls: he declared independence from Persia, advanced on Kandahar and crushed intriguers under the feet of elephants, then set about creating for the first time the *vilayet* – in this case meaning the state – that later became Afghanistan. Exploiting the mayhem in Persia and India, he emulated Nader in his conquests but learned from the folly of the Hotaki: he would build an empire around an Afghan core. Marching east, he annexed territory down to the Indus in Sindh (Pakistan), then moved westwards to take Mashhad and Nishapur (Iran) where – honouring his promise to Nader – he established Big Daddy's blind grandson Shahrukh as puppet.

Durrani was not the only player who benefited from the downfall of Nader:* in Arabia, two dynasties emerged who still rule today. When the news of Nader's killing reached Arabia, the Iranian garrison in Oman was invited to a banquet by his local ally, Ahmed bin Said. In his fortress at Barka, he slaughtered them all, founding a new empire that would ultimately extend from the coasts of Pakistan to the shores of Africa. In

---

* Nader's Georgian ally King Hercules II, who had accompanied him to Delhi, united Kartli and Kakheti to create the first united Georgia for many centuries.

1749, he was elected imam,* a rise that was regarded with hostility by his Arabian rivals – the Saudis, who were building their first kingdom. Ever since Saladin, a single family – founded by Qatada, a sharif, descendant of Muhammad – had ruled Mecca, Jeddah and Hejaz, controlling the revenues of pilgrimage; their position was confirmed by Selim the Grim in 1517. But the Ottomans never ruled the interior of Arabia, Nadj. A typical tiny oasis town, Diriyyah, with just a few hundred inhabitants, was the fief of al-Saud, now led by Muhammad ibn Saud, landowner and merchant. Then in 1744 a former date farmer named Muhammad ibn Abd al-Wahhab, son of a line of religious notables, arrived in Diriyyah. Wahhab had started to preach after his return from the *hajj*, disgusted by the impure pollution of Mecca and Medina, tainted by the cults of saintly tombs and holy men. Any mediation between God and man was heresy. Visiting Basra, he had seen Christians and Jews living together under the heterodox Nader.

This firebrand preached holy war to purify Islam, assert *tawhid* – the doctrine of one God – and create a sacred amirate, based on the return to the origin – *salaf* – of Islam. Unambitious for himself, Wahhab was adept at forming political alliances while inspiring awe among his followers. 'What is there beyond truth but error?' he asked, disowning his father, his brother and some of his children. There was no compromise in his Manichaean worldview: 'unsheath the sword' against idolaters, charlatans, Shiites. Any mixing with infidels was evil. He shocked his home town of Uyayna by stoning an adulteress. He was expelled and escaped to Diriyyah, where he made the alliance that changed world history.

'This oasis is yours,' said ibn Saud. 'Don't fear your enemies. We'll never throw you out!'

'You're the town's chieftain,' replied Wahhab. 'Promise me you'll wage jihad against Unbelievers. I'll be leader in religious matters.'

The imam and sheikh immediately launched their jihad, conscripting all men aged eighteen to sixty, later joined by Bedouin cameleteers, conquering the towns of Nadj one by one, and assassinating opponents. After the death of Saud in 1764, his son Abdulaziz, advised by Wahhab, took Riyadh. The Saudi–Wahhabi alliance had boundless ambitions, aiming to conquer not just Mecca and Medina but Iraq, to vanquish even the Ottomans. But first they threatened the Hashemites of Hejaz and the loathed Ibadites of Oman.

---

* The Omanis were Ibadites, followers of an eighth-century scholar who rejected certain Sunni and Shia doctrines, and were ruled by elected imams from a single family who had expelled the Portuguese and returned to their traditional trade on the Swahili coast of Africa.

Ahmed bin Said and his immediate successors were expanding, making Muscat the entrepôt between India and Africa. As the French expanded their sugar and coffee plantations on Mauritius (Isle de France) and as the military conflict intensified in India, the Omanis supplied the slaves from their east African empire based at Zanzibar, then seizing Kilwa. The sultans of Oman annually traded 50,000 slaves, but even this was dwarfed by what was happening in the Atlantic.

AGAJA, THE VICEROY OF OUIDAH AND THE MONSTER OF JAMAICA

In west Africa, Agaja, the *dada* (king) of small but aggressive Daho-mey, attacked Ardra and Ouidah, Fon kingdoms that traded slaves to the French and British. Agaja, son of the founder Houegbadja, faced constant challenges from his dominant neighbour, the Oyo Kingdom. Its *alafins* (kings) commanded a formidable cavalry and were enriched by their huge trade in slaves with the Europeans. Dada Agaja accepted Oyan tributary status, but that did not stop him deciding to seize a slice of the Franco-British slave trade that was now reaching a terrible intensity. Agaja watched how the ports of Ouidah and Allada (Ardra) generated massive profits. 'The king [Haffon of Ouidah] is an absolute boar,' noted an English naval surgeon. 'If he can't obtain a sufficient number of slaves he marches an army and depopulates. He and the king of Allada adjoining commit great depredations inland.'

Ruling from Savi, his capital, surrounded by the factories of the Euro-peans, Haffon sat on a throne given by the *Compagnie Française des Indes Occidentales*, wearing a crown presented by the British RAC, sourcing and controlling his human merchandise. In 1724, Agaja of Dahomey first seized Allada, then in 1727 Ouidah, killing Haffon and shattering his occult power by eating his sacred pythons. When Agaja purged dis-sidents, he sold them as slaves to Brazil. Amassing a regular army of 10,000, he expanded the existing female bodyguard, recruiting female prisoners, manumitted slaves, runaways, whom he trained to kill and seize slaves to sell to the Europeans. Based at Agaja's capital at Abomey, these forces terrified their neighbours with attacks on innocent villages in which old and young were slaughtered while strong males and fe-males were kidnapped and marched to the slave markets. Even today, their descendants recount stories of these exploits. The female guards only reflected the power of women at the Dahomean court, where all the inhabitants of the Big House palace were called *ahosi* – royal wives

– including the male ministers, while the actual princesses, all of whom had special roles at court, sat as a Council of Wives, which could over-rule the *dada*. (In Oyo, when an *alafin* was unpopular, he was strangled by his wives.)

Agaja and his son Tegbesu, who succeeded him in 1740, ran a slave-trading monopoly, earning an estimated £250,000 per annum. Tegbesu killed or enslaved his rivals including his brother Truku, who was sold to Brazil. Tegbesu negotiated deals with the Europeans, receiving them 'on a handsome chair of crimson velvet, ornamented with a gold fringe, smoking tobacco, with gold-laced hair, a plume of ostrich feathers, a rich crimson damask robe'. Under the Dahomeans, Ouidah became west Africa's busiest slave port: after 1700, between twenty-five and fifty ships sailed annually to the Americas.

Nearby, west of Dahomey, inland from the Gold Coast (Ghana), an Akan leader, Osei Tutu, united bands of hunters and farmers, using Dutch guns, to defeat a rival gold-rich kingdom, Denkyira, and crown himself *asantehene* – king. In 1680, creating a capital inland at Kumasi, Osei Tutu advised by his priest Anokye adopted a curved seat of solid gold, the *Sika Dwa Kofi*, delivered from the sky, as the mark of his king-ship and the spirit of the Asante people. After the founder's death in 1719, his successor Opoku Ware 'ruled violently as a tyrant, delighting in his authority', noted the Gonja people, who were victimized by Asante. 'People of all horizons feared him greatly.'

The *asantehenes* were chosen from the family by an assembly of 200, dominated by four families, advised in power by a council of eighteen officials and the queen mother – *ohemmaa*. Their palace was 'an immense building'; their craftmanship in gold trophy heads and jewellery was exquisite. Among their medical traditions, they had long practised a form of inoculation against smallpox. By the end of the century, 25,000 lived in their capital (at a time when Glasgow had 77,000, New York 40,000) and they ruled around one million. The Asante initially imported Portuguese slaves from Angola to work their mines and farms, serve at court and, at the death of *asantehenes*, suffer sacrifice. But now they raided the interior to supply slaves to the Brit-ish and Dutch, trading gold, cloth and nuts in return for weapons and metals.

The enslaved were force-marched, chained in atrocious coffles by Afro-European agents, many of them female. At Cacheu, Portugal's west African slave port, the most powerful trader was Bibiana Vaz, who launched a coup against another female slave trader, Crispina Peres, who was accused of 'fetishism' (surely a syncretized version of

Catholicism and African religion) and deported to Lisbon to be tried by the Inquisition.

These agents delivered their victims to the fearsome slave castles where the transatlantic slave trade, dominated by the British, French and Dutch, was intensifying. It is currently estimated that 6,494,619 slaves were traded across the Atlantic in the period 1701–1800, over half the total of the entire Atlantic slave trade between 1492 and 1866. British ships transported over three million persons between 1618 and 1807, mostly during the eighteenth century. The French transported over two million between 1625 and 1848. It was a well-tried coercive system, but there was resistance.

Out of 36,000 voyages, there were 500 rebellions. The story of the Dutch slaver *Neptunus* demonstrates why they so rarely succeeded: on 17 October 1785, off the west African coast, 200 enslaved prisoners were delivered via canoes by African slave traders to *Neptunus*. The prisoners rebelled and seized the ship, but African slave hunters – paid to recapture escapees – surrounded it, aided by British slavers. Faced with recapture, the courageous rebels lit the gunpowder in the hold and committed mass suicide.

The diabolic cruelties of the British plantations were so much part of settler life that a planter on Jamaica, Thomas Thistlewood, recorded his atrocities cheerfully in his diary. Younger son of a Lincolnshire farmer, he arrived aged twenty to become overseer of a large plantation in Jamaica named Egypt. The island was still recovering from a prolonged revolt by runaway slaves led by two armed Maroon communities under Queen Nanny and Colonel Cudjoe, both Akan from Gold Coast, who worsted the British enough to win their freedom – in return for their aid in crushing future slave revolts. Like many planters, Thistlewood hired the Maroons to hunt down runaways, describing Cudjoe's 'majestic look' with 'a feather'd hat, Sword at his Side, gun upon his Shoulder . . . Bare foot and Bare legg'd'. Nine years after he arrived, Thistlewood witnessed another slave revolt led by Tacky and Queen Akua, both of whom were hunted down by soldiers, settlers' militiamen and Cudjoe's Maroons.

The revolts shocked the British – the first of the rebellions that, as much as the abolitionist campaign, gradually discredited slavery. Buying his own estate, Breadnut, Thistlewood lived the genteel life of a gentleman of the Enlightenment, ordering scientific books from London and living with and having children with a female slave, Phibbah – while simultaneously ruling his slaves with demented sadism, punishing them with whippings, shacklings, picklings (when the escapees would beaten, with salt pickle and pepper rubbed into their wounds) and a penalty he proudly invented for a slave called Derby who had eaten sugar cane. He called it 'Derby's Dose', and in January 1756 recorded: 'Had Derby well whipped, and made Egypt [a fellow slave] shit in his mouth.' When another slave, Port Royal, ran away, Thistlewood 'Gave him a moderate whipping, pickled him well, made Hector shit in his mouth, immediately put a gag whilst his mouth was full & made him wear it 4 or 5 hours.' Thistlewood recorded 3,852 of his own rapes (including gang rapes) of 138 women, many underage, carelessly spreading VD.

Most of the Enlightened luminaries – from Diderot in Paris to Samuel Johnson in London – were horrified by slavery. Voltaire had a mixed record, deploring the institution, regarding Africans as cousins – 'no one could treat their relative more horribly' – and in his novel *Candide* asking, 'At what price do we eat sugar?' Yet he regarded Africans as having a different origin to Europeans.* Diderot and Guillaume Thomas Raynal denounced slavery in their *Histoire philosophique des deux Indes* and approved slave rebellion. Yet the German *philosophe* Kant opposed any 'fusing of races' and in his essay 'On the Different Races of Man' supported slavery, believing it reflected a hierarchy of races with the whites at the top, Asians and Africans in the middle ('the Negro can be disciplined and cultivated, but is never genuinely civilized . . . he falls of his own accord into savagery') and Native Americans 'far below the Negro'. Kant's racist ideology was unusual in these circles, yet Euro-American slavery required a theoretical justification for its unchristian dominance, the violence necessary to maintain it and the luxurious lifestyle and vast profits it delivered to its masters. Racialized ideas about Africans were not invented by European slave masters in the eighteenth century: medieval people were obsessed with heredity and breeding; Arab slave traders and intellectuals like Ibn Khaldun propagated racialized ideas about Africans not that different from those of European slave owners at a time when slavery was not based on racism at all since slaves were as likely to be white as black. But now, in a more scientific age, a more systematic approach was on the rise: in 1774, Edward Long, English judge and Jamaican planter, furnished a racist ideology in his *History of Jamaica*, suggesting that Africans were a separate 'race of people' who were 'indistinguishable from the animal', with 'bestial manners, stupidity and vices'. This new strain of an old idea was designed to justify chattel slavery. 'Slavery was not born of racism,' wrote Eric Williams. 'Racism was born of slavery.'

---

* Voltaire was even ruder about Jews, whom he described as 'an ignorant and barbarous people, who have long united the most sordid avarice with the most detestable superstition'.

In London and Paris, slave-owning sugar barons now fused with the nexus of aristocrats, merchants and India nabobs: Henry Lascelles, scion of Yorkshire gentry, arrived in Barbados at twenty-two, collecting Caribbean plantations while maintaining a British life, becoming an EIC director and MP. By the time he committed suicide in 1753, he was the richest man in England, leaving half a million pounds, a fortune that funded the establishment of a classic British dynasty – the estates, mansions and earldom of Harewood.

Unlike the laws in the Americas, British common law did not recognize slavery. In 1729 slave owners petitioned the attorney-general, who backed them, giving his opinion that 'a slave coming from the West Indies to Great Britain does not become free'. Slaves were openly advertised: 'To be sold. A pretty little Negro boy about nine years old' reads one in the *Daily Advertiser*. Yet, despite the 1729 opinion, while slavery was entirely legal on ships making the Atlantic crossing and in the colonies, its status was ambiguous in the metropolis. It was the same in France, where a slave could sue for freedom in the Admiralty court.

In both countries, there were many freed slaves and even more people of mixed race. We will look at Paris later, but there may have been 15,000 black Britons by mid-century. And there were rare exceptions to the horrors: in 1752, a slave owner, Colonel Bathurst, sold his Jamaican estates and returned with a seven-year-old slave called Francis Barber, probably his natural son, whom he freed in his will. After a short adventure in the navy, Barber became the much loved servant of Samuel Johnson, the closest British equivalent of Voltaire, rambunctious lion of the London Enlightenment, wit and lexicographer. An opponent of slavery, he educated Barber, making him a figure in literary London and, on his death, one of his heirs.*

But these were exceptional characters: most enslaved persons were not rescued by duchesses or scholars but died young on ships mid-Atlantic or on Caribbean plantations.

The Atlantic trade was one part of a world of bondage, but its record-keeping allows historians to estimate that in total over four centuries around 12.6 million were enslaved. The Portuguese/Brazilians transported almost half of the 12.6 million; the British a quarter; the French

---

* More outrageous was Julius Soubise, a manumitted slave originally named Othello who became the fencing teacher of an ageing society beauty, Catherine Hyde, duchess of Queensberry. Treated as her adopted son, renamed after a French duke, he became a fop, seducer and rake among the society dandies known as the Macaronis for their European style (Soubise was called the 'Mungo Macaroni' by the news-sheets), and probably her lover But when he was accused of raping a housemaid, the duchess sent him to India, where he founded a Calcutta riding school, dying after a riding accident.

10 per cent, the Dutch 5 per cent. During the four modern centuries, it is likely that over thirty million people were enslaved: twelve million across the Atlantic, approximately ten million from east Africa across the Indian Ocean, and ten million Turks, Russians, Georgians and Circassians from the Eurasian steppes. That does not include the Barbary–Moroccan trade in western Europeans nor the several million Serbs and Albanians enslaved by the Ottomans: some of these enslaved children became viziers and *valide sultans*, but that does not diminish their tragedy. Many Islamic slaves were females who served in households – but domestic service almost always included sexual abuse. It is estimated that the Crimean khans alone enslaved four million. Since there is no paperwork whatsoever for any of these trades, it is likely they are grossly underestimated.

From Ouidah and other slave castles, the ships were loaded with hundreds of slaves in their holds 'crammed together like herrings in a barrel' and set off on the dread trip to Portuguese Brazil, French Saint-Domingue or the British 'Old Dominion' – Virginia.

THREE AMERICAN FAMILIES: HEMINGSES, JEFFERSONS AND TOUSSAINTS

In 1735, a newly arrived 'full-blooded African' woman, in the words of her great-grandson, who had been enslaved in west Africa, was either raped or seduced by an English sea captain named Hemings at Williamsburg, possibly arriving as a captive on his slave ship. Slaves preserved their African origins as baKongo or Akan as long as they could. Masters, fearful of such affinities, were keen to sever any dangerous links, granting fresh enslaved identities with new, often classical names: there were many Hannibals and Caesars. Her name might have been Parthenia.

She became pregnant. In 1662, the Virginians had ruled that *partus sequitur ventrem* – if the mother was a slave, the child was. So when she delivered a daughter, Elizabeth known as Betty, Captain Hemings offered 'an extraordinarily high price' for his 'own flesh', but her owner refused.

Hemings tried to kidnap the baby but finally gave up. Betty Hemings found herself owned by Martha Eppes, who had inherited her from her father, himself descended from founding settlers who had acquired lands. In 1746, Martha married a self-made frontier lawyer and slave broker named John Wayles, born in Lancashire, England, who had been brought over as a gentleman's indentured servant and had gained an estate and wealth – an early version of what would one day be called the American Dream. All the American colonies had elected assemblies – Virginia's was called the House of Burgesses – dominated by planters of tobacco who created a legal infrastructure to protect their human property and their lives against any rebellion: 40–50 per cent of Virginians were slaves. In 1723, Virginia decreed that 'no negro, mulatto, or Indian slaves shall be set free upon any pretense'. Wayles became the owner of Elizabeth Hemings.

Two years after the marriage, Martha Wayles died giving birth to a second daughter, named Martha after her. Wayles married two more wives, both of whom died young, after which he took Betty Hemings, described as a 'bright mulatto' woman – 'bright' meaning light – as a 'concubine'. Although society disapproved, this was so common it was almost universal. 'The pervasive doctrine of white supremacy supposedly inoculated whites against interracial mixing,' writes Annette Gordon-Reed, but that proved 'unreliable when matched against the force of human sexuality'. Wayles and Hemings had six children together. It is clear that sexual bondage was always a part of enslavement, whether in pagan Rome, Islamic Istanbul or here in Virginia: sex between owners and slaves was 'on the terms of the males, beyond the eyes and scrutiny of the outside world . . . either through rape, using outright or implied force, or, in some cases, when men and women were genuinely attracted to each other'. It is impossible to evaluate such relationships on our terms: 'enslaved women practically and legally could not refuse consent' and testimony 'makes clear the prevalence of rape during slavery'.

When Wayles died, Betty, her children and the rest of his 124 slaves would be inherited by his daughter Martha – and by her future husband, one Thomas Jefferson, who had been born in 1743, not long after Betty.

Jefferson, scion of the Virginian slave-owning elite, was growing up nearby. His father Peter was an adventurous second-generation frontiersman who managed to survey new lands, pushing the frontier westwards, mapping a route to the Allegheny Mountains. He served in the House of Burgesses and as a justice of the peace, while amassing 7,000 acres and sixty slaves, and creating the genteel, intellectual lifestyle that produced Thomas. A child of the Enlightenment, Thomas read Locke, Newton, Voltaire and played the violin, telling his daughter that 'there's not a sprig of grass that shoots uninteresting to me nor anything that moves'. Six foot two, slim with light red hair, hazel eyes, pointed nose, Jefferson was sociable yet inscrutable, polite and ostentatiously frank yet privately ambitious. Behind his charming gloss, he was also passionate and highly strung, suffering stress-induced migraines.

On his father's death, he inherited 5,000 acres. At twenty-six, after training as a lawyer, Jefferson was elected to the House of Burgesses. Martha Wayles meanwhile had married and been widowed. In the compact colonial society, it was only a matter of time before he came to call.

Just as Elizabeth Hemings's mother arrived in Virginia, Hippolyte, enslaved son of an Allada governor, probably captured and sold by King Agaja of Dahomey, was delivered to the French colony of Saint-Domingue, half of the island of Hispaniola (the other half being a Spanish colony, Santo Domingo). In one of slavery's millions of daily tragedies, Hippolyte's wife Affiba and their children were also captured but traded separately to Saint-Domingue. Without knowing they were toiling on a nearby estate, Hippolyte married a woman named Pauline, a fellow Allada. When Affiba discovered this, she died of sorrow. Hippolyte and Pauline had five children, the first of whom was a son: Toussaint.

'I was born a slave but nature gave me the soul of a free man,' recalled Toussaint, who grew up on the Bréda sugar estate owned by an absent French aristocrat, Count Pantaléon de Bréda, that gave him his name Toussaint Bréda. Working from a young age as a cattle herder, he was trained by his father in Allada medicine and baptized as a Catholic while also revering voodoo; he spoke Fon, French and creole. Toussaint knew the tragedy of slavery 'to tear son from his mother, brother from sister'.

Both his parents died young, after which Toussaint was 'adopted' by an Allada freedman and African-born friend of his mother, an example of the informal affiliations that made the unbearable bearable. Most slaves in Saint-Domingue were worked to death before they reached thirty-seven, then replaced by new arrivals from Africa known as *bossales*. Sixty per cent of male slaves, who on average survived three years, were worked to death – approximately 500,000 in total. It was an environment that encouraged what the Haitian intellectual baron de Vastey later called 'crapulous debauchery'. The *Code Noir* was widely ignored, and French masters treated their slaves atrociously: many were raped and tortured in ingenious ways, including by packing them with explosives to blow them up, known by the French as 'a little powder in the arse', buried alive, burned in furnaces, genitally mutilated, routinely forced to wear muzzles.

The French *colons* lived a life of luxury on Saint-Domingue,* but all

* A typical French plantation owner, Gaspard Tascher, bought estates in Martinique and La Pagerie in Saint-Domingue, providing him with an aristocratic surname and funding a lifestyle that allowed his son to serve as a page at Louis XVI's court. His granddaughter,

the while they were terrified of being murdered by their slaves, whom they characterized as both lazy livestock and menacing aliens. Society was strictly divided between the whites, the growing population of mixed-race people and black freedmen who often owned slaves themselves – and the slaves.

The way to survive was to become a coachman or a servant in the planter's mansion:* Toussaint was promoted by his estate manager Bayon to coachman. As he grew up, he witnessed the rebellion of François Makandal, a one-armed holy man (*oungan*) from west Africa – he spoke some Arabic – who practised rituals that, merged with Catholicism, became Haitian voodoo. The *colons* claimed that Makandal had poisoned them though new research shows this was an outbreak of anthrax. Nonetheless Makandal led an insurgency that was a lethal threat, so he was captured and burned alive in Port-au-Prince. The slaves believed that his spirit escaped the flames.

'The virtuous Bayon de Libertad' manumitted Toussaint, who leased his own slaves on his own farm. Although he married his godfather's daughter Suzanne and had children with her, he was a prolific lover who had many paramours, black and white. Meanwhile he joined the underground of slave brotherhoods and voodoo believers who started to dream of revolution. Yet Toussaint's worldview was never racialized. A product of both Makandal's world of African voodoo and *kalinda* combat dances mixed with his Catholic faith and his Enlightenment, he believed in the potential of human nature.

At the same moment, these two remarkable Americans, Toussaint and Jefferson, were reading the same books – Voltaire, Diderot, Raynal – and yet dreaming of different versions of freedom.

Maria Theresa did not know much about America but a remote American massacre led by a young colonialist now gave her the opportunity to destroy Frederick the Great.

Marie Josèphe Rose Tascher de La Pagerie, brought up by slaves, ruined her teeth eating sugar, so that when the creole arrived in Paris to marry an aristocrat her mouth was just full of black stumps; she was barely educated, yet she possessed conquering charm. Later known as Empress Josephine, she and Toussaint would cross paths.

* As in Virginia, female house slaves, often teenagers, were the prey of their proprietors. In Guadeloupe, on his Saint-Georges plantation, a French planter called George de Bologne had a son with a maid, Nanon, aged seventeen. The son Joseph could not inherit nobility but, indulged by his father, he was educated in music, classics and philosophy and was later sent to boarding school, where it turned out he was a musical prodigy, virtuoso violinist and composer.

MIMI AND ISABELLA: YOUR ARCHANGELIC LITTLE BUM

On 28 May 1754, in the vastness of Ohio County, a young British officer led his force of 300 Americans and Mingo Native Americans in an ambush of French and Iroquois troops under Sieur de Jumonville. French and British officers were competing to colonize the American interior.

The officer, George Washington, aged twenty-two, six foot tall and strapping, was, like Jefferson, the son of a wealthy planter descended from the first settlers who owned thousands of acres and many slaves. Washington's father died young, his mother was frostily overbearing and he grew up reticent, solid and cautious. But like Cromwell he was much more canny and ambitious than he ever let on.

Thanks to his friendship with the Fairfax family, descendants of Cromwell's commander in the civil war, who controlled five million American acres, Washington at sixteen had started surveying the Shenandoah Valley. By the time he was twenty, he owned 2,000 acres. During these early years, he fell in love with Sally Fairfax, the dazzling wife of his best friend and patron, the singular passion of a phlegmatic life that he later referred to as 'a thousand tender passages'. After this romantic crisis, he married a rich, plain widow, Martha Custis, who brought with her land and three hundred more slaves, making him one of the richest men in the colonies. Jefferson noted that Washington 'always ruled severely'. Indeed he was 'first brought up to govern slaves, then an army then a nation'. Washington constantly watched for his slaves' laziness, complaining that 'there's not to be found so idle a set of rascals'. When his slaves ran away – 7 per cent of them did – he was tireless in recapturing them. He sent badly behaved slaves to early deaths in Caribbean plantations.

Tracking the enemy in Ohio County, Washington earned the nickname Conotocaurius – village destroyer – from his Mingo auxiliaries. When his force caught up with the French and Iroquois, they ambushed and slaughtered them: many were scalped. While Washington was interrogating Jumonville, one of his Mingo allies split the captive's head with a tomahawk.*

When the news reached London, the flappable prime minister, Thomas Pelham, duke of Newcastle, one of the brothers who had continued Walpole's system, studied the map, struggling to find these obscure places. 'Annapolis must be defended to be sure,' he huffed. 'Where is Annapolis?' Newcastle had run British foreign policy for

---

* A month later when the French counter-attacked and captured Washington, he was lucky not to get a tomahawk in the head himself.

thirty years, but it was the first time a British statesman had needed to master America. Now even he realized that a colonial war against France was inevitable: the French were challenging British interests in America, India and west Africa. Newcastle had always backed Maria Theresa against Prussia – his 'Old System' – but in a dizzying change of dance partners he ended up backing Frederick the Great against Maria Theresa, who in turn found some surprising allies who were threatened by Prussia. Louis XV and his mistress Pompadour loathed Frederick, as did Peter the Great's steely blonde daughter, Empress Elizaveta of Russia: Frederick did not help his cause by calling Pompadour and Elizaveta 'the whores'.* Maria Theresa dramatically switched alliances, allying herself to her traditional enemy, France, and they were joined by Russia.

Funded by British subsidies but now facing a lethal coalition, Frederick launched a pre-emptive strike into Bohemia and besieged Prague, unleashing the first world war. At Kolín on 18 June 1757 Maria Theresa's armies smashed Frederick's: as his troops wavered, he cried, 'Rascals, you want to live for ever?' Forty per cent of them were killed and the king barely escaped with his life. 'Phaeton has finally crashed to the ground,' sneered his jealous brother Prince Heinrich. 'We don't know what will become of us.' But Frederick, aided by Austrian inertia and Russian unreliability, darted at the French, defeating them at Rossbach, then routed the Austrians at Leuthen, his greatest victories.

But the Cossacks were coming. 'I mean to continue this war,' said Elizaveta, who owned 5,000 dresses, 'even if I'm compelled to sell all my diamonds and half my clothes.' Pompadour agreed: 'I hate the king of Prussia . . . let's demolish this Attila of the North.' Maria Theresa just called him 'the Monster'. Frederick sneered at 'the first three whores in Europe united together'. In August 1758, at Zorndorf, he fought the ferocious Russians, a gruelling draw of a butchers' battle. At year later, at Kunersdorf, the Russians smashed him. 'My coat is riddled with musket balls,' he wrote, 'and I've had two horses killed beneath me.' He considered suicide: 'It's my misfortune to be alive . . . I've only 3,000 men out of 48,000 left . . . Everything is lost . . . I shan't outlive the downfall of my fatherland. Farewell for ever.' Russian cavalry raided

---

* Elizaveta, a dashing blonde amazon wearing a breastplate and riding a sleigh, had seized power in a coup. She had inherited her father's ruthlessness and proved a capable if inconsistent and whimsical autocratrix, while enjoying many simultaneous affairs with young lovers. Chief of these was the handsome Ukrainian Cossack chorister Alexei Razumovsky, whose brother Kyril she appointed as the grand hetman of the Cossacks: he was the last semi-independent hetman before 1918.

Berlin. Frederick's position was desperate: 'My only motto now is conquer or die.' Gambling was all that was left: 'I must embark on a great
adventure and play double or quits.'

Maria Theresa, anxiously charting the slow manoeuvres of her
generals and the intermittent ferocity of her Russian ally, watched
his demolition with satisfaction. Meanwhile in 1760 she arranged the
marriage of her impressive but dogmatic nineteen-year-old son Joseph
to Isabella of Parma, aged eighteen, a dark-eyed, olive-skinned sensual
brunette, who for a short time illuminated his obstinate egotism and
sparked passion among the Habsburgs. Isabella, a clever, wild, brooding romantic who wrote on philosophy and economics, was instantly
adored by the empress-queen and her husband (sharing his love of
music and philosophy). Yet neither noticed Isabella fall in love with
Joseph's cleverest sister Mimi, still only seventeen, her mother's confidante and favourite.

'Believe me, my greatest, I can say only, joy, is to see you and be with
you,' Isabella told Mimi in one of more than 200 love letters. 'Never in
heaven or earth, neither because of absence or anything or anyone else,
shall I change in this.' Her passion was volcanic: 'I adore you, I burn
for you.' After sending one of her letters, she wrote, 'Here I am again,
my all too cruel sister, on tenterhooks until I know the effect of what
you have been reading . . . I can think of nothing but that I am head
over heels in love like a fool. Because you are so cruel, that you really
shouldn't be loved yet how can one help it if one knows you?'

After giving birth to a daughter, she emerged even more passionate, her
mind a jumble of 'Philosophy, morals, stories, profound reflections . . .
and rapture for you'. They arranged secret meetings around Joseph. 'If
the archduke goes out, I'll be at your house,' Isabella told Mimi.

'I love you furiously and yearn to kiss you,' Mimi wrote. 'To kiss and
be kissed by you. I kiss your archangelic little bum.'

'Pray for fine weather if you wish to possess me,' wrote Isabella. 'I
kiss everything you let me kiss.'

Isabella called Mimi 'the most adorable creature' whom she was 'very
inclined to suffocate by kisses'. Yet she was weirdly macabre: 'Death is a
good thing.' Mimi was triggered by Isabella's fatalism: 'Allow me to tell
you that your great longing for death is an outright evil thing. It means
either you are selfish or want to seem a heroine.' Did Isabella crave
death as an escape from an unbearable love or did her wild love express
her edgy fatalism?

At the height of this intense relationship, the Habsburgs invited a
musical family to perform for them. The empress adored music and

singing in public. Joseph played the keyboards, Leopold and Marie Antoinette the harpsichord and all the girls could sing.

On 13 October 1762, the Habsburgs gathered at Schönbrunn to watch
the little pianist Wolfgang Mozart play. The six-year-old was accompanied by his family. His father Leopold, a gifted, driven but morose
violinist and assistant *Kapellmeister* of the prince-bishop of Salzburg,
descended from a creative family, early recognized that his son was a
prodigy: at five, Mozart composed his first piece. Now Leopold played
violin, then Wolfgang played harpsichord and, when challenged by
Emperor Franz, he placed a cloth across the keys and played perfectly.
Archduchess Isabella played violin. 'Suffice to say that Wolferl [Mozart]
sprang on to the lap of the empress, put his arms around her neck and
vigorously kissed her,' wrote Leopold Mozart. The next day the Mozarts
received a big payment. Maria Theresa was so delighted by Wolfgang
that she sent him a special lilac brocade costume that surely contributed
to his future taste for sartorial extravagance.

Mozart was 'a fundamentally happy man', writes Jan Swafford, witty,
exuberant, energetic, constantly infused with musical ideas of power and
beauty – very different from the cliché of the brooding genius expected
by the Romantics in the next century. 'Wolfgang is extraordinarily jolly,'
wrote his stern father, 'but a bit of a scamp too.' Leopold was moody,
disappointed by his own career – 'All men are villains,' he told Mozart
– but his wife was playful and scatological. In his teens, Mozart found
a mischievous partner in his cousin Maria Anna Thekla: 'The two of
us are made for each other because she's a bit of a rogue too.' Their
sexual explorations inspired his pungent letters: 'I'll kiss your hands,
face, knees and your ... whatever you permit me to kiss.' Even while
performing for aristocrats he privately guffawed as 'a number of high
nobility were present: Duchess Kickass, Countess Pisshappy, also Princess Smellshit with her two daughters'. But he was already composing:
'The concerto I'll write him in Paris, it's fitting / For there I can dash it
off while I'm shitting.'

Inspired by Vienna, Leopold took Mozart on a European tour to Paris
(where traumatically his mother would later die of typhus), London and
back to Vienna. There Joseph would become his patron.

Joseph was already wildly in love with Isabella when she played so
well with the Mozart family. Isabella managed him excellently while,
perhaps for Mimi, writing a treatise on men as 'useless animals', looking forward to female empowerment.

Then: disaster. After the premature birth of a second daughter whom
Isabella named after Mimi, she caught smallpox. Her last letter was to

Mimi: 'God is too benevolent not to let me have the pleasure of kissing you again . . . Goodbye, be well.' Isabella died aged twenty-one, then the baby followed.

Mimi was poleaxed – though she later married happily – but Joseph was inconsolable: 'I have lost everything, the object of all my tenderness, my only friend.' He told his mother, 'I'll never marry again . . . my existence is strained to breaking point.' The queen-empress immediately ordered him to marry a Wittelsbach princess, Josepha of Bavaria. He resisted. Mimi, placing the dynasty first, showed Joseph her letters from Isabella in order to shatter his illusions, though he did not understand them. Acquiescing, he hated his new wife – 'short, without a vestige of charm, her face covered in spots, her teeth horrible' – and complained to a friend, 'My wife is unbearable, they want me to make children. How can I? If I could put the tip of a finger on the tiniest part of her body not covered with spots, I would try.' Observing her brother's meanness, Mimi reflected, 'If I were his wife, I'd hang myself on a tree in Schönbrunn,' but even their mother conceded that Josepha was 'not agreeable'. Within two years, Josepha too was dead of smallpox, that relentless killer.

As Frederick manoeuvred and negotiated desperately, William Pitt, the new prime minister, grandson of John 'Diamond' Pitt and son of Robert who had smuggled the jewel out of India, orchestrated a multi-front war that delivered an astonishing array of victories from America and Africa to India.

Romanovs and Durranis, Pitts, Comanche and Kamehamehas

PITT'S WAR: THE GREAT COMMONER

A born performer, melodramatic, tempestuous and hard-drinking, Pitt, after an early spell of soldiering, had made his name with vicious attacks on Walpole and the Pelhams, skewering their domestic corruption and global inertia. While raging against venal factions (and brilliantly coordinating them), Pitt sat for the constituency Old Sarum, an uninhabited ruin bought by Diamond Pitt. Married to Lady Hester Grenville, daughter of a powerful clan, he was supported by his own faction: this tiny clique of Pitt–Grenvilles dominated politics for the next half-century.

George II loathed Pitt, but in December 1756, realizing that Newcastle was out of his depth, he accepted that the preeningly vain orator had a plan and acquiesced in a Pitt ministry, nominally under the Duke of Devonshire. 'I am sure I can save this country,' boasted Pitt, now secretary of state for the south, 'and no one else can.' When he was manoeuvred out of power, Pitt launched a national campaign that revealed the new importance of public opinion and forced his recall, now popularly acclaimed as the Great Commoner; this time he was in partnership with Newcastle.

Pitt masterminded the country's first global conflict, the Seven Years War: his strategy was to win 'Canada on the banks of the Rhine', paying Frederick to fight France while his swashbuckling protégés – 'Pitt's boys' – attacked French colonies. He seized French slaving castles in Senegal and Gambia, and stormed Guadeloupe; in America, Louisburg and Quebec fell. But not everything went right: at Monongahela, in the Ohio valley, a bunglingly arrogant British general, Edward Braddock, ignored the advice of his Virginian deputy, Colonel Washington, expert in colonial warfare, and was routed by French–Iroquois forces. Braddock was killed; Washington had two horses shot from under him. It was decisive in a different way: Washington noted British insouciance and resented his superiors' refusal to recognize or promote him and his colonial troops. But that was a rare setback.[*]

In India, a new game was opening: a voracious and brutal foreign invader was about to ravage the land.

INDIAN WARLORDS: DURRANI AND CLIVE

His name was Ahmed Durrani, the extraordinary Afghan shah, former bodyguard of Nader. In January 1757, just as Pitt was orchestrating his world offensive, Durrani marched into Delhi. It was far from his first invasion of India, and altogether he would invade India eight times and loot Delhi twice.

The Afghan predation of India had started ten years earlier, in December 1747, when Durrani attacked the opium-addled Mughal emperor Rangila, who got lucky when the invaders' gunpowder magazine exploded. A year later, Durrani seized Sindh and Punjab (Pakistan), then conquered Kashmir, drawn into the vortex of India by the advance of the Marathas under the *peshwa* Balaji Rao, who after Shahu's death ruled through a puppet *chhatrapati*. In 1749, the seventy-six-year-old Nizam of Hyderabad, a legend having survived eight emperors, one shah and eight battles, died, sparking a struggle between his heirs that drew yet more players into the vacuum. These princelings manipulated – and were manipulated in turn by – British and French soldier-merchants, aggressive adventurers attracted to a region that was politically chaotic but still commercially rich. Both the Nizam dynasts drew in rival Europeans: one was backed by a flashy French governor-general, Joseph, Marquis Dupleix, a veteran of the *Compagnie des Indes Orientales*, who was married to a part-Indian beauty known as Joanna Begum, a useful intermediary with the Indian potentates. Dupleix led his army of Indian sepoys dressed as an Indian nawab. The rival dynasty hired a redoubtable EIC major, Stringer Lawrence. Then Balaji Rao and his Marathas joined the carve-up – and Durrani had to defend his new empire. None of the players in this mayhem – Indian, Afghan, French or British, Muslim, Hindu or Christian, white or brown – were scrupulous or peace-loving, and all were greedy and merciless.

Shah Durrani marched into Delhi, looting its treasures and collecting its concubines, but he did not seize the throne, telling the helpless

---

[*] The brutality of the American colonial war is best grasped by the bounty offered by the Massachusetts governor William Shirley for native American scalps: £40 for adult males, £20 for women and children under twelve.

Emperor Alamgir II, 'I bestow on you the crown of Hindustan: come see me tomorrow morning in royal dignity.' Afterwards he expressed his restraint in poetry:

I forget the throne of Delhi
When I remember the mountain tops of my beautiful Pashtunkhwa.

Holding court with his harem in the imperial apartments in Delhi, Durrani married his son Timur to the emperor's daughter while he himself married Rangila's daughter. Returning through Punjab, he and his son dealt with a new challenge: the Sikhs had been repressed by generations of Mughals, their gurus executed, but they had reacted by becoming a military-religious order, divided into armies and divisions, commanded by elected commanders, the *sirdars*. Durrani and Timur destroyed the Sikh holy cities of Kartarpur and Amritsar, razing the temples of the Chak Guru, desecrating them with cow blood, and soiling the sacred lakes. Sikh insurgents harassed the Afghans, who slaughtered Sikh civilians en masse.

As Durrani held court in the Mughal capital, a young British warlord was manoeuvring to destroy French power and dominate a distant but rich province: at nineteen, Robert Clive, a Shropshire vicar's son, had joined the EIC as a bookkeeper. Gifted with manic energy interspersed with bouts of mental illness, Clive was a fighting accountant who craved action – 'a man not born for a desk' in Pitt's phrase – and joined the EIC army, where he rose fast. At the time, 90 per cent of EIC profits came not from India but from China.* Yet the chaos in India was an opportunity none of the players could resist. Just as in the west Durrani and Balaji Rao converged on Delhi, so in the east, during the 1740s, Dupleix and the French *Compagnie des Indes Orientales* launched an offensive against the passive British. Inspired in part by Dupleix, Clive won his first command. In 1751, he had made his name – and announced a new British dynamism – by seizing a fortress, holding it and then defeating an Indian potentate backed by the French. Pitt praised him. He married

---

* Almost an exact contemporary of Frederick the Great, born in 1711, the Qianlong Emperor was the eleven-year-old prince who had been so loved by his grandfather Kangxi. After the death of his father Yongzheng, probably of an overdose of the mercury-based Taoist elixirs that killed so many Chinese monarchs, he expanded the empire westwards into Xinjiang (New Province) to the edge of the Himalayas (wiping out the Dhungars almost completely and slaughtering Uighur Muslims after a rebellion, caused by mass rapes of Uighur women by Chinese officials) and enjoyed vast revenues from selling porcelain and tea to the EIC and other European traders while writing over 40,000 poems. But at the heart of his glory was a sadness: he never stopped loving his first wife, Lady Fuca, whose her death at thirty-six from smallpox broke his heart: 'Ah, that ill-fated third month of spring,' he wrote, 'seventeen years have passed yet my grief remains unappeased.'

an eighteen-year-old girl who had come to Madras on her brother's advice specifically to marry Clive, and they had nine children. When Clive suffered a nervous collapse, they returned rich to London, where he was elected an MP and bought a baronetcy. But he returned to India just in time for Pitt's war.

'A scene of anarchy, confusion, bribery, corruption and extortion,' said Clive, 'was never seen or heard of in any country except Bengal.' He was not the only predator tempted by Bengal: Balaji Rao saw it too, raiding Bengal six times, killing 40,000 people. But Clive's temperament was ideal for fighting the French and Indian warlords of the time, his aggressive spirit best summed up by a note to a subordinate facing a superior force: 'Dear Forde, fight them immediately; I will send you the order of council to-morrow.' Now a series of disasters befell British interests. The young nawab of Bengal, Siraj ud-Daula, grandson of Alivardi Khan who had grabbed the province from the Mughals, seized the profitable British fort of Calcutta, where his sixty-four British prisoners were locked in a dungeon in the heat. Forty-three of them died.

On 5 February 1757, Clive marched his tiny army through the vast Indian camp – running the so-called Calcutta Gauntlet – to retake the fort. On 23 June, his decisive 'battle' of Plassey was a pantomime. The safest way to win a battle is to negotiate the outcome. His army – 1,100 Europeans, 2,000 sepoys – was minute; the nawab's ministers and army mostly changed sides thanks to Clive's negotiations; the rain soaked the gunpowder; and he lost only twenty-two sepoys (and no Europeans). Having undermined the French, he also defeated the Dutch, reporting to Pitt, 'I've made it pretty clear to you that there will be little or no difficulty in obtaining the absolute possession of these rich kingdoms; and that with the Mughal's own consent.' He secured Bengal for the EIC. In Parliament, Pitt praised 'Clive . . . that heaven-born general' who fought with 'an execution that would charm the king of Prussia'. Enjoying their nabobian fortune of £300,000 (a billion pounds today) the new Lord and Lady Clive of Plassey bought the duke of Newcastle's estate and shocked London with their ostentation: her pet ferret wore a £2,500 diamond necklace and her pet prodigy – Mozart – performed in their salon. Clive remained fragile: addicted to opium, he suffered another breakdown.

Yet Bengal was just one province. Back in Kandahar, Durrani, now rich from his looting of Delhi and the revenues of Punjab and Khorasan, was happy to leave the Mughals alone, provided the Marathas did the same. But a Maratha general, accompanied by Balaji Rao's teenaged son Vishwas, marched into Delhi and placed his own emperor on the throne, provoking Durrani. On 14 January 1761, the two armies met at

Panipat, where Babur had won India in 1526. Durrani killed the general, Vishwas, and 28,000 Marathas, enslaving 22,000 women and children. The battle confirmed the end of Mughal India – which, following occupations by the Persians, Marathas and Afghans, was now no more than a symbolic entity.

Durrani celebrated with a triumphant entry into Delhi then looted the city for the second time in five years. But in his absence the Sikhs had rebelled – their guerrilla tactics and aggressive impetuosity made them hard to defeat. The Afghans launched a campaign of annihilation against Sikh civilians since they could not catch the warriors. On 5 February 1762, Durrani slaughtered around 20,000 Sikhs, mainly women and children. The Sikhs still call this *Vadda Ghalughara* – the Great Massacre – an imperialist atrocity unparalleled in modern Indian history. Travelling with fifty carts of Sikh heads, Durrani again blew up the Harmandir Sahib shrine in Amritsar, desecrating the sacred lake with the bodies of men and cows. But as the temple exploded, a fragment hit him on the nose – a wound that would eventually kill him – but it looked as if the new hegemon of India would be Durrani or the Hindu *peshawas*.[*]

Back in London, Pitt's *annus mirabilis* had delivered the first British empire but Frederick seemed finished – until he got lucky. Empress Elizaveta left the Russian throne to a poxy Germanic coxcomb, Peter III, who worshipped Frederick and immediately recalled Russian armies. Frederick was amazed: 'What dependence may be placed on human affairs if the veriest trifles can change the fate of empires? Such are the sports of fortune.' Frederick privately mocked the 'divine idiocy' of Peter III, who swiftly offended the Russian army, the nobility and, most unwisely, his clever, charismatic wife Catherine. Maria Theresa's monarchy was exhausted; the French were near bankrupt and grieving over their losses at the expense of a sated Britain, which had cleaned up on the continent where the war began – America. Fort Duquesne, taken by Colonel Washington and his Virginia Regiment, was renamed Pittsburgh. By 1763, Britain's American empire was won[†] – but it would last scarcely a decade.

---

[*] In modern histories, focused narrowly on the British empire, this is usually blamed on Britain and its East India Company, and Plassey is presented as momentously important – yet the British would not control Delhi or most of India for half a century. Durrani the Afghan conqueror, who does not fit the conventional narrative of 'Afghanistan, graveyard of empires', is much neglected. And it was the huge Maratha empire that would now dominate most of India for many decades.

[†] The other winner was Spain, which received swathes of New France – the vastness of Louisiana, much of the central-southern USA – to add their existing New Mexico, California and Texas.

EMPIRE BUILDERS: COMANCHE WARLORDS AND
PITT THE SNAKE

Yet the American vastness had scarcely been penetrated by British-Americans, French or Spanish. Europeans just occupied the Thirteen Colonies on the east coast. Elsewhere, tiny posses of European adventurers sheltered in wooden palisades and traded in furs, negotiating with the Native Americans who controlled the interior. While snuff-snorting bewigged aristocrats in European capitals traded these lands on maps, this made little difference on the ground. That expanse was ruled by an ever-changing map of indigenous nations who did not measure power in terms of boundaries and kingdoms. Yet they were not at peace with each other; they too were empire builders.

The greatest of them were the Comanche, an offshoot of the Shoshane, distant relatives of the Mexica, speaking a similar language and also worshipping the sun. Decisions of war and peace were made by assemblies at which the older men were the most influential, but younger bloods and women sat in an outer circle and could voice their views. They elected a *paraibo*, a warlord, to lead confederacies of warbands.

Their world had been changed by the arrival of the Spanish, who brought guns and horses that had never existed in the Americas: after an uprising by the peoples of the south-east, the Pueblo Revolt of 1680, the Spanish lost control of thousands of horses. The Comanche, using guns, bows and spears and wearing leather armour, mastered equestrianism, breeding as many as 80,000 of the small Arab horses, trained for heat and dust. The traditional narrative of indigenous peoples inevitably defeated by triumphant Europeans is belied by the rise of the Comanche, who over 150 years thrived in the south/south-west by adapting skilfully. The horses and guns allowed them to slaughter the bison herds, over 200,000 annually, and also to smash their rivals, the Apache, who were vulnerable because they farmed as well as raided, and to raid into Spanish territory, often on the night of the full moon – the Comanche Moon.

The Spanish controlled these territories on European maps, but their governors called this Comanchería, and negotiated deals with Comanche *paraibos* to desist from raids and instead trade: the Comanche traded in enslaved captives, fellow natives and Europeans. At the Taos fairs, the Spanish governors exchanged horses and guns for bison, beaver pelts and slaves, especially girls. Once sold, the Comanche 'deflower and corrupt [the girls] in the sight of innumerable assemblies of barbarians and Catholics ... saying to those who buy them, "Now you can take her – now she's good."' On Comanche raids, men were usually killed, eyes gouged out, scalped, penises often stuffed in their mouths; if they were kept alive, they were taken back to the villages where the women tortured them. Girls were raped, but they and their children were kept as slaves.

There was another side to this ferocity: the Comanche and other Native Americans often adopted the European prisoners who survived these early torments. Once these prisoners had learned how to live and ride like them, their captors were colour-blind, incorporating Europeans and captured black slaves into their families. One of their greatest warlords would be half-European.

By the 1760s, the Comanche numbered around 40,000, each family owning around eight horses, and ruled much of New Mexico and Texas, which was virtually purged of European settlers. The nominal rule of Comanchería changed when the Europeans negotiated the end of the war, but it made little difference to the Comanche.

On 25 October 1760, the twenty-two-year-old George III, the first of his family to speak English without a guttural Germanic accent, inherited the throne. He was determined to be a 'patriot king', reinvigorating royal power by removing the venal Whig oligarchs who had ruled since 1688: the sovereign was still the head of government, appointing ministers who, although led by a premier, responsible for managing royal business in parliament, were accountable to the crown. Democracy was still far away. Full-lipped, small-headed with bulbous watery-blue eyes, industrious and sincere, George called Newcastle 'a knave' and Pitt 'the snake', while his views on slavery were radical. Slavery, he wrote in an essay for his mentor, the earl of Bute, was 'as repugnant to the civil law as to the law of nature'.

The serpentine Pitt was mobbed by fans at George III's coronation, but in the row over the peace he resigned, bursting into tears. Instead George appointed his unworldly mentor Bute, who so mismanaged parliamentary and diplomatic business that the king realized that he had to compromise. He and his new prime minister, George Grenville – brother-in-law of Pitt – agreed that the American colonists, 2.5 million of them (of whom a quarter were enslaved African-Americans), must contribute to the cost of the war. In 1765 they therefore imposed new taxes – a stamp tax – on colonial goods which provoked American resistance under the slogan 'no taxation without representation'. George and his ministers blinked and after only a year repealed the Stamp Act, encouraged by Pitt, who declared, 'I rejoice that America has resisted.' But London also honoured promises to Native American allies by banning

American expansion over the Alleghenies, which Washington and Jefferson, typical land-hungry magnates and members of the Virginian House of Burgesses, regarded as their right.

The crisis brought Pitt, now fifty-eight, back to power, raised to earl of Chatham, but he was suffering from agonizing gout and a nervous breakdown, for which his doctor appallingly prescribed alcohol. At a vital moment in the American crisis, Britain was run by an alcoholic manic depressive hiding in a dark room who was too unstable to govern but too prestigious to fire.

Unlike Britain, Maria Theresa had failed to make gains from her victories. Frederick kept Silesia, and two years later she was heartbroken by the sudden death of the Little Mouse, Franz, which meant she had to involve Joseph, now emperor, in government. The two clashed continually, Joseph pushing for power, advocating radical, Enlightened reform and aggressive expansion, travelling and inspecting peripatetically, while the queen-empress, now overweight, sometimes despondent and always in mourning black, tried to improve and restrain him through a mix of sharp reprimands and abdication threats.

Joseph himself suffered, desperately missing Isabella and then losing his adored daughter too: 'I miss her in everything.' Embittered but filled with reforming energy, he grumbled about the longueurs of his mother's priggish court, 'an assemblage of a dozen married old ladies, three or four old maids ... Yet no society at all ... the intelligent bored to death with stupid women.' Joseph himself was not one for extravagance or debauchery, falling in love with his daughter's older governess, then with a grand princess, and finally consoling himself with random pick-ups on his travels, whores (one visit to a Viennese brothel ended badly with Joseph hitting a girl and being thrown out) and regular visits to his gardener's daughter. His greatest pleasure was music.

Yet Maria Theresa had not lost her exuberance. When Leopold gave her a grandson – a future emperor – she ran through the Hofburg on to the stage of its theatre and, stopping the actors in mid-sentence by clapping for silence, cried, 'Our Leopold has had a son!' More urgent was the problem of her youngest, Marie Antoinette.

THE RULE OF COCK AND CUNT:
CATHERINE THE GREAT AND POTEMKIN

The queen-empress had, like a prim headmistress, carefully managed the education of her children, but she could never control Antoinette. In

1770, Maria Theresa saw off the sobbing fourteen-year-old, blue-eyed, oval-faced, porcelain-skinned, auburn-haired, leaving mama for the last time, to marry Louis, the fifteen-year-old French dauphin, an obstinate plodder and enthusiastic hunter, obsessed with the navy, who was happiest tinkering with locks in his workshop and torturing cats. The old king Louis XV, an incorrigible sex addict with paedophile tendencies, was dismayed by Louis's oafishness and his unBourbon lack of interest in sex, while Antoinette immediately made a fool of herself by refusing to greet the royal mistress, Madame du Barry.

Soon Antoinette's politics and sex life were worrying her anxious mother. She reported on her regular periods to Maria Theresa, who soon learned that the marriage had not been consummated on the wedding night – nor for eight years thereafter. 'As for the dauphine,' Maria Theresa grumbled, 'nothing!'

In April 1774, Louis XV died of smallpox, his passing followed by a 'thunderous roar' – the stamp of courtiers' feet as they ran from the death chamber towards the new king. Louis XVI appointed a veteran navy minister, the comte de Maurepas, as his *principal ministre d'état*, whose advice he generally took. In economic matters he often said, 'It seems to me to be the general wish and I want to be loved,' but despite his passive image he was clear what he wanted: to build the navy until he found an opportunity to overturn British gains.*

Antoinette craved masques and spent exorbitantly on gambling at *faro*, magnificent towering hairstyles, jewels and new palaces. 'I am apprehensive about my daughter's youth,' wrote Maria Theresa, 'her susceptibility to flattery, idleness, disinclination for any serious activity,' and arranged for spies to watch her in Paris. She expected Antoinette to look after Austrian interests: her state chancellor Prince Kaunitz called Antoinette a 'bad payer' when she did not deliver. Louis himself warned her that 'The ambition of your relatives is going to upset everything' and boasted 'I've no intention of letting women [for example, his Habsburg wife] have any influence.' He was referring to foreign policy. At court, Antoinette first sought revenge on the courtiers who had humiliated her as dauphine. Promoting her best friend Yolande de Polignac and her family, Antoinette tried to diminish the high nobility by bringing in her own coterie, behaviour that alienated the grandees.

Early in her father-in-law's reign, Antoinette boasted that she had had a minister sacked. 'I asked the king to send him away,' she told a close

---

* The secretary to the royal council was a young man who had left his peasant family at fourteen and risen in the royal bureaucracy: his name was Bernard-François Balssa and he later changed his name to Balzac. He was the father of the novelist.

friend, mocking Louis as that 'poor man'. This outraged her mother. 'Where is the good and generous heart of Archduchess Antoinette?' she asked her. 'I see only intrigue, vulgar spite, delight in mockery and persecution.' She added, 'All the winter long I have trembled at the thought of your too easy success and the flatterers surrounding you while you have thrown yourself into a life of pleasure and preposterous display.'

It was unfortunate that this couple faced the challenges of a monarchy on the verge of bankruptcy. France had never been as absolute as Louis XIV claimed, always undercut by the medieval rights of the parlements and by a creaking taxation system that did not tax the aristocracy. Even as crisis threatened the regime, courtiers greedily grabbed every franc they could. Ruled by ravening factions and sclerotic formality, even a Mazarin would have struggled to navigate the problems faced by the royal locksmith.

'Your luck can all too easily change,' Maria Theresa warned Antoinette. 'One day you will recognize the truth of this and then it will be too late. I hope I shall not live until misfortune overtakes you . . .'

Antoinette was chastened: 'I love the empress but I'm afraid of her.' While worrying about Antoinette, Maria Theresa had to cope with an ebullient and ambitious upstart to the east: Catherine the Great. It is ironic that this chauvinistic era boasted more female potentates than the twenty-first century.

In 1762, the man who had saved Frederick, Tsar Peter III, had paid for this folly with his life when his long-suffering German-born wife Catherine organized a coup with the help of her lover and his friends in the Guards. Peter was arrested then strangled by her lover, a regicide that horrified Maria Theresa, who was also appalled by Catherine's lack of sexual inhibitions: she advanced her lovers to official court positions, like a king with his mistresses. Worse, Catherine turned out to be politically brilliant, adeptly expanding Russian power. She was a passionate enthusiast for the Enlightenment and even wrote a reforming plan, convening a commission to debate the abolition of serfdom.

'A woman is always a woman,' Frederick told his brother Heinrich, 'and in feminine government, cunt has more influence than sound reason.' In fact, reason of state was paramount for Catherine. Blue-eyed, auburn-haired, curvaceous, radiantly charming and politically rapacious, Catherine was a master of publicity, corresponding with Voltaire, who acclaimed her the Great (as he had Frederick), and hosting Diderot in St Petersburg. But she was too shrewd to impose their ideas, turning instead to empire building, dominating first Poland, where she orchestrated the election of an ex-lover, Stanisław Poniatowski, as king, then fighting the Ottomans and Girays in the south, where she gained new territories.

In 1772, Catherine manoeuvred Frederick into a carve-up of Poland–Lithuania, and together they offered Maria Theresa a bite. Maria Theresa hated any collusion with the monstrous Frederick and the lascivious Catherine but could not resist. 'One must know,' she sighed, 'when to sacrifice oneself.' After Joseph had travelled to meet Frederick ('That man is a genius,' he said), she joined the partition that would demolish the Polish kingdom. 'Catherine and I are simply brigands, but I wonder how the queen-empress managed to square her confessor,' sneered Frederick. 'She wept as she took; the more she wept, the more she took.'

This was only the beginning for Catherine, but faced with a long Ottoman war and a dangerous peasant revolt, she promoted an irrepressible, flamboyant and larger-than-life visionary, her lover Grigori Potemkin, who became her secret husband and political partner – the greatest minister of the Romanov dynasty. 'This is what happens', reflected Frederick, 'when cock and cunt rule.'*

The unusually wholesome George III, happily married to a German princess, sought a very different approach. In 1770, he appointed a genial, competent childhood friend untainted by faction to lead the government who proved the most successful manager of parliament since Walpole, though he was less proficient in America. Lord North, thirty-eight years old, was so modest he refused to call himself prime minister. But he could not escape the truth that British parliamentary government was badly designed to conduct wars in faraway places. Frederick the Great, master of united command, scoffed that 'The King of England changes his ministers as often as he changes his shirts.'

The British now ruled an extensive empire from Canada to Bengal in

---

* Potemkin led the expansion of the Russian empire around the Black Sea, long ruled by the semi-nomadic khans of the Giray family, descended from Genghis, and the Ottomans. Catherine had abolished the hetmanate in 1764. Now Potemkin annexed the old Cossack republic, the Zaporozhian Sech, assuming the title grand hetman and making the Cossacks into a Russian national legion. He directed the conquest of what is now south Ukraine. Calling it New Russia, he founded a series of new cities, starting with Kherson. In 1783, he annexed Crimea, where he built a new naval base, Sebastopol, and Russia's first Black Sea fleet. Kherson was followed by Mariupol, Ekaterinoslav (Dnipro) and Nikolaev (Mykolaiv). Then he conquered Ottoman lands, where he founded Odessa. The Russians had now conquered a vast territory sparsely populated. Russian viceroys, Potemkin and his successor the French aristocrat the duc de Richelieu, attracted Greeks, Italians, Ukrainians, Poles and Russians to settle in the new cities, and many Jews who were unable to live in the big cities but settled in huge numbers in Odessa. When Ukraine became the breadbasket of Russia, Odessa became its entrepôt. But there was a dark side to Russian settlement and conquest: Muslim Tatars, Turks and other peoples such as the Circassians and Chechens were ethnically cleansed or massacred if they resisted.

eastern India. Durrani, shah of the Afghan empire, installed a Mughal puppet, Alam II, in Delhi, writing to the British conquistador, Lord Clive, ordering him to recognize his poodle emperor. In 1765, Clive returned as the first governor-general of Bengal. Clive had left General Hector Munro in command as Alam and an anti-British coalition challenged EIC power in Bengal. In October 1764, Munro crushed a sepoy mutiny. The British had early on adopted the Mughal punishment of firing rebels from cannon. 'The upper part of the back is resting against the muzzle,' observed a shocked officer. 'When the gun is fired, the head is seen to go straight into the air forty feet, the arms fly off right and left, high up in the air, the legs drop to the ground . . . and the body is literally blown away.' Munro executed twenty rebels in this way. Then he routed the Mughal army, killing 2,000 to his own losses of 289.

When Clive returned, he was happy to support the powerless emperor in return for Bengal. On 12 August 1765, he received a *firman* from Alam giving Bengal to the EIC as well as granting some powers in the Carnatic and Deccan. The transaction, marking the start of British hegemony in east India, was a contrast to what Durrani was doing in Punjab in the west.[*]

DURRANI'S MAGGOTS: EMPIRE IN INDIA

'Let's destroy these people,' ordered Durrani, 'and enslave their women and children!' The Afghans killed Sikh and non-Sikh in a frenzy before Durrani departed and galloped westwards to receive the tribute of the emir of Bukhara – his empire extended into today's Uzbekistan. But the fifty-year-old Durrani was now sick, the Amritsar fragment having infected his face. In summer 1772, maggots infested his nose and nasopharynx, dropping into his mouth, until he could no longer speak or eat. The epigraph on his octagonal tomb in Kandahar claims that 'the lion lay with the lamb', such was the peace won by his greatness. Yet he spread little peace: he was a ferocious, peripatetic, poetry-writing conqueror who perpetrated atrocities in Punjab but also laid out the modern cities of Kabul and Kandahar and created a new country, where he is still known as *Baba-i-Afghan* – the Father of Afghans. Although he lost Punjab to an independent Sikh kingdom, his son Timur held

---

[*] Clive again returned home on the verge of nervous breakdown. Both Munro and Clive had sons who joined the EIC and served in India. Munro's sons became famous because one was killed by a tiger, the other by a shark.

Durrani's empire together, but seventy years later Durrani's grandson would contribute to Britain's first Afghan fiasco.

Back in London, Lord North now faced a crisis in Bengal where the EIC was going bankrupt, thanks to soaring military expenditure, as Bengals starved, thanks to EIC taxes. Clive and his fellow nabobs were already notorious for their fortunes. There had been talk of appointing Clive to command British troops in America, but all factions were uneasy about his methods and wealth. In 1772, he was attacked by political enemies in Parliament for his rapacity. 'A great prince was dependent on my pleasure; an opulent city lay at my mercy . . . I walked through vaults which were thrown open to me alone, piled . . . with gold and jewels!' he retorted. 'Mr Chairman, I stand astonished at my own moderation.' No one else was astonished by it. But when the nabob was exonerated by a parliamentary vote, George told North that even though 'no one thinks his services greater than I do' he was 'amazed' that the MPs' judgement 'seems to approve of Lord Clive's rapine'.[*]

In 1773, North took government control of the EIC, appointing a governor-general and council: the effective rule of Bengal by the armed company had lasted little more than ten years. But he also faced a crisis in his other colonies, in America, and his solution linked the two. To help the EIC, he abolished duties on Indian tea exported to America, where the colonists objected to undercutting their own merchants. In November that year, Americans – wearing blackface and Mohawk head-dresses – raided tea-bearing ships in Boston harbour. North overreacted by passing the so-called Coercive Acts and dispatching troops.

On a mountain top in rustic Virginia, Jefferson moved his wife Martha Jefferson into the Honeymoon Cottage, the small but finished wing of Monticello. Three years earlier, just after his election to the House of Burgesses, Thomas Jefferson had come to call on Martha Wayles Skelton, twenty-three years old and a widow. In January 1772, they married and, when her father died the next year, they inherited 11,000 acres heavily encumbered with debts, as well as 135 slaves, including Betty Hemings and her six children by Wayles. The youngest was a newborn baby, a daughter named Sally, who would play a special role in Jefferson's life.

---

[*] On 22 November 1774, Clive, in agony from gallstones and depressed by his critics, overdosed on opium then cut his throat with a penknife. He was forty-nine. Samuel Johnson noted that the conquistador 'had acquired his fortune by such crimes that his consciousness of them impelled him to cut his own throat'. His son Edward was given the earldom of Powis, allowing him to keep his father's treasures in Powis Castle, where many remain today. Returning to India, he governed Madras for five years.

RADICALS: JEFFERSON AND THE HEMINGSES; THE ENGLISH
QUEEN OF DENMARK AND THE DOCTOR'S FALL

Jefferson was already obsessed with two difficult missions – building his new mansion, Monticello, atop a hill, and 'a city on a hill', his vision of Enlightenment in America. 'Architecture is my delight,' he said, 'and putting up, and pulling down, one of my favorite amusements.' Monticello would be his lifelong obsession. Hired slaves levelled the mountain; the house itself was built by enslaved (his own and hired) and free labour, white and black, over the years. He designed it himself, filling it with novelties and charms, and having his study built around his bedroom. His ideas of liberty clashed with the reality of a lifestyle based on chattel slavery: as a lawyer, he represented the sons of slaves seeking freedom and proposed that masters should free their slaves, yet he did not free his own and did not believe black and white could live together. However liberal the slave master, the institution only worked because it was based on violence. He allowed his overseers to beat his slaves, but he was considerably less strict than, say, his contemporary and fellow grandee Colonel Washington. It was one thing to talk enlightenment and another to practise it.

Domestic slaves who lived close to the planter's mansion were in some ways privileged over those who toiled in the plantations, but they were more likely to be raped by the masters. The Hemingses were treated differently – they were three-quarters white and half-siblings to Mrs Jefferson.

As Martha had two daughters with Jefferson, the Hemingses played the traditional role of house slaves in helping her raise the children, who grew up with their contemporary enslaved cousins. The youngest, Sally Hemings, was thriving at Monticello as Jefferson wrote his *Summary View of the Rights of British America*. 'Kings are the servants,' he wrote, 'not the proprietors of the people . . . Let not the name of George III be a blot in the page of history.' In this tract, he toyed with a definition of the rights of man and proposed the abolition of slavery – just not yet.

Not everyone was as measured in their reforms as those pillars of the Enlightenment, Catherine, Frederick – and Jefferson. At almost the same moment, in Denmark, a scandalous ménage à trois of a radical doctor, his lover the queen and her husband the king launched the most Enlightened reform anywhere in the world.

The experiment had started in in November 1766, when George III sent his fifteen-year-old sister, Caroline Matilda, to marry her first cousin, Christian VII, king of Denmark, Norway and Iceland. The groom, a gawky, pinheaded and unstable seventeen-year-old, a public masturbator, self-harmer and denizen of Copenhagen brothels, treated his wife coldly. The isolated teenaged queen, modest, passionate and intelligent, was desperate. She was bewildered and frightened by Christian's sexual eccentricities, yet she charmed the Danes: 'her appearance allowed her to avoid criticism of women, but still captivate the male eye'.

When she gave birth to a son, Frederick, her husband showed no interest. He was sometimes manic, often enervated. His veteran ministers enquired about treatment and were recommended to a young German doctor, Johann Friedrich Struensee, aged thirty-one, dashing, worldly, the scholarly son of a Pietist minister. Struensee had met the *philosophes* in Paris and embraced the ideas of Jean-Jacques Rousseau, their most radical thinker. Rousseau had just published *The Social Contract*, in which he argued that man was born pure and became corrupted by society, and *Émile, or Treatise on Education*, in which he declared, 'Everything is good as it leaves the hands of the Author of things; everything degenerates in the hands of man.' So he proposed that children should be 'denatured' to prepare them for citizenship. Struensee, who wrote his own Rousseauesque treatises, blew into the disturbed court like a breath of fresh air, calming the king, reassuring the queen. Christian came to trust him passionately as did the queen, especially after the inoculation of their son. Struensee reconciled the teenagers, encouraging the king to return to the queen's bed, while supervising the upbringing of Prince Frederick according to Rousseau's rules.

Still only nineteen, Caroline fell in love with Struensee, starting a wild affair right in front of the king. In September 1770, infected with the vision and authority of the doctor, Christian sacked the chancellor and promoted Struensee to count and Privy Cabinet Minister with the power to sign royal orders: Enlightened dictator. When the queen mother confronted her, Caroline retorted, 'Pray, madam, allow me to govern my own kingdom as I please.' Her mother-in-law bribed the servants to chronicle Caroline's adultery with Struensee, scattering flour outside her bedroom to record male footprints. They also found her garters in Struensee's bed.

In July 1771, the queen gave birth to a daughter, Louise Augusta, who resembled Struensee. The king became suspicious and unsettled. Meanwhile the count-doctor signed over a thousand decrees that abolished torture, noble privileges, censorship and the slave trade.* He created

---

* The *Vestindisk Kompagni* traded 3,000 slaves annually from Fort Christiansborg, the Castle of the Gold Coast. Denmark was the first European country to abolish the slave trade.

foundling hospitals funded by a gambling tax and increased peasant land ownership. Denmark was now the most progressive kingdom in Europe.

On 16 January 1772, in Copenhagen, Struensee danced with his mistress the queen, watched by her husband, at a masquerade ball at the Court Theatre in the Christiansborg Palace. In the early hours after the ball, he was arrested by royal guards, in a coup organized by a cabal backed by the queen mother. While the queen was interrogated in Kronborg Castle, Struensee himself denied a sexual relationship, convinced that the king would back him and the queen defend him. But both lovers were tricked into confessing the relationship, she hoping to draw the guilt on to herself, he in response to being offered his life if he admitted the truth. She recanted her confession but too late. Condemned to the amputation of his right hand – signer of treasonous decrees – and then to losing his head, Struensee was convinced he would be spared until almost the last minute when he saw his closest associate beheaded before him. 'I would have liked to have saved them both,' said the king, but he did not. After three clumsy blows, Struensee was beheaded with an axe – now on display in Copenhagen – then quartered. Struensee's decrees were abolished, the slavery of the Danish East Indies Company restored.

Although he was embarrassed by his sister's 'criminal conduct', George III warned the Danes not to punish her and dispatched the Royal Navy to threaten Copenhagen.* But the king was now facing revolution in America.

George and North might have devised any number of solutions to the crisis. George could have declared himself king of America (his father had considered moving his younger brother to the colonies as duke of Virginia) and announced that he was protecting American rights – as he now did with his Canadian subjects; he could have called the Americans' bluff by giving them seats in Parliament (as had happened with Scottish and Irish union). Instead, North decided to crack down,[†]

---

* The Danes negotiated Caroline's exile. George settled her at Celle Castle, Hanover: she never saw her children again, dying at the age of twenty-three. As for the daughter of the English princess and the Enlightened doctor, Louise Augusta, cultured and beautiful, was brought up as a royal daughter, married within the royal family and saw her daughter married to a future king. But she had inherited one thing from her parents: among many lovers, she had a romance with the royal doctor who solved her infertility (it was actually her husband's) by fathering her children himself. She lived into another age, dying in 1843.
† British insouciance was personified by the fourth Proprietor of Maryland, Frederick, Lord Baltimore, a psychopathic predator who in 1751 inherited the family's fortune and American estates, and almost provoked an early revolution by ordering taxes to be raised in Maryland – but not on his own estates. Baltimore killed his first wife (sister of the duke of

provoking the American Patriots to hold their first Continental Congress in Philadelphia, attended by Washington. The delegates founded a Continental Association that linked the colonies in one organization. While Jefferson watched from Monticello, the lofty, taciturn Washington decided 'to devote my life and fortune in the cause', taking command of a Virginia militia.

George and North believed that the colonists were incapable of political coordination and would back down. 'The die is now cast,' George wrote to North; 'the colonies must either submit or triumph . . . we must not retreat.'

In April 1775, at Lexington, British redcoats were defied by a posse of colonials – an escalation that led to a second Congress at which Washington was elected commander-in-chief – his appointment owing as much to 'his tall stature', noted John Adams bitchily, as to his 'gift of silence'. Washington was toasted by Jefferson and the most famous colonial, the sixty-nine-year-old Benjamin Franklin, polymathic luminary of the Enlightenment, but so far the general was the only soldier in the Continental Army. Jefferson was elected to a Committee of Five to draft a Declaration of Independence, approved in July 1776: 'all men are created equal', this asserted, 'with certain unalienable Rights', among which 'are Life, Liberty and the pursuit of Happiness' – though not for everyone. The aspirations of the American founders – all males, writing about 'men' being equal – set high moral standards for democracy, but they did not live up to them. Jefferson wanted to abolish the slave trade but other slave masters resisted, so they compromised and agreed to revisit this after twenty years. In London, Samuel Johnson mocked American humbug: 'How is it we hear the loudest yelps for liberty among the drivers of Negroes?'

Rushing to New England, Washington drove the British out of Boston but then had to defend New York with his small army of 8,000, which soon buckled under British attack. In the retreat, Washington unusually lost his composure, shouting, 'Are these the men with which I'm to

---

Bridgewater, the future canal magnate) by pushing her out of a speeding carriage, then set off to live in Constantinople like a Turkish pasha with a harem, stoned on opium and aphrodisiacs (observed by James Boswell, who described him as 'living a strange, wild, life'). He returned to London where in 1768 he kidnapped and raped a beautiful milliner, Sarah Woodcock, leading to his arrest and trial, at which he was acquitted, the victim blamed for not escaping more efficiently. Baltimore then travelled in Europe accompanied by 'eight women, a physician, and two negroes, which he called his *corregidores*, who were entrusted with the discipline of his little seraglio. One of his mistresses then published *Memoirs of the Seraglio of the Bashaw (Pasha) of Merryland, by a Discarded Sultana* who revealed that he struggled to satisfy his eight girlfriends.' In 1771, he died in Naples, leaving Maryland to his illegitimate son, Henry Harford, the last Proprietor.

defend America?' But they were and he did, withdrawing to New Jersey as the British took Philadelphia.

North believed victory was assured, and hired 18,000 Hessian mercenaries, a traditional measure since British armies were small. Catherine the Great and Potemkin, who had just crushed a massive serf rebellion on the Volga, offered George a Russian army to destroy the Americans, an intriguing possibility. Had George and North really been 'tyrants', as the Patriots alleged, they would have launched a total war like Catherine's against her rebels with massive forces, or they would have retaliated with the brutality used by the king's uncle the duke of Cumberland against Scottish rebels in 1745. Instead they hoped to win over the Americans, never sent enough troops, underestimated the rebel resolve, skills and numbers and exaggerated Loyalist sentiment. North barely interfered with his colonial secretary, Lord George Germain, who divided British forces into three under rival commanders which ultimately allowed the Americans to defeat them one by one. It was difficult enough to run a war five weeks away. North, depressed, begged to resign, but George, having secretly paid his massive debts, forced him to stay. In May 1778, a cadaverous Pitt (Chatham) hobbled into the Lords, aided by his son, to advocate American conciliation, only to collapse. He died in the arms of his eighteen-year-old son William, who would be the greatest premier of the century.

Louis XVI watched Britain's American fiasco with satisfaction, though he agonized over whether or not to intervene. But he had bigger problems: failing debts in his kingdom and sexual failure in his boudoir, both of which were the talk of Europe.

ANTOINETTE AND LOUIS: IMPERIAL SEX THERAPY AT VERSAILLES

In November 1776, Antoinette, unhappy and bewildered, appealed to her brother Emperor Joseph, a most unlikely sex therapist, whose latest marriage and personal relationships were disastrous. In June 1777, Joseph visited his sister in Paris where he investigated the astonishing situation at the most sexually unbuttoned court in Europe: no one had explained to either the king or queen how to make love. But the emperor was perhaps the only man the king of France could confide in. Joseph took the king – 'rather weak but not an imbecile' – on a walk. 'Imagine! In his marriage bed. He has strong perfectly satisfactory erection . . . introduces the member, stays there for two minutes without moving,

withdraws without ever discharging but still erect and bids goodnight,'
Joseph wrote to his brother Leopold. 'Ah! If I could have been present
once, I should have arranged it properly. He needs to be whipped to
make him discharge in a passion like donkeys. Furthermore my sister
is pretty placid and they're two incompetents together.'

Somehow Joseph arranged it, saving the alliance and the marriage.
As Louis made love to Antoinette, she thought of Maria Theresa: 'My
dear mother . . . it has already been more than eight days since my
marriage was perfectly consummated; the proof has been repeated and
yesterday even more completely. At first I thought of sending my dear
mama a courier . . .'

The first birth – a daughter – was nightmarish: at the words 'The
queen is about to give birth,' courtiers filled the hot chamber; she haemorrhaged and passed out as Louis tried to open the window. When later
he did not make love to her, Maria Theresa presumed he had a mistress:
'My rule is the woman must just patiently endure her husband's lapses.
No point making an issue of it.' Yet their marriage was much better:
Louis told her he loved her and would never take a mistress. Two sons
followed quickly. Joseph boasted: 'They both [king and queen] have written to thank me.' The kaiser adored his sister, reflecting that he could
be happily married to her himself, but she worried him, for 'the vortex
of dissipation around her prevents her from seeing and thinking about
anything but going from one pleasure to another'. Joseph predicted,
'The revolution will be cruel.'

The American revolution too had become cruel, with a racial undercurrent. The British governor of Virginia, the earl of Dunmore,
immediately appealed to enslaved African-Americans: 'all servants, negroes and others' were to be freed 'if able and willing to bear arms' they
joined 'His Majesty's troops'. Three hundred freedmen in Dunmore's
Royal Ethiopian Regiment fought under the banner 'Liberty to Slaves',
while a Black Brigade under a remorseless guerrilla commander, Titus
Cornelius, known as Colonel Tye, harassed American forces. Fifty
thousand slaves escaped to the British. The Iroquois and other Native
Americans planned to back the British against the colonials.

Washington tried to hold the army together at Valley Forge as he intimidated Iroquois leaders and trained his 'exceedingly dirty and nasty'
troops whose naivety he blamed on 'an unaccountable kind of stupidity
in the lower class of these people'. He hoped that an extended war with
overlong supply lines would undermine British resolve.

The ideals of the American revolution marked a new epoch – the
fruition of both the English civil war and the Enlightenment.

Yet without a game changer, the Americans seemed unlikely to win.

SHOOT OFF YOUR ARROW: KAMEHAMEHA AND COOK

At Valley Forge, Washington was joined by a young French aristocrat, Gilbert du Motier, marquis de Lafayette, who had fitted out a ship with his own money and, in June 1777, arrived in America to fight for freedom aged only nineteen. The Americans quickly understood Lafayette's potential influence in Paris, elevating him to major-general. Washington offered to be his 'friend and father'. His skirmishes with the British, recounted in his excited letters home, were closely followed by Louis and Antoinette.

Many a ruler has dreamed of that ultimate panacea: a short victorious war. Louis XVI was no exception. He knew he could not afford a war, but his new finance minister, the Swiss banker Jacques Necker,* advised that if he won the war in a single year loans without higher taxes would fund it. Lafayette returned to advocate for America and, after a victory at Saratoga had shown that Americans could beat British–Hessian troops, Louis agreed to intervene, backed by his Spanish cousins. A short victorious war would restore royal fortunes. On 6 February 1778, the octogenarian American envoy Benjamin Franklin negotiated the alliance. Antoinette supported the war, and her first lover would play a role in the American revolution.

Soon after her arrival in Paris, Antoinette had met this special friend at a masque ball, a very eighteenth-century event that allowed incognito monarchs to meet masked strangers – and everyone to meet new lovers. She encountered a flaxen-haired Swedish count, Axel von Fersen, the same age as her, who had talked to her without realizing who she was. Now in 1778 Ferson returned to Paris. 'Ah, here's an old acquaintance,'

---

* Necker was a bold speculator who made a series of fortunes on the bourse and in the *Compagnie des Indes Orientales*. As he made his money during the 1760s, he paid court to a French widow, Madame de Vermenou, who had hired a young Swiss governess, Suzanne Curchod, a pastor's daughter. Suzanne had fallen in love with a young British gentleman, Edward Gibbon, a child of the Enlightenment, on his travels and become engaged. When both families vetoed their marriage, Gibbon returned home. Not unlike one of his trades, Necker switched out of Vermenou into Curchods and married Suzanne: their daughter would be the writer and provocateur Germaine de Staël. Now, just as Necker became Louis's finance minister, Gibbon published his elegantly written and entertaining *Decline and Fall of the Roman Empire*, recasting history with the Enlightened idea that the superstitions of Christianity had undermined the pagan pragmatism of Rome, while implying that modern Europe was the heir of Roman civilization.

she said; an equerry noticed that 'her hand trembled with visible emotion'.

After her disappointing marriage, she fell in love. Fersen thought the heavily pregnant queen 'the prettiest and most amiable princess'. Asking him to wear his smart Swedish uniform, she welcomed him at her informal villa, Petit Trianon, on the Versailles estate, where 'The queen couldn't take her eyes off him . . . eyes full of tears.' It was the beginning of a loving liaison that endured for the rest of her life, but they were not yet physical lovers. 'I love you and will love you madly all my life,' he wrote later, while she called him 'the most loved and loving of men', affirming 'My heart is all yours.'

In America, Washington was now becalmed for another anxious winter at Middlebrook, New Jersey. Yet, while the Atlantic world focused on the rebellion, a Polynesian potentate – whose island would form another part of America, was encountering his first European.

On 26 January 1779, at Kealakekua Bay, Kaleiopuu, *alii-nui* (king) of Hawaii island, one of the last lands outside European knowledge, made a visit to the captain of one of two British ships, accompanied by his son Kiwalao. Also among his entourage of young nobles, towering over both of them, was the third man of the kingdom, his nephew Kamehameha; a hefty giant of seven foot, with low brows, penetrating, heavy-lidded eyes and an air of menacing power who would soon unite the Hawaiian islands.

The old *alii-nui*, wizened from his addiction to the narcotic *awa* but still an enthusiastic lover of his young boyfriends, arrived wearing a gorgeous scarlet, black and yellow *ahuala* cloak, made from 400,000 feathers taken from 80,000 birds, and a feathered *mahiole* helmet. While the regalia was impressive, the Hawaiian leaders were weakened by the ferocity of their political struggles.

Around 1735, an ambitious prince of the ruling clan, Alapai the Great, had overthrown and killed rivals, sacrificing them to gain their spiritual power, *mola*, uniting several islands into a single kingdom, which he ruled for twenty years.

When his niece, the noblewoman Kekuiapoiwa, became pregnant, she asked for the eyeball of a shark, a signal that the baby would be a king slayer, at which Alapai ordered the baby to be killed. Unsure what to do, the baby boy's mother placed him on Naha, the sacred stone: if he cried, he would be killed – but he did not. The warrior king sent assassins, but Kekuiapoiwa hid the baby. Finally Alapai, confident in his power, lifted the death sentence and recalled the baby Kamehameha to court. When Alapai died around 1754, his kinsman Kaleiopuu seized power.

Now boarding the European ship with his king, Kamehameha sized up the ships and their cannon along with the European chieftain who combined the scientific pursuits of an Englishman of the Enlightenment with the imperial mission of a British conquistador: James Cook.

As a boy, Cook had been miserable, working on his father's Yorkshire farm and in a grocery store, until he joined the Royal Navy, distinguishing himself as a pilot in time to guide General Wolfe up the St Lawrence River to capture Quebec. In August 1768, Cook, now thirty-nine, shy, impatient and quick-witted, tall and handsome, self-taught and self-driven, had been chosen by the Royal Society to command HMS *Endeavour* and observe the transit of Venus across the sun in Tahiti, transporting an astronomer, along with a rich young botanist called Joseph Banks, round Tierra del Fuego to the Pacific. In Tahiti he met a Polynesian navigator and priest Tupaia, a haughty refugee from Raiatea, who taught him how Polynesians had navigated the ocean, helped him map the islands, and accompanied him across the Pacific in 1770 to land on Aotearoa – which the Dutch had called New Zealand – where they encountered Maori people.

Sailing to Australia, Cook landed at what he called Stingray Bay on the eastern coast, renaming it Botany Bay in honour of Banks, who collected 30,000 samples on the trip and spotted an extraordinary animal – a kangaroo – the first sign that this continent had been isolated for many millennia. Claiming eastern Australia – New South Wales – for Britain, Cook encountered Gweagal aboriginals of the Botany Bay area, sailing 'so near the shore as to distinguish several people upon the sea beach; they appear'd to be of a very dark or black Colour'. Unfortunately the Gweagal resisted Cook's landing, throwing spears until they were shot at and one man injured. They did not wish to communicate. Tupaia died at Batavia on Cook's voyage home.

On their return to London, Cook and Banks became celebrities flaunting their exploits, their 1,400 new plants including eucalyptus and acacia, and their Tahitian passenger, Omai, who was introduced to George III and painted by Joshua Reynolds. But Cook was bored at home. His thoughts roaming boundlessly, he claimed that he had travelled 'farther than any man has been before me, but as far as I think it is possible for a man to go' – true at the time.

In July 1776, Cook's patron the earl of Sandwich, first lord of the Admiralty, commissioned a voyage on HMS *Resolution* and *Discovery* to take Omai home but really to find a north-west passage to the Pacific – and beat France.

Cook returned Omai to Tahiti, then sailed on to 'discover' Maui and

Hawaii, which he named the Sandwich Islands. Unbeknown to the British, it was the Makahiki season, the festivities to celebrate harvest and the god Lono, one of the four primal deities, and boatloads of Hawaiians canoed out to visit the Europeans. The men wished to trade and offered pigs and fruit; the girls danced on deck singing a *hula*:

> Where oh where
> Is the hollow stemmed stick, where is it,
> To make an arrow for the hawk?
> Come and shoot . . .
> A penis, a penis to be enjoyed:
> Don't stand still, come gently . . .
> Shoot off your arrow.

The Protestant British were amazed by their sexual generosity. Never himself partaking of the Hawaiian girls (loyal to his wife at home with their six children), Cook wrote that he allowed sexual contact 'because he could not prevent it'. But he tried to limit the spread of venereal disease from his men to the Polynesians, inspecting them and allowing only healthy ones loose on the islands. It was not understood at the time that men with STDs might be asymptomatic but still infect others, and he was agonized to see Hawaiian women with syphilitic sores.

On the *Discovery*, the *alii-nui* Kaleiopuu took off his cloak and helmet and presented them to the Englishman, who could not have known how valuable they were. But both sides were quickly disillusioned with each other: Britons had sex with women on what to the Hawaiians was holy ground, while prudish sailors were shocked to learn that Kaleiopuu kept a string of teenaged boys as his *aikane* (lover of the same gender) whom he liked to ejaculate on to him. When one of Cook's officers, William Bligh,* ordered Hawaiians to perform some tasks and tried to beat them when they refused, Cook wisely sailed away – to explore the coast of California.

On Cook's return, his men infuriated the Hawaiians by mistakenly purloining idols for firewood. Sensing peril, he decided to emulate Cortés and kidnap King Kaleiopuu at gunpoint, but he was foiled when

---

* Bligh's career was a chronicle of naval stupidity. Ten years later, in 1789, as captain of HMS *Bounty*, he was ordered to Tahiti to gather breadfruit saplings which Sir Joseph Banks believed would serve as food for Caribbean slaves. There he was overcome by mutineers, who were partly dazzled by the idyllic Tahitian life, and set adrift, surviving a journey of 4,160 miles. In Tahiti the mutineers aided a chieftain named Pomare to unite the islands as a single kingdom which they ruled until a French protectorate was imposed. Sailing on, they settled on the uninhabited Pitcairn Island, named after a British officer later killed in battle with the Americans at Bunker Hill. As for Captain Bligh, he was promoted to vice-admiral and appointed governor of New South Wales. That did not go well either.

his wife Kanekapolei raised the alarm. In the melee, Cook shot a Hawaiian and his marines killed several more before a nobleman smashed Cook on the head with a shark-tooth mace. The Hawaiians then stabbed Cook and four marines.

While the king hid, his nephew Prince Kamehameha sent a pig as a gesture of reconciliation to the *Discovery*. After the British had bombarded a village, Kaleiopuu delivered Cook's skull, scalp, feet and hands.* The remains were buried at sea.

In 1782, when Kaleiopuu died, his son Kiwalao succeeded him, with Kamehameha as keeper of the war god: offering humans to the war god was the royal prerogative, but Kamehameha sacrificed a rebellious nobleman to the god himself. When Kiwalao tried to stop him, Kamehameha captured and sacrificed him, and then made himself *alii-nui* of the main island. To conquer the other islands, he needed cannon – and soon afterwards two Americans blundered murderously if providentially to deliver them. Similarly Washington needed the French fleet if the Patriots were to win, but Louis moved with glacial slowness.

THE INTERVENTION: ANTOINETTE AND FERSEN

Louis sent a contingent under the comte de Rochambeau to America in 1780; and to stop the gossip and seek adventure, Fersen joined him. Yet this intervention in America was too little, too slow. Louis had also dispatched a Franco-Spanish armada of sixty-five ships-of-the-line bearing 30,000 troops to invade Britain, an enterprise that narrowly failed thanks mainly to the weather. Necker had borrowed massively to pay for it. It was the murkiness of the royal finances that made French borrowing so expensive: British finances were much more transparent, allowing the British government to borrow at a full 2 per cent less than France. Necker produced a false budget that concealed the desperate financial crisis now exacerbated by war, then resigned in a sulk.

Not until two years into the war did Louis order his full fleet under Admiral de Grasse to back the Americans. In September 1780, Washington and Lafayette met Rochambeau and Fersen to coordinate. As the toughest British general, Charles Cornwallis, marched his 9,000 troops into Virginia, Washington and the French, supported now by the formidable fleet under Grasse, gave chase.

---

* In death, Cook was treated like a chieftain by the Hawaiians. He was scalped, his heart excised, his body eviscerated and some flesh preserved, then the rest was placed in a traditional underground oven, and the bones collected to preserve his *mana*, sacred charisma.

In early 1781, Cornwallis dispatched units to hunt down Governor Jefferson of Virginia. Jefferson abandoned the capital, Richmond, to British predations, and fled to his western plantation. Twenty-three of his slaves escaped – as Jefferson put it, 'joined the enemy' – as did fourteen of Washington's.

Jefferson was no warlord. His delicate wife Martha gave birth to six children, though only two daughters survived their childhood; each time her health had declined.* Now he devotedly nursed her.

Suddenly the war accelerated. Washington, Rochambeau and Grasse converged on Virginia, where Cornwallis confidently fortified his camp at Yorktown.

In November 1780, as Antoinette awaited news from America, her mother Maria Theresa, aged sixty-three, lay dying at the Hofburg in Joseph's arms.

'Is Your Majesty uncomfortable?' asked Joseph.

'Yes,' replied the queen-empress, 'but in a good enough position to die.' Now Joseph could patronize his beloved musicians, Salieri and Mozart, and reform the monarchy with ideas that even Jefferson would approve of. 'All men,' Joseph declared, 'are equal at birth.'

MOZART, JOSEPH AND HIS CONTINUAL ERECTIONS

Joseph, now forty, far from being a long-jawed, slathering Joseph Habsburg, was slim, handsome, informal, witty and self-deprecating, the most extraordinary of his family – a radical visionary: 'We inherit from our parents no more than animal life, hence there's not the slightest difference between king, count, bourgeois and peasant.' He embarked on endless tours and inspections, with a tiny entourage, eschewing ceremony, enjoying his incognito as Count von Falkenstein, dressed plainly in military coat and boots, and indulging in sexual adventures which he complained were a 'choice between ugly peasants and falconers' wives'. Visiting Paris, he was randomly recruited to stand godfather at a christening where the priest asked his name:

'Joseph.'

'Surname?'

---

* While others were fighting, Jefferson, once his term as governor was over, worked on his *Notes on Virginia* on race and slavery, reflecting on the inferiority of black reasoning, which could be improved by white blood. He argued that hurried liberation of slaves would unleash a race war against whites.

'Second.'

'Occupation?'

'Emperor.'*

When the American revolution was discussed, Jefferson claimed Joseph joked, 'I'm a royalist by trade.' But he was also obsessional, tactless and in a hurry. 'As a prince he'll have continual erections,' his dear friend, the prince de Ligne, predicted, 'and never be satisfied. His reign will be a continual priapism.' Believing reform was possible only from above, Joseph was an indefatigable legislomaniac, promulgating 6,206 mostly admirable laws: his *Toleranzpatent* delivered religious tolerance to Protestants and Jews – while imposing measures to rationalize what he regarded as Jewish superstition. The kaiser was a great reformer but also a militaristic disciplinarian, believing that 'Everything exists for the state.' He abolished serfdom, reduced censorship and diminished the nobility. Nonetheless as emperor he lacked both balance and empathy.

In 1784, he banned extravagant funerals and to save space and decay ordered people to be buried in sacks in communal graves, designing a reusable coffin that opened to drop the body into the grave. The Viennese so hated this that Joseph sparked funeral riots. 'He had no idea whatever of the art of government,' wrote Casanova, who met him, 'for he hadn't the slightest knowledge of the human heart.' But, for musicians, Joseph was a boon: he lived for music, himself playing clavier and cello, and adored Italian comic opera.

In 1781, Mozart, now twenty-five and court organist in Salzburg, was ordered by his master the prince-archbishop to meet him in Vienna for the celebrations of Joseph's accession. Mozart could not wait to rid himself of the prince-archbishop who, jealous of his minion, screamed at him. Mozart, small, thin, with large eyes and a nimbus of blond hair, was outraged by the prince-archbishop's arrogance: 'my body was trembling all over, and I staggered about the street like a drunkard'. Mercifully sacked, 'my main goal now is to meet the emperor . . . I'm determined he should get to know me. I would be so happy if I could whip through my opera for him and then play a fugue or two, for that's what he likes.' By December, Joseph had invited Mozart to play in a piano competition and was backing his career as pianist and as

* Joseph also enjoyed being mistaken for his own servant. Asked what services he provided the emperor, he said straight-faced, 'I sometimes shave him.' Although his brother Leopold, grand duke of Tuscany, was his heir, Joseph trained his conscientious but lumpy nephew Franz for the future, complaining that the 'stunted' boy was 'backward in bodily dexterity' and 'a spoiled mother's child'.

composer of concertos and of operas, starting with *The Abduction from the Seraglio*.

In a city of music, favoured by a music-crazy emperor, Mozart bubbled with ideas. 'The music reigns supreme,' he wrote. Just as he had once written about sex and shitting, now it was all about music as he describes how he wrote his opera: 'Now about Bellmont's [sic] aria in A Major. Oh how anxious, oh how passionate? Do you know how I expressed it? – even expressing the loving, throbbing heart? – with two violins playing in octaves.' Mozart, whose amorous instincts had been restrained by a terror of venereal disease ever since seeing a childhood friend afflicted with syphilis, was boarding with a musical family, the Webers, whose nineteen-year-old daughter Constanze he fell in love with. They married happily and had six children, losing half of them. Mozart was heartbroken when their first boy died: 'We are both very sad about our poor, bonny, fat darling little boy.' He never stopped flirting, but as he wrote to a playboy friend, 'Don't you think the pleasures of unstable capricious love affairs don't even come close to the blessing of true affection?' Walking in the Augarten, spotting Mozart and Constanze japing around, Joseph strolled up and teased them: 'Well, well, married three weeks and fisticuffs already.'

It was at the premiere of the opera that Joseph supposedly said, 'Too beautiful for our [Viennese] ears, my dear Mozart, and a monstrous quantity of notes,' but the emperor admired and supported Mozart. He was joking, as he often did, about cloddish Viennese audiences, though earlier he had said that Mozart 'has only one fault in his pieces for stage, and his singers have often complained of it, he deafens them with his full accompaniment'.

At the premiere of his D-minor Piano Concerto, Joseph waved his hat and shouted, 'Bravo, Mozart!' It was mutual. 'There's no monarch in the world, I'd prefer to serve than the emperor,' said Mozart, 'but I shan't go begging for a post.' His real frustration was that Joseph had appointed an Italian composer, Antonio Salieri, six years older, as imperial chamber composer, blocking his way. Salieri's operas were more successful than Mozart's. Joseph backed both composers; when Gluck died, Joseph promoted Salieri to *Kapellmeister* and Mozart to imperial chamber composer.

Yet the Habsburg dreamed of conquest. Joseph outmanoeuvred old Frederick to negotiate a new alliance with Catherine the Great, planning to attack and partition the Ottoman empire. The Romanovs had always aspired to conquer Constantinople, which they called Tsargrad

– Caesarcity.* Their plan depended on Britain and France being distracted in America.

Instead of defying the rebels at Yorktown, Cornwallis was trapped there. When the Royal Navy tried to rescue him, the French defeated it in Chesapeake Bay. On 19 October 1781, Cornwallis surrendered to Washington.† Fersen helped with the negotiations while enjoying the Americans. 'The women are pretty, amiable and available,' he wrote. 'That's all I need.' Louis and Antoinette had much to celebrate. Three days later at Versailles, she delivered a dauphin, heir to the throne. This time only ten people were allowed to attend the birth – and Antoinette feared it was another daughter until the king said, 'Monsieur le Dauphin requests permission to enter!'

Without informing America's French allies, Ben Franklin started to negotiate American independence.‡ Loyalists fled to Canada or back to Britain; the escaped slaves who had fought for the British were now in peril. Washington, marching on New York, ordered that his runaways be recaptured: 'Some of my own slaves ... may probably be in New York ... I'll be much obliged by your securing them so I may obtain them again.' Seventeen were hunted down. It is not known how many of Jefferson's slaves were recaptured. At the last moment, in scenes not unlike Saigon in 1975 and Kabul in 2021, Loyalists crowded on to British ships to escape. But, unlike the betrayals of Kabul 2021, the British, despite Washington's demands to reclaim slaves, refused to renege on their promises to rescue all of them: 75,000 Loyalists, including many ex-slaves, were evacuated from New York, Savannah and Charleston.

'Oh God,' gasped Lord North, 'it's over!' George III wanted to fight on, but North was broken.

Scorning those who asked him to take power or become king of America, Washington resigned his command and retired to Mount Vernon. 'If he does that,' said George, who had spent his whole reign seeking an honest politician, 'he'll be the greatest man in the world.'

Shaken by the debacle, George sought fresh leaders untainted by the

---

* The Ottoman carve-up was not Joseph's only scheme. His main one was to swap the Austrian Netherlands (Belgium) with Bavaria to create an even larger German monarchy. But twice the plan was foiled by Frederick, who mobilized his army, and by Joseph's brother-in-law Louis failing to back him despite Antoinette's lobbying. Instead, Louis settled the dispute by paying millions to Joseph, payments that would cost Antoinette dearly.

† Yorktown was the harbinger of modernity in a different way too: among the young French aristocrats fighting with Lafayette was Henri, comte de Saint-Simon, an American general at twenty, who forty years later developed the idea of socialism.

‡ To win leverage in negotiations, Washington ordered the kidnapping of George III's son Prince William (the future William IV), who was still with the navy in New York, but his commander bungled the plan.

loss of America, and turned to an unusual young man, William Pitt, second son of the victor of the Seven Years War. After Cambridge, where his friend William Wilberforce recalled, 'No man ever indulged more freely or happily in playful facetiousness,' Pitt arrived effortlessly in Parliament. He argued that America must be granted its freedom, and in 1782 became chancellor of the exchequer, still only twenty-three, in the short-lived government that negotiated US independence. The loss of America diminished royal power decisively, forcing George to accept an unholy alliance of North and the sybaritic radical Charles James Fox – one of the first times a British king was obliged by parliamentary votes and public opinion to accept a minister totally against his will. But he soon dismissed them.

Desperate to break the pattern of corrupt government, George offered Pitt the premiership thrice before at Christmas 1783 he accepted: wags believed that Pitt and his 'mince-pie ministry' would scarcely survive Christmas. But Honest Billy or William the Great – punctilious, eloquent, incorruptible, but also tightly wound, hard-drinking (prescribed booze for his nerves by his idiotic doctor, as his father had been) and asexual (he probably died a virgin) – was a sublime orator and efficient manager, demanding control of his ministers from the king. George agreed, marking the beginning of what became cabinet government under a powerful prime minister.

America was gone, but the death of the British empire was exaggerated. Politically divided, the transatlantic Anglo-states remained interconnected by culture, language, commerce and migration.* Pitt was about to appoint a new warlord in India who would found a British raj there. It happened that in the home island three extraordinary entrepreneurs were driving the changes that would propel Europe to global power and remodel the very shape of the family.

---

* In 1783, when the US became independent, north America contained around three million people; Spanish America fifteen million. Britain's population was nine million; Spain's ten million. The Spanish world was twice as large as the Anglo-world. Yet the Brits were catching up: between 1640 and 1820, 1.3 million migrants – British, French and German – settled, around 70 per cent of them British. In the next long century massive migration to north America, as well as to Australia and South Africa, completely reversed the trend: by 1930, the Anglo-world was twice the size of the Spanish.

ACT THIRTEEN
990 MILLION

Arkwrights and Krupps, Habsburgs, Bourbons and Sansons

In 1786, George III knighted an irascible, grouchy Lancashire entrepreneur who had started as a barber inventing waterproof periwigs: Sir Richard Arkwright, now fifty-four. Fifteen years earlier, Arkwright, a sturdy tailor's son, had created a small factory using the new technology of a spinning frame to spin cotton, then set up a water-powered mill at Cromford that was so successful that he founded a new type of workplace, the factory, bringing in more workers, among them children as young as seven, whom he organized in thirteen-hour shifts, policed by ringing bells that enforced strict timekeeping: latecomers were not paid.

The 'bag-cheeked, pot-bellied' Arkwright amassed a fortune of £500,000, enabling him to buy a country castle, as he aggressively opened more factories that revolutionized the British textile industry. For a long time, the factories were small cottage industries where women could work while still caring for the growing numbers of children who also joined the workforce. Woolmaking – in England, Flanders, Florence – had helped create the European mercantile class, but Indian textiles still dominated. For millennia, the essentials of life had not changed greatly; for centuries, work had remained essentially the same. But super-shifts require a dynamic nexus of coalescing forces: revolutions and wars combined with new technologies and ideologies. Arkwright's use of technology was as radical as his creation of the factory system that changed the way people worked. Now everything would change – and fast.

Steam-driven engines were first used to drain coal mines; now deployed in cotton mills, they increased productivity by two hundredfold. Like computers in the 1990s, they powered changes in the very mindset of a generation. Steam power, like the textiles it produced, became a core technology so universal that it attained invisible ubiquity. Such technologies, writes Mark Weiser, 'weave themselves into the fabric of everyday life until they are indistinguishable from it'. But the inventions would not have worked without the proximity of fossil fuel – Britain's plentiful coal was essential. Now the coal had to be transported to the factories.

The entrepreneur who created the means of transporting the coal was as far from being a harsh former wig-maker as you could get: Francis Egerton, duke of Bridgewater, was one of those lucky landowners who discovered coal on his estates. But he had to get the coal to the factories. In 1776, aged forty, he completed his first canal, started in 1771, linking Worsley to Manchester, while he built another between Liverpool and Manchester. He was a serious and unhappy, rather plump boy who had inherited his titles at twelve. He became engaged to a society star, Elizabeth, duchess of Hamilton, one of the Irish Gunning sisters,* It-girls of the time, famous for their amateur acting. Yet the engagement was cancelled, she married another magnate and Bridgewater closed down his London mansion, never married and retired to collect art and design the canals that made him £2 million – the richest British nobleman.

In 1781, this coal power was harnessed by a maniacal ironmaster, John Wilkinson, a potfounder's son nicknamed the Iron-Mad Titan, using steam engines to fire up blast furnaces for casting iron to make artillery and sponsoring the Coalbrookdale iron bridge – the world's first – cast by Abraham Darby III, scion of another iron-mastering family. By now Wilkinson was making an eighth of all British iron, his 'iron madness' culminating in his casting of his iron coffin and the iron obelisk over his grave.

The principles of the new technologies had been known for centuries. Steam technology was not itself new; Arkwright's spinning machine was just an improvement on the work of a long line of inventors, from James Watt and Matthew Boulton back to Thomas Newcomen in 1712, who was inspired by a Frenchman, Denis Papin, who had published his ideas in 1687. The Greeks had had a steam pump in the first century; the Han Chinese had puddled iron. Their development owed less to 'genius' inventors than to centuries of accumulated knowledge, small modifications, accidental revelations and now a quickening exchange that allowed educated minds and interconnected networks to experiment, innovate and apply the technologies – and then compete with one another. Many of these British inventors were members of the Lunar

---

* The other sister, Maria, countess of Coventry, died at twenty-seven of cosmetics poisoning, having overused Venetian ceruse, which gave girls fashionable alabaster skin but contained lead and mercury. When Maria's skin burst out in rashes, she covered them up with more ceruse, which soon killed her: death by cosmetics.

Society, which met in provincial Birmingham to debate 'the first hints of discoveries, the current observations, and the mutual collision of ideas'. It was that 'collision of ideas' – they corresponded with Ben Franklin in America and the *philosophes* in Paris – that now became the engine of innovation and the reason henceforth why so often inventions were being worked on simultaneously in different places.

Yet the knowledge would never be developed without the demand of a market to pay for it, a political system fluid enough to foster it and a society supple enough to reward it: all three were combined in one figure – the king's son George, prince of Wales, the oldest of an egregious royal brood of depraved, amoral scapegraces.

In 1783, the twenty-one-year-old prince received his own household at Carlton House. Greedy, dissipated, delusional, shameless and running to fat, though refined and artistic, he was scarred by the generational loathing and neglect built into the Hanover family. The king, he said, 'hates me; he always did, from seven years old'. Allying himself with the opposition against the king and Pitt, he fell in love with a streak of beautiful paramours. When forced to give one of them up, he swooned spasmodically on the carpet, shrieking, 'How I love her! I'll go distracted! My brain will split!' When he finally married a coarse Brunswick princess, Caroline, it was partly to get access to parliamentary money to pay his prodigious £630,000 debts. When he first saw her, he muttered, 'I'm not well; pray, get me a glass of brandy,' but drunkenly managed to consummate the marriage perhaps a week after the wedding night – enough to conceive an heiress, Princess Charlotte.

Yet no one so championed and personified the new consumer society as much as 'Prinny' and his much younger friend, George 'Beau' Brummell, the handsome, self-promoting grandson of a servant, son of Lord North's secretary. As an Etonian schoolboy then a teenage Guards officer, Brummell had captivated Prinny with his sense of style, replacing sumptuous coats, knee breeches and cotton stockings with a white cravat, pressed shirts, tailored dark coats and trousers, while grooming himself with an elaborate toilette, washing with soap and brushing his teeth – all of which cost a fortune. 'Why, with tolerable economy, it might be done with £800,' said Beau at a time when a gentleman could live well on £200 per annum – and a worker on £12.

Prinny and Brummell were the trendsetters for the fashionable elite, known as *le ton*, who spent their time calling on each other, feuding, frizelating with each other's wives, fornicating with courtesans, gambling at *faro*, commissioning art, planning new houses and gardens, travelling to Italy on Grand Tours (returning as fashionable 'Macaronis') and promenading around London which would now, thanks to the new manufacturing, become a world capital.

Elite clubs – both exclusively male and exclusively female – existed to exclude but tempt the aspirational middle class. Female trendsetters led by the duchesses and countesses flaunted their fashions and affairs and influenced politics through their salons: the five lady patronesses of the female club Almack's revelled in their whims and lovers. Their fashions were reported in news-sheets and cartoons, then copied by the middle classes who shopped for drapes, hats, gloves, dresses in new shops that sold accessories manufactured in the factories of Manchester, often by female and child workers paid half what men earned. The middle classes could now afford servants, usually poor women from the countryside. This contrast encouraged a cult of middle-class women who not only did not work, protected by their industrious husbands, but personified frail, idealized virtue.

In London, such people could afford to eat out in restaurants; public eating was not just about nourishment but about entertainment, ostentation and gratification. Public pleasure was just as delicious as the private variety. At Vauxhall Gardens, on the south bank of the Thames, an entrepreneur created a shady pleasure dome where nightly 2,000 punters, sometimes 12,000, high and low, mixed to eat, walk, frizelate and find sex. Cities had dark sides. Slums – known as rookeries – were filthy, gin-soaked stews. Prostitution boomed – there were said to be 80,000 part-time prostitutes in London, personified by the artist William Hogarth's provincial girl Moll Hackabout, to say nothing of famous courtesans.

No one understood this new market as well as a one-legged Staffordshire pottery manufacturer, Josiah Wedgwood, born into a Nonconformist family of potters, who encouraged these first influencers – whom he called 'legislators in taste' – to buy his pottery.

As a young man a bout of smallpox gave him the opportunity to develop new potting techniques, but it damaged his leg, preventing him from throwing pots (from then on he walked with a crutch) and made him into a designer. Twenty-five years later, it led to the amputation of a leg, without anaesthetic, and his workers took to calling him Owd Wooden Leg.

Wedgwood understood that it was women who bought luxuries: 'Fashion is infinitely superior to merit,' he mused. 'You've only to make choice of proper sponsors.' In 1765, when George III's consort Queen Charlotte ordered a set, he called himself 'Master Potter to Her Majesty' and advertised it as 'Queen's ware', producing cheaper sets for the middle classes and pioneering catalogues, money-back guarantees and special offers – in other words, he was the inventor of marketing. In 1767 he built a new modern pottery, Etruria, in Stoke, beside the route of the planned Trent and Mersey Canal in which he invested and which transported his wares.* As his pottery conquered the world – even Catherine the Great ordered sets – Wedgwood opened a showroom in Mayfair, where he displayed 'various Table & dessert services complete-ly ... on two ranges of Tables ... in order to do the needful with the Ladys in the neatest, genteelest & best method'. It was the start of a new commercialism that would develop into monumental department stores and, two centuries later, into the online shopping and influencers of today.

Few aristocrats were as entrepreneurial as Bridgewater. Titled mag-nates were positioned to dominate the emerging new world but they did not. While their incomes were colossal, they frittered their riches away on country houses, addictive gambling and expensive courtesans, while middle-class industrialists invested in new technologies. Many of the textiles for middle-class shoppers were manufactured by Robert Peel, the hard-working, harsh son of Lancashire yeomen who for generations had 'put out' cloth to small cottage weavers. Now in his mid-twenties, he used Arkwright pumps to set up a cotton-spinning mill and then at thirty founded the first industrial complex at Radcliffe, housing his workers in a barracks and using child labour to toil ten hours a day.

This intense commercial system offered families undreamed-of opportunities and penalties. The affluent became more restricted by bourgeois convention and the need to earn salaries: men had to work long hours at offices and obey a new sort of master, now known as the 'boss' – from the Dutch *baas*; virtuous middle-class women were confined to work unpaid at home; and the regimented poor, including women and children, toiled in unrelenting factories, often under abu-sive bosses.

Peel, the seventh richest man in Britain, soon a baronet and MP, was decent enough to realize his factories were cruel, and fostered the first legislation to improve working conditions. Determined to make

---

* Wedgwood's closest friend was a rambunctious doctor, Erasmus Darwin – they were both luminaries of the Lunar Society – who also invested in the Trent and Mersey Canal and advised him to power Etruria with steam engines. Darwin was a brilliant, fat, promiscuous physician, investor and scientist, a founder of the Lunar Society who notoriously fathered many children, including with some of his servants. His son Robert, a six-foot-two giant of twenty-four stone – married Josiah's daughter Susannah Wedgwood. Their son Charles Darwin, born in 1809, started to study medicine, then, funded by Wedgwood money, switched to learning taxidermy and natural sciences.

his eldest son Robert a gentleman, he trained him not for business but to join Britain's rulers, making him repeat sermons after church and sending him to Harrow School. The boy would be the first of the new middle class to rule Britain.

North-western Germany was not far behind Britain. It was now that a woman started the dynasty that would power the rise of German industry. In 1782, Helene Amalie Krupp, fifty-two-years old, whose husband Jodocus had died thirty years earlier, bought out of bankruptcy an iron forge north of Essen in the Ruhr and invested in coal mines to fuel her blast furnace, employing her son as her accountant. The Krupps were an old Ruhr mercantile family – one of them, Anton, had manufactured cannon during the Thirty Years War – sometimes serving as burgermeisters of Essen. But, like Merseyside in Britain, the Ruhr possessed the essential matrix of science, innovation and commerce coupled with coal, water and communications. Widow Krupp's blast furnace was soon manufacturing kitchenware and cannonballs that she sold to German principalities including Prussia. After the early death of her son, she steadfastly trained her grandson, Friedrich Krupp. When Widow Krupp died at ninety-seven, she left him a fortune – which he managed to lose. The Krupps seemed to have failed, but they would recover.

This industrial 'revolution' took over a century to modernize human life in a way we would recognize. 'The Englishman of 1750,' wrote David Landes, 'was closer in material things to Caesar's legionaries than to his own great-grandchildren.' It was a century that changed human life more than all those before it and that made humans, long the most powerful animal on earth, so dominant that they started to change earth itself, even its climate – an anthropocene age.

In 1700, an alien could have been certain that China and India would continue to dominate the world. Yet the alien would have been wrong. It was not enough for Europe to succeed; the giants of the east had to fail. The Mughals had already collapsed and, though no one yet knew it, China would follow.

There was something about Europe that qualified it for what happened next. No hegemon dominated Europe, a gallimaufry of 500 kingdoms, city states and republics locked in ferocious competition that stimulated independence and ingenuity, propelled by rival civic and economic power centres, cults of aspiration, Enlightened culture – and nuclear families who, like the Wedgwoods and Krupps, intermarried with each other, sharing values and passing on wealth. The idea of a Protestant work ethic has been overdone – Catholic France was also sophisticated – but these northern nations had developed the spirit of self-starting motivation, creating a singular European psychology that favoured individualism, self-improvement and a society of trust. 'Wherever manners are gentle there is commerce,' a *philosophe*, the baron de Montesquieu, reflected in 1749, 'and wherever there is commerce, manners are gentle.' Not just manners but standards. 'Whenever commerce is introduced,' wrote a Scottish *philosophe*, Adam Smith, in 1766, 'probity and punctuality always accompany it – the principal virtues of a commercial nation.'

It was financial capitalism in its widest sense that funded the revolution. The international esprit of Britain, Holland, France and the new US republic stimulated manufacturing and trade. The economic life of the world was shot through with slavery, thanks to sugar, tobacco and cotton. Its profits were embedded in the wealth of those powers, ready to invest in new businesses; it touched everything. Yet there was plenty of wealth that was not linked to slavery, from Bridgewater's coal and canals to Wilkinson's iron and Wedgwood's china – and then there were the German Krupps and other entrepreneurs of the German kingdoms, which had minimal slavery and empire. Slavery was a significant source of capital but far from the only one.

A sudden spurt in the British population – fuelled by rising food production, which doubled between 1600 and 1800 – provided a market of workers and consumers. People poured into cities: between 1790 and 1850, the city dwellers more than doubled from 9.7 per cent to 22.6. By 1800, there were a million Londoners. In thirty years, that doubled; by the 1870s, it had doubled again. The surge was nourished by better food and conditions, but certainly not by medical advances. An eminent case was now to demonstrate how doctors remained an iatrogenic menace – even to the most privileged.

On 16 October 1788, the fifty-year-old George III went mad – at least partly poisoned by his own doctors.

SALLY HEMINGS AND MARIE ANTOINETTE: THE DIAMOND NECKLACE AND THE LOVE CABBAGE

'I wish to God I may die,' cried George, 'for I'm going mad.' Suffering stomach pains and fever, he started to jabber incessantly, deteriorating until he was demented and in the full grip of psychosis. Sometimes he was violent, oftentimes he ran away from his courtiers and had to be pursued. His appalling doctors treated him with an array of lethal medicines and damaging treatments, including scarification (cutting the skin), blistering (creating pustules on the skin), cupping (applying heated glass cups to the skin), venesection (bloodletting), the application of leeches and dosages of laudanum, purgatives and emetic tartar laced with arsenic.

The king's madness was later diagnosed as hereditary porphyria, but modern doctors now believe he suffered from bipolar disorder, possibly sparked or exacerbated by chemical poisoning.* In 1788, doctors had no understanding of mental illness or the properties of their own medicines. Finally a 'mad-doctor', Francis Willis, a sixty-year-old vicar and physician who treated 'wrongheads' not just with the traditional coercion but also with the 'health and cheerfulness' of serene rustic exercise, arrived at Windsor. But although he reduced the poisonous tonic, he deployed his trademark kindness with the use of gags and straitjackets that if anything increased the stress on the patient.

Pitt was forced to pass a Regency Act that allowed for the prince of Wales to become prince regent. Prinny was thrilled at the thought of power – dismissing Pitt and promoting his Whig allies – and more spending. But George recovered, allowing Pitt to avoid dismissal. For now, Pitt increased the prime minister's authority, partly thanks to the madness, partly thanks to America – where the new republic, chaotic and indebted, was governed by a confusion of committees and states. As Washington tried to restore his declining estates and recapture fugitive slaves, Rochambeau and Fersen returned in triumph to Paris, where Antoinette welcomed the Swede for the most intense period of their relationship. A new American minister soon followed them: Jefferson.

It was an escape from tragedy. The jubilation of American liberty was bittersweet for Jefferson. Just after Yorktown, in May 1782, his wife Martha gave birth to a daughter (who later died young of whooping cough), but after six pregnancies she deteriorated, cared for by Betty Hemings, surrounded by the Hemings children, her enslaved half-siblings, her two daughters with her husband and a distraught Jefferson. Taking Martha's hand, Jefferson 'promised her solemnly he'd never marry again'. When she died on 6 September, he gave her eleven-year-old half-sister, Sally Hemings, Martha's handbell, an ambiguous keepsake that was a tribute to intimacy but also a tool of service. After ten years of 'unchequered happiness', he collapsed.

---

* At a time when doctors had prescribed port for both Pitt and his father, turning both into alcoholics, George's massive doses of emetic tartar contained as much as 5 per cent arsenic: when his hair was recently tested, it contained seventeen times the level that counts as arsenic poisoning, enough to aggravate his stomach aches, delirium and psychosis.

America's relationship with its chief ally France was paramount: the Continental Congress asked Jefferson to become minister in Paris. He set off, taking his daughter Patsy and James Hemings, who would be trained as a French chef.

Jefferson relished the life of enlightened Paris, where, in his rented Hôtel de Langeac, he engaged with liberal society, became entangled in a passionate affair with a young married woman, Maria Cosway, and a frizelation with Angelica Church (later sister-in-law and intimate friend of another American luminary, Alexander Hamilton), able to live in a way every enlightened American could only dream of.

Antoinette's delivery of a dauphin, Louis-François, three days after the British surrender at Yorktown was soon followed by the arrival of another son. A happy family life had brought the king and queen closer together, giving Antoinette more influence. The dauphin was sickly, but the birth of a son had increased her power; the American victory had boosted Louis too. It was most likely now, after the delivery of a son, that Antoinette, probably with Louis's acquiescence, took Fersen as a lover.

The Swede enjoyed an array of mistresses, but he loved Antoinette. 'I don't want the ties of marriage which are against nature,' wrote Fersen to his sister. 'I can't marry the only person I would want to, the only one who really loves me, so I can be no one's.' An invoice shows that Antoinette now paid a locksmith to create a pulley system that enabled her to lock and unlock the door from her bed in her secret Versailles apartments. Fersen's logbook notes their 'plan to lodge upstairs'. If he saw Fersen, Louis would withdraw 'with infinite tact . . . so she didn't have to fear being surprised'. In his letters to her, Fersen called her 'Josephine' – her full name being Marie Antoinette Josèphe. Fersen was always with her. 'Farewell,' he wrote to his sister, 'I must go to the queen.' It is possible her second son, her favourite whom she nicknamed *Chou d'Amour* – Love Cabbage – was Fersen's love child. 'The fashion for looking after your own children,' wrote the aristocratic bishop and future premier Talleyrand, who as a lame child had been rejected by his parents and passed over in his inheritance, 'had not yet arrived. The very opposite was true.' Yet Antoinette – influenced perhaps by Rousseau's *Émile* – now spent much time with her children, who caused her great anxiety. The eldest daughter displayed Habsburg–Bourbon arrogance; the sweet, fragile eldest dauphin suffered TB of the spine; but 'Love Cabbage is charming and I love him to distraction . . .'

Yet the victory against Britain had come three years too late, costing 1.5 billion francs and bankrupting the kingdom, leaving it stricken with debt, food shortages leading to famine and a surging resentment at the isolated court where the stolid king was seen to be overwhelmed by the exuberant frivolity of his Austrian queen – who now forced her husband to let her buy yet another palace at Saint-Cloud.

Strong states are not undermined by trivialities, but scandal can destroy a weak regime as fast as gunpowder. It started with the Parisian jewellers who had created a mountainous diamond necklace to sell to Louis XV for his mistress du Barry. Louis having died, they were desperate to sell it. Back in 1775 Antoinette had spent 500,000 livres on diamonds, but now a mature queen was not interested when her husband offered it to her, saying such money would be better spent on battleships.

Instead the jeweller was manipulated by a grifter called Jeanne de la Motte, a married woman but mistress to an array of grandees and hucksters including Cardinal de Rohan, *grand aumônier* at the royal court, disliked by Antoinette for sneaking about her follies to her mother. Motte offered Rohan the necklace. He hoped to win Antoinette's favour by delivering it. Motte used forged letters to trick him into believing that Antoinette was interested and deployed a prostitute dressed as the queen to persuade him. The jeweller gave the necklace to Rohan, who gave it to Motte to present to Antoinette. Instead Motte instantly sold the stones in London, leaving the cardinal dangerously exposed.

In May 1786, Louis was informed of the heist and ordered Rohan, Motte and the charlatan Cagliostro* arrested. 'Sire, I've been tricked,' Rohan told Louis. The mess should have been examined secretly by a commission of the council. But 'the public assumes I got the necklace without paying for it', said Antoinette, who pushed for a public acquittal in the Paris parlement. Motte was flogged naked and branded – though she bit the executioner. Yet the parlement was filled with Antoinette's enemies, who on 31 May 1786 acquitted Rohan of disrespect to the sovereigns. For the monarchs, calumnied then humiliated, it was a double fiasco.

A young artillery lieutenant, third son (out of eight children) of a prominent Corsican lawyer and his wife, impoverished nobles, whose worshipful love gave him an invincible self-confidence, followed the scandal closely, later seeing it as a grave step towards disaster. 'The

---

* This sleazy cast would not be complete without 'Count Cagliostro', a charlatan who, claiming to be several thousand years old (born in ancient Egypt) and to have met Jesus personally, thrived in this time of self-invention, social mobility and mystical credulity. Born Joseph Balsamo in Palermo, this mountebank conned a rich gold dealer, then, adopting his exotic title, travelled through Europe with a lissom teenaged wife Serafina, whom he lent to his patrons. Rohan was one of them, but you cannot trick a trickster: he showed Cagliostro the contract faked by Motte: 'A forgery!' said Cagliostro.

queen's death must be dated from the diamond-necklace trial,' concluded Napoleon Bonaparte, who believed that 'Some little thing always decides great events.'

After Jefferson had been in Paris for a year, he summoned his younger daughter Polly, aged nine, who was to be accompanied on her transatlantic journey by her fourteen-year-old enslaved cousin, Sally Hemings. The girls travelled via London, where the priggish American minister John Adams and his wife Abigail were shocked that the beautiful Sally was joining Jefferson. 'The old Nurse whom you expected to have attended her,' wrote Abigail to Jefferson, 'was sick and unable to come; she has a Girl about 15 or 16 with her.' They advised sending Sally back to Virginia. Jefferson overruled them.

In Paris, Sally joined Jefferson's household. She was 'very handsome' and 'mighty near white', a fellow slave, Isaac Jefferson, recalled, with 'straight hair down her back'. Unusually Jefferson paid wages to James and Sally Hemings, revealing both the different circumstances of Parisian life but also the special status of the Hemingses, siblings of his darling wife. As his affair with Maria ended, Jefferson paid for the expensive inoculation not just of his family but of the Hemingses too by a celebrity doctor to kings, Daniel Sutton. Jefferson also organized French lessons for Sally and bought her clothes.

Jefferson, aged forty-four, who had written on how racial intermixture delivered 'improvement in body and mind', now started a relationship with Sally, still only fifteen. 'During that time,' as their son Madison put it, 'my mother became Mr Jefferson's concubine.'

SAINT-GEORGES, DANGEROUS LIAISONS AND THE ABOLITIONISTS

In the spring of 1789, Jefferson, his daughters and surely the Hemingses attended a concert by a remarkable mixed-race violinist, the eleven-year-old George Bridgetower, marketed as 'the African Prince'. Many African and mixed-race people lived in Paris, as they did in London. Just as British law was ambiguous about slavery, French law too was confused about whether slavery could exist in France itself. Slaves could register at the Admiralty court and could claim freedom.

Born in Poland, George was the brilliant son of a Barbadian servant of the Esterházy princes, patrons of Haydn. Jefferson and his household would also have followed the career of the most famous mixed-race man in Paris 'who was close to both political intrigue and the new French abolitionist movement: Joseph Bologne, chevalier de Saint-Georges, a champion fencer, violinist and composer. Saint-Georges was hired by the powerful Orléans family, the king's cousins, to run their Masonic *Concert Olympique* which played at their Palais Royal. His opera *L'Amant anonyme* was successful and he premiered a new one just after Sally's arrival. Saint-Georges was now friends with the young, liberal, rich Philippe, duc d'Orléans, first prince of the blood, who was not only conspiring against the king but a supporter of a radical cause: the abolition of slavery.

Orléans, his chief of staff Laclos, his adviser the *philosophe* Jacques-Pierre Brissot and his musician friend and *homme de couleur* Saint-Georges regularly visited London for politics and pleasure.* Orléans, always juggling multiple paramours, was friends with Prinny, the prince of Wales, with whom he shared the Scottish courtesan Grace Elliott. After giving birth to a royal bastard, Grace accompanied the duke back to Paris. Laclos based the libertinism of his novel *Les Liaisons dangereuses* on Orléans's complicated love life. Orléans admired Britain's parliamentary monarchy and hoped, by replacing his cousin Louis as regent if not as king, to establish such a system in France. But all of them were also vehement opponents of slavery, now at its diabolical zenith for both Britain and France.

In 1778, France was trading 13,000 Africans annually to the Caribbean; Britain was far ahead, trading 80,000. In both countries, a growing section of the elite was appalled by slavery, though the slave-owning lobby known as the Interest remained extremely powerful. In France the movement would be backed by the first prince of the blood, in London by the prime minister himself.

On 12 May 1787, at Holwood House, Pitt's suburban home in Bromley, the twenty-seven-year-old prime minister sat under a tree chatting with two MPs, his cousin William Grenville and William Wilberforce, a rumpled Yorkshire merchant's son. Wilberforce had been Pitt's friend at Cambridge and together they had gone on a

---

* Saint-Georges had become a sensation twenty years earlier by winning a duel against a racist fellow pupil. He won a place in the royal guard of honour but made his name as a musician, rising to direct Paris's *Concert des Amateurs*. He had been in line to direct the Opéra when its sopranos complained to Queen Antoinette, 'assuring Her Majesty that their honour and delicate conscience could never allow them to submit to the orders of a mulatto'. But Antoinette favoured Saint-Georges, summoning him to Versailles, where he was 'invited to play with the queen' – she liked to play piano, he no doubt played violin. Saint-Georges started to write opera with a literary artillery officer, Pierre Choderlos de Laclos, but their *Ernestine*, attended by Antoinette, was not a hit. This 'mulatto man', wrote the American John Adams when he visited Paris in 1779, 'is the most accomplished man in Europe in riding, shooting, fencing, dancing and music.'

Grand Tour of Europe. It says something about the tininess of the oligarchy of merchants and landowners who ruled the industrializing nation that both Pitt and Grenville were the sons of prime ministers, and both would head governments themselves. 'I remember a conversation with Mr Pitt,' recalled Wilberforce, 'under the root of an old tree.'

'Wilberforce,' said Pitt, 'why don't you give notice of a motion on the subject of the Slave Trade?'

Wilberforce had been recruited to the abolition campaign by a Cambridge contemporary, the Reverend Thomas Clarkson, who visited him weekly.

The campaign had been gathering momentum since 1765 when a slave named Jonathan Strong, brought to London from Barbados, was beaten by his master, a lawyer, David Lisle, and left to die, but was spotted and rescued by a remarkable doctor, Granville Sharp, a civil servant and member of a talented family of accomplished professionals and amateur musicians. Sharp threatened to charge the slave master with assault if he tried to repossess Strong. Sharp won Strong's freedom, though the Barbadian died at twenty-five, probably of his injuries. Sharp began to campaign against 'the injustice and dangerous tendency of tolerating slavery'. But the lord chief justice, William Murray, earl of Mansfield, tried to avoid any change that would challenge the ownership of property until in 1772 he finally ruled that the Interest could no longer enforce slavery in Britain.*

Then in 1781 an atrocious case intensified anti-slavery feeling. A Liverpudlian slave ship, the *Zong*, owned by William Gregson, a mayor of Liverpool and slaving mogul, sailed from Cape Coast Castle, the RAC headquarters (Ghana), with 442 slaves crammed into its hold, double the number for which it was designed. Sixty-two Africans died at sea. When water and supplies ran out with disease rife, the captain, aware that slaves who died onshore could not be claimed on insurance, murdered 142 men and women by throwing them into the sea. Another ten killed themselves. The murders allowed Gregson to declare that the slaves had 'perished just as a cargo of goods had perished', claiming £30 per drowned slave from the insurance. It is likely that such murders and insurance payments were common, but this time the story was spotted

---

* Mansfield had more experience of this world than he let on for he had adopted Dido Belle, the daughter of his sailor nephew and an enslaved woman, bringing her up with his children (painted with Lady Elizabeth Murray by David Martin) and leaving her an annuity in his will. She later married a Frenchman and had two sons – both of whom worked for the EIC – dying in 1805.

by a freed slave, Olaudah Equiano, an abolitionist campaigner, whose autobiography *Interesting Narrative* charted his kidnapping from Benin and enslavement in America, the Caribbean, Europe and Asia, traded by three owners, until he emerged free in 1780s London.

Starting in 1783, Equiano and Sharp publicized the outrage. The first trial found in favour of the slave traders, but when the insurers challenged this, Mansfield gave an ambiguous judgment, acknowledging property rights while ruling on a technicality that the insurers were not liable.

Ten days after Pitt's conversation with Wilberforce, on 22 May 1787, he joined Clarkson, along with Sharp and Equiano, at the first meeting of the Society for Effecting the Abolition of the Slave Trade, funded by the designer Josiah Wedgwood, along with other radical entrepreneurs, often Dissenters.* Wilberforce would lead the campaign in Parliament, tabling his first bill in 1791. His strategy was to abolish the trade first, avoiding the issue of how to confiscate human property.† The abolitionists were vigorously opposed by the Interest, led by George Hibbert MP, Jamaican slave trader and builder of the West India Docks in London, but also a botanist, antiquarian and founder of the Royal National Lifeboat Institution, who called the slave trade 'indispensable', explaining that 'The colonies would not exist without the African trade. The Manchester & Sheffield Manufactories would instantly go to ruin & their people set a starving.'

In London, in November 1787, the *philosophe* Brissot was invited to attend Sharp's Abolition Society. Brissot was supported by a free-spirited young playwright, Olympe de Gouges, who was also a member of the Orléans coterie. De Gouges had already started campaigning against slavery with her play *L'Esclavage des noirs*, but now published *Réflexions sur les hommes nègres*. Brissot was prompted to found a French *Société des Amis de Noirs* which was soon joined by de Gouges and the marquis de

---

* Wedgwood designed an anti-slavery medallion that showed a kneeling black man, hands raised to heaven, inscribed 'Am I not a man and a brother?'
† Yet even Wilberforce did not believe the slaves were ready for liberation, telling Parliament in 1805 that before they 'could be fit to receive freedom, it would madness to attempt to give it to them'. At his dinners for the African and Asiatic Society, black activists ate behind a screen. Opponents of slavery in both America and Britain founded new settlements of returned black slaves in west Africa. In 1787, Sharp and others involved in the Committee for the Black Poor backed a plan to settle several hundred black Londoners in a Province of Freedom in Sierra Leone not far from the slaving castles on the coast. Despite backing by Pitt, then chancellor, most of the settlers died. In 1792, a flotilla of black Loyalists from Nova Scotia, including Harry Washington, an escaped slave of the US president, founded Freetown.

Lafayette.* Brissot admired Jefferson, whom he knew well, and invited him to join the *Amis de Noirs*. 'I'm very sensible of the honour,' replied the ever-supple Jefferson on 11 February 1788. 'You know nobody wishes more ardently to see an abolition not only of the trade but of the condition of slavery: and certainly nobody will be more willing to encounter every sacrifice for that object.' But he refused because 'it might render me less able to serve [the cause] beyond the water'. Orléans sent Saint-Georges to London to talk to Prinny and the abolitionists,† but soon he was immersed in exploiting the deepening crisis faced by Louis and Antoinette. Behind the dazzle of the court, Louis was bankrupt – and he now took his greatest gamble.

REQUIEM: JOSEPH AND MOZART

Faced with his financial crisis, Louis embraced reform and summoned an assembly of Notables to demand real taxes for nobility and the empowering of the parlements. 'The peasants pay everything,' said the king, 'the nobles nothing.' His plan was not impossible but required the skilful building of a coalition. Instead Lafayette, American paladin, one of the Notables, attacked the court; the Notables rejected Louis's reform, accelerating the credit crisis. Louis collapsed, his crack-up exacerbated by the death of their tiny daughter Sophie, nursed for weeks by the queen. The couple were both under terrible pressure. Louis turned up at Antoinette's apartments in tears. She herself leaned on Fersen, with whom she corresponded in lemon juice or invisible ink.

Louis drew her into high politics. As Antoinette made cuts to court expenditure and virtually ran the government from her personal palace at Petit Trianon, confiding to her best friend Polignac that 'The personage above me [Louis] is in no fit state,' unrest spread. Treason started in the family and spread to the nobility: Orléans led a *révolte nobiliaire* that undermined the regime from within. Antoinette was blamed for

---

* France, like Britain, oscillated between the ideal that slavery could not exist in a law-based homeland and the reality of the slave owners' profits. After Louis XIV had freed two escaped slaves in 1691, slave owners won an edict in 1716 that allowed slave masters to bring slaves to France; this was overturned in 1738 and it became routine to free the enslaved until in 1777–8 a procurator at the Admiralty, Guillaume Poncet de La Grave, warned against racial pollution by the growing number of free people of colour, persuading Louis XVI to decree a Police des Noirs to prevent them entering France and marrying whites. Yet slaves could still appeal for freedom at the Admiralty court.

† In London, Saint-Georges endured the whims of the prince of Wales, who insisted on organizing a fencing competition between the mixed-raced composer and the French transvestite the chevalier d'Éon.

everything in a spiral of conspiracy theories, denounced as *Madame Déficit* for her extravagance, *La Austrochienne* (Austro-bitch) for giving millions to the Austrians. *Le Godmiché Royal* (The Royal Dildo) and other pornographic pamphlets depicted her having sex with Yolande de Polignac.* 'Do you know a woman,' she asked, 'more to be pitied than me?'

The people demanded the return of Necker, the speculator whose wheeler-dealings had overpromised and worsened the crisis. Louis reluctantly reappointed Necker. 'I tremble,' admitted Antoinette. If Necker failed, 'I'll be detested even more.' Necker kept the regime afloat by more borrowing, yet even the king realized that he now had no choice but to call the *États Généraux*. This elected assembly of nobles, clergy and commoners, which had prospered during medieval crises and not been called since 1614, would herald the end of the absolutist monarchy created by Richelieu, Mazarin and Louis XIV. 'All men's minds are in a ferment,' noted Fersen. 'Nothing's talked of but a constitution. The women especially are joining in the hubbub . . .'

At Versailles, on 5 May 1789, the Estates met. Louis and Antoinette swiftly lost control as the Third Estate – filled with provincial lawyers outraged by Bourbon decadence – seized the initiative, swearing to create a constitution. Louis tried to dismiss it, but the Third Estate convened in a tennis court as the National Assembly, joined by the renegade Bourbon Orléans and the renegade noble Lafayette, who became Antoinette's most hated traitors. Amid this nightmare, Louis and Antoinette were facing the greatest horror known to a parent: the dauphin died in agony of spinal TB, and Love Cabbage became the new heir.

In Paris, bad harvests threatened famine. A crowd shouting 'Bread! Bread!' stormed the Bastille prison, symbol of royal injustice and now of impotence, seized weapons, decapitated royal officials and terrorized the countryside. Louis's only hope was to assume leadership of a liberal revolution himself. As troops guarded Versailles, the king's brothers and many aristocrats fled into exile, but Louis dithered: 'Do I stay or do I go? I'm ready for neither.'

Antoinette's brother, Emperor Joseph, watched with horror. In

---

* Antoinette was already hated. Ten years before, at the Parisian Opéra, she had endured faltering applause. 'Why was I scarcely clapped?' she asked. Bursting into tears, she added, 'What have I done to them?' She could not help being a Habsburg, but in 1784 she backed payments to buy off her brother Joseph's menaces to Holland. She was extravagant – though her extravagance hardly approached that of Catherine the Great – and she never said, 'Let them eat cake.' She was, writes John Hardman, 'the scapegoat of an irrational age suffering a nervous collapse, the so-called rationality of the Enlightenment shot through with the charlatanism of Cagliostro, Mesmer [celebrity hypnotist] and Necker'.

1787, Joseph had joined Catherine the Great and Prince Potemkin on a dazzling, festive tour of New Russia and Crimea, the Tatar khanate just annexed by the Romanovs, but its showmanship provoked the Ottomans to counter-attack: the resulting war was a triumph for the Romanovs, who gained south Ukraine and the Black Sea coast, but not for the Habsburgs. Joseph, at the Ottoman front in Wallachia (Romania) and Moldavia, faced defeats and epidemics, consoling himself by singing the score of Mozart's new opera.

Mozart was flourishing in fun-loving Vienna, but he overspent on clothes and luxuries, conducting rehearsals wearing a crimson cloak and a cocked gold-laced hat. In 1785, still only twenty-nine, he brought Beaumarchais's play *Marriage of Figaro* to Joseph's favourite librettist, Lorenzo da Ponte, a Jew born in the Venetian ghetto who became a dissolute priest and brothel-keeper. *Figaro* the opera delighted Joseph. Next, Mozart and da Ponte started to work on *Don Giovanni*, joined by da Ponte's friend Casanova, who helped with the libretto. 'My opera *Don Giovanni* was performed,' wrote Mozart from Prague where it was premiered, 'with the greatest of applause.'

Mozart was in a frenzy of creativity – in 1788, he wrote three symphonies in six weeks. Although the war was destroying Joseph, he loved *Don Giovanni*: 'The opera is divine, possibly just possibly even more beautiful than *Figaro*.' Mozart borrowed too much and went on tour to raise money, writing to Constanze, 'Dearest little wife of my heart. Are you thinking of me as often as I'm thinking of you? I look at your portrait every few minutes, and cry half out of joy, half out of sorrow ... I'm writing this with tears in my eyes.' But his debts were out of control; he was tormented both by Constanze's flirtations and by her illnesses. And his patron Joseph was suffering TB, malaria and a revolt in Flanders – just as his sister Antoinette faced destruction in Paris.

Lafayette consulted his friend Jefferson on a French *Déclaration des droits de l'homme*. Like all the revolutionaries, they were influenced by Rousseau, whose *Du contrat social* argued that the people expressed themselves through '*la volonté générale*' – the general will. 'The law,' Lafayette wrote, 'is the expression of the general will.' The Assembly passed the *Déclaration* along with a draft constitution. In Paris, royal authority had almost vanished.

'Is it a revolt?' asked Louis.

'No, sire,' replied a courtier. 'It's a revolution.' The king was appalled when Lafayette was elected commander of the militia, renamed the *Garde National*, but he was now too paralysed to take advantage of a stalemate between moderates and hardliners. The latter broke the impasse by dispatching a Parisian mob to Versailles, which stabbed two bodyguards and burst into the palace crying, 'Cut off her head and fry her heart and liver!' Antoinette hid in a secret passageway: her hair turned grey that day. She and her husband nonetheless appeared on the balcony with Lafayette to face the people, before Louis and Antoinette were dragooned to the Tuileries Palace in Paris by a mob bearing the piked heads of their bodyguards. 'I was witness of it all and I returned to Paris in one of the carriages of the king's suite,' wrote Fersen. 'God keep me from ever again seeing so afflicting a sight.' The terrorized king tearfully approved the abolition of old feudal taxes and rules and the *Déclaration des droits*, drafted by Jefferson.

As Jefferson was enthusiastically watching the revolution, he learned that Sally was now pregnant. Her view of Jefferson is mysterious. 'Oppressed people . . . often develop their own internal narratives . . . contemptuous of their overlords,' writes Annette Gordon-Reed, but 'the way Jefferson treated Hemings and her family probably made her more favorably disposed toward him than hostile.'* Sally knew enough about French slavery laws to understand that she had a choice: she could stay and claim freedom via the Admiralty court, or she could return with Jefferson to slavery at Monticello. So, her son Madison recalled, she did a bold thing: 'She refused to return with him,' demanding concessions for their children. Jefferson 'promised her extraordinary privileges . . . a solemn pledge'.

Then they set off for America, landing in December 1789, to find an offer from the new president of the United States of America. On 30 April, in New York, Washington had been inaugurated after winning the first election under the new constitution, created by a convention in Philadelphia. His ex-secretary Colonel Hamilton had pushed for an English-style mixed system with a ruler for life called the governor, but others had resisted that as too monarchical: the compromise was a strong presidency, balanced by a bicameral congress and an independent judiciary. Here was a state founded on the principle of freedom,

---

* 'Every enslaved woman who ever had sex with a white man during slavery in the US', writes Gordon-Reed, in *The Hemingses of Monticello: an American Family*, was 'a rape victim'. Yet 'whether Jefferson used violence or employed his well-known charming manner with women to win Hemings over, his power was such that he could never be sure of her true desires . . . She did not – because she *could* not – consent.' Yet 'the profanity of slavery does not define the entirety of the lives of enslaved people . . . we find enough signs that these two people were emotionally attached to each other . . . Saying that works no fundamental change in the nature of American slavery', because 'the idea of their love has no power to change the basic reality of slavery's essential inhumanity'.

its democracy an example to the world – 'It astonishes me to find this system so near perfect,' said Franklin.*

Washington, who rejected the title 'His Highness', preferring 'Mr President', offered the secretaryships of state to Jefferson and of the treasury to Hamilton. Among the first items of business was the choice of a new capital and the creation of a state bank. In June 1790, in New York, Jefferson, Virginian aristocrat-planter, invited Colonel Hamilton, penniless self-made West Indian bastard and war hero to dinner, cooked by his French-trained chef-slave James Hemings. In 'the room where it happens', they agreed that, after a temporary stay in Philadelphia, they would build a new capital on the Potomac. That December, Hamilton founded a state bank.

At Monticello, Sally Hemings gave birth to her first child by Jefferson, assisted by her mother Betty, but the child soon died (though five more would live to adulthood). In Philadelphia, Jefferson and Hamilton, who loathed one another, clashed over the future of the republic. Washington† was alarmed by the violence in France. Hamilton was pro-British; Jefferson, pro-French, pontificated that one could not move 'from despotism to liberty in a featherbed'.

Back in Paris, as foreign powers started to arm against the revolution, encouraged partly by the royal couple, using Fersen as intermediary, Antoinette had not dared to correspond with her brother, Emperor Joseph, but now sought help. Joseph planned to rescue the Bourbons, but, ignored by his Russian friends who were seizing Ottoman lands round the Black Sea, he returned to Vienna, covered in agonizing sores. 'I'm unfortunate in everything I undertake,' he wrote, writing his own epitaph: 'Here lies a prince whose intentions were pure but who had the sorrow of seeing all his plans collapse.' So much of politics is waiting and silence. 'He governed too much,' wrote Ligne, 'and reigned too little.'

---

* The president and vice-president were separately and indirectly elected by an electoral college; the Senate was indirectly elected by state legislatures; the House of Representatives was directly elected. The system's noble aspirations and universal male suffrage contained a colossal flaw: slaves had no vote. The slave owners of the south negotiated a double triumph that both protected slavery and yet, for the purpose of the proportional representation of the House of Representatives, made their slaves count in their favour as three-fifths of a person. 'I'd never have drawn my sword in the cause of America,' said Lafayette, 'if I had conceived I was thereby founding a land of slavery.'

† The law of Pennsylvania ruled that any slave resident for over six months was automatically freed. In Philadelphia, Washington was always accompanied by his manservants Billy Lee and Christopher Sheels, his cook Hercules and five other slaves. But he shuttled his slaves back and forth from Mount Vernon, without revealing the real reason. 'I wish,' he said, 'to have it accomplished under pretext that may deceive both them [the slaves] and the public.' It is notable that slavery was the only matter in which Washington compromised his famous honesty.

On 20 February 1790, shortly after Mozart premiered *Così fan tutte*, Joseph died in despair and Mozart lost his patron, whose brother Leopold, the new emperor, now worked to save the monarchy. As he composed his masonic opera *Die Zauberflöte*, Mozart missed Constanze: 'There's a sort of emptiness, which hurts somehow.' That year he wrote two operas in three weeks, but when he received the commission for a requiem, he told Constanze, 'I know I must die'; the Requiem 'is for myself'. Yet he now received the lucrative post of Viennese *Kapellmeister*. Even Salieri praised him, and he was spending time with his son Karl: 'So delighted I took him to the opera. He looks great.' He planned an opera of Shake-speare's *Tempest*. Everything was looking up, but then Mozart fell ill. Horribly swollen, he kept scribbling multiple scores. On 5 December 1791, he died. Constanze believed he worked himself to death, that his only fault was 'too soft a heart' and not knowing 'how to handle money'. He was buried according to Joseph's decrees in a communal grave.

In Joseph, Antoinette lost her dearest ally, but she still saw her lover, Fersen. 'I'm a little happier,' he wrote. 'Sometimes I see her quite freely and this consoles us for all the unpleasantries she has to tolerate.'

ANTOINETTE, THE EXECUTIONER AND THE GUILLOTINE MACHINE

In July 1790, at her chateau Saint-Cloud, Antoinette secretly negotiated with the moderate revolutionary, Honoré, comte de Mirabeau, a sybarit-ic colossus and president of the Assembly who wanted to be the premier under an English constitutional monarchy. Antoinette, though horrified by the gigantic, messy count, offered him a salary for backing the king. 'Madame, the monarchy's saved!' he boomed; she was 'the only man the king has'. But Mirabeau died, succeeded in his mission to make consti-tutional monarchy work by his handsome, slim young deputy, Antoine Barnave. Louis and Antoinette offered the vain, ambitious Lafayette an ancient rank, that of constable, yet the swanning paladin, aspiring to be a Cromwell–Washington, refused – missing the chance to seize the leadership. Without a clear leader, the Assembly laid the foundations for modern society: Jewish rights and equality were granted, leading to the lifting of repression across Europe. But women were neglected; and slavery was positively supported by many of the revolutionaries. The As-sembly's abolition of nobility alienated 250,000 nobles; its persecution of priests sparked a Catholic counter-revolution in western France; its torment of the king mobilized the monarchs of Europe.

Extreme times offered extreme opportunities for those with extreme solutions. The Assembly's delegates discussed a penal code, adopting Dr Guillotin's proposal to create a rational instrument of humane execution. 'Now with my machine,' boasted Guillotin, 'I'll knock your head off in the twinkling of an eye and you'll never feel it.' He was not actually inventor of the guillotine, just its advocate, but many who laughed would 'in the twinkling of an eye' experience his 'machine'. The hereditary executioner, known as Monsieur de Paris, was Chevalier Charles-Henri Sanson, who tested the guillotine on sheep and dead convicts. A medical student until he inherited his father's position as a teenager, he was the fourth in this killing dynasty. Already executioner for three decades, he had supervised the gruesome punishments – by sword, axe and wheel – of the ancient regime. In 1757, when he was eighteen, he had executed an attempted royal assassin, Damiens, whom he tortured, castrated and, harnessing four horses to his limbs, tore apart, slicing his tendons to ease the dismantling, before burning him alive. Sanson recommended the guillotine to the Assembly. His expertise would be much used.

'At last,' Fersen told his sister, 'on the 24th [December 1790] I spent a whole day with Her. It was the first. Imagine my joy.' Antoinette's beautiful day with 'the lovable personage' touched her. 'The personage and I managed to see each other safely once,' she told Yolande de Polignac. 'You can judge our happiness.'

Louis and Antoinette now agonized over the constitution that the Assembly expected them to approve and demanded the right to move from Paris to Saint-Cloud. When permission was refused, Antoinette ordered Fersen to plan their escape to a fortress, Montmédy, where Louis could manage both the revolutionaries and his exiled brothers, who were inviting Austria to attack the Assembly.

On the hot night of 20 June 1791, two children and two monarchs jumped into a carriage bought by Fersen, with the king disguised as the servant of a Russian baroness (Antoinette). The dauphin thought he was going to a play 'since we've all donned these odd dresses'. Their disappearance was noticed, couriers dispatched; they missed a rendezvous with loyal Hussars, and Antoinette's hairdresser did not turn up, always a bad sign. When the carriage galloped into Varennes, they were recognized and arrested. The Bourbons were escorted triumphantly back to Paris by a delegation including the sympathetic thirty-year-old Barnave. An attraction flickered between him and Antoinette, the start of a secret correspondence about installing a moderate monarchy. When a priest showed support in the street, the crowd dismembered him and presented his hands and head to Antoinette.

The foiled escape exposed royal duplicity. 'In that single night,' noticed a courtier, Antoinette's already greying hair 'turned white as that
of a seventy-year-old woman'. Imprisoned in the Tuileries Palace, Louis
railed against Voltaire and Rousseau – 'these two men have been the
ruin of France'. Antoinette corresponded with Barnave, ascendant in the
Assembly, and, through Fersen, with her brother Leopold. 'Don't worry
about us. We're alive,' she told Fersen in code. 'The Assembly leaders
seem to want to treat us gently.' But then: 'Speak to my relatives about
outside help.' Two days later, she told him, 'Look after yourself for me. I
won't be able to write any more. But nothing in this world can stop me
adoring you until I die.' Fersen was jealous of Barnave, noting, 'It's said
the queen sleeps with Barnave.' Louis and Antoinette staggered between
desperate plans. She ordered Fersen to stop the intervention by Austria
and Prussia: 'Force will only do harm.' In September, the agonized Louis
took the oath to obey the constitution – which still empowered him to appoint ministers and veto laws – as Antoinette and Barnave hoped to steer
a moderate course. 'If I find myself in treaty with some of them,' she reassured Fersen, 'it's only to use them.' But the arming of Habsburgs and
Hohenzollerns undermined Barnave – and condemned the Bourbons.[*]

   In January 1792, a vanquished Barnave retired to the provinces, his
vision of a constitutional monarchy discredited, overthrown in the Assembly by a pro-war government of the more radical Girondin faction,
led by Brissot. A month later, Fersen, planning another rescue, crept
into Paris in disguise (staying with one of his other mistresses) and,
dodging the guards, penetrated Antoinette's apartment. They spent
the night together, their last meeting. 'I am going to close,' she wrote
afterwards, 'but not without telling you, my dear and very tender friend,
that I love you madly . . .'

   In February, the advance of the German monarchs threw Paris into

---

[*] The Romanovs too were ready to destroy the revolution which had thrilled the Poles,
hoping to create a strong monarchy and rid themselves of Russian hegemony. The old king
Stanisław August placed himself at the head of their own revolution. Catherine the Great
was horrified by Paris and Warsaw – 'Better the tyranny of one man than the madness of
the multitude.' Potemkin planned to become king of Poland, but his dramatic death on
a Moldavian steppe left Catherine both heartbroken and flint-hearted. First she cracked
down on dissent in Russia, then she bloodily crushed the Polish revolution: 20,000 Poles
were killed as Russian troops stormed Praga, a suburb of Warsaw. Shortly before her death,
the Habsburgs and Hohenzollerns joined her in the final carve-up of Poland. Lvov and
Galicia – southern Poland, now western Ukraine – were ruled by Austria for the next two
centuries. Three million Jews now found themselves under hostile Russian rule; Potemkin
had been a philo-semite but the ageing, repressive Catherine confined the Jews to a 'pale
of settlement', banned from cities to avoid clashes with her Orthodox subjects. Her successors increasingly repressed the Jews. Poland would not exist again until 1918.

a crisis that destroyed the Girondins. It was a colourless, awkward, myopic and ascetic lawyer from Arras with a reedy voice who filled the vacuum. The thirty-three-year-old Maximilien Robespierre, elected leader of the Jacobins, a more radical faction, had gradually emerged as the incorruptible voice of virtue and the interpreter of the general will: 'Legitimately, sovereignty always belongs to the people,' but a select elite must decide the general will of the people, who 'want what is good but don't always see it'. It was an idea that would justify much bloodshed. This puritanical guardian – possibly a unique virgin among swaggering womanizers – increasingly guided the people or rather the radical artisans, the Parisian sans-culottes (they wore trousers instead of breeches). 'That man will go far,' Mirabeau had joked; 'he believes everything he says.' Robespierre had argued against war, claiming it would strengthen the king. Now the crisis swept Robespierre to power and destroyed the Bourbons. The war, which would last – with short interludes – for twenty-three years, encompassing all Europe and much of the world, intensified the fanaticism and intolerance of the revolution. 'Your friend,' wrote Antoinette to Fersen, scarcely encoding her meaning, 'is in the greatest danger. His illness is making terrible progress ... Tell his relations about his unfortunate situation.'

As the Bourbons endured this crisis, a French subject, far away in Saint-Domingue in the Caribbean, was disappointed by the French revolution for very different reasons. Toussaint, the former slave, was launching the greatest slave rebellion since Spartacus and the *zanj*.

TWO REVOLUTIONS – HAITI AND PARIS: CÉCILE AND TOUSSAINT, ROBESPIERRE AND DANTON

In August 1791, a cabal of slave leaders, Dutty 'Zamba' Boukman, Georges Biassou and Cécile Fatiman, coordinated by Toussaint, met by night in secret at Bois Caïman, to launch a rebellion on behalf of the 500,000 slaves. They swore vengeance with voodoo rituals, supervised by the twenty-year-old Cécile Fatiman, who acted as *mambo* (priestess).* A pig was sacrificed, its blood drunk.

---

* Fatiman was a central figure in Haitian history: the green-eyed daughter of an enslaved African and a French Corsican who had been a courtier of the adventurer Theodore von Neuhoff, briefly king of Corsica in the 1730s. During the Haitian revolution, she married a general, Jean-Louis Pierrot, raised to baron and prince under King Henry Christophe, before being elected president in 1845 and then appointed grand maréchal under Emperor Faustin. Cécile died at 112 in 1883. Her daughter married Haiti's war minister and later president Pierre Alexis.

Toussaint was unimpressed by the French revolution: for all its liberal measures, the Assembly was dominated by slave owners who refused to abolish slavery. Now in Saint-Domingue 10,000 slaves joined
the rebel army, which was soon 80,000 strong, overcoming the 40,000
whites and 28,000 free black people to conquer much of the colony as
slave masters were killed, estates burned. Biassou appointed himself
viceroy, but Toussaint 'directed all the strands of the plot and he organized the revolt and prepared the explosion'. Most wanted abolition of
slavery; the radicals wanted to 'kill the whites'; but Toussaint envisioned
a multiracial community that kept sugar estates intact. The revolutionaries positioned themselves as loyalists supporting Louis against the
pro-slavery lobby in the Assembly: this was partly a revolution against
the French revolution.

In July 1792, Toussaint helped draft a '*Lettre originale des chefs des
Nègres révoltés*', advocating abolition of slavery on the basis of 'universal
natural rights' and creation of a non-racialized community of equals in
a multiracial Saint-Domingue.

In August 1792, rallying against the slave-owning Assembly, Toussaint celebrated the birthday of Louis XVI, just as murderous panic
– sparked by the fear of foreign invasion and internal betrayal – crackled
through Paris. On 9 August, the urban militants of Paris elected an
insurrectionary Commune which, in cooperation with Robespierre,
organized an insurgent mob that the next day attacked the Tuileries,
killing 900 Swiss Guards, and overthrew the constitutional monarchy.
'What can do they to me?' cried Antoinette. 'Kill me, today's as good as
tomorrow.' Louis and Antoinette fled to the Assembly, where through
a grille they witnessed the suspension of the monarchy before they
were arrested and jailed in the forbidding Temple fortress. There Louis
humbly taught his son Latin and geography every morning. As elections
by universal suffrage were held for a new assembly, the Convention, the
hysteria – encapsulated by the slogan '*La Patrie en danger*' – was now
murderous.

Ten days after the Tuileries attack, the Prussians invaded France.
When they reached Verdun, Paris spun into a vicious frenzy. In September, as the new Convention gathered, Robespierre's charismatic ally,
Georges Danton, a shaggy lawyer's son from Champagne, rallied the
deputies. 'Anyone who refuses to serve must be punished by death!'
he cried. To conquer their enemies, 'Dare, dare again, always dare, and
France is saved!' Then came amazing news: on 20 September, at Valmy,
the French revolutionary army had defeated the Prussians. On the 22nd
the deputies abolished the monarchy. Although there was a stand-off in

the Convention between the Girondins, led by Brissot among others, and the more radical Montagnards, so named because they sat on the highest benches of the Convention, now led by Robespierre, the fear and panic drove squads of killers, some spontaneous, inspired by Danton, some probably organized by the Jacobins, to raid prisons, slaughtering 1,300 courtiers and priests, while prostitutes were gang-raped. Antoinette's friend the princesse de Lamballe was disembowelled and her head displayed to the queen, who fainted.

Yet the government, overseen by the Convention, was totally chaotic as it struggled not only against external enemies but against Catholic and royalist counter-revolution in the Vendée and moderate republican revolt in Lyons. As Robespierre emerged as the personification of republican virtue in the Convention, the new state was blooded with a royal sacrifice – the start of a modern era of mass national politics that remodelled both dynasty and private family. At 5 a.m. on 21 January 1793, Louis was awoken by drums.

ACT FOURTEEN
790 MILLION

Bonapartes and Albanians, Wellesleys and Rothschilds

ANTOINETTE, JOSEPHINE AND THE NATIONAL RAZOR

The night before, Louis XVI – forewarned – told the family that he would say goodbye in the morning, but when the morning came he could not bring himself to see them. His seven-year-old son, the dauphin, sobbed, 'Let me out!' The jailer asked him where he wished to go. 'To talk to the people so they don't kill my father.'

Robespierre had revealed the Bourbons' treasonous correspondence with the invaders and called for their execution. Tried before the Convention, Louis answered each of the thirty counts, calling them 'absurd', and ultimately declared, 'I always acted for the people.' Ironically he was accused of supporting the Saint-Domingue revolution.

Robespierre had demanded death, boasting: 'I'm inflexible to oppressors because I'm compassionate toward the oppressed.' The Convention, including Louis's cousin Orléans who had absurdly changed his name to Philippe Égalité, voted for death. Louis found a confidence in tragedy that he had scarcely known in glory. When his weeping lawyer informed him of the vote and proposed a counter-revolution, Louis replied, 'Such proceedings would incite civil war. I'd rather die. Order them to make no effort to save me – the king of France never dies.'

The streets were so crowded it took two hours to reach the gallows in the packed Place de la Révolution, where the executioner Sanson awaited Louis with his sons, Gabriel and Henri. Louis started to speak – 'I die innocent . . . I pray to God that the blood you shed may never be visited on France' – but the beating drums drowned him out. Sanson cut his hair and tied to him to the contraption. The blade decapitated him, and Sanson showed the head to the people. '*Vive la nation!*' cried the crowd. Antoinette and the children heard the roar. Baying citizens bathed in his blood, spattering it on each other.

Antoinette was given Louis's wedding ring, engraved 'M.A.A.A. [Marie Antoinette, Archduchess of Austria] 19 Aprille 1770'. In a scene of agonizing drama, played out in their filthy cells, Antoinette, with her daughter Marie Thérèse, curtsied to her son as Louis XVII. But the boy was emaciated and ill. Soon afterwards the children were separated from their mother. 'My child, we are about to part,' said Antoinette, gripping Louis XVII. 'Never forget God who thus tries you, nor your mother who loves you. Be good, patient and kind and your father will look from heaven and bless you.'

Louis's execution was 'the foulest and most atrocious deed which the history of the world has yet had occasion to attest,' said Prime Minister Pitt, who resolved to use British wealth – 'Pitt's gold' – to fund a series of coalitions of European powers in wars against France.* At home, he feared revolution, legislating to ban trade unions. As French revolutionary armies overran Belgium then invaded Holland, the Convention declared war on Britain.

On 6 April 1793, as the Vendée uprising threatened Paris, the Convention created an emergency *Comité de Salut Public* (Committee of Public Safety) under Danton 'to grasp the weapon of the Revolutionary Tribunal'. A democratic constitution was passed in June, but thanks to the war it was never implemented. That month, Danton retired to the country as the Convention announced 'a revolutionary government until peace', which gave full powers to the Committee, twelve revolutionaries, mainly provincial lawyers, re-elected every two months by the Convention. On 2 June, Robespierre orchestrated the arrest of Brissot and the Girondins and next month he was elected to the Committee, which ruled from the king's green study in the Tuileries. The twelve directed the war, and instituted what came to be called *La Terreur* as a manifestation of 'justice . . . severe and inflexible . . . the emanation of virtue'. On 23 August 1793, a massive conscription programme, the *levée en masse*, created the first real national army, directed by the ablest of the Committee, Lazar Carnot, 'organizer of victory'. It was 'a new era', said the poet Goethe, 'in the history of the world' – the time of nations and ideologies, expressed in mass politics. The end of sacred monarchy inaugurated the cult of the nation and its institutional doppelganger, the nation state, still the basic unit for organizing governments today. Power is the mother of ideology. Nationalism, the identification with a bigger community that shared language, fortified by race and history

---

* An observer of all this, the Anglo-Irish MP Edmund Burke, predicted in his *Reflections on the Revolution in France* that its consequences would be very different from its intentions, forging an unfailing rule of history. 'That which in the first instance is prejudicial maybe be excellent in its remoter operation and its excellence may arise from the ill effects it produces in the beginning,' he wrote. 'The reverse also happens: and very plausible schemes, with very pleasing commencements, have often shameful and lamentable conclusions.'

– both often invented and garnished with plangent myths – developed to justify the nation state. If it looked like reason and virtue would remove families from power, that did not happen: dynasties, old and new, shapeshifted easily and adapted to the new dynamics.

On 17 September, a Law of Suspects granted the Committee powers of summary execution as they assumed total command of the economy and then declared a new revolutionary calendar. Public hysteria, military chaos, factional rivalry and brazen corruption intensified the Terror. On 31 October, Brissot and twenty-eight Girondins sang republican songs on their way to the guillotine. Sixteen thousand victims, many denounced in a frenzy of fear and cowardice, and most guilty merely of being 'aristos', would be guillotined. The Terror did not kill people for religious reasons, as had been the practice in Europe for centuries, but to enforce loyalty. Robespierre investigated a Foreign Plot against the revolution that was really a case of peculation of *Compagnie des Indes Orientales* funds by elite revolutionaries close to the twelve. The law of 14 Frimaire (December) gave the Committee the power to crush opposition, a power that can be said to define the sovereignty of a nation. This was as significant an effect of the revolution in the creation of modern politics as the Rights of Man: one endorsed an omnipotent state; the other heralded the rule of individualism.

The Committee's envoys travelled across France, executing traitors. 'These monsters must be unmasked and exterminated,' said Robespierre of the Lyons rebels. 'The city of Lyons shall be destroyed,' ordered Robespierre. Two thousand were killed there, tied together before cannon and shot to pieces. At Nantes, 2,000 were locked into barges that were then sunk.

In Paris, Sanson – now beloved as Charlot, or the National Avenger – and his sons frantically beheaded 2,900 of Robespierre's victims. Sanson became so exhausted that he handed over to his son Gabriel. In a telling moment of the Terror, Gabriel was beheading so many people that, holding up a head to the crowd, he slipped on the blood, fell off the scaffold and broke his neck. 'Like Saturn,' wrote an observer, 'the revolution devours its children' – and the feasting had begun. Philippe Égalité voted for the Terror, but when his son, Louis Philippe, disgusted by the king's killing, defected to the coalition, the duke was guillotined.[*]

---

[*] That tainted his fencer-composer Saint-Georges who, accompanying the duke, backed the revolution and joined a black unit, *La Légion Nationale des Américains et du Midi*, funded by the richest free black planter of Saint-Domingue, Julien Raymond, who owned hundreds of slaves but had become an abolitionist. Here he met another mixed-race officer who became famous. Thomas-Alexandre Dumas was born in Saint-Domingue; his father was a French

So was Barnave. Among those arrested was a young slave owner's daughter, Marie Josèphe Rose Tascher de La Pagerie, the future Empress Josephine, who aged fifteen had arrived from Martinique to marry Vicomte Alexander de Beauharnais. Now in crowded cells, both awaited death.

Little Louis XVII, separated from his mother, half starved and plied with booze, was brainwashed and forced to denounce his mother for sexual abuse. When he heard their footsteps in the cell above, the boy sneered, 'Have those fucking whores been guillotined yet?' Antoinette's eldest child, Marie Thérèse, and her sister-in-law, Madame Élisabeth, remained with the queen. Then they too were parted.

On 14 October 1793, wearing mourning black but red high heels from another era, Antoinette was tried, found guilty of spying for Joseph II, of paying him money and of sexually abusing her son. When informed of her son's allegation that she was a 'new Agrippina', who had taught him to masturbate so hard that one of his testicles had swollen and had then fornicated with him, she replied, 'Nature refuses to answer such a charge, but I appeal to all the mothers who are here.' Robespierre feared that her dignity would 'make her an object of pity'. The daughter of Maria Theresa disdained her tormenters: 'I was a queen and you dethroned me. I was a wife and you murdered my husband. I was a mother and you've torn my children from me. I have nothing left but my blood – hurry up and take it!' Her last letter to her sister-in-law and daughter testified to her regret at her parting from her children and begged Élisabeth to forgive her son's allegations – 'Think how easy it is at that age to make a child say anything' – asking her to kiss her 'poor

---

planter and slave owner, the Marquis Antoine Davy de la Pailleterie, while his mother was the enslaved Marie Cessette Dumas, so that he was born a slave. His father was the elder but useless brother of the successful planter Charles, for whom Antoine worked until they argued at which Antoine bought Marie Cessette, then left the white plantations and vanished for thirty years, running a small cacao estate, where Marie Cessette gave birth to Alexandre in 1762. Returning to France to claim his title and estates, Antoine sold Marie Cessette and the children to a baron, then rebought Alexandre, enrolled him in the army and funded his lavish lifestyle. Dumas was a titanic swashbuckler who rose fast in the revolutionary army. Saint-Georges served as colonel of his own Saint-Georges Legion, under Dumas. At the height of the Terror, Saint-Georges, accused of peculation, denounced Dumas. The composer was jailed, and Dumas was about to be arrested when Robespierre fell. Both were lucky to avoid the guillotine. Afterwards Dumas was promoted to général-en-chef – the first general of colour since the Russian general, Abram Gannibal, a protégé of Peter I. Saint-Georges travelled to Saint-Domingue, hoping to find a peaceful revolution of colour. Instead he found Saint-Domingue in a vicious civil war and escaped back to Paris, where he consoled himself with music. 'I was particularly devoted to my violin,' wrote this swordsman, violinist, soldier and friend of princes before he died of cancer aged fifty-one. 'Never before did I play it so well!'

and dear children'. Her letter was not delivered but given instead to Robespierre.

When her executioner, Henri Sanson, who had succeeded his brother, arrived at the Conciergerie prison to bind her wrists she asked if she could relieve herself in private. He refused and she squatted in a corner in front of the jailers. Dressed in white, Antoinette, thirty-seven years old but looking like an old lady, was transported in an open tumbril, mocked by the crowd. At some point, she scribbled a note to Fersen that was later smuggled out to him: 'Adieu, my heart is all yours.' She died courageously.

'I was devastated,' wrote Fersen. 'I thought about her constantly, all the horrible circumstances of her sufferings, the doubt she might have had about me, my attachment . . . tormented me.'

Louis XVII deteriorated in a cell awash with faeces. 'My brother is sick,' wrote his sister Marie Thérèse. 'I've written to the Convention for permission to nurse him.' But Robespierre was implacable. When the boy died, his doctor smuggled his heart out in a handkerchief for sacred burial.

'If the basis of popular government in peacetime is virtue, its basis in revolution is both virtue and terror,' declared Robespierre on 5 February 1794: 'virtue, without which terror is disastrous; terror, without which virtue has no power.' His whirlpool of virtue would be the template for all similar self-righteous, secular witch-hunts; the Committee was the first modern war cabinet, the first government designed to purify and reshape society.

In March, the return of Danton – demanding an end to the Terror, warning of dictatorship and proposing peace negotiations – threatened Robespierre's rule and vision. The Sea-Green Incorruptible – the epithet applied to him by the historian Thomas Carlyle – denounced him and his supporters for defeatism, stealing funds from the *Compagnie des Indes Orientales* and interceding for Marie Antoinette. On 5 April, Danton and the others went to the guillotine. 'What annoys me most', Danton supposedly reflected in Sanson's carriage, 'is I'm going to die six weeks before Robespierre.'

Robespierre had won, but now no one was safe. He and the Committee accelerated the executions by the 'national razor'. The war speeded the rise of a generation of young officers. In the south, where British and royalist forces had seized Toulon, Robespierre sent two legates to retake the port, his brother Augustin and an ex-vicomte, Paul Barras, who were impressed by a young Corsican captain called Napoleon Bonaparte, energetic, thin and sallow, who in December 1793 commanded the artillery during its successful recapture. At the age of twenty-four, Bonaparte was promoted to general. In Saint-Domingue, another brilliant young general was taking command of a revolutionary army.

Three years into the revolution, the Convention outlawed racial discrimination but refused to abolish slavery, sending out 6,000 French troops to retake the Jewel of the Caribbean.

BLACK SPARTACUS AND THE TYRANT OF VIRTUE

As the French tried to crush the ex-slaves, Toussaint travelled to the Santo Domingo half of Hispaniola to negotiate an alliance with the Spanish, who duly made him a general. Meanwhile Biassou and several leaders were themselves trading in slaves, whom they sold to the Spanish. Biassou ordered Toussaint's murder; he then stayed with the Spanish, and Toussaint emerged as paramount leader.

Wiry, tall, tireless, sporting 'a blue jacket, large red cape, red cuffs with eight rows of lace on the arms, large gold epaulettes, scarlet waistcoat, pantaloons, half-boots, round hat with a red feather', he 'managed to make himself invisible where he was and visible where he was not', an enemy recalled. 'He borrowed his spontaneity of movement from the tiger.' Infused with his African culture and slave traditions of voodoo occultism along with Catholicism, the French language and the Parisian Enlightenment, witty, playful and always surprising, Toussaint was a master of military tactics, manoeuvring between France, Spain and Britain. 'Say little,' he said, 'but do as much as possible.' Presenting himself as a cross between a god of war, Ogoun Fer, and a shapeshifting voodoo spirit of the crossroads, Papa Legba, he adopted a new name, Louverture – the Opening.

After two years 'behind the curtain', Toussaint proclaimed, 'I am Toussaint Louverture: you have perhaps heard my name. You are aware, brothers, that I have undertaken vengeance and I want freedom and equality to reign in Saint-Domingue . . . to establish the happiness of us all.'

As commander he gathered around him the henchmen who would dominate Haiti. Jean-Jacques Dessalines, future emperor, was one of the slaves Louverture had managed after his own manumission, while Henry Christophe, future king, had worked as slave, stableboy and waiter, and as a drummer boy had fought at Savannah with the black French regiment *Chasseurs-Volontaires de Saint-Domingue* and with the Americans against the British. Most of Toussaint's men were

African-born slaves, particularly Kongos from Angola, but his chief of staff, General Agé, was white. Louverture boasted that he 'put ninety Spaniards to the sword' after one battle and sent heads to the French, yet he disliked 'warriors with a fondness for spilling blood', often protecting the *colons*.

On 4 February 1794, in Paris, Robespierre backed the Convention's decree to abolish slavery: '*La Convention Nationale déclare que l'esclavage des Nègres dans toutes les colonies est aboli*', acknowledging that the slave rebellion was irreversible. Toussaint hailed this 'great consolation for all friends of mankind'. Ending his tactical alliance with the slave-trading Spanish, he negotiated with the French governor Étienne de Laveaux and promised to become 'devoted to crushing enemies of the republic'. Toussaint praised Laveaux for his 'exceptional love of black people'; Laveaux raved to Paris, 'I can't speak highly enough' of Toussaint's 'virtues, talent, martial qualities; he is full of humanity, indefatigable as warrior'.

Robespierre now embraced a vision of a state of virtue.* 'If God didn't exist,' he said, quoting Voltaire, 'it'd be necessary to invent him.' On 8 June, at a turgidly solemn ritual atop a man-made mountain on the Champ de Mars, Robespierre presided over the launch of a new religion, '*le Culte de l'Être suprême*'. As virtuous potentate and hierophant of the Supreme Being, he was at his murderous zenith – but he was overreaching, his prominence resented by his colleagues. Two days later, a law granted Robespierre and the Committee powers to kill all public enemies. In July, sixty victims were beheaded daily; one of them was Josephine de Beauharnais's husband, and she expected death herself. Now even the Sansons had doubts: the old father suffered 'terrible visions . . . Perhaps I'm punished by God for my cowardly obedience to mock justice.' Henri Sanson was arrested. But the Committee was reduced to nocturnal screaming rows. Robespierre retired to his lodgings to recover and plan the arrest of all his enemies. On 26 July, he delivered a disastrously misjudged speech, defending his revolution, 'the first founded on the theory of the rights of humanity and the principles of justice', and menaced its enemies – 'the monsters' – before reflecting, 'Death is not an eternal sleep . . . Death is the start of immortality.' But his threat to 'crush all factions' united both moderates and radicals in

---

* Women were missing from Robespierre's vision: the Jacobins associated them with intrigue and the vice and luxury of courts. Olympe de Gouges, one of the first French abolitionists, one of the few revolutionaries to back the Haitian revolution and one of the first feminists, did not live to see the abolition of slavery. Her *Déclaration des droits de la femme et de la citoyenne* had challenged the patriarchy of the revolution: 'A woman has the right to mount the scaffold. She must possess equally the right to mount the speaker's platform.' Robespierre sent her to the guillotine where her 'courage and beauty were unparalleled'.

a conspiracy against him that night. Next day, 9 Thermidor in the revolutionary calendar, when they tried to launch their purge, he and his
epigones were accused of planning to 'murder the Convention'.

'Down with the tyrant,' cried Robespierre's critics.

He tried to speak but fear stole his voice.

'Danton's blood', came the shout, 'chokes you!'

'Is it Danton you regret?' Robespierre replied. 'Cowards! Why didn't
you defend him?'

Arrested then freed in the chaos, Robespierre and his henchmen fled
to the Hôtel de Ville where, besieged by militia, Robespierre shot himself, but merely shattered his jaw. Watched by baying crowds, his face
bandaged, he was conveyed to the national razor where Henri Sanson,
reinstated, ripped off his bandage. Robespierre emitted a high-pitched
shriek and fainted before Sanson removed his head. This was not a
revolution but an internecine coup within the Committee, where the
Jacobin faction continued to rule in partnership with the now empowered moderates. Prisoners, including Josephine, were released.* Among
Robespierrists arrested in Nice was General Bonaparte, who was fortunate to be released. Meanwhile his patron, Barras, a bisexual Provençal
bon vivant who had fought the British in India, helped dismantle the
machine of terror.

On 5 October 1795, faced with a revolt in Paris, Barras summoned
Bonaparte, who sent a Gascon innkeeper's son, Joachim Murat, a jet-
haired, six-foot-tall, blue-eyed eighteen-year-old, to get forty cannon.
'The rabble must be moved by terror,' said Bonaparte, ordering Murat
to fire 'a whiff of grapeshot' into the crowd. The cannon fire killed 300
and won for the general the gratitude of Barras, who was now chosen as
the president of a five-man *Directoire*. France, fighting the Habsburgs,
the Hohenzollerns and the British in Italy, Germany and the Netherlands, was holding its own, efficiently organized by one of the *directeurs*,
Carnot. Released from the Terror, enjoying their power, self-made
revolutionaries and returning aristocrats celebrated their survival in a
florescence of libidinous luxury and venal dealmaking: none more so
than Charles Maurice de Talleyrand, a languid, lame libertine, who in
British and American exile had met Pitt and Hamilton, and who became
the wily and witty foreign minister.

Barras, whom Carnot described as possessing 'the tastes of an opulent
prince, generous, magnificent and dissipated', embarked on an affair

---

* One of them was a minor aristocrat, Jean-Baptiste de Gaulle, great-grandfather of the
twentieth-century president.

with Josephine de Beauharnais. When she became too demanding and expensive, he said he was 'tired and bored' of that 'cajoling courtesan'. He promoted the pale, long-haired Bonaparte, whose 'emaciated thinness was converted into a fullness of face' and 'a smile always agreeable' and now encouraged Josephine to focus on his protégé. After sending her little son Eugène to deliver a message, she finally met Napoleon and he fell wildly in love with her. She was six years older than him but much less innocent – her charm, chestnut hair and hazel eyes, allied with a sophisticated sexual technique that Bonaparte called *le zigzag*, outweighed the toothlessness that prevented her from smiling, her incontinent extravagance and her supposed lack of intelligence: 'No one,' laughed Talleyrand, 'ever managed better without it.'

'I awake full of you,' wrote Bonaparte that December. 'Your image and the memory of last night's intoxicating pleasures has left no rest to my senses.' In March 1796, Barras presided over their marriage and, convinced of Bonaparte's devoted loyalty, chose him to command the Army of Italy. Left in Paris, Josephine started an affair with a young hussar and tried to regain possession of her estates on Saint-Domingue.

In April, Toussaint celebrated his alliance with Laveaux, who called him 'the black Spartacus, the leader announced by the *philosophe* Raynal to avenge the crimes perpetrated against his race', and appointed him deputy governor. Toussaint was much favoured by the wives of the French *colons*. Married to Suzanne and father of beloved sons, Toussaint was the lover of Madame Fisson, 'a white girl of rare beauty', whose *colon* husband became one of his agents, and of Marguerite Descahaux, another *colon*'s wife. He was bombarded with locks of blonde hair and notes that called him 'my prince' from planters' wives and he encouraged his white officials to marry black women, including his own paramours.

Yet his real challenge was to unite his people, most of them *bossales* from Africa still identifying as Kongos or Ibos. 'I'm the person black people see when they look in the mirror,' he said, 'and it's to me they must turn if they wish to enjoy the fruits of liberty.' Yet the *Directoire* distrusted Toussaint, who retorted that Africans had 'used their weapons and bare hands to keep the colony French'. Barras was not convinced, sending a general named Hédouville to disarm the black militias. 'Who's the greater defender of your freedom?' Toussaint asked his people, 'General Hédouville, former marquis, or Toussaint Louverture, the slave from Bréda?'

Toussaint's revolt was terrifying a nearby coterie of slave owners. 'I feel sincerely those sentiments of sympathy,' wrote President

Washington, 'for the distresses of suffering brethren [slave masters].' In February 1793, he signed the Fugitive Slave Act, permitting the pursuit of escaped slaves. Jefferson too, convinced that 'all the West India islands will remain in the hands of the people of color', declared that 'we should foresee the bloody scenes which our children certainly, and possibly ourselves (south of Potomac), will have to wade through'.

British slave owners were afraid too, but Pitt had held up Wilberforce's 1792 Slave Trade Bill, instead focusing on fighting France and seeking imperial gains. In September 1793 he sent a large expedition to seize a rich French asset, Saint-Domingue, and re-establish slavery in order to safeguard British sugar plantations in Barbados and Jamaica. Toussaint led furious resistance, defeating two British expeditions with the aid of rampaging yellow fever.

In May 1796, turning to India, where the French were conspiring against Britain, Pitt appointed a close friend from Eton and Oxford, the thirty-seven-year-old Richard Wellesley, earl of Mornington, as governor-general of the presidency of Fort William (Calcutta). One of Pitt's first acts, in 1784, had been to take control of the EIC: henceforth the prime minister would appoint the India Board of Control and the governor-general who actually ran the three Indian presidencies.* Although Clive had secured Bengal, Britain's territories were limited and most of India was ruled by the Marathas, enjoying huge revenues. It was only now that Wellesley, dynamic and autocratic, libertine and spendthrift, studied how to lay 'the foundations of our Empire in Asia', aided by two younger brothers, one serving as his adjutant, the other as trusted commander. Arthur, the future duke of Wellington, handsome, frosty, laconic and talented, complemented Richard's overblown schemes and explosive impetuosity. Between them the two sons of an undistinguished Anglo-Irish landowner would establish British power in India and Europe.

---

* Among those who joined the EIC's forces during Wellesley's rule were two brothers, William and Christopher Biden, who became captains of Indiamen. While William died in Rangoon in 1843 aged fifty-one, Christopher retired to Madras (Chennai), settling with his wife to become a marine storekeeper. A son, Horatio, rose to become colonel of the Madras Artillery, and there were other Bidens out there. One of them, George Biden, was an EIC captain who married an Indian woman, most probably the founder of the Indian Bidens. They are likely to be related to Joe Biden, US president, who called George his 'great-great-great-great-great-grandfather'.

A HEAP OF EYEBALLS: TIGER TIPU, THE WELLESLEY
BROTHERS AND THE AVENGING EUNUCH OF PERSIA

Once in Calcutta, Wellesley played the proconsul, parading in a fancy carriage and with an armed retinue, building a new resplendent Government House and pursuing sexual escapades. Asia had changed since Clive's day: a Sikh *sirdar*, Ranjit Singh, was carving out a kingdom in Punjab, having expelled the heir of the Afghan conqueror Durrani, who had also lost his Persian and central Asian provinces thanks to the conquests of a ferocious eunuch intent on avenging humiliations national and testicular.

Wizened, wrinkly and tiny with a high voice, Agha Muhammad Khan had been castrated at five by Nader Shah's nephew to prevent any threat from his Qajar tribe, and was then kept as a prisoner at court for decades until 1779 when a change of regime enabled the eunuch to escape, raise his tribal army and conquer Shiraz, Isfahan and Tabriz. When he pivoted into Khorasan he captured Nader's blind grandson, Shahrokh, personally torturing him by filling his crown with molten lead. He had the body buried under the doorway of the palace in his new capital, Teheran. In 1791, he invaded the Caucasus, expelling Russian forces and recapturing Yerevan. When he took Kumani, he had the eyeballs of its 20,000 people gouged out and collected in heaps.

In August 1795, he attacked Georgia, where its king Hercules II, who had served in Nader's entourage, begged Catherine the Great for protection. Just before she died, Catherine abandoned Georgia. In September the eunuch routed Hercules and razed Tbilisi, building towers of bodies before taking 15,000 slaves back to Teheran, where he was crowned shah.

His reign was short. In June 1797, when he heard his valets arguing, he sentenced two of them to death but put off the executions until the next morning. Overnight they crept into the royal tent and stabbed him. But the monster had united Iran: his successor, his nephew Fath-Ali Shah, held it together, and the family ruled until 1925.

While the Persians, Afghans and Sikhs were busy in the east, Wellesley was determined to be the founder of the British empire in India where the British were just one part of a cosmopolitan melange of Europeans and Indians who mixed together on equal terms: one in three Britons on the subcontinent were married to Indian women. In Hyderabad, where the British ensured the Nizam did not ally with the French, the British Resident (representative), James Kirkpatrick, was married to the beautiful princess Khair-un-Nissa. Wellesley was said to disapprove, but he focused on Britain's chief enemy, Mysore, a kingdom recently carved out of the southern Vijayanagar empire by a warlord, Haidar Ali Khan. His French-trained son Sultan Tipu, a tigerish showman whose sultanate was known for its social stability, economic prosperity and harmony between Hindu and Muslim citizens, hired French officers to conquer the Carnatic and Malabar and defeated a British army – believing the French would back him. But they let him down. Having succeeded in 'drawing the Beast of the jungle into the toils', Wellesley unleashed his brother Arthur, who stormed Seringapatam and killed Tipu. Wellesley used Mysore to turn on the Marathas. In September 1803, at Assaye, General Arthur Wellesley defeated the maharaja of Gwalior, which he later regarded as a greater victory than Waterloo – 'the bloodiest for the numbers that I ever saw' – while in the north another British army defeated the Marathas, commanded by French officers, outside Delhi, which then joined the British sphere. Many of the rulers, including the Mughal emperor, were allowed to rule while the British controlled foreign policy. India had frequently been conquered by war bands from the east, but this was its first conquest by a sea power – and it gave Britain mass and span. By the time Wellesley arrived home with a marquessate and £100,000, the real architect of the British Raj had more than doubled London's territories and planned to become prime minister. Arthur too entered politics.

Further east, the EIC again tried to penetrate China, the most powerful Asian state, ruled by the octogenarian Qianlong, emperor of 300 millions, who had expanded Chinese power into central Asia: the biggest ever Chinese empire. But he had lived too long and suffered from the success curse: past success makes present reform unthinkable.* The trade balance was vastly in China's favour, with the British, confined to Canton, paying in silver, but the EIC hoped to pay for Chinese tea with a new Indian crop, opium. In September 1792, they dispatched an envoy, Earl Macartney, to request 'a small unfortified island for the residence of British traders'.

Qianlong, slim in build, aquiline of face, serene and majestic, dressed in 'a loose robe of yellow silk, a cap of black velvet with a red ball on the top, and adorned with a peacock's feather', received Macartney, who presented gifts to show off British technology: a telescope, barometer,

---

* The Ming had ruled 1.2 million square miles; by 1790, the Qing ruled 5.7 million – nearly five times larger. The Qing territory was an empire, mainly consisting of ethnically Han Chinese with some non-Chinese attached to its periphery. Since the Shang, Chinese kingdoms had faced the threat of nomadic war bands from the north. Now the threat had vanished, and the triumph of Chinese empire fostered self-congratulatory complacency.

air pump, planetarium and six Wedgwood pots. Qianlong mocked the air pump – 'enough to amuse children' – but it was the Wedgwood that should have alarmed him. With the British sending china to China, the world had changed, yet Qianlong rejected British pretensions, reflecting the worldview of his prime: 'Our Celestial Empire possesses all things in prolific abundance,' while Britain's 'evil request' was a 'flagrant infringement of the usage of my empire'. For now the British looked irrelevant in China.

Britain could no longer deport criminals to America, but Captain Cook's naturalist Banks suggested that New South Wales was ideal for a new penal colony. Pitt and his home secretary Viscount Sydney dispatched a fleet of eleven ships under Captain Arthur Phillip to secure the colony on the vast continent of Australia, the home of hundreds of thousands of indigenous peoples, most of whom had had no contact with Europeans except for a few Dutch and British sailors over the last century.

In January 1788, Governor Phillip raised the flag on the coast, naming the settlement Sydney Cove and delivering the first 732 convicts, thieves from London. By 1792, when Phillip returned to London, 4,221 Britons – of whom 3,099 were convicts – were settled in New South Wales. Its convicts worked in chain gangs, while its indigenous peoples were culled by diseases and broken by settler land grabs.*

The British were not the only conquerors carving out a Pacific realm. In 1790, it was the predations of an American family of fur traders who unknowingly helped Kamehameha create a Hawaiian kingdom. An American trader, Simon Metcalfe, sailed his *Eleonora* to the Hawaiian islands, where after a dispute he flogged a Hawaiian chieftain, slaughtered 100 Hawaiians with his cannon and sailed on towards China. A little later, when his nineteen-year-old son Thomas arrived in the ill-named *Fair American*, the Hawaiians took revenge, storming the ship and killing him and his crew – except one artillerymen.

On a nearby island, his father Simon waited and sent a boatswain ashore to find out what had happened to Thomas. When the sailor was taken prisoner, Simon sailed away to China.

The two British sailors were invited by Kamehameha to operate his newly acquired cannon: wisely they not only agreed but became

---

* Phillip was formally in charge of Aotearoa (New Zealand), which was not yet under British control. While a few convicts escaped there and whalers regularly stopped there, Aotearoa was home to the Maori *iwi* (tribes), descendants of the waves of Polynesians who had settled there as late as 1300, ruled by their *rangatiras* (chiefs) and often at war with one another.

his intimate courtiers. Isaac Davis from Wales and John Young from Lancashire began as his gunners, then helped command his armies and ultimately married into the dynasty. After buying guns from British and American traders and learning how to manufacture gunpowder from saltpetre – easily found on Hawaii – Kamehameha, assisted by Davis and Young, stormed Maui. Five years later, in May 1795, he led 1,000 war canoes and 10,000 troops, along with cannon operated by his Lancashire and Welsh artillerymen, to seize Oahu, winning a battle at Nu'uanu and then sacrificing its ruler. Next this remarkable conqueror would take on American and European traders at their own game.

In December 1793, Jefferson resigned from Washington's cabinet, leaving the field to his rivals from the conservative Federalist Party, Hamilton and Vice-President Adams, claiming disingenuously, 'The little spice of ambition . . . has long since evaporated,' while plotting remorselessly. 'He's as ambitious', noted Adams, 'as Oliver Cromwell.' Jefferson hated direct confrontation, assuming an Olympian gentility, at the same time manipulating newspapers to destroy Hamilton – and refusing to denounce Robespierre's Terror. In Monticello, he pulled down and restarted his domed mansion and resumed his relationship with Sally. In 1795, still only twenty, Sally gave birth another daughter, who also died young.

After two terms, Washington returned to Mount Vernon to salvage his fortunes.* Jefferson's 'retirement' was short-lived and illusory: he carefully transformed himself from Parisian–Virginian aristocrat into austere man of popular virtue and ran against Adams, who won the presidency. As vice-president, his reward for finishing runner-up, Jefferson spent as little time in the capital Philadelphia as possible and as much as he could at home, where in 1797 Sally gave birth to a son, Beverly. While Adams's presidency deteriorated, Hamilton, high-handed, brilliant but self-destructive, had ruined himself by admitting an affair

---

* As Washington ended his second term, he contemplated emancipating all his slaves – yet never did while he doggedly also pursued escapees: Oona Judge was a young mixed-race maid, a favourite of George and Martha, but in May 1796, knowing that the Washingtons were returning and fearing she would never be manumitted, she escaped. Martha was upset – 'The blacks are so bad in their nature, they have not the least gratitude for the kindness showed to them' – and the couple were convinced that she had been 'seduced by a Frenchman'. Washington ordered his treasury secretary to use customs officials to kidnap her in Portsmouth, New Hampshire. Instead Oona persuaded the customs official that she had not been seduced and would return if she was promised manumission. Any such deal, said Washington, was 'inadmissible' and he tried one more time to capture her. Finally he stopped, fearing bad publicity, at which the brave Oona insisted, 'I am now free now and choose to remain so.' On 14 December 1799 Washington died aged sixty-seven, leaving 317 persons to Martha. They were finally manumitted in Martha's will.

with a married woman, Maria Reynolds. Jefferson doubtless revelled in the implosion of these Federalist rivals, but as he got closer to the presidency his own secrets became political dynamite.

In 1800, Jefferson, running with an amoral New York lawyer Aaron Burr, was (just) elected president and moved into the President's House in the new capital Washington – shortly before Sally gave birth to a daughter, Harriet. In September 1801, the *Virginian Federalist* published revelations about 'Mr J', claiming that he 'has a number of yellow children and that he is addicted to golden affections'. Then a year later James Callender, a racist scribbler used by Jefferson in his battles with Adams, revealed in the *Richmond Recorder*, 'It is well known that the man, whom it delighteth the people to honor, keeps . . . as his concubine one of his own slaves. Her name is SALLY.' Jefferson ignored the story.

Initially welcoming Saint-Domingue as part of the age of revolution, Jefferson changed his view when he heard about the killing of white people, warning that the 'cannibals of the terrible republic' could spark the 'combustion' of a US race war. Yet he tried to avoid the subject of slavery, concentrating on his life's work – the creation of the new American nation. His greatest opportunity was ironically accelerated by Toussaint's success.

In return for not encouraging slave revolts, Toussaint now cultivated good relations with the US and Britain. Believing that the best route to freedom lay through Paris, he sent his sons to be educated in France and had just invaded Spanish Santo Domingo, liberating its slaves and uniting the two sides of the island, when news arrived that a French general had seized power in Paris.

Just after his March 1796 wedding to Josephine, the twenty-six-year-old Bonaparte arrived in Italy to fight the Habsburgs, who were defending their northern Italian provinces. Bonaparte manoeuvred with vertiginous grace on the fields both of battle and of publicity. Like Germany, Italy was a 'merely geographical expression', as a Habsburg minister would say, ruled in the north by the Habsburg emperor and the Savoyard king of Piedmont–Sardinia, in the centre by the popes and in Naples–Sicily by a Bourbon king. As Bonaparte conquered Milan that May and moved south, he set up new republics to mirror France itself, imposing the principles of the Enlightenment, abolishing the Inquisition and noble assemblies and freeing the Jews from centuries of anti-Jewish restrictions.

Intoxicated by the excitement of power and the exercise of French superiority, 'I no longer regarded myself as a simple general,' Bonaparte confessed later, 'but as a man to decide the fate of peoples.' None of his ambitions would have mattered without the victories he won, which would have impossible without the unshackled force of France, *la Grande Nation*, its large population, its remarkable military organization and its generals, sons of innkeepers and coopers promoted on merit, combined with its republican fervour and a sense of French superiority. Their coalition of enemies, the Habsburgs now joined by the Romanovs and funded by Pitt, was overextended and ill-coordinated.*

Bonaparte dreamed of power and of Josephine, begging her to join him, writing daily, swinging from the practical – 'I'm a little tired, every day on horseback' – to the erotic – 'a kiss on your breast and then a little lower, then much, much lower'. When he discovered that she was sleeping with a 'very pretty' hussar, he dived into a romantic swoon: 'You don't love me any more, I have only to die.' Holding court in a Milanese palace, joined by his mother, Bonaparte adopted regal ways, promoting his brothers, marrying his sisters to French generals and Italian aristocrats, while joking disarmingly to the *Directoire*: 'If months ago I wished to be duke of Milan, today I desire to be king of Italy.' '†

After signing a peace that won northern Italy and Belgium for France, Bonaparte advised the *directeurs* that they should aim to attack Britain 'or expect to be destroyed by the corruption of these intriguing and enterprising islanders'. He added, 'Let's concentrate all our activity upon the naval side and destroy England. That done, Europe is at our feet.' At a Paris triumph, Barras and the *Directoire*, all absurdly wearing Roman togas, compared Bonaparte to a new Caesar, who now planned an oriental adventure to knock Britain out of the war, found an Alexandrian empire, champion French Enlightenment and make himself invincible: Egypt.

As suggested by Talleyrand, Bonaparte promised that 'as soon as he'd conquered Egypt, he will establish relations with the Indian princes and, together with them, attack the English in their possessions'. On

---

* When Pitt accused an MP of obstructing the defence of the realm, he was challenged to a duel. On 27 May 1898 the men fought at Putney Heath. No one was harmed, but he was not the last premier to fight a duel.

† Bonaparte cultivated the legend of his Olympian acumen and sleepless energy – 'Different subjects and different affairs are arranged in my head like a cupboard; when I wish to interrupt one train of thought, I shut that drawer and open another. If I wish to sleep, I close all the drawers and I sleep.' His talents varied from a logistical mastery and tactical virtuosity to a personal touch with his *grognards* (veterans) that won him longstanding loyalty. He revelled in his new power: when the king of Sweden sent him Fersen, Queen Antoinette's lover, as an envoy, he told the Swede he was 'mocking the first nation of the world'. Later raised to marshal of the Swedish court, Fersen, entangled in the fall of the Vasa dynasty, was stomped to death by a mob in 1810.

19 May 1798, Bonaparte and his 280 ships sailed out of Toulon with an army of 38,000, accompanied by 167 savants (historians, architects, mathematicians and botanists), his brother Louis, his stepson Eugène and his mixed-race cavalry commander General Dumas, plus 800,000 pints of wine.

EGYPTIAN POTENTATES: BONAPARTE AND MEHMED ALI

Bonaparte, immersing himself in the ancient history of pharaohs, Alexander and Caesar, arrived in a semi-autonomous province of the Ottomans. Egypt, like most Ottoman territories, was now semi-independent, ruled by rapacious Mamluk-Turkish pashas. 'This horde of slaves, bought in Caucasus and Georgia, has tyrannized the most beautiful part of the world,' said Bonaparte, who ordered his troops to be tolerant of Egyptian culture: 'Treat them as you treated the Jews and the Italians. Respect their muftis and imams.'

After landing at Alexandria, the vanguard under General Dumas, whom the Austrians nicknamed the Black Devil, rode south. But this irrepressible giant, 'the handsomest man you ever saw', resented Bonaparte's ambitions and started plotting against him.

On 20 July 1798, just outside Cairo, Bonaparte defeated the Mamluks. The publicity maestro named this his 'Battle of the Pyramids', declaiming, 'Soldiers, remember that, from these pyramids, forty centuries of history contemplate you' – even though they were not actually in view. Dumas's cavalry pursued the Mamluks. The French occupied Cairo, Africa's largest city, but ten days later Bonaparte's fleet, moored in Aboukir Bay, was destroyed by an impetuous one-eyed, one-armed British admiral, Horatio Nelson. Bonaparte was nonplussed, but his options were now limited. In October, the Cairenes rebelled; Bonaparte and Dumas crushed the revolt, killing 5,000 rebels and trapping the last of them in the Al-Azhar Mosque, which they bombarded with artillery and then stormed, with Dumas himself galloping into the mosque on horseback. But now Bonaparte learned of Dumas's intrigue: he threatened to shoot him, but allowed him to return to France.* Dumas was replaced by Murat, that Gascon fighting cockatoo, his sword engraved 'Honour and the Ladies', who several times saved the French from Mamluk cavalry.

---

* On the way home, Dumas was captured by papal forces and imprisoned; his health broken, he retired. His son was Alexandre Dumas, author of *The Three Musketeers* and *The Count of Monte-Cristo*; his grandson the younger Alexander wrote *La Dame aux camélias*.

But an Ottoman army was approaching through Syria, supported by the pasha of Acre. Bonaparte marched north and besieged Acre. The expedition was a disaster: he massacred his prisoners, killed his own wounded soldiers and failed to take Acre. While pumping out mendacious bulletins about his achievements and gaining a rallying song, 'Partant pour la Syrie', Bonaparte was finally informed that Josephine had been unfaithful all along. 'I've lost faith,' he sobbed, 'in human nature.'

In October 1799, Bonaparte abandoned his entire army (not for the last time) and slipped past British ships. 'Bah! We'll get there,' he said. 'Luck's never abandoned us!' Accompanied by his Georgian slave-bodyguard Roustam, he arrived in Paris to exploit his political prestige. Back in Egypt, British and Ottoman forces converged on the French army, which was finally evacuated.* Sultan Selim III had ordered Egypt's recapture, massing an army that included a Turkish-Albanian, Mehmed Ali, the exact same age as Bonaparte, who would become the Islamic Napoleon.

Born in Kavala (Greece), Mehmed Ali was the son of an Albanian Ottoman official and nephew of the governor, 'brought up a gentleman'. But 'when Napoleon invaded Egypt, his uncle enrolled him in a unit commanded by his own son. He arrived in Egypt in 1801 as the French withdrew and just as Cairo descended into chaos. The Ottomans failed to control the Mamluks. Yet Mehmed Ali, taking command of 4,000 aggressive Albanians, skilfully outmanoeuvred both. In May 1805, Cairene grandees dispatched a delegation to see him.

'Who,' he asked, 'have you chosen as governor?'

'We'll accept no one,' they replied, 'but *you*.' It was only now that he sent for his sons and family from Greece. After just four years in Egypt, scarcely speaking Arabic, illiterate until he was forty, Mehmed Ali ruled Egypt. Like Napoleon, he burnished his legend, often speaking in the Caesaresque third person; but, unlike the Corsican, he created a state and dynasty that endured. The most successful Islamic potentate in modern times, Mehmed Ali would dominate Egypt for forty-three years, conquering (like Napoleon) a vast but short-lived empire, almost causing a European war, but then creating the first industrial economy outside Europe and a dynasty that ruled Egypt until 1952.

In October 1799, arriving back in Paris, Bonaparte found the *Directoire* falling apart, and – aided by two allies, his spidery brother Lucien,

---

* The expedition's most lasting effect was archaeological. In July 1798, just after their arrival, Bonaparte's scientists discovered at Rosetta a stele of Ptolemy V, engraved in three languages – Greek, hieroglyphic and demotic – that, later handed to the British, allowed the translation of hieroglyphic, opening up the study of ancient Egyptian writing.

president at twenty-three of the legislature's lower house, the Council of Five Hundred, and Talleyrand – he agreed to be the 'sword' for a coup. At first the coup on 18 Brumaire (9 November) went wrong. Bonaparte strode into the Council of Ancients, the upper house, but fluffed his speech. The Council of Five Hundred refused to be dismissed. As Bonaparte wavered, Murat and his grenadiers expelled the Five Hundred and bullied the Ancients. Bonaparte emerged as first consul, ruler of France, approved by 99.95 per cent in a plebiscite. 'If he lasts a year,' said Talleyrand, reappointed foreign minister, 'he'll go far.'

After much screaming and sobbing, the first consul forgave Josephine's infidelities (while embarking on many of his own with enthusiasm but never virtuosity: 'Three minutes and it's over,' he told his staff). They moved into the royal apartments of the Tuileries. Bonaparte enjoyed their transformation. 'Come on, little creole,' he joked, lifting his wife into Antoinette's boudoir, 'get into the bed of your masters.' Josephine had the decency to confess, 'I can feel the queen's ghost, asking what I'm doing in her bed.'

The consul now turned to the anti-French coalition, as the Austrians took the offensive in Italy. Bonaparte led his army over the Alps, a Hannibalesque exploit with cannon instead of elephants, then, by superb manoeuvring and pure luck, defeated the Austrians at Marengo, pulling off a peace with both Austria and Spain that won France more territories – including the interior of America, Louisiana, which he planned to make the centre of a new empire. It gave Bonaparte a chance to consider what to do with France's rebel slaves.

TWO GENERALS: TOUSSAINT AND NAPOLEON

Toussaint had also emerged with a fancy new title along with the leadership of his country. Winning a vicious War of Knives in which he fought against a rival biracial warlord, André Rigaud, in July 1801 his Assembly approved a constitution entitled 'concernant la liberté des Nègres, des gens de couleurs et des Blancs' that appointed him Liberator, Protector and Governor-for-Life with the right to choose his successor. But he carefully examined Bonaparte's new French constitution: article 91 allowed some slavery to be reimposed in the Caribbean.

Protector Toussaint was keen to preserve the wealth of the plantations that were now disintegrating without slave labour: he and his generals Dessalines and Christophe now ran their own estates (Dessalines owned thirty), while imposing martial law to enforce indentured labour. Toussaint even discussed importing indentured labourers from Africa. But his regal powers inspired opposition, led by his own venal nephew General Moyse. When the latter tried to seize power, Toussaint had him shot and forty rebels fired out of cannon.

Toussaint assured Consul Bonaparte of the colony's loyalty, but 'under the administration of a black man'. Bonaparte approved, briefly. While he was in Egypt, Josephine had requested the return of her plantations. Toussaint restored them, sending her the income; Josephine entertained Toussaint's sons for dinner, and became fond of Placide. Bonaparte told the young men their father was 'a great man who'd rendered eminent services to France' and decided to recognize him as captain-general, hoping that he would lead a French army against British Jamaica and possibly America. Instead the Protector appeased the US and Britain; meanwhile, given that Spain was now a French ally, his occupation of Santo Domingo interfered with Bonaparte's Spanish relations

Canvassed by the slave masters' lobby, Bonaparte decided to restore slavery and destroy Toussaint, warning that his rule failed to recognize the 'sovereignty of the French people'. Refusing to 'tolerate a single epaulette on the shoulders of these negroes', Bonaparte told the Council of State, 'I'm for the whites, because I'm white and for no other reason . . . How could we have granted freedom to Africans, these men without civilization?' He added, 'If the . . . Convention had understood what they were doing and known about colonies, would have they abolished slavery? I very much doubt it.' He mustered an army of 20,000, later finding 23,000 reinforcements, his biggest overseas expedition, under Victoire-Emmanuel Leclerc, to whom he had married his most beautiful sister, Pauline. Bonaparte gave Leclerc detailed secret orders to first charm Toussaint, then, if he resisted, to eliminate him while publicly threatening that persons of colour who resisted would be 'devoured by fire like dried sugar cane'. Yet travelling with the French were two Saint-Domingue generals, and future leaders of Haiti, Alexandre Pétion and Jean-Pierre Boyer, both sons of French *colons* and enslaved women, who had been defeated by Toussaint and now backed the French. Realizing that the French aimed to restore white supremacy and chattel slavery, as they would soon do in Martinique and other colonies, Toussaint trained his 20,000 men, but declared, 'If I have to die under these circumstances, I'll face death honourably – like a soldier.'

The reality was worse. In January 1802, Toussaint watched Leclerc's troops disembarking. 'We must perish,' he concluded. 'All of France has come to Saint-Domingue.' Leclerc bungled his landing, but Toussaint ordered Dessalines and Christophe to destroy the town of Cap (once 'Paris of the Caribbean') and unleash 'fire and destruction . . . Destroy and burn everything so that those who come to re-enslave us always have before their eyes the image of hell they deserve.' The war was merciless: Leclerc ordered mass drownings of black prisoners and built a gas chamber on a ship using volcanic sulphur to suffocate 400 Haitians; Toussaint corkscrewed the eyes out of French captives.

Leclerc swung from genocidal fury to flaccid despair, barely coping with Pauline, though she was safe aboard his flagship; he told Napoleon that the surrounding chaos 'wore her down to the point of making her ill'. Reduced to a brigade of 4,000 that included devoted white officers and African-born female fighters, Toussaint fought a guerrilla campaign, travelling in disguise, sleeping on a plank; whites were massacred. 'Spare no one,' he ordered. 'We must conquer or die!' The French suffered punishing losses. By March 1802, half the French were dead or sick of yellow fever. Leclerc proposed a policy of mass killing; Pauline begged Bonaparte to recall him. Tormented by Pauline, who took a series of lovers from the few French soldiers not dying in the epidemic, Leclerc begged her to go home, but she consoled herself that 'Here I reign like Josephine; I hold first place.' But she reigned over desolation.

Yet the French advanced. Toussaint haemorrhaged men, and his generals Christophe and Dessalines negotiated pardons and then defected. Toussaint, forced to negotiate, met Leclerc, afterwards celebrating the ceasefire at a banquet attended by the commander and four future Haitian rulers. Toussaint retired to one of his estates, but Bonaparte demanded his capture. Leclerc, aided by his nemesis Dessalines, suborned a trusted ally to lure Toussaint to his estate where he was arrested and, along with his wife, sons (including Placide, who had joined the fight against the French) and devoted mixed-race servant Mars Plaisir, handed over to Leclerc. The chained Liberator was dispatched to France.* Between

---

* Toussaint warned Bonaparte, 'In overthrowing me, you've done no more than cut down the trunk of the tree of black liberty in Saint-Domingue. It will spring back from the roots, for they are numerous and deep.' He begged Bonaparte to free his wife Suzanne, but he never saw her or his sons again. While they were kept in captivity, Toussaint and Mars Plaisir were imprisoned in the Fort de Joux, a medieval fortress in the Jura Mountains, where Bonaparte systematically destroyed him: no contact with his family, no visitors, no reading materials, no medical care. Leclerc was terrified that he would escape to 'set the colony alight'. Bonaparte sent an aide who reported that the prisoner was 'self-possessed, cunning and skilful'. As Toussaint's health collapsed, he felt himself 'buried alive' but managed to dictate a testament, justifying his policies, pointing out that no 'white general' would have been treated like this: 'Does the colour of my skin get in the way of my honour and bravery?' But the winter was cruel: in April 1803, he was found dead in his cell.

May and July 1802, Bonaparte restored slavery in some Caribbean territories, which sparked a new war of liberation in Saint-Domingue. This
was led by Dessalines, who was elected commander-in-chief and joined
by Christophe, Boyer and Pétion. Dessalines slaughtered Toussaint's
white and black supporters. The French, Leclerc proposed to Bonaparte,
should 'destroy all the negroes of the mountains, men and women, and
keep only children below twelve, destroy half the blacks on the plains
and leave not a single man of colour who has worn an epaulette'. But
then he himself perished of fever.

In November, Pauline sailed back to Paris with his body;* his replacement, Donatien, vicomte de Rochambeau, son of Washington's ally,
deployed terror – mass drownings and public burnings, crucifixions
and feeding humans to dogs. He held a ball in Port-au-Prince for elite
mixed-race women, who banqueted in a black-lined hall after which their
host opened doors to a chamber where their husbands, just executed,
were displayed. Rochambeau ordered genocidal measures, the killing of
every black adult over the age of twelve and the import of new African
slaves. But on 18 November 1803, at Vertières, Dessalines vanquished
the French. Next day, Rochambeau opened negotiations. Dessalines
gave him ten days to evacuate 8,000 men. France's richest colony was
lost: Bonaparte was astonished – 'the greatest error I ever committed' –
reflecting later that he should just have appointed Toussaint as viceroy.
In the third of the three great revolutions, Toussaint and Dessalines
had changed the world: after the death of 30,000 French and 350,000
Haitians, Dessalines had defeated a European great power. But it was
decisive in another way too: it convinced Napoleon to sell the interior
of America.

Jefferson had first supported Bonaparte's crushing of Toussaint's
rebels, but when he discovered that the consul had regained Louisiana, the core of north America, this Francophile plotted to remove the
French, convinced that America needed the port of New Orleans. Jefferson threatened Bonaparte that he would ally with Britain if he did not
get it. He dispatched James Monroe to Paris just as Bonaparte realized
that he was losing Haiti.

---

* Bonaparte ordered Pauline to return to 'the consolation in the love of your family', but
she was 'a less than desolate widow'. Proud of her dynasty and beauty (Canova made the
plaster cast of her breasts which can be seen in the Museo Napoleonico, Rome), she was
determined to live passionately. Napoleon arranged her marriage to a feckless Roman
aristocrat, Prince Camillo Borghese – 'an imbecile', she thought – whom she cuckolded
wildly. Her brother tried to restrain her, advising, 'She should not indulge in these bad
manners.'

In April 1803, uninhibited by his suspicion of presidential power and imperial diplomacy, Jefferson purchased Louisiana for $15 million: 'It is the case of a guardian, investing the money of his ward in purchasing an important adjacent territory; & saying to him, when of age, I did this for your good.' Jefferson had doubled the size of America, swallowing what would be fifteen states and enabling the expansion of the nation into a continental power.* Fascinated by the stories of Captain Cook, he formed a Corps of Discovery, dispatching an expedition, led by Meriwether Lewis and William Clark, to explore the west and reach the Pacific. Soon afterwards, Jefferson met a rough, crude German immigrant whose trade in pelts, Chinese luxuries and Manhattan property would dovetail with American prosperity. The president thought the dour merchant, John Jacob Astor, aged forty, 'a most excellent man'.

Son of a butcher in Walldorf, near Heidelberg, Astor first moved to London to trade in music instruments, then, following a brother who joined the British Hessian mercenaries to America, he set up a music shop in New York, switching to the lucrative trade in beaver, ermine, mink and otter furs.

Setting out by canoe and cart, Astor bought pelts from Native Americans around the Canadian border, sometimes winning them over by playing the flute, sometimes selling rum and weapons, earning 1,000 per cent profits when the furs sold in London. After marrying a well-off New Yorker, Sarah Todd, with whom he soon had a large family, he started to send a network of trackers into Jefferson's newly opened lands and on to the Pacific, where California remained Spanish and where Russia had just claimed Alaska.

Astor, coarse, red-faced and avaricious, but a tireless organizer, lobbied politicians, lending money to Vice-President Burr and cultivating President Jefferson, who approved his plans. Often his trackers were massacred by Native Americans, but his American Fur Company prospered.

In April 1804, the president rushed home to Monticello where his daughter, Maria, was ailing. She died in his arms; but, while there, he conceived a child with Sally Hemings. When she gave birth to a son, Jefferson followed his tradition with Sally that each of their children were named after one of his friends: Dolley Madison, wife of the secretary of state, promised Sally a present if the son was named after her husband.

---

* Jefferson was later tempted by Cuba. 'I cordially confess', he wrote, 'that I have ever looked upon Cuba as the most interesting addition that could ever be made to our system of States.'

No present ever arrived, but the boy was named James Madison Hemings.*

Ironically, Jefferson's best service to mankind was linked to his dubious attitude towards slavery. He was aware that the greatest killer was smallpox. In Paris he had had Sally Hemings and her brothers inoculated. In May 1796, an English country doctor, Edward Jenner, noticing that milkmaids were immune to smallpox, scraped pus from a milkmaid's cowpox blister and injected it into a boy, who himself became immune: he called this vaccination, after *vacca*, cow. As with many advances, the discovery was not recognized by most doctors. It took amateurs and then leaders to deliver the benefits to the public, and that often required decades. In 1801, Jefferson heard about vaccination from a Harvard professor who – astonishingly – had received the vaccine by post across the Atlantic and sent it in a corked vial to the president. Jefferson realized there was 'no discovery in medicine equally valuable' and 'inoculated about 70 or 80 of my own family . . . Our whole experiment extended to about 200,' including some of his children and three slaves, of whom two, his butler Burwell Colbert and blacksmith Joseph Fossett, were immunized successfully. The shock of vaccination was that it was a medicine for people who were not yet sick, leading to an anti-vaxxing movement. 'As mindboggling as it is to contemplate a sitting president conducting experimental drug trials in his spare time', writes Steven Johnson, it was appropriate that a non-doctor should defeat anti-vaxxers and promote the most important cure of modern times. Jefferson publicized his findings, leading Congress to pass the Vaccine Act in 1813. It took forty years for Britain to catch up.

Back in Paris, Bonaparte, still only thirty-three, was sitting in his bath when his brothers Joseph, the eldest, and Lucien attacked his decision to sell Louisiana. 'I know the price of what I abandon,' he shouted, standing up starkers. 'I renounce it with the greatest regret.' Now his chief American preoccupation was the marriage of his youngest brother

---

* President Jefferson immediately faced a challenge from the slaving dynasties of Tripoli, Algiers and Tunis, the 'Barbary States' that benefited from the trans-Saharan slavery and the seizure of western cargoes and 'white slaves'. Britain and Spain, even Sweden and Denmark, were perennially at war with these predators or paying them tribute. Tripoli had been ruled since 1711 by a dynasty founded by an Ottoman officer Ahmed Karamanli. In May 1801 his descendant Yusuf Pasha demanded tribute from the US and declared war. Jefferson sent a naval squadron into Tripoli harbour and in April 1805, while Europe was distracted by Bonaparte's campaigns, the former US consul, William Eaton, led eight Americans and 500 Berber, Arab and Greek mercenaries from Alexandria to take Yusuf's town of Derna. Yusuf backed down and freed his white slaves. It was America's first Islamic war.

Jérôme, a feckless naval officer, to an heiress, Betsy Patterson, in Baltimore. Napoleon furiously ordered Jérôme to return, complaining about his avaricious family. The Bonapartes were jealous of Josephine and her Beauharnais children – her charming son Eugène, who served on Napoleon's staff, and her intelligent, beautiful daughter Hortense – though Napoleon himself preferred them to his own fissiparous brothers. But he tried to reconcile the families by marrying his brother Louis to Hortense. Whatever their faults – and they were legion – he planned to found the greatest dynasty since Charlemagne.

ONE EMPEROR AND FIVE KINGDOMS

On 2 December 1804, at Notre-Dame, in a ceremony at which Pope Pius VII officiated, Bonaparte crowned himself emperor, wearing a long satin gown chased with gold, a scarlet ermine mantel and a golden laurel crown. He whispered to his brother Joseph in Italian, 'If only Daddy could us now,' but their mother Letizia, who had survived thirteen pregnancies, was there to see their apotheosis. Joseph had tried to stop Josephine being crowned empress, because Louis and Hortense's offspring would thereby be imperial grandchildren while his would be grandchildren of a bourgeois. The Bonaparte sisters refused to carry her train, but Napoleon insisted: 'My wife's a good woman. She satisfies herself with diamonds, nice dresses and the misfortunes of her ageing . . . If I make her an empress, it's act of justice. I am above all a fair man.' He then crowned a kneeling, weeping Josephine, wearing a white robe and a gilded satin mantel, with diamonds spangled across her coronet, belt, necklace and earrings, and 'so well made up, she looked twenty-five'.

The emperor, at war with Britain, Russia and Austria, felt that the title would enable him to negotiate with Romanovs and Habsburgs. In August 1802, he had clinched the first consulate for life, and France had already conquered a European empire from Belgium to Italy. In January 1804, a Bourbon assassination conspiracy had focused his attention on monarchy. 'They seek to destroy the Revolution by attacking my person. I will defend it for *I am* the Revolution,' he proclaimed, adding, 'The hereditary principle could alone prevent a counter-revolution.'* In May,

---

* 'An end should be put to the hopes of the Bourbons,' Napoleon said, ordering the kidnap and execution of a Bourbon prince, the duc d'Enghien, who had no connection to the plots. He later claimed it had been Talleyrand's idea, but the foreign minister denounced

the French endorsed him as *empereur des français*, a new monarchy approved by plebiscite, its stability assured by dynasty – which he briskly designed, borrowing as his emblem the bees of the Merovingians and creating a meritocratic aristocracy and marshalate. Joseph was raised to grand elector and Louis to constable of France, but Napoleon grumbled bitterly about their irresponsible squabbling: as 'the sole instrument of my destiny, I owe nothing to my brothers'. Murat was rewarded by marriage to his sister Caroline, a grand dukedom, a marshal's baton and the title *premier chevalier d'Europe*. Napoleon annulled the American marriage of Jérôme, whom he forgave, while the demands of his sisters made him laugh. 'To listen to my sisters,' he joked, 'you'd think I'd mismanaged the inheritance of our father, the late king.' Soon afterwards, Napoleon, who was already *il presidente della Repubblica Italiana*, was crowned king of Italy. '*Pourvu que ça dure*,' muttered their mother. 'Long may it last.'

Most politicians struggle to differentiate between their own interests and those of the state, but dictators believe the two are identical. In Napoleon's case, this delusion justified the deaths of hundreds of thousands in battles to secure his personal rule during a tumultuous decade. But his coronation outraged many. One of them was a young south American admirer, in Paris that day, Simón Bolívar, who fulminated, 'Henceforth, I viewed him as a hypocritical tyrant.' In Vienna, the composer Beethoven ripped the title page of his Third Symphony in half. 'Is he then, also, nothing more than an ordinary man?' he asked. 'He'll exalt himself above all others and become a tyrant.' Beethoven changed the dedication *Entitled Bonaparte* and renamed it the *Heroic*, 'in memory of a great man'.*

Napoleon now wanted peace with Britain, hoping that London would

---

it acutely as 'Worse than a crime, it was a mistake.' Much of Europe was disgusted by the murder and by the coronation, which intensified the hostility of the European dynasties: the Russian emperor Alexander called him 'the Corsican Ogre'.

* Beethoven, grandson of a wine merchant and musician, son of an alcoholic court singer for the elector of Cologne, settled in Vienna in 1794, writing pieces for aristocratic patrons, but he targeted an altogether grander audience – the people, his times and posterity. He was singular, sociable with friends, but never married and was, said Goethe, 'completely intractable'. Now he was alone in another way: he was going deaf: 'Ah how could I possibly admit an infirmity in the one sense which ought to be more perfect in me than others,' he wrote to his brother. 'I must live almost alone like an exile.' He contemplated death: 'It's only my art that held me back. Oh it seemed impossible for me to leave this world before I had produced all I felt capable of producing and so I prolonged this wretched existence.' He wrote tortured letters to an unknown woman, his 'Immortal Beloved': 'No one else can ever possess my heart never never . . . Vienna is now a wretched life.' He consoled himself with visits to 'fortresses' (brothels). Beethoven personified the suffering genius, hero of the Romantic movement.

be satisfied with its world empire while he dominated Europe, but it was British policy, starting with William III and continuing into the twenty-first century, to challenge any single power dominating Europe. In May 1804, Pitt, now forty-five, returned to power, after a short hiatus. Power had aged him: he had achieved much, including in 1801 the addition of Ireland to join England and Scotland in the United Kingdom. Now an alcoholic, nicknamed the Three-Bottle Man for his port compulsion, prescribed by his doctor, he was determined to stop Napoleon, funding Austrian, Prussian and Russian armies on land and deploying the Royal Navy at sea. Napoleon decided to invade – 'it is necessary for us to be masters of the sea for six hours only and England will have ceased to exist' – and ordered his Franco-Spanish fleet to smash the Royal Navy.

When Austria joined the third coalition, Napoleon performed what he called a 'pirouette' and dispatched his *Grande Armée* into Germany. In September 1805, he conducted a virtuoso campaign in which he outmanoeuvred his enemies ('I've destroyed the Austrian army simply by marches,' he told Josephine) and then in December, after taking Vienna and spending a night at Schönbrunn, he joined his army at Austerlitz, taking advantage of sluggish Austrian commanders, the jejune bungling of the overconfident Russian emperor Alexander and poor coordination between the two, while displaying his masterful ability to apply maximum force at the right point and the right time to smash the Austrian and Russian armies: 'Let's finish this war with a thunderclap.' On the battlefield he wrote to Josephine: 'I've beaten the Russian and Austrian army commanded by the two emperors. I am a little tired.'

Yet just as he won European hegemony by land, his fleet was routed at Trafalgar by Nelson, who was himself killed in the battle. The British victory limited the sustainability of Napoleon's empire and established British naval dominance for a century. At a dinner in London, Pitt, exhausted and ailing, responded to acclamation as 'saviour of Europe' with laconic eloquence: 'Europe is not to be saved by any single man. England has saved herself by her exertions, and will, as I trust, save Europe by her example.' But when he heard of Austerlitz he realized the momentum lay with Napoleon: 'Roll up that map; it will not be wanted these ten years.'

The day after Austerlitz, Napoleon met the Habsburg emperor Franz, grandson of Maria Theresa, whose Habsburg wholesomeness amused the peripatetic Corsican. He was 'so moral', laughed Napoleon, 'he never made love to anyone but this wife'. Trained by his 'second father' Emperor Joseph, who thought him dutiful but unimaginative, Franz spoke Viennese German, as well as Czech and Italian, cultivating a style of folksy familiarity and giving general audiences (open to the public) twice a week while wearing a plain military coat, Joseph-style. But he was also suspicious and jealous of his brothers, particularly the fine commander Karl, whom he spied on. He was almost capable of wit: when told of a Tyrolese patriot fighting the French, he replied, 'I know he's a patriot – but is he a patriot for me?' He preferred uxorious life with his wives – he married four times – and toffee-making to detailed politics. Horrified by the swaggering conqueror but agonizingly polite, Franz bitterly acquiesced in Napoleon's reordering of Europe: the Roman empire was replaced by a Rhine Confederation led by Napoleon. Franz had already changed his own title to emperor of Austria.

On 23 January 1806, Pitt died aged forty-six of a burst ulcer (saying either 'Oh my country' or 'I think I could eat one of Bellamy's porkpies'), succeeded by his cousin Grenville, the first of a succession of 'friends of Mister Pitt' who were all determined to destroy Napoleon.* The emperor designed a blockade to cut off the income of the 'nation of shopkeepers' while he remained at war with the Russian tsar, who was joined by Prussia. 'Your Majesty', Napoleon warned the Prussian king, 'will be defeated.' In October 1806, Napoleon routed the Prussians at Jena (where Hegel, seeing him riding past, marvelled at witnessing 'the World-Spirit ride out of town . . . an individual on horseback raising his arm over the world and ruling it'), then the Russians at Eylau and Friedland. 'And what are two thousand men killed in a great battle?' mused Napoleon.

The victories forced Russia to negotiate. On a raft at Tilsit, the emperor was charmed by the strapping, blue-eyed and fair-haired Tsar Alexander, an inscrutable master of duplicity who had survived the courts of his grandmother Catherine the Great and his tyrannical father Paul the Mad, in whose murder he had colluded. Now the chastened Romanov collaborated with the Corsican Ogre in a carve-up of Europe, gaining Finland among other territories.

Napoleon locked in his victories by elevating his family: his brothers

---

* Grenville was also forced to preside over the *Delicate Investigation* into the scandalous conduct of Princess Caroline, wife of the prince of Wales, which ruled that while, as a footman testified, 'The princess was very fond of fucking,' none of it was provable nor was the rumour that a boy she had adopted was her own illegitimate child. Caroline was as popular as George was hated, remaining a lightning rod of radical opposition until her death in 1824.

became kings – Joseph of Naples, Louis of the Netherlands, Jérôme of Westphalia; his stepson Eugène became viceroy of Italy.* Napoleon bullied and lectured his royal brothers, telling his favourite Joseph, 'You must be a king and talk like a king,' something Joseph never quite managed, and reprimanding Jérôme for being funny: 'Your letter was too witty. You don't need wit in war.'

King Louis, married to Josephine's daughter Hortense, went native, announcing, 'From the moment I set foot on Dutch soil, I became Dutch.' This outraged the emperor, who said, 'If you continue to govern by whingeing, if you allow yourself to be bullied', he would be of no use. Napoleon went on, 'You tire me needlessly . . . Only women cry and complain; men act; you'll make me regret your weakness. More energy, more energy!' The brothers in turn were jealous and resentful; no one had Napoleon's energy, certainly not Louis, whom the emperor soon sacked as Netherlands king – but he was more useful dynastically. Hortense gave birth to a boy, Louis-Napoleon, but then flaunted her affair with Talleyrand's natural son with whom she had an illegitimate son, Charles de Morny. Long afterwards, Louis-Napoleon would sit on the French throne – and Morny would put him there.

As Napoleon reordered the smaller states of Germany, he unknowingly launched the career of the Jewish banker who became known as the Napoleon of Finance.

THE KINGS OF CAPITAL: THE ROTHSCHILDS

Nathan Mayer Rothschild was the son of Mayer Amschel Rothschild, the court agent of Wilhelm IX, prince-elector of Hesse-Kassel, who had made a fortune renting out Hessian mercenaries (usually to Britain, for which they fought in America) and now had made the mistake of backing Prussia. Napoleon punished Wilhelm by giving Hesse to his brother King Jérôme. Wilhelm entrusted his money to Rothschild to conceal it from the French emperor. Rothschild had already dispatched Nathan to Britain, where he used the Hessian capital to set up a family who

---

* The only enduring Bonapartist crown is the one he did not initiate: his marshal Bernadotte, once a fanatical republican with 'Death to kings' tattooed on his chest, was competent, haughty and unimpressed by Napoleon, who in turn was unimpressed by him: 'Very mediocre; I've no faith in him.' But he was semi-family, married to Désirée Clary, Napoleon's first love, and sister of Joseph's wife, Julie. When in May 1810 the heir of the last Vasa king of Sweden died, the Swedes offered the throne to Bernadotte. Clever enough to betray Napoleon at the right moment, in 1812, he ruled Sweden as King Carl Johan until 1844. The Bernadottes still reign.

would personify the new era of international capitalism and become the richest in the world.

'A rather big man who wore a round unpowdered wig and small goatee beard', Mayer Rothschild had been born in the Judengasse – Jews' Lane – of the Frankfurt Ghetto, created by Frederick the Fat in 1458 to protect and squeeze Jews. Given that Jews were banned from owning land, prohibited from entering parks, bars and promenades and forced to wear yellow rings and step off the pavement and doff their hat if any non-Jew said to them, 'Jew, do your duty,' they had little choice but to concentrate on their faith and work in commerce. Rothschild, originally a dealer in coins and textiles, became *Hoffaktor* – court fixer – to Wilhelm IX and then to Emperor Franz. Although Joseph II and the French revolution had started the process of relieving Jews from their restrictions, Rothschild worked to win civil equality for 'our nation', whose people craved liberty but refused to give up their Judaism. This would be an enduring Rothschild mission.

Now that Napoleon had cancelled Hesse-Kassel, Rothschild smuggled four chests of coin to Britain, where, first in Manchester, then in London, Mayer's third son Nathaniel invested Wilhelm's money, giving the family a powerful foundation as they transformed themselves from court Jews and textile traders into bankers. Mayer's wife Gutle, who had survived ten pregnancies, was tough enough to withstand a French raid and interrogation in pursuit of the Hessian treasure. But women were excluded from the family business: when Mayer died at sixty-eight, he left a moderate fortune and a will specifying that property must pass through the male line only, which encouraged marriage among family members. Nathaniel, aggressive and ingenious, emerged as the leader of the five brothers, honouring their father's insistence on the family's 'unbreakable unity' by placing his brothers in different European capitals. 'My brother in London is the commanding general,' said Salomon Rothschild, who covered the Habsburgs in Vienna, 'I'm his field marshal,' adding, 'No disapproval shall be expressed by either of us at the conduct of the other since we act always for the joint interest.'

The move to London placed them perfectly: the Rothschilds would be beneficiaries of three world-changing movements. First was industrial expansion, based on British textiles and steel and powered by coal and steam, soon spreading to Germany and France. Next was the opening up of society to talent and the start of mass politics fostered by Napoleon, who by removing restrictions on Jews allowed them to take part in western communities for the first time. Finally, Napoleon's war obliged nations to deploy armies so large that they had to be financed by a grow-ing capital market that this family would shape – and dominate – for a century.

Their opportunity arrived fast as Napoleon, having settled the east, turned westwards, determined to force Portugal and Spain to join his war against Britain. The emperor resembled a shark who had to keep feeding to stay alive. But each new conquest opened the possibility of another which he could not resist but which further stretched his resources. Spain was ruled by an inept ménage à trois of a bluff oft-cuckolded Bourbon king, Carlos IV, his impulsive queen María Luisa and her preposterous lover, Manuel Godoy, nicknamed El Chorizo – the Sausage – in a nod to his province of Extremadura, known for its meat, and to his formidable sexual equipment. The queen one day saw the Sausage strumming his guitar and fell in love. In 1792 the king jovially appointed the twenty-eight-year-old popinjay as secretary of state, later garlanded with two dukedoms and then with the preposterous title *príncipe de la paz* (prince of peace). Godoy was soon the most hated sausage in Spain.*

Napoleon smelled blood in the water. When he wrote to warn Carlos of Godoy's cuckoldry, the Sausage intercepted it but just passed it on to Carlos – who ignored it. Napoleon easily manipulated the three, along with the embittered heir, Fernando, into joining him in an invasion of Portugal that inserted French troops into Spain; next he persuaded the royal couple to abdicate their throne altogether. He appointed Joseph as king, replacing him in Naples with his brother-in-law Murat. The *premier chevalier* – whom Napoleon called 'the bravest man in the world . . . decked out in gold and feathers that rose above his head like a church tower' – was in Spain at the time commanding the French army. He occupied Madrid, but on 2–3 May 1808 the Madrileños rebelled. 'French blood has spilt,' said Murat. 'It demands vengeance. All arrested will be shot.' The crackdown unleashed a ferocious insurgency, its atrocities gruesomely sketched by Goya in his *Disasters of War*. Napoleon called this 'my Spanish ulcer', admitting 'the injustice was too cynical . . . it remains very ugly'.

In Portugal, he had provoked something just as extraordinary. On 29 November 1807, as French troops advanced on Lisbon, the *príncipe regente*, João VI, a long-faced, fat-lipped, bleary-eyed, pot-bellied

---

* Juggling the attention of a wife, an armada of girlfriends and the queen, Godoy com-missioned the court painter, Francisco Goya, to paint his paramour Pepita, the contessa di Castillo Fiel, in *La maja vestida* but also naked in the sensuous *La maja desnuda*, which he kept in an alcove behind a curtain alongside Velázquez's *Venus*.

vacillator who lived in the palace-monastery of Mafra accompanied only by priests and a force of bats deployed to kill the raging insects, left for Brazil.

Zulus and Saudis, Christophes, Kamehamehas and Astors

TROPICAL MONARCHIES: KINGS OF HAITI AND BRAZIL

João had long ruled in place of his insane mother Queen Maria, a religious hysteric haunted by the devil and treated vainly by George III's 'mad-doctor' Willis. João's real enemy was his Spanish wife, Carlota Joaquina, skinny, sharp-faced, warty, moustachioed and lame, who, while fiercely riding horses, learning to fire cannon and relishing love affairs, tried to overthrow her husband and rule in Spain's interest. This did not enhance marital harmony.

Now João agonized for months then courageously decided to defy Napoleon and move his court to Brazil. As panicking courtiers mobbed the docks at Belém loading their belongings, ladies abandoned their carriages and waded fully clothed out to the ships, some of them drowning. João arrived disguised as a woman and boarded the *Príncipe Real* accompanied by his treasonous wife, seven children and the demented queen, who kept saying, 'Go slower! They'll think we're running away.' When over 12,000 Portuguese had embarked on a British fleet of fifteen warships and forty smaller vessels, they sailed, playing cards all the way to Rio.

On arrival, the Brazilians were unimpressed by the royal family: although bathing was prized by creoles in Rio, the *príncipe regente* never fully washed. But the people of Rio – the Cariocas (from the Tupi Kara-i-oka) – were excited to share the first American capital of a European dynasty.

This was a city run on slavery. Slaves worked as casual labourers, sold food and carried masters in sedan chairs, while new slaves arrived from Africa at the docks. The *príncipe regente* owned 38,000 slaves. The Braganzas embraced Brazil's eclectic culture, forming a theatrical company of enslaved African musicians, but they were shocked by the chaotic informality of 'this infamous Babylon', African in appearance, its festivals combining Portuguese Catholicism with African ritual. The king, after the death of Maria the Mad, was happy to remain in Brazil

– as British troops under Wellington fought the French in Portugal – a decision that would lead to an independent south American monarchy.

It would not be the only one. On 1 January 1804, Governor-General-for-Life Dessalines declared the independence of a new republic that he called Haiti, its Taíno name – a nation of freed slaves, the second free republic in the Americas and the first country to abolish slavery. 'It is not enough to expel the barbarians that drenched it in blood,' he declaimed. 'Soldiers! give all nations a terrible but just example of vengeance.' He promised 'to kill every Frenchman who soils the land of freedom'. Five hundred were hanged in a row, and hundreds of men, women and children* were paraded to the port, the women raped, then all drowned in front of foreign merchants. Pregnant women were killed to prevent the birth of more Frenchmen. The killings – somewhere between 600 and 4,000, mainly butchered with knives – were designed to ensure the French would never return. The bloodshed was brutal, yet it was a small atrocity compared to the 350,000 killed by the French.

'I've avenged America,' said Dessalines, but the killing of all whites helped destroy the Haitian economy. On 6 October, he was crowned Emperor Jacques I of Haiti. His empress Marie-Claire Heureuse Félicité cared for wounded Frenchmen, begged her husband to spare the whites and hid some of them in their house (while also raising their own seven children and those of his many paramours). The emperor protected and gave a job to his old French slave master, but he backed the 90 per cent of black Haitians against the mixed-raced elite, a rivalry that still undermines the country in the twenty-first century.

The emperor rightly feared that France would try to regain the colony: he ordered his general Henry Christophe to start the building of the huge fortress La Citadelle and other defences. Jacques himself, rapacious ruler of plantations, used his army and the Haitian whip, the *coco-macac*, to enforce the labour of the *cultivateurs* who now toiled in the fields. His generals conspired against him; in October 1806, the

---

* The author of the Haitian Declaration of Independence was the first Haitian intellectual, Louis Boisrond-Tonnerre, a carpenter's son who had been educated in France, known as Tonnerre (Thunder) because his cradle had been hit by lightning. He encouraged the massacre: 'For our declaration of independence, we should have the skin of a white man for parchment, his skull for an inkwell, his blood for ink, and a bayonet for a pen!' One of the killers was Jean Zombi, whose name spread the spectre of 'zombies' in western imaginations. The idea of zombies derived from west Africa, particularly Dahomey, where nothing was so terrifying as the undead deadness of slavery: the enslaved, it was believed, became half dead but still alive. Zombi's killings reversed the sorcery. The only whites spared were the Poles in the French army, whom Dessalines, aware of the Russian massacres of Poles in Warsaw, called 'the White Negroes of Europe'.

emperor marched to crush the rebels but, lured to Alexandre Pétion's house in Port-au-Prince, he was shot and stabbed and his head was sliced open. A crowd then paraded his dismembered body, shouting, 'The tyrant is dead!'

After Jacques, Henry Christophe, English-speaking, veteran of the American War of Independence, former waiter, drummer boy and paladin, became president, with the mixed-race Pétion, sometime French ally and enemy of Louverture, as Senate president, but they quickly fell out. Pétion ruled the south leniently, breaking up the estates while favouring his own mixed-race elite. Nicknamed *Papa Bon Coeur*, he was advised by one of the most remarkable women in American history, his paramour Marie-Madeleine Lachenais, daughter of a French colonel and an African woman. Later in Pétion's rule, she became the lover of his secretary and heir General Boyer and so was known as *La Présidente de Deux Présidents*. But the Haitians were far from finished with monarchy.

In the north, President Henry Christophe came to power just as Wilberforce and the British abolitionists who were finally making progress.

On 23 February 1807, Grenville, the prime minister who with Wilberforce had backed abolition in Pitt's garden, ensured that the Act for the Abolition of the Slave Trade was passed in the Commons by 283 votes to 16. Britain was not the first: Denmark had abolished the trade four years earlier at the second attempt. But Britain had the power to impose abolition, sending warships, soon upgraded to the West Africa Squadron based at Freetown, that seized 1,600 slave ships, freeing 150,000 slaves. Haiti was the only country that had so far abolished slavery itself. Wilberforce and Clarkson were soon in contact with Christophe.*

On 26 March 1811, Christophe was crowned King Henry I (*premier monarque couronné du Nouveau-Monde* as well as defender of the faith) by a white priest, alongside his queen Marie Louise,† whose free father had owned the Crown tavern where they had met. They were enthroned on a

---

* Across the world, in Britain's penal colony in Australia, a military coup had just taken place. Since the foundation of the colony, the Wales Corps had served as a garrison, increasingly trading in 'rum' – wheat-based booze from Bengal. With a shortage of coins, this moonshine was used as currency. When a new governor, Admiral Bligh, who had accompanied Captain Cook then survived a mutiny on his ship *Bounty*, became governor, he tried to end the commercial dealings of the so-called Rum Corps. In 1808, irate soldiers marched on Government House, arrested Bligh and seized power, which they held for two years – the first military coup in the British empire since Cromwell. When a new governor arrived, civilian power was restored and the corps was disbanded.

† Queen Marie Louise was a half-sister of Cécile Fatiman, the voodoo *mambo* who had started the rebellion in 1790.

platform seventy feet high under a scarlet canopy in a church shrouded with sky-blue silk. At the celebrations afterwards, King Henry toasted 'my dear brother George III – invincible obstacle to the unbridled ambition of Napoleon', though, like the emperor, he created a Christophean aristocracy led by four princes and eight dukes: his commander-in-chief became the duc de Marmelade and he co-opted Emperor Jacques's nephews as barons and equerries. Yet he also promoted intellectuals of the Haitian Enlightenment. The writer Julien Prévost became foreign minister and comte de Limonade, and his ideologist was the historian Valentin de Vastey, now a baron.

The king and queen ordered royal carriages and regalia in London – engraved 'Liberty, Equality and Henry', their crest declaring 'Reborn from the ashes', their court revelling in its gold braid and spectacular uniforms. The queen led her own unit of Royal Amazons who paraded at annual fetes, celebrating with lightshows and pyramids, creole songs, *kalinda* and *samba* dancing.

Autocratic and short-tempered, the king was irrepressibly energetic, the first great black statesman of modern times, dreaming of creating an orderly rich and educated Haiti that would show whites that a black kingdom could equal or overtake them. He faced the constant threat of internal rivals and French invasion, enforcing his power with a Royal Corps of Dahomey – 4,000 troops imported from west Africa – while completing Emperor Jacques's fortress, Citadelle La Ferrière, where thousands of labourers reportedly perished. His Sans-Souci Palace in Milot, featuring marble floors cooled by water from mountain springs, was just one of his fifteen chateaux, 'erected by the descendants of Africans', wrote baron de Vastey, 'to show we have not lost the architectural taste and genius of our ancestors who covered Ethiopia, Egypt, Carthage and old Spain with their superb monuments'.

Son of a French slave owner and a free black woman, Vastey, a cousin of Bonaparte's general Dumas, reacted against Enlightened apologies for slavery and racism, placing the stories of Haitian cruelty in context by exposing France's 'unheard-of crimes that made nature shudder', in works that were widely read in Europe and America – the first intellectual of colour to win a world readership, the first to write black history. Wary of a new French invasion and keen to unite Haiti, King Henry raided Pétion's rival state and created his own navy under a British admiral. He was an Anglophile who consulted Clarkson on his vision of teaching Haitians English literature and language. Clarkson sent English teachers to the king, who in turn supported Clarkson's campaign to abolish slavery altogether.

Grenville's Act was far from the end of the slave trade. Some 700,000 people remained enslaved on British plantations, 300,000 in Jamaica. Brazil, Cuba and the French colonies still demanded more slaves, as new technical developments made them even more important in the USA.

Jefferson had survived the revelations about his family with Sally Hemings to be re-elected president in 1804.* In 1807, a month after Grenville's Act, he signed an Act Prohibiting Importation of Slaves, but he remained uncertain about how to abolish slavery itself and suspicious about real liberation, refusing to recognize Haiti and allowing slavery to be extended into the Louisiana Purchase.

Just when it looked as if the profitability of slavery was ebbing, an invention suddenly placed slavery at the centre of American prosperity. In 1793, Eli Whitney, a Savannah schoolteacher, helped create a machine with a more effective system of rollers for clearing the seeds from the cotton. This cotton engine – a gin – helped make cotton planting vastly profitable. Southern planters switched to cotton growing, the cotton sent to New England mills or via New York to British Manchester. In 1793, a total of 500,000 pounds was exported. By 1810, it was 85 million, 20 per cent of US exports. Ten years later it had doubled. Slavery had become essential to the south.

Further west, Astor's trackers were exploring river and coast in their pursuit of pelts. Astor founded his own Pacific town, Astoria, and dispatched ships to Alaska, then to Hawaii and China to trade pelts for sandalwood, tea, opium and spices. He poured the profits from his American Fur Company into New York property, buying Burr's estate and much else. By the 1820s, Astor was America's first millionaire. Surprisingly, his rival in the Pacific trade was neither American nor European but a Hawaiian conqueror.

---

* Jefferson decided to drop his vice-president, Aaron Burr, from the ticket. When Burr ran for New York governor, his old ally Hamilton called him an 'unprincipled voluptuary' and backed his opponent. Burr lost. On 11 July 1804, the men met to duel for their honour: Hamilton fired in the air but Burr shot him lethally in the stomach, shattering his liver. Burr fled but was never tried. Instead, rejected by the republic he had helped create, he planned to found an empire in the south-west, carved out of the Louisiana Purchase and Spanish Mexico. The details are murky, yet he probably imagined himself as emperor. If it seems preposterous now, this was a time when an obscure Corsican had made himself emperor of Europe. But when he approached the US commander, the latter informed Jefferson, who backed his prosecution. When Burr was acquitted, he left America, travelling in Europe, returning only in old age.

WIVES OF THE CONQUERORS:
KAMEHAMEHA AND NAPOLEON

Far to the west, Kamehameha, king of Hawaii, who resided at his villa in Kailua-Kona with his thirty wives and twenty-five children,* was completing the conquest of Hawaii, aided by his British gunner John Young, whom he raised to the nobility and married to his niece. While he still ruled as a warrior conqueror, wearing the yellow *ahuala* cape made up of 250,000 feathers of the (now extinct) mamo bird, leading his armies and personally making human sacrifices, he always appreciated European technology. After trading sandalwood with the Europeans and Americans, he constructed his own fleet of twenty ships to trade with China, America and Russian Alaska – an extraordinary performance that contradicts the traditional narrative of European imperialism. As Kamehameha was at his peak, so was Napoleon.

In September 1808, at Erfurt in Germany, Tsar Alexander, four kings and a glittering entourage of aristocrats and nobles paid court to the hegemon of Europe.

Napoleon believed that 'There must be a superior power which dominates all the others with enough authority to force them to live in harmony' and that power was France. Britain and the rest of Europe disagreed. Napoleon had already overreached – his brothers lacked grip, Habsburgs and Romanovs were conspiring and Talleyrand, whom he cordially hated as 'shit in a silk stocking', was betraying him. 'It is for you to save Europe,' Talleyrand told Alexander, 'to resist Napoleon. The French are *civilized* – their sovereign is *not*.' Alexander despised the Ogre but played his vanity sublimely. 'I'm happy with Alexander,' Napoleon told Josephine. 'Were he a woman, I think I'd take him as my lover.'

In March 1809, Emperor Franz dispatched armies into Germany, Poland and Italy to restore Austrian pride and the balance of power in Europe, but in a series of battles culminating at Wagram, just across the Danube from Vienna, Napoleon defeated Franz's brother, Archduke Karl. 'My enemies are defeated, thrashed, in full rout,' he told Josephine. In Vienna, Beethoven sheltered from Napoleon's shelling in his brother's basement with cushions over his ears. Napoleon occupied the capital, imposing stringent terms on the Habsburgs. He also survived

---

* Kamehameha married for both love and prestige: he married Keopuolani, daughter of King Kiwalao, whom he had sacrificed, but they lived separately. She had fourteen children, four by the king, ten by her lovers. But his chief adviser was his favourite, Queen Ka'ahumanu, funny, clever and weighing 500 pounds, whom he appointed regent.

an assassination attempt. This, along with close misses in battle, the death of his heir and nephew, Louis's eldest son, and his own fathering of two illegitimate sons by different paramours, combined to convince him that he must divorce Josephine, now forty-six. As she cried and fainted, he told her, 'You have children, I have none. You must feel the necessity of strengthening my dynasty.'

Napoleon proposed marriage into the Romanovs – to Alexander's beloved sister Catherine. Alexander was horrified by the Ogre's presumption. Catherine was quickly married off, leaving a younger sister Anna. But Napoleon switched from the Romanovs to Europe's grandest dynasty, the Habsburgs.

'I pity the poor princess he chooses,' laughed the eighteen-year-old Maria Ludovica, better known as Marie Louise, pretty, sunny, fair-haired daughter of Emperor Franz – before she knew it was her. When she did, she sighed, 'I resign myself to Divine Providence.' The newest dynasty was marrying the oldest. The marriage took place by proxy before the archduchess set off for France. When she arrived at the Compiègne Palace, the couple were mutually impressed, she exclaiming, 'You are much better-looking than your portrait,' and he so delighted that he consummated the marriage before the formal celebrations. 'She liked it so much,' boasted Napoleon, 'she asked me to do it again.'

WELLESLEYS, ROTHSCHILDS AND THE WOMAN
WHO RIDES UPON THE BEAST

Napoleon was so keen on the empress, he retired his favourite mistress and spent every night with Marie Louise, though he reflected, 'I loved Marie Louise . . . I loved Josephine better; that was natural; we'd risen together; she was full of grace.' Marie fell in love with him, telling her father, 'I assure you, dear papa . . . the better one knows him, the better one appreciates and loves him.'

'Ought princesses to fall in love?' Napoleon wondered later. 'They are political chattels.'

In March 1811, as Napoleon advised his obstetrician to 'Pretend you're not delivering the empress but a bourgeois from the rue Saint-Denis,' Marie gave birth to a king of Rome, Napoleon François, after an agonizing labour. 'I'm not soft-hearted, yet I was much moved how she suffered,' he said, boasting tactlessly to Josephine, 'My son is big and healthy.' He was ecstatic: 'My family's allied to all the sovereigns of Europe.' That was true, but all of his new relatives were conspiring to bring about his downfall. Designed to destroy Britain, his blockade known as the Continental System was neither continental nor systematic. Britain was defiant under a 'friend of Mister Pitt', Spencer Perceval, an evangelical who regarded Napoleon as 'the woman who rides upon the beast' in the Book of Revelations. Marquess Wellesley had fancied his chances at becoming prime minister, but a vicious feud with his ex-actress wife and a sex addiction that embarrassed even his brother Arthur meant that he had to settle for foreign secretary. Perceval and Wellesley, seeking a way to attack the French–Spanish alliance, were persuaded by a south American adventurer to send an army to Venezuela.* Arthur Wellesley, tempered by his Marathan victories, was designated commander, but the army was redirected to support the Spanish insurgency. After quickly defeating the French at Talavera, the general, raised to Viscount Wellington, became loved by his soldiers, who called him Beau; he called them 'the scum of the earth' as well as 'fine fellows': 'I don't know what effect these men will have upon the enemy, but, by God, they frighten me.' Despising vainglory, he said, 'There's only one thing worse than a battle won and that's a battle lost' – though he never discovered what losing was like.

Wellington was constantly short of funds. Nathan Mayer Rothschild, trading in bullion with the continent and lending it to the government, now offered to smuggle it to Wellington to pay his army. The 'government didn't know how to get it to Portugal', he explained. 'I undertook all that and I sent it to France.' This vast and secret work laid the foundation for the family fortune – 'the best business I ever did'. The youngest Rothschild brother, James, handled the delivery across the Channel and on to Wellington. 'Mister Rothschild', said Lord Liverpool, the war secretary who appointed him Wellington's supplier, was 'a special friend . . . I don't know what we should have done without him.' NM, using his own secret couriers and informants, communicating with his brothers using codes for gold such as 'fatman', 'fish', 'beer' and 'children', was soon delivering not only British gold to Wellington but the subsidies to Russia, Prussia and Austria – £42 million between 1810 and 1815. Constantly in

---

* This Francisco de Miranda was one of the most extraordinary characters of his time. Born into privilege – until his father, a Spaniard noble who migrated to Caracas, was denounced for having impure (Jewish) blood; ultimately his father's certificate of *limpieza de sangre* was confirmed but the disgusted young Miranda left Caracas, fighting for Spain, travelling to America where he befriended Washington and Jefferson, and to Russia, where he charmed Catherine and Potemkin, before fighting for the French revolution then being imprisoned by Robespierre. Surviving the Terror, he travelled for a decade to promote his vision of a revolt against Spain to create a united south America under a hereditary Inca, advised by himself.

and out of Downing Street to see Liverpool, the prime minister, he raised the money on the markets that made Britain a world power.*

As Wellington bled the French in Spain, Napoleon's relations with Alexander were so strained that both were massing new armies. 'But for my marriage with Marie, I never should have made war on Russia but I felt certain of the support of Austria . . .' claimed Napoleon who decided to invade Russia.

ARABIAN CONQUESTS: MEHMED ALI AND THE SAUDIS

In Cairo, in 1811, at the height of Napoleon's power in Europe, the pasha of Egypt, Mehmed Ali, invited 450 Mamluk amirs dressed in their yellow turbans, robes and chainmail, red pantaloons and red pointed slippers, to a ceremony at his divan in Saladin's Citadel. He received them respectfully, but as they left through a passageway, its gates slammed shut and his troops slaughtered every one of them. As their heads were gathered, their households were raided, their women raped and a thousand more hunted down. He was master of Egypt.

The Ottoman sultan Mahmud II recognized Mehmed as Egyptian governor but set him a test that would kill two birds with one stone. Ever since 1517, the sultans had proudly guarded the *hajj* as Protectors of the Two Sanctuaries, Mecca and Medina, but now an obscure family of puritanical fanatics, from the deepest Najd, had stormed the cities. The family were the Saudis, who starting in 1744 as amirs of Diriyyah had made an alliance with the ascetic Sunni preacher Wahhab to liberate Islam from polytheism, magic, corruption and Shiite heresy, in order to reassert its origins. The Saudi amir Abdulaziz, who took Riyadh, accepted the allegiance of Qatar and Bahrain, then attempted to overthrow the al-Saids of Oman, dispatching an army under a black Nubian amir that failed to dislodge the family. In 1802, he sent his son Saud the Butcher into Ottoman Iraq, to storm the Shiite sanctuary of Karbala, where he massacred thousands of Shiites. Karbala was avenged when a Shiite stabbed Abdulaziz. The Butcher advanced into Hejaz, where

---

* In February 1811, George III, increasingly blind and bewildered and heartbroken after the death of his daughter Amelia from TB, became permanently mad. Perceval activated the Regency Act; Prince George became prince regent. Like many a young radical, the prince had become more conservative with age. When Perceval was assassinated by a lunatic, he appointed the earl of Liverpool as prime minister, betraying his furious Whig friends. When the regent cut his former pals Beau Brummell and Lord Alvanley at a ball, Beau delivered the best put-down in royal history: 'Alvanley, who's your fat friend?' Living in French exile for another twenty years, Brummell died half mad and penniless.

he was resisted by Gahlib, amir of Mecca, one of the Hashemites descended from the Prophet: it was the start of a feud between the two first families of Islam that lasted into the twentieth century. The sultan ordered Mehmed to destroy the Saudis.

Mehmed's son Tousson retook the Holy Cities but struggled to beat the Saudis, and became downhearted. 'Don't give up and don't despair,' advised the father, 'for despair is a disgrace not befitting you.' When Tousson died of the plague, Mehmed himself galloped into Arabia to counter-attack, assisted by his red-haired eldest son Ibrahim, possibly adopted, who had slaughtered the Mamluks. Ibrahim now proved a superb general, chasing the Saudis to Diriyyah, where he captured the young amir Abdullah and sent him to Constantinople. After being made to listen to the lute – a painful punishment for a Wahhabist – Abdullah was publicly beheaded. Everyone presumed they would never hear of the Saudis again.

Having added Arabia to his fiefdom, Mehmed now planned to conquer Sudan. At home, he embarked on visionary reforms, took personal ownership of Egyptian land, reformed the law, created schools for women, traded sugar and cotton – he micromanaged everything, his ambitions Napoleonic. 'I'm well aware that the [Ottoman] empire is daily heading toward destruction,' he said. 'On its ruins, I'll build a huge kingdom . . . up to the Euphrates and Tigris.' In Paris, the Mehmed Ali of Europe was mustering the biggest army ever seen in Europe to conquer its biggest country.

NAPOLEON, MARIE AND MOSCOW: THE FRENCH ARE LIKE WOMEN – YOU MUSTN'T STAY AWAY TOO LONG

In May 1812, Napoleon left Marie Louise as regent in Paris, looking after the king of Rome, and invaded Russia with his multinational *Grande Armée* of 600,000. 'The game', he said, 'is always with him who makes the fewest mistakes.' Despite advice from those who knew better, Napoleon underestimated the vastness of Russia, the passion of Russian patriotism, the ferocity of Russian soldiery and the toughness of Alexander. Expecting Alexander to negotiate, he advanced deeper, the Russians retreating until the beleaguered tsar was forced to appoint a revered marshal, Prince Mikhail Kutuzov, an unflappable one-eyed veteran, to stand and fight. More men were killed in the few hours of grindingly bloody butchery at Borodino than in any engagement until the first day of the Somme in 1916. It was a stalemate, but Kutuzov retreated and abandoned Moscow.

Napoleon found himself in a deserted burning city, waiting for a sur-render that never came.* As brutal winter descended that October, he left Moscow and fought his way back across Russia before abandoning his men to save his throne. 'The French are like women,' he joshed. 'You mustn't stay away too long.' Galloping across Europe, he reached Paris in December, having lost 524,000 men, more of them killed by typhus than by Russians.

'What a career he's ruined,' Alexander exclaimed. 'The spell is broken.' Now it was Alexander's turn for vengeance. Russia and Prussia joined a coalition funded by Britain, but Napoleon raised new armies and dazzled his gathering enemies with virtuoso manoeuvres. 'Write to Papa François once a week,' he told Marie, 'send him military particulars and my affection.' At Lützen in May 1813, after defeating the Russians and Prussians, he told her, 'I am very tired, I've gained complete victory over . . . Emperor Alexander and the King of Prussia.' He added in a message to her father Franz that she 'continues to please me in the extreme. She's now my prime minister . . .'

Yet Franz, advised by his gifted but vain, neurotic, pleasure-loving minister Klemens von Metternich, was moving inexorably against his son-in-law. Blond, blue-eyed and cosmopolitan, Metternich was friendly with Napoleon, had slept with his sister Caroline Murat and had nego-tiated Napoleon's marriage to Marie Louise, but he was a believer in strategic balance, and he realized Napoleon would never accept com-promise.

'Metternich strikes me as an intriguer directing Papa François very badly,' Napoleon told Marie, but he faced the dilemma of self-made warlords: 'I owe everything to my glory. If I sacrifice it, I cease to be.' In August 1813, the Habsburgs switched sides. 'Deceived by Metternich, your father's joined my enemies,' he told his loyal wife. At Dresden he defeated Austrians, Prussians and Russians, informing Marie that 'Papa François had the good sense not to come,' while 'Papa François's troops have never been so bad.' But at Leipzig in October, Napoleon's 200,000 men were defeated by 300,000 Russians, Austrians and Swedes – the biggest European battle until the First World War. France was invaded by the coalition, led by Alexander from the east and Wellington from the south-west. Even the king and queen of Naples – Murat and his

---

* Amid the bleakness, only the flashy courage of Marshal Murat, king of Naples, raised French morale – 'a stage king in the studied elegance of his attire', wrote an eyewitness, 'a real king in his bravery and inexhaustible activity'. Easily 'recognized by his dress', recalled Napoleon, 'he was a regular target for the enemy, and the Cossacks used to admire him on account of his astonishing bravery'.

sister Caroline – betrayed Napoleon, while Talleyrand negotiated the restoration of the Bourbons in the obese shape of the guillotined king's brother, Louis XVIII. 'Treason,' Talleyrand said, 'is a matter of dates.' As his house of cards collapsed, Napoleon admitted (like Louis XIV), 'I've waged war too much.' He reassured his anxious Marie, 'I'm sorry to hear you are worrying. Cheer up and be gay. My health is perfect, my affairs, none too easy, aren't in bad shape . . .' But Marie was perhaps focused more on herself than on Napoleon's crisis, writing in her diary as if she wondered what was keeping her husband so busy, 'I have no news from the emperor. He is so casual in his ways. I can see he's forgetting me.'

As a mark of the disintegration of the empire, in March 1813 Napoleon's brother tried to seduce Empress Marie. 'King Joseph', she complained to Napoleon, 'says very tiresome things to me.'

'Don't be too familiar with the King,' Napoleon warned her. 'Be cold to him . . . No intimacy . . . Talk to him only in the presence of the duchess and by a window.' Later he confided, 'All this depresses me rather; I need to be comforted by members of my family.' He warned Joseph pathetically, 'If you want the throne, take it . . . but leave me the heart and love of the empress,' before instructing him, 'Don't allow the empress and the king of Rome to fall into enemy hands.' Referring to the boy, he added grimly, 'I'd sooner see him drowned in the Seine.'

As the allied armies surrounded Paris, Empress Marie fled, spoiling any chance of her baby king succeeding to the throne. Talleyrand assumed power. The Russians occupied Paris eighteen months after Parisians had occupied Moscow; Alexander had fought from Moscow to Paris, thus overseeing Russia's emergence as a great power.* The tsar stayed at Talleyrand's mansion, joined by Wellington, newly minted duke. Alexander was charmed by the Empress Josephine; Wellington enjoyed the favours of the actresses who had once favoured Napoleon.

Lafayette arranged Napoleon's exile to America. Instead, at Fontainebleau, Napoleon abdicated in favour of his son, who technically became

---

* Napoleon had tried to create a European empire; Russia and Britain too were building empires but against much weaker opponents outside the core of Europe. Britain's triumph at Trafalgar was to confine Napoleon within Europe, where he had to fight the most powerful militaries in the world. Now full victory over Napoleon propelled Britain to world eminence: by not seeking European hegemony, merely enforcing a balance of power, it could deploy its relatively small population and formidable resources of naval power and industry in an aggressive pursuit of world empire. The victory also granted Russian tsardom a confidence that masked its primitive weakness. Nonetheless 1814 along with 1945 are the moments of Russian imperial triumph. In April 1945, when Soviet troops liberated Berlin from the Nazis, US ambassador Averell Harriman congratulated Stalin. 'Yes,' replied the dictator, 'but Alexander took Paris.'

Napoleon II, and accepted instead the title emperor of the small island of Elba, and for Empress Marie, the Italian duchy of Parma. 'You're to have . . . a beautiful country,' he wrote. He hoped that 'When you tire of Elba and I begin to bore you, as I can but do when I'm older . . . you'll be content with my ill-fortune if you . . . can still be happy sharing it.' That night he attempted suicide with his poison kit, carried since Moscow.

WATERLOO: THE BRITISH CENTURY; NAPOLEON II
AND THE RISE OF THE ROTHSCHILDS

After a night of vomiting, Napoleon survived. The Royal Navy delivered him to Elba, where he was soon joined by his mother and sister Pauline. Card games bored him.

'You're cheating, son,' Madame Mère said.

'You're rich, mother,' he replied. In Paris, Josephine died of pneumonia aged fifty, while his second empress, Marie, was scooped up by Austrian cavalry and reunited with her father. She still hoped to follow Napoleon to Elba. 'I am in a very unhappy and critical position; I must be very prudent,' she wrote. 'There are moments when I think the best thing I could do is to die.' Franz sent her and the infant ex-Napoleon II to Vienna, where she was assigned Count Adam von Neipperg, a one-eyed bravo, as chamberlain to prevent her joining Napoleon. 'Within six months I'll be her lover,' Neipperg boasted, 'and soon her husband.' Marie fell in love with him – then fell pregnant.

Marie was soon joined in Vienna by the potentates and grifters of Europe as her father Emperor Franz and Chancellor Metternich presided over a congress to reorganize the continent. 'When I arrived yesterday,' wrote Metternich, 'I found all Europe in my antechamber.' The congress was the world's biggest junket, a diplomatic summit, an interminable ball, a social carousel, a feast of gourmandism, a VD-infested super-brothel, attended by Alexander, Wellington, Talleyrand and hundreds of diplomats, spies, bankers, mountebanks and panders, as well as thousands of prostitutes and 18,000 members of the public, with a soundtrack by Beethoven: his 'Wellington's Victory' was its anthem. It opened with a ball at the Hofburg for 10,000 guests.*

---

* The diplomacy was negotiated in ballrooms and bedrooms, particularly in the Palm Palace where two female grandees held court. Metternich was in love with an intelligent, libertine potentate, Wilhelmine, duchess of Sagan, whose lands were in the Russian sphere; Alexander tormented the chancellor by sleeping with her. Metternich's own part-time affair with the White Pussycat, the Russian princess Catherine Bagration, also known

Yet there were a hints of a new age. One of the favourite salons, attended by Metternich, Wellington and Talleyrand, was held by a sophisticated banker's wife, Fanny von Arnstein, who was Jewish – a first for a salonnière. Metternich created one of the first secret-police bureaucracies to watch the players: these were soon essential tools of statehood. Baron Franz von Hager's *Oberste Polizei und Zensur Hofstelle* employed an army of spies from princesses to the *Grabennymphen*, prostitutes of the streets: daily *rapporte* were presented to kaiser and chancellor. Metternich's other indispensable aide was his publicist, Friedrich von Gentz. 'The greatest evil is the press,' Metternich told Gentz. But mass politics was on the threshold of the palace.

The exhausted grandees restored what they regarded as balance: the Habsburgs headed a German Confederation and secured northern Italy; the Romanovs were restored in Poland, the Bourbons in France; and outside Europe, Britain kept Cape Colony, and slave trading was abolished in the northern hemisphere.* Just after the treaty was finally signed, the magnates received astonishing news.

In February 1815 Napoleon, infuriated by the failure to pay his pension and the diverting of Marie, escaped from Elba, rallied his veterans, who flocked to his banner unmoved by the fat, arrogant Louis XVIII, and retook Paris. He was at once declared 'a disturber of the world'. He advanced into Belgium to knock out the Anglo-Prussians before the Austro-Russians arrived. He started well. 'Napoleon has humbugged me, by God,' said Wellington, leaving Vienna to take command. On 18 June, at Waterloo, Napoleon, now forty-five, pot-bellied, dog-tired and haemorrhoidally aggra-vated,† failed to master the battle and lost 25,000 men – more than at any other battle except Borodino.‡ 'A damned close-run thing,' said Wellington.

---

as the Naked Angel thanks to her see-through dresses and concupiscent techniques, was ruined when she switched to Alexander, feeding him intelligence. Metternich wept with frustration. Talleyrand was accompanied by his niece-mistress Dorothea, later duchess of Dino, thirty-nine years his junior, who supported his restoration of France while juggling her own young lovers.

* In the east, a young EIC conquistador, Stamford Raffles, son of an EIC sea captain born at sea, had just defeated French–Dutch forces and taken Java. In 1815, when the Dutch lost the Cape but kept the East Indies, Raffles, a fluent Malay-speaker, persuaded the weak sultan of Johor to cede to Britain a strategic island which Raffles developed into a thriving colony: Singapore.

† 'My brother,' he wrote to King Jérôme in 1807, 'I hear you suffer from piles. The simplest way to get rid of them is to apply three or four leeches. Since I used this remedy ten years ago, I haven't been tormented since.'

‡ The bodies were, like all of the 500,000 or so killed in Napoleonic battles, stripped naked, often by their own comrades while dying. Then scavengers extracted teeth with pliers and sold them to denture makers – 'Waterloo Teeth' being especially popular – and collected bones that they sold to bone grinders to use as fertilizer.

Nathan Rothschild heard of Waterloo before Lord Liverpool, benefiting from his own intelligence network, but contrary to the myth that the Rothschilds made a fortune with the information, the quick victory wrongfooted him, exposing his holdings, just as the closing of the great French war ended his subsidy-delivery business. 'I feel my spirits very low,' Nathan told this brother Carl two weeks later. Their brother Salomon raised funds for Kaiser Franz and lent cash to Metternich (codenamed Uncle). Metternich was the first statesman to dine regularly with Jews chez Rothschild. In 1816, Emperor Franz elevated the brothers to the nobility, awarding the title baron, though he joked pointedly that they were 'richer than I am'. Carl in Naples was advising the ex-empress Marie Louise; Amschel in Frankfurt covered Prussia; Nathan, ascetic and intense, directed the family from London.

The pleasures of family were their real treasure. 'After dinner, I usually have nothing to do,' Nathan wrote to Saloman in Vienna. 'I don't read books, I don't play cards ... My only pleasure is my business and in this way I read Amschel's, Salomon's, James's and Carl's letters.' In 1806, Nathan had married a Dutch merchant's daughter, Hannah Barent Cohen,* with whom he had seven children and who described him as her 'best friend'. Her sister Judith married an Italian immigrant, Moses Montefiore, a Sephardi banker, who lived next to Nathan and above the bullion business in St Swithin's Lane in the City of London. They shared family and business, and increasingly collaborated in campaigns for Jewish rights and liberal reforms.

Nathan was expert at making bets on the future. 'Mr Rothschild has been a very useful friend,' said Liverpool, who was capable enough to remain prime minister for over fourteen years.† The wars cost Britain much in blood and treasure, but ultimately they slowed the European economy – over three million died – but quickened the British. The war was the engine that drove British growth. And the Rothschilds provided the fuel: capital.

In Europe their judgement was just as acute. They lent money to Louis XVIII and Talleyrand. Months after trundling back into Paris, Louis sacked Talleyrand and failed to restrain a purge of Bonapartists.

* Ironically for the royal family of capital, Barent Cohen's first cousin was Karl Marx's grandmother.

† Bland and managerial, Liverpool was also part Indian, Britain's only mixed-race premier. His grandmother was the part-Indian, four-times-married Frances 'Begum' Johnson, daughter of a Portuguese-Indian Isabella Beizor and a British governor of St David's (Chennai) – it was a time when many Britons in India married Indian women. Frances's daughter Amelia married Charles Jenkinson, first earl of Liverpool, but died aged nineteen giving birth to the future prime minister.

In Marseilles, 300 of Napoleon's Mamluks were slaughtered in their barracks. After the assassination of the king's nephew, thousands were prosecuted for supporting Napoleon – inspiring the story of Dumas's novel *The Count of Monte-Cristo*. 'They've learned nothing', warned Talleyrand, 'and forgotten nothing.' The Rothschilds also supported the king's liberal cousin Louis Philippe, duc d'Orléans. 'A court is always a court,' said James de Rothschild, 'and it always leads to something.'

In London, Nathan backed an urbane German prince, Leopold of Saxe-Coburg, who, after spending time at the courts of Napoleon and Alexander, pulled off his marriage to the British heiress Princess Charlotte. But in 1817 she died after giving birth to a stillborn child. Leopold had no prospects, yet Salomon advised Nathan, 'We should show even more friendship towards a man who fell on hard times than before.' The death of Charlotte meant that the British succession now passed to one of the prince regent's despicable brothers, the duke of Kent, who, marrying late, managed to father a girl, Victoria. But both the bets on Louis Philippe and Leopold would pay off.

In London, Nathan was trusted by all players from George IV (as the prince regent became in 1820)* to Lord Liverpool and Wellington, the apex of the new nexus of finance, power and society, his standing enhanced when he helped rescue the Bank of England. But the Rothschilds' success did not make them loved. They were the vanguard of newly emancipated Jews who, once hidden in the Judengasse counting houses, now thrived in a strange brash world of stock markets, factories, newspapers and bourgeois values, social-climbing their way into aristocratic drawing rooms and Christian families. The success spawned new strains of medieval anti-Jewish racism, partly jealousy at parvenu wealth, partly suspicion of power, encompassing both nationalist fervour and conservative fear.

Jews still faced discriminatory laws across Europe: they were increasingly persecuted in Russia, and even in Britain they could not be elected to Parliament, attend university or hold office. Nathan and his brother-in-law, Montefiore, campaigned for Jewish rights. However Olympian their social lives and however palatial their mansions, they were still family-minded observant Jews: of Nathan's seven children, four married Rothschilds, one a Montefiore, another a cousin, and only one married out. But in 1827 Montefiore embarked on a dangerous visit to Jerusalem, now a half-deserted monumental village neglected by

---

* When the deluded George IV boasted that he had led a charge at Waterloo, Wellington semi-tactfully replied, 'I have often heard Your Majesty say so.'

voracious Ottoman pashas, and there embraced a religious belief in the traditional Jewish dream of a return to Zion that dovetailed with a new Christian interest in the Holy City.

On 5 May 1821 while Metternich presided over the balance of power in Europe, a sickly retired soldier died in a damp house on the forsaken Atlantic island of St Helena and no one cared. 'Not an event,' quipped Talleyrand. 'Just news.' As the fifty-one-year-old Bonaparte succumbed to stomach cancer, three conquerors – south, east and north – were founding new African empires.

SHAKA ZULU, MOSHOESHOE AND DONA FRANCISCA: THE *MFECANE*

In 1816, Shaka bewitched his father, *nkosi* (king) of the minor Zulu chiefdom of the White Mfolozi River, an Ngumi people of southern Africa,* then, on his death, killed his half-brother, the rightful successor, and claimed the throne. Shaka was mercurial, creative and charismatic, but ultimately even his own family regarded him as terrifying and unpredictable.

He was the unplanned, perhaps unwanted, eldest son of King Senzangakona, and a chief's daughter, Nandi – Sweet. When Senzangakona succeeded to the throne, he married many times and fathered eighteen sons, resenting his first son. Nandi and Shaka fled, protected by the king's sister, Mnkabayi, a shrewd power broker who became arbiter of the kingdom in a culture where female power was respected. Nandi remarried, while Shaka, bitter and alienated, returned to his father's household. When it was clear he was going to make trouble the father decided to kill him.

Shaka fled into the wider world, which was divided between two Nguni kingdoms – Mthethwa led by King Dingiswayo and the Ndwandwe under King Zwide – who were already locked in a deadly rivalry that would explode into a broader conflict, the *Mfecane* – the Crushing. Aged twenty-two, Shaka joined King Dingiswayo of the Mthethwa, who, declaring 'there should be one great king to exercise control over the little ones', recognized the potential in the bastard prince and promoted him to commander; Shaka soon became known as Dingiswayo's Hero. Together they plotted for Shaka to seize the Zulu chiefdom. In 1816,

---

* The name Zulu derived from a warlord, Zulu kaMalandela who had founded the tribe a century earlier. Zulu meant heaven or sky and they called themselves *Abantu Bezulu* – the People of the Sky.

when his father visited, Shaka arranged the bewitchment, a powerful tool in Nguni society, that led to Senzangakona's death. The king was succeeded by a younger son, Sigujana. Dingiswayo lent Shaka a regiment so that he was able to put Sigujana to death. His aunt Mnkabayi, acting as his regent, arranged his invitation to become *nkosi* of the small Zulu realm. Shaka danced the *ukugiya*, washed in the royal enclosure and then emerged to be hailed *nkosi*. But in 1818 Zwide attacked and killed Dingiswaya, telling Shaka, 'Now I've removed your head, why don't you just bring the whole body before me, or I'll chuck the body into the River Thukela.'

'The body had two heads like the great river snake Nkanyamba,' replied Shaka. 'You're just too stupid to see the other one.'

Shaka expanded his own kingdom, training a new army using the methods he had developed with his patron: swift manoeuvring by intensively drilled regiments behind walls of shields, commanded by himself, to act like the horns of cattle in battles of envelopment. They used both the traditional long spear and the mace, but also a new short stabbing spear. They had no horses, which died after being bitten by the tsetse fly, and no rifles, which they disdained. Shaka demanded celibacy from his active troops, who were trained to fight barefoot, hardened by dancing on devil-thorns. Any disobedience was punished with death. Creating a hierarchical nation with his family at the top, and conquered nations further down, he fostered an esprit de corps in the Zulus, parading his *amabutho* – regiments – who danced in animal skins singing 'You're a wild animal! A leopard! A lion!', believing they were the People of the Sky empowered by the gods and the spirits of ancestors. Witches could take control of a person by procuring snippets of the body, fingernails or hair or urine – so these had to be carefully disposed of. After battle, warriors risked contamination from their enemies, whose bodies were therefore disembowelled to cleanse the killer. No prisoners were taken. 'Let no one remain alive,' said Shaka, 'not even a dog or a child on its mother's back.'

In 1819, Shaka defeated King Zwide, who escaped to Mozambique.* The Zulu killed Zwide's mother by sealing her in a hut with ravening hyenas.

Shaka moved on to new conquests. The king was not regarded as handsome – his head 'peculiar', his eyes red, with two prominent teeth

---

* The northern Nguni included the Zulus and Swazis; the southern became the Xhosa peoples. In the *Mfecane*, their leader Ngubengcuka, related to Zwide, led his clan south into the eastern Cape, where he founded the kingdom of abeThembu, before dying in 1832. The children of his junior wife were the Mandelas. Nelson Mandela was his great-grandson.

and a way of laughing 'outside his mouth', his body unusually hirsute – and he was aware of it. 'Though it's said I'm in the habit of killing people, never will I kill you,' he menacingly told a handsome warrior. 'Were I to do so, Zulus would laugh at me, saying I'd killed you for being handsome and because I'm ugly.' Later he ordered Europeans to bring him Macassar hair oil to dye his beard and hair black.

In his various capitals, he lived among hundreds of women – senior wives and his *isigodlo* of concubines, who styled their hair in topknots and wore short leather pleated skirts and carved ivory earplugs. Shaka 'was a man of great feeling and used frequently from grief or excessive joy to burst into a crying fit'. He fathered no known children, though that may have been deliberate; those who got pregnant were ordered to abort or be killed. On most mornings, after being shaved, he came out and summoned his commanders and addressed the people. 'Do you hear the king?' shouted his courtiers.

'Yes, Father!' Healers (*sangoma*) and diviners (*izangoma*) were consulted to 'smell out' evil wizards: if they were clever, they divined Shaka's wishes; but if they pointed out his favourites, he had the diviners killed. When he pointed with his staff saying, 'Kill the wizards,' the victims were dragged off to be impaled through their bowels and then smashed with a cudgel or had their necks broken, while women were strangled. 'See vultures flying above,' Shaka cried. 'Wu! The birds of the king are hungry.' He was said to have eviscerated a pregnant woman to 'see how her child lay' – stories that are told by more than one source and may have been true. The cruelties were becoming more capricious. His half-brothers Dingane and Mhlangana and his powerful aunt watched him closely. Even his mother Nandi, the Great She-Elephant (female monarch), questioned his excesses.

As Shaka's conquests intensified the *Mfecane*, he was just one player in a multi-ethnic tournament for power and resources. To the north-east, the Portuguese forged a unique model of European empire. Portuguese kings granted titles and estates to Luso-African warlords, the *prazo senhors*, who ruled alongside African magnates.* These Luso-African lords – the *prazeiros*, commanding private armies of African *colonos* and

---

* When the men died, the estates were inherited by female mixed-race potentates: in Zambezia (parts of Zambia, Zimbabwe, Mozambique) these Luso-Africans were known as the *Zambezi donas*. Dona Francisca de Moura Meneses was a mixed-race heiress who, born in 1738, ruled a massive Zambezian estate, owning several thousand slaves, presiding over many thousands of free Africans and deploying a private army that at times threatened the Portuguese governor. The Africans called her *Chiponda* – She Who Tramples All Underfoot. There was no equivalent of the *Zambezi donas* back home in Europe, let alone in any other empire.

chicundas (slave-soldiers) – hunted deeper into Africa for cattle, slaves and ivory to sell in Lourenço Marques (Mozambique); further north, Omani and Swahili slave traders hacked their way into central Africa, selling their captives around the Indian Ocean as Mehmed Ali raided into Sudan. To the south, the mixed-race Griqua raided into the northern Cape; Xhosa kings conquered the east Cape; and behind them came the Dutch and the British.

The Dutch traders of the VOC had founded Cape Town, where they settled thousands of poor Boers – farmers, devout Calvinists – who soon encountered the hunter-gatherer Khoikhoi (Bushmen or Hottentots to the Europeans), descended from the original inhabitants of the continent, pushed southwards by the Bantu who migrated from west Africa. The Dutch imported slaves from Dahomey, Angola and Mozambique to work their plantations while breaking the Khoikhoi, who, crushed between Bantu and Dutch, decimated by smallpox and reduced to indentured labour close to slavery, almost ceased to exist. The settlers, who called themselves Afrikaners, expanded northwards and eastwards, thus encountering the Nguni, herders of long-horned cattle, who were moving south conquering their own kingdoms.

The Afrikaners developed into skilled frontiersmen, who raided the herds and hunted elephants for ivory, but they also settled with African women with whom they had children, sometimes living more like Nguni royalty than Europeans. They became expert fighters in mounted units called *commandos*, and trained their mixed-race sons to serve as auxiliary fighters. When the British seized the Cape, it was a colony of 75,000 people – 15,000 semi-hostile Afrikaners, 13,000 black slaves, 1,200 freedmen and the rest mixed-race Khoikhoi-Dutch Griqua, known as the 'Bastards'. As new British settlers arrived in the Cape, moving north and eastwards, they encountered resistance from the amaXhosa kingdom led by Tshawe warrior kings Ngqika, Hintsa and Mgolombane Sandile. The Xhosa were formidable fighters whose acumen is often neglected by historians: they halted the British empire for seventy years.

Now in 1818 as the British were fighting the amaXhosa under Hintsa, a group of frontiersmen founded Port Natal on the east coast and travelled to Shaka's capital kwaBulawayo. The king mocked their strange fair hair – comparing it to cattle tails – but granted them rights to the port and recruited them as military advisers. Yet Shaka's conquests were reaching their limit.

In 1824, while the British hunters were still in his *kraal*, Shaka was dancing when a would-be assassin speared him in the side. Shaka hunted down the hitmen, who were beaten to a pulp by the people, then he massacred the Qwabe tribe whom he decided to blame – though he rightly distrusted his own family. In 1827, his mother Nandi died mysteriously. She had disapproved of his purges, and may have protected a male baby born of his concubines: he either killed her in a rage or had her killed, like Nero. She was buried as Zulu royalty, sitting up supported by the bodies of sacrificed henchmen, servants and concubines, strangled or buried alive. Killing anyone suspected of disloyalty, Shaka supposedly killed 7,000 people. After Nandi's death he appointed his aunt Mnkabayi as Great She-Elephant.

As the British and Afrikaners probed Zulu lands, and Shaka launched his terror, southern Africa was in ferment. In 1828, needing another victory, Shaka ordered an expedition against Soshangane, formerly one of Zwide's generals, who led the tribe founded by his grandfather Gaza eastwards to find their own realm. Emulating many of Shaka's military tactics, Soshangane routed the Zulus, weakening Shaka. 'I'm like a wolf on the plain, at a loss for a place to hide his head in,' Shaka said, encouraging the diviners to smell out witches among his half-brothers, Dingane and Mhlangana. Great She-Elephant Mnkabayi began to suggest that he was mad and had killed his mother. But while he was protected by his devoted *inceku* (warrior/bodyguard) Mbopha, no one could touch him.

Less meteoric than Shaka but more remarkable was Moshoeshoe, born the same year as the Zulu, leader of the Sotho, herdsmen who suffered bitterly from predations by Nguni and Griqua. Moshoeshoe led his Sotho on a perilous migration to the Qiloane plateau (Lesotho) where he created a stronghold – the Night Mountain, said to grow in the day and shrink in the night – where he withstood attacks by all his rival leaders to create a rich cattle-owning kingdom. Cleverly exploiting the British, he offered himself as a balance to Afrikaners and Zulus, buying rifles and hiring a French missionary, Eugène Casalis, as consigliere.

In a fifty-year reign (it ended in 1870), Moshoeshoe defeated the British, Afrikaners, Zulus and Ndebele. More humane and constructive than Shaka, he was 'majestic and benevolent. His aquiline profile, the fullness and regularity of his features, his eyes a little weary made a deep impression upon me,' wrote Casalis. 'I felt at once I was dealing with a superior man, trained to think, to command others and, above all, himself.' Out of these wars emerged the present shape of southern Africa.*

---

* Mosheshoe's family still rules Lesotho. Shaka accused Mzilikazi, a grandson of Zwide, of keeping cattle prizes for himself. The punishment was death. Mzilikazi escaped with his Ndebele clan into Transvaal and then Zimbabwe, where his Matabele kingdom confronted

Further north, an ex-general of King Zwide and cousin of Shaka, Zwangendaba, led his Ndwandwe on a 1,000-mile trek through Mozambique and Zimbabwe that took fifteen years. After the Zambezi parted for them during an eclipse, they ended by settling in today's Tanzania where an Omani sultan, Said the Great, was conquering an empire from Somalia to Mozambique, from Kenya to Pakistan.

It all started with two Arab sheikhs duelling with daggers in the Arabian desert.

EMPIRE BUILDERS OF EAST AFRICA: MEHMED ALI AND SAID

In 1832, Said bin Sultan, sultan of Oman, moved his capital to Africa, creating his court on Zanzibar, where he built a palace, Bait al-Mtoni. His rise had started two decades earlier when his father was assassinated; his cousin Badr was appointed regent, backed by the Saudis. In 1806 Said lured the regent to his desert fortress and then ambushed him. The al-Said princes duelled to the death – and the teenaged Said won. As the bleeding Badr staggered into the desert, Said's cameleteers beheaded him.

Having sliced up his cousin, Said seized Muscat, which his father had helped make one of the entrepôts of the Indian Ocean, then set about the conquest of the Swahili coast of Africa. The al-Said family already owned Zanzibar, which Said had visited as a child. He built a thalassocratic empire, taking Pemba in 1823. In the Gulf he took Bahrain and Qatar but failed to keep them. He then seized the ports of Gwadar (Pakistan) and Bandar Abbas and Hormuz (Iran). In 1837, he seized Mombasa.

But there was a problem: slavery. Said sold slaves to Indian princes, and French planters in Réunion and Mauritius, and kept some for his own cloves plantations. Afro-Omanis hacked their way into the African interior on murderous elephant and slave hunts around Lakes Tanganyika and Victoria, into Uganda and Congo. At Kazeh (Tanzania), the Zanzibari slave lords lived sultanically with slaves and concubines, ruling their own Congolese fiefdoms. Later in Said's rule, Tippu Tip, the twenty-year-old son of an aristocratic Omani mother and Swahili father, led a hundred gunmen into Africa to launch his career as slaving

the Shona: the two tribes dominate Zimbabwe today. Shoshangane turned his victory into the Gaza kingdom in southern Mozambique, forcing the Afro-Portuguese *prazeiros* to pay tribute. Sobhuza, ruler of the Dlamini, also migrated to avoid Shaka, founding Swaziland (Eswatini), named after his son and successor Mswati. It likewise is still ruled by his family.

warlord, trader of cloves and much later a player in the European carve-up of Africa.

In 1820, understanding that the British craved security for India, Sultan Said negotiated an alliance with Britain in return for a personal exception to the slaving ban.

The Omani also sold slaves to his northern neighbour Mehmed Ali, who had rescued Oman from the predations of the Saudis and was now determined to conquer his own African empire. In 1820, Mehmed sent an expedition under his son Ismail to destroy the kingdom of Sennar and conquer Sudan. 'You're aware your mission has no other aim than to gather negroes,' Mehmed told Ismail. 'Slaves are worth more than jewels to us.'

Holding court in his half-lit Cairene divan like 'a spider in a web', Mehmed Ali Pasha cultivated an air of mystery, staring at his visitors, speaking portentously. 'The only books I read,' he said, 'are men's faces.' Setting up his own printing press, he refused to print Machiavelli, joking that the Italian 'had nothing to teach him'. He ran everything, promoting his sons but beheading any opposition.[*]

Mehmed Ali founded Khartoum in Sudan as his southern base, whence his henchmen seized 30,000 slaves of whom two-thirds perished as they were being driven northwards 'like sheep with the rot'. His rash son Ismail was killed, but Egyptian raids were now delivering 10,000 Sudanese slaves annually. Yet Mehmed Ali, ruler of Arabia, Egypt and Sudan, coveted Europe's new technologies, cultivating cotton and building mills to process it – the first non-European state to join the industrial revolution. He invited French officers to train his modern army, modelling himself on Napoleon while cultivating a special relationship with Bourbon Paris – where the weary, bloated Louis XVIII struggled to compete with the glory of Napoleon. The legend of the emperor grew. After Waterloo, Napoleon's Marie Louise set off with Neipperg to rule Parma, where she secretly bore him children, but she was ordered to leave her young son Napoleon in Vienna.

The boy was given a new name: having been both king of Rome and Napoleon II, his grandfather Franz renamed him Napoleon-Franz, duke of Reichstadt.[†] Worshipping his father, he was shocked to discover his

* It ran in the family. When Mehmed Ali's daughter Nazli noticed her husband flirting with a female slave, she presented him with the slave's head on a platter. The husband walked out and Mehmed Ali ordered one of his grandsons, Abbas, to execute Nazli, but Abbas persuaded him to let her live.

† His closest friendship, possibly a love affair, was with Sophie, the high-spirited, ambitious Bavarian princess married to Emperor Franz's dull son Franz Karl. Her eldest son, Franz Josef, was a future emperor whose reign would extend into the First World War.

mother's love life with Neipperg. 'If Josephine had been my mother,' he told a friend, 'my father wouldn't have been buried on St Helena, and I wouldn't be in Vienna. My mother is kind but weak . . . not the wife my father deserved.'

Napoleon-Franz trained as a soldier but his grandfather and Chancellor Metternich were terrified that he could rally Bonapartists in France or revolutions elsewhere. In 1814, Tsar Alexander had conceived a conservative alliance to guide a rules-based Europe – an autocratic version of the UN Security Council – with Metternich and Lord Liverpool's Britain, to crush the spread of revolutionary spirit. Or at least, as Metternich put it, 'Events that can't be prevented must be directed.'

Yet Metternich and his allies struggled to hold the line in Iberia: one of the peninsula's kings, João, was in Rio, while the other, the inept king of Spain, Fernando, was trying to restore absolute rule. Fifteen years earlier, the sixteen-year-old Fernando had played tennis with a skinny colonial boy from Caracas, Simón Bolívar, aged seventeen, who, losing a point, hit the prince of Asturias over the head. 'Who'd have guessed that this accident was a harbinger,' Bolívar later boasted, 'and I would rip the most precious jewel from his crown?' The 'jewel' was America – and Bolívar, along with two Haitian monarchs and a Brazilian prince, would liberate a continent and open an era.

ACT FIFTEEN
1 BILLION

Braganzas and Zulus, Albanians, Dahomeans and Vanderbilts

THE LIBERATORS: BOLÍVAR AND PEDRO

Around 13 October 1822, high in the Andes, at Loja (Ecuador), a desiccated, exhausted and feverish soldier inspected his troops. Later in a delirium he dreamed of climbing the volcano of Chimborazo, 'giant of the earth'. On reaching its summit, 'I fell in a swoon . . . I felt as if inflamed by strange, supernatural fire. The God of Colombia had taken possession of me. Suddenly Time stood before me . . .'

'I am the father of centuries!' said the God.

'Surely, oh Time,' he replied, 'the miserable mortal who has climbed this high must perish!'

'Hide not the secrets which Heaven has revealed to you! Speak the truth to mankind!'

The delirious dreamer was not some tripping pre-hippy but Simón Bolívar, *El Libertador*, the thirty-nine-year-old president of the vast Republic of Gran Colombia, who in the most extraordinary career of his time had liberated much of south America and was now focusing on Peru, Ecuador and Bolivia. He had conquered a million square miles, an area larger than Europe, mastering jungles, deserts and mountains, freeing millions from slavery. Few, other than an Alexander, a Genghis, a Napoleon, had experienced such triumphs, but Bolívar was more sensitive, less coarse, more aesthetic than the others.

Born into luxury, Bolívar, five foot six, wiry with burning eyes and skinny legs, was exuberant, passionate and boundlessly confident: he had tempered his slight body in order to compete with hardened cowboys, once mounting his horse with his hands bound behind his back and another time riding into a river with both his hands tied to show his virtuosity: 'Don't think this sort of thing isn't useful in a leader.' He had given away his money; he lived on horseback with the roughest *gauchos*. 'What?' cried a Spaniard who wanted to see the Liberator. 'That little man . . . riding the mule?'

After each victory, Simón was mobbed by female admirers who

dressed in white to greet the Liberator as he took each town, every victory celebrated with a ball. 'There are men who need to be alone and far from the hubbub to think,' he said, but 'I deliberated best when I was the centre of revelry, amid the pleasures of a ball.' He never doubted his destiny. 'A strong man delivers a single blow,' he wrote, magniloquently, 'and an empire vanishes.'

Bolívar's father, Juan Vicente, bitterly resented the corrupt direction of their Spanish masters. 'Injustice,' whispered the colonials, 'means Revolution.'* Juan begged his friend, the radical Francisco de Miranda, to lead a revolution against Spain, a dangerous enterprise.†

Simón Bolívar lost both parents young, leaving him a wealthy orphan, raised by a black slave Hippolyta, educated by Enlightened scholars and running wild with street children. Bolívar 'thought of little else' other than liberating Latin America: 'I was fascinated by stories of Greek and Roman heroes,' while 'Washington awoke a desire in me to be just like him.' Many creoles were restrained by fear of race war: one in ten Venezuelans were enslaved. Yet Bolívar was proud of a pedigree that included an enslaved girl. 'Our people are nothing like Europeans or North Americans,' he mused, 'we're more a mixture of Africa and America.'

At fifteen, Bolívar sailed to Madrid, where he met Queen Luisa because her latest lover was a Venezuelan – this was when he hit the crown prince with his racket. After a spree of love affairs, Bolívar married a young Caracan *mantuano*, but his wife soon died of yellow fever. She was the love of his life, 'but had I not become a widower', he wrote, 'I'd never have been General Bolívar, *El Libertador*. The death caused me early in the road of politics to follow the chariot of Mars.'

In 1807, Napoleon's drubbing of the risible Spanish king broke the fear necessary for the survival of empires: the Caracas grandees set up a junta loyal to the king, sending Bolívar to London where he pleaded in vain for support from Marquess Wellesley and met his ageing hero

---

* The father, a super-rich procurator, illustrated the sexual predations of the white elite, the *mantuanos*. Even by the standards of slave-owning rapists, he was a predator: two enslaved sisters reported to the bishop of Caracas that he regularly raped them – 'this infernal wolf trying to take me by force and consign me to the Devil'. The bishop investigated and arranged the marriage of Don Juan Vicente, fifty years old, to Maria, a fourteen-year-old *mantuano* girl, who was soon pregnant – with Simón.
† All remembered the 1781 rebellion against Spanish oppression in Peru by Tupac Amaru II, an educated Amerindian descended from the Incas. He led an army of 70,000, including female fighters led by his wife, against Cuzco, massacring Spaniards. When it was crushed, 100,000 Amerindians were killed and the Inca himself had his tongue cut out, before being pulled apart by four horses and displayed on the same square in Cuzco where his great-great-great-grandfather Inca Tupac Amaru I had been executed.

Miranda. The pair joined forces, sailing home to launch revolution, but Generalissimo Miranda, now sixty, offended everyone and was outmanoeuvred by the Spanish. Bolívar probably betrayed the eclipsed dictator, arresting him just before the Spanish swooped. Miranda died in a Spanish jail, and Bolívar took command of a rebel army.

Like the French in Haiti, the Spaniards fought differently in the colonies: they massacred 12,000, flaying rebels, wearing their ears on their hats. 'Spaniards, count on death,' declared Bolívar, 'even if you've been indifferent. Americans: count on life even if you have been guilty!' In August 1813, he took Caracas, but the *llaneros*, the mixed-race cowboys of the plains, backed the Spanish. Their Army of Hell routed the rebels. Bolívar escaped Caracas with his family, mistress and beloved manumitted nurse Hippolyta. Executing 1,000 Spaniards on the way, he made his way to Haiti, where President Pétion – the *Papa Bon Coeur* of the Haitian revolution – befriended him. 'I could feel his greatness,' said Pétion, who demanded nothing except the liberation of all slaves.

'European ambition forced the yoke of slavery on the rest of the world,' agreed Bolívar, already an abolitionist, 'and the rest of the world was obliged to answer.' He never forgot that 'Pétion is the true liberator.'

In December 1816, armed with Haitian guns, Bolívar returned to Venezuela. 'I decree full liberty to all slaves,' he declared, launching a war of elimination of his own, uniting armies of creoles, ex-slaves, *llaneros* and British mercenaries in a tireless campaign against Spain. *El Libertador* took the war into New Granada (Colombia), winning at Boyacá on his horse Palomo, capturing Bogotá.

In June 1821, Bolívar won the decisive battle at Carabobo that expelled Spain from Caracas and was then elected president of a new republic called Gran Colombia. Exhausted, drawn, greying, he admitted, 'I am consumed by the demon of war, determined to finish the struggle.' As he explained, 'My doctor often told me my spirit needs to feed on danger. This is so true. When God brought me into the earth, he brought a storm of revolutions to feed off. I am the genius of the storm.'

In Spain, a revolution had undermined the rule of King Fernando. Now the storm-born Liberator crossed over snow-capped Andes and tropical jungles to attack the Spanish in Peru. Sharing the tribulations of his troops, he defeated the Spanish at Bombona and contemplated Chimborazo, just as a very different Liberator was declaring the independence of Brazil in a splurge of dysentery.

The other Liberator would never have conquered a half a continent nor spoken to a god on a volcano – and he was neither a revolutionary nor an abolitionist. In fact, he was a Braganzan prince and the owner of thousands of slaves, and the liberation of Brazil could not have been more different.

Prince Pedro was playful and informal, keen on singing and playing guitar, usually dressed in a boater, white cotton trousers and a striped jacket. Nine years old when he arrived in Rio, he relished the city's hedonistic informality, chatting to passers-by in the streets and plunging in semi-disguise into its bars and bordellos; he also took a French actress as his mistress. Unlike his father King João, Pedro had adopted the Brazilian taste for washing. But while he counted himself a sort of liberal, he beat his slaves and revelled in his sexual mastery over enslaved women, whom he often spotted and bought in the street.

João remained in Brazil and negotiated his son's marriage to an Austrian Habsburg. Kaiser Franz had already married one daughter to Napoleon; now he agreed to marry Marie Louise's younger sister, Leopoldina, a fair, slim, dutiful and cheerful twenty-year-old, to the louche Pedro, nineteen at the time. Metternich was exasperated by the negotiations – 'The Portuguese are the slowest people in the world!' – and then by the archduchess herself: 'I've never seen a more spoilt and foolish child . . . If I was her father, I'd beat her.'

Leopoldina, close to her sister Marie Louise, was excited by the adventure of Brazil, learning Portuguese, studying botany and the works of the travelling naturalist Alexander von Humboldt, though her views were romanticized. 'Europe has become unbearable,' she wrote, while Brazilian 'savages' were 'children of nature not yet corrupted by luxury'. Sensing the 'corruption' of Brazil, she declared, 'I'll conduct myself with all possible modesty,' eschewing 'any literature that excites sensuality'.

As she arrived in November 1817 to popular excitement, King João had just put down a revolt in Pernambuco and sent away Pedro's French actress. After a wedding night when she was undressed by her mother-in-law and sisters-in-law, Leopoldina was shocked by the pettiness of the palaces, the stink of her ill-washed father-in-law and her husband's coarseness.

Pedro swore blindly, sketched pornography, loathed his 'bitch' of a mother, urinated off verandas, defecated in full view of his troops. 'I am entranced by the country,' Leopoldina wrote bravely. 'I spend my days making music with my husband.' But to her sister Marie Louise, she admitted, 'In all honesty, he speaks his mind with a certain brutality; he's accustomed to doing exactly what he wants,' but 'he loves me tenderly'. She added, addressing the woman who had survived Napoleon: 'You are indeed right, true happiness doesn't exist.' The couple's attitudes to their slaves were different: 'She was always very kind when she passed us slaves,' recalled a slave at their country house. 'He was arrogant, walked around with a silver-topped cane and beat us.' She was perpetually pregnant and depressed.

Then suddenly in 1820 revolution broke out in Portugal, the start of a long struggle between constitutional liberalism and royal absolutism exacerbated by Braganza feuds. The king agonized, before finally agreeing to return home, leaving the twenty-two-year-old Pedro as regent of Brazil. In Rio, the crowds shouted, 'Let the people rule Brazil!' and demanded that João embrace a liberal constitution yet remain in America. Pedro ordered his troops to shoot into the crowds. In April 1821, as he departed for Lisbon after thirteen years away, King João awkwardly told him, 'Pedro, if Brazil breaks away, better it be by your hand, with the respect you have for me, than by the hand of one of these adventurers.' Strangely the Brazilian revolution was now led by Pedro. When the *Cariola* crowds demanded he remain, he declared, 'Tell the people, I stay.'

In August 1822, Regent Pedro visited São Paulo. Pedro had vacillated between independence and loyalty to his father, writing warm letters to him, telling him about his grandchildren and boasting about his sexual exploits with *Carioca* girls. Enduring his brutish behaviour, Leopoldina also pushed him towards independence. Toying with the idea, Pedro travelled through the provinces, winning support for himself and statehood, while enjoying the girls procured by his pandering secretary, 'Fruity' Gomes.

Near São Paolo, he 'happened' to encounter a litter borne by two slaves that contained Domitila de Castro, a beauty married to a provincial bully and sister of one of his courtiers. Dazzled, he dismounted, praised her and then insisted on bearing her litter himself.

'How strong you are, Your Majesty,' said Domitila.

'Never again,' he said, 'will you be attended by little negroes like this.'

When he headed back to Rio, Domitila joined him in the great affair – selfish, passionate, destructive – of Brazilian history. The political pressure was rising. Out riding, he was just suffering a spasm of diarrhoea when he was handed a letter from Rio: Portugal was preparing to reconquer Brazil, just as Brazilian aristocrats were demanding full independence. There was not much of a choice, since he faced arrest if he resisted. Between spasms of dysentery, at a river called Ipiranga, he tore off the colours of Portugal, throwing his hat to the ground, drawing his sword and crying, 'The time has come. Independence or death. We've separated from Portugal.'

In October 1822, Pedro was declared emperor of Brazil. 'From Portugal we want nothing, absolutely nothing,' Pedro wrote to his father. 'Brazilian independence triumphs ... or we die defending it.' At his coronation on 1 December, Emperor Pedro fused Habsburg, Braganza and Amerindian themes, dressed in a green silk tunic, spurred boots and a green and yellow cloak made of toucan feathers. But his was not the first American monarchy.

QUEEN MARIE LOUISE OF HAITI AND THE GRAND LORD OF PARAGUAY: DR FRANCIA'S RACIAL EXPERIMENT

In Haiti, the visionary King Henry still ruled his northern kingdom; in the south, Bolívar's ally 'Papa Bon Coeur' Pétion died, leaving power to his ally, Boyer, son of a French tailor and an enslaved Kongo woman.

In October 1820, Boyer orchestrated a coup against Henry. The king, autocratic and unpopular, suffered a stroke at Palais Sans-Souci and on 8 October shot himself with a golden bullet. He was swiftly buried up at his Citadelle. His heir, the sixteen-year-old prince royal, Victor Henry, was bayoneted; baron de Vastey was stabbed, then hurled down a well. Boyer, advised by his paramour Marie-Madeleine Lachenais, *La Présidente de Deux Présidents*, united north and south, then annexed Spanish Santo Domingo and welcomed 6,000 free African-Americans as colonists, an experiment that failed: 2,000 of them soon returned home.* Yet France still claimed Haiti.

Haiti was not the only new state pioneering a post-slavery society.

Paraguay was trying a racial experiment unique to the continent, though ultimately with catastrophic consequences.

In October 1820, as Bolívar was conquering the continent and King Henry was facing mutiny, a studious and frugal doctor of theology, José Gaspar de Francia, who had become first a teacher then a lawyer, discovered a plot to assassinate him. The fifty-four-year-old had recently declared himself supreme dictator of a new state named Paraguay. Now he ordered his secret police, the *Pyraguës* (Hairy Feet), to arrest all the plotters and virtually everyone who was either educated or had played any political role. They were to be tortured in the Chamber of Truth and then killed. Since he prided himself on his husbandry, each executioner

---

* Boyer was kind to Queen Marie Louise, granting her some property. But, as she came to fear for her life, she was rescued by the Royal Navy and conveyed to London. She and her daughters Améthyste and Athénaïre stayed with Clarkson: a black queen and princesses in Regency London..

was permitted one bullet. Francia watched the killings sitting on a stool under an orange tree outside his palace. Beneath the death lists, Francia wrote unironically: '*Pax Francia*'.

Severe, dutiful and solemn, black-eyed with a penetrating and suspicious demeanour, often wearing his official uniform of blue-laced coat, waistcoat, breeches and white stockings, the doctor lived in his tiny, bungalow palace with just his widowed sister, two mixed-race maids (occasional mistresses), a young black barber-valet, a creole doctor and three Guaraní guards, trusties occasionally accused of treason and executed.

Francia was almost singlehandedly responsible for Paraguay, named after a Amerindian tribe, the Payaguá, which had resisted the early conquistadors. The remote Spanish territory Provincia Gigante de Indias was a backwater where a tiny elite of semi-educated creoles (Francia was one of only two university-educated doctors in the whole country) ruled *encomienda* estates, worked by African and Guaraní slaves. Ruled by Spanish viceroys in faraway Río de la Plata (Argentina), its capital Asunción contained just 3,500 creoles and 1,500 black people. Though the new republic was enriched by tobacco, its prosperous tranquillity was threatened by indigenous tribes, slave rebellions and Portuguese advances from Brazil.

El Supremo ruled the nation with barely a minister, observing the stars with astrolabes, studying and sketching botany, smoking his cigar and sucking up the national delicacy, the stimulating *yerba mate* tea, with a straw.*

The creoles were heavily intermarried with the Guaraní but defended their racial superiority with touchy arrogance. When he entered public life in a bid for the chair of theology at the seminary, Francia, son of a creole officer and cruel estate manager, was accused of being mixed-race but insisted on his *limpieza de sangre*. After Spanish rule had been overthrown in Buenos Aires, the Paraguayans declared independence and Francia rose to power by shrewd patronage along with regular resignations and retirements to his little *chacra* (farm). In 1813 he was elected joint consul, setting up the first military division under his command, and then, outmanoeuvring rivals, in June 1816 he was elected perpetual dictator. The Guaraní were encouraged to call him the sacred *Caraí Guazú* (Grand Lord).

* Francia never married and loved no one but recorded his sexual partners in a book, fathering seven children. When he discovered his own illegitimate daughter Ubalda was having sex for money, he declared the nobility of prostitution, which he regulated by ordering prostitutes to wear the gold comb, sign of a respectable Spanish lady. Only in Francia's Paraguay were sex workers honoured.

An obsessive micromanager, he was determined to create a Rousseauesque state of racial equality and national virtue. He controlled the trades of sugar cane, tobacco, cigars and *yerba mate*, which funded his new army, and decided to legislate a solution to racial caste by ending white supremacy. He banned any creoles or Spanish-born *peninsulares* from marrying other whites: they were ordered to marry only Amerindians or persons of colour. Enforced rigorously, Francia supervised every wedding, this terminated centuries of Spanish racial rule and produced a new mixed Paraguayan nation. Slavery was abolished, yet Francia's forced labour in the plantations was not so different.

This sociological experiment created the most orderly nation in South America, which would endure under a quasi-monarchy for sixty peaceful years. Francia gloated over the disorder in the rest of the continent: 'My policy for Paraguay', he said, was 'a system of non-intercourse with other Provinces of South America' to prevent 'contamination by that foul restless spirit of anarchy and revolution that has desolated and disgraced them all'.

MANUELA, THE LIBERATOR AND KING COTTON

In Peru the other Liberator, Bolívar, was watching the advance of a rival warlord. José de San Martín, commander of the Army of the Andes, dispatched by the rulers of Río de la Plata, had liberated Chile and advanced into Peru. But there he had run out of supplies. In July 1822, in a prickly meeting of titans, Bolívar outplayed San Martín. High in the Andes, Bolívar defeated the Spanish and then fell in love like never before.

Riding into Quito (Ecuador) the Liberator looked up at a balcony to see a young woman, Manuela Sáenz, who was watching his arrival. Soon afterwards they met at a ball. Manuela, an aristocrat's illegitimate daughter married to a dull English merchant, was a gorgeous life force who now joined her life to his. She fought beside him in battle: 'If my soldiers had your marksmanship,' said Bolívar, promoting her to colonel, 'we'd have routed Spain long ago.' She served as his secretary, but infuriated him with her erotic adventures, taking female lovers including her two maids, black ex-slaves whom she dressed as Mamluks. Her passion exhausted him. 'I want to answer, most beautiful Manuela, your demands of love,' he begged. 'My passion for you is wild,' but 'Give me time.' In August 1824, leading his men into the mountains, Bolívar drove out the Spanish and was elected dictator of Peru and president of a new country named for himself, Bolivia. But Peru 'contains two elements that are the bane of every just and free society', said Bolívar, 'gold and slaves. The first corrupts all it touches; the second is corrupt in itself.'

He might have been talking about America.

On 9 February 1825, the outgoing President James Monroe attended a dinner with his successor, president-elect John Quincy Adams – son of the second president – and his defeated rival, a rough frontier general named Andrew Jackson, in honour of the visiting marquis de Lafayette at which Bolívar was toasted as the 'Washington of South America'. But their toasts to American liberty scarcely concealed the rising tensions between the spirit of continental conquest, Christian mission and the institution of slavery on one hand and the liberal values of American democracy on the other.

The abolitionists of the northern states tried to stop the slave owners of the south from extending slavery into the new states. Between 1820 and 1830, cotton production doubled in the south, requiring more slave labour. The slave trade had been banned, which meant that slaves were no longer worked to death and replaced; slaves lived longer and had children, making the trade less urgent. But the cruelties were no less atrocious as around 875,000 slaves were 'sold down the river' (the Mississippi, transported in steamships or coffles on foot) to toil in the cottonfields. But American slaves were inspired by the liberations achieved by Bolívar and Dessalines. Southern slave owners presented themselves as a courtly aristocracy in pillared mansions, but the genteelness was skin-deep, founded on racial violence – rebellions were savagely crushed. At the same time their culture of human ownership diminished their work ethic; they never invested in industry, and thus the enslaved society bore the seeds of its own defeat.

In 1820, a compromise was negotiated by which Maine as a non-slavery and Missouri as a slavery state joined the Union. 'We have the wolf by the ear, and we can neither hold him nor safely let him go,' Jefferson reflected.* 'Justice is in one scale, and self-preservation in the

---

* When Jefferson retired to Monticello in 1809, the grand Virginian returned to his courtly lifestyle, cared for by his paramour Sally Hemings, who was bringing up their four children. Although one of her sisters, Thenia, had been sold to James Monroe, Jefferson had freed two of her brothers, one of whom, his French-trained chef James, he had invited to be his White House chef; James refused; later he committed suicide. As for his own enslaved children, Jefferson had the boys trained as carpenters, and Harriet as a weaver, though they also learned violin. Their training as artisans was very different from the education of white Virginians.

other.' The compromise, 'like a fire bell in the night, awakened and filled me with terror. I considered it at once as the knell of the Union . . . hushed indeed for the moment, but this is a reprieve only.'

Lafayette went on to Monticello to see Jefferson, and the two burst into tears as they hugged. Jefferson showed Lafayette around his university of Virginia, which he had designed as an invitation to youth to 'come and drink of the cup of knowledge'. Yet his remodelled Monticello and his university campus were built by slaves, a fact that made Lafayette uneasy. On 4 July 1826, Jefferson died aged eighty-three, manumitting Madison and Eston, his two younger children with Sally (the two eldest children having already left Monticello) but not formally freeing Sally herself, and leaving catastrophic debts of $100,000 that led not just to the sale of Monticello but to the tragic auctioning of his slaves and the break-up of their families. Patsy, Jefferson's daughter, allowed Sally to live in Charlottesville with Madison and Eston until she died. The two older Hemings children identified as white, and the younger ones as black, and they vanished into those two communities.

It was the end of a certain sort of America. Yet Lafayette also visited a very different sort of hero – General Jackson, at his Hermitage plantation in Tennessee. He represented the brash aggression of the frontier and the realm of King Cotton who sent his harvests to the Cottonopolis of Britain.

That spirit of liberty was abroad. Even affluent, victorious Britain seemed close to turmoil: protests seethed; armed rebellions were planned in Yorkshire and Shropshire; conspirators devised terrorist atrocities.

ROMANTICS AND THE MODERN NATION: LORD BYRON'S GREEK ADVENTURE AND BEETHOVEN'S NINTH

Lord Liverpool feared a British revolution. Britain was far from a democracy: around 400,000 men, a small proportion of the male population, enjoyed the vote. Grandees owned tiny 'rotten boroughs' that selected MPs: one estimate was that, of 515 MPs, 351 were chosen by 177 grandees. A typical rotten constituency, Higham Ferrers, owned by Earl Fitzwilliam, had only one voter, yet sent an MP to Westminster.

The movement for reform was propelled by the growth of the industrial cities. Manchester was the Cottonopolis and a dystopian 'chimney of the world'. Every human invention has both improved life and endangered humanity and the environment: the factories created a new environment, a harsh, smoking and cruel world of 'dark satanic mills' for a new working class. As a visitor later put it, 'Rich rascals, poor rogues, drunken ragamuffins and prostitutes form the moral; soot made into paste by rain, the physique, and the only view is a long chimney: what a place! The entrance to hell realised.'*

In Manchester, on 16 August 1819, a crowd of 60,000 demanded reform of the franchise. Cavalry charged the crowd, killing seventeen and wounding over 400 – the Peterloo Massacre (only in Britain could eighteen deaths be called a 'massacre' or be compared to Waterloo) – which sparked more protests. Anxious to suppress radical propaganda, Liverpool cracked down with his Six Acts, which in February 1820 provoked a conspiracy to kill and behead the prime minister and prince regent. Police spies betrayed the thirteen conspirators, who were arrested in a raid by the early police force, the Bow Street Runners. Five of the conspirators, including William Davidson, son of a British planter in Jamaica and a black woman, were hanged, then after their death beheaded. Britain held on, but the pressure for reform was becoming unstoppable. In Europe, Metternich and his allies found it hard to repress a soaring spirit of freedom and sense of nation that combined into the thrilling, brooding movement of the Romantics.

On 6 March 1821, a Greek officer in the Russian army, Prince Alexander Ypsilantis, leader of a secret Greek organization, *Filiki Etaireia*, rode across the border from Russian Kishnev into Ottoman Jassy to announce a Greek revolution. 'The hour has come,' he wrote. 'The enlightened peoples of Europe eagerly await the liberty of the Hellenes.' In the following months, Greeks rebelled against the Ottoman sultan across the Greek world, which encompassed Phanar in Constantinople, Moldavia and Wallachia, as well as mainland Greece.† The sultan cracked down:

---

* In its biggest slum, Angel Meadow, families lived amid heaps of garbage and clouds of smoke. In Liverpool, home to 80,000 and Britain's second largest city by 1800, some 60 per cent of children died before the age of five, and life expectancy was twenty-six. Even as food improved, pushing up the population (the average height of an Englishman increased by two inches between 1750 and 1900), the industrial cities – seething with TB, cholera and typhoid – were killing the new working class in vast numbers. These new industries also widened the gap between classes, and changed the shape of families. The factories required managers and clerks, a new caste, mainly male, though aided by literate female assistants, who all worked in a new location: the office. While the workers sweated on the factory floor, these managers signed papers and enforced the new timetable – the working schedule that set the pace of western urban life until the Covid pandemic of 2020. Office workers wished to show their seniority to the foreman and their proximity to the proprietor. To promote the cult of industry, now associated with virtue and status, office workers wore dark shortened jackets and trousers, a costume that became the suit. Starting as Beau Brummell's cravats, ties – the most futile item of clothing ever invented – developed as part of the uniform of working sobriety.

† The rebellion placed Tsar Alexander in an awkward position: his entourage was filled

the Phanariots were publicly beheaded, the Orthodox patriarch was hanged from his own gate, the Greeks routed and massacred. But in Greece itself a medley of klepht brigands and Phanariot princes fought on – a spur to Romantic revolution. A thousand philhellenes rushed to fight for Greece – most famously the outrageous Romantic poet Lord Byron.

A lame, curly-haired, poetic celebrity, described as 'mad, bad and dangerous to know' by one of his female lovers, delighted Romantics with his epic of the adventures of wild young man *Childe Harold* and had shocked British bourgeois by having affairs with boys and girls, culminating it was said in the seduction of his half-sister. In the wake of the ensuing outcry, he left to support Italian radicals in Italy, where he lived the Romantic dream, defining man as 'Half dust, half deity, alike unfit / To sink or soar'. He hated Metternich and Liverpool.* If the words were by Byron, the music was by Beethoven, whose wild-haired, half-mad, deaf genius personified tempestuous Romanticism. In May 1824, he premiered his Symphony No. 9, a celebration of freedom, using Schiller's 'Ode to Joy', that could only be a criticism of Metternich's system. 'All men shall be brothers!'†

In August 1823 the thirty-five-year-old Byron arrived in Cephalonia, Greece. Early the next year on the mainland, accompanied by his small Byron Brigade, he took joint command of Greek forces while falling passionately in love with his Greek page. The Romantic hero was planning an attack on Lepanto when he unromantically perished of dysentery. The rebellion intensified, watched with alarm by the Ottoman sultan and with uneasiness by Metternich, Liverpool and the new Russian tsar

with Greeks, and his foreign minister was the Corfiote aristocrat Ioannis Kapodistrias, who left Russian service to become the first governor of independent Greece. Not only Greeks joined the Orthodox revolt: the Serbian warlord Đorđe Petrović, known as Black George (*Karađorđe*) joined the *Filiki Etaireia*. In 1804, this sheep trader led a successful but short-lived rebellion against the Ottomans. He was assassinated in 1817 by his rival warlord, Miloš Obrenović, who had won concessions from the sultan. The two families, Obrenovići and Karađorđevići, fought for power in Serbia until 1903.

* When the foreign secretary, Viscount Castlereagh, a manic depressive, committed suicide, Byron was elated:

  Posterity will ne'er survey

  A Nobler grave than this:

  Here lie the bones of Castlereagh:

  Stop, traveller, and piss!

† Sitting at the front of the orchestra who had been instructed to follow the conductor not the composer, Beethoven 'threw himself back and forth like a madman. He stretched to his full height . . . crouched down to the floor . . . flailed about with his hands and feet as though he wanted to play all the instruments and sing all the chorus.' As he died in 1826, he said, like Augustus, 'Applaud, friends, the comedy is over.' At his funeral, crowds lined the streets of Vienna.

Nicholas I, a brother of Alexander. On his succession in December 1825, Nicholas – an imperious and magniloquent, strappingly good-looking, pewter-eyed martinet – faced a coup by liberal officers. It was a moment when Russia could have taken another route. Instead Nicholas crushed it with artillery and hangings. He took no chances at home, founding the first Russian political police, the Gendarmes, and the secret police, the Third Section of his personal chancellery, which started with just 416 employees. Such covert bureaucrats increasingly were not only tools of state power but represented its fearsome mystique too.

Starting with Alexander and continuing with Nicholas, the Romanov family beat the odds of biology by producing four conscientious, capable emperors in a row. Contemptuous of Britain's chattering Parliament, loathing liberal views, despising his millions of Jews, Nicholas, a torch-bearer for Russian autocracy, nationalism and Orthodoxy, embraced a mission of empire. Using his total command to outplay the inconsistent western democracies, he was an adept player of the World Game, crushing a Polish rebellion in 1830, seizing back the Caucasus from Persia, fighting a long war against Chechen jihadists and plotting to seize Constantinople.

His first chance came when Sultan Mahmud II recruited the dynamic Egyptian ruler Mehmed Ali to crush the Greek rebels. Mehmed dispatched his talented son Ibrahim the Red – named for his beard and his ferocity – to Greece where he systematically slaughtered the rebels, breaking the rebellion. The Greeks appealed to the Russians, the French and the British, who were all now sympathetic, for different reasons.

Nicholas, the Orthodox champion, saw the Greeks as a way to crack the Ottomans; in Britain, Parliament was dominated by George Canning, the bald, nervy, brilliant son of an impoverished Anglo-Irish vintner and an actress, who was tentative about reform at home but saw an opportunity for Britain in the new nations abroad – from Gran Colombia to Greece. 'Our foreign policy cannot be conducted against the will of the nation,' he said. In Greece, he joined forces with Nicholas, sending fleets to protect the Greeks. Mehmed Ali advised the sultan to be cautious, but was ignored.

At Navarino, on 20 October 1827, the Anglo-Franco-Russian fleet sank the Egyptian–Ottoman fleet – and Ibrahim returned to Egypt. Mehmed was incensed by the Ottoman folly. Canning and Nicholas now backed a new country – Greece – that was a new type of state, formed by self-determination, which aspired to recreate an ancient history, language and nation. It was the first of many which, over the next century, were relaunched out of the dynastic empires. A new way of imagining politics, it became the only way.

Canning celebrated Bolívar's new nations. 'Spanish America is free,' he said, recognizing Bolívar's Gran Colombia. He added melodramatically, 'I called the New World into existence to redress the balance of the Old.'

Bolívar had won the war, but he struggled to control the peace.

ARE YOU STABBING ME, KING OF THE WORLD?
BOLÍVAR AND SHAKA

In 1828, Bolívar, inspired by both America and Britain to devise a way out of 'anarchy', assembled a congress at Ocaña to agree a constitution for Gran Colombia, but when the meeting broke up he imposed his own Organic Decree declaring himself president for life with the right to name his successor. Cadaverous and sick, Bolívar struggled to control his colossal state. His paramour Manuela refused to return to her English husband and rejoined Bolívar, scandalizing society with her power (nicknamed *La Presidenta*), dancing and frizelations while he dreamed of more conquests. Seizing power in Bogotá, he was declared president-Liberator. 'The republic will be lost,' he declared, 'unless it gives me the fullest authority.' Yet, to his horror, he was now hated as a tyrant.

As Bolívar's enemies in south America planned his murder, in south Africa intimate killers stalked Shaka.

On 22 September 1828, Shaka was sitting on the mats outside his house at KwaDukuza admiring his cattle herd and receiving delegations, served by his *isigodlo* women, when suddenly his half-brothers Dingane and Mhlangana appeared, spears hidden under their cloaks. Shaka had established his kingdom using new military tactics and unpredictable terror, but his king-making aunt Mnkabayi, shocked by his Neronian matricide, now regarded him a 'madman'. He had to be culled.

Shaka's bodyguard Mbopha diverted the king's attention by dispersing the gathered crowd. The king watched with amusement as Mbopha returned to take up his position behind him. But then, as the brothers approached, Mbopha speared Shaka in the back; Prince Mhlangana joined in, but Dingane, careful not to be a king slayer, held back. 'What's the matter with my father's children?' cried Shaka. 'Are you stabbing *me*, king of the world? You'll come to an end through killing one another.' Mhlangana jumped over the body to claim the throne.

The crowd watched in amazement. The assassins gathered to hear the sacred ballad and sacrifice a black ox to honour the deeds of ancestors and give thanksgiving to their father Senzangakona – and to purify the killers against wizardry.

Shaka was buried sitting up with a slice of buttock in his mouth to suppress the anger of his spirit; ten courtiers and women were sacrificed with him. The assassins banned mourning for the 'madman', then while Mbopha ran the kingdom, the Zulu family met to choose the new *nkosi*. Dingane was popular with the army, but Mhlangana had killed Shaka and jumped over his body. Dressed as a man, clad in robes of blue monkey tails and a feathered headdress, and brandishing a bundle of spears and a war shield, the Great She-Elephant Mnkabayi, who had made Shaka king and then agreed to his murder, denounced Shaka who had become chief only 'through demented strength'. She decided that 'the one with the bloody assegai' – Mhlangana – 'shall not rule' and nominated Dingane, who called himself 'the Mediator'. The She-Elephant ordered Mhlangana's killing. Dingane invited Mhlangana to swim with him in the river, where the Great She-Elephant's posse ambushed him.

Strapping and handsome with a small beard, agile in dance and war, Dingane, forty years old, executed Mbopha, eighty commanders and all his brothers except one and then crushed Tsonga opposition in southern Mozambique, as well as the Ndebele and Swazis. As for the Europeans at Lourenço Marques and Fort Natal, renamed Durban after the British governor of the Cape, Sir Benjamin D'Urban, he sent impis (Zulu regiments) to punish them, while persuading white hunters to train some of his men with rifles.

Shaka was dead, but in Bogotá, three days later, the assassins coming for Bolívar encountered a force of nature: Manuela.

In the early hours of 25 September 1828, a hit squad burst into the palace. Manuela, awakened, defended the door and, when Bolívar prepared to fight, ordered him to escape. Bolívar jumped out of the window; Manuela held the assassins at bay. Frustrated, they beat her as *El Libertador* hid under a bridge. Bolívar thanked Manuela, 'Liberatrix of the Liberator', but the humiliation had shattered the Genius of the Storm whose state now fell apart as Peru, Bolivia, Ecuador, Venezuela and Colombia grasped independence. Like Gran Colombia, Bolívar was dying.

In January 1830, Bolivar, still only forty-seven, faced reality: 'Colombians! Today I cease to govern you . . . Never, never, I swear, have my thoughts been tainted by lust for kingship.' Cadaverously consumptive, he retired to his house, La Quinta, near Cartagena, spluttering, 'How will I get out of this labyrinth?'

There was no way out.

REVOLUTION: PEDRO AND DOMITILA

Bolívar died with a curse: 'America's ungovernable; he who serves a revolution ploughs the sea. The country will pass into the hands of an indistinguishable string of tyrants of every colour.'

Just as Bolívar was losing control of Colombia, Metternich was losing control of France, the sparkwheel of revolution. 'When Paris coughs,' said Metternich, 'Europe catches cold.'

On 30 July 1830, revolution returned to the streets of Paris. The last of Louis XVI's brothers, Charles X, aided by his minister the duc de Polignac, son of Marie Antoinette's best friend, attacked the liberals in the Assembly, opposed by Lafayette – now seventy and back in France after being voted a fortune of $200,000 by the US Congress. From the start of his reign, Charles had been determined to promote absolutism at home and empire abroad. On 17 April 1825, he dispatched fourteen battleships to force Haiti to pay an indemnity to compensate France for the loss of its slaves and the 1804 massacre – in return for recognition. President Boyer was blackmailed into paying 150 million francs but was forced to take out a loan with a French bank to pay it. The money was sent to France in cash. The double debt impoverished Haiti.*

As opposition seethed, Charles sought a Napoleonic distraction in an African conquest: it started as a farce but would in the twentieth century almost destroy France itself. When a ruler of Algiers touched a French envoy with his fly-whisk, Charles used this *opéra bouffe* moment as his pretext to invade the Barbary State, the start of what became the largest empire in Africa. On 5 July 1830, French troops seized Algiers. On the 9th, at Palais Saint-Cloud, Charles announced that he would now rule by *ordinance* and, as trouble began in Paris, on the 25th he cancelled the free press, dissolved the Assembly and cut the franchise. Two days later, the newspapers defied the king, launching the first media revolution.

---

* The families of slave owners – including the Duke of Leutchenberg (Empress Josephine's son Eugene) – received Haitian payments for many generations, the only case of the descendants of liberated slaves themselves forced to compensate the descendants of their own masters. In 1843, Boyer was overthrown in popular protests; Santo Domingo rebelled and fought a war of independence to create the Dominican Republic; and, paying its last instalment in 1888, Haiti took out loans from US banks that it could not service.

Crowds built barricades in the streets of Paris, shouting '*À la guillotine!*' Fighting spread; on the 29th the mob stormed the Tuileries. As Lafayette rushed to the city and assumed the leadership of the National Guard, Charles abdicated. The Assembly invited Lafayette to rule; instead he proposed the king's liberal cousin, Louis Philippe, as king of the French.

Louis Philippe's father Philippe Égalité had been guillotined; he himself had fought the Austrians and had then defected from the revolution, travelling through Europe and America, staying with George Washington, teaching geography at a German school and maths at an English one, before returning to France with his Bourbon cousins.* The duc d'Orléans was bluff, unpretentious and unregal, mocked by Talleyrand who quipped, 'It's not enough to be someone – you have to be something.' But the king had lived an amazing life and even Talleyrand's mistress-niece, Dorothea de Dino, said, 'There's no more interesting conversation than the king.' But he played the citizen king, eschewing a court, while his friend James de Rothschild funded the regime and supported him in discouraging wars. Rothschild also backed the first railways, launching his *Chemins de Fer du Nord* by taking 1,700 Parisians to lunch in Lille and dinner in Brussels.

James held court in Talleyrand's old mansion in Paris, where his dinners were cooked by Carême, a *chef de bouche*, philosopher of haute cuisine who had served Talleyrand, Alexander I and George IV. The banker was able to celebrate wins by his racehorses with his own Lafitte wines. Witty, caustic and vigilant, he was happily married to Betty, his beautiful Viennese niece, who had her five children taught piano by Chopin and held an almost royal salon, herself friends with Queen Marie Amélie. When his brother Nathan died in 1836, James became the leader of the family. He still spoke French with a heavy German accent and when his London niece married out of the faith, he insisted she be ostracized. Yet he personified a new interconnected capitalist world. At

---

* Alexandre Dumas, the son of Thomas-Alexandre 'Black Devil' Dumas, Haitian revolutionary general, was Louis Philippe's librarian/secretary during the 1820s and took part in the 1830 revolution. Now he started to write stories based on his father's adventures, including his uncle's smuggling via a small Caribbean island, Montecristo. In 1844, his novel *The Count of Monte-Cristo* chronicled the perils of the ever-changing regimes in France. It was published in eighteen instalments in the *Journal des Debats*. Dumas became one of the commercial super-novélists who benefited from improved literacy and the proliferation of reader-hungry newspapers. The sales were colossal, but thanks to juggling a family and a lifestyle that involved building a Château de Monte-Cristo and forty mistresses, the irrepressible novelist was always broke, despite hiring a stable of writers to pump out bestsellers. Dumas flourished under Louis Philippe, though constantly confronting racism about his origins. 'My father was a mulatto, my grandfather was a Negro,' he would reply, 'and my great-grandfather a monkey. You see, Sir, my family starts where yours ends.'

his salon he entertained not only princes but also Honoré de Balzac, the rambunctious novelist who observed characters, high and low, surviving in the new realm of industry and money. Balzac's father had made it from peasant boy to royal secretary, then became a revolutionary organizer and idiosyncratic essayist, only at fifty-three marrying a beautiful, well-off shopkeeper's daughter who became Balzac's mother.

After an internship in a law firm,* Balzac embarked on a quixotic pursuit of fortune in multiple fields, from publishing to Sardinian slag-heaps and Ukrainian forestry, unable to resist a *'bonne speculation'*.

His first bestseller, *Eugénie Grandet*, portrayed a daughter overshadowed by the avarice of her rich farmer father; then in *Père Goriot* he introduced Rastignac, a young provincial making it in a turbulent Paris: 'the streets of Paris possess human qualities'. Paris was always a character – 'the city of a hundred thousand novels, the head of the world'.

Balzac's novels, *'faits pour tout le monde'*, written for everyone and about everyone, made him, like Dumas, vast sums. He lived as he thought a Parisian writer should live, enjoying love affairs with duchesses and courtesans, writing all night, overweight, breathless, gradually poisoning himself on overdoses of coffee (a warning to all writers). But he was also a romantic, falling in love with a Polish countess whom he knew only through letters signed *L'Étrangère*.

Balzac accepted loans from James de Rothschild, but he perhaps resented the banker's power, repaying his help with his character baron de Nucingen who bore resemblances to James. 'The secret of all great fortunes, when there is no obvious explanation for them,' wrote Balzac in his *Le Père Goriot*, defining a rule of modern capitalism, 'is always some forgotten crime . . . forgotten because it's been properly handled.' Balzac was fascinated by all of society, analysed in his realistic novels, which he called *'Études des Moeurs'*, 'that no longer believes in anything but money'. But it was through family that this indefatigable dynamo followed the threads.

After Paris, revolution spread to Habsburg Italy, Romanov Poland, the Netherlands and, in April 1831, Braganza Brazil. In 1824 Emperor Pedro had been granted a prerogative – the Moderating Power – to oversee an assembly elected by a broad suffrage of white males in a

---

* Balzac chronicled and rejected the horror of the new office life, an institution that dominated the days of millions in the west into the twenty-first century, fearing that as 'a clerk, a machine . . . eating and drinking and sleeping at fixed hours, I should be like everyone else.' He became, before Dickens, the first observer of the lives of clerks in his *Les employés* and his essay *La physiologie de l'employe*. 'Bureaucracy,' he said, 'is a giant mechanism operated by pygmies.'

hybrid constitution. Soon afterwards, in December 1825, his ill-treated Habsburg empress Leopoldina gave birth to a son, Pedro, duke of Braganza, but Pedro also flaunted his devotion to Domitila, now raised to marquess of Santos, who had herself just given birth to a daughter, Isabel, recognized by the emperor as duchess of Goiás.

Wildly in love with Domitila, he imposed his paramour on his depressed wife who, now hating 'dreadful America', wrote to her sister Marie Louise about the 'barbarous' Pedro: 'He's just given me proof of his negligence to me, mistreating me in the presence of the person who is the cause of all my afflictions.' She was pregnant again. In December 1826, while her husband was away fighting a southern rebellion, Leopoldina miscarried; weakened by emetics and laxatives, she died. Pedro was horrified by his own behaviour, haunted by her ghost. He even jumped out of the bed he shared with Domitila: 'Get off of me! I know I live an unworthy life. The thought of the empress doesn't leave me.' He sobbed over his son Pedro: 'Poor boy, you are the most unhappy prince in the world.' He decided to remarry.

It was not easy – in Brazil and Europe, his cruelty and promiscuity were notorious. He compromised, choosing Princess Amélie, the seventeen-year-old daughter of Josephine's son Prince Eugène. So his first wife was Habsburg, his second Bonapartist. He became a loyal husband. Meanwhile, he struggled to establish Brazil. First he defeated the northern Confederation of the Equator before leading a war in the south: in 1825, the remote Brazilian province of Banda Oriental (East Bank) rebelled, encouraged by the United Provinces of the Río de la Plata. Pedro fought the Argentines on land and sea in small skirmishes (both the Argentine and Brazilian fleets on the River Plate were commanded by British mercenaries). At the same time, his father João of Portugal died, making him king there too. But he abdicated that throne in favour of his little daughter Maria II, who, with the negligence of dynasties, was dispatched to Portugal. But the Liberator's war failed; he lost part of the province, which became Uruguay.

Hated for his marital cruelty, challenged by the liberal Assembly, facing rebellion from cariocas shouting 'Death to the Emperor!', Pedro abdicated and left for Europe, characteristically treating Brazil like a girlfriend. 'Everything is over,' he said, 'between me and Brazil – for ever.'

His five-year-old son, now Emperor Pedro II, was raised in the seclusion of a country estate while Brazil was ruled by regents. Although the first constitution had promised a 'gradual emancipation of African slaves', the next one in 1824 ignored slavery, which was booming:

40,000 African slaves arrived annually in the first half of the 1820s, and 60,000 a year after 1826. British abolition of slave trading and its West Africa Squadron had reduced the Atlantic trade. Yet between 1807 and 1865, 3.5 million enslaved Africans were bought and transported across the ocean.

THE GLADSTONES — QUAMINA AND SIR JOHN: SLAVE REBELS AND SLAVE MASTERS

As Britain fought Napoleon and debated political reform, even Wilberforce said little about slavery, though 700,000 people remained enslaved on British plantations. Jamaican slavery was consolidated by the acquisition of Dutch Guiana on the mainland, where plantations in Demerara used slaves to make the world's best brown sugar. Sir John Gladstone, devout Presbyterian son of a Scottish trader, who had moved to Liverpool and made a fortune in commodities, corn, sugar and cotton, trading with India, US and Brazil, already owned plantations in Jamaica but had bought a new one in Demerara that helped make him the biggest British slave owner and chairman of the West India Association, the Interest. Yet it was just at this moment that the slaves themselves placed their suffering back at the centre of politics.

In August 1823, Quamina and Jack Gladstone, an enslaved father and son, led a revolt starting on the Success plantation, owned by Gladstone. They were not, however, related to the nabob of Liverpool, whose three sons, including William, the future prime minister, were already at Eton. Quamina, in his late forties, who had been trafficked from the Gold Coast, was Gladstone's head carpenter; his son Jack, a cooper, was handsome, 'well-made' and six foot two. Forced·to work thirteen-hour shifts, Quamina had been prevented from nursing his dying wife Peggy, and returned to find her dead. Encouraged by an English pastor, John Smith, whose church Quamina attended, Jack organized a revolt which was joined by 13,000 slaves. They almost seized the colony.

The British rushed their West India Regiment, made up of freed Caribbean slaves, to crush the rebels. Hundreds were killed; nineteen were sentenced to death, their heads displayed on spikes, a warning to the African-born slaves who believed only complete bodies would return to their homes after death. Quamina was cornered, shot and strung up on a gibbet, where a 'colony of wasps built a nest in the cavity of the stomach and were flying in and out of the jaws that hung frightfully open'. After a letter from Gladstone in England requesting mercy, Jack was exiled to St Lucia, but the death in prison of the Reverend John Smith ignited the abolitionist cause as much as killing the enslaved. As abolition gathered momentum, so did the resistance of the Interest.

The duke of Wellington, now prime minister,* was determined to resist abolition, parliamentary reform and the lifting of restrictions on Catholics and Jews. Yet his lieutenant Robert Peel, the textiles heir, persuaded him to end Catholic restrictions.† The duke claimed Parliament had no right to free slaves. 'We must not plunder the proprietors in the West Indies,' he said, 'to acquire popularity in England,' while the removing of Jewish restrictions was out of the question.

British manufacturing was booming, aided by the first railways, which used steam power to transport passengers and goods at perilous new speeds: on 15 September 1830, Wellington opened the Manchester–Liverpool line. Former cabinet minister William Huskisson was chatting to the duke in his official locomotive, when another, *The Rocket*, careened towards him. Huskisson tried to climb into the ducal train, but fell under *Rocket*'s wheels, his leg smashed as the duke watched. 'I've met my death,' said Huskisson. 'God forgive me!' The accident did not act as a deterrent, and railways quickly united Britain: train journeys rose from 5.5 million in 1838 to 111 million twenty years later. In Manchester, Wellington was booed by millworkers, but he still refused parliamentary reform – a policy which destroyed his ministry just as the fat old king, George IV, died. His only child, the adored Charlotte, had died in childbirth at twenty-one in 1817. So his heir was his brother, the Duke of Clarence, a bluff former sailor, with ten illegitimate children by his actress paramour, who was doubtful about reform and abolition. He became William IV aged sixty-four and was forced to offer the premiership to Charles, Earl Grey, a veteran advocate of reform and abolition. Out of power since 1807, this septuagenarian Regency roué and landed magnate boasted that 'The acreage of his cabinet surpassed any previous record.' Yet Grey would revolutionize the British world in two acts.

---

* When Lord Liverpool suffered a stroke after the longest premiership of the last two centuries, the snootier grandees believed Canning could never succeed him. 'The son of an actress is, ipso facto,' said Earl Grey, 'disqualified from becoming prime minister.' But George IV appointed him. On his death after just 119 days, the next government collapsed after just 144 days and in January 1828 the king appointed Wellington.

† Such was the rancour inspired by Catholic emancipation that Wellington challenged a critic, the earl of Winchilsea, to a duel, held on 23 March 1829 in Battersea Fields. Both discharged their weapons harmlessly and honour was satisfied. This was the last prime ministerial duel.

LORD CUPID AND THE LADY PATRONESSES

Grey's partner was his irrepressible foreign secretary, the Anglo-Irish landowner Harry Temple, Viscount Palmerston, now forty-six. Originally notable for his tireless sexual adventures, Palmerston, who dominated governments from 1830 to 1865, was more than anyone else the architect of British world power in a new age of empire.

As a Harrow schoolboy, he had been known as a philistine boxer; as a young man, he was nicknamed Lord Cupid, an unreconstructed Regency buck who had first attracted attention as the lover of three of the five lady patronesses of the elite Almack's club, starting with the Russian ambassador's wife, Dorothea Lieven, who had also been Metternich's paramour. Now, unrestrained by being foreign secretary, he kept a diary of his almost daily sexual encounters, sometimes in the morning, sometimes in the evening and often in the middle of the day, with a diverse cast of courtesans, prostitutes and countesses, scarcely concealed, in a very English code, as reports of the weather. 'A fine night in the garden' was a typical entry.

Lord Cupid had been in Tory governments since 1809 as secretary at war, but in 1828 he switched to the Whigs as a protégé of Canning, a supporter of cautious reform and the abolition of slavery. From now on, serving almost permanently as foreign secretary, he backed liberal measures at home while implacably promoting British power abroad. 'We have no eternal allies, no perpetual enemies,' he declared. 'Our interests are eternal and perpetual, and those interests it is our duty to follow.' He insisted, 'Those who desire to see the principles of liberty thrive and extend through the world should cherish, with an almost religious veneration, the prosperity and greatness of England.' When a Frenchman, thinking to be highly complimentary, said to Palmerston, 'If I weren't a Frenchman, I'd wish to be an Englishman,' he replied, 'If I weren't an Englishman, I should wish to be an Englishman.' His endurance in detailed negotiations earned him another nickname: Protocols Palmerston. A mediocre speaker, the exuberant, shrewd and bewhiskered ruffian became a public icon, portrayed in the press as Pam the prize fighter. It was Lord Pumicestone who now forged Britain's idiosyncratic combination of liberal mission and gun-toting imperialism – a policy which resembled that of the US in the second half of the twentieth century. It was built in his own image. He first coped with the aftermath of the 1830 revolutions in which the former Austrian Netherlands rebelled against the Dutch king. Palmerston created a new kingdom, Belgium, that he hoped would restrain France and guard the balance of power.

He offered its throne to a favourite prince, Leopold of Saxe-Coburg, widower of the British heiress Charlotte. Leopold became the first king of Belgium, where his family still reign.

Metternich was shaken by 1830 – 'My entire life is destroyed' – and he hated Palmerston: 'Palmerston is wrong about everything.' Palmerston enjoyed baiting the old chancellor. 'I'd like to see Metternich's face,' he said. But the 1830 revolutions proved less disastrous than first feared: the tsar crushed the Poles, Metternich held Italy; Louis Philippe and Leopold stabilized France and Belgium, where both proved vigorous patrons of industry, and both were intimate allies of the Rothschilds. Louis Philippe appeared the very model of a modern monarch; the Bonapartes were clearly finished.[*]

As Palmerston projected his new world vision, at home he backed reform and abolition, which were now becoming inevitable.

RATHER DIE THAN LIVE AS A SLAVE:
DADDY SHARPE AND ABOLITION

In December 1831, 60,000 Jamaican slaves rebelled, led by a captivating Baptist millenarian preacher, Samuel 'Daddy' Sharpe, 'the most intelligent, remarkable slave, his fine sinewy frame handsomely moulded', recalled a missionary, with 'an eye whose brilliancy was most dazzling'. Only fourteen whites were killed but, aided as usual by the Maroons, whom planters paid by the numbers of black ears delivered, the Christmas Rebellion was crushed. Six hundred slaves died in battle or were murdered by planters, 340 sentenced to death, some just for stealing a pig or a cow. 'I'd rather die upon yonder gallows,' declared Sharpe, 'than live as a slave.'

As Grey appointed a committee of inquiry filled with slave owners, rioters demanded electoral reform and attacked Wellington's mansion. On 7 June 1832, Grey and Palmerston passed the Reform Act, a partial measure that raised the electorate by 250,000 voters to around 650,000 – almost the same number as the Caribbean slaves whose liberation

---

[*] Louis Philippe's lack of glamour encouraged Bonapartist dreams, centred around the heir, known as the Eaglet. In Vienna, Emperor Franz gave Napoleon's son a regiment but prevented him from serving anywhere. On 22 July 1832 Napoleon-Franz died of TB, aged twenty-one. The young Adolf Hitler was obsessed with the duke of Reichstadt: in 1940, one of the first things he did on conquering France was to order Napoleon II's reburial in the Invalides in Paris next to his father, as a gift to the French people.

became the issue in the general election at the end of that year. Young William Gladstone denounced abolition, arguing that slavery was 'not necessarily an evil', and claimed that the conditions of slaves were no worse than those of child labourers in England, while liberation would 'exchange the evils now affecting the negro for others which are weightier'. The king, who had visited slave plantations as a sailor, also insisted that the 'state of the negroes' was 'humble happiness'.

Yet, horrified by the slave rebellions, the reformed Parliament finally had a majority for abolition. Grey's colonial secretary, Edward Stanley, Lancashire grandee, future earl of Derby, later thrice prime minister, promised abolition 'without palliative or compromise'. But if it was to pass, it required *both* palliative and compromise – 'to be fair to the slave', said Palmerston, 'as to the planter'. The votes of the Interest blocked abolition unless the government paid compensation, buying the slaves from their owners in order to liberate them.

The Slavery Abolition Act had its third reading in the House of Commons in August 1833, just after William Wilberforce died, and came into force a year later. But it was so flawed that some abolitionists contemplated voting against.

The compromise egregiously enriched slave owners for owning humans, yet without the compensation it would not have passed. Slaves became indentured 'apprentices' for six years before full liberation. The slave owners, who varied from titled grandees to persons of colour, a quarter of them women, were, for example, paid £20 a slave in Jamaica, £15 in Guiana, a total of £15 million.* Sir John Gladstone received the biggest payment, £106,769 for his 2,508 slaves, and his son William, the future prime minister, acknowledged abolition: 'God prosper it.'†

---

* In 1833, this compensation formed '40 per cent of the government's annual expenditure', writes Michael Taylor, 'and until the banking rescue package of 2008 it remained the largest specific payout in British history'. Baring Brothers initially bid to raise the vast loan, but its size was daunting. Grey turned to Nathan Rothschild and his brother-in-law Moses Montefiore, both supporters of abolition who deplored slavery as akin to the racist persecutions of Jewish people over many centuries. They regarded the raising of the loan as essential to delivering liberation, while they campaigned hard to overturn restrictions against Jews. Days after abolition passed, Parliament rejected the Jewish Civil Disabilities Repeal Bill. Britain 'is a Christian country and a Christian legislature', said Wellington. 'This measure would remove that peculiar character.'

† Just after abolition, a young amateur naturalist set off on the Pacific voyage of HMS *Beagle* that was both imperial project and scientific inquiry. Born at the heart of the interrelated industrial families of Wedgwoods and Darwins, Charles Darwin was partly chosen for his study of marine invertebrates and partly because his wealth covered his expenses. His father Robert vetoed the trip until persuaded by his brother-in-law, the pottery king Josiah Wedgwood II. On the five-year voyage, Darwin studied the long-isolated animals of the Galapagos Islands and, noting the variety of natural life, developed the idea that 'It

Yet not everyone was delighted by abolition. In Africa many rulers obstinately resisted the end of this profitable trade and, strangely, abolition coincided with an intensification of conflict and of slavery itself across the continent.

THE FEMALE FIGHTERS OF DAHOMEY, THE VICEROY OF OUIDAH, THE CALIPH OF SOKOTO AND COMMANDANT PRETORIUS

Four years after abolition but out of British reach, the caliph of Sokoto, Muhammad Bello, died, leaving a new empire that was now the second largest slave state in world history with around 2.5 million slaves – compared to 3.5 million in the largest, the USA. Bello's father, Usman dan Fodio, a tall, charismatic Hausa born in Gobir (Nigeria), a Muslim city, had in 1774 at the age of twenty launched a jihad, inspired by mystical trances and visions, going on to conquer the largest empire in sub-Saharan Africa and in 1803 declaring himself the caliph. On his death in 1817, his son Bello continued the holy war, expanding from northern Nigeria to Burkina Faso, Cameroon and Niger.

Wars between African polities continued as they fought and expanded, no different from Eurasian states; wars captured slaves, who were less easy to export, creating a surplus. 'After abolition,' writes John Reader, 'the use of slaves in Africa became more common than ever before and enslavement actually increased.'

Further south, King Ghezo of Dahomey, assisted by the notorious 'viceroy of Ouidah' and his female army, resisted abolition. One visitor to Ghezo's palace in the capital Abomey passed 'three human heads ... the blood still oozing' on each side of the doorway. 'The slave trade has been the ruling principle of my people,' Ghezo told British envoys. 'It's the source of their glory and wealth. Their songs celebrate their victories and the mother lulls the child to sleep with notes of triumph over an enemy reduced to slavery.'

Ghezo intensified his slave trading, selling 10,000 slaves annually. He sent expeditions to seize slaves from neighbouring peoples, and turned

---

is absurd to talk of one animal being higher than another.' In 1859 he published *On the Origin of Species*, in which he argued, 'As many more individuals of each species are born than can possibly survive; and as, consequently, there is a frequently recurring struggle for existence, it follows that any being, if it vary however slightly in any manner profitable to itself . . . will have a better chance of surviving, and thus be naturally selected.' He concluded that 'from so simple a beginning, endless forms most beautiful and most wonderful have been, and are being, evolved'.

his female bodyguard into the crack Ahosi, or Mino (King's Wives, or Mothers, in Fon), vanguard of 3,000–6,000 girl soldiers who fascinated European visitors raised on tales of Herodotos' Amazons. Joining as early as eight and banned from sex or marriage (except with the king), the women were trained to endure pain by barefoot tramping over thorns. They wore striped armless tunics and a crocodile-emblazoned cap, and carried daggers, short swords, maces and rifles. They would chant:

> As blacksmiths forge iron and change its nature,
> So we change ours!
> We're no longer women, we are men.

Some were recruited from palace women, some forcibly enrolled by their own families, many were widows of killed or enslaved captives. Ghezo used them not only as shock troops and slave raiders but also as his executioners; visitors chronicled hundreds of scalps collected by the warriors. Their commander, Seh-Dong-Hong-Beh, was drawn by a visiting British envoy, holding a rifle in one hand and a bleeding severed head in the other.

In 1818, this young Dahomean prince had seized the throne from his brother, King Adandozan, with the help of an Afro-Brazilian slave trader, Francisco de Sousa, scion of the first Portuguese governor of Brazil. Adandozan increased his slaving expeditions while using slaves to work his plantations of palm olive that now became profitable in Nigeria. He even sold possible dissidents within the royal family as slaves. The grizzled, gruesome de Sousa, who combined Catholic and voodoo faith, was originally so poor that he stole cowrie shells from voodoo temples, but ultimately he thrived as a slave trader, living in sultanic splendour in a family compound, Singbomey in Ouidah, amid a harem of African women with whom he fathered 201 children. When he went to reclaim a debt from Adandozan in Abomey, the king imprisoned him. But he was visited in jail by Prince Gakpe (the future Ghezo), whose mother Sousa had rescued from Brazilian slavery, and they made a blood pact to destroy the king. Aided in his escape by the Afro-Dutch widow of King Agonglo, he delivered guns to the prince, who seized power, taking the name Ghezo, and promoted Sousa to *chacha*, an invented title derived from his habit of saying '*Já, já!*' – Soon, soon! in Portuguese. Ghezo installed his mother, Agontime, as *kpojito* (queen mother) and, using rifles supplied by Sousa, broke the Oyo kingdom, thus expanding his power. Before long Britain blockaded his ports in a bid to restrict his slaving.

Ghezo and Bello were far from the only African potentates who resented abolition.* Slavery was booming in east Africa too, and in southern Africa a white tribe was also outraged by the abolition of slavery.

In 1836, Dutch-speaking Afrikaners, who regarded the enslaving of Africans as a God-given right, started to migrate from the Cape, to escape British rule and conquer a new homeland. These 14,000 Voortrekkers, righteous, heavily armed and well organized, accompanied by a similar number of enslaved Africans who, after abolition, had been retitled 'apprentices' but were often trained to fight beside them, clashed with the African kings. The Afrikaners became another tribe in the chain-predation of the *Mfecane* for land and cattle – but with better weaponry. Some attacked King Mzilikazi of the Ndebele, driving him north into Zimbabwe; others led by Piet Retief reached the Zulu court of King Dingane. Shouting 'Kill the Wizards!', Dingane had them cudgelled to death before attacking their encampments, killing 40 Voortrekkers, 250 black auxiliaries and 185 children, while another regiment under Prince Mpande eliminated an entire British unit from Natal, killing the sixteen whites and several thousand black auxiliaries and raiding Port Natal itself. But the Afrikaners rallied under the skilled fighter Andries Pretorius, elected chief commandant, who in December 1838, deploying 472 Boers and 120 African troops, defeated 12,000 Zulus, killing 1,000 of them with just three Boers wounded. Pretorius founded a republic around a new town of Pietermaritzburg in Zulu territory. Dingane, defeated by the Swazis and humiliated by the Boers, was planning to kill his remaining brother Mpande. Accompanied by his son Cetshwayo, Mpande escaped to recruit Pretorius's help.

In 1840, Mpande and Pretorius attacked and defeated Dingane, who retreated to the mountains, only to be murdered by his own courtiers. Fat, indolent and good-natured but aware that 'the Zulu people are ruled through killing', Mpande had no choice but to divvy up the booty of cattle with Pretorius, to whom he ceded two-fifths of his kingdom. Britain, whose appetites and resources exceeded those of all local players, Dutch and Nguni, was on their tail, soon consuming the Afrikaner Republic of Natal.

As for Pretorius, invited north to aid the Sotho king Moshoeshoe,

---

* The *oba* of Lagos, Kosoko, a Dahomean vassal, refused to cooperate until in 1851 the Royal Navy bombarded the city and deposed him, replacing him with another ruler: the first step towards a new colony. In 1862, fear of French encroachment persuaded Palmerston to annex the city. Further west, on the Gold Coast, the Asante now used slaves to work their gold mines and plantations, many living in villages around the capital Kumasi; unlucky slaves were sacrificed in annual rituals.

he founded a new South African (later Transvaal) Republic, while other Voortrekkers created the Orange Free State. When Pretorius died, his son Marthinus was elected president of Transvaal – its capital named Pretoria after his father – and later of the Free State too, all the while hunting elephants for ivory, rustling and wrangling cattle and seizing African slaves. Soon the discovery of diamonds and gold would spark another tournament of power.

Further north, in Egypt, slavery was still essential to the project of Mehmed Ali, who had hired French officers to train an army of enslaved Georgians and Sudanese, conscripted Egyptian *fellahin* and Turkish officers and rebuilt his fleet. Infuriated that the sultan had lost him his fleet at Navarino, he demanded Syria in return. When it was not forthcoming, he seized his chance to conquer an empire.

MEHMED ALI'S GAMBIT: NAPOLEON OF THE EAST

On 31 October 1831, Mehmed Ali's son Ibrahim invaded Syria, seizing Jerusalem and Damascus. 'If the sultan says I can keep Damascus,' mused Mehmed Ali, backed by Louis Philippe, 'I'll stop there ... and if not, who knows?' Then, in May 1832, Ibrahim crossed the Taurus Mountains into the Turkish heartland. As Mehmed Ali considered placing Ibrahim on the throne of Constantinople, Sultan Mahmud granted Egypt to him and ceded Syria. As Ibrahim moved closer to the Great City, the sultan appealed to his ancestral enemy, Tsar Nicholas, who sent an army to defend Constantinople, and in July he accepted a Russian protectorate. Nicholas claimed he wished to preserve the Ottoman empire: 'If it falls, I don't desire its debris. I need nothing.' No one believed him.

In May 1838, Mehmed Ali, who now ruled Sudan, Arabia, Syria, Israel and most of Anatolia, declared independence from Constantinople. Sultan Mahmud had recently eliminated the overmighty Janissaries – massacring 5,000 of them – and hired western officers to train his own modern army.* But now, at Nezib, Ibrahim routed the new Ottoman army and advanced on the Great City. Encouraged by his evangelical son-in-law Lord Shaftesbury, and the campaigns of Montefiore, both

---

* The best of the Ottoman advisers was a young Prussian captain from a Danish–Mecklenburger family who would later transform war and the shape of Europe: he advised the vizier not to fight at Nezib. The vizier ignored his advice with fatal consequences. The adviser was Helmuth von Moltke, who was a very untypical Prussian officer, thoughtful, literary and cosmopolitan, author of romantic novels, history books and now his *Letters from Turkey*.

believers in a Jewish Return to Zion, Palmerston dispatched a British consul to Jerusalem to protect Jews, long the target of persecution. He was determined to save the Ottoman, undermine the Romanov and stop Mehmed Ali. In July 1840, Palmerston threatened Louis Philippe, Mehmed Ali's backer, with war and rescued the Ottomans, sending in the fleet to bombard Beirut and Acre: Mehmed Ali accepted hereditary rule in Egypt and Sudan in return for withdrawing from Syria, Türkiye, Crete and Arabia.

Further east, Lord Cupid faced a crisis of Britain's own making in Afghanistan, where the grandsons of the great king, Durrani, ruined their empire by fighting each other, allowing another Pashtun clan, the Barakzais, led by Dost Mohammad, to seize Kabul. Durrani's deposed grandson, Shah Shuja, went into Indian exile.

Palmerston and his Indian proconsuls monitored Russian advances in central Asia. The buffer states between the two empires – the khanates of Bukhara and Khiva, Persia, Afghanistan and the Sikh kingdom – became the arena for a clandestine tournament, the so-called Great Game, in which daring Britons and Russians, often in local disguise, tried to recruit the rulers. Russia backed a Persian attack on Herat while a Russian force tried to take the khanate of Khiva (Uzbekistan). Britain backed the Sikh maharaja Ranjit Singh, inveterate enemy of the Afghans.* The Afghan amir Dost Mohammad resisted British demands to hand over control of foreign policy. Exaggerating his defiance, manipulated by the Sikh maharaja, the Indian governor-general Lord Auckland lied to London, demanding an invasion to install Shah Shuja when he should simply have negotiated a security arrangement. Palmerston reluctantly approved.

In February 1839, the Army of the Indus – 55,000 strong, with British officers and Indian sepoys, aided by Sikh troops – marched on Kabul, where, in August, Shah Shuja Durrani was acclaimed shah. Withdrawing most of the British forces, Auckland left 8,000 to back Durrani, their number reduced further when the new British prime minister, Robert Peel, cut costs. In Kabul, the sexual liaisons of Afghan women and British troops outraged the Afghans as much as the cruelties of Shah Shuja, regarded as a puppet of the British, and of the Sikhs, hated since Durrani's Punjab wars. Tensions were further aggravated when a British soldier raped an Afghan girl. Around Kandahar, the Ghilzai launched a jihad against the British.

---

* When Shah Shuja was deposed as a boy, he was given asylum by the empire builder Ranjit, who demanded in return his treasured diamond, the Koh-i-Noor.

On 2 November 1841, the amir's son Akbar Khan led insurgents into Kabul, where they attacked and killed the British within the town, then besieged the military cantonment. When Akbar tricked the British into negotiations, he personally gutted their envoy. After a defeat at Bibi Mahru, 690 Britons, 3,800 Indians and 12,000 women and children were forced into a retreat from Kabul.

As they passed through narrow defiles, Akbar, deploying masterful Afghan snipers, orchestrated the slaughter of the entire column in eight days. A single survivor, Dr Brydon, staggered into Jalalabad. Shah Shuja turned against the British but was assassinated.

In 1842, two British armies invaded Afghanistan, leaving a trail of destruction and slaughter, and retook Kabul, where they dynamited the bazaar and pillaged the city before departing. Despite the unprecedented loss of 4,500 soldiers, British power had been reasserted, and was confirmed by the fate of the Sikh empire: its maharaja had died during the invasion. In 1849, his son Maharaja Duleep Singh signed the Punjab over to the British. In 1855, the Afghan amir Dost Mohammad agreed to be 'friends' with Britain.

The retreat was a disaster, but a small one for a global empire. The lesson was not that Afghanistan was 'the graveyard of empires' – an erroneous cliché – but simply that invaders should get in and get out fast, which is what happened in 1842. Afghanistan remained a client state – with a blood-spattered interlude in 1878 – until 1919. Ironically, imperial Britain handled Afghanistan much more wisely than democratic America and Britain in the twenty-first century.

Back in the Mediterranean, Palmerston had successfully saved the Ottoman sultanate from Mehmed Ali and from the Russians. As he sank into senility, fantasizing about an invasion of China, Mehmed Ali, the greatest leader of Egypt in modern times, left an independent state, with a cotton industry and a modern army, that would be ruled by his family into the 1950s.

To the west, another cotton-producing, slave-trading empire under a successful warlord was planning its own expansion.

Into Texas.

AMERICAN WARLORDS: JACKSON'S BULLETS AND SANTA ANNA'S LEG

On 30 January 1835 in Congress, a mad assassin fired two pistols at President Jackson, then aged sixty-seven, and both misfired. Old Ferocious had lost none of his ferocity: he felled the assassin with his cane and would have beaten him to death had he not been pulled off by a fellow frontiersman, Davy Crockett.

The presence of the beaver-hatted Crockett was no coincidence. The member of the House of Representatives was planning his own personal expeditions to seize Texas.

The grizzled president founded his entire career on expansion into British, Spanish and Native American territory. Craggy, six foot one with blue eyes and wild red hair, this tough son of Ulster raised in the Carolinas was a harsh frontiersman and saloon brawler who had two bullets in his body from duels. His men called him Old Hickory, Native Americans dubbed him Sharp Knife and Old Ferocious – and the story of his life was the story of the voracious march of American power. 'I was born for the storm,' he said, 'and a calm does not suit me.'

As a teenager, he fought in the War of Independence; as a young man, he won fortune enough to buy his Hermitage, Tennessee, cotton estate and 150 slaves, yet also adopted a Native American orphan. He defended with his pistols the virtue of his wife Rachel against accusations of bigamy: he killed a man who insulted her. On the frontiers he commanded militias of settlers and their Native American auxiliaries, keen to 'conquer not only the Floridas but all Spanish North America'. In 1812, when Britain's harassment of American ships and encouragement of Shawnee resistance led to war, Colonel Jackson struck at Muscogee (Creek) Native Americans who had attacked American colonists, and on 8 January 1815 General Jackson became a national hero by saving New Orleans and routing a British army. During the war, enslaved African-Americans fled to the Seminole Indians and formed their own free community at Fort Negro in Florida. In 1816, Jackson, assisted by Creek auxiliaries, raided Florida, destroyed Fort Negro and defeated the British-backed Seminole.* In 1818, ignoring President Monroe, he finally seized Florida, executing two captured British agents. Spain, coping with Bolívar in south America, sold Florida to the US; Jackson later became governor of the new state. He despised the hifalutin presidents Monroe and Adams, Virginian aristocrats and Massachusetts lawyers, laughing that 'It's a damn poor mind that can think of only one way to spell a word.'

* A separate community developed of Black Seminoles – half African, half Seminole – who developed a hybrid culture combining Native American and African culture, and speaking the Gullah language, fusing west African Krio with Seminole. During the Slave Revolts of 1835, Black Seminoles joined African-American slaves in attacking plantations. Later many Black Seminoles served as scouts with the US or Mexican armies.

In 1822, Jackson, wounded and exhausted, collapsed after his victories, coughing blood, but he recuperated then built his Democratic Party, and ran for president against John Quincy Adams. He lost the first campaign but won the second in 1828, which was viciously fought: Jackson was accused of being the cannibal son of a prostitute and a 'mulatto', married to a bigamist. Warning that 'the most important powers of government have been given or bartered away' and that he would reclaim them for the people, Jackson achieved 56 per cent of the popular vote, growling, 'Desperate courage makes one a majority.' But Rachel, anguished by the abuse, died of a heart attack just afterwards. Jackson had to be prised off the body, and at her funeral at Hermitage he warned, 'God Almighty forgive her murderers, as I know she forgave them. I never can.'

Jackson's politics like his life was visceral: he regularly swore to kill his rivals; he loathed bankers and told a delegation, 'You're a den of vipers and thieves, and by the eternal God, I will rout you out.' Taking the oath on 4 March 1829, Jackson invited the public to his inaugural party in the White House and supposedly escaped the ensuing carnival through the window. In office he purged the bureaucracy of 'unfaithful or incompetent hands', launching the system of presidents appointing their own civil services. Jackson's government was no cleaner than his predecessors': he preferred to rule through his cronies, nicknamed the Kitchen Cabinet, instead of his ministers, the Parlour Cabinet, who infuriated him by protesting against the morality of his war minister's wife.

Jackson aggressively pushed forward the American frontier, passing his Indian Removal Act that forced Native Americans on to reservations in Oklahoma – thousands of Cherokee died on the way in their 'Trail of Tears'. In the west, fur traders, some working for Astor, pioneered the Santa Fe and Oregon trails, guided and protected by Mountain Men: James Kirker, an Irish immigrant, came to personify the feral darkness of frontier life. A younger colleague, Kit Carson, later became its glamorous face, hero of 'dime novels' and newspaper articles. Both were illiterates who started as fur traders, dabbling in silver and copper mining. They lived like natives, often married native wives – and killed natives. Kirker, the older of the two, had commanded an American privateer against the British in 1812, then, hunting furs, lived beside the Apache, even joining their raids. Carson, joining a western expedition, killed his first Native Americans at nineteen. They had stolen his horses. 'During our pursuit for the lost animals, we suffered considerably,' he wrote, 'but the success of having recovered our horses and sending

many a redskin to his long home, our sufferings were soon forgotten.'
The Americans scalped their victims just as the natives would scalp
them. Yet Carson married two Native American women, Singing Grass
and Making Out Road.

Jackson's Indian policy was linked to his expansionist plans for
Spanish America. He hoped to buy Texas from a new country that
had emerged from the Spanish provinces of New Spain: Mexico. His
opponent was Antonio López de Santa Anna, whose career, based on a
famous victory against a European imperial power, resembled his own.
Six times president, Santa Anna dominated Mexico for fifty years.*

As Santa Anna built up his estates in Veracruz and rose to general, he
made his name in 1829 defeating a final Spanish attempt to retake New
Spain, after which he declared himself Napoleon of the West. In 1833 he
was elected president, but he was happiest either holding court at his
hacienda, seducing women (he married two heiresses, the second being
sixteen when she married the forty-something general; he recognized
four illegitimate children) or leading an army. But Mexico was vast,
stretching from California to Texas and encompassing most of central
America. Comanche and Apache ranged across its northern provinces,
fighting for its prizes, cattle and human. A Comanche *paraibo* Iron
Jacket raided into Texas: in 1820, he had a son Peta Nocona, who would
play a special role in American history. Both the Mexicans and American settlers struggled to cope with the free-ranging Comanche who had
mastered horse and rifle warfare across their realm of Comancheria.

Santa Anna disdained his Amerindian and mixed-race citizens. 'A
hundred years to come,' he told an American, 'my people won't be fit for
liberty. They don't know what it is; a despotism is a proper government
for them, but there's no reason why it shouldn't be a wise and virtuous
one.' He believed he was the man to provide it. The president enforced
a new centralized government, but he faced Jackson, who hoped to do
in Texas what he had done in Florida. The American capture of Texas

---

* In 1821, as a young officer fighting for Spain, Santa Anna switched sides to join the revolution along with a general, Agustín de Iturbide. The two manifested the contradictions
of Mexico: the revolution was started by a priest of mixed race but now its leaders were
white Catholic officers. Iturbide offered the Compromise of Iguala, based on three guarantees – independence, Catholicism and equality between white and mixed-race Mexicans.
It would establish a monarchy, possibly Bourbon. But in October 1821 Iturbide's victory
was so heady that his backers suggested he take the crown: 'I had the condescension – or
call it weakness – of allowing myself to be seated on the throne I'd created for others.'
Iturbide was crowned Emperor Agustín but quickly faced resistance. In December 1822,
the twenty-nine-year-old Colonel Santa Anna rebelled and marched on Mexico City, leading
to the emperor's exile and the creation of a republic. When Agustín returned to retake the
throne, he was executed.

was once presented as a noble enterprise against primitive Mexicans. In fact, in 1829, Mexico had abolished slavery; the Americans wished to restore it.

In 1825, Stephen Austin, whose father had dreamed of colonizing the territory, settled 1,200 families in Texas under a contract with the Mexican government. They were slave owners. 'The idea of seeing such a country as this overrun by a slave population almost makes me weep,' said Austin. 'It is in vain to tell a North American that the white population will be destroyed some fifty or eighty years hence by the negroes, and that his daughters will be violated and butchered by them.' Hence 'Texas must be a slave country.'

Austin, joined by Davy Crockett, demanded autonomy for his colony, then in October 1835 declared independence. Santa Anna arrested him and marched into Texas but was held up by Crockett and other frontiersmen at the old mission at Alamo. During the thirteen-day siege, Santa Anna killed 188 frontiersmen, then slaughtered Crockett and 342 prisoners. His wars were usually combined with sex: during the Alamo, Santa Anna seduced a beautiful girl who refused to sleep with him unless they married. The caudillo dressed a colonel as a priest and held a fake wedding ceremony to trick her.

Yet the delay at the Alamo enabled a remarkable late-coming Texan settler to emerge as leader. Sam Houston, who had spent years living with the Cherokee people and had fought with Jackson against the Creek, had qualified as a lawyer and been elected governor of Tennessee before arriving in Texas, where he swiftly rivalled Austin as leader. At San Jacinto, Houston defeated and captured Santa Anna (though he himself was wounded) and was elected president of the Republic of Texas. At the end of his presidency, Jackson offered Mexico $5 million for Texas and considered seizing it. President Houston knew the Cherokee and other tribes well and planned to negotiate a border between Texas and Comancheria, but he lost power to Mirabeau Buonaparte Lamar,* a Georgian cotton planter's son, poet, lawyer and warrior. Lamar had led the cavalry charge at San Jacinto and now armed the republic's own paramilitary killers, the Rangers, to destroy the Comanche and Cherokee, whom he called 'red n——' and 'wild cannibals', demanding their 'total extinction'. The Rangers, aided by Indian auxiliaries, the cannibal Tonkawa and mixed-race black Indians, fought the Comanche and Apache, the two sides mirror-images of the other.

---

* Lamar's parents named their children after their French revolutionary and Roman heroes: his brother was Lucius Quintus Cincinnatus Lamar.

These masters of murderous frontier war embarked on fifty years of ferocious conflict.

In May 1836, Iron Jacket and his teenaged son Peta Nocona joined 500 Comanche and allies on a raid into eastern Texas, where they attacked Fort Parker, the log-cabin stronghold of a seventy-seven-year-old frontiersman, John Parker, and his family. The Comanche killed, scalped and castrated the male Parkers and captured two women and three children, including Cynthia Ann Parker, aged eight, who was adopted by Comanche and renamed Foundling, learning the language and embracing their culture. A few years later, she was chosen by Peta Nocona as a wife. Comanche were polygamous, but Peta loved her, and they had three children, the first being a son, Quanah. Cynthia was not alone. By the 1840s, the Comanche owned 5,000 Mexican slaves.

In 1849, Kit Carson helped track an American woman, Mrs Ann White, captured by the Apache, who killed her at the last moment. 'Mrs. White was a frail, delicate, very beautiful woman,' wrote one of the soldiers, 'but having undergone such usage as she suffered nothing but a wreck remained . . . covered with blows and scratches.' If they survived the initiation, these prisoners could be freed to become Comanche themselves.

The Texans never gave up on trying to find each of the captives taken during the raids. Although hundreds were either ransomed or eventually rescued in Texas Ranger and Scout expeditions, many others remained in the hands of the Comanche; some wished to remain. The Rangers launched reprisal attacks against Comancheria. Comanche chiefs became willing to negotiate peace, restoring white slaves in return for recognition of Comancheria.

In March 1840, sixty-five chiefs, accompanied by women and two children, arrived at the Council House in San Antonio to negotiate, bringing with them one white captive, a girl. Suddenly the windows of the Council House opened and hidden Texan militiamen opened fire on the Comanche, who had left their guns and lances outside the town. Thirty-five Comanche (including three women and a child) were shot down, along with seven Texans. As vengeance, a war chief, Buffalo Hump, amassed a war band of around 500, including Iron Jacket, who in July raided towns on the coast, killing slaves, capturing 1,500 horses and bloodying Texas units – even the Rangers, who managed to kill twelve Comanche at Plum Creek. When Sam Houston was re-elected as Texan president, he negotiated a peace recognizing Comancheria, but the Senate refused to ratify it. Meanwhile the Comanche *paraibos* Buffalo Hump and Iron Jacket led 800 warriors to raid Mexico.

The Mexicans responded by hiring James Kirker, that agile, long-haired Mountain Man. The fur trade was dying, and in 1834 Astor sold out. 'Beaver was getting scarce,' said Kit Carson. 'It became necessary to try our hand at something else.' Carson became an army scout and guide for the thousands of migrants heading west. Hired by Mexico, Kirker became a professional killer, leading (with a Shawnee deputy named Spybuck) a crew of 200 psychopaths – whites, Indians, escaped black slaves. They were joined by John Horse, a legendary Black Seminole, son of an enslaved mother and Seminole father, who had fought the Americans, afterwards escaping both American and Seminole slavery, to reach Mexico where he became a frontier auxiliary and scalp hunter. These chilling predators, sporting necklaces of ears, were paid by 'scalps with an ear on each end' (100 pesos for an adult male, 50 for a woman, 25 for a child). Kirker himself killed over 500 Apache.* The Comanche joined in killing their Apache rivals.

Released by the Americans, Santa Anna redeemed himself in blood when the French king Louis Philippe sent an army to Veracruz to avenge Mexican ill treatment of a French *pâtissier* – was there ever a more Gallic pretext for war? In 1839, Santa Anna defeated the French, though in the fray he lost a leg and a hand; ever the showman, he granted his leg a military funeral. His lost limbs restored his power but not for long. A rebellious mob overthrew his presidency and, exhuming his honoured leg, smashed it in the streets of Mexico City. The general retired to Cuba, but he was soon back.

In February 1845, the outgoing President John Tyler, Virginian slave holder, annexed Texas as many Americans embraced the idea that the continent was their providential empire, its conquest their 'manifest destiny'. Over thirty years, 400,000 poor migrants trekked westwards in wagons along the dangerous Oregon trails. Mexico mobilized as the incoming president James Polk, who had campaigned for expansion, provoked war then ordered a full-scale invasion which blooded many of the generals of the future civil war; the Mountain Men Carson and Kirker served as scouts. In the army of General 'Old Rough 'n' Ready' Zachary Taylor as he won the first US victories served a young officer, Ulysses Grant, the reticent, intense son of a loudmouth Ohio entrepreneur, a West Pointer married to Julia, daughter of a curmudgeonly southern slave owner. Grant disapproved of this 'most unjust war', as did an Illinois congressman, Abraham Lincoln, who attacked Polk's

---

* Their atrocities inspired the classic novel *Blood Meridian* by Cormac McCarthy. Kirker served later as a scout for the American invasion of Mexico, then escorted 49ers (participants in the 1849 Gold Rush) into California, where he settled and died peacefully.

quest for 'military glory – that attractive rainbow, that rises in showers of blood'.

When Polk became jealous of Rough 'n' Ready's laurels, he appointed Winfield 'Old Fuss 'n' Feathers' Scott to land at Veracruz. As Scott advanced on Mexico City, Grant, a cavalry virtuoso, served with his future opponent, Robert E. Lee. Mexico turned to their one-legged hero Santa Anna, whose fortified position halted Scott's advance until Lee found a way to bypass it. Santa Anna escaped, 'pursued so closely', Grant told his wife Julia, 'that his carriage, a splendid affair, was taken and in it his cork leg and $30,000 in gold'. On 8 September 1847, Scott fought through the streets into Mexico City, and afterwards promoted both Grant and Lee.*

On 2 February 1848, in a treaty signed at Guadalupe Hidalgo, America won California and new territories larger than western Europe; Mexico lost 55 per cent of its land. The victory opened opportunities for American settlers, who rushed westwards to find land and gold, but this expansion now raised the question: would slavery expand with it? 'The United States will conquer Mexico,' wrote Ralph Waldo Emerson, 'but it will be as the man who swallows the arsenic, which will bring him down in turn. Mexico will poison us.' Grant saw the coming catastrophe as 'largely the outgrowth of the Mexican war. Nations, like individuals,' he wrote, 'are punished for their transgressions.' There were now over three million slaves in the cotton-growing southern states, while the industrial north attracted waves of immigrants from Ireland, Germany and later Italy who poured into its growing cities.

The settler nation now extended from ocean to ocean, even though the central section was, writes Pekka Hämäläinen, 'a seemingly disordered, uncontainable world of grasslands, deserts, buffalos, and Indians'. Thousands rode in wagons, prey to the elements and Native Americans. In February 1847, a party of eighty-seven members of the Donner family tried a new route from Missouri but, getting lost in mountains and desert, were decimated by hunger and reduced to cannibalism. Only forty-eight survived. Two years later, the discovery of gold in California launched the first gold fever: the village of San Francisco grew from 1,000 souls to 30,000; altogether 300,000 settlers rushed to California. For almost a century, few settlers had arrived in America – in 1820,

---

* Santa Anna again retreated into exile, but in 1853 he returned as dictator for life and 'Serene Highness', toying with the crown until forced to resign, replaced by a new sort of Mexican leader, an Amerindian Zapotec lawyer, Benito Juárez, who had once served him barefoot as a waiter. Santa Anna denounced Juárez, the 'dark Indian' who had 'to be taught to wear shoes, jacket and trousers'.

just 8,000 came – but now, thanks to steamships, crises in Europe, land rushes and gold rushes, immigration tripled: 1.6 million Irish, escaping a famine at home, immigrated,[*] the start of a rush of settlers that transformed America, creating new cities and bringing more Europeans into contact with Native Americans, who still controlled much of the interior.

In California, militias of gold miners and other settlers attacked and slaughtered Native Americans, collecting ears and scalps to earn bounties. The Indian Protection Act, meanwhile, forced Native Americans and their children into servitude. Survivors were driven into reservations, but these masters of the interior were able to defy the Euro-American settlers: the Lakota still ruled the northern plains, the Comanche the Texan–Mexican borderlands of Comancheria. The Native Americans, armed with guns and horses, had intensified their hunting of bison. The Comanche alone had annually killed 280,000 of the animals, but now settlers were wiping out the herds. Among the Comanche lived the chief Peta Nocona and his wife Naduah (once known as Cynthia Ann Parker, the girl kidnapped from Fort Parker) with their son, Quanah. Quanah had no idea that his mother was white; he had been trained as a Comanche fighter by his father, whom he regularly accompanied on raids.[†]

---

[*] Irish famine also rearranged British politics. In 1845, a blight in Ireland destroyed the potatoes that had been, since the crop was imported from America, the staple diet of an impoverished Catholic peasantry toiling under British Protestant landlords who refused to repeal the Corn Laws that protected their grain prices. But as the famine intensified and as a million Irish people died, the Tory prime minister, Peel, joined with Gladstone and other Whigs to repeal the laws. Peel was opposed by his own party, led by an unlikely figure to represent the Tories – a novelist and dandy, born Jewish of Moroccan origins, called Benjamin Disraeli. Out of the crisis emerged the Liberals led by Palmerston and the Conservatives, soon led by Disraeli.

[†] A similar process was taking place in another continental settler nation, Australia. Here the conquest was easier; on the one hand, the indigenous peoples were much less organized, their resistance much less fierce, and there were no other rival European powers present. On the other hand, the settlers were less divided, untainted by slavery but deploying no less injustice, violence and bigotry. British settlers and outlaws, inspired by vast spaces and an adventurous spirit, expanded aggressively. In 1851 the discovery of gold attracted an influx of immigrants who demanded representation. In 1854, the revolt of gold miners at Ballarat, Victoria, was crushed, with twenty-seven miners killed, but it was followed by the granting of limited self-rule and universal male suffrage, with an innovation – the 'Australian' secret ballot, later copied throughout the world. A generation of outlaws called the Bushrangers roamed over the vast territories. Captain Thunderbolt – Fred Ward – personified the type. A labourer turned cattle rustler, Ward was arrested and sent to Cockatoo Bay, whence he escaped. During the 1860s, he launched a spree of heists, and was chased by government troopers. Admired by many as the 'gentleman bushranger', the bushy-bearded Thunderbolt defied capture until 1870 when, aged thirty-five, he was hunted down and shot.

AMERICA TURNS WEST: THE KING OF HAWAII, QUEEN EMMA
AND COMMODORE VANDERBILT

As thousands of Americans settled in California, the nation was drawn towards the Pacific, trading in China, infiltrating Hawaii and keen to open Japan, closed for centuries under the Tokugawa dynasty of shoguns. In July 1853 the US president Franklin Pierce dispatched a commodore, Matthew Perry, veteran of the Mexican war, to Japan to force open the closed nation. Perry sailed into Edo Bay with four heavily armed steam cruisers to demand a trade treaty with Japan at the end of a gun barrel.

In Hawaii, the reign of Kamehameha III, son of the Conqueror who had united the islands, had been dominated by the struggle between his desperate love for his sister and the influence of American missionaries.* Hawaiian kings had often married their siblings, but the Conqueror's widowed queens had banned sacrifices and then, in a radical reform, abolished the traditional *kapu* system of idolatry and converted to Christianity. They also welcomed American missionaries, who started to marry into Hawaiian families, buy estates and interfere with local sexual customs.

The young king initially devoted himself to sexual adventures with Kaomi, an ex-Christian, half-Tahitian male lover, the traditional *aikane*. Kamehameha appointed him co-ruler until pressure forced his removal. His real agony, however, was not his affair with Kaomi, but the great love of his life: his full sister Nāhiʻenaʻena – luminous in her scarlet feather cloak in a portrait by the painter Robert Dampier – who was also in love with him. In Hawaiian tradition, their marriage could only strengthen the dynasty, but the missionaries managed to ban it. Married to another aristocrat, she and the king became lovers anyway and when she gave birth to a son in 1836, Kamehameha declared the child his heir.

Yet, like the Habsburgs, the family was being genetically destroyed by incestuous marriage: the child died within hours. The king was heartbroken. Nāhiʻenaʻena died soon afterwards, aged twenty-two. When he finally married another relative, Kamala, both their children died in infancy.

The kings had always employed half-Hawaiian or European ministers.

---

* In 1819, when Kamehameha the Conqueror died, his dissipated son, Liholiho, Kamehameha II, had neglected his father's fleet and spent a fortune on an American luxury yacht which he named *Cleopatra's Barge* and on which he languished too drunk even to speak. He and his soused crew soon wrecked it – before he set off to visit George IV in Britain, where he died of measles. His brother succeeded him as Kamehameha III.

The family of John Young, the Conqueror's gunner, played a special role. Young's son John Young II, brought up with the king, served as his premier. But then in 1839 the premier was caught 'fastening his pantaloons' in the bedroom of Queen Kamala. He was sentenced to death, a penalty only commuted at the plea of the queen dowager. Amazingly John Young II remained interior minister. Kamehameha III maintained Hawaiian independence, but Americans and Europeans were increasingly interested.

In December 1854, when Kamehameha III died suddenly, his nephew, Alexander Liholiho, succeeded as Kamehameha IV.* While he resisted American encroachment, he fell in love with another member of the Young family, a granddaughter of the Conqueror's gunner, Emma Rooke, regarded as startlingly beautiful by both Europeans and Hawaiians. Once they had married, the couple spent much time with the king's good-looking American secretary, Henry A. Neilson. After the queen gave birth to a son in 1858, the king started to drink and become jealous of the American: in September 1859, he shot Neilson in the chest. Neilson, grievously wounded, survived for two years during which the king tried to redeem himself by caring for him. Shortly afterwards, the couple lost their son, aged four. They were poleaxed; Emma assumed the name Flight of the Heavenly Chief.

As America turned west, a pugnacious but visionary entrepreneur, Cornelius Vanderbilt, who already operated steam-powered ferries in New York, switched to steamships, which became the fastest way to reach California: passengers would cross the Panamanian isthmus by boat and then rail, before re-embarking on his steamships to reach San Francisco. Hefty and menacing, Vanderbilt, descended from the pirate's son Janszoom of Salee, had started working on his father's boats, owning his first at sixteen. A superb predictor of the market and exploiter of new technologies, autocratic and harsh, dubbing himself the Commodore, he punched his enemies, bullied his family, betrayed his friends, bribed judges and politicians, manipulated the stock market and ruined his rivals: 'I for one will never go to a court of law when I have the power in my own hands to see myself right.' Intense and vigilant, he existed in a world of vigorous competition: 'I'm not afraid of

---

* Although he had been raised by American missionaries, Kamehameha IV loathed them – and American racism. He and his brother Lot had travelled to meet President Taylor in Washington and Queen Victoria in London. On the train to New York, 'the conductor . . . took me for somebody's servant just because I had a darker skin. Confounded fool – the first time I've ever received such treatment. In England an African can . . . sit alongside Queen Victoria' but Americans, though they 'talk and think a great deal about their liberty, were often remiss with strangers.'

my enemies, but by God, you must look out when you get among your friends.' The first American railways were built in 1827; by 1840, there were 2,700 miles of track; by 1860, there were 30,000, built, floated and controlled by aggressive entrepreneurs led by Vanderbilt, who soon joined the octogenarian Astor as the richest men in America.

In New York, the Commodore and the brash railway barons were forgiven for their wealth and invited into the refined quasi-British world of the older families in return for philanthropic donations to institutions still controlled by American aristocrats. The older families were not afraid of commerce; they were just not as good at it. The Roosevelts, descended from the first Dutch settlers, had made money in linseed oil and Manhattan property, but they also entered public life, serving as aldermen and US congressmen; they built mansions upstate and tended to marry within a genteel circle. That changed with Cornelius Van Schaack Roosevelt, born in the eighteenth century and the last Dutch-speaking member of the family, descended from Schuylers and Van Schaacks. CVS, short, red-haired, solemn and energetic, had demonstrated his spirits as a boy one Sunday by jumping on the back of a male pig, one of those that still wandered Manhattan streets at the start of the century, and riding it until it bucked him off. Aiming to become 'a man of fortune', he manufactured plate glass, essential for the building boom to house new immigrants, then invested in property, making over $3 million.

As CVS aged, he bought his five children houses around his mansion on East 20th Street and Broadway: one son became a congressman while the youngest, Theodore, was less interested in glass. Described by his namesake son as 'a handsome, good-natured lion' and 'best man I ever knew', Theodore funded charities and founded the Metropolitan Museum of Art. When he was nineteen, he travelled through the south where the northern Knickerbocker heir met Martha 'Mittie' Bulloch, a Georgian planter's daughter, brought up at Bulloch Hall, a pillared mansion. Like all daughters of planters, she had grown up sharing her room with an enslaved companion, known as her 'shadow' – Lavinia, nicknamed Toy. The teenagers came from different worlds that were about to collide.

As America gained an empire, the monarchies of Europe were shaken by revolution. Twenty days after Guadalupe Hidalgo, on 22 February 1848, Parisian crowds, crying *'Vive la réforme!'* and *'Vive la République!'*, took control of Paris – an upheaval that heralded the return of the Bonapartes and the moment when mass politics and public health remodelled family dynasty and state power to reform Europe.

ACT SIXTEEN
1.1 BILLION

Bonapartes and Manchus, Habsburgs and Comanche

REVOLUTIONS AND MASS POLITICS: LOUIS NAPOLEON AND LOLA MONTEZ

'I have a firm seat on the horse,' insisted Louis Philippe, who now suppressed dissent and resisted British-style reforms: only 1 per cent (240,000 voters) of the French population could vote for the Assembly as workers toiled in drear factories and the bourgeois craved the freedoms granted in Britain, which now had a million voters. Louis Philippe tried to distract the French with Bonapartist *gloire*: in 1840, he staged the return of Napoleon's body from St Helena, attending its entombment at Les Invalides.

In January 1848, riots started in Palermo and then spread to Paris, where on 22 February crowds took to the streets. The following day, soldiers killed fifty-two protesters. Crowds of socialist workers and liberal bourgeois soon commanded the streets and besieged Louis Philippe in the palace. The king abdicated in favour of his grandson, and after a full day of riots he escaped in a cab in disguise. His fall marked the end of the Capet family, which had ruled France – with a few minor intervals – since 922.

The radical poet Alphonse de Lamartine declared a Second Republic, which enfranchised all nine million adult males (granting universal male suffrage before Britain or America), created National Workshops to employ workers, and finally, on 27 April, fifteen years after Britain, abolished slavery by compensating the slave masters.*

The news was relayed by a new medium, the telegraph, that accelerated world events: revolution spread through Europe. As the ex-king Louis Philippe sailed for Dover under the name 'Mister Smith', Prince Louis Napoleon Bonaparte, the conqueror's forty-year-old nephew, son of his brother King Louis, sailed for Calais.

The prince had seen Napoleon only once – at a parade in the weeks

---

* Since British abolition, the prices for slaves were higher, so that the cost of compensating owners for their 240,560 slaves was even higher, totalling 120 million francs.

before Waterloo – and for twenty years his escapades had been a European joke. But he possessed invincible self-belief. 'From time to time,' he wrote, 'men are created into whose hands the fate of their country is entrusted. I am such a man.' His rise illustrates that mysterious process of politics, momentous inevitability, by which the preposterously impossible becomes plausible, then – as alternatives are rejected and other routes closed – likely, and finally, imminent. Yet Louis Napoleon was a herald of the modern world: he helped create new mass politics and founded the last version of French empire.

His mother Hortense, Josephine's daughter, 'an exquisite blonde with amethyst eyes' and a talented songstress who wrote '*Partant pour la Syrie*', the Bonapartist anthem, had always treated him as a man of destiny, while his mean-spirited father Louis never quite trusted that the prince was his real son. Educated in Switzerland and trained as a gunner at military school, he was shy and taciturn, brown-eyed, big-nosed and full-lipped, with a big head and torso on stubby legs in an age when tight breeches made the male leg essential for masculine beauty. Yet he possessed a romantic mystique appealing to women. 'It's usually the man who attacks,' he boasted. 'As for me, I defend myself, and I often capitulate.'

As soon as his cousin the duke of Reichstadt – Napoleon II – had died in 1832, he became the Bonapartist pretender. At twenty-five, he published his manifesto *Rêveries politiques*, gathering a crew of motley adventurers who always included a devoted female patroness, a few officers and his manservant Thélin. They were joined early by Jean Fialin, the *soi-disant* vicomte de Persigny, a seedy ex-soldier, part-time journalist and political promoter of genius, one of the first of the spin doctors who would become the spirits of modern democracy. In 1836, Louis Napoleon had tried to seize power from Louis Philippe in Strasbourg, hoping to lead a march on Paris, but instead he was humiliated, arrested and expelled from France. Europe laughed, and his father and uncles, who had given up on Bonapartism, desperate to receive pensions from Louis Philippe, were furious.

Yet Louis Napoleon never gave up, embarking on years of exile in London and New York. When Louis Philippe brought Napoleon's body back to France, Louis Napoleon considered doing a Ptolemy – hijacking the body. Instead, he launched his second coup attempt, which ended with him sentenced to 'perpetual imprisonment' in the Fortress of Ham near the Somme. 'In France,' he joked, 'is anything perpetual?'

At what he called Ham University (not the last prisoner to use prison as an academy), he read books and pursued love affairs (fathering two sons with a clog dancer), then escaped with the aid of Thélin. In London, he inherited his father's fortune, embarking on a further series of love affairs. Once his money was gone, he hooked up with a courtesan-actress performing under the name Harriet Howard; she had run off with a jockey, then settled down with a nabob who left her a fortune. She fell in love with the prince, and, believing in his destiny, backed him all the way.

As Louis Napoleon arrived in revolutionary Paris, the Viennese were rebelling against their bewildered emperor: Ferdinand, aged forty-two, child of double first cousins, had been born with encephalitis and epilepsy and was glad to leave politics to his antique chancellor, Metternich. Ferdinand had failed to consummate his marriage due to a wedding night interspersed with fits, and lived for his beloved apricot dumplings – shouting when told they were out of season, 'I am the emperor, and I want dumplings!' He was mentally stable but incapable of ruling. Now, when Metternich told him about the revolution, he asked, 'Is that allowed?' It was not, but that is the thing about revolutions: Hungarians and Italians and even the Viennese turned on the Habsburgs, who tried to protect Metternich, then, as troops shot demonstrators, sacrificed him. The Coachman of Europe faced the reality that the monarchy was galloping out of control. 'I'm no longer anybody,' he said after thirty-nine years in power. Dressed as a woman, he escaped to London with his young wife and family: 'I've nothing more to do, nothing more to discuss.'

The revolutions were a howl of rage directed at the old hierarchy in a new era of seething cities, billowing factories, careening railways, rollercoasting stock markets, multiplying newspapers, bestselling instalment-novels and news-bearing telegraphs. British railways – in 1840, they had laid 1,498 miles of line, tripling to 6,621 by 1850 – now linked British cities; France was far behind with 2,000 miles. Railway entrepreneurs considered adding a transatlantic route to their networks: in 1840, a Canadian entrepreneur, Samuel Cunard, sailed on his first steamship, *Britannia*, from Liverpool to his native Nova Scotia in twelve days, launching a service that linked the continents, soon enabling millions of poor people from many countries, from Ireland to Germany, to migrate to seek new opportunities in the settler nations of the Americas and Australia. At the bottom of society, urban working classes toiled in hellish factories that produced goods for the newly confident bourgeois consumers: the first department store, Bon Marché, had opened in Paris in 1838 and its own proprietor was planning a larger version – an age of emporia as well as empires. Workers now confronted industrialists, forming unions and embracing a new ideology that placed the working class at the centre of society: socialism.*

Twice fleeing their capital, as ministers were lynched and hanged from lampposts, Kaiser Ferdinand and the Habsburgs still possessed the will for power that is essential to keeping it, deploying their loyal armies to crush Italy and then storm Vienna. They held a secret family conference where 'the only man at court', Archduchess Sophie, the emperor's sister-in-law, the Bavarian princess who had flirted with Napoleon's son in the 1820s, stiffened resolve: she persuaded her husband, the emperor's brother, to renounce the succession. She had trained their eighteen-year-old son Franzl, fair-haired, blue-eyed, serious and dutiful, for the throne. At Olomouc, the handover was recorded poignantly by the outgoing kaiser. 'The affair ended with the new Emperor kneeling before his old Emperor and Lord, that is to say, me,' wrote Ferdinand, 'and asking for a blessing, which I gave him, laying both hands on his head and making the sign of the Holy Cross . . . then I kissed our new master . . . After that I and my dear wife packed our bags.'

Assuming the name Franz Josef, the new emperor resumed the reconquest of the empire, first in Italy, then in Austria. Many dynasties tottered. In Bavaria, one of the oldest, the Wittelsbachs, resembled an *opéra bouffe*: King Ludwig, at the age of sixty-two, who had ruled for twenty-three years, had recently fallen under the sway of a dazzling Irish courtesan, Eliza James, who claimed to be a Spanish dancer named Lola Montez. 'I love you with my life, my eyes, my soul, my body,' he wrote, raving about her 'black hair, blue eyes, graceful form . . . I'm young again.' Lola dominated Munich: 'I'm on the point of receiving the title of countess!' she boasted to a friend. 'I have a lovely property, horses, servants . . . surrounded by the homage of great ladies, I go everywhere, all of Munich waits upon me,' and 'The king loves me passionately.' But the reign of Lola was short. She amused herself by having affairs with students just as the revolution ignited Bavaria, forcing Ludwig

---

* The idea of socialism had been developed by a French aristocrat, Henri, comte de Saint-Simon. After fighting for the Americans at Yorktown at the age of twenty with his friend Lafayette, Saint-Simon had supported the French revolution, was arrested and almost guillotined under Robespierre, then planned with Talleyrand to dismantle Notre-Dame and sell the lead from its roof. Living splendidly during Napoleon's reign, he lost his money and started to study the industrial world. In 1817, at the age of fifty-seven, he wrote *L'Industrie*, in which he declared two principles: 'The whole of society rests upon industry' and 'Politics is the science of production.' He grew so depressed by the lack of support that he shot himself six times in the head, but only lost the sight in one eye. A decade after his death, the word socialism was coined.

to exile her and accept a constitution. 'My very beloved Lolitta,' wrote the cuckolded king, 'Luis [himself] is no longer loved, only your heart remains to me . . . I will renounce the crown.'* His abdication calmed the revolution.

Further north, in Frankfurt, an excited National Assembly promoted a united, constitutional Germany, dispensing with the 'German Confederation' chaired by Austria and offering the crown to the timorous Prussian king Frederick William IV. At first a Berlin revolution had forced the Flounderer to agree a constitution. His conservative younger brother, Wilhelm, went into British exile; when he returned, he used gunpowder to restore order in the streets. Now the Flounderer refused to 'pick up a crown from the gutter, disgraced with the stink of revolution, defiled with filth'. Yet he then flirted with leading a German union. But Austria had recovered and reasserted its power; the Assembly was closed down; the Hohenzollerns had been at once humiliated and shown to be essential.†

The Flounderer's performance had infuriated the Junker nobles, none more so than a strapping landowner from Pomerania, Otto von Bismarck, who, provoking liberals with his talk of divine monarchy, fantasized about leading an army to overthrow the king and encouraged the 'rattling of sabres in their scabbards'. The backlash against the rebellion deeply disappointed two young German radicals planning socialist revolution.

COURTESANS AND *DAS KAPITAL*: NAPOLEON AND MARX

Frederick Engels, the son of a German industrialist who owned textile factories in Manchester, had met a fellow radical, Karl Marx, in Paris

---

* Lola was graceless in her narcissism, turning on the heartbroken king. 'After all I've suffered for you, chased from Munich for my devotion to you, your conduct appears strange and heartless,' she wrote to him. Ludwig died in exile. She went on tour in America.

† There was a darker chauvinism within the German revolution. In Dresden, the court conductor of the Saxon king, Richard Wagner, thirty-five-year-old son of a police clerk in Leipzig, where he was brought up in the Jewish Quarter, and already the writer of a successful opera *Rienzi*, supported a socialistic German nationalism – 'I, poor artist, swore eternal fidelity to my German fatherland' – and joined the revolution. Driven into exile, he anonymously wrote a vicious denunciation of '*Das Judenthum in der Musik*' (Jewdom in Music) that helped invent the new strain of racism, calling the Jews 'the evil conscience of our modern civilization'. Aiming to 'explain to ourselves the involuntary repellence possessed for us by the nature and personality of the Jews, so as to vindicate that instinctive dislike', he coined a trope that compared Jews to 'a swarming colony of insect life' on the noble body of the German nation.

in 1844 when they were aged twenty-three and twenty-six, and together they developed the idea that the working class – which they called the proletariat – would become the engine of world revolution. Marx was the son of a Jewish lawyer from Triers, Herschel Marx, descended from a line of rabbis, who converted to Protestantism and changed his name to Heinrich. Marx was both heartbroken and impoverished by his father's death, but he married a well-connected, intellectual aristocrat, Jenny von Westphalen, with whom he had already had three children. While her husband planned revolution, her brother was the Prussian interior minister who helped suppress it.

As both an industrialist and a lover – guided by his paramour, an Irish millworker named Mary Burns – Engels knew Mancunian workers, and he had money, enabling him to take Marx on a study tour of Manchester. Marx and Engels observed how industrialized cities were killing the working class: even after the improvements of medicine and food, life expectancy was falling. Liverpudlians died at twenty-five. Working-class Britons now lived seventeen years less than the upper classes, many of them killed by cholera. Doctors believed this was caused by 'miasma'. In the USA, life expectancy had fallen by thirteen years between 1800 and 1850; in New York City child mortality was almost 50 per cent. Many mothers now gave birth in maternity units in hospitals, but as many as 10 per cent of mothers were dying – and it turned out that it was doctors themselves who (with the best intentions) were killing them.*

Just as improvements in healthcare and urban hygiene were about to launch a massive improvement in life expectancy, the two Germans, adapting Saint-Simon, saw the new system of capitalism as the culprit.

---

* Since the seventeenth century, most European cities had maternity units within their hospitals, but these had catastrophic death rates from puerperal fever and it remained safer to give birth at home with traditional midwives. Male physicians were increasingly involved in childbirth. For a long time, a few doctors had suspected that they themselves were responsible for the women's deaths. In 1843, the American professor Oliver Wendell Holmes (father of the judge) identified lack of hygiene as the cause. Three years later, Ignaz Semmelweis, a Hungarian doctor at the Vienna General Hospital, noticed that at its First Clinic, operated by doctors, 10 per cent of mothers died; at the Second Clinic, operated by midwives, only 4 per cent died. When a doctor died after accidentally stabbing himself with a scalpel used in an autopsy, Semmelweis realized that the doctors were constantly going from autopsies to births. Semmelweis's measures of hygiene at once reduced deaths dramatically. But doctors mocked both the idea that they as gentlemen could be unclean and the very theory of germs. Simultaneously the 1848 revolution, including the Hungarian rebellion, made Semmelweis a suspect figure. He was stymied and forced to resign. He moved to Pest in Hungary, but while the British tentatively welcomed his ideas, German and Austrian doctors attacked him. He went mad, talking incessantly about childbed fever, and died in a lunatic asylum. It was only with germ theory that Semmelweis was proved right and childbed fever and infant mortality sharply reduced.

In January 1848, they wrote their *Communist Manifesto*, developing a 'critical theory' that explained an interconnected world: 'The philosophers have only interpreted the world in various ways; the point is to change it.' They argued that 'The history of all hitherto existing society is the history of class struggles.' Weeks later, Europe was in revolution. The two threw themselves into the tumult, Engels transporting rifles, Marx using an inheritance to arm Belgian workers.

In Vienna, Milan and Prague, Franz Josef overpowered the rebels, but Hungary embraced national independence, as did the Ottoman provinces of Wallachia and Moldova, aspirations that could easily spread to Nicholas's Polish and Ukrainian subjects. The tsar occupied Bucharest and Moldavia and offered to crush Hungary. Franz Josef humiliatingly agreed; 190,000 Russian troops hacked their way into Budapest, and the young kaiser never forgave the arrogant tsar for his help. In Berlin, the Flounderer revoked his constitution and restored a limited version of his earlier power. Having enforced order in their own kingdoms, the dynasts watched France. The one name they did not want to hear was Napoleon.

Louis Napoleon, staying in a Parisian hotel in a country he scarcely knew and whose language he spoke with a German accent, had always believed in the magic of the name Bonaparte. At first he let his old uncle, the ex-king Jérôme, and two other cousins run for the National Assembly while he returned to London, where Chartist crowds, infected with the spirit of revolution, demonstrated for more democracy. Wellington, now seventy-nine, massed troops, and Bonaparte registered as a special constable. In Paris, Jérôme and the others were elected. Persigny stuck up posters across the city with Louis Napoleon's picture and the message '*Lui!*' Him!

The workers of the National Workshops armed themselves, adopting red as the colour of revolution; the bourgeois panicked at this Red Menace. 'The spectre of 1792, the sound of the guillotine, was heard,' observed Gustave Flaubert, a young writer.* The war minister, General Cavaignac, crushed the rebels, who resisted fiercely. In the fighting, thousands were shot. Cavaignac became the favourite to win the first presidential election, but Louis Napoleon ran too, aided by a new brother he scarcely knew he had. When he was three, his mother had vanished

---

* Flaubert, a Norman surgeon's son, escaped the revolutionary chaos by embarking on an aesthetic and sexual tour of Greece, Egypt and Constantinople, sampling boys and girls in exploits recounted in his letters. He disliked both the revolution and its backlash, calling himself a 'romantic, liberal old dunce'. It was only later in 1857 that he wrote his study of society's cruel treatment of an unfaithful wife, *Madame Bovary*.

to give birth to Auguste de Morny, who, a debonair player in politics, sex, finance and the Jockey Club, had supported Louis Philippe while he made a fortune in sugar beet. But now he joined his half-brother. Persigny and Morny offered all things to everyone – order and security, socialism and glory.

In December 1848, after the Assembly cut the franchise, Napoleon won 5.5 million votes to Cavaignac's 1.1 million. The prince-president, moving into the Élysée Palace, behaved as if he was constantly running for office, travelling by railway around the country, declaring that 'The name Napoleon is a complete programme in itself. At home it means order, authority, religion and the welfare of the people; abroad, the dignity of the nation,' and promising to represent the ordinary man against the Red Menace of socialism. He was just awaiting the chance to show his Napoleonic acumen. First, he sent troops into Italy to rescue Pope Pius IX from Italian nationalists, brandishing his Napoleonic, conservative and Catholic credentials.

The next step was led by men but partly organized and funded by women: on 1 December 1851, after attending the theatre and then the Jockey Club, Morny launched a Napoleonic coup, Operation Rubicon, funded by Napoleon's paramour Harriet Howard and his own, the Belgian ambassador's wife. Friendly generals arrested 26,000, shot 400, deported 9,000 to Algeria and overthrew the constitution. After he had restored universal suffrage, 7.5 million voters approved Louis Napoleon's dictatorship for ten years. 'It seems France desires a return to empire,' he declared, adding, in order to reassure Europe, 'The empire means peace.' In December 1852, approved again by 7.5 million, he was proclaimed Emperor Napoleon III.*

The revolution was over but it had changed everything. Marx escaped to London. Now sporting the beard of a biblical prophet, struggling to survive in dingy Soho digs, short of money, boozing heavily, cursed by boils and headaches, he survived on Engels's gifts and meagre earnings from journalism for the *New-York Daily Tribune*, grumbling bitterly about

---

* In 1849, soon after Napoleon's election, Faustin Soulouque, the Haitian president, declared himself Emperor Faustin. Born in 1782, of Mandinka descent, he was freed and then fought the French, rising to chief of the presidential guards. On the death of the president, the 'mulatto elite' chose the unambitious sixty-five-year-old Soulouque as a frontman. Instead, he formed a militia, the Zinglins, executed any opponents, then founded a new Haitian empire. Since he and Empress Adelina had only a daughter, he chose his nephew as heir. The emperor tried to reconquer the Dominican Republic, independent since 1844. But Haiti was not allowed to keep its conquest. In 1859, the emperor was overthrown by his henchman, General Fabre Geffrard, duc de Tabara, who became president. It was the end of Haitian experiments in monarchy.

'the wretchedness of existence'. But he also neglected his long-suffering wife, got his housekeeper pregnant and persuaded Engels to take responsibility for his lovechild, who was given away to foster-parents.*

Yet in the British Museum's reading room Marx was devising an all-embracing ideology in a masterwork, *Das Kapital*: capitalism was doomed by its own internal contradictions because history was ruled by dialectical materialism, a progression towards, first, the rule of the proletariat and, then, a stateless, classless communism of total equality. In the certainty of his scientific research, Marxism offered an orthodoxy that would replace religion for the many excluded from the spoils of capital at home and empire abroad. A small band of radicals started to follow him. When the working class voted for order and liberty instead of revolution, Marx denounced them as *Lumpenproletariat* whose views displayed 'false consciousness'.

Napoleon gloried in the creation of a new empire but, like his uncle, the Nephew required an heir.† The erotomane emperor picked up women at Élysée balls or ordered his cousin-chamberlain, Felix Baciocchi, to procure them. At the palace, they were instructed to await the emperor naked with the words, 'You may kiss His Majesty anywhere except his face.' His mistresses attested to his brazen dexterity, his selfishness as a lover and the melting of his waxed moustaches. One girl recalled that she 'didn't even have time to make a token protest before he laid hold of me in an intimate place'. After failing to marry a German princess, Napoleon encountered Eugénie de Montijo, countess of Teba, an icily elegant Spanish redhead. Instructed by her mother,‡ Eugénie resisted until he was in love.

---

* Disgusted by the rise of Napoleon III, 'the Nephew', Marx joked grimly, 'Hegel remarks somewhere that all great world-historic facts and personages appear, so to speak, twice. He forgot to add: the first time as tragedy, the second time as farce.' In their letters, in which they vehemently denounced their many enemies and rivals, he and Engels traded racist abuse ('n——' was a favourite); Engels called Marx 'the Moor' for his swarthiness; Marx called Engels 'the General'.

† Napoleon was accompanied back to splendour by his uncle Jérôme, whose two children were the heart of the family: the heir, the inept and petty Plon-Plon, thought he should be emperor and consoled himself by stealing Napoleon's mistresses and demanding money; his sister Mathilde was the opposite, artistic and unpretentious, laughing, 'If it weren't for Napoleon I, I'd be selling oranges in the streets of Ajaccio.' Jérôme, king of Westphalia, commander of a corps in Russia and at Waterloo, was now president of the Senate. Jérôme's son by Betsy Patterson, Bo Bonaparte, had stayed in America where his son Charles served in Teddy Roosevelt's Cabinet.

‡ Eugénie's mother Manuela was an Irish wine merchant's daughter who had married a Spanish grandee and then become mistress of an array of European luminaries, including the British foreign secretary, Lord Clarendon. Her friend Prosper Mérimée based his novel *Carmen* on her life, later adapted for opera by Bizet.

'How can I reach you, mesdames?' Napoleon jokingly called up at her when he saw Eugénie and her mother on a balcony at a ball.

'Through the chapel, Sire,' answered Eugénie.

The Bonapartes disapproved. 'Louis,' said Uncle Jérôme, 'will marry the first woman to refuse him.' But Morny approved and Baron James de Rothschild spotted her early. In January 1853, Eugénie turned up on Rothschild's arm for a ball during which she told the vacillating emperor that if he did not propose she would leave for London. 'Madame la Comtesse,' he wrote to her mother, 'for a long time I have been in love with Mademoiselle your daughter . . .' After his patroness Harriet Howard had been paid off, Napoleon married Eugénie, who turned out to hate the sex that he relished – 'Really, why do men never think of anything but *that*?' she mused – but she was pregnant.

SPLENDEURS ET MISÈRES DES COURTISANES

On 16 March 1856, after an agonizing labour, in which Napoleon begged the doctors to use 'any sedative modern science has devised', Empress Eugénie gave birth to the heir, the prince imperial.

Napoleon was an energetic modernizer. He envisioned a modern Paris that would set new standards for the hygiene and layout of cities everywhere, including London. On 23 June 1853, he had appointed a provincial official, Georges Haussmann, as prefect of Paris – 'one of the most extraordinary men of our time', said Persigny, 'big, strong, vigorous, energetic, and at the same time clever and devious, full of ingenuity'. Napoleon ordered Haussmann to '*aérer, unifier et embellir Paris*'. As Napoleon planned the works on a huge model in his office, Haussmann demolished slums and laid out the boulevards, parks, squares and stations of today's Paris. More important than the beauty was the hygiene. 'The underground galleries are an organ of the great city, functioning like an organ of the human body,' the prefect said. 'Clean fresh waters circulate; the secretions removed mysteriously.'*

---

* Lionel de Rothschild, head of the British bank, visiting his uncle James, was impressed: 'I wish we had a man like the emperor to make a few alterations in old London.' Twenty years earlier, Lionel had succeeded his father NM, who at his death in the 1830s was probably the richest private individual in the world: 'his personal fortune', estimates Niall Ferguson, 'equivalent to 0.62 per cent of British national income'. Now, Lionel was close friends with the man who commissioned a 'few alterations in London': Benjamin Disraeli. Five years later, in the summer of 1858, London, also suffering frequent cholera epidemics, emulated Paris after a faecal stench – the Great Stink – had overwhelmed the city. The Conservative chancellor, Disraeli, denounced the 'Stygian pool, reeking with ineffable and

Napoleon promoted railways. Trains encouraged travel and trade, but steam was also about power and conquest – it accelerated the divergence between north-western Europe plus the settler republic of America, and the rest of the world. In Europe, railways facilitated military deployment, pioneered by France but later perfected by Prussia. Abroad, steamships empowered empire, enabling Britain and France to rush troops to Africa or the east.[*]

Napoleon's railway boom was accelerated by his brother Morny but was guided by James de Rothschild. In the railway boom, the Rothschilds prospered greatly, fighting off challenges from rival bankers. By 1870, France boasted 14,000 miles of track.

In 1855, James commissioned a neo-Renaissance palace at Ferrières, built by the same architect who had designed Mentmore for his English cousins. 'Build me a Mentmore,' James ordered, 'but twice the size.' It was a palace fit for a master of the world, its eighty suites fitted out with every luxury, its colossal hall 120 feet long and 60 feet wide and topped with a glass skylight. It was a 'fairyland, a palace of Aladdin', declared his cousin Charlotte de Rothschild, wife of Lionel, while the antisemitic writers, the Goncourt brothers, decried this 'idiotic and ridiculous extravagance – a pudding of every style'.

At its opening, Napoleon arrived by train, stepped on to a green carpet embroidered with Bonapartist bees and travelled to the palace in carriages fluttering with Rothschild blue and yellow to admire the

intolerable horrors', and launched the construction of London's magnificent sewers by a visionary engineer, Joseph Bazalgette, who created 82 miles of brick-lined sewers and 1,100 miles of street sewers with pumping stations as splendid as palaces. It took twenty years but it ended the stink and reduced cholera too. Cholera had probably originated in India centuries before it was identified on its arrival in Britain in 1831. Known as the Blue Death – lack of oxygen in its last stages turned patients blue – it was caused by a bacterium in the drinking water of industrial cities contaminated by human faeces. At exactly this time, late 1854, John Snow, a doctor who had anaesthetized Queen Victoria with chloroform during the delivery of her eighth child, was tracking a cholera outbreak that killed 127 in Soho, London, when he realized that a street pump was the key contaminator. Closing the pump ended the epidemic, proving that cholera was passed by water.

[*] To keep up with steam, the telegraph was developed, and in 1851 a line was laid between Britain and France. In July 1858, an American tycoon, Cyrus West Field, who had made a fortune supplying paper to newspapers, orchestrated the laying of a transatlantic telegraph cable, 2,000 miles long, that allowed President Buchanan and Queen Victoria to exchange greetings. Field's achievement contributed to the link between Britain and America and accelerated the globalization of the world. By 1865, a message from London to Bombay took thirty-five minutes. The smaller world made news more urgent: after Charles-Louis Havas, a Jewish writer from Rouen, had founded the first press agency, one of his employees, Israel Josaphat, a rabbi's son from Kassel, defected to start his own agency, first using pigeons, then paying steamships to throw canisters with American news off ships at the first Irish port and finally, after moving to London and changing his name to Reuter, his new company used telegraphy to become a global news agency.

chateau filled with works by Rubens and Velàzquez. As he left, James joked with his poker face, 'Sire, my children and I will never forget today. *Le mémoire* will be dear to us' – *le mémoire* also meant the bill.

Napoleon frequently consulted James, who now supervised a global financial empire, raising loans for dynasties from the Brazilian Braganzas to the Ottomans, while his American agent, August Belmont, funded American railways and the US war against Mexico. Yet James discouraged Napoleon from fighting wars. 'It's a principle of our house not to lend money for war. It's not in our power to prevent war,' he wrote. 'We at least want to retain the conviction we haven't contributed to it.' Antisemites tried to blame Jewish financiers for European wars, yet continental powers had been fighting wars constantly since the Goths, long before the Rothschilds, and would continue long after they ceased to be pivotal players. James mocked Napoleon's slogan '*L'empire c'est la paix*', preferring '*L'empire c'est la baisse*' – The empire means a crash – adding, 'The emperor was right when he said the empire means peace; but what he doesn't know is the emperor is done for if we have war.'

James lived for family, but even he could scarcely resist the Parisian phenomenon of the courtesan. In *Splendeurs et misères des courtisanes* – one of Balzac's last novels before he died of overwork and coffee-poisoning – the Rothschildian baron de Nucingen pays to sleep with the adorable but fragile Esther. More than James, the emperor's brother the duc de Morny became the arbiter of pleasure, finance and fashion. Napoleonic luxury was sybaritic and sultanic, but so was the venality in a city of grinding and miserable poverty, crowded with thousands of street prostitutes and middle-ranking *grisettes*. But the richer courtesans, the *grandes horizontales*, often ex-prostitutes or actresses who were paid for their favours by aristocrats, plutocrats and playboy *cocodès*, became celebrities – appearing on stage, their pictures, using the new medium of photography, sold as postcards, their antics recounted in newspapers. They were viciously exploited from childhood, their lives often ending tragically, yet they were also defiantly independent, mocking the restrictions of respectable women. It was a world with music, art and literature, but the *horizontales* were centre stage. Jacques Offenbach, son of a synagogue cantor from Cologne, was the empire's trademark composer, with librettos by Ludovic Halévy. In 1855, when Napoleon opened his *Exposition Universelle*, visited by over five million people, Offenbach launched his first *opéras bouffes*, debuting Hortense Schneider, who became La Snéder, the personification of Parisian beauty and pleasure. The courtesans starred in his operas, particularly *Orphée aux enfers*, in which the 'Galop infernal' – the can-can – became the theme of its time. La Snéder started as one of Offenbach's mistresses and became the paramour of Napoleon, Morny and a succession of princes. The brashest *horizontale* was British: the daughter of Irish musicians from Plymouth, Cora Pearl (real name Emily Crouch) appeared half naked as Cupid in *Orphée*.*

Novelists and artists were fascinated by the drama and tragedy of the girls' lives. In 1863, at the Salon des Refusés, created by Napoleon specifically for innovative artists, Édouard Manet exhibited his painting *Olympia* of a bold, nude courtesan, modelled by Victorine Meurent, who was his lover and an artist, accompanied by her fully clothed black maid, based on a model named Laure. It shocked the bourgeois but helped launch a new genre that was criticized as too 'impressionistic': the name caught on.

The sensitive, talented doyenne of the courtesans, Valtesse de La Bigne, nicknamed *Rayon d'Or*, was friend and lover of Manet and Offenbach, patroness of painters and writers, actress and author of a novel *Isola*, but it was her magnificent gilded, canopied bed – still displayed in the Musée des Arts Décoratifs – for which she is best known. A young half-Italian critic, Émile Zola, at the age of twenty-eight launched a series of novels inspired by Balzac chronicling a single family in Napoleonic Paris, *Les Rougon-Macquart* – a seminal work of family history: 'I want to explain how a family, a small group of regular people, behaves in society . . . Heredity has its own laws, just like gravity.' After interviewing Valtesse and viewing her bed, he created the first novel about celebrity sex appeal, personified by the irresistibly destructive Nana, that 'good-natured child' who rises to wealth in her palatial bed, 'a throne, an altar where Paris came to admire her sovereign nudity' – a dazzling erotic meteor like the empire itself. Valtesse hated *Nana*, calling its heroine 'a stupid vulgar whore'.[†]

---

* Cora became a courtesan by accident, starting out with a 'horror of men', but became the lover of Morny and a series of high-born young men including Tsar Alexander II, the Prince of Orange, Napoleon, Plon-Plon and later the British prince of Wales. She held court in a Paris mansion nicknamed Les Petites Tuileries and a country chateau, her bedrooms and bathrooms fitted in gold. Once she had herself borne by four giants into a dinner party on a silver salver which was then opened to reveal Cora, inviting the guests to 'cut into the next dish'. Typically, the story ended tragically: a young man, ruined by Cora, shot himself in her mansion. Her luck turned, her chateaux and jewels were sold and she died in poverty.

† Alexandre Dumas, son of the author of *The Three Musketeers*, asked Valtesse if he could call on her. 'Sorry, monsieur,' she replied, 'it's not within your means.' Valtesse was one of the few *horizontales* who survived into old age, keeping her fortune and dignity. Dumas immortalized his love affair with Marie Duplessis and her death from TB in his novel *La*

In 1853, the delights of Paris changed the life of an impressionable visitor from south America, the heir to the dictator of Paraguay, who was entertained by Napoleon and fell in love with a courtesan who would become the most powerful woman in south America and the world's biggest landowner.

ELIZA LYNCH AND QUEEN VICTORIA:
TWO FEMALE POTENTATES

Francisco Solano López was the son of the ruler of the small, isolated, socially and racially egalitarian republic created by the Grand Lord, Dr Francia, who had ruled for twenty-six years until his death in 1840. After a short interlude, he was succeeded by his cousin Carlos Antonio López; 'this great tidal wave of human flesh, a veritable mastodon', based his hopes on his eldest son Francisco, whom he dispatched to Europe to buy arms for his outsized army. Francisco, twenty-eight years old, ordered British ships and French artillery, and while in Paris in 1854 'gave full rein to his naturally licentious propensities and plunged into the vices of that gay capital' – until he met the nineteen-year-old Eliza Lynch, red-haired courtesan daughter of an Irish naval doctor.

General López returned to Paraguay with his new steamship and a pregnant Eliza Lynch, who was determined to bring the razzmatazz of Second Empire Paris to his minuscule country, where she gave birth to the first of five children. Meanwhile her lover was promoted to war minister and vice-president. If the Paraguayans were fascinated by Eliza, whom they called La Lynch, the López family were horrified by *La Concubina Irlandesa* – but it would be Francisco himself who would destroy Paraguay.

Just after Napoleon's marriage to Eugénie, a vicious skirmish with daggers and pistols broke out between Catholic and Orthodox monks in Jerusalem's Church of the Holy Sepulchre. The coenobite brawl ignited a European war that gave Napoleon the chance to ally with the only country liberal enough to associate with the parvenu emperor: Britain. Nicholas and Napoleon competed to bully the Ottoman sultan

---

Dame aux camélias, coining the term demi-monde for this world between the street and the palace. Reality and theatre merged as the play became a hit, watched by the entire demi-monde; Verdi later turned it into an opera, *La Traviata*. Out of this cruel, implacable world emerged a real genius. Sarah Bernhardt was the daughter of a Dutch-Jewish courtesan, Julie, who was a lover of Morny (possibly Sarah's father). Morny arranged for Sarah to join the Comédie-Française where, playing roles like the heroine of *La Dame aux camélias*, she became the world's most famous actress.

Abdülmecid into conceding their protection of Christians and influence. Napoleon sent a gunboat to assert French 'sovereign authority'
over the Holy Places. Abdülmecid accepted that authority until Tsar
Nicholas threatened war, at which the Ottoman agreed the Romanov
was the protector of Orthodox Christians.

The tsar then invaded Ottoman Moldavia and Wallachia, hoping
to advance further south to seize Istanbul; as Europe's chief exporter
of grain from Odessa, he aspired to control the Straits. He called for
a Balkan Slav revolt, influenced by a new ideology of pan-Slavism,
through which Slavs under Russian leadership would defy the hatred
and hypocrisy of the democratic west. But Nicholas, spoilt by success,
rigid and ailing, miscalculated. He counted on Habsburg support and
western divisions. Instead Franz Josef betrayed him. And then there
was Palmerston's loathing for Nicholas's expansionist autocracy. Pam
was a reforming liberal home secretary, a scourge of global slavery,
reducer of child labour, protector of women by creating civil divorces
and pioneer of the state role in fighting pandemics by making the vaccination of children against smallpox compulsory.* Now he rushed to
Paris to coordinate with Napoleon.

On 27 February 1854, when Nicholas would not retreat, Pam guided
Britain and France into a joint war against Russia. In September, 30,000
French and 26,000 British troops, aided by the Italians of Piedmont
and the Ottomans, landed in Crimea to seize Potemkin's naval base Sebastopol and destroy Russian power in the Black Sea. It was the first of
the mid-century wars in which the chivalry and ineptitude of aristocratic
commanders clashed with the murderous efficiency of modern weaponry. Both sides were blunderingly incompetent, using cavalry charges
against massed artillery and exposed infantry against fortified positions;
both were commanded by negligent, arrogant martinets.

Palmerston suggested that Queen Victoria and her husband Prince
Albert, the quintessence of a new bourgeois prudishness, should do
the unthinkable: invite Napoleon, heir to the ancestral enemy and notorious emperor of the fleshpots of the new Babylon, to visit Windsor.
Palmerston had welcomed Napoleon's coup, his enthusiasm outraging

---

* The advances of medicine could save the lives of millions only thanks to the public measures of leaders like Palmerston, combined with international cooperation. In 1851, the
first international health organization had been founded when twelve European nations
each sent a diplomat and a doctor to the International Sanitary Conference in Paris to
agree quarantine measures against cholera. In 1907 the conference metamorphosed into
the *Office International d'Hygiene Publique*. But it took decades to coordinate measures to
prevent infection. For almost a century, smallpox was the only disease treated with vaccination.

Albert, whose complaints forced Pam's resignation as foreign secretary. The royal couple disapproved of Palmerston, but Napoleon was beyond the pale.

The British queen had succeeded to the throne in 1837 when she was an untried and nervous teenager. The monarchy was no longer powerful, but Victoria, pale, blonde, dumpy with a round face and blue eyes, behaved as if she was the ruler, deploying her influence and prestige with obstinate grandiloquence unencumbered by self-doubt. Her sturdy grandeur provided a reassuring figurehead for her brash, ambitious and prosperous people; her sanctimonious virtue dovetailed with the values of Britain's self-righteous middle classes. But it was Palmerston and a cast of aristocrats and oligarchs who actually led Britain to world power.

Victoria's chief job was to marry and provide an heir. The small principalities of Germany had long acted as the matchmaking service for European dynasties, but her uncle, King Leopold of Belgium, had made his family, the Saxe-Coburgs, into what Bismarck called the 'stud farm of Europe'. Leopold was overbearing and sophisticated, avidly developing the newly invented Belgium, aided by his Rothschild friends, into a wealthy modern economy, but he was also the arch-matchmaker. In 1840, he guided his solemn, cerebral and breezy nephew Albert towards the world's most eligible girl. Albert had reacted against his unbuttoned parents, the duke and duchess of Saxe-Coburg. The duke had taken young Albert and his brother Ernst to sample the courtesans of the Parisian Babylon: Ernst became a sex addict, Albert a prig. Their mother repaid the whoremongering duke by taking her Jewish-born chamberlain as lover, supposedly Albert's natural father, and was divorced; she was never allowed to see her children again. Albert dazzled Victoria: 'full of goodness and sweetness,' she wrote, 'very clever and intelligent . . . extremely handsome; his hair is about the same colour as mine; his eyes large and blue, a beautiful nose, very sweet mouth . . . but the charm of his countenance is his expression, which is most delightful'. Victoria thanked Leopold 'for the prospect of *great* happiness you have contributed to give me'. She was pregnant for much of their marriage, starting with a daughter, Vicky, followed by a boy, Bertie, prince of Wales, and a further seven children.*

---

* Albert was a reforming visionary filled with ideas to improve palace and public. He was one of the creators of the Great Exhibition of the Works of Industry of All Nations in the Crystal Palace in 1851 – its exhibits included the Koh-i-Noor diamond just procured by the annexation of the Sikh Punjab – which was visited by six million people. It was filled with the technological wonders of progress but also with those of destruction. A Prussian ironmaster named Alfred Krupp displayed a Krupp cannon and a 43,000-pound ingot of steel, a technical wonder. (The eccentric did not sell any cannon and Prussia remained a minor

Victoria and Albert regarded Palmerston and Napoleon as disgraceful fornicators. Now happily married to his long-time mistress, Countess Cowper, Palmerston had never retired from the arena: his venturing into the bedroom of a lady-in-waiting at Windsor shocked the queen, who disliked 'that strong, determined man with so much worldly ambition'. Albert called him 'unscrupulous'.

On 16 April 1855, Napoleon and Eugénie arrived at Windsor. Surprisingly, the incorrigible emperor and his parvenu empress charmed the prim Saxe-Coburgs. 'There is something fascinating, melancholy and engaging, which draws you to him,' thought Victoria. Soft-spoken, urbane, inscrutable, Napoleon flirted with Victoria, who was, noted foreign secretary Clarendon (a descendant of James I's favourite Buckingham who happened, in the tiny world of European society, to be the lover of Eugénie's mother), 'mightily tickled by it, for she had never been made love to in her life and his love-making was of a character to flatter her vanity without alarming her virtue; she enjoyed the novelty'. Napoleon spoke German to Albert, indulging his pedantic lectures on his worthy plans for museums and charities.

In Crimea, artillery and disease killed 450,000 Russians, 120,000 Ottomans, 100,000 Frenchmen and 40,000 Britons, but the westerners proved marginally less inept, defeating the Russians and finally taking Sebastopol. Tsar Nicholas died miserably, Russian backwardness exposed; his attractive son Alexander II was forced to negotiate the Paris treaty that temporarily extinguished Russian power in the Black Sea.*

power still crippled by the recent revolutions. There seemed little use for his colossal guns.) Albert used the Exhibition's profits to build his next project, Albertopolis, still London's quarter of museums. Yet he was often stymied by courtiers, politicians and even his own wife. 'I'm very happy and contented,' he said, 'but the difficulty in filling my place with the proper dignity is that I am only the husband, not the master in the house.'

* Alexander II, genial, lascivious and urbane, saw himself as a European cosmopolitan like his uncle Alexander I rather than as a despotic nationalist like his dread father. Russia's first defeat since 1812 convinced him that his country needed reform. In 1861, he liberated twenty-three million serfs whose lot was similar to slavery; he created local self-government bodies and jury trials, raising hopes of deeper reforms. Yet he was every inch a Russian autocrat, completing his father's war against the Chechen jihadis and purging the Circassians, both in the Caucasus. Then in 1863 the Poles launched a rebellion; to European outrage (though he was backed by Prussia) Alexander crushed them; 22,000 Poles were hanged or deported, and he ordered Russification policies, banning the use of Polish, Ukrainian and Lithuanian languages in schools and offices. As in 1830, Russian society, even liberals, backed the suppression of Poland and of Little Russia (one of the three Russian governates that comprise today's Ukraine), an attitude that the dissident writer Alexander Herzen called 'patriotic syphilis'. Yet Alexander also promoted the use of the Finnish language and offered Finland its own constitution. He redirected Russian expansion into central Asia, where he ruled through Islamic institutions and notables. Frustrated in Europe, he dreamed of an attack on British India.

As for the Ottomans, Palmerston had again saved their empire: Palmerston and Napoleon encouraged reformers around Sultan Abdülmecid to modernize their state and promise equal legal rights for non-Muslims, thus protecting Jews and Christians, and the abolition of black slavery – though not of white slavery: brutal Russian operations against the Circassian minority in the Caucasus would now lead to a boom in the sale of Circassian slaves to Istanbul. Ottoman *Tanzimat* – reorganization – fostered a new 'Ottomanism', in a bid to create a multi-ethnic identity to hold the empire together. Palmerston established a special British protection of Ottoman Jews, while the French protected the Maronites of Lebanon. European influence had guided Ottoman tolerance, but this age of cosmopolitanism lasted just three decades.

On 18 August 1855, Napoleon met Victoria and Albert at Dunkirk and escorted them to Paris to visit his *Exposition Universelle*, his version of their Great Exhibition.* The first British sovereign to visit Paris since Henry VI, Victoria brought her thirteen-year-old son Bertie, who was enraptured by the pleasure city. 'I wish,' the prince of Wales told Napoleon, 'I were your son.' Plump, ginger-haired Bertie both craved his father's approval and loved to shock him: he would return to the Parisian Babylon as soon as he got the chance. Crimea was not the only Anglo-French project – both nations were suddenly drawn into conflicts against the dynasties of the east.

On 11 May 1857, the Mughal monarch Bahadur Shah Zafar, eighty-one-year-old descendant of Tamerlane, Babur and Alamgir, received alarming news: a revolt had started against the British and now the first rebel sepoys were arriving in Delhi to acclaim him as ruler and kill any Christian they could find.

REBELLION: LAST OF THE TAMERLANIANS AND THE FIRST OF THE NEHRUS

Bahadur possessed little power outside his residence, the Red Fort in Shahjahanabad, Delhi. Like all educated Mughals, he was a calligrapher

---

* In 1858, Albert negotiated the marriage of their eldest child, pretty, fair Vicky, aged seventeen, to the impressive Prince Frederick (Fritz) of Prussia, five years her senior: 'the 2nd most eventful day in my life', wrote Victoria. 'I felt almost as if it were I that was being married again, only much more nervous.' Vicky was soon pregnant, enduring an almost fatal breech birth, in which the breathing of the baby, born with a withered left arm, was obstructed. The child was named Wilhelm, the future Kaiser of Germany.

and poet in Persian and Urdu, but he ruled only 'from Delhi to Palam' (a Delhi suburb), his court funded by an EIC pension. Britain, which had just taken control of the Punjab in the west and Burma in the east, now dominated India, the first time the subcontinent had ever been ruled by one power. The British aspired to the Mughal realm and, as with the Mughals, theirs was a makeshift structure, run by London, some parts nominally governed by the EIC, much still ruled by Indian princes. Clumsy British arrogance had infuriated both Hindus and Muslims. The early cultural mixing had been replaced by a British racist superiority that closed top positions to Indians and an evangelical mission that raised fears of forced conversion. Princes and landowners resented British annexations. Proto-nationalists resented foreign rule. In early 1857, in the Bengali army, new cartridges, greased with cow or pig fat, alarmed both Hindus and Muslims, who, resenting the punishments of oafish British officers, mutinied in Meerut and now rushed to Delhi.

Zafar felt the expectation of millions as rajas and sepoys turned to him as the traditional authority in India. In Delhi, sepoys joined the Meerut rebels and an underground network of jihadis; the British fled the city or hid in the palace as a popular revolt exploded across Uttar Pradesh and Madhya Pradesh as well as Rajasthan and Bihar.

As a mixture of rajas, warlords, peasants, sepoys and preachers – Muslim and Hindu – attacked British soldiers, murdering women and children, the British responded with equal ferocity, aided by the three new technologies that gave them the ultimate advantage: the telegraph allowed them to deploy reinforcements, at home railways rushed troops to ports and steamships conveyed them to India. British security was fragile: there were 45,000 British troops, some EIC, some royal, and 311,000 sepoys. A single unifying Indian leader might have seized the entire country. Yet the mutiny was very regional, with mass support only in western Uttar Pradesh, while the vast majority of the population, most Indian merchants, the port elites and most princely states in the north and centre remained loyal, as did two of the three EIC armies. Without the aid of Indian soldiers, the British could never have crushed the rebellion.

'I didn't call for you, you've acted wickedly,' Zafar told the rebel sepoys, but they rushed around him, shouting, 'Unless you join us, king, we're all dead men.'

'I have neither troops,' replied Zafar, 'nor magazine nor treasury.'

'Just give us your blessing.'

Zafar blessed them, resumed the durbars for the first time since Nader's conquest and appointed his energetic son Mirza Mughal as commander-in-chief. Mirza Mughal urgently built defensive positions. The sepoys, along with his own servants, hunted down Europeans. Mirza Mughal colluded in the massacre of fifty-two Britons in the Red Fort. Within the city, the emperor's *kotwal* – chief of police – was Gangadhar Nehru, son of an EIC scribe and now father of four children, who avoided involvement in the rebellion. Ultimately his family would dominate a united India.

In Awadh, south-east of Delhi, Begum Hazrat Mahal, widow of the last king, seized power in the capital Lucknow and enthroned her adopted son, Nana Sahib. Four hundred Britons were slaughtered. Further south, Lakshmi Bai, the beautiful thirty-year-old widow of the last raja of Maratha Jhansi and accomplished fencer and horsewoman whose principality had been annexed by the British, sympathized with the rebels but tried to protect British civilians. Facing invasions from rival Indian princes and British intervention, she joined the rebellion, supervising the casting of cannon and emerging as a glamorous but harsh military leader, fascinating the British with her 'high character' and 'remarkably fine figure'.

Palmerston, prime minister at last, was relieved that the Madras and Bombay armies were loyal, as were the rulers of Kashmir and Hyderabad, along with the Sikhs and Pathans of the Punjab. Appointing Charles Canning, son of the prime minister, as governor-general, he ordered the rebellion to be crushed. Extreme violence on both sides unleashed mutual savagery.

FLAY, IMPALE, BURN: THE BRITISH RECONQUER INDIA

In Awadh in summer 1857, British civilians and troops were besieged in Lucknow. In Kanpur, Nana rescued 200 women and children from a massacre. As British forces advanced from Allahabad, sepoys refused to kill them, whereupon five butchers from the bazaar slaughtered the 200 Britons with cleavers, while babies were brained against nearby trees. The bodies were then thrown down a well. Britons were sometimes fired out of cannon. Altogether, in the rebellion, 6,000 were killed.*

The killing of British civilians and the supposed rapes of British women luridly reported in the home press were used to justify British vengeance. William Hodson, a vicar's flaxen-haired son, part scholar

---

* In Madras, retired EIC official Christopher Biden, beach magistrate, author of a manual on naval discipline and relative of a twenty-first-century US president, 'fell by the hands of a band of fanatics'.

fluent in Persian, Latin, Greek and Hindi, part butcher enthused by killing with sword and his favourite weapon, hog spear, formed an Anglo-Sikh militia, Hodson's Horse, who prided themselves on their butchery. 'I never let my men take prisoners,' Hodson said, 'but shoot them at once.' An Anglo-Irish brigadier, John Nicholson, was dining with fellow officers when he learned of the rebellion. 'Mutiny's like smallpox,' he said. 'It spreads quickly and must be crushed as quickly as possible.' Nicholson, 'a commanding presence, six foot two inches in height, with a long black beard and dark grey eyes with black pupils that would dilate like a tiger's', hardened by wars against the Sikhs and Afghans (during which he found the mutilated body of his brother with its genitalia stuffed in its mouth), formed a 'strong movable column' of British regulars and Punjabi auxiliaries and started to hunt rebels. He proposed 'flaying alive, impalement or burning' for 'murderers and dishonourers of our women', boasting, 'I'd inflict the most excruciating tortures I could think of with a perfectly easy conscience.' After hunting down rebels in Peshawar, he hanged the chefs who had tried to poison British officers, saying as he entered the mess, 'Sorry, gentlemen, to have kept you waiting for your dinner, but I've been hanging your cooks.'

Nicholson and Hodson headed for Delhi. In September, they joined the British forces camped on the ridge above Delhi, skirmishing with the rebels but paralysed by the vacillations of their inept colonel, Archdale Wilson. Nicholson, always accompanied by his giant Punjabi bodyguard who stood behind him at meals and slept across his doorway, had become a legend. When, thanks to his aggressive tactics, reinforcements fought their way through, the British stormed the city. In the fighting, Nicholson was shot, still outraged by the dithering colonel, waving his pistol: 'Thank God I have the strength yet to shoot him, if necessary.' It wasn't. Nicholson died as the emperor and his sons retreated to Humayoun's Tomb.

Hodson galloped with his Sikh horsemen through a hostile Delhi, forcing 2,000 rebels to surrender, then surrounded the tomb and demanded Zafar's surrender. Taking Zafar prisoner on promise of his life, Hodson returned next day for the surrender of the prince Mirza, his brother and son. As they were conveyed in a bullock cart into Delhi, Hodson stopped and, drawing his Colt, shot all three dead, stripping them, removing their swords and signet rings, then hanging up the naked bodies at Khooni Darwaza, Blood Gate. 'I can't help but be pleased with the warm congratulations I received for my success in destroying the enemies of our race,' he wrote. Most of the emperor's sixteen sons were killed. 'I disposed of the principal members of the house of Timur the Tartar,' boasted Hodson. 'I'm not cruel, but I did enjoy the opportunity of ridding the earth of these wretches.'

In November, the British retook Kanpur and in March 1858 relieved Lucknow, where, under fire from the Sikandar Bagh stronghold, troops bellowing 'Kanpur! You murderers!' slaughtered 2,000 rebels, their bodies piled 'in a heap as high as my head', recalled a future field marshal, Frederick Roberts. 'A heaving, surging mass of dead and dying inextricably entangled.' When British troops discovered the bodies of murdered civilians, they went berserk, raping women, sewing Muslim sepoys into pigskins before execution, having Hindu Brahmins killed by Dalits (once known as Untouchables, the oppressed stratum below the four castes). Ten thousand Indians were killed at Kanpur and Lucknow. Hodson, under investigation for corruption, was killed storming the begum's palace; the begum escaped.*

After Jhansi had been retaken with a massacre of women and children, Lakshmi Bai rode to Gwalior to make a final stand. In June, the British attacked. Sporting a cavalry uniform, she was wounded and unhorsed by a British sabre, then, as she fired her pistol, shot dead. At home, the British public thirsted for blood; hundreds of thousands of Indians were killed before Canning halted the bloodletting. Mocked as 'Clemency' Canning, he now assumed direct control from the EIC, ruling India as the first viceroy in tandem with a secretary of state for India. Victoria became queen of India and the viceregal relationship with princely rulers was promoted in majestic durbars, ceremonies presided over by imperial proconsuls.†

In 1862, dying in Burmese exile at eighty-seven, Zafar was the last of the Tamerlanians. At the same time, another dynasty was born: as the British shelled Delhi, the emperor's police chief Gangadhar Nehru had escaped with his wife Jeorani and four children, to settle in Agra. Shortly after the death of Gangadhar, Jeorani gave birth to a son, Motilal. When his elder brother qualified as a lawyer, the family moved to Allahabad,

---

* Buried in Lucknow, his epitaph read: 'Here lies all that could die of William Stephen Raikes Hodson.'
† All empires are based on fear: the killing enabled Britain to dominate India with relatively few officials for around seventy years. A frosty British sense of racial superiority now reigned over the British Raj: marriage and indeed mixing between British and Indians diminished; British girls sailed for India to find husbands. British civil servants and officers governed, excluding Indians from the senior positions, with a new sense of seigneurial responsibility. Railways and telegraphs were useful for suppressing any future rebellions but also provided the infrastructure of India as a single political unit, raising rural incomes by as much as 16 per cent. By 1900, Indian railways were the world's third largest network. Schools, universities and a British-style judiciary started to train an Indian middle class.

where Motilal too became a successful lawyer and married his second wife Swarup Rani Thussu. On 14 November 1889, she gave birth to a son, Jawaharlal. Motilal, a dapper raconteur with waxed moustache and resonant voice, flourished, in 1900 buying a towered mansion where Jawaharlal was educated, until he was sent to the same British boarding school as Palmerston – Harrow.

India was not Pam's only eastern crisis. Some of the troops that crushed the Indian rebellion had been on their way to attack China, where British merchants, making fortunes selling Indian opium to Chinese addicts, had been assaulted. In April 1856 as the Crimean war ended and the Indian rebellion started, an imperial concubine in Beijing, the twenty-one-year-old Cixi, gave birth to a boy, the only son of the Xianfeng Emperor.

She would bestride Chinese politics into the twentieth century.

LIMPING DRAGON, IRON-HEADED OLD RAT AND LITTLE AN: THE RISE OF CIXI

Cixi was born into a colossal empire on the verge of catastrophe. She grew up in a comfortable household, the strongminded daughter of a Manchu officer and junior duke; unlike Han Chinese, Manchus did not bind female feet. In 1839, when she was seven, the Daoguang Emperor ordered the seizure and destruction of an illegal British commodity. 'Opium,' he said, 'is poison, undermining our good customs and morality.' For 200 years, the Aisin Gioro family of the Manchus had ruled an ascendant China, allowing Europeans, first the Portuguese then the British, Americans and others, to trade through Guangzhou (Canton). The Qianlong emperor and his successors resisted European demands for ports and had no interest in British mill cloth. When their cotton business was undercut by the American south, Bengal farmers started to grow opium which was sold in Guangzhou. Since the EIC was banned from trading it, the opiate was bought in Calcutta by entrepreneurs, some of them Parsees and some British, led by a tough Scotsman, William Jardine, an EIC ship's doctor, who had founded the company Jardine Matheson and become the most successful opium trader, nicknamed Iron-Headed Old Rat by the Chinese. Jacob Astor and other Americans joined the trade.

When the Chinese destroyed British opium, Jardine lobbied Palmerston, foreign secretary, who in Parliament mocked Chinese 'moral habits' and ordered war to defend British opium. British warships, armed with Congreve rockets, routed the Chinese war junks. 'There's no doubt that this event, which will form an epoch in the progress of the civilization of the human races,' Palmerston wrote to Iron-Headed Old Rat, 'must be attended with the most important advantages to the commercial interests of England.' In 1842, China granted Hong Kong and 140 acres north of Shanghai to the British, then ports to France and the USA.* For China, this was the devastating end of a two-century ascendancy.

When the shattered emperor ordered corruption investigations, Cixi's father was fined but could not find the money. Cixi, a teenaged girl, suggested which assets to sell. 'This daughter,' said her father, 'is more like a son.'

In 1852, Cixi, wearing an embroidered Manchu dress and bejewelled headdress, stood among a group of Manchu (not Chinese) girls in a hall at the back of the Forbidden City for the first selection of concubines for the harem of the new Xianfeng emperor, a lame melancholic nineteen-year-old opera lover known as the Limping Dragon. Tiny, with perfect skin, large lips and radiant eyes, now known as Concubine Yi, Cixi was not the most beautiful but she was chosen as a low-ranking concubine to join the eight ranks of the harem.

At the top rank stood Empress Zhen, a year younger than Cixi and nicknamed the Fragile Phoenix: she had ten maids, a private cow, plentiful meat and many eunuchs. At the bottom of the ranks, Cixi had four maids and no cow. But it was not enough for Limping Dragon to enjoy his Manchu concubines in the Forbidden City; he also smuggled into the more relaxed Summer Palace prostitutes with bound feet, a delicacy that he relished. When he wanted sex he marked a concubine's name on a bamboo tablet which he gave to his chief eunuch; the concubine was then brought to one of his two bedrooms naked in the arms of a eunuch. After sex, she returned to the harem. Cixi was summoned and became

---

* It was a time when British conquistadors could still seize new provinces for the empire. In 1838, a young adventurer called James Brooke, son of an EIC judge in Calcutta, chartered his own ship and intervened in the internecine politics of the sultanate of Brunei. His defeat of Malay pirates and Dayak tribesmen in 1842 persuaded the sultan, Omar Saifuddien II, to appoint him hereditary raja of Sarawak. 'The white raja' tried to ban Dayak headhunting, but he also used Dayak auxiliaries to crush opposition. In London, accused of atrocities, he defied his critics but struggled to organize the succession to his strange monarchy. As a boy Brooke may have fathered a child, but he was a secret homosexual who fell in love with a Brunei prince, Badruddin, and a series of young English aristocrats and street children to whom he wrote feverish love poems. Since he had no legitimate sons, he appointed a nephew as heir, then fell out with him. The raja spent his old age in Totnes, pursuing and being blackmailed by local boys. When he died he left his raj to a younger nephew, Charles Brooke. The dynasty ruled Sarawak until 1946.

pregnant. In 1854, she was raised to rank five. When she gave advice to the emperor, he was unnerved, complaining to his wife Zhen that she was 'cunning'. Zhen formed an alliance with the pregnant Cixi. When, as her palace file read, 'Concubine Yi gave joyous birth to a grand prince,' the emperor was thrilled, promoting her to Noble Consort Yi, number two after the empress, and marrying his brother Prince Chun to her sister.

Xianfeng needed good news. Soon after his accession, ten years after the defeat by Britain, a peasant revolt started in the south, led by a charismatic peasant, Hong Xiuquan, who called himself 'the Sun' and 'brother of Jesus Christ'. His mystical God Worshipping Society, the Taiping, overran the south, where he founded a Heavenly Kingdom, based in Nanjing. When he heard of the revolt, Xianfeng wept. But worse was to come.

His father had chosen him, his fourth son of nine, as successor (sealing his name in a lacquered box with the words 'Ten Thousand Years') because of Xianfeng's hatred of the British, French and Americans. The foreigners had more than tripled opium deliveries in a decade, building new ports at Hong Kong and Shanghai as their missionaries were penetrating the country. Xianfeng appointed officials to crack down on his father's concessions and restrict the missionaries. In October 1856, as Cixi's son was born and trouble started in India, a Chinese attack on a British ship, the *Arrow*, triggered confrontation. Palmerston refused to 'abandon a large community of British subjects at the extreme end of the globe to a set of barbarians – a set of kidnapping, murdering, poisoning barbarians'. It was war.

Fresh from his joint victory with Britain in Crimea, Napoleon, using the murder of a French missionary in China as his pretext, joined the attack on China.

Xianfeng strengthened his defences around Beijing, but the Anglo-French forces, under the command of James Bruce, earl of Elgin, and Charles Cousin-Montauban, landed troops and advanced to the Dagu fortresses. The emperor agreed to British demands but then reneged. When the British tried to storm the Dagu Forts, they were repulsed. In August 1860, Elgin and Montauban successfully stormed the fortresses. In revenge Xianfeng had British envoys arrested and tortured, fettered with their hands and feet tied tightly behind them: twenty-one of the thirty-nine died in agony. But at Ba-li-qiao (Palikoa) on 21 September the Manchu cavalry was annihilated, and the Europeans took Beijing. Xianfeng and his court, including Zhen and Cixi, moved northwards, releasing the surviving captives to such western outrage that Elgin and Montauban ordered the looting then burning of the beautiful Summer

Palace, built by Qianlong. The troops engaged in 'indiscriminate plunder and wanton destruction', wrote a young British officer, as they became 'seized with a temporary insanity' fixated on 'plunder, plunder'. Elgin and Montauban – now comte de Palikoa – looted gold and jade staves for Victoria and Napoleon, while an old courtesan who died during the attack left five Pekinese dogs that were taken back to Britain; the queen was given one, crassly named Lootie, who lived in Windsor for ten years. The peace treaties signed by the emperor's brother ceded Kowloon to Britain, promised indemnities and granted Russia a section of coast, where an eastern port, Vladivostok, was soon built.

Napoleon believed in France's *mission civilisatrice* as much as any British statesman believed in his own nation's imperial destiny. In Algeria, now home to over 100,000 French *colons*, Napoleon's forces used brutal methods, massacres and deportations. The French were defeated for a while by a mystical sheikh and then on his death by a female leader, Lalla Fatma N'Soumer, until she was captured and died in prison. Napoleon, visiting Algeria, attempted to counter *colon* racism and envisioned a French colony and an Arab kingdom with him as *roi des Arabes*: 'I'm just as much emperor of the Arabs of Algeria as I am of the French.' As in Britain, aggressive businessmen drove imperial expansion. When Napoleon was canvassed by the Prom family of shipping tycoons from Bordeaux to move into Africa, he ordered his governors to expand from Saint-Louis on the coast into the interior of what became Senegal. Keen to exploit the French presence in east Asia, he grabbed a naval base in China, then sent a flotilla to attack Annam (Vietnam) where Catholic missionaries had provoked a backlash, with the emperor Tu Duc trying to reject Catholic infiltration by executing two Spanish priests. In September 1857, French troops seized Da Nang and Saigon; both were repelled by the Vietnamese, but Napoleon dispatched reinforcements that in June 1862 retook Saigon. Thus was established the French colony of Cochinchina.

Then in 1863 Napoleon turned on Cambodia. Its kings had long since abandoned Angkor, moving their capital to Phnom Penh, but, weak and divided, it was fought over by the emperors of Vietnam and the kings of Siam (Thailand). In 1848 a Cambodian prince Duong expelled the Vietnamese, backed by Siam, and re-established the Khmer kingdom. But he made the mistake of asking for Napoleonic protection in 1853: 'What would you have me do? I have two masters as my neighbours, and France is far away.' Not for long. Duong's son Norodom was forced to accept a French protectorate. Napoleon had established Indochine, a French Asian empire that lasted until 1954.

In Beijing, the debacle broke Xianfeng, who was succeeded in 1861 by his five-year-old son with Cixi, the Tongzhi emperor, and eight regents, led by a Manchu prince, Sushun, and his brother, while Empress Zhen acted as his formal mother and dowager empress. As the funeral neared, Cixi, still officially Consort Yi, persuaded Zhen to canvass for her promotion to joint dowager empress, adopting the name Joyous – Cixi. Secretly gathering support from her husband's brothers, Princes Gong and Chun, who encouraged her to 'listen to politics behind the curtains', and artfully getting control of the royal seals, she manipulated the regents into shouting disrespectfully at her while she and Zhen cradled the boy-emperor. Sushun ordered Cixi's murder.

At her husband's funeral, when half the regents accompanied the coffin and half the new emperor, Cixi orchestrated a coup, hiding the decree to dismiss the regents by sewing it into Zhen's robes. Some of the regents burst into the harem shouting, 'We are the ones that write decrees.' Cixi coolly ordered their arrest. Sushun, in charge of the coffin, was arrested in flagrante with two concubines, unbecoming conduct during royal obsequies. As Cixi fixed the trial, blaming the regents for signing the foreign treaties and falsifying her husband's will, two 'received silk' – the white scarf with which to hang themselves; Sushun was beheaded.

After her son's coronation, wearing yellow brocade illustrated with dragons, on a nine-dragon throne in the Hall of Supreme Harmony, Cixi was ruler of China, rising each day with Zhen (with whom she nominally ruled for twenty years) to sit in their phoenix-patterned robes, pearl-encrusted shoes and gate-towered hairdos behind the little emperor while they discussed matters of state with the Grand Council. Most urgent was the Taiping rebellion, whose leaders now ruled thirty million in an area larger than all of Europe. The Heavenly King, Jesus' Brother, had died, but the Heaven Worshippers fought on as bubonic plague raged. Cixi mustered a western-supplied Ever Victorious Army under a civil servant, Li Hongzhang, assisted by two extraordinary adventurers, the American Frederick Ward and the Briton Charles 'Chinese' Gordon.* Li invited Taiping leaders to a dinner where they

---

* Ward was a filibuster, a commander of American private armies who had served in the navy, then joined the filibuster William Walker in his attempt to conquer a private empire in Mexico before travelling to China, where he enrolled as a pirate hunter. Next he set up a small Colt-wielding group of mercenaries, the Shanghai Foreign Arms Corps, which developed into an army, until he was killed aged thirty. His successor was a blue-eyed general's son and fervid evangelical with a Jesus complex who regularly conversed with St Paul. Gordon served in the Crimean War before serving in China. He was disgusted by what he heard of Elgin's 'vandal-like' sacking of the Summer Palace. Joining Cixi's war

were offered a mandarin's hat, but as they knelt and bared their heads, they were decapitated. The Taiping was, with the eighth-century An Lushan rebellion, the bloodiest civil war in history: thirty million died, maybe more.

Cixi launched a 'Self-Strengthening Movement', commissioning modern warships, steamers and railways. But her power had its price. As a widow, in her early thirties, Cixi was not allowed to wear make-up nor bright reds, instead favouring orange robes, pale-blue waistcoats and, as she got older, a toupee. It was hard for her to have friends, let alone lovers, her companions being eunuchs. Cixi fell in love with a young, sensitive eunuch, An Dehai. When she rashly commissioned Little An to direct the selection of a wife for her son Tongzhi, he proudly set out with an entourage – breaking a rule that eunuchs were not allowed out of Beijing. The princes Gong and Chun ignored Cixi's authorization. Little An was arrested with six other eunuchs; he was then beheaded and exposed naked. One of Little An's friends, a fellow eunuch, criticized Cixi for failing to support him. She had him strangled, then collapsed into bed for a month of insomnia and vomiting. She always chose power over love. When her only son Tongzhi died in 1875 just two years after assuming full powers, she adopted and enthroned her baby nephew, the Guangxu emperor, removing him from his father, her enemy Prince Chun, whom she humiliated. Taking the title empress mother she made the emperor call her Papa Dearest. She would now dominate China into the twentieth century.

Napoleon had won wars against Russia and China, had secured Algeria and expanded into Senegal and Indochine. Now a beautiful countess turned his focus on Italy.

IF NECESSARY, SEDUCE THE EMPEROR: NAPOLEON, QUEEN OF HEARTS AND THE RISORGIMENTO OF ITALY

Contessa Virginia 'Nini' di Castiglione was no ordinary diplomat. 'I've enrolled the beauteous countess in the diplomatic service of Piedmont,' said Conte Camillo Cavour, premier of Piedmont, the north Italian

---

against the Taiping, 'this splendid Englishman' won thirty-three battles, surrounded by his blue-clad bodyguard, showing unusual mercy in a brutal conflict and earning promotion from the emperor. On his return to England, he became a social worker among the poor boys of Gravesend, inviting these 'scuttlers' to stay in his house. Often wishing he had been castrated, he was probably a repressed homosexual.

kingdom. In order to bring about the unification of Italy, she was 'to flirt and if necessary seduce the emperor', obtaining Napoleon III's support against the Habsburgs. Green-eyed and jet-haired, 'a miracle of beauty, Venus descended from Olympus', in the words of the Austrian ambassador's wife Paulina Metternich, but also insouciant and saucy, Castiglione was a Florentine aristocrat recently married to an older count with whom she had a son before a short affair with the Piedmontese king, Victor Emmanuel II. 'An imbecile', concluded Lord Clarendon, but Cavour, a long-haired playboy with flying moustaches and six mistresses, believed she was his secret weapon. 'Succeed, my cousin, by any methods you like.'

Paris was already filled with ambitious beauties, but Castiglione made herself the cynosure and was swiftly noticed by Napoleon, who had her smuggled into the Tuileries. While Empress Eugénie was pregnant, Castiglione appeared at a ball as Queen of Hearts in a costume 'entirely open at the sides from hips downwards, her hair flowing loose over neck and shoulders', with a heart strategically positioned over her pubis.

'Your heart seems a little low,' observed the empress. Yet 'every movement was contrived and she began to get on one's nerves', said Paulina Metternich.

'Very beautiful,' Napoleon told his cousin Princess Mathilde, 'but she bores me to death.' Napoleon moved on to Marie Anne, wife of his foreign minister, Comte Alexandre Walewski, who was the son of Napoleon I with his Polish paramour Marie Walewska. Once when the imperial train was chuffing along to Compiègne, a door slid open to reveal the emperor kissing Marie Anne, in full view of her husband. In the Tuileries, when courtiers caught Napoleon *en bonne fortune*, he simply saluted and continued; when the empress surprised him, she would snap, '*Sortez, mademoiselle,*' and the girl would dress and leave fast.

Where sex had failed Italy, murder succeeded. In January 1858, Italian nationalists, disgusted by Napoleon's neglect of their cause, tossed bombs at Napoleon and Eugénie on their way to the theatre, killing eight. The monarchs, lightly wounded, bravely watched the play, but the near-death experience made Napoleon recall his youth as an Italian patriot. Now, combining his romantic nationalism, compulsive plotting and military ambitions, he backed Cavour and Italian *risorgimento*, provoking war with Austria.

On 24 June 1859, at Solferino in Habsburg Italy, Napoleon, chainsmoking in the saddle, defeated the Austrians under Franz Josef in one of the first battles of modern warfare and the last commanded by sovereigns. A total of 300,000 soldiers fought and 29,000 were killed – more than at Waterloo. 'The poor fellows! What a terrible thing war is!' sighed Napoleon, vomiting at the sight of a heap of amputated limbs. Later he joked grimly but wisely, 'I've had enough of war. There's too much luck in it.' In a hut outside Villafranca, he met Franz Josef and agreed a compromise that ceded most of the Habsburgs' Italian territories to the new kingdom. But, again betraying his Italian allies, Napoleon took Savoy, today's Riviera, for France. Many Italians were infuriated. A swashbuckling patriot, Giuseppe Garibaldi, a sailor from Nice who became a professional liberator,* now led his army of volunteers, the Thousand, to seize Sicily, where he was acclaimed dictator. In Milan, Victor Emmanuel declared himself king of Italy, hailed by Garibaldi, who now turned to a new war.

In 1861, Garibaldi offered his services to the newly elected US president, Abraham Lincoln, in the crisis over slavery ignited by the moral contradiction at the heart of the world-changing democracy.

Just months earlier, in April 1860, an ex-officer, fallen on hard times, started work as a clerk in his father's leatherwear store in Galena, Illinois, where he served customers and collected invoices. Sometimes Ulysses Grant entertained friends with stories of the Mexican war. But there was a shadow in his past: six years earlier Captain Grant had been forced to resign from the army for being drunk on duty. 'When I have nothing to do,' he confessed, 'I get blue and depressed, I've a natural craving for drink.' His father Jesse, now a rich tanner and store owner, gave him a job as shop assistant, and it was from this unlikely perch that Grant observed the rising crisis.

He never grumbled, but he was obviously destined for obscurity, and there was little sign he would soon emerge as one of the greatest Americans.

---

* Garibaldi had earlier fought for Uruguayan independence. While in south America, he had sought out Manuela Sáenz, Bolívar's paramour. Garibaldi had lost his own Manuela: during the Uruguayan war, he had fallen in love with a Brazilian gaucho, Anita de Sousa, who joined his freedom fighters. She combined 'the strength and courage of a man and the charm and tenderness of a woman, manifested by the daring and vigour with which she had brandished her sword and the beautiful oval of her face that trimmed the softness of her extraordinary eyes'. They had four children together and in 1848 she returned with him to fight for Rome, dying of malaria as French and Austrian troops crushed the revolution. Garibaldi always wore her poncho and scarf.

LICK 'EM TOMORROW: ULYSSES AND ABRAHAM

The next month, the recently formed Republican Party chose as their presidential candidate a little-known prairie lawyer and former congressman, Abraham Lincoln. Six foot four, grey-eyed, simian and loquacious, born in a Kentucky log cabin, Lincoln had been promoted as Honest Abe and the Railsplitter (a backwoodsman used to splitting logs) who had won national attention in the debates for an Illinois Senate race.

The American schism was already simmering into war. It had started in Kansas where a half-mad abolitionist, John 'I'm the instrument of God' Brown, led an anti-slavery militia that fought slave owners. In October 1859 Brown invaded Virginia, for which he was hanged. Lincoln loathed 'the monstrous injustice of slavery' and the moral decay of 'slave power'. Although the presidential candidate of the new Republican party acquiesced in its existence in the southern states, he would not countenance its spread. Southerners feared that any limit would ultimately threaten their power to expand. Suddenly the forty-year quest for compromise seemed to exhaust itself.

On 6 November 1860, Lincoln was elected president. In December, South Carolina seceded from the Union, followed by six other slavery states. Together they declared a Provisional Confederacy of the United States, which elected a slave-owning former general and senator, Jefferson Davis, as president and Alexander Stephens as his deputy. At a speech in Savannah, Georgia, Stephens defined the Confederacy through slavery: 'its cornerstone rests upon the great truth, that the negro is not equal to the white man; that slavery – subordination to the superior race – is his natural and normal condition. This, our new government, is the first, in the history of the world, based upon this great physical, philosophical, and moral truth.' The gentlemen planters of the Confederacy created a myth of Southern gentility that Grant mocked: 'Southern slave-owners believed that the ownership of slaves conferred a sort of patent of nobility.' The rebellion was about slavery, not about states' rights. The ensuing war revealed that slavery was not only morally repugnant but economically disastrous. The Confederacy was less populous, because slavery drove down the wages of poor whites and therefore did not attract new immigrants; and its slave-owning entitlement did not foster industry. Yet this would be a war of conscript armies and industrial slaughter.

As Grant offered his services and took command of a regiment in Missouri, Lincoln offered Robert E. Lee, a handsome Virginian patrician married to Martha Washington's great-granddaughter, the post of commander-in-chief. Lee, who believed that 'The blacks are immeasurably better off here than in Africa . . . The painful discipline they are undergoing is necessary for their instruction as a race,' refused and took command of Confederate forces. Lincoln turned to a young general, George McClellan, who despised him as a 'well-meaning baboon', wanted to maintain slavery and harboured Caesaresque ambitions, telling his wife, 'I seem to have become *the* power of the land . . . I almost think that were I to win some small success now, I could become Dictator . . .' Lincoln appointed him to command the Army of the Potomac and then as overall commander, but McClellan prevaricated as the Confederates attacked. Lincoln was soon dissatisfied. 'If General McClellan doesn't want to use the army,' he said, 'I'd like to borrow it for a time.'

The Confederacy controlled Virginia, and its best chance of beating the more populous north was to strike fast. Lee advanced, but not quickly or forcefully enough. The war that followed demonstrated the destructive power of the new technologies on the flesh of men who were deployed as if they were fighting traditional wars of cavalry and courage. Instead, artillery barrages and long-range rifles marked a new era that required new generals: at Antietam, 20,0000 were killed or wounded, the single bloodiest day in American history. Lincoln soon noticed that Grant, fighting in the west, was a winner. Even when he was almost defeated, at Shiloh, he just said, 'We'll lick 'em tomorrow.' Generals needed the nerve to take punishing casualties, but Grant also possessed the sangfroid and strategic foresight to win. 'I saw an open field,' he recalled of the aftermath at Shiloh, 'so covered with dead that it would have been possible to walk across the clearing, in any direction, stepping on dead bodies, without a foot touching the ground.'

The end of Lee's offensive empowered Lincoln, on 22 September 1862, to order the emancipation of the 3.5 million slaves in the Confederate states, effective from 1 January the following year. Frederick Douglass, the once enslaved African-American leader, had wondered if Lincoln would ever deliver: 'Can any colored man . . . ever forget the night which followed the first day of January 1863, when the world was to see if Abraham Lincoln would prove to be as good as his word?'*

---

* Douglass was born enslaved on a Maryland plantation, to an African-American mother while 'My master was my father.' Escaping from his bondage, he made it to Massachusetts, where he started to campaign against slavery. There Douglass, handsome and charismatic, a beautiful writer and superb speaker, celebrated his freedom with 'joyous excitement': 'I felt as one might feel upon escape from a den of hungry lions.' He added, 'I lived more in one day than in a year of my slave life.' But he felt he had no part in American democracy: 'I have no country. What country have I?' His autobiography, published in 1845, rallied the anti-slavery movement.

More than 179,000 African-Americans escaped the south and joined Unionist forces. Not all Union generals welcomed them, but Grant did.*

Lincoln finally demoted McClennan, but Grant was criticized for his bloody battles and alcoholic lapses. 'I think Grant has hardly a friend left except myself,' said Lincoln. 'What I want is generals who fight battles and win victories. Grant's done this.' Grant took Vicksburg in Mississippi, while another competent general, deploying the Union's superiority in men and material, defeated the Confederates in a bloody battle at Gettysburg in Pennsylvania. When Lincoln visited the battle-field, he defined the American ideal of 'government of the people, by the people, for the people'. As he planned his re-election, he feared that Grant would run against him. Once he had checked that Grant had no such ambition, he promoted him to command the Union armies, and the two finally met.

'Why, here is General Grant,' said Lincoln at the White House. 'Well, this a great pleasure, I assure you.' Grant, laconic, sturdy, intense, admired the gangly, yarn-spinning Lincoln – 'a very great man', he said – but loathed the attention, telling Julia, 'I heartily wish myself back in camp.' Yet they had much in common: both were underrated, plain-spoken prairie pragmatists who abhorred slavery yet had married into self-important slave-owning families. Both had crosses to bear: for Lincoln, it was depression; for Grant, drink. Lincoln's operational orders were simple. 'He wished me to beat Lee,' said Grant, 'but how I did it was my own duty.' Grant and Lee were opposites: Lee a patrician who manoeuvred like a Virginian Napoleon; Grant 'the quietest little fellow you ever saw', noted an officer. 'The only evidence you have that he's in any place is that he makes things git.' He soon made things git, advancing in Virginia and Georgia.

Lincoln ordered conscription, though the first drafts led to riots in Manhattan. Civil wars divide families, and the Roosevelts were typical: the ageing millionaire CVS Roosevelt and his son Theodore were pas-sionately abolitionist and Yankee, but the latter's wife, Mittie, was an equally passionate Confederate. In 1860, Mittie gave birth to Theodore junior, Teddy, by which time America was in crisis. Mittie secretly sewed clothes for Confederate troops, and her brothers were Confed-erate agents plotting to assassinate Lincoln and buying new battleships

---

* It was typical of Grant too that when Ely Parker, born Hasanoanda, a full-blood Seneca Native American, who was trained as lawyer and engineer, offered to raise a Native Amer-ican regiment and was turned down by Lincoln's war secretary, he was employed and promoted by Grant.

in Britain. Her husband Theodore refused to fight her family, instead, like many of his class, paying a surrogate to fight in his place. Little Teddy admired his mother, yet he worshipped Lincoln and dreamed of fighting for the Union.

The self-destruction of the USA was an opportunity for its rivals. Out in the west, the native peoples started to raid again. Comanche bands attacked Texas; in September 1860, Governor Houston dispatched a unit of Rangers and their Tonkawa auxiliaries to hunt the Comanche raiders, ambushing Peta Nocona's village and massacring men, women and children. Peta Nocona and his son Quanah were away, but the Rangers captured a fair-haired, blue-eyed woman and her baby daughter.

CYNTHIA PARKER AND PETA NOCONA; FRANZ JOSEF AND SISI

When she was questioned, the blonde woman said, 'Me Cynthia,' at which one of the Rangers exclaimed, 'Why, Tom, this is a white woman, Indians don't have blue eyes.' She was taken back to Fort Belknap, where her surviving brother Isaac Parker could not identify his long-lost sister – who could barely remember any English. But finally the Parkers adopted her. Yet Cynthia grieved for Peta and her sons, whom she believed were dead. When her daughter died of influenza, she tried to kill herself, cutting her breasts, and finally starved herself to death.

Out on the prairie, her husband Peta Nocona mourned her too, dying of wounds soon afterwards. Their son Quanah, now fifteen, learned for the first time that his mother was American. Determined to fight for his people, he joined another war band and planned revenge.

Napoleon and Palmerston also saw opportunities. Ironically the first Old World potentate to back Lincoln was Alexander II. The virtuous backwoods lawyer and the concupiscent Romanov emperor had something in common: in February 1861 Alexander had liberated Russian serfs, two years before Lincoln's emancipation. In both cases, the measure raised radical expectations that proved disappointing – and both would pay with their lives.

Surprisingly, Britain and France leaned towards the Confederacy. Palmerston had been re-elected in 1859 at the age of seventy-four, his vigour confirmed by rumours of illegitimate children and his citation in a divorce case, which only added to his roguish popularity. Pam was exasperated by his chancellor, the melodramatic, wild-eyed, self-righteous Gladstone, who stalked the streets of London seeking prostitutes to redeem: this involved long, titillating conversations about Christ with ladies of the night after which Gladstone tried not to masturbate. 'Whenever he gets my place,' said Palmerston, 'we'll have strange doings.' Palmerston had orchestrated the navy's anti-slavery campaigns, yet the British and French textile industries were dependent on southern cotton. Gladstone proposed an armed intervention,* and Palmerston came close to recognizing the Confederacy – as did their ally Napoleon, who was restrained in part by his American dentist, Thomas Evans, certainly the most powerful dentist in history.† But Napoleon, in the midst of expanding in Asia and Africa, saw the chance to found an American empire – in Mexico.

Halved in size by American gains, and hobbled by misrule and racial and economic inequality, the republic was struggling, but its president Benito Juárez, a lawyer risen from the humblest Zapotec origins, had restored order after Santa Anna but suspended payments on its European debts. Encouraged by Morny, who held Mexican bonds, Napoleon assembled an Anglo-French coalition to exploit American chaos. Although Palmerston backed French intervention, he limited his involvement. In December 1861, Napoleon's troops, conveyed in steamships, landed in Mexico, expelled Juárez and in June 1863 took the capital. Eugénie introduced her husband to Mexican grandees, who proposed a European monarchy. In July, Napoleon sought an emperor for Mexico and found him among the Habsburgs: Maximilian, the brother of Franz Josef.

The young emperor had faced defeat at Solferino and lost Italy, but

---

* Gladstone, son of Britain's biggest slave owner, was still conflicted about slavery. He described 'the principle of the superiority of the white man and his right to hold the black in slavery' as 'detestable' and favoured emancipation of slaves, yet he supported the Confederacy, claiming that 'Slaves would be better off if the States were separated,' and that the Confederacy 'had made a nation of the South'. Even in 1864, when the war was almost over, he criticized the 'negrophilists' who 'sacrifice three white lives in order to set free one black man'.

† Evans was living the Empire life in Paris, with a mansion (Bella Rosa), an art collection and of course a courtesan, Manet's model Méry Laurent. It was a long way from Philadelphia, but in 1850 the twenty-seven-year-old dentist was called in to treat Napoleon. 'You're a young fellow, but clever, I like you,' the emperor said. Evans became his doctor surgeon, developing the first fillings and the use of laughing gas, and was soon consulted by Tsar Alexander II and the Ottoman sultan. Visiting Napoleon weekly, he admired Haussmann's plans for Paris, enabling him to buy property that soon made him a fortune. When Eugénie first came to Paris, one of Napoleon's adjutants spotted her in Evans's waiting room and reported her arrival to the emperor. The dentist became her confidant. In 1864, Napoleon sent him to America to report on the civil war.

he had survived it all. Until recently Archduke Maximilian had been his heir, but their mother Sophia had arranged Franz Josef's marriage to her Bavarian niece, the twenty-three-year-old Princess Sisi. The dour kaiser fell madly in love with her. 'Dear Angel', he always called her, 'My sweet dearest soul, my heart's love', signing himself 'your little man'. As he recovered from the loss of Italy, Sisi gave birth to two daughters. But she was unmoved by the stolid emperor, stifled by the pompous court and harassed by her strident mother-in-law, who commandeered the babies and mocked Sisi as a 'silly young mother'. When a daughter died of typhus aged two, Sisi sank into depression, refusing to eat. Setting up gyms in her palaces, she exercised, dieted and binged obsessionally.

Tall, slim, beautiful, she prided herself on her waist (16½ inches), strapping herself into tightly laced corsets. She craved freedom, fame and love like a modern woman, riding and hunting manically, making herself Europe's fastest equestrienne. Growing ever more self-absorbed and self-indulgent, she had little time for Franz Josef and not much for her children: 'Children are the curse of a woman, for when they come, they drive away Beauty.' She adored Heinrich Heine's verses and wrote poems herself, often mocking her enemies; she hated royal life – 'this drudgery, this torture', she called it. 'She espoused the view that freedom was everyone's right,' wrote her future daughter-in-law Stephanie. 'Her picture of life resembled a beautiful fairy-tale drama of a world without sorrow or constraint.' In 1858, she gave birth to a son, Crown Prince Rudolf, fulfilling her chief duty, after which she travelled the world, pursued pleasure and avoided court, husband and children.

Maximilian was a problem. Recently married to Leopold of Belgium's daughter Charlotte, another Saxe-Coburg splicing, he craved a crown. The emperor appointed him naval commander but sacked him for liberalism. Now, in the summer of 1863, as the American civil war raged, he was offered the throne of Mexico. Charlotte pushed him to accept. It was not quite as absurd as it seems today: there was already a successful Brazilian monarchy, ruled by his cousins, and the Habsburgs had ruled Mexico for centuries. Napoleon turned his charm on to Maximilian, who disdained him as a 'circus ringmaster . . . with bow legs, a sidling walk and a furtive look out of half-closed eyes, running after every pretty woman'. But Napoleon played on Maximilian's sense of liberal mission. 'It is a question of rescuing a whole continent from anarchy,' he said, 'of setting an example to the whole of America.' He promised, 'France will never fail the Mexican Empire.'

Embroiled in civil war, Lincoln warned against a plan that contravened American paramountcy in south America, expressed in the Monroe

Doctrine, but he was in no position to stop it. Franz Josef encouraged it but insisted that Maximilian renounce his rights to Austria. A furious Maximilian had second thoughts, but Charlotte insisted, and Napoleon wrote, 'It's impossible you should give up going to Mexico. The honour of the House of Habsburg is at stake.'

Maximilian and Charlotte sailed for Mexico.

AMERICAN WARS: PEDRO AND LÓPEZ; CHARLOTTE AND ELIZA

In May 1864, the couple arrived in Mexico,[*] setting up their court at the vast but ruined Chapultepec Castle, once a shrine for the Mexica *tlatoani*, more recently stormed by US troops, and now extravagantly restored. Maximilian favoured universal education and workers' rights, which alienated conservatives; French support discredited him with liberals. He pivoted to the right, backed by his tiny Mexican forces, French troops and a black Sudanese regiment, dispatched by Napoleon's Egyptian ally, Said, son of Mehmed Ali. But Juárez, the elected president, rallied a national insurgency.

Maximilian could look southwards to his first cousin, Pedro II, in Brazil with some envy: there the young emperor was beloved. Aged fourteen, the grandson of Franz of Austria, nephew of Napoleon I – very Habsburgian, blond, big-chinned – had been crowned as constitutional emperor with sceptre, toucan cloak and epaulettes of galo-da-serra feathers, attended by black and mixed-race courtiers. 'The monarchy,' writes Lilia Schwarcz, 'was tropicalizing itself.'

Moving between Rio and a summer palace at his new resort, Petropolis, Pedro directed but did not dictate government, diligently promoting American monarchy and new technology, steamships and railways, and becoming the first royal photographer, buying daguerreotype equipment. 'If I wasn't emperor, I'd love to be a teacher,' he said, sometimes adding, '*La science, c'est moi.*' Breezy, studious, multilingual, studying Greek, medicine, astronomy and engineering, dutifully married to a Bourbon princess, discreetly devoted to his mistress, he embraced Afro-Brazilian culture, backing the Rio carnival and paying homage to its

---

[*] Maximilian spent the trip writing a detailed Habsburgian court etiquette with Mexican trappings ('At this point, the Emperor will hand his sombrero to the attending Field-Adjutant . . .'). He was not the first emperor: Maximilian appointed the grandsons of Emperor Agustín as princes and possible heirs, while selecting a descendant of the last *tlatoani* as lady-in-waiting.

elected black leaders, the Three Kings and the Emperor of the Divine Holy Spirit.

Yet this was a society still based on coffee plantations, worked by slaves. Between 1841 and 1850, at least 83 per cent of African slaves went to Brazil, with the rest going to the USA and Cuba. But the British Royal Navy was seizing ever more ships. Brazilian planters still feared a Haitian-style revolt – in 1849 in Rio there were 110,000 slaves to 266,000 whites. The area around Rio's palace was so filled with slaves that it was known as Little Africa and, for all the mixing of races, the Brazilian elites were all white. Countesses attended royal balls and shopped in the Parisian emporia of the Rua do Ouvidor, as recounted in the stories of the novelist Machado de Assis, whose character Cândido Neves is a slave hunter proud of his work. In 1850 Brazil banned the trade but not slavery. Yet it was not a slave revolt that challenged the monarchy but a war.

In 1864, Marshal Francisco López, president of Paraguay since his father's death* and partner of Eliza Lynch, mother of his five sons, attacked Brazil. In the seven years since she had arrived from Paris, La Lynch had taught the locals how to enjoy French food, cooking and fashion, while amassing twelve million acres of state land transferred to make her the world's greatest landowner.

On his deathbed, the marshal's father had warned him to avoid war with Brazil. Yet with 55,000 troops armed with the latest technology, López, known as El Mariscal, using the independence of Uruguay as pretext, attacked both Argentina and Brazil. His folly was astounding: Paraguay's total population was smaller than the Brazilian National Guard. As Brazil, Uruguay and Argentina counter-attacked and Maximilian struggled to survive in Mexico, General Grant was strangling the Confederacy from north and south.

LINCOLN AND GRANT: WE'RE ALL AMERICANS

In Washington, DC, on 4 March 1865, as black soldiers marched in his inaugural parade, Lincoln was sworn in for the second time, promising 'malice toward none; with charity for all; with firmness in the right', but warning, with exquisite eloquence, that the war would continue if

* He was the first of a modern phenomenon prevalent particularly in Latin America and Asia: the dynastic republic, a hereditary dictatorship founded not on the pre-1789 sacred monarchy but on a cosplay democracy and presidential constitution with rigged elections. The succession was usually father–son but sometimes husband–wife.

necessary 'until every drop of blood drawn with the lash, shall be paid by another drawn with the sword'. Vice-President Andrew Johnson got drunk. 'Don't let him speak,' ordered Lincoln – but he did anyway. Among the guests was a fanatical Confederate actor, John Wilkes Booth, invited by his girlfriend, a senator's daughter. He had recently acted in a production of *Julius Caesar* and considered killing Lincoln at the inauguration. Instead he started to put together a conspiracy to kidnap or kill the president.

On 9 April, at Appomattox in Virginia, Grant outmanoeuvred Lee, who finally agreed to negotiate terms. At the local courthouse, Lee, dapper in immaculate grey uniform, with buckskin gauntlets, silk sash and polished boots with red silk toppings, offered his sword to Grant, who was chewing on a cigar wearing a 'common soldier's blouse, un-buttoned, on which, however, the four stars; high boots, mud-splashed'. Grant made chitchat. 'I met you once, General Lee, while we were serving in Mexico.'

'Yes, I know, but I've never been able to recollect a single feature,' retorted Lee grandly. 'I asked to see you to ascertain upon what terms you'd receive the surrender of my army.' Grant scribbled his terms, which were written out by his adjutant, General Ely Parker, the full-blood Tonawanda Seneca converted to Christianity, who handed them to Lee. The Confederate blushed and hesitated, believing Parker was black. Then he offered his hand.

'I'm glad to see one real American here,' said Lee.

'We're all Americans,' replied Parker. Lee signed. Three million Americans had fought, including about 180,000 black soldiers and 20,000 black sailors; 750,000 had died. The Union had won, 3.5 million slaves had been freed and would soon be granted the vote. Lincoln welcomed the south back: 'Let 'em up easy.' Not everyone was convinced he would defend the freed slaves: Lincoln, said Douglass, was still a 'white man's president'.

At the White House, on 14 April, Grant recounted the surrender to Lincoln and his cabinet, after which the president invited the Grants to Ford's Theatre that evening to watch *Our American Cousin*. When Booth visited the theatre, he learned that the Lincolns and Grants would attend that night; he and his cohorts planned to save the Confederacy – which still had one active army in the field – by decapitating the Union. But Julia Grant, who did not get on with Mary Lincoln, vetoed the invitation. 'Dear Husband,' said Mary Lincoln to Abraham that afternoon, 'you almost startle me by your great cheerfulness.'

'And well I may feel so, Mary,' said Lincoln. 'I consider this day the war has come to a close.' Mary Lincoln was unwise, inconsistent, unstable and possibly bipolar, a trial for her husband, but they had lost one son aged three, and another, Willie, aged eleven, died of typhoid; during the war, they had endured appalling stress. The president added, 'We must both be more cheerful in the future – between the war and the loss of our darling Willie – we have both been very miserable.'

As the Lincolns prepared for the theatre, the Grants headed to the station. On the way, a horseman – Booth – galloped alongside and peered into their carriage, confirming that they would not be at the theatre. At 10.13 p.m., at Ford's Theatre, Booth sneaked into the president's box and shot him in the back of the head with a Deringer pistol, then jumped out of the box on to the stage, shouting '*Sic semper tyrannis!*' before fleeing. One other conspirator ambushed the secretary of state, William Seward, who was sick in bed, and stabbed him, while the third failed to find Vice-President Johnson – and got drunk. Lincoln died next morning. Booth was killed in a shoot-out; the other conspirators were hanged.

Johnson, a long-haired, hard-drinking and pugnacious mediocrity, was sworn in. As the only southern senator to support the Union, he had been selected for the vice-presidency by Lincoln as a sign of reconciliation, but he was a diehard racist: 'This is a country for white men, and by God, as long I'm president, it'll be a government for white men.' The Civil Rights Act of 1866 promised the vote for all citizens 'without distinction of race or color, or previous condition of slavery'; Johnson vetoed it, but his veto was overridden. Amendments to the constitution abolished slavery and granted citizenship to all ex-slaves. African-Americans delighted in their ability to vote. As Congress passed the Reconstruction Acts, which detailed the terms under which the rebel states would be readmitted, Union armies occupied the south and Grant ordered his generals to enforce the new laws. The Union had won the war, but it would lose the peace.

The fightback by white supremacism started at once. Southerners passed Black Codes to stop the freedmen voting. In Memphis and New Orleans white mobs murdered black people. In Pulaski (Tennessee), Confederate veterans founded a clandestine militia, named Ku Klux Klan after the Greek *kuklos* (circle), sporting white hoods to represent the ghosts of dead comrades.

As President Johnson tainted Lincoln's legacy,* his paladin Grant

---

* Johnson's only real achievement was to order Secretary Seward to buy Alaska from Russia for $15 million, a good deal for America.

announced, 'Now for Mexico,' since he regarded Napoleon 'as an active part of the rebellion' and Emperor Maximilian as a 'foothold' of 'European monarchy . . . a direct act of war'. His Mexican war would be 'short, quick, decisive' but his plan was derailed by his deteriorating relationship with the egregious President Johnson.

Grant did not need to fight Napoleon in Mexico: Napoleon lost his nerve as his position in Europe deteriorated. 'The French army is full of enthusiasm for Max,' Empress Charlotte told her father, but in February 1866 Napoleon, agonized by the successful insurgency against his puppet, exposed by Union victory, started to withdraw – a move which, he wrote to Maximilian, 'may cause Your Majesty temporary embarrassment'. Emperor Maximilian planned to abdicate, but Charlotte sailed for Europe to appeal to Napoleon, who received her on three tearful but painful encounters: 'We've done our best by Maximilian but all we can do now is help him escape.' Charlotte, proudly half Bourbon, half Coburg, shrieked, 'Bourbon blood flows in my veins . . . I ought not have dishonoured my forebears and myself by treating with a Bonaparte.' But no one would help. 'All is useless,' she cabled Maximilian, then sank into madness, hiding in the Vatican and claiming that she was being poisoned. She was later locked up in a Belgian castle, where she came to believe she was empress not just of Mexico but of many other places too. Maximilian refused to flee as Mexican forces closed in.

Further south, the other Napoleonic protégé, Marshal López, was convinced he had triumphed against Brazil and Argentina, while his lover Eliza Lynch commanded her own battalions of female warriors, *Las Residentas*. López's first offensive into Brazil's Mato Grosso was successful but the second against Argentina was disastrous. Emperor Pedro declared himself Volunteer Number One and rushed to the front. Brazilian ironclads advanced up the Paraná River as the Triple Allies attacked. Brazil had a tiny army of 18,000, but Pedro recruited more, offering slaves their freedom in return for service: 'More and more strength should be given to [General Baron] Caxias; speed up the buying of slaves and increase our army.' Twenty thousand slaves joined up.

In May 1866 an allied army invaded and destroyed most of López's forces in a series of routs in which Paraguayans were mowed down as they charged artillery. Soon the marshal was so short of men, he too had to recruit slaves, and his men went into battle 'semi-nude without shoes or boots, covered with shoddy ponchos – even colonels go barefoot'. As Paraguay starved and suffered epidemics, the invading army of the Brazilian general Caxias besieged the massive fortress of Humaitá unaware that it was virtually empty – until it finally surrendered in August

1868. Now López was doomed: despite terrible Brazilian losses, Emperor Pedro insisted on hunting down 'the tyrant' as the cast changed in Europe.

Napoleon and Palmerston had directed European affairs for twenty years. At eighty, still riding every day, Old Pam finally went into decline. On 18 October 1865, as he sank into a coma, he imagined he was still negotiating treaties: 'That's Article 98; now go on to the next.' Victoria had always been unsure about the old rogue, who 'often worried and distressed us, though as Pr. Minister he behaved *very well*'. Palmerston, granted a rare state funeral, had shaped the British century. 'Death,' wrote Gladstone, 'has indeed laid low the most towering antlers in the forest.'

As his partner Pam was exiting, Napoleon, tired, unwell and chastened by Mexico, was holidaying at Villa Eugénie in Biarritz. There he entertained a giant German visitor who ate and drank Brobdingnagian quantities: at one session he downed 'a glass of madeira, ditto of sherry, one whole flask of Yquem and a glass of cognac', and he so enjoyed the turbot that he exclaimed, 'For a sauce like that I'd give twenty banks of the Rhine.' Napoleon and his entourage mocked his hulking Prussian coarseness – but, learning from Napoleon's success and exploiting his own remorseless virtuosity, he was about to reorder European power. 'They treat me like a fox,' Bismarck said later. 'A cunning fellow of the first rank. But the truth is that with a gentleman I am always a gentleman and a half, and when I have to deal with a pirate, I try to be a pirate and a half.' The Prussian pirate planned to create a new power: Germany.

ACT SEVENTEEN

1.2 BILLION

Hohenzollerns and Krupps, Albanians and Lakotas

THE MAD JUNKER, THE CANNON KING AND
THE TOURNAMENT OF MODERN POWER:
I'VE BEATEN THEM ALL! ALL!

In 1865 Otto von Bismarck had been minister-president of Prussia for three years, and he had come to the Villa Eugénie to analyse Napoleon and learn his price for not intervening in his planned war against Austria. The Prussian had admired Napoleon's use of universal suffrage to win conservative support and was now planning to do the same himself. Nationalism had replaced religion to provide a sense of belonging and meaning for millions; nation states, run by impersonal bureaucracies, became awesome organizers of resources; civil societies grew ever more complicated – but dynasties could adapt and provide stability and leadership. Nations were like families, monarchs their fathers and mothers.

Many believed that the shrewd Napoleon would outwit Bismarck and only hindsight can justify the contempt historians show to Napoleon and the respect shown to the minister-president. 'We can imagine the eccentric volubility with which M. Bismarck would develop his sanguine schemes,' wrote a British diplomat, 'and the covert irony and silent amusement of the subtle sovereign.'

Bismarck was subtler than he looked. He was the brilliant, misanthropic son of an archetypical but ineffectual Junker and his intellectual wife, who was the daughter of an adviser to Frederick the Great. Bismarck despised his ordinary father – 'How often did I repay his . . . good-natured tenderness with coldness and bad grace' – and sneered at his mother: 'As a small child I hated her.' He grew up boundless in his confidence.

While at Göttingen University, he was nicknamed Mad Junker for his wild hunting, drinking and duelling (he insulted everyone and sought duels, managing to fight twenty-five in three terms), but he was curious and cosmopolitan, multilingual, well read and drawn to foreigners – his best friend was an American and he fell in love with an Englishwoman.

After a crush on a friend's wife, he married the demure Johanna von Puttkamer, with whom he had three children, including a son he bullied horribly, and later consoled himself in a platonic passion for a Russian princess. He delighted in conflict, yet never served in the Prussian army; he was an evangelical Pietist Christian without an ounce of Christian generosity. A soft-voiced but impressive speaker, he was a beguiling wit and a superb writer.

Horrified by the 1848 revolutions, he thought Frederick William the Flounderer was too weak, offering his services to his conservative brother Prince Wilhelm, while making provocative speeches in the Landtag (the Prussian assembly). But he saw politics with absolute clarity, a skill honed by spells as ambassador to Frankfurt, Paris and Petersburg: 'Why do great states fight wars today? The only sound basis . . . is egoism, not romanticism.' Bismarck learned his essential lesson from Napoleon III: nationalist populism was conservative. 'Prussia is completely isolated. There's but one ally for Prussia if she knows how to win and handle them . . . The German people.' He would find a way: 'Politics is less a science than an art.' He revelled in its risks: 'This trade teaches that one can be as shrewd as the shrewdest in the world and still go like a child into the dark.'

When Wilhelm succeeded as king, he found the monarchy paralysed, unable to get the Landtag to pass his military budget. The immoderate Bismarck, once unthinkable, had now, by a process of momentous inevitability, become the only choice left. Unlike Napoleon III, Bismarck did not depend on either election or coup, he did not lead a political party; his entire career depended on the favour of one old Hohenzollern officer, Wilhelm, who could dismiss him at any moment. Their relationship was like a stormy twenty-six-year marriage, interspersed with Bismarckian spasms of shouting, weeping and threats of resignation. 'It's not easy,' joked Wilhelm later, 'to be kaiser under Bismarck.' This solitary, indefatigable giant was manic, petty, paranoid and vindictive – but the dynamic executor of plans that were the fruit of brutally clear analysis of the alchemy of power.

Bismarck's plan was bold but not secret: 'I'll soon be compelled to undertake . . . the Prussian government,' he told Disraeli, visiting London in June 1862. 'My first care will be to organize the army,' then 'I shall seize the pretext to declare war against Austria . . . and give national unity to Germany under Prussian leadership.'

'Be careful about that man,' said Disraeli. 'He means what he says.' As minister-president, Bismarck enjoyed shocking Prussian liberals: 'The great questions of the time will be resolved not by speeches and majority decisions – that was the great mistake of 1848 – but by iron and blood.'

War was risky – Bismarck called it 'rolling the iron dice' – but he was a risk-taker: 'My entire life has been spent gambling for high stakes with other people's money.' Bismarck had Jewish confidants but, like many Junkers and many conservative nobles from Russia to France, despised Jews socially and regarded them as harbingers of dangerous liberalism. Yet his schemes required finance. The Rothschilds were close to Austria and France, but he went to dine at the Frankfurt mansion of Mayer Carl von Rothschild, sneering at the 'real old Jew haggler, tons of silver, golden spoons and forks', who recommended Gerson Bleichröder, a Rothschild ally. Bleichröder became Bismarck's banker, diplomatic fixer and arguably one of his few friends.

Bismarck and Wilhelm were aided by the third remarkable Prussian: Alfred Krupp, the Cannon King, founder of a dynasty that would dominate German industry through the rule of Hohenzollerns, Hitler and the European Union.*

Widow Krupp's grandson, Alfred's father, had founded the great steel works in Essen, but he had driven them into the ground, even losing his mansion and being forced to move to a small cottage that stood beside the furnaces. Alfred was as extraordinary as Bismarck, a spidery, stick-thin, neurotic, pointy-faced, hypochondriacal crank who wore a shabby red toupee and was obsessed with steel, technology and weirdly the smell of horse manure.

When his father died in 1826, Alfred, then aged fourteen, brought up 'with the fear of total ruin', inherited the works, travelling to Yorkshire to spy on the making of Britain's finest Sheffield steel. On his return, barely sleeping, constantly ill – 'I celebrate my birthday in my own way, last year with cough medicine, this one with enemas' – he single-handedly propelled Krupp: 'I myself acted as clerk, letter writer, cashier, smith, smelter, coke pounder, nightwatchman at the converting furnace,' where 'I succeeded in the important invention of a completely weldable crucible steel.' First he made money manufacturing spoons for the Austrians, then, riding the railway boom, he started selling his cast-steel axles and springs, and the first weldless steel railway wheels; soon he would be supplying railway track to Europe, America, Asia. Then he tried making rifles with steel.

In 1853, the steel-mad entrepreneur married the twenty-one-year-old

---

* In 1815, Prussia had received the Ruhr, with its yet unknown reserves of coal – and the Krupps would benefit from the exponential growth of the German economy and the growth of population: twenty-two million Germans had doubled to forty by 1870.

Bertha, a blonde fellow neurasthenic whom he romanced with steel: 'Where I supposed I had nothing but a piece of cast steel, I had a heart.' She gave birth to a son, Friedrich, but suffered in their dreary soot-smeared cottage. 'One should be downright simple,' he lectured her. 'Knowing you have clean underwear under your dress should be enough.'

Soon she could bear it no longer. But in 1852 Krupp met the other essential relationship in his life: Prince Wilhelm admired a Krupp gun so much that he came to inspect the Essen factory and, as king, ordered 100 sixty-pound cannon. After Bismarck's 'blood and iron' speech, Wilhelm sent him to Krupp, who would provide the iron. At the works, they dined together, Bismarck saying of Napoleon, 'What a stupid man he is.' When Krupp designed a breech-loading cannon, Wilhelm and Bismarck bought it, but so did Russia, Britain, Austria. 'We must,' wrote Krupp, 'put all our energy into serving Prussia.' Bismarck waited to use his new guns.

In November 1863, the death of a Danish king enabled Bismarck to exploit a traditional dynastic puzzle. Denmark claimed the German duchies of Schleswig and Holstein. In January 1864, Bismarck formed a Germanic alliance with Franz Josef to defeat Denmark, each occupying one of the duchies. Bismarck appreciated a moment of felicitous conjunction: Russia was won over by Prussian acquiescence in the crushing of the Polish rebellion; Britain was distracted by India, and France by Mexico.

Bismarck briefed Bleichröder to inform James de Rothschild in Paris that 'The intimacy with Austria had reached its term. A chill will follow.' Bismarck visited Napoleon in Biarritz, vaguely dangling bits of Belgium, Luxembourg and the Rhineland, but nothing was agreed. Napoleon thought Belgium 'a ripe pear which one day will fall into our mouth', but Bismarck compared him to 'an innkeeper holding out his hand for a tip'. The emperor was 'a sphinx without a riddle'. King Wilhelm received Krupp, warning him not to sell guns to Austria: 'Come to your senses while there's still time.'

Bismarck engineered the confrontation with Austria. Eugénie encouraged Napoleon to mobilize but, wearied by the corrosion of power and bamboozled by Bismarck, he saw no need.* The Habsburgs had been

---

* Bismarck's ally, the Prussian war minister Albrecht von Roon, watched him 'construct a parallelogram of forces . . . of that which has already happened, then he assesses the nature and weight of the effective forces which one cannot know precisely – through which I watch the work of the historic genius who confirms that by combining it all'. The gift of a statesman is precisely in 'combining' so much that is moving and unpredictable with what can be assured.

the 'presiding power' of the German Confederation, the replacement for the Holy Roman Empire, since 1815 (with a short interlude during the years 1848–9). To defend this paramountcy, Franz Josef confidently went to war against Prussia, backed by the kings of Bavaria, Saxony, Hanover, all fielding Krupp cannon. Prussia's needle gun was superior to Austria's Lorenz gun, but astonishingly the Habsburg believed in his slower guns because rapid fire encouraged soldiers to waste ammunition. The Prussian chief of staff, Helmuth von Moltke, had noted the use of railways by Napoleon III, then by the Americans in the civil war, and mastered their use himself.

On 3 July 1866 at Sadowa (Königgrätz in Czechia), Moltke routed the Austrians.* Bismarck ended Austria's nominal German leadership and created a North German Confederation, headed by King Wilhelm of Prussia, who wanted to carve up the Habsburg empire. But after a tantrum, tears and screaming, Bismarck won his point, predicting that Austria would become Prussia's natural ally: indeed, House Habsburg became its chief ally until 1918.

Bismarck relished 'playing a game of cards with a million-dollar stake he didn't really possess. Now the wager had been won, he felt depressed.' Later he was elated, banging his desk: 'I've beaten them all! ALL!' Krupp too had mixed feelings – one of his cannon had exploded, killing its gunners. After a semi-breakdown, not helped by his wife's separate, luxurious life and affairs, he offered to swap the old guns for new, demonstrating a new generation of guns to an enthusiastic Wilhelm and Bismarck.

The defeat at Sadowa was a sign for Napoleon to exercise caution, especially as the French were watching the Mexican endgame. Maximilian withdrew to Santiago de Querétaro, where Juárez besieged him. When he attempted to break out, Maximilian was betrayed. Juárez sentenced him to death. 'I always wanted to die on a morning like this,' murmured Maximilian as he was taken out before 3,000 troops. He boldly addressed them: 'Mexicans! Men of my class and race [he meant the Habsburgs] are created by God to be the happiness of nations or their martyrs. Long live Mexico!' Refusing a blindfold, he choreographed his martyrdom with two of his generals on either side of him like Christ.

---

* At Sadowa, a young Prussian lieutenant, Paul von Hindenburg, blond and six foot six, son of a Junker landowner and a descendant of Martin Luther, was proud to serve. 'If I fall,' he wrote to his father, 'it's the most honourable and beautiful death.' He was almost killed when a bullet lodged in his helmet and knocked him out. Hindenburg would be a key figure in world history: he ruled Germany in the First World War, and it was he who appointed Hitler as chancellor.

Franz Josef said nothing about his brother's death except that he would be missed at the next shoot, where 'we may still look forward to some good sport'.

Waiting for a chance to unite Germany, Bismarck pivoted like a Krupp howitzer towards France. In April 1867, the world celebrated the apogee of Napoleonic France at the second *Exposition Universelle*, attended by seven million. The novelist Victor Hugo, usually a Napoleonic critic, wrote the brochure.

On 12 April, Hortense Schneider, the sexual icon of Paris, starred in Offenbach's *La Grande-Duchesse de Gérolstein*, a performance attended by Napoleon, King Wilhelm and Bismarck, Tsar Alexander II and Kaiser Franz Josef. Besieged by monarchs, La Snéder would not get into bed for less than 10,000 francs. Bertie, the twenty-five-year-old pinguid prince of Wales, representing his mother, dived into Parisian lubricity.* But the host would have done better to pay attention to Krupp at the Exposition, where his display of a colossal fifty-ton cannon, 1,000-pound shells and a giant steel ingot of 80,000 pounds was visited by Bismarck and Wilhelm. No wonder that at the theatre Bismarck had laughed at Offenbach's portrait of power and war: 'That's exactly how it is.'

ISMAIL THE MAGNIFICENT AND EUGÉNIE: THE EMPIRE IS AN OLD WOMAN

On 17 November 1869, Empress Eugénie opened the Suez Canal, the work of her cousin Ferdinand de Lesseps.† The project of a canal to link the Indian Ocean and the Mediterranean, cutting the distance between Europe and India, was an ancient idea but the British role in restraining

---

* Bertie's erotic adventures had shocked his prim father Albert, who had died, probably of colitis, in 1861. Queen Victoria blamed Bertie: 'I'll never look at him without a shudder.' She orchestrated Bertie's marriage to a beautiful and long-suffering Danish princess, Alexandra. But this trip to Paris changed his life. He visited Schneider and Sarah Bernhardt and fell for the Italian courtesan Giulia Barucci, who, told to curtsey on meeting him, instead just shook off her dress: 'What, didn't you tell me to behave properly to His Royal Highness? I showed him the best I have!' Bertie sent her love letters that his courtiers later had to buy back from her. As his spree of sex and gambling scandals shamed his mother, he became an honorary Parisian, designing his own *fauteuil d'amour* (love chair) for his favourite brothel, Le Chabanais, where he felt at home since it was run by the Irish-born Madame Kelly. Much later, as an admirable king, he turned his Francophilia into a political alliance.

† Mehmed Ali died in 1848, and his favourite son Ibrahim the Red died soon afterwards, leaving the throne to a vicious grandson, Abbas, who so adored his horses that he once punished his groom by shoeing him with red-hot horseshoes. Unsurprisingly, a servant assassinated him.

Mehmed Ali's conquests led him to favour a French plan. Lesseps was a diplomat, not an engineer, but he had served in Cairo, meeting Mehmed and his successors to pitch a project personally backed by Napoleon. Cairo's relations with the emperor were so close that the Egyptians had sent a Nubian regiment to fight in Mexico. During the American war, Egyptian cotton supplied British factories; money poured in and thousands of labourers perished building the canal.

Ismail, aged thirty-three, the reigning khedive of Egypt, grandson of Mehmed, son of Ibrahim the Red and his Circassian wife, was a life force who embraced the Suez project, supervised by Lesseps from his villa (still standing) in the new town, Ismailia. Ismail the Magnificent, imaginative, impatient and energetic, was also in the audience for *La Grande-Duchesse de Gérolstein* and shopped in Paris, splurging on Krupp's cannon – and on the Parisian courtesan, Blanche d'Antigny, who joined him in Cairo. Egypt, he said, 'is no longer in Africa; we're now part of Europe', and he built railways, palaces, bridges, theatres.

Eugénie* and Franz Josef each moored their yachts beside Ismail's *Mahrousa*. 'Magnificent!' Eugénie telegraphed to Napoleon. At Ismailia, Ismail built a sultanic encampment of 1,200 tents with chandeliers and paintings and commissioned Giuseppe Verdi's *Rigoletto*, performed at his new opera house. But his real ambition was an African empire and his gambit helped unleash the European carve-up of Africa.

At home, Eugénie found Napoleon suffering from gallstones and exhaustion. His shrewd brother Morny was dead and he tried to appease mounting opposition by conceding some power to ministers and the Assembly – reform is always a dangerous moment.

In February 1870, Spain offered its throne to King Wilhelm's cousin Prince Leopold von Hohenzollern-Sigmaringen. Now Leopold consulted King Wilhelm: should he accept Spain? Wilhelm banned it, but Bismarck persuaded him to change his mind, planning to use the offer as bait for Napoleon: 'Politically a French attack would be very beneficial.'

The French were outraged, forcing Napoleon to react. His sexual energy endured longer than his political will. He had enjoyed a last affair with a circus acrobat but, in agony from his gallstones, he struggled to resist escalation. 'It's a disgrace,' said Eugénie. 'The empire's turning into an old woman.'

---

* Ismail flirted clumsily with Eugénie, presenting her with a golden chamber pot with an emerald at its centre. 'My eye is always on you,' the khedive told the unamused empress.

THE MOUSETRAP: NAPOLEON'S DEBACLE

Harassed by Eugénie, panicked by public war fever, Napoleon allowed his foreign minister to demand that Wilhelm reject the Spanish offer.* When Wilhelm did so, instead of banking this success his ambassador insisted on a written rejection, possibly seeking a pretext for war. If so, he succeeded only too well: the irritated old king dictated a telegram. Bismarck doctored it to make it positively rude. Napoleon's honour was impugned. France declared war. In July, the French mobilized an army forged in Algeria and Mexico that had beaten Russia and Austria; many expected it to beat Prussia. Wilhelm mobilized, joined by Bavaria and other kingdoms, 1.1 million men in all. 'We've been shamelessly forced into this war,' Crown Princess Vicky told her mother Queen Victoria. Both deplored Napoleonic aggression and admired Prussian honour, oblivious to Bismarck's gambit.

Napoleon insisted on taking command of one army in Lorraine accompanied by the fourteen-year-old prince imperial, Loulou, while leaving Eugénie in Paris as regent; the other army mustered in Alsace. Yet the mobilization was incomplete, the emperor in pain and not in control. On the Prussian side, the cerebral, meticulous chief of staff von Moltke, *Der Grosse Schweiger* – the Great Silent One – manoeuvred brilliantly over specially built railways, deploying Krupp cannon with twice the French range.† The sick Napoleon could barely mount a horse let alone command a war and he and his marshals were repeatedly confused by the direction taken by the Prussians. After narrowly escaping Metz, which was besieged by the Prussians, Napoleon tried to relieve his other army and cover Paris, falling into a Prussian trap. After tearfully hugging Loulou, he sent him to safety.

At Sedan, on 1–2 September 1870, Moltke's 250,000 troops with 500

---

* Leopold did not become Spanish king, but his second son Ferdinand became king of Romania. Ironically this branch of the Hohenzollerns was descended from the Beauharnais and its members were friendly with Napoleon, who had in 1866 joined the Russian tsar Alexander II in promoting Leopold's elder brother Karl to *domnitor* (prince) of a new country made up of Wallachia and Moldavia, now called the Romanian United Principalities – the future Romania. Karl, who became King Carol of Romania, had no sons and was succeeded by his nephew, Ferdinand.

† Obsessed with history, Moltke had spent ten years planning a war against France, but he had also long been obsessed with railways, making a fortune from investing in them, joining the board of the Berlin–Hamburg line and advising on the laying of Prussian railways with military use in mind. Later he added to the general staff a railway section plus a historical one too. Now he had just completed instructions for Prussian officers: 'No plan of operations extends with certainty beyond the first encounter with the enemy's main strength,' he ruled. 'Strategy is a system of expedients' in which officers must use their initiative. 'A favourable situation will never be exploited if commanders wait for orders.'

guns, and with Bismarck and Wilhelm spectating, trapped Napoleon and 110,000 men. 'We have them,' said Moltke, 'in a mousetrap.'

'We're in a chamber pot and they're shitting on us,' exclaimed General Ducrot. Krupp guns scythed through French cavalry charges.

'Agh!' gasped King Wilhelm. 'Brave fellows.'

'Why,' asked Napoleon, riding out into the battle to find death, 'does this useless struggle go on?' But, unable to die, he ordered surrender. Bismarck was astonished that Napoleon was present. As the emperor rode painfully towards the Prussian headquarters, Bismarck cut him off: 'I gave the military salute. He took off his cap whereupon I took off mine.' Led to a cottage, Napoleon lamented that he had 'been driven into war by public opinion'. Bismarck was amazed by Napoleon's decrepitude, muttering, 'There's a dynasty on the way out.'

Meeting at a nearby chateau, Wilhelm treated Napoleon courteously. 'I congratulate you on your army, above all your artillery,' said Napoleon. Krupp had won. As Napoleon sobbed, Wilhelm blushed and looked away.

In Paris, Eugénie received Napoleon's telegraph. 'Surely you don't believe that abomination,' she cried in a 'torrent of incoherent mad words'. 'A Napoleon never surrenders. He's dead! Why didn't he kill himself? . . . What a name to leave to his son!' Outside, rebellious crowds surrounded the Tuileries chanting 'La déchéance!' Dethronement! On 4 September, the Third Republic was declared at Paris's Hôtel de Ville, launching a new 1792-style war effort against Prussia. Eugénie, insisting that she had 'no fear of death' but that 'I dreaded falling into the hands of the viragoes who'd defile my last scene,' fled to the house of her American dentist, Evans, who escorted her to England. She settled in Kent, and a dying Napoleon joined her. Their son Loulou longed to enlist in the British army.

La Débâcle coincided with the triumph of the tropical emperor Pedro over Marshal López, who had so admired Napoleon.

KKK AND GREASY GRASS: GRANT AND SITTING BULL

Pedro camped with his soldiers and resisted any move towards peace as the Brazilians fought their way into Paraguay, hunting the tyrant. 'What sort of fear could I have? That they take the government from me?' asked Pedro. 'Many better kings than I have lost it, and to me it is no more than the weight of a cross which it is my duty to carry.'

After the Brazilians had taken Asunción, López twice moved his capital. Pedro appointed his twenty-seven-year-old French son-in-law Gaston, comte d'Eu, as commander-in-chief. Gaston, a grandson of Louis Philippe, had initially been disappointed by his wife, Princess Isabel, but he turned out to be affectionate and capable. The public relished his exploits as he not only won battles but liberated 25,000 Paraguayan slaves – though many were then conscripted into the allied army. The desperate López murdered his own two brothers, his brothers-in-law and hundreds of foreigners; his English engineer committed suicide by injecting nicotine. Short of ammunition, he had his victims lanced to death. Finally at Cerro Corá, López, accompanied by Madama Eliza Lynch and their son Colonel Juan, aged fourteen, her *Residentas* and a guard of 400 half-dressed youths, was trapped, wounded and abandoned. Brazilian soldiers found him washing his wounds in a stream and shot him. 'A Paraguayan colonel never surrenders,' cried his son – also shot. Madama threw herself on to his body shouting, 'Is this the civilization you promised?' They forced her to bury both Lópezes with her bare hands.* Between 800,000 and 1.3 million Paraguayans were dead, a toll from which Paraguay never recovered.

Emperor Pedro was triumphant. Yet the war had exposed inefficiency, injustice and corruption; in particular, the bravery of black regiments had highlighted the infamy of slavery. Pedro was an unhurried abolitionist who lacked the constitutional power to overrule his slave-owning elite.† But in the wake of his victory, in September 1871, he orchestrated the Law of Free Birth: the babies of slaves were born free. Brazil, with its 1.6 million slaves, was now the last slave society in America. As Pedro was hosted in Washington by a new president, America's ex-slaves were in danger of losing their liberty all over again.

As Johnson's presidency was disintegrating, General Grant had resigned from the government. Johnson, widely despised, had dismissed his secretary of war whose tenure was protected by congressional legislation, leading to the first impeachment. Johnson survived

---

* Madama Lynch's estates were confiscated, but she was allowed to sail for Europe. She later returned to Paraguay to reclaim her property after she had been promised safety but was tried and expelled, dying in Paris in 1886 still only fifty-two. Bizarrely Madama later became a national hero: the vicious dictator and friend of Nazis General Stroessner brought her body back to Paraguay and entombed her in the national cemetery.

† The French minister in Brazil was the racist ideologue Arthur de Gobineau, inventor of the term 'master race', who was disgusted by Brazilian society: 'a population totally mixed, vitiated in its blood and spirit, fearfully ugly . . . Not a single Brazilian has pure blood because the pattern of marriages among whites, Indians and Negroes is so widespread,' leading to what he called 'genetic degeneracy'. Yet he regarded the blue-eyed Pedro as a perfect Aryan. Pedro befriended Gobineau until, after the diplomat disgraced himself in a brawl, he requested his recall.

his Senate trial but was too damaged to run for the presidency a second time.

Diffident and reticent, but at the height of his prestige, Grant was ambivalent. 'I didn't want the presidency,' he said. 'But it couldn't be helped . . .' In November 1868, Grant, backed by Douglass, won the election – the youngest president so far, and one determined to defend the 3.5 million freed African-Americans of the south at any cost.

At his inauguration, Grant promised that black suffrage would be protected in a Fifteenth Amendment to the Constitution, inviting the first African-American senator, Hiram Revels, an Episcopal minister who had helped arrange black regiments during the war, to the White House. In February 1870, he ordered the firing of a hundred cannon to celebrate the Fifteenth Amendment – 'the most important event,' said Grant, 'since the nation came to life.' While only three black officials had ever been elected in America, sixteen were now elected to Congress, over 1,000 others elected to other positions; black churches and schools were created across the south; and black families – divided by the anti-family mechanism of slavery – were reunited and consolidated in a quest for lost relatives.

Great gains had been made, yet the former slave masters of the south were determined to claw back their power, and they would ultimately be supported by the leaders of the north in pulling off an astonishing reversal of the victory of the war.

All freed slaves were promised forty acres and a mule, but former slave masters refused to deliver – even though their ancestors had received free land by headright. The freed slaves' poverty made them vulnerable. 'When you turned us loose,' Frederick Douglass declared ten years later, 'you gave us no acres: you turned us loose to the sky, to the storm, to the whirlwind, and, worst of all, you turned us loose to the wrath of our infuriated masters.' Across the south, the KKK assassinated and intimidated freed slaves and white campaigners for black rights. The KKK's Invisible Empire of racist paramilitaries threatened a new conflict and a new oppression. Two thousand African-Americans were killed in lynchings – extrajudicial murders of African-Americans, supposedly guilty of crimes, often celebrated by whites as part of 'southern' culture.

The violence was just the vanguard of a deeper counter-attack. The ex-Confederate vice-president Alexander Stephens and many of his racist cohort had been elected to Congress. When the African-American Senator Revels took his seat, southern Democrats tried to stop him. They gradually reimposed supremacy over their ex-slaves but, above all, they wished to prevent black people, 36 per cent of the southern votes, from exercising their rights. Even in the north, only parts of New England gave African-Americans the vote. Connecticut, Wisconsin and Minnesota refused; most southern states now passed 'Black Codes'. Murder sprees by the KKK and its allies, the Knights of the White Camellia, escalated, and the racists seized power in some counties.

Grant denounced the 'force and terror' designed to 'reduce colored people to a condition akin to slavery', oversaw the passing of the KKK Act and three Enforcement Acts and dispatched federal troops plus Justice Department marshals and the new Secret Service to destroy these domestic terrorists. In South Carolina, 2,000 Klansmen were arrested. In 1873, the KKK and another paramilitary group, the White Man's League, rampaged through Colfax, Louisiana, killing around 300; in 1876 in Ellenton, South Carolina, 150 black people were massacred. In both cases, Grant sent in the army, crushing the KKK, but the struggle was just beginning.

Grant proposed another solution, pursuing Lincoln's idea to buy a new state that would be a safe home for southern black people from 'the crime of Ku Kluxism'. When Congress failed to ratify the treaty, he sent Douglass down to the Caribbean to investigate the US annexation of the Dominican Republic, the formerly Spanish colony that had won its independence after defying attempts by Haitian President Boyer and Emperor Faustin to conquer their own little empire. Supported by Douglass, Grant bought it for $1.5 million, but Congress stymied the purchase. Douglass was both disappointed and infuriated by the betrayals of the civil war victory.

During his two-term presidency, Grant's noble work in the south and his decent intentions towards Native Americans were undermined by his personal naivety in high politics, and by his inability to restrain America's imperial voracity in the west. He backed a Peace Plan, offering the Native Americans 'civilization, Christianization and citizenship' when what they wanted was freedom to hunt and raid. The civil war had reinvigorated the Lakota and Cheyenne in Colorado and the Dakotas, while in the south the Comanche had returned to raiding.

Now both fronts deteriorated in tandem. Grant was sympathetic but many of his generals shared the view of General Sherman: 'The more Indians we kill this year, the less we'd have to kill next.' In early 1870, US cavalry burned alive and hacked to pieces 173 Piegan Blackfeet, mainly women and children, in Montana, exposing the army's genocidal instincts.

On 27 June 1874, Quanah Parker, son of Peta Nocona and his Anglo wife Cynthia Ann, led a unit of 300 fighters to attack a hundred buffalo hunters at Adobe Walls in the Texas Panhandle. Quanah was accompanied by a new spiritual leader, Isa-tai, a medicine man who in May had envisioned during a sun dance the destruction of the white settlers, uniting many of the Comanche into a newly powerful war band of a thousand fighters. 'There was never a more splendidly barbaric sight,' recalled Billy Dixon, one of the buffalo hunters. 'Hundreds of warriors, the flower of the fighting men of the southwestern Plains tribes, mounted upon their finest horses, armed with guns and lances, and carrying heavy shields of thick buffalo hide, were coming like the wind.' But their buffalo guns held Quanah at bay and a lucky shot by Dixon killed Isa-tai; Quanah was wounded.

Out west, army predation and a gold rush of settlers raised tensions and forced a reluctant Grant to order the removal of the Lakota. In November 1864, at Sandy Creek (Colorado), US troops killed and scalped 160 Cheyenne. In 1868, a treaty recognized the Black Hills, sacred land, as territory of the Lakota people, the Oglala Sioux, but six years later the army sent in a flashy colonel, George Armstrong Custer, and a thousand troopers of the Seventh Cavalry who confirmed the presence of seams of gold. Prospectors poured into the Hills, founding Deadwood and other raucous mining camps. In June 1876, Sitting Bull, supreme chief of the Sioux and holy man, performed a sun dance and in his trance saw 'soldiers falling into his camp like grasshoppers from the sky'. He and fellow leader Crazy Horse put together a multitribal alliance and launched a war.

Down south, in Texas, the Comanche kidnapping of a white boy now provoked military action. America, said General Sherman, must not 'submit to this practice of paying for stolen children. It is better the Indian race be obliterated.' Troops, backed by Tonkawa scouts, attacked Comanche villages, hunting down Quanah, whose surrender marked the end of Comancheria.*

In the Dakotas, several army columns converged on Lakota villages. Grant loathed the insubordinate, narcissistic self-publicist Custer, a daredevil with long blond hair and fringed buckskin costumes, who had opposed Reconstruction, had been court-martialled for shooting deserters and had recently murdered more than 100 southern Cheyenne women and children. Grant banned this 'not very level-headed man'

---

* Quanah settled on the Kiowa–Comanche–Apache Reservation in Oklahoma where, leaving his traditional lodge, he built his European-style Star House, took the surname Parker, embraced his own adaptation of Christianity, combined with imbibing the hallucinogenic peyote, and became a successful rancher.

from the expeditions, but acquiesced when the general in command requested his presence.

On 17 June, Crazy Horse defeated a column under General Crook. At Greasy Grass, on 25 June, the overconfident Custer and his men were ambushed by Sitting Bull, Crazy Horse and several hundred braves and wiped out in thirty minutes, with 267 killed. Custer was found shot in the head, stripped naked, an arrow through his penis.

The defeat led to the systematic destruction of Native American villages across the Great Plains; afterwards the tribes entered reservations. The Black Hills were seized; the pre-eminent beneficiary of the gold rush was a straggly-bearded Missouri-born mining engineer, now based in San Francisco, called George Hearst. A veteran of the '49 gold rush, whose Homestake Mine helped make him the richest mining baron, Hearst afterwards won election as a senator and in 1880 accepted, as payment for a poker debt, a failing newspaper, the *San Francisco Examiner*, which he then presented to his son, William Randolph.

Hearst was just one of the robber barons who surfed the wave of muscular American capitalism. While black sharecroppers struggled to survive, cotton production recovered. Railways reached across the continent, doubling in length from 35,000 miles in 1865 to 70,000 by 1870. Railways became America's business, enriching the titanic oligarchs of what the writer Mark Twain called the Gilded Age:* Vanderbilt switched into railway building, fighting rivals Jay Gould and E. H. Harriman. It was in his relations with businessmen that Grant, who had coolly overseen the army, now displayed a high-handed naivety that tainted his presidency.

The Gilded Age was coal-fuelled and steam-powered, but an angular and meticulous young man was investing in another carbon fuel that seemed useful only for illumination. In fact it would change the world. On 10 January 1870, the thirty-one-year-old John D. Rockefeller founded an oil refinery in Cleveland, Ohio, that he called Standard Oil. At the end of the civil war, he had started to buy out other oil refiners. Rockefeller's ascetic nature, manifested in an obsession with order and tidiness, was a reaction against a father who was an itinerant huckster, bigamist and

---

* Twain was himself one of the ornaments of the Gilded Age, a self-invented boy named Samuel Clemens from Hannibal, Missouri, who had worked the steamboats of the Mississippi, toiled in silver mines and then in 1876 published his *Adventures of Tom Sawyer*, based on his exploits and taking his nom de plume from the cry 'mark twain' of the leadsmen who measured the depth of the river. An abolitionist and liberal, he travelled the world to file travelogues, and later produced his other great novel *Huckleberry Finn*, also starring Tom Sawyer. Twain became rich and famous, usually sporting a trademark white suit, but constantly lost his money, though never his wisdom or wit.

snake-oil salesman. Houses had long been lit by whale oil, extracted by whalers, but in 1857 oil was discovered seeping out of the ground in Oil Creek, Pennsylvania, starting a switch to Rockefeller's chief product, kerosene, now used to light private houses and the streets of the growing cities. Rockefeller played what he called his 'great game', an aggressive integration of the oil business into one 'trust' that controlled everything from the gushing oil via ships and refineries to the customers who bought their kerosene tins from the local store. The by-products of refining oil were useful for making lubricants for machinery, skin products and something called gasoline, but it was not lucrative. There seemed no use for it.

Money was Grant's weakness. The president was entertained by the omnivorous Gould, who, gobbling up railways, was also attempting to corner the gold market. Gould personified the glamour and sleaze of the predatorial capitalist: Americans, wrote Twain, had 'desired money' before, 'but he taught them to fall down and worship it'. If Grant's misjudgements spoiled his reputation, his real achievements were squandered by his successors.[*]

'You say you've emancipated us. You have; and I thank you for it,' said Douglass at the Republican convention in 1876, but 'What does it all amount to, if the black man's unable to exercise that freedom, and, after having been freed from the slaveholder's lash, he is to be subject to the slaveholder's shot-gun?'

In 1876, Grant steered the country through a viciously contested election that was ultimately won by an Ohio Republican, Rutherford Hayes, thanks to a deal that withdrew federal troops from the south and allowed southern Democrats to 'redeem' their states, passing a slew of repressive laws (known as Jim Crow after 'Jump Jim Crow', a white theatre act portraying black people) that enforced segregation of schools, entertainment and transport and prevented black people from voting, encouraging an atmosphere in which persecutions were normal, none more malignant than lynchings, which became ever more frequent. Some 6,500 black people (and 1,300 whites, usually immigrants) were lynched between 1865 and 1950. Hayes's dark deal was scarcely redeemed by his appointment of the ageing Douglass as the first black US marshal in DC. The Union had won the war; the Confederacy won the peace.

---

[*] Nor did Grant learn from his presidency: in his retirement, humiliated by his own lack of capital, he lent his name and prestige to an outrageous fraudster who bankrupted him. Dying of cancer, Grant was forced to write his memoirs, and was rescued by Mark Twain, who turned publisher for the deal. Dictated tirelessly by the old general, the memoirs proved both a classic and a bestseller.

On 5 January 1871, Bismarck finally got his way and Moltke's Krupp guns started to bombard besieged Paris.

THE IRON CHANCELLOR AND DIZZY

After the fall of Napoleon, Paris was quickly surrounded. Bismarck and Wilhelm made themselves comfortable in the most luxurious residence in western Europe, the palace of James de Rothschild at Ferrières. 'Here I sit,' boasted Bismarck to his wife, 'under a picture of old Rothschild and his family.'

'I'm too poor to buy myself such a thing,' grumbled Wilhelm. 'Folks like us can't rise to this; only a Rothschild can achieve it.' As Bismarck negotiated a unified Germany with the German kings, the mood darkened at Prussian headquarters. The new French government refused the moderate terms and attacked the Prussians; French peasants joined an insurgency. Moltke ordered villages destroyed, civilians shot, but refused to bombard Paris. Three months later, moving with the king into Versailles, Bismarck got his way: Krupp cannon lobbed 12,000 shells into Paris. In the besieged city a worker's rebellion seized power and declared the Paris Commune.

Bismarck needed a German monarch to make the request that Wilhelm should become German emperor, and the best candidate was the king of the largest kingdom after Prussia: the twenty-five-year-old Ludwig II of Bavaria. A grandson of Lola Montez's patron, Ludwig was an unbalanced dreamer who on succeeding to the throne immediately invited to Munich his washed-up, indebted hero, the composer Richard Wagner, who since the 1848 revolution had left a trail of adulterous and indebted adventures. Ludwig identified with the mythical Lohengrin, Knight of the Swan, one of the German heroes that inspired Wagner, who was writing a new operatic cycle, *Der Ring des Nibelungen*. Ludwig was dazzled by the masterful, wild-haired, sharp-chinned Wagner, who shamelessly flirted with the homosexual monarch. Ludwig sponsored his new opera *Tristan und Isolde*, but Wagner shocked the Bavarians with a wild affair with his conductor's wife, Cosima Liszt, and then demanded the dismissal of the kingdom's ministers. An offended Ludwig sent him away, but ultimately he funded Wagner's own *Festspielhaus* and mansion in the small town of Bayreuth, where he presented his *Ring*, showcasing the soaring range and musical barrage of what he called *Gesamtkunstwerk* – total artwork – which in its way defined Germanness just as much as Bismarck's new empire, the empire for which he now wanted Ludwig's help.

The Swan King preferred a loose Germany under his Habsburg cousins and resisted Wilhelm's request until Bismarck secretly paid him six million gold marks. Ludwig signed his *Kaiserbrief* asking that Wilhelm 'extend presidential rights across the German states . . . with the title of German Kaiser'. On 18 January 1871, at a convocation of princes and ministers at Versailles, Bismarck 'came forward in the grimmest of humours' and read his 'address to the German People', after which a grand duke cried, 'Long live Kaiser Wilhelm!' A 'thundering hurrah at least six times shook the room'.* It was 'the dream of German poets', exulted the new kaiser's son Fritz. 'Germany has her emperor again . . .' The guns thundered as they bombarded Paris. Finally the French Third Republic agreed to German terms, the loss of Alsace and Lorraine and payment of five billion francs, raised by James's sons Gustave and Alphonse de Rothschild, who had helped defend Paris during the siege.

Bismarck designed an experimental German state, a hybrid of absolutism and democracy in which the king of Prussia, Wilhelm, presided over the many German kingdoms and principalities as kaiser, balanced by a Reichstag, elected by universal male suffrage – a mixed monarchy so complicated that it could be directed only by Europe's most brilliant manipulator, Bismarck himself. Its contradictions made it unstable, probably unworkable, but it was instantly an economic powerhouse. Krupp, master of the greatest industrial complex in Europe, celebrated. The victorious war was his best advertisement. 'Cast steel has won its present position as the most indispensable material in war and peace,' the Cannon King crowed to the German kaiser. 'Railways, the greatness of Germany, the fall of France, belong to the steel age.' Now residing in a new 300-room palace Villa Hügel outside Essen, employing 20,000 workers drilled in special Krupp uniforms, Krupp trained his son Fritz as heir.

Bismarck, appointed chancellor and raised to prince, feared the death of his octogenarian kaiser Wilhelm: his heir, Fritz, who had distinguished himself in the war, was a liberal, influenced by his English wife Vicky. Bismarck hated both as obstacles to his plans. The strain of managing his incoherent invention was compulsive but draining even for the cynical, ingenious chancellor. Into his seventies, he could dictate memoranda for five hours while micromanaging his own multiple

* The ceremony was attended by the strapping Prussian officer Paul von Hindenburg. *La Débâcle* in Paris also united Italy: as French troops withdrew from Rome, the Eternal City fell to the Savoyard king, Victor Emmanuel. Italy, now a constitutional kingdom, was united for the first time since Theodoric. Pope Pius IX refused to recognize Rome as Italian capital, launching a long papal sulk.

conspiracies. Yet the stress led to a spiralling psychosis of paranoia, gluttony and insomnia that almost killed him – only saved by a doctor who lovingly placed him on a diet, relaxed him by wrapping him in blankets and held his hand until he finally slept.

The Iron Chancellor allied Germany with the other two conservative emperors, Franz Josef and Alexander II of Russia. The tsar, who had ac-quiesced in the unification of Germany in return for lifting the limitations imposed by the Crimean War, now focused on Ottoman disintegration as the Orthodox Slavs of eastern Europe sought independence. Serbia and Romania were already autonomous. In 1877, Alexander attacked the Ottomans to forge a new country, Bulgaria – and seize Constantinople and the Straits. As Romanov armies galloped towards the outskirts of the Great City, Disraeli, now prime minister, stopped Russian aggres-sion and saved the sultanate by sending in the Royal Navy. Bismarck supported him, fearing a Russian conquest of Istanbul.

They were from different worlds. Disraeli, son of a bookish Jewish immigrant from Morocco, was the first outsider to rule Britain since the Romans, a rise achieved with brazen intrigue and brilliant wit but without money, land or connections. 'Mr. Disraeli is Prime Minister!' Queen Victoria wrote to her daughter Vicky. 'A proud thing for a man "risen from the people".' He celebrated: 'I've climbed to the top of the greasy pole.'

Slim and dandyish with dark eyes and curling ringlets, often sporting green trousers and a primrose, Disraeli had dabbled in shady finance and lived for a time in a ménage à trois with a scandalous potentate and his young mistress before his novels made him famous. Now de-voted to a well-off if fey wife, twelve years his senior, who called him Dizzy and who 'didn't know', he joked, 'who came first, the Greeks or the Romans', he was the first modern Conservative, an advocate of the unity of aristocracy and the people in 'One Nation', and an enthusiastic promoter of British world power, all with shameless panache.*

In 1867, he outmanoeuvred Gladstone's Liberals to pass a Reform Act that doubled the number of male voters, the start of a real British democracy in which most male adults had the vote. Winning a land-slide in 1874 and raised to earl of Beaconsfield, now wizened, weary and

---

* Disraeli is the wittiest of British leaders: 'There are three types of lies,' he said. 'Lies, damn lies and statistics.' Joking that he was 'the blank page between the Old and New Testaments', he deflected antisemitic attacks in the House of Commons with biblical grandeur: 'Yes, I am a Jew, and while the ancestors of the right honourable gentleman were brutal savages in an unknown island, mine were priests in the temple of Solomon.' He re-mains an inspiration to all writers. 'When I want to read a good book,' he said, 'I write one.'

languid, he was Britain's most cosmopolitan leader, having travelled to Cairo and Jerusalem – the first prime minister from an ethnic minority. Now at a Berlin congress he and Bismarck joined forces to restrain Russia, save Constantinople and rearrange eastern Europe.

The two admired each other. 'Bismarck soars above all,' wrote Disraeli. 'Six foot four, proportionally stout with a sweet and gentle voice which singularly contrasts with the awful things he says, a complete despot here.' Bismarck declared, 'The old Jew is the man.' The congress granted Cyprus to Britain, censured antisemitism and created a band of new national states: Serbia and Romania became kingdoms; Bulgaria and Montenegro independent principalities, each aspiring to recreate vanished, often imaginary realms.* But the decay of the Ottomans, the ambitions of the new Slavic states and the rivalry of Russia and Austria meant that the Balkans now became the sparkwheel of European conflict. 'One day,' predicted Bismarck, 'the great European War will come out of some damned foolish thing in the Balkans.'

Disraeli was welcomed home: 'I've brought you back peace – but a peace I hope with honour.' This delicate balance in Europe now forced the powers to fight their rivalries outside Europe in a new arena: Africa.

---

* As Carol now became the Hohenzollern king of Romania, the creation of Bulgaria yielded the House of Saxe-Coburg its last throne: the etiolated Prince Ferdinand was chosen as Bulgaria's king. The tiny ethnically Serbian Montenegro had been ruled under the Ottomans by a hereditary Petrović dynasty of *vladikas* or prince-bishops, inherited from uncle to nephew until the prince-bishop Danilo transformed himself into a married hereditary prince. When he was assassinated in 1860 his nephew, the giant Nikola, succeeded him; Nikola declared war on Constantinople in 1876 and then married two daughters to Romanov grand dukes, ensuring Russian protection.

ACT EIGHTEEN
1.3 BILLION

The Houses of Solomon and Asante, Habsburg and Saxe-Coburg

SALAMA, PRINCESS OF ZANZIBAR, AND KING CORPSES OF KATANGA

On 24 December 1871, at his Cairo opera house, Ismail the Magnificent presided over the premiere of the opera *Aida* for which he had paid Verdi 150,000 francs. Its story of an Ethiopian princess captured and enslaved by an Egyptian paladin was not completely fictional. Ismail was determined to conquer east Africa, starting with Ethiopia. The European scramble for Africa was in many ways kicked off by the ruler of Egypt.* To win western support, he backed the anti-slavery crusade, sending armies southwards to seize Darfur (Sudan). Although Atlantic slavery had diminished, it was booming within Africa. African and Arab potentates and, so far, a motley scattering of Europeans, were all players in a tournament of power and resources. In the west of the continent, the caliphs and slave masters of Sokoto owned 2.5 million slaves – a quarter of the region's population;† in eastern Africa, the mayhem was intensifying.

On the death of the remarkable Omani sultan, Said, conqueror of an African–Arabian empire, in 1856, his sultanate of Zanzibar and Oman was split between two sons: one ruled Oman, while the other, Sultan Majid, backed by the British, took Zanzibar and much of Kenya and Tanzania, dispatching slave-hunting and ivory-collecting raids deep into the continent. East African slavery now reached its height. In the course of the nineteenth century, 1.6 million slaves, two-thirds of them women, were traded to Arab and Indian masters; 60,000 slaves annually were traded to the Mkunazini slave market in Zanzibar, confined in seventy-five hellish slave chambers.

---

* Married to four wives, keeping 200 odalisques, Ismail fell in love with a beautiful harem slave only to find that she had had her arm amputated for stealing; nonetheless he married her and she became the mother of King Fuad, living into the 1930s.
† The Sokoto jihadi empire would help inspire others in Africa later in the century, first the Senussi in Libya and then the Mahdi in Sudan. In the twenty-first century, it is the inspiration for the jihadist insurgencies in Nigeria, Mali, Chad and Niger.

In Zanzibar itself, where 100,000 slaves toiled, Majid enjoyed massive income from slaves, cloves and ivory, converting a Confederate warship, the *Shenandoah*, into a luxurious yacht, the *Majid*. But the sultan's younger brother Bargush loathed the rising British influence and in 1859 planned a coup, assisted by his fifteen-year-old sister, Salama bint Said.* This failed, but Bargush succeeded as sultan anyway; he bought steamships and founded his own shipping line between Africa and India. While he agreed to close the Mkunazini slave market, he secretly profited from the slave raiding and empire building of a fearsome phalanx of warlords, some African, some Arab, others European, all trading in slaves who were used to carry an even more valuable merchandise: ivory.†

One Omani–Zanzibari warlord, Tippu Tip, hacked out an empire of 250,000 square miles. He was 'a tall, black bearded man, of negroid complexion, in the prime of life, straight and quick', wrote a journalist. 'He had a fine intelligent face, with a nervous twitching of the eyes,' always dressed in dazzling white with a silver filigreed dagger. He had a dictum: 'Slaves cost nothing; they have only to be gathered.' When a boatload of enslaved women and children were lost over a waterfall, he just said, 'What a pity – it was a fine canoe.'

Not all the slave trade was in the hands of Arabs: two Nyamwezi warlords ruled swathes of Congo for decades. One of those warlords, Mytela Kasanda, fought the Omanis, adopting the name Mirambo – Corpses – and leading his *ruga-ruga* militiamen who wore shirts of flayed human skin, caps of human scalps, belts of human intestines and teeth necklaces. His rival Msiri ruled his Yeke kingdom in Katanga, armed by his Afro-Portuguese ally Coimbra from Angola whose elegant sister, Maria de Fonseca, was a player in her own right. Msiri married his daughter to Tippu Tip to confirm their alliance.

* Singular, passionate, beautiful and intelligent, Salama had taught herself to read and write. On the death of her mother, Jilfidan, a Georgian slave bought by her father in Constantinople, she had inherited three clove plantations worked by slaves. Majid defeated the coup, exiling Bargush to Bombay, though their sister was not punished. When Bargush succeeded as sultan, Salama broke convention by spending time with Europeans, attending their parties and falling in love with a German trader, Heinrich Ruete. When she became pregnant, the sultan was enraged and ordered her execution. A Royal Navy frigate conveyed her to freedom. She converted to Christianity as Emily, marrying Ruerte and bringing up two children in Hamburg. When her husband was killed in a tram accident, Emily/Salama lost her security, was unable to claim her Zanzibari estates and, settling in Beirut, wrote her *Memoirs of an Arabian Princess from Zanzibar*, perhaps the first Arab woman to write a modern autobiography.
† By 1890 Bargush was selling 75 per cent of global ivory, overseeing the killing of 60,000 elephants annually. The ivory was traded east and west. In the latter it was used to construct, among other things, the pianos – 'supreme symbol of Victorian female gentility', in Neil Faulkner's words – that embellished European homes.

In the south-east, the chief potentate was Mutesa, *kabaka* (king) of Buganda (Uganda), a strapping but psychotic dictator, his body embellished with copper rings and jewellery, who held court for thirty years from 1856 at a royal capital of huge huts, attended by his mother, 400 wives, ministers and executioners, deploying a vast army and a fleet of canoes that traded ivory and slaves. Winning power aged nineteen with a family massacre, Mutesa, whose dynasty had ruled for two centuries, maintained his dominance with capricious killings and tortures, sanctified by seasonal human sacrifices of 800 victims.

Ruling around two million people, the *kabaka* played off Muslims and Christians, Zanzibaris and Egyptians, as he expanded his kingdom. Further south, a fearsome Goan warlord, Manuel de Souza, known as Gouveia, leveraged his uncle's plantations into a personal slaving and ivory fief in Portuguese Zambezia, building a private African army and taking over the Gasa kingdom to become Lord of Manica; he married the daughter of a Barue king, their son becoming heir to the throne. All of these were slave states locked in a frenzied spasm of predatory wars for land, slaves and ivory that now attracted the biggest African power: Egypt.

ISMAIL AND TEWODROS:
THE BATTLE FOR EAST AFRICA

After taking Sudan, Ismail pushed further into central Africa, annexing Equatoria (northern Uganda), where as governor he hired General 'Chinese' Gordon, last seen fighting the Taiping for Empress Cixi. Even though Ismail was a slave lord, Gordon took the job to fight slavery.

Then Ismail turned to Ethiopia, a vast multi-ethnic region divided up into Christian kingdoms and Islamic sultanates, nominally ruled by a *negus negust*, king of kings – or emperor – of the Christian dynasty, claiming descent from King Solomon and the Queen of Sheba, though certainly descended from its medieval founder Menelik. In 1855, a minor nobleman, Kassa Hailu, conquered the kingdoms of Tigray, Gojjam, Showa and Wollo, imprisoned their Solomonic princes in his mountain fortress Magdala and crowned himself *Negus Negust* Tewodros II. 'Of medium stature but possessing a well-knit muscular frame capable of enduring any amount of fatigue', Tewodros had 'a noble bearing and a majestic walk, and he was the best shot, the best spearman, the best runner, and the best horseman'.

At his Magdala eyrie, he favoured one prisoner, a young Showan prince named Sahle Maryam – later known as Menelik – to whom he married his daughter. Menelik had revered Tewodros, 'who educated me, for whom I'd always cherished filial, deep affection'. After the death of Tewodros's beloved wife, the emperor started to unravel. Menelik escaped, while Tewodros tossed his prisoners off a cliff, then killed and tortured many more. In 1862, the erratic emperor requested British aid against Muslim potentates and, when it was not forthcoming, he imprisoned British envoys and missionaries. Disraeli dispatched 13,000 troops under Sir Robert Napier, quintessential soldier of empire, who had fought Sikhs, Indians and Chinese. In April 1868, Napier defeated Tewodros outside Magdala, killing 900 Ethiopians to two British losses after which the desperate emperor released his British hostages, threw his Ethiopian prisoners off the precipice and then, as Napier stormed the fortress, shot himself. Rewarded with a peerage, Lord Napier of Magdala looted Ethiopian treasures but withdrew* as rival princes led by Menelik of Showa and Kasa Mercha of Tigray vied for the throne. Kasa won, and was crowned Yohannes IV.

This British raid was covered by an American journalist who chronicled the predations of British soldiers, but now fell in love with Africa and came to personify the spirit of European adventure and exploitation: Henry Morton Stanley. In fact he was neither American nor called Stanley; he was born John Rowlands, an illegitimate Welsh boy, abandoned by his mother and raised in workhouses. At eighteen, he sailed for America, adopted a new name, worked on Mississippi riverboats, fought for both the Confederacy and the Union, then, embracing sensationalist war journalism, was hired by the New York Herald to cover Napier's little African war.

Stanley ignored African history and culture, calling it 'unpeopled country' and seeing it as a blank canvas, a commercial opportunity, a fantastical arena for this mendacious and indefatigable adventurer to display Victorian machismo and defy 'that shallow life which thousands lead in England where a man isn't permitted to be real and natural'. Now he needed a greater story.

His famous contemporary, the indomitable missionary Dr David Livingstone, was lost, feared dead. Stanley, still in his late twenties, proposed to his editor-proprietor in New York City to manufacture his own newspaper sensation: by finding Livingstone.

---

* The empress asked the British to protect Tewodros's young son Alemayehu, who was brought up as an English gentleman.

Livingstone was already celebrated for a different approach to Africa, where he had led a typically Victorian mission to spread Christianity, destroy east African slave lords and find the origins of the Zambezi and Nile. He too was an attention-seeker, a humourless and obsessional self-made man, a working-class Glaswegian, now a father of five who was bored at home and craved the solitary, righteous drama of his missions. Starting as a missionary in South Africa aged twenty-seven, he was restless and tireless, becoming the 'explorer' who travelled across the continent (a feat hailed in the British press, though two slave-trading *pombeiros* had crossed Africa in 1806). Seething within Livingstone was a Victorian cult of death: 'Am I to be a martyr to my own cause?' The booming newspapers of London and New York followed his exploits, the ladies attended his lectures. His abolitionist passion was noble and genuine but it was linked to his own vanity and his conviction that opening Africa to 'commerce' – British business – was the best antidote to slavery.

Many of the African 'adventurers', mostly British and French, believed in a 'civilizing mission' based on racist views of African inferiority; and even before the states arrived, it was hard to differentiate between Christian missionaries, scientific-geographic explorers and empire builders, mercantile adventurers, predatory mercenaries and sex tourists – but they were all risk-takers. Their journeys were often lethal. When Stanley later crossed Africa from the Indian Ocean to the Congo, some 7,000 miles, every white member of his party (except himself) and 173 Africans perished.

In 1866, Livingstone set off from the east African coast with just thirty-five bearers to find the source of the Nile, but found himself in an imbroglio of war and slave hunting in which his men died or deserted. He was driven by his Nilotic obsession: 'The Nile sources are valuable only as a means to enable me to open my mouth with power among men . . . to remedy an enormous evil.' At the mercy of slave lords, almost out of supplies, he somehow survived, although suffering dysentery. The news of his vanishing fascinated the world.

In March 1871 Stanley set off to 'rescue' Livingstone, accompanied by columns of African bearers and a formidable arsenal, as he played the warlord, fighting his way through conflicts between African and Arab slavers, picking off passing Africans with his rifle. At last, in November, he found the lost explorer in a setpiece of myth-making imperial adventure. 'Dr Livingstone, I presume?' said Stanley, initiating this encounter of noble mission and shameless hucksterism. Toothless and emaciated, Livingstone was by then 'just a ruckle of bones'. Stanley rushed back to file his story, and Livingstone, characteristically, insisted on pushing on towards the Nilotic source, dying of dysentery.

Yet Stanley's story made him world famous. More importantly it publicized the 'great human woe' of east Africa's slave trade, leading the British public to demand its abolition, a campaign that would – along with imperial ambition – draw in the European powers. London sent the navy to intercept slave traders and forced Sultan Bargush of Zanzibar to cease the trade.

After this sensation, Stanley travelled to west Africa where a British expedition demonstrated how, for the first time, new technological and scientific advances made a European advance into internal Africa feasible. In the four centuries since the Portuguese had built Elmina, Europeans had rarely attempted to conquer the interior, except for the Anglo-Dutch in the Cape and the Portuguese in Angola and Mozambique. They remained confined to the coast, restrained by terrain, climate and above all malaria and yellow fever, which killed most Europeans. In 1824, a British attempt to challenge the kingdom of Asante ended with the British governor's head served as a goblet for the *asantehene*. Only around 5 per cent of Africa had been colonized. That was about to change dramatically: telegraph speeded up communications; steamships meant troops could be concentrated; new weaponry delivered devastating firepower; and, the game changer, the availability of quinine, found in the bark of the Andean cinchona tree and now grown in Java, to treat malaria meant that Europeans could survive within Africa.

In 1871, the Asante challenged the British purchase of Dutch Gold Coast, under Afua Kobi, queen mother, the essential decision maker in the matrilineal Asante kingdom. After orchestrating the killing of rival princes, Afua Kobi had placed her son Kofi Karikari on the throne. 'I'm only a woman,' she said, 'but would fight the governor with my left hand.' Unbeknown to her, new technologies had changed the dynamic. In February 1874, Garnet Wolseley – one of those Anglo-Irish generals indispensable to British empire building – used steamships to land 2,500 British troops and built roads into the interior. Then, allied with thousands of African Fante auxiliaries, he advanced on the capital, Kumasi. Afua Kobi and the Asante were defeated in intense fighting, covered by the celebrated Stanley. As Afua retreated, Wolseley destroyed the capital and forced her to pay an indemnity in gold, liberate thousands of Asante slaves and ban human sacrifice – though the British did not capture the sacred Golden Stool. Queen Afua Kobi now deposed Kofi and placed another son on the throne. Wolseley – who said, 'There's only one way for a young man to get on in the army – he must try to get killed in every way possible' – became the imperial troubleshooter, his competence coining a saying: 'All Sir Garnet' – meaning 'Everything under control'.

Back in the east, the chaos in Ethiopia was an opportunity for Khedive Ismail, who occupied Massawa (Eritrea) and Zeila (Somalia) on the coast, and tried to seize Zanzibar, but was repelled by the sultan. In 1875, an Egyptian army led by the khedive's son Hassan, and American, Swiss and Danish officers, invaded Ethiopia but was ambushed and annihilated at Gundet and Gura by Emperor Yohannes; Prince Hassan was captured. The victory empowered Yohannes.* Nearby, Gordon, Ismail's governor-general, was expanding the Egyptian empire 3,000 miles down the Nile all the way to the great lakes and Buganda, where the *kabaka* Mutesa resisted his advance. Travelling tirelessly through the vastness of Sudan on camels and Nilotic steamers, the saintly paladin Gordon declared: 'I'm striking deadly blows against slavery' – but he was struggling. The Sudanese slave lords – *khabirs* who enslaved 50,000 a year – resisted strongly.

Ismail the Magnificent had failed in Ethiopia and Buganda, but he now ruled an enormous empire, the first of the carve-up for Africa. Yet after ten wars, 1,200 miles of railway, French courtesans and Krupp cannon, Ismail could not cover his debts. He considered the sale of his shares in the Suez Canal, shares which Dizzy coveted. The prime minister turned for help to one of his best friends, Lionel de Rothschild.† At cabinet in November 1875, Disraeli proposed the purchase, then popped his head out of the meeting. 'Yes,' he said to his secretary, Montagu Corry, who rushed by carriage to New Court. Rothschild was waiting. Disraeli needed £4 million 'tomorrow'. 'Rothschild picked up a muscatel grape, ate it, threw out the skin.'

'What's your security?' asked Rothschild.

'The British government,' said Corry.

---

* Yohannes's rival Solomonic prince, Menelik, submitted and was crowned as king of Showa; his daughter Zewditu was married to his emperor's son. Menelik would become the formative emperor of modern Ethiopia; Zewditu would be empress; and her regent would be Haile Selassie.

† Back in 1844, as his novel *Coningsby* first became successful, Dizzy had met Lionel de Rothschild, Nathan's heir as head of the British bank. He was fascinated by Lionel's power and by his wife, Charlotte, intelligent daughter of the Neapolitan branch. 'The young bride from Frankfurt,' he wrote, 'was tall, graceful, dark and clear.' In *Coningsby*, Disraeli based his Sephardic Jewish potentate Sidonia on a mixture of Lionel, Montefiore and himself. While running the bank, Lionel raised funds for the Irish famine and with his uncle Montefiore led the long campaign to win Jews the right to serve in the House of Commons, winning three elections (without being allowed to sit in the chamber) before the Jews Relief Act was finally passed in 1858.

'You shall have it.' As Rothschild telegraphed the money to Ismail, Disraeli was received by Victoria.

'It's settled,' said Disraeli portentously. 'You have it, Madame.'

CETSHWAYO'S VICTORY AND THE LAST NAPOLEON

'The Fairy' – as he called Victoria – 'is in ecstasies,' boasted Disraeli. A year later, he consolidated the Raj by making her 'Empress of India' whose border he was then forced to defend. Empire is always a charade of power, a confidence trick, pulled off with the mystique of hegemony that can only be sustained by the threat of swift force. But the European powers – Portuguese, Dutch, British – were small nations that particularly needed the empire bluff to control far-flung colonies and vast populations. Yet empire was expensive. Armies and infrastructure soon ate the profits, and it was hard to avoid the imperial vortex: each new conquest required more war to hold what you had and then further annexations to deny prizes to your rivals. Disraeli bought the Canal to keep out France, but Russia was Britain's chief enemy, the Romanovs the most successful empire builders since Genghis. In 1865 Russia took Tashkent, in 1868 Samarkand, while the amirs of Bukhara and the khans of Khiva became vassal rulers. After an astonishing ten-year advance, Alexander II had reached the Afghan border. Prevented by Britain from taking Constantinople, Alexander discussed an Indian invasion with his generals.

As the Romanovs nervously probed the Afghan amir Sher Ali and the British demanded proof of his loyalty, he swung between fraught insecurity and proud defiance. When he refused British demands, Disraeli agreed to an invasion, which, better planned and armed than that of 1839, took Kabul and installed Sher Ali's son with a British plenipotentiary to guide him. Meanwhile the prime minister faced disaster in Africa.

In January 1879, Cetshwayo, *nkosi* of the Zulus, son of Mpande, nephew of Shaka, ordered an impi of 20,000 men against an advancing British army of 18,000 redcoats, who were encamped insouciantly at Isandlwana.

The war was not the first to be provoked by Lord Carnavon, the colonial secretary in London, who after making Canada a self-governing dominion hoped to erect a similar structure in South Africa, ruled by the white settlers. But South Africa was not Canada: the Zulus, Xhosas and white Afrikaners had no intention of cooperating. The arrogant demands of the high commissioner Bartle Frere soon drove the Xhosas into rebellion. After crushing them, he turned on Cetshwayo, 'a man of considerable ability, much force of character, a dignified manner, sagacity'. As Cetshwayo retrained his armies, Frere demanded he give up territory and reduce his forces. The *nkosi* refused and massed his warriors. Frere was ready.

British aggression reflected the new stakes in South Africa. Eight years earlier, near the Vaal River, north-east of Cape Town, prospectors had found diamonds on the farm of the de Beer brothers in Griqualand, home of the mixed-race Griquas, who were ruled by their hereditary *kaptein*, Andries Waterboer. As diamond fever struck, 50,000 fortune hunters poured in to work the so-called Big Hole. Among the brilliant-seekers were an East End Jewish boxer, Barney Barnato, and an asthmatic English vicar's son, Cecil Rhodes. Both the Griqua *kaptein* and the Afrikaner presidents of Transvaal and Orange Free State claimed the mines, but the British swiftly annexed the New Rush camp, which was soon named after colonial secretary Lord Kimberley. Now Frere planned moves not just against Cetshwayo but also against the Afrikaner Transvaal, which he annexed. The Afrikaners did not immediately resist for they too were nervous of the resurgent Zulus.

In January 1879, Frere sent in 18,000 men under General Lord Chelmsford, who led one column of 1,500 himself. Cetshwayo targeted Chelmsford with 24,000 fighters under his brother: 'March slowly, attack at dawn, eat up the red soldiers.' The overconfident Chelmsford established his column at Isandlwana without a fortified camp, convinced that his 1,000 British redcoats and 500 African auxiliaries with their Martini–Henry rifles would easily overpower the Zulus. He was absent on a surveillance mission when the Zulus ambushed his troops, killing 1,210 soldiers – 739 white and 471 Africans, all with their stomachs ripped out – though losing a similar number themselves. Later Zulu troops besieged a British unit at Rorke's Drift that managed to hold out for twelve hours. In March, at Intombe, Cetshwayo destroyed a British column, killing eighty; but a rash assault on a fortified camp, although it killed eighty-four Britons and a hundred Africans, cost him 2,000 Zulus. In London, Disraeli was furious, but Chelmsford redeemed himself by reinvading with 25,000 men, armed with a new weapon: the Gatling gun.[*]

---

[*] An American inventor Richard Gatling created this first machine gun to save lives during the civil war: 'If I could invent a machine – a gun – which could, by its rapidity of fire, enable one man to do as much battle-duty as a hundred, it would . . . supersede the necessity of large armies, and consequently, exposure to battle and disease.' It did not work like that.

A young Frenchman rushed from London to join the British forces: Louis Napoleon – the twenty-two-year-old Loulou, only son of Napoleon III and Eugénie. Loulou begged to enlist. Disraeli vetoed it, but Eugénie appealed to Queen Victoria. 'What can you do,' sighed Disraeli, 'when you have two obstinate women to deal with?' Loulou – nicknamed PI (prince imperial) – was keen to fight, saying, 'If I had to fall, I'd prefer an assegai to a bullet.' Out scouting, his small unit was ambushed by thirty Zulus; his horse bolted with him clinging on until he fell and he was left behind, firing his pistol, until he was overwhelmed, sustaining eighteen assegai wounds.

Victoria visited Eugénie at her Kentish home to offer comfort. Later when Cetshwayo offered peace, he returned Loulou's Napoleonic sword. At home in England, his death, marking as it did the end of the Bonapartes, fascinated the public almost as much as Rorke's Drift.

On 4 July 1879, Chelmsford advanced on the royal kraal at Ulundi, where, facing the Zulu army in a hollow-square formation, his two Gatling guns and artillery scythed down 1,500, wounding thousands in thirty minutes. Afterwards he burned Ulundi. The king was captured and dispatched to London, the kingdom broken up.* The fall of Cetshwayo unleashed the Afrikaners, sharpshooting maestros of commando warfare, who defeated the redcoats. Britain recognized their independence, but the diamonds, soon followed by gold, would transform South Africa.

'The terrible disaster,' Disraeli remarked of Isandlwana, 'has shaken me to the centre' – and so did his other fiasco in Kabul. On 3 September, a mutiny of unpaid Afghan soldiers escalated into an insurgency: the British plenipotentiary was murdered, 7,000 British troops besieged and defeated. Isandlwana and Kabul demonstrated how a great empire is one that can be defeated on more than one front simultaneously, without any loss of prestige.

With an election campaign underway Disraeli's rival William Gladstone, an indefatigable seventy-year-old, attacked the imperial impresario for his showy vainglory, while Disraeli, five years older, suffering gout and asthma, mocked that 'sophisticated rhetorician, inebriated with the exuberance of his own verbosity'. But the verbosity worked: in April 1880, Gladstone won a landslide, exulting that Disraeli's defeat was 'like

---

* Cetshwayo was exiled, but when his kingdom dissolved into civil war he was returned as king. But, now sixty and wounded in battle, he was poisoned by rivals. His son Dinuzulu recruited Afrikaner commandos to restore his kingdom, but was captured and exiled by the British to St Helena. The kingdom was incorporated into South Africa, but the house of Shaka still reigns.

the vanishing of some vast magnificent castle in an Italian romance'.

Gladstone – nicknamed GOM (Grand Old Man) – was committed to granting Home Rule to troublesome Ireland, where Catholic peasants raged against Protestant lords. But he could not avoid the imperial vortex: Afghanistan had to be stabilized. This time the British were better led by General Frederick 'Bobs' Roberts, small, wiry Anglo-Irish veteran of India and Ethiopia, who repulsed the siege of his palisade then retook Kabul. In July 1880, a British force of 2,500 mainly Indian troops was routed by Afghans under Sher Ali's son. But Bobs led his Kabul and Kandahar Field Force to save Kandahar, where in September he routed the Afghans in turn. As in 1842, the British understood the principle of Afghan war: strike hard and then get out fast, leaving a friendly ruler. 'It may not be very flattering to our amour propre,' wrote Bobs, 'but . . . the less the Afghans see of us the less they'll dislike us.' The new amir, Abdur Rahman, agreed that Afghanistan would have foreign relations only with Britain and then spent twelve years crushing rebellions. When in 1885 Russian troops assaulted an Afghan unit at Panjdeh, bringing Russia and Britain to the brink of war, the amir and his British backers held their nerve. The debacles of 1878 won Britain another forty years of protectorate over Afghanistan.

Gladstone's other imperial vortex was Egypt, where in 1882 British interference provoked a nationalist revolt. To protect the Canal, Gladstone reluctantly sent Wolseley to occupy the country, but further south in Sudan, Britain's anti-slavery mission had unleashed a jihadist insurgency under a Nilotic boat builder's son, Muhammad Ahmed, who after a life of austere hermitage experienced divine visions and claimed to be the Mahdi. 'We shall destroy this and create the next world,' he said. 'Whoever doesn't believe in my messianism shall be purified by the sword.' He then ordered his adepts, the Ansaris (after the followers of Muhammad who went to Medina), 'Kill the Turks [Egyptians], pay no taxes.' The Mahdi's rebellion was backed by the reactionary slave traders who had been threatened by well-meaning British abolitionism.

As fanatical Ansaris defeated British and Egyptian troops, the British press demanded: 'Send Gordon!' Gladstone reluctantly appointed the righteous maverick Gordon to evacuate Sudan, only for the general to follow his own divine mission. When the Ansaris closed in, Gordon continued to hold Khartoum with 7,000 Sudanese. 'I feel so very much inclined to wish it His will might be my release,' he told his sister. 'Earth's joys grow very dim, its glories have faded.' As the publicity-seeking martyr flaunted his courage, a public outcry forced Gladstone to send an expedition under Wolseley. 'Better a bullet to the brain,' wrote Gordon, 'than to flicker out unheeded.' The doomed Gordon chain-smoked, beat his servants with a cane and ranted, 'Go, tell all the people of Khartoum that Gordon fears nothing, for God has created him without fear!'

On 26 January 1885, the Mahdi stormed Khartoum, butchering Gordon's troops. Gordon himself was speared on his veranda; his head was cut off and taken to the Mahdi, who hung it from a tree in Omdurman: 'his blue eyes half-opened', noted a European prisoner. The British admired this display of Christian heroism and demanded revenge; Gladstone was swept from office (GOM now said to mean Gordon's Own Murderer). The Mahdi ruled Sudan, making slavery a government monopoly, assisted by Arab slave masters who enslaved hundreds of thousands. On his death the *khalifa* (successor) Abdullahi, served by fifteen enslaved boys and 400 concubines, took command, treating Darfur and Equatoria as hunting reserves for slaves. Keen to expand his empire, in 1888 the *khalifa* invaded Ethiopia, slaughtering or enslaving thousands then sacking the capital Gondar. Emperor Yohannes counter-attacked into Sudan. In March 1889 at Gallabat – a neglected moment, perhaps because it was an encounter between Africans, but one of the biggest battles ever fought on the continent – 150,000 Ethiopians chastened 80,000 Sudanese, who tore victory out of defeat by killing Yohannes IV, the last monarch to be killed in battle, sending his head back to dangle next to Gordon on that grisly tree in Omdurman.

This battle, in which as many as 30,000 were killed, was just one sector in the carve-up that would be unleashed in part by the ambition of one king.

BUTCHER LEOPOLD, HANGMAN PETERS AND MAD CAPTAIN VOULET: AFRICAN CONQUESTS

Angular and awkward, long-nosed and bushy-bearded, Leopold II of Belgium was an oddball manipulator who had always craved an empire. Son of Victoria's uncle Leopold of Saxe-Coburg and a daughter of Louis Philippe, the young duke of Brabant was embarrassed by being 'king of a small country and small-minded people', but claimed that 'When men are great, however narrow the frontiers within which they live, they always find the means to do great things.' He tried to buy Crete, Cuba, Fiji, Sarawak, Philippines, Vietnam and parts of Texas and China. Inspired by Ismail the Magnificent, he thought Egypt 'a gold mine and we must spare no effort in our attempt to develop it', then suggested,

'One could purchase a small kingdom in Abyssinia.' His father married the boy to a Habsburg archduchess, Marie Henriette, who was obsessed with horses: it was a marriage 'between a stable boy and a nun', joked Pauline Metternich, 'and by nun I mean the duke of Brabant'. After his accession in 1865, Leopold declared that his ambition was to make Belgium 'strong, prosperous, [and] therefore have colonies of her own'.

As soon as he heard of Stanley's trans-African journey, he announced, 'I'd like to see Stanley.' He charmed Stanley, the journalist who fancied himself a warlord. Setting up his *Comité d'Études du Haut-Congo*, its name designed to sound philanthropic, the king hired Stanley, who understood that the 'clever' king, 'under the guise of an international Association, wants to make a Belgian dependency of the Congo basin'. In Africa, Stanley started to found Belgian 'stations', the most important being Leopoldville (Kinsasha), beating a French explorer Comte Savorgnan de Brazza in the race to claim territory. 'I don't want to miss,' said Leopold, 'a share of this magnificent African cake.'

In 1882, he set up the *Association Internationale du Congo* to front his acquisitions, which he called 'Free States', claiming swathes of 'central Africa abandoned by Egypt where slave trading continues. To allow these to be administered by a new State would be the best way to get at the root of the trouble and eradicate it.'

'Swindle! Fantasies!' sneered Bismarck, disgusted by Leopold, who 'displays the pretensions and naive selfishness of an Italian who considers his charm and good looks will enable him to get away with anything and give nothing in return'. The Iron Chancellor, facing resentment even from social democrats that Germany was missing out on empire, was being pressured by a sinister clergyman's son from Hanover, Carl Peters, a twenty-six-year-old philosophy graduate who, after hearing of British colonial gains while staying in London, founded a German East African Company and travelled to Zanzibar to claim territories. Twice Bismarck refused to accept Peters's claims over parts of Rwanda, Burundi and Tanzania. But in November 1884 he invited all the African contenders to Berlin for the dissection of a continent, as Leopold waited in Brussels. Europe, particularly in the Balkans, was so tense that the powers, accustomed to fierce competition, pivoted their rivalries on to Africa: British and French 'explorers' – usually imperial soldiers – raced to claim slices of the 'cake' if only to deny it to the other. Ideology and religion always reflect political contingency: Christian mission and *mission civilisatrice*, justified by theories of racist superiority and eugenics, dovetailed perfectly with imperial ambition and commercial avarice.[*]

Yet at that very moment, in the same city, a scientist was laying the foundations that would disprove this pseudo-science. In 1869, in Tübingen, Germany, a Swiss scientist, Friedrich Miescher, had borrowed pus-soaked, bloody bandages from a local hospital and, analysing the white blood cells, had identified a new substance that he called nuclein. He did not yet know it but nuclein contained deoxyribonucleic acid – DNA – that revealed how family and heredity really descended through ancestral lines over thousands of years. While Bismarck was dividing up Africa at the Berlin chancellery, a chemistry professor across town at the university – Albrecht Kossel – sensed the importance of these nucleins. 'The processes of life are like a drama,' Kossel said, 'and I'm studying the actors, not the plot.'

The plot remained in the hands of Bismarck. Germany, Britain and France each backed Leopold to prevent Congo going to the others. The Belgian king took personal possession of Congo, a million square miles, seventy-six times the size of Belgium with ten million inhabitants. Almost declaring himself 'emperor of Congo', he called it Congo Free State, but first he had to conquer it. Ordering its commercial exploitation, he formed a private army, the *Force Publique*, hiring Belgians and many other European adventurers as officers to command 20,000 Congolese auxiliaries, to direct ivory hunting and to manage a new source of income, rubber. In 1888, John Dunlop, an Irish vet, invented the rubber tyre, used on bicycles and soon on motor cars. Leopold's thugs, wielding rifles, *chicotes* – hippo-hide whips – and machetes, hunted down any opposition and executed workers who failed to deliver their rubber quotas. 'As soon as it was a question of rubber,' recalled a Leopoldine official, Charles Lemaire, 'I wrote to the government: "To

---

[*] Such ideas were developed simultaneously by British, German and French thinkers. The biologist-sociologist Herbert Spencer, whose *Progress: Its Law and Cause* (1857) came out just before Darwin's *On the Origin of Species*, argued that human species perfected themselves by fighting for mastery – 'survival of the fittest'. A wealthy cousin of Darwin, Francis Galton, obsessed with how to breed *Hereditary Genius* (the title of his 1869 book), believed that admirable characteristics could be encouraged by selective breeding: 'superiors' must be encouraged to breed; 'inferiors' – who lived off charity or in lunatic asylums – should not be allowed to breed or they would overrun society. He called his theory eugenics and it came to be widely held. Simultaneously the French diplomat Gobineau, disgusted by the 'age of national mediocrity', had invented modern scientific racism in his *Essai sur l'inégalité des races humaines*, published in 1855, in which he argued that 'The white race originally possessed the monopoly of beauty, intelligence and strength,' and in which he used the term 'Aryan' to describe a master race, *la race germanique*. The theories were embraced by his friend Wagner, whose wife wrote to Gobineau, 'My husband is quite at your service, always reading *The Races*.' The American racists Josiah C. Nott and Henry Hotze, as well as Kaiser Wilhelm II, espoused his views, which later inspired Hitler.

gather rubber, one must cut off hands, noses, ears."' The *Force Publique* enforced cheap rubber collection and cheap labour with violence, killing those who refused to work or punishing those who resisted by cutting off limbs for minor infringements: its units even had a Keeper of Hands since some soldiers were paid bonuses for hands collected (and bullets saved); others collected them as trophies. Leopoldine officers sometimes shot Africans for fun, killed their mistresses if they slept with other men, raped women and traded chained 'volunteers', effectively slaves. Though the number of deaths is now impossible to calculate, millions died. But this was not enough.

Leopold wanted to expand eastwards to grab Sudan. He ordered Stanley to reach the beleaguered governor of Egyptian Equatoria, Emin Pasha, a German-Jewish doctor convert to Islam, but to do so they needed Zanzibari help. Leopold and Stanley joined forces with the warlord Tippu Tip, appointing him a local governor. Emin was rescued and Equatoria claimed. 'Now what do you say,' the king asked Stanley, 'about taking Khartoum?' As host of the Brussels Anti-Slavery Conference, Leopold was criticized for his alliance with Tippu. The ailing Tippu soon retired to Zanzibar, succeeded by his son Sefu and nephew Raschid, who ruled large parts of Congo with other slaver-warlords. In 1890, Msiri, king of independent Katanga, was approached by British, French and Belgian emissaries, who negotiated with his Luso-African wife, Maria de Fonseca.

Leopold won by being more ruthless: when the sixty-year-old Msiri drew his sword against a Belgian lieutenant named Omer Bodson, he shot and then beheaded the warlord, shouting, 'I've killed a tiger! *Vive le Roi!*' Msiri's guards then killed Bodson. But Msiri's adopted son Mukanda accused Maria of betraying Msiri to the Europeans. Pushing her to her knees, he beheaded her with a machete. 'I'm Mukanda who walks over enemies!' he said, but he had lost his independence: Leopold got Katanga.

Bismarck accepted lesser prizes, ranging from Cameroon to South West Africa* – while Peters, broad-hipped, soft-skinned and pasty, sporting self-designed military gear and bearing an array of guns, tried to seize Uganda from the *kabaka* of Buganda, and Tanganyika from the sultan of Zanzibar. He was successful in Tanganyika, where as Reichskommissar, known as *Mkono wa Damu* – Bloodsmeared Man – he ruled murderously. When his favourite concubine slept with his manservant, he hanged both and liquidated their villages, shocking even the

---

* The first governor of German South West Africa was Heinrich Göring, father of Hitler's Reichsmarschall.

Germans, who recalled Hangman Peters and sent troops to crush the
resulting rebellion.[*]

The lion's share of Africa was secured by Britain and France, the
Third Republic proving every bit as hungry for empire as the Napole-
ons. The era of popular nationalism that doomed pure monarchy and
aristocracy fostered both bourgeois values and increasingly representative government at home, but security, profit, and prestige demanded
empire abroad. In 1873, France – with a monarchist majority in the
Assembly – offered the throne to the comte de Chambord (grandson of
Charles X), who lost the crown by refusing to accept the tricolour flag.
In the absence of a monarchy, the army came to symbolize stability,
Catholicism and *l'ordre moral* – against the other France, secular, liberal,
socialist. The army was the unifying symbol of a divided country, the
empire its consolation.

'The higher races,' said the premier Jules Ferry to the Assembly
on 28 March 1884, 'have a duty to civilize the inferior races.' Ferry, a
heavily bewhiskered lawyer, annexed the last Barbary State, Tunis, and
expanded Indo-China, taking Cambodia, Laos and the rest of Vietnam,
though the latter absorption was challenged by China. Ferry defeated the
Chinese, a war that helped discredit the premier – but not the empire.
While killing many thousands in an endless war to subjugate Algeria,
the French military were spearheaded by their cosmopolitan vanguard,
the Foreign Legion, with its cut-throat cult of victory. 'You, legionnaires,
became soldiers to die,' their general Oscar de Négrier told them as they
seized more of Vietnam, 'and I'm sending you to do just that!'

In west Africa, France crushed the Wassoulou kingdom in Mali and
Guinea, then turned on Dahomey. Its king, Glele, son of Ghezo, had maintained power through military raids, using slaves to work his palm-oil
estates, but his granting of the towns Cotonou and Porto-Novo to France
undermined his authority. The Berlin conference granted Dahomey to
Paris. After Glele was assassinated, his son Kondo, taking the regal name
Béhanzin, became a warrior king in the Dahomean tradition, propagat-
ing his image in the form of wooden statues decorating Abomey. In 1889,
he returned to slaving in French territory, using his female vanguard, the
Minon, as slave raiders. In 1892, the French invaded, commanded by a
tough colonel of mixed French, African and Amerindian descent, Alfred-
Amédée Dodds, who had fought at Sedan and in Indo-China. At Adégon,

***

[*] Yet Peters remained a hero to many in Germany, keeping a job at the Colonial Office, embarking on expensive 'explorations' and writing a book expounding racist social Darwinist
philosophy, *Willenswelt und Weltwille* (The Will to Power and the Power to Will). In 1914 he
was pardoned by Kaiser Wilhelm and after his death rehabilitated by Hitler.

King Béhanzin was routed by Dodds, and 400 of his female fighters killed. In January 1894, as Dodds closed in, the king burned Abomey, and was exiled to Martinique. France seized massive territories using its harsh *Armée d'Afrique*, composed of Berber and Arab cavalry – the *Spahis* – and cameleteers from the Maghreb, along with 200,000 west African sharpshooters, the *Tirailleurs Sénégalais*, and *Tirailleurs* from Indo-China and Madagascar. These troops helped to conquer a French empire from southern Congo to Chad and most of north-west Africa.

While France celebrated its conquests abroad, at home the nation edged towards civil war over a case of grotesque injustice. On 5 January 1895, a Jewish officer, Captain Alfred Dreyfus, son of a self-made Alsatian textile manufacturer, was found guilty of spying for Germany and sentenced to life on the hellish Devil's Island off French Guiana. Yet the army command knew that he was innocent and knew the identity of the real culprit, an aristocratic officer. The Dreyfusard novelist Zola exposed the outrage in '*J'accuse*', an open letter to the president – for which the novelist may have been poisoned by anti-Dreyfusards. The army falsified more evidence, finding Dreyfus guilty again, but the president pardoned him. *L'affaire Dreyfus* had exposed the fragility of France – and the special role of the army in holding together *patrie* and empire.[*]

The British too were seizing as much as they could – as cheaply as possible – through the usual armed companies. 'British policy,' said the prime minister, the marquess of Salisbury, formerly Disraeli's foreign secretary, 'is to drift lazily downstream occasionally putting out a boathook to avoid collision.' But his hand was repeatedly forced by imperialistic ministers and entrepreneurial conquistadors. In east Africa, when the empire-building *kabaka* Mutesa died in 1884, his son's murder of Christian converts provoked a dynamic British merchant-soldier, Frederick Lugard, yet another vicar's son, veteran of the Afghan and Sudan wars, to outmanoeuvre the German psychopath Peters and take control of Uganda; his successors added the Kikuyu lands (Kenya).

---

[*] In November 1898, two psychopathic officers – Captain Paul Voulet, known for his 'love of blood and cruelty', and Lieutenant Julien Chanoine, 'cruel out of hard-heartedness and pleasure' – embarked with a mainly African force of *Senegalese Tirailleurs* and Berber *Spahis*, armed with Gatling guns and artillery, to complete the conquest of Mali and Chad. Having made their names taking Ouagadougou and been given carte blanche by the war minister, their 'infernal column' burned villages and killed thousands, with men suspended so they were eaten by hyenas and vultures, women raped and hanged, children roasted – until their own officers denounced them. When a colonel was sent to stop them, Voulet and Chanoine murdered him. 'I'm no longer a Frenchman,' declared Voulet, 'I'm a black chief. With you, I'll found an empire.' But French officers and *Senegalese Tirailleurs* killed the two men. As in the case of Dreyfus, the army proved untouchable: an inquiry decided that these monsters had merely suffered the madness of '*soudanite aiguë*' – African heat.

When the sultan of Zanzibar, Khalid, poisoned his British-backed uncle Bargush and defied the British, the Royal Navy opened fire as 150 marines stormed the palace and overthrew him in thirty-eight minutes – the shortest war in history. Khalid's successors agreed to Zanzibar becoming a British protectorate, freed 60,000 slaves and kept their throne.

In west Africa, a secretive, sex-obsessed, hard-drinking Scottish-Manx merchant, Sir George Goldie, was conquering an empire north of the British colony of Lagos. 'I conceived the ambition of adding the region of Niger to the British empire,' said Goldie, who had once lived 'a life of dissipation', including some years with an Arab paramour in Egypt. On African visits, he fathered children with an Igbo woman. He was a master of political canvassing, orchestrating a charter for his Royal Niger Company on the Niger River run by Lugard, fresh from the conquest of Uganda, enforced by the Royal Niger Constabulary, a militia of British officers and African auxiliaries, which regularly launched raids and executed any opposition. The prize was palm oil, which was used to make industrial lubricant and soap.

In 1895, in the Gold Coast, the British forced a protectorate on the *asantehene* Agyeman Prempeh, who was exiled to the Seychelles. But just five years later the crassness of a British governor demanding to sit on the sacred Golden Stool of the Asante sparked a rebellion led, in the absence of the *asantehene*, by a sixty-year-old female leader, Yaa Asantewaa, queen mother of the Fon fiefdom of Ejisu, who took command of 12,000 Asante warriors. After ferocious fighting, she was captured, but the Golden Stool remained hidden.[*]

In 1897, Goldie's militia attacked and conquered the two amirates of Bida and Ilorin, partly to stop their slaving raids but also to beat the French. The next year, Goldie advised London to conquer the northern slave-owning emirates of Sokoto, and then to merge the multi-ethnic, multi-religious region into one colony. He was bought out (his company later became the conglomerate Unilever), but his plan was executed: Lugard and his West Africa Frontier Force conquered Sokoto, liberating two million slaves. It was Lugard's wife, Flora Shaw, who argued that the colony should be called Nigeria, of which he became the first governor-general.

---

[*] The *obas* of Benin also could not avoid the British. In January 1897, members of a delegation to force Benin to open to British trade were murdered, providing the pretext for an invasion already mustering. After bombarding Benin City with artillery, the officers captured and exiled the *oba*, Overami, and looted 2,000 of his ivory, wooden and bronze sculptures, keeping some for themselves and sending others to the queen and various museums: some are now being returned.

By now, France ruled the largest portion of Africa, followed by Britain. In terms of population, Britain ruled almost 30 per cent of Africans, France 15 per cent. The more aggressive imperialists in both countries aspired to contiguous empires: the French east–west, from Senegal to the French colony of Djibouti; the British north–south, from the Cape to Cairo. But their visions were about to clash.

As Leopold's profits poured out of Congo, so did stories of his atrocities, first publicized in the novel *Heart of Darkness* by Joseph Conrad, a Polish steamboat officer in Congo, and then in the damning report of the British consul Roger Casement. In London, Leopold was named in court as the paedophilic patron of a 'disorderly house' to which he paid £800 per month for a supply of virgins, aged ten to fifteen. In Paris, the sixty-five-year-old king fell for a prostitute, Blanche Delacroix, aged fifteen, 'plump but graceful', dispatching his female pander with a message: 'Madame, I am sent to you by a gentleman who's noticed you. He's a very high personage, but his exalted position obliges me to withhold his name.' Summoned for a comical interview at which the 'high personage', whom she mistakenly called 'King Oscar', examined her in silence, she passed the test. Blanche became his paramour, mother of two sons and proprietress of millions of Congo shares; she was also created baronne de Vaughan.

Yet he had not completely neglected his family. In 1880, he had triumphantly married his daughter Stephanie to the Habsburg crown prince, Rudolf, at a wedding in Vienna, attended by Bertie, prince of Wales, and Wilhelm, crown prince of Prussia. But Rudolf was wild, if not insane; Stephanie grew desperate, but no one could have predicted the tragedy that followed.[*]

RUDOLF AND MARY AT MAYERLING; INSPECTOR HIEDLER AND ADOLF AT BRAUNAU

Long ignored by his self-obsessed mother Sisi and coldly lectured by Franz Josef, who had refused to let him study at university, Rudolf was intelligent and surprisingly liberal with republican tendencies, seeking out liberals, even Jews, writing anonymous articles attacking the nobility

---

[*] In 1906, the outcry against Leopold's brutal proprietorship of Congo led the Belgian state to negotiate the takeover of the colony, spending 45.5 million francs to finish his building projects and paying the king himself 50 million francs: yet the cost of buying out the predator was to be raised from Congo itself. Leopold, one of the richest men in the world, died in 1909 – though it was far from the end of Belgian predations in Congo.

and an ethnographic study of the empire that his father approved. When-ever Sisi swept into his life on one of her visits to the court, 'The crown prince's eyes glowed . . . he's very like his mother, whom he worships.'

Franz Josef was bemused by his untameable wife and alienated son. Sisi spent most of her time hunting in England, obsessively slimming and exercising, both seeking privacy and courting publicity, but she had at least helped him in Hungary where the reconquest of 1848–9 had never been forgiven. Cultivating an intimate friendship, possibly an affair, with a dashing Hungarian ex-rebel who favoured the gold-embroidered, tiger-skinned Attila dress of the nobility, Count Gyula Andrássy, she orchestrated the negotiation of a new arrangement, a Dual Monarchy of Austria–Hungary. Andrássy became foreign minis-ter, drawing Austria close to Germany, but the rise of the Hungarians, coupled with the emergence of new Slavic countries, encouraged the seething nationalism of Czechs and other Slavs.

Sisi encouraged her plodding husband, now fifty-three, to console himself with a married actress, the thirty-year-old Katharina Schratt, whom he had admired from the imperial box in the Burgtheater. The kaiser's seduction was glacial. 'I didn't have the courage,' he wrote to her, 'while one is observed from all sides through opera glasses and the press hyenas are everywhere.' But finally their affair was consummated. 'Yesterday it was exactly six weeks since I left you in your bed, hoping in two days I should be sitting on it again!' wrote Franzl to Kathi. 'We'll have a wonderful reunion.' Sisi helped him by visiting Kathi herself. 'You will control yourself,' Franzl assured Kathi, 'so will I, though it will not be easy for me,' adding, 'The empress has repeatedly expressed herself in favourable terms about you.' Privately Sisi thought Schratt bovine, but as their daughter Marie Valerie put it, 'Her calm, very natural ways are attractive to papa.' Soon Schratt was part of the inner Habsburg family, the only thing except shooting that made Franz Josef cheerful: 'Poka [Hungarian for turkey, her nickname for Franz Josef] is happy tonight,' Sisi told her daughter. 'I've invited his friend.'

Neither parent had much time for Rudolf, who resented Sisi's slick hunting boyfriend Bay Middleton and ridiculed her spiritualist fortune tellers. Sisi did not help by bullying her daughter-in-law, calling her a 'mighty bumpkin'.

The crown prince, needy and heedless, became 'mad about women', addicted to drugs and courtesans, keeping a ledger of sexual conquests (virginities taken in red ink), and established a hierarchy of gifts for his con-quests, depending on whether they were royalty, nobility or commoners.

Rudolf and Stephanie were becoming estranged. After the birth of a daughter, Rudolf returned to his mistresses, falling in love with Mitzi Kaspar, teenaged actress and courtesan from Madame Wolf's Viennese bordello. He soon infected Stephanie with gonorrhoea. Unsurprisingly she turned against him, and started an affair with a Polish count. Pursuing his liberal views, Rudolf was friendly with the open-spirited Bertie, who was friends with Rothschilds and other Jewish magnates. Both were connoisseurs of courtesans, but even Bertie thought, 'For a young man of his age, Rudolf knows a lot about sexual matters.' Rudolf loathed his grotesque fellow heir, Wilhelm of Prussia, whom he called 'a diehard Junker and reactionary', joking to Stephanie that he would 'only invite Wilhelm along . . . so as to hasten him out of this world through an elegant hunting adventure'.

Rudolf meanwhile watched the tragedy of his cousin, Ludwig of Bavaria, who for twenty years had spent extravagantly on swan castles and Wagnerian operas, ignoring state business and having love affairs with male favourites. Only his cousin Empress Sisi was sympathetic. 'The King wasn't mad,' she believed, 'just an eccentric living in a world of dreams.' Ludwig planned to dismiss his ministers, who appealed to Bismarck. In 1886, a psychological report by doctors declared him insane. That June, when ministers and doctors arrived to depose him, a loyal baroness tried to beat them off with an umbrella and Ludwig took them prisoner, then tried to escape. Since he had no children, his uncle Luitpold became regent. 'Have you declared me insane?' Ludwig asked Dr Bernhard von Gudden, director of the Munich Asylum. 'You've never examined me.' Next day, transferred to Berg Castle on Lake Starnberg, Ludwig and Gudden did not return from a walk around the lake shore. Found dead in the water, Gudden had been strangled, the king's cause of death still unknown.*

Rudolf fantasized about watching someone else die and proposed a suicide pact to Mitzi, not least because he was sure his own succession was hopeless. 'On the day Papa closes his eyes for ever, things will grow very uncomfortable in Austria,' he warned his sister. 'I advise you to emigrate' – as millions of Germans were doing.†

He had already had an affair with a promiscuous married woman of

---

* In the royal palace in Munich, the princes were being tutored by a respected local schoolmaster, Gebhard Himmler, an enthusiastic royalist whose favourite pupil was Prince Heinrich. When he had a son, he named him Heinrich after the prince, who became a godfather of the future Reichsführer-SS.

† Much of Bavaria was poor. Between 1881 and 1890, 1.4 million Germans immigrated to the USA, many of them Bavarians. A typical example of these migrants, leaving in 1885, was Friedrich Drumpf, whose family would travel from the village of Kallstadt to the White House, a quintessential American story. Later Drumpf changed his name to Trump.

recent nobility, Baroness Helene Vetsera, who had slept with him when he was barely out of his teens. Now she introduced him to her teenaged daughter, Mary, who grumbled about her mother: 'Ever since I was a little girl she has treated me like something she means to dispose of to the best advantage.' Mary fell wildly in love with Rudolf, who was captivated by 'the power of her full and triumphant beauty, her deep black eyes, her cameo-like profile, her throat of a goddess, and her arresting sensual grace'. He declared, 'I can't tear myself away from her.' But she was far from his only paramour.

On 29 January 1889 Rudolf slept with Mitzi, his real love, but the next day he and Mary set off for his shooting lodge at Mayerling. 'If I could give him my life,' wrote Mary, 'I should be glad to do it, for what does life mean for me?' Rudolf wrote to his mother, describing Mary as 'a pure angel who accompanies me to the hereafter'.

The next day in the early hours, the seventeen-year-old Mary lay down on the bed, her hair around her shoulders, holding a rose; Rudolf, now thirty, shot her in the temple or gave her poison to drink – the details are still mysterious – then spent several hours with her body before shooting himself. When they were discovered, Sisi was told first; she received the news icily, insisting that 'the girl poisoned him', but calling Schratt and instructing her to soothe Franz Josef as she gave him the news. Sisi then summoned Stephanie, telling her maliciously, 'Things would have been different if he'd had a wife who understood him.'* Mary's mother Helene turned up wanting to know if anyone had seen her daughter. Sisi told her. Helene sobbed: 'My child, my beautiful child!'

'But you do know Rudolf is dead too?' said Sisi.

Helene fell to her knees: 'My unhappy child, what has she done?'

'Remember,' Sisi said. 'Rudolf died of a heart attack.' Back at Mayerling, courtiers were frantically covering up: Rudolf's body was sent back to the Hofburg, but Mary's two uncles smuggled out her body, dressed and seated upright in their carriage. The court announced that Rudolf had killed himself while insane, which meant that he could be buried in the Capuchin Chapel. Sisi returned to her travelling, her behaviour ever more idiosyncratic.

While decadent Vienna reflected the Habsburgs' multi-ethnic empire,

---

* As Rudolf was buried, his 'friend' Wilhelm, the new German kaiser, reflected that 'lunacy was lurking in the background and the monomania of suicide has done its silent but sure work on the overexcited brain'. Stephanie survived the malice of Sisi to remarry and settle in Hungary, but in a surprising initiative for a Habsburg crown princess, in 1908 she invented the hostess trolley – 'a new chafing dish and spirit lamp combined' – taking out US and British patents.

the archaic kaiser ruled the *k. und k.* (*kaiserlich und königlich* – imperial and royal) monarchy through its rigid hierarchy of nobility and bureaucracy. A typical example of this species was Alois Hiedler, inspector of customs at Braunau am Inn. Born illegitimate when his mother Maria Schicklgruber got unexpectedly pregnant, he later assumed the name of his stepfather (probably his real father) Hiedler.

Alois was an irascible, taciturn, hard-drinking bully but also capable. Lacking the usual education, he rose by merit, proud of his uniform, demanding to be addressed as *Herr Oberoffizial* Hiedler. His hobbies were beekeeping, beer drinking and skirt chasing: his love life was chaotic and semi-incestuous, as he fathered children with various women, of whom a daughter Angela survived, before he began an affair when he was already married with a cousin or half-niece hired as a maid called Klara Pölzl, twenty-three years his junior. After the death of his wife, he married Klara. Their first three children died young, two of the same bout of diphtheria. In April 1889, when Hiedler (now spelt Hitler) was fifty-one, Klara gave birth to a third, Adolf, followed by a daughter Paula. Another son died of measles. Far from having a harsh childhood, Adolf enjoyed a comfortable upbringing on Alois's generous salary. Alois occasionally beat him but such discipline was almost universal at that time. Adolf found schoolwork 'laughably easy' and bathed in his mother's passionate love, which granted him boundless self-confidence and self-indulgence. If anything, he was loved too much.

Oberoffizial Hiedler retired to a farm aged fifty-eight but dropped dead in 1903 when Adolf was thirteen, Paula six. Adolf had disdained his father's bureaucratic pomposity, believing himself destined to be an artist. Moving to Linz, Klara, affectionate and devout, raised the children, encouraging Adolf's indolent dreaming and supporting his yearning to study art. Hitler's relations with his sisters were cool – 'stupid geese', he called them – though he was closer to Angela. Early on, adults noticed his 'remarkable eyes': 'He had his mother's light-coloured eyes ... her penetrating stare.' Escaping from his dull family, he set off to become a famous artist in Vienna, where there was a new heir: Franz Ferdinand.

MODERN MONARCHS: FRANZ FERDINAND AND SOPHIE, PEDRO AND ISABELLA, DARLING WILLY

He was son of the emperor's brother, who, in yet another blow, had died on pilgrimage to Jerusalem after drinking the waters of the River Jordan.

Franz Ferdinand was fixated on royal hierarchy and shooting anything, from elephants to the 272,511 birds and beasts listed in his diary, but he was at least conscientious. Even so, he shocked the emperor by falling in love with a non-royal noblewoman, Sophie Chotek. Franz Josef finally allowed them to marry morganatically (meaning their children would be excluded from the succession).

A short-tempered, arrogant but intelligent champion of autocracy, Franz Ferdinand travelled the world to prepare himself. Setting up a military chancellery at his residence the Belvedere Palace, he thought about the problems facing the monarchy. He believed the empire needed to offer the Slavs a partnership similar to that of the Hungarians: 'Irredentism in our country . . . will cease immediately if our Slavs are given a comfortable, fair and good life.' Franz Ferdinand repeatedly warned against confrontations with Serbia that would bring in Russia.

Franz Josef's first cousin Emperor Pedro had now ruled Brazil for fifty-eight years, and Brazil was almost the last Atlantic slave-owning society. Weary of power, Pedro travelled the world and left his daughter, Isabel, in charge, but her French husband Gaston became hated as an avaricious foreigner. In 1881, the royal jewels were stolen from the palace, and when two servants were suspected, Pedro protected them – to public outrage. Pedro aimed to abolish slavery slowly to avoid revolts and an agricultural crash. In 1885, the Sexagenarian Law freed slaves at sixty. Finally, on 13 May 1888, Isabel abolished slavery and freed 700,000 slaves, generating a surge of popularity as Redeemer of the Blacks. While black people supported the monarchy, forming a Black Guard to defend it, many planters became republican.

Politics was stalemated. Everyone looked to the army, whose commander Marshal Deodoro de Fonseca was still devoted to Pedro. On his return, Pedro was jubilantly received, but it did not last. In November 1889, the old emperor held a ball for the visiting Chilean navy. But when Pedro arrived, he tripped. 'The monarchy stumbles,' he joked. 'But doesn't fall.' Marshal Fonseca discouraged republican officers – 'I want to accompany the emperor's coffin. He's old; I respect him' – but they went ahead anyway. A provincial government declared a republic. At the palace, Pedro waited for the marshal, who was too embarrassed to come. The empress panicked. 'Nonsense, my lady,' said Pedro. 'It's a tempest in a teapot – I know my fellow Brazilians. Monarchies don't fall that easily.' But they do.

In the early hours, junior officers arrived to inform Pedro that he had been deposed and banished. 'I'm not an escaped slave,' he said as he boarded a ship. 'I won't leave in the middle of the night.' But he did.

'Gentlemen,' he exclaimed, 'you're all mad!' As the emperor sailed for Europe, Fonseca became the first president of Brazil.

Pedro had once been celebrated for his modernity, but now in Europe a bumptious young kaiser, who prided himself on his knowledge of technology and ethos of medieval chivalry, was taking centre stage.

In March 1888, on the death aged ninety of Wilhelm I, his son Friedrich III – Fritz, the able commander of 1870 – succeeded to the throne with his British wife Vicky, daughter of Queen Victoria, knowing he was already far too ill to realize their vision of a liberal Germany. When German Jews were attacked in an antisemitic campaign, Fritz and Vicky had supported them by going to a synagogue in Berlin.

Bismarck plotted their destruction, focusing his hatred on Vicky – 'a wild woman . . . who terrified him by the unrestrained sexuality which speaks through her eyes'. But the chancellor was fortunate: Fritz was already suffering from throat cancer and filial betrayal. His son Willy, long indulged and funded by his grandfather 'Wilhelm the Great', despised his weakened father and liberal mother and could not wait to become absolutist kaiser and arbiter of Europe.

Kaiser Friedrich ruled for just ninety-eight days, dying on 15 June 1888, succeeded by twenty-nine-year-old Wilhelm, whom the ageing Bismarck called 'the young man'.

Willy's breech birth damaged his left arm. Educated at a normal school, he was happiest in the Guards, adoring the male companionship and the fetishistic trappings of Prussian virility, uniforms, high boots, eagle helmets. He travelled to Vienna for sexual adventures, having a child with one mistress before embarking on another affair with a Berlin courtesan who called herself Miss Love – both of whom indulged his fetish for women wearing gloves. At twenty-two, Willy married Dona (Augusta Victoria) of Schleswig-Holstein, who likewise indulged his fetish for gloves. 'I shall see you have all your little pleasures,' she promised. 'I always have gloves on at night now . . . You naughty little husband . . . You know how awfully much I love you and . . . how willing I am to do everything. You won't be disappointed.' They had seven children, but Willy was bored by her.

Wilhelm inherited Bismarck, creator of the hybrid Reich which only he could truly manage, striving to control the rise of socialists in the Reichstag and the brash young kaiser. Both were challenging: the Supreme Warlord was almost gifted, interested in everything, but also unbalanced, bombastic, impetuous, magniloquent and hyperactive, a manic babbler who scarcely stopped talking and travelling for the next thirty years, telling his entourage, 'All of you know nothing. I alone know something.'

Willy bullied and persecuted his mother Vicky, who smuggled out her letters to England. 'W fancies he can do everything himself,' she wrote to her mother Queen Victoria. 'He cannot. A little modesty and self-knowledge would show him he's not the genius or Frederick the Great he imagines. I fear he'll get into trouble,' thanks to his 'love of playing the despot and showing off'. She added, 'It's indeed a misfortune for us all that W . . . is imbued with prejudices, false notions and mistaken ideas . . . so unripe of character and judgement . . . Power was put into his hands which he so often abuses.' Vicky had foresight too: 'The worst of it is that we shall perhaps *all* have to pay for his ignorance and impudence.' She meant war.

Germany was booming, in one sense the most modern state in Europe, its Reichstag filled with middle-class socialists; its industries, particularly steel and chemicals, overtaking those of Britain and France. In another sense it was antiquated, ruled by the absolute prerogative of the Prussian king, surrounded by high-booted Junkers, to whom he said he would 'always be mindful that the eyes of my forefathers look down upon me from the next world and I shall one day have to answer to them for the glory and honour of the army'. Willy believed his power was bestowed by God. 'Forever and forever there's only one *real Emperor* in the world,' he wrote, 'and that is the *German* regardless of his person and qualities but by *right of a thousand years'* tradition. And his Chancellor has to *obey!*'

Bismarck had to buy Willy's love letters off Miss Love, but Willy soon resented the chancellor's dominance. 'I am accustomed to being obeyed,' said Willy. 'I don't enter into discussions.'

Willy gathered around himself a coterie of harsh Junker generals and worshipful, secret homosexual friends, led by his favourite Count 'Phili' zu Eulenburg, singer, poet and spiritualist, and a married father of six, who was twelve years older. When they met at a shooting house party in 1886, they were instantly dazzled by one another. Together they sang Nordic mystical ballads, rowed on lakes, shared seances, discussed race and gossiped about Ludwig of Bavaria, where Phili was a diplomat. But most of all they planned the Wilhelmine reign. Kaiserin Dona was immediately jealous, accusing her husband of having an affair with Phili.

The kaiser ignored her, confessing he was happiest with 'the nice young men' of his Potsdam regiments. He prized his summer cruises on the yacht *Hohenzollern* with male company, indulging in manly pranks that usually involved rectums and sausages. At sea in 1894, Phili was awoken by the 'loud, laughing, shouting, pealing voice of the Kaiser outside my door: he was chasing the old excellencies

Heintze, Kessel, Scholl, etc., through the corridors of the ship to *bed*'.[*]

Eulenburg adored Willy, whom he called *Liebchen* – Darling – even to his face, and 'the kindest of Kaisers, most sympathetic of friends' for whom he 'yearned'; Willy called him 'my bosom friend, the only one I have'. Yet the repressed kaiser knew little of the secret lives of Phili's intimates. When rumours about one of them, Count Kuno von Moltke, commandant of Berlin, reached Willy, he stopped another of the coterie. 'The *Liebchen* accosted me in the Tiergarten the day before yesterday,' wrote Baron Axel von Varnbüler. 'After he duly admired my yellow boots and colour-coordinated riding costume, he asked me "Do you know anything about Kuno?"'

Willy mocked Bismarck's alliance with Russia, which was designed to ensure peace and prevent the encirclement of Germany. 'That young man wants war with Russia,' complained Bismarck, 'and would like to draw his sword straight away if he could. I shall not be a party to it.' Now Phili saw his Darling as the 'personification of Germany', and praised the way 'The kaiser combines in himself two different natures –the chivalrous . . . and the modern.' He now advised Willy to dismiss the domineering old monster. In March 1890, when kaiser and chancellor clashed about workers' rights, Willy duly dismissed Bismarck, appointing in his place a more compliant general.

Willy wanted to be 'my own Bismarck', making full use of the awesome powers of kaiserdom. Abroad, his dream, he told Eulenburg, was German domination, 'a sort of Napoleonic supremacy . . . in the peaceful sense', but he also embraced the racial ideologies of Teutons (Germans) versus Slavs (Russians). Phili had had an affair with Gobineau, the racist ideologue, and Willy embraced his theories about the Aryan master race, which were becoming popular.

Willy sustained Bismarck's alliance with Austria–Hungary, recently joined by Italy, but his bombast sowed confusion and alarm: he was both jealous of Britain's liberalism and power (represented by his mother and her brother Bertie) and awestruck by its empire and navy (represented by his revered grandmother Victoria).

---

[*] Willy loved bullying his Junker generals. 'It's a curious sight,' chuckled Phili. 'All those old military fogeys having to do their knee-jerks with strained faces! The Kaiser sometimes laughs out loud and eggs them on with a dig to the ribs.' Willy encouraged his courtiers – Junker officers – to dress as poodles or ballerinas. 'You must be paraded by me as a circus poodle! – that will be a "hit" like nothing else,' Count Georg von Hülsen wrote to a fellow courtier. 'Just think: behind shaved tights . . . at the back a genuine poodle tail, a marked rectal opening and, when you "beg", in front a fig-leaf. Just think how wonderful when you bark, howl to music, shoot off a pistol or do other tricks. It is simply splendid! . . . I can already see H.M. [His Majesty] laughing with us . . . H.M. must be satisfied.'

A similar contradiction distorted his approach to Russia. On 1 March 1881, the sixty-seven-year-old emperor of Russia, Alexander II, was riding in his carriage through the streets, surrounded by Cossacks and secret policemen, on his way to review his Guards when a radical threw a bomb. It was a special day: the Romanov had just signed a decree to form Russia's first consultative assembly of elected delegates, which 'I don't hide from myself, is the first step towards a constitution'. Yet his slow reforms had inspired, then lethally disappointed, Russian radicals, whose People's Will faction launched four assassination attempts. Now Alexander was unharmed, yet against advice he insisted on comforting the wounded. As he did so, another terrorist dropped at bomb at his feet, blowing off his leg. He died a few hours later, watched by his Brobding-nagian son, now Alexander III, and his stunned grandson, Nicholas.

Alexander III, six foot three, coarse, hard-drinking, who favoured wearing *muzhik* blouses and boots, ended his father's reforms, re-pressed both nationalist and liberal aspirations and embraced the other tradition – police autocracy, imperial expansion and messianic nation-alism linked to Slavophilism. Russification – the banning of the use of Georgian, Finnish and Ukrainian languages – drove those peoples to join nationalist or socialist parties. Jews, the bottom of the ethnic hierarchy, were intensely persecuted. The Colossus was a masterful, competent autocrat who always knew what he wanted: he once bent a fork and told the Austrian ambassador, 'That's what I'm going to do to your army corps.' He thought nothing of grabbing his ministers by the scruffs of the neck and bullied his shy slight son, Nicky, whom he called a 'child'. But he also backed business, creating an economic boom of railway building and industrial development.[*]

Willy tried to charm the Colossus (who was repelled by him), but then discontinued Bismarck's alliance with the tsarist empire. Even Phili struggled to understand what Willy really wanted. Britain and Russia were rivals for Asian power, but did Willy want an alliance with Russia against Britain or one with Britain against Russia?[†] Yet for twenty-four years this unstable narcissist was, said his ally Franz Ferdinand, 'the grandest man in Europe'.

Alexander III reacted with two far-sighted decisions that produced

---

[*] This was funded by raising loans on the markets but also selling grain. When this caused a famine on the Volga, Alexander denied it existed, continued exporting grain and 350,000 perished – a precursor of the famines of 1932/3.

[†] Willy was so inconsistent that at various times he planned to seize Iraq, China and Latin America, and in 1903 he even ordered the Admiralty to prepare an invasion (Operations-plan III) for Cuba, Puerto Rico and New York, while seeking alliances with and against virtually every other state.

world-changing consequences. In July 1891, he allied Russia to republican France, effecting the very envelopment that Wilhelm had meant to avoid; and around the same time he commissioned the building of the 5,772-mile Trans-Siberian Railway, projecting Russian power towards disintegrating China.

Willy was too gripped by the emergence of what the racist Gobineau called 'the Yellow Peril'. On 17 September 1894, at the mouth of the Yalu River, a new naval power, Japan, sank eight (out of ten) Chinese battleships and then invaded China, seizing Port Arthur and massacring civilians.

The Houses of Hohenzollern and Roosevelt, Solomon and Manchu

That July, the seventy-year-old Dowager Empress Cixi, retired for five years, was informed by her nephew the Guangxu Emperor that a war was about to start with Japan. Guangxu was rattled: ignorant, insouciant, terrified of thunder (during storms the eunuchs shouted to drown out the sound), the emperor had reversed Cixi's reforms and neglected her navy while his teenaged Consort Zhen was selling offices to the highest bidders. The Manchu monarchs, ruling 400 millions, regarded the forty million Japanese as racially inferior *wojen* – dwarves. When the clash came, Guangxu announced, 'The Dwarves have broken all the laws of nations and exhausted our patience: we command our armies to tear the Dwarves out of their lairs.' But the Japanese had changed.

Thirty years earlier, in November 1867, the hereditary shogun, whose Tokugawa family had ruled Japan for the three centuries since Tokugawa Ieyasu, handed back power to the emperor. After a short conflict, a new *tenno* (emperor) declared the Restoration of Imperial Rule, which was to 'enrich the country, strengthen the military'.

When the teenaged prince, Mutsuhito, succeeded to the throne, he took the name Meiji – Enlightened Rule – and served as figurehead for an elite coterie of reformers who wished to overthrow the old order and forge what was really a new state. The capital was moved from Kyoto to Edo (renamed Tokyo); a young samurai reformer, Ito Hirobumi, drafted a new constitution, a hybrid of those of Germany and Britain, with a premiership and elected assembly, that would serve the 'sacred' and 'inviolable' emperor of the 'Sacred Throne established when heavens and earth separated'. The *tenno* 'must be reverenced'. Yet 'knowledge', stated Ito's Charter Oath, 'shall be sought throughout the world so as to invigorate the foundations of imperial rule'. British and German officers arrived to train a new military infused with technical modernity and medieval bushido that, along with the emperor himself, would form the heart of *kokutai*, a matrix of monarch, Shinto religion and society that would rule until 1945.[*]

In twenty years, Japan was transformed into Asia's most industrialized economy, just as China was disintegrating and so providing an irresistible target for the European empires – both a temptation and a warning to Japan.

Korea would be on the front line in the race between the Europeans and the Japanese to exploit the decline of China. If the Europeans took Korea, it would be 'a dagger pointed at the heart of the Japan'. Korea, ruled since 1392 by the Joseon family, was traditionally a Chinese vassal. Advised by his charismatic wife, Queen Min, its king Gojong navigated a middle way. Their marriage had been arranged by the king's domineering father, the *daewongun* – the prince of the great court – who as regent tried to exclude all foreign influence, a policy that was becoming impossible with expansionist Japan and Russia targeting the Hermit Kingdom.

At first the couple loathed each other and she refused to consummate the marriage on their wedding night, but they grew closer, despite losing their first child. 'A slim woman with a very elegant figure', Queen Myeongseong – Min – was scholarly and strikingly beautiful, observed an English visitor. 'The hair shiny ebony, and the skin transparent and pearly . . . and she had a sparkling intelligence.' After the *daewongun* had ruled for a decade, Gojong came of age and, fortified by Min, retired him. Negotiating with China and Russia, and opening the Hermit Kingdom to modernization, Min resisted Japanese control. But now in April 1894 a peasant rebellion provoked both China and Japan to intervene.

In Tokyo, there was no choice, said Premier Ito Hirobumi, 'but to go to war' to keep China out. Emperor Guangxu was 'surprised by this treachery', admitting, 'It's difficult to reason with the Dwarves' – who efficiently landed 240,000 Japanese troops in Korea. Japan captured Pyongyang and King Gojong, then smote China on land and sea, its officers comparing the Chinese to 'dying swine'. In April 1895, at Shimonoseki, Ito forced China to grant Korea 'independence' under Japanese influence and cede the prosperous island of Taiwan and the strategic northern city Port Arthur (Lüshunkou) to Japan. Out of nowhere, Japan

---

[*] Centuries of almost Habsburgian intermarriage had led to high infant mortality, spinal deformities and mandibular prognathism, though Meiji concealed his jaw under a beard. Meiji's wife was childless, but of the fifteen children conceived with his concubines ten died young and his crown prince, Yoshihito (later Emperor Taisho), was an invalid. Yet Taisho married and fathered a healthy family, starting in 1901 with the birth of a son, Prince Miji, later known as Hirohito.

had grabbed China's choicest morsels, much to the outrage of Willy.

The kaiser feared a 'consolidated Asia, the control of China by Japan', and appealed to St Petersburg, where Alexander III, only forty-nine but an incorrigible boozer who hid banned vodka receptables in his boots, was dying of liver cirrhosis. He was succeeded by his twenty-six-year-old son Nicholas, who sobbed, 'I'm completely unprepared. What's going to happen to Russia?' It is hard to be prepared for power – most democratic leaders have no experience of it when they are elected – and there was no training for the array of gifts necessary to rule as autocrat. He was no colossus like his father, nor a showman like Willy, but his handsome inscrutability, agonizing politeness and uxorious devotion belied his determination to promote Orthodox autocracy and Russian power. In the Japanese victory, Nicky saw the opportunity to do what Romanovs did: expand.

Willy had known Nicky and his half-English, half-German wife, Alexandra of Hesse-Darmstadt, granddaughter of Queen Victoria, all their lives: they were both cousins of his. Nicky and Alix had met as children and fallen in love as teenagers, but the pious Protestant Alix refused to convert to Orthodoxy – until April 1894, when both attended the wedding of her brother, along with Queen Victoria and Kaiser Wilhelm. After Alix turned down Nicky's proposal, she consulted Willy, who encouraged her to accept. In the miserable days after Alexander's death, Nicholas married Alexandra.

Now Nicky embraced his own vision of Asian empire along the Trans-Siberian Railway. Willy sent him a letter with a sketch entitled 'Against the Yellow Peril'. 'I'll certainly do all in my power to keep Europe quiet and guard the rear of Russia,' Willy wrote to Nicky in April 1895, 'so nobody shall hamper your action towards the Far East. For that is clearly the great task of the future for Russia to cultivate the Asian Continent and defend Europe from the inroads of the Great Yellow race.'

Nicky, backed by Willy, forced Japan to surrender some of its gains, and bribed China to grant concessions to France and Germany – and Port Arthur to Russia. After consulting Tibetan and Mongolian mystics, the tsar planned to seize Manchuria and Korea, with Queen Min keen for Russian backing in order to escape Japanese dominance. Embittered at losing their Chinese prizes, the Japanese were determined on vengeance, launching Operation Foxhunt. Min was the fox.

At dawn in October 1895, fifty assassins broke into the Gyeongbokgung Palace. They secured the king, then hunted for Min: her femininity provoked their special fury. They found her hiding among her ladies-in-waiting. The women were killed. The *ronin* gang-raped and slashed the forty-three-year-old queen, slicing off her breasts, then displayed her body to the Russian envoys, before taking her to the woods and burning her remains with kerosene. The king was horrified and heartbroken. In a backlash against the killing, Korean rebels attacked the Japanese. The fight was now on for hegemony in the east.

In Beijing, Emperor Guangxu invited Cixi back into power. 'We should comprehensively adopt western ways,' he decided, and create a constitutional monarchy. Yet he and his ministers also feared female power and ordered Cixi's murder. Instead she swept them aside, beheaded the reformers and imprisoned Guangxu. Manchu misrule now inspired a Cantonese medical student to overthrow the dynasty.

'We mustn't miss the opportunity of a lifetime,' declared Sun Yat-sen, aged twenty-nine, who loathed the Manchus and believed that he should be the revolutionary leader of a free Chinese republic. Son of a tailor and porter, the young Christian doctor helped found the Revive China Society, backed by a Shanghai businessman called Charlie Song, a former Christian preacher, one of whose daughters would one day marry Sun. Their rebellion ended in disaster. Cixi had captured rebels beheaded.

Single-minded, obsessional and politically as remorseless as he was supple, Dr Sun escaped to join his wealthy brother in Hawaii – where another female potentate, a remarkable queen, was fighting for its independence against the other new Pacific power: America.

QUEEN LILI'UOKALANI AND TEDDY ROOSEVELT: THE ABUNDANCE AND INGENUITY OF AMERICA

A singer-songwriter, a ukele player, an amorous enthusiast and Hawaiian patriot, Lili'uokalani was fifty-five when she succeeded her jovial brother Kalākaua as queen, but she had long dominated Hawaii as regent. Lili'uokalani, unhappily married to an American merchant's son with whom she lived at a pillared mansion Washington Place, was a cousin of the Conqueror's dynasty, a long-serving courtier to the kings and a rich landowner. She wrote her best song 'Aloha Oe', about one of her many affairs.[*]

Lili'uokalani was determined to halt American expansion and defeat the American sugar barons. In 1887, their Annexation Club, backed by a

---

[*] 'Farewell to thee, farewell to thee, / The charming one who dwells in the shaded bowers, / One fond embrace, / Ere I depart, / Until we meet again.'

settler militia, the Honolulu Rifles, forced Liliʻuokalani and her brother to accept the so-called Bayonet Constitution that further weakened the monarchy and granted the vote to all whites but only some Hawaiians – and no Asians.

Yet America, like Japan, was projecting its new naval power across the Pacific. In 1867, it took advantage of its Guano Act* to annex the Hawaiian island of Midway, while the queen's brother, King Kalākaua, also granted Pearl Harbor to America. Now in Washington, DC, a new assistant secretary of the navy watched, and planned to join the Pacific carve-up.

Teddy Roosevelt, the boy who had watched Lincoln's cortège from his window, was a weak asthmatic who had been home-schooled. Aspiring to be a scientist, he filled his room at home with stuffed creatures, nicknamed the Roosevelt Museum of Natural History by his siblings. Recovering his health, he learned to box at Harvard, emerging as an eccentric with the maniacal energy that is often the antidote to depression. After the death of his father, this irrepressible, pugnacious dynamo with round spectacles, rasping voice and 'castanet-like snapping teeth' entered 'the arena': 'I intended,' he said, 'to be one of the governing class.'

At his graduation party, his much older cousin, 'Squire' James Roosevelt, met a haughty young woman, Sara Delano, daughter of a rich China trader, whom he married. Soon afterwards she gave birth to a son, Franklin, whose life would be inspired by the career of cousin Teddy. Squire Roosevelt had made his fortune in railways and coal in a booming America personified by the Wizard of Menlo Park, who in later years would record Teddy's voice and support his politics.

In 1882, Thomas Alva Edison, a half-deaf teachers' son from Ohio who had started as a telegraphist during the civil war and aged twenty-two registered his first patent, threw a switch in the office of his banker, J. P. Morgan, which started generating electrical power for use in the lighting of fifty-nine homes in Manhattan, launching the utility that became Edison Illuminating Company.

Edison, who patented 1,093 inventions, was a one-man hub of scientific ingenuity at the moment when the technical improvements of the last century really began to improve the daily lives of ordinary

---

* Guano was, for a short time, a valuable commodity: it was bird and bat excrement, used as fertilizer but also to manufacture gunpowder. Found on the coasts of Peru and Bolivia and on Pacific islands, it was in such great demand that wars were fought, fortunes made and lands annexed for it. The 1856 Guano Act allowed America to annex any islands where guano was found. In 1879, Chile defeated Bolivia and Peru, seizing Bolivia's coastline, in the Guano War – the world's only faecal conflict – just before new chemical methods of producing fertilizer and gunpowder made the droppings worthless.

people. Ruthlessly competitive and intolerant of any opposition,* he was registering an average of one patent every four days, playing with his inventions in his crumpled, soiled suit, a vegetarian who lived on milk, sometimes working for seventy-two hours and often sleeping four hours a night. His family took second place. His first wife died of an accidental morphine overdose, after which he married a twenty-year-old. But he neglected his children and was exasperated by his alcoholic huckster sons, whom he refused to employ in his labs.

Edison personified the convergence of scientific invention and practical application that had been missing before. 'We've got to keep working up things of commercial value,' he said. 'We can't be like the old German professor content to spend his whole life studying the fuzz on a bee!' He created a new environment for thinking creatively: using profits from one of his inventions, a multiplex telegraphic system, he founded a laboratory in Menlo, New Jersey, dreaming up the concept of research and development. 'I never made a single discovery,' he said, and joked that 'Genius is 1 percent inspiration and 99 percent perspiration.'

Edison's electrical company was not based on a sudden discovery. Only recently electricity had been regarded as a form of entertainment, but he was just one of a phalanx of inventers who were experimenting with light bulbs that could illuminate houses and streets, competing with oil lamps.† Then he worked on the technology to generate and distribute the electricity. He did not get everything right. He insisted that direct current was the safe way to distribute electricity, but he employed a talented young Serb, Nikola Tesla, who left to work for his rival, George Westinghouse, to develop alternating current. Tesla was right. Edison was overtaken by Westinghouse and his bankers merged his businesses with others to create Con Edison and General Electric. But he was also experimenting with recording sounds (the phonograph that launched the music business) and transmitting voices (the carbon telephonic transmitter that became the telephone), the rechargeable battery and the movie camera (the Kinetograph, which created the film industry). He even founded Black Maria, the first movie studio, which made 1,200 silent movies.

---

* A new biography accuses him of murdering one of his competitors.
† Edison's success drove one rival into a different business: killing. His rival in creating the light bulb was Hiram Maxim from Maine, a sufferer from bronchitis whose first invention was a puffer but whose installation of light bulbs in a building was just ahead of Edison. Yet Edison beat Maxim, registering his own patent and going public. Leaving America, Maxim settled in Britain and started to work on another invention, a machine that would revolutionize warfare: the machine gun. Edison later said, 'I'm proud of the fact that I never invented weapons to kill.' Yet both were simply improving on the work of others.

Later he toyed with a contraption for speaking to the dead. Perhaps he was joking, but it was only a matter of time before other electrically powered gadgets would radically change life. The refrigerator so improved nutrition that in the next decades the height of the average American increased by 5.1 per cent. Across the world, at almost the same time, in February 1882, a New Zealander pioneered a refrigerator ship that conveyed frozen lamb from Dunedin to London which was edible after ninety-eight days at sea.* All of these became so ever present that their ubiquity was almost invisible; the skills to live without them were lost. Yet without them, modern life would collapse in a second. These improvements in nutrition coincided with advances in healthcare and agricultural productivity that together unleashed the biggest surge in population in world history.

Light bulbs made kerosene obsolete – just as Rockefeller won control of the US kerosene market. It looked as if Rockefeller would become a synonym for an impoverished businessman who had taken over a worthless industry, but the chief engineer of Edison Illuminating in Detroit had a vision that would change all this, resigning to work on a vehicle that used a gasoline by-product to power the combustion engine of a horseless carriage.

At first motor carriages were so slow that wags would shout, 'Get a horse!' Edison had encouraged Henry Ford, a Michigan farmboy who had long tinkered with gasoline-fuelled farm engines to create the self-propelled Ford Quadricycle. Like Edison himself, Ford was far from the only visionary: an engineer in Mannheim, Germany, Carl Benz, had developed a petrol engine in 1885 and designed the Benz motor car. These inventors were male, but in August 1886 Mrs Bertha Benz stole her husband's contraption with her two sons on board, and drove sixty-five miles, buying gasoline from pharmacies, to visit her mother. It was the first road trip, but Bertha also made driving safer by using a garter to insulate a wire, wielding a hairpin to unblock a pipe and inventing brake pads. Ford took note. At his Ford Motor Company, he developed

---

* These electrical goods – telephones, fridges, radios – needed to be made in a substance that was light, mouldable, cheap and insulated from electric currents. It did not exist until 1907, when a Belgian physicist, Leo Baekeland, who had already made a fortune creating the first photographic paper, experimented with combinations of phenol and formaldehyde to create Bakelite, the first of what he called plastics from the Greek for mouldable – *plastikos*. Baekeland took out a patent and made another fortune with his General Bakelite Company. It turned out that plastics could also be used for packaging and preserving food and for holding water in bottles – and that they lasted almost for ever. This was the start of the Age of Plastics that became a curse on the world: since the 1950s it is estimated a billion tons of plastics have been dumped, destroying the environment, killing animals and penetrating to the bottom of the seas – and even into human bloodstreams.

mass production of affordable automobiles – as did his rival Benz in Mannheim. Edison and Ford – a virulent antisemite and conspiracy theorist – became friends, holding annual motoring expeditions.*

As new oilfields were discovered in Texas and California, and in Persia, automobiles – followed by buses and trucks – opened the world up and swiftly became so popular that gasoline became essential. And Rockefeller became the richest man in the world – just as Teddy Roosevelt, the politician who would challenge his monopoly, was first elected to the New York State Assembly.

The bumptious, wealthy, toothy Republican attracted the hostility of the Democrats, who planned to humiliate him with a blanket-tossing. 'By God, if you try anything like that,' Teddy warned, 'I'll kick you, I'll bite you, I'll kick you in the balls.' One day he was called out of a session by a desperate telegram.

Rushing back to his house in Manhattan, he faced a double tragedy: his mother Mittie had died of typhoid; his adored young wife, Alice 'Sunshine' Lee, had given birth to a daughter, Alice, and then died of Bright's Disease. 'The light,' he wrote in his diary, 'has gone out of my life.' He was close to a breakdown. Dumping his daughter Alice with relatives, he consoled himself in the lawless, thrilling Badlands of the Dakota Territory where the Native Americans had been broken, the buffalo herds hunted to extinction and fortunes could be made in cattle raising and gold mining. There he befriended Quanah Parker, the last of the Comanche chiefs.

A wealthy poseur, Teddy bought the Elkhorn ranch in North Dakota, dressing the part of cowboy – 'I wear a sombrero, silk neckerchief, fringed buckskin shirt, sealskin chaparajos, alligator-hide boots, and [carry] my pearl-hilted revolver and a beautifully finished Winchester rifle,' plus a Bowie knife engraved 'T.R.'. Elkhorn was not far from where Sitting Elk, Lakota leader, now faced the vengeance for Custer's massacre.

On 29 December 1890, at Wounded Knee, South Dakota, the Seventh Cavalry were disarming a Lakota village when a deaf warrior who

---

* Another mechanical development changed daily life: in 1880, a sixteen-year-old Virginian schoolboy, James Bonsack, attracted by a prize offered by tobacco growers, left school and invented a machine that could roll 200 cigarettes a minute. He granted a monopoly to a North Carolinian cigarette maker, James Duke, who, forming British American Tobacco, launched a marketing campaign that made cigarettes fashionable: by the mid-twentieth century, much of the world was hooked on cigarettes (80 per cent of British males, 40 per cent of females) which caused lung cancer to increase twentyfold, a connection only fully proven in the 1950s. Heath warnings were only put on US cigarette packets in 1965 – the first country to do so. Even today, tobacco kills nine million annually.

couldn't hear the orders discharged his rifle, seemingly by accident. Mayhem ensued. Soldiers shot the ailing chief Sitting Elk. Afterwards soldier Hugh McGinnis recalled that 'helpless children and women with babies in their arms had been chased as far as two miles from the original scene of encounter and cut down without mercy by the troopers ... The soldiers simply went berserk.' Three hundred Lakota were killed; twenty-five soldiers died too. 'I can still see the butchered women and children lying heaped and scattered all along the crooked gulch,' remembered Black Elk, a Lakota survivor. 'A people's dream died there.'

The US, both liberal democracy and conquest state, had grown by a factor of ten since independence: this was the end of the continental conquest made irresistible by the sheer numbers of settlers. Wrangling his cattle in thirteen-hour days on horseback and hunting down cattle thieves at gunpoint, Roosevelt learned that 'By acting as if I wasn't afraid, I gradually ceased to be afraid.' He played out an aristocratic version of the frontier, but lower down the social ladder, millions were arriving by steamship, a wave sparked by the assassination of Alexander II.

Rumours spread that the assassins were Jews (though in fact none of them were). In Kyiv, Warsaw and Odessa, and around 200 other places, Jews were attacked by Russian crowds, probably hundreds raped and killed in pogroms (from the Russian *pogromit* – to destroy). Alexander III hated the Jews and blamed their disloyalty for their persecution, launching new repressive laws, maintained by his son Nicholas II, who shared his bigotry. This drove many Jews in the Russian empire to become Marxist revolutionaries and millions more to emigrate, some to return to Jerusalem, embracing a new Jewish national movement, and even more, during the next twenty years, to go west: 140,000 arrived in Britain but the majority – 2.5 to 4 million – travelled to America.*

This vast wave of voracious, risk-taking settlers was no longer 'an act of desperation' but, writes James Belich, 'an act of hope'. Some 4.5 million Irish men and women, 3 million Italians, 2 million Poles, 2 million Germans† and 1.5 million Scandinavians arrived. It was not

---

* In 1888, a typical Jewish immigrant, Benjamin Wonskolaser, a Jewish cobbler from Romanov Poland, arrived with his sons, moving between London, Ontario and Youngstown, Ohio, and making a living by mending shoes, selling pots and pans, running a grocery store and bicycle shop before opening a bowling alley. This would lead to their opening a theatre in New Castle, Pennsylvania, funded by pawning a horse; the theatre became a cinema that tempted them into the movie business. Benjamin changed his name to Warner; his sons Szmuel, Hirsz and Aaron changed their names to Sam, Harry and Albert, and, joined by their brother Jack, a 'song and dance man', would become the kings of the Hollywood film business.
† A typical Bavarian immigrant, Friedrich Drumpf, first worked as a barber in Manhattan, then, like Roosevelt, headed west, establishing the Poodle-Dog, a brothel-cum-milk-'n'-booze

just the US: altogether during the long nineteenth century, thirty-six million people arrived in Australia and North America, a movement of mainly English-speakers that should be seen alongside the Macedonian, Arab, Mongol and Spanish conquest-migrations.* Most of these immigrants poured into cities. In 1830 there were fewer than a hundred people in Chicago; in 1890 there were a million; within the same span, Melbourne grew from zero to 378,000. New York had a million people by 1850; by 1900, it had 3.5 million, which had almost doubled by 1930. Over twenty million immigrants arrived in America between 1850 and 1920 – the greatest migration in history, which in a frenzy of righteous destruction and crusading creativity powered the rise of the USA – and a truly interconnected global market. But the new world market presented new risks too. The failure of a reckless British bank, Barings, sparked the first ever global economic crisis that inspired millions to turn to Marxism and anarchism. Starting with the assassination of the French president in 1894, anarchists killed a cavalcade of western leaders. A world depression encouraged what the poet Emma Lazarus in 1883 called 'your huddled masses yearning to breathe free, / The wretched refuse of your teeming shore. / Send these, the homeless, tempest-tost to me.' America welcomed families like the Bavarian Drumpfs and the Jewish Wonskolasers.

Drumpf and the Wonskolasers were rough but just legal. When Teddy Roosevelt returned to 'the arena' in New York, he confronted the power both of immigrant criminals and of rich plutocrats. After losing a lot of capital and making some back with a bestseller, *Hunting Trips of a Ranchman*, he married a childhood sweetheart, Edith Carow, with whom he had five sons. He then persuaded President Benjamin Harrison to appoint him to the Civil Service Commission in New York. In 1894, the pugnacious Roosevelt became NYC police commissioner, relishing raids on vice dens and clashes with city bosses. But after befriending the muckraking journalist Jacob Riis, author of *How the Other Half Lives*, he

---

bar ('Rooms for Ladies') in Seattle, before following the latest gold rush to Monte Cristo in Washington State and then Klondike in Canada, where his Arctic Hotel offered gold-dust scales and rooms by the hour, expanding to the White Horse Hotel that served 3,000 meals a day. Drumpf returned to Kallstadt to marry a tinker's daughter, Elizabeth Christ, whom he brought to the Bronx, where in 1905 his son Fred, Donald Trump's father, was born.

* Anglo-American history is filled with piously monumental moments – Magna Carta, *Mayflower*, Glorious Revolution, Declaration of Independence. But it was all about population and migration: between 1790 and 1930, global English-speakers multiplied sixteen-fold from 12 to 200 million, not including the 400 million colonial subjects. Britain dominated the world not just by industrialization and conquest, but by migration and breeding. 'The remarkable explosion of the nineteenth century,' writes James Belich, 'put the Anglophones on top of the world.'

also tried to improve the appalling conditions of the immigrants. 'For two years,' recalled Riis, 'we were brothers in [Mafia-ridden] Mulberry Street.' Thousands of immigrants were pouring into New York, first the Irish, then Italians, Germans, Jews. By 1901, New York was the biggest port on earth, but the hardscrabble fostered another quintessential American culture that is usually left out of world history: crime.

Not long after Roosevelt began patrolling Little Italy, a good-looking and flashy teenager, whose parents had just arrived from Sicily where his father had toiled in a sulphur mine, threatened a tiny, frail Jewish boy if he did not pay protection money of ten cents a week. The Jewish boy, who had just arrived from Grodno in the Russian empire, refused. Impressed, the Sicilian, Salvatore Lucania, invited the Jew, Meier Su-chowlański, to join his Five Points Gang. Lucania now called himself Lucky Luciano; Suchowlański shortened his name to Meyer Lansky, and together they formed a partnership with Lansky's violent, dapper friend, Benjamin Siegel, a psychotic killer with bright-blue eyes nicknamed Bugsy, who was already running a protection racket on Lafayette.

They were tiny street players, but Luciano knew that Sicily had a long history of criminal societies, developed among peasants, who, denied justice by aristocrats and kings, enforced their own rules, and created their own rituals that were pastiches of Catholicism, though the name Mafia may have originated from the Christian subjects of the Arab emirate who, claiming to be *ma'afi* or exempted, refused to pay the *jizyah* tax. In Roosevelt's New York, Italian crime was ruled by Giuseppe 'Clutchhand' Morello, a ruffian from Corleone, who defeated the Nea-politan Camorra, stuffing his victims in barrels, but he was arrested and jailed, ultimately making way for the man who invented the US Mafia: Giuseppe 'Joe the Boss' Masseria. For now the three boys, Luciano, Lansky and Siegel, made money in pimping, theft and protection, but ultimately the three would organize national crime in America, corrupt politics in New York City and Cuba, and create the casino and entertain-ment industry in Las Vegas.

Patrolling this underworld while publicizing his exploits in the New York press brought Roosevelt to the attention of the new president, William McKinley, who in 1897 appointed him assistant secretary of the navy. Roosevelt was influenced by a book by an American officer called Alfred Mahan: *The Influence of Sea Power upon History*. Nothing so demonstrated the benefits of naval power as what was happening in Hawaii.

In 1893, Queen Lili'uokalani tried to overturn the power of American sugar barons by rewriting Hawaii's constitution, a move that provoked a

Committee of Public Safety led by Sanford Dole, a descendant of American missionaries, to order the Honolulu Rifles to attack the palace. Charles Wilson, the royal marshal, an American loyalist in command of the 500 Royal Guards, defended the queen. The Committee appealed to the US consul, who called in the Marines. Watching them from the balcony as they set up two cannon and two Gatlings, Lili'uokalani agreed to negotiate but refused to abdicate. Dole was declared president; but President Cleveland denounced 'the lawless occupation of Honolulu under false pretexts by US forces' and ordered the queen's restoration if she amnestied the rebels. But she refused.

In January 1895, guns for a counter-coup were found at Lili'uokalani's Washington Place. She was arrested, tried and sentenced to five years' hard labour. Dole threatened to execute her supporters unless she abdicated. 'For myself, I'd have chosen death,' she said, but she signed. President McKinley had promised 'no wars of conquest', but 'We can't let those islands go to Japan.'* Congress annexed the islands, while Roosevelt saw the next opportunity in the rebellion of one of the last Spanish colonies, Cuba: its 350,000 slaves had been freed only ten years earlier, and the Spanish were brutally repressing rebels whom many Americans supported – even more when their leader, the poet-philosopher José Martí, was killed in battle. McKinley and Roosevelt sent a battleship, the *Maine*, to Cuba, where on 15 February 1898 it exploded in Havana harbour, killing 266 officers and men. 'If that wasn't wrong,' Roosevelt remarked to his sister, 'I'd rather welcome a foreign war.'

ROOSEVELT AND THE ROUGH RIDERS

A Spanish war would be 'taking one more step toward the complete freeing of America from European dominion', Roosevelt said, and would also benefit 'our people by giving them something to think of which is not material gain'. He guided McKinley into the war, aided by the war-hungry newspapers of Willie Hearst, son of the gold mogul. Using his chain of newspapers from the *San Francisco Examiner* to the *New York Journal*, Hearst pursued readers (at his apogee, thirty million of them) with brash headlines, emotive stories and lurid gossip. Now his 'yellow' journalism stoked a Spanish war as Roosevelt formed his own regiment, the 1st Volunteer Cavalry, which he called the Rough

---

* Japan did consider occupying the islands. In 1917 Lili'uokalani died aged seventy-nine. Pearl Harbor was only fully developed as a naval base in 1931.

Riders, a mix of east coast aristocrats, real cowboys and Texas Rangers.

In July 1898, landing in Cuba and advancing against the Spanish at San Juan Ridge, Colonel Roosevelt, riding his horse Little Texas, gave the order to charge, riding ahead as eighty-nine of his men were killed. Roosevelt shot a Spaniard: 'I made a vow to kill at least one,' he said. 'Look at all those Spanish dead.' Hearst promoted his exploits in that 'crowded hour' in the liberation of Cuba, while across the Pacific, Roosevelt's fleet routed the Spanish in Manila Bay, then seized the Philippines. Spain ceded Puerto Rico, Guam and the Philippines to the US, but the Filipinos, under national leader Emilio Aguinaldo, declared independence. Promising what he called 'benevolent assimilation' – a new euphemism for imperial conquest – for 'the greatest good of the governed', McKinley unleashed a colonial war, deploying waterboarding torture, killing and camps, to crush Filipino resistance. Some 200,000 were killed. Roosevelt, now McKinley's vice-president, had helped make America a naval and Pacific power. He was not the only one obsessed with the navy.

Kaiser Wilhelm too had read Mahan, telling his mother, 'Nelson is for me "the Master" and I shape my naval ideas and plans from his.' Frustrated by his failure to win over Britain, he launched his *Weltpolitik* – power policy: 'I have learnt most of my military principles I adopt and follow from Napoleon,' he informed Vicky. If it wanted to conduct *Weltpolitik* along these lines, Germany had to equal British naval power. To pursue this *Flottenpolitik*, Willy recruited his friend Fritz Krupp to build nineteen battleships, eight armoured cruisers, twelve large cruisers and thirty light cruisers.

In autumn 1898, he extended his *Weltpolitik* to the east, setting off with a large entourage (including eighty maids and servants), a new wardrobe of arabesque uniforms (boots, whips and veils feature prominently) to visit the sultan, Abdulhamid II, who had removed a short-lived liberal constitution to restore Ottoman autocracy over an empire that had lost most of its European provinces. Tiny, vigilant and neurotic, his beard reddened with henna, Abdulhamid was a skilled carpenter, pianist, operatic composer and champagne-quaffing fan of Sherlock Holmes novels and French theatre, and a technical modernizer. Now he presented himself as caliph, encouraging Islamic nationalism to unite his restless Arab and Turkish subjects. He murdered reformers, using a secret police based on his Russian neighbours', and was an adept player of ethnic politics. Infuriated by Russian championing of Armenians and Bulgarians, Abdulhamid repressed a revolt by the Kurds, a Sunni mountain people spread across Ottoman Iraq and Syria, then armed Kurds in new Hamidiye regiments and unleashed them against Christians. He carefully watched the new Arab clubs that discussed the awakening of an Arab nation, hoping to project Ottoman power by building new railways to Baghdad and into Arabia.

There, two families, the Hashemites and the Saudis, rivals for three centuries, appeased Abdulhamid but deplored his power. Both would produce kings of many kingdoms; both rule into the twenty-first century. A Hashemite and a Saudi would remake the Arab world.

ABDULAZIZ – THE RETURN OF THE SAUDIS

In Mecca, the Hashemite amir, Ali Awn al-Rafiq, promoted by the sultan, was one of a family descended from Muhammad that had governed the holy city since Saladin – except between 1803 and 1818 when another family, the Saudis, had expelled them.

Knowing Hashemite prestige, Abdulhamid had noticed that the amir's nephew Hussein was plotting against the amir and summoned him to Istanbul, where the secret police reported his meetings with his relatives, describing him as a 'wilful recalcitrant person whose views on the rare occasions he consented to express them revealed a dangerous capacity for original thinking'. The sultan warned him to be careful but appointed him to the Council of State. Hussein, at home in the small oases of Arabia, the desert encampments (where he hunted with falcon and studied the fauna) and the coffee houses on the Bosphoros, was diminutive and obstinate, courtly, shrewd and aware of his lineage. He awaited his opportunity.

Across the peninsula in Kuwait, another extraordinary prince, Abdulaziz ibn Saud – known in the west as Ibn Saud – planned to regain his lost patrimony. Brought up in a world of conspiracy and chaos, his family, in partnership with the Wahhabi sect of Salafist purists, had already won and lost two kingdoms. In 1890, when he was fifteen, Abdulaziz had seen his father driven out of Riyadh by a rival, losing everything; but the refugees were granted asylum by their friends, the al-Sabah, once brigands in Iraq until, driven out by the Ottomans, they had seized Kuwait. These tiny Gulf fiefdoms, once controlled by Iran, were allied with the British viceroy of India, who cared little what happened within Arabia. Abdulaziz, aquiline, strapping and six foot four, an expert cameleteer and sharpshooter, was brought up partly by his aunt. 'She loved me even more than her own children,' he recalled. 'When we were alone she told of the great things I'd do: "You must revive the glory of the House of Saud," she told me again and again, her words like a caress.'

When he was twenty-six, Abdulaziz, wielding scimitar and Martini–Henry rifle, led a series of attacks into Nadj. In one raid, he and six men raided Riyadh where he murdered the governor and took the fortress. Abdulhamid sent troops to expel Abdulaziz, who was wounded but did not give up: he raided again, this time killing his rival and taking Nadj: the Saudis were back but Abdulhamid had plans to control Arabia with Willy's help.

In October 1898, the manic kaiser arrived in Constantinople bursting with ideas to discuss with Abdulhamid: the building of his railways, the training of his army – and Zionism. Back home, Wilhelm had been approached by a Viennese journalist, Theodor Herzl, who had observed the rise of antisemitism – a word for anti-Jewish racism coined only in 1880 – not just in Russia but in Paris and Vienna, and concluded that the Jews would never be safe in Europe. 'The idea I've developed' – he called it Zionism – 'is a very old one: the restoration of the Jewish State.' Judaea had been ruled by Jews for the millennium before Christ's birth; Jews everywhere had revered Jerusalem and Judaea since the fall of Simon Bar Kochba in 135 and had dreamed of return. A small, impoverished Jewish community, often persecuted and limited in rights, had long lived in Jerusalem and Ottoman Palestine. Between the 1560s and 1860s, Jerusalem was neglected and pillaged, a monumental but half-empty walled village, prey for local Turkish despots, home to a few thousand Arabs and a few hundred Jews until the conquest of Mehmed Ali and Ottoman reforms had reignited the reverence of British and European powers, who rebuilt the city with churches and hostels. The Romanovs sent thousands of Russian pilgrims annually – yet it was their antisemitic measures within their empire that also attracted Russian Jews to Jerusalem. Arabs and Jews moved into the city. In 1860, Moses Montefiore built the first Jewish borough outside the walls, just as the Husseinis, Arab grandees, built the first Arab settlement. In 1883, Edmond de Rothschild, youngest son of James, helped Russian immigrants found a Jewish town, Rishon LeZion, and by the 1890s there was a slight Jewish majority in Jerusalem. Herzl, imagining an aristocratic Jewish republic led by the Rothschilds, turned to Europe's most civilized, modern state, Germany, and through an introduction to Phili Eulenburg reached Willy.

Willy and Phili were rabid Jew-haters. 'I'm very much in favour of the Mauschels [a pejorative for Jews] going to Palestine,' responded Wilhelm. 'The sooner they clear off there the better.' But when he mentioned this to Abdulhamid, busy promoting his caliphal credentials in the Arab world, he brusquely dismissed it. Next Willy proceeded to Jerusalem, where he opened a hulking German church, mocked impoverished Jews as 'greasy and squalid, cringing and abject . . . Shylocks by the score' – and received Herzl, telling him his idea was 'a healthy one'. But as for funding, he sneered, 'Well, *you* have plenty of money!'* In Damascus, Willy declared himself 'protector of all Muslims', backing the Ottomans and stealing a march on the British, who had overextended themselves in Africa.

At first the British had seemed unstoppable, thanks to an invincible new piece of killing technology. On 25 October 1893, British paramilitaries, controlled by the diamond mogul Cecil Rhodes, deployed a new weapon – Maxim's machine gun – against charging Matabele warriors for the first time.

RHODES, THE MAXIM GUN AND LOBENGULA

Rhodes did not expect to live long. Like Clive and Lugard, he was a clergyman's son, this time from suburban Hertfordshire, who had a weak heart and chronic asthma. He craved adventure; his family believed South African heat would save his life, and as a teenager he set himself up in the rough Kimberley mining camp. There, he outplayed competitors and amalgamated claims, then won Rothschild backing to turn his De Beers company into the dominant diamond producer. Unmarried and awkward with women, manipulated by a female grifter who almost broke him, he was probably gay and was devoted to his secretary, Neville Pickering. But his passion was the British empire and its extension along a planned railway line from the Cape to Cairo, African peoples dominated by the white race. 'I contend that we are the finest race in the world,' as he wrote in his will, 'and that the more of the world we inhabit the better it is for the human race.'

In 1886, the stakes rose when gold was discovered in Transvaal, the Afrikaner republic, which was soon overwhelmed by British gold seekers, the *uitlanders*. In 1890, Rhodes, now thirty-seven, was elected premier of the Cape, and moved to limit African rights. 'The native is to

---

* 'The energy, creativity and efficiency of the tribe of Sem,' wrote the kaiser, 'would be diverted to worthier goals than sucking dry Christians, and many Social Democrats would clear off East.' But he added, 'Given the immense, extremely dangerous power which International Jewish Capital represents, it would be of huge advantage to Germany.' Antisemitism already contained a contradictory duality: poor Jews in Polish *shtetls* and Jerusalem's Old City were despised for their alien faith and filthy poverty, Rothschilds and 'International Jewish Capital' for their mystical power.

be treated as a child and denied the franchise,' he said. 'We must adopt a system of despotism.' Then, chartering a paramilitary British South African Company, he pushed British power into Transvaal and north-wards into the African kingdom of Lobengula, king of the Ndebele, son of the founder Mzilikazi, ex-general of Shaka, who had conquered the kingdom during the 1820s. Commander of 20,000 warriors, husband of twenty wives, ruler since 1868, Lobengula had successfully limited British infiltration, but Rhodes and his paramilitaries, organized by his irrepressible henchman Leander Jameson, a gun-toting doctor,* pro-voked war. Lobengula mobilized. At Shangani, 6,000 fighters, armed with Martini–Henrys and spears, attacked Rhodes's posse, who had a singular advantage: the Maxim.

Arriving in England in 1882 from the United States, after losing the electric bulb war to Edison, Maxim had met an American who advised, 'Hang your chemistry and electricity! If you want to make a pile of money, invent something that will enable these Europeans to cut each other's throats with greater facility.'

At Shangani, five Maxims killed 1,500 Matabele in minutes, 'like mowing grass'; a week later, they killed another 2,500. 'The shooting,' said Rhodes, 'must have been excellent.' The public was impressed with British technology. 'Whatever happens,' wrote Hilaire Belloc, 'we have got / The Maxim gun, and they have not.' But the trouble with new technology is that competitors can buy it too, and soon the British would be on the receiving end. His prestige shattered, Lobengula was poisoned, the kingdom's destruction aided by a shrewd neighbouring Tswana king, Khama the Great. British settlers poured in, naming the territory Rhodesia, but when Rhodes turned to break Khama, he was outwitted. Khama, a Christian convert, travelled to London and appealed to the government, which shamed by Rhodes's predations, allowed the king to keep Bechuanaland (Botswana).† 'It's humiliating,' grumbled Rhodes, 'to be utterly beaten by these n*****s.'

In December 1895, Rhodes orchestrated an invasion of Transvaal, backing Dr Jameson and 600 mercenaries, who were easily shot down by Afrikaner farmers. The prime minister Lord Salisbury was incensed. Rhodes resigned as Cape premier. Jameson took the blame.‡ Kaiser

---

* Jameson combined a colonial career with his medical one, treating not just Rhodes but also King Lobengula and President Kruger of Transvaal.
† Khama's grandson Seretse would be the first president of a new country, Botswana; his great-grandson would be president in the twenty-first century.
‡ Later Jameson was rehabilitated and elected Cape premier; he went on to receive a baron-etcy. Rudyard Kipling wrote 'If . . .' about his optimism in the face of adversity.

Wilhelm ordered German troops to intervene against Britain but was restrained by his ministers.

Weeks after the Jameson raid, an African monarch proved the limits of European conquest. On 1 March 1896, at the valley of Adawa, 14,000 Italian troops attacked the Ethiopian army.

MENELIK AND EMPRESS TAYTU: AFRICAN VICTORY

Like Germany, Italy was a touchy new country, desperate to catch up with the Anglo-French. Its premier Francesco Crispi, an authoritarian nationalist and dramatic populist known as the Loner who had fought with Garibaldi, was an aggressive imperialist. 'Crispi wants to occupy everywhere,' joked the king Umberto, 'even China and Japan,' adding, 'Crispi's a pig but the essential pig.' Close to Bismarck, with whom Italy was allied, Crispi seized Massawa, a territory he named Eritrea (from the Latin term for the Red Sea, *Mare Erythraeum*), but when he planned to expand into Ethiopia, he encountered the most talented African leader of the imperial age: Menelik II.

He was the young prince who had been a prisoner and son-in-law of the capricious Emperor Tewodros. After Tewodros's suicide, he mourned the emperor but submitted to Emperor Yohannes, who installed him as king of Showa. For seventeen years he was married to an untameable noblewoman, Princess Befana, who promoted her sons by previous marriages and repeatedly tried to overthrow him. After their divorce, he grieved for her: 'You ask me to look at these women with the same eyes that once gazed upon Befana?' Third time lucky, he married Taytu Betul, a potentate from Gojjam and Gondar in the north who had been married three times before and could field her own regiment.

In 1889, after Emperor Yohannes had been killed by the Mahdists, Menelik, claiming direct male descent from Solomon and Sheba, finally became emperor. A mix of regal grandeur and accessible geniality, he 'showed great intelligence' and 'boyish curiosity', especially about western weaponry: 'very friendly', noted an Italian visitor, 'a fanatic for weapons'. Fast-talking and laconic, he answered all petitioners with 'Yes maybe.' Having trained his troops to use French, British and Russian artillery and rifles, some captured, some purchased, he expanded from the Amhara region in the centre, in ten years of conquest, incorporating Tigray and other northern provinces, but also smiting the southern kingdom of Kaffa and others, massacring enemies and enslaving thousands. Headquartered in a new capital, Addis Ababa, founded by his wife, Menelik created an Ethiopian empire which endured, with notable interludes, until the 1970s. Those wars and the introduction of Italian cattle brought rinderpest and a famine that may have been Africa's worst ever, killing ten million people.

Menelik was happy to leave Eritrea to the Italians, but now Crispi ordered the annexation of Ethiopia, trying to trick Menelik. 'This country is mine,' he declared, 'and no other nation can have it.' Crispi boasted that Italy would rout the African 'barbarians' and bring the emperor to Rome 'in a cage'.

'An enemy has crossed the sea,' declared Menelik, 'burrowing under our territories like a mole ... I negotiated with these people,' but 'Enough! I'll repel the invader.' The Italian general Oreste Baratieri underestimated Menelik, who quickly defeated one Italian unit and then, mustering a huge army, marched north, riding on a scarlet saddle, clad in white robes and sheltering under a golden parasol. Crispi reprimanded Baratieri for being defeated by African 'monkeys': 'This is military phthisis, not a war ... We're ready for any sacrifice whatever the cost to save the honour of the army and the prestige of the monarchy.' Baratieri with his 20,000 men, including his Eritrean allies, attempted a surprise assault on the heights at Adowa, sending three brigades up mountain paths in darkness and hoping to draw Menelik into battle. Commanding from a mountain top with Empress Taytu, the emperor defeated each Italian brigade separately. Suddenly Empress Taytu jumped up. 'Courage!' she said. 'Victory is ours! Strike!' She sent in her men and Menelik followed with 25,000 reserves, killing 43 per cent of the Italians and three out of five generals, an African triumph unprecedented in colonial history. Crispi fell from power. Menelik continued his conquests as he played the Europeans against each other. He now backed construction of a railway from Addis to the French port of Djibouti, granting the franchise to his powerful Guadeloupian doctor, Vitale.* As the Italians dreamed of 'the vengeance of Adowa', in neighbouring Sudan the British were avenging General Gordon.

On 2 September 1898, at Omdurman, outside Khartoum in Sudan, a young cavalryman with his regiment, the 2nd Lancers, prepared to charge the khalifal army, an intimidating force of 50,000 spearmen and cavalry, waving banners, wearing jibbahs and chainmail. Earlier he

---

* Menelik's planned successor had been his cousin, Ras (duke) Makonnen Wolde Mikael, a grandson of a king of Showa, his top commander at Adowa, but he died first, leaving a son, Tafari Makonnen, later Emperor Haile Selassie. When the emperor had a stroke in 1904, his wife Taytu ruled for him and on his death vainly attempted to stop the succession of his grandson, Lij Iyasu.

had scanned the enemy ranks through his binoculars. 'Never shall I see such a sight again,' wrote the twenty-three-year-old Winston Churchill, a brash, bumptious Old Harrovian journalist, descendant of John Churchill, duke of Marlborough, and son of a maverick politician Lord Randolph, who had died of syphilis.

Herbert Kitchener, *sirdar* of the Egyptian army, did not want Churchill there, but his mother, Jenny Jerome, glamorous daughter of an American Gilded Age speculator, and lover of the prince of Wales and many others, pulled strings – and Churchill joined Kitchener's 25,000 Anglo-Egyptian troops.

Ice-cold, solitary and obsessional, Kitchener, six foot two, blond, with pewter eyes (and a cast in one of them) and a face like a mask, was a self-made Anglo-Irish officer, a celibate, probably a repressed homosexual, who combined steely acumen, vindictive ambition and porcelain collecting. Now this meticulous operation would win him the nickname the Sudan Machine. When the British Lancers charged, Churchill rode with them.

GANDHI, CHURCHILL AND THE SUDAN MACHINE

'The event seemed to pass in absolute silence,' remembered Churchill of one of the last cavalry charges. 'The yells of the enemy, the shouts of the soldiers, the firing of many shots, the clashing of sword and spear were . . . unregistered by the brain.' As he fought, 'Men, clinging to their saddles, lurched helplessly about, covered with blood from perhaps a dozen wounds. Horses, streaming from tremendous gashes, limped and staggered . . .' When the Mahdists charged, the Maxim guns scythed through them, before the troops advanced shouting, 'Remember Gordon!'

'Well, we have given them a damn good dusting,' said the Machine, killing the enemy wounded. Churchill thought the British were 'disgraced by the inhuman slaughter of the wounded'. Twelve thousand Sudanese lay dead. As a witness observed, 'It was not a battle but an execution . . . The bodies weren't in heaps – bodies hardly ever are; but they [were] spread evenly over acres and acres.' There were just forty-eight British dead. Churchill was further 'scandalized' by Kitchener's 'desecration of the Mahdi's Tomb and the barbarous manner in which he had carried off the Mahdi's head in a kerosene can as a trophy', planning to use it as his inkstand. Although an outcry forced him to bury it, Kitchener was raised to the peerage, the khalifa defeated and killed.

South Sudan was the last corner of Africa unclaimed by Europeans. Kitchener learned that a French captain and 120 Senegalese *Tiraill-eurs*, travelling all the way from Brazzaville, had reached the village of Fashoda in a bid to secure a French transcontinental empire. Kitchener sailed down the Nile and faced off the French as his subaltern Churchill rushed down to South Africa, where Britain would be humiliated by very different enemies.

In October 1899, as British *uitlanders* demanded voting rights within the Afrikaner republics, the latter's commandos, expert fighters armed with their own Maxim machine guns, launched pre-emptive attacks on British towns, besieging Kimberley and Ladysmith and defeating cumbersome British forces. Rhodes helped defend Kimberley. Churchill, covering the war for a newspaper, was captured but managed to escape, his adventures making his name. Meanwhile, in a very different milieu, an Indian lawyer worked as a stretcher-bearer for the British at the battle outside Ladysmith. Mohandas Gandhi, middle-class son of the chief minister of a small fiefdom in Rajasthan, had been called to the Bar in London, but in 1893, when he was twenty-three, he was invited to take a case in South Africa. He moved to Durban, where, dapper in starched collar, trimmed moustache and suit, he would spend twenty-one years, representing Indians' rights. While Churchill returned to London as a hero of empire and was elected to Parliament, Gandhi developed his concept of non-violent protest, *satyagraha* (truth force), which he would later apply to the cause of Indian independence.

As inept British forces floundered, Salisbury sent in the Sudan Machine. In December 1899, Kitchener arrived to break the Afrikaners, burning their farms, 'concentrating' their families in new camps, in which around 26,000 children and women died of disease, and finally capturing their capitals and defeating their armies.* Kaiser Wilhelm and Tsar Nicholas were delighted by the near humiliation of Queen Victoria's empire – just as the crisis of that other empress, Cixi, gave them a chance to gobble up more of China.

TWO ANCIENT EMPRESSES: CIXI AND VICTORIA

'I've often thought I'm the cleverest woman that ever lived,' Empress Cixi said later, but she admitted she was about to make 'the only

---

* Just after the war, Rhodes died, aged forty-eight, leaving North and South Rhodesia (Zambia and Zimbabwe) named after himself. Buried with the salute of Ndebele warriors in today's Zimbabwe, he left his fortune to educate Rhodes scholars at Oxford.

serious mistake I made in my life'. Unable to kill her loathed nephew the Guangxu Emperor, who still reigned while under house arrest, she turned on his Consort Zhen, exposing her corruption and forcing her to watch the torturing of her eunuchs. But the national humiliation of the war against Japan sparked a new rebellion led by a Society of Righteous Harmonious Fists, who practised martial arts in the belief that they made them invulnerable to European bullets. Aiming to 'exterminate the foreigners', these so-called Boxers, 250,000 pike-wielding peasants in red bandannas, advanced on Beijing to expel the Europeans. As westerners sheltered in their legations, many Chinese and Manchu paladins sympathized and cooperated with the Boxers. 'The Boxers were sent by heaven,' said Cixi, 'to rid China of hated foreigners.'

As Cixi herself wavered, the eight great powers, led by a German general, intervened to save their subjects. 'Should you encounter the enemy, give no quarter, take no prisoners,' the kaiser told his troops. 'Just as a thousand years ago the Huns under their King Attila made a name for themselves . . . may the name German be affirmed by you in such a way that no Chinese will ever again dare to look cross-eyed at a German.' Even Eulenburg was privately worried about Willy, because he 'is no longer in control of himself when seized by rage. I regard the situation as highly dangerous.'

Cixi backed the Boxers: 'Perhaps their magic isn't reliable but can't we rely on the hearts and minds of the people?' She declared war on the eight greatest nations on earth, even though 'China is weak', arguing that 'If we just fold our arms and yield to them, I'd have no face to meet our ancestors after death. If we must perish, why not fight to the death?' As the eight nations fought their way into Beijing, Cixi, accompanied by the Guangxu Emperor, fled northwards, saying to her imprisoned enemy Consort Zhen, 'You're young and pretty, likely to be raped by the foreign soldiers. I trust you know what you should do' – she meant suicide. But instead she had Zhen thrown down a well. Fleeing to Xi'an, at times sobbing as she suffered cold and hunger, she sued for peace – and returned to the Forbidden City.

Far away in London, the other empress was sinking. In January 1901, Victoria's doctor sent a secret telegram from her palace at Osborne, Isle of Wight, to Kaiser Wilhelm: 'Disquieting symptoms have developed.' Willy had always craved Victoria's love – 'People have no inkling how much I love the Queen, how intimately she's linked to my memories' – and now confessed his fear that 'she's hopelessly ill . . . without my being able to see her again'. He rushed to London where Bertie tried to divert him, but Victoria's condition deteriorated, so uncle and nephew hurried to Osborne. When the blind, semi-conscious queen awoke, her children didn't mention that Willy was there. He was hurt, but finally the doctor led him to the sickbed on his own, after which she whispered, 'The emperor's very kind.' Willy knelt next to the bed, supporting her with his right arm, 'his eyes immovably fixed on his grandmother'. The kaiser and Bertie, now King-Emperor Edward VII, lifted the tiny queen into her coffin.

'Although I've heard much about Queen Victoria,' reflected Cixi, 'I don't think her life was half so interesting and eventful as mine . . . She had nothing to say about policy. Now look at me. I have 400 million dependent on my judgement.' Cixi ordered elections for an assembly and reforms banning foot-binding and death by a thousand cuts, while founding schools for girls and awarding scholarships for girls to study abroad. Among the scholarship girls were Qingling and Meiling Song, the daughters of the Christian businessman Charlie Song, who now set off for Wellesley College, Massachusetts. Song's secret ally, Sun Yat-sen, tried to launch further revolutions – which again failed. Sun waited in Japan.

Cixi had survived, but Tsar Nicholas kept his armies in Manchuria and accelerated his infiltration of Korea.* The Japanese regarded both Manchuria and Korea as theirs. The two sides started to negotiate. Nicholas could have struck a deal, taking Manchuria, ceding Korea, but instead, deluded by his visions of Asian empire and divine mission, he mocked Japanese challenges to Russia, insisting, 'There will be no war,' because 'those macaques' could never defeat Russians.

Nicky's reign had so far been a limited success. His economy was booming, his Baku oilfields were producing half the world's oil, but the workers pouring into the cities to work in the new factories and refineries† lived in appalling conditions and began embracing Marxist revolution. The tsar's refusal to countenance any reform left the opposition no choice but to embrace revolution. His policy of promoting Orthodox Russians to rally support for the Romanovs alienated half his

---

* It was what a Russian leader did. Since the Romanovs had come to power in 1613, Russia had expanded an average 55 square miles a day, 20,000 a year, from 2 million square miles to 8.6, which, with only a few setbacks in 1856 and 1878, made it one of the most successful conquest machines in world history.

† In 1873 a successful gunmaker named Ludwig Nobel, son of a Swedish inventor who had made his fortune in Russia and brother of Alfred who had invented nitroglycerine dynamite first for mining then for war, arrived from St Petersburg and bought a refinery in Baku. Nobel invented the first oil tanker, appropriately called the *Zoroaster*, to transport this 'black gold'. The Nobels soon had competition: Alphonse de Rothschild of Paris invested in a railway to get the oil to the Black Sea port of Batumi, where he built an oil refinery.

subjects: Catholic Poles, Protestant Finns, Jews, Armenians and Georgians.

In 1901, a young Georgian started to work at the Rothschild oil refinery in Batumi, secretly organizing strikes and sabotage: his name was Josef Djugashvili, son of a drunken, abusive cobbler and a devoted, pious mother who, determined that he should become a bishop, would do anything to get him into the Tiflis seminary where the use of Georgian was banned: the boys were beaten for speaking it. There, like thousands of other young people, Josef Djugashvili embraced a different faith – Marxism. He joined the Social Democratic Party, drawn to one of its leaders, Vladimir Ulyanov, who called himself Lenin, a cultured, well-off nobleman ferociously dedicated to revolution, who adapted Marx to fit Russia, creating a tiny vanguard to exercise a 'dictatorship of the proletariat' backed by terror. Djugashvili hero-worshipped Lenin: 'my mountain eagle'. Later he adopted the name Stalin.

Nicky's interior minister Vyacheslav von Plehve suggested that 'What this country needs is a short, victorious war to stem the tide of revolution.'* Many politicians wish for a 'short, victorious war', but few are granted. Nicholas was sure that he was close to securing Manchuria and Korea.

The crisis was watched from Washington, DC, by a new president. In September 1901, speaking in Buffalo, President McKinley was shot by an anarchist. Vice-President Roosevelt, holidaying in Vermont, visited the recovering McKinley in hospital, then returned to the Adirondacks. Then suddenly McKinley deteriorated. Roosevelt was president.

DU BOIS, WASHINGTON AND ROOSEVELT

This bumptious show-off was a new sort of president, revelling in the plenitude and spectacle of growing American power, presenting the presidency as a guide to the nation, lecturing from his 'bully pulpit' with the moral confidence possessed only by those of inherited grandeur.

He ruled through his intimates, known as the Tennis Cabinet.

---

* Plehve's nationalist agitations contributed to a new spasm of anti-Jewish pogroms, starting on Easter Day 1903 in Kishinev (Moldova), which encouraged more Jews to emigrate. Plehve was assassinated, but among those leaving fast was a Jewish dentist, Max Jaffe, and his son Henry, who left Vilnius, buying tickets for New York. A few days later, they landed in Ireland. When they grumbled, it turned out they had bought tickets for New Cork. They settled in Limerick in a neighbourhood known as Little Jerusalem until January 1903, when a local priest, Father Creagh, incited local peasants to attack the Jews, most of whom left for England. Henry Jaffe was a grandfather of this author.

Meanwhile, the family became celebrities, widely photographed. Teddy insisted on family games and hikes, on which they chanted, 'Over, under, through but never around!' His bear hunting even spawned a toy: the Teddy Bear. But he struggled to control his wild, vivacious eldest daughter Alice, who danced late, smoked, flirted and wore a snake around her neck. He tried to channel her exuberance by sending her on a trip to China and Japan, during which she met Empress Cixi but caused further scandal by flirting with a congressman, Nicholas Longworth. Even though she later married Longworth, Roosevelt was exasperated.

Alice grumbled that her father 'wants to be the bride at every wedding, the corpse at every funeral, and the baby at every christening', while he exclaimed, 'I can do one of two things: I can be president . . . or I can control Alice. I can't possibly do both.'

Roosevelt turned on the overmighty trusts, the first president to believe that the state had to limit the power of monopolies. 'Of all forms of tyranny,' said Teddy, 'the least attractive and most vulgar is the tyranny of mere wealth.' He rightly believed that it was the state's duty to limit the plutocracy. 'Like all Americans I like big things,' he said, 'big prairies . . . wheatfields, railways, factories, steamboats. But . . . no people were ever yet benefited by riches if their prosperity corrupted their morals.' The president, assisted by his attorney-general Charlie Bonaparte,* struck at Rockefeller, forcing the break-up of Standard Oil, along with banks, railways and tobacco trusts.

Yet Roosevelt's most enduring achievement was a giant step forward in public health that saved millions of lives not just in America. Pharmacies still sold a selection of semi-poisonous snake-oil potions as medicines, many of them containing generous portions of arsenic, cocaine, heroin. In 1906, encouraged by socialist activists and doctors, Roosevelt created a national agency to enforce standards of medicine and food, work which demonstrated that scientific discoveries were essential in the saving of lives, yet useless without the leaders, organizers and activists who could actually deliver the improvements to the people. In 1863, a French scientist, Louis Pasteur, experimenting in his Lille laboratory, had discovered the bacterium that caused wine to spoil. When he expanded his experiments to milk, he found it could be made safe by heating – a revolutionary discovery. Yet it took forty years for pasteurization to save lives.

For decades, thousands of children had died after being poisoned by

---

* Crookbuster Charlie, who founded the Bureau of Investigation (the future FBI), was the grandson of King Jérôme and great-nephew of Emperor Napoleon.

'swill milk', produced by cows which had been fed the waste created by distilling grain to make whisky. Poisonous milk went on killing until Nathan Straus, Jewish owner of Macy's department stores, started to pasteurize milk and sell it cheaply to the poor. Roosevelt backed Straus and ordered an investigation that led to the endorsement of pasteurization. It was a similar story with other life-saving discoveries.* But he was less bold in taking on racism.

Soon after becoming president, Roosevelt invited the black leader Booker T. Washington to dinner with his family in the White House – the first such occasion. Washington, born a slave, head of Tuskegee College in Alabama, backed by white millionaires, was a revered moderate who had proposed the Atlanta Compromise that southern black people should leave politics to whites in return for education and legal equality, acquiescing in Jim Crow. He supported a cohort of black businessmen, led by Ottawa W. Gurley, son of Alabama slaves, who moved to Greenwood, a section of Tulsa, Oklahoma, to build what Washington called 'Negro Wall Street'. Gurley built the Gurley Hotel, developed property and became the first black millionaire. But he was an exception: the Jim Crow laws still imposed segregation and removed the black right to vote across the south.

The invitation to Washington outraged southerners. The White House, fulminated James Vardaman, soon to be Mississippi governor, was now 'so saturated with the odor of the n***** that the rats have

---

* In 1882, a German professor in Berlin, Robert Koch, had discovered that tuberculosis, one of the biggest killer diseases, was caused by a bacterium, often passed to humans in milk. Koch was building on Pasteur's work. Koch also discovered the bacterium that causes cholera. Germ theory changed the world – since, along with the development of anaesthesia and anti-septis and sterilized equipment, it enabled the development of invasive surgery for the first time. Yet it was widely questioned. It was a young Jewish Russian microbiologist, Waldemar Haffkine, born Vladmir Chavkin in Berdiansk, trained in Odessa, who was the first to create and use vaccines against cholera and the plague. When the pogroms started in 1881, Haffkine, aged twenty-one, helped defend Jews in Odessa but was wounded and arrested, before being released with the help of his professor. Escaping antisemitism and joining the Pasteur Institute, he tested his vaccines on himself. Frequent epidemics in India led him to start his programmes there. In 1896 Bombay suffered a bubonic outbreak, spread from Chinese ports in an outbreak exacerbated by the Taiping Rebellion via Hong Kong, where Alexandre Yersin finally discovered the plague organism. The plague killed over ten million Indians as the British tried to control it. Haffkine ultimately vaccinated millions of people and helped wipe out these diseases. In 1902, a contaminated vial led to nineteen deaths, which prompted accusations of misconduct in an atmosphere of antisemitism and he was dismissed. But the accusations were disproven and he returned to work in India. His Haffkine Institute is Mumbai's main bacteriology research centre and he appeared on Indian stamps. Yet pasteurization was not fully accepted in the US until 1915, while the anti-TB Bacillus Calmette–Guérin (BCG) vaccine was not used until 1921 – forty years after Koch's discovery.

taken refuge in the stable'. Roosevelt trod timidly. 'The very fact,' he
admitted, 'I felt a moment's qualm on inviting him made me ashamed
of myself,' but he did not repeat it.

Washington's compromise was attacked by his ex-supporter, the visionary polymath W. E. B. Du Bois, the first African-American to earn a
doctorate from Harvard, who had then studied in Berlin. In his twenties
Du Bois had investigated the high death rates from TB of poor African-
Americans in Philadelphia, revealing that their mortality – people of
colour were likely to die fifteen years earlier than white people – was
thanks to the way they were directed to live in the least sanitary districts.

Publishing his *Souls of Black Folk*, a sociological study of the
African-American experience, he denounced Washington as 'the great
accommodator' and, at Niagara, launched a counter-attack, campaigning against not just the Jim Crow laws but also what he later called the
invisible 'color-line', the 'veil' that African-Americans felt they had to
wear and the 'double-consciousness' they were forced to adopt.* Yet the
lynchings continued, and when whites in Brownsville, Texas, framed
black soldiers, Roosevelt unjustly dismissed 167 of them.

He was braver abroad. 'I've always been fond of the West African
proverb,' he said. '"Speak softly and carry a big stick; you will go far."'
He took control of the building of the Panama Canal, and saw an opportunity in the crisis between Russia and Japan.

On 8 February 1904, the Japanese fleet under Admiral Togo Hei-
hachiro launched a surprise attack on the Russian naval base at Port
Arthur, besieging the city, as other Japanese forces seized Korea and
then attacked Russian troops in Manchuria. The Japanese had been
facilitated by their ally Britain, so suspicious of Russian threats to India
that British forces were mustering to invade Tibet.† Initially, Marquess
Ito, who had been premier four times, had supported a compromise

---

* Du Bois invented the idea of 'white supremacy', proposing that the word coloured rather
than black be used to describe 'dark-skinned people everywhere', and later he expanded his
campaign to support black women.
† Nicky's obsession with a Russian empire in east Asia alarmed the British viceroy of India,
George Curzon, an unusual Etonian grandee who had travelled through Iran and central
Asia. Just before the Japanese attacked Russia, Curzon dispatched a punitive expedition,
3,000 mainly Sikh and Pathan troops under Colonel Francis Younghusband, to secure
Tibet against Romanov interference. On 31 March 1904, Tibetan troops, armed only with
muskets, blocked the invasion, at which Younghusband open fire with his Maxims: 'I got
so sick of the slaughter that I ceased fire, though the general's order was to make as big a
bag as possible,' recalled the commander of the Maxims. 'I hope I shall never again have to
shoot down men walking away.' As the ruling Dalai Lama fled to Mongolia, Younghusband
took Lhasa. Tibet agreed to become a British protectorate. Yet it was unnecessary. The
Japanese war ended Russian ambitions in east Asia.

with Russia and travelled to Petersburg to negotiate, but the tsar's feckless arrogance convinced the *genro* – grandees who had become oligarchs – to go to war. A young Japanese prince, Hirohito, watched the drama. His grandfather, Meiji the Great, now fifty-one, was far from a warm paterfamilias for Hirohito and his brother Chichibu, receiving them in military uniform standing to attention. 'Never did I experience the warm unqualified love an ordinary grandfather gives his grandchildren,' declared Chichibu.

'There will be no war,' repeated Nicholas. He was at the theatre when he learned he was wrong. He rushed troops along the Trans-Siberian, but they arrived far too slowly and their command was chaotic, while the Japanese were well organized. Port Arthur surrendered after a siege, Admiral Togo routed the Russian fleet in the Yellow Sea, and the Russians were defeated at Mukden. The quick war to avoid revolution caused one: by spring 1905, the tsar had lost control of Poland, the Caucasus and the Baltics. Soon after the exciting birth of an heir, Alexei, Nicholas desperately ordered his Baltic Fleet to embark on a global voyage through the English Channel, around Africa, across the Indian Ocean to defeat the Japanese. Instead in May at Tsushima the Japanese annihilated it, sinking eight Russian battleships, killing 5,000 sailors. Even though the Russian army was unbroken and only approaching full strength in Manchuria, Nicholas's reputation and Romanov prestige sank with his ships.

Roosevelt offered to mediate. In August 1905, he welcomed Russian and Japanese delegates but found the negotiations tortuous. 'The more I see of the tsar, the kaiser and the mikado,' said Roosevelt, 'the better I am content with democracy.' He had initially leaned towards the underdog Japanese, but he gradually grasped that Japan was a coming threat. Nicholas was forced to give up Port Arthur, evacuate Manchuria and recognize Japanese control of Korea. The peace deal 'is a mighty good thing for Russia and for Japan', exulted Roosevelt, 'and for me!'

On St Patrick's Day 1905, he attended the wedding of his niece, Eleanor, to their ambitious cousin, Franklin Roosevelt. 'Well, Franklin,' said the president, 'there's nothing like keeping it in the family.'

FRANKLIN, ELEANOR AND HIROHITO

They were an unexpected couple. Eleanor had endured a miserable childhood, half abandoned in the madhouse of a drunk, demented uncle. Her father Elliott, the president's brother, was a violent alcoholic who called her Little Nell; her mother, who had died young, called her Granny, while the president's wife just said, 'Poor little soul, she's very plain.'

It was only when Eleanor studied in London that she discovered herself. Home-schooled then educated at Groton and Harvard, Franklin was the opposite, genial and urbane, athletic and exuberant with a leonine head and dazzling smile but very precious and spoilt. He had grown up a Little Lord Fauntleroy, adored by his father – Squire James who died in 1900 – and his forceful mother Sara, who gave him absolute confidence. But his mother loathed Eleanor, who in turn worried, 'I'll never be able to hold him. He's too attractive.' Although she thought sex 'an ordeal to be endured', six children followed. Franklin's choice of bride partly reflected his hero-worship of Teddy: he too dreamed of being president.

Teddy rashly promised that he would follow Washingtonian tradition and not run for a third term, so when he left the White House in 1908 he was just fifty – and set off to hunt big game and travel in Latin America. It was a decision that he would bitterly regret, and that his cousin Franklin would cheerfully avoid. It was Franklin who would cope with the aggressive Japan created by its Russian victory.

Young Hirohito was tutored by the war heroes General Nogi and Admiral Togo. In 1907, Meiji signed General Military Ordinance No. 1 granting the military 'the authority to act independently of the cabinet' while laying down that the guiding rule of policy would be 'the rights and interests we planted in Manchuria and Korea'.* In 1912 when Meiji died and his sickly son succeeded, Hirohito's tutor Nogi and his wife bowed to portraits of the *tenno*, then she stabbed herself in the neck and he disembowelled himself. Ritual suicide, until recently regarded as medieval, was again fashionable in Japan's new war cult.

In October 1905, the rolling revolution forced Tsar Nicholas to concede a constitution. His adored heir Alexei turned out to have haemophilia, making his early death likely, a secret that Nicholas and Alexandra struggled to bear. Their pain was eased by a mystical Siberian, Grigori Rasputin, whose peasant simplicity, religious conviction and tsarist devotion restored their confidence. While determined to

---

* In 1910 Japan annexed Korea altogether, declaring 'enlightened administration' while suppressing the rising resistance. Many Koreans escaped Japanese oppression by crossing the border into China's northern province of Manchuria. Among them were a couple of Korean Presbyterians, Kim Hyong-jik and Kang Pan-sok, with their eight-year-old son, Kim Song-ju, who would in his teens join an anti-imperialist organization and later converted to Communism using the name Kim Il-sung. His grandson still rules North Korea into the 2020s.

claw back autocracy to hand over to his son, besieged in his palaces as terrorism and chaos stalked the empire, Nicholas had retained the loyalty of his army. Now, he presided over a bloody reconquest of his own empire, and his gleeful rival, Wilhelm, saw a chance to force the tsar into a world-changing alliance.

Relishing the eclipse of Russia, Willy invited Nicky to meet on their yachts in the Baltic. Still advised by Phili, Willy was at his zenith, appointing Eulenburg's insinuating protégé, Bernhard von Bülow, as chancellor. 'Since I have Bülow,' Willy told Phili, whom he raised to prince and ambassador in Vienna, 'I can sleep peacefully.' Bülow was not nicknamed the Eel for nothing, flirting with Phili as much as he flattered Willy.*

After a rebellion by Herero, Nama and San peoples in South West Africa, Willy encouraged his commander, Lothar von Trotha, to pursue genocide. 'I believe the nation should be eliminated,' said Trotha. The exact numbers are unknown, but from October 1904 as many as 60,000 men, women and children were slaughtered, a decision approved by Alfred von Schlieffen, the elderly chief of staff. 'Racial war,' Schlieffen said, 'once commenced, can only be ended by annihilation or the complete enslavement of one party.' But he was also working on a plan for a European war.

On their yachts in the Baltic, Willy bamboozled the tsar into an alliance that contradicted Russia's French alliance. Afterwards, Nicky was forced to cancel it. Willy's aggressive fleet building – he planned a home fleet of sixty battleships by 1918 – backfired, provoking Britain into intensifying the construction of its Dreadnought battleships and moving towards France, just six years after the two countries had almost gone to war over Fashoda. In 1904, that urbane Francophile Edward VII encouraged an *entente cordiale*, soon militarized with secret clauses aimed at Germany.

Schlieffen believed the only way Germany could win a European war was to smash France, possibly crashing through neutral Belgium, while holding off Russia. Schlieffen's plan became even more essential and yet risky when in August 1907 Britain and Russia signed an alliance, ending a half-century of central Asian rivalry. Willy's failures had achieved the envelopment of Germany.

Yet there was no need for war. The German economy, driven by steel

---

* In 1901, Phili introduced Willy to a racist disciple of Gobineau, Houston Stewart Chamberlain, son-in-law of Wagner, who preached racial superiority: 'If we don't decide to think resolutely' about 'our utterly Jew-ridden artistic life, our Germanic species will be lost'.

and chemicals, was set to overtake Britain and dominate Europe.* It was only in Wilhelm's strutting court that men oscillated bewilderingly between war fever and enervation, fearful of challenges from other nations and races – most urgently the Slavic Russians. In the great republic of America, Teddy Roosevelt believed that 'No triumph of peace is quite so great as the supreme triumphs of war' – that was how great statesmen were made. In Vienna, Constantinople and St Petersburg, leaders were convinced that only war could reinvigorate senescent dynasties; in Belgrade, Athens and Sofia, thrusting new nations were convinced war would deliver new empires; even in the democracies, men trained jovially in military brigades for a coming conflict. When it came it would destroy the dynasties it was designed to save and, out of blood, dynamite and mud, remould the family, in power, at work and at home.

In Berlin the crisis of masculinity was exacerbated by scandals at the apex of the kaiser's macho war machine.

---

* Germany was especially advanced in chemicals, now linked to medicine and agriculture. In 1897, a single German chemist, working at a dye-manufacturing company, Bayer, in Elberfeld, created two of the essential drugs of modern life: that August, Felix Hoffman, twenty-nine, synthesized an ancient pain-killing tonic, salicin, extracted from willow tree bark, to produce aspirin, the antipyretic, anti-inflammatory, analgesic drug that enriched Bayer and conquered the world. He also synthesized diamorphine to create a less addictive version of morphine, which he called heroin after *heroisch* – 'heroic' – for its euphoric effects. (Heroin was marketed as a cough mixture until after the First World War and was only banned in the USA in 1924.) In 1907, Paul Erlich, a German-Jewish associate of Koch, seeking what he called a 'magic bullet' that killed a bacterium but not other cells, discovered that synthetic compounds could cure first sleeping sickness and then syphilis; he teamed up with the chemical conglomerate Hoechst to mass-produce the first synthetic antibiotics. In 1908, the German-Jewish chemist Fritz Haber created ammonium nitrate to replace natural nitrates such as guano for use as fertilizers. The chemical magnate Carl Bosch developed the Haber–Bosch process to manufacture a substance that helped intensify modern farming and enable it to feed billions. This truly was an intense agro-revolution that improved nutrition and, combined with better healthcare, cleaner water, vaccination, electricity, refrigeration and petrol engines, powered an exponential rise in population. It is believed food production increased eighteen-fold, mostly after 1900. In 1800 there were 900 million on earth; by 1900, there were 1.65 billion – and it went on rising: in 2022, there were 8 billion. The growth in cities, particularly those in the English-speaking world, was remarkable. In 1890, London and New York were the two clear million-peopled cities, though Chicago was close behind. By 1920, there were twenty million-plus mega-cities; fifty-one by 1940; and 226 by 1985.

It is estimated that the Haber–Bosch process helps generate a third of global food production, which in turn feeds around three billion people. Yet these same life-giving chemicals were also essential for killing. The fertilizers were used in manufacturing explosives; Haber developed chlorine used as a weapon in the First World War; Bosch went on to head the BASF chemicals group and in 1925 founded IG Farben, a new conglomerate that also merged with Mayer and which later manufactured Zyklon-B, the gas used to murder Jews during the Holocaust. Such are the multiple possibilities of science.

ACT NINETEEN
1.6 BILLION

Hohenzollerns, Krupps, Ottomans, *Tennos* and Songs

It started with Friedrich Krupp, son of the great cannoneer, Wilhelm's partner in the arming of his forces and the building of his ships, *Meister* of 50,000 workers at Essen. Krupp was married with children, but he spent much of his time enjoying a promiscuous gay life at Capri and in Berlin hotels. In Germany, as in every other European country, homosexuality was illegal and could be prosecuted under the Criminal Code's inhumane paragraph 175. It was also taboo in this macho Pietist society, leaving gays vulnerable to both arrest and blackmail.

When the socialist press started to spread rumours, Wilhelm advised Krupp to avoid Capri, but then the *Meister*'s wife, Margarethe, received anonymous letters and photographs revealing Krupp's orgies. She appealed to the kaiser and tried to seize the company. Instead the kaiser colluded in her confinement in a lunatic asylum, Krupp thanking him for 'the kind and gentle way in which Your Majesty intervened on my behalf'. In November 1902, socialist journalists exposed 'Krupp on Capri', naming a young barber as his lover. A week later Krupp committed suicide. The kaiser, having been assured that Krupp was 'asexual' even if he had 'an exceptionally soft' nature, attended the funeral of this 'truly German man', attacked the socialists and then, recognizing the Krupp dynasty as a strategic asset, presided over the succession. Krupp had left two daughters: the fourteen-year-old Bertha was the sole heir. Wilhelm chose her husband, Gustav von Bohlen und Halbach, a diplomat, who on their marriage in 1907 assumed the name Krupp and proved a skilful magnate, providing the guns for the First World War – nicknamed Big Berthas by the troops – and then embracing Hitler.

In 1907, a socialist journalist aided by an embittered bureaucrat in the Foreign Ministry exposed an aristocratic homosexual circle, led by 'the Harpist' (Eulenburg) and his lover 'Sweetie', General Kuno 'Tutu' von Moltke. As Princess Eulenburg understood, 'They are striking at my husband, but their target is the kaiser.' Willy ordered his friends to sue for libel. In October 1907, Moltke launched the first of seven court cases that unveiled a secret realm of saucy nicknames, fabulous costumes, secret power and sexual assignations with a cast of grandees, waiters and fishermen. Advised by the chief of his Military Cabinet, General Dietrich von Hülsen-Haeseler, a harsh critic of Phili's camarilla, the kaiser dismissed Moltke and dropped Phili, who had introduced him to 'gentlemen of dishonourable reputation'. Phili collapsed and was then arrested. Another journalist alleged that Chancellor 'the Eel' von Bülow, though married, was a secret homosexual, nicknamed Concettina in their coterie, and had appointed his young lover to the Privy Council.

Willy had a nervous collapse. While recovering with friends in England, he gave a provocative interview which would almost destroy him. At home his anachronistic hatred for the elected politicians, unions and press, indeed for much of the modern world, combined with the louche Phili scandal, undermined his supremacy – just as tensions rose in the Balkans.

Germany's ally, Austria, struggling to control its restless Slavs, was challenged by Serbia under its pro-Russian king Peter Karađorđević,* guided by a nationalist public and a secret coterie of powerful irredentists who dreamed of a greater Serbia carved out of Habsburg territory. Willy's friend Franz Ferdinand regarded Serbia as an existential threat, but now Tsar Nicholas started to back the Serbs.

If there was an answer to this conundrum it was to be found in Vienna, where after fifty years on the throne the antique emperor, Franz Josef, still went about his usual routine. He 'still stands upright', wrote his daughter Valerie, 'a simple and just man', after so many tragedies and defeats.

In September 1898, Empress Sisi was getting off a ferry in Geneva when a passer-by brushed against her. She fell but got up again and walked 100 yards chatting. 'What did that man want?' she asked a courtier. 'Perhaps he wanted to take my watch?' Then she suddenly gasped,

---

* Serbia was dominated by the two rival dynasties, Obrenovići and Karađorđevići. King Alexander Obrenović had been hated for his pro-Austrian policy and for divorcing his popular queen to marry Draga, an experienced engineer's widow twelve years older than him. An officer codenamed Apis founded a secret organization, the Black Hand, that decided to kill the king. Apis was Dragutin Dimitrijević, bald, muscle-bound and bullish (his codename was the Egyptian bull-god), who on 11 June 1903 stormed the palace and, finding Alexander and Draga hiding in a cupboard, shot them and then mutilated their bodies, cutting off her breasts and tossing them out of the windows into a heap of manure. Apis installed the Black George family as kings and would play a special role in the tragedy of the First World War.

'Oh no, what's happened to me now?' and collapsed. An anarchist had stabbed her in the heart with an iron file. 'How can you kill a woman who's never hurt anyone?' asked Franz Josef. 'You don't know how much I loved this woman.'

As this bowed, grey, bewhiskered monarch grieved, Franz Ferdinand sought a solution while all around their booted, braided and epauletted Habsburg court – the dullest in Europe – seethed Vienna, the most exciting city, a laboratory for the ideas of race, revolution and art that made the twentieth century.

VIENNA: FRANZI, FREUD, KLIMT, HITLER AND OTHER ARTISTS

The feeling that the empire was ending gave the city a nervy, feverish, almost sexual charge, expressed by writers, doctors and artists, many of them Jewish.

A Galician Jewish doctor, Sigmund Freud, son of a wool merchant, was both typical and exceptional. Adored by his mother, highly educated and multilingual, Freud first studied the effects of cocaine, almost losing himself to coke addiction before he settled for cigar smoking. In 1886, now married to a rabbi's granddaughter and father of a family, he set up a private practice specializing in nervous disorders, treating a patient suffering from mysterious ailments, 'Anna O' (actually a wealthy Jewish feminist named Bertha Pappenheim), by encouraging her to discuss sexually charged incidents from her childhood that eased her neurotic symptoms, a process he called 'psychoanalysis' which ultimately changed the consciousness of the twentieth century. His *Interpretation of Dreams*, published in 1899, argued that a subconscious coexisted with the conscious. He followed that up with the idea that character, governed by the libido and the death drive, was formed by psychosexual experiences in childhood. In particular, he identified the Oedipus complex of paternal hatred and maternal attraction, along with castration anxiety for boys, penis envy for girls.

Just as Freud was first publishing on dreams, another Jewish doctor, Arthur Schnitzler, son of a Hungarian throat surgeon, who knew Freud, was writing *La Ronde*, which, starting and ending with a prostitute, told the story of ten sexual liaisons in decadent Vienna. Schnitzler was accused of writing pornography, but replied, 'I write about love and death. What other subjects are there?' Working in the War Ministry's archive, an aspiring writer, son of a Jewish banker, Stefan Zweig, a committed cosmopolitan who in a cosmopolis glowing with rabid racism and universalist liberalism disdained all sides, wrote in his autobiography *The World of Yesterday*, 'From the start, I was sure in my heart of my identity as a citizen of the world.' Son of an Austrian gold-engraver, Gustav Klimt painted seething erotic paintings *The Kiss* and *Woman in Gold*, agleam with gold leaf, depicting his lover Adele Bloch-Bauer, a Jewish financier's daughter married to an older banker. Klimt became famous, but many aspiring artists were penniless.

The Austrian official's son Adolf Hitler wanted to study art at the Vienna Academy of Arts but, twice failing to win a place, he moved to the city in 1907 aged eighteen, living in a bed-and-breakfast, reading in bed – 'books were his whole world' – about Frederick the Great and Germanic mythology, and attending Wagner operas.

That December, Hitler was poleaxed by the death of his forty-seven-year-old mother, Klara, from cancer. He kept her portrait in his pocket and a painting of her in his room until his own death. He was grateful to the Jewish doctor who cared for her, promising he would never forget; much later, Dr Bloch was the only Jew he protected. For a while he lived cushily on his mother's inheritance. When her money ran out, he lived in workers' hostels, doing menial work and lived by selling his sketches on postcards, all the while observing the tensions between Germans, Jewish bourgeoisie and Slavs.

The native Viennese were almost overwhelmed by a deluge of immigrant Czechs, Jews and Poles. Between 1880 and 1910, the city's population doubled; a fifth of the inhabitants were Czech, while 8.7 per cent were Jewish, higher than in any other European city. A new German nationalism targeting these immigrants was rallied by 'Handsome Karl' Lueger, the long-serving mayor who horrified Franz Josef with his vulgar racism: the Habsburgs were the only dynasty whose multi-ethnic empire meant they could not embrace nationalism. 'Vienna mustn't become Jerusalem!' said Lueger. Yet he joked, 'I decide who's a Jew,' adding, 'Some of my best friends are Jewish.'

Young Hitler respected Handsome Karl, whom he recalled as 'an excellent speaker', but he particularly admired Georg Ritter von Schönerer, aristocratic Führer (leader) of an antisemitic, anti-Catholic movement who favoured the Roman salute. Hitler often watched debates in the Imperial Council, disgusted by the jabbering Slavic parliamentarians, and noticed the senescent Emperor Franz Josef conveyed in his carriage between palaces.

In the same streets and cafés, Josef Djugashvili, the Georgian Bolshevik, nicknamed Koba, was living in a boarding house next to

Schönbrunn, working on an article for Lenin about the nationalities of the Russian empire. Djugashvili, a student priest, failed poet, prolific lover and handsome if pockmarked loner with a withered arm and hazel-coloured eyes, was a fanatical Marxist who had spent years in Siberian exile, frequently escaping. The tsar's secret police, the Okhranka, the only efficient organization in the Russian empire, had smashed the revolutionaries, sending many to Siberia and even more into exile.

In late 1912, Djugashvili went to visit Lenin in Kraków, in Habsburg Galicia. In his Bolshevik faction, filled with garrulous windbags whom he called 'the tea-drinkers', Lenin appreciated the toughness of Djugashvili and his brigands. He funded his Party by ordering Koba to raid banks: in June 1907, in Tiflis, Djugashvili had pulled off a spectacular (but bloody) heist. Lenin praised this 'wonderful Georgian' as 'exactly the type we need'. For his Viennese article, Djugashvili chose a new name, emulating Lenin, by adopting a proletarian pseudonym: Stalin – Steelman. While in Vienna, he met a bouffant-haired, barrel-chested Marxist journalist, a glamorous if arrogant hero of 1905, Leon Trotsky, son of a rich Jewish farmer in Ukraine. The two hated each other on sight. Neither of them met Hitler.

Down the road, in his gorgeous Belvedere Palace, Franz Ferdinand sought a creative solution to the Slavic problem. In 1906, he promoted a new chief of staff, Franz Conrad von Hötzendorf, who was equally obsessed with destroying the Serbs and annexing Bosnia to save the empire. But the tsar and his nationalistic public supported their fellow Orthodox Slavs. Both worm-eaten empires looked to ferocious and uncontrollable Balkan nations to bolster their obsolescent swagger.

In September 1908, Franz Ferdinand orchestrated a deal with Russia that bypassed Serbia: if Russia got a free hand over the Straits of Constantinople, Bulgaria, also a Russian protégé, would become independent,* and Austria would annex Bosnia. Franz Ferdinand boasted to Willy that 'he was involved in it everywhere. Its driving force.' A month later, Franz Josef announced the annexation of Bosnia, at which Russian Slavophiles, outraged by the betrayal of Serbia, forced Nicholas to deny the pact. Serbia threatened war, backed by Russia, forcing the Habsburgs to appeal to their ally, Kaiser Wilhelm. 'I stand by you,' Willy

* Thanks to the Bosnia deal, the Bulgarian prince Ferdinand declared himself tsar. Chosen in consultation with Russia, Ferdinand of Saxe-Coburg was mocked in the family for his long proboscis (Willy called him the Nose), effete eccentricity and open bisexuality. When he was chosen as prince in 1887 aged twenty-six, Queen Victoria thought this 'should be stopped at once' since he was 'totally unfit . . . delicate, eccentric and effeminate', but 'Foxy' Ferdinand turned out to be shrewd. Wilhelm loathed the Nose, almost causing a diplomatic incident by smacking him on the bottom at a family wedding.

promised Franzi, 'through thick and thin.' Europe was close to war.

In late October, the London *Daily Telegraph* published the kaiser's outrageous interview, given months earlier, assuring the British that his fleet was aimed at the Yellow Peril and claiming that he had protected the British, who were 'mad as March hares'. Britain was alarmed by Wilhelm, and at home his rule was threatened; he sacked 'traitor' Bülow and promoted the steady Theobald von Bethmann Hollweg. The kaiser not only backed the Habsburgs but encouraged war: 'Get on with it!'

In November, Willy went shooting with 'dear Franzi' and then on to a hunting party given by his new best friend, the Austro-German Prince Max von Fürstenberg, at Donaueschingen Castle. There, as everyone was having cocktails before dinner, General Count von Hülsen, the strapping moustachioed chief of the kaiser's Military Cabinet, emerged wearing a bright-pink ball dress belonging to their hostess and a hat decked with ostrich feathers. As a witness recalled, he was 'dancing gracefully to the music, holding a fan coquettishly in his hand. Rewarded with resounding applause, stepping backwards throwing kisses to the ladies,' he retired – then collapsed. 'The man who had just been so full of the joys of life – dead! And by his head stood the Kaiser, by the body of the man who had been closer to him than any other.' While this flamboyant death was being hushed up, Russia threatened to back Serbia. At this, in February 1909, Wilhelm warned France that 'In the event of Russian's intervention against Austria, the *casus foederis* [triggering a treaty obligation] arises for us immediately: mobilization.' Facing war with Germany and a European conflict, Nicky, weakened by revolution, blinked. 'The role Germany's played is odious and disgusting,' he told his mother. 'We won't forget it.' Willy and Franzi were elated at Russia's retreat. 'It was a real pleasure to me to be a good second to you for once,' Willy told his friend. 'A wonderful trial-run for the showdown.'

A sense of desperation and of diminishing time encouraged extreme solutions. Reclaiming his autocratic powers, Nicholas rebuilt his army; next time he would have to fight. In Belgrade, Apis sought a way to accelerate Serbian resurgence. In Constantinople, Ottoman officers sought to halt the dismemberment of their empire. In Thessalonica, a cosmopolitan Ottoman city, home to 90,000 Jews, soldiers backed by merchants of an abstruse religious minority* joined a secret Com-

---

* The Dönme were a heretical sect which, fusing Muslim and Jewish rituals, believed that a seventeenth-century messianic Jewish mystic, Sabbatai Zevi, was indeed the messiah. Accepted by neither Jews nor Muslims, the Dönme had become wealthy textile merchants in Thessalonica, where many of the Young Turks – including the future rulers Enver, Talaat and Kemal (Atatürk) – were based.

mittee of Union and Progress – Young Turks – that took over the Third Army and forced Abdulhamid to accept a parliament. The last Ottoman autocrat abdicated; a parliament was elected; a passive sixty-five-year-old Ottoman, Mehmed V, was enthroned. Among the Young Turks, a dashing young officer, Enver Bey, disdained democracy: only war could restore empire. As Mehmed clutched at the reins of power, another decaying empire was losing its veteran monarch: that November, Empress Cixi realized she was dying and reached for the arsenic.

I WANT NANNY: THE BABY EMPEROR, DR SUN YAT-SEN AND THE SONG SISTERS

First Cixi ordered the poisoning of her nephew Emperor Guangxu,* then she sent eunuchs to seize without warning the Manchu toddler Prince Puyi, two-year-old son of Prince Chun, taking him away from his mother (whom he did not see again for seven years) and, with the child screaming, convey him by palanquin to the empress. 'I remember suddenly finding myself surrounded by strangers,' wrote Puyi, 'while before me was hung a drab curtain through which I could see an emaciated, terrifying, hideous face. This was Cixi. I burst into loud howls. Cixi told someone to give me some sweets, but I threw them on the floor.'

'I want nanny,' shouted Puyi.

'What a naughty child,' said Cixi. 'Take him away.'

Two weeks after her death, in the Hall of Supreme Harmony, Piyu, terrified by the drums and music, sobbed all the way through his coronation as Xuantong Emperor. 'Don't cry,' said his father, Regent Chun. 'It'll be over soon.' Xuantong grew up into a capricious hell-child – 'Flogging eunuchs was part of my daily routine,' he later admitted, and he fired his airgun at courtiers.

That tireless hatcher of conspiracies Dr Sun Yat-sen, now forty-four, determined 'to expel the Tatar barbarians [Manchus], revive China, establish a republic and distribute land equally', watched this from his exile. He had travelled for a decade, seeking backers and ideologies to help win him power in China. At one point the government trapped him in the London embassy, and he was about to be sent home for beheading when a press outcry forced his release. He had launched at least seven failed revolutions and, on 10 October 1911, he was in the

---

* Forensic tests on his body were carried out in 2008, revealing 2,000 times the usual amount of arsenic.

USA planning his next when soldiers in Wuhan mutinied. The regent sent Cixi's long-serving general Yuan Shikai, appointed prime minister, to crush them, but rebellion spread quickly. Sun rushed home.

In December, revolutionary delegates in Nanjing elected Sun Yat-sen as provisional president of the first Chinese Republic. Arriving in Shanghai, Sun set up headquarters in the mansion of Charlie Song, whose daughters Qingling and Meiling were still studying in America, but the eldest, the twenty-three-year-old Ailing, charmed the new president, who was married with several concubines, all of whom he treated appallingly. Ailing did not reciprocate. And Sun was powerless: he was not the only president of China.

In Beijing, General Yuan Shikai was offered the leadership by the revolutionaries if he deposed the monarchy. On 12 February 1912, he orchestrated Puyi's abdication – the end of 250 years of Manchus and two millennia of emperors – and, as Sun resigned, became president.* Yuan, born into the gentry, lived in a traditional Chinese household with a wife and nine concubines with bound feet, while for his health he drank human milk, delivered by wet nurses. Now this conservative paladin, who disdained Dr Sun as a cosmopolitan amateur, embraced power and its trappings, being escorted around by a corps of giant bodyguards in uniforms trimmed with leopard-skin. A mix of agitators, generals and gangsters seized power. In Shanghai, elegant fulcrum of capitalism and fashion, the criminal Green Gang bestrode business and politics; a revolutionary, Chen Qimei, linked to the gangsters, captured Shanghai for Sun. When Sun was challenged by a former supporter, Chen ordered a henchman to assassinate him. The assassin was a follower of Sun named Chiang Kai-shek, son of a poor family who had been educated in Japan. Chiang would become the ruler of China.

In China's first real elections, forty million voted and Sun's nationalist KMT party won the most seats in a national assembly that now sat in Beijing. Both sides, allied to the criminal gangs, tried to kill each other. Yuan survived one attempt and hired the Green Gang to kill Sun. In March 1913, he murdered Sun's nominee for premier and dismissed the assembly.

Sun fled to Japan, accompanied by Charlie Song, joined by his

---

* Puyi, that vicious toddler-tyrant, went on terrorizing his eunuchs in the Forbidden City. Permitted to live as emperor within the Forbidden City and the Summer Palace, he did not know for some time that he had abdicated. He had been missing maternal affection, but the arrival of an English tutor, Reginald Johnston, who gave him the name Henry, changed his life. The court arranged his marriage to a Manchu princess, Wanrong, which was unhappy but long-lived.

daughters, who became the leader's secretaries. Sun fell in love with Ailing, but when she married someone her own age, he moved on to his new assistant, the middle sister, Qingling, fresh from Wellesley College, Massachusetts: 'I just can't get Qingling out of my head,' he confessed. 'I have encountered love for the first time.' Qingling flirted, warning him she might marry President Yuan and 'be an empress'. Sun appealed to her father, who stated pointedly, 'We're a Christian family; no daughter will become anybody's concubine, king, emperor or president.' But Qingling, aged twenty-one, started an affair with the fifty-year-old Sun, her 'Big Busy Man'. They eloped to Tokyo and married.

Sun's return looked unlikely as President Yuan dismissed parliament and declared himself emperor.

A FAMILY WEDDING: THREE EMPERORS AND THREE PASHAS

Yet Yuan was not dictator for long. When he died of uraemia, the Central Country splintered into pieces, ruled by three weak governments while real power rested with the warlords and gangsters, led by a man who was a cross between the two. Zhang Zuolin, who called himself the Mukden Tiger, had started as a skinny brigand, nicknamed Pimple, but now he dominated northern China with his own army of 300,000. Taking control of Beijing, he toyed with restoring the Manchu. But they were irrelevant now.*

Yet in Europe the dynasties remained central. In May 1913, the kaiser, babbling about the imminence of war, hosted his cousins Tsar Nicholas II and King-Emperor George V, at the 1,000-guest wedding in Berlin of his only daughter, Viktoria Luise, to Prince Ernst August of Hanover, first cousin to the British and Russian monarchs.

George, a dutiful but splenetic martinet, arrived with Queen Mary, but Nicholas came alone. Georgie and Nicky both wore Prussian Dragoon uniforms with spiked pickelhaube helmets, Willy dressed as a British dragoon with a Russian order; but behind dynastic swagger and sartorial ententes, the three emperors tensely surveyed a quaking Ottoman empire. The trepidation had started in 1911 when Italy, desperate for colonies after its Ethiopian humiliation, seized Tripoli and Benghazi. The Young Turk Enver tried to hold Tripoli, then rushed to defend the

---

* Zhang restored Puyi as emperor for a matter of weeks then deposed him again. In 1924, Puyi was expelled from Beijing and fled to Japanese protection with the empress. Happiest with a male lover, he treated his wife and mistresses cruelly. Wanrong became an opium addict.

Turkish homeland as the hungry new kingdoms of the Balkans – Bulgaria, Romania, Greece, Serbia and Montenegro – joined the carve-up. In this first Balkan war, Bulgarian troops grabbed the most territory.

In January 1913, believing himself to be the Turkish Napoleon, Enver seized power with two comrades, Talaat and Jemal – the Three Pashas – who embraced a toxic mix of Turkish ultra-nationalism, social Darwinism, including eugenics and a hierarchy of racial superiority taught them by their German military instructors, and militaristic warmongering, to save race and empire. They loathed Christian minorities, particularly Armenians and Greeks, and their views were not that different from those later espoused by the Nazis. Enver joined the dynasty, marrying the sultan's daughter.

At the Hohenzollern wedding, 'There was absolute unanimity between George V, the emperor [Nicholas] and me,' Willy boasted to Franz Ferdinand (who was not at the wedding), that the Balkan kingdoms could attack Bulgaria.* The kaiser dragged George's private secretary aside. 'The Slavs have become unrestful and will want to attack Austria,' he predicted ominously. 'Germany is bound to stand by her ally. Russia and France will join in and then England.'

Many in Britain were convinced that war was now inevitable. The Liberal chancellor, David Lloyd George, a self-made silver-tongued lawyer known as the Welsh Wizard (as a priapic dynamo he was also nicknamed the Goat), had delighted in baiting and taxing the aristocracy to fund social welfare for the working classes, but now he warned that Britain would fight if peace became 'a humiliation intolerable for a great country'. His friend Winston Churchill, aged thirty-seven, newly appointed first lord of the Admiralty, ordered four more battleships 'to prepare for an attack by Germany as if it might come the next day', and made a key decision: he converted the navy from coal to oil, purchasing 51 per cent of a company, Anglo-Persian Oil, that had struck oil four years earlier. Iran, ruled by the Qajar shahs, recently weakened by a revolution, became vital to British power, as the possession of oil now became essential to great powers. 'Mastery itself,' declared Churchill, 'was the prize.'

Even in his wedding toast, Wilhelm could not resist combining family with race. 'My darling daughter, I want to thank you from the bottom of my heart for all the joy you have given me,' he proclaimed. 'As long as the German tongue is spoken, it will tell of the prominent role played

---

* Greenlighted by the tsar, Greece, Romania and Serbia now attacked Bulgaria; Enver joined in. In this second Balkan war, Bulgaria lost its gains and Enver got back Adrianople (Edirne).

by the Guelphs and Hohenzollerns in the historic development of our fatherland.' At the end of the ball, Nicholas approached the bride. 'I hope,' he said gently, 'you'll be as happy as we have been.'

The three emperors would never meet again. Willy kept close to Franz Ferdinand, writing after the wedding to express 'staunch confidence in you, dear Franzi' and encouraging the Austrian commander, General Conrad, to destroy Serbia. Conrad, chomping at the bit, in 1913 asked twenty-three times to go to war. 'I go along with you!' said Willy, who was infuriated by the glacial slowness of Austrian decision-making, which was still ultimately in the hands of Franz Josef. 'The struggle between Slavs and Germans can no longer be avoided and will surely come,' he raged. 'When? We shall see.'

In mid-June 1914, Wilhelm stayed with Franz Ferdinand at Konopischt Castle, Prague. The kaiser recommended war; if the Austrians 'didn't strike, the position would get worse'. Two days after his return, he told Chancellor Bethmann Hollweg that Russia planned a pre-emptive strike. On 28 June, in Kiel, Willy, accompanied by Gustav Krupp, boarded his yacht *Meteor* to prepare for a race, while Franzi and Sophie headed to Sarajevo to open a museum.

Hohenzollerns, Habsburgs and Hashemites

As they drove through Sarajevo in an open Gräf & Stift Double Phaeton motor car, a Serbian terrorist, Nedeljko Čabrinović, a member of a Serbian hit squad (three of them teenagers, always the best age for terrorists) organized by Colonel Apis, threw a bomb at the car; the driver accelerated to the governor's residence. 'So *that's* how you welcome your guests,' shouted Franzi, '– with bombs!'

Another terrorist, Gavrilo Princip, nineteen years old, waiting with a pistol on another part of the route, realized the attempt had failed and, giving up, decided to eat in a café. At the governor's house, Franzi insisted on visiting those wounded by the bomb. Since it was obvious that there might well be further assassins – after all, Tsar Alexander II had been killed in May 1881 when he survived the first bomb and ignored the possibility of a second – the planned route was changed. But when Franzi and Sophie climbed into the Double Phaeton, the dazed driver mistakenly followed the original itinerary. Backing down a side street to turn, the driver stalled, delivering Franzi and Sophie in front of the very café where Princip sat. Jumping up, he crossed the street, drawing his pistol, and fired, hitting Sophie in the stomach, then Franzi in the neck. As the car restarted, lurched backwards and raced to the town hall, a streak of blood ran down Franzi's cheek.

'For heaven's sake! What happened to you?' Sophie said, then, haemorrhaging internally, fell between his knees.

'Sophie, don't die, darling,' he begged her. 'Live for our children.' His hat fell off and he toppled sideways, but was caught by his adjutant Colonel von Harrach.

'Is Your Imperial Highness suffering very badly?' asked Harrach, trying to unbutton his collar.

'It's nothing,' Franzi repeated. 'It's nothing.' Both of them bled out quickly. When he heard that his unloved nephew was dead, Franz Josef, who had lost two wars and his brother, wife and son to violent deaths, just said, 'One mustn't defy the Almighty.' Then he mused, 'A superior power has restored that order which I unfortunately was unable to maintain.' But how to react to Serbia?

'Do you think we'd better cancel the race?' Willy asked at the Kiel regatta. He rushed to Berlin just as, in Vienna, Franz Josef and General Conrad decided to attack Serbia and the old emperor wrote to Willy asking for support. 'The Serbs need sorting out – and soon,' wrote Willy. 'Now or never.' He immediately told the Austrians, 'We mustn't wait to take action.' Indeed Franz Josef would regret it 'if we don't make use of the present moment'. Impulsive and incoherent, Wilhelm embodied the centre of German decision-making, assisted by Bethmann Hollweg and his neurotic chief of staff, Helmuth von Moltke the younger, who owed his position to his all-conquering uncle. At minimum, they envisioned the liquidation of Serbia; at maximum, a European war to defeat France via the adapted Schlieffen Plan, taking their empire and industrial regions, converting Belgium into a satellite state, breaking up Russia into principalities and establishing Germanic hegemony.

'Military action against Serbia,' Bethmann Hollweg reflected on 6 July, 'could lead to world war.' Although there were arguments about tactics during the exceedingly stressful weeks ahead, there was surprising agreement among the German leaders as well as among their Austrian counterparts that the opportunity must be taken, for honour – which we would now call credibility – but also for cold power. 'It'll be a hopeless struggle,' Conrad confided in his mistress, 'but it must be pursued because so old a monarchy and glorious an army can't go down ingloriously.' Even at the zenith of their military power and righteous superiority, empires are haunted by anxieties about fading potency and imminent decline. These empires were far past noon; it was dusk.

Wilhelm set off on his annual Norwegian cruise in order to provide a diplomatic alibi, telling Krupp, 'This time I shan't topple over.' But in Austria Franz Josef waited at his Alpine schloss at Bad Ischl as ministers and generals in Vienna drafted a brutal ultimatum to Serbia, only to delay it when they realized that the French president Poincaré was in Petersburg visiting his ally Nicholas. They delayed the ultimatum until he was back at sea, a delay that made war more likely. On 23 July, the Habsburg ultimatum was delivered to Serbia, setting off a fatal sequence. In a complex diplomatic matrix conducted mainly by the toneless slow medium of the telegraph (and occasionally, for the first time in world affairs, by telephone), no statesman mastered the consequences or the multifaceted course of the unravelling crisis.

'Ruthlessly and under all circumstances,' Bethmann Hollweg told Wilhelm on 26 July, 'Russia must be made into the source of injustice.' Wilhelm hoped the Russians would blink, but instead Nicky prepared for war. Willy presumed the British would remain neutral, sending his brother Heinrich to see George V at Buckingham Palace. But British monarchs had no authority. On 25 July, Serbia rejected the ultimatum. On the 27th, the kaiser returned to Berlin and met with Bethmann Hollweg, who insisted on waiting for Russian mobilization because 'We must appear to be the ones who are forced to go to war.' On the 30th, Franz Josef declared war on Serbia, murmuring, 'I can't do anything else,' and telling Conrad, 'If we must perish, we should do so with honour.' Nicholas ordered mobilization. Wilhelm telegraphed the tsar to appeal for restraint, dishonestly since he had insisted Austria attack Serbia.

'Am glad you're back,' telegraphed Nicky. 'An ignoble war has been declared on a weak country ... I'll be overwhelmed by pressure and forced to take measures that will lead to war. I beg you in the name of our old friendship to stop your allies ...'

'Russian military measures,' Willy telegraphed, 'would precipitate a calamity.' Nicky asked Willy to mediate. Lifting a new-fangled invention, the telephone recently installed at the Peterhof Palace, Nicholas halted his mobilization – to the exasperation of his generals. But in one of his telegrams to Willy he stated that he had five days earlier started 'military measures' – a misstatement that underlines the importance of clear drafting and the dangers of personal diplomacy.

'That's almost a week ahead of us!' cried Willy. 'I can no longer involve myself in mediation ...The tsar who was calling for it was secretly mobilizing behind my back. My task is finished!' He added, 'That means I've got to mobilize too.' He demanded that Russia cease any such measures. The tsar, watching Austria mobilize, could not delay, and allowed his foreign minister to telephone the chief of staff to restart mobilization.

'Henceforth,' said the general, 'my telephone's out of order.'

'Smash your telephone,' replied the minister, as millions of Russians were called to their units. France too now had to mobilize. At his Neues Palais, Potsdam, Willy was encouraged by his bombastic sons and the kaiserin, all 'frightfully warlike' and all hoping that Russian aggression would allow Britain to stay out – even though Britain had twice made clear it would never tolerate French destruction.

On 31 July, confirming Russian mobilization, Wilhelm used his new telephone to unleash Moltke. Leaving one army to defend against

Russia, Moltke ordered his forces to smash through Belgium into France and take Paris. Wilhelm practically ordered Franz Josef to declare against Russia: Serbia was now 'a side issue'. Only the role of Britain was uncertain: when British intervention became likely, Moltke panicked so much that Wilhelm sneered, 'Your uncle would have given a different answer.' Moltke was falling apart from the strain, weeping, 'I'm happy to wage war against the French and Russians but not against such a kaiser.' A conciliatory telegram arrived from George, at which an 'elated' kaiser toasted British neutrality with champagne. But on 4 August, when German forces invaded Belgium, Britain declared war as hysterical crowds celebrated across Europe: the tsar and Alexandra appeared on the balcony of the Winter Palace; the kaiser told the crowds, 'I see no parties, just Germans'; while on Munich's Odeonsplatz, the twenty-five-year-old Hitler, having moved to Munich flush with his father's inheritance and having been rejected by the Austrian army for medical reasons, joined the exultant throng. 'Overcome by tempestuous enthusiasm,' he recalled, 'I sank to my knees and thanked heaven . . . I was fortunate enough to live in these times.' He quickly joined the Royal Bavarian Army, and 'the most unforgettable and exciting time of my life had begun'.

The kaiser, exhausted, spent forty-eight hours in bed. 'A little nerves rest cure,' he said. While the Russians advanced on the eastern front, Moltke took the Liège fortress, then swung down towards Paris. A veteran general in the east, Paul von Hindenburg, recalled from retirement and assisted by an ambitious self-made officer, Erich von Ludendorff, encircled the Russian armies at Tannenberg, just as in the west German armies were stopped at the Marne. The Schlieffen–Moltke Plan had failed. On 14 September, after six weeks of wartime command, Moltke had a nervous breakdown; Wilhelm sacked him and appointed the war minister, Erich von Falkenhayn. But Falkenhayn persisted with the plan and launched the 'race to the sea', hoping to encircle the French, who were soon joined by a massive British force. The cerebral British prime minister, Herbert Asquith, a Liberal lawyer who daily spent hours writing love letters to his aristocratic young paramour, appointed Earl Kitchener as war minister. The Sudan Machine was one of the first to spot that the war would last years and require 'new armies' of conscripts who would fight 'to the last million'. His pewter-eyed stare and slogan – 'Your Country Needs You' – attracted hundreds of thousands of volunteers. The scale of the war reflected the surging world population, the mystique of nationalist ideas, the panoply of modern power, the extent of the European empires and the ability of trains and steamships to transport vast numbers around the world to fight: the Mass Age.* On the western front the combatants became locked in a savage and bloody stalemate; this was the horror of the trenches, where green countryside and mass armies of millions of civilians, mobilized in numbers never before seen, were mulched into mud and splinter, flesh and limb, by Vickers machine guns and Krupp howitzers.

A GERMAN PRIVATE ON THE WESTERN FRONT: MASS KILLING IN THE MASS AGE

'We took up positions in large trenches and waited,' remembered a German private at one of these battles, the first clash at Ypres, writing one of most vivid accounts of the universal experience on both sides of the western front. 'Finally came the command "Forwards". We climbed out of our holes and sprinted . . . Left and right shells were exploding, English bullets were humming . . . Now the first of our numbers were falling. The English had trained their machine guns on us. We threw ourselves on the ground . . . We couldn't stay there for ever.' They raced across the field and jumped into the British trenches: 'By my side were men from Württemberg and under me were dead and wounded Eng-lishmen. I suddenly realized why my landing had been so soft.' There followed hand-to-hand combat. 'Anyone who didn't surrender got cut down.' The dead were everywhere. The guns formed a 'hellish concert', all around them 'the howling and cracking of shells'. Yet there was a sort of beauty: 'Only the flares still gleam and in the distance to the west you can see the searchlights and hear the constant artillery fire of the heavy armoured ships.' He was the only soldier left alive in his group; then 'A bullet tore its way through my right sleeve, but miraculously I remained without a scratch' – the first of many lucky escapes that convinced him providence was protecting him. Private Hitler had survived his baptism of fire.

In the east, as Franz Josef's forces drove the Serbian king into exile

---

* Sixty-five million soldiers served – 12 million Russians, 11 million Germans, 7.8 million Austrians, 2.8 million Ottomans, while Britain and France deployed 8.9 and 8.4 millions, armies that included recruits from their African and Asian empires and dominions – Canadians, Australians, 1.3 million Indians and over 2 million Africans. Canadians and Australians were committed enough to the British metropole or the national-imperial idea to die for it. Given the scale of the colonial presence on the Allied side, one wonders if the war could have been won at all without Canadians and Australians, not to speak of Indian and African volunteers. As African troops helped roll up German colonies in Africa, some fought on the western front.

and advanced into Russian Galicia, he invited his new heir and family to join him in Schönbrunn. When the twenty-six-year-old Karl heard that Franz Ferdinand was dead, he was understandably shaken. 'I saw his face go white in the sun,' recalled his young wife, Zita. 'I'm an officer, body and soul,' Karl told her, 'but I don't see how anyone who sees his dearest relations leaving for the front, can love war.' He commanded armies first against Italy and then against Russia and Romania, and was admired for his dutiful geniality. When Zita celebrated an early Austrian victory, Franz Josef, now eighty-four, shrugged. 'Yes, it is a victory, but that's the way my wars always begin, only to end in defeat. And this time it'll be even worse . . . Revolutions will break out and then it will be the end.'

'But that's surely not possible,' cried the twenty-two-year-old Zita. 'It's a just war!'

'Yes, one can see you're very young, that you still believe in the victory of the just.'

The western front was now 'A web of dugouts, trenches with embrasures, saps, wire entanglements and landmines – almost impregnable', recalled Hitler. In Europe the eastern and western fronts fluctuated in harmony, movement on one coinciding with stalemate on the other. Falkenhayn attacked across Flanders but was repelled with massive losses; in the east the Austrians and Germans took Poland and Galicia; then, back in the west, Falkenhayn tried to bleed the French army at Verdun in a grinding bloodbath – 145,000 Germans and 163,000 Frenchmen were killed. In July–November 1916, on the Somme, an Anglo-French offensive designed to break the deadlock was a new low in mechanized butchery: 20,000 British soldiers were killed on the first day; over the five months of the battle there were 420,000 British empire killed or wounded, 200,000 French and 500,000 German.

Hitler, now serving as a runner who 'risked his life every day' and won the Iron Cross, Second Class, was at the Somme, where the British tried a new diesel-powered weapon, initiated by Churchill in a bid to achieve a breakthrough: a steel box with gun turret on tracked wheels that he called a 'caterpillar'; others preferred 'landship'. Instead it was given a bland codename: tank. Improved models of tanks, mounted with howitzers, revolutionized warfare, recreating the momentum of charging cavalry for the mechanized era just as improved flying machines, aeroplanes, were first used for reconnaissance, though mocked by macho generals. '*Tout ça, c'est du sport,*' spluttered Marshal Foch. But within months the planes were hand-dropping bombs and then, fitted with machine guns and later bomb payloads, duelling with enemy aircraft for mastery of the air. At sea, another new contraption, Krupp-built submarines – U-boats – tried to starve Britain into submission by sink-ing food-bearing ships.

Germany had counted on support from Italy and Romania. Instead Italy joined the Allies, fighting the gruelling Alpine 'white war' against Austria. To Wilhelm's outrage, his Hohenzollern cousin Carol of Roma-nia refused to back him.

On 29 October 1914, Enver, glorying in the titles 'Vice-Generalissimo, Commander-in-Chief of the Armies of Islam, *Damad* [son-in-law] of the Caliph', joined Germany. In the Caucasus he lost 80,000 men in an of-fensive against the Russians, who were backed by their fellow Orthodox Armenians. His partner Jemal's attack on British Egypt failed.

Yet elsewhere on their massive panorama the Ottomans performed well. Churchill believed that the deadlock on the western front and the Russian retreat could be reversed by knocking out the Ottomans, so he instigated a landing in the Dardanelles to seize Constantinople. But an able colonel, Mustafa Kemal – later Atatürk, the creator of Türkiye – routed the ill-coordinated military and naval forces (though with huge Ottoman losses), a debacle that made Kemal and brought down Church-ill. As British forces protected the new oilfields in Persia, an Allied army advanced from Basra towards Baghdad, but at Kut the Ottomans sur-rounded it and forced its surrender. *

Arab nationalists in Damascus, Beirut and Jerusalem, finally seeing a chance to escape Ottoman rule, plotted against the Three Pashas, who launched a genocidal campaign against ethnic traitors. In January 1915, blaming the Armenians for their earlier defeats, Enver, Talaat and Jemal ordered the killing of all Armenians, whom they suspected of pro-Russian sympathies. First they murdered notables in Istanbul, then they unleashed their paramilitary Special Organization, which killed around a million Armenians.† 'The Armenian question,' Talaat boasted, 'no longer exists.' The Assyrians – a Christian sect – were also slaughtered by the Special Organization. The Kurds in the Hamidiye regiments joined the killing; other Kurds were deported and killed. In Damascus and Beirut, the pashas hanged Arab nationalists, while in Arabia two dy-nasties made their moves: Hussein of Mecca, thirty-seventh in descent

---

* Yet the suicide in February 1916 of Crown Prince Yusuf Izzedin, fifty-eight, who person-ally confronted Enver about Ottoman losses, was an ominous sign.

† Many Armenians managed to escape and emigrate to the west. A typical example was a young Armenian whose family had long lived close to Kars, part of Russia since 1878, and who left just before the war to settle in Los Angeles. Tatos Kardashoff married within the Armenian community, thriving in garbage collection and changing his name to Thomas Kardashian, great-grandfather of Kim, who, eighty years later, demonstrated the peculiar opportunities of American consumerism and entertainment.

from Muhammad, had waited a long time to get power in Hejaz, the western coast. Obstinate, vain and autocratic, the sixty-one-year-old Hussein believed that he and his Hashemite family should succeed the Ottoman sultans not just in Arabia. He sent his energetic eldest son, Abdullah, to offer the British an Arab revolt against the Turks. But his intrigues alarmed the rival Saudi family in Najd, eastern Arabia, where Abdulaziz ibn Saud, the tall, energetic sheikh who hated the Hashemites, pushed the British to recognize his fiefdom as independent.

In 1915, the British, facing slaughter in Flanders, defeat at Kut and in the Dardanelles, encouraged both Hashemites and Saudis to join the Allies. Abdulaziz resisted, but Hussein, negotiating through his sons Abdullah and Faisal, now demanded a vast hereditary kingdom encompassing not just Arabia but also today's Iraq, Syria, Lebanon and Israel. The British excluded Jerusalem and slices of Palestine but agreed in principle.* Simultaneously, the British started to negotiate a Jewish homeland in Palestine with a Zionist leader, a Russian-born chemist, Chaim Weizmann, who, aided by two Rothschild wives, Dolly and Rózsika,† discovered that Lloyd George and the aristocratic ex-prime minister, now first lord of the Admiralty, Arthur Balfour were already sympathetic to a Jewish return to Judaea.

Both negotiations were designed to maximize support at a desperate time, and both were subordinate to traditional imperial power plays in which the British, French and Russians agreed, in a Sykes–Picot–Sazanov pact, to divide the Ottoman empire, with the British getting Palestine and Iraq, the French Damascus and Beirut, and the Romanovs swathes of Ottoman territory plus the jewel, Constantinople.

THE KAISER'S SCROTUM: HINDENBURG AS DICTATOR

In June 1916, as the fighting was at its most desperate on the western front, Tsar Nicholas's forces shattered the Austrians, who were rescued by

---

* At the same time, the British promised an independent Kurdish state to the Kurdish leader, Sheikh Mahmud Barzani.
† The Jewish banking families were divided by Zionism: Walter, the new Lord Rothschild, was unsure; Sir Francis Montefiore was a supporter; Claude Montefiore an opponent; Edwin Montagu, secretary of state for India, was vehemently opposed. Weizmann spotted that in this generation the Rothschild women were the real potentates. The Hungarian Rózsika was the first to meet Weizmann, who then wrote to Dolly, twenty years old and married to James, a son of the Frenchman Edmond de Rothschild, already a Zionist benefactor. The two advised Weizmann on British society, but most importantly they won over their relative Lord Rothschild, regarded as the leader of the Jewish community.

the Germans just in time. Decisively, Nicholas's Guards – the Romanov praetorians – were obliterated. In every country, sluggish politicians were replaced by warlords, ready to wage total war. The kaiser had lost control almost immediately, preposterously instructing, 'Issue the order to fix bayonets and drive the bastards back,' in a war dominated by mud and dynamite. But he did understand the new savagery, demanding that French civilians should 'be ruthlessly strung up', Russian prisoners left to starve. Willy remained sequestered at headquarters. Suffering a swelling on his scrotum, twelve and a half inches in circumference, until his doctors managed to operate, he was simultaneously suffering furuncles (boils) on his face, possibly signs of porphyria. His condition was exacerbated by disillusionment with Falkenhayn, who questioned whether his rival, the sixty-four-year-old Hindenburg, commander in the east, 'has the desire and the courage to take the post' of chief of the general staff in his place.

'The desire, no,' retorted Hindenburg. 'But the courage – yes.' In August 1916, Willy appointed Hindenburg as chief of staff, with Ludendorff as quartermaster-general. The duo ran Germany from head-quarters at Pless Castle in Poland and later at Spa, Belgium, reporting daily to the Supreme Warlord. In London, Asquith had never mastered arms production and could not control Kitchener and the generals. A shell shortage was solved by Lloyd George; the Kitchener problem solved itself when the field marshal was drowned on the way to Russia; and in December Lloyd George became prime minister, determined to win. In Russia, the process was reversed: Tsar Nicholas appointed a passive incompetent – himself – as commander-in-chief, and a foolish hysteric – his wife Alexandra, advised by an ignorant, venal and debauched Sibe-rian mystic, Rasputin – to manage the complexities of an empire at war. The Habsburgs too were collapsing. Wilhelm forced them to recognize Hindenburg as supreme commander. In November 1916, Franz Josef, sick with bronchitis, sighed, 'Why does it have to be now?' and died. Karl was emperor.

On 30 December 1916, a cabal of Romanovs and aristocrats used a beautiful princess to lure Rasputin to a palace where he was poisoned and then shot before being pushed under the ice of the Neva. The lecherous peasant was blamed for the incompetence of the Romanov couple but the responsibility was theirs, and his death diminished their decaying authority. As Nicholas returned to headquarters, bread short-ages sparked spontaneous demonstrations that overran the capital. The tsar ordered rioters to be shot, but the troops changed sides. Rushing back, he was isolated in a railway carriage and forced by his generals to abdicate. But he was replaced by a Provisional Government determined to fight on against Germany.

The fall of the Romanovs coincided with the operation on the Wilhelmine scrotum. As he recovered, Wilhelm was stunned by Nicky's downfall but exhilarated as German armies advanced into Russia: 'Victory and, as its prize, the first place in the world, is ours if we can revolutionize Russia and break up the coalition.' His Foreign Ministry identified the perfect bacillus to infect Russia: Lenin, the Bolshevik leader who was in Zurich, had almost given up on the revolution. 'I don't think,' he said, 'it will happen in our lifetime.' When it did, he asked, 'Is it a hoax?'

Now the Germans arranged a sealed train (that is, without passport controls) to deliver the Bolshevik with thirty comrades to Petrograd – as the capital had been renamed to avoid the German overtones of Petersburg. On the train, Lenin immediately assumed autocratic control, dictating smoking and lavatory rotas. His arrival in Russia changed everything.

In July 1917, as more grinding western front battles bled both sides, the Hashemite prince Faisal and his adviser Colonel T. E. Lawrence took Aqaba.

A KING IN ARABIA, A BOLSHEVIK IN PETROGRAD

Sharif Hussein launched his revolt by firing a rifle out of the window of his Meccan palace, then sent his sons to attack the Ottoman forces in Arabia, Abdullah taking Jeddah on the coast while Faisal seized Wejh on the borders of Syria. Deluded about his power and appeal, Hussein declared himself king of the Arabs, a move that outraged his rival, Abdulaziz ibn Saud, who complained to the British: they forced Hussein to demote himself to the modest role of king of Hejaz.

The British sent an intelligence officer who became the family's champion. Thomas Lawrence, aged twenty-nine, was a classic inside outsider, an Arabist who despised the British elite yet revered the empire, a reticent recluse who was a self-promoting fabulist, a baronet's illegitimate son, a scholar of Arab history, a beautiful writer whose great love was an Arab boy. It turned out he was also a born desert fighter. Meeting the Hashemite princes, he was bowled over by the thirty-two-year-old Faisal, his ideal of Arab knighthood, gushing: 'He's a ripper.' Lawrence backed the Hashemites, but as a servant of empire he expected Faisal to display the appropriate gratitude. 'The tribes', said Lawrence, were 'lively, almost reckless', the war 'one of dervishes against regular forces – and we're on the side of the dervishes. Our text-books don't apply.' But he exaggerated his exploits. In November, he was captured and raped by the Ottomans yet somehow escaped: 'That night the citadel of my integrity had been irrevocably lost.' As one British army took Iraq, another, now joined by the Hashemites, advanced from Egypt into Palestine where Falkenhayn, sent by Hindenburg, stiffened Ottoman resistance.

Wilhelm and Hindenburg now faced food shortages and political discontent as socialist and liberal parties demanded reforms. In January 1917, the kaiser unleashed his U-boats against civilian shipping in order to starve Britain, but their sinking of American ships and Berlin's encouragement of Mexican aggression provoked America. In April, the US president Woodrow Wilson asked Congress to declare war, parading American righteousness over European avarice. 'We have no selfish ends,' he declared. 'We are but one of the champions of the rights of mankind' – though his morals were less evident at home. He did nothing to challenge the Jim Crow laws and intervened militarily across the Americas.[*]

A classical historian, president of Princeton University and a latecomer to politics, Wilson, son of a South Carolinian theologian, won the presidency in 1912 because Teddy Roosevelt, estranged from his successor William Taft, had founded a third party that split the Republican vote. But he appreciated the glamour of the Roosevelt name and appointed Franklin, just elected a New York State senator and obsessed with ships, to Teddy's old position, assistant navy secretary. As America mustered its army, Franklin Roosevelt assiduously enlarged the navy fourfold.[†]

---

[*] American banks had taken over from France as Haiti's chief creditor. Haiti, unable to service the loans, endured rising turbulence; in the four years after 1911, four presidents were killed or deposed as America feared German influence in Haiti and Wall Street demanded action. In December 1914, Wilson dispatched US Marines to raid Haiti's National Bank and seize $500,000 of bullion. When the Haitian president Guillaume Sam was overthrown and gruesomely dismembered, sparking two weeks of chaos, Wilson again sent troops into Haiti, starting a nineteen-year occupation stained by corruption, racism and repression. An insurgency was led by Charlemagne Péralte, a general's son and official, whose fighters defied American troops and planes. Péralte was finally betrayed and displayed, nailed to a door like a Ku Klux Klan crucifixion. Watching American violence and promotion of the mulatto elite over the black majority inspired a belief in African empowerment and culture in a Haitian judge's son who qualified as a doctor, François Duvalier, later nicknamed Papa Doc by his patients. When the long-serving Mexican dictator Porfirio Díaz, once a general opposed to Emperor Maximilian, was deposed in a revolution, Wilson sent troops into the bloody civil war.

[†] Roosevelt was aided in Quincy, Massachusetts, by a brash young businessman, Joseph Kennedy, whose energy and ambition were boundless: his father PJ, son of immigrants

There was another reason for Franklin's dedication: the former governess of his children, Lucy Mercer, now worked with him – and they fell
in love. 'Franklin deserved a good time,' said Alice Roosevelt after she
spotted the couple. 'He was married to Eleanor.'

'Isn't she lovely?' said Franklin. Alice cruelly tormented Eleanor,
hinting that Franklin had a mistress.

The Americans arrived in Europe just in time. France was wavering, mutinies spreading through its army; Russia was disintegrating
as Lenin prepared to seize power. On 2 November 1917, Balfour, now
British foreign secretary, sent a letter to Lord Rothschild promising a
'Jewish national home' in Palestine while offering the assurance that
'nothing shall be done which may prejudice the rights of existing non-
Jewish communities', namely Palestinian Arabs. The letter, which was
approved by President Wilson and repeated in a similar French declaration, was designed to appeal to the Jewish communities in America
and Russia. Hussein and the Hashemites had been promised much of
the Arab world. Neither promise would have been made in any other
circumstances than the bleeding stalemate, now exacerbated by a collapsing Russia.

As Lawrence raided along the Ottoman railway, a British army advanced on Jerusalem. Lloyd George encouraged the capture of the Holy
City as a 'Christmas present' for the British people, which they duly
received when its mayor, waving a blanket as a white flag, farcically
tried to surrender thrice to surprised Tommies before the capitulation
was finally accepted. Colonel Lawrence and British officers respectfully
walked into the city.

On 8 November, in Petrograd, Lenin, disguised in a wig, was turned
away from his own headquarters at the Smolny Institute by his own
Red Guards. But, finally convincing them it was indeed him, he took
command of Bolshevik forces and launched a coup.

Since his arrival in April, he had harassed the premier, Alexander
Kerensky, a diminutive but dynamic socialist lawyer, with a shrewd programme of 'Land, Bread, Peace'. In July, Kerensky, who fancied himself
a Napoleonic warlord, launched offensives against the Germans, but
their failure played into the disintegration of the state, a vacuum Lenin
determined to fill. Kerensky hunted Lenin, who went underground.

from County Wexford, had become wealthy as a saloon owner, serving in the state House
of Representatives. In 1913, his twenty-five-year-old son Joe had used his father's stake
in a local bank to become what he called 'America's youngest bank president'. Already a
Democrat, opposed to the WASP Brahmins who traditionally controlled Boston, Joe was
just starting, but he would later leverage his meeting with Roosevelt into a political career.

Marshalling his radical henchmen, Trotsky and Stalin, Lenin orchestrated the taking of the Winter Palace.* It was barely defended, but the Bolsheviks who finally stormed it raided the tsar's wine cellars and got so drunk that the fire brigade were called to smash the bottles, only to get drunk themselves. The Bolsheviks secured Moscow too, but the rest of the empire was grabbed by the Germans and Ottomans. Meanwhile Poles, Georgians, Finns, Ukrainians, Armenians and many other peoples declared independence.

Faced with unbearable decisions by unstoppable German advances, Lenin negotiated a peace with Germany that ceded much of Ukraine, the Baltics and the Caucasus, thrilling the kaiser. 'The Baltic lands are indivisible and I'll be their ruler. I've conquered them,' Willy bloviated as he assigned kingdoms (Catholic Lithuania for a Habsburg, Finland for a Hessian prince), though he called the Bolsheviks 'Jewboys', denouncing this 'Jewish International for the sake of which the Christians are expected to beat each other to death'.† Hindenburg had replaced the kaiser as the national symbol, issuing a statement for his seventieth birthday: 'Muscles tensed, nerves steeled, eyes front!' When Hindenburg gave a respectful order to Wilhelm, the kaiser replied, 'I don't need your parental advice' – but he obeyed.

On 16 November 1917, France, beset by mutinies and close to collapse, turned to a ferocious critic of its leadership and former premier, Georges '*Le Tigre*' Clemenceau, aged seventy-seven,‡ who rallied France with rhetoric that clearly inspired Churchill twenty years later: 'At home,

---

* The three leaders formed a highly intellectual if murderous clique who were about to achieve supreme power: when they were already ruling the empire and were asked their professions in a Party questionnaire, each of them described himself as a man of letters or a journalist.
† In Kyiv, German troops threw out a Central Rada (Council) which had declared Ukrainian independence and installed a new hetmanate under Pavlo Skoropadsky, a Russian general from the family of Peter the Great's hetman. A Transcaucasian republic took control in Tiflis, which after a few months broke up into independent Georgia, Azerbaijan and Armenia. Georgia was ruled by the Mensheviks, rivals to the Bolsheviks.
‡ One of the sharpest of modern leaders, it was Clemenceau who said, 'War is too serious to leave to generals.' He had had an extraordinary life. When he worked as a riding instructor in America, he fell in love with and married his student. He flaunted his paramours, but when back in France his wife took a lover, he had her arrested and sent back to America. Training as a doctor, he became a radical journalist, covering the American civil war then criticizing Napoleon III, who imprisoned him. He was a friend of Monet and Zola and a supporter of Dreyfus, but he mocked the French literary elite: 'Give me forty arseholes and I'll give you the *Académie Française*.' When he sacked Marshal Joffre, he commented, 'Stripes and a cap aren't enough to transform an imbecile into a clever man.' Even in his seventies he prided himself on his love life. 'The best moment in a love affair,' he mused, 'is as one goes up the stairs.' When he was shot by an assassin, he mocked him for missing with all but one of his bullets and carried on walking.

I make war; abroad, I make war; everywhere I make war.' He added, 'To die isn't enough, we must conquer!' Practising his fencing and meeting his mistress daily, the Tiger sacked generals, arrested critics and promised *'la guerre jusqu'au bout'* (war to the end). Churchill compared him to 'a wild animal pacing'. France held on as a million Americans started to arrive.

On the other side, the Ottomans were tottering. In early 1918, the Ottoman crown prince Mehmed arrived in Germany with his top general Kemal to inform Wilhelm and Hindenburg that the empire could not carry on, blaming Enver. In March, triumphant in Russia, frustrated in the west, wilting at home, Ludendorff launched Operation Michael to break the Allies, advancing forty miles. 'The battle is won,' crowed the kaiser, 'the English totally beaten.' German losses were punishing: Hitler's unit lost half of its men just in April; Corporal Hitler won the Iron Cross, First Class. But the killing brutalized the soldiers. 'You can only defeat death with death,' concluded Hitler, a convinced social Darwinist. 'Life is a constant terrible struggle which serves to preserve the species – someone has to die so others may survive.' Yet he also loved the camaraderie with the soldiers (and with a terrier, Foxl) – the family he lacked – though when they planned to celebrate their survival in a French bordello, Hitler exclaimed, 'I'd die of shame if I saw a French woman naked,' convincing the others that this teetotal, non-smoking virgin was a 'little bit eccentric'. When Hitler visited starving Berlin he heard the conspiracy theories that Jews were undermining the armies, even though Jews were serving like everyone else. In July, the French counter-attacked; the Germans started to crack, their reserves expended; and at Amiens in August, 456 new British tanks shattered German lines, then started to advance, reinforced by the Americans.

In October, Prince Faisal, supported by Lawrence, rode into newly liberated Damascus; in Arabia, his brother Abdullah besieged the Ottomans in Medina. But already there were tensions between the Hashemite aspirations and the reality of the Anglo-French carve-up. Damascus was in the French sphere, but Faisal defiantly claimed Syria first in the name of his father King Hussein. That month, Wilhelm visited Gustav Krupp (wartime slogan: 'The greater the foe, the greater the honour!') at his Essen works. Wearing his golden eagle helmet and field marshal's uniform, the kaiser addressed the workers from a slagheap and ranted against 'traitors', exhorting, 'Be as strong as steel!', unwisely adding, 'Each worker has his duty, you at your lathe, me on my throne.' After a long silence the workers shouted, 'Hunger!' and 'Peace!' Willy was shaken.

At headquarters, Ludendorff had a nervous breakdown, and was led ranting out of a meeting by Hindenburg, who refused to sack him: 'Often has the soldier's calling exhausted strong characters.' But now the duo told Wilhelm the truth. 'The war,' said a stunned Willy, 'must be brought to an end.'

THE FALL OF THE KAISERS

The fighting ground on. In October 1918, Hitler was in hospital, having been temporarily blinded by mustard gas, as Wilhelm appointed a liberal prince, Max of Baden, ironically a cousin of Napoleon III, as chancellor, with the task of requesting an armistice. But the power now moved to the Social-Democrats (SPD), headed by a tailor's son and long-serving Reichstag leader, Friedrich Ebert, who favoured the survival of the monarchy but feared Communist revolution. When the navy rebelled at Wilhelmshaven, Ebert accepted that the monarchy needed to go. As Communist Spartacists created workers' councils in Berlin, Max visited Spa to ask for Wilhelm's abdication. 'I wouldn't dream of quitting my throne for a few hundred Jews or 1,000 workers,' sneered Willy.

'If the Kaiser doesn't abdicate,' Ebert told Max, 'social revolution's inevitable. But I don't want it, I hate it like sin.' On 9 November, Ebert demanded the chancellorship, asking Prince Max to serve as regent for Willy's second son. But that afternoon Ebert's comrade Philipp Scheidemann appeared on the Reichstag balcony. 'The old rotten monarchy's gone,' he declared. 'Long live the German Republic!'

'You've no right,' shouted Ebert, 'to proclaim the republic!' But it was done. The next day Wilhelm left for Dutch exile* as the twenty-two German dynasties fell too. 'Well then,' said the Saxon king Friedrich August III as he abdicated, 'take care of this crap yourselves!' The 'crap' was imminent Marxist revolution.

In Vienna, Karl offered a federal state for the different nationalities with independence for Poland. But the Monarchy disintegrated into new states (Czechoslovakia, a democratic republic; Yugoslavia, a monarchy under Peter Karađorđević) and older ones. Poland – arising out of Habsburg and Romanov lands – declared independence under Józef Piłsudski, an irrepressible patriot, a nobleman turned socialist who had

---

* One Hohenzollern throne remained – Romania – where after the death of the founding monarch King Carol his nephew Ferdinand had joined the Allies and been pummelled by the Germans but now kept his throne. The Coburgs still ruled Belgium – and Bulgaria where Foxy Ferdinand abdicated in favour of his baby son Boris.

escaped from Russian prisons, had served as a minister in a German client 'kingdom' and was now elected head of state, envisioning Poland as a multi-ethnic 'home of nations'. Hungary and Austria turned against the Habsburgs.

On Armistice Day, 11 November, Karl relinquished his 'participation in administration' but lingered at Schönbrunn until the socialist leader Karl Renner came calling: 'The taxi is waiting, Herr Habsburg.' The ex-emperor left but insisted, 'I didn't abdicate . . .' Hitler, still in hospital, learned the news of the Armistice from the chaplain: 'Everything went black again and I stumbled my way back to my sickbed . . . Everything had been in vain.'

The meatgrinder of the war changed everyone, its scale propelling the Mass Age. 9.7 million soldiers had been killed; perhaps 10 million civilians.* Returning men expected a say in the future. It changed the shape of families: afterwards women, even middle-class ones, worked and wanted to work. There were shortages of men, which handed power back to women. It was only now that full democracy – universal suffrage for men and increasingly women – was instituted in many places.†

Like many others, Hitler asked himself, 'Had everything happened only so that a band of criminals could get their hands on our fatherland? . . . My hatred grew.' Only the *Dolchstoss* – 'stab in the back' by traitors and Jews – could explain the German collapse. At that moment, 'I decided to become a politician.'

THE TIGER, THE GOAT AND JESUS CHRIST

Franklin Roosevelt, dispatched to Europe to inspect naval facilities, visited Paris and London, where he met Churchill – 'one of the few men,'

---

* Among the soldiers, Britain lost 800,000 killed with 2 million wounded; also killed were 2.2 million Russians, 2 million Germans, 1.3 million Frenchmen, 1.2 million Austrians, 550,000 Italians, 325,000 Ottomans, 115,000 Americans; in addition, 74,000 Indian and 77,000 African soldiers were killed.

† Women received the vote in Russia; Germany; Britain (men over twenty-one and women over thirty – 5.6 million men and 8.4 million women – were enfranchised); and the USA. 'We've made partners of women in this war,' declared Wilson: the Nineteenth Amendment enfranchised 26 million women, though 75 per cent of African-Americans remained voteless. France did not enfranchise women until 1944, yet pioneered fashions that reflected new freedoms. In 1919, Gabrielle 'Coco' Chanel, thirty-seven – a captivating ex-singer born in a provincial orphanage, daughter of a laundrywoman and a pedlar – founded her Parisian *atelier*, funded by two wealthy lovers, one French, one English. The *couturière* rejected corsets, hobble-skirts, long dresses and, often using knitwear, promoted casual shorter dresses, trousers and her No.5 perfume, that – in a long, controversial career – helped change the way women dressed.

recalled FDR, 'who was rude to me'. Sailing back to the USA as Germany collapsed, Roosevelt fell ill with a fever, probably suffering from influenza A virus subtype H1N1 – the flu – the name itself deriving from an Italian outbreak in 1743 supposedly caused by the *influentia* of the stars. It was a new strain, first registered in an army camp at Fort Riley, Kansas, then spreading through the American troops to Europe where the illness of King Alfonso XIII earned it its name, Spanish Flu (though in Africa it was called Brazilian Flu, in Poland Bolshevik Flu). The transoceanic movements of soldiers helped it race across the world, its first wave mild, its second lethal, killing multitudes of young children and those in the 20–40 age group. Half a billion people caught it; thirty million died. In Moscow, it killed Lenin's henchman Yakov Sverdlov; in Arabia, three of Abdulaziz's sons and a favourite wife died; in Ethiopia, the young regent, Ras Tafari Makonnen – soon to be Haile Selassie – survived it.*

On USS *Leviathan*, many died; Roosevelt was stretchered off the ship, and recovered.† Examining his baggage, Eleanor discovered love letters from his lover Lucy Mercer. Deeply hurt she offered to divorce him, but Franklin's new political adviser, a tiny hideous, obstreperous journalist, Louis Howe, warned him that he would never be president if he divorced, and his mother Sara threatened to cut him out of her will. FDR promised never to see Lucy again; but he didn't keep the promise.

In January 1919, President Wilson sailed for Europe, determined to impose American morality – self-determinism expressed in his Fourteen Points – on Britain and France, both of them semi-bankrupted by war yet focused by habit, mission and ambition on empire. Roosevelt and Eleanor, rebuilding their marriage, which their son James described as 'an armed truce until the day he died', joined Wilson in Paris.

Lloyd George and Clemenceau, the Goat and the Tiger, agreed to Wilson's principles – promising 'the complete and final liberation of the peoples' – and his proposal for a new international organization to avoid future wars, the League of Nations. But the two lascivious radicals proved enthusiastic empire builders. 'Wilson bores me with his Fourteen Points,' laughed Tiger. 'God only had ten!' Wilson thought LG 'slippery' but preferred him to Clemenceau. 'I did as well as might

---

* After Menelik's death, the Ethiopian succession had not gone smoothly. Emperor Iyasu's religious fluctuations and pro-German policies had led in 1916 to his deposition and replacement by Menelik's daughter Zewditu. She was forced to nominate as regent and heir Ras Tafari Makonnen.

† Frederick Trump, Bavarian-born gold-rush brothel keeper and grandfather of the president, now died of Spanish Flu aged just forty-nine. He had invested in property in Queens, New York. Now his widow Elizabeth took over the business, which she called E. Trump, soon joined by her sons. The second one, Fred, was eighteen when he built his first house.

be expected,' joked LG, 'seated between Jesus [Wilson] and Napoleon [Clemenceau].'

'Three all-powerful, all-ignorant men', observed Balfour, 'carving up continents', decided a lot – though much was left up in the air: their Versailles treaty reconstituted Poland and recognized multi-ethnic amalgamations Czechoslovakia and Yugoslavia created out of the fiefs of Hohenzollerns, Romanovs and Habsburgs, punished Austria and Hungary, shrinking them drastically. They diminished Germany, returning Alsace to France, demilitarizing the Rhineland, charging reparations and placing millions of ethnic Germans in new Slavic countries. It was impossible to satisfy everyone, but Italy and Japan had fought for the Allies and received little. In Asia, the three Allied powers did not apply Wilson's principles at all: in China, they awarded German treaty ports to Japan, but when Prince Konoe, the Japanese delegate, demanded a statement that non-white peoples were equal, the powers refused, infuriating both Japanese and Chinese.* And what to do with the Ottoman empire? LG and Clemenceau bargained for what they called 'mandates' over Arab lands like this:

Tiger: 'Tell me what you want.'

Goat: 'I want Mosul.'

Tiger: 'You shall have it. Anything else?'

Goat: 'Yes, I want Jerusalem too.'

Tiger: 'You shall have it.' Clemenceau claimed Syria because the Crusader kings were French and both imperial Napoleons had sent troops to the region. Lloyd George planned to find a kingdom for Faisal, whom Lawrence introduced as 'the greatest Arab leader since Saladin'. The Turkish heartland would be divided between an international Constantinople, a Turkish rump and two new countries, Kurdistan and Armenia, while Smyrna (İzmir) and western Anatolia would join a new Greek empire.†

---

* A Vietnamese socialist in Paris wrote to the three powers to demand independence for Vietnam from France, signing his appeal Nguyen Ai Quoc (Patriot Nguyen). Aged twenty-eight, Nguyen Sinh Cung was the son of a rural teacher and magistrate who loathed French rule, though he had attended a French school. He had applied to study at the French Colonial Administrative School and travelled to France, but his application was turned down – one of the biggest mistakes in French imperial history, even if he was probably already a socialist. Instead he worked as a waiter and dishwasher, maybe even as a pâtissier, writing articles and studying, travelling on to study in Bolshevik Russia. Later he adopted the name Ho Chi Minh.

† This was the *Megali Idea*, the Great Idea, an irredentist scheme to re-establish the Eastern Roman empire on the ruins of the Ottoman sultanate – promoted by Eleftherios Venizelos, who dominated Greece, serving as premier eight times, and who at Versailles enchanted Lloyd George with his tales of ancient Greece and his own exploits on Crete in 1897, fighting the Ottomans.

Versailles had many flaws but the biggest was that it excluded Europe's two eastern powers, Germany and Russia. It was always doomed. Lloyd George admitted that the 'mandates' were 'a substitute for the old imperialism'. Yet the war also mobilized imperial resistance. In April 1919, Gandhi, now forty-nine, announced a *satyagraha* campaign against the British across India, but it was British violence that was to revolutionize his non-violent campaign. In Amritsar, two of his followers were arrested, leading to riots. On the 11th, the British fired on the crowds; rioters killed five Europeans; but two days later a crowd, some celebrating the Baisakhi festival, gathered at Jallianwala Bagh, where a bone-headed British general, Reginald Dyer, arrived with ninety Indian soldiers determined to 'to punish the Indians for disobedience'.

AS LONG AS WE HAVE INDIA: GANDHI AND NEHRU

Gandhi was back after twenty-one years in South Africa, where he had analysed British power: it only worked, he argued in his book *Hind Swaraj* (Indian Home Rule), because most Indians cooperated with the British; it was Indian soldiers and police who provided the coercion. Gandhi transformed himself from besuited elite barrister to half-naked activist, wearing *dhoti* and shawl, homespun Indian cottons, as part of his *Swadeshi* self-sufficiency movement – in which he called for the population to spin and weave their own handwoven *khadi* and boycott the fabrics coming from British factories that had undermined the Indian textile industry. A Congress Party, approved by the viceroy, had been founded twenty years earlier but was split between moderates and radicals, and many Indian grandees disdained the movement. Motilal Nehru, a wealthy lawyer, Brahmin pandit (an honorary Hindu title), descendant of Mughal officials, brother of a chief minister, who lived in an Allahabad mansion, believed in Anglo-Indian cooperation and sent his son Jawaharlal to become an English gentleman at Harrow.

But Jawaharlal, after Cambridge and the Bar, now living in the mansion with his wife Kamala, embraced socialism and joined Congress, excited by the return of Gandhi: 'All of us admired him for his heroic fight in South Africa, but he seemed very distant, different, unpolitical.' When the thirty-year-old Nehru met Gandhi, 'We saw that he was prepared to apply his methods in India also, and they promised success.' Initially keeping out of Congress, Gandhi – known as Mahatma (Great Soul) – proved that his methods could work. The British offered limited Indian participation in local government, but most leaders in London regarded India as essential to British power. 'As long as we rule India,' said the ex-viceroy Curzon, now foreign secretary, 'we're the greatest power in the world,' and 'We haven't the slightest intention of abandoning our Indian possessions.' When the British imposed emergency limits on Indian protests, Gandhi organized his first boycott.

On 13 April 1919, at Jallianwala Bagh, General Dyer ordered his Indian troops to fire into the crowd, killing between 500 and 1,000, wounding 1,200.* The massacre shattered the facade of British benevolence and competence: Motilal Nehru burned his English suits, his homburgs and his London furniture in the garden, watched by Jawaharlal's two-year-old daughter, Indira. Gandhi, backed by Nehru, assumed leadership of Congress.

Yet there was a flaw: the Indian Muslims were a huge minority: the British understood Islam better than Hinduism and based their Raj on the Mughals; in the First World War, 1.3 million Indians, mainly Muslims, volunteered. Ascetic, brilliantly empathetic and charismatic, Gandhi saw himself as a religious figure, seeking *moksha*, self-perfection, through 'mortification of the flesh', freed from normal rules. 'It's not necessary for me to prove the rightness of what I said then,' he asserted later, 'it's essential only to know what I feel today.' He was determined to unite the communities of India, but Congress, for all its secularity, became 97 per cent Hindu. When a movement of Dalits demanded their own representatives, Gandhi fasted to stop them. 'The caste system,' he argued, 'isn't based on inequality,' but was the structure that held Hindu India together. Gandhi personified peaceful protest but knew that the 'communal problem' might only be solved by violence. 'I'd rather be witness to Hindus and Mussulmans doing one another to death,' he wrote in 1930, 'than I should daily witness our gilded slavery.'†

Having recast the world, Wilson had returned to DC exhausted. On 2

---

* This was not the end of Dyer. Just after the massacre, the amir of Afghanistan Amanullah invaded British India with regular troops, aided by Pashtun uprisings and Indian army mutinies – designed to restore Afghan independence after eighty years as a British protectorate. The British easily repelled the invasion with Dyer commanding one of the brigades. Amanullah nonetheless won Afghan independence, taking the old Durrani title shah. But his western reforms led to his overthrow and civil war. In October 1929, a royal cousin, Nader Khan, emerged as king.

† Another British-trained lawyer, Ali Jinnah, a slim, dapper, whisky-drinking Ismaili in Savile Row suits, was shouted down by Congress and walked out, committing himself to a new Muslim League. Not all Hindus followed Gandhi's inclusivity: the ideal of *Hindutva*, Hindu nationalism, was invented by Vinayak Damodar Savarkar, who had started a violent campaign against the Muslims and for independence; he was arrested in 1910 and imprisoned by the British, later founding the Hindu Mahasabha, initially within Congress. In 1925, he was one of the founders of the paramilitary Hindu RSS organization that wore uniforms, provided protection at rallies and aimed to create a *Hindu Rashtra* (Nation).

October 1919, he suffered a stroke, leaving him semi-paralysed and half blinded. Keeping his health a secret, his second wife, Edith Galt, managed the presidency – 'I, myself, never made a single decision; the only decision that was mine was what was important . . . when to present matters to my husband.'

Like Wilson, Americans turned decisively inwards. That September, in Elaine, Arkansas, when black sharecroppers tried to organize a union, white lynch mobs and a new version of the KKK, backed by the governor, claimed that a 'Negro Insurrection' was afoot and killed 200 black people in three days of riots. Seventy-three more black innocents were tried for murder and insurrection, twelve sentenced to death. The NAACP (National Association for the Advancement of Colored People) campaigned against the injustice, and the convictions were eventually overturned by Arkansas's Supreme Court. In Tulsa, Oklahoma, in May 1921, after a black shoeshiner was accused of attacking a white girl, an attempt to lynch black prisoners led to a shoot-out at the jail. A white mob stormed and burned 'Negro Wall Street', killing many, while Gurley and other entrepreneurs lost everything. The National Guard interned 6,000 black people; 100,000 lost their homes. Among those who witnessed a lynching in rural Georgia was a young Baptist, Michael King, future father of Martin Luther King Jr, who decided to qualify as a minister in order to combat racial injustice.

Beside the racial tension, a new American puritanism vied with a wild *joie de vivre* that exploded after the years of war and pandemic.

THE BRAIN, THE DUMB DUTCHMAN AND LUCKY LUCIANO

In October 1919, the Volstead Act, propelled by an evangelical awakening, banned alcohol, a decision that criminalized much of society but legitimized a new criminal coterie whose members killed the traditional Sicilian *padrini* – godfathers. Lucky Luciano, aided by his Jewish allies Meyer Lansky and Bugsy Siegel, ran just one of the networks of criminals operating in all major cities ready to import alcohol and serve it in new secret bars. A fellow member of the Five Points Gang, Al Capone, known as Snorky for his dapperness and Scarface for his gashed cheeks, moved to Chicago where he assassinated the *padrino* and became boss himself. Luciano was mentored by an extraordinary uptown manipulator named Arnold Rothstein, son of a law-abiding Jewish businessman and a gangster more by choice than necessity. Known as the Brain, Rothstein made money by gambling – he supposedly fixed the 1919 baseball World Series – before importing Scotch on his own ships and trucks: crime run like a corporation.

The Brain backed Luciano, even teaching him how to dress, and coordinated influence, corrupting a network of judges, police and politicians. The alcohol business, dovetailing with their other interests – casinos, brothels, drugs, gambling, unions, docks and protection – suddenly made these rough immigrants into crime magnates.

Back in the White House, run by Edith Wilson, Assistant Navy Secretary Roosevelt was horrified to see the crippled president: his own sporty vigour was part of his charm. At the election of 1920, he ran as vice-presidential candidate, but the Democrats lost.* Planning his next move, in August 1921, FDR, now thirty-nine, went for a sailing holiday at his seaside house on Campobello Island, Canada, where he felt a surging ache in his muscles and spine. He collapsed with fever and paralysis. Suddenly he could not move at all, even to empty his bowels. He struggled desperately to survive, while doctors argued over the diagnosis, finally identifying polio – 'a children's disease', said FDR. When the fever lifted, he was paralysed from the waist down. He almost vanished from the lives of the children. 'This was the time of the second father,' said his son James, 'the father with dead legs.'

Aided by his 'first-class temperament', FDR focused on rebuilding himself, spending months in Florida and then searching for a cure in Warm Springs, Georgia, which he bought and turned into a hydrotherapy centre, presiding over the patients with his remarkable jovial confidence: 'Have you been good boys and girls while Papa was away?'

FDR learned to propel himself tortuously with crutches, building powerful chest and shoulder muscles, and to stand using leg braces. But his legs remained useless and his progress was precarious. When he tried to return to his law practice, he fell in front of everyone. 'Nothing to worry about,' he said, smiling as he was helped up. 'Give me a hand there.' He conquered his ailment with a determination cloaked in an irresistible but inscrutable breeziness, the shallow aristocrat hardened by the grit of suffering and warmed by the empathy it engendered. Eleanor nursed but let him go, his new companions being his spin doctor Howe

---

* The new Republican president Warren Harding appointed Teddy Roosevelt's eldest son, Ted, as assistant naval secretary, the third member of the family to serve there. Ted Roosevelt, who lacked his father's exuberance but shared his ambitions, was eager to be president too, but his involvement in the Teapot Dome oil scandal ruined his career. He and his sister Alice Longworth resented the rise of cousin Franklin and tried to stop him. Alice was already the grande dame of Republican Washington, a role she would play until the presidency of Nixon. 'If you can't say something good about someone,' she liked to say, 'sit right here by me.'

(who called him the Master or sometimes 'you dumb Dutchman') and a young secretary, 'Missy' LeHand, who worshipped him. Eleanor sought her own life as a campaigning liberal, and was taught public speaking by Howe.

'I believe someday,' Howe told Eleanor, 'Franklin will be president.' As FDR struggled to rebuild himself, the Wilsonian peace in Europe was already falling apart. It looked as if Germany, if not much of Europe, was about to fall to the Bolsheviks.

In Russia, the withdrawal of German forces sparked a ferocious civil and ethnic war, but Lenin, a master pragmatist, defeated his challengers one by one, then launched a reconquest of the Romanov empire. Moving the capital of his Soviet state (named after the revolutionary councils that had sprung up in most Russian cities and were now used as a figleaf for his dictatorship) to Moscow, he commissioned Trotsky to muster a new Red Army and an ascetic Polish nobleman, Felix Dzerzhinsky, to form a secret police, the Cheka, to liquidate enemies.

Lenin's enemies were not imaginary: in August 1918, he just survived a coup by his own radical allies; and he was shot during a speech but survived. His Reds fought for survival against conservative Whites. National revolutionaries declared independence for Georgia, Ukraine, Finland and Poland, along with Estonia and the Baltics. Ill-coordinated and insubstantial interventions by America, Britain, France and Japan contributed to the shattering of the ex-tsarist empire. But Trotsky, holding the central, most populous region, conscripting five million men by 1921, enforcing strict command, managed to defeat each enemy separately.*

All sides deployed ingenious cruelties on a massive scale: twelve million people perished. While the Whites offered no land to the peasants and a new Russian empire, Lenin rallied workers, bamboozled the peasants and offered national autonomy to the minorities. Lenin abandoned Finland and the Baltics but fought for the Ukraine, essential for his new state as the producer of a third of Russia's grain, two-thirds of its coal and most of its steel.† In April 1920, Marshal Piłsudski, agreeing with the

---

* 'In war, as in prostitution,' Napoleon supposedly said, 'amateurs are often better than professionals.'

† After the Germans withdrew, in December 1918, their Ukrainian puppet hetman Skoropadsky was overthrown by a nationalist Directorate named after the French revolutionary government. It was dominated by a socialist journalist and Ukrainian nationalist named Symon Petliura, who took the title great ataman (*otaman*) and in May 1919 was elected dictatorial head of the Directorate. Ukraine was invaded by the Bolsheviks and the White Russian armies, both keen to re-establish Russian control. Petliura fought both but could scarcely control his subordinates, warlords who launched pogroms against Jews. The Ukrainians were not the only ones killing Jews – Bolshevik Cossacks and White Russians played their part too – but around 65 per cent of the killing was by Ukrainian warlords.

Ukrainian hetman Petliura to create aligned Polish and Ukrainian states similar to a new Polish–Lithuanian Commonwealth, invaded Ukraine, taking Kyiv that May. Lenin counter-attacked. Kyiv fell in June. Once Ukraine was controlled by Moscow, Poland and Germany were next.

As Lenin fought for Ukraine, German Communists tried to seize power in Berlin and occupied Munich, but the president Ebert appeased German soldiers, telling them, 'You were undefeated.' Ebert allied with the army and paramilitary freebooters, the Freikorps, who killed Marxist leaders in Berlin, then in April 1919 retook Munich, killing 600.*

Still a soldier and now twenty-nine, Hitler shared the fury at German defeat, and began embracing German racial supremacy and rabid antisemitism. At an army instruction course, he spoke publicly for the first time. 'I saw a pale drawn face,' remembered one of the instructors, 'underneath a decidedly unmilitary shock of hair with a trimmed moustache and remarkably large, light-blue, fanatically cold, gleaming eyes,' and heard the guttural voice as he addressed his fellow students: 'I had the strange feeling that he had got them excited and at the same time that their interest had given *him* his voice.' The observer remarked to a colleague, 'one of your trainees is a natural-born public speaker'. Hitler embraced the 'stab in the back' theory, claiming that the traitors were Jews, with whom he conflated the Communists: Judaeo-Bolshevism.

'We must probe with bayonets,' Lenin said, 'whether the social revolution in Poland has ripened.' In summer 1920, he invaded Poland, appointing his secret policeman Dzerzhinsky as dictator designate. Warsaw seemed doomed. Europe held its breath.

Their excuse was that some of the Bolshevik leaders – most prominently Trotsky, a Ukrainian Jew from Kherson – were Jewish. The Bolsheviks tried to stop such killings. On the Ukrainian side, only the anarchist warlord Nestor Makhno, diminutive and brave, who for a while controlled the region between Kharkiv and Donbas, fighting at times the Whites, at other times the Reds, tried seriously to stop them. Around 150,000 Jews were killed, dwarfing the notorious tsarist pogroms and anticipating the Holocaust. Petliura banned the pogroms but did little to punish their perpetrators. He went into exile where he was later assassinated by a Jew as revenge.

* In Hungary, a Bolshevik insurance clerk named Béla Kun seized power, launching a Red Terror, but in November 1919 he was swiftly overthrown by a former ADC to Franz Josef who had in May 1917 won a skirmish against the Italian navy with a tiny Habsburg fleet. After swearing to restore Kaiser Karl in both Vienna and Budapest, Admiral Miklós Horthy, a nobleman who, in command of the National Army, rode into Budapest on a white horse, slaughtered around 6,000 Communists and Jews ('Stop harassing small Jews,' he ordered. 'Kill some big Jews' – he meant Bolsheviks) and set up a conservative–military dictatorship under himself as regent for a non-existent king. He always said that when he had a problem he asked himself what Franz Josef would have done. But, as he wrote, 'Concerning the Jewish question, all my life I have been an antisemite.' He immediately started to negotiate diplomatically to restore lost Hungarian lands – and to repress Hungary's huge Jewish community through anti-Jewish laws.

PROBING WITH BAYONETS: THE KINGS OF MUNICH,
SYRIA AND IRAQ

On 16 August 1920, Piłsudski, advised by British and French officers, including a young French officer named Charles de Gaulle, shattered the Bolshevik offensive. Lenin absorbed the devastating blow. To the south, Stalin seized independent Georgia, Armenia and Azerbaijan, with its Baku oil.* The Bolsheviks would not take Europe, not yet anyway, but now Lenin had to make his state work, just as in Munich, bloodily liberated from Communist rule, Hitler, a spy for army intelligence, was monitoring a small *völkisch* German Workers' Party. He left the army as Lenin's forces were routed on the Vistula and took over the Party, renamed the National Socialist German Workers' (Nazi) Party. 'It was a wonderful time,' he said later. 'The best time of all.'

Hitler developed his oratory, practising his wild gestures like an actor, mastering the phrases and themes, a mix of racial pseudoscience, fake history, medieval chivalry and religious imagery, that resounded with his audiences in crowded Bavarian cellar bars, attacking the 'November criminals', corrupt politicians and Jews. 'Why are we antisemites?' he asked, answering that the Jews 'were parasites on other peoples', driven by 'Mammon and materialism ... the only Jewish goal – world domination' and the only solution 'the removal of Jews from our people'. In early 1921, he formed the paramilitary *Sturmabteilung* – Stormtroop – fitting them out in brown uniforms, to fight 'our enemy the Jew'. The Nazis attracted two well-connected war heroes, the thrice-wounded, scar-faced Captain Ernst Röhm and Hermann Göring, son of a governor of German South West Africa and bemedalled star pilot married to a baroness. As hyperinflation, riots and strikes created an atmosphere of dystopic freefall, Hitler became the 'King of Munich', and was joined by General Ludendorff himself in a plan to seize power. Their inspiration was Italy.

In October 1922, a bullish, squared-jawed veteran and journalist,

---

* The Soviets managed to conquer three new countries that had not been formal parts of the Romanov empire. In 1920 they reconquered central Asia and seized the independent emirate of Bukhara and the khanate of Khiva – where the Mongol khan Sayid Abdullah, a scion of a dynasty, the Khongirads, was the last member of the Genghis Khan family to rule. The khanate was included in the new Soviet republics Uzbekistan and Turkmenistan. In the bizarre last act of the civil war, a demented Baltic officer, Baron Roman von Ungern-Sternberg, who believed he was Genghis reincarnated, seized Mongolia, massacred Jews and Bolsheviks and declared a Buddhist empire, until Russian and Mongolian Bolsheviks attacked his new realm. In August 1921, his invasion of Siberia ended with his capture and execution. Instead of Poland, Mongolia became the first Soviet client state.

Benito Mussolini, leader of his National Fascist Party, backed by the paramilitary *Squadrismo*, the Blackshirts, threatened to march on Rome to seize power in the kingdom which was falling apart after brutal losses in the war. Mussolini insisted that the 'plutodemocracies' (Britain and France) had prevented Italy's receiving its deserved spoils. Mussolini's Fascism was named after the *fasces*, a bundle of wood and an axe that symbolized the authority of Roman consuls; he advocated a new Roman empire to replace democracy and vanquish Marxism. It impressed many businessmen and aristocrats. When Mussolini threatened a march on Rome, King Victor Emmanuel III invited him to Rome, no march being necessary.

The king, five feet tall and nicknamed *Sciaboletta* (Little Sword), saw Mussolini as an essential 'strong man' like Crispi.* Mussolini, in a characteristically phallic image, disdained the king as his 'contraceptive', adding that the king was 'too tiny for an Italy destined for greatness'. Mussolini believed his bullish libido was an extension of his power, boasting 'genius lies in the genitals'. He arrived in Rome by train, was appointed premier and went on to use terror to subdue Italy. But the new cult of the superman-dictator was a transcendent rejection of petty routine and projection of the extraordinary in which the mass could share. Hitler believed he could do the same: he planned to seize power.

To the east, Faisal and Lawrence were also trying to overturn Allied decisions. On 7 March 1920, in Damascus, Faisal was hailed as king of a greater Syria that would include today's Syria, Lebanon and Israel.

Faisal knew this was the French mandate and tried to negotiate with Clemenceau, but the Syrians rejected the French and forced his hand. Embracing Britain's Zionist promise within this Arab kingdom, Lawrence arranged meetings between the Zionist leader Weizmann and Faisal, who backed Jewish immigration but only if it was subject to his authority. This was all part of Lawrence's plan, while Faisal's elder brother Abdullah would get Iraq.

But the French were determined to claim their new empire and they defeated Faisal's ragged army. While he believed in 'take, then ask', Faisal understood 'the art of flexible politics: the Syrians lost independence by insisting on all or nothing'.

On 12 March 1921, at the Semiramis Hotel, Cairo, Churchill, now LG's colonial secretary, revelled in a gathering of his 'Forty Thieves', experts

---

* Victor Emmanuel's father King Umberto, before his assassination by an anarchist in 1900, had advised him: 'To be a king, all you need to know is how to sign your name, read a newspaper and mount a horse.'

who would redraw the map of western Asia, including Lawrence, Sir
Percy Cox and Gertrude Bell. She however, thought 'you might search
our history from end to end without finding poorer masters of it than
Lloyd George and Winston Churchill'.

Churchill's first task was to crush the anti-British rebellions in Iraq,
by Shiites, Sunnis and Kurds, the latter's sheikh Mahmud Barzani
having declared himself king. While Churchill ordered the RAF to
bomb the rebels ('a wonderful training ground'), he devised a cheaper
way to govern the mandates. Britain would run Palestine directly –
welcoming Jewish immigrants though there was no actual plan for a
'Jewish Homeland' – and offer Iraq to the Hashemites. Yet Churchill
learned fast that the Hashemites were not what they claimed: 'I hadn't
appreciated the weakness inherent in King Hussein's position . . . Ibn
Saud's much stronger.'

King Hussein, an Arabian King Lear, raged from his Meccan palace
not only against British betrayal but also against filial betrayal. Hussein
had arrogantly disdained Abdulaziz, but the Saudi sheikh now deployed
a fanatical Wahhabi army, the *Ikhwan* – the Brethren – whose war cry
was 'The winds of heaven are blowing!' The Saudi boasted that his
Wahhabism 'is the purest of all religions in the world', adding, 'I am the
Ikhwan – no one else.'

In May 1919 Abdullah advanced towards the Saudi capital Riyadh.
Hearing rumours that the British were giving Iraq to Faisal, Abdulaziz
reflected that the British 'have surrounded me with enemies'. His
Ikhwan crept into the encampment of the overconfident Abdullah,
shouted, 'The winds of heaven are blowing!' and slaughtered most of
his 8,000 men, while the prince escaped only by slitting open the back
of his tent and galloping away in his nightshirt. Hussein was finished,
the Saudis ascendant.

Now Churchill offered Iraq's throne to Faisal, who would be confirmed by plebiscite but rule under British protection. Faisal accepted:
in August 1921, he was crowned king in Baghdad with the British
proconsul Cox shouting, 'Long live the king!' as soldiers of the Dorset
Regiment fired a salute. Faisal, long-faced, sad-eyed and wise, ruled
through cabinets of Sunni notables, Jewish grandees and his lieutenant
from the Arab Revolt, Nuri al-Said, who would dominate Iraq until a
macabre downfall three decades later.

Abdullah raged against Faisal. Infuriated by the loss of Iraq, 'even
if it belonged to his brother', he led thirty officers and 200 Bedouin
into the eastern section of Palestine, Transjordan, seizing the town of
Maan (Amman). Abdullah was a *bon vivant*, 'attractive and delightful in

speech and enjoys joking and laughing', said Faisal, 'a connoisseur of poetry' who liked shooting apples off the heads of his servants.

Churchill gave him his fiefdom. 'Amir Abdullah is in Transjordania,' wrote Churchill, 'where I put him one Sunday afternoon in Jerusalem.' He turned out to be the most capable Hashemite – his family rule Jordan into the twenty-first century – but they swiftly lost Arabia.*

In March 1924, Hussein declared himself caliph, outraging most Muslims after his mismanagement of Mecca and embarrassing his own sons. Abdulaziz ibn Saud attacked Mecca's resort town, Taif. The *Ikhwan* drove out Hussein's son Prince Ali and slaughtered 300 civilians. Ali fled to his father, who screamed at him, but the writing was on the wall. Hussein abdicated in favour of Ali, now king of Hejaz, while he left in a convoy of cars, stacked with kerosene cans filled with coins, his black bodyguards riding on the running boards.

King Ali waited in Jeddah as Abdulaziz's cameleteers burst into Mecca, crying, 'The peoples of Mecca – neighbours of God – are under the protection of God and Ibn Saud.' That November, Abdulaziz rode into Mecca on a camel, before kneeling as a humble pilgrim to the Holy City. He carefully portrayed himself as the new Guardian of the Two Sanctuaries. When King Ali fled by boat, Abdulaziz was proclaimed king of Nadj and sultan of Hejaz. After 112 years, the Saudis were back.

The Arab arrangements of Lloyd George and Clemenceau lasted for twenty years, but their Ottoman partition, granting an empire to Greece, was already collapsing: the dashing Ottoman general, Kemal, led a Turkish awakening that destroyed their plans.

---

* The mandates were based on amalgamated Ottoman *vilayets* that did not cohere and had never existed before: French Syria encompassed three *vilayets*, Damascus, Aleppo and Beirut, inhabited by Maronite Christians, Shia and Sunni, Druze and Alawites. The French planned to divide their mandate into four – a Sunni Syria around Damascus, a Christian state named Lebanon based in Beirut, an Alawite state at Latakia and another for the Druze. Later, much to the fury of the Alawites and Druze, they amalgamated these into Syria and Lebanon. One of the Alawite chiefs was Ali al-Assad (the Lion), who wrote to the French premier: 'The Alawite people have kept their independence for generations, people of different religious beliefs, traditions and history from the Sunni Muslims . . . The Alawites refuse to be attached to Muslim Syria.' His son Hafez would rule the very Syria Ali hoped would never exist. British Iraq was created out of three *vilayets*: Baghdad, Basra and Mosul, a mix of Shia, Sunni, Kurds, Yazidi and Jews that has proved as unmanageable for the Iraqis as it was for the British. LG and Clemenceau are rightfully criticized for this late imperial carve-up, though they were wise not to hand over the entire region to one family. The Ottomans ruled ruinously for four centuries: the Anglo-French ruled ineptly for twenty-five years. In seventy years of independence, Iraqis, Syrians, Lebanese, Israelis, Saudis, Palestinians and Jordanians have hardly proved paragons of governance.

Pahlavis and Songs, Roosevelts, Mafiosi and Kennedys

ATATÜRK, REZA, LENIN: FATHER OF THE TURKS, LIGHT OF THE IRANIANS AND GREATEST OF GENIUSES

Blond, blue-eyed and lithe, Kemal was the son of a Turkish soldier and an Abkhazian mother, raised in Thessalonica, who joined the Young Turks and fought the Italians when they seized Libya in 1911 and then the Bulgarians in Thrace in 1912. He had warned Enver not to join Germany in the war, but made his name at Gallipoli before halting the Russians in the Caucasus and holding back the British in Syria. Now he faced the Anglo-French partition of the Ottoman heartland that granted swathes of territory to the Great Idea, the new Greek empire, much favoured by the enthusiastic Classicist LG.

In September 1921, Marshal Kemal, speaker of a Grand National Assembly in Ankara, halted the Greeks, then in August 1922 in a clash of 400,000 men routed them at Dumlupınar, bursting into the cosmopolitan Graeco-Turkish city of Smyrna where, in scenes of infernal slaughter, the Greeks were driven out in what they called the Catastrophe. The fiasco brought down Lloyd George. In November, Kemal abolished the monarchy: the last sultan, Mehmed VI, departed on a British warship, though a cousin was temporarily installed as caliph. The forty-three-year-old Kemal, elected president of a new republic of Türkiye, was acknowledged by the Allies, agreed a population swap of 350,000 Turks and 1.1 million Greeks* and cancelled independent Armenia and Kurdistan.

---

* Self-determination was a noble ideal, still universally accepted as the correct basis for the organization of the modern world, but in practice, it was painful. The new nation states had to be hacked out of territories long ruled by multi-ethnic empires. In Ireland, Britain, faced with a Catholic Irish revolt and civil war, would now negotiate a partition between an independent Catholic republic in the south and a Protestant province in the north. Just as the creation of Greece in the 1820s had led to the departure of Muslims, now the creation of Türkiye brutally expelled the Greeks. After the Second World War, such brutal partitions created new states in Germany and Poland 1945; India and Pakistan 1947; Israel 1948.

Kemal was implacable to his opponents, who were assassinated or hanged,* and he massacred and bombed the Kurdish rebels who threatened his regime.

Kemal had a vision of a Turkish nation. He rejected Ottoman decadence, separated religion from politics, commissioned a Turkish alphabet in Latin letters, founded Ankara university, liberated women from the veil and granted female education and suffrage. He moved the capital to Ankara and in the formally renamed Istanbul he converted the Hagia Sophia (the former church built by Justinian, converted into a mosque by Mehmed II) into a museum. He also ordered Turks to take surnames for the first time: he became Atatürk – Father of Turks.

Atatürk was a sultanic autocrat who lived in the old Ottoman palaces, cruising in his presidential yacht; although he was a raffish epicurean, a womanizer with a complicated love life and a hard drinker of rakı, he was also a generous paterfamilias, adopting thirteen orphans.† He never became a sultan, but he inspired another general to become a shah.

On 25 April 1926, in the hall of the Golestan Palace in Teheran a tall soldier of obscure origins placed the crown on his own head and was hailed as shah of Iran. In a few years he had gone from stableboy to monarch, creating a dynasty that would rule until the 1970s, temporarily restoring Iran to power and wealth. A harsh, uneducated martinet, grandson and son of soldiers, ramrod straight and irascible, Reza had been born in the Mazandaran Province on the Caspian Sea and had joined the Persian Cossack Regiment set up by Russian advisers. Adept on horseback and expert with Maxim guns, he rose to the rank of commander and married the top general's daughter – just as Persia was falling apart. Its oil was essential to British power. In 1906, the Qajar shah had been forced to grant a constitution, but the kingdom was dominated by Britain and Russia. After Lenin's revolution, the Soviets were pushed out by the British general Edmund Ironside, who sought a strongman. Then he met Reza for the first time. 'Well over six foot, with

---

* Enver, once Ottoman vice-generalissmo but now outmanoeuvred by Kemal, left for Berlin then Moscow and Central Asia where he declared himself amir of Turkestan and launched a Turkic uprising, resisted by Lenin's Red Army, which was seeking to secure central Asia. Not far from Dushanbe (Tajikistan), he was killed by the Bolsheviks in a skirmish. The other two pashas, Talaat and Jemal, were assassinated by Armenians.

† During the war Atatürk's secretary Fikriye Hanım was his main lover, but now he met the cultured Latife Uşaklıgil, forming a triangle that ended with Fikriye shooting herself (with a pistol that was a gift from Kemal). In 1938, just fifty-seven, Atatürk died of cirrhosis at the Ottoman Dolmabahçe Palace in Istanbul. His vision, guarded by the army, which intervened repeatedly to seize power, endured until 2003 when the Islamist Recep Tayyip Erdoğan, first as premier, then as president, enforced an Islamist autocracy, symbolically reconverting the Hagia Sophia into a mosque.

broad shoulders,' noted Ironside, 'his hooked nose and sparkling eyes gave him a distinguished look.'

Reza seemed an ideal frontman. In 1921, he proposed to seize power. When the British approved, 'He began dancing, whistling,' recalled one of his officers, 'and snapping his fingers.' Reza and 600 horsemen rode into Teheran and overthrew the premier, setting up a replacement and becoming war minister himself; he announced his arrival with posters that began, 'I command'. After crushing rebellious warlords, Reza emerged as a visionary reformer, a passionate patriot and a paranoid autocrat, while the ineffectual young shah sulked in Europe.

In October 1925, when the Majlis (parliament) debated the end of the Qajars and the installation of Reza as shah, two future potentates were present: a rich Paris-educated landowner, Mohammad Mosaddegh, aged forty-three, who had already been foreign minister, warned that Reza was too capable to serve as a constitutional monarch; while a twenty-three-year-old student of Islamic scholarship and history at the Qom seminary, and sometime poet, Ruhollah Khomeini, watched the debates, disgusted by foreign interference as much as by the rise of this irreligious general. Reza's henchmen assassinated an opponent of his accession on the steps of the Majlis. Though they killed the wrong man, it did the trick. In December, the Majlis approved a new monarchy.

At the coronation, an urbane aristocrat, Abdolhossein Teymourtash, presented the crown to Reza, now forty-eight, sporting uniform and royal cloak. Teymourtash, a womanizing, gambling and boozing sophisticate, educated in Petersburg, designed the new monarchy: Ferdowsi's *Shahnameh* was recited, Cyrus and Darius quoted. Inspired by his ally Atatürk, Reza ordered Persians to adopt surnames and wear western dress, while women were to remove veils and go to school; he also built railways, factories, roads, secular schools and a university in Teheran. Wielding his cane, he barked at his nation of 'bigoted and ignorant' subjects and beat anyone who contradicted him. He kicked insubordinates in the groin; and although he paid lip-service to the powerful mullahs, when an ayatollah commented on the dresses of the shah's daughters, Reza slapped him.

One thing mattered to Reza: his son Mohammad, aged six, born with a twin sister Ashraf, must succeed him. He nicknamed the prince Bird of Good Omen. But regarding any indulgence as likely to encourage homosexuality, Reza and son called each other 'sir', and Mohammad thought his father 'most frightening'. But his mother Tadj ol-Molouk taught him that he was a man of destiny.

Teymourtash was influential too – Mohammad's first love was the minister's daughter. Teymourtash recommended that the boy study at Le Rosey in Switzerland, enabling him to escape his father. Here from the age of eleven the crown prince discovered the joys of western sybaritism – and finally found a friend, Ernest Perron, the school's twenty-three-year-old gardener and assistant poetry teacher who introduced him to Rabelais and Mozart. This was not quite the virile instruction that Reza had envisioned for his heir.

As Atatürk and Reza shaped their new states, the third creator, Lenin, was forging a new Russia, unafraid of the human cost. 'A revolution without firing squads is meaningless,' he said, and in his orders to henchmen he frenziedly demanded mass killings. Now he devised a state, ruled by himself as chairman of the council of people's commissars (premier), controlled exclusively by a small Communist Party and actually governed by a tiny cabal of leaders. The cabinet, known as the Political Bureau (Politburo), dominated by the talented Trotsky and Stalin, assumed a quasi-sacred prerogative of omniscient decision-making on behalf of the people that Lenin called 'the dictatorship of the proletariat'. As Lenin temporarily instituted a soft capitalism to cope with a country ruined by war, he and Stalin debated its ethnic shape with a view to keeping Ukraine and controlling what they called the 'limitrophes' (border-countries from Roman *limitrophus*). Stalin, a Georgian, proposed a Russian Soviet federation; the Ukrainian, Georgian and other ethnic Bolsheviks wanted independence from Russia. Lenin, who loathed 'Great Russian chauvinism', agreed with them. He aimed to keep Ukrainians in and Poles out, proposing a Union of Soviet Socialist Republics of Europe and Asia in which the four main peoples had their own republics. This was designed to satisfy the aspirations of Ukrainians and Georgians who had supported the revolution to escape the tsarist 'prison of nations'. Its genius was that technically the peoples could 'check out' any time they liked, but they could 'never leave'. Its flaw was if the Party was ever weakened, the republics could seize theoretical independence and become ready-made countries. But no one considered that. It was never likely to happen.*

The effort had broken Lenin. In May 1922, resting at a dacha outside Moscow, he suffered a stroke, leaving him half paralysed and unable to speak. At the Bolshoi Theatre, on 28 December, Stalin oversaw the

---

* 'The right of the republics to secede freely from the Union was included in the text,' wrote a Russian historical essayist in 2021, but 'by doing so, the authors planted in the foundation of our state a dangerous timebomb'. The essayist was Vladimir Putin. The original four republics were Russia, Ukraine, Belarus and Transkavkazia (Caucasus). The central Asian republics were then added and Transkavkazia broken up. After 1940 there were fifteen.

creation of the Union of Soviet Socialist Republics, in which national cultures such as the Ukrainians or Georgians were encouraged within their republics. When Lenin returned to the Kremlin, he had another stroke. Like all leaders, he believed he was irreplaceable: he appointed Stalin, his high-handed but self-deprecating Georgian henchman, as general secretary, to balance the haughty, flashy Trotsky, war commissar. Now he begged Stalin to give him cyanide so he could commit suicide. Stalin refused. Yet while Trotsky did little to create a faction, Stalin, sociable, accessible and modest, cultivated allies among the tough provincial *praktiki* who preferred his dourness to Trotsky's arrogance. Besides, the Russians would never support a Jewish leader. When Stalin's coarse will to power emerged, the paralysed Lenin tried to remove him, but it was too late. While Trotsky and other hifalutin ideologists continued to underestimate Stalin, he was already making decisions: in January 1923, he supported Sun Yat-sen who, after thirty years, finally found a backer who could deliver.

THE SONG SISTERS: SUN, CHIANG AND MAO

Sun and his young wife Qingling Song had lived for five years see-sawing between power and disaster. In 1917 Sun, backed by the Germans, seized power in Guangzhou and declared himself grand marshal, but he was swiftly deposed. As Lenin fell ill, Sun returned to Guangzhou as president, until in June 1922 one of his generals tried to assassinate him. Sun fled for the port, ruthlessly leaving his young pregnant wife Qingling as bait to cover his escape: it was 'a life-and-death struggle', she recalled; 'we were literally buried in a hell of constant gunfire', after which 'I disguised myself as an old countrywoman with a guard disguised as a pedlar . . .' She suffered a miscarriage, but she and Sun were reunited and protected by a young KMT general, Chiang Kai-shek, who arranged their sanctuary in Shanghai as Sun appealed to Moscow.

Soon after Lenin's coup, Sun had telegraphed his admiration to the 'great man'. There was something about Sun and Lenin that was similar. 'Do you know,' said Meiling Song, 'I've noticed the most successful men are usually not the ones with great powers as geniuses but the ones who had such ultimate faith in their own selves that invariably they hypnotize others as well as themselves.' Lenin had ordered the founding of the Chinese Communist Party, but it was tiny: Moscow backed Sun.

On 21 January 1924, Lenin, just fifty-three, died, having ordered a plain burial. Stalin, the ex-seminarist, recited 'We vow to you, Comrade

Lenin', a credo of devotions to 'the greatest of geniuses of the proletariat', and had Lenin embalmed and displayed as a Christlike Soviet *tsar-batiushka* – little father – in a red porphyry mausoleum. 'We Communists are people of a special mould,' said Stalin. 'We're made of a special stuff.' That was already apparent. As he played off his Party rivals and promoted 'socialism in one country', he sent cash to Sun, enabling him to found the Whampoa Military Academy and train his military; in return Sun allowed him control of Mongolia and Xinjiang and folded the new Chinese Communist Party into his ruling KMT. Sun, advised by Qingling and her brother T. V. Song, armed by Stalin, planned to conquer warlord-infested northern China, in a campaign under thirty-seven-year-old Chiang Kai-shek. Among the Communists who now arrived at KMT headquarters was a tall, dishevelled figure with shaggy hair: Mao Zedong, aged thirty-one. Together with Sun, these two would decide the fate of China for the rest of the century.

Violent, irascible, skin-headed yet emotional, Chiang, a poor salt merchant's son empowered by a worshipful mother whom he adored, had been trained in the Japanese army, before joining the Green Gang of Shanghai in 1911 and embracing Sun's cause. Now Sun dispatched him to Moscow, where he developed a loathing for the arrogant Bolsheviks (particularly Trotsky), their dogma and their veiled ambitions in China. Concealing his misgivings, he sent his only son, by his first wife, Chiang Ching-kuo, to study at the newly created Sun Yat-sen University in Moscow. Although her brother was an enthusiastic capitalist, Qingling embraced Marxism.

Just as Sun, now fifty-eight, was preparing his Northern Expedition, he was diagnosed with liver cancer. As he lay dying, he backed the Soviet alliance and told Qingling, 'I wish to follow the example of my friend Lenin in having my body embalmed,' and insisted his tomb be built on the Purple Gold Mountain in Nanjing next to Zhu Yuanzhang, founder of the Ming. Sun was almost deified as Father of China and Liberator of the Nation, echoing Lenin's cult – and Chiang emerged as a contender for the leadership. 'I have position,' Chiang told his wife, 'but I lack prestige,' adding, 'I need to get close to the Song family.' The Song family agreed.

In June 1926, the eldest sister Ailing – married to the wealthy banker H. H. Kung – invited Chiang to a dinner where he sat between the hostess and her youngest sister, Meiling, both glamorous in bright *cheongsams*. Meiling was surprised to find that the crude, short-tempered general was serious and sensitive, while Chiang saw the chance of marriage to the sister-in-law of Sun.

Soon afterwards Chiang, now commander-in-chief, led the Northern Expedition, pushing his power into the north, but his successes empowered the Communists within the government. Mao Zedong, both a radical Marxist and a nationalist, worked with the KMT as an alternate member of its Central Executive Committee: a group photograph shows him standing behind Qingling and T. V. Song. Son of a well-off peasant from Hunan – he never lost his accent – Mao had clashed with his father, but he admitted, 'I worshipped my mother,' a Buddhist with bound feet, 'three-inch golden lilies', a definition of beauty at that time. Bathing in her indulgence, he enjoyed a carefree youth, writing poetry, then joined a republican army, before training as a teacher and reading about history and struggle: 'When Great Heroes give full play to their impulses they are magnificently powerful, stormy and invincible . . . like a hurricane from a gorge, a sex maniac on heat, prowling for a lover.' The excitement of conflict and of power over life and death has never been better expressed. 'Revolutionary war is an anti-toxin which not only eliminates the enemy's poison,' he argued, 'but also purges us of our filth.'

When the Communist Party was founded in Shanghai, he attended its first meeting. Even while cooperating with the KMT, he focused on land reforms, his views and nature implacably radical. Impulsive and unscrupulous, a supreme manipulator of personalities with a fine turn of phrase, a relentless reader and history buff, with a superb memory, he possessed an unyielding will to dominate. Influenced like so many by social Darwinism, which dovetailed with Marxist class struggle, Mao believed that 'Long-lasting peace is unendurable to humans'; rather 'We love sailing on a sea of upheavals.' China had to be 'destroyed and reformed' to rise again.

When Chiang captured Wuhan, the Communists, backed by Madame Sun, took over, launching a reign of terror as small Red armies seized territory. The KMT congress was hijacked by its Communist minority, and Communists in Shanghai, led by a subtle young leader, Zhou Enlai, seized businesses: Chiang was losing control of China. The Songs urged action: recruiting his gangster-boss ally 'Big-Eared' Du, Chiang planned a counter-coup and compiled death lists: Mao and Zhou were on them.

Chiang's son was still in Moscow, but Chiang said, 'I can't sacrifice national interests for my son.' On 12 April 1927, he pounced: 'Big-Eared' Du and his gang members beheaded Communists in the streets of Shanghai. Ten thousand were killed. 'Better to kill 1,000 innocent people,' said Chiang, 'than let a single Communist escape.' Mao escaped and met up with a Communist army, later launching an uprising that was obliterated. Demoted for 'military opportunism', Mao fled to a Communist enclave in Jiangxi, but he learned the lesson of Chiang's purge, telling Stalin's envoy, 'Power comes from the barrel of a gun.'* Taking command in Jiangxi, he spotted a skinny, neurotic graduate of the Whampoa Academy, the twenty-one-year-old Lin Biao, who later became the best Communist general and the chosen heir but who died trying to overthrow him. Mao felt the ferocity of the struggle when his wife was beheaded by the KMT, though he swiftly married a young comrade, with whom he had more children. While Zhou organized clandestine work in Shanghai, Mao held public executions of landlords at Party rallies, declaring, 'Revolution's not a dinner party, nor an essay, nor a painting, nor embroidery,' but 'an act of violence by which one class overthrows another'. Stalin noticed that Mao was 'insubordinate but successful' and started to back him.

Now Chiang courted Meiling Song, inviting her on a series of dates. He agreed to study Christianity and dismiss his concubines. In September 1927, they were engaged, marrying in December, the 'biggest wedding Shanghai ever saw', wrote Meiling, who tamed Chiang, emerging as his chief adviser, eschewing western clothes and always sporting a silk *cheongsam*, slit to the knee on both sides. It was never a passionate romance. 'Here was my opportunity,' she wrote. 'With my husband, I would work ceaselessly to make China strong.'

Chiang set up his dictatorship at Nanjing styled as chairman of the State Council and generalissimo. He disdained Chinese people as 'lazy, indifferent, corrupt, decadent' and 'walking corpses', and he trusted no one, setting up rival secret-police organs whose operatives assassinated his rivals and tortured his enemies. When Chiang had a Communist comrade executed, Madame Sun screamed at him, 'Butcher!' Afterwards, he planned her assassination in a faked car crash, but cancelled it.†

Yet in the north an aggressive empire was keen to expand. The Tiger of Mukden, Grand Marshal Zhang Zuolin, still ran Manchuria, with Japanese backing. On 25 December 1926, Hirohito became emperor at a time when his generals sought to guide the nation. The army's

---

* Mao channelled the fifth-century BC philosopher Sun Tzu: 'When the enemy advances, we retreat. When the enemy rests, we harass him. When the enemy avoids battle, we attack. When the enemy retreats we advance.'
† 'There's no genuine friendship or kindness or love under heaven,' wrote Chiang in his surprisingly emotional diary. 'The relationship of mother and son is the only exception.' He trusted only Meiling: 'Apart from my wife, not a single other person can share a little responsibility or a little work with me.' Chiang granted subsidies to the warlords who backed him and Meiling organized payments, while T. V. Song and H. H. Kung served as premier and finance minister. When assassins tried to kill Generalissimo and Madame Chiang, they shouted, 'Death to the Song Dynasty!'

Imperial Way faction saw the new reign as an unmissable opportunity to remove cautious liberal politicians and bring in a militaristic nationalist dictatorship under the emperor: a Chinese empire was Japan's right as a great power.

Two men stood in their way: in Manchuria, Marshal Zhang; and in the rest of China, Chiang Kai-shek. Without any permission from Tokyo, Japanese generals solved the first problem. On 4 June 1928, they blew up the marshal's train. Manchuria was inherited by the Tiger's opium-addicted son, known as the Young Marshal, but his grip was much weakened. Next they needed to deal with Chiang, who had emerged as national leader at the same time as the man who would ultimately back him.

On 6 November 1928, Franklin Roosevelt pulled off an astonishing rebirth. The Democratic presidential nominee, Al Smith, had proposed that FDR run for New York governor, presuming that a crippled man would never be able to challenge him at a national level. Though he was lifted out of cars and helped to rostrums, Roosevelt proved him wrong. 'Well, here's the helpless cripple my opponent is speaking about,' he said on the pitch. 'This is my sixteenth speech today.'

JAZZ: ROOSEVELT, JOSEPHINE BAKER, LUCKY LUCIANO AND THE ROARING TWENTIES

To everyone's surprise, even his own, Roosevelt won the governorship, and Smith lost the presidency resoundingly to Herbert Hoover. A reporter asked Eleanor how she felt. 'I'm not excited about my husband's election. I don't care. What difference can it make to me?' Roosevelt promised 'an era of good feeling'.

Although America had stayed outside Wilson's League of Nations, the economy was booming, the stock market soaring, the Twenties roaring and American 'good feeling' conquered the world. At home, where alcohol was still banned, Americans drank in blind tigers – covert bars or speakeasies – to the sound of jazz, a word that originated in jasm, which among black musicians in New Orleans meant sexual energy. Jazz, a fusion of African-American blues, ragtime and jig piano, was developed there in New Orleans. Its seminal ballad, 'Strange Fruit', sung by Billie Holiday, recounts a lynching: most of the musical movements that swept twentieth-century Euro-America would be rooted in the horror and passion of the African-American experience. F. Scott Fitzgerald, a young novelist who chronicled the careless wealth and mysterious pasts of the new grandees in his novel *The Great Gatsby*, called the period the Jazz Age. In Chicago and New York at the same time, vertiginous sky-scraping towers were built. Jazz was now embraced by white Americans spending money made in industry, on the stock market or from crime in glamorous clubs controlled by Italian, Irish and Jewish gangsters where Scottish and Canadian whisky was served. Lucky Luciano was recruited as a hitman by the pudgy, epicurean New York *padrino* Joe Masseria; Meyer and Bugsy often assisted at his killings. Masseria was confronted by challengers and survived (with only two bullet holes in his hat) a gun-blazing assassination attempt, with hitmen firing tommy-guns while riding on the running boards of a motor car. He emerged as *capo di tutti capi* – boss of bosses – forcing other Mafiosi from Detroit and Buffalo to pay tribute.

'The Brain' Rothstein was the quintessential Roaring Twenties man of elegant violence, holding court at racetracks, restaurants and blind tigers surrounded by his bodyguards, but even he could not control his gam-bling addiction, and he accumulated a debt that led to his shooting. Dying in hospital in 1928, he refused to reveal his killers. 'You stick to your trade,' he told the police, 'I'll stick to mine,' joking, 'My mudder did it.'

In Paris, the end of war and pandemic sparked a *joie de vivre, les années folles* – Crazy Years – when a black ex-soldier Jim Europe and his Harlem Hellfighters brought American ragtime and the Charleston to the city in their *Revue Nègre*. Paris was dazzled by a nineteen-year-old American mixed-race dancer, Josephine Baker from Missouri, who had started dancing on St Louis street corners but hated American racism. 'I just couldn't stand America,' she said, 'and I was one of the first colored Americans to move to Paris' – which she took by storm, dancing almost naked except for a loincloth of bananas. 'The most sen-sational woman anyone ever saw,' recalled an American novelist, Ernest Hemingway. It was not just music: in 1927, Baker was the first African-American to star in a movie, a silent French production *La Sirène des tropiques*, but it was American cinema that now conquered the world. If a family of Russian immigrants pioneered the 'talkie', it was a piratical Irish banker who made the first movie fortune that helped launch his family as an American political dynasty.

RIN TIN TIN: KENNEDY, LITTLE CAESAR AND FDR

On 6 October 1927, at a Warner brothers' cinema in New York, the Warner brothers premiered their first talkie movie, *The Jazz Singer*, using the new Vitaphone system. When the star, Al Jolson, delivered his trademark 'Wait a minute, you ain't heard nothing yet,' the audience were first astonished and then almost hysterical. The movie made the Warners $2.6 million and opened a new era.

Edison's patent had allowed him to claim a film monopoly until 1915, when it was overturned, but already others were making silent movies. By the time Edison died in 1918, a generation of Russian Jews – furriers, glovers, cobblers – had moved to Hollywood, attracted by the sunny climate, ideal for filming. In 1917, the four Warners had founded Warner Brothers, which first made money in a film about German atrocities, then lost more in a story about venereal disease and then made it big with a series featuring a dog named Rin Tin Tin whom Jack Warner thought was cleverer than most of his actors.

As 15,000 theatres across America showed movies and millions listened to the radio, the business attracted a banker from Boston, Joe Kennedy, the fair-haired Bostonian dynamo who had proclaimed himself 'America's youngest bank president' while making a fortune on the stock market. Kennedy understood that movies along with radio would change life. 'This is another telephone,' he said, 'and we must get into this.'

He was not alone. Randolph Hearst, heir to the Deadwood gold fortune and newspaper mogul, was making movies to help his actress paramour Marion Davies. Kennedy met Hearst and proposed an amalgamation – to 'foment the talkie revolution and a model of corporate control and vertical integration' – but when the newspaper baron did not bite, he bought into a bankrupt studio, moved to Los Angeles and soon controlled three studios. Married wholesomely to Rose Fitzgerald, daughter of Honey Fitz, long-serving Boston mayor, Kennedy had nine children, including four boys, but he left them in Boston so that he could enjoy Hollywood where he swiftly beguiled the lost, gamine movie star Gloria Swanson. An insatiable womanizer, often asking his henchmen for 'good-looking girls' because he had to be 'fed on wild meat', his seduction techniques resembled his business style: he burst into Swanson's bedroom, announcing, 'No longer, no longer! Now!' Gloria recalled. 'He was like a roped horse, rough, arduous, racing to be free' and reaching a 'hasty climax'.

In October 1928, Kennedy merged his studios into RKO, then cashed out with $5 million, selling his last studio to Pathé for $4 million. Abruptly abandoning Swanson and LA, he returned to New York where the stock market was soaring in frenzied trading. Kennedy liked to claim that when a shoeshine boy gave him share tips, he knew it was time to sell all his holdings.

On 29 October 1929, 'Black Tuesday', shares crashed on Wall Street, then on stock markets globally, followed by a grinding depression, economic and psychological, a massive sell-off, then falls in prices, demand and credit, leading to the devastation of US industry and agriculture, with thirteen million unemployed. America lost its confidence.

The Crash accelerated a crisis in another American industry: organized crime. Joe the Boss's rival, Salvatore Maranzano, a murderous braggart from Sicily's Castellammare del Golfo who saw himself as the Julius Caesar of crime, persuaded Luciano to kill the *padrino*. In April 1931, Luciano invited Joe to play cards at a Coney Island restaurant. When Luciano went to the bathroom, Bugsy Siegel burst in with three others and killed the Boss, marking the end of what came to be called the Castellammarese War. Pompously declaring himself *capo di tutti capi*, 'Little Caesar' Maranzano organized the Mafia into five New York 'families' along with city 'families' across America.* Obsessed with the Julio-Claudians, suspicious of the Jewish Meyer and Bugsy and jealous of his deputy, Maranzano ordered a hit on Luciano. Instead, in September, Bugsy and Meyer sent four Jewish hitmen dressed as policemen to Maranzano's Park Avenue office where they stabbed him to death. Crime was so big that Luciano made millions a year, but he did not declare himself godfather, instead creating a commission to act as a board of directors which supervised organized crime for the next fifty years.

In respectable New York, Governor Roosevelt tried progressive measures to fight the Depression as President Hoover floundered in Washington. In 1932 FDR ran against Hoover. 'I pledge you, I pledge myself to a new deal for the American people,' he declared, promising vast spending and the repeal of Prohibition. Hoover called him 'a chameleon in plaid', but America was desperate for hope: FDR won the presidency. Even before his inauguration, a lunatic tried to shoot him, but Roosevelt reassured Americans that 'The only thing we have to fear is fear itself.' In a blizzard of legislation that enacted his New Deal, he restored faith in the banks and spent lavishly. Setting up a new Stock Exchange Commission to impose rules on the stock market that had caused the crash, he chose as its chairman one of the most successful speculators, Joe Kennedy, who had put his gains into property and, after

---

* Each family had a hierarchy of boss, captains and soldiers. In a quasi-Catholic ritual, the finger of a 'made man' was pricked, blood dripping on to a picture of St Francis of Assisi which was then lit as he swore *omertà* – silence – with the words: 'As this saint burns so shall my soul. I enter alive and I only leave dead.' Crime families recreated the loyalty of real families, though their bosses were actually elected; only the Trafficante family of Florida passed from father to son.

Prohibition had been overturned by Congress, into Scotch whisky. Kennedy planned to run for president himself, but FDR privately mocked the 'red-haired Irishman'.

FDR exuded a breezy confidence with his sonorous voice and debonair cigarette holder, backed up by his own story of recovery. Broadcasting aristocratic radio lectures from his people's fireside, he proved the ultimate political thespian, scarcely hinting at the devious player behind the urbane smile.

FDR encouraged Eleanor to become the 'conscience of the New Deal', which she popularized in a daily column. As she travelled around the country, Eleanor was invaluable for Franklin: she tapped the perfect man to direct the Works Progress Administration that created three million jobs, a social worker named Harry Hopkins who, after Howe died of cancer, became Roosevelt's essential aide. Roosevelt needed his family at his court, but he understood that 'One of the worst things in the world is being child of a president.' Jimmy became stressed by serving as his assistant; Elliott became a shady playboy; Anna married twice, but later returned as his favourite companion.

'I realize FDR's a great man and he's nice to me,' Eleanor confessed, 'but as a person I'm a stranger and I don't want to be anything else.' This was perhaps a coping mechanism after the heartbreak of FDR's affair, but she found warmth in a special friend, a sturdy cigar-chomping ex-reporter called Lorena Hickock, known as Hick, with whom Eleanor enjoyed something close to love. 'I couldn't say *je t'aime* and *je t'adore* as I longed to do,' she wrote, but 'I go to sleep thinking of you.' It was probably sexual: 'I'd never do what I did to you with anyone else,' wrote Eleanor. Roosevelt's White House was a presidential court: Missy LeHand taking notes in her nightgown, Hick, who moved into the White House, following Eleanor 'like a St Bernard'.

On 30 January 1933, as Roosevelt prepared for his inauguration, Adolf Hitler called on the German president, Field Marshal Paul von Hindenburg, who at 11.15 a.m. swore him in as chancellor of Germany. Like his polar opposite Roosevelt, Hitler was made by the Crash, but although he insisted his rise was providential, it was far from inevitable. It was made possible by the titanic Old Man, the greatest living German.

THE FIELD MARSHAL AND THE CORPORAL

'It was against my inclination,' declared Hindenburg, who had retired to write his memoirs, farm his estate and enjoy his hunting, 'to take any interest in current politics.' That was not quite true. In 1919, the ambitious old Junker had testified that Germany had not been defeated – just 'stabbed in the back' by mysterious traitors. In 1920 he wanted to run for president, but he had been distracted and heartbroken by the death of his wife.

Then in late 1923 his old quartermaster-general Ludendorff approached him with an extraordinary idea: he was going to seize power with a vulgar rabble-rouser. Hindenburg firmly rejected such impertinence.

On 8 November that year, Hitler, Ludendorff and 2,000 Nazis marched on the Munich Beer Hall where the Bavarian government commissioner was speaking. Firing his pistol into the ceiling, Hitler jumped on a chair yelling, 'National revolution has broken out! The hall's surrounded . . . Nobody can leave.' After a long night of confusion, Ludendorff and Hitler led the revolutionists towards the Bavarian Defence Ministry, but at the Odeonsplatz soldiers manning a barricade opened fire. Fourteen Nazis and four policemen fell dead; Hitler ran down a side street, jumped into a car and, when the car broke down, limped to a supporter's house. 'I opened the door,' wrote Helen Hanfstaengl. 'There he stood pale as a ghost, without a hat, his face and his clothing covered in dirt . . .' He promised to kill himself.

Hindenburg called for national unity. Hitler was sentenced to a five-year jail term for treason. His nine months in Landsberg Prison were 'my state-university', and it was there that he wrote his essential work, *Mein Kampf* (My Struggle), dictated to his devoted secretary Rudolf Hess, son of a wealthy businessman. This laid out with brazen clarity his stupendously ambitious and murderously vicious programme, from the 'eradication' of the Jews to the conquest of Aryan 'living space' in Russia and Poland, achievable only by war and killing under his providential leadership. The instant bestseller made him rich, and after its publication none of his backers could ever claim to be ignorant of his intentions.

As Hitler emerged from prison, Germany was recovering, even thriving, aided by the US Dawes Plan, under President von Hindenburg, who in 1925 had secured the permission of the ex-kaiser – his 'king and lord' – to run for the presidency.

Hitler had to reconquer his own Party, bringing in a young socialist journalist, Joseph Goebbels, who was dazzled by 'those large blue eyes like stars' and helped him build his personal leadership, founded on a quasi-messianic cult, with its own bible, *Mein Kampf*, its own official greeting 'Heil Hitler!' and its own bodyguard, the black-clad

Schutzstaffel (SS). The SS was commanded by Heinrich Himmler, a failed Bavarian chicken farmer with nervous stomach ailments, the gawky, myopic son of a headmaster and royal tutor. Hitler believed his time would come: 'I have been the prophet of many things.' In October 1929, the Crash threw Germany into a desperate economic spiral of inflation, unemployment and violence.

In March 1930, Hindenburg, advised by the camarilla of his son Oskar and his wartime adjutant Colonel Kurt von Schleicher, rejected parliamentary government and resorted instead to autocratic rule through Article 48 of the constitution, appointing a chancellor and ruling by decree. Hindenburg was repudiating parliamentary democracy just as Hitler's extremism, along with proliferating rightist movements, became popular not just among the threatened middle class but among the elite who hated the socialists, feared the Communists, resented Versailles and craved authoritarianism. Prince Wilhelm August, a son of the kaiser (still living in Holland), was one of the first of many aristocrats and tycoons to join the Nazis.*

In the elections of September 1930, Hitler won 18.3 per cent of the vote, second only to the Social Democrats. While the SA terrorized the streets, the Nazis, led by Göring, dominated the Reichstag. The Nazis expected power, but none came. Instead Hitler suffered a familial blow. His niece Geli Raubal, cheerful daughter of his half-sister Angela, nineteen years his junior, was his frequent companion on his tireless political tours, but when she fell in love with his chauffeur, Uncle Alf banned the relationship. Hitler admired women, often praising them as 'big and blonde and wonderful', but unlike his priapic father he was awkward, asking at least two girls, 'Don't you want to kiss me?' to which they answered, 'No, Herr Hitler.' But he probably loved the omnipresent Geli, encouraging her to become a singer, and he certainly preferred younger girls, as his father had. 'There's nothing better than educating a young thing,' he reflected, 'malleable as wax.' In September 1931, Geli shot herself with a pistol given to her by Uncle Alf. No one knows why she killed herself, but most likely she found herself suffocated by Hitler's control.

'The days are sad right now,' a poleaxed Hitler told Winifred Wagner, the composer's daughter-in-law and one of the devoted hostesses who served as surrogate mothers. The suicide made him a vegetarian and confirmed that love and family mattered little to him. 'I'm the most

---

* The kaiser's eldest, the ex-crown prince Wilhelm, supported Hitler initially, hoping to run for president himself and restore the monarchy.

limited person in the world in this area,' he said, 'I am a fully non-familial being.' Soon afterwards, Hitler, now forty, met the eighteen-year-old Eva Braun, a schoolteacher's daughter and assistant to his photographer Hoffmann, who fitted Hitler's ideal of 'big and blonde and wonderful'. When she too attempted suicide, it won her a permanent place in his life – 'This girl did this out of love for me' – but her discretion allowed him to declare frequently, 'I have another bride. I *am* married: to the German people.' That marriage looked like it might never happen. In autumn 1931, Hindenburg met Hitler at a conference. Hitler thought him 'an old fool' while Hindenburg hated 'that Austrian corporal'. It seemed unlikely he would ever come to power and it was not Germany but Japan that became the sparkwheel of world conflict.

On 18 September 1931, Japanese officers blew up a bridge outside Mukden that pushed the emperor and his generals into sending more troops into China. Hirohito backed the seizure of much of Manchuria, where he allowed the last Manchu, Puyi, to be crowned puppet emperor. The success encouraged ultra-nationalists and expansionist generals who were convinced that a Japanese empire in China was their country's right. Force was the only way: at home they assassinated the premier and planned coups; abroad they provoked fighting with Chinese troops in Shanghai.

Chiang Kai-shek realized that a Japanese war was inevitable but sought 'Domestic Stability First' – the eradication of Communist Jiangxi. He also tried to get his son back from Stalin. 'I've been longing to see my son more than ever,' he wrote. 'I dreamed of my late mother and cried out to her twice ... I've committed a great sin against her.' Advised by German generals, he launched five campaigns to destroy Mao's Communist base, encircling it with blockhouses. Stalin punished Chiang by sending his son to work in the mines.

In October 1934, as Chiang closed in, Mao broke out on a long twisting trek during which he lost, by disease, war and defections, 80,000 of his 100,000 followers. Mao himself abandoned his own brother as well as a wife and several babies, but in January 1935 at Zunyi he won power over the Party Secretariat. The trek was later mythologized as the Long March, with many of its heroic battles invented by Mao's propagandists. He was no military genius, his leadership quixotic and costly – Chiang was bewildered by this 'wandering in circles'. Finally, when Mao and just 4,000 troops set up headquarters at Shaanxi, on the Yellow Earth Plateau close to the Yellow River, he was joined by his former superior Zhou Enlai, sophisticated, French-speaking and feline, as lieutenant and backed by the comrade who would one day rule China, Deng Xiaoping, a diminutive, peppery Sichuan landlord's son aged thirty-one.* Setting himself up at Yan'an in comfortable cave houses filled with his books, Mao built up military power, determined to destroy Chiang. He would remain at this base for ten years as Japan advanced into China, disdaining the League of Nations.

In March 1932, Hindenburg beat Hitler in the presidential elections. Hindenburg, who now faced soaring Nazi violence, was determined to be the leader of the right. 'I won't abandon my efforts for a healthy move to the right,' he promised, appointing a new chancellor, Schleicher's wartime friend Franz von Papen, a rich Catholic nobleman, prize-winning equestrian and decorated wartime officer who during the First World War had tried to orchestrate a Mexican attack on the USA. Schleicher, now defence minister, controlled this 'cabinet of monocles', but Hindenburg offered the vice-chancellorship to Hitler, leader of the largest Reichstag party, who overreached by demanding the chancellorship. 'I can't entrust the empire of Kaiser Wilhelm and Bismarck to a corporal from Bohemia,' growled the president, but he received Hitler regally: 'I want to extend my hand to you as a fellow soldier.' The corporal and the field marshal had different styles but much in common: both were German nationalists, both loathed the republic and Versailles, both planned to dismantle Poland.† Both believed they personified the German nation (though Hindenburg revered the monarchy and preferred a Hohenzollern restoration), both believed in the 'stab in the back' by socialists and Jews, both revered a militaristic *Volksgemeinschaft* – national community – and despised democracy, as did the Japanese generals who now accelerated conflict in the east.

Schleicher and Papen were already negotiating with the Nazis, hoping to exploit their thugs on the streets and their votes in the Reichstag.

---

* At fifteen, Deng had travelled to study and train as a fitter in France, where he became a Marxist and met Zhou Enlai, afterwards returning to join the army of a warlord allied to Chiang. When the general turned against the Communists, Deng fled to Mao and accompanied him on the Long March. At his new base, Mao also promoted Xi Zhongxun, son of a local Shaanxi landowner. Xi's work during the Forties included United Front work to win over KMT leaders and territory. He met a young girl from Beijing whose father was a KMT official, but she joined the Communists and they married in 1943. When he moved to Beijing, she went with him, working in the propaganda department. Their son Xi Jinping would rule China in the twenty-first century, and his mission would be to complete his father's work by reclaiming the last KMT bastion, Taiwan.

† After defeating the Bolsheviks in 1920, Piłsudski had retired, returning in 1926 in the face of growing instability, to rule as minister of military affairs. Unusually in a Europe seething with antisemitism, Piłsudski welcomed Poland's many Jews into his national project, a policy he called 'national assimilation'. Aware of Polish vulnerability to Hitler, he may have suggested to France launching a pre-emptive strike – before his death from cancer in 1935, which left Poland as a dictatorship without a dictator.

Schleicher regarded them as a vulgar but essential manifestation of the nation, yet the Nazis had passed their peak: in November 1932 they lost votes. By Christmas Hitler was in despair.

As Papen struggled to maintain order, Hindenburg fired him and appointed Schleicher. Papen, still close to Hindenburg, craved the chancellorship. On 4 January 1933, he met Hitler at the Cologne house of the Nazi banker Baron Kurt von Schröder, typical of the magnates now backing Hitler. The Nazi was back in the game. Papen still insisted on the chancellorship, but finally, on 23 January, meeting at the house of a Nazi champagne salesman, Joachim von Ribbentrop, Papen agreed to propose Hitler as chancellor.

When Schleicher resigned, the president, despite his promises never to appoint 'the corporal', asked Papen to form a cabinet that included Hitler. Even though Papen learned that Hitler would dismiss the Reichstag and assume absolute powers, he persuaded Hindenburg to appoint Hitler to the chancellorship with himself as deputy, both men supporting the principles of Hitler's openly stated programme – 'removal [from society] of Social Democrats, Communists and Jews' and 're-establishment of order' – while convinced they themselves could stop any excesses. Papen recruited Alfred Hugenberg, former Krupp executive, leader of the National People's Party and media baron, who agreed to become economics minister. 'We've bought Hitler,' claimed Papen. Hugenberg agreed that Hitler was their 'tool' and they would 'limit his power as much as possible'.

At the last minute, Hitler, securing the police and military portfolios, shook hands with Hindenburg. It was, thought Goebbels, who arranged a torchlit parade, 'like something out of a fairy tale', while Hitler believed it was 'nothing less than the renewal of a millennial condition'. Moving into the chancellery, Hitler confided to a henchman, 'Now we can really get started. I am never leaving here.'

In February, Hindenburg agreed to curtail free speech and assembly, cracking down on leftist parties. On the 20th, Göring hosted a meeting between Hitler and twenty-two industrial tycoons, led by Gustav Krupp, chief of the armaments dynasty favoured by Wilhelm II, now a convinced Nazi, who contributed a million of the total three million Reichsmarks raised from business magnates to fund the election that would deliver the votes to seize absolute power. On 28 February, a fire at the Reichstag, lit by a Communist lunatic, provided the excited Hitler with the excuse to crush and ban the Communists. In March, Hindenburg ordered the Nazi insignia, the swastika, to become the official flag alongside the old imperial banner, while the SS commander Himmler

and his sidekick Reinhard Heydrich, from a well-off musical and intellectual family that had lost its standing (he himself was an ex-naval
officer cashiered for immorality), moved from Munich to create Hitler's
security organs, founding the first concentration camp, Dachau. In
April, Göring, Prussian police minister, formed the Gestapo – *Geheime
Staatspolizei* – secret police – later handed over to Himmler. At a ceremony in the Garrison Church in Potsdam, Hitler, in black coat, bowed
before a tearful Hindenburg, who, in marshal's uniform, prayed in the
crypt of Frederick the Great. Addressing the president, Hitler acclaimed
'your wonderful life' – a fusion of Hohenzollerns and Nazis.

Two days later, the Reichstag passed the Enabling Act that made
Hitler dictator – and a week later he ordered a boycott of Jewish
businesses and embarked on antisemitic legislation that excluded 'non-
Aryans' (defined as those with one Jewish grandparent or more) from
the civil service, culminating in the 1935 Nuremberg Laws that removed
German citizenship from Jews and banned them from relationships
with Aryans. Hindenburg agreed, provided Jewish veterans were
excluded. From the start, Hitler looked abroad to destroy Versailles, renouncing membership of the League of Nations, and planned to reunite
the German peoples, starting with his own homeland, Austria, where
democracy was already compromised. Of the new nations of Versailles,
Hitler particularly hated Poland and Czechoslovakia. But his interest in
Austria clashed with the ambitions of his early hero, Mussolini.

When the two met in Venice, Il Duce was unimpressed by Der
Führer – 'more mule-headed than intelligent', Mussolini believed. But
Hitler's first Austrian move failed when local Nazis attempted a coup
that collapsed. Mussolini was furious, but he was busy building up his
forces in Eritrea and Somaliland to attack Ethiopia. Hitler meanwhile
reduced unemployment by spending profusely on autobahns and other
big projects, but the economic miracle could not last. When Krupp
expelled Jews from the Reich Industrial Board, his wife Bertha was
dubious. 'The Führer's always right,' replied Krupp. Hitler appointed
him Führer of Industry.

In June, Papen, finally glimpsing reality, denounced Hitler. When
Goebbels refused to report the speech, Papen complained to Hindenburg, who suddenly threatened to dismiss Hitler: he could have done
so. The industrialists and generals feared the SA, whose chieftain
Röhm hoped to supplant the army and nationalize industry. Krupp
appealed to Hitler, who in June 1934 visited the Krupp factories. The
Prussian generals now backed Hitler. They were essential, the SA
dispensable.

Hitler agonized at his vertiginous eyrie on the Obersalzberg. It was his self-fulfilling belief that made his speeches so alluring and his personality so compelling. Inscrutable and secretive – his codename for himself was Wolf – Hitler was ruled by a conviction that he might die young, often reflecting, 'When I'm no longer here . . .' He was a reckless gambler whose dreams defied conventional sense: 'I go the way that providence dictates with the assurance of a sleepwalker.'

Two heroes particularly inspired him as warlord-cum-artist, Frederick the Great and Wagner. Portraits of Frederick hung in all his offices; his stays with the Wagners at Bayreuth were sacred. All politicians exist twice – as individuals representing just their personal qualities and as phenomena representing something more: the magic lies in the fusion of the two. Capable both of insinuating charm and of foam-flecked rages, Hitler played many roles, joking that he was 'the greatest actor in Europe'. As performer and manipulator, he was capable of overawing and co-opting aristocrats and workers, Germans and foreigners, while also skilled in balancing his intimate 'familial' court of devoted henchmen in what his architect Albert Speer called 'a carefully balanced system of mutual enmity'.

Although he slept late and rarely sat at a desk, he was capable of sustained concentration, whether dictating speeches to several secretaries simultaneously or later directing the war. Vegetarian and teetotal, an obsessive germophobe with bad teeth, rotted by Bavarian cakes, which later caused eyewatering halitosis, he was most relaxed with certain families, his early patrons and friends in Munich, followed by the Wagners, later the Goebbelses and Eva Braun. But he increasingly embraced the ultimate test of power: the dictator's reversal of time. Hating solitude, he treated his retainers to long monologues that first fascinated and later bored them. Armed with his autodidact's omniscience and the adventurer's braggadocio, he despised experts and always knew better. 'My life,' he said, 'is the greatest novel in history.'

LONG KNIVES; GREAT TERROR; MASS MOMENTUM AND PERSONAL POWER: HITLER AND STALIN

'In God's name,' exclaimed Hitler. 'Anything's better than this waiting around. I'm ready!' On 30 June 1933, the killing started small. Hitler approved the death lists compiled by Himmler and Heydrich, giving the codeword Hummingbird to Goebbels, who telegraphed it to Göring and Himmler in Berlin.

Hitler flew to Munich. Röhm was arrested in bed (with a male lover) by a splenetic Hitler, holding a whip; several other SA leaders were also caught in homosexual clinches, much to Hitler's horror. All were then shot by the SS; in Berlin, Schleicher (and his wife) and Nazi rivals were killed; perhaps 180 died altogether. Hindenburg was shocked by the killing of the Schleichers, but Hitler apologized, claiming the general had drawn a pistol. Hindenburg, now dying of cancer, approved.

Hitler arrived back in Berlin, revelling in the drama: 'Brown shirt, black tie, dark brown leather coat, high black military boots, everything dark upon dark,' wrote a witness. 'Above it all, bareheaded, a chalkwhite, sleepless, unshaven face . . . from which a pair of extinguished eyes stared through some clotted strands of hair.' Next morning, Hitler told his secretary, 'I've just had a bath and feel like I've been born again.' On 2 August, Hindenburg died, leaving letters pleading for the restoration of the monarchy – and praising Hitler's 'historic mission'. Hitler now combined the presidency with the chancellorship; the army swore allegiance to him as 'Führer of the German People'.*

'That Hitler is quite a fellow,' said an unexpected admirer, Stalin, to his Kremlin epigones, impressed by the Night of the Long Knives. A born extremist, backed by a murderous secret police, now called the OGPU, and a network of concentration camps, the GULAG, Stalin mastered the propulsive politics of the Mass Age, mobilizing millions of people, particularly the young, in the Bolshevik project to destroy the old and build a new, more just world in the thrilling drama of revolution. But he also appreciated that modernity was a struggle of geopolitics, driven by mass weapons, mass killing, mass production and mass spectacle. He combined his Marxist mission with his own personal power and Russia's exceptional imperial destiny. The more he mobilized the masses, the less power they had and the more he wielded – the irony of mass politics. Stalin had embarked on a radical and colossal gamble to industrialize Russia at breakneck speed, using American advisers and technology to collectivize agriculture in Ukraine and other regions,

---

* A visitor from another world witnessed these events. A delegation of American Baptists was touring Germany that month: Michael King, a Baptist minister in Atlanta and father of a boy Michael Jr, aged five, was inspired by visiting Martin Luther's house in Wittenberg but horrified by Hitler's antisemitic racism. On his return, he changed his name and that of his son to Martin Luther King and helped draft a declaration by the Baptist World Alliance that 'This Congress deplores and condemns as a violation of the law of God the Heavenly Father, all racial animosity, and every form of oppression or unfair discrimination toward the Jews, toward coloured people, or toward subject races in any part of the world.'

mercilessly collecting grain to pay for the industrialization. Initially the Bolsheviks had promoted Ukrainian culture, as part of their policy of *korenizatsiia* (indigenisation), providing Moscow was paramount. But when the peasants in Ukraine resisted, Stalin 'broke their backs' by repression and famine. Remembering the Polish invasion and fearing that 'We may lose Ukraine', he cracked down on Ukrainian language and culture, arresting, shooting or deporting 4–5 million people. Yet neither the repression nor the famine were limited to that republic: the starvation also hit the lower Volga, the north Caucasus and Kazakhstan. Later Stalin casually told Churchill ten million had starved, and demographic research confirms the vanishing of eight and a half million people. Four million peasants died of starvation in Ukraine – one in eight people – the atrocity today known as the *Holodomor* ('Death by Hunger') that was, writes Serhii Plokhy, 'a man-made phenomenon, caused by official policy', resulting from 'policies with a clear ethnonational coloration'. Simultaneously, it was part of a wider Soviet famine – 1.2 to 1.4 million Kazakhs starved to death: 'This,' writes Stephen Kotkin, 'was the highest death ratio in the Soviet Union.' Stalin's self-made calamity could have destroyed the USSR, but instead the cruel gamble paid off: the USSR emerged with collectivized farms worked by 100 million farmers as oppressed as serfs – and modern industry that could soon outproduce Germany.

Benefiting from the exceptional moment of Marxist internationalism in a realm usually dominated by ethnic Russians, this Caucasian, pockmarked and compact, with a withered arm, a Marxist-Leninist fanatic who always spoke Russian with a heavy accent, now ruled the tsar's empire. But within the Party Stalin's comrades mocked his obscurity, challenged his dictatorship, questioned his collectivization and, he believed, encouraged his manic-depressive wife, Nadezhda, to commit suicide. If Russia faced a new war against Hitler, Stalin needed to enforce total supremacy. Killing was his way to do it. 'Our system,' he told a confidant, 'is bloodletting,' later explaining that his method was 'quicker but requires more blood'.

Five months after the Night of the Long Knives, on 1 December 1934, Stalin's ally and Leningrad (formerly Petrograd) leader Sergei Kirov was assassinated, most likely by an unstable comrade whose wife he had seduced – though it also possible that Stalin organized it. Always a master improviser, Stalin took emergency powers and launched a Terror, ordering arrests, deportations and killings to purge the Party not just of traitors but even of those who might *think* disloyal thoughts. Terror was part of the DNA of the Communist Party; autocracy was part of the DNA of the Russian state; and killing was Stalin's essential political tool but also part of a personality shaped by his underground life, the savagery of the civil war and, above all, by the experience of power and insecurity in the Kremlin. Dictatorship makes its own monsters. The bizarre mayhem of the Terror was the creation of all of these, driven by Stalin's ferocious darkness, implacable will, political skill and his cool but totally reckless violence. No great power has ever mutilated itself in such an extraordinary frenzy of chaos and murder. Suspicious of veteran Bolsheviks and generals, Stalin orchestrated a national witch-hunt, staging melodramatic show trials at which respected leaders confessed to outlandish plots. He and his NKVD commissar, a dwarfish myrmidon called Nikolai Yezhov, drew up death lists known as 'albums' of thousands of comrades whom Stalin often knew intimately; meanwhile hundreds of thousands of unnamed victims, singled out via quotas of place, race and background, were also targeted: in the 'national operations', Poles and Koreans were decimated; within the republics, the terror hit Ukrainians most intensely. The vindictive torture of old enemies, the killing of friends and families and the paranoid scenarios of lurid conspiracies all reflected the strangeness of Stalin himself, but he believed that terror was the only way to ensure total loyalty. 'Better that ten innocent people should suffer than one spy get away,' he said. 'When you chop wood, chips fly.' During his reign, eighteen million innocents passed through the atrocious GULAG camps. Starting from a mere 79,000 slave labourers in 1930, rising to a million in 1935 and around seven million by 1938, these slaves toiled on canals or in mines; yet, as in the American south, slavery was not only diabolical but economically inefficient. During 1936–8, a million victims were officially liquidated but real numbers were much higher. Forty thousand officers were executed, including three out of the five marshals. The total killed during Stalin's rule will never be known but it was probably close to twenty million.

Watching Stalin's self-destructive 'meatgrinder', Hitler was convinced that the Soviet Union had been severely weakened. He revelled in the messianic mystical union of *Volk und Führer*, performing at vast theatrical rallies at Nuremberg. 'Once in the days of yore you heard the voice of a man,' Hitler told the rally in September 1936, 'and . . . it awakened you, and you followed it . . . When we meet here we are suffused with wonder at our coming together. Not all of you can see me, and I can't see all of you. But I can feel you, and you can feel me.'

ETHIOPIA WITH OR WITHOUT ETHIOPIANS:
HAILE SELASSIE AND MUSSOLINI

In December 1934, as the Führer turned to Europe and Stalin launched his Terror, the Duce turned to Ethiopia to avenge Adowa.

Five years earlier, its thirty-seven-year-old regent, Ras Tafari, had been crowned as *Negus Negust* Haile Selassie in St George's, Addis, a ceremony attended for the first time by guests from all the European powers, designed to dazzle with traditional Ethiopian glory and independent modernity. Haile Selassie annexed the last of the Muslim sultanates and created a constitution with an assembly that established an absolutist monarchy.* But Ethiopia's position between Italian Eritrea and Somaliland made it an ideal place to launch Mussolini's new Roman empire.

'Only he and I knew what was going to happen,' boasted General Emilio De Bono, promising the Duce that its conquest 'wouldn't be difficult'.

'Full speed ahead,' ordered Mussolini.

In Addis, as the Italians tried to provoke the Ethiopians at the remote Ogaden oasis of Wal-Wal, Haile Selassie refused to mobilize and appealed to the League of Nations. Britain and France, already alarmed by Hitler and keen not to drive Mussolini into a German alliance, disgraced themselves by acquiescing in the Duce's predation.

On 3 October 1935, without any declaration of war, De Bono from Eritrea and Rodolfo Graziani from Somaliland invaded Ethiopia with 476,000 men, including 60,000 Eritrean Royal Colonials, 17,000 members of the irregular *Gruppo Bande Eritrea* and Somalians under Sultan Olol Dinle, along with 500 tanks and 350 planes. Of Haile Selassie's 250,000 soldiers, only the 20,000 Imperial Guards were fully armed; he had eight operative planes, and the Italians had suborned some Ethiopian magnates.

Outside the Menelik Palace, to the beat of drums, the khaki-clad *negus negust*, calm and poised, reviewed his troops, his Guardsmen armed with Vickers machine guns on mules but many with sticks, spears and empty ammunition belts. As the Italians bombed Adowa, Mussolini sacked De Bono and appointed Marshal Pietro Badoglio, whom he ordered 'to use gas and flamethrowers even on a vast scale', adding, 'Use

---

* Ras Tafari's coronation, together with Marcus Garvey's Return to Africa movement which predicted that 'Kings would come out of Africa', inspired a new movement, Rastafarianism, in Jamaica whose adherents believed that Haile Selassie marked a black Second Coming of Christ.

all means of war.' Mussolini's pilot sons Bruno and Vittorio revelled in their bombing raids and boasted of slaughtering Ethiopians.

The emperor counter-attacked in southern Tigray but was thrown back, his troops poisoned with gas. 'Of all the massacres,' he recalled, 'of this terrible and pitiless war, this was the worst. Men, women, animals were blown to pieces or burned with mustard gas, the dying, the wounded, screamed with agony.' In March 1936, Haile Selassie and the last army in the north were defeated at Maychew by Badoglio, with 11,000 killed. The emperor retreated to pray at Lalibela's subterranean rock-cut cathedrals before halting at Addis, where his advisers begged him not to fall into Italian hands. Badoglio declared a March of the Iron Will from the north, while Graziani, who like Badoglio had made his name massacring Libyans in north Africa, advanced from the south. In May Haile Selassie escaped Addis three days ahead of Graziani, who became viceroy. Four days later, in Rome, Mussolini appeared on the balcony of the Palazzo Veneziano. 'Ethiopia is Italian!' he told ecstatic crowds. 'Adowa is avenged.' Victor Emmanuel was proclaimed emperor of Ethiopia.

In July, Mussolini and Hitler received envoys from a rebel general in Spain. The country had been damaged by dictatorship, inequality, depression and bewilderment at the loss of empire. Its Bourbon king Afonso XIII was exiled, with the impoverished republic lethally divided between secular socialists and Catholic conservatives. Now when socialists won the election, the general, Francisco Franco, joined the rebellion. Tiny, broad-hipped and high-voiced, cautious and cunning, Franco had become the country's youngest ever general as commander of the brutal African Legion fighting in Spain's Moroccan colony, but now his legionaries were stuck in Morocco, allowing the Republican government to retain control of much of the country.

His envoys were lucky to find Hitler staying with the Wagners at Bayreuth. 'That's no way to start a war,' the Führer exclaimed, fearing that 'Jewish Bolsheviks in Moscow' would seize Spain. Hitler and Mussolini airlifted Franco's troops to the mainland, followed by 50,000 Italian troops and 16,000 Germans. The fight against Fascism attracted 40,000 volunteers, known as the International Brigades. Slowly, Stalin came round to backing the Republic, sending 3,000 advisers and armaments and launching a terror in Spain to match the one he was conducting in Russia. Franco, a murderously plodding generalissimo, failed to take Madrid but, aided by Italian and German bombing, he saw himself as El Caudillo of the Last Crusade, annihilating godless socialists. Both sides killed civilians: the Republicans shot around 38,000, but Franco shot

200,000.* There were similarities between Spain and Ethiopia.

Graziani, now marquess of Neghelli, banned 'racial commingling' and, after an assassination attempt in Addis on the day Ethiopians recall as Yekatit 12 (February 1937), he unleashed Italian soldiers and Black Lion militiamen who, shouting 'Duce! Duce!' and 'Civiltà Italiana!', butchered 20,000 people. 'Whole streets were burned down,' their occupants machine-gunned or stabbed.

'The Duce will have Ethiopia,' said Graziani, 'with or without the Ethiopians.' The year before, while inspecting a church at Jijiga, the viceroy fell through a hole concealed under a carpet, a humiliation he was determined to avenge. At Debre Libanos, Graziani ordered: 'Execute summarily all monks without distinction, including the vice-prior.' Two thousand monks were killed. Altogether the Italians killed 400,000 Ethiopians. The League of Nations passed then cancelled sanctions. 'Italy considers it an honour to inform the League,' Mussolini's foreign minister and son-in-law, Count Ciano, boasted, 'of her efforts to civilize Ethiopia.' In Geneva, Haile Selassie, serene and solemn, warned the League, 'It's not merely a question of Italian aggression; it's collective security,' and asked, 'What reply shall I take back to my people?'

There was none – and Hitler was not the only one who understood that the League was toothless. On 25 November 1936, Japan signed an anti-Soviet pact with Germany, soon joined by Italy – the future Axis alliance. Emperor Hirohito's own views remain opaque, but it is likely that he along with his courtiers and generals became convinced that it was the time to conquer China.

In February 1936, a coup by nationalist officers had placed further pressure on Hirohito. The rebels were executed, but Hirohito, his generals and the *genro*, his political veterans, intensified the cult of militaristic nationalism, laced with bushido chivalry, Shinto ritual and

---

* Franco was not the only autocrat in Iberia, but Portugal followed an entirely different model. After the Portuguese monarchy was overthrown in 1910, the country was ill managed and impoverished, though maintaining its empire in Angola, Mozambique, Guinea and Goa. But after a military coup in 1926 officers did an unusual thing: instead of appointing a general, they recruited a talented economics professor, António Salazar, son of a provincial estate manager who had almost become a priest, as finance minister. Salazar balanced the budget, then as premier, creating what he called a pluricontinental, imperialist Catholic *Novo Estado* (New State), he stabilized Portugal as a conservative dictator, based on God, Country and Family, suppressing opposition at home with the help of his secret police the PIDE and rejuvenating the empire by sending settlers to Angola and Mozambique. He was illiberal and authoritarian but also professorial and cerebral; there were few rallies and minimal racism. But the PIDE operated a camp on Cape Verde where prisoners were tortured and killed. Salazar kept out of the Spanish civil war and the Second World War, but he was willing to fight to maintain the Portuguese empire.

imperial cult. Hirohito privately did not regard himself as divine, but he believed that the emperor was synonymous with nation and state. In May 1937, he backed *kokutai no hongi* – the fundamentals of national polity – which saw the emperor as a 'living god'. Everyone must 'live for the great glory of the emperor, abandoning the small ego and thus expressing our true life as a people': this was *kodo*, the imperial way. Hostile to western democracies, this Pan-Asian ideology was conditional on Japanese supremacy. The *genro* regarded China as racially subhuman, merely a territory that Japan, thanks to the blood sacrifices of 1895 and 1904, was fated to rule.

On 7 July 1937, an unplanned exchange of fire between Japanese and Chinese troops at the Marco Polo Bridge which provided access to Beijing provided the pretext to invade China – the start of a struggle that would kill fourteen million Chinese (only Russia would lose more) and provide a spark for world war.

ACT TWENTY
2 BILLION

Roosevelts, Suns, Krupps, Pahlavis and Saudis

HIROHITO INVADES CHINA

Hirohito, consulting with his generals, led by his great-uncle Prince Kotohito, chief of staff, and his premier Prince Konoe was assured the war would be 'finished up in two or three months'. Konoe, cultured and pragmatic, a fan of Oscar Wilde, was convinced, after attending the Versailles conference, that the western powers were racist colonialists determined to break Japan.

'Wouldn't it be better to concentrate a large force at the most critical point,' asked Hirohito, 'and deliver one overwhelming blow?' The war minister agreed: it must be 'total war' but 'undeclared' to avoid western or Soviet intervention. On 28 July 1937, the correct date for the start of the Second World War, the Japanese launched a full offensive against Beijing and the port of Tianjin. On 8 August, the old capital was captured along with much of northern China.

Chiang Kai-shek was agonizing over when to resist 'the dwarf bandits', asking 'Existence or obliteration?' If he did not resist, he risked losing power; if he did, he risked defeat. He agreed to negotiate with Mao on a united front against Japan. In Xi'an, Chiang met Mao's lieutenant Zhou Enlai. But the Communists manipulated the patriotism of the Manchurian warlord, the Young Marshal, Zhang Xueliang, who, disgusted by the generalissimo's vacillations, devised a plot to force Chiang's hand. The Young Marshal's troops stormed Chiang's villa, killing his guards, and discovered the generalissimo hiding on a mountainside in his nightshirt and without his dentures. His wife, Meiling Song, considered attacking the town but instead rushed to join her husband. Mao wanted Chiang killed, but Stalin, afraid of Japanese attack, ordered his release. Chiang agreed to Stalin's plan for an anti-Japanese alliance, receiving his son back as a prize.

On his release, chastened and humiliated, Chiang defended Shanghai with 500,000 men. Hirohito agreed with his generals to order Japanese forces 200,000 strong to storm Shanghai. Nine thousand Japanese were killed as against almost 250,000 Chinese. The Japanese were outraged by their losses, and their troops were ordered to treat civilians and non-civilians the same: they took no prisoners, butchering thousands in Shanghai. On 13 December, they seized the capital Nanjing. General Matsui Iwane, commander of the front, and Hirohito's uncle Prince Yasuhiko Asaka as commander of the Shanghai Expeditionary Force ordered harsh reprisals as a preliminary to a parade. On the first day, 32,000 people were killed. Asaka's order was 'Kill all captives'. All told, Asaka's troops may have killed as many as 340,000 Chinese; some 20,000 women were raped, mutilated and killed.* The killing, an expression of rage for Chinese resistance and a demonstration of Japanese racial superiority, continued for six weeks. Hirohito and his generals were responsible, but even General Matsui became 'depressed', adding, 'I feel sorry for the tragedies, but the Army must continue unless China repents.' Matsui and Asaka were recalled, but Hirohito praised Matsui and decorated Asaka.

Chiang took a stand at Wuhan but was routed, moving his capital to Chungking in the interior. In his Shaanxi fiefdom, Mao settled down for a long guerrilla war, remarking on the irony that 'Those who've seized the latrine pit can't shit while the people who are bloated have no pit.' In his capital, Yan'an, he increased his forces from 30,000 to 440,000, but left frontal warfare to Chiang. By 1938, the Japanese controlled most of coastal China, with Chiang and Mao holding out in the interior, but they were committed to a war they would never finish and could not afford. In this rapidly changing kaleidoscope, there was only one certainty understood by all players: the coming conflict, said Stalin, would be a 'war of machines', and that meant that 'mastery of oil' in Churchill's words 'was the prize'. Those who controlled it would be the masters.

OIL KINGS — THE CONQUEST OF ARABIA: ABDULAZIZ AND REZA

The shah had clashed with the British, demanding a bigger share of Iranian oil. By threatening to cancel the concession altogether, he got better terms. It was the beginning of a transfer in power from

---

* It is said that two Japanese officers Toshiaki Mukai and Tsuyoshi Noda of the Japanese 16th Division held a public contest with *shin guntō* swords to see who could behead 100 Chinese first before the city fell: by the time Nanjing had fallen, Noda had killed 105, Mukai 106, and they started another race to 150.

Europe to Asia. But the friction poisoned Reza's court.*

Reza hoped to secure the dynasty for his son, Mohammad, who now arrived home from Swiss boarding school with the effete school odd-job man Ernest Perron, eleven years older: 'a curious fellow', wrote a British diplomat, 'dressed like a musical comedy bohemian who also writes characters from the palm of your hand and makes the most surprising statements about your *vie sexuelle!*' The shah, terrified of homosexuality, was horrified and attacked Perron with his whip, ordering his expulsion until his daughters persuaded him to let him stay. The shah appointed him gardener. Whatever Perron's role it was emotional, not sexual: the crown prince had lost his virginity to a Swiss maid, and embarked on a lifetime of womanizing.

The shah, rushing to arrange his son's marriage, chose an Egyptian princess: the House of Mehmed Ali was the oldest dynasty in the region, even though it was Sunni. In March 1939, at Abdeen Palace in Cairo the crown prince was married to Princess Fawzia, sister of young King Farouk of Egypt, before the ceremony was repeated in Teheran in the presence of the shah. Fawzia, whose mother Queen Nazli was part French, had 'a perfect heart-shaped face and strangely pale but piercing blue eyes'; raised in the hedonistic luxury of Egypt, she was horrified by the uncouth shah, bored by the bourgeois parochialism of the Persian court and unhappy with her awkward husband. Sensing the coming war, the shah hoped to secure his kingdom by balancing Britain against Germany.

To the south, on 3 March 1938, an American oil company struck oil at the Dammam 7 well in the new kingdom of Saudi Arabia. Until then, the rise of Abdulaziz ibn Saud and his Wahhabis had been a minor security issue for the British, defending their Hashemite kings in Iraq and Transjordan. Now Arabia joined Iran and Iraq as increasingly potent masters of oil.

The king depended on pilgrim tolls in Mecca, but his revenues sank during the Depression. The *Ikhwan* had made him, but now they threatened him and he had to destroy them. In March 1929, at Sabilla, Saudi machine-gunners, aided by RAF planes, mowed down several hundred cameleteers, ending the *Ikhwan* as a force. On 23 September 1932,

---

* The shah's potentate Teymourtash started the negotiations. But Reza increasingly distrusted the minister. Teymourtash privately criticized Reza's 'suspicion of everyone and everything', and the shah's secret-police chief, probably channelling British disinformation, suggested that Teymourtash was a Soviet spy. In 1933, Reza suddenly arrested him and had him murdered in prison by a prison doctor, Ahmadi, using air injection.

Abdulaziz declared himself king of a new country, Saudi Arabia.* The rewards emerged immediately: his engineers fitted out his new Murabba Palace with electricity and lavatories, the start of the transformation of the Saudis from desert warlords into international potentates. Encouraged by a byzantine Englishman, St John Philby, a former British diplomat who on converting to Islam was named Sheikh Abdullah by the king, western oil companies (all of them paying Philby) started to prospect for oil.† In Riyadh, Philby played the sheikh, in the clubs of St James's, the British civil servant. Now he negotiated the first Saudi oil concessions, signed in 1933 with SoCal, joined in 1936 by Texaco, in a joint venture with Abdulaziz's Aramco. As international tensions rose, every power – but particularly Germany and Japan, which controlled no oilfields – sought 'the prize'.

THAT'S HOW IT'S DONE: HITLER'S PLAN

On 20 April 1937, his forty-eighth birthday, Hitler revealed his real vision for empire to his two confidants: Albert Speer, a suave young architect, presented him with a model of his gigantomaniacal new capital, Germania (Berlin). 'Do you understand now why we plan so big?' asked Hitler as he, along with Goebbels, admired a People's Hall that was seven times the size of St Peter's, designed to hold 180,000 people; the fortress-like Führer Palace; a 260-foot Victory Arch to dwarf the Arc de Triomphe; and a station bigger than New York's Grand Central. 'I did these sketches ten years ago,' Hitler had said when he commissioned Speer. 'I knew some day I'd build them.' Speer planned to complete Germania in 1950. Afterwards he showed his father. 'You two have gone completely mad!' his father said. But now Hitler confided in Speer that

* Abdulaziz gathered a trusted court: it was now he met a young Yemenite, a porter in Jeddah, rough, uneducated but capable, who started to organize building work at the shrines, winning the king's trust. The builder became the richest contractor in Arabia: Muhammad bin Laden. The king's doctor, Muhammad Khashoggi, became so trusted that he too brokered deals: later his son Adnan would become the richest man in the world, while his grandson Jamal, a journalist, would fatally cross the House of Saud.
† Philby was a poisonous but creative maverick – explorer, socialist, antisemite, a man of masks who promoted the Saudis as Lawrence did the Hashemites. Philby, who delighted in his duplicity, had named his eldest son Kim after Kipling's spy. At Cambridge, Kim and his circle were attracted to Communism. Several of them joined the diplomatic service. In 1934, in Regent's Park, London, Kim was introduced by his Austrian girlfriend, a Communist, to a mysterious 'man of importance' who recruited him as a Soviet agent. He became a journalist for *The Times*, covering the Spanish civil war. Then in 1940, thanks to the help of one of his Cambridge friends who was now a British diplomat and Soviet agent, he joined British intelligence, MI6, and became one of the most significant Soviet assets.

Germania would be 'the capital of the Germanic empire'. Later he told Goebbels of his imminent plans for Austria and Czechoslovakia: 'We'll get them . . . Hence the Führer's great construction plans.' At a secret gathering, Hitler explained, 'I always go to the extreme of what I feel I can risk and no further . . . I say, "I want to destroy you. And now I'll ask my wits to help me manoeuvre you into a corner so that you can't lash out at me because you would suffer a fatal blow to the heart."' And then he bellowed: '*That's* how it's done.'

Hitler started to increase the pressure on Austria, summoning its chancellor Kurt Schuschnigg in February 1938 to threaten invasion. 'My task is preordained,' he told him. 'Surely you don't think you could put up even an hour's resistance? Who knows? Maybe I'll be in Vienna to-morrow morning like a spring storm.' Schuschnigg tried to beat Hitler at his own game, calling a referendum on independence which provided Hitler's pretext for massing the Wehrmacht on Austrian borders.

In Vienna, Baron Alphonse de Rothschild was unsure whether he should leave or not, but his wife, an elegant Englishwoman named Clarice Sebag-Montefiore, heard from her lover in the Foreign Ministry that the Nazis already had a list of Jews to arrest. They packed up their car and drove into France. The eighty-two-year-old Sigmund Freud refused to leave. 'In the Middle Ages, they'd have burned me,' he insisted. 'Now, they're content with burning my books.'

Schuschnigg cancelled the plebiscite and resigned, handing over power to his Nazi interior minister. On 12 March, German forces entered Austria. Driving in a motorcade of open-topped Mercedes through ecstatic crowds, Hitler passed through Linz, where he looked up at the window of his Jewish doctor Eduard Bloch who nodded back at him, and then into Vienna, where he appeared on the balcony of the Hofburg before visiting the grave of his niece Geli Raubal. This *Anschluss* – Union – unleashed a host of tragedies: Nazi thugs forced Jews to clean the streets. Himmler's Jewish expert Adolf Eichmann, a former Dachau guard and son of an accountant who now ran the SD's Jewish Department, Section II/112, commandeered one of the five Rothschild palaces for his Central Agency for Jewish Emigration, to oversee the confiscation of Jewish wealth, particularly that of 100,000 Jews who wished to leave.

Baron Louis de Rothschild, debonair brother of Alphonse, polo player, botanist, aesthete, married to an Austrian countess, was visited by SS officers who were told by his butler to return after lunch. When he tried to leave, he was arrested at Aspern airport. Göring and Himmler vied with each other to extract a Rothschildian ransom. Himmler won, visiting Rothschild in jail to negotiate the handover of $21 million of assets in return for freedom. Louis joined his brother in America.* Freud refused to leave.

In the Nazis' wake followed the profiteers, led by Krupp, who now, aided by Göring, seized the chief Austrian steelworks. Just as the Wagners were Hitler's cultural dynasty, the Krupps were for him industrial royalty. When Mussolini visited, he showed him round Krupp's Essen works. Krupp celebrated Hitler's fiftieth birthday by presenting him with a swastika-spangled steel table engraved with a *Mein Kampf* quotation. Hitler was thrilled. Gustav's son Alfried, hook-nosed, cadaverous and sunken-eyed, an SS member since 1931, joined the board, developing tanks for the new, mobile warfare.

'Now it's the Czechs' turn,' a euphoric Hitler told Goebbels, preparing for war against Czechoslovakia on behalf of its German minority in the Sudetenland. On 17 September 1938, the British prime minister, Neville Chamberlain, beakily uninspiring, now determined to save European peace, arrived at the Berghof, the Führer's spectacular Alpine home, where he was treated to foam-flecked rants and rational negotiations. Chamberlain disdained Hitler – 'entirely undistinguished', he said, 'you'd take him for the housepainter he once was'. Hitler mocked Chamberlain as 'schoolmarmish' and 'a worm'. After subsequent meetings, Chamberlain boasted that he would try to avoid war 'because of a quarrel in a far-away country between people of whom we know nothing'. At a Munich conference mediated by Mussolini, Chamberlain and the French premier Daladier agreed the 'cession to Germany of the Sudeten German territory' of Czechoslovakia.

Chamberlain flew home triumphantly. 'My good friends,' he said at the airport. 'I believe it's peace for our time. Go home and get a nice quiet sleep.' Wise men did not sleep. 'You were given the choice between war and dishonour. You chose dishonour, and you will have war,' warned Churchill, calling Munich an 'unmitigated defeat'. Watching from Washington, Roosevelt privately agreed, noting the 'blood on their

---

* Freud's patient, friend and fellow psychoanalyst Princess Marie Bonaparte, descended from Napoleon's brother Lucien, rich thanks to her grandfather, the casino king of Monaco, and married to the gay Prince George of Greece, begged him to leave. After exploring her sexuality in a spree of affairs with the French premier (among others) during the First World War, she had consulted Freud in 1925 for her inability to achieve orgasm in the missionary position. 'The great question that has never been answered,' said Freud to Marie, 'is "What does a woman want?"' She became a psychoanalyst and sexual researcher. Now, when Freud's daughter, Anna, forty-three, was arrested, Freud agreed to leave, his escape and ransom paid by Marie Bonaparte. Freud settled in London near his architect son, Ernst, whose son Lucian was starting to study art. Sigmund Freud died in 1939. Marie Bonaparte tried to rescue Freud's elderly sisters – but in vain.

Judas Iscariot hands'. Keen to divert Joe Kennedy from a presidential bid at home, FDR promoted him to London as ambassador. There the cocksure Irishman revelled in society but supported the antisemitic coterie around Viscountess Astor, who favoured appeasement of Hitler. The German 'kikes', Kennedy said, 'had brought it upon themselves', telling a friend that 'individual Jews are alright but as a race they stink. They spoil everything they touch.' FDR was horrified by Hitler – 'His shrieks, his histrionics and the effect on the audience – they did not applaud – they made noises like animals,' FDR told his confidante and cousin Daisy Suckley. 'Europe is full of world dynamite.'

The Sudetenland was not enough for Hitler, who, cheated out of war, planned to 'rapidly occupy' the rest of Czechoslovakia, then, 'When the time is right, we'll soften up Poland using tried and tested methods.'

Weeks later, after the shooting of a German diplomat in Paris by a Polish Jew, Hitler and Goebbels organized an anti-Jewish pogrom, *Kristallnacht* (Night of Broken Glass), across Germany. On 9–10 November, Jews were beaten, around 100 were killed and 30,000 were arrested and sent to camps; 1,000 synagogues were burned, Jewish shops smashed. Hitler discussed 'the Jewish question' with Goebbels. 'The Führer wants to drive the Jews entirely out of Germany. To Madagascar or somewhere like it.' On 30 January 1939, speaking to the Reichstag, Hitler linked the fate of European Jews to the war he was planning to start. 'I've very often in my lifetime been a prophet and been mostly derided,' he said. 'I want today to be a prophet again: if the international Jewish financiers ... succeed in plunging the nations once more into a world war, the result will be not the Bolshevization of the earth and thus the victory of Jewry, but the annihilation of the Jewish race in Europe.'

In March, he summoned the old Czech president Emil Hácha to force the surrender of the rest of Czechoslovakia. Hácha suffered a stroke. German troops then occupied Prague, now capital of Hitler's Protectorate of Bohemia and Moravia, while a Slovak client state under a Fascist priest was granted independence. Hitler gave the Škoda works to Krupp. Days later he forced Lithuania to hand over the Baltic port of Memel. Finally Britain and France, realizing their mistake in appeasing Hitler, guaranteed the borders of his next target, Poland. Hitler had delivered a streak of successes. 'It's the miracle of the age that you found me among so many millions,' he told a rally. 'And that I have found you is Germany's great fortune.' Believing war was inevitable and desirable, he turned to the other anti-Versailles power that had lost its Polish lands, led by his Bolshevik enemy Stalin. Only the Soviet dictator could prevent Hitler fighting a war on two fronts.

In May, as Hitler brooded at the Berghof, Ribbentrop, his foreign minister, played him footage of Stalin in Moscow reviewing the May Day military parade from Lenin's Mausoleum. Stalin, said Hitler, 'looked like a man he could do business with'.

It was mutual – but always temporary.

Stalin had been sending signals of detente for some time. The Terror was spinning out of his control. On 25 November 1938, Yezhov, sinking into binges of drinking and fornication with both sexes and trying to cover up his own excesses, was replaced by a highly competent myrmidon, Lavrenti Beria, a toadish Georgian, a sadist and rapist, who oversaw a last spasm of killing that now included Yezhov himself. 'I die with Stalin's name on my lips,' said Yezhov, before he was shot. Stalin, facing a resurgent Hitler in Europe and an aggressive Japan in Asia but master of a terrified Party and weakened state, entertained the approaches of both the Nazis and the Anglo-French democracies. Distrusting the British, who had long tried to destroy Soviet Russia and 'want to use us like farmhands' to 'pull their chestnuts out of the fire', Stalin had no illusions about Hitler's ultimate hostility. He had read *Mein Kampf* in translation but found Hitler's detente more plausible, and more profitable. As for Hitler, never forgetting his promise in *Mein Kampf* to eradicate Judaeo-Bolshevism, he ordered war against Poland – a decision that was dependent on an alliance with Stalin. Courted by all contenders, time was on Stalin's side.

In August 1939 Hitler sent a telegram to Stalin suggesting Ribbentrop's immediate flight to Moscow. When Stalin's reply was brought in to Hitler at dinner, he banged the table: 'I have them!' As the Führer briefed his generals that Germans would now get their 'living space', Ribbentrop flew to Moscow and drove to Stalin's office in the Kremlin, the Little Corner, where the general secretary was ready to negotiate the carve-up of eastern Europe. While Stalin was hosting Ribbentrop, he was directing battles against the Japanese on the Mongolian border. Two days before Ribbentrop arrived, Stalin's newly promoted commander, Georgi Zhukov, attacked the Japanese with 50,000 troops at Khalkhin Gol. The battle would decide the future of the world war every bit as much as the conversations in the Little Corner.

At the Berghof, Hitler dined with Eva Braun and retinue, then stayed up with Goebbels, sleepless, hollow-eyed, almost feverish. At the Little Corner, Stalin and Ribbentrop traded quickly – one advantage of dictatorship. 'Germany and Russia will never fight again,' exulted Ribbentrop, toasting Stalin with champagne.

'That *ought* to be the case,' said Stalin, beaming but vigilant. At 4 a.m.

Hitler received Ribbentrop's telegram: he and Stalin had divided Poland; Stalin was promised ex-Romanov limitrophes, parts of Finland, Baltics and Romania.* Hitler greeted Ribbentrop as 'the new Bismarck' and ordered the Polish invasion. On 25 August, far away in Mongolia, Soviet tanks encircled Japanese forces, a victory that changed Japanese plans. Instead of attacking Russia, Japan would assault Britain and America. As for Stalin, he had found a winner: Zhukov, strong-willed, coarse, tough, would be the greatest general of the Second World War.

Until victory was secured, 'I want nothing more than to be the first soldier of the Reich,' Hitler, in a field-grey tunic, told the hushed Reichstag on 1 September, or he 'would not live to see the end' – a public warning of suicide. He compared himself to Frederick the Great, who had also 'confronted a great coalition' but 'triumphed'.

As 1.5 million troops smashed into Poland that morning, Hitler ordered his henchmen to fight a new type of war. 'Annihilation of Poland,' he specified in notes kept by a general. 'Hearts closed to pity. Brutal action . . . Maximum severity.' Hitler despised democracies – 'Worms! I saw them at Munich' – but this time the worms turned: Britain and France declared war; Chamberlain sent an expeditionary force of 390,000 troops to support the French and reluctantly brought the indomitable but masterful Churchill back as first lord of the Admiralty.

FDR, realizing Chamberlain was damaged, wrote to 'my dear Churchill' secretly, encouraging him to 'keep me in touch personally with anything you want me to know about'. But he was restrained by 62 per cent of Americans who wanted neutrality, by widespread antisemitism and by Ambassador Kennedy: 'always has been an appeaser and always will be an appeaser', said FDR. 'Pain in the neck.'

Hitler ordered 'a bitter ethnic struggle' in Poland with 'no legal bounds'. While annexing ex-Prussian provinces and creating a General Government to run the rest, he explained, 'all we want there is to harvest labour' and 'cleanse the Reich of Jews and Polacks'. Around 1.7 million Polish Jews fell into German hands. The army was followed by five, later seven, special murder squads, SS Einsatzgruppen, created by Heydrich, now head of the Reichssicherheitshauptamt (Reich Main Security Office / RSHA),

---

* Stalin annexed the three Baltics (which became Soviet republics) and forced Romania to hand over Bessarabia (taken from Russia after the First World War, which became the Soviet republic of Moldavia). Beria's secret police deported 140,000 people from Estonia, Latvia and Lithuania. But the Finns, until 1918 a Romanov grand duchy, refused to hand over the territory Stalin demanded. Stalin invaded, calling the war a mere policing operation. But the Finns routed the huge Soviet army, killing 131,476 troops before they finally succumbed. Stalin ordered reforms of his army but the humiliation convinced Hitler that the USSR would collapse fast.

combining the SD with battalions of ordinary policemen. They murdered all those on a death list (Special Prosecution Book) of 40,000 elite Poles. 'There must be no Polish leaders,' said Hitler. 'Where Polish leaders exist they must be killed, however harsh that sounds.' Some *Einsatzgruppen* commanders were coarse thugs with criminal backgrounds, but many were highly qualified – three commanders were doctors, as were nine of seventeen officers in *Einsatzgruppe* A – and middle class if not aristocratic. After the war, German generals propagated a myth that the Wehrmacht had played no part in Nazi atrocities. In fact, most officers not only acquiesced in and sanctioned the 'ethnic–political tasks' but assisted them; ordinary soldiers joined in and even took photographs. A very few, very brave soldiers refused to take part. Himmler attended some of the executions, telling the murderers, 'I can be frank – I do nothing without the Führer's knowledge.'*

Although thousands of people were already involved in killing, it all depended on Hitler's leadership. In November he flew to Munich to give his annual speech to 'old fighters' of the Beer Hall Putsch, ending his speech early and leaving – just as a bomb, planted by a lone assassin, Georg Elser, exploded. Hitler believed providence had spared him – 'The fate of the Reich depends on me alone' – which made his mission even more urgent: 'We can only confront Russia if our hands are free in the west.'

A race between Britain and Germany to seize Norway was lost by the British. Chamberlain, no warlord, lost his authority. At 10.15 a.m., on 9 May 1940, he met the two contenders for his succession. Chamberlain and the Tory grandees preferred the foreign secretary, the earl of Halifax, nicknamed the Holy Fox, ex-viceroy of India. Halifax, a desiccated, self-righteous aristocrat with one withered arm lacking a hand, leaned towards negotiation with Hitler. Churchill, regarded as a piratical, bumptious, half-American warmonger, brooded in pugnacious silence until Halifax gave way.

Churchill, an aristocratic imperialist, was an eccentric throwback, extravagant and *bon vivant*, heavy-drinking and cigar-chomping, irascible, cutting and witty, with a taste for idiosyncratic uniforms – his self-designed siren suit resembled a baby's romper suit. Yet not only had he recognized the nature of Hitler, but his martial temperament, visionary creativity, exuberant energy, unrivalled ministerial experience,

---

* Stalin invaded eastern Poland, where Soviet depredations were equally bleak. Soviet forces arrested and deported 400,000 Poles; 22,000 elite prisoners were imprisoned in camps near Katyn Forest. On 5 March 1940, Stalin and the Politburo ordered Beria to execute these 'nationalists and counter-revolutionaries', who were then buried in the woods.

knowledge of war and history, and mastery of language made him singularly qualified to ensure British survival. 'Poor people, poor people,' murmured Churchill. 'They trust me, and I can give them nothing but disaster for quite a long time.'

On 10 May, after months of 'phoney war', Hitler, skittish and nervous, announced a battle that would decide 'the fate of the German people for a thousand years' and struck west through Belgium and Holland. But he aimed his main thrust further south through the Ardennes, boldly using his tanks in a lightning war – Blitzkrieg. 'We've been defeated,' the French premier Paul Reynaud, told Churchill, who flew out to stiffen French resistance. When Churchill asked, 'Where's the strategic reserve?', the French commander-in-chief replied, 'Aucune.' None.

Reynaud appointed the Verdun hero, Marshal Pétain, aged eighty-four, to his government along with a general who had led three failed counter-attacks and believed that France should never surrender: Charles de Gaulle, under-secretary of war, was an ungainly, six-foot-four soldier-scholar of minor nobility with a small head and long nose nicknamed Le Grand Asparagus. On 9 June, he flew to see Churchill at Downing Street and requested the commitment of the RAF to the battle of France. Churchill refused. But he admired the 'young and energetic' de Gaulle: hardened by his German imprisonment as a First World War PoW, he believed in 'a certain idea of France', a France of grandeur, preferably led by a regal leader who might one day be himself.

Two days later Churchill returned to France to meet a despondent Reynaud, and there observed de Gaulle's 'vigour'; Pétain was already a defeatist. Back in London, Churchill proposed an Anglo-French union, but on 10 June Reynaud resigned and Pétain became premier to negotiate with Hitler. As Mussolini joined the war, invading France from the south, de Gaulle escaped to London, 'alone and deprived of everything . . . I was entering into an adventure.' On 14 June, Paris fell. Four days later 'I, General Charles de Gaulle, currently in London', broadcast to France. He asked, 'Has the last word been said? Must hope disappear? Is defeat final? No! . . . Nothing is lost for France.'

As Pétain opened negotiations, the British army was surrounded on the beach at Dunkirk. The victory was so total that Hitler wavered. 'Führer's terribly nervous,' wrote his chief of staff. 'Frightened by his own success'. While Hitler vacillated, 300,000 British soldiers were rescued by a flotilla of small boats.

Hitler received the French surrender – technically an armistice – in the same carriage at Compiègne where the Germans had surrendered in 1918; and left southern France and the French empire intact under Pétain ruling from Vichy. The ex-kaiser and his sons congratulated Hitler.

At dawn on 23 June, accompanied by Speer, Hitler flew into Paris for sightseeing in an open Mercedes, stopping at the Tour Eiffel and standing before Napoleon's tomb at Les Invalides, where he ordered the return of the body of the emperor's son, the duke of Reichstadt, one of his stranger historical obsessions. 'Wasn't Paris lovely?' he said to Speer. In July, Hitler arrived in Essen to celebrate Krupp's seventieth and to thank him in person for the panzers.* At Bayreuth, he watched an operatic *Götterdämmerung*. 'I hear,' he told Winifred Wagner, 'the wings of the goddess of victory.' He was about to order the greatest gamble of a gambling life.

He expected the British to surrender. Halifax suggested negotiations. Churchill held his nerve, telling the British people, 'I have nothing to offer but blood, toil, tears and sweat' in a war 'against a monstrous tyranny never surpassed in the dark and lamentable catalogue of human crime'. Sneering at 'Britain's hopeless military situation', Hitler ordered a sea assault (Operation Sealion), but his admirals warned that such an operation would be possible only with air superiority. In July 1940, Hitler commanded his chosen heir, Göring, the Luftwaffe commander recently promoted to Reichsmarschall, to 'beat down the RAF' then 'eliminate the English motherland and . . . occupy the country completely'. But he was already turning to the crusade of his life: 'Once Russia has been destroyed, England's last hope will vanish.'

In August, Hitler unleashed the Luftwaffe but delayed Sealion after plucky British pilots and superior aeroplanes, aided by new radar, combined with eloquent Churchillian defiance, won the battle for Britain. Churchill's other victory was transatlantic. Kennedy, denouncing the 'actor' Churchill, believed (in Roosevelt's words) that his 'small capitalist class was safer under Hitler', reporting to Washington that Britain was doomed and 'democracy is finished'. But Churchill won over Roosevelt, urgently requesting help – 'I must tell you in the long history of the world this is the thing to do now.'

HITLER AND THE YOUNG KING

FDR delivered fifty destroyers to Britain and recalled Kennedy, whom he slyly neutralized by offering to support his future presidential bid. FDR,

---

* Krupp, joined by Ferdinand Porsche and his son, developed the gigantic Panther, Leopard and Tiger tanks demanded by Hitler.

running for an unprecedented third term, won by a landslide,* freeing him to help Britain with a Lend-Lease plan. 'Suppose my neighbour's home catches fire. If he can take my garden hose,' he artfully explained in a Fireside Chat to the Americans, 'I may help him put out his fire.' America would be 'the arsenal of democracy'.

On 22 June 1941, Hitler, now widely regarded in Germany as a genius, invaded Russia in what he called Operation Barbarossa, a campaign that he had first envisioned in *Mein Kampf* and had planned since the fall of France. 'The demolition of Russia', he had explained to his generals, would force a British surrender but also enable Japan to 'concentrate all its strength against the United States', which would prevent America fighting Germany. He ordered the generals to prepare post-Barbarossa for an 'invasion of Afghanistan and conflict with India'. Barbarossa was to be a war of annihilation, 'a fight to the finish' in which 'Bolshevist rabble-rousers, partisans, saboteurs and Jews' were to be instantly liquidated and Russian prisoners of war were to be deliberately starved to death. 'Once we've achieved victory, no one will ask about our methods,' he said, reflecting that 'No one remembers the Armenians now.'

Hitler was exhilarated by the scale of this 'mass attack on the grandest scale, the most enormous that history has ever known. The example of Napoleon won't be repeated.' The USSR would collapse 'in four months'. Even for Hitler, there were moments of doubt about the 'great risk' he had taken: 'The beginning of every war is like opening the door into a dark room. One never knows what is hidden in the darkness,' he admitted to his secretaries. 'Uncanny' Russia was like the 'ghost ship in the *Flying Dutchman*. Nothing at all can be known . . . It could be a gigantic soap bubble but it could be completely different . . .' And it was.

The invasion had been delayed by the contingencies of proliferating war. Hitler's successes attracted bottom feeders: Generalissimo Franco of Spain met Hitler to demand British Gibraltar and French colonies. 'I'd rather have two or three teeth pulled,' grumbled Hitler, 'than meet him again.' Mussolini wanted Nice and French Tunisia but overestimated

---

* Sitting with some cronies (who included the future president Lyndon Johnson) FDR phoned Kennedy: 'Joe, how are ya? Just sitting here with Lyndon thinking about you. I want to talk to you, my son. Can't wait . . . Make it tonight.' Then he hung up the phone smiling at Johnson: 'I'm gonna fire the sonofabitch.' Kennedy helped win FDR the Irish vote, backing him in the election, only realizing later that he had been handled. He placed his own presidential hopes in his eldest son, Joe Jr, who had visited Germany where 'Hitler's building a spirit in his men that could be envied in any country.' His second son Jack had also travelled around Europe, preparing for a political career, but questioned his father's pro-German politics. Both studied at Harvard and the LSE. While Kennedy was despised as a defeatist, his children had charmed the British: his daughter Kick would soon marry Billy, marquess of Hartington, the heir to the duke of Devonshire.

Italian capabilities: he invaded Albania, ruled since the 1920s by a self-made king, Zog, who fled to London; then, without consulting Hitler, he invaded Greece, where his troops ran into trouble. The British, fielding 375,000 African troops, liberated Ethiopia, restoring Haile Selassie, then attacked Mussolini's Libya, where the Italians collapsed. Hitler sent an Afrika Korps to halt the Italian retreat and threaten British Egypt and also had to rescue Italy in Greece.

Hitler was anxious about the Balkans, source of Romanian oil as well as the base for Barbarossa. Stalin had been pushing for Soviet influence in Bulgaria and Romania, which made Barbarossa even more urgent. The Führer admired the Romanian despot, Ion Antonescu, a splenetic martinet, nicknamed Red Dog for his ginger hair and furious temper, who had made his name fighting for the Allies in the First World War. King Mihai, last of the Hohenzollerns, haunted by his narcissistic, sexually incontinent and politically catastrophic father Carol II, endured the bullying Red Dog, who now delivered Romania to Hitler.

The eighteen-year-old Mihai, gentle and decent, brought up by his responsible mother, was powerless, forced to grant Antonescu the Führeresque title of *Conducator*. 'We had a strange relationship,' the king told this author. 'He treated me as a child, excluded me. I hated having a dictator.' In early 1941, Mihai lunched with Hitler, who was 'stiff and unfriendly. He'd suddenly get on to a subject, his eyes would go glassy and he would start declaiming. I tried to speak but couldn't interrupt.' Hitler kept talking: 'The last thing I remember him saying was "I guarantee America will never enter the war against us." I didn't believe him.'

Antonescu was a vicious antisemite. 'Satan is the Jew,' he told his cabinet. 'Ours is a life-and-death struggle. Either we win and cleanse the world or they win and we'll be their slaves.' Antonescu keenly embraced Hitler, who even allowed Red Dog to lecture him on Romanian history. Antonescu promised troops for Barbarossa. Hungary, Bulgaria and Yugoslavia joined Hitler's Axis, until a pro-British coup in Belgrade threatened to delay his Russian invasion.

Hitler, enraged, ordered a war of 'pitiless harshness' to 'destroy Yugoslavia', dividing it to create an independent Croatia under the ultra-nationalist Ustashe, led by Ante Pavelić. Once in power – nominally under an Italian king Tomislav II – Pavelić, assuming his own Führeresque title *Poglavnik*, unleashed a frenzy of killing, supported by Catholic priests. Aiming to kill all Croatian Jews plus a third of all Serbs, his butchery exposed the hatred of intimate neighbours: 300,000 Serbs, 30,000 Jews and 20,000 Roma were killed in such ghoulish bedlam that the Nazis called the Ustashe 'monsters'* and Himmler complained to the *Poglavnik*.

Yugoslavia delayed Barbarossa by a few key months. 'In four weeks,' said a euphoric Hitler, now ensconced at the Wolf's Lair, a gloomy, mosquito-infested headquarters of hulking concrete bunkers at Rasten-burg, East Prussia, 'we will take Moscow . . .' At 3 a.m. on 22 June, three million soldiers† and 3,000 tanks crossed the border.

THE GREATEST BATTLE IN HISTORY: HITLER'S WAR OF ANNIHILATION; HIROHITO'S GAMBLE

The surprise was almost total. The day before, Stalin listened tensely to growing reports of massing German forces and his generals' unease. Allowing only minor preparations, he had scarcely fallen asleep at his home, the Nearby dacha when he was awoken by the phone. Zhukov reported that the Germans were attacking on all fronts.

It was the biggest mistake of Stalin's career. Intelligence had poured in from his superb espionage network in Berlin and Warsaw, as well as from Churchill and even Mao, but particularly from his spy in Tokyo, Richard Sorge, a raffish half-German, half-Russian playboy. Sorge, best friends with the German attaché whose wife was one of his many lovers, learned the date of the invasion. 'There's this bastard who's set up fac-tories and brothels in Japan and even deigned to report the date of the German attack as 22 June,' sneered Stalin. 'Are you suggesting I believe him too?' Dictatorship and Terror can suppress priceless intelligence and common sense. 'Send your source to fuck his mother,' he wrote on one report. Stalin could be as mulishly obtuse as he was lupinely astute and felinely flexible. 'An intelligence officer,' he said, 'ought to be like the devil, believing no one, not even himself.' In this case, the devil out-devilled himself. He knew that Hitler was his enemy and that war

---

* 'The Ustashe have gone raving mad,' reported Nazi plenipotentiary General Edmund von Horstenau. The guards at the Jasenovac camp preferred to kill using hammers, axes and specially designed *Srbosjek* (Serb-cutter) knives strapped to the hand, indulging in demo-niac tortures, eye gougings, impalings and castrations. Visiting the village of Crkveni Bok near the Jasenovac camp, Horstenau reported the ravages of teenaged Ustashe torturers: 'People were killed everywhere, women raped then tortured to death, children killed . . . I saw in the Sava River the corpse of a young woman with her eyes dug out and a stake driven into her sexual parts . . . aged twenty when she fell into the hands of these monsters. All around, pigs devoured unburied human beings.'
† Not as cosmopolitan as Napoleon's *Grande Armée*, they were mainly Germans but also included 500,000 Romanians (the largest contingent), 300,000 Italians, 200,000 Hun-garians and 18,000 Spaniards.

would come but believed the pact would delay it until 1943. As tension rose, he should have probed an alliance with Britain. His mistake was to regard Hitler as a conventional statesman, while in fact the Führer was the self-declared 'sleepwalker' who sought wars of annihilation.

Rushing to the Kremlin, Stalin ordered counter-attacks on all fronts. They were disastrous, drawing millions of Soviet soldiers into German encirclements, as the Germans powered forward, taking Minsk, then Smolensk. When Stalin and his retainers visited headquarters and demanded the latest reports, Zhukov, a general of adamantine hardness, had to admit the fronts were in disarray and burst into tears. 'Lenin left a state and we've fucked it up,' said Stalin, returning to his mansion for two days to collect himself and, like Ivan the Terrible, test the loyalty of his boyars. On the third, his grandees arrived to insist that he take command. The Georgian ex-choirboy who, like Hitler, believed he was a born soldier, assumed the title Supremo and, mustering Russia's unparalleled resources of human and industrial power, fielding an awesome 4.2 million troops, rallied his own people with a mix of patriotism, terror and Marxism to engage Hitler in a 'life-and-death struggle'.

'Brothers and sisters, my friends!' Stalin began, addressing his people. 'History shows there are no invincible armies.' Hitler disagreed.

'The war is fundamentally won,' the Führer told Goebbels a week later. 'The Kremlin will fall.' He assured the Japanese ambassador that 'Resistance won't last longer than six weeks.' Stalin's interference in the war was disastrous: he lost 3.5 million men and most of European Russia in just over a year. Occupied territories were divided into Ukraine and Ostland. Hitler's plan was that 'Moscow will be wiped off the face of the earth.' The Russian population of 194 million would be starved until there were just thirty million left; his German empire would extend to the Urals; German governors would live in palaces, German farmers would live in beautiful villages in Ukraine, Crimea and the Baltics while enslaved Slavs toiled, with the rest driven into Siberia. Nazi invaders instantly started to murder large numbers: out of 5.7 million PoWs, 3 million were starved, the greatest crime of the war after the killing of European Jews. 'I'm approaching this matter ice-coldly,' Hitler said. 'I feel myself to be but the executioner of the will of history. Once we are the lords of Europe, we will hold the dominant position in the world.'

Roosevelt, surveying a broiling world from the serenity of the White House, concentrated first on London, sending his devoted aide Harry Hopkins, cadaverous yet buoyant, who promised a tearful Churchill, 'Whither thou goest, I will go.' Hopkins flew on to Moscow to meet

Stalin and promise aid, then back (exhausted) to join FDR for his summit with Churchill on board the *Prince of Wales* in Placentia Bay off Newfoundland.

'At last we've gotten together,' said FDR to Churchill, later writing to Daisy Suckley, 'He's a tremendously vital person. I like him.' After agreeing a Wilsonian programme of democracy later (the Atlantic Charter), both were moved when at a Sunday morning service on the great battleship, the Protestant aristocrats sang the rousing hymns of their boarding schools with the (doomed) crew. It was the first of many meetings.

In September, Hitler's Army Group Centre was approaching Moscow, but Soviet resistance was intensifying, winter stirring, and Russia had still not collapsed 'like a house of cards'. When it dawned on him that his Blitzkrieg could fail, Hitler became quieter, more short-tempered, as he forced his generals to seize the rich resources of the south and Leningrad in the north, delaying the storming of Moscow. In the south, Kyiv fell, trapping 665,000 Soviet troops, while in the north he besieged Leningrad, where a million civilians starved to death, planning to raze it:* 'The nemesis of history,' he ranted.

'This,' crowed Goebbels, 'will be the biggest drama of a city in history.' Keen to avoid 'the second Mongolian storm from a second Genghis Khan', Hitler ordered 'the greatest battle in world history', the storming of Moscow. But the temperature plummeted; Soviet fighting stiffened; then came a thaw; vehicles languished in mud. Hitler told Count Ciano that winter heralded 'a repetition of Napoleon's fate but for Russia not Germany'. In Moscow, on 16 October, Stalin evacuated the main commissariats to the rear; disorder broke out; his train was packed with his library – but on the 18th he stayed to fight. On the 30th the Germans halted. On 7 November, Stalin presided over the October Revolution parade and summoned Zhukov to take command. Stalin had a reserve that Hitler had not registered: his Far Eastern army of a million men, 17,000 tanks, to cover against Japanese attack.

Hirohito too was agonizing over strategy. In July 1940, with Hitler's acquiescence, the Japanese, overstretched by their war in China,

* Among those struggling to survive was Maria, a factory-worker and the wife of a working-class submariner, Vladimir Putin. The couple, married in 1928 in their twenties, had two sons. They had already lost one child to the epidemics of the 1930s. Now as Vladimir, son of an NKVD servitor, served in an NKVD punishment battalion (later transferred to a regular Red Army unit), Maria lost her two-year-old son to starvation or diphtheria in besieged Leningrad. Vladmir was wounded but survived the war, later becoming a foreman and Party committee secretary of a train-making factory. It was only at forty-one that Maria gave birth to a lastborn son: Vladimir Vladimirovich Putin.

occupied French Indo-China. President Roosevelt punished Tokyo, banning iron and steel supplies and some fuel. Just after Barbarossa, the Japanese Imperial Conference had leaned against any more fighting with Russia, signing a neutrality treaty with Stalin. If America threatened oil supplies, Japan would have to fight the USA as well as attack Dutch and British colonies. 'Our empire won't be deterred by war with Great Britain and USA,' said Prince Konoe, though 'If the German–Soviet war should develop to the advantage of our empire, we will settle the northern question.'

The hawkish war minister, General Tojo, had a clear plan – and simplicity is often mistaken for lucidity. This general's son, nicknamed the Razor, a veteran of the Russian civil war, then commander in Manchuria, was a humourless disciplinarian who routinely slapped the faces of his officers as a means of instilling bushido. He proposed attacks on the USA and Britain.

'Do you have any plans for a protracted war?' retorted Hirohito. Tojo had to win at once – or not at all. His Southern Plan would send 185,000 men to seize oil and resources in the Dutch East Indies and British Malaya. But first the Japanese had to knock out America, so they were planning an attack on the US fleet at Pearl Harbor in the tradition of the 1904 raid on Port Arthur. To cover themselves they would also have to take the American Philippines and Guam, an expansive offensive across the Pacific, with a second operation advancing to Australia. But their best admiral, Yamamoto Isoruku, a veteran of Tsushima, warned it 'wouldn't be enough if we take Guam and the Philippines, nor even Hawaii and San Francisco', and wondered if Tojo and the hawks had 'confidence as to the final outcome and are prepared to make the necessary sacrifices'.

'The Japs are having a real drag-down,' said FDR, who hoped to avoid provoking Tokyo, 'trying to decide which way they're going to jump. No one knows what the decision will be.' Prince Konoe suggested negotiations; FDR agreed, but by September 1941 the shortage of oil threatened to incapacitate Japan altogether. Konoe proposed 'to start a war if by early October we can't achieve our demands through negotiations'. He asked Hirohito to make a decision: he could have refused to go to war, negotiated with America and made temporary concessions, while awaiting developments in the European war. Prince Konoe consulted Admiral Yamamoto.

'I'll run wild considerably for the first six months or a year,' replied the admiral, 'but I've utterly no confidence for the second and third years.' Konoe preferred negotiation but, as he recalled, 'His Majesty . . .

leaned towards war.' In an astonishing conversation, Hirohito, now forty-four, and his commanders decided to risk everything rather than give up any of their expansionist ambitions.

'If we open hostilities,' asked Hirohito, 'will our operations have a probability of success?'

'Yes,' answered General Hajime Sugiyama, his chief of staff.

'At the time of the China Incident [invasion] the army told me we'd achieve peace after one blow. Sugiyama, you were army minister then.'

'We met unexpected difficulties . . .'

'Didn't I caution you?' asked Hirohito. 'Are you lying to me, Sugiyama?'

'Your Majesty?' asked naval chief Admiral Nagano.

'Proceed.'

'There's no 100 per cent probability of victory . . . Assume there's a sick person and we leave him; he'll die. But if the doctor's diagnosis offers 70 per cent survival if we operate, then don't you think we must try surgery? And if after surgery the patient dies, one must say it was meant to be.'

'All right.'

Stalin, desperately holding out in Moscow, was waiting to see what Hirohito would do. 'The possibility of a Japanese attack, existing until recently,' the spy Sorge reported to Stalin on 14 September, 'has disappeared.' It was the most decisive jewel of intelligence in the Second World War.* Stalin took notice, secretly bringing his fresh Siberian army to Moscow.

Konoe opened negotiations with America, but Roosevelt still demanded withdrawal from China and Indo-China. 'If we yield to America's demands,' warned Razor Tojo, 'it will destroy the fruits of the China Incident' – the Chinese empire. On 17 October, Konoe resigned and Hirohito appointed an 'absolutely dumbfounded' Tojo. 'I'm just an ordinary man possessing no shining talents,' said the Razor. 'Anything I've achieved I owe to hard work and never giving up.' But he accepted. It was war. 'If the Emperor said it should be so,' said the Razor, 'then that's it for me.'

'Now next,' said Hirohito, 'when does the navy plan to open hostilities?'

---

* It was Sorge's last service to Moscow. Shortly afterwards, the *Kenpeitai*, Japanese military intelligence, arrested him and rolled up his network. He was hanged in 1944. Among his lovers was his German fellow agent Ursula Kuczynski, who having moved to London, codename Agent Sonja, handled the nuclear scientist Klaus Fuchs, one of the Soviet spies who helped Stalin get the Bomb.

'On 8 December,' said Admiral Nagano.

Razor compared the risk to jumping off a cliff with his eyes closed: 'There are times when we must have the courage to do extraordinary things.'

Razor checked with Hitler whether he would join the war against the USA. Hitler had no obligation but America was 'a mongrel society' of Jews, black people and Slavs that 'couldn't possibly create an indigenous culture or operate a successful political system'. He believed he was already at war with Roosevelt. Besides, 'the Soviet Union was finished', his spokesman announced.

'Never before,' Hitler told his veteran comrades, 'has a gigantic empire been so quickly smashed.' But the frosts came again; the Germans halted again, just outside Moscow. On 6 December, Zhukov counter-attacked. Moscow was indeed 'the greatest battle in world history' – the decisive battle of the war that marked the end of Hitler's winning streak.

Two days later, before dawn on X-Day, 8 December, Japanese planes took off for Pearl Harbor, Singapore and Guam while the army invaded British Malaya and the Dutch East Indies. 'Throughout the day, the emperor wore his naval uniform and seemed in a splendid mood' as the first reports came in from the War of Greater Asia. At dawn, 353 Japanese planes hit Pearl Harbor, aiming to destroy four battleships and, especially, the three aircraft carriers. The battleships were sunk and 2,467 men were killed, but the carriers were at sea. The planes returned without finding them. Hirohito celebrated, but Yamamoto realized that Japan had not done enough.

Shaken and ashen, Roosevelt addressed Congress on this 'date which will live in infamy', but he was still not at war with Hitler. On 11 December, in the Reichstag, Hitler declared war on America, accusing Roosevelt of leading 'the Jews in all their satanic treachery'. He looked triumphant, but that moment was the beginning of the American Century. Outside Moscow, Zhukov pushed the Germans back. Their generals panicked. Hitler ordered them 'not to retreat a single step'. The generals begged him to permit retreat. 'Do you think Frederick the Great's grenadiers died gladly? They'd have liked to stay alive but the king had every right to demand the sacrifice.' Hitler claimed that if he had 'shown weakness even for a moment, a catastrophe that would have far overshadowed Napoleon's would have been at hand'. But as he told the Danish foreign minister in November, 'If the German people prove not strong or willing enough to make sacrifices and shed their blood for the sake of their existence, they deserve to die out and be destroyed by another stronger force.'

In January 1942, the other overconfident, autodidactic supremo, Stalin, insisted on a multifront offensive that, overstretching his armies, allowed the Germans to recover. And the failure of Hitler's Blitzkrieg accelerated the tragedy of the Jews.

I SEE ONLY ONE OPTION – TOTAL EXTERMINATION: HITLER AND THE HOLOCAUST

Returning to his 'prophecy', Hitler declared that 'The result of this war will be the destruction of Jewry.' The murder had started not with Jews but with Germans.

In spring 1939, Hitler had ordered the liquidation of the elderly, the mentally ill and the deformed to ensure 'survival of the fittest'. Hitler had often talked at dinners of his plan 'to eradicate the incurably ill and not just the mentally ill'. He commissioned his personal doctor Karl Brandt and a Reich Committee for the Scientific Registration of Major Genetic Disease and Suffering, made up of radicalized doctors, to create a secret system denoted T4 (Tiergartenstrasse 4, Berlin – headquarters of the euthanasia programme). In September 1939 Hitler ordered 'mercy killings of ill people deemed incurable', using Luminal, or Phenobarbital, then, at the suggestion of the SD, carbon monoxide. Over 65,000 were killed.

Although there were only 200,000 terrified and impoverished Jews left in Germany, there were 1.5 million in Hitler's Poland. He planned to deport them to French Madagascar, where many would presumably perish, but in the meantime, in 1940, the Germans started to wall up ghettos in Polish cities, entrapping over 400,000 Jews. But the Russian war provided the fatal arena for slaughter. At a conference in December 1940, Himmler announced that Eichmann had calculated there would soon be 5.8 million Jews in Nazi hands, offering the chance for a Final Solution to the Jewish Problem. In early 1941, Hitler asked Heydrich to produce 'a proposal for a final solution'. In May just before Barbarossa, with Hitler's agreement, Himmler created four *Einsatzgruppen* that were to follow the Army Groups, each led by trusted RSHA officers. Göring ordered Heydrich to make 'all preparations' for 'a total solution to the Jewish question'. So far 'Jews who occupy Party and state positions' were the victims, but the *Einsatzgruppen* immediately started to kill all Jews, including women and children, in the Baltics and Ukraine,

assisted by Lithuanian, Latvian and Ukrainian fascists* – and enthusiastically joined by the Romanians.

In June 1941, Antonescu ordered, 'Cleanse Iaşi of its Jewish population: 13,000 Jews were butchered. When Odessa, the great cosmopolitan
Black Sea city, entrepôt of Russian grain, fell in October after a siege that
exposed Romanian ineptitude, the Romanians killed 30,000 Jews in the
streets, while the surviving 200,000 were concentrated at Bogdanovka
and murdered so chaotically that Himmler and Eichmann became
vexed. Cooperating with German *Einsatzkommandos* (*Einsatzgruppen*
units) and Ukrainian Germans, the Romanians killed over 300,000
Jews and were responsible for more Jewish murders than anyone except
the Germans.

Himmler and Heydrich visited the sites of the massacres and approved them, including the burning by Order Police of 500 women and
children in a synagogue in Białystok. On 29–30 September 1941, at Babi
Yar, near Kyiv, *Einsatzgruppe* C, aided by Ukrainians, killed 33,771 Kyivan
Jews. 'The action itself proceeded smoothly,' said the official report.
'The Wehrmacht welcomed the measures.' Army officers registered
the Jews, marked them with white armbands and concentrated them,
providing trucks for transportation, cordoning off execution zones, even

---

* Around 35,000 Ukrainians, many of them members of the OUN, the Ukrainian Nationalist Organization, joined the *Ukrainische Hilfspolizei* or Ukrainian Auxiliary Police, who
wholeheartedly murdered Jews. The OUN was founded in 1929 in Poland, splitting into
rival factions, one (OUN-M) under Andriy Melnyk, another (OUN-B) under the younger
Stepan Bandera. Melnyk was an old-fashioned nationalist, Bandera a radical nationalist
with fascist tendencies. Both were armed by the Nazis after the invasion of Poland. At the
start of Barbarossa, Bandera followed the Nazi invaders with two German-supported units
of militia, the Nachtigall (under his lieutenant Roman Shukhevych) and Roland battalions,
and declared Ukraine independent. In Lviv, in early July 1941, Bandera's OUN and Nachtigall henchmen killed over 5,000 Jews with *Einsatzgruppe* C, followed by another carnival
frenzy, the Petliura Days, in which militias and farmers used guns and farm tools to kill
2,000 Jews. In September, Bandera, refusing to retract the declaration of Ukrainian independence, fell out with the Germans, was arrested and was sent to a concentration camp.
Shukhevych and many of the members of the Ukrainian battalions enrolled in German
Schutzmannschaft 201, an auxiliary police battalion – part of the *Ukrainische Hilfspolizei*
who killed tens of thousands of Poles – and joined the Nazi killers in the murder of more
than 200,000 Jews.

A typical operation took place in the industrial town of Kryvyi Rih, where the Ukrainian
Auxiliary Police murdered most of the Jews, including members of a typical Jewish family,
the Zelenskys. There were four Zelensky brothers. Semyon Zelensky escaped to join the
Soviet army and, rising to colonel, fought all the way to Berlin. In 2020, on a visit to the
Yad Vashem memorial in Israel, his grandson, Volodymyr Zelensky, called this a 'story of
a family of four brothers. Three of them, their parents and their families became victims
of the Holocaust. All shot by German occupiers. The fourth survived. Two years after the
war, he had a son, and thirty-one years later he had a grandson. In forty more years, that
grandson became president [of independent Ukraine] and he is standing before you today.'

participating in the slaughter themselves. By the end of the year *Einsatz-gruppen* had killed 500,000 Jews in Ukraine and the Baltics.*

That August, Himmler had attended an execution, which may have been filmed by Hitler's personal cameraman, though it is unknown if the Führer watched it, after which he asked the *Einsatzgruppe* commander Arthur Nebe to find a less 'psychologically burdensome' means than mass shootings. Nebe turned to the doctors who had euthanized Germany's disabled and who were now free since Hitler had cancelled the programme when the Bishop of Münster denounced it.

In November 1941, SS-Standartenführer Walther Rauff tested gassing by carbon monoxide in special trucks which were then provided to *Einsatzgruppen*. In October, Himmler had ordered SS police chief Globocnik to create a death camp at Belzec – as Hitler ordered all Jews to wear yellow stars and decided to deport all Jews from Germany. The RAF's bombing of German cities and, above all, the failure of the Russian war justified this path towards physical extermination. At meetings with his paladins, Hitler constantly called for the liquidation. As Goebbels recorded, 'The Führer has decided on a total clean-up. He prophesied to the Jews that if they started a world war they would experience their own destruction. This is not just a turn of phrase . . . the destruction of Jewry must be the result.' At a meeting with Hitler on 18 December, Himmler noted: 'Jewish question. To be exterminated as partisans.' Himmler later remembered that 'The Führer placed the execution of this very difficult order on my shoulders.' It is likely that the decision to launch the Holocaust was taken by Hitler between 12 and 18 December 1941 – the moment the Russian counter-attack was revealing that the war might not be won.

On 20 January 1942, at a lacustrine SS villa at Wannsee in Berlin, Heydrich held a meeting with fifteen civil servants (from the Interior, Justice, Foreign and other ministries) and SS and Nazi Party officials, including Eichmann of the RSHA Jewish Department to decide 'a consistent approach among the central organs' to the 'final solution'. After reminding everyone pompously that Göring had given him and Himmler responsibility for this '*Endlösung*', Heydrich reported that of eleven million Jews in Europe the able-bodied could be worked to death,

---

* A million Jews were murdered in Ukraine, but that was part of a multifaceted bloodbath. Over five million Ukrainians –one in six – were killed, including Jews. The butchery was made more complex by a three-way war: in March 1943, many Ukrainian Auxiliary Police, who had aided the Nazi killing, as well as other patriots, joined Bandera's Ukrainian Insurgent Army (UPA) under Shukhevych and launched an insurgency against the Nazis, killing Jews, Poles and Germans. As the Nazis retreated, they fought the Soviets. Between 1918 and 1950, Ukraine was the most murderous place on earth.

'eliminated by natural causes', while the rest, the strongest, would have to be 'treated accordingly' since they would be 'the product of natural selection and if released act as a seed of a new Jewish revival'. The representative of the General Government suggested that his 2.5 million Jews should be liquidated immediately, then Heydrich explained that the rest of the Jews would be transported to 'transit ghettos from which they would be transported to the east' – a euphemism for mass murder. Jews would be gathered across Europe, transported to death camps and ultimately killed. Afterwards, Heydrich invited Eichmann for a cognac.

Five days later, at the Wolf's Lair, Hitler told Himmler and others, 'This has to be done quickly . . . The Jews must leave Europe . . . I see only one option: complete extermination . . .' On 14 February, he told Goebbels, 'No sentimental feelings. The Jews deserve the catastrophe they're now experiencing . . . We must accelerate this process with unemotional ruthlessness.' Three days later the first victims, Jews from Lublin, were gassed at Belzec. In a month 70,000 were killed. New killing camps were built at Sobibor and Treblinka, where by autumn 1942 a total of 1.7 million Polish Jews had been murdered.* A new killing camp, Birkenau, was added to the existing Auschwitz complex, where in September 1941 a new poison, Zyklon-B gas, was tried out on Russian prisoners.

On 27 May 1942, Heydrich, now protector of Moravia, whom Hitler was planning to appoint as French governor, was being driven out of Prague when his Mercedes was struck by grenades, thrown by brave Czech commandos. Fragments of the car seat peppered his spleen. Although penicillin, being developed in America, would have cured him in a week, he died days later. But the Final Solution continued.

THE SLAVE MASTERS: KRUPP

Auschwitz-Birkenau became the killing and slavery centre for European Jews outside Poland and the USSR. Heydrich's system called for local police to register their Jews, then summon them for entraining for 'evacuation to the east', yet the reaction of Hitler's vassals was unenthusiastic and defiance was entirely possible: Mussolini had passed Racial Laws but refused to deport any Italian Jews; the Hungarian regent Horthy, who had persecuted Jews through a series of Nazi-style

---

* The vast data on Jews and their transport by rail to Auschwitz and Treblinka was tabulated by a computing company that used hole-punching machines. It was called Dehomag, a wholly owned subsidiary of an American company, IBM.

Jewish Laws from 1938 and was fully informed about the Final Solution, sent 100,000 Jews to the killing camps but refused to surrender the majority of his large Jewish community. There were 300,000 Jews in France plus another 400,000 in Algeria. Few were touched in Algeria, but in the metropolis, ordinary French police rounded up 75,000 Jews and sent them to the killing camps, where virtually all were killed, a particularly horrific record in the home of the Enlightenment. The Danes managed to hide virtually all their Jews, saving 90 per cent by spiriting them to Sweden. The Dutch on the other hand cooperated with the killing: 107,000 out of 140,000 Jews were deported and virtually all were killed – a higher proportion than in any other country in western Europe including Germany.

On arrival at Auschwitz, the Jews faced the 'selection' by an SS doctor, Joseph Mengele, who determined who could be forced to work and who should be exterminated at once. Mengele, an elegant ghoul who conducted vicious 'experiments' on Jewish children, would send children, women and elderly to the 'showers' (sealed and fitted with invisible gas siphons) where they were stripped of their belongings and clothes, then gassed, their bodies dragged out by Jewish slave workers who, after extracting gold teeth, fed them into the crematoria that coughed sickly smoke out of towering chimneys.* In July 1942, Himmler watched Mengele make a selection of Dutch Jews in total silence before dining with the commandant in 'the finest, radiant mood'. One Viennese family personifies the intricate scale of trans-European murder: four of Sigmund Freud's elderly sisters were now dispatched on death trains to be slaughtered in distant killing camps – Mitzi and Paula Freud were gassed at Maly Trostenets (Belarus), Rosa at Treblinka, and Dolfi was starved at Theresienstadt.

Between 5.9 and 6.1 million Jews were killed in total, including the near million murdered by *Einsatzgruppen*. An entire world was destroyed, a culture vanished. Romani and Sinti (denounced as 'mongrel Gypsies') were also targeted: 500,000 were killed in the *Porajmos* (Devouring) along with 5,000–15,000 homosexuals and several million Gentile Poles and Russians. Although trains and barbed steel had made possible vast deportations and concentration camps since 1890s, and although other regimes particularly Stalin's in Russia and later those

---

* 'As I arrived with my parents, the Jewish *kapos* [camp trusties] whispered to me, "Say you're Catholic" because I was blond and blue-eyed,' a Hungarian Jewish boy, Yitzhak Yaacoby, then aged thirteen, told this author. 'I remember so well how Mengele looked at me. "Are you Jewish?" he asked. "Catholic," I said. "Pah! Go on then!" laughed Mengele, hitting me with his baton, but not sending me to the "showers".' Yaacoby survived.

in Communist China and Cambodia killed many, none did so on such a scale and using industrial means. It was a crime, based on race, unequalled in history, for which no word existed: in 1944, a Jewish Pole invented 'genocide' to describe its enormity – a word that like the Holocaust itself should never be misused.

There is always money in mass murder: Nazi viceroys living in luxury enjoyed sadistic and sexual control over innocent people whose property they looted. But they also enforced slavery on Slavs and Jews. The Krupps, consuming businesses all over conquered Europe, were typical of the German businesses that embraced this diabolic order. Krupp owned factories in twelve nations from Dnepropetrovsk (Dnipro) in Ukraine to Paris where he seized Jewish firms, colluding in sending one of their owners to the death camps. In April 1942, visiting Hitler at the Wolf's Lair, Krupp praised the liquidation of Jews, 'but could see no reason they shouldn't contribute before they went', requesting an assignment of slaves and offering the SS a commission per slave.

In three years, twelve million slaves – Poles wearing 'P' on their clothes, Russians 'SR' (Soviet Russian) or 'OST' (for *Ostarbeiter* – eastern worker) and Jews '*Judenmaterial*' (Jewish property), later superseded by the yellow star – were imported to the Reich or worked in slave camps. Some 30,000 Slavic women toiled in German military brothels. The numbers are imprecise but colossal. After the war, 5.2 million slaves were repatriated to Russia and Poland.

In July 1942, Krupp worked closely with Speer, armaments minister, and history's greatest slave master accepted '45,000 Russians, 120,000 prisoners, 6,000 civilians' for his steelworks and coal mines. But this was just the start. Krupp got Hitler's permission to use Auschwitz's Jewish slaves to build the Berthawerk factory (named after his mother) in Silesia and soon more arrived in Essen, where signs read: 'Slavs are slaves'. Corporate memoranda openly reported that 'slaves' had arrived from the 'slave market', with Alfried Krupp designated the *Sklavenhalter* – slave owner. Krupp controlled thirty-eight camps guarded by SS and his own Kruppstahl guards with blackjacks. 'You must be careful History doesn't call you a slave trader,' warned one of his directors.

In October 1942, Krupp opened a gun-fuse factory at Auschwitz 'to make use of the people there', the details worked out by Krupp and the commandant Rudolf Höss. 'As regards the cooperation of our technical office in Breslau, I can only say that, between that office and Auschwitz, the closest understanding exists,' wrote Krupp in September 1943, 'and is guaranteed for the future.' Right to the end of the war, noted one of his managers, 'Krupp considered it a duty to make 520 Jewish girls, some of them little more than children, work under the most brutal conditions in the heart of the concern, in Essen.'

These crimes were made possible by the collaboration of hundreds of thousands of people, each of whom bears precisely the same guilt as Hitler himself. It was quickly known to the leadership and most of the German public via events on their streets, if not via the stories of soldiers. Many who should have known better did nothing; Pope Pius did scarcely anything. Yet there were many brave people, many but not enough, who protected Jews, some of them rogues – the profiteer Oskar Schindler saved 1,400 Polish Jews – but most were ordinary people of courage, and some were royal. In Romania, King Mihai visited Odessa with Antonescu, impotently protesting against the massacres. But when Himmler ordered the killing of all Romanian Jews, he and his mother Queen Helena refused to countenance it. 'By 1942,' Mihai said, 'I was convinced something had to be done.'

'Keep quiet,' barked Antonescu, 'you're still a child.' But Mihai won the release of Romanian Jewish leaders and stopped the deportations to Belzec, a notable achievement in the midst of the appalling Romanian crimes.*

Meanwhile Hitler had a more immediate concern. 'If I don't get the oil of Maikop and Grozny,' he said, 'I'll have to liquidate this entire war.'

HITLER'S BATTLE FOR OIL

That summer of 1942, Hitler was planning Operation Blue, an offensive against Russia to secure Stalingrad on the Volga and the oilfields in Baku, Maikop and Grozny. The capture of Russian fuel depots did not help: Russian tanks ran on diesel, German on gasoline. Stalin was the master of industrial production, moving entire industries eastwards: his T-34 tank, simple and manoeuvrable was, agreed German generals, 'the best tank in the war', its largest factory in Leningrad being totally moved to Chelyabinsk which became Tankograd (Tank City), soon producing

---

* In Greece, Princess Alice (mother of Prince Philip, later duke of Edinburgh) hid a Jewish family and was honoured at Yad Vashem as a 'righteous Gentile'. Even the countries where there was most collaboration with the Nazis, there were also people of great courage and decency: the most 'righteous Gentiles' were in Poland (7,177), Holland, France and Ukraine (2,619), but also include two Arabs, the Egyptian doctor Dr Mohamed Helmy and the Tunisian farmer Khaled Abdelwahhab who saved Jews in Vichy north Africa.

1,300 a month, outstripping German production under Speer.* But it all depended on oil.

In June, General Erwin Rommel forced the surrender of thousands of British troops in Tobruk, and his forces were soon heading for Egypt. If Hitler seized the Caucasus, he would secure the oil in Iraq and Iran – and win the war. Palestinian Jews were afraid as Rommel approached Egypt.† British forces, aided by Jewish fighters, including the young Zionist Moshe Dayan, had seized Syria from the Vichy French: Dayan lost an eye in the battle. Churchill took no risks with his oilfields. In Iraq, where King Faisal's grandson Faisal II, aged six, was too young to rule, the British had overthrown a pro-German general. In Iran, Reza Shah tried to play Britain off against Germany, but in August 1941 Stalin and Churchill invaded, swept aside his vaunted army (at which the shah beat his general with his cane) and forced his abdication and exile, replacing him with his son Mohammad Reza, now twenty-one.

In July 1942, Hitler arrived at his Ukrainian HQ in Vinnitsa – Werewolf – to launch Blue, which again wrongfooted Stalin and achieved astonishing advances, as the Axis forces, having mopped up Crimea,‡ charged across the sweltering steppes, reaching Stalingrad in September. While Churchill sought a winning general to stop Rommel, Stalin, ordering 'Not one step back' and placing blocking units to execute any retreating troops, turned the ruins of Stalingrad into a fortress. As the German Sixth Army fought its way into the city, the Soviets held out in a cauldron battle. Sensing he was close to victory, Hitler determined to take it: 'a battle of the giants' was what Goebbels called it. Stalin barely

---

* It was only now that Hitler grasped the scale of Stalin's industrial achievement that would win the war: 'they have the most monstrous armament humanly conceivable – 35,000 tanks!' Hitler told the Finnish Marshal Mannerheim on 4 June 1942, in his only private conversation to be recorded. 'If a general of mine had told me a state could have 35,000 tanks, I'd have said, "That's crazy! You're seeing ghosts!"' But they were real.

† The leader of the Palestinian Arabs, Amin al-Husseini, mufti of Jerusalem, travelled to Berlin where he met Hitler and Himmler and backed the Holocaust. In summer 1943, Himmler boasted that the Nazis had 'already exterminated more than three million [Jews]' – which astonished Husseini. 'It's the duty of Muslims generally and Arabs in particular to drive out all Jews,' said the mufti in November. 'Germany . . . has very clearly recognized the Jews for what they are and has resolved to find a definitive solution for the Jewish danger that will eliminate the scourge that Jews represent in the world.'

‡ The taking of Sebastopol in July 1942 was aided by a giant cannon with a twenty-five-mile range built on Hitler's personal orders by Krupp. 'My Führer,' wrote Alfried Krupp, delivering the letter in person at the Wolf's Lair, 'the big weapon manufactured thanks to your personal command has proved its effectiveness . . . Krupp gratefully recognizes the confidence displayed in the family by you, my Führer . . . Following an example of Alfred Krupp in 1870, my wife and I ask the favour that the Krupp Works may refrain from charging for this product . . . Sieg Heil!' In 1943, at Gustav's request, Hitler passed a special Lex Krupp to ensure that the firm remained within the dynasty.

slept, spending the night on a sofa in the Little Corner, as the Russians fought ferociously, an astonishing resistance encouraged by terror but truly inspired by the quasi-sacred cults of patriotism, sacrifice and heroism. '*Za Rodina, za Stalina!*' they cried as they fought. 'For Motherland, for Stalin!' Soviet losses in the entire war were unparalleled: twelve million soldiers and over fifteen million civilians perished.

Roosevelt, far from the grim, micromanaging intensity of Hitler's and Stalin's headquarters, was hosting Churchill in his idiosyncratic White House, which FDR grandly called 'the backyard'. There, theatrically wielding his cigarette holder, he faced global decisions on a vast scale, tempered by the mixing of martinis and the company of resident cronies Harry Hopkins, the pretty young Crown Princess Märtha of Norway and his devoted cousin Daisy Suckley, along with Fala the Scottish terrier: 'You're the only one I don't have to entertain,' FDR flattered Daisy and often talked of retiring with her to his cottage at Hyde Park. The pressure was astonishing. 'I'm going over to the office and will spend the day blowing various people up,' FDR told Daisy, to whom he found time to write indiscreet letters. His guest, Churchill, who had suffered a minor heart attack during an earlier White House stay in December 1941, reeled from British military disasters, the fall of Singapore and defeat at Tobruk. But over the next weeks, he and FDR delayed any invasion of France and agreed instead to land in north Africa and attack Hitler's 'soft underbelly' in Italy. Churchill flew to Moscow to inform Stalin there would be no invasion of France. Stalin accused him of cowardice – but the two warhorses ended up drinking together into the night.

Hitler boasted that Stalingrad was about to fall and 'No one will drive us from this place again,' adding, 'The Jews once laughed at my prophecies . . . I can assure you they'll choke on their laughter everywhere.'

In the Pacific, Tojo was celebrating a roll of victories, sinking the British battleships *Repulse* and *Prince of Wales*, taking Malaya and Hong Kong from Britain, the East Indies from Holland, Guam and the Philippines from America. In February 1942, British Singapore had surrendered. The Japanese bombed Australia and the Imperial Navy had proposed an Australian invasion. Tojo preferred to attack the British Raj, starting with Burma. Backed by the Thais and by insurgents led by an anti-British nationalist Aung San, Tojo conquered most of the country, cutting Allied supplies to China. Aung was typical of Asian nationalists who embraced Japan's Pan-Asian policy against European empires.*

---

* In the Dutch East Indies, a charismatic teacher's son and trained architect, Sukarno,

But Japanese cruelty exposed the reality; Allied prisoners suffered slave labour, death marches, torture, beheadings and starvation. One in four Filipinos were killed. In China, the Japanese killed four million civilians in their 'Burn to Ash Strategy', known as the 'Kill All, Burn All, Loot All' policy, signed off by Hirohito. Overall during the war, fourteen million Chinese died.

MAO AND THE SHANGHAI ACTRESS

FDR decided 'Europe First', which called for limited aid to Chiang, who he hoped would tie down 700,000 Japanese troops. Roosevelt sent a peppery American general, 'Vinegar Joe' Stilwell, who soon loathed Chiang (whom he called Peanut); Chiang hated him back. Incapable of understanding China, Stilwell resented Chiang's dictatorship, enforced by a secret-police chief, Dai Lai, who threw prisoners into cauldrons. Madame Chiang flew to America to address rallies and win over FDR, charming the Americans with her Wellesley accent and chic *cheongsam*. As British and Indian forces retreated in Burma, Stilwell demanded that Chiang help; Chiang sent troops, but they were routed. In the comfortable caves of Yen'an, his rival Mao Zedong fought a guerrilla war against the Japanese, deploying new units north into Manchuria – among the cadres a young Korean, Kim Il-sung, whom the Japanese nicknamed Tiger on account of his small-scale but ferocious attacks.

Revelling in Chiang's defeats, Mao launched a Rectification Campaign, a Stalinesque terror of what he called 'pain and friction' managed by Kang Sheng, a sadistic myrmidon who always wore a black tunic and boots and rode a black horse. Kang had escorted Mao's two sons to be educated in Moscow, where in 1937 he had helped Stalin's hatchet man Yezhov liquidate Chinese Trotskyites. Now attaching himself to Mao, with whom he enjoyed talking about sex and terror, sharing erotica and devising tortures, he tortured and shot thousands while staging the 'struggle and confession' sessions that would characterize Maoist terror.

Mao played mahjong, read history books and frolicked with a harem of Shanghai actresses until a dazzling film star, Jiang Qing, twenty-seven-year-old daughter of a concubine and an alcoholic innkeeper, arrived in

who had served four years in Dutch jail for his nationalist activities, joined the Japanese to promote his vision of a new national concept based on the European colony: Indonesia. But not all nationalists followed this path: Ho Chi Minh and his Viet Minh resistance, which encompassed Communist and nationalist elements, fought the French and then the Japanese, winning the aid of the USA and Britain.

Yen'an. In Shanghai she had been arrested for Leftism but had flirted if not slept with her KMT interrogators. Mao's comrades criticized his 'imperial concubines', but, addressing a meeting, he spotted her in the front row and lent her his coat. Later she arrived at his residence to return the coat and stayed the night. Mao abandoned his respected wife, who had endured the Long March, and insisted on marrying Jiang Qing, backed by Kang Sheng, whose alliance with her lasted until the 1970s. Mao's son Anying now arrived back from Russia, with a pistol given by Stalin, joining his four-year-old sister Li Min in their troglodytic ménage. In 1940, Jiang Qing gave birth to a daughter, Li Na, but family was always at the mercy of power. Mao declined to rescue his brother Zemin, who was excuted by the KMT; Jiang meanwhile denounced Li Na's nanny for poisoning their milk, shrieking, 'Poison! Confess!' Mao recognized that Jiang Qing was 'as deadly poisonous as a scorpion': one day she would almost rule China.

After Rangoon fell, the Japanese threatened India where Nehru, charming, quicksilver, elegant, had emerged as the leader of Congress, respectfully following his 'Bapu' Gandhi. In 1928, Nehru had declared, 'India must sever the British connection and attain Purna Swaraj – total independence.'* Nehru was in jail when his wife Kamala died of TB. He had devoted himself to politics – admitting, 'I almost overlooked her' – though she had been jailed for her campaigning. It was their daughter, Indira, often alone while her father was in jail, who became his political confidante.†

Nehru and Gandhi, frustrated by years of British obfuscation, disagreed on the war: Gandhi, a pacific pragmatist, wanted neutrality; Nehru, an internationalist socialist, supported Britain against fascism. But the British refusal to promise post-war independence reunited them again. 'Some say Jawaharlal and I were estranged,' said Gandhi. 'It will require much more than difference of opinion to estrange us . . .

---

* The British responded with the Roundtable Conferences of 1930–2 – attended at times by Gandhi and Jinnah – which led to the limited elections, mocked by Nehru as 'a machine with strong brakes but no engine'. The process outraged Churchill, who fulminated, 'It's alarming and nauseating to see Mr Gandhi, a seditious Middle Temple lawyer, now posing as a fakir, striding half-naked up the steps of the Vice-regal palace to parley on equal terms with the representative of the King-Emperor.' Nonetheless, following the 1935 Government of India Act, there were elections in 1937 leading to the establishment of provincial Indian governments – though the viceroy still ruled. When the Second World War began, the process of negotiations was abandoned altogether.

† Both men disagreed with the president of Congress, Subhas Chandra Bose, a wealthy lawyer and a socialist who favoured a Hindu–Muslim alliance in Bengal – until he was defeated by Gandhi. Now he escaped to Germany before emerging from a Japanese submarine to lead an Indian National Army of 60,000 which fought against the British in Burma.

Jawaharlal will be my successor.' But many Muslims as well as Hindus volunteered to fight for Britain, increasing the size of the Indian army tenfold to 2.5 million, and the British recognized Jinnah as representative of Indian Muslims: 'After I was treated on the same basis as Mr Gandhi, I was wonderstruck.' In Lahore, Jinnah declared, 'Muslims are a nation according to any definition of a nation and must have . . . their states.' Gandhi was agonized by this dilemma.

Now Chiang Kai-shek, keen to help Britain but also to show Asian solidarity, flew to Delhi to meet Nehru and Gandhi, whom he urged to join the war. They both cordially ignored him.

In August 1942, they launched a Quit India campaign, which, far beyond civil disobedience, destroyed hundreds of police and railway stations, sabotaging railways and telegraphs. The British responded by deploying troops and mass arrests but the campaign failed. Indians continued to volunteer for Britain.

During Chiang's visit, two famines were killing many in the two greatest Asian countries, both exacerbated by governmental incompetence and wartime priorities. Three million Indians died in a famine in Bengal.* Six hundred miles to the east, in Henan, noted Chiang, 'People are starving, dogs and animals are eating corpses.' He added, 'Our social reality is scarred. We're exhausted after six years of the war.' Two million Chinese died.

In May 1942, Razor Tojo was planning an extravagantly Japanese Pacific – as fantastical as Hitler's visions – dominating China, giving eastern India to a new Burmese kingdom, ruling Australia, Hawaii, Alaska, even Canada. But Admiral Yamamoto resisted this 'victory fever', writing to his favourite geisha, 'The first stage has been a kind of children's hour and it will soon be over; now comes the adult's hour.'

---

* In rural Bengal, run by an elected Indian government, a catastrophic shortage of rice came about as a result of a cyclone, the fall of Burma (which had exported rice to India), the destruction of coastal boats to prevent them falling into the hands of the Japanese and widespread hoarding by speculators and merchants. Relief efforts were hampered by both intra-Indian politics and the incompetence, negligence and lethargy of the viceroy, Lord Linlithgow. Churchill and the London cabinet, whose priority was to feed the army, failed to act until it was too late. The famine was not intentional but Britain as the imperial power bore responsibility. Similar famines raged in Japanese-occupied Vietnam (where two million died) and in newly liberated Greece and Netherlands.

THE FUTURE OF MANKIND:
ROOSEVELT, STALIN AND JACK KENNEDY

In June, Yamamoto and the fleet, including four carriers, sailed to take Midway Island, on the way to Hawaii, but instead the Americans, aided by breaking Japanese codes, sank all four, losing only one of their own. In April 1943, the Americans decrypted Yamamoto's flight plan and shot down his plane. Now the initiative passed to the Americans, who launched their first offensive across the vast Pacific distances far to the south at Guadalcanal and the Solomon Islands, where at 2.27 a.m. on 2 August a patrol torpedo boat, *PT-109*, commanded by Lieutenant Jack Kennedy, twenty-six-year-old son of the ambassador, was rammed by a Japanese destroyer. *PT-109* exploded and sank, and two of his crew were killed instantly. Ten men survived, three badly burned. 'Fight or surrender?' he asked them. 'You men have families . . . I've nothing to lose.' They chose to fight. Kennedy had already endured much ill health, including Addison's Disease (diagnosed after the war), and the incident damaged his back. He nonetheless rescued two others, towing them to the nearest island, then several times swimming miles until Polynesian scouts finally arrived to rescue and feed the starving crew. Ambassador Kennedy made sure Jack's heroism was celebrated. 'KENNEDY'S SON', the *New York Times* announced, 'IS HERO IN PACIFIC'.*

At the Wolf's Lair, Hitler declared that Stalingrad's fall 'was only a matter of time', boasting privately that he would advance into Iraq – 'thoroughly within the realms of possibility' – but his eagerness blinded him to a growing vulnerability. In Moscow, Stalin and Zhukov, looking at the map, saw an opportunity and, unusually, the ice-cold dictator shook hands with the harsh general. As the cauldron battle raged in Stalingrad, throughout October and November, General Montgomery mustered superior forces and defeated Rommel at El Alamein; on 8 November 107,000 Anglo-American troops landed in Morocco and Algeria, rolling up German, Vichy and Italian forces.

On 19 November, Zhukov sprang Operation Uranus, a million Russians in two pincers smashing through the weaker Romanians to surround Hitler's Sixth Army around Stalingrad. 'No matter what,' shouted Hitler, 'we'll hold out at all costs.' On 2 February 1943, the Sixth Army surrendered. The myth of Hitler's invincibility was shattered. While Hitler believed he was a military genius, Stalin learned the art

---

* JFK was still undergoing treatment for his back injuries when, in August 1944, his elder brother, Joe Jr, a bomber pilot, was killed on a mission.

of command: find talented generals and work with them. He promoted himself and Zhukov to marshal. Ten million Soviet soldiers started their two-year multi-fronted, thousand-mile-long counter-offensive that, against stubborn resistance and at unspeakable cost, drove the Nazis out of the devastated motherland.* On 9 July, Anglo-American troops landed in Sicily. After losing tens of thousands of men in Russia and Africa, Mussolini was crippled with stomach cramps. On 25 July, Victor Emmanuel dismissed and arrested Mussolini. Hitler immediately occupied Italy, and had the Duce rescued by commandos.

The road to victory had to be agreed in person. FDR, Stalin and Churchill travelled to Teheran – Stalin had never flown before. On 28 November FDR met Stalin for the first time, the two striking up an affinity, personal and strategic, at the cost of Churchill, the weaker player whose Indian empire seemed old-fashioned to the progressive American. Stalin persuaded FDR, who was staying at the US legation, that a Nazi assassination plot meant he must be protected in the more secure Soviet legation; keen to build on his relationship with Stalin, FDR agreed. Stalin naturally bugged FDR's room.

'In our hands, we have the future of mankind,' said Churchill, opening their summit, 'the greatest concentration of world power that has ever been seen in the history of mankind.'

'History has spoiled us,' Stalin acknowledged. 'Let's begin our work.' They agreed that the Anglo-Americans would invade France in May 1944 (later delayed by a month) and that Stalin could keep the three Baltic states, given to him by Hitler. At dinner Stalin suggested that 50,000 German officers be executed. FDR agreed. When Churchill walked out, Stalin insisted he was joking.

The least important leader in Teheran was the young shah of Iran. Churchill did not bother to visit him; Stalin visited. The shah already craved Iranian power and asked for tanks; Stalin agreed, provided Russian troops operated them. The king collected cars, learned to fly and chased girls. Unhappy with his Egyptian wife, Fawzia, he depended on his mystical-poetical Swiss adviser, Perron, now promoted from gardener to royal secretary. But he had learned the meaning of power.

---

* Stalin was obsessed with treason: 600,000 *Hilfswilliger* – Russian auxiliaries – known as *Hiwis* or *Askaris* (Africans) fought for Hitler, while 120,000 formed a Russian Liberation Army under German command. In 1943–4, Stalin punished potential traitors with deportations of entire smaller peoples – Muslim Tatars, Chechens, Kalmyks, Karachays, Volga Germans, Ingush. Out of 480,000 Chechen deportees, 30 to 50 per cent died. When the survivors returned to Chechnya, they nurtured a deep hatred, inbred from their long insurgencies the century before, for Russian rule.

On D-Day – 6 June 1944 – 156,000 Anglo-American troops under the American Dwight Eisenhower landed in Normandy – Operation Overlord.* By the end of the month 850,000 troops were ashore, breaking out into France as other forces fought their way up through Italy. The D-Day landings marked an even greater victory: the infections of its wounded were treated with a new miracle drug, penicillin.†

As Anglo-American forces fought their way up through Italy and across France, Hitler ordered that Paris 'must not fall into the enemy's hands except lying in complete debris', but his generals disobeyed him. Dodging German snipers, de Gaulle marched through Paris, celebrating 'Paris outraged! Paris broken! Paris martyred! But Paris liberated!' He was determined to restore *'la grandeur'* of *'France éternelle'* with himself as a republican monarch.

Stalin's armies burst into Poland; days later, on 20 July, Hitler was leaning over his maps in the wooden operations hut at the Wolf's Lair when a bomb exploded.

Among the shattered walls and dead officers, Hitler had a cut leg and a burst eardrum, but he was alive, protected by the table leg. Exhilarated at this further evidence of providence, Hitler learned that the assassin was a decorated colonel who had just left the hut: Count Claus von Stauffenberg, who had lost an eye and a hand in the war which he, like most Junker officers, had supported, with all its horrific atrocities, until Russian defeat. Yet he was one of the courageous few who dared resist Hitler. Hearing the explosion, Stauffenberg escaped from the Wolf's Lair and, convinced that Hitler was dead, flew to Berlin to find

* On his return to Washington, FDR secretly sought out his lover, Lucy Mercer, who had just lost her long-time husband, Winthrop Rutherford. He had written to her all along but they had only met once during her long marriage. He asked his daughter Anna to arrange their meetings, some of them in the White House, others in Georgetown. Lucy and his daughter became friends, but Eleanor was furious when she discovered.

† Penicillin had been discovered sixteen years earlier by a British scientist, Alexander Fleming. Keeping a messy laboratory, Fleming had returned to find his experiments overgrown with a fungus which had destroyed bacteria; using the fungus and the tears and snot of his assistants, he developed penicillin, the first natural antibiotic. 'One sometimes finds what one isn't looking for,' he said, yet it was not really an accident as he was an enthusiastic innovator: 'I play with microbes.' He published his findings, but no one appreciated it until 1939, more than ten years later, when a Jewish-German refugee, Ernst Chain, and his colleague Howard Florey at Oxford infected eight mice with streptococci and gave four of them penicillin. Those four lived. In 1941, they tried it on a patient dying of infection, who then recovered. Now realizing its potential, they flew to New York where the Rockefeller Foundation created a team, backed by the US army, which included a scientist, Mary Hunt (nicknamed Mouldy Mary), who found penicillin in a rotting cantaloupe, which formed the basis of streptomycin. Antibiotics changed the world: people no longer died of minor infection, and the drugs later enabled doctors to limit infection even after massive surgery.

his coup falling apart. The Führer proved he was alive by talking on the phone to the key conspirator, who then arrested and shot Stauffenberg to save his own skin. Himmler then rounded up suspects, whom Hitler ordered to be 'hanged like meat', their agonies filmed – and possibly later watched by the dictator. Already suffering from Parkinson's disease, and stimulated by a pharmaceutical cornucopia injected by his quack Theodor Morell (who had made millions from his own branded delousing 'Russia Powder' issued to the army), including Pervitin (a methamphetamine) and Eukodal (the opioid oxycodone), Hitler had been injured, his cuts filled with splinters from the bomb. Morell saved his life by administering penicillin found on captured American troops. Hitler had deteriorated, and now he was red-eyed, deathly pale, limping, his leg and arm shaking. Although he tightened his grip on Germany through his campaign of vengeance, he was losing allies fast as the Red Army approached his borders.

In July, Stalin halted his forces near Warsaw as 20,000 Polish resistance fighters launched their uprising, timed to establish themselves before the Soviets arrived. Obsessed like all Russian leaders with the danger of an independent Poland and keen to establish his own Communists in power, Stalin called their bluff and did not help, leaving Hitler's SS and assorted Ukrainian auxiliaries of diabolical depravity to slaughter 15,000 Polish rebels and 200,000 civilians and raze Warsaw itself.

'I planned a coup,' King Mihai of Romania told this author, 'against Marshal Antonescu.' The Soviets were on his border. On 23 August 1944, the Hohenzollern invited Red Dog for an audience and ordered an armistice. Red Dog raged. Mihai drew his pistol. Four officers disarmed Antonescu. At gunpoint, the king 'led him into the king's safe where my father used to keep his stamp collection. I locked him in there' and sued for peace. It was Mihai's finest moment, but it was too little too late.

Next door in Bulgaria, Hitler had already poisoned a reluctant ally, Tsar Boris III. In Hungary, Horthy also attempted an anti-Nazi coup at which Hitler's commandos kidnapped the regent's son, who was held hostage to force Horthy to relinquish control. In the wake of German troops came Eichmann, who organized the deportation of 400,000 Jews in just three months. Most were murdered at Auschwitz.

In February 1945, after American bombers shattered the Berlin Chancellery, and Allied forces converged from east and west, Hitler, accompanied by Eva Braun, moved into the nearby *Führerbunker* just as Stalin, Roosevelt and Churchill set off for a conference at Yalta in

Crimea, once the tsar's holiday palace, recently liberated. In the twilit, dank concrete gloom of the Berlin bunker, Hitler's mother's portrait hung in his bedroom; his tiny office was dominated by a portrait of Frederick the Great whose last-minute reprieve on the death of Tsarina Elizaveta obsessed him. 'He too was cut out not for the Seven Years War,' murmured Hitler, 'but for dalliance, philosophy and flute-playing, yet still had to live up to his historical mission.' Frederick's coat was always covered in snuff stains. Eva Braun noticed mess on Hitler's grey tunic. 'You don't have to copy everything to do with Old Fritz!' she teased him.

His afternoons were spent in meetings, meals were taken with Braun; his four secretaries still had to endure 'tea' until 4 a.m. as the supine dictator droned on – a routine interspersed with embers of hope and spasms of rage.

FDR AND THE THREE KINGS

On 4 February, Stalin, travelling in Nicholas II's train carriage, arrived at Yalta, as in Berlin, Eva Braun, determined to remain and if necessary die with Hitler, celebrated her thirty-third birthday with her lover and his courtiers upstairs in an intact section of the Chancellery.

In the tsar's white palace of Livadia, Stalin presided with calm, gleeful and inscrutable potency, master of his brief though weary after years of sixteen-hour days. FDR, the youngest of the three, was exhausted, having just been elected president for an unprecedented fourth time. But he now suffered arteriosclerosis and felt 'tired and listless', his mouth sometimes gaping. Churchill too was worn out, 'woollier than ever', complained a participant; but even past his best he was still better than most. Revelling in his new power, Stalin was moved by FDR and suspicious of Churchill. FDR, accompanied by his daughter Anna and a depleted Hopkins, leaned towards Stalin, naively believing their progressive powers could remake a post-imperial world; Churchill craved his old partnership with FDR. But Britain, bankrupt and overstretched by imperial obligations, was overshadowed by the new superpowers. The Three decided that Germany must surrender unconditionally; they would create a stronger international organization called the United Nations. Stalin would enter the war against Japan. But that grim realist, whose armies were liberating eastern Europe, already knew that 'Borders will be decided by force,' and was sending in cohorts of local Stalinists to be his vassals. Only in

Yugoslavia and Albania did local partisans seize power without Soviet troops.*

FDR told Stalin he was a Zionist and asked if he was one. 'In principle,' replied Stalin. Talking of Palestine, FDR joked that he had 'three kings waiting for him'.

'I'm a bit exhausted but really all right,' FDR told Eleanor before sailing from Yalta on USS *Quincy*. Moored in the Great Bitter Lake in Egypt, sitting on deck in a dark cape, he met the epicene young Egyptian king Farouk, descendant of Mehmed Ali, then Haile Selassie, now rebuilding Ethiopia after Italian depredations; finally Abdulaziz ibn Saud arrived, conveyed on USS *Murphy* with a herd of sheep to slaughter and guards wearing scimitars. Abdulaziz was lame. President and king sat together on deck in their wheelchairs. Citing German atrocities, FDR asked him to approve rising Jewish migration to Palestine. 'Jews and Arabs could never cooperate,' replied Abdulaziz. 'Give the Jews the best German lands.' FDR's voyage home took nine days.

On 19 March Hitler ordered the destruction of all German infrastructure, the Nero Decree, but in many areas reasonable officials were already ignoring fanatical orders; across the sinking empire, SS guards blew up the killing camps and forced starving prisoners westwards on death marches. On the 20th, Hitler emerged from the bunker to review young fighters of the Hitler Youth – one was twelve – pinching cheeks, tweaking ears as he moved down the line, his last appearance on film. Goebbels retained Hitler's favour, while Göring dreamed of the succession and Himmler tried to trade Jewish lives in secret negotiations.

'Well, who's going to take Berlin?' Stalin asked his top commanders in the Kremlin on 1 April, 'we or the Allies?'

'It's we who'll take Berlin,' barked bullet-headed Marshal Konev.

'Whoever breaks in first, let him take Berlin,' ordered Stalin. Konev and Zhukov raced for their planes to fly to the front.

While the Soviets were marshalling their vast forces, FDR was with Daisy Suckley at Hyde Park but he 'looks terribly badly – so tired . . . He just can't stand this strain indefinitely.' Boarding the train to Warm Springs (the Little White House) with Daisy, he was 'joking and laughing as usual', perhaps because Lucy Mercer was joining him. On 12

---

* When told that Pope Piux XII was concerned about Polish independence, Stalin quipped, 'How many divisions has the pope?' Pleased with his definition of hard power, Stalin repeated it on other occasions. 'You may tell my son Josef,' Pius later joked, 'he'll meet my divisions in Heaven.'

April, sitting with Daisy and Lucy, FDR raised his hand to his head, saying he had a headache, and died.*

'The great miracle!' cried Hitler, convinced this was the replay of Frederick the Great's reprieve. 'Who's laughing now? The war's not lost.'

WE CAN STILL WIN: HIROHITO'S OFFENSIVE

Stalin was strangely moved by the president's death: 'Roosevelt was clever, educated, farsighted,' even if 'he prolonged the life of capitalism'. At the White House, minutes after Eleanor heard the news, the vice-president Harry Truman, an obscure but loyal Missouri senator, arrived for a drink. She placed her hand on his shoulder: 'Harry, the president is dead.'

Pause.

'Is there anything I can do for you?' Truman asked Eleanor.

'Is there anything we can do for *you*?' she replied. Later Truman placed a placard on his Oval Office desk: 'The buck stops here!'

On 16 April, Zhukov and Konev unleashed 2.5 million men, 41,000 guns and 6,250 tanks against Berlin, with the former given the honour of taking the city. When Zhukov was delayed by German resistance, Stalin rang Konev: 'Turn your tank armies on Berlin.' A cauldron battle was fought, street by street, as they converged on the Chancellery. In Germany alone, an estimated two million girls were raped by Russian soldiers.† Down in the bunker 'The artillery fire can already be heard,' wrote Eva Braun, who practised pistol shooting in the garden. As Soviet tanks reached the outskirts, Hitler celebrated his birthday with Göring, Himmler and Goebbels. When they flew out of the city, he insisted on dying there. That night, Eva Braun had a party for him upstairs, dancing, singing and drinking champagne. But at the next day's meeting he learned that his order to SS-General Steiner to counter-attack had been disobeyed, at which a flushed, foam-flecked Hitler denounced the treachery before collapsing in his chair: 'The war is lost, but if you believe I'm leaving Berlin, gentlemen, you're sadly mistaken. I'd rather

---

* To avoid scandal, Lucy quickly packed and left the Little White House.
† 'You have of course read Dostoevsky?' Stalin said to a Yugoslav Communist leader, Milovan Djilas, who confronted him with the Russian army's mass rapes. 'Do you see what a complicated thing is man's soul? ... Well, then imagine a man who fought from Stalingrad to Belgrade ... And what is so awful about his having fun with a woman after such horrors?'

put a bullet in my head.' His SS doctor recommended a 'pistol and poison' combination for his suicide.

Outside Berlin, Göring claimed the succession and was dismissed, while Himmler was disgraced for talking to the Allies. Himmler's representative, Hermann Fegelein, married to Eva Braun's sister, was found drunk with a mistress and shot in the garden. The Russians captured Vienna; the Americans took the Ruhr, arresting Alfried Krupp at Villa Hügel. Russian tanks were closing in. The Goebbels family now moved into the Bunker with their five children. Eva Braun wrote a letter, a 'final sign of life', to her best friend; as death drew 'perilously nearer' she was suffering 'because of the Führer. Maybe everything will turn out all right but he's lost faith . . .'

On the night of 28 April, Hitler and Eva married – he wearing a grey tunic with medals, she a dark silk dress. She signed the certificate, 'Eva Hitler née Braun', and celebrated with champagne as the groom retired to dictate 'my political will', in which he blamed 'Jewish interests' who had been 'made to atone for their guilt albeit through more humane means', an oblique reference to the Holocaust. As the couple sat up until 4 a.m., the staff partied wildly. 'An erotic fever seemed to take possession of everyone,' recalled Hitler's secretary. 'Everywhere even in the dentist's chair I saw bodies interlocked in lascivious embraces. The women had discarded all modesty . . . freely exposing their private parts.'

Rising late, Hitler learned that Russian tanks were just 500 yards away. In Milan, Mussolini and his lover had been shot and hung upside down by their feet. After lunch on 30 April, Hitler tested his cyanide on his Alsatian dog Blondi, who died instantly; he then shook hands with his staff and the Hitlers withdrew into their study. The staff waited until the sounds of partying upstairs were interrupted by a shot. The valet peeped inside, then re-emerged. 'It's happened,' he said. Eva Hitler sat, legs drawn up, on the sofa, suffused with the smell of almonds, a sign of cyanide, while Hitler leaned the other way, a finger of blood at his forehead, pistol at his feet, blood spattered on the wallpaper. The bodies were wrapped in a carpet, carried out and burned in the garden as Russian shells exploded nearby. Just over twelve hours later, Zhukov phoned Stalin's Kuntsevo mansion.

'Comrade Stalin's just gone to bed,' said the bodyguard.

'Wake him,' ordered Zhukov.

Stalin picked up the phone. 'So,' said Stalin, 'that's the end of the bastard. Too bad we couldn't take him alive. Where's Hitler's body?'*

---

* On 4 May, SMERSH military intelligence found the charred remains, identified from

Germany surrendered three days later as Stalin sent Soviet and Mongolian armies to attack the Japanese in Korea and north China. As American forces fought their way across the Pacific, Hirohito repeatedly demanded Japanese counter-attacks. 'There's no sign of any attacks. Why aren't you carrying them out? Isn't there some way some place we can win a real victory over the Americans?' he asked. 'Do this for me so I can have peace of mind.'

As American bombers immolated Japanese cities in frequent air raids, Hirohito criticized his generals: 'We have to do the attacking.' In January 1944, his troops had attacked India unsuccessfully; in April, his Ichigo offensive, deploying 700,000 Japanese troops, shook Chiang's government; but in July he dismissed Razor Tojo, promising his new premier that he would 'remain in this divine land and fight to the death'. In October, when the Americans under General Douglas MacArthur landed in the Philippines, Hirohito demanded resistance. 'I agreed to the showdown battle of Leyte,' he admitted afterwards, a decision that cost the lives of 80,000 Japanese troops. In early 1945, he consulted his ex-premiers, all of whom favoured fighting on except Konoe. 'If we hold out long enough,' said Hirohito, 'we may be able to win.' Konoe complained that 'Considering our *kokutai*, unless the emperor assents to it, we can do nothing.' The ex-premiers were 'madmen'. In June, Hirohito was so nervous, he fell ill. 'I desire that concrete plans to end the war be swiftly studied,' he ordered, 'and efforts made to implement them.' But the Allies demanded unconditional surrender.

On 17 July, as the Americans approached Japan, Stalin travelled by train to meet Harry Truman and Churchill (the latter had just faced a general election) in Wilhelm II's mock-Tudor Cecilienhof Palace at Potsdam.* They agreed on partitions and population transfers that confirmed Stalin's annexation of Lviv and south-western Poland – added to Soviet Ukraine – and Moldavia and the Baltics.† 11.5 million German

---

Hitler's jawbone, which along with fragments of his skull are in Moscow. In 1970, the rest of the body was secretly and anonymously buried under a Soviet military base in Magdeburg.

* Among the press covering the conference was Jack Kennedy, whose father got him the job working for Hearst.

† There was talk among Polish Stalinists of Poland joining the USSR. Stalin never considered this, partly because of the importance of Poland to the Allies. But like the tsars before him Stalin was determined to control Poland. Stalin was granted the great Prussian city of Königsberg, renamed after Stalin's puppet president Kalinin and ethnically cleansed of Germans; it became a Soviet enclave. In Ukraine, as the war ended, Bandera managed to escape from German captivity and with US support settled in Munich, while his ally Shukhevych led a multi-year war against the Soviets, winning some victories (in February 1944, he killed top Soviet general Vatunin); 130,000 Ukrainians and over 30,000 Soviets

refugees trudged westwards. The three men were masters of a new world, although none yet understood that their dominion would be overshadowed by a new force. On 17 July, Truman learned that a baby had been born: 'Doctor has just returned most enthusiastically and confident that the little boy is as husky as his big brother.' But it was not a baby: it was a bomb.

were killed, until in 1950 Shukhevych was finally trapped and killed. In Munich in 1959, the KGB managed to assassinate Bandera. In the Baltics, anti-Soviet insurgents known as the Forest Brothers fought on for ten years. Stalin orchestrated massive purges of Ukraine, Belarus and the Baltics, so by 1950s the GULAG camps reached their peak of 2.5 million enslaved labourers. In his new west Ukraine, Stalin executed around 200,000 and deported 400,000. Between 1940 and 1953, around 10 per cent of the Balts were deported. One could argue that Stalin, Marxist pontiff and Russian imperialist, fatally overreached by consuming the Baltics. In 1990–1, it was the Balts, even more than the Georgians, who accelerated the break-up of the Soviet Union. Had Stalin not consumed these territories, one wonders if the USSR would have survived in 1991.

ACT TWENTY-ONE
2.3 BILLION

Nehrus, Maos and Suns, Mafiosi, Hashemites and Albanians

RADIANCE OF A THOUSAND SUNS: TRUMAN'S NON-SURPRISE AND THE AMERICAN CENTURY

The day before, 16 July 1945, as he watched the mushroom cloud of Operation Trinity, the exhilarated director of the secret Manhattan Project, Robert Oppenheimer, quoted the *Bhagavad Gita*: 'If the radiance of a thousand suns were to burst at once into the sky, that would be like the splendor of the mighty one.' But the 'splendor' had a fearsome power: 'I am become Death, destroyer of worlds.'

The Bomb had been in the making for forty years.* In 1943, at Quebec, FDR and Churchill merged their countries' nuclear research into the Manhattan Project based at Los Alamos in New Mexico. Now as Stalin arrived to visit Truman (finding him 'neither educated nor clever'), neither man mentioned the test. 'I didn't know then,' said Stalin, 'at least not from the Americans.' He had known since 1942, informed by Soviet spies. Until the explosion neither Stalin nor Truman could conceive of Trinity's world-shattering significance. Learning from their spies about Trinity and knowing that their agents had secured uranium from Nazi laboratories near Berlin, Stalin and Beria twice discussed how to react if

---

* In 1898, a Polish physicist, Marie Skłodowska, born in Romanov Warsaw, and recently married to a French colleague, Pierre Curie, developed the theory of what she called 'radio-activity', revealing the enormous energy within her newly discovered elements polonium and radium, which would have immense implications for both war and medicine. In 1905 a German-Jewish physicist, the twenty-six-year-old Albert Einstein, son of a failed technical entrepreneur from Württemberg, had written a paper demonstrating the physical reality of atoms and molecules, which had been known about since the early nineteenth century. He showed through his theory of relativity that energy and matter are equivalent and provided a precise equation to show how much energy is contained in a particular amount of matter. After 1933, when Einstein had escaped Germany and moved to the US, physicists had discovered that certain isotopes of uranium had the potential to sustain a chain reaction that split atoms. The energy this released could be calculated from Einstein's formula of decades earlier. In 1939, realizing that this energy could be prodigious, Einstein had advised FDR to develop its potential. Hitler decided not to concentrate on the development of a nuclear bomb, perhaps his biggest mistake, while persecution of Jewish scientists meant that many of its creators were German refugees.

Truman informed him; they agreed to 'pretend not to understand'.

On 24 July at Potsdam, Churchill attacked Stalin for his aggressive actions in Romania. 'An iron fence,' he said, trying out the phrase that would become the Iron Curtain, 'has come down.'

'Fairy tales,' replied Stalin, getting to his feet. Truman hurried after him; Churchill, pre-warned, watched.

'The USA,' said Truman, 'has tested a new bomb of extraordinary destructive power.'

Not a muscle moved in Stalin's face. After the fanatical Japanese resistance on Okinawa and the expectation that attacking Japan itself could cost 268,000 American dead, Truman planned to use the new weapon against Japan.

'A new bomb!' said Stalin. 'Of extraordinary power. Probably decisive on the Japanese! What a bit of luck!' Back in Ludendorff's house, Stalin briefed his henchmen that Britain and America 'are hoping we aren't able to develop the Bomb ourselves, but that's not going happen'. Stalin had already put Beria in charge of the nuclear project, but now this was 'Task No. 1'. The race to catch up was on.

On 6 August a B-29 bomber named *Enola Gay*, after the mother of its pilot Colonel Paul Tibbets, took off from Tinian, Mariana Islands, and flew six hours to Hiroshima where at 8.15 a.m. it dropped the first atomic bomb, Little Boy, on Hiroshima. Only three of *Enola Gay*'s crew knew they were dropping the device. 'It was hard to believe what we saw,' said Tibbets. 'My God!' gasped the crew. On the ground, 100,000 were killed instantly, 100,000 horribly burned, survivors experiencing a flash, a boom, then a firestorm that ravaged the city as black radioactive rain fell in a new vision of hell on earth.

Hirohito was shaken but did not immediately surrender; he procrastinated, seemingly more shocked two days later when Stalin invaded Manchuria. At dawn on 9 August, another American B-29 – *Bockscar* – dropped Fat Man on Nagasaki as Hirohito was meeting his generals to discuss negotiations, insisting that if divine *kokutai* was not preserved he would fight on. Within two days, the Bombs convinced him to accept unconditional surrender; the hawkish war minister, General Anami, reluctantly agreed. The emperor planned a speech to the people. The speech, recorded by radio technicians, contained the greatest understatement in history: 'The war,' said Hirohito, 'has developed not necessarily to Japan's advantage.' His 'jewel-voice' was faint, so he had to record it again. Before it could be broadcast, officers, encouraged by Anami, attacked the palace in a bid to seize the recording. They killed the commander of the Imperial Guards, but failed to find it and committed suicide. Next day, General Anami himself committed ritual disembowelment, leaving a note: 'I – with my death – humbly apologize to the emperor for the great crime.' And at noon the Japanese heard their *tenno* for the first time. 'Our people believed too much in the imperial country,' Hirohito wrote to his eleven-year-old son, Crown Prince Akihito, who was staying outside Tokyo for his safety. 'Our military men knew how to advance not retreat. If we'd fought on, we'd have been unable to protect the three imperial regalia [mirror, sword, jewel] and more of our countrymen would have had to die. Repressing my emotions, I tried to save the seed of the nation.'

On 30 August, General MacArthur arrived in Tokyo, charged by Truman with preserving Japanese stability, while trying the militarists for war crimes. Tojo was executed, but MacArthur then decided to keep Hirohito, undoubtedly guilty too, by recasting him as a non-divine constitutional monarch.

The only one of the aggressors to remain in office became the figurehead of a thriving democracy, reigning until 1989 (his grandson, Naruhito, succeeded in 2019 as 126th *tenno* of the most ancient dynasty). In the west, the victors agreed to put the Nazis on trial at the International Military Tribunal in Nuremberg, a partnership between democratic and Stalinist judges. Ribbentrop was sentenced to hang; Göring killed himself; and Speer charmed his way off the gallows. The chief murderers of the *Einsatzgruppen* and the killing camps were hanged – Himmler had committed suicide – but few lower ranks were punished. Krupp was tried and sentenced to twelve years. Antonescu was shot. Chastened by these horrors, a more rules-based world, created by a combination of a court of human rights and the authority of the United Nations, fostered supranational law, a measure of civilized conduct and a legal definition of genocide.* Antisemitism became morally unacceptable; the Enlightenment was restored.

By the time the Bombs were dropped, Churchill was no longer prime minister, a victor's defeat that surprised Stalin. 'One party,' he said, 'is much better.'

'A blessing in disguise,' said Clementine Churchill.

'At the moment,' replied Churchill, 'it seems very effectively disguised.' The defeat was soothed partly by George VI's offer of the

---

* A World Health Organization was founded that through a massive vaccination programme – 150 years after Jenner – managed to eradicate smallpox globally. As Steven Johnson writes, 'Global eradication was as dependent on the invention of an institution like the WHO as it was on the invention of the vaccine itself.' The Covid pandemic only underlined this.

dukedom of Dover, a title he refused. The Labour prime minister Clement Attlee ('a modest man', quipped Churchill, 'with much to be modest
about') created a system that paid unemployed people and offered free
healthcare, the prototype of an ambitious vision of the state as guarantor
of comfort that western citizens came to regard as more important than
its traditional roles of order and security. Previously only revolution
could redistribute wealth and protect the poor: the British achievement
was to do it peacefully. At home, Attlee offered what he called a 'New
Jerusalem'; abroad, his vision would spark war for the old Jerusalem
– and sanguinary independence for India. In December 1945, Indians
voted for a legislative assembly.

The problem was: there were two winners.

THE DEATH OF ONE INDIA: NEHRU,
JINNAH AND THE VICEREINE

Nehru and Congress won the election. But so did Jinnah and the Muslim
League who, campaigning on one issue – the creation of Pakistan – won
every seat reserved for Muslims. Nehru formed the first Indian government, an interim one, in tense coalition with the League.

Freed from prison in 1944, Nehru aspired to inherit the entire British
Raj, the first time in history India had ever been united. The British
agreed, keen to hand over the Raj complete to a single leader, Nehru,
which would embellish the Anglosphere as a British dominion.

Nehru was a romantic who had embraced a vision of gorgeous India
that this lover of women always compared to a beautiful girl. 'India
was in my blood,' he wrote, like a romantic novelist; 'she is very lovable
and none of her children can forget her . . . for she is part of them in
her greatness and failings and they are mirrored in those deep eyes
of hers . . .' Overlooking much of Indian history (Gandhi disdained
history as 'an interruption of nature', an instant in the cycles of life and
reincarnation) as well as the differences between Hindus and Muslims,
he believed in a single secular liberal democracy represented by Congress. 'There is no cultural conflict in India,' he insisted. There was just
one India and Nehru dismissed the prospect of a Muslim challenge.
'The idea is absurd,' he wrote in 1935, 'hardly worth considering.' But
the decline of British power and the new electoral politics promoted a
new ethnic and religious nationalism: the electoral results undeniably
revealed two visions of India.

Attlee proposed an Indian federation that might have prevented partition. Initially both sides accepted the idea, but then Nehru rejected it, believing Congress could receive the Raj complete. Jinnah in revenge called a Direct Action Day in Kolkata, where Muslims slaughtered Hindus, unrestrained by Bengal's Muslim League government. Gandhi rushed to Kolkata to fast for peace.

In March 1946, Nehru travelled to Singapore to review Indian troops. When the soldiers mobbed him, the forty-four-year-old Edwina Mountbatten, wife of the Allied supremo in East Asia, Lord Louis 'Dickie' Mountbatten, was knocked over in the excitement. Nehru and Mountbatten helped her up. The three got on so well that when Attlee sought a viceroy to oversee independence, Nehru probably suggested Mountbatten. Attlee appointed Viscount Mountbatten of Burma (as he had become) as the last viceroy – 'the most powerful man on earth' in his own words. He was debonair, capable and vain. Edwina was a sharp-tongued, free-spirited heiress, combining an exciting extramarital sex life (her lovers included women and men, a favourite being Hutch the Grenadian cabaret star) with intelligent public service. Mountbatten admired her as a force of nature.*

The couple frequently invited Nehru and Indira to the Viceroy's House in Delhi. Indira was Nehru's indispensable companion in the vertiginous months ahead. Mountbatten became 'real friends with Nehru'. Mountbatten's daughters sometimes burst in to find Nehru on his head doing yoga. Gradually, an intimate friendship, all the more touching for its maturity, developed between the widowed Nehru and the married vicereine Edwina. 'Suddenly I realized (and perhaps you did also),' wrote Nehru later to Edwina, 'that there was a deeper attachment between us, that some uncontrollable force of which I was only dimly aware, drew us to one another. I was overwhelmed and at the same time exhilarated by this new discovery.' She agreed: 'You left me a strange sense of peace and happiness. Perhaps I brought you the same?' Mountbatten noticed, telling his daughter, 'Please keep this to yourself but she and Jawaharlal are so sweet together. They really dote on each other ... Mummy's been incredibly sweet lately.'

Mountbatten leaned strongly towards Nehru, and both mocked Jinnah: 'a psychopathic case', said Mountbatten; 'a paranoid', said Nehru. 'Hitlerian.' Yet Jinnah's landslide had exposed the myth of Nehru's one nation.

---

* Mountbatten was a great-grandson of Queen Victoria, descended from an illegitimate son of a Hessian prince, the marquess of Milford Haven, who had made his career in Britain, rising to command the Royal Navy. Edwina was granddaughter of a German-Jewish magnate, Sir Ernest Cassel, banker of Edward VII.

Mountbatten could have explored a federation, which as the US demonstrated could be powerful and democratic. Gandhi proposed Jinnah as premier of a united India. It was just such a federal compromise that might have avoided bloodshed. But a federation would take time to forge. Instead Nehru accepted Jinnah's demand for a partition in which Congress would receive the larger part of British India – its capital, army, bureaucracy – in return for Dominion status for both of the new countries. 'We were tired men,' he admitted later. 'Partition offered a way out and we took it.'

Mountbatten embraced the plan for two states, India and Muslim Pakistan.* Gandhi knew this would provoke violence. 'The only alternatives,' he told Mountbatten, 'are a continuation of British rule to keep law and order or an Indian bloodbath. The bloodbath must be faced and accepted.'

On 3 June 1947, accompanied by Nehru and Jinnah, Mountbatten announced 'the transfer of power to a fifth of the human race' and partition, creating Pakistan in two unconnected parts. This pleased no one: Jinnah wanted the whole of Punjab and Bengal along with Kashmir, and requested a strip of India to link the two. The exact maps, to be drawn up by a British judge who had never been to India, would be announced just after independence, stoking up tension.

Then Mountbatten announced Britain would leave in ten weeks, a breakneck departure, unveiled with Mountbattenesque showmanship. It is a reality of all power that the moment departure is decided, the magnet of new power exerts its own visceral attraction and repulsion. The speed and uncertainty were likely to cause a bloody cataclysm, the only excuses being that British power was diminishing by the second; that he was unwilling to allow British troops to die keeping order; and that no ruler of India had ever voluntarily handed the subcontinent to another power before. Millions of people started to panic, anxious not just about what country they would live in but for their safety. 'We're living in the midst of crises,' said Nehru. A further complication was that the princes still ruled 40 per cent of India: the Croesan nizam of Hyderabad, Sir Osman Ali Khan, Asaf Jah VII, sixty-year-old descendant of the paladin of Aurangzeb, saw himself as a Muslim monarch and

---

* Pakistan means Land of Purity in Urdu, but it is also an acronym for Punjab, Afghania (North-West Frontier Province), Kashmir and Indus-Sind, combined with the -stan suffix from Baluchistan, coined in 1933 by a law lecturer of Emmanuel College, Cambridge, Rahmat Ali, and his three colleagues at the time of Round Table negotiations between Britain and Indians, none of whom embraced it. It was only after 1940 that Jinnah co-opted the idea. Rahmat got little credit and when he arrived in 1948 in the new state he had conceived, he was expelled, dying penniless soon afterwards at Cambridge.

had married his son to the daughter of the last Ottoman caliph. Now he refused to join India and planned his own independence.

On 14 August 1947, in Karachi, Jinnah, aged seventy-one and already suffering from TB, announced Pakistani independence, becoming premier and governor-general and hailed as supreme leader. The next day, Nehru announced India's 'tryst with destiny . . . at the stroke of the midnight hour', his Britannic rhetoric underlining how much he, the Harrovian Brahmin for all his socialism, was the successor and heir of the British Raj. India took possession of three-quarters of the Raj and the colonial administration, always overwhelmingly run by Indians, was transferred to the new state, just without the British. A vast crowd watched the raising of the Indian flag, which used the *dharmachakra*, symbol of Ashoka. Nehru had to rescue the viceregal daughter, Pamela, who almost got crushed by the crowds. 'He was very nimble with his sandals,' she recalled. 'He said, "Come on." I said, "I can't, I've got high heels." "Well, take them off," he said' – and the two of them were passed by hand over the crowd.

Away from this excitement, Muslims, Hindus and Sikhs attacked each other, sparking migrations of terrified refugees. Two million were killed in a frenzy of slaughter, rape and arson. Trains of refugees arrived with every single passenger already slaughtered. Over ten million people moved homes in the largest single migration in history. As the killing started, Gandhi, his life's work covered in blood, threatened to fast to death, while Nehru filled his residence with refugees, saying, 'I know, *mere bhai* [my brother], it is my sorrow too.' When Indira saw a Muslim about to be lynched, she dismounted from her train and shouted at the mob, overawing them into releasing him.

Nehru was determined to seize as much of India as possible. Kashmir, Muslim but ruled by a Hindu maharaja, was strategically vital, but to Nehru, descended from Kashmiri pandits, it was like 'some supremely beautiful woman'. In October, Muslim Pathans and Pakistani troops invaded, prompting the maharaja to agree that Kashmir should accede to India, allowing him to request troops. Four days later, Nehru sent in his army.

When Gandhi arrived in Delhi, Nehru, as well as Indira and her elder son Rajiv, aged three, visited him nightly. On 30 January 1948, the day after Indira and Rajiv visited, Gandhi, walking as usual to prayers, was shot thrice in the chest by a Hindu nationalist, linked to the paramilitary RSS. Nehru rushed to Gandhi's Birla House, falling to his knees beside the tiny body, sobbing. That night, to calm the growing crowds surrounding his house, Gandhi's body was sat up and illuminated on the roof. 'The light has gone out of our lives,' said Nehru, 'and there's darkness everywhere.'

The love between Nehru and Edwina intensified in the last months. 'We talked more intimately as if some veil had been removed,' wrote Nehru in May 1948, 'and we could look into each other's eyes without fear or embarrassment.' Whether it was sexual or not matters little. Sometimes it caused tensions with Nehru's younger sister, Krishna: 'Edwina could do no wrong . . .' When Nehru told her off for wearing too much jewellery, she replied, 'You don't get angry with Edwina, in fact you keep admiring her jewellery . . .' Edwina wept when the Mountbattens left India; Nehru wandered through her rooms in the Viceroy's House to 'lose myself in dreamland'.*

In September 1948, as Indian forces, the cream of the Raj's army, defeated Pakistan in Kashmir, Nehru invaded his other troublesome princely state, Hyderabad, where the nizam had declared independence. In Operation Polo, a five-day war, India defeated the Hyderabad forces, while Hindu mobs massacred 40,000 Muslims – the biggest bloodbath in modern Indian history. As Nehru dominated an India thriving in its first ten years, he was assisted by Indira, who, living at his residence Teen Murti House, raised her children for the dynastic life. 'One mustn't be afraid of getting hurt,' she told Rajiv and Sanjay. 'I want both of you to be courageous . . . there are millions of people in the world, but most just drift along, afraid of death and even more afraid of life.' Jawaharlal, Indira and her sons – who would rule the greatest democracy for three generations – would not be like that.

As the British left independent India and Pakistan (while planning to keep their African possessions), the Dutch and French, bruised by defeats in the Second World War, were determined to reclaim their Asian empires, French Indo-China and the Dutch East Indies. In Vietnam, Ho Chi Minh and his Viet Minh declared independence in Hanoi, joining the French initially in a purge of Trotskyites and nationalists. But in 1946, when the French reoccupied the country, Ho and his brilliant general, Vo Nguyen Giap, a history teacher who now put his lessons into practice as an Asian Trotsky, fought a formidable French army in a brutal war. In Jakarta, East Indies, the ex-architect Sukarno declared

---

* Later, accompanied by his daughter Indira and her daughter Pamela, Nehru and Edwina holidayed at Orissa; Nehru also visited Broadlands, Mountbatten's house, eight times. Edwina Mountbatten died in 1960. In 1981, Earl Mountbatten of Burma, who had met his cousin Tsar Nicholas II as a child before the First World War and served as Britain's chief of the defence staff under both Conservative and Labour governments up to 1965, was assassinated by IRA terrorists while fishing near his Irish castle in Sligo.

himself president of a new state, Indonesia, framed by the Dutch colony, but based on his five principles, *pancasila*, fusing democracy with nationalism. In July 1947, as Nehru and Jinnah assumed power, the Dutch attacked Sukarno, then exploited a Communist insurrection to reconquer much of the archipelago. Sukarno, aided by his top officer Suharto, crushed the Communists himself but struggled against the Dutch. This European imperial war worried Truman, who threatened to cut aid to the Netherlands. The Dutch withdrew, recognizing the vast new country, which Sukarno, flirting with a large Communist presence, transformed into a Guided Democracy with himself as monarchical president for life.

The British, meanwhile, were also leaving Palestine, where in a multifaceted conflict, two Arab kings vied with a nascent Jewish state and Palestinian militias.

TWO KINGS: FAROUK, ABDULLAH AND THE CARVE-UP OF PALESTINE

The vicious ethnic war at the heart of Palestine was exacerbated by the ambitions of the two leading Arab dynasts, the cunning Hashemite king Abdullah of Jordan, and flashy King Farouk, scion of House Mehmed Ali, king of Egypt, to expand their kingdoms and bid for the leadership of the Arab world.

Most of the states of west Asia – Syria, Israel, Lebanon – were created out of the old Ottoman empire in the two years after the Second World War. In April 1946, the French granted independence to two newly crafted countries, Syria and Lebanon;* Britain did the same to Transjordan, and in Egypt withdrew British troops to the Canal. Palestine was more complicated: in 1917 the British had promised a 'Jewish homeland', but there was no promise of a state and even the promise of a 'homeland' did not mean it would ever happen. The Kurds, Armenians, Alawites and Druze had also been promised states – which had never materialized. The Palestinian Arabs had long been the majority alongside a small Jewish community – both ancient. But there had been a Jewish majority in Jerusalem since the 1880s.

* Neither country had ever existed before and both are failed states. Lebanon, a fragile concoction of Christian Maronite, better-off Sunnis, poor Shiites and martial Druze, was designed by the French to protect their Christian favourites, storing up resentment of the Shiites. Syria was a conglomerate of Sunnis, Alawites, Kurds and Druze. Lebanon, ruled by venal magnates and sectarian warlords, has been cursed with civil wars, Palestinian intervention, Israeli invasion, state capture by a Shiite resistance movement and, in the 2020s, collapse. And in 2012, Syria dissolved into civil war.

The Arabs resented the arrival of Jewish immigrants, who soon formed a thriving agricultural community. British backing for a Jewish homeland did not last twenty years: as the conflict intensified, Britain totally reversed and in 1937 promised independence to the Arabs, just as they launched an insurgency that was crushed by British arms. Now, as independence was granted to new Arab states, the 600,000 Jews, led by a diminutive pugnacious Polish-born pragmatist with a shock of white hair, David Ben-Gurion, launched a Jewish rebellion against the British to win their own state. The Jewish experience was unique, as were the circumstances in Palestine, but in other ways, as Stalin put it, Zionism was simply 'Jewish national expression'. The suffering of the Holocaust persuaded many to support a Jewish state. But not Britain: Attlee banned Jewish immigration into Palestine and hoped to hand it over to an Arab state. Jewish militias attacked British troops: Israel, like Türkiye in 1922, was forged by an anti-imperial rebellion against British wishes. Attlee desperately passed the problem to the United Nations.

On 29 November 1947, in Resolution 181, the UN voted to partition Palestine into Arab and Jewish states, a plan not unlike those in Ireland and India. President Truman backed it. 'I am Cyrus,' he joked, referring to the Persian king. Ben-Gurion, believing in 'a state at any cost', accepted the compromise; the Palestinians preferred to fight for the whole. Arab paramilitaries attacked the Jewish community, defended by its well-organized militia, Haganah.

Watching this was Farouk, the young ruler of the greatest Arab nation, Egypt. King at sixteen, six foot and matinee-idol handsome, he had been educated in Britain and was vastly rich, owning 75,000 acres; he was so sheltered he had never visited the Pyramids but quickly became the Beloved King, *al-malik-al-mahbub*. During the Second World War, he had been humiliated by the British proconsul who had imposed his will on Farouk by surrounding Abdeen Palace with tanks; now he was keen to assert Egyptian power.

Farouk, who was married, was addicted to showgirls, nightclubs, fast cars and casinos, his Egypt a cosmopolitan mix of Turks, Circassians, Copts, Jews, Greeks and Lebanese. He 'was fascinated by the fact I was a Jewess', recalled his mistress Irene Guinle. 'The only person Farouk ever listened to was his father, Fuad ... [who] told him that the best women in the world were Jewish women.' But all Farouk's girlfriends agreed that he was a lazy man-child who was so lonely that his best friend was the grifter son of the palace electrician, Antonio Pulli, known as the Stork for his ability to fall asleep standing up in nightclubs.

Still in his late twenties, Farouk was learning politics, embracing the new Arab nationalism while warily monitoring the rise of an Islamicist sheikh, Hassan al-Banna. The sheikh's followers, the million-strong Muslim Brothers, believed that 'Islam is the solution' and were infuriated by Faroukian decadence and by Jewish immigration to Jerusalem. They started to assassinate Farouk's ministers. Farouk tried to promote a Muslim monarchy, but when he made the *hajj* it was on his yacht *Mahrousa*. Now he hoped to neutralize the Brothers by fighting Jews and annexing south Palestine. After all, Mehmed Ali had ruled the lot.

In Cairo, in December 1947, Farouk hosted a new Arab League of the seven independent Arab countries, who decided on war. 'It doesn't matter how many [Jews] there are,' said the League's Egyptian secretary Azzam Pasha, 'we'll sweep them into the sea.' Setting up the mufti of Jerusalem as Palestinian president, Farouk commanded 40,000 soldiers, but when he was warned that only half were equipped and of those only his Sudanese guard was ready for combat, he insisted that forty-five million Arabs could obliterate 600,000 Jews, who fielded just 35,000 fighters. But he had an Arab rival in the carve-up.

Abdullah, king of Transjordan, descended from Muhammad, mocked Farouk's dynasty: 'You don't make a gentleman of a Balkan farmer's son simply by making him a king.' But he also possessed a crack unit of 10,000, the British-officered Arab Legion. Abdullah was determined to seize swathes of Palestine by war or guile, secretly negotiating a partition of Palestine with the Jews while publicly denouncing the Jewish state. Abdullah got himself elected supreme commander of Arab League forces and massed his legionaries; Farouk reviewed Egyptian troops on horseback and promoted his sisters to general.

On 15 May 1948, as the British evacuated, Ben-Gurion declared the establishment of the State of Israel,* just as Farouk and Abdullah were joined by the Syrians plus Iraqi and Saudi contingents. Stalin, who was already arresting and shooting Soviet Jews, accusing them of split loyalties, was the first to recognize Israel. The Egyptian plan was to race up the coast and take Tel Aviv. Instead, in a ferocious war, accompanied by atrocities on both sides, the new Israeli army, well led by disciplined officers, armed with shipments of Soviet weaponry, defeated all the Arab armies. More than 700,000 Palestinians fled or were expelled during the war, but their Catastrophe – the *Nakba* – was the birth of Israel, aided by the expulsion by Arab states of 800,000 Sephardic Jews,

---

* The new country was going to be called either Judaea or Israel and they chose Israel.

communities that had thrived in Alexandria, Damascus, Marrakesh and Baghdad for millennia, who now arrived in Israel, shaping its culture.

As the war progressed, the total commitment of the Israelis and the influx of Sephardic immigrants allowed them to field 115,000 men by early 1949, the Arabs still only 60,000. While Abdullah successfully invaded the West Bank and seized the Old City of Jerusalem, Farouk's troops were routed, let down by the Stork, who had procured faulty Italian weapons. Two Egyptians distinguished themselves: General Mohamed Naguib was wounded three times, but was disgusted by Farouk, whose excesses he knew well. When 4,000 Egyptians were trapped for four months in the Faluja Pocket, one of them, a tall handsome postman's son, Colonel Gamal Abdel Nasser, wounded in the siege, was so incensed by Faroukian incompetence that he wrote *Philosophy of the Revolution*, and planned a coup.

In February 1949, Farouk agreed to an armistice, withdrawing from the Negev desert. Israel was established as a liberal democracy with a Jewish majority and an Arab minority – the only democracy in the region then and now. The Palestinians, like the Jews before them, did not give up their dream of Return.

Arab soldiers found it hard to forgive their inept leaders. In Syria, the fragile democracy left by France was overthrown by General Husni al-Zaim – the first of many Arab military coups. Leaders across the region would shamelessly use reckless violence, ethnic rivalries and kinship favouritism instead of building democracy and civil societies, with fatal consequences. The other winner was Abdullah of Jordan, as he called his kingdom, which doubled in size. Now that he possessed the Holy City, he declared himself king of Jerusalem, the first actually to rule there since the short visit of Emperor Frederick II in 1229. Many could not forgive his successful game of thrones: in 1951, he was assassinated in the al-Aqsa Mosque on Jerusalem's Temple Mount – in front of his grandson and later successor, Hussein, a seventeen-year-old Harrovian schoolboy who never forgot the sight. In Egypt, a cholera epidemic exposed Farouk's ineptitude, while the Muslim Brothers planned his downfall, assassinating his premier. Instead Farouk had al-Banna assassinated and banned the Brothers. Bald, obese and absolute but with a thriving economy and almost rid of the British and the Brothers, Farouk had survived.

Stalin had ordered his Czech vassals to provide Israel with the armaments that won the war, while in China he was transferring huge caches of weaponry that would change the world.

MAO, JIANG QING AND RED SISTER SONG

The victory of Mao was not inevitable. As soon as Stalin withdrew Soviet troops from Manchuria in May 1946, essential for his relations with the USA, Chiang, now deploying 4.3 million troops, seized most of the province, driving back 1.27 million Communists. Mao panicked and prepared to return to guerrilla warfare but was saved by the Americans. Truman's envoy General George Marshall, wartime chief of staff, was deceived by Mao, who played down his links to Stalin and played up his openness to American friendship. Marshall forced Chiang Kai-shek to stop the civil war and negotiate a ceasefire – a fatal mistake. Stalin had starved Mao of arms during the war, helping Chiang against the Japanese. Now Stalin pivoted towards Mao, transferring stashes of Japanese and Soviet arms, training the Japanese-allied Manchukuo army as Red soldiers and lending 200,000 Koreans from the Soviet northern sector of Korea.

At home, Stalin deported tens of thousands from his retaken regions, causing – though denying – a second Ukrainian famine in which almost another million died: he joked that he would have deported the entire Ukrainian nation but there were too many of them. He now saw the world divided into 'two armed camps' and envisaged, one day, war against the capitalist states led by America. Close to getting the Soviet Bomb – he tested his first in August 1949 – Stalin forced his own vassals onto eastern Europe, believing as he told the Yugoslavs that 'Each side will impose their own system.' For a Russian leader, Poland was the first and most important of those countries to secure. In Romania, Mihai of Romania, still only twenty-six, was forced to appoint a Communist-dominated government that arrested and tried liberal leaders and supporters, decrees he refused to sign. In November 1947, after attending the London wedding of his cousins, Princess Elizabeth of England and a naval officer Prince Philip of Greece, where he met his future wife, he returned home. There on 30 December he was summoned to the Elisabeta Palace. The Communist leader Gheorghe Gheorghiu-Dej and Stalin's henchman Andrei Vyshinsky, the shrieking prosecutor of the show trials, threatened, 'If you don't sign this [an instrument of abdication] immediately, we're obliged to kill more than 1,000 students in prison.' But Mihai refused to abdicate, hoping to call in loyal troops.

'Your guards have been arrested,' said Dej, 'the telephones have been cut and artillery are pointed at this office.' He drew a pistol. 'I looked out of the window,' Mihai recalled, 'and saw the howitzers. I signed.' Dej declared a 'people's republic' that day. Bulgaria* had fallen much earlier, but now similar coups, orchestrated by Stalin, were taking place in Poland, Hungary and Czechoslovakia; in the latter country the former foreign minister and son of the country's founder, Jan Masaryk, either committed suicide or was defenestrated. Yugoslavia and Albania, the countries that had liberated themselves from the Germans, were more idiosyncratic: the regal Josip Tito, half Croat, half Slovene, who had survived the Terror in Moscow, reunited Yugoslavia, purging enemies. But Tito resisted Stalin's bullying. Infuriated by such lese-majesty, Stalin ordered his killing. In a very rare example of anyone defying Stalin, Tito wrote him a letter: 'Stop sending assassins to kill me ... If you send another, I'll send one to Moscow and I won't have to send another.'†

As he secured this unprecedented Russian empire, larger than the Romanovs', Stalin calculated that the capitalist democracies lacked the will to fight for eastern Europe and he was right: the peace of the next forty years was based not just on the rules of international law but on the western recognition that half of Europe belonged to Moscow. On Europe's western extremity, Spain was still ruled by Franco, who frantically trimmed his Fascistic dictatorship to win American favour as an anti-Communist crusader, calling himself 'Caudillo of the War of Liberation against Communism' and restoring the Bourbon monarchy with himself as regent. His less rebarbative Portuguese ultranationalist neighbour, Salazar, delivered stability at home and vigorously maintained the empire abroad, sending thousands of white settlers to his African colonies.

European democracy was limited to the centre and even there it wavered. Impoverished Italy looked likely to embrace Communism. In France, where a weak fourth republic proved unmanageable, Premier de Gaulle retired to his bleak Colombey house. Governments were short-lived. France, like Portugal, consoled itself with empire.

---

* Tsar Simeon of Bulgaria, Foxy's grandson, was deposed by plebiscite in 1944. Bulgaria, run by Stalin's trusted henchman Dmitrov, became a people's republic.
† Tito helped an obscure Communist schoolteacher, Enver Hoxha, to seize power in his minuscule neighbour, Albania. Hoxha was handsome, tall, garrulous and strangely literary, writing diaries and memoirs – sixty-five volumes in all. Ruling through a tiny intermarried cabal that lived in an ugly heavily guarded street in mid-Tirana called *Blloku* (the Block), Comrade Enver systematically murdered all rivals: 'Irfan Ohri must be tracked down and killed,' read a typical note. 'I believe he's staying at a house near the Rex Cinema.' Even as he took power in November 1944, he ordered, 'Set up prisons and concentration camps; don't show mercy to anyone,' adding, 'Stop, arrest and execute influential individuals.' Hoxha worshipped Stalin, whom he met for long conversations.

Both Stalin and Truman were uncertain whether Germany, divided between Soviet and western zones, should ever be reunited. As the Cold War intensified, Truman was sceptical; Stalin initially favoured reunification. But Berlin, deep in Stalin's eastern zone, remained divided between the powers. In 1948, hoping to solve the German conundrum by driving the Americans out of Berlin, Stalin blockaded the western zones; Truman instead ordered an airlift to Berlin. Stalin now realized that America would resist Communist advances on all fronts and that a united neutral Germany was impossible, so he installed a Soviet vassal state in his eastern sector. The Americans fostered a West German democracy and needed German sophistication to use against the Communists. Hitler's anti-Soviet intelligence chief Gehlen set up West Germany's intelligence service, his missile expert Werner von Braun worked on US missiles; several of the Holocaust Wannsee planners were released.* Krupp was restored to run his industrial empire. America prescribed a bold tonic for European sickness: a massive aid programme, the Marshall Plan. Stalin rejected it and launched new repressions. His blundering threats led the western democracies, recovering thanks to US aid and sharing a growing confidence in their open societies, to form the North Atlantic Treaty Organization, a military alliance against the Communists, who would soon form their own. America, inspired by its missionary religious origins, embraced the conviction that openness, elections and markets would ultimately produce progress towards democracy and capitalism everywhere. Stalin's USSR, fusing its Marxist quasi-religious mission with traditional anti-western Russian nationalism, was convinced it too would lead the world towards its version of progress.†

Stalin's success in the west encouraged him in the east, where Korea became the Asian Berlin. Soviet troops occupied the northern half, the Americans the south. Planning a Communist client state, Stalin struggled to find vassals. Finally Beria discovered a Korean-born Communist whose Christian parents had founded one of the first anti-Japanese groups, and who had fought during the 1930s in Mao's armies before escaping into Russia. The thirty-three-year-old Kim Song-ju was unknown in Korea, but he cleverly adopted as nom de guerre the name

---

* Some of the most evil escaped down the 'Ratline' to South America where a new Argentine dictator, Colonel Juan Perón, an admirer of Hitler, gave refuge to Adolf Eichmann, Josef Mengele and Ante Pavelić. Pavelić died two years after an attempted assassination; Eichmann was kidnapped by Mossad and hanged in Jerusalem. Mengele drowned.

† 'Not since Athens and Sparta, not since Rome and Carthage,' Deputy Secretary of State Dean Acheson told US senators, 'have we had such a polarization of power.'

of a famous, possibly mythological fighter: 'Tiger' Kim Il-sung. Kim embraced Stalinism mixed with Korean nationalism.

In March 1948, when Marshall's truce collapsed, Chairman Mao seized Manchuria from Generalissimo Chiang, who in turn captured Mao's headquarters at Yen'an. Mao rode away with his wife Jiang Qing and lieutenant Zhou Enlai. Basing himself near Beijing, he ordered his best general, Lin Biao, to advance southwards. The Japanese war had hollowed out Chiang's China; victory destroyed him. Although he was uninterested in lucre, the Songs were a study in malversation: Madame Chiang lived like an empress, her brother, premier T. V. Song, made $300 million in currency speculations. Chiang sacked T.V. but promoted commanders so inept they may have been Communist moles. Chiang ranted against the Songs; Meiling flew to New York.

In April 1949, Mao took the capital Nanjing. After Chiang prayed tearfully at his mother's tomb, he flew to Taiwan where, months later, Meiling joined him.* Mao invited her sister, Madame Sun – Qingling – whom he addressed as 'Dear Elder Sister', to join him in Beijing: 'Show us how to build a new China.' Mao met her at the station, and appointed her vice-chairman; Premier Zhou Enlai gave her the palace where Puyi had been born ('I'm getting the royal treatment,' she boasted).†

Mao decided to move the capital to Beijing, setting up his home – a comfortable villa, the Library of Chrysanthemum Fragrance, with a giant bed piled with books – in the heavily guarded Zhongnanhai compound of the Forbidden City that became his Kremlin. Zhongnanhai is still the metonym for the Chinese leadership. Mao was interested not in money but in comfort and security, using around fifty refurbished villas, ordering the army to choose girls from their theatrical groups to serve in his own troupe, available for sex with the chairman, which his defence

---

* Chiang established an independent republic ruled by the Song and Chiang families. Chiang had lost 550 million people and now ruled six million, subdued by waves of terror and ruled by mainlanders for the next half-century. Reigning there as dictator for the rest of his life, he was succeeded like an emperor by his Russian-educated son, Ching-kuo, who introduced democracy. Taiwan's liberal democracy, home to a sophisticated semiconductor industry, was protected by the USA into the 2020s. But it remains the last Chinese entity outside Beijing's control.
† Puyi on the other hand was not getting the royal treatment. In 1945, Japan's puppet emperor had abdicated and then been captured by the Soviets, who repatriated him. He was forced to perform menial jobs, though Mao encouraged him to write his memoirs. In 1960, Premier Zhou Enlai received him: 'You weren't responsible for becoming emperor at the age of three or the 1917 attempted restoration coup. But you were fully to blame . . . when you agreed to become Manchukuo Chief Executive.' Puyi agreed, wishing he could say sorry to all the eunuchs he had thrashed. In 1967, the last emperor died aged sixty-one.

minister Marshal Peng called 'selecting imperial concubines'. His wife, Jiang Qing, did not interfere.

On 1 October 1949, Mao, accompanied by Madame Sun, announced the people's republic from the top of Tiananmen Gate to 100,000 people. The triumph of Mao combined with Stalin's explosion of the Bomb that August shocked America, destabilized President Truman and unleashed a witch-hunt against secret Communist infiltration (so-called Un-American Activities), led by an alcoholic senator, Joseph McCarthy, who, backed by the omnipresent Joe Kennedy, hired Kennedy's younger son, Bobby, as a lawyer on his committee. As Mao turned to Stalin to industrialize China, he launched a ferocious terror 'to suppress counter-revolutionaries', specifically ordering 'massive arrests, massive killings', criticizing his underlings 'for being much too lenient and not killing enough' and complaining that 'Many places don't dare kill counter-revolutionaries on a big scale with publicity. The situation must be changed.' Many were shot in front of parades, the brains spattering the crowd. Although Mao boasted that 700,000 were shot, the real number was around three million, and a further ten million were sent to *Laogai* – Reform by Labour – camps, where unknown millions died during his reign. He also attacked kinship traditions, banning polygyny, concubinage and foot-binding.* No sooner was this campaign over than he devised a new purge known as the Three Antis (targeting bureaucratism, embezzlement, waste), telling his henchmen, 'We must execute tens of thousands of embezzlers ... Whoever disobeys is either a bureaucrat or an embezzler himself.' Killing, said Mao, was 'extremely necessary. Only when done properly can our power be secure.'

Always reading history, particularly about the First Emperor, with whom he identified, Mao's real priority was to win great-power status for China, particularly possession of the Bomb. In December 1949, he travelled by train to Moscow for Stalin's seventieth birthday. Here the fifty-six-year-old Mao courted the grizzled Stalin, calling him 'the Master'. When Stalin kept him waiting for weeks, he grumbled, 'Am I here just to eat, shit and sleep?' Stalin kept his influence in Manchuria; Mao got industrial aid and overlordship of Asian Communists.† The meetings of these gifted, paranoic megalomaniacs were awkward,

---

* Cixi had banned foot-binding in 1902, as had the new republic in 1912, and the practice was already declining. This time it was final.

† Stalin and Mao together received Ho Chi Minh in Moscow. Mao started to train and arm 70,000 Viet Minh fighters. Mao invited other Indo-Chinese Communists for training in Beijing: one was a Cambodian teacher, trained in Paris, called Saloth Sar, who later changed his name to Pol Pot.

ending in a dinner at Stalin's dacha where the Red Tsar tried to get the Red Emperor to dance to his gramophone. Mao refused; Stalin glowered; and the Bomb was out of the question – but Mao had a merciless plan to ensure that he got it.

In April 1950, Stalin received Kim Il-sung, who asked permission to attack American-backed South Korea.

TIGER KIM AND STALIN'S PROXY WAR

Kim was already expert at manipulating his titanic patrons: a year earlier he had asked Stalin to start the war; when Stalin refused, he went to Mao, who promised to back him. Then Kim probed Stalin, who again refused; Kim added that he would consult Mao. Stalin summoned him to Moscow and approved 'a more active stance in the unification of Korea' – war – provided he 'rely on Mao who understands Asia beautifully'. But he warned him, 'If you get kicked in the teeth, I shan't lift a finger. You'd have to ask Mao for help.' Stalin knew this might launch a world war – 'Should we fear this? I should not' – but more likely Kim would test America and 'spend several years consuming several hundred thousand American lives'. Stalin was forging the Cold War template: the proxy war, locally lethal, safe from nuclear jeopardy.

On 25 June 1950, Kim's 75,000 Koreans attacked the American-backed South Korea, quickly occupying most of the peninsula, but Truman, supported by the UN, poured in American troops, under the bombastic, Caesaresque MacArthur, who routed Kim's army and took his capital, Pyongyang.

Kim begged for help from Stalin, who told Mao, 'Move 5–6 divisions across the 38th Parallel . . . Call them volunteers.' Mao refused to intervene; Stalin received Zhou and Lin at his Black Sea villa. Sitting up late in the hot Georgian night, Stalin teased Mao that the chairman did not have to fight, but promised air cover. Mao felt obliged to intervene.

'With or without Soviet air cover, we go in!' On 25 October, 450,000 Chinese attacked the bewildered Americans in human waves; the southern capital, Seoul, fell in January 1951.

A million American troops, under MacArthur, counter-attacked, pushing the Chinese back. MacArthur threatened to use tactical nuclear weapons; Truman sacked him. Crushed between Stalin–Mao and the Americans, Kim Il-sung was desperate for peace. Stalin and Zhou discussed whether to liquidate the panicking Korean, but Stalin agreed with Mao that the war must go on. 'The war's shown American weakness,' said Stalin. 'They want to subjugate the world and can't subdue little Korea,' adding chillingly, 'The North Koreans have lost nothing except casualties.' Mao had lost a little more: 400,000 men, and his son Anying, who, working as Marshal Peng's Russian interpreter, died in an American air raid. When told, Mao was silent, then just said, 'In a war, how can there be no deaths?'

In February 1953, the newly elected president Dwight Eisenhower, the general who had commanded D-Day, explicitly threatened China with nuclear weapons. Korea had shown Stalin that China needed the Bomb. On the 28th, Stalin sat up jovially drinking with his henchmen until the early hours.* He was planning a new Terror against his grandees, linked to the arrest of mainly Jewish doctors in a murder plot he had himself invented. But that night he suffered a stroke; his comrades and his doctors were too terrified to treat him in case he was merely drunk: he was left on the floor soaked in his own urine. After the embalmed Stalin had joined Lenin in the Mausoleum, Beria dominated the state as first-vice-premier, security chieftain and nuclear supremo, freeing vast numbers of GULAG slave labourers and proposing a withdrawal from East Germany – 'It's not even a real state,' he said, 'but only kept in existence by Soviet troops' – and political liberalization, much the same programme later proposed by Gorbachev.

The new leaders made peace in Korea. Kim Il-sung had lost the war and ruined the country, but he executed rivals and devised a particularly Korean concept of Communism and nationalism, *juche* – self-reliance and isolation – infused with a sacred cult which involved the quasi-divine birth of his son Jong-il (actually born in the USSR) on Korea's holy mountain. Out of it he would spawn a hereditary dynasty which ruled North Korea into the third generation.

Beria, who had not received the top offices, nonetheless appeared to be the real power, yet his ghoulish vices and risky politics alarmed his coarse, lumpy and warty comrade Nikita Khrushchev, whom Beria fatally underrated. Khrushchev warned his comrades, 'Beria's sharpening his knives.' Beria controlled the security organs who guarded the grandees, so Khrushchev recruited Marshal Zhukov, who on 26 June 1953 led a posse of loyal officers, including Leonid Brezhnev, deputy army commissar favoured by Stalin, into the Kremlin. At a Presidium session, Khrushchev orchestrated the denunciation of Beria; Zhukov's

---

* To celebrate the tricentenary of Hetman Khmelnytsky's treaty of allegiance to the Romanov Tsar Alexei in April 1654, Stalin decided to grant Crimea to Ukraine. The new leaders made the transfer the next year. This meant that when in 1991, the Soviet Union broke up, Crimea remained part of Ukraine.

posse burst in, pistols drawn, and arrested the Georgian. Beria was later tried for rape and treason and, his mouth stuffed with a towel, shot in the forehead.

Khrushchev, a pugnacious semi-literate miner and devout Marxist-Leninist, impulsive and irrepressible, was Stalin's protégé, who had killed many when he ran Ukraine and Moscow. Yet he brought to an end government by killing, though the secret police – renamed KGB – remained omnipresent and vigilant. After war and terror, there was such a shortage of men that women were encouraged to work, and abortion, illegal since 1935, was legalized. The porcine Khrushchev now confronted the polished Eisenhower in a bipolar tournament of power, fought out in proxy duels across the world. After Communist victories in China then in Indo-China, Eisenhower feared 'what you call the "falling domino" principle. You knock over the first one and . . . the last one . . . will go over very quickly.' America and Russia, the two nuclear superpowers, now enjoyed truly global reach, each seeking local clients and using war, espionage, credit and culture to defeat their ideological rivals. Both showered spending and technology on their military industries. Both the KGB and America's new intelligence agency, the CIA, became huge, potent and often murderous global bureaucracies, though the KGB was also responsible for oppressing its own citizens and those of its vassals.*

At home, the US thrived, its economy – now a third of global output – stimulated by mass consumerism, military production and technical ingenuity, boundlessly innovative and confident in its righteous mission to promote capitalist democracy. In the richest country that had ever existed,† the appetite of its well-off consumers for flashily advertised

---

* A world game of espionage was played out as each side tried to burrow agents, single, double and triple, deep into the institutions of the other. This bleak, amoral world was exquisitely rendered and turned into literature in the masterpieces of human frailty and betrayal, *The Spy Who Came in from the Cold* and *Tinker Tailor Soldier Spy* by an ex-intelligence officer who became one of the great post-war novelists: John le Carré. Both sides used clandestine and kinetic methods to overthrow their rival's proxies all over the world. Yet in both camps the control of local actors by Moscow and Washington were as exaggerated as the rare successes of the KGB and CIA. Later a myth grew up that the CIA had successfully launched multiple coups. This anti-imperialist narrative underplayed the agency of local potentates. One rare case of a CIA plot that succeeded was greenlit in June 1954 by Eisenhower in Guatemala, where US auxiliaries overthrew the socialist president.
† Housing was needed and property prices were rising in the expanding cities. In New York, Fred Trump, son of Drumpf the Bavarian gold-rush brothel-keeper, built thousands of houses and apartment, seeking government loans to offer cheap housing, often keeping much of the money. Telling his agents 'not to rent to blacks' and, if they were already tenants, to 'get rid of the blacks', he was found guilty of bias against the black tenants. He was the personification of hard-nosed American capitalism, bullying his three sons. Fred Trump left a billion-dollar fortune, a huckster flamboyance and a personal philosophy to his second son Donald, who embraced the old man's philosophy: 'In life there are killers

fashions, cars and fridges stimulated efficient production; its films and music reverberated across the world as compulsive as the pelvic thrusts of Elvis Presley. A handsome boy with an invincible sex appeal and a creamy baritone who, channelling the African-American gospel and blues he heard in his dirt-poor upbringing in Mississippi and later in Memphis, promoted a new sound – rock 'n' roll – selling 500 million records to make him 'The King'. Radio and television had diminished community – promenades and theatres were no longer essential – but the home theatre of television tied families together and helped build nations through the sharing of beloved drama series and trusted anchormen, and yet televised scenes of political strife and warfare could also divide them. Some leaders were better on television than they were at ruling.* TV became a powerful political tool for all states, democratic or autocratic. It was television that helped expose the bullying bombast of US Senator McCarthy, who had orchestrated witch hunts against supposed Communists in arts and governments.

It was not just goods that travelled: cheaper flights allowed millions to go on holiday to foreign lands, and many Americans now flew down to their own American Babylon: Cuba.

MEYER LANSKY'S HOTEL NACIONAL;
FIDEL CASTRO'S FAILED REVOLUTION

In 1952, Meyer Lansky, the Russian-born gangster who had started in the backstreets of Little Italy, met a former Cuban dictator, Colonel Fulgencio Batista, at his suite in the Waldorf-Astoria, Manhattan, to plan a new seizure of power and division of casinos in Havana. An illegitimate ex-labourer, Batista, part-Taíno, African, Chinese and Spanish, the only mixed-race president Cuba has ever had, had early befriended Lansky, who, starting in 1933, helped turn Havana into the pleasure dome of the western world.

Lansky and Bugsy Siegel had survived the arrest and trial of their boss Lucky Luciano, sentenced to fifty years for pandering,† but the Mafiosi

and there are losers ... We're killers ... you're a king, you're a killer.'
* A paradox of populist televised politics is that the best performer may not be good at anything else: 'The qualities rewarded in the rise to eminence,' wrote Henry Kissinger, 'are less and less the qualities required once eminence is reached.'
† After Luciano's arrest, his own organization was taken over by underboss Vito Genovese; the Five Families that dominated New York crime continued as before, as did the Mafia's governing body, the Commission, founded by Luciano. Lansky's partner was a cunning younger Mafioso in New York, Carlo Gambino, consigliere of the most terrifying Mafia

had negotiated his release through a deal, Operation Underworld, in which he and his longshoremen would prevent Nazi infiltration of New York Harbor. On his release, Luciano set up headquarters in Havana, where, in 1946, he and Lansky held a Mafia conference of kingpins at the Hotel Nacional, where they were entertained by a young singer, blue-eyed son of a New Jersey bar-owner, fixer (and occasional abortionist) and a boxer, called Frank Sinatra, whose feral sex appeal, transcendent baritone and extended phrasing would make the idol of the first teen-ager 'fanatics' of the consumer age, the bobby-soxers. The first problem on their agenda was their oldest friend: Bugsy Seigel.

As Havana boomed, Lansky and Siegel pursued their vision of an American pleasure city, investing in a hotel–casino, the Flamingo, at the village of Las Vegas in the Utah desert, attracted by legal gambling and off-track betting. Siegel was basing himself in Los Angeles, where the rich gangster became friends with the movie stars and producers of the Hollywood industry that was purveying the glamour of American cap-italism to the world. After several murder cases, Bugsy was keen to go legitimate, reassuring his builder at the Flamingo, 'Don't worry, we only kill each other.' But Siegel spent too much money buying jewellery for his girlfriend. After blowing $6 million on the Flamingo, he attracted his friends Clark Gable and Judy Garland to the launch, but Lansky and Luciano now suspected him of 'skimming' profits – a capital offence in their milieu. Lansky signed off: on 20 June 1947, as Siegel held court in his Beverly Hills mansion, a sniper shot him through the eye.

Batista, allowing Lansky to open hotels and casinos and American industry to control Cuba's sugar, asked the diminutive gangster to bribe the island's president to resign and then seized power again as dictator. As the Mafia ruled Havana and the American fruit companies dominat-ed Cuban agriculture, the CIA backed Batista. Wiser Americans worried that his corruption would encourage revolution.* Batista and his secret

chieftain of his day, Albert Anastasia, who ran a hit squad out of the City Democratic Club which the newspapers called Murder Inc, with Anastasia as lord high executioner. But when Anastasia tried to create his own casinos in Havana, Lansky and Gambino ordered him hit: on 25 October 1957, Anastasia was at the Park Sheraton Hotel, Manhattan, reclining in his barber's chair, covered in warm towels, when he was shot, creating one of the famous images of a Mafia hit. Gambino took over the Family that later produced John Gotti.

* Batista was typical of the leaders backed by the US who became even more essential in the struggle against Communism. 'He may be a bastard,' FDR supposedly said about the US ally Anastasio Somoza of Nicaragua, 'but he's our bastard.' Somoza and his son ruled until 1979. On the island of Hispaniola, the US backed Rafael 'El Jefe' Trujillo, Dominican tyrant since 1930, who in 1937 had ordered the slaughter of thousands of black Haitians in a massacre known as El Corte. In Haiti, it tolerated the election of a popular doctor who made his name treating yaws, a common disease, then as a progressive health minister, François

police the Bureau for Repression of Communist Activities soon demonstrated how easily he would crush any Communists.

On 26 July 1953, Batista foiled a pathetic Communist attempt to seize the barracks in Santiago. Many of the 165 rebels were shot, their amateurish leader, a young lawyer named Fidel Castro, imprisoned and unlikely to be heard of again. Cuba was safe, but now the CIA worried about two friendly kings in danger.

FAT FUCKER AND THE BOY SCOUT:
NASSER AND THE SHAH SEIZE POWER

In 1952, Kim Roosevelt, a thirty-five-year-old American spy, arrived in Cairo to see King Farouk, whom he had befriended during the war, keen to bolster the monarchy. Kermit, grandson of President Teddy, who had joined CIA forerunner the OSS during the war and believed America should back Arab nationalists to counter Soviet subversion, personified the tweedy jauntiness of the early CIA. That tone was also echoed in the name of his Egyptian mission: Project FF (Fat Fucker). King Farouk was the Fat Fucker. Roosevelt had a second mission related to another young king, the shah of Iran. In Egypt, control of the Canal was essential for oil supplies; in Iran, the oilfields were in peril, and the two were connected: Farouk's sister Fawzia was married to the shah. Roosevelt, chief of the Near East and Africa Division, was ordered to save both.

Roosevelt started with Fat Fucker, but Farouk refused to reduce his extravagance or dismiss the Stork and other favourites, leading the American to probe a coterie of young officers who loathed the inept monarchy. These Free Officers were led by Colonel Nasser and his ally Anwar Sadat, son of a fellahin, a poor Nilotic farmer, who had been imprisoned in the war for pro-German conspiracy. Giving up on FF, Roosevelt encouraged Nasser, who he believed was pro-American.

Farouk, who hated the British, declared that the Canal belonged to Egypt, elevated himself to a new title, king of Egypt and Sudan, and faked a descent from Muhammad: 'If there was any Arabic blood in

'Papa Doc' Duvalier. In a country long dominated by the mulatto elite, Duvalier was black, promising to protect 'the great unacknowledged'. Distrusting the army, he created his own *Milice de Volontaires de la Sécurité Nationale*, a militia of murderous machete-wielding secret policemen nicknamed Tontons Macoutes after the bogeymen who in voodoo mythology would catch victims in a sack. Led by a henchman known as the Vampire due to his trade in blood plasma, the Macoutes burned, shot and dismembered Papa Doc's enemies, whose remains were often displayed in trees as a warning; Washington had nonetheless initially trained them. In 1964 Duvalier declared himself president for life.

Farouk's veins, it was so diluted that it couldn't possibly have been traced back to Muhammad,' fulminated General Naguib. 'A sacrilege.' Farouk divorced his queen, the popular part-Turkish aristocrat Farida, to marry a teenager, Narriman, chosen in part because she was Arab and middle-class; but the combination of cold-heartedness and extravagance made the obese sybarite unpopular. When Peter Ustinov played Nero in the new film *Quo Vadis*, the resemblance to the king was so strong that the film was banned in Egypt. Farouk was losing control: on 26 January 1952, rioters burned down cinemas, hotels and nightclubs.

Now Farouk promoted his brother-in-law, Ismail 'Pretty Boy' Chirine, a playboy who had married Fawzia after her divorce from the shah, to defence minister. It was the last straw for Nasser who, chain-smoking and listening to Rimsky-Korsakov's *Scheherazade*, accelerated his coup, recruiting Naguib as figurehead. When some officers betrayed the plot to Farouk he mocked them as 'a bunch of pimps'. On the night of 23 July 1952, Nasser seized Cairo's army headquarters. Farouk was at an Alexandrian casino, but he appealed to the US ambassador for help against Communist mutineers. Nasser and Sadat debated whether to execute him, but, deciding to let him live, they dispatched two columns to arrest him.

Brandishing a machine gun, Farouk drove Narriman, his son and Pulli the Stork to the fortified Ras el-Tin Palace, defended by Sudanese guards. When the rebels attacked the palace, he shot four with a hunting rifle; but neither the Americans nor the British backed him and he signed the abdication, in favour of his son Fuad. Dressing up in his white admiral's uniform, Farouk with his family boarded the *Mahrousa*, which had taken his grandfather Ismail into exile in 1879. Naguib, embarrassed and moved, kissed his hand. 'It isn't easy to govern Egypt, you know,' said Farouk, ending 146 years of his family's rule.

The Free Officers appointed Naguib as president, but as his conservatism became apparent, the dashing, tall and exuberant Nasser, who had already become premier, replaced him as president, winning massive popularity with his land reforms and powerful oratory, first in Egypt but ultimately as the voice of secular pan-Arab nationalism. There was always another route in the Arab world: religion. Religious and secular power were always in contact, sometimes clashing, sometimes combining, but like all ideologies always contagious and fluid.

Nasser consulted a leader of the Muslim Brothers, Sayyid Qutb, a pale, heavy-lidded bachelor who had been disgusted by American decadence during his studies in Colorado and preached jihad against the materialistic west. The modern history of the Arab world can be written through these two men. Once Qutb realized Nasser was opposed to his views, he ordered his assassination. In October 1954, while Nasser was speaking live on the radio in Alexandria, a Brother shot at him and missed. Nasser, a born thespian, played it to the hilt. 'Let them kill me,' he cried, 'so long as I've instilled pride, honour, and freedom in you. If Gamal Abdel Nasser should die, each of you shall be Gamal Abdel Nasser.' Nasser, advised by the CIA but also employing ex-Nazis, now used his General Intelligence Service, the *Mukhabarat* – the essential tool of all Arab rulers – to purge the jihadists. He hanged Qutb, but his works were read across the House of Islam by all sects – including the Shiite lecturer in philosophy and sharia in Iran, Ruhollah Khomeini.

As Farouk settled into luxurious Italian exile with a new starlet, Kim Roosevelt arrived to advise his ex-brother-in-law, Shah Mohammad Reza, who at thirty-four was in danger of being exiled or murdered. He had suffered bitterly from the humiliations of his father's downfall and Anglo-Soviet occupation, but he had the acumen to govern. 'There's no more lonely unhappy life,' said the shah, 'than that of the man who decides to rule instead of reign.' He gained stature first in 1946 when Tabriz was recovered from the Soviets, and then in 1949 when, visiting Teheran University, he was shot in cheek and shoulder by an assassin who was himself shot on the spot. A wave of sympathy permitted the shah to pass new powers to appoint governments, a first step in his mission to modernize Iran and make it a great power.

The shah had to deal with a rising Communist Party; the Tudeh, a mercurial ayatollah Kashani, who backed a terrorist movement called Fadayan-e Islam or Devotees of Islam; a conservative army; and, in the parliament (Majlis), the return of a veteran politician, Mohammad Mosaddegh and his National Front, who spearheaded the call to nationalize British oil. In the face of anti-British fury, the shah appointed a forceful general, Ali Razmara, to negotiate with the British, but he was assassinated by Fadayan-e Islam. The shah sought another premier, but the Majlis voted to nationalize British oil and then for Mosaddegh, now backed by the religious leader Ayatollah Kashani, to succeed Razmara. On 28 April 1951, the shah duly appointed Mosaddegh, who three days later nationalized the Anglo-Iranian Oil Company. Mosaddegh, now sixty-nine, was an unlikely revolutionary. Educated in Paris, he was a semi-royal, super-wealthy landowner – his mother was a Qajar princess, his wife granddaughter of a shah – but he was also a valetudinarian who, pyjama-clad, governed from bed. Detesting the British – 'You have no idea how crafty they are, how evil,' he told an American envoy – this neurotic funambulist tried to balance the Communists on one side, shah, army and ayatollahs on the other. The only way to do so was to assume autocratic powers himself.

In July 1952, Mosaddegh challenged the shah's control of the army; the shah dismissed him but, faced with riots organized by both the Communists and the ayatollahs, recalled him. Mosaddegh, now taking command of the military, backed by the ayatollahs and the Communists, assumed emergency powers. He tried to appease the Communists but only succeeded in disappointing them while convincing everyone else that he was either becoming a despot or turning Communist. In January 1953, Ayatollah Kashani turned against him. The Communists attempted to seize power. An army conspiracy plotted with the shah. Abroad, Winston Churchill, seventy-eight, prime minister for the second time, agreed with Eisenhower that Mosaddegh was in danger of being overwhelmed by the Communists.

The shah felt beleaguered – 'The bastard was out for blood,' he later recalled of Mosaddegh – consoled only by Soraya, his half-German, half-Iranian second wife, the love of his life. The queen dispensed with his Swiss mentor Perron, whom she called a 'woman-hating homosexual who spread poison'. Shah Mohammad was shy and yet sexually voracious, his eyes revealing: 'Dark brown, almost black, shining, at times hard, at times sad or gentle, they exuded charm and reflected his soul.' Soraya calmed him with sex, the only thing, along with flying planes, that soothed him. He slept with a pistol under his pillow.

Mosaddegh, talking in riddles in his barricaded mansion, had alienated all sides. 'Our authority throughout the Middle East,' said Churchill, 'has been violently shaken.' Eisenhower agreed; his advisers, Secretary of State John Foster Dulles and his brother Allen, founding director of the CIA, believed that Mosaddegh was an ineffective dictator who would be forced into the arms of the Soviets. 'Is there,' asked Eisenhower, 'any feasible course of action to save the situation?'

In July 1953, Roosevelt drove into Teheran with a million dollars in cash to arrange a coup against Mosaddegh: Operation Ajax. An ambitious if venal general, Fazlollah Zahedi, Mosaddegh's former interior minister and cousin, also married to a Qajar shah's granddaughter, was already planning his own coup and was happy to receive western help. The shah distrusted everyone, particularly the Anglo-Americans.

On 1 August, Roosevelt was smuggled on the floor of a limousine into the Golestan Palace to see the shah. Coups do not usually have soundtracks but Roosevelt chose Sinatra's 'Luck be a Lady' as his theme song. He and his British SIS colleagues Woodhouse and Darbyshire massively exaggerated their own importance and competence amid this welter of conspiracies. Their portrait of all Iranians, starting with the shah and Zahedi, as childish, corrupt panickers and themselves as ice-cool, swashbuckling manipulators was delusional braggadocio and racist orientalism of the worst sort. Roosevelt revealingly codenamed the shah Boyscout, Mosaddegh Old Bugger and himself Rainmaker.

On 16 August, outside Teheran, the shah signed decrees that dismissed Mosaddegh and appointed Zahedi, but Mossadegh mobilized a mob with the aid of Communists and tried to arrest Zahedi. A mob funded by Roosevelt was vanquished, but Zahedi went underground. The coup had failed; the shah, now in danger of assassination, flew Soraya to Baghdad then to Rome.

Norodoms and Kennedys, Castros, Kenyattas and Obamas

THE YOUNG KING OF CAMBODIA

Yet Zahedi and his cohorts were at large; Mosaddegh's refusal to arm the Communists lost him their support, while his negotiations with the westerners alienated Kashani. On 19 August the ayatollah brought a mob to the city, aided by $100,000 of CIA funds, just as Zahedi re-emerged, sending troops to bombard Mosaddegh's house. Old Bugger fled over his wall in his pyjamas, but was quickly arrested. In Rome, at the Excelsior Hotel, Soraya wept with relief. 'I knew,' said the shah, 'they loved me.'*

Flying home, Shah Mohammad spared Mosaddegh, who was confined to one of his estates, and dismissed Zahedi within a year, revealing himself as a steelier player than the west had expected. Vigilant and paranoid, he privately hated both superpowers, but played off the Soviets and Americans to the extent that Khrushchev ordered his assassination and Eisenhower threatened his deposition. He believed he could out-fox them both. At home he emulated Mosaddegh, commandeering his land reforms and nationalist rhetoric for a modern monarchy, planning to launch his own revolution.

Nasser too was playing the superpowers against each other – 'Food from the Americans, money from the Arabs, guns from Russia, a veritable magician,' joked the shah later. Now Nasser demanded funding

---

* Roosevelt spent the rest of his life advertising his dashing role. But the generals and ayatollahs were probably much more important than the Americans. There were several conspiracies: it was Zahedi's troops who seized power and Ayatollah Kashani's crowds that ruled the streets. Roosevelt did recruit some criminals, but it is unlikely that their crowd of gangsters and prostitutes were decisive and even by his own account he scarcely spent his own budget. Indeed he gave Zahedi the remaining $900,000 of Ajax funds. Eisenhower remarked that the CIA man's report 'seemed more like a dime novel than historical fact'. The preposterous self-promoter was the novelist. Yet the coup became an iconic crime of American imperialism, its myth encouraged by both the CIA, to boost the mystique of its power, and the shah's enemies, Iranian nationalists and the Islamic republic, to demonize and taint the Pahlavis. When the shah heard Roosevelt's vainglorious claims, he just laughed, a scene recounted in the diaries of his court minister Asadollah Alam.

for a huge project, the Aswan Dam. At first Eisenhower and Dulles were sympathetic, but, suspicious of Nasser's Soviet links, they withdrew. As Nasser encouraged Palestinian attacks on Israeli borders, in July 1956 he nationalized the Suez Canal, using the resulting funds for the Dam. The British prime minister Anthony Eden, who after waiting for fifteen years to succeed Churchill was now addicted to painkillers and too ill to do the job, absurdly regarded Nasser as a new Hitler – a regular flaw in leaders of the Second World War generation. Meanwhile the French were suffering even more than the British from imperial decline.

On 7 May 1954, the commander of 11,000 French troops at Dien Bien Phu in Vietnam sent a final message – 'The enemy has overrun us. We are blowing up everything. *Vive la France!*' – and surrendered to the forces of Ho Chi Minh. Faced with French reconquest, Ho and Giap had always believed that however much blood was spilt they would defeat the westerners. 'You can kill ten of my men for every one I kill of yours,' Ho supposedly told a Frenchman. 'But even at those odds, you'll lose and I'll win.' Giap had exploited French incompetence by secretly using thousands of bearers to convey artillery through jungles to surround a French army – winning independence for North Vietnam.[*]

In neighbouring Cambodia, an extraordinary young king was also striving for independence. Blessed with good looks, impulsive spirit, limitless ambitions and boundless egotism, King Norodom Sihanouk had spent his youth riding horses, playing football, studying films and chasing girls, fathering many children by many lovers from two of his own aunts to actresses and courtesans, and playing saxophone and clarinet in his own royal band. But he was determined to escape French rule. For the next fifty years, Sihanouk would variously be king, premier, president, autocrat as well as figurehead, victim and prisoner of Pol Pot, a career that started in 1941 when Paris selected Sihanouk to be king because he combined the two rival branches of the royal Norodom family.

As the prince was growing up, he was closely connected to a boy who would one day control him and kill a million of his people, including several of his children. Saloth Sar, son of well-off peasant farmers, arrived from the countryside with his brother to live with their cousin, who was a ballerina and mistress of then King Monivong; for eighteen

---

[*] Ho's paternal charm belied his Stalinist ferocity. Rivals were quietly executed: 'All those who don't follow the line I've laid down will be broken.' In North Vietnam, 200,000 innocent well-off peasants were executed by quota, laid down in May 1953 – 'fixed in principle at the ratio of one per one thousand people of the total population'.

months he trained as a novice Buddhist monk. Later, after an education at a privileged new boarding school, the future Pol Pot won a scholarship to study electronics in Paris.

The French–Vietnamese war helped push the playboy King Sihanouk into front-line politics. After triumphantly winning independence in 1953 following a tour through France and the USA, Sihanouk leaned towards socialism and rejected American hegemony. 'Had I been born to an ordinary family,' he said, 'I'd have been leftist, but I was born a prince . . . I can't detach myself.' Yet Saloth Sar did detach himself. In Paris, he read Stalin, Mao, Rousseau, Sartre, and met his best friend Ieng Sary; they married sisters, and returned as fanatical Marxists. Saloth immediately joined a Viet Minh unit, but then emerged in Phnom Penh as a teacher. It seemed as though Saloth had returned to normal life.

A natural showman, Sihanouk revelled in the limelight but craved real power. On 2 March 1955, he suddenly abdicated (succeeded by his father) and, coining the title *Samdech Upayuvareach* – Prince Who Was King – he won the premiership. France was gone, and Sihanouk planned to navigate neutral peace for Cambodia.

Defeated in Asia, France was not willing to give up Africa, but many of its soldiers fighting the Vietnamese were Algerians. Algeria, French since 1830, was part of Metropolitan France; a million French settlers, the *pieds-noirs* or *colons*, lived there, but in 1945, in Sétif, Algerians demonstrated for rights, and French troops and *colons* fired into the crowds. Revenge attacks on the *colons* provoked the French to murder thousands of Algerians. On 1 November 1954, the Algerian FLN – *Front de Libération Nationale* – murdered Frenchmen across Algeria. The French army and the *colon* militias responded with brutality in a war that would rebound to threaten the very existence of French democracy.

While France struggled, Khrushchev and Mao were prevailing on all fronts. But now the Soviet leader almost destroyed his own empire.

AN ISRAELI IN PARIS

On 25 February 1956, Khrushchev defined his own supremacy by denouncing Stalin's crimes to the Central Committee, a 'secret speech' that provoked first Polish unrest then, on 23 October, a Hungarian revolution against Soviet rule. Barely sleeping for weeks, facing the loss of Stalin's empire, Khrushchev threatened to invade Poland, restrained himself, but then, nervously consulting Mao and even Tito, prepared to invade Hungary. Its revolution thrilled America: Stalin's empire was tottering. Yet, the very next day, three powers met secretly in Paris to collude in a plan that let Khrushchev off the hook.

On 24 October, in a villa in Sèvres, the representatives of the old world – the declining empires Britain and France – and the new world – the energetic, tiny Israel – cooperated to humble another new force, Nasser, who had signed a massive arms deal with the Soviet Union and nationalized the Suez Canal. His troops were increasingly clashing with the Israelis – and he was backing Algerian rebels against France.

The British, French and Israelis shared the same enemy. An Israeli, Shimon Peres, protégé of Ben-Gurion, born Szymon Perski in Poland before arriving in Palestine in 1934, a master negotiator with a poetical streak, was already buying French weapons. 'I was seduced by the French, nation of seduction,' he told this author. 'To me, a rough kibbutznik, Paris was the most beautiful city of dreams and literature.' The US had refused to sell arms to Israel; France supplied them.

Now in Sèvres, Ben-Gurion, accompanied by his one-eyed chief of staff Moshe Dayan and Peres, secretly agreed with the French premier Guy Mollet and the British foreign secretary Selwyn Lloyd to kill several birds with one stone: in an operation appropriately codenamed Musketeer, Israel would attack Egypt, whereupon France and Britain would intervene to impose peace. Within the secret Sèvres negotiations lurked a deeper secret. Peres explained that Israel was a tiny new state taking a risk: 'We need a force of deterrence,' he said. 'France can give us this deterrent.' France agreed. A country eight years old was getting the Bomb, developed at Dimona in the Negev. Peres never admitted that Israel had the Bomb. 'War and peace are always a dance of the mysteries,' he told this author, but it changed the balance of power in west Asia.

On 29 October, Ben-Gurion sent his army racing across Sinai; Anglo-French paratroopers seized the Canal; Nasser and his commander Abdel Hakim Amer bickered about the imminent downfall of Egypt. But the plan fell apart: Eden had not consulted Eisenhower, who, fearing that the Arabs would rally to the Soviets, demanded an Anglo-French withdrawal, sparking a run on the pound and the resignation of Eden. Ironically, Khrushchev also demanded their withdrawal, threatening nuclear war if they did not. Suez helped doom the Hungarians and save Khrushchev.

THE MINER AND THE SWIMMER: KHRUSHCHEV AND MAO

On 4 November, Khrushchev ordered Soviet forces to invade Hungary: they killed 10,000 rebels and restored Soviet rule before the capitalists could intervene. Yet his political bungling and drunken jabbering had alarmed his Stalinist comrades, who tried to overthrow him. Khrushchev was rescued by Marshal Zhukov, who flew in regional leaders to back him. But Zhukov was too popular, and Khrushchev soon denounced him for 'Bonapartism'. Initially self-deprecating, Khrushchev, now both Party secretary and premier, changed into a swaggering autocrat who never stopped talking and believed himself expert on all matters, from literature to science. Now he was ready to break the impasse with the west. 'Like it or not, history is on our side,' he told ambassadors after the crushing of Budapest. 'We will bury you!' His nuclear threats during Suez had worked: 'The winner has the strongest nerves.'

Yet he failed to keep the Communist world together. Mao was both horrified by and contemptuous of the cloddish Khrushchev, regarding himself as the paramount Marxist leader. His performance in Korea had demonstrated that China needed nuclear protection; now his shelling of Taiwanese territory provoked a nuclear threat from Eisenhower. 'In today's world, if we don't want to be bullied,' said Mao in January 1955, 'we have to have this thing.' In 1957, Khrushchev started to hand over nuclear technology to Mao, a process that led to the explosion of the Chinese Bomb. 'If the worst came to the worst [nuclear war], and half of mankind died,' Mao told the Russians in Moscow, 'the other half would remain, imperialism razed, and the world would become socialist.' Khrushchev was aghast. 'I couldn't tell if he was joking.' He was not.

Mao was ungrateful. When Khrushchev requested listening posts on the Chinese coast, Mao reacted so menacingly that the Russian flew to Beijing. In a series of screaming rows, Mao humiliated and mocked him. 'You've talked a long time,' said Mao, 'but you still haven't got to the point,' then forced him to come swimming where the floundering Russian struggled like a drowning pig to keep up with the Chinese shark. 'I'm a miner, he's a prize-winning swimmer,' said Khrushchev. Mao, noticed his doctor Li Zhisui, 'was deliberately playing the emperor, treating Khrushchev like a barbarian come to pay tribute.'

Khrushchev realized that Mao was like Stalin: 'They were the same.' Human life meant nothing. Challenged from within, Mao now launched a terror that took China out of the world game for a decade. Back in Moscow, the arrogant Khrushchev was scarcely chastened by this setback in Beijing. He backed the production of missiles to catch up with America – using the technology to launch space exploration, in October 1957, sending a satellite, *Sputnik*, then Laika the dog, the first mammal to orbit the earth (though she was probably already dead), and four years later the *Vostok 3KA*, in which a cosmonaut, Yuri Gagarin, first man in space, orbited and returned. Eisenhower, in response, established NASA to catch up. Khrushchev decided the way to defeat the west was a monumental bluff that would take the world to the edge of cataclysm.

Suez destroyed Eden, but it empowered Nasser. In July 1958, the Egyptian leader's reach was demonstrated when the Iraq mob played football with the head of the young king Faisal of Iraq . . .

DISEMBOWELLED IN BAGHDAD:
EL RAIS AND THE LAST KING OF IRAQ

Nasser – wildly popular as *El Rais*, the Boss – threatened western allies, the Saudis of Arabia and the Hashemites of Jordan and Iraq. In Arabia, the founding king, Abdulaziz, died in 1953, choosing as heir, out of his forty-five sons, Saud, unwise and extravagant, who was soon embroiled in a costly war in Yemen against Egyptian troops. Saud and Nasser planned each other's assassinations. In the Saud family, the brothers removed Saud and put the steely Faisal in control.

The Hashemites were more vulnerable. On 1 February 1958, Nasser and the Syrian president agreed to fuse their states into a single United Arab Republic with Nasser as panjandrum. The Hashemites panicked and planned a united kingdom of Jordan and Iraq, but this British-backed Arab Union was unpopular, especially in Baghdad. Its king Faisal II, a genial twenty-three-year-old, happiest playing cricket at Harrow, was dominated by the Anglophile strongman Nuri al-Said, who had fought with Lawrence of Arabia and been premier fourteen times. The Arab Union accelerated the plot of Iraq's Free Officers, encouraged and inspired by Nasser.

On 14 July 1958, the night before King Faisal's wedding, officers led by Abd al-Karim Qasim stormed the Rihab Palace. Faisal surrendered but was forced with his aunt, uncle and mother to stand in the court-yard, where they were machine-gunned down. 'All I did was remember Palestine,' said one of the assassins, 'and the trigger on the machine gun just set itself off.' The bodies were dragged down al-Rashid Street, stripped, mutilated, beheaded, stomped on, dismembered, gutted and dangled from balconies before being burned.

As the mob stormed his mansion, Premier Nuri escaped in women's clothes, but his male shoes were spotted and he was shot and buried, only to be exhumed by the mob, emasculated, hanged and driven over repeatedly by buses. Nasser was delighted. The west was shocked, sending troops into Lebanon, while Khrushchev warned against any interference. In neighbouring Jordan, Hussein, now the last Hashemite monarch and surrounded by Nasserist officers, submitted himself to Nasser as Iraq was enveloped in a spiral of extremism. Qasim and his successors struggled to control a Baath (Resurrection) Party, founded in Syria by a Christian, which preached a violent mix of socialism, nationalism and anti-imperialism.

Within five years, in February 1963, the Baathists seized power in Syria and then in Iraq, where the bluff new premier, Colonel Ahmed al-Bakr, used his implacable cousin for special murderous tasks: the thirty-one-year-old Saddam Hussein.

Suez accelerated the African crisis that France and Britain handled very differently. Their vast African empires had existed for only around seventy years, but their power was haemorrhaging. Now France suffered an existential crisis that led to a military coup and the near destruction of democracy.

LA GRANDEUR: DE GAULLE AND HOUPHOUËT

In 1956, an Ivorian leader, Félix Houphouët-Boigny, joined the French cabinet as a minister, the first African, the first person of colour, in any European or North American government ever, something that would have been unthinkable in London, let alone in the US. Formidable, playful and shrewd, Houphouët was a phenomenon, son and successor of a tribal chief, who had converted to Catholicism and qualified as a doctor; he had served as a *chef de canton* in the Côte d'Ivoire, became *grand propriétaire* of a cocoa plantation and then in 1945 was elected to the French Assembly to represent his country, campaigning for independence with Machiavellian artistry. When he allied with the French Communists, he teased anyone who accused him of Communism: 'How can we say I, Houphouët, traditional leader, doctor, *grand propriétaire*, Catholic, am a Communist?'

France had traditionally been brutal in crushing any challenge to its empire, but after Indo-China and Suez the French embraced Houphouët and other black African nationalists and, instead of fighting the rise of African potentates in British style, they chose their favourites and promoted them. Houphouët, soon president of independent Côte d'Ivoire and known as *Papa* or *Le Vieux*, became the intimate of French presidents as did the absolute kings of Morocco.* But there was a glaring exception to this generous approach: the agony of Algeria.

As de Gaulle watched and waited in his Colombey house, the Algerian revolt deteriorated into a sectarian bloodbath. Yet it was Algeria that had brought him back to power. The French army and *colons* destroyed and deported whole villages, waterboarded and electrocuted prisoners or threw them out of helicopters, and assassinated leaders, while the FLN murdered, kidnapped, mutilated, raped civilians, terrorized Algerians and executed their own activists: in eight years, around 900,000 Algerians, 25,000 soldiers and 10,000 *colons* were killed. On 13 May 1958, as Parisian governments failed to cope, in Algiers French generals, backed by *pieds-noirs*, launched an insurrection against Paris and declared a Committee of Public Safety, feeling out de Gaulle, whom they called *Le Grand Charles*. He regarded the restoration of France as his destiny: 'There was no moment in my life when I wasn't certain one day I would rule France.' It was not easy: 'How can one govern a country,' he said, 'that has 258 cheeses?' Now that country was on the verge of disintegrating. This strange-looking giant was born for conflict. 'To be great,' he paraphrased Shakespeare, 'is to sustain a great quarrel.' He believed that 'France cannot be France without *la grandeur*.' His definition of grandeur was himself. The Napoleons were on his mind: 'I want 18 Brumaire [Napoleon's 1799 coup] without the methods of 18 Brumaire.' Yet by inclination and conviction he was a monarch. 'The leader is he,' he wrote while held in a German prisoner-of-war camp in 1917, 'who does not speak.'

His inscrutability allowed both sides, the floundering politicians and the rebellious generals, to believe he was theirs. A maestro of clandestine intrigue, much of it organized by a plump, bland ex-spy, Jacques Foccart, he kept the military threat simmering until the politicians accepted his return. 'The national crisis', he announced, could be 'the start of a resurrection . . . Now I'm going to return to my village and hold myself at the disposal of the country.'

---

* In 1957, Paris handed over Morocco to Sultan Muhammad Alawi descendant of the terrifying seventeenth-century monarch Ismail ibn Sharif. Muhammad had resisted Vichy demands to send Moroccan Jews to the death camps, then after the war had demanded the reuniting of Morocco and independence. Paris exiled him to Madagascar. Now he and his son Hassan negotiated the French and Spanish exit from Morocco. As king in 1961, Hassan promoted the dynasty as sherifians, assuming the title Amir al-Muminin, and assuming absolute power while allowing a multi-party parliament. Able, haughty and ruthless, he crushed opposition, often with French help, seized Western Sahara and succeeded in making Morocco a stable hybrid monarchy.

On 1 June 1958, as premier, he asked the National Assembly for full powers for six months, which they approved – giving his coup legality. Three days later he flew to Algeria to tell the ecstatic crowds: 'I've understood you.' He had, but not in the way they hoped. Eighty-five per cent of the French 'Community' (France and the African colonies) ratified a constitution that created what he called 'a kind of popular monarchy which is the only system compatible with the character and perils of our epoch'.*

One of his first acts was to invite the chancellor of West Germany, Konrad Adenauer, to Colombey, where these two old men created a new Europe. His predecessor Mollet had already forged a European Economic Community. Initially de Gaulle was suspicious but a partnership with Adenauer placed France at the centre of an increasingly federal Europe. He kept Britain out with a haughty 'Non!' – and America at a distance, while he created France's own nuclear *force de frappe*.

His priority was Algeria, where he surprised the *colons*, coolly betraying Algérie Française and granting Algeria independence. 'We move,' insisted the president, 'or we die.' In response, in April 1959, generals, paratroopers and Foreign Legionaries took over central Algiers, while at home the army planned to seize power. Addressing the nation in uniform, de Gaulle denounced this 'handful of retired generals . . . We see the state flouted, the nation defied, our power degraded . . . Alas! Alas! Alas!' He added, 'Look where France risks going, compared to what she is in the process of becoming.' The brutality intensified in Algeria and France; the FLN launched terrorist attacks in Paris; the *pied-noir* terrorist organization, the OAS, tried to kill de Gaulle. On 22 April 1961, French generals launched a coup d'état in Algiers against the French president. Soon afterwards French terrorists tried to kill him with a bomb. A year later on 22 August 1962, de Gaulle's Citroën was ambushed by terrorists with a bullet narrowly missing his head. In Paris, on 17 October 1961, French police attacked an Algerian demonstration

---

* De Gaulle's 'politics of grandeur' reflected his personality and life. 'Of course I wouldn't redo the Second Empire,' he reflected, 'because I'm not Napoleon's nephew and one doesn't become emperor at my age.' His view of life was one of struggle: 'Life is a combat and each of its phases includes both successes and failures . . . Success contains within it the germs of failure and vice versa.' His view of humanity was low: 'There are only two motors to human action, fear and vanity. Either there's a state of catastrophe and fear dominates. Or calm and then it is vanity.' De Gaulle won a plebiscite that approved his Fifth Republic, creating a powerful presidency like a republican monarch, successor to the Bourbons and Bonapartes. When he met the young British queen Elizabeth II, she asked his advice and he perfectly defined constitutional monarchy for her: 'In the place where God has placed you, be who you are, Madam. I mean be that person around whom, thanks to your legitimacy, everything in your kingdom is organized, around whom your people see their *patrie* and whose presence and dignity contribute to national unity.'

with such savagery that over fifty were killed, an atrocity unparalleled in any western democracy.

'Napoleon said that in love,' remarked de Gaulle, 'the only victory is flight. In decolonization too, the only victory is to leave.' On 1 July 1962, Algeria became independent. Yet if France was to remain great, the general said, 'It is thanks to Africa.'

The general placed his *éminence grise* Foccart in charge of *Françafrique*, and Foccart duly became the godfather of the Francophone autocrats, most of whom worshipped de Gaulle. For thirty-five years under four presidents, Foccart policed African politics, sending in French troops and spies whenever French-backed autocrats were threatened. 'Let's put an end to this comedy,' de Gaulle said to Foccart, who ordered troops into Gabon. When African dictators faked their elections, they were told, 'The General finds 99.8 per cent a bit too much.' In 1966, in the Central African Republic, a murderous officer, Jean-Bedél Bokassa, who worshipped de Gaulle as 'papa', seized power: Foccart advised that he was 'reliable'.

'Yes,' answered de Gaulle, 'but an idiot.' Bokassa was backed by France as he crowned himself a Napoleonic emperor: only after thirteen years of tyranny, when he murdered hundreds of schoolchildren, did French troops remove him.*

There was success too: Papa Houphouët did not expel French colonialists, praised 'the human relationship between the French and Africans' and ruled for thirty-three years as a French-backed autocrat, masterfully cooperating with French presidents. He was so close to de Gaulle that he helped draft the 1958 constitution. Houphouët, accompanied by his beautiful, free-spirited wife Marie-Thérèse, twenty-five years younger than *Le Vieux*, frequently saw de Gaulle and Foccart (the latter was godfather to their adopted children). The two Frenchmen backed Houphouët even when in old age he moved the Ivorian capital to his home village, where he built a cathedral larger than St Peter's. It was said its French architect became too close to Marie-Thérèse: he died soon afterwards in a helicopter crash. Unembarrassed by his wealth

---

* In 1966, in tiny, oil-rich Gabon – part of France's central colonial federation, *Afrique-Équatoriale française* – de Gaulle interviewed a dapper, diminutive ex-officer who spoke beautiful French, Albert-Bernard Bongo. At just thirty, de Gaulle blessed him as vice-president and then backed him as president, in return for favoured access to Gabonese oil and uranium. Bongo, who later converted to Islam, ruled like a monarch for forty-two years, enriched by oil and French subsidies, intimate with every French president up to Sarkozy. His many children were promoted to government. In 1980, his daughter Pascaline had an affair with Bob Marley, the Jamaican Rastafarian singer whom she invited to play in Gabon; later she was promoted to foreign minister. When Bongo died in 2009, his son Ali Bongo succeeded him. The Bongos ruled for over fifty years.

– 'People are surprised that I like gold; it's simply that I was born in it' – Houphouët helped Foccart overthrow Communist leaders all over Africa. Even in the twenty-first century, French troops were fighting in west Africa and presiding over successions. Such was France decolonization: 'Everything had to change,' writes Julian Jackson, 'so everything could stay the same.'*

Britain's world-weary, unflappable new prime minister, Harold Macmillan, did things very differently – with a dance.

BURNING SPEARS: KENYATTA, NKRUMAH AND BARACK OBAMA (SENIOR)

On 18 November 1961, the first independent ruler of British Africa asked an English woman to dance the 'high life' shuffle at a ball held at Ghana's State House – formerly the slave castle Fort Christiansborg. The occasion, the location, the characters could not have been more fitting for this moment, which marked a new era in the relations between Europe and Africa. She was Queen Elizabeth II, aged thirty-five, beaming in a bare-shouldered dress; he was the fifty-one-year-old president, Dr Kwame Nkrumah, exuberant in black tie.

He was a Marxist, pan-Africanist autocrat and yet he admired the 'young girl'. When her visit had been cancelled on a previous occasion because Elizabeth was pregnant, he exclaimed, 'If you told me my mother had died, you couldn't have caused greater shock.' As Nkrumah

---

* Salazar, the dictator of Portugal, did not espouse the French embrace of independent Africa. In February 1961, Angolan rebels, spearheaded by the People's Movement for the Liberation of Angola (MPLA), backed by Moscow and Havana, started to fight for independence, soon followed by the Liberation Front of Mozambique (Frelimo) in Mozambique. Salazar regarded the empire as essential to Portugal, embracing the singular theory of 'Lusotropicalismo' which held that the Portuguese empire was especially multicultural and multiracial and claiming that an African could in theory become president of Portugal. He encouraged Portuguese settlement in the colonies – between 1960 and 1975, 200,000 Portuguese left for Africa, and soon there were 400,000 colonists in Angola, 350,000 in Mozambique. Now he was the only European leader willing to fight a full-scale war to keep his colonies. Fifty thousand Portuguese troops crushed the African revolts, increasingly aided by units of elite African commandos who by 1970 made up 50 per cent of the Portuguese army (the most decorated officer in the army was Colonel Marcelino da Mata, a Guinean soldier who rose to command the crack Comandos Africanos). Salazar's dictatorship was showing strain: in 1958, a charismatic opposition leader, Humberto Delgado, almost won the presidency, which would have allowed him to dismiss Salazar. He went into exile, and in 1965 the secret police PIDE murdered him in Spain. Salazar's African wars were fought brutally – with massacres and beheadings – but within ten years the insurgencies had been almost crushed. US president Kennedy later advised Salazar to give his colonies independence. Salazar refused.

drove a restless Ghana towards a one-party state, seeking a Soviet alliance, Macmillan worried that the queen could be killed. 'How silly I'd look if I was scared to visit Ghana and then Khrushchev went,' she grandly told the prime minister. 'I'm not a film star. I'm the head of the Commonwealth – and I'm paid to face risks.'*

The dance was the last act in a long movement between Britain and African independence leaders. Until Suez, London had counted on keeping many colonies and imprisoned African leaders and repressed rebellions, though its rule was increasingly undermined by energetic African resistance. But, with Britain bankrupted by world wars and now focused on European defence against Russia, Macmillan released them and allowed elections. This process was very different from what had gone wrong in South Africa. In Cape Town, on 3 February 1960, Macmillan had pointedly welcomed the 'winds of change'. But South Africa was now ruled by white Afrikaners through a racist system of apartheid. Africans had never had the vote there under British rule, but in 1948 the Afrikaner National Party, campaigning on the slogan *die kaffer op sy plek* ('the African in his place'), won power with the backing of the three-million-strong white electorate and proceeded to segregate thirteen million black Africans, to disfranchise mixed-race peoples and to ban interracial sex, measures similar to Jim Crow laws in the southern US states.

Four years earlier, the British had handed Ghana to Nkrumah; ten years before that, he had been in a British prison. An Akan goldsmith's son who had attended the British Prince of Wales School in Accra as a boarder, then qualified as a teacher before studying in the US and Britain, Nkrumah regarded himself as a philosopher and historian. On his travels, he embraced Marcus Garvey's dream of a one-state Africa and had met W. E. B. Du Bois.† Winning elections in 1951, becoming premier of the newly independent Gold Coast in 1957, he renamed his country after the kings (*ghanas*) of medieval Wagadu. Attacking 'tribalism' and sidelining the Asante kings,‡ Nkrumah, a lonely, isolated man,

---

* Afterwards, Macmillan proudly called on the US president Kennedy to back the Upper Volta dam: 'I've risked my queen,' he said. 'You must risk your money.'

† As president, Nkrumah invited the ninety-three-year-old Du Bois, who had lost his US passport thanks to McCarthyist investigations into his socialist connections, to compile the *Africana* encyclopaedia in Ghana. Du Bois arrived in 1961, becoming a Ghanaian and dying in Accra, shortly before the US Civil Rights Act, the culmination of his life's work.

‡ Few of the African monarchs became rulers, partly because their prestige had been diminished by decades as figureheads. There were exceptions. In Swaziland and Lesotho, the descendants of the successful warlords of the *Mfecane* ruled as king, having shrewdly avoided being swallowed by South Africa. In Bechuanaland, Sir Seretse Khama, grandson of King Khama III, heir to another of the kingdoms that had emerged out of the *Mfecane*,

quickly instituted a one-party dictatorship with a semi-messianic cult (taking the title *Osagyefo* – Redeemer) and launched a crusade to make himself president of the united states of Africa.

At the London School of Economics, where he studied anthropology, he had encountered the other great African inspired by Du Bois, Johnstone Kamau, who changed his name to match his country.

Jomo Kenyatta, the strapping son of a Kikuyu farmer, was larger than life: educated by missionaries, he had studied in Moscow – where he disliked Marxism – and the LSE where he dazzled fellow students with his fez, cloak and silver-topped cane, and defined a new Kenyan nation in his anthropological study *Facing Mount Kenya*. After spending the war raising chickens in Sussex (where he was nicknamed Jumbo in the local pub) he went home. The British had carved several new-fangled entities out of British East Africa: one was Uganda but the largest was Kenya, named after its largest mountain. Farmed by 80,000 British settlers, famed for their cocktail-fuelled swinging (and occasional socialite murders), Kenya could have become a settler state like South Africa, but British land grabs fatally offended the Kikuyu, sparking an insurgency in 1952, called the Mau Mau uprising by the British, that killed thirty-two settlers and 2,000 Africans. The British crushed the rebels, killing 11,000, hanging 1,000, in their last colonial war in 1952, and they arrested Kenyatta – wrongly accused of leading the Mau Mau. He was in prison for seven years.

Kenyatta – known as the Burning Spear – was aided by a charismatic labour leader, Tom Mboya, a Luo, who was arranging scholarships for Kenyan youngsters. In 1960, Mboya helped send an exceptional Luo economics student named Barack Obama to study at Hawaii University.

His father, Hussein Onyango Obama, was a Luo farmer, elder and medicine man, living in western Kenya, near Uganda, so restlessly intelligent the villagers joked he had 'ants up his anus'. But he had a son, Barack, by his fourth wife, Akumu. Educating himself, Hussein moved to Zanzibar, served in the British King's African Rifles in Burma and returned at fifty with a gramophone. 'How can the African defeat the white man,' he asked, 'when he can't even make his own bicycle?' Arrested and released by the British during the Mau Mau rebellion, he became friends with Mboya. Hussein adored Barack 'because he was

---

caused a scandal in both his homeland and Britain by marrying in 1948 a white English woman, Ruth Williams – the first prominent mixed-race couple of modern times – but on his return he campaigned for independence, emerging as Botswana's first president. Khama and later his son dominated a tolerant and orderly Botswanan democracy into the twenty-first century.

so clever' but could not tolerate his independence, beating him when he was expelled from school. Barack married a local girl, Kezia, but hated the clerk's job his father arranged for him in Mombasa. After his father threw him out, he attend independence rallies, was arrested and released. He became close to Mboya, who had just got back from America, where he had been welcomed by the American Committee on Africa, led by Eleanor Roosevelt, meeting Sidney Poitier and Martin Luther King and, at the family compound at Hyannis Port, a young senator and Democratic candidate called Jack Kennedy, who agreed to fund student exchanges.

Mboya chose Obama, who left for Hawaii; Kennedy won the presidential election.

NIKITA AND JACK, MIMI AND MARILYN

Joe Kennedy was still pulling the strings but he had faced unbearable blows: his eldest son Joe had been killed in the war; his daughter Kick perished in a plane crash; and Jack was (secretly) cursed with ill health, suffering back pain, Addison's disease and hyperthyroidism, treated with steroids, amphetamines and hormones.

His father guided him into Congress straight after the war. In 1953, just after Jack's election as senator, he married an elegantly ice-cool socialite, Jackie Bouvier, with whom he had a boy and a girl, but soon after his marriage he underwent massive back surgery. Ill health and Kennedy machismo encouraged a life of risk taking and womanizing; he often joined his friend Sinatra – supercool maestro of Swing – and his Rat Pack of actor pals, including Kennedy brother-in-law Pat Lawford and African-American Sammy Davis Jr – in Vegas, where singer and senator shared girls and jinks. Kennedy was already the best-prepared candidate for the presidency: a Harvard graduate who had studied at the LSE, travelled all over the world and met everyone, war hero and Pulitzer-prize winning author. Yet he had never run anything, his sex life was recklessly priapic, his health dubious, and his career had been funded by his rich father. He was already running for president when he first encountered Khrushchev.

In September 1959, the Russian visited the US, the first Russian leader to visit the continent. He had learned from the Suez crisis that nuclear threats won him respect and an invitation from Eisenhower. His pugnacious joviality – after the morose, saturnine Stalin – amazed the Americans. On the trip, he saw into the future when he visited the

research campus of International Business Machines, IBM, but characteristically was more impressed by their canteen than their technology
and understandably more excited by meeting Marilyn Monroe. But he
also met Kennedy.

After the successful visit, Khrushchev's detente with Eisenhower was
destroyed by his discovery of US spy flights over the USSR. Outraged,
he went on a hypomaniacal rampage that made his own comrades
wonder if he was completely sane. He ordered a U2 spy plane shot down
but then ranted at the Americans. When Macmillan visited Moscow to
mediate, Khrushchev screamed at him, afterward boasting that he had
'fucked the prime minister in the arse with a telephone pole'. At the
UN, he banged his fists on the table and then smacked it with his shoe
(to the embarrassment of his own comrades). 'It was such fun!' he said
afterwards. Loathing Eisenhower and his vice-president Richard Nixon,
he believed his strength had undermined the latter's campaign, not only
welcoming the election of the Massachusetts princeling but claiming,
'We helped elect Kennedy.'

What looked like glamour to the Americans appeared to Khrushchev
to be callowness. The Kennedy takeover of Washington was compared
to a family of *condottieri* seizing a small town in Renaissance Italy. But
they were better than that, bringing Camelot – the father's vulgarity
refined by one generation at Harvard into American class spangled with
showbusiness – to Eisenhower's dull Washington. It was very much
a macho family business with brother Bobby as attorney-general and
chief henchman, and an entourage of family retainers and friendly
stars led by Sinatra, champion of civil rights, Mafia intermediary and
Inaugural Gala organizer, who arranged lovers. 'If I don't have sex every
day,' he told the cerebral, asexual Macmillan, 'I get a headache.' His
lovers varied from a courtesan, Judith Exner, introduced by Sinatra, and
pop singer Phyllis McGuire, both shared with Sinatra's friend, Chicago
Mafia boss Sam Giancana, to Marilyn Monroe, shared with his brother
Bobby, as well as his two secretaries nicknamed Fiddle and Faddle and
a tall posh intern, Mimi Alford.

On her fourth day in the White House, Mimi was invited by the First
Friend and presidential procurer Dave Powers to a swimming party,
which led to cocktails and then to a euphemistic invitation: 'Would
you like a tour of the residence, Mimi?' A tour of the residence usually
included a tour of JFK. Mimi 'cannot describe what happened that night
as making love' – she called him 'Mister President' even when naked
in Jackie's bed – but it was 'sexual, intimate, passionate', and later he
introduced amyl nitrite poppers into their assignations.

JFK displayed his nastier side when, at the White House pool, he ordered her to give oral sex to Powers: 'I don't think the president thought I'd do it, but I'm ashamed to say that I did. The president silently watched.' Calling himself 'Michael Carter' when he phoned her, she called him 'the Great Compartmentaliser', a quality essential for any leader. Indeed, 'There was always a layer of reserve.'

Kennedy's court was tightly controlled. JFK's confidence allowed him to appoint the most gifted advisers and aim high at the essential reforms. A century after the civil war, racial apartheid still ruled the south, where African-Americans were segregated and could not vote. JFK was no liberal on race but he gingerly embraced long-overdue civil rights, pushed by a rising movement led by Martin Luther King, the son of the Atlanta pastor who had visited Berlin in 1934.

The pastor had often thrashed Martin junior, but 'Whenever you whipped him, he'd stand there, and the tears would run down, and he'd never cry.' His father had joined the National Association for the Advancement of Colored People, committed to campaigning against 'the ridiculous nature of segregation in the south', telling a rally, 'I ain't gonna plow no more mules. I'll never step off the road again to let white folks pass.' His son recalled how when a policeman stopped him for a traffic offence and called him 'boy', his father pointed at Martin junior: 'This is a boy. I'm a man and until you call me one I will not listen to you.' So dapper he was nicknamed Tweedy, Martin junior studied in Boston, attending classes at Harvard and showed off his resonant eloquence on a musical student, Coretta Scott, with whom he was set up.

'I'm like Napoleon at Waterloo,' he said on the phone, 'before your charms.'

'You haven't even met me yet,' she laughed. When they were married, he tried to keep her out of the campaign, looking after their children. Serving as co-pastor of their Atlanta church with his father, he campaigned with him, in 1955 looking for a case to challenge segregation laws: when Rosa Parks, an African-American woman in Montgomery, Alabama, refused to give up her seat on a bus to a white person and was arrested, the case sparked a campaign against Jim Crow. MLK organized a bus boycott; his house was bombed, but he emerged as the leader of the Southern Christian Leadership Conference, pushing JFK to cancel the Jim Crow laws. When MLK was arrested during the presidential election campaign, the Kennedys rang to support Coretta and got him released. But once in power the Kennedys allowed the FBI to bug King's phones to discover any Communist connections – and to chronicle his adulterous affairs. Repeatedly arrested, during the spring of 1963 King

moved his campaign to Birmingham, Alabama, where the police brutally crushed protests. From a Birmingham jail, King argued that only
lawbreaking would bring change: 'The Negro's great stumbling block
in his stride toward freedom is ... the white moderate, who is more
devoted to "order" than to justice'; he added, 'Everything Hitler did in
Germany was legal.'

On 28 August, after Bobby Kennedy had ordered his release, he led
his March to Washington for Jobs and Freedom, backed by JFK. In front
of the Lincoln Memorial he addressed hundreds of thousands: 'I have a
dream that one day on the red hills of Georgia the sons of former slaves
and the sons of former slave owners will be able to sit down together at
the table of brotherhood.' Kennedy's first attempt at a Civil Rights Bill
failed, but he tried again.

As King campaigned, the young Kenyan, Barack Obama senior,
a scholar partly funded by Kennedy, had enrolled as the first African
student at Hawaii University. In early 1960, in a Russian class, Obama
met a white American anthropology student who gloried in the name
Stanley Ann Dunham. 'He was black as pitch,' wrote their son Barack
Obama later, 'my mother white as milk,' yet they were welcomed by his
grandparents. The Dunhams from Kansas, descended from a Union
soldier, a cousin of Jefferson Davis, and a Cherokee, were freethinking
liberals. After Ann brought a black girl home to play and a neighbour
said, 'You best talk to your daughter, Mr Dunham. White girls don't play
with coloreds in this town,' they moved to Hawaii.

'Brilliant, opinionated and charismatic', Obama, scholar, talker and
dandy, favouring blazers, ascot hats and smoking a pipe, was masterful,
irrepressible but also reckless and unpredictable: when a friend nudged
his pipe off a cliff, Obama senior 'picked him clear off the ground and
started dangling him over the railing'. On 4 August 1961, Ann gave
birth to a son, Barack junior, but Obama was restless and the marriage
failed. Ann started a relationship with an Indonesian student that took
mother and son to Indonesia. 'Your father could handle just about
anything,' the boy's grandfather told Barack junior later. Nonetheless,
Barack senior hardly saw his son again, moving to Harvard, where he
married a young Jewish student. But the career of the son would change
the USA – while his father, intense and troubled, returned to Kenya,
where Kenyatta, finally released by the British, and Mboya were negotiating independence.

While the new states struggled to establish themselves, Africa had
an emperor whose country – apart from six years of Italian occupation
– had never been colonized.

THE LION OF JUDAH — AND THE AFRICAN PIMPERNEL

On 13 December 1960, when Haile Selassie, now sixty-eight and in power since 1916, was visiting Brazil, a junta of his courtiers seized most of his cabinet at the Menelik Palace and launched a coup – Africa's first. Outside Ethiopia he was an African hero, the Lion of Judah; at home, he was an isolated autocrat who was building an empire.

Everything was centred in his person at the Menelik Palace, where in Amharic it was said you had to 'let your face be slapped' and 'wait a long time outside the gate' if you wanted to be noticed by the emperor.

The *negus* had formed interlocking security agencies, the Department of Public Security and the even more secret Imperial Private Cabinet which watched his own ministers, who were constantly moved from job to job, except for the devoted minister of the pen. But this tight control blinded him: he promoted a talented officer, Workneh Gebeyehu, from head of the security agency to chief of chancellery. But then the favourite suggested that the old *negus* should abdicate in favour of the crown prince. 'Workneh,' replied the *negus*, 'we're dismayed to find you're still a child. We'll continue to exercise power the Almighty has vested in us to the end. Besides: have you ever heard of anyone voluntarily relinquishing power?' Workneh conspired with two of the emperor's other favourites to overthrow the Lion. Crown Prince Asfaw Wossen agreed to broadcast a 'revolutionary proclamation' that he was now regent of a constitutional government: 'Today is the start of a new era.' But the emperor rushed back from Brazil.

At the airport, his son lay in the dust at his feet. Raising him, Haile Selassie said, 'We would have been proud of you if We were coming to attend your funeral. Get up!' Their relationship never recovered. The Lion's troops attacked the rebels in the streets of Addis. Two thousand were killed. When imperial tanks attacked the palace where the ministers were held, the rebels killed fifteen ministers and generals. The ex-favourite Workneh shot himself, and his body was strung up outside St George's Cathedral.

'There'll be no change in the system,' announced the Lion, who now moved into the new Jubilee Palace. The heir to Menelik II, he was an empire builder: after the British had occupied the Italian colony of Eritrea in 1946, the UN placed it in a federation with Ethiopia, but Haile Selassie annexed it in 1962 and banned political parties that disagreed. Like all empires, Ethiopia was held together by force. Rebellions in Eritrea and the Somalian Ogaden became festering wars of conquest.

Yet Haile Selassie was the iconic African leader. In February 1962, he invited African freedom fighters to a Pan-African Freedom Movement conference in Addis Ababa, at which, wearing a gorgeously braided, bemedalled uniform, he was the first speaker. He was followed by a South African lawyer, travelling for the first time: Nelson Mandela. The forty-three-year-old Mandela was fascinated by 'how small the emperor appeared, but his dignity and confidence made him seem like the African giant he was'. This was so even though Ethiopia was no democracy: 'Only the emperor was supreme.'

Mandela – clan name Madiba – was a prince of the Xhosa people of Thembu, in Transkei, northern Cape, descended from King Zwide. His father, counsellor of the Thembu king, was sacked for defying the British, but Mandela was adopted by his people's charismatic regent and raised with the princes. 'My later notions of leadership were influenced by observing the regent,' who groomed him to be counsellor, sending him to Methodist boarding schools. After qualifying as a lawyer and marrying a nurse Evelyn, the tall, handsome Mandela joined the African National Congress (ANC), because 'To be an African in South Africa means one's politicized from birth.' Mandela devoted his life to the campaign against apartheid. He was repeatedly arrested, his dedication leading to the estrangement of his wife, with whom he had a son. Then: 'As I passed a bus stop, I noticed out of the corner of my eye a lovely young woman waiting for the bus.' Mandela fell in love with Winnie Madikizela – 'her passion, her youth, her courage, her wilfulness' – and 'My love for her gave me added strength for the struggles that lay ahead,' and two children.

In 1960, police in Sharpeville killed sixty-nine protesters and wounded 249, igniting further protests for which Mandela was arrested. But when he was acquitted 'I became a creature of the night,' nicknamed the Black Pimpernel. He now founded the ANC's military wing – Spear of the Nation – which started a bombing campaign. Haile Selassie invited Mandela and his comrades for military training. But when he got home from Addis, the Pimpernel was arrested.

In prison, 'The officer turned a blind eye [to him and Winnie] and we embraced and clung to each other.' At his trial for high treason and terrorism Mandela, dressed not in a suit but in a Xhosa leopard-skin *kaross*, declared in a speech, 'I am prepared to die.' On 12 June 1964, he was sentenced to life imprisonment. Confined on Robben Island – from where only one prisoner had ever escaped to the mainland – the guards greeted him by chanting in Afrikaans: 'This is the island. Here you will die!' When he was defiant, they threatened, 'Look, man, we'll kill you, no fooling, your wives and children will never know what happened.'

Mandela deployed steely discipline and daily meditation to survive, writing to Winnie that prison was 'an ideal place to learn to know yourself . . . At least, if for nothing else, the cell gives you the opportunity to look daily into your entire conduct, to overcome the bad and develop whatever is good,' adding, 'Never forget a saint is a sinner who keeps on trying.' While he was away, his eldest son was killed in a crash, and Winnie often arrested. In his letters to her, he acclaimed 'your devastating beauty and charm . . . Remember, hope is a powerful weapon when all else is lost . . . You're in my thoughts every moment.' His twenty-seven years in prison corroded their marriage yet burnished his legend.

Meanwhile, on 25 May 1963, in Addis, Haile Selassie, paragon of African rulers, invited his rivals to the first meeting of his Organization of African Unity: Nkrumah, Anglophone Marxist, hoped to lead a United States of Africa with its own army; Francophone Papa, Houphouët of Ivory Coast, mocked his ambitions. Haile Selassie held the balance between the two, leading the organization before handing over to Nkrumah the Redeemer.

'I know decolonization is disastrous,' said de Gaulle privately. 'They're again going to experience tribal wars, witchcraft, cannibalism,' yet 'The Americans and Russians think they've a vocation to free colonized populations and are outbidding each other.' Khrushchev was the first to spot the opportunity of 'uprisings against rotten reactionary regimes, against colonizers', promising 'to march in the front rank with peoples fighting national liberation struggles'. The proxy wars of the superpowers – a second scramble, this time in the name of decolonization and freedom – would kill more Africans than the first.

It started in early 1960, when the Belgians had suddenly lost control of Congo. After the *Force Publique* shot demonstrators in the streets, they held elections and King Baudouin (great-grandson of Leopold II) praised Belgium's 'civilizing mission' as he conceded independence in June 1960. Meanwhile Belgium, hoping to keep control of military and resources (Congo possessed uranium among other mineral treasures), organized the overthrow of the elected first premier, Patrice Lumumba, thirty-five – a talented pan-Africanist but also a Soviet ally – by Colonel Joseph Mobutu, *Force Publique* officer, now chief of staff. Mobutu was the first of many politicised generals who demonstrated how often in the new African states, conglomerated by the colonial powers into huge new entities, the army emerged as the embodiment of the nation. Astonishingly, the Belgians ordered Lumumba's '*elimination definitive*', their agents seizing, torturing then shooting him before dissolving him in acid. A Belgian agent took one of his teeth home as a trophy. Khrushchev was infuriated as Mobutu, backed by the USA, established a baroque, kleptocratic dictatorship of Zaire that lasted for thirty years.*

JFK had promised in his inaugural address that 'In the long history of the world, only a few generations have been granted the role of defending freedom' – code for fighting Communism – 'in its hour of maximum danger. I don't shrink from this responsibility – I welcome it.' Khrushchev too sought a way to raise the stakes, but unexpectedly he found his opportunity in the Americas when another pair of brothers took power just ninety miles from Miami.

BROTHERS: THE CASTROS AND THE KENNEDYS

On 9 January 1959, the thirty-three-year-old cigar-chomping, bearded Fidel Castro, *El Comandante*, assisted by his dourer brother Raul, who directed the military, rode into Havana. The Castros were illegitimate but well-educated sons of a sugar planter, a self-made Spanish immigrant who had amassed 25,000 acres; they had been taught by Jesuits, imbibing St Ignatius' 'All dissidence is treason.' Fidel became a doctor of law but embraced revolution ('if I could be Stalin'), first joining an abortive coup in Bogotá, then, disgusted by Batista's return to power, leading the attack on the Moncada Barracks, Santiago. The brothers were captured.

Castro became famous, treating the court to a grandiloquent oration – 'History will absolve me' – but the brothers only escaped being shot thanks to their connections: Castro's wife was the sister of Batista's interior minister. When he discovered after his imprisonment that she too had joined the Interior Ministry, he divorced her; politics was all. He was verbose and loquacious, even his brother Raul complaining that in prison he never stopped talking for weeks on end.

When American pressure forced Batista to release him, Fidel fled to Mexico City, where he met Ernesto 'Che' Guevara, a handsome,

---

* Unbeknown to anyone, undetected in the confusion of Belgian withdrawal, a new disease that attacked the immune system had leaped from monkeys to humans in Congo. The first identified case of the new disease was found there in 1959, probably spread through west and central Africa after the Second World War by unclean vaccinations and sexual contact, often via blood exchanged in anal sex and through the prevalence of genital ulcers during vaginal sex. It probably reached the USA soon afterwards: Richard R, a young man who died of pneumonia in 1969, was the earliest confirmed case. Only identified in 1981, it became a pandemic that killed millions. It was later called human immunodeficiency virus (HIV) and acquired immunodeficiency syndrome (AIDS).

asthmatic doctor, son of a rich Argentine family. 'Extraordinary', said Castro, 'a person of great culture, great intelligence ... a doctor who became a soldier without ceasing to be a doctor'. The two talked all night.

In November 1956, the brothers plus eighty-one half-trained fighters boarded a leaky boat, the *Granma*, and landed in Cuba. They were heavily bombarded, and only nineteen of the eighty-one survived, but the Castros and their *barbudos* – bearded ones – launched a guerrilla war in which they were three times almost annihilated but, aided by the remoteness of the Sierra Maestra, survived. Thanks to Batista's corruption, arrogance and ineptitude, plus surprisingly some misguided CIA funding, the legend and successes of the *Fidelistas* grew. Castro himself met a young guerrilla, Celia Sánchez, a doctor's daughter, who became his lover and aide. At the darkest moments, when they had just twelve fighters left, 'Celia was with me.'

As Batista fled with millions, in January 1959 Castro set up headquarters in Havana's Hilton Hotel, ruling with Raul as war minister, Che as education minister and Celia, in whose tiny apartment he lived, as secretary of the council of ministers. Those on a death list of enemies were shot. 'We're not executing innocent people,' Fidel insisted, just 'murderers and they deserve it'. American fruit tycoons and Mafia kingpins were driven out.

The Castro brothers ruled together, but they were opposites: Fidel, an egomaniac showman and bloviating strategist; Raul, cautious and meticulous. Fidel was nicknamed *El Caballo* – the Horse – favouring one-night stands with admirers from abroad, particularly dazzled French liberals; Raul was inseparable from his wife Vilma. Yet they spoke several times a day and, when the regime was settled, they lived next to each other on Punto Cero, a heavily fortified *estancia* outside Havana. Fidel's office contained a portrait of José Martí, a signed photograph of Ernest Hemingway ('I read *For Whom the Bell Tolls* three times') and one of his own father.

Castro initially saw himself more as a Latino Alexander the Great (he named several of his sons Alexander) than as a Lenin, but, he explained, 'I had a compass – Marx and Lenin.' In February 1960, Khrushchev sent his ally Anastas Mikoyan to Havana. Mikoyan, a tough Armenian ex-seminarist who had survived the inner circles of Lenin and Stalin, advised Khrushchev to support Castro. The combination of the impulsively manic ex-miner Khrushchev and the highly strung, narcissistic Cuban intellectual was about to bring the world to the edge of catastrophe.

Kennedy inherited CIA plans to invade Cuba. On 17 April 1961 his invasion, using 1,400 Cuban émigrés and a few American planes, landed at the Bay of Pigs but was easily repelled by Castro: although hundreds of Castro's militia were killed, he captured a thousand of the émigrés, and executed hundreds. 'Thanks for Playa Girón,' he wrote to JFK, referring to the beach where the raiders had landed. 'Before the invasion, the revolution was weak. Now it's stronger.' JFK soon sacked Allen Dulles from the CIA.* Although he had despised the Mafia corruption in Havana, even sympathizing with Castro, he ordered the Cuban's liquidation – with Mafia assistance. The CIA recruited Meyer Lansky, Santo Trafficante and Giancana. At least eight attempts, including poisoned diving gear, cigars, toothpaste, failed. 'There were dozens of plans,' said Castro, 'some close to succeeding,' but 'chance sometimes intervened against them'. Khrushchev was unimpressed by Kennedy.

Inconsistency was the only consistent thing about Khrushchev. On 4 June 1961, the two men met in Vienna, where the pugnacious Khrushchev almost crushed JFK, twenty-three years younger but medicated for his back pain. 'If the US starts a war over Germany,' Khrushchev shouted, 'let it be so' – a chilling moment in a depressing encounter. 'It's going to be a cold winter,' concluded JFK. He was crestfallen. 'He just beat the hell out of me,' he said. But he hardened himself.

Khrushchev mocked JFK as 'very inexperienced, even immature'. He first hoped to force Kennedy out of west Berlin. 'Berlin is the testicles of the west,' said Khrushchev, 'every time I want the west to scream, I squeeze.' But the testicles survived the squeezing. It was his frontline satellite, East Germany, a grim totalitarian dystopia policed by the omniscient Stasi, that was fragile. So many citizens were escaping to western plenty that Khrushchev ordered the building of the Berlin Wall to confine its people. Now he mulled over Kennedy's threat to Cuba. 'The most important consideration in the power struggle of our time', he decided was that 'those with weak nerves go to the wall'. He would test those nerves. 'It's like playing chess in the dark.'

INSTALL NUCLEAR WEAPONS IN CUBA: THE MILLIONAIRE'S WHORE AND THE IMMORAL GANGSTER

After the Bay of Pigs, 'one thought', recalled Khrushchev, 'kept hammering away at my brain, "What if we lose Cuba?"' In May 1962, he

---

* 'How could I have been so stupid?' he exclaimed, reflecting the danger of self-delusion among isolated potentates. 'You get walled off from reality when you want something to succeed too much.'

had an idea for his comrades: 'Fidel would be crushed if another inva-sion were launched,' but if he placed ballistic missiles on Cuba 'such a disaster' could be prevented, plus they would 'equalize the balance of power': the Americans had just installed missiles in Türkiye, right on his borders. The grandees acquiesced before the bombastic Khrushchev, but Mikoyan had a question. The Americans would strike the missiles: 'What are we supposed to do then – respond with a strike on US soil?' Mikoyan was overruled. 'Install nuclear rocket weapons. Transport se-cretly. Disclose later,' recorded the minutes. 'This will be an offensive policy.'

Within days, the Castros were informed. 'The best way to safeguard Cuba,' replied Fidel. 'We're willing to accept all the missiles.' Khrush-chev told his comrades he was stuffing 'a hedgehog' down Uncle Sam's pants. In July as plans were made, Raul Castro and Che Guevara visited Moscow, asking, 'What precautions have you taken in case the operation is discovered?'

'Don't worry,' beamed Khrushchev, 'there'll be no big reaction and if there is, I'll send the Baltic Fleet.' Later he suggested, 'I'll grab Kennedy by the balls and make him negotiate,' adding that, like a peasant who brings his goat into his hut for winter and gets used to the stink, Kenne-dy would 'learn to accept the smell of the missiles'.*

On 26 July 1962, a Soviet armada departed from Odessa bearing 44,000 troops and six atomic bombs, along with eighteen nuclear cruise missiles, three divisions of tactical nuclear weapons and six bombers. In August they started installing the missiles: it is likely Khrushchev permitted his commander to use the tactical weapons – if necessary. American intelligence noticed activity in Cuba but had missed massive activity in Odessa and never realized the full extent of the Soviet deploy-ment.†

---

* It was a moment when modern humans started to glimpse the implications of their total domination of the planet. In 1960, an American scientist, Charles David Keeling, taking temperature measurements in Hawaii, revealed how rising CO_2 and 'greenhouse gases' in the atmosphere, emitted by the burning of coal and oil, as well as deforestation and intense agriculture, the result of industrialization over the last two centuries of human development, were causing the earth to heat up, a process, predicted in his Keeling Curve, that could produce irreversible and catastrophic damage. Simultaneously, Herman Kahn, a systems theorist, was warning of nuclear war, publishing on 1 January 1962 a book entitled *Thinking about the Unthinkable*, which posited sixteen (later raised to forty-four) stages culminating in 'Spasm/Insensate War'.

† On 19 May, JFK had celebrated his forty-fifth birthday at a fundraiser where Marilyn Monroe, in a beaded dress, breathily sang 'Happy Birthday', the apogee of Kennedy Camelot. Monroe had been introduced by her ex-lover Sinatra, who occupied a unique place in US culture at the nexus of entertainment, presidential power and organized crime. She had affairs with both JFK and Bobby (father of eleven children with a long-suffering

On 14 October, a US spy plane revealed some of the missiles in Cuba, throwing JFK into an existential world crisis. He had found the hedgehog in his pants. 'He can't do this to me,' he said, calling Khrushchev 'a fucking liar', an 'immoral gangster'. It was the biggest crisis any president would face, and ultimately he proved his acumen, telling his Executive Committee, 'Gentlemen, we're going to earn our pay today.'

Kennedy listened as his hawkish aides proposed surgical attacks on the missiles, a plan supported by nine members of his Executive Committee against seven who supported a blockade. But he quickly switched to blockading Cuba and announced a press conference. In the Kremlin, Khrushchev panicked: 'That's it! Lenin's work has been destroyed.' Mikoyan and the Presidium, all Second World War veterans fearful of war, were alarmed by his recklessness. Khrushchev was afraid that an invasion was imminent, and admitted, 'The tragedy is they can attack and we'll respond. This could escalate into large-scale war.' Khrushchev urged his commanders to 'Make all efforts initially not to use atomic weaponry,' and now stressed that Moscow's authorization would be required for their deployment.

In Washington, JFK announced instead a quarantine of Cuba and demanded removal of weapons. At the ExComm, 'we'd taken the first step,' recalled Bobby, '– and we were still alive.' JFK permitted his trigger-happy generals to plan air strikes – all of them unaware that a full nuclear arsenal was on the island – but 'it looks like hell', he told Bobby, 'doesn't it!' JFK was obsessed with a history book, *The Guns of August* by Barbara Tuchman, about the start of the First World War, which he and his aides had read. 'They somehow seemed to tumble into war,' he said, through 'stupidity, individual idiosyncrasies, misunderstandings, and personal complexes of inferiority and grandeur'. Never has a historian been so important.

In Moscow, a jumpy Khrushchev ordered some of the Soviet ships to turn back; in Washington, keen to test the quarantine, JFK was delighted to see the six ships turn, but ordered the stopping of all of them. 'His face seemed drawn, his eye pained,' noted Bobby. The order to stop the other ships, which would have led to confrontation, was withdrawn just in time. 'For a moment the world had stood still and now it was going

wife) between failed marriages to baseball star Joe DiMaggio and playwright Arthur Miller. Marilyn suffered bitterly from the wounds of a desolate childhood in foster homes, and she was cold-shouldered when she fell for Bobby. In August, she was found dead of an overdose of sleeping pills, the Kennedys suppressing any evidence of their liaisons. Her life personified American glamour at the height of the American Century, her death the fragility of beauty and the darkness of fame.

round again.' In Moscow, a sleepless Khrushchev 'swore at Washington, threatened to nuke the White House', but then calmed down and led his comrades off to watch *Boris Godunov* at the Bolshoi. 'It'll have a calming effect,' said Khrushchev. 'If Khrushchev and other leaders are sitting in the theatre, then everyone can sleep soundly.' But the next morning, when he learned of a tightening of the blockade, he cursed 'like a bargeman', stamping his foot. 'I'm gonna crush that viper!' he bellowed. JFK was 'a millionaire's whore'.

While Khrushchev was calming down, Kennedy sent Jackie and the children out of Washington and raised DEFCON (Defence Readiness Condition) to Level 2,* just short of war, a move that so alarmed Khrushchev that he told Mikoyan he was withdrawing the missiles in return for 'promises the Americans won't attack Cuba'. He dictated a long, meandering letter offering a mix of peace and defiance. But the crisis was still escalating: Castro ordered the shooting down of any US aeroplanes and prepared for an imminent American invasion, staying up all night at the Soviet embassy, drinking beer and eating sausages. It was now he decided that the best course was nuclear war.

Khrushchev had been reading translations of articles by the powerful *Washington Post* columnist Walter Lippman, who had suggested a solution: removal of American missiles from Türkiye in return for removal of Soviet missiles from Cuba. No journalist in history has ever been so influential. With this idea, Khrushchev sent a second less conciliatory letter to JFK, who dispatched his brother to discuss the plan with the Soviet ambassador. As the president relaxed somewhat, Special Assistant Dave Powers summoned his teenage lover, the intern Mimi. Yet though he chatted to her, JFK's 'expression was grave . . . even his quips had a half-hearted, funereal tone': 'I'd rather my children were red than dead,' he said before sending her alone off to bed while he watched a movie, *Roman Holiday*.

* Since 1959, the Pentagon had been working on a 'survivable' communications system that would function if a nuclear strike destroyed telephone cables and radio networks. Paul Baran, a Polish-born Jewish scientist whose family had arrived in America in 1928 and who now worked for the Rand Corporation, had just created a cheap, quick new way of sending data separated into what he called 'message blocks', findings he published in his *On Distributed Communications*. Demonstrating how 'discoveries' are the result of cumulative knowledge, a British engineer, Donald Davies, simultaneously developed the same idea though he called the data 'packets'. In 1967, the two shared their 'packet switching' ideas, Baran telling Davies, 'You and I share a common view of what packet switching is all about, since you and I independently came up with the same ingredients.' In 1969, the Pentagon's Advanced Research Projects Agency used their work to create a network to communicate between computers. Over the next twenty years, a galaxy of scientists developed the technology out of which came the internet and email.

The leaders were moving towards the deal, yet soldiers and weapons were still moving towards war. Khrushchev now received Castro's letter: 'the imperialists might initiate a nuclear strike against the USSR', suggested Fidel, so the 'moment would be right' to launch nuclear strikes on America. 'However difficult and horrifying this decision may be, there is I believe no other recourse.' It remains the most terrifying letter ever written by a leader. Khrushchev was horrified: 'When this was read to us, we, sitting in silence, looked at one another for a long time.'

'You proposed we carry out a nuclear first strike,' he wrote to Castro. 'This wouldn't be a simple attack but the start of a thermonuclear world war.'

'We knew we'd be exterminated . . . should a thermonuclear war break out,' responded Castro, 'and if such an event occurred, what would one do with the madmen who unleashed the war?'

Soviet troops were permitted to resist with anything non-nuclear – and they shot down an American plane and killed a pilot. Bobby told the Soviet ambassador that his brother could withdraw the Turkish missiles in '4–5 months' but 'can't say anything public', adding, 'Time is of the essence.' This was no exaggeration: off Bermuda, US ships dropped non-lethal depth charges to signal to a nuclear-armed Soviet submarine, the B-59, that it should surface. Yet the officers of B-59 had had no contact with Moscow and only knew of negotiations from American radio. Around midday on 27 October, Captain Savitsky, believing the two superpowers were at war, ordered the launch of a T5 nuclear missile: 'Prepare [nuclear] torpedo tube 1 and 2 for firing!' But his commander, Akhipov, using the sub as a command centre, overruled him and convinced him to surface, where an American ship flashed its searchlights in a friendly gesture. Savitsky understood and ordered: 'Stop preparations for firing.' It was the closest the world came to nuclear war.

At his dacha at Novo-Ogarevo outside Moscow (later Vladimir Putin's residence), Khrushchev persuaded his comrades, Mikoyan and his protégé, the titular head of state Leonid Brezhnev, to take JFK's offer of Cuba for Türkiye: 'To save humanity, we should retreat.'

In Washington, JFK was so relieved 'I feel like a new man,' he told Powers. 'Do you realize we had an air strike all arranged for Tuesday. Thank God it's all over.' But when Khrushchev informed Havana, Castro was incandescently defiant. Khrushchev suggested 'we offer friendly advice: show patience, restraint and more restraint', and sent Mikoyan, even though his wife Ashken was dying in Moscow, to Havana, where he told Castro the missiles were going home. In private, Castro called

Khrushchev a 'bastard . . . asshole', and ranted, '*No cojones!* No balls! *Maricon!* Homosexual!' At a later meeting on 22 November, Castro refused to allow UN inspections and raged at Mikoyan: 'We didn't agree with the removal of the missiles . . . What do you think we are? A zero on the left, a dirty rag.' Then he bid for nuclear weapons.

Castro: We took the risk . . . We were even prepared for a nuclear war . . .

Mikoyan: We were also prepared to make sacrifices for Cuba.

Castro: Doesn't the Soviet Union transfer nuclear weapons to other countries?

Mikoyan: We've a law prohibiting the transfer of any nuclear weapon.

Castro: Would it be possible to leave the tactical nuclear weapons in Cuba . . .

Mikoyan: No, Comrade Fidel, it would not be possible.

Mikoyan learned his wife had died, and sent his son Sergo[*] home to attend the funeral, which Khrushchev oafishly refused to attend himself: 'I don't like funerals, it's not like attending a wedding is it?' The ballistic weapons were removed, even the atom bombs and tactical nuclear weapons – the ones the Americans hadn't known about.

The crisis was over.

Khrushchev denounced the Cuban: 'Because he's young, he couldn't behave himself.' But the crisis had shown, he said, 'we are members of the World Club' and defended himself: 'It's not necessary to act like the tsarist officer who farted at the ball and then shot himself.' It had been a bit more than a fart at a ball. 'I cut his balls off,' exulted JFK, who resumed the affair with Mimi. Kennedy and Khrushchev, who had terrified each other, hinted through aides that it was time to reduce nuclear weapons and agreed to establish a hotline – actually a teleprinter – to avoid future crises. Each side tested the hotline – the US quoting Shakespeare, the Soviets Chekhov: it would be used sooner than anyone guessed.

'We have a problem making our power credible,' said JFK, 'and Vietnam looks like the place.' Khrushchev regarded Ho Chi Minh as a Red 'saint' but gave limited backing to the Vietnamese, monitoring more US personnel arriving in Thailand and South Vietnam. Kennedy, riding high after Cuba, hated – and was hated by – the two Asian leaders who most resembled him.

---

[*] Sergo Mikoyan, who had accompanied his father as his aide, recounted the drama of the journey to this author. 'My father said, "The future of the world requires that my mission succeed. That's it." You can appreciate it was a very tense flight but my father was always calm. He was used to high tension: after all, he had lived with Stalin for thirty years!'

SIHANOUK AND THE SHAH

Prince Sihanouk, charismatic playboy, now in love with a teenaged Eurasian beauty queen named Monique who became his chief but not only lover, often compared to Jackie Kennedy, was trying to keep Cambodia neutral. Sihanouk joined the non-aligned movement, led by Nasser, Nehru and Sukarno, which leaned strongly towards the Soviets. But in Indo-China, where even the US and USSR agreed to a neutral Laos, there was little space for real neutrality. After a breathing space following the French withdrawal, Ho Chi Minh and his younger more aggressive comrade Le Duan ordered General Giap to infiltrate South Vietnam, now ruled by another set of siblings, President Ngo Dinh Diem and his brothers.[*]

Kennedy raised the number of American military advisers from 1,000 to 16,000, and pressured Sihanouk to resist Communist encroachment. The CIA approved Sihanouk's assassination, organized by the Ngos, but the prince survived the bomb. Kennedy himself was exasperated by the Ngos, who were brutally crushing mounting Buddhist protests. In November 1963, just twenty days before JFK went to Dallas, the Ngos were deposed by their generals and bayoneted, though Madame Nhu survived because she was abroad. Sihanouk, growing close to China, resented JFK's menaces.

Similarly, JFK had much in common with the shah – the same age, both athletic playboy sons of domineering self-made moguls, both married to cool-blooded fashion icons. But tragically Queen Soraya could not have children; after the shah, now forty, had begged her to allow him

---

[*] In the tiny elite of Vietnam, Ho Chi Minh and the younger General Giap had both attended the French lycée, Quoc Hoc, in Hue founded by the Catholic Vietnamese official who was father of President Ngo Dinh Diem. Giap and President Ngo were pupils at the same time. After rising to provincial governor, Ngo collaborated with the Japanese against the French. Appointed as premier by the last emperor of Annam, he removed the monarchy and as president the celibate, puritanical Catholic, who surrounded himself with handsome young men, led a murderous kleptocratic dynasty. One of his brothers, Nhu, Hitler admirer and drug addict, ran Ngo's party and secret police, which he modelled on the SS; his wife Madame Nhu was beautiful, fiery, always gorgeously attired and packing a pistol. Of the others, Thuc was archbishop of Hue, Can ran Hue, and Luyen was ambassador to London. But all of them lived in the presidential palace. The irrepressible Madame Nhu terrorized the president and her husband, declaring, 'Power is wonderful, total power totally wonderful,' and adopted a moralistic programme, burning pornography and trying to ban prostitution – while complaining that her husband neglected to have sex with her. When monks burned themselves alive in protest at Ngo predations, Madame Nhu called them 'barbecues': 'Let them burn!' she said, and menaced her enemies: 'We'll track down and exterminate all these scabby sheep.' Vietnamese were horrified by her; Americans half appalled, half fascinated.

to take a second wife, they divorced and in 1959 he married a young, high-spirited architecture student, Farah Diba, wearing a wedding dress by Yves Saint Laurent. Farah was more liberal, more open to change than he was. They had two sons and two daughters, and her elegance too was compared to that of Jackie Kennedy. Both JFK and Moham-mad Pahlavi were risk-taking womanizers and clients of the Parisian Madame Claude.*

Yet president and shah hated each other. In the ten years since the fall of Mosaddegh, the shah had emerged as the rising power of the region. While coping with a welter of conspiracies, he renegotiated the oil deals with the west and in 1960 he was one of the founders of OPEC, the oil producers' organization, managing to be close to both Saudis and Is-raelis, whom he respected and liked. Playing the Americans against the Soviets, he chose the former as allies but resented their interference. He created a secret police, SAVAK, to hunt Communists, many of whom he executed, and to confront the constant plots against him.

JFK regarded the shah as an inefficient tyrant, advising that he appoint a Kennedy ally as premier. Bristling with pride and planning revolution and rearmament, the shah was incensed but agreed, convinced JFK was trying to overthrow him. When the shah and Farah visited Kennedy at the White House, the meetings were chilly. On the shah's return, his firm treatment of the ayatollahs finally convinced JFK that he could be a useful ally.

On 9 January 1963, the shah launched his Shah and People Revo-lution, to industrialize, distribute land and grant female rights, but it outraged the *ulema* – Islamic jurists – led by Ruhollah Khomeini. The glowering ayatollah, sixty-three years old, seemed the very model of a medieval mullah, but he was also an innovator. Backed by Fadayan-e Islam, the secret network of terrorist extremists who had assassinat-ed several ministers, Khomeini was developing an extraordinary idea that involved rejection of secular rule altogether: as Shiites awaited the messianic emergence of the occulted Mahdi, they should adopt rule by an Islamic judicial guardian – *velayat-e faqih* – and probably Khomeini

---

* 'There are two things that people will always pay for: food and sex,' Madame Claude said. 'I wasn't any good at cooking.' Claude (Fernande Grudet), proprietor of Paris's leading *maison close*, specialized in sophisticated middle-class girls, often second-rank actresses and models, who were not full-time professionals. Almost the carnal division of the French intelligence services throughout the 1960s, her clients included film stars (such as Marlon Brando), plutocrats (Rothschilds, the Italian Fiat magnate Agnelli, the Greek shipping tycoon Aristotle Onassis, who later married Jackie Kennedy) and potentates from the shah and Saudi fixer Muhammad Khashoggi to President Kennedy, who on his visit memorably requested a girl 'like Jackie. But hot.'

was already thinking of himself. Most of the *ulema* regarded the idea as eccentric if not bizarre.

On Ashura, 3 June 1963, Khomeini denounced the 'wretched miserable' shah, comparing him to the Umayya caliph Yazid who had killed the first imam Husain on that day. The shah turned to his trusted premier, Asadollah Alam, a debonair landowner who had given away his estates and prosecuted corrupt officials. 'Guns and cannon are in my hand . . . I'll tear their mothers apart.' On 5 June, Alam arrested Khomeini, sparking days of riots that were suppressed by the army, which shot 400 dead. Temporarily moving his trusted Alam aside, the shah appointed a new premier, Hassan Ali Mansur, who berated Khomeini and slapped his face. Dispatched into exile in Iraq, Khomeini ordered Mansur's assassination. Yet the shah had triumphed. Khomeini was irrelevant and obsolete.

The shah, appointing his friend Alam as court minister, a job more important than premier in an absolute monarchy, had won time to put his revolution into practice. His aims were admirable, his execution flawed, yet the shah successfully promoted Iran as 'the key to a vast region', receiving massive US armaments, while supporting western allies Morocco, Jordan and Israel.* Iran countered a radical Iraq by backing a rebellion by its Kurds.

The shah was admired by Alam as 'a determined, demanding reformer', a meritocrat who liked to say, 'Where did the Pahlavis begin? My father was a simple soldier from the provinces.' Negotiating everything himself, the shah trusted no one, and complained of the stress. His recreation was hardly different from that of any other potentate, but Alam's diaries reveal the details. The marriage with Farah was happy, yet he and Alam enjoyed flying in 'visitors' – Madame Claude's call girls, who were paid in jewels. Sounding exactly like JFK, he said sex was his 'only relaxation . . . If it weren't for this little indulgence of mine, I'd be an utter wreck.' Queen Farah, intelligent, sensitive, 'a moderating influence', disliked Alam, knowing that 'her husband and I go philandering together'.

At home, the shah's policies had created a literate middle class, and millions of peasants moved to the cities to work. Yet the shah offered

---

* Israel was still dependent on French weaponry, though de Gaulle had ended any nuclear assistance. America was just starting to supply Israel with weaponry but JFK was infuriated by its nuclear programme. When Shimon Peres, its mastermind, visited the White House, JFK asked him about the nuclear weapons; he replied with deliberate vagueness, 'I can tell you clearly that we shall not introduce atomic weapons to the region. We shan't be the first to do so.'

no participation in government, the oil money was frittered away on luxury, corruption and armaments instead of alleviating poverty, while SAVAK resorted to torture to crush dissent. But as his friend the duke of Edinburgh, who stayed with him, told this author, 'The shah shows it is dangerous and difficult if you try to do everything yourself.' The shah, spoiled by success and ever more grandiose, felt his rise was providential – a view confirmed when his enemy in the White House went on campaign to Dallas.

EXIT KENNEDY: LBJ AND MLK

In Dallas, on 22 November 1963, JFK, riding in an open limousine with Jackie, chic personified in a pink Chanel suit, was shot in the skull and throat by an assassin, Lee Harvey Oswald, probably operating alone. As sections of his brain spattered her suit, Jackie crawled out of the back of the limousine and was rescued by a bodyguard as the convoy sped to the hospital, where the president was declared dead. His successor Lyndon Johnson, a Brobdingnagian tough, self-made Texan machine-politician and congressional maestro who had hated the vice-presidency ('not worth a bucket of warm spit', said LBJ, quoting one of FDR's veeps) and the smug Kennedys, took the oath of office on Air Force One beside Jackie in her bloodied Chanel.

LBJ ordered the hotline used for the first time to inform Moscow of the assassination. Khrushchev, who feared the Soviets would be blamed, believed that JFK had been killed by conservatives to stop any detente with Moscow. Khrushchev sent Mikoyan, who had been a bearer of Lenin's coffin in 1924, to Kennedy's funeral.

LBJ, whose style of leadership was 'If you can't fuck a man in the ass, then just peckerslap him – better to let him know who's in charge than to let him get the keys to the car,' proved a surprise, determined to force through civil rights. He resented the respect he owed the Kennedys. Now Bobby mourned Jack in a romance of grief with his widow Jackie. LBJ hated Bobby and his 'Harvards'; Bobby hated him back. 'Bobby, you don't like me,' Johnson had once said to him. 'Your brother likes me . . . Why don't you like me?' Bobby admitted that LBJ was 'the most formidable human being I've ever met. He just eats up strong men,' but he regarded him as 'almost an animal'. LBJ kept Bobby as attorney-general, in charge of civil rights.

'Until justice is blind to color, until education is unaware of race,' promised LBJ, 'until opportunity is unconcerned with the color of

men's skins, emancipation will be a proclamation but not a fact.' Yet
his decency was always infected with oafish pragmatism: 'I'll have those
n*****s voting Democrat for the next 200 years.' On 2 July 1964, the
Civil Rights Act outlawed racial discrimination and segregation. In
March 1965, Martin Luther King launched a campaign for voting rights
in Selma, Alabama, where police brutality on Bloody Sunday exposed
how much Jim Crow, like slavery, was based on violence. Two days after
King had led a prayer session on the Edmund Pettus Bridge, LBJ, the
most successful legislator in presidential history, backed the Voting
Rights Bill, signed into law on 6 August 1965. King wept: after 300
years of slavery and apartheid, the liberation of African-Americans had
started. But it would take more than two statutes to overturn the prejudices of centuries.

The shah did not mourn JFK, even drafting a critical letter to LBJ that
Alam refused to send, but he too lived under the gun. He had already
been shot once by an assassin. Soon after JFK's murder, an Islamicized
bodyguard tried to shoot the shah in his office: after dodging machine-
gun fire, he carried on coolly with his day, commenting, 'Thieves never
hit the same house twice.'

In the Kremlin, Johnson faced a new team. Castro, safe but humiliated, had no choice but to forgive Khrushchev, whose own comrades
could not. At 4 p.m. on 13 October 1964, the seventy-year-old Khrushchev walked into the Presidium in the Kremlin. He had been on holiday
in Abkhazia on the Black Sea when Brezhnev had suddenly called
him back: 'We can't decide without you!' Khrushchev flew back. At the
meeting Brezhnev suddenly denounced him for dictatorship, blundering, boozing, 'contradicting Lenin', 'making decisions over lunch' and
calling the Presidium a pack of 'male dogs peeing on kerbstones'. Now
the pee was aimed at him.

The fifty-seven-year-old Leonid 'Lyonia' Brezhnev, ursine and bushy-
browed, unpretentious and jovial, had been Khrushchev's protégé
since the 1930s, a Russian lathe worker's son from east Ukraine who
had served on the Ukrainian front with his patron, then been selected
by Stalin for promotion. He was one of the team that arrested Beria,
backing Khrushchev against the Stalinist grandees (and fainting in the
middle of the drama), and was promoted to deputy Party leader. But
he disapproved of the denunciations of Stalin, was embarrassed by
Khrushchev's tantrums and was most appalled by the disaster of Cuba.
'Before the war,' Khrushchev said mockingly of Brezhnev, 'the boys
nicknamed him the Ballerina' because 'anyone who wants can turn
him around'. In June 1964, Brezhnev started to plot but was so nervous

that he almost wept – 'Khrushchev knows everything. All is lost. He'll shoot us' – and even wrote fake diary entries: 'Met Nikita Sergeievich. Joyous pleasant meeting.' Brezhnev recruited the KGB and suggested they murder Khrushchev or arrange an accident for his plane. But in October 1964, when Khrushchev was enjoying his holiday at Pitsunda, Brezhnev set the trap, calling to order his return to Moscow.

'You're suffering from megalomania,' a grandee shouted at Khrushchev, 'and the illness is incurable.' But Cuba was his ultimate sin. 'Juggling the fate of the world,' said another. 'Neither the Russian nor the Soviet army,' said a third, 'had ever suffered such a humiliation.'

'I can't make bargains with my conscience,' concluded Brezhnev. 'Dismiss Comrade Khrushchev from the posts he holds and divide them up.'

'You gathered together and splattered shit on me,' said Khrushchev, 'and I can't object . . . I'm old and tired.' But his real achievement? 'The fear is gone and we can talk as equals. That's my contribution.' Khrushchev was not shot. While Mikoyan became head of state, the veteran Alexei Kosygin became premier and Brezhnev became Party leader, soon taking Stalin's old title of general secretary. But he was no Stalin – and no Khrushchev either.

Hashemites and Kennedys, Maos, Nehruvians and Assads

LYONIA THE BALLERINA: BREZHNEV IN POWER

Brezhnev was energetic and sharp, good-natured and humorous, a cautious realist, always making jokes, giving nicknames and laughing loudly. His judgements on American politics and foreign leaders were surprisingly on point, and in the Kremlin he tried 'to win over his interlocutors and create a free and open atmosphere for conversation', recalled the young secretary of Stavropol, Mikhail Gorbachev, whom he always teased about his 'sheep empire'. A hard-drinking, hard-hunting *muzhik* and womanizer, both vainglorious and self-deprecating, Brezhnev collected fast cars and undeserved medals: visiting Berlin, when given a new Mercedes by his East German vassal Honecker, he drove so recklessly he crashed it on a sharp right turn.

After promoting himself to the marshalate, he was derided for bellowing, 'Make way for the marshal,' but on Marxist scholarship he joked, 'You don't expect Lyonia Brezhnev to have actually read all that.' He kept a diary, Habsburgian in its dullness: 'Killed 34 geese' was a typical entry. 'With Lyonia, all I had to do was tell a few jokes,' recalled KGB chief Semichastny, 'and that was it.' While the Americans were convinced that the Soviets were the puppet masters, the Vietnamese made their own decisions, and Mao was now asserting himself.

In Hanoi, as the venerable Ho retired, Le Duan escalated their war, infiltrating 40,000 regular troops into the south to join 800,000 Viet Cong guerrillas. 'The Communist threat,' said Johnson 'must be crushed with strength.'* By the end of 1965, he had deployed 200,000

---

* LBJ saw Communist advances everywhere: like JFK, he was terrified of a 'new Cuba' in south America, encouraging a military coup – '*Golpe de 1964*' – against the leftist president of Brazil, João Goulart, who in April 1964 was overthrown by a junta that ruled for twenty years, arresting over 40,000 and killing at least 333, all supposedly Communists, and probably several hundred more. In Indonesia, a similar process sparked the bloodiest Cold War coup of all. The maverick showman Sukarno defied American influence but also mocked the Soviets for being white and arrogant, meanwhile consolidating his own dictatorship backed by a popular Communist Party. LBJ ordered the CIA to overthrow him, but Sukarno

troops and was bombing the north. He underplayed US escalation: 'If you have a mother-in-law with only one eye . . . in the center of her forehead,' he explained, 'you don't keep her in the living room.' Sihanouk, now Cambodian head of state, was at his height, ruling absolutely, giving long speeches, boasting of sexual conquests, performing his own jazz songs with his band and presenting ballets starring his own beautiful daughter. He also assassinated opponents, and allowed Monique's family to make fortunes as the Vietnamese cauldron overflowed into Cambodia.

The Viet Cong used the Cambodian and Laotian borderlands as supply routes into South Vietnam – the Ho Chi Minh Trail. In 1964, Sihanouk, close to Zhou Enlai, who visited Phnom Penh, allowed Chinese supplies to be delivered through Cambodia to the Vietnamese – the Sihanouk Trail – in return for a share of military equipment. As America deployed more troops, Sihanouk tacked left, recruiting into his government Khieu Samphan, a Marxist intellectual educated at the Sorbonne who was a member of the secret Maoist faction led by the teacher named Saloth Sar. When Sihanouk accused him of backing a peasant rebellion and arranged his public debagging, Khieu Samphan vanished. Many thought he was dead. He was joined in the jungle by Saloth Sar, who flew to Beijing where he was hosted by the deputy premier Deng Xiaoping. But it was Mao's secret-police chief Kang Sheng who grasped his grim potential. In 1966, as China turned against Sihanouk, he realized something was happening in Beijing.

THE SCORPION'S BITE AND THE FALL OF LITTLE CANNON: MAO UNLEASHES JIANG QING

In November 1965, the seventy-one-year-old Mao, after enduring three years of rising opposition, summoned his wife Jiang Qing, the ex-actress turned cultural commissar who admired classical movies and operas yet had become the enforcer of Party kitsch, and ordered her to draft a manifesto of revolution. Culture was the tool, the aim 'to punish this Party of ours', the target 'the black line opposed to Mao Zedong Thought'. Watching him cavorting with his harem of dancers, Jiang was

revelled in his own drama, calling 1965 'the year of living dangerously'. But when a Communist coup killed six generals, Sukarno lost control to his own general Suharto, who launched a purge of Communists and their ethnic Chinese supporters, killing 500,000 people, many by beheading. Suharto remained dictator for the next thirty-one years. In 2001 Sukarno's daughter Megawati was elected president.

hurt. 'In political struggle,' she remarked, 'no leaders can beat him,' but 'in private conduct, nobody can restrain him either'. When she discovered Mao, in his mid-sixties, in bed with a nurse, she yelled at him and left. On reflection she sent him a note from the novel *Journey to the West*: 'My body is in Water Curtain Cave, but my heart is following you.' Mao had his lovers, she wanted a career. Mao had privately come to loathe Jiang – 'poisonous as a scorpion' – but for years she had been disdained by Party grandees. Now she had her revenge. 'I was Chairman Mao's dog,' she said later. 'Whoever Chairman Mao asked me to bite, I bit.'

Mao ordered her to recruit Lin Biao, the vicious, hypochondriacal and cadaverous marshal recently promoted to vice-chairman, who had compiled a red book of Mao's sayings. Now Mao promised to make him his successor. Lin and his equally neurotic wife, who was embittered by sexual gossip about her past, joined Mao's cabal along with the black-clad security boss Kang Sheng. The wives were to be players; jealousies would play their part; vengeance was savoured.

Mao's crisis was self-inflicted. In 1958, he had launched a Great Leap Forward, a frenzied, demented industrialization campaign designed to help China 'overtake all capitalist countries' at breakneck speed by forcing peasants and workers to produce surplus food to pay for more steel, more ships, overruling the advice of experts: 'Bourgeois professors' knowledge should be treated like dog farts.' The food was sold to pay for new technology and weaponry. Ninety million Chinese were forced to build steel furnaces that produced worthless metal. Soon the peasants were starving: in three years, thirty-eight million perished, the worst famine of the century.* 'Working like this,' said Mao in May 1958, 'half of China may have to die.' He added, 'This happened before a few times in Chinese history.' In 1959, the defence minister Peng criticized the Leap but was removed and replaced by Lin Biao. By 1962, even President Liu Shaoqi, Mao's deputy, was attacking the Leap: 'People don't have enough food.' Liu, Premier Zhou and the pragmatic vice-premier Deng Xiaoping, who would be the other key figure of the Chinese century, moderated the requisitioning of food.

Abroad, while jousting with the bewildered Russians, Mao was projecting power, the start of a new version of history in which China

---

* The advances in food production and intensive agriculture mean that even though the world population has surged, famines are much rarer. Five million died between 1980 and 2020, while fifty million had died between 1940 and 1980, some famines caused by droughts, some by wartime failures of food distribution, but most by deliberate political policies adopted by Marxist-Leninists in the USSR, China and Ethiopia, and by the Nazis in Europe.

appears as a perpetual paramount power of east Asia – a role it had played for the climaxes of the Tang, Ming and Manchu interspersed with centuries of fragmentation. In 1959, Mao swallowed Tibet, driving out its young sacred king, the Dalai Lama, who was welcomed by Nehru in India. Mao decided to teach Nehru a lesson in Chinese power.

Nehru had presided over the world's biggest democracy for a decade, pursuing socialistic planning projects and developing power and steel production, officially 'non-aligned' but effectively allied with the Soviets: he criticized the Anglo-French invasion of Egypt but simultaneously refused to criticize Khrushchev's crushing of Hungary. His challenge was 'creating a just state by just means' and 'creating a secular state in a religious country', yet he did little to challenge poverty or the caste system, which he regarded as part of Hindu culture. His approach to the people was aristocratic. 'I rather enjoy these fresh contacts with the Indian people,' he told Edwina Mountbatten. 'The effort to explain in simple language . . . and reach the minds of these simple folk is both exhausting and exhilarating.' Yet his inherited British Raj was bedevilled by armed rebellions, all brutally suppressed, and by the ulcer of Kashmir. In 1961, he seized Goa from Portugal and in the next year received Pondicherry from France.

Nehru had started to procure the Bomb for India. 'We must have the capability,' he said. 'We should first prove ourselves and then talk of Gandhi, non-violence and a world without nuclear weapons.' Khrushchev had visited Delhi, but Nehru got on best with Zhou Enlai; he was fascinated by China, which he saw as India's great partner in the coming Asian century. Yet now Mao challenged the Indian–Chinese border, ill defined by the Manchus and Victorians. 'Not a yard of India is going out of India,' responded Nehru, who appointed an inept Kashmiri crony as chief of staff and ordered him to remove Chinese troops.

In October 1962, Mao's troops routed the Indians and advanced. Nehru, who had revelled in his Chinese alliance, desperately rang Washington and begged for US bombers. Indira's forty-ninth birthday party the following month was miserable. When the family asked Nehru how he was, he just replied, 'The Chinese have broken through the Sela Pass.' Mao could have continued all the way to Kolkata, but he halted. 'Nothing grieved me more,' Nehru said. Indira noticed his decline: 'The strain is tremendous.' On 27 May 1964, Nehru, after eighteen years as prime minister, died of a heart attack aged seventy-four. Indira had lost her closest companion and even her home, for she had lived in Nehru's residence since independence. As she considered leaving India and running a boarding house in London, Congress grandees chose Lal

Shastri as prime minister, who appointed Indira information minister. Her time would come sooner than she expected.

Successes abroad did not secure Mao at home. In April 1966, he unleashed Jiang Qing and her 'kill culture' manifesto, an 'anti-Party clique' were denounced and Lin Biao declared that anyone who criticized Mao should be 'executed . . . the whole nation must call for their blood'. As Mao unlocked a seething resentment against Party barons, in private at the Politburo Lin Biao answered the poison-pen letters signed 'Montecristo' that accused his wife of sexual adventures by bizarrely reading out a declaration that Madame Lin 'was a virgin when she married me' and 'had no sexual amorous relationship'. In May, once he had secured the backing of Premier Zhou, Mao orchestrated the Terror in detail through his Cultural Revolution Group,* ordering students to punish any 'bourgeois ideas' among teachers and suspending lessons. Professors at Beijing University were beaten by gangs of so-called Red Guards.

In July, Mao signalled his power by swimming in the Yangzte. 'I wanted to show off,' he admitted afterwards, but if he had not been surreptitiously helped by his guard, 'I'd have died.' At Zhongnanhai, the reinvigorated septuagenarian moved into a new residence, the Poolside House, next to his own indoor pool. Within Zhongnanhai, when Mao summoned his courtiers, the guards would say, 'You're wanted at the swimming pool.'

That August, Mao himself wrote a letter to the nation's students, attacking 'poisonous' Party leaders and 'the arrogance of the bourgeoisie' and ordering, 'Bombard the headquarters.' He then appeared with Lin at a parade holding his *Little Red Book*. He instigated a public witchhunt: the minister of coal was beaten, bent forward with his arms pulled back – the torture known as jet-planing – and then stabbed with knives. Across China, gangs of students and brigands attacked their bosses, from teachers to Party leaders, holding 'struggle sessions' in which the victims were beaten up but forced to incriminate themselves – a new template for leftist intolerance.

Mao, like Stalin, a maestro of Mass Age mobilisation, directed the terror, promoting Lin Biao as his heir apparent as both his wife and Lin's joined the Politburo. He preserved those he might need later. The president, Liu, was dismissed as 'No. 1 Capitalist Roader', then he and his wife were jet-planed and beaten to the ground. Later Liu was left to

---

* Mao's daughter Li Na, by Jiang, worked as his secretary during the Cultural Revolution, witnessing struggle sessions for him. She became ever more haughty, threatening staff. Mao promoted her to director of the Small Group that ran the campaign. But in 1972 she had a nervous breakdown and Mao lost interest in her.

die of cancer, refused all treatment. Yet Mao respected Deng Xiaoping, the tough, capable ex-favourite who was running China, nicknaming him Little Cannon. But now Deng was denounced as 'No. 2 Capitalist Roader', dismissed and dispatched to a tractor factory in Jiangxi; his son Pufang was tortured and thrown from the top of a building, surviving as a paraplegic.* His ally, Xi Zhongxun, a vice-premier, was denounced by Kang Sheng, demoted to a tractor factory, then publicly tormented and imprisoned, while his ten-year-old son, Xi Jinping, raised in privilege, witnessed his father's downfall, and Red Guards smashing his home. His wife Qi Xin was forced to denounce her husband in a terrifying struggle session. Their daughter committed suicide. Qi chose to accompany Xi into exile, where he read Adam Smith and Churchill, but he was embittered and damaged by the trauma and by more than ten years of disfavour. The boy was forced to join Mao's Down to the Countryside Movement but escaped to Beijing, was arrested and sent back. He did not see his parents again until he was almost twenty. When he became China's autocrat, he remembered the Terror. 'I see the bullpens [Red Guard detention camps],' he said fifty years later. 'I understand politics on a deeper level.' China was chaotic: three million killed, a hundred million sacked, seventeen million deported or rusticated for 're-education', a billion *Little Red Books* brandished.

Brezhnev was fascinated but bewildered by Mao. 'What kind of person is he?' he said wonderingly to Castro. 'Is he a Communist or a Fascist? Or perhaps the new Chinese emperor?' Eschewing Maoist lunacy, Brezhnev defended Stalin's empire – 'When forces hostile to socialism try to turn some socialist country towards capitalism, it becomes ... the common problem of all socialist countries' – but, after Cuba, he was keen to limit nuclear weapons with the USA while fighting the hot struggle through African proxies.

NASSER AND THE KING: SIX DAYS IN JUNE

Africa was fertile territory for the Soviets, but western rivalry and political instability were a challenge. Nkrumah the Redeemer travelled frequently to Moscow, Havana and North Vietnam, but Papa Houphouët, coordinating with de Gaulle's African mastermind Foccart, backed a conspiracy against the Redeemer, who was redeemed by his

---

* During the 1990s, this author met Deng Pufang in Beijing. 'Yes, let us say we have come through struggles to get here,' is how he described his trajectory, sitting in his wheelchair.

own army and deposed, sending Ghana into a spiral of dictatorship and corruption. Houphouët was one of many inclined towards the west. On 12 December 1964, the sixty-six-year-old Kenyatta, only recently freed from house arrest, was elected president. Genial, pleasure-loving and theatrical, Burning Spear was polygamous, marrying four times, lastly to Ngina, thirty-four years younger, who was as extrovert as he was but shamelessly amassed a fortune. Ultimately forging a one-party state, hailed as the *mzee* – elder master – brandishing his flywhisk and often sporting head-to-foot leopard-skin robes, he dominated Kenya* through a court of Kikuyu henchmen, carving up the spoils of government, making his own family the country's largest landowners and clashing with his ally, Tom Mboya, the Luo minister of finance.

At the same time, Mboya's protégé, Barack Obama, returned from Harvard to join the elite. As his ex-wife Ann, now a qualified anthropologist, lived with her new Indonesian husband in Jakarta, accompanied by his son Barack junior, senior was joined in Nairobi by his new wife, Ruth Baker, white and Jewish. Dr Obama became a senior economist at Mboya's Finance Ministry. He was set to thrive. Yet he did not – and he would meet Barack junior only one more time.

Kenyatta kept the Soviets out of Kenya; Egypt was more receptive. Brezhnev backed Nasser with Soviet arms, advisers and intelligence in order to confront the western ally, Israel. Nasser prepared for war, promoting his long-serving crony Abdel Hakim Amer to war minister and marshal. Amer, lean and raffish but contumacious, resisted Nasser's attempts to control the army. He partied heavily with girls and drugs, while Nasser, diabetic with heart problems, suffered from stress and insomnia. At home, his favourite daughter fell in love with a flashy young engineer, a general's son called Ashraf Marwan, whom the dictator distrusted. But Mona got her way and his new son-in-law joined the presidential office, living for a time in London luxury until Nasser, furious about their extravagance, humiliated Marwan: he would take his revenge.

---

* While Kenyatta was consolidating his power in Kenya, the British withdrew from Tanganyika and Zanzibar. In January 1964 the sultan of Zanzibar – the Arab monarch whose cousin ruled Oman – faced an invasion by a demented messianic Ugandan Christian, John Okello, who seized the island with 600 revolutionaries and tried to capture Sultan Sir Jamshid bin Abdullah, who fled on his yacht. Okello ordered the killing of all Arabs between eighteen and twenty-five, gang-raping all women, though banning the rape of virgins. Two thousand Omanis were killed – vengeance for centuries of slave trading. But Field Marshal Okello was outmanoeuvred by saner leaders who, after trying to impose a Marxist republic, expelled him and negotiated a union with Tanganyika to form Tanzania. The sultan ultimately retired to Oman: his cousins still rule Oman today.

Darling of the crowds, Nasser escalated the threats of annihilation against Israel, encouraged by Amer's promises of military power. The dictator who believes his own myth will be consumed by it. In early 1967, as Israel struck back against raids by militias of Palestinian exiles, and duelled with the Syrian army, Nasser dismissed UN peacekeepers from Sinai and heralded the liquidation of Israel. Brezhnev forwarded to Nasser intelligence that claimed Israel planned to attack Syria. The intelligence was flawed, but Nasser used it to stoke the Syrians for war.

On the central front in Jordan, the diminutive Hashemite king Hussein, still only thirty-two, had already been denounced by Nasser as an 'imperialist lackey' and was stalked by Nasserite assassins. Named after his great-grandfather, the amir of Mecca, educated at Harrow and Sandhurst, Hussein was cunning, jaunty and sporty, with an eye for beautiful women. He prided himself on his guardianship of the Haram al-Sharif in Jerusalem, but his survival was doubtful. He still mourned his gibleted cousin Faisal of Iraq. While Hussein ruled the West Bank, Nasser endorsed the newly founded Palestinian Liberation Organization (PLO), dominated by a young radical named Yasser Arafat, born in Cairo but partly brought up in the Maghrebi Quarter of Jerusalem, as the legitimate representative of the Palestinians.

Now Nasser summoned the little king. Nasser might arrest or kill him in Cairo, but Hussein acquiesced. Nasser, towering over him, joked ominously that he was not arresting him but demanded command of Jordanian forces. Hussein submitted. 'Our basic objective,' said Nasser, 'will be to destroy Israel.'

Across the border, the Israelis were in a fever of panic. Their premier Levi Eshkol was indecisive, elderly and unnerved. The chain-smoking, laconic, fair-haired chief of staff, Yitzhak Rabin, special forces commander in 1948, was close to breakdown. Surrounded by popular existential anxiety, Eshkol bowed to public demand and appointed the piratically eye-patched Moshe Dayan as defence minister. 'Original, handsome', in Peres's words, 'and a brilliant mind', Dayan was a kibbutznik born in Israel, a compulsive lover of women, amateur archaeologist and fluent Arab-speaker with many Arab friends. He had been trained by British commandos during the Arab revolt. Dayan and Rabin devised a pre-emptive strike to hit Egypt, then Syria, warning Hussein to keep out of the conflict.

At dawn on 5 June 1967, Israeli planes – Mirages supplied by France – obliterated the Egyptian air force, then Israeli troops smashed through Egyptian defences to take Sinai and reach the Suez Canal; Marshal Amer ordered counter-attacks, claimed victory, then panicked and retreated.

Dayan switched northwards to smash Syria and take the Golan. Hussein watched tensely; Amer boasted of historical victories and ordered Jordan to attack Israel. Hussein sent in his Arab Legion. Dayan swiped them aside, occupying the West Bank, then, in a moment of almost mystic excitement, reunited Jerusalem under Jewish rule after two millennia. The Six-Day victory changed much: as Jews across the world celebrated and thousands prayed at the *Kotel* – the Wall, a surviving section of the Jewish Temple – Israel enjoyed a burst of overconfidence. Cool strategy suggested that some of Judaea and Samaria along with Golan and Sinai should be retained to give the narrow state some strategic depth. But the triumph brought many Palestinians under Israeli rule and awakened a religious nationalism beneath Israel's secular, socialist tradition which demanded that Israelis should settle the lands of the ancient kingdoms. For many Israelis, Jerusalem – sacred Zion – became the 'indivisible' and 'perpetual' Israeli capital.

Nasser rushed to army headquarters where he and Amer almost came to blows, after which *El Rais* broadcast his resignation. Millions gathered outside his palace, crying, 'We're your soldiers, Gamal!' Nasser, restored to power, sacked Amer, who supported by his officers tried to seize power. Nasser, at his own house, confronted Amer, ordering his arrest and exit: Amer either committed suicide or was liquidated. *El Rais* mourned his 'closest man' and visited Brezhnev to procure arms. 'If I were the Israeli leader,' Nasser told Brezhnev, 'I'd never give up the occupied territories.' Brezhnev, facing the rout of his allies, used the hotline to confirm that LBJ would not intervene.

THE ASSASSINATIONS: RFK, MLK, MBOYA

LBJ was in no position to do so, destroyed by his Vietnamese war and challenged by his enemy, Bobby Kennedy, now New York senator, who had transformed into an inspirational liberal and channelled the rising disgust felt for the president. 'Some men see things as they are, and ask why,' he said. 'I dream of things that never were, and ask why not.'

A total of 525,000 US troops were fighting in Vietnam; thousands of young Americans, rallied by Kennedy and MLK, protested against an unjust and misconceived war. Long hair, bell-bottoms and miniskirts were the costumes, marijuana the tonic and Marxist critical theory the vision, Mao and Che Guevara the heroes, for a radical new world that promised a utopian dream of love, tolerance and equality for the small numbers of young people in the Americas and Europe who actually experienced the short period known as 'the Sixties'.

Its real chroniclers were poets first and foremost: Bob Dylan and Leonard Cohen, both Jewish children of middle-class families – one from Minnesota, the other from Montreal – who put their poems to music. Rock music provided the Sixties' soundtrack, particularly a wave of British bands, led first by The Beatles but personified by the Rolling Stones, fronted by the lithe strut and full-lipped sexual insolence of Mick Jagger and the riffing guitarist Keith Richards, who wrote their own songs, channelling American blues, and now 'conquered' America; few songs encapsulated the rebellion, promise and cynicism of the Sixties as well as '(I Can't Get No) Satisfaction'. The British establishment feared these hedonistic radicals, arresting Jagger and Richards, who were sentenced to jail for drug possession. But they were rescued by a *Times* editorial entitled 'Who Breaks a Butterfly upon a Wheel?' After their release came apotheosis: they and other rock stars – gifted musicians from obscure origins now rich from selling millions of records and playing to stadiums, flying the globe in customized airplanes accompanied by their own retinues of paramours, courtiers and drug dealers – attained, for the next fifty years, the apex of a new global social prestige, shared with film and sports stars, in the West's mass-consumer age, comparable to that of princes, paladins and popes of earlier centuries.

The era had its own distinctive visual backdrop too: news footage of sweaty, stoned American troops and Chinook helicopters in the first televised war, Vietnam. The great artistic manifestation of this alienated world was the distorted brilliance of the paintings of Lucian Freud, grandson of Sigmund, which were more considerably exciting than the concept-laden 'abstract expressionists' of the Fifties.[*]

The rebellion of youth was happening just as the reality of family had been proven: in 1962, two scientists, one British, one American, won the Nobel Prize for discovering the structure of DNA. Nine years earlier, a balding boffin walked into his local Cambridge pub, the Eagle, and announced to the bemused boozers, 'We've found the secret of life.' The thirty-six-year-old Francis Crick, working with a young American, James Watson, just twenty-four, had discovered the double-helix of DNA – but not on their own. In fact they had been racing another researcher,

---

[*] Lucian Freud, who had only known the famed psychoanalyst, his grandfather, in old age, lived like an eighteenth-century street-fighting rake, horseplayer and libertine, holding court with a harem of lovers and fathering at least twelve children. In 1966, painted his first reclining nude portrait, *Naked Girl*. His own raw, alienated, sensual and harshly impastoed style over the next fifty years mastered and gloried in the flesh, the soul and the human condition: 'I want paint to work as flesh,' he said. 'My portraits to be of the people, not like them. Not have the look of the sitter, being them.'

Rosalind Franklin, a thirty-two-year-old Anglo-Jewish chemist, whose essential discovery of the key properties of DNA they had obtained without her knowledge, passed to them by a colleague at King's College London. 'When we saw the answer,' Watson recalled, 'we had to pinch ourselves. Could it really be this pretty? It was so pretty.' Franklin died of cancer at just thirty-seven and therefore did not share the Nobel Prize won by Crick and Watson.

The discovery confirmed that DNA itself was the carrier of hereditary information, and further study showed that humans were virtually all the same; differences were tiny and everyone was a walking collection of family histories and a member of a deeper, broader family. It confirmed that race as a social category was neither based on scientific differences nor reflective of genetic ancestry. It was a social construct, but that did not it make any less powerful. Unravelling human DNA helped reveal the twists, migrations, settlings and clashes of the human story, as well as launching a biological revolution that changed the world, from the treatment of diseases and the investigation of crime to a new passion for family history.

In 1960, a birth-control pill, using hormones to inhibit ovulation, freed women from male control of sex for the first time: it could be enjoyed for its own sake. New household gadgets, washing machines, fridges, vacuum cleaners, made female servants obsolete, but also liberated women – encouraged by a movement of female empowerment, feminism – to pursue independent careers. They had fewer children, but now most of those survived to adulthood, leading to a new cult of childhood, particularly in the middle class, where the desire for women to work clashed with the virtues of attentive parenting. The feminist movement was the great success of the Sixties and early Seventies, the Great Liberal Reformation that delivered the right to abortion, curtailed capital punishment, legalized homosexuality and later gay rights.

Female sexual freedom shocked a gerontocracy of starchy male leaders. In 1965 Franco and Tito both reached seventy-three, de Gaulle seventy-five.* 'One must not reduce women to machines for making love,' declared de Gaulle, denouncing the Pill that year. 'A woman is made to have children . . . Sex will invade everything!' So it did. Two years later, he legalized the Pill, but on 3 May 1968 radical students seized Sorbonne University in Paris and started to build barricades, calling for Marxist revolution and 'adieu de Gaulle!' Workers went on strike;

---

* In September 1968, Salazar, aged seventy-nine, fell over in his bath and suffered a stroke. Yet Portugal's *Estado Novo* did not fall. A loyalist was appointed prime minister, who continued the dictatorship at home and the brutal colonial wars abroad.

students occupied their campuses. The president called this *'chienlit'* – or havoc, literally shit in the bed – and sent in his riot police: 'When a child gets angry and oversteps the mark, the best way of calming him is to give him a smack.' The violence only intensified *les événements.* Madame de Gaulle wept at dinner, the president ranted, 'The French have never recovered from defeat at Waterloo and Sedan,' and warned, 'I'm not Louis Philippe.'

Instead he contemplated a solution unique in the modern democracies: on 29 May, the president set off for home in Colombey but instead, taking an aide and his son, he commandeered the helicopter and flew to French NATO headquarters in Baden-Baden. 'It's all over,' he told General Massu, testing the loyalty of the army for a military coup.

'This is impossible,' replied the general. 'This is madness.' De Gaulle was not the only potentate under siege. In Czechoslovakia, a reformer launched a Prague Spring against the Soviet imperium. In America, LBJ, broken, announced he would not run for a second term. Bobby Kennedy was expected to win. Yet in France, as elsewhere, the majority – hailed by the US presidential candidate Richard Nixon as 'the silent majority' – was willing to tolerate young radical excess only for a while. When de Gaulle flew back to the Élysée Palace to call new elections, opinion had turned against the students. But he was fatally damaged, and resigned soon afterwards.

On 21 August, Brezhnev sent 200,000 troops to crush the Prague Spring, gaining Stalin's empire another twenty years. In America too, the loving feast of the Sixties was spoiling. Martin Luther King was bombarded with threats: in Memphis, on 3 April 1968, he talked about his death. 'I just want to do God's will,' he preached. 'And He's allowed me to go up to the mountain. And I've looked over. And I've seen the promised land. I may not get there with you.' Next day, on the balcony of his motel, MLK was assassinated by an attention-seeking criminal. RFK denounced 'this mindless menace of violence', saying, 'No martyr's cause has ever been stilled by his assassin's bullet.' Three months later, in June, Kennedy, forty-two years old, close to clinching the Democratic nomination, spoke at the LA Ambassador Hotel where, walking through the kitchens, he was shot by an unbalanced Palestinian. 'Everything,' he said as he lay dying, 'is going to be OK.' But it was not.

On 5 July 1969, in Nairobi, Tom Mboya, exuberant finance minister serving the ageing President Kenyatta, was walking down Government Road when he bumped into his protégé Barack Obama. He had tried to help Obama, but that irrepressible maverick had criticized his policies, then lost other jobs, becoming an abusive alcoholic. While driving drunk, he killed his passenger and best friend, the first of several car crashes, while his marriage broke up. Now he chatted with Mboya and moved on. Moments later he heard shots: Mboya, the Luo, had been assassinated by a Kikuyu. Before he was hanged the killer asked, 'Why don't you go after the Big Man [Kenyatta]?' Kenyatta liked to say, 'T. J. [Mboya]'s my favourite son,' but his Kikuyu courtiers may have ordered the hit, which, like the shootings of RFK and MLK in America, marked the start of a harsher, more tribal politics in Kenya. It also accelerated the decline of Dr Obama: he was convinced his next booze-fuelled car crash was a hit ordered by Kenyatta. As his family later told his son, Kenyatta dominated Kenya – 'That's where it all starts. The Big Man' – and Obama 'forgot what holds everything together here'.* But he had not forgotten his American son: 'I left a baby bull in America. Someday I'll go get him.'

One day, Obama, now thirty-seven, turned up in Hawaii to see his long-lost son, who was back there after his time in Indonesia. Ann was still married to her Indonesian husband and had a job in Jakarta. Aged ten, Barry went to stay with his grandparents in Hawaii to attend the best prep school in the state. Later Ann joined him. Now the boy encountered his famous father once again: 'a tall dark figure . . . thinner than I expected', sporting 'a blue blazer and white shirt, scarlet ascot, horn-rimmed glasses', limping with an ivory-headed cane. He taught Barry to dance – and addressed his class at school. But he had come to take Ann and Barry back to Nairobi. Ann refused.

Barry and his father never met again; his mother, only eighteen years older than him, was everything to him – 'the kindest, most generous spirit I've ever known,' he wrote; 'what is best in me I owe to her.'

In Nairobi, Dr Obama was given a job at the Finance Ministry, finally finding the respect he deserved, while Barry studied in LA before getting into Columbia Law School. On 23 November 1982, Dr Obama, just forty-eight, was killed in a car crash. 'After my twenty-first birthday, a stranger,' wrote Barack Obama junior, 'called to give me the news.' He craved to know the real story of his father and to construct his family history: he had a dream of his father, and looked to Africa to define himself.

As Obama started his studies and his search for himself, America was at its lowest ebb, divided at home, stalemated by Soviet Russia,

---

* Kenyatta died in 1978 aged eighty-four, leaving his family one of the richest in Kenya, but his sons were too young to succeed him. He selected a henchman, Daniel Arap Moi, who ruled for twenty years. Kenyatta's son Uhuru served as president from 2013 to 2022 – another African dynasty in a flawed but functioning democracy.

haemorrhaging men and prestige in Vietnam. 'You think you're the most powerful leader since God,' an exhausted LBJ told his successor, Richard Nixon, reluctantly welcoming him into the Oval Office, 'but when you get in that tall chair, as you're gonna find out, Mr President, you can't count on people.'

THE APHRODISIAC OF POWER: KISSINGER AND NIXON'S TRIANGULAR GAME

Nixon was just as hard-scrambled as LBJ but slightly more polished. The prickly, awkward, misanthropic, emotionally strangulated son of a mean-spirited bankrupt grocer, his mother 'a Quaker saint', Nixon had overcome defeat by JFK, then run disastrously for California governor. 'You won't have Richard M. Nixon to kick around any more,' he told the press after the latter failure. But then, watching LBJ's Vietnam fiasco and the national divisions it sparked, he reinvented himself as the representative of 'the silent majority'. His first challenge on taking office in January 1969 was how to get out of Vietnam.

'My rule in international affairs,' he said to the Israeli prime minister, Golda Meir, 'is "Do unto others as they would do to you."'

'Plus ten per cent,' added his national security advisor, Dr Henry Kissinger. The two were an unlikely but effective double act. The forty-five-year-old Kissinger was instantly more important than the secretary of state. A Jewish refugee from Fürth, Bavaria, who escaped in 1938, he had come closer to the tragedies of European extremism than any other American statesman: 'Having lived through totalitarianism, I know what's it like.' It made him a connoisseur of power. After serving in the US army he became a Harvard historian, writing his thesis on Metternich. Inevitably he compared himself to Metternich and America in 1969 to Austria in 1809: 'a government that had lost its élan and its self-confidence, which knew its limits but hardly its goals', goals that could only be achieved by 'the subtlety of its diplomacy'.

Coming from different worlds, Nixon and Kissinger were both secretive and pragmatic, both impressed and repelled by the other, both adroit players of the World Game. But while the president was morose and solitary, the gravel-voiced, German-accented Kissinger was a showman who, during a long career, delighted in analysing the personalities he had known: at regular dinners for the antique Alice Roosevelt Longworth, daughter of Teddy, Nixon encouraged his Harvard professor to perform and Kissinger became the most glamorous wonk since Palmerston, revelling in being the cynosure of attention, joking that 'Power is the greatest aphrodisiac' as he dated film stars. 'The focused energy of the first months in office,' Kissinger told this author, 'are always vital and we had a grand design.' Perhaps the conjunction was right: on 16 July 1969, 650 million people watched two American astronauts walk on the Moon.* 'The Heavens,' Nixon told them from the White House, 'have now become part of man's world.' Astronaut Buzz Aldrin described the Moon as 'magnificent desolation'. First Nixon had to deal with the desolation of Vietnam.

'A sudden withdrawal might give us a credibility problem,' said Kissinger, who sought to change the relationship with Russia and China. 'The challenge for the US was to make sure it always has more options than either of the other two parties within the triangle.' He planned to negotiate with Brezhnev, reach out to Mao and leave Vietnam in a blaze of gunpowder. He managed all three. But in the process Nixon's flaws tainted American democracy as much as the bruises of Vietnam had done.

In March, Nixon ordered the secret bombing of Communist trails in Cambodia. Prince Sihanouk had failed to keep Cambodia out of the war. As thousands of anti-war students protested across America, Nixon and Kissinger launched counter-offensives as a basis for starting secret negotiations, yet the policy expanded the war before it ended it. Sihanouk, trying to keep the Americans and Communists out, did not wish to lose the eastern part of his country to the Vietnamese nor to encourage his local Communists, whom he called Khmer Rouge. Instead he was ground between the two.

In early 1970, the ex-teacher and French student Saloth Sar, general

---

* That week, a British art and drama student and singer-songwriter from Brixton named David Bowie (né Jones) released a song, 'Space Oddity', that told the story of a stranded astronaut, Major Tom, who orbited earth forever. Fascinated by space travel, Bowie – a figure of cadaverous beauty and vampirical glamour – now chronicled the messianic strangeness of fame in the age of mass consumerism in his album *The Rise and Fall of Ziggy Stardust and the Spiders from Mars*. His only equal as a songwriter and showman was his contemporary, also a working-class Londoner, Elton John (né Reggie Dwight), who also chronicled the space world in his 'Rocketman' and whose masterwork 'Goodbye Yellow Brick Road' expanded what was meant by pop music. Their fusion of theatre, fashion and music showed that rock was becoming the dynamic wing of art, while their exploration of sexual androgyny (both caused much shock by admitting to being bisexual), exotic hedonism and their near destruction through cocaine addiction marked the end of the utopian Sixties and the dawn of the darkening Seventies. But it was the Rolling Stones, whose 'Sympathy for the Devil' – the best history song of all time – confronted the Age of Aquarius with the satanic forces of history. The Sixties unofficially died on 6 December at the Stones concert at Altmont, California, when a fan was stabbed to death by marauding Hells Angel security. But the Stones survived it all and played to vast stadiums for the next fifty years.

secretary of the Cambodian Communists, adopted a new name, Pol Pot, and arrived in China, where Mao promised military aid for a revolution that was no longer an obscure dream.

KILLING B-52: MAO AND POL POT

While Pol was in Beijing and Sihanouk – the Prince Who Was King – was visiting Moscow, his pro-American commander Lon Nol seized power in Phnom Penh. Yet such was the prestige of the monarchy that peasants rebelled and killed Lon Nol's brother in revenge for the coup, reportedly eating his liver. Lon Nol knelt at the feet of the queen mother to ask forgiveness for overthrowing her son, but his attacks on the North Vietnamese brought not just more Viet Cong but American troops into Cambodia – an operation ironically codenamed Freedom Deal. Determined to get power back, Sihanouk flew straight to Beijing, where Mao and Zhou welcomed their friend, whom they persuaded to join in an alliance with their other Cambodian guest, Pol Pot. Sihanouk's vanity helped bring about a tragedy. Mao kept Sihanouk in Beijing and sent Pol Pot to Cambodia – just as he faced his own crisis.

In September 1971, Mao arrived back in Beijing unaware that his heir, Marshal Lin Biao, and son 'Tiger' Lin Liguo were planning to assassinate him in a drama that would mystify the outside world for decades.

After Mao had declared the end of his Cultural Revolution, he noticed that Lin was pursuing his own ambitions, exerting influence even over his personal bodyguards and criticizing Madame Mao. Lin was also alarmed by Mao's warmongering: in March 1969, Chinese and Soviet troops clashed on the Ussuri River, encouraged by Mao, who toyed with launching a full-scale war. The Helmsman tested Lin by demanding a self-criticism. Marshal Lin refused. Lin's secret views of Mao were reflected in the plans of his beloved son Tiger, playboy deputy chief of the air force command who came to loathe the 'paranoid sadist . . . the biggest feudal tyrant in Chinese history' whom he codenamed B-52 after the American bombers.

Tiger planned the assassination of B-52, just as the Chairman briefed allies that Lin 'can't wait to seize power'. The Lins decided to divebomb Mao's train, but B-52 kept changing his plans. Now Tiger's latest plan clashed with the news that Mao had turned on the marshal. They planned their escape, but Tiger hoped to kill Mao first. Foolishly he confided in his sister Dodo, a fanatical Maoist, who snitched to Mao's bodyguards. When Mao was informed, he was so alarmed he had to be sedated. As Lin Biao, his wife and the pistol-brandishing Tiger raced for the airport, they were chased by Mao's guards but just managed to board their half-fuelled plane and take off.

Two hours later, Mao learned that a plane had crashed in Mongolia, and that his paladin was dead. Frantic and feverish, quaffing mao-tai and sleeping pills, he was suddenly old and his doctors discovered a heart condition. He had long believed in 'one united front' against Moscow, but now the old manipulator planned a final world-changing reversal. 'We must win over one of the two hegemons,' he said; 'never fight with two fists.' That dovetailed with Kissinger's plan.

It started with ping-pong. Mao directed the moves through his nephew Mao Yuanxin, son of his brother Zemin executed in 1943. He had long found his wife Jiang Qing unbearable. Once when she talked her way into his compound he threatened to arrest her unless she got out. So it was his young nurses-cum-lovers who interpreted his orders. The Helmsman 'came to trust women far more than men', his doctor, Li, recalled. Bingeing on sleeping pills, he said: 'Words after sleeping pills don't count.' Now the order was so surprising that his favourite nurse, whom he called Little Wu, had to double-check.

'You've taken sleeping pills,' said Little Wu. 'Do the words count?'

'Yes! Do it quickly!' ordered Mao. 'Or there won't be time.' Zhou was to coordinate the plan, suddenly inviting the American ping-pong team to play in Beijing. 'You've opened a new chapter,' Zhou told the bemused paddlers, 'in Chinese–American relations.' Via Pakistan, Mao invited Kissinger to Beijing. 'This,' said Kissinger to Nixon, 'is the most important communication to an American president since the Second World War.' In July 1971, as India and Pakistan clashed, Kissinger flew in.

CALL ME SIR – DUMB DOLL DOMINATES INDIA

Nixon called Indira Gandhi 'the Bitch' and sometimes 'the Witch'. 'The Indians are no goddamn good,' he told Kissinger; he preferred the Pakistanis, who were 'straightforward' if 'sometimes extremely stupid'. Nixon was not the first to underestimate Indira, although he did realize how ruthless she could be. When Shastri died of a heart attack in January 1966, the Congress powerbrokers chose Nehru's attractive daughter, now forty-eight, as their puppet prime minister: a socialist politician nicknamed her Dumb Doll. But the Doll outplayed them all and then won an election.

Neglected during her lonely childhood when her father was often in prison or on campaign, she was born to rule, combining a longing for love with the entitlement of power. She had sat with her grandfather Motilal, with Gandhi and then with Nehru hosting world leaders; she had studied at Oxford and had followed her father's advice: 'Be brave and the rest follows.' When asked what the US president should call her, she replied, 'He can call me Prime Minister or Mr Prime Minister. You can tell him my ministers call me Sir.' But Indira's grandeur, recalled Kissinger, 'brought out Nixon's insecurities'. Graceful in her saris with her greying hair, she was masterful but paranoid and suspicious. When the press tried to find out if Indira had a lover, she reflected privately, 'I don't behave like a woman; the lack of sex in me partly explains this.'

In March 1971, promising to *'Garibi Hatao!'* (Abolish poverty!), she had won an election victory so sweeping that westerners nicknamed her Empress of India. Now she saw an opportunity in the disintegration of Pakistan. The resulting war, like the Arab–Israeli conflicts, was a sequel to the unfinished business of partition, which had created a new nation, Pakistan, that had inherited little of the stabilizing British-trained bureaucracy, its identity shaped by its army and Islam, united by visceral hatred for India. It was divided into two, Punjab in the west, Bengal in the east, 1,600 miles apart. Now the easterners rebelled, seeking independence from the arrogant grandees of Islamabad, driving millions of Hindu refugees into India.

The Pakistani military dictator Yahya Khan set his troops loose in the east's capital Dhaka, machine-gunning students, mass-raping women, murdering children, killing 10,000 in days, 500,000 within months. Indira prepared for war, skirmishing with Pakistani forces in the east. But on 3 December 1971 the Pakistanis, inspired by their enemy Israel, launched air strikes on eleven Indian air bases. Indira liberated Dhaka and attacked western Pakistan too, routing its forces in a thirteen-day war. The east declared independence as Bangladesh; Indira was triumphant.* Indians, exultant that their country had won their first

---

* Pakistan smarted from the disaster, its president ceding power to its dynamic foreign minister, Zulfiqar Ali Bhutto, a socialist heir to 250,000 feudal acres in the family power base Sindh, educated at Oxford and Berkeley. Two weeks after taking office he summoned Pakistani scientists: 'We're going to have the Bomb. How long will it take?' But Indira Gandhi was pursuing the Bomb too. Aided by the Soviets, in 1974 she tested an Indian device that, feared Bhutto, would establish Indian 'hegemony in the subcontinent'. He accelerated the Pakistani project, promoting a young scientist, A. Q. Khan, who started to buy plans and equipment for an Islamic Bomb. 'Christian, Jewish and Hindu civilizations have this capability,' said Bhutto. 'Islamic civilization is without it.' He tried to combine Pakistan's different sides. 'Islam is our faith, democracy our policy,' he declared, 'socialism our economy.' But he was overshadowed by a military which regarded itself as the guardian of the precarious state. In the east, the founding leader of Bangladesh, Sheikh Mujibur

victory in centuries, hailed her as Durga, invincible ten-armed goddess. 'India is Indira,' declared the Congress president. Having inherited the throne herself, she now started to groom her favourite son for the crown.

Nixon and Kissinger watched morosely. Earlier in the year, Kissinger had flown in to encourage conciliation, but that was his cover. Pakistan was backed by China and America, a link that brought them together. Secretly, Kissinger flew on to Beijing to meet Mao, preparing the way for the president himself . . .

I LIKE RIGHTISTS: AMERICAN METTERNICH AND THE PHILOSOPHER-KING OF CHINA

On 21 February 1972, Nixon and Kissinger were received by Mao in his book-heaped study at the Swimming-Pool House that resembled 'more the retreat of a scholar than the audience room of the all-powerful leader'.

'I voted for you,' joked Mao to Nixon. 'I like rightists.'

Kissinger told Mao he recommended his books to his Harvard students.

'These writings of mine,' said Mao, 'aren't anything.'

'The Chairman's writings,' answered Nixon, 'moved a nation and changed the world.'

'I've only been able to change a few places,' smiled Mao, 'in the vicinity of Beijing.' He damned Nixon with faint praise: 'Your book *Six Crises* isn't bad.' When the Americans tried to negotiate – offering to drop recognition of Taiwan as official China, Mao grandly dismissed them: 'Troublesome problems I don't want to get into.' Kissinger could not help but admire 'the philosopher-king'.

Brezhnev watched this encounter with horror and invited Nixon to Moscow, believing that in war 'everyone loses'. Perhaps perversely he trusted Nixon more than any other US president and admired, almost envied, Kissinger. 'There was never a good president,' Brezhnev told Castro, 'and probably never will be. The difference between Republicans and Democrats is unsubstantial.' As for America, Brezhnev thought it was 'a sick society' where 'gangsterism, racism and drug addiction have reached enormous proportions. The monopolies are robbing the people,

---

Rahman, nicknamed *Bangabandhu* (Friend of Bengal), ruled the new state until his assassination in 1975; he founded a dynasty – his daughter Sheikh Hasini ruled autocratically into the 2020s.

having grabbed political power.' Yet he admired Nixon and thought Kissinger 'a cunning, smart guy', though Kissinger was unimpressed by Lyonia. In one of their encounters, Brezhnev, a metalworker turned tsar, dressed Kissinger, German-Jewish schoolteacher's son, in boots and khaki and took him wild-boar hunting. Kissinger refused to shoot; Brezhnev killed one boar and wounded another. Brezhnev also drove Nixon at high speed in his ZiL limousines and his speedboats. 'Enjoy good things with impunity,' he bellowed. When he visited Washington, Nixon gave him a Lincoln Continental. Brezhnev insisted on driving it, which the Secret Service vetoed.

'I'll take the flag off the car, put on dark glasses,' said Brezhnev, 'so they can't see my eyebrows and drive like any American would.'

'I've driven with you,' replied Kissinger. 'I don't think you drive like an American!'

In May 1972, Nixon and Brezhnev signed a first agreement – Strategic Arms Limitation Treaty (SALT) – the start of thirty years of negotiations. Surfing on these successes, the duo now negotiated American withdrawal from Vietnam. Yet Nixon could not restrain his own Manichaean paranoia. A month after SALT, he ordered a henchman to send five myrmidons – 'the Plumbers' – to burgle and set up wiretaps in Democratic headquarters in the Watergate Building, only for them to be arrested. Nixon lied to conceal his role, but it is not true that he was solely destroyed by the cover-up. The original crime was bad enough. Two journalists at the *Washington Post* unveiled a web of paranoid conspiracies and secret payments that corroded Nixon's presidency.

Moreover, the Soviet detente was fragile. On 24 October 1973, just months after a jovial US–Soviet meeting, Brezhnev threatened military intervention.

Houses of Solomon and Bush, Bourbon, Pahlavi and Castro

WILD BEASTS AND LIONS: THE ASSADS OF DAMASCUS

On 6 October 1973, Yom Kippur – holiest day in the Jewish calendar – Egyptian and Syrian troops attacked Israel across the Suez and Golan, taking the Israelis by surprise, despite warnings from their agent in the Egyptian president's office.* Two new leaders, in Egypt and Syria, had changed the Arab response to Israel: one would prove a peacemaker of courage and pay for it with his life; the other founded a gangster dynasty that would cost his country the lives of many.

The change of the guard had started with the biggest funeral in world history. On 28 September 1970, Nasser, only fifty-two, died of a heart attack with his vice-president and fellow Free Officer Anwar Sadat at his bedside. As over ten million Egyptians mourned him, King Hussein sobbed for the man who had almost killed him, but he was himself fighting for survival against the PLO under Arafat, who tried to kill him and convert Jordan into its base. Hussein was aided by Israel, Arafat by Syria, until a ceasefire was brokered by Nasser.

There had only been one Nasser, but there were several pretenders to his throne. The new contenders paraded their credentials at the funeral. The first mourner, sobbing ostentatiously, was the twenty-nine-year-old Lieutenant Muammar Qaddafi, a good-looking Libyan Bedouin who had been trained in Britain, where he played football in Hyde Park and promenaded down Piccadilly in Arab robes. He had worshipped Nasser and founded his own Free Officers, who in 1969 deposed King Idris. Promoting himself to colonel and president, Qaddafi rushed to Cairo. 'A nice boy,' Nasser had thought, 'but terribly naive.' He was much worse than naive.†

---

* They were aided by contingents from allies: Castro sent 4,000 Cubans to aid the Syrians; Bhutto sent a squadron of Pakistani fighter jets, one of which shot down an Israeli plane.
† Qaddafi proposed a pan-Arabist merger with Egypt. Rich on oil revenues, he backed Palestinian and anti-western radicals, buying arms from Moscow. 'Qaddafi's just a boy . . . they have no idea about Lenin or socialism,' said Brezhnev to Castro. 'What they do have is

A more formidable contender was also at the funeral: a tall, slim Syrian defence minister, General Hafez al-Assad, fair-haired with a bulging forehead. Just after the funeral, Assad withdrew Syrian forces from Jordan, helping to save Hussein; and then on 12 November 1970 he seized power in Damascus.

Assad was one of eleven children from a tough clan of Alawites, the sect that lived around Latakia on the coast, traditionally opposed to the Sunnis in Damascus. His grandfather had been nicknamed al-Wahhish – Wild Beast – and his father, Ali, champion of independent Alawite Latakia, took the name al-Assad – Lion – and Hafez became the Sphinx of Damascus.

He had hoped to become a doctor but instead qualified as a pilot, trained in Egypt and the USSR, before joining the nationalist Baathists, who in March 1963 seized power. He delivered the air force. Navigating fissiparous Baathist feuding, in 1964 he was promoted to air force chief while his brother Rifaat created a praetorian Baathist unit. In 1966, an Alawite faction under the leftist Salah Jadid seized power, appointing Assad defence minister. But the Assad brothers rejected internal revolution to confront Israel.

Assad promoted Alawites and Assads to run Syria. His brother Rifaat commanded his guards, the Defence Companies. Himself long married to Anisa Makhlouf, who was mother of five children, Hafez promoted her brother to run his security, the *Mukhabarat*; her nephew became the family's financier. Rifaat was married to Salma Makhlouf, a cousin of Anisa.

Hafez and Anisa's favourite son, Bassel, was eight when his father became president. 'We saw father at home but he was so busy that three days could go by without us exchanging a word with him,' Bassel later told his father's biographer. 'We never had breakfast or dinner together, and I don't remember ever having lunch together as a family.' Yet film footage records family holidays: 'As a family, we used to spend a day or two in Latakia in the summer, but then too he used to work in the office and we didn't get to see much of him.' For the moment, Hafez's brother, Rifaat, was his heir.

a lot of money. Simultaneously he's a fanatical Muslim.' 'My impression,' replied Castro, 'is that he's crazy.' Inflating himself in a cult of personality, preaching his own Marxist–Muslim ruminations in his *Green Book*, living in a luxurious Bedouin tent pitched at his military headquarters, protected by female bodyguards, he sought to conquer an empire in Chad and lead a pan-African union, having himself crowned king of kings. He backed IRA and Palestinian terrorists but also funded Nelson Mandela's ANC in South Africa. He degenerated into a radical Arab Nero, organizing terrorist atrocities such as the Lockerbie plane explosion, while murdering dissidents, ravishing young girls and grooming his son al-Saif for the succession.

As soon as he was president, Assad flew to Moscow to ask Brezhnev to rearm Syria – in return for the Tartous naval base. Brezhnev agreed. The Assads would be Moscow's Arab ally into the 2020s.

The last candidate to be Nasser's heir was the most overlooked: his Egyptian successor Sadat. But the poor farmer's son quickly won popularity by toning down the vicious secret police and expelling Soviet advisers, and he had a plan to humble Israel that coincided with Assad's ambitions. Assad quickly learned that Sadat too was planning a war: they met secretly and planned a surprise attack, though they concealed their ultimate aims: the refreshing and courageous Sadat was positioning himself to negotiate peace; the irredeemably radical Assad was aiming to eliminate the Zionist entity. Sadat consulted the Saudi king Faisal, the second of Abdulaziz's sons to reign, who was overseeing the kingdom's astonishing oil wealth and supervising improvements at the Holy Sites by his friend the builder Muhammad bin Laden. Faisal sent detachments to fight with the Egyptians, but he also believed the Arabs had never used the oil weapon. Now was the time.

As the Arabs trained for war, the Israelis cultivated close relations with a local friend, the shah, who admired the state, supplying its oil, buying its weapons and welcoming its leaders to Teheran. The shah was at his apogee.

On 12 October 1971, the shah held the party of the century to celebrate 2,500 years of Iran's Great Civilization.

IMPERIAL PEACOCKS: THE SATANIC FEAST AND THE ANGEL

The shah linked his own achievements to an unbroken line stretching back to pre-Islamic Persia. Oil revenues funded his status as the hegemon of the Gulf, aided by his close relationship with Nixon, while he outplayed Iraq by backing Kurdish rebels.

'Cyrus! Great King, King of Kings, you immortal hero of history,' intoned the shah portentously at the opening ceremony before the tomb of Cyrus. 'Today as in your day, Persia bears the message of liberty and love of mankind in a troubled world.' But he also warned his enemies: 'We are vigilant and will remain so.'

The shah welcomed 600 guests – including the US vice-president Agnew, the Soviet president Podgorny, Hussein of Jordan, Prince Philip and his daughter Princess Anne, and Emperor Haile Selassie – to Persepolis, where they stayed in a specially built Golden City of luxurious circular tents, marked with the insignia of the Cyrus Cylinder and lined with Persian carpets woven with the face of each potentate. As 50,000 specially imported songbirds trilled, the guests of honour ate a feast, prepared by Maxim's of Paris and featuring *paon à l'impériale* (imperial peacock) and 330 pounds of caviar, off Limoges plates, at a 230-foot table, lubricated by 2,500 bottles of Dom Pérignon champagne, 1,000 bottles of Bordeaux and 1,000 bottles of Burgundy, then they watched thousands of Iranian troops dressed in newly fashioned uniforms play Iranian heroes from Darius and Khosrow to Qajars and Pahlavis.

Yet there was disquiet: the songbirds dropped out of the sky, dead from the heat, there was a fight between French and Swiss waiters, Princess Anne murmured that she never wanted to eat peacock again. Farah hated 'these ghastly celebrations', later admitting the party had outraged religious Iranians 'without our being really aware of it'. 'Should I serve heads of state bread and radishes instead?' asked the shah. In his Iraqi exile, Ayatollah Khomeini raged against that 'Satanic feast'.

The shah had been spoiled by success. 'For twenty-seven years, I've been at the centre of international affairs,' he told Alam; 'it's hardly surprising I should be blessed with foresight.' He still had a sense of humour, teasing his mother about her sex life with Reza Shah.

Yet Alam 'noticed alarming changes': rigidity and arrogance. 'The Iranian people love me,' he said 'and will never forsake me.' In February 1971, the shah made the self-congratulatory declaration that 'Iran's leadership of the Middle East is acknowledged across the world.' Unsurprisingly he functioned in a conspiratorial world, convinced America was run by 'an organization working in secret powerful enough to dispose of the Kennedys and anyone else who gets in its way'. He believed he was protected by a murderous providence: 'I've learned by experience a tragic end awaits anyone who crosses swords with me: Nasser's no more; John and Robert Kennedy died by assassins, their brother Edward disgraced, Khrushchev toppled . . .'

In October 1967, he had promoted himself to *shahanshah* – king of kings. Yet Alam begged him to liberalize the autocracy. When Farah suggested elections, he mocked her: 'You're becoming quite the revolutionary yourself. I'd like to see you run this country . . .' The shah micromanaged SAVAK: 2,000 political prisoners were arrested and tortured. 'Sophisticated societies have efficient systems of interrogation,' he later explained. 'In cases of betrayal of one's country, anything goes.'

Even his love life spun out of control: 'A girl named Gilda,' wrote Alam, 'is spreading rumours around Teheran that His Majesty is head over heels in love with her.' Gilda was 'a beauty but vain and ruthlessly ambitious'.

'Bloody woman,' said the shah. 'I met her a few times ... The ru-mours are getting close to the Queen.' Farah's mother then threatened him with divorce 'to the effect that her daughter had not become accus-tomed to luxury'.

'Crap,' said the shah. 'After much debate,' wrote Alam, 'we agreed the bloody girl Gilda must be found a husband.' But the shah still lived for his 'visits': 'I passed on a letter addressed to His Majesty by a charming young creature,' recorded Alam. 'He was greatly flattered,' until Em-press Farah came to ask what they were talking about.

'Affairs of state,' replied the shah with a straight face.

In March 1972, the shah entertained a secret female visitor who *was* there to discuss affairs of state. The seventy-three-year-old Golda Meir, Israeli prime minister, a tough Zionist veteran (née Golda Mabovich in Kyiv) whom Ben-Gurion had predictably called 'the only man in my cab-inet', found much in common with the shah, and together they backed the Kurds against Iraq.

Golda Meir was now receiving warnings of war from an extraordinary agent right at the centre of Egyptian power. Sadat promoted Nasser's son-in-law Dr Ashraf Marwan, married to Mona Nasser, to be his chief adviser on foreign affairs. Yet a month later, in December, Marwan met a Mossad agent at London's Royal Lancaster Hotel to offer his services to Israel. Mossad called him the Angel. His motives were family bit-terness, frustrated ambition and conspiratorial glee. Now he began to warn that Sadat was planning a surprise attack. The intelligence was compelling, but Sadat twice delayed the war, undermining Marwan's credibility.

Meir had focused on the rising terrorism against Israel. On 6 Sep-tember 1972, Palestinian terrorists seized eleven Israeli athletes at the Munich Olympics. The terrorists were members of Black September, a unit formed by Arafat to hit Israel after King Hussein's defeat of the PLO in September 1970. At least one hostage was castrated; all eleven Israelis and nine terrorists were killed when the West German rescue attempt ended in a catastrophic shootout. Two days later Meir formed Committee X to direct Operation Wrath of God to assassinate the twenty leaders behind Black September: in October, as the assassinations start-ed, the Angel's warnings became urgent.

Sadat and Assad met in Alexandria and summoned King Hussein, concealing the imminence of the planned assault but inviting him to join. On 25 September 1973, the king flew to Tel Aviv and warned Golda that the Syrians would attack. 'Are they going to war without the Egyp-tians?' she asked.

'They'll cooperate,' replied the Hashemite. It sounded like a trap. Golda and Dayan believed the Arabs would never dare attack so soon after 1967.

On 6 October, the Arab armies caught Israel by surprise, pushing back Israeli forces from the Suez Canal and storming Israeli positions on Golan. Their air forces hit their targets, their hand-held Soviet Sagger missiles crippled Israeli armour, their anti-aircraft missiles brought down Israeli planes. The Syrians broke through Israeli positions; in desperate fighting, a few Israeli tanks just held the Syrians. But the Egyptians, with different aims, halted and dug in, letting Israeli throw everything at the Syrians.

By 8 October, Dayan was so downhearted he told Golda that Israel was in peril, asking, 'Is it the end of the Third Temple?' – his coded way of suggesting they might need to use nuclear weapons (code: Temple). Meir ordered the arming of thirteen tactical devices. Meir desperately asked Nixon for military supplies; Sadat and Assad requested more weapons from Brezhnev; both airlifted weapons to their proxies. But the worst was over: on the 9th the Syrians retreated. On the 11th, Israeli tanks counter-attacked and broke through, heading towards Damascus. On the 15th, Israeli forces crossed the Canal into Egypt and surrounded Sadat's Third Army. Suddenly Cairo was imperilled. Sadat panicked, appealing to Nixon and Brezhnev, together or separately, to send soldiers to stop the Israelis, who kept advancing.

On the evening of 24 October, Brezhnev told Nixon, 'I will say it straight that if you find it impossible to act jointly with us in this matter, we'd face the necessity to consider taking appropriate steps unilaterally.' Brezhnev dispatched airborne divisions towards Egypt. Kissinger rushed to the White House. 'What's going to stop them,' he asked, 'flying in paratroopers? Shall I wake the president?' But the soused president had passed out, 'distraught' about the growing clamour for his impeachment. Kissinger, now secretary of state, asked Sadat to withdraw his request for Soviet and American intervention and reassured Brezhnev, but he moved nuclear readiness to DEFCON 3. Brezhnev was shaken. Sadat withdrew his request; Brezhnev sent a conciliatory message as Kissinger shuttled between the combatants, finding Meir a 'preposterous woman', Assad surly and Sadat admirable. Assad and Sadat had both won respect but used it differently. Assad had moved to extend Syrian power into Lebanon, position himself as chief enemy of Israel and found a dynasty. As for Sadat, Kissinger thought he 'had the wisdom and courage of the statesman and occasionally the insight of a prophet'. Now he would risk everything to make peace.*

King Faisal now unsheathed the oil weapon, orchestrating an OPEC price rise and production cut. The ensuing oil crisis threatened to break the west. American vulnerability meant that in future it would fight to maintain access to oil. As for the Saudis, price rises showered Croesan wealth on the family as they embraced the double life of Wahhabi puritans at home and decadent sybarites abroad, splurging on yachts, palaces and call girls as well as monumental modernization and new armaments, much of the latter fixed by the son of Abdulaziz's doctor, Adnan Khashoggi, a globe-trotting playboy nicknamed the Pirate whose commissions made him the 'richest man in the world'. The House of Saud had joined the arbiters of the world, just as the House of Solomon was disintegrating.

On 12 September 1974, at his Jubilee Palace, the eighty-one-year-old Emperor Haile Selassie was amazed to confront a posse of young radical officers: what were they doing in his apartment? They told him he was under arrest. He did not believe them.

DID KING DAVID RETIRE?
THE *NEGUS* AND MAJOR MENGISTU

When the emperor returned from the shah's party, he faced a continuing war against Eritrean rebels in the north and Somalians in the south, while a famine raged in Wollo and Tigray in the north-east. The superpowers played proxies in the Horn of Africa: Moscow backed Siad Barre of Somalia, whom it armed to attack Ethiopia, which was supported in turn by Washington; Eritrean rebels, trained by China, attacked from the east. The emperor was losing his grip at home. When a loyal nobleman asked him to retire, he replied, 'Tell me, did King David retire?' Challenged by a female journalist, he shouted, 'Democracy! Republic! What do these words mean? Illusions, illusions,' before stalking out, grumbling, 'Who's this woman? Enough, go away.' But the illusions were his.

---

* As for the Angel, Marwan served in Sadat's office until 1976, when he retired to make a fortune, playing roles in the takeover battles for Harrods and Chelsea Football Club. His espionage was revealed much later by retired Israeli agents. On 27 June 2007, Marwan was killed, impaled on railings beneath his fifth-floor apartment in London. Egyptian potentates and intelligence chiefs attended his funeral. 'Marwan carried out patriotic acts,' claimed President Mubarak, implying Marwan was a double agent who had misinformed Israel. Naturally his death was blamed on Mossad, but it is likely he was liquidated by Egyptian intelligence, alarmed that he was planning an autobiography.

As 50,000 starved, the *negus* denied the famine: 'Everything is under control.' His ally, the shah, offered help, but 'He refused,' noted Alam, 'denying anyone was suffering or even that there was a drought.' The emperor's delusions reminded him of the shah: 'Inevitably one thinks of the parallels.'

Students protested; young officers conspired. In February 1974, after riots in Addis, Haile Selassie addressed the nation on television, calming the demonstrators, but his rule was subsiding rather than collapsing as generals, students, NCOs and Marxists planned a takeover. General Aman Andom, who had been sacked by the emperor, assumed leadership of a Provisional Military Administrative Council (nicknamed the Derg) to which each rebel unit sent three delegates.

On 12 September, the Derg easily took control of the Jubilee Palace and arrested the emperor, now a wizened old man, who was bizarrely conveyed in a VW Beetle to the military barracks – 'What? In here?' murmured the emperor at the sight of the car – before being imprisoned in the Grand Palace. Technically the rebels recognized the crown prince, abroad for medical treatment, as 'emperor-designate', but then appointed General Aman as first president. Aman had been the mentor of a young soldier of poor background who would emerge as leader. Mengistu Haile Mariam, now thirty-seven, had been sent to join the Derg by his commander, who wanted to get rid of a troublemaker. Instead the troublemaker took over the country. He had been trained in the USA but had suffered racism there. At home, this dwarfish servant's son burned with hatred for the racism of the imperial elite. 'In this country, some aristocratic families automatically categorize persons with dark skin, thick lips, and kinky hair as *barias* – slaves,' he told the Derg. 'Let it be clear to everybody that I'll soon make these imbeciles crawl and grind corn!' Now a convert to Marxism, he remained behind the scenes, but started to organize the Derg and push for Leninist revolution, encouraging the crushing of opposition within the military. In October, the killing started. Aristocrats and generals were arrested. When Mengistu's old patron, General Aman, resisted, he was denounced and killed in a shootout. In March 1975, Mengistu proposed that Derg leaders should be elected by secret ballot, and he emerged as joint vice-chairman with another major Atnafu Abate. For two years, the two majors Mengistu and Atnafu ruled Ethiopia.

In November 1974, after mass arrests of the elite, Mengistu proposed the execution of sixty princes, generals and aristocrats. The Derg approved. Mengistu arrived to interrogate the emperor, accusing him of stealing $14 billion: 'Where would I get this money? And for what?' he replied. 'To live in exile? We have experienced exile . . .' Living alone, cared for by his butler, the ex-monarch looked out of the window and wept. 'Oh Ethiopia, do you ever harbour ill towards me?' He was right to sense peril.

On 27 August 1975, Mengistu lingered outside his bedroom. The butler was sent away. Mengistu and three others chloroformed the old emperor, then suffocated him. 'We tried our best to save him,' lied Mengistu later, 'but we could not keep him.' Mengistu buried the last Lion of Judah under a slab outside the latrines in the palace yard.

With the Soviets challenging America in Africa, Kissinger ran foreign policy as Nixon faced impeachment. 'People have got to know,' Nixon said on television, 'whether or not their president is a crook. Well, I'm not a crook. I've earned everything I've got.'

His main enemy could not believe it: 'Nixon's in a difficult position,' said Brezhnev, chatting to Castro, 'but we think he'll get himself out of the problem. He has Kissinger, that cunning guy, he'll help him.' Castro hated the president – 'Nixon's a son of a bitch,' he said – but Brezhnev was so sympathetic he wrote to Nixon: 'We see how tendentiously and shamelessly your opponents manipulate this or that . . . I can't say it all. I think you understand everything the way I want you to understand it.' Brezhnev never sent the letter, but Nixon, losing even Republican support in Congress, faced imminent impeachment. On the night before he resigned, he asked Kissinger to kneel and pray.

On 9 August 1974, he resigned: 'Sometimes I've succeeded, sometimes I've failed, but always I've taken heart from what Theodore Roosevelt once said about the man in the arena, "whose face is marred by dust and sweat and blood . . ."'

BROTHER NO. I AND THE GANG OF FOUR

Watching from Beijing, the ageing Mao sympathized with Nixon, musing on the fall of emperors. Yet he was disappointed by the results of his American detente, grumbling to Kim Il-sung that Kissinger (secretary of state for the new President Ford) was 'a bad man' who had used China to seduce Moscow. He needed to protect his revolution but time was short; his henchmen Kang Sheng and Zhou Enlai were dying of cancer; Lin was dead; but he had his wife, 'the scorpion' Jiang Qing. He promoted her and her epigones, whom he nicknamed the Gang of Four. Of these he favoured a suave Shanghai security guard turned Red Guard leader, the thirty-seven-year-old Wang Hongwen, whom he appointed vice-chairman, his heir apparent.

Yet even Mao realized that the Gang lacked the authority to rule China, so he brought back Deng Xiaoping – Little Cannon – to command the army. As Mao, diagnosed with Lou Gehrig's Disease, started to wither and choke, he still micromanaged the leadership, refusing to allow Zhou any surgery for his cancer. The dying Zhou pressured Mao into appointing Deng first vice-premier, something Mao resented.*

Mao waited his moment to again unleash the Scorpion while celebrating the triumph of another of his vicious protégés, Pol Pot, bizarrely backed by ex-king Sihanouk.

On 17 April 1975, the young fighters of the Khmer Rouge, wearing black pyjamas and red scarves, emerged out of the jungle to occupy the elegant and Frenchified capital Phnom Penh, which resembled a sinking ship as the Americans choppered out, the government fled and the last premier was beheaded. The Khmer Rouge – only 68,000 of them – immediately ordered the capital's 370,000 people to leave within three days. On 23 April, Pol Pot arrived in a deserted Phnom Penh.

Pol Pot, forty-five years old, ascetic, soft-spoken and neurotic, a fan of French poetry, was 'very likeable, really nice, friendly', recalled a comrade, 'very sensible'. Formed by years of clandestine life in the jungles, 'he'd never blame you or scold you', usually holding a fan like the Buddhist monks who had taught him, yet he was a micromanaging fanatic obsessed with a vision of radical revolution to outpace even his patron Mao. General secretary of the Party since 1963, Pol led a tiny cabal of fanatical teachers so secretive that he rarely used a name, usually just Brother No. 1 or Brother No. 87, and so tight-knit that he and Brother No. 3, his old friend from Paris, Ieng Sary, were married to sisters Khieu Thirith and Khieu Ponnary, privileged daughters of a judge, whom they met at their private lycée before the sisters departed to study Shakespeare at the Sorbonne. Their Paris friend, another teacher Son Sen – Brother No. 89 – ran the secret police the *Santebal* (Peacekeepers) while his teacher wife ran education. This sixsome of homicidal pedagogues dominated *Angkar* – the Organization, the faceless government. Together, aided by the veteran intellectual Khieu Samphan, No. 4,

---

* But Mao allowed some of the purged to be rehabilitated: one of those was the Xi family. In 1972, the premier Zhou Enlai, who had himself survived Mao's terror only by slavish submission, orchestrated a family union for the purged Xi Zhongxun, who had not seen his son Jinping for a decade. It was still hard for the young Xi Jinping: he was rejected seven times when he applied to join the Communist Youth League, ten times when he applied to join the Party. But finally he enrolled to study engineering in Beijing. The hell of the Cultural Revolution was almost over for the family of the future ruler of twenty-first-century China.

they planned to forge 'a precious model for humanity' by murdering all educated and privileged classes, emptying the capitalistic cities and forcing Cambodians to return to a pre-industrial classless society in a Year Zero of Democratic Kampuchea. 'We'll burn the old grass,' said Pol, 'and the new will grow.' Two and a half million people trekked out of the cities, 20,000 died or were killed on the way, with executions starting immediately.

Yet the new head of state was a sacred king descended from four centuries of monarchs: Sihanouk broadcast from Beijing to tell the peasants to support the Khmer Rouge. Earlier he had trekked into the jungle to meet Pol Pot, his ego tickled, his suspicions disarmed by Brother No. 1's calm humility. Sihanouk returned to Phnom Penh to the royal palace; Pol Pot lived for a while in the Silver Pagoda where the leadership held its meetings, then moved to the old State Bank Building, codenamed K-1. As he orchestrated Year Zero, 'bad elements' were told, 'To keep you is no profit, to destroy you is no loss.' Then, to save ammunition, they were beaten to death with cudgels. Children were removed from families. Son Sen supervised the slaughter with 'a schoolmasterish eye for detail', his *Santebal* torturing and killing thousands at their headquarters, a converted school codenamed S-21, and at 150 lesser killing centres. The Khmer Rouge sometimes ate the livers of victims, used unborn foetuses as talismans and buried bodies as fertilizer. Over a million were executed; 2.5 million died in all.

Sihanouk defended Democratic Kampuchea publicly. The Khmer Rouge's brutality was known even before they took Phnom Penh, but in this Faustian compact Sihanouk embraced a benumbed strategic ignorance to ensure his survival and as part of his manoeuvrings to oust the myrmidons when he got the chance. Taken on a rural tour by No. 4 Khieu Sampan he saw what was happening, but it was too late. He tried to resign but was kept under house arrest. He had colluded not just in the slaughter of his people – 33 per cent of males died – but in that of his own family: five of his own children were liquidated. The pressure was punishing even for *Angkar*. Paranoiac stress drove Pol's wife insane, until she was finally incapacitated with schizophrenia. Phnom Penh was the first of America's toppling dominos; next, on 30 April 1975, Saigon fell to the Viet Cong; on 23 August, Vientiane, capital of the kingdom of Laos, fell to the Communist Pathet Lao, its last king worked to death in prison camps.

After unleashing the Killing Fields, Pol flew to meet Mao, who praised Year Zero: 'One blow and no more classes . . . a splendid achievement'. But, just as Stalin had lectured him, he lectured No. 1. 'You're right. Have you made mistakes? Certainly you have. Do rectification.' Pol privately disdained both Khrushchev and Mao; the latter's revolution 'has faded and is wavering' unlike 'the brilliant red' of his own. But Mao's warning was shrewd. Pol Pot aggravated the pro-Soviet Vietnamese, who fresh from their defeat of America would tolerate no lessons from their own former province.

Soon after meeting Pol, in January 1976, Mao's elegant premier Zhou Enlai died. The Helmsman himself could barely move or speak without the interpretation of his nurses, but was still acute and vigilant. When students used Zhou's funeral to protest, he dismissed Deng, again, but placed Little Cannon under house arrest, specifying that he was not to be harmed. After planning to crown his wife's acolyte, Wang Hongwen, one of the Gang, he surprised everyone by choosing Hua Guofeng, governor of his home province, whom he had met when he inspected the shrine at his birthplace. His nurses read him Sima Guang's history and, as he sank, Jiang Qing barged in, massaging his limbs, giving orders to doctors. But the master of the deathbed does not always inherit the kingdom.

THE CRUSADER AND THE PRINCE:
EUROPEAN TYRANTS AND DEMOCRATS

As Mao listened to the histories of the emperors and toyed with his heirs, a European monarch was arranging his own succession. On 30 October 1975 Francisco Franco, now eighty-two, fell into a coma. He saw himself as a ruler in the tradition of Ferdinand and Isabella and Philip II, so only a king could succeed a Franco. It helped that he had no son, just a daughter Carmen. He planned a royal succession of the Bourbons, the ancient French Capet family that had ruled Spain from 1714 until the revolution of 1931, balancing both branches along with his own *Movimiento Nacional*.

The count of Barcelona, son of the last king, had asked Franco if his sons could study in Spain. Franco agreed. In 1956, the two princes, the elder son Alfonso and Juan, were fooling around with what they assumed was an unloaded pistol. Juan pointed it at Alfonso and pulled the trigger. It was loaded, and the prince was killed. 'Say you didn't do it on purpose?' screamed their father. As he toyed with the two branches of the Bourbons, Franco took an interest in the handsome Juan, who, advised by his father, promised the generalissimo to respect his authoritarian vision.

In 1962, Franco invited Prince Juan and his wife to move into the Zarzuela Palace; seven years later, he asked Juan to swear loyalty to the

Movimiento Nacional and declared him the heir, advising him to take the name Juan Carlos. Franco had another condition: the prince must raise his daughter Carmen to duchess. Juan agreed. Courtiers warned Franco that the prince was a secret liberal and louche libertine, but Juan Carlos treated Franco like an old king; the Caudillo trusted him. In 1968, the dictator, ageing and controlled by his daughter and her husband, handed over Spain's last possession, tiny Equatorial Guinea, to Macías Nguema, a Fang witchdoctor's son, who had seen his father murder his brother before being bludgeoned to death by a Spanish colonial official; his mother committed suicide; and he himself was mentally ill, a drug user, who had sought treatment in Spanish mental hospitals. At a meeting in Madrid to discuss the country's future, he claimed that Hitler had meant to liberate Africa but had conquered the wrong continent. He often lost his thoughts during speeches, which voters interpreted as charming fey-ness, but soon after winning the first presidential election, he threw his foreign minister out of a window and embarked on a reign of terror of astonishing intensity. Seeing himself as the Unique Miracle and glorified with the motto 'No other God than Macías Nguema', he organized mass executions of around 50,000 victims, sometimes drowned out by loud English pop music. He kept the entire treasury in suitcases in his house, looting the tiny oil-rich country and killing or exiling a third of the popu-lation. Equatorial Guinea was so tiny that Nguema ruled with the help of his family, who were the only people strong enough to destroy him.*

The Spanish succession went more smoothly. On 20 November 1975, Franco died, and Juan Carlos succeeded him as king, promising 'I swear to God and on the holy Gospels to . . . remain loyal to the principles of the *Movimiento Nacional*' and making the dictator's daughter Carmen the duchess of Franco.

No monarch in Europe had enjoyed such power since 1918. Far from being a Francoist, the thirty-seven-year-old Juan Carlos, a compulsive hunter of big game and blonde women, was a democrat. For six years, he carefully guided Spain to democracy, sacking the Francoist premier, appointing in his place an ex-Francoist turned democrat, Adolfo Suárez, who in June 1977 won the first real elections for forty years. Suárez's new constitution converted Juan Carlos into a constitutional monarch.

---

* When his brother and nephew demanded money to pay the presidential guard, Nguema had them killed. The nephew's brother, Teodoro Obiang, decided to kill Nguema before he was killed: he arrested and executed him. Obiang has ruled ever since, promoting to vice-president and heir apparent his son Teodorín, who spent his Californian university days living at the Beverly Hills Hotel and running a $100 million yacht. The country has been ruled by one family since 1968.

But the king's achievement would be tested: in November 1978, a military coup – Operation Galaxia – was foiled, but the officers, believing that Juan Carlos could be controlled, planned another putsch to restore the dictatorship.

In India, it was Indira Gandhi who launched a coup.

INDIRA AND SON

The world's biggest democracy was becoming a hereditary dynasty: Indira Gandhi now promoted her favourite son, Sanjay, for the third generation of Nehrus.*

While her elder son Rajiv was a serene Indian Airlines pilot with an Italian wife, Indira adored her haughty second son Sanjay, an impulsive, spoilt and authoritarian princeling with a will to power that equalled Indira's own. A playboy who raced cars and piloted planes, he wanted to be an Indian industrialist, founding a car factory that survived on government favours. Indira worried about him and was fascinated by him. 'Rajiv has a job,' she wrote, 'but Sanjay doesn't . . . He's so like I was at that age – rough edges and all – that my heart aches for the suffering he may have to bear.'

Indira's imperious style, the rise of Sanjay, Congress's corruption and the oil crisis provoked strikes and riots in the country. By 1975, all these crises had converged. Court cases exposed the seamy cash payments of Indira's henchmen and used technicalities to challenge her own election victory. Morbid and suspicious, trusting no one, seeing a 'deep and widespread conspiracy . . . forces of disintegration . . . in full play', Indira now overtrusted Sanjay, to whom this ice-cold potentate wrote preposterous ditties: 'Sanjay, ferocious being / . . . Whose judgements almost always bite.'

In June 1975, a legal challenge citing electoral corruption invalidated her election. Sanjay warned her of a 'conspiracy' and told her not to resign. 'You know the state the country was in,' she said. 'What would have happened if I hadn't been there to lead it? I was the only one who could, you know.'

---

* Indira's husband, the editor and politician Feroze Gandhi (no relation), had died ten years earlier. It was not easy being married to Indira Nehru. For twenty years, the couple had lived with her father, Nehru. Feroze often found himself ignored, murmuring, 'Look at me! I'm husband to Indira Nehru.' But as a parliamentarian he was one of the first anti-corruption crusaders, a critic of corporate scandals engineered by business houses of Kolkata connected to Nehru.

On 25 June, Indira declared an emergency 'to bring about a situation of calmness and stability'. Using old British legislation kept in force by India's Constituent Assembly, Indira arrested opponents and censored the press, comparing India to a sick child and herself to its mother: 'However dear a child may be, if the doctor prescribed pills, they have to be administered . . . When a child suffers, the mother suffers too.' Her own child, Sanjay, who had disdained 'lily-livered' Indians who 'lacked guts', downplayed democracy: 'Future generations won't remember us by how many elections we had, but by the progress we made.' Sanjay boasted of his power – his mother 'obviously listens to my views, she listened to them when I was five' – and launched a twenty-five-point programme of radical reforms to fight poverty, clear slums and control the rise in population. Indira promoted him to leader of Congress Youth and overlord of Delhi. He revelled in his power, living right next to Indira and constantly with her. They sneered at democracy, which 'only throws up the mediocre person'.

Their arrogance led to abuse: fortunes were made in property development; 140,000 were arrested including 40,000 Sikhs; the same fate befell all opposition leaders. Sanjay oversaw a sterilization campaign to reduce the population: 8.3 million men underwent vasectomies, some of them by force, with the result that many died of infections. 'Indira is India and India is Indira,' declared her Congress courtiers, in 'a form of oriental excess to which I pay no attention'. But Sanjay's antics undermined her. 'Those who attack Sanjay attack me,' she said. 'He isn't a thinker, he's a doer.' Yet Sanjay was loathed. When Indira ended the emergency and called an election in March 1977, she was defeated so badly that she lost her own seat in the Lok Sabha – lower house – while Sanjay failed to win one. Soon afterwards she and then Sanjay were arrested. Indira and son were surely finished – just as Mao's wife soared.

On 9 September 1976, just after midnight, attended by his nurse-girlfriends, his wife Jiang Qing and nonentity heir Hua, Mao died. The Gang of Four controlled the Party. Jiang Qing demanded that she succeed Mao as chairman.

LITTLE CANNON, THE EIGHT IMMORTALS AND THE SCORPION'S GANG

Hua Guofeng, now chairman and premier, was alarmed; so were Mao's veteran henchmen, who secretly contacted Little Cannon, Deng, under house arrest in the leadership compound, Zhongnanhai. While Jiang suspected a conspiracy, Deng and her enemies planned a coup, recruiting the Central Guards, Unit 8341, the praetorians. On 6 October, Hua invited some of the Gang to discuss a new volume of Mao's works. Two were arrested as they arrived; Mao's nephew was nabbed in Manchuria; the vice-chairman Wang Hongwen resisted arrest, killing two guards; then Unit 8341 surrounded Jiang's mansion on Fisherman's Terrace and arrested her.

Hua had the top jobs but power flows fluidly to authority, not to office: unlike water, it always flows upstream. Deng held court at home, yet he held no office. Six months later, the seventy-three-year-old Little Cannon, as vice-chairman and chief of staff, took command, making decisions that would change the world: Mao, he decreed, was 'seven parts good, three parts bad', but the mistakes would be blamed on the Gang of Four, who were put on trial, Jiang Qing sentenced to death.* But his titanic decision was to open Chinese markets while maintaining the Party's monopoly of power. 'It doesn't matter whether a cat's black or white; if it catches mice, it's a good cat.' The cat was good. His reforms, he said, were China's 'second revolution'.† He recalled his old ally, Xi Zhongxun, in disgrace for sixteen years, only just out of prison, whom he appointed to run Guangzhou (Canton). Xi proposed an innovation: a trading region. 'Let's call them special zones,' agreed Deng, adding a phrase from the Long March: 'You have to find a way in, to fight a bloody path out.' Xi Zhongxun's son Jinping, who had spent years among the peasantry, returned to join the children of the elite – the princelings – who were aware that they would one day help rule China. Xi's special economic zones would power China's economic explosion. But in foreign policy 'We should act calmly. Don't be impatient.' Britain watched anxiously: the lease on Hong Kong would run out in 1997. Here too Deng was flexible, conceding 'one country, two systems' while saying that China would 'hide its capabilities and bide its time'.

Jovial, peppery, diminutive, foul-mouthed, the Little Cannon was now the Paramount Leader. Deng soon gave up most of his positions,

---

* Madame Mao was reprieved, then, diagnosed with cancer, released. Before she hanged herself at the hospital in 1991, she wrote: 'Today the revolution's been stolen by Deng's revisionist clique ... Chairman Mao exterminated Liu Shaoqi, but not Deng, unleashing endless evils ... Chairman, your student and fighter is coming to see you!'
† At the same time Deng approved another way to make China richer by reducing the population: in 1980, he enforced a One-Child Policy banning families from having more than one child and forcing an astonishing 108 million women to be sterilized and 324 million to have intrauterine devices installed. But Chinese families wanted sons more than daughters, and they used abortion and infanticide to tip the gender balance, so that by 2009, there were thirty million more boys than girls. By the time the law was abolished in 2016, the Party believed it had reduced the population by 600 million people.

deciding everything during meetings at home with veterans – known as the Eight Immortals after eight heroes of Chinese mythology – smoking, playing chess and expectorating into a spittoon, while his youngest daughter Deng Rong took notes. In world affairs, he advised, 'Observe calmly, secure our position.' The west was charmed by Deng* but, impatient for a thaw, Chinese students hoped for pluralism. Little Cannon was flexible about ideology and economics but never about power: that still came from the barrel of a gun.

In November 1975, the last empire, Portugal, suddenly withdrew from Africa, as a new foreign power arrived: the Cubans.

CASTRO'S AFRICA

Castro's anti-colonial war was an almost symmetrical inversion of history, the irony of which he appreciated: as the son of a Spanish colonialist, he dispatched his overwhelmingly black army to fight US-backed forces all over Africa. Cuba, he said, was 'repaying Africa for the slave trade'. He regarded Africa as 'the weakest link in the imperialist chain' and was willing to impose Marxism – a European ideological antidote to European empire – on the continent. His intervention was jump-started by a coup in Lisbon: in April 1974, a cabal of captains, weary of domestic oppression and African wars, seized power. Their Carnation Revolution, establishing democracy in Portugal, ended five centuries of empire and thirteen years of colonial wars – but accelerated a bloody scramble for Angola.

On 11 November 1975, Agostinho Neto, Marxist leader of the MPLA liberation movement, a Lisbon-trained doctor and son of a Methodist pastor, declared Angolan independence and seized the capital Luanda just as two rival anti-Communist factions occupied other parts of the country. Neto, married to a Portuguese, was a veteran revolutionary who had met Castro and Che in Havana and been regularly imprisoned by

* Deng was just as suspicious of Russian perfidy as Mao, telling the Americans, 'We believe the Soviets will launch a war.' In Cambodia, the genocidal Pol Pot, the Chinese proxy who had been groomed by Deng, clashed with the Soviet ally, Vietnam, reflecting traditional nationalist rivalries. In December 1978, when Pol Pot expelled ethnic Vietnamese and probed his neighbours, the Vietnamese drove him back into the jungles, where he survived as an isolated warlord until 1998. Deng decided to teach Vietnam (and the USSR) 'a lesson': in February 1979, China attacked Vietnam, but its forces were humiliated. As for Cambodia, the Vietnamese later installed a former Khmer Rouge commander, Hun Sen, who became premier. In 1991, Sihanouk returned as 'constitutional king', abdicating in 2004 for his son Norodom Sihamoni; but Hun Sen's harsh autocracy would endure for almost forty years. In 2022, Hun declared that his successor was to be his son.

Salazar, while continuing to practise medicine. After the colonial wars under Salazar's right-wing dictatorship and centuries of Portuguese predation, the war was brutal. Neto executed any opposition, declaring a one-party Soviet-style state, and appealed to Moscow and Havana for help. 'We accepted the challenge,' said Castro, who pointedly called it Operation Carlota after an enslaved female who, 'in 1843, led one of many risings against the stigmas of slavery and gave her life'. The Americans backed the other factions, and their covert ally, South Africa, occupied South West Africa and then invaded Angola. Thirty-six thou- sand Cubans were rushed to prevent the fall of Luanda, soon boosted to 55,000. 'Few times in history,' boasted Castro, who flew in to visit the front, 'has a war – the most terrible heart-rending human action imaginable – been accompanied by such a degree of humanity on the part of the victors.' Cuban troops, he added, were there for fifteen years. As late as spring 1988, some 40,000 Cuban, Communist Angolan and Namibian troops defeated Angolan rebels and their South African allies at Cuito Cuanavale, the largest modern battle in African history. Over 300,000 Cuban troops served in the country.

Angola became the ferocious front line in a proxy war raging across southern Africa from ocean to ocean. In the west, Castro backed in- surgents in South West Africa; in the east, in Portugal's other colony, Mozambique, Samora Machel, a well-off farmer's son whose grandfa- ther had fought for the last Gaza king, declared independence, backed by Castro and fighting counter-revolutionaries backed by South Africa. After centuries of Portuguese rule, and forty years of ferocious right- wing dictatorship, Machel nationalized property, tortured opponents in 're-education centres' and executed 30,000 class enemies. In the centre, the 270,000 white Rhodesians defied British plans to grant in- dependence to six million Africans. Backed by apartheid South Africa, the Rhodesians fought against the overwhelmingly black majority,* who were claiming independence decades after most of Africa for the country they called Zimbabwe in honour of the ruined thirteenth-century city.

In early 1977, Castro received requests for help from Mengistu in

---

* Its insurgents were themselves divided between tribal allegiances and superpower back- ers: the mainly Matabele ZAPU led by Joshua Nkomo was backed by Russia and Cuba; the ZANU – overwhelmingly Shona – led by Robert Mugabe, was backed by China. In 1980, Rhodesia became independent under a British-negotiated deal. Mugabe was elected prime minister and, aided by his secret-police chief Emmerson Mnangagwa, slaughtered 30,000 Nbedeles in massacres known as the *Gukurahundi* between 1983 and 1987. The killings won Mnangagwa the nickname *Ngwena* – Crocodile – and established Mugabe's dictatorship, which ruinously endured until his overthrow in 2017. His successor was the Crocodile.

Ethiopia, and sent 16,000 troops. 'We felt obliged to help the Ethiopians,' he said, 'and do our bit.' Soon after the suffocating of Haile Selassie, Ethiopia started to disintegrate: insurgents in Tigray and Eritrea intensified their rebellions at the centre. The revolution consumed its children. 'We'll tackle our enemies that come face to face with us,' said Mengistu, 'and we won't be stabbed in the back. We'll arm the comrades and avenge the blood of our comrades double and triple fold.' Mengistu and Atnafu drew pistols on each other in meetings as their rivalry simmered. On 3 February 1977, Mengistu carried out a purge of the Standing Committee of the Derg, pulling out a machine gun and personally mowing down his comrades, killing fifty-eight Derg officers. He was then elected chairman and emerged as dictator, basing his Terror – *Qey Shibir* – on that of Lenin in 1918. Brezhnev and Castro were impressed. 'Mengistu strikes me as a quiet, honest and convinced leader,' Castro concluded. 'He's an intellectual personality who showed his wisdom on 3 February . . . He had the rightists arrested and shot.' His rival Atnafu had been out of town on 3 February, but he was executed later that year.

'We want to assure you, Comrade Brezhnev,' said Mengistu on a visit to the Kremlin, 'we'll sacrifice everything for the revolution.' This was not hyperbole. 'Death to counter-revolutionaries,' he cried at a rally, dementedly smashing bottles of red fluid. But his Terror was also an imperial fight-back: 'We fought them when they sought to dismember the nation.' Mengistu was responsible for 750,000 deaths. But the Somalians were advancing towards Harar in eastern Ethiopia; in Tigray, a talented scholar called Meles Zenawi, just twenty-two, who had won the top Haile Selassie prize at the best school in Addis, founded the Marxist–Leninist League of Tigray that bizarrely supported Enver Hoxha in Albania against all the great powers; in Eritrea, a Marxist fanatic, Isaias 'Isu' Afwerki, trained in Beijing, was armed by China. Soviet Ethiopia was in jeopardy; Castro airlifted more troops.

After a triumphant progress across Africa visiting Neto and Mengistu, Castro flew on to Moscow to join Brezhnev celebrating yet another success: Communists had seized power in Afghanistan.

Shah Zahir, son of the founding monarch of the dynasty, had successfully navigated the Cold War as Soviets and Americans bid to back Afghan projects, but he was much closer to the Soviets: Kabul had been Khrushchev's first South Asian visit. The KGB funded a Communist Party that was divided between Pashtun- and Farsi-speaking factions just as the shah's reforms sparked an Islamicist movement. In 1973, the shah was overthrown by his cousin and long-serving premier, Prince

Daoud, who was supported by the Communists. But his reforms disappointed while his claims of Pashtunistan in Pakistan led its premier Bhutto to start funding Islamists through his secret service ISI. When Brezhnev complained about American interference in Afghanistan, Daoud defied him and started arresting Communists.

In April 1978 Communist troops stormed the palace and machine-gunned Daoud and family, including women and children, tossing them into a mass grave. Nur Muhammad Taraki – a veteran writer of Afghan socialist-realist novels who combined *bon vivant* womanizing with fanatical Marxism – took control and proclaimed himself 'the Genius of the East'. He grew so overconfident and out of touch that he boasted to the KGB, 'Come back in a year – the mosques will be empty!'

Brezhnev regarded Taraki as a fellow Leninist and backed his programme of secular education, land reform and female rights – much of it not dissimilar to what the Americans would try to impose after 9/11. But their radical reforms alienated the conservative Afghans, while the Pashtun faction started murdering their moderate Tajik rivals. The Soviets advised them to stop killing each other, yet 'They continue to execute people who disagree with them,' said Soviet premier Kosygin. As *mujahedin* (Islamicist guerrillas) launched an anti-Communist jihad, Taraki begged for Soviet troops and massacred any opposition, his premier Hafizullah Amin killing around 30,000 in the first eighteen months. Then in September 1979 Amin arrested Taraki and, claiming that Brezhnev had given him permission, had the old man strangled. Brezhnev was upset; the countryside seethed with jihadis; the Russians were losing control and the KGB chairman, Yuri Andropov, had an old-fashioned solution – poison.

Brezhnev, now seventy-two, had just suffered a stroke, but his fellow geriatrics in the Kremlin leadership felt no need to retire him in a system as sclerotic as his arteries. His decline was quick. Sickly and addicted to sleeping pills, drinking heavily, Brezhnev struggled to control his family, his daughter Galina smuggling Siberian diamonds and brazenly having affairs with gangsters and lion tamers. The horizon of this world potentate shrank. Often Brezhnev was alone all day: '16 May 1976. Went nowhere. No one called. I called no one. In the morning I had my hair cut, shaved and washed my hair. Walked a bit. Watched Central Army [football team] lose to Spartak. The lads played well.' But the diaries reveal who was rising. 'Yu. Andropov phoned. He came. We talked.' Andropov supplied sedatives for him. More importantly, they discussed what to do with the murderous Afghans.

THE SPYMASTER: ANDROPOV AND HIS PROTÉGÉ GORBACHEV

'A committee's been set up,' Andropov wrote to Brezhnev, 'to liquidate Amin.' The KGB had a department – the Camera – dedicated to poisons. Andropov infiltrated into Amin's kitchens an Azeri assassin, codenamed Patience, trained as a cook.

Andropov had a vision to reform the Soviet Union. As ambassador in Budapest he had orchestrated the crushing of the Hungarian revolution in 1956 and then, appointed KGB chairman in 1967, he had supervised the invasion of Czechoslovakia, as well as the new repressions against dissidents and Jewish refuseniks, devising the use of psychiatric hospitals to 'destroy dissent in all its forms'. Implacable, teetotal and incorruptible, Andropov was a Dostoevskian inquisitor who knew everything about everyone. Interviewing a subordinate who said, 'Let me tell you about myself,' Andropov replied, 'What makes you think you know more about yourself than I do?' But Andropov had a family secret: he had been brought up by a stepfather and had worked on Volga barges, a perfect proletarian background, but he was actually the son of a Jewish jeweller, Karl Fainshtein, killed in an anti-German riot during the First World War and his wife Evgenia – a fact he concealed in order to join the Communist Party in 1937. His secret Jewishness did not discourage his persecution of Jewish dissidents.

Abroad, Andropov disdained the corruption and weakness of western democracies and pursued sophisticated programmes of disinformation that are the real origins of today's 'fake news'. This diehard Leninist, who loved detective novels and jazz, believed that harsh measures were required while the dictatorship reformed itself. He realized that the Soviet state, increasingly interlinked with the world economy, needed to change. Its military expenditure – 15 per cent of its GNP – was not outrageous for a superpower. In 1977, its new West Siberian oil field made it the world's biggest producer. Yet it was overdependent on oil profits, which it spent on importing grain instead of western technology, and on subsidising Cuba and other vassals, which Andropov called 'vulgar robbery'. 'The task is to work out a system of logistical, economic and moral steps,' he said, 'that would encourage renovation of equipment and managers.' He foresaw the peril presented by Lenin's structure of fifteen 'independent' republics. 'Let's get rid of the national partition,' he said. 'Draw me a new map of the USSR.'

'In twenty years,' he said in 1975, 'we'll be able to allow ourselves what the west allows itself now, freedom of opinion and information, diversity in society and art.' But he believed that political power must remain the monopoly of the Communist Party. Like Deng in China, he envisaged a rising economic freedom but steely political control. He was 'the most dangerous', noted a reformer, Alexander Yakovlev, 'because he was the most smart'.

Andropov had recently befriended an energetic new Party leader in Stavropol whom he visited for holidays, hikes and singalongs of songs forbidden by his own KGB: Mikhail Gorbachev. The upcoming Gorbachev praised Brezhnev and did what was necessary to rise. But he and his auburn-haired wife Raisa, both children of families killed by Stalin, were appalled by the inertia of Brezhnev.

Andropov guided the rise of Gorbachev, who knew that the system was failing. Gorbachev found a kindred spirit in the tough but intelligent Georgian Party chief, Eduard Shevardnadze, blue-eyed with a plume of white hair, who walking along the Black Sea beach suddenly said to him, 'You know, everything is rotten.' In 1978, Brezhnev, prompted by Andropov, promoted Gorbachev to the Politburo in Moscow. 'Do we really need this?' asked Raisa.

'We can't go on,' replied Gorbachev, 'living like this.'

In the Kremlin, he was amazed to see the general secretary fall asleep in Politburo meetings. The leadership functioned like 'a scene from Gogol'. Gorbachev complained to Andropov, who replied that 'the stability of Party, country and even the world' required they 'support Leonid'.

Further down, in the lower ranks of the KGB, Andropov fostered an esprit of knightly loyalty. In 1969, he promoted a new cult of the secret policeman, the Chekist, backing a TV mini-series *Seventeen Moments of Spring* featuring a Soviet super-spy, Colonel Isayev, who penetrates Nazi headquarters using the name Stierlitz.* It worked. Stierlitz became a Soviet hero. Brezhnev so loved the series he changed the timing of Central Committee meetings to watch it, and it inspired many – including a Leningrad law student named Vladimir Putin – to join the KGB. Putin hero-worshiped Andropov and wanted to be Stierlitz. 'My notion of the KGB,' he remembered, 'came from romantic spy stories.'

In 1975, Putin joined the KGB at the age of twenty-three, working in both counter-intelligence and internal surveillance. Later he was trained at the Yuri Andropov Institute. His background was conventional. He had

---

* Modern spies, part old-fashioned killers, part covert bureaucrats, symbolized the mystical power of surveillance and violence controlled by the modern bureaucratic states, celebrated in the genre of spy thrillers and movies. The British version was James Bond, a debonair and sadistic killer-seducer, created by a former British banking scion and security agent, Ian Fleming, whose creation dovetailed with his own aristocratic and sado-masochistic tastes. The most successful James Bond movie, *Thunderball*, released in 1965, appeared at the height of the Cold War.

grown up in the impoverished, leaky apartments of a decaying Leningrad block, running with street children, but his mother, Maria, forty-one at his birth, had lost a baby in the Siege and cosseted him with the special attention that can sometimes endow a child with great self-confidence. Vladimir – known as Vova – was rescued by the kindness of a Jewish neighbour who fed him while his parents worked, and by his sports training as a karate fighter. But he had a deeper secret-police connection: his grandfather Spiridon had worked in the NKVD service staff, cooking for both Lenin and Stalin; his father had served with NKVD units in the war.

Now the poisoning of the Afghan tyrant proved more difficult than Andropov had hoped: Brezhnev and the Politburo agonized over what to do. Andropov initially advised restraint. Let poison do its work. But if intervention became necessary, surely it would be quick and easy.

In August 1978 the shah of Iran was telephoned by his neighbouring potentate, Saddam Hussein, Iraqi vice-president, who asked if he would approve the killing of that troublesome Iranian exile in Iraq, Ayatollah Khomeini. Saddam explained that Khomeini was making trouble among Iraqi Shiites. Saddam could kill him or exile him. Which would the shah choose?

IMAM, SHAH AND SADDAM

By now even the shah's courtiers were suggesting reform. In June 1974, Alam asked him, 'How can we expect people to go without bread when we're telling them we're in the midst of a golden age?' The shah 'seemed thoroughly taken aback and ordered me to set up a committee'. Yet the shah's gambit to make Iran the hegemon of the Gulf and break up Iraq was working. He had backed a bloody Kurdish insurgency, led by the latest warlord of the Barzani family, which forced the Iraqis to recognize their autonomy.* But the emergent leader of Iraq – Saddam Hussein – feared that the loss of Kurdistan would break the country up.

---

* The Kurds' leader was Mustafa Barzani, the latest of the dynasty to lead their struggle. The Barzanis were Sufi sheikhs and landowners from Sulaymaniyah (Iraq). After the disappointed promise of an independent Kurdistan, Sheikh Mahmud Barzani rebelled against the British and Hashemites in Iraq and in 1923 declared himself king of Kurdistan. He was captured in 1932, and the struggle was continued by young kinsmen, Sheikh Ahmed and his brother Mustafa. During the Second World War, Barzani was backed by Stalin to carve a Kurdish republic out of western Iran, but one of the terms of Yalta was Soviet withdrawal. The republic collapsed and Barzani escaped to the Soviet Union, returning to Iraq after the fall of the monarchy. In 1971, Saddam tried to kill him, so now aged seventy he launched a new insurgency. Once again, it looked as if Kurdistan was about to be born.

The shah and Alam regarded Saddam as a 'slim, handsome young man of considerable intelligence'. Born in the town of Tikrit, he had not been spoiled by an admiring mother nor had he clashed with an aggressive father. Instead his father had died after his birth and his mother Sabha had collapsed, sending the child to be raised in Baghdad by her brother, Khairallah Talfah, a radical Arab nationalist. Khairallah introduced the boy to the Baathist Party, which in 1963 seized power in both Iraq and Syria, though it was soon crippled by feuds and purges. 'The Baathists,' said Khrushchev, watching the killings, 'borrowed their methods from Hitler.' Saddam earned kudos with the attempted assassination of an Iraqi president and fled to Egypt, but in 1968 he returned when his cousin General Ahmed al-Bakr, who was in turn married to Uncle Talfah's sister, seized power in the latest spasm of Baathist faction fighting, appointing Saddam as secret police supremo.

When Saddam married his uncle's daughter, Sajida, a teacher, he placed himself at the centre of a tiny clan, soon joined by his uncle's son and his half-brothers. As the shah spent billions on American armaments, Saddam, vice-chairman of the Revolutionary Command, cultivated Moscow. In April 1972, Baghdad signed a treaty with the Soviets, while Saddam became close to the KGB spy Yevgeny Primakov – sometimes codenamed Maxim though his real name was Finkelstein (he was Jewish) – who admired in the Iraqi a 'firmness that often turned into cruelty, a strong will bordering on implacable stubbornness'. Al-Bakr fell ill just as the shah's Kurdish rebels threatened to detach northern Iraq. Saddam was not strong enough to stop them; he had to negotiate.

At a meeting in Algiers in March 1975, the shah pulled off a coup when Saddam conceded Iranian control of the Shatt al-Arab waterway in return for abandoning the Kurds. Success discourages reform, and the shah was triumphant. By July the following year, Alam was desperate: 'We claim to have brought Iran to the verge of a Great Civilization, yet it's hit by power cuts and we can't even guarantee water in the capital . . .' The shah denied it all: 'The only thing wrong with the economy is the extraordinary rate at which it's growing.'

Power is corrosive; the shah had been playing the game since 1941, almost forty years. 'There's no firm hand on the tiller,' warned Alam, 'the captain is overworked.' Meanwhile, 'The People want more than material progress, they demand justice, social harmony, a voice in political affairs. I'm gravely apprehensive.' But by January 1977 vast revenues had been frittered away. 'We're broke,' said the shah to Alam.

One of the shah's Swedish lovers got food poisoning, but when the court minister sent the royal doctor he went to Alam's 'French girlfriend' instead. 'His Majesty nearly wept with laughter.' But Iranians were not laughing. Millions of peasants had poured into the cities where, anchorless and impoverished, neglected by venal elites, they turned to traditional mullahs and listened to tapes smuggled in from Ayatollah Khomeini in Najaf that called the shah 'the American serpent whose head must be smashed with a stone'. Now Saddam offered the shah the head of Khomeini: the king of kings rejected the offer. Saddam expelled the ayatollah.

Khomeini sought refuge in Paris. The French president Giscard d'Estaing consulted the shah, who did not object. In October, Khomeini settled in Neauphle-le-Château, a Parisian suburb. His media appearances, sitting berobed under an apple tree, the antithesis of the gold-braided flash of the shah, were managed by an alliance of educated liberals, Shiite moderates and leftist revolutionaries, trained by the PLO in Lebanon. Each believed they controlled the old man. None did.

The shah discounted the threat, calling his opposition 'a few corrupt scoundrels'; SAVAK continued arresting and torturing suspects. But the trouble with a one-man regime is that it depends on the survival of one man: the shah, feeling exhausted, was secretly diagnosed with lymph cancer, while his trustee Alam was himself dying of cancer. Treated with steroids, depressed and passive, Shah Mohammad vacillated. He ignored the start of regular demonstrations and fundamentalist attacks. Then in August 1978 a fire at the Rex Cinema in Abadan, started with petrol, incinerated 420 people – the doors were found to be locked. It was a provocation by Islamic terrorists, and it worked: SAVAK was blamed, and the protests snowballed.

The sick shah lost the will to fight, refusing to shoot protesters. But he consulted his ally, America, where the backlash after Watergate had washed into the White House an inexperienced, sanctimonious and toothsome Democrat, Jimmy Carter, a peanut farmer from Georgia. Carter was the anti-Kissinger, but his mere presence weakened American power. He signalled that he did not support the shah, while Khomeini's envoys confided that the ayatollah would never threaten US oil. As millions seethed in the streets, the shah was astonished by the American betrayal and struggled to find anyone who would become premier; as his army wilted, his monarchy crumbled like rotten wood. On 8 September 1978, security forces fired on mass protests, killing around 100: Black Friday provided martyrs and momentum.

On 16 January 1979, the Shah, frail, pale, yet straight and dignified, boarded his plane as a young officer fell to his knees to kiss his hand,

and Farah, sedated, wept silently. The shah flew to Egypt where Sadat welcomed him. Two weeks later, on 1 February, Khomeini took off from Paris on a plane filled with his leftist advisers and American news journalists who asked him how he felt. *'Hichi'* – Nothing – he replied, rejecting American sentimentality and instead expressing the mystical grandeur of God. Six million people – one of the largest crowds ever – almost crushed him as his convoy drove to the Martyr's Cemetery, where he had to be rescued by a military helicopter. 'I will decide the government,' he told the crowds. 'I will punch this [provisional] govern-ment in the teeth.' The decisive moment came fast: his secular allies had arranged for him to stay in the Refah girls' school, but the next morning the mullahs, allies and former pupils, burst in and conveyed Khomeini, now hailed as the infallible imam, to their headquarters.

Although he appointed a moderate Islamicist as premier, he had tricked the leftists, the moderates and the Americans: Khomeini del-egated power to a Council of the Islamic Revolution, where many of his pupils, men who had been in and out of prison for years, joined the inner circle: one of them, a forty-year-old Najad clergyman called Ali Khamenei, trusted by Khomeini, organized a new army, the Islamic Revolutionary Guards. These two – first Khomeini, then Ali Khamenei – would rule Iran as imams into the 2020s.

Khomeini's real nature was revealed at once as his supporters won shootouts with the Imperial Guard and arrested all the generals and ministers. These they brought to the Refah school, where the chief revolutionary judge, Sadeq Khalkhali, a plump, murderous giggler, a Khomeini disciple since 1955 and long-time leader of the Fadayan-e Islam, shot them on the roof. When he received a phone call asking him to delay the execution of the shah's long-time premier, he asked them to wait and then personally shot him before returning – 'Sorry, the sentence's already been carried out.' Later he boasted, 'I killed over 500 criminals close to the royal family . . . I feel no regret,' except that the shah had escaped. In October, the shah arrived for medical treatment in America, inspiring a 'Death to America' campaign: 400 students stormed America's Teheran embassy. They took sixty-six Americans hostage, backed by Khomeini, who used the episode to remove the moderates and impose his unique theocracy: the Supreme Leader – by the Law of the Guardian – was an absolute sacred monarch, superior to an elected president and assembly.

Humiliated, Carter dispatched commandos in Operation Eagle Claw to rescue the hostages, but the choppers crashed in a sandstorm, kill-ing eight soldiers, whose wizened bodies became props in a macabre

Iranian show. 'Who crushed Mr Carter's helicopters?' asked Khomeini. 'We did? The sands did! These sands are agents of God. Let them try again.' They did not. American commanders-in-chief require the laurels of victory: Carter was tainted with defeat and misfortune, but he did nurture the first Arab–Israeli peace treaty.

On 19 November 1977, Sadat, confident after his early successes against Israel, had courageously flown to Jerusalem.

JJ OF GHANA AND SADAT IN JERUSALEM

Sadat told the Knesset: 'Let's put an end to war.' His Israeli host, Menachem Begin, a dour Polish-born nationalist who had used terrorism to undermine the British Mandate, had overturned thirty years of Labour government, winning the votes of the neglected Mizrahi Jews from Arab countries. Begin returned Sinai to Egypt in return for a peace that outraged the rest of the Islamic world. In March 1979, when the deal was signed in Washington, Assad of Syria and Qaddafi of Libya denounced Sadat's betrayal along with Imam Khomeini.

Khomeini's first foreign visitor was Yasser Arafat, the Palestinian leader, who had trained many Iranian radicals in his Soviet-funded Lebanese camps. Faith is contagious and fungible: the revolution of 1979 changed the world as much as those of 1789 and 1917. Secular westerners saw Khomeini as a spectre from the obscurantist, intolerant past. Actually, he was the future. Khomeini's ambitions were pan-Islamic, unbounded by Shiism or Iranian history, embracing the secular Palestinians ('Today Iran, tomorrow Palestine') as well as Sunnis. Khomeini had been inspired by the Egyptian Sunni, Qutb, hanged by Nasser; now Qutb's followers were inspired by him. President Sadat had granted asylum to his friend the dying deposed shah, who moved from America to Panama, pursued by Khomeini's agents demanding his murder or extradition. When he died in Cairo, Sadat buried him in al-Rifai Mosque beside Ismail the Magnificent and Farouk. Sadat's peace with Israel and loyalty to the shah aroused Islamicist hatred.

In Pakistan, on 4 April 1979, the elected former prime minister Bhutto was hanged on the orders of the Islamicist general who had deposed him. The chief of staff, General Muhammad Zia, had in July 1977 deposed Bhutto, whose high-handed autocracy and manoeuvres between socialism, Islam and the feudal lords, not to speak of the murder of his opponents, had alienated all sides. Bhutto himself had appointed Zia and encouraged the brisk, moustachioed British-trained officer to promote Islam in the army, but the general loathed him, later trying him for murder. Now the Shiite Iranian revolution encouraged the Sunni Zia to Islamicize Pakistan and impose sharia law.

Khomeini's influence was powerful, but he faced a present threat: he despised Saddam Hussein and called for the destruction of the 'godless Baathists'. Saddam despised him back.

On 22 July 1979, Saddam Hussein, newly minted president of Iraq, puffing on a cigar, strolled on stage at a meeting of the Revolutionary Command Council to launch a purge, videotaped and later shown throughout the country. After Sadat's peace with Israel, President al-Bakr had proposed a union with Assad, his fellow Baathist in Syria: al-Bakr would be president, Assad his deputy, and Saddam would lose his position. Saddam therefore undermined the deal. This led to a schism with Assad of Syria, who instead made an alliance with Iran, an alliance that would ensure the survival of his dynasty into the 2020s.

After finessing al-Bakr's retirement, Saddam emerged from the shadows, a half-educated radical whose easy rise, ingenious cruelty and sycophantic court convinced him of a providential destiny to be a new Saladin and Nasser, Nebuchadnezzar and Stalin rolled into one. On taking the presidency, he arrested his enemies and tortured them to incriminate others in 'the Syrian plot'.

Now on stage, he presided over the naming of 'brothers who betrayed us' in the audience with the insouciance of a diabolical game-show compere. As they were named, Saddam shouted 'Get out!' and the cameras showed suited *Mukhabarat* agents escorting them out of the room as the survivors displayed their loyalty by cheering, shouting and hailing Saddam. When it was over, Saddam and his henchmen wept, dabbing their eyes with handkerchiefs, and later led the survivors down into the cellars where they were given pistols and forced to shoot some of the prisoners; others were reprieved and forced to kill more.

Khomeini and Saddam were not the only leaders who sought to use murder to cleanse their nations. On 26 June 1979, a thirty-two-year-old Ghanaian flight sergeant, Jerry Rawlings, set up a line of stakes on the beach in Accra, Ghana, and invited the press to a macabre spectacle. 'There were six stakes, each with a rope dangling from it,' recalled a journalist. 'Sandbags were piled behind each stake.' Then an ambulance drew up. 'The door was flung open' and out stepped two ex-presidents, Generals Akuffo and Afrifa, and four top officers. 'A sudden hush fell on the teeming spectators' as the men were tied to the stakes. 'Hardly anyone saw the firing squad enter the tents, all attention was on the condemned officers . . .'

Son of an Ewe mother and a Scottish pharmacist from Galloway, 'JJ' Rawlings was a flashy, tall pilot disgusted by the venality and incompetence of the military and civilian rulers who had followed Nkrumah. But, recently married to Nana and with three children, he kept failing his officer examinations and was about to be dismissed from the military. Capricious and impetuous, Rawlings joined a secret organization, the Free Africa officers, planning coups across the continent.

His own coup was devised by him and his best friend from Accra's famous British-style Prince of Wales boarding school, Major 'JC' Kojo Boakye Djan; as boys they had rebelled against the English headmaster. In May 1979, Rawlings burst in on his friend: 'JC, let's go for a drink.'

Over cocktails at the Continental Hotel, Rawlings suddenly declared, 'JC, we're ready to take over.'

'You and who?' asked JC.

'I've got a lot of boys,' said JJ. JC warned him against it. 'You temporize too much,' warned JJ, 'you risk being seen as a coward.'

The coup was a disaster. Rawling and his 'boys' were captured, and were facing execution. 'The options were clear,' said JC. 'We had to release Rawlings before he was executed.'

On 4 June 1979, JC stormed the prison and liberated Rawlings; they then seized the Castle and overthrew General Akuffo. Setting up an Armed Forces Revolutionary Committee, Flight Sergeant Rawlings declared 'a house-cleaning exercise', arresting three ex-presidents and five generals. The first shootings were in private, but on the beach in Accra crowds were gathered.

'There was no audible order to fire,' recalled the journalist. 'Just a sudden: *ko.ko.ko.* I could see the blood soaking through . . .' Years later, Rawlings reflected that it was 'very painful and regrettable, but there was no other way out'. A hit list of 300 was compiled and all were killed, before Rawlings amazed everyone by letting a free election take place, won by a respectable diplomat and Nkrumahite, Dr Hilla Limann. Rawlings returned to the barracks, but after two years of weak, corrupt rule, on 31 December 1981 he retook the Castle. 'Fellow Ghanaians,' he announced, 'this isn't a coup. I ask for nothing less than a revolution . . . Nothing will be done from the Castle without the consent of the people.'

Rawlings presided over the revenge killing of three judges who had dared to challenge his repressions during his first rule. Faced with an outcry, Rawlings arrested his own junta henchman and had him shot. Meanwhile he ruined the economy with Marxist nationalizations, encouraged by his allies Castro and Qaddafi. Rawlings resembled many of the pro-Soviet tyrants in Africa, but he was not one of them: ultimately this maverick would surprise everyone.

Back in the Gulf, Saddam and Khomeini had long hated each other. Saddam had almost had Khomeini assassinated; instead he killed the Shiite ayatollah al-Sadr. The Iraqis had long resented Iranian superiority and the shah's power: Saddam's surrogate father Uncle Talfah had written a pamphlet, *Three Whom God Should Not Have Created: Persians, Jews and Flies*. Now Saddam flew down to Riyadh to get Saudi support. Khomeini detested the Saudis, whom he had mocked as 'the camel-grazers of Riyadh and the barbarians of Najd'. Fahd, Saudi crown prince and son of Abdulaziz, promised Saddam a billion dollars a month. The Americans greenlighted the war; so did Brezhnev, who had just taken a fatal decision.

OPERATION 333 IN KABUL

Operation Storm-333 was the most successful commando mission of modern times. At 19.15 on 27 December 1979, more than a thousand Soviet commandos, disguised in Afghan uniforms, stormed the Tajbeg Palace ten miles outside Kabul, to liquidate the Afghan general secretary Hafizullah Amin, whose radical policies and murderous purges, admiration for Stalin, and American education, alarmed the Soviets. Brezhnev's senile elation was disturbing: he tangoed with typists and waitresses, but in public he could not finish a sentence, becoming a national joke. But the omnipotent geriatrics agonized about Amin. 'Under no circumstances,' said Andropov, 'can we lose Afghanistan.'

The generals had warned against invasion. Privately Gorbachev thought it 'a fateful mistake', but on 12 December Andropov won the argument. As troops were mustered, Amin had moved out of the Presidential Palace to the heavily defended Tajbeg. Andropov's Agent Patience was now Amin's chef. If he could kill Amin, an Afghan invasion could be avoided.

On 13 December, Agent Patience poisoned Amin, but his nephew ate most of the poisoned food and had to be flown to Moscow and treated with an antidote. Then a sniper tried to shoot him but could not get close. Andropov ordered a quick surgical strike to liquidate Amin and pacify the country. On 25 December, Soviet forces started arriving with Amin's approval. On the 27th, just hours before Storm-333, Amin presided over a banquet where he was poisoned again: he and his guests were all ill. Amin went into a coma but his Coca-Cola addiction diffused the poison and a Russian doctor, unbriefed by the KGB, revived him. Once news reached the hit squad that Amin was alive, 700 commandos led by twenty-five assassins of the Thunder unit of Alpha Group along with KGB and GRU contingents backed by 700 paratroopers and *Spetsnaz* operators stormed the palace, defended by 1,500 troops, who fought back.

'The Soviets will save us,' said Amin as Andropov's commandos blasted their way in.

'They *are* the Soviets,' replied his adjutant.

'It's all true,' said Amin. Once inside the palace, the assassins slaughtered Amin and virtually his entire family, his wife and son aged eleven and 350 guards; a daughter was wounded but survived. The parquet floors were awash with blood. A pro-Soviet president Karmal was installed; 80,000 troops with 1,500 tanks seized the cities, soon rising to 125,000; and at its peak over 600,000 personnel were drawn into the war. The invasion sparked a growing insurgency by around 250,000 mujahedin under tribal and religious leaders,* backed first by Pakistan, then by the CIA and the Saudis.

Afghanistan provided perfect cover for Saddam. On 22 September 1980, he invaded Iran, calling it 'Saddam's Qadisiyya', referring to the 638 Arab defeat of the Persians. Yet Saddam failed to destroy Khomeini; on the contrary, the Arab attack rallied Islamic zealotry and Iranian nationalism behind the imam, saving the regime. Thousands of Iranians volunteered to wear the red bandannas of martyrdom and were sent over the top of the trenches, often unarmed except for the key to the gates of heaven, in human waves that halted the Iraqi advance. As Khomeini executed Marxists and liberal 'traitors' in massive numbers, he rushed 200,000 recruits to his new army, the Revolutionary Guards. America and Russia lavished military aid on the Iraqi dictator. 'It's a pity,' said Kissinger, 'both sides can't lose.' The war would last ten years and kill a million young men – a forgotten catastrophe that encouraged Khomeini to consolidate his theocracy and Saddam to take more risks, funded by the Saudis.

King Fahd, fourth of Abdulaziz's sons to be king, reacted to the Iranian challenge – and an attack by Islamicist rebels on the Mecca shrine – by tightening religious observance in the kingdom, changing his title to Guardian of the Two Sanctuaries and funding a Wahhabi campaign

---

* One of these, a Pashtun mullah named Jalaluddin Haqqani, created a terrorist dynasty that would play a special role over the next forty years. Haqqani was the son of a chieftain. He had studied at the Haqqania seminary in Pakistan in the 1960s, funded by the ISI, and on his return adopted the named Haqqani.

across the Arab world to confront Khomeini in a battle of faith that intensified a competition of fanaticism. His brother Salman, the intelligent, wilful, irascible governor of Riyadh (later king in the 2020s),* who often punished the impertinent with a slap across the face, took over the funding of Islamic charities – channelling the money to fund the Afghans – and the small coterie of Saudis who went to fight for them.

Osama bin Laden, now twenty-two, was one of the fifty-six children of the king's builder, Muhammad bin Laden, a Yemenite who had started as a porter in Jeddah, then in 1930 won the favour of Abdulaziz and befriended Faisal, rebuilding Mecca and Medina for the Saudis. The family were experts at cultivating not only the royal family but also American grandees.

Muhammad bin Laden educated most of his children in Britain or the USA: his heir Salem was at a British boarding school. When his father died in a plane crash, Salem bin Laden built on his relationship with Faisal but also bought houses in Florida and became friends with a useful patrician family. In April 1979, he invested in the oil start-up of George W. Bush, the swaggering and hard-drinking son of an upper-class politician, George H. W. Bush, who was planning to run for president.

POPPY, OSAMA AND W

Tall, reedy-voiced and preppy, inarticulate and bereft of 'the vision thing', George senior suffered from the clash between his upper-class decency and his voracious ambition. A scion of the type of American family that owned its own 'family compound', the Bushes were descended from English blacksmiths, teachers and prospectors; they were radical abolitionists and supporters of female suffrage but also members of an east coast business elite. George's grandfather Samuel, son of an Episcopalian vicar, made money by managing a steel company that manufactured parts for the Gilded Age robber baron E. H. Harriman. His son, Prescott, worked at the Harriman Brothers investment bank and married the daughter of the bank boss George Herbert Walker. From Walker the Bushes inherited their Maine compound, Kennebunkport, where like other WASPs they embraced the double hell of spartan domestic arrangements and cold outdoor sports.

Nicknamed Skin for his skinniness and Poppy after his grandfather

---

* His son, Muhammad bin Salman – future ruler of Arabia – was born in 1985 in the middle of this campaign.

Pop Walker, Bush followed his father to Yale and into the posh Skull and Bones drinking society, then married an indomitable daughter of a successful publisher, Barbara Pierce, descended from one of the first Massachusetts settlers. Soon after his marriage, George joined the air force and survived being shot down by the Japanese in 1944. Moving to Houston, he made money in oil while he and Barbara had six children. Heartbroken by losing a daughter to leukaemia, they indulged their eldest son, George W. – known as W – who grew up as a raffish cross between booted Texas princeling and Yalie Bonesman. It was he who got the bin Ladens to back his business.

George senior had followed his father into politics, and Nixon rewarded his loyalty with the ambassadorship in Beijing; Ford made him CIA director. More networker than meteor, Bush wrote thank-you notes to every person he met. Now he was ready to run for president. Meanwhile W was making money in oil and had invested in the Texas Rangers baseball team, but he was drinking heavily, and was arrested for Drinking under the Influence. W's marriage to Laura Welch, a virtuous librarian, led him to change his life: he gave up alcohol and embraced God, sobriety and politics. Not only was Laura 'elegant and beautiful, [she was] willing to put up with my rough edges', he said. 'And I must confess she's smoothed them off.' W moved from the Episcopalians to Laura's evangelical United Methodists.

That other princeling, Osama bin Laden, six foot four, striking and charismatic, embraced the ideas of Sayyid Qutb, and attended the lectures of his brother in Jeddah. Above all, he believed that only holy war against godless European infidels – Soviets, Americans, Zionists – and the restoration of sharia law would return Islam to its ancient and pure origins. Having inherited $25 million from his father, he left college without graduating and, backed by King Fahd and Prince Salman, travelled to Pakistan where, aided by the ISI, he used his fortune to gather around 2,000 Arab fighters for the struggle against the Russians. While he was in Peshawar, he met a bespectacled multilingual Egyptian surgeon, Dr Ayman al-Zawahiri, aged thirty, a member of a terrorist faction, Islamic Jihad, also keen to organize Afghan resistance. Al-Zawahiri would become his doctor, adviser and successor, but for now he returned to Cairo, where his comrades were planning to murder President Sadat.

In September 1981, Sadat ordered mass arrests of jihadists, Muslim Brothers and intellectuals, even Copts, but he missed a network of conspirators within the army command. They infiltrated a platoon led by a jihadist lieutenant named Islambouli into a parade of artillery and tanks to celebrate Sadat's 1973 war against Israel. On 6 October, as Sadat took the salute of fighter jets, Islambouli seized one of the army trucks taking part in the review while his posse, with grenades hidden in their helmets, jogged towards the stand. Thinking they were part of the review, Sadat stood and saluted, whereupon they threw grenades and opened up on the president, hitting him in the chest. As all hell broke loose, Islambouli climbed on to the stand and emptied his magazine into the prone president – the best Egyptian leader since Mehmed Ali. The vice-president Hosni Mubarak was wounded, but he succeeded to the presidency, ruling Egypt for thirty years, maintaining the Israeli peace and surviving an assassination attempt by Islambouli's brother. The assassins were executed – and Dr al-Zawahiri was arrested. When he was released, he rejoined Osama bin Laden in Pakistan fighting the Soviets. Together they founded a jihadi terror organization, the Base – al-Qaeda.

Sadat was not the only one facing a jihadi challenge, but Assad dealt with his differently: on 2 February 1982, his howitzers started to bombard his own city of Hama.

Assad, ruling a small country with a centralized Soviet-style economy, had created a greater Syria by intervening in Lebanon. Beirut was famed for its decadent charms and weak state, its domination by Maronite Christians resented by a downtrodden Shia minority recently empowered by a ferocious militia, Hezbollah – Party of God – funded by Khomeini. Its collapse was exacerbated by two other players – a Druze warlord, Walid Jumblatt, a pistol-packing playboy spouting Marx from the back of his Harley-Davidson, and Arafat's PLO, which had built its own fiefdom and helped spark a civil war. In 1976, Assad sent in troops to staunch the bloodletting, while his brother Rifaat and other princelings made fortunes there. But Assad's secular dictatorship, suppression of Islamicists and Alawite heresy infuriated the Muslim Brotherhood.

In June 1980, as Islamicist disturbances hit Hama, Homs and Idlib, jihadists tried to kill Assad; in response, on 27 June his brother Rifaat slaughtered a thousand Muslim Brotherhood prisoners at Tadmur (Palmyra) prison and assassinated their leaders. In February 1982, after Sadat's assassination, the brothers decided to liquidate the Islamicist problem: Rifaat surrounded the insurgency's centre, Hama, with 12,000 Defence Company troops and attacked with helicopters and howitzers, then stormed the city with tanks, possibly using gas, killing around 40,000 people.

The Assad brothers carefully monitored their Lebanon province, which the PLO was using as a base for attacking Israel. The brothers

loathed Arafat and undermined him by championing their own Palestinian factions, but their attacks on Israel drew the Jewish state into the
imbroglio. On 6 June 1982, Menachem Begin, inspired by his swaggering defence minister, Ariel Sharon, a veteran general, hero of the 1973
war, ordered an invasion to expel the PLO; as Syrian and Israeli pilots
duelled overhead, the Israelis besieged Beirut. In August, Arafat and
the PLO were forced out of Lebanon, and an Israeli ally, the Christian
Bachir Gemayel, was elected president.

The Israelis had occupied half of Lebanon and their ally was president, but their successes provoked a reaction that turned their triumphs
to ashes: the Assads ordered the assassination of President Gemayel.
Furious Christian militias slaughtered Palestinians in the Sabra and
Chatila refugee camps, watched by Israeli forces, while Hezbollah
launched a murderous bombing campaign against the Israelis. Begin
fell into depression; Sharon was sacked and condemned; and the
Assads' Shiite ally Hezbollah gradually took over Lebanon, with disastrous consequences.

The Assads had restored their influence in Syria. Then in November
1983 Hafez had a heart attack. Rifaat bid for power, attempting a coup
in March 1984, but Hafez recovered, foiled Rifaat, dismissed him from
command of the Defence Companies, 'promoted' him to vice-president
and exiled him. He now turned to his eldest son, Bassel. The Assads
were not to be troubled by Islamicists for another twenty-five years.

As the Assads were crushing jihad in Syria, the Americans ironically
were investing in holy war in Afghanistan.

MAGGIE AND INDIRA

A new US president, Ronald Reagan, rejected Nixon's detente with
the Soviets and saw an opportunity to hit the 'empire' in Afghanistan.
Elected at the age of sixty-nine, Reagan shaped a more theatrical, majestic and military presidency. Born in Illinois, a debonair yet folksy
son of a boozy, sometimes violent salesman and sunny mother who
'always expected to find the best in people and often did', he became
a radio announcer, film star, union official and then Californian governor, whose mellifluous voice, athletic figure, instinctive lightness,
cowboy swagger, Christian wholesomeness and anti-Communism
restored faith and confidence after the Manichaean contrasts of Nixon
and Carter. Nicknamed Gipper after a football player he portrayed in a
movie, Reagan combined his breezy western appeal with the uptight

east coast aristocrat George Bush, who became his vice-president.* No one could equal his wisecracking suaveness under pressure. Soon after taking office,† he was shot by a lunatic but managed to joke to his wife, Nancy, 'Sorry, honey, I forgot to duck.' In the ensuing crisis, Bush won his trust by not exploiting his temporary incapacity.

Once the Iranian hostages had returned, Reagan deployed American power to confront what he called the Soviet 'evil empire' on all fronts, from Angola and central America to space, where he promised a fantastical high-tech Strategic Defence Initiative which alarmed the Soviets – even though it did not yet work. While Reagan appeared placid, his swashbuckling lieutenants were recklessly cynical in their shenanigans, his presidency almost destroyed by their illegal plot to pay for the release of the Iranian hostages and fund anti-Communist guerrillas in Nicaragua, selling Israeli weapons to Iranian ayatollahs in one phantasmagoric conspiracy. Yet nothing seemed to touch the schmaltzy, slick-feathered president who had restored American confidence in their 'city on a hill'.

Afghanistan quickly proved a quagmire for the Soviets, who struggled to defeat the mujahedin insurgents in the rough Afghan terrain. In the Panjir Valley, the Soviets launched nine offensives, but rarely controlled more than the main cities. Carter had started Operation Cyclone in Afghanistan, but Reagan expanded it, spending $3 billion to bleed the Soviets while challenging them all over the world. The Americans romanticized these 'freedom fighters', thinking they shared their anti-Communism; but the jihadists detested any infidel intruders. The money was channelled through President Zia's ISI, which favoured jihadist groups as an insurance that Afghanistan would never fall under Indian influence.

---

* But there was a dark side to Reagan's sunlit America: in 1981, doctors started to treat a cluster of pneumonia and skin cancer cases among gay men and drug users. Initially fear and ignorance led to wild rumours about a 'Gay Plague', but doctors soon realized they were facing a new disease, AIDS, passed mainly by unprotected sex, particularly anal, by contaminated syringes and also from mother to child in pregnancy. In the next forty years, it killed thirty-six million people. Initially AIDS cut a swathe through the US and European gay communities, defining the 1980s as a time of desperate suffering. In southern Africa, it spread through the entire population, exacerbated by a stigma against using condoms, and even presidents encouraged irresponsible conspiracy theories and false cures that hugely increased the death toll: over fifteen million Africans died. Although preventative education is lowering infection rates and patients now usually survive thanks to retroviral drugs, in 2011 there were 23 million people living with AIDS in Africa, where each year 1.2 million die and 1.8 million are infected. Those rates are now improving.

† Sinatra, an old friend, now a Republican, sang at his Inaugural Gala. It was now too that the FBI finally broke the power of the Mafia's Five Families, using new legislation, the Racketeer Influenced and Corrupt Organizations (RICO) Act, to link the bosses of the criminal conspiracies to their soldiers. The godfathers were sentenced to over 100 years in prison.

'We are neither pro-Russia nor pro-America,' said Indira Gandhi, back in power and watching the Afghan war. 'Just pro-India.' She ruled with her son Sanjay, now MP and general secretary of Congress, and clearly her heir. But on 23 June 1980 he took out an aeroplane from the Delhi Flying Club; looping the loop over his office, his chappal shoes became entangled with the pedals and the plane crashed. Indira rushed to the scene and saw his mutilated body; it took doctors three hours to reconstruct it so that it could be displayed. Her sangfroid was invincible: when a relative wept, Indira said, 'Now now, *puphi*, we don't cry.'

Four days later she was back at her desk, but with Sanjay gone she turned to her eldest son Rajiv as heir. He was happily married to Antonia Maino, a pretty builder's daughter from near Turin, who, knowing nothing of India, had worked as an au pair in England and then as a flight attendant, which was when she met Rajiv, a pilot. 'As our eyes met, I could feel my heart pounding,' she recalled. 'Love at first sight.' Taking the name Sonia, she worked as a picture restorer and quickly became Indira's favourite. 'I don't know much about politics,' Rajiv said. 'But Mummy had to be helped.'

Soon afterwards in April 1981, Indira flew to London to discuss Afghanistan with another female leader.

'People think it strange Mrs Gandhi and I got on so well personally,' said Margaret Thatcher, British prime minister. Gandhi, pro-Soviet socialist, and Thatcher, anti-Communist conservative, were opposites, though they had much in common, both graduates of Somerville College, Oxford, both natural commanders in war and peace, women who had succeeded in male worlds. 'I am in no sense a feminist,' wrote Indira, 'but I believe in women being able to do everything.' Thatcher agreed: 'The feminists hate me, don't they?' she said. 'And I don't blame them.' When Thatcher said Indira 'had this combination of things of being both very feminine but nevertheless capable of making very tough decisions', she could have been talking about herself. And like Indira, it took a war to make her.

On 2 April 1982, Argentina, long ruled by military dictators who had killed or 'disappeared' thousands of leftists over recent decades, invaded and seized a distant British possession, the Falkland Islands. Within three days, Thatcher had mustered and dispatched a task force that sailed 8,000 miles to retake the islands. When an Argentine cruiser, *General Belgrano*, sailed into what Thatcher had declared to be an exclusion zone, she ordered its sinking, a decision that removed the Argentine navy from the battle. On 21 May, British forces landed; on 14

June, the capital fell. The operation had been a risk. Before the war, her premiership had looked doomed. Instead she had pulled off every leader's dream: a short, victorious war. Yet she was a born war leader. 'You can't retake islands I'm afraid without loss of life,' she told a schoolboy interviewer (this author) in Downing Street soon afterwards. 'We lost 255 lives in Falklands. The Russians shot down a Korean airliner and lost 269 lives in one act.' The victory restored confidence in her vision of British exceptionalism: 'I don't believe you can be over-patriotic when you stand for a country that stands for honesty, integrity, freedom, justice.'

Thatcher, née Margaret Roberts, was a Grantham grocer's daughter who graduated from Oxford as a chemist and became a barrister. Cleverer than most of her opponents, mastering her briefs and dominating her male colleagues and rivals, she was both a radical, favouring the brashness of self-made entrepreneurs, and socially conservative. Her operatically posh accent, her bouffant blonde hairstyle, her swinging handbag became props of her theatrical regality. She prided herself on her industry and energy, surviving on just four hours' sleep a night. 'I was born that way, I was trained that way,' she told this author. 'I've gone on acting that way ... You must be born fairly fit and then you must train yourself to work extremely hard. I'd need to sleep a lot more than I do if I made a habit of more sleep.' Long married to a whisky-sniffing golf-playing retired company director, she, like Indira, shamelessly favoured a jackanapes son.

During the 1970s, Britain had joined the European Economic Community (later the European Union), but membership had not stopped a steep spiral of decline, as unemployment soared, overmighty trade unions bullied employers, who themselves were stuck in an obsolete culture, and Irish terrorists, the Provisional IRA, launched a murderous campaign, partly funded by Qaddafi. Elected in 1979, Thatcher confronted the unions, deregulated the stock market and promoted 'self-reliance, initiative, hard work', a new confidence in entrepreneurial energy and a patriotic view of Britain's democratic and imperial past: 'In this enormous empire we tried to take the best of our law and the best of our honesty to nations we administered. It wasn't a bad record.' But she never saw herself as Churchillian: 'No one can see themselves as Churchill. That would be too arrogant and conceited for words ... but he saw clearly, warned clearly, acted clearly, and I try to do the same.' If Indira was her avatar as warrior-queen, Reagan was her geopolitical partner. Reagan and Thatcher performed on a political stage dominated by television, a media that would never have worked for earlier leaders: 'I can't remember Churchill ever doing a TV interview,' mused Thatcher. She and Regan mastered the medium, henceforth essential for all leaders in all systems.*

Closely allied to Reagan, Thatcher surveyed a world that appeared to be unchangeably divided between the Soviets and the Americans; it is easy to forget that Iberian democracy was new and that half of Europe was still ruled by Leninist dictators. On 23 February 1981, a conspiracy of 200 Spanish soldiers, led by a colonel, tried to halt Spain's advance to democracy. They attacked the Cortes (parliament), seized hostages and fired shots while officers sent tanks on to the streets of other cities, in a bid to restore Francoist dictatorship in the name of the king. After eighteen hours, at 1.15 in the morning, Juan Carlos, wearing the uniform of a captain-general, addressed the nation: 'The Crown won't tolerate the interruption by force of the democratic process.' It was 'my decisive moment and I knew what to do', he told the author.

In the east, the Communist dictatorships were grimly permanent and sometimes still capable of murderous terror. In December 1981, Enver Hoxha unleashed a terror against his own comrades that culminated in the deaths of the prime minister and two other ministers – all thanks to a love affair between two teenagers.

Regarding himself as the sole judge of Marxist virtue, Hoxha feuded first with his Yugoslav backer Tito, then denounced Khrushchev and embraced Mao before rejecting Deng's reforms, making a cult out of his righteous isolation and building a network of 170,000 fortifications to repel capitalistic and heretical invaders. As cultists expressed loyalty with the Hoxhaist Salute – right fist to the heart – he supervised every detail of Albanian life, backed by the ferocious *Sigurimi* secret police. In August that year, Hoxha's trusted henchman Mehmet Shehu, who had been premier for twenty-seven years, was visited by his son Skender, who told his father he was in love with a pretty volleyball player, Silva Turdiu. They were going to marry. 'Oh dear, why did you get involved with them?' asked the premier, knowing that Silva was related to a writer who had mocked Hoxha for secret homosexuality, not least with the line 'Glory to your ass, oh dandy!'

After suffering a heart attack, Hoxha became distrustful of Shehu, suspecting him of planning the succession of his sons. Now Hoxha and his drear wife Nexhmije crossed the street of the Block to congratulate Shehu and his wife Fiqirete in the presence of the young couple, but

---

* After the interview by this author, Mrs Thatcher decided that the interview had been 'cheeky' and resolved to do no more schoolboy interviews.

the dictator was seething because his permission had not been sought. Eight days later, the engagement was cancelled. 'I called Mehmet,' wrote Hoxha on 11 September, 'to ask about his son's engagement to a family teeming with war criminals, some executed, some exiled. The city is buzzing with the news. Mehmet was fully cognizant of the fact. A grave political error.'

In the tiny cabal of the Block, Hoxha toyed with his premier and family. On 17 December, Shehu was attacked at the Politburo. 'Reflect on the criticism,' warned Hoxha. That night, Shehu wrote a long letter to him, reflecting on their struggle against the betrayal of the 'Iago–Khrushchev plot' – a mix of Marxist and Shakespearean jargon – and later was found shot in his bedroom. 'You can say Mehmet died "accidentally",' Hoxha wrote. It is not known if Shehu killed himself or was liquidated, but Hoxha had his wife arrested and tortured, and his son Skender shot, along with the interior and health ministers.[*]

Thatcher and Reagan knew little of these secret murders in tiny, impoverished Albania, but, alarmed by Soviet gains in Angola, Afghanistan and Nicaragua and by a build-up of Soviet nuclear weapons, they intensified the competition. Atop his decaying system, Andropov worried about strikes and protests in Poland and feared that the trigger-happy cowboy Reagan planned a pre-emptive nuclear strike. 'The US is preparing for nuclear war,' he warned in May 1981 as a succession battle raged around Brezhnev. Andropov faced competition from a geriatric mediocrity, Konstantin Chernenko, the Silent One, who had started as a Stalinist executioner before becoming Brezhnev's deputy, trying, noticed Gorbachev, to 'isolate Brezhnev from any direct contact'. But in July 1982 Brezhnev telephoned Andropov: 'Why do you think I transferred you to the Central Committee apparatus? I put you there to lead . . . Why don't you act?' At the next Politburo, Andropov seized the chair, but he was already suffering kidney failure, undergoing regular dialysis. On 10 November, when Brezhnev died in his sleep, Andropov succeeded as the tension with America mounted.

On its way to the lying-in-state, Brezhnev's body fell through the bottom of his coffin.

---

[*] When this author visited Albania, the then premier Sali Berisha, who lived in Shehu's old house in the Block, showed him the room where Shehu was shot. 'We still don't know,' he said, 'exactly what happened.' Soon afterwards, on 11 April 1985, Hoxha died, succeeded by a chosen disciple. His original patron and later rival Marshal Tito had died in 1980 aged eighty-seven. Even in eastern Europe the guard was changing.

THE NEHRUVIANS: THIRD GENERATION

On 15 November 1982, at Brezhnev's traditional kitsch funeral, attended by Castro, Assad, Mengistu and Indira Gandhi, the coffin-lowering mechanics failed and the coffin fell into the grave beside the Kremlin Wall with a loud crash that caused the assembled mourners led by Vice-President Bush to struggle to conceal their laughter. It was the sound of an empire dying. Yet a sinking power is more dangerous than a rising one, and it was now that the world came close to cataclysm.

The red imperium was as atrophied as the furry arteries of Brezhnev's successors. Andropov, disturbed by Reagan's deployment of Pershing II nuclear missiles in Europe, believed that the US president was keen on 'unleashing nuclear war', a hankering that 'isn't just irresponsible, but insane'. As he monitored NATO exercises and the increase in encrypted communication between Reagan and Thatcher, he ordered heightened vigilance and instant counter-strike.

On the night of 31 August/1 September 1983, this trigger-happiness led Soviet defences to shoot down a South Korean airliner, killing 269. Andropov mocked his 'blockhead generals'. At midnight on 26 September, Stanislav Petrov, a lieutenant-colonel in Air Defence Forces, was on duty in a bunker near Moscow when he was informed by satellites that a missile was approaching; Petrov questioned this since a single missile seemed unlikely. Then the system identified four more missiles, still too little for a massive American attack. Petrov believed the new computers were unreliable. While he did not have the authority to launch a counter-strike, he had seven minutes to report a missile attack to Andropov, but the ruler was incommunicado on a dialysis machine.

Petrov delayed and did not report the missile: he was right. The computers were actually reacting to a rare synchronicity of sunlight and cloud. 'I think that this,' said Petrov, who was not rewarded since he had revealed technical failings in a Soviet system, 'is the closest our country has come to accidental nuclear war.' Weeks later, Andropov believed an Anglo-American exercise with tactical nuclear weapons codenamed Able Archer 83 might cover a real attack; the generals waited in their bunkers.

Thatcher and Reagan shared a vision even if their styles were very different. Thatcher was abrasive and haughty – the Soviets called her the Iron Lady, while the French president Mitterrand admired 'the eyes of Caligula, the mouth of Marilyn Monroe'. She was certainly unafraid of confrontations with supercilious colleagues, rioting unions or Irish terrorists. On 12 October 1984, while she was staying at the Grand

Hotel in Brighton for the Conservative Party conference, the IRA tried to assassinate her, blowing up the hotel. Five were killed, but Thatcher reacted with the sangfroid she shared with Indira Gandhi.

'It doesn't matter to me,' said Indira, a few days later on 30 October, when she faced increasingly alarming death threats from the Sikhs of Punjab, 'if I live or die.' The next day, wearing an orange sari, the prime minister kissed her granddaughter Priyanka, told her grandson Rahul to be brave when she died and walked from the family residence towards her office, approaching two of her Sikh bodyguards, who reached for their guns.

The Sikh challenge was played out in her own house. Her relationship with Sanjay's feisty widow Maneka, twenty-five, swiftly deteriorated. Maneka, a Sikh general's daughter who aspired to succeed her husband, defied Indira's orders to refrain from politics; Indira threw her out of the house, telling her, 'You're not taking anything out apart from your clothes.' As Maneka was leaving, the two women screamed at each other and Indira tried to keep hold of her baby grandson. 'It's alien to Indian culture to kick your daughter-in-law out,' Maneka declared. Indira insulted Maneka's Sikh family – 'You came from a different background . . .'

The Sikhs – some of them campaigning for an independent Sikh homeland – had already led the opposition to Indira's emergency. Now Indira, hoping to split the Sikh Akali Dal party, promoted a Sikh leader, Jarnail Singh Bhindranwale, but she had chosen an extremist and he quickly spun out of her control, arming his followers, demanding the creation of a Sikh state and fortifying the Akal Takht, the second most holy shrine of the Golden Temple at Amritsar, while sending gangs of killers to terrorize his enemies.

On 3 June 1984, Indira ordered the army to storm the complex. The ferocious fighting that followed destroyed the Akal Takht, killing 780 militants and 400 troops. Sikhs swore vengeance against Indira, who responded, 'India has lived a long long time – thousands of years – and my sixty-six years hardly count . . .'

On the morning of 31 October, as Indira walked to her office, her bodyguard Sub-Inspector Beant Singh drew his pistol and shot her five times in the stomach before urging his colleague Constable Satwant Singh to join him. Satwant Singh fired twenty-five bullets from his Sten gun into the dying Indira. Sonia Gandhi was in the bath when she heard the shots, and for a moment thought they were Diwali fireworks. Then she ran out in her dressing gown, shouting 'Mummy!', and knelt over Indira. Beant and Satwant surrendered. 'I've done what I had to do,' said Beant. 'You do what you want.' The guards killed him and shot Satwant, who survived.

On the plane back from Kolkata, Rajiv was asked to become prime minister. 'I have no interest,' he replied. 'Don't bother me.' But he was cooler by the time he joined Sonia at the Delhi hospital. She tried to persuade her husband not to accept the prime ministership. 'They were hugging each other and he was kissing her forehead,' telling her, 'It's my duty, I have to do it.' Sonia said he would be killed. Rajiv replied that he 'would be killed anyway'. Such is the grinding logic of hereditary power. Heir to a family whose leadership went back to his great-grandfather if not to the police chief of the last Mughal, Rajiv was the third generation of the Nehruvians to rule the world's greatest democracy.

Thatcher flew to Delhi. As Hindu mobs chanted 'Blood for blood', Rajiv lit his mother's pyre. On the night of the murder, Hindu mobs had poured into the streets of Delhi, searching for Sikhs: 8,000 were killed, a pogrom almost justified by Rajiv who, a few days later, reflected, 'When a mighty tree falls, it is only natural that the earth around it does shake a little.' Thatcher attended the cremation: 'She looked so small.'

At home, she and Reagan watched Moscow's cadaverous succession. 'How am I supposed to get any place with the Russians,' quipped Reagan, 'if they keep dying on me?'

On 9 February 1984, Andropov died of kidney failure, encouraging Gorbachev to succeed him. Gorbachev grieved. 'We owed him everything,' said Raisa. But the sclerotic cabal instead chose Brezhnev's waxen sidekick Chernenko the Silent, who spent most of his reign in sepulchral silence in hospital while the Soviet Union itself was on life support. Its flaws – economic failure, global overreach, Afghan defeat, repression and inequality – were grave but not necessarily fatal. No one predicted what was about to happen.

As Chernenko declined, Gorbachev was invited to London by Thatcher, who was studying Russian history. The two admired each other. Thatcher challenged Gorbachev about the Soviet lack of enterprise and freedom and he debated with her. Thatcher was impressed with Gorbachev's well-cut suit and Raisa's fashion sense – 'the sort of thing I might have worn myself'. Afterwards Thatcher flew to Washington to tell Reagan a new era was opening: 'I like Mr Gorbachev.'

On 10 March 1985, Chernenko succumbed and Gorbachev became general secretary, promising *glasnost* (openness) and *perestroika* (restructuring). As he wrote in his notes, he also planned to 'exit Afghanistan' – slowly. 'We'll be out in two or three years,' he said, 'but the result mustn't look like a shameful defeat as if after losing so many young men [13,000 Soviet troops] we just gave up.' Everything about him was refreshing: charming, optimistic, indefatigable, Gorbachev smiled, his eyes sparkled and he listened to ordinary people. Even the birthmark on his forehead seemed a mark of honesty. But he was a devout Leninist, studying Lenin for lessons on how to reform a modern state in a global economy. The USSR was the world's biggest oil producer, reaching its height in 1987 just as a glut sent prices falling and the Soviet economy into shock. Abroad, he knew he had to reduce Moscow's global expenditure and at home attack 'the dictatorship of the bureaucracy'. To challenge the supremacy of Lenin's Party or the Soviet state was unthinkable. Yet his confidence was overwhelming: he felt he could do it all.

First he appointed an ally, the Georgian Party secretary, Eduard Shevardnadze, as his foreign minister. 'But I'm a Georgian,' replied Shevardnadze, 'not a diplomat.' Nonetheless, Gorbachev liked his fierce intelligence and 'Oriental affability'.

Gorbachev also summoned a strapping, ebullient reformer from the Urals to be Moscow Party secretary: Boris Yeltsin. Both men were fifty-four, both the children of parents arrested by Stalin, both hard-driving, proud and vain, both craved the limelight, both had climbed the Communist Party and been appointed regional leaders by Brezhnev, yet they were opposites. Almost teetotal, Gorbachev was austere, sometimes verbose and pompous, Yeltsin was wild, obsessive, social, exuberant – and an alcoholic. Gorbachev was a literature student married to an outspoken student of philosophy, Yeltsin was an athletic engineer, a volleyball and tennis player, married to a self-effacing engineer. Yeltsin was moreover a born leader, but also impulsive, volatile, unstable and (often) inebriated, a man of appetites on a Russian scale. As a child, he had blown off some fingers playing with a grenade; now he did the same in Gorbachev's Politburo.

Almost immediately, Gorbachev's *glasnost* was challenged. On 26 April 1986, the core in No. 4 nuclear reactor at Chernobyl melted down and exploded. The catastrophe was a symbol of imminent Soviet decay – just as America reached its apogee as the unipower and its technology changed the way families everywhere lived and thought.

ACT TWENTY-TWO
4.4 BILLION

Yeltsins and Xis, Nehruvians and Assads, Bin Ladens, Kims and Obamas

As hundreds of thousands were endangered and finally evacuated from the environs of Chernobyl, Gorbachev tried to suppress the news, only announcing it almost a month later. The costs placed more pressure on the economy and on Gorbachev, who now pivoted to plan his own radical explosion. His first reforms to free the economy from Party supervision did not immediately solve his problems. In January 1987, going further than Andropov, he took an astonishing decision that was almost romantically delusional: he would not only reform the economy but set up a sort of one-party *demokratizatsiya* through a real election to produce a Congress of 2,250 people's deputies that would outrank the Politburo and government. He was misunderstanding Lenin, who always asked, 'Who controls whom?' Lenin had commandeered, then neutered, the Soviets in order to concentrate awesome power in his own hands. Gorbachev was trying to withdraw from the empire, and reform the economy simultaneously with political liberalization, a move bound to stimulate nationalism among the many peoples in the USSR, and political disintegration in Moscow. To try all three was so ambitious as to be either naive or hubristic, almost suicidal.

Abroad, Gorbachev realized that he could not reform the state while engaged in ferocious competition with America. He proposed the phasing out of all nuclear weapons by 2000: in October 1986, he and Reagan met in Reykjavik and almost abolished nuclear weapons. The two got on well, though their wives disliked each other. Later Gorbachev announced that the Soviets would withdraw troops from eastern Europe, embracing not world revolution but 'all-human values'. The Americans were unsure if this was real or just window dressing, but Reagan kept up the pressure. When he visited the Berlin Wall he said, 'Mr Gorbachev, tear down this wall.'

At home, Yeltsin trailblazed through Moscow, walking to work or taking the Metro, visiting cafés, shops and factories, handing out watches – his devoted bodyguard Korzhakov kept spares in his pocket. Gorbachev sneered at this self-promotion; Yeltsin found the general secretary 'patronizing'. In January 1987, he criticized Gorbachev for being over-optimistic about *perestroika*; Gorbachev shot back at Yeltsin's 'loud, empty, ultra-leftist words'.

'I'm still new in the Politburo,' said Yeltsin apologetically. 'This is a good lesson for me.'

'You're an emotional man,' warned Gorbachev. At home Communist diehards resisted the reforms. Yeltsin pushed for more, admitting that he had begun 'to abuse sedatives and become enamoured of alcohol'. In September 1987, when conservatives reprimanded Yeltsin for allowing small demonstrations, he suddenly resigned from the Politburo. 'Wait, Boris,' said Gorbachev, 'don't fly off the handle.' But in October Yeltsin attacked Gorbachev at the Central Committee. Infuriated, Gorbachev denounced his 'immaturity' and 'illiteracy' – 'You couldn't tell God's gift from an omelette!' Gorbachev now hated him: 'He wants to be the popular hero.' Yeltsin drank and fell into wild depression, cutting his chest and stomach with scissors. 'What a bastard!' sneered Gorbachev. 'He bloodied his own room.' He had Yeltsin hospitalized, then forced him to face ritual denunciations. Yeltsin never forgave this 'immoral, inhuman' treatment. Accompanied only by Korzhakov, who resigned from the KGB to support him, Yeltsin retired to a sanatorium. 'I looked inside,' said Yeltsin, 'there was no one there. I was only nominally alive.'

The KGB asked Gorbachev if he wanted something to happen to Yeltsin. Gorbachev declined the offer.

In February 1988, Gorbachev's reforms loosened Moscow's control over the fifteen republics of the Soviet Union that were never designed to become independent. In Nagorno-Karabakh in Azerbaijan, Christian Armenians fought Islamic Azeris who then slaughtered thousands of Armenians. Georgians, seized by Lenin after a short independence, craved freedom. In the north, the Lithuanians, Latvians and Estonians – Nordic and Germanic peoples, not Slavs, who had been forcibly annexed by Stalin after twenty years of independence – started to campaign. The best way for them to win independence was to win it for all the fifteen republics created by Lenin and Stalin. Some, like Georgia, were ancient nations, others were Soviet inventions that had never existed before. Russia was the largest, followed by Ukraine, which, apart from the many regimes of the civil war, had been ruled variously by Russia since 1654, the 1780s and 1945. Kazakhs, Uzbeks, Tajiks had originally been ruled by ancient khanates, but Kazakhstan and the other four 'stans' of central Asia were Soviet inventions carved out of Romanov provinces. Before it was White Russia, Belarus had belonged to Lithuania.

As Gorbachev relaxed the Soviet hold over his client-states, he was also trying to negotiate a compromise exit from Afghanistan, where he installed a subtler ex-secret-police chief, Najibullah, to create a government of reconciliation, but conciliation was impossible in the midst of retreat. In May 1988, the Soviet army withdrew unilaterally and Najibullah's regime started to wilt. A peaceful retreat was afoot in Europe: in December, Gorbachev started to withdraw 500,000 troops from his European vassals, promising 'freedom of choice'. No empire lasts without the threat of violence.

Gorbachev was now a funambulist attempting not just one tight-rope walk but four simultaneously – economic reform, challenging the Party, defending the Union and sustaining Soviet world power. In May 1989, he presided over the first elected Congress, which chose a ruling Supreme Soviet with him as its chairman. At the height of his fame and confidence, an increasingly autocratic Gorbachev hoped to guide reform as an omnipotent parliamentary speaker, but in fact this ponderous, often verbose apparatchik immediately struggled to control diehard Communists, republican nationalists and liberal intelligentsia. Worse, he lost the menacing mystique of a Stalinist general secretary; Moscow lost its power over its vassals. His humane aversion to violence was both his greatness and his tragedy for it doomed his achievements to failure. 'They don't know that if they pull strongly on the leash,' he said, 'it would snap.' But the Poles, who had lost their ancient independence, were the first to test the leash. Helmut Kohl, the West German chancellor, asked Gorbachev what would happen. 'Everyone,' came the reply, 'answers for themselves.'

Across Europe, in the brittle vassal-states from East Germany to Hungary, crowds demonstrated for freedom. Within the Union, Georgia and Lithuania pushed for independence. Yeltsin, on a visit to America, got publicly drunk but was astonished by the plenty in American supermarkets. On his way home, he questioned Bolshevism. 'What,' he asked, 'have they done to our poor people?'

While Gorbachev was attempting to manage all these shocks, Deng Xiaoping was watching in amazement from Beijing, where he demonstrated that there was another way. Deng was tougher, more blood-soaked, more cautious than the naive Gorbachev. The economy could be liberated, but Little Cannon knew power rested on the gun. Lose the gun, lose everything. Gorbachev, said Deng, 'is an idiot'.

In May 1989, Gorbachev's arrival in Beijing embarrassed Deng, who was losing control of his own capital. Almost a million protesters, most of them students, were camped in Tiananmen Square, gathered around a huge papier-mâché statue, the Lady of Liberty, demanding democracy as the leadership agonized about what to do. The eighty-five-year-old Deng was still chairman of the Central Military Commission, but he was semi-retired, having handed over to chosen successors who had failed to restrain widening protests against corruption and nepotism. In April, after anti-reformers had ordered that Deng's ally Hu Yaobang be fired, Hu died of a heart attack, sparking pro-democracy protests at his funeral. A Deng protégé, the general secretary Zhao Ziyang, went to talk to the students. After Gorbachev had left, on 17 May, Deng, convening the Party grandees nicknamed the Eight Immortals in Zhongnanhai, said he feared that 'Their goal is to establish a totally western-dependent bourgeois republic,' and warned, 'There's no way to back down now without the situation spiralling out of control.' Little Cannon reached for his gun: troops were massed; Zhao spoke to the protesters in tears and was promptly dismissed by Deng. The Eight Immortals – all men except Zhou Enlai's widow, Deng Yingchao – voted to crush the rebels.

On 2 June, Deng commanded that 'order be restored to the capital . . . No person may impede the advance of the troops.' The soldiers 'can act in self-defence and use any means to clear impediments'. The 'impediments' were the students, who had built barricades. The army retook the streets. A soldier was killed, stripped naked and suspended from a bus, but then the army started firing. One student stood in front of a column of tanks, halted them and climbed on to the turret to denounce the soldiers. Hundreds were killed.

Appointing new leaders, Deng retired, keeping only the chairmanship of the China Bridge Association. But he remained Paramount Leader, and confirmed his policy of political power with economic freedom before he died at ninety-two. Deng had created a template for Chinese power, Gorbachev an accelerating momentum towards Soviet disintegration. Only force could stop it.

NEW AFRICA: MANDELA AND JJ, MENES AND ISAIAS

In September 1989, Poland elected a non-Communist premier; East Germans probed the borders; within the USSR, Georgians, led by a mad-eyed Shakespeare professor and former dissident, Zviad Gamsakhurdia, voted for independence as their own minorities, Ossetians and

Abkhazians, fought for their own states; Armenians and Azeris clashed. At least Gorbachev's rival, Yeltsin, was disintegrating too. On the 28th, he turned up extravagantly drunk at Gorbachev's birthday party with a bouquet and tried to gate-crash. Bodyguards roughed him up and threw him into the Moskva River. 'The water was terribly cold,' said Yeltsin. 'I collapsed and lay on the ground . . . I staggered to the nearby police station.' Gorbachev's allies claimed that Yeltsin's mistress had thrown a bucket of water over him; his allies saw an assassination attempt. The Yeltsin threat was clearly over.

At 11.30 p.m., Berlin time, on 9 November, East German leaders, pressured by the opening of the Austria–Hungary border and then by huge demonstrations, planned quietly to open the gates in the Wall, but bungled the announcement, sparking joyous demonstrations as people suddenly poured through the gates and started to tear down the Berlin Wall with axes and bare hands. In Dresden, as crowds stormed Stasi headquarters across East Germany, an astonished KGB colonel, Vladimir Putin, aged thirty-seven, burned secret files and then started the miserable drive home to Leningrad. In Poland, Hungary and Czechoslovakia, the Communists were swept away in velvet revolutions. Some were less velvety than others: on Christmas Day 1989 in Bucharest, Romania, a frightened but defiant sexagenarian couple were dragged out of the belly of an armoured personnel carrier. Nicolae Ceaușescu and his wife Elena had ruled Romania since 1965. Now Ceaușescu was overthrown by his own comrades and the people in a shootout with his *Securitate* agents and quickly sentenced to death. Four soldiers were assigned to shoot them separately, but they insisted on dying together, singing the Internationale. They died mid-verse.

In February 1990, the US secretary of state, James Baker, discussed the reunification of Germany and the expansion of NATO. In September, Gorbachev agreed to the reunification and allowed Germany to join NATO. He could have extracted much more while he still had 300,000 troops in the country, but he needed the western loans to run his state. Now he had missed his chance. The Americans were dizzy with victory. When Gorbachev tried to lay down the parameters of Germany's relationship with NATO, Bush (now president) told Kohl, 'To hell with that. *We* prevailed and *they* didn't.' It showed a lack of imagination. Russia could have been coopted into the EU, even NATO. After all, victories do not last for ever. 'In victory,' advised Churchill, 'magnanimity.'

The 'Wall' fell in Africa too. On 5 July 1989, Nelson Mandela, almost seventy-one, newly fitted with a suit after twenty-seven years behind bars, was driven out of prison and taken to meet *Die Groot Krokodil*

– the South African president, P. W. Botha – at his residence Tuynhuys, where Rhodes had stayed, for a secret chat. To Mandela's surprise, the Crocodile, who as coloured affairs and defence minister had enforced apartheid for decades, was 'courteous and deferential' as they discussed history. 'Now I felt there was no turning back.'

Mandela was right: the fall of the Iron Curtain meant the end of proxy war in Africa. America and the USSR no longer supported their egregious allies, yet their downfall often destroyed the existence of their states: in Zaire – Congo – the fall of America's long-reigning ally, Mobutu, triggered a scramble for power and for minerals that lasted for thirty years.*

Mandela was returned to prison; Crocodile resigned in favour of a new Nationalist premier, F. W. de Klerk. On 13 December, 'I was taken again to Tuynhuys,' wrote Mandela, where he realized de Klerk 'was a man we could do business with'. On 9 February 1990, de Klerk told Mandela 'he was making me a free man' and then poured them both a tumbler of whisky: 'I raised the glass in toast but only pretended to drink; such spirits are too strong for me.' The day after at 4 a.m., Mandela rose. He had befriended and charmed his Afrikaner guards, who had 'reinforced my belief in the essential humanity even of those who kept me behind bars'. He embraced them. At 3 p.m., Mandela, joined by Winnie, walked out of the prison. 'When a TV crew thrust a long dark furry object at me, I recoiled.' He had never seen one. 'Winnie explained it was a microphone.'

As he emerged to meet his ANC comrades, 'I could see the question in their eyes: had he survived or was he broken?' His marriage was

---

* In Latin America, the end of the struggle against Communism accelerated the fall of juntas in Argentina and Brazil, which then became democracies; in Paraguay, the vicious Hispano-Bavarian tyrant Stroessner, who had protected Josef Mengele, was deposed; in Haiti, 'Baby Doc' Duvalier, who at nineteen had inherited the throne from his father Papa Doc, claimed he was 'firm as a monkey tail' but, rocked by protests and pressured by Washington, flew into exile. In Colombia and Mexico, America feared a new export, not Communism but cocaine. In 1989 in Colombia, the rise of a minor Colombian cigarette smuggler from Medellín in the late 1970s had transformed the cocaine business: Pablo Escobar, paunchy and moustachioed, had created a business – offering his victims 'money or lead' – that manufactured cocaine and delivered it to its American markets. Now at his height, he exported eighty tons a month, bringing in $70 million a day, so much that he subverted and corrupted the fragile Colombian state. When threatened, he launched a murderous terror in which his assassins killed 25,000 people with bullet and bomb, even blowing up a civilian airliner while, worth $30 billion and commanding his own army, he lived in splendour at his spacious ranches. When Escobar was arrested, he was so powerful he was able to build his own prison, and escape when he wished. America intervened to help Colombia: on 2 December 1993, Escobar, at the age of forty-four, was finally hunted down and killed by American and Colombian commandos, his business commandeered by a more discreet cartel from Cali. After they too were arrested, the business was taken over by Mexican *narcotraficantes* who lethally undermined the Mexican state.

broken: Winnie, unable to resist the strain of loneliness, the bruise of repression and the temptations of power, had had affairs and led a vicious gang terror in Soweto where her bodyguards, the Mandela United Football Club, had killed opponents, even children. 'She married a man,' said Mandela graciously, 'who soon left her, became a myth,' but then the myth came home and was 'just a man'. It was his greatest regret: 'When your life is a struggle, there's little room for family.' His children had lost their father and when he returned 'he was father of the nation'. Mandela divorced Winnie and, at eighty, he met someone else, Graça, the widow of Machel, dictator of Mozambique, announcing, 'I've fallen in love.'

Mandela embarked on a world tour, meeting his old backers Castro and Qaddafi, who had funded the ANC, and new backers, led by Harry Oppenheimer, the liberal magnate, owner of De Beers diamonds and Anglo American gold mines, who helped buy his new house. Mandela had started as a Thembu prince, become a Communist revolutionary and then developed into a humanist liberal democrat who, inspired by Gandhi and MLK, was determined to create a 'rainbow nation' of white and black people. Astonishingly, after forty years of vicious repression, he achieved this without any massacre or flight of whites – an achievement without parallel that was the fruit of his personality. A peace and conciliation committee listened to testimony about the repression by South African security agents – and forgave their predations. Where Gandhi had failed to achieve peaceful transition, Mandela, elected president in April 1994, succeeded.

Soviet allies fell too: in Ethiopia in 1984–5, Mengistu's atrocities, along with a drought, had caused a famine that affected over seven million people. He deliberately restricted food supplies to Tigray and Wollo, where resistance to his rule was most effective. Over a million died. Now in May 1991 Mengistu, abandoned by Gorbachev, fled into exile, leaving a civil war that was swiftly won by an alliance of ethnic rebels led by the Tigrayan Meles, who had rejected Hoxhaite Marxism and formed an alliance with the Eritrean Maoist Isaias Afwerki, which captured Addis. Meles embraced the zeitgeist, promising liberal democracy but ruling as autocrat for twenty years. He soon fell out with the demented Isaias, who converted Eritrea, an independent state for the first time, into a regimented personal domain, in which the entire population were conscripted and terrorized by secret police, a system the UN called a form of slavery: Afwerki ruled into the 2020s. After Meles's death, the Tigrayans lost power to an Oromo, and the country again dissolved into ethnic fighting.

There was only one Mandela, but another gifted African leader, much less well known outside the continent, rescued his country after almost destroying it. JJ Rawlings, ruling from the Castle for a decade, was the dictator who in 1979 had shot his generals on the beach in front of the press. Now he reacted to the fall of the Wall. Economically he took advice from the World Bank, while politically he fostered a liberal democracy. The showman Rawlings, sporting fancy suits or traditional robes, founded his own political party and ran for president. On 3 November 1992, he won a free election with 60 per cent of the vote, winning a second term in 1996. Succession is the test, but when he had served his permitted two terms he retired at fifty-four, leaving Ghana as a thriving democracy and economic force – one of the successes of Africa. 'At the risk of sounding immodest,' reflected Rawlings, 'Ghana wouldn't have been brought out of the abyss without a visionary' – a very flawed one for sure.

In Russia, the fall of Communism was also the work of a visionary – but it wasn't Gorbachev. In March 1990, Gorbachev's election to a post, the presidency of the USSR, sparked a cascade of new aspirations in the most surprising places: in Alma Ata, a former steelworker, now first secretary, Nursultan Nazarbayev,* had himself elected president of the Kazakh republic. 'I thought we'd agreed there's only to be one president,' said Gorbachev.

'People in Kazakhstan,' explained Nazarbayev, one of the key movers in what happened next, 'say can't we have a president too?'

Nazarbayev switched patrons, following the flux of power to a different source. On 29 May 1990, Yeltsin was elected chairman of Russia's Supreme Soviet. Gorbachev could not understand it: 'Here and abroad he drinks like a fish. Every Monday his face doubles in size. He's inarticulate . . . but again and again the people keep repeating "He's our man" and forgive him everything.' On 12 July, Yeltsin stormed out of a Communist Congress, resigned from the Party and then claimed sovereignty in Russia. Hated by Communist diehards and despised by frustrated liberals, undermined by a collapsing economy and raging nationalism, Gorbachev saw his power wither as he ranted about the 'scoundrel' Yeltsin: personalities matter and their rivalry helped destroy the state. In August, Gorbachev negotiated the price of German reunification in return for billions of dollars in loans to the USSR which, grumbled

* Nazarbayev was an astute player of the system, orchestrating the overthrow of his boss to become the youngest premier in the Union. 'I was an ambitious young man and Party membership was the route to all advancement,' he explained. 'If I had thought that it would have helped my ambition in those days to be a Buddhist I would have become a Buddhist.'

Gorbachev, were instantly stolen: 'It's just gone.' President Bush was delighted that 'The day of the dictator is over, the totalitarian era is passing, its old ideas blown away like leaves from an ancient, lifeless tree,'* but he was alarmed by Soviet turbulence. Now the adventure of a real suicidal nationalist – Moscow's closest Arab ally – would further undermine Gorbachev.

On 2 August 1990, Saddam invaded Kuwait. He counted himself the victor of the war against Iran, in which the ageing Khomeini had finally agreed to a ceasefire. 'Happy are those who have lost their lives in this convoy of light,' said the ayatollah. 'Unhappy am I that I still survive and have drunk the poisoned chalice.' He brought with him to Teheran Ebrahim Raisi, a young mullah who had studied under his deputy Khamenei, and heading the 'death committee' personally tortured and oversaw the executions of thousands of opposition activists. When the imam died at eighty-six, his funeral ranked with Nasser's as the largest ever: millions of frenzied mourners overran the cortège, knocking the flimsily wrapped body to the ground, tearing the shroud to shreds and leaping into the grave, until guards fired overhead and rescued the body by helicopter to be buried later in the day. Yet his creation proved stronger: his henchman, President Ali Khamenei, was chosen as Supreme Leader,† and ruled for thirty years during which Iran achieved power greater than that of the shah.

Saddam, with a bloated army, mountainous debts, a rapacious family and a splintered country, also sought extreme solutions. At home, he liquidated 180,000 Kurds and Assyrians in Anfal who had assisted the Iranians, slaughtering civilians, using chemical weapons, while he procured nuclear weapons with French help. In 1981, Israel bombed his facility; when he hired a Canadian gunmaker to build a supergun, Big Babylon, Mossad assassinated him.

Saddam struggled to control his sons and cousins. His pimp and food taster, Hana Gegeo, son of his chef and his daughters' governess, introduced him to a blonde doctor Samira, who became his mistress and then his wife, which naturally made enemies of his first wife Sajida and her sons. His trusted half-brothers wanted their sons to marry Saddam's daughters but in the mid-1980s his rising young cousins Hussein and Saddam Kamel won the girls, Raghad and Rana. A boy who flirted with his favourite daughter Hala was killed.

---

* Except in Albania, still a Communist dictatorship. Hoxha had died in 1985 but his chosen heir Ramiz Alia was still hoping to hang on – which he did until December 1990.
† In 2020, the Supreme Leader orchestrated the election of his former pupil, the Butcher of Teheran, Raisi, as president.

Even Saddam was unable to manage his eldest son, Uday, whom he had appointed to run the Olympic Committee and the Football Association, clearly heir apparent. Yet this Caligularian psychopath with a speech impediment regularly beat up men and raped women. In 1988, he burst into a party given for the wife of the Egyptian president Mubarak and beat Gegeo to death with an iron bar. Afterwards he tried to kill himself, then, summoned by Saddam, told his father, 'Stay with your real wife.' Infuriated, Saddam almost killed him: he 'was lucky I was unarmed'. An attempt to flee to America was foiled by his brothers-in-law, the Kamel brothers, igniting a feud that would end in bloodshed. Saddam exiled Uday to Switzerland and switched his favour to the less demented Qusay, who ran the SSO secret police.

Now Saddam was broke. Kuwait had lent him $30 billion and wanted it back. Tiny Kuwait had the same 20 per cent share of world oil as Iraq. Saddam claimed it as part of the old Ottoman *vilayet* of Basra. He probed America: 'We've no opinion on Arab–Arab conflicts,' the US ambassador told him, mistakenly greenlighting his plan, 'like your border disagreement with Kuwait.' Saddam's 120,000 Iraqi troops and 850 tanks rolled into Kuwait. The amir fled; his brother was shot, then gleefully pulped by one of Saddam's tanks. Unleashing Uday, back from exile, and the ravening Tikriti clan in a looting frenzy, Saddam annexed Kuwait.

Gorbachev was infuriated and sent his spymaster Primakov to restrain Saddam, but the Iraqi leader threatened the foundation of the west – oil – not to speak of international law. Bush vacillated; 'This is no time to go wobbly,' Thatcher told him. Bush won a UN resolution and recruited an unprecedented coalition, from Thatcher* to Assad, which mustered in Saudi Arabia. Saddam had achieved the impossible: uniting most of the fissiparous Arab world against himself. Only Arafat – and a reluctant King Hussein – backed him.

On 17 January 1991, Bush launched the first bombardments of Desert Storm, encouraging Iraqis to rebel against Saddam. Saddam fired Scud missiles at Israel before invading Arabia, temporarily taking the town of Khafji. In the first video war, watched live on the new twenty-four-hour news channel CNN, Bush's grand army of 956,600 troops used overwhelming air and land power to rout the Iraqis, incinerating entire divisions of tanks and trucks while Kurds, Shiites and Marsh Arabs all rebelled. But once Kuwait had been liberated, Bush, wary of

---

* In November 1990, Thatcher, having won an unprecedented three elections, but showing signs of deluded grandeur, promising to 'go on and on', was overthrown by her own cabinet – she was the longest serving twentieth-century PM and the ablest since Churchill.

entanglement, halted the invasion, leaving Saddam in power in central Iraq with all destructive weapons banned. Saddam had grossly miscalculated but, after two decades of terror, his camarilla remained loyal, even more concentrated on his family. His negotiators won American permission for Iraqi forces to fly helicopters, which they then used to slaughter the rebels. Just 292 coalition troops had been killed compared to 85,000 Iraqis. American apogee coincided with Soviet perigee.

At 4.30 p.m. on 18 August 1991, Gorbachev, on holiday at his Foros dacha in Crimea, was interrupted by his bodyguard: a mysterious delegation had arrived. Gorbachev found his phone lines had been cut. 'Something bad has happened,' he told Raisa. 'Perhaps terrible.' It was a coup: the State Committee on Emergency Rule, led by the KGB boss and defence minister, had seized power to stop the rolling disintegration of the USSR. In December 1990, Shevardnadze had resigned, warning of a coup. Lithuania had been the first to declare independence, followed by Estonia and Latvia, but Gorbachev himself had lost control since 13 January when his Spetsnaz commandos had shot civilians at a TV station in the Lithuanian capital, Vilnius, a crime that only consolidated its defiance. In March, Gorbachev had won a referendum to create his new Union of Sovereign States. Nazarbayev agreed to be its first premier. But the same month, Georgia embraced freedom. On 10 July, Yeltsin was democratically elected president of Russia, a legitimacy that the unelected Gorbachev could not equal. Then Ukraine delayed agreeing to the new Union. On 1 August, President Bush tried to save the USSR, visiting Kyiv to warn Ukraine against 'suicidal nationalism'.* Gorbachev, himself half Ukrainian, desperately tried to keep Ukraine within his new Union, warning that Ukraine would be too unstable to survive as a state and telling Bush it existed as a republic only because Ukrainian Bolsheviks had crafted it to increase their own power and 'added Kharkiv and Donbas'. Stalin had organized the actual borders. Crimea was added by Khrushchev. Those Russian regions, Gorbachev explained, would undermine any independent Ukraine.†

Now at his villa, Gorbachev asked the group who had sent them.

'The Committee.'

---

* The US and UK were in denial. This author was travelling through the Caucasus and central Asia at this time; on his return to Moscow he was debriefed by both British and US intelligence officers who enquired if he had seen any nuclear weaponry while assuring him that 'The USSR is here to stay.'

† Sometimes Bush's entourage was more realistic than Gorbachev's. When Jim Baker, secretary of state, discussed Ukraine with Politburo member Alexander Yakovlev, he wondered if there would be war. There were twelve million Russians in Ukraine, replied Yakovlev, 'many in mixed marriages, so what kind of war would that be?' Baker replied: 'A normal war.'

'What committee?'

When they started to explain the Committee's aims, Gorbachev shouted, 'Shut up, you asshole. Scumbag!' KGB forces had surrounded the mansion; ships on the Black Sea trained their guns. Raisa Gorbachev suffered a minor stroke. Unbeknown to the Gorbachevs, the Committee had made a series of unforced errors in Moscow. First they had planned to arrest Yeltsin and had surrounded his dacha, but he escaped to the Russian Supreme Soviet – nicknamed the White House – where he was joined by several military units. Then the conspirators held a farcical press conference at which at least two of them were drunk. The White House was defended by crowds of people and Yeltsin's units. Yeltsin then appeared and climbed defiantly on to a tank. The conspirators rushed to Crimea to beg forgiveness, while Yeltsin sent his own units to rescue Gorbachev. After arresting the conspirators, Gorbachev phoned Yeltsin. 'So you're alive,' boomed Yeltsin. 'We've been ready to fight for you!' Two conspirators killed themselves. When Gorbachev arrived back in Moscow, his power had haemorrhaged and he resigned as general secretary on 24 August. At the Supreme Soviet, Yeltsin launched his own coup, humiliating Gorbachev at the rostrum and forcing him to admit that his own ministers had backed the coup.

On 1 December, Ukraine voted for independence. Yeltsin tried to make it stay inside his new version of the Union but failed; Ukraine's secession was decisive. On the 8th, at a Belarusian Belavezha hunting lodge, beloved of tsars and general secretaries, Yeltsin secretly met the Ukrainian and Belarusian leaders and pulled off their own coup to end the USSR. Nazarbayev and the Central Asians joined them in a new Commonwealth of Independent States.

'Who gave you the authority?' shouted Gorbachev. 'Why didn't you warn me? . . . And once Bush finds out, what then?' But Yeltsin had already called Bush. On 9 December, Gorbachev received Yeltsin and the Kazakh president Nazarbayev.

'OK, sit down,' Gorbachev told them. 'What are you going to say to the people tomorrow?'

'I'm going to say,' replied Yeltsin, 'I'm going to take your place.'

Afterwards Nazarbayev claimed he 'wished I hadn't been there', but now he became dictator of a vast new state, Kazakhstan, so absolute that he ruled for thirty years, acclaimed himself Leader of the Nation and named the capital Nursultan.

At 5 p.m., on Christmas Day, Gorbachev rang Bush. 'Hello, Mikhail,' said Bush, at Camp David with his family.

'George, my dear friend,' said Gorbachev. 'I finally decided to do it today, at the end of the day.' He meant his resignation. 'The debate in our union on what kind of state to create took a different track from what I thought right.' This was one of history's great understatements.

At 7 p.m., as Gorbachev addressed the nation, a general arrived to collect the nuclear briefcase and delivered it to Yeltsin. Afterwards Gorbachev told his aides he was going to ring his old mother who 'has been saying to me for ages "Throw it all over. Come home"'. Gorbachev took his mother's advice. Down the Kremlin corridors, Yeltsin searched Gorbachev's office – the Little Corner, once occupied by Lenin, Stalin and Andropov – then demanded, 'Bring us glasses.' He and Korzhakov downed their whiskies. 'Now,' growled Yeltsin, president of the new Russian Federation, 'that's better.'

THE *FAMILIA*: BORIS, TATIANA AND RASPUTIN

Yeltsin, advised by a cohort of young reformers, banned Communism, opened many archives, pell-mell converted the command economy to free-market capitalism and launched a privatization programme. But almost immediately the economy crashed, Mafia criminals ran amok and the privatizations were fatally rushed and corrupted as a well-connected plutocracy of ex-Communists and self-made robber barons, together known as the oligarchs, bought oil companies for a fraction of their true value. Yeltsin, who combined the liberal instincts of a democrat with the habits of a drunken tsar, revealed the crimes of Stalin and encouraged exposés of history, yet he never dispensed with the security services. Instead of dissolving the KGB, he divided it into two new agencies. Meanwhile he played two entourages off against each other: on one hand, he championed his young westernized reformers; on other hand, he spent time with his swaggering, hard-drinking security chieftain, Korzhakov, now a general.

As Yeltsin took power in Moscow, Shevardnadze, the former Soviet foreign minister, was metamorphosing into a Georgian leader. In May 1991, Zviad Gamsakhurdia, who had been persecuted by Shevardnadze when he was Soviet proconsul there in the 1970s, was elected president by 86.5 per cent in a free election, promising to end all Russian interference. But within weeks Gamsakhurdia, manic, hollow-eyed and neurotic, managed to offend liberals with his despotism, Moscow with his Russophobia and ethnic minorities with his chauvinistic 'Georgia for Georgians'. By September the president was a lonely Shakespearean figure besieged in his palace. 'I'm the victim of the infernal, diabolic machinations of the Kremlin,' he told this author in his office. 'If Shevardnadze ever returns, we'll shoot him like a poodle.' Yet the rebels now surrounded the palace. 'Yes, I'm like a king in a Shakespearean play.' Henry V became first King Lear, then Richard II.

His chief enemy was an even more extraordinary personality, a former gangster boss, GULAG prisoner and playwright, Jaba Ioseliani, who during Stalin's reign had raided a bank. He now formed a private army, *Mkhedrioni* (the Knights), to defend Georgian territory and overthrow Gamsakhurdia. In December, Ioseliani, the kind of maverick who thrives in the chaos of fallen empires, drove out Gamsakhurdia and formed a State Council that invited Shevardnadze to return. The Grey Fox, once a world arbiter with Bush and Gorbachev, now became an embattled patriot in a tiny, impoverished state in disarray where he was backed by a warlord who had been in jail when he sat in the Politburo. Shevardnadze swallowed his pride. Watching Jaba and his entourage swagger by, he smiled grimly: 'How I miss Thatcher and Bush now.'

Spasms of killing inspired by medieval dreams of lost empires demonstrated what could happen when neither empires nor superpowers balanced the world. Yugoslavia was shattered by its feuding nationalities, incited to confrontation by vindictive nationalists, leading first to a war between Serbia and Croatia, then to a Serbian campaign to exterminate Bosnian Muslims, complete with concentration camps, mass rapes and massacres. After three and half years of war, in November 1995, Bill Clinton orchestrated a peace deal at Dayton, Ohio, that formed a tortuously complex multi-ethnic Bosnian state, but the Serbs switched to crushing Kosovan Albanians until March 1999, when Clinton unleashed NATO airstrikes that forced Serbian withdrawal and further infuriated Russia.

In Africa, no one intervened. In April 1994, Hutu tribesmen in Rwanda launched a carefully planned slaughter of their Tutsi neighbours, aiming to annihilate them completely. The colonial powers, Germany and Belgium, had long favoured the Tutsi, stirring Hutu resentment that led to massacres just before the country became independent. But France, always keen to promote *Françafrique*, adopted Rwanda as a sort of colonial foster child, backing the Hutu leadership and training its militias. When the Tutsi Rwandan Patriotic Front, led by a gangly general named Paul Kagame, rebelled, France regarded this as a British-backed challenge to *Françafrique*. Although Paris did not abet the coming slaughter, it had certainly done nothing to restrain it. When the Rwandan president was shot down by the RPF, Hutus embarked on genocide, killing, often with machetes, over 500,000 Tutsi in a few days. France intervened only partially and very late before the RPF invaded from the Uganda–Congo borderlands and installed Kagame as dictator. The ambitions of Rwanda and Uganda now blew back to support Congo's own warlords and elite in a continental blood bath, Congo's Great African War an atrocious struggle for minerals and power.* Neither European powers nor western intelligentsia showed much interest as the catastrophe killed around 5.4 million.

Back in Moscow, Yeltsin was challenged by a new breed of authoritarian ultra-nationalists in the Russian Supreme Soviet, who defied him from a fortified White House and criticized his pro-American free-market liberalism that had sent the economy into freefall – GDP dropped by 50 per cent; law and order collapsed, with Mafiosi openly assassinating their enemies and infiltrating business. As the White House voted to depose Yeltsin, its forces occupied the TV station at Ostankino and built barricades in the streets; Moscow emptied. Yeltsin's security chief Korzhakov advised sending in the tanks. 'Fascist–Communist armed rebellion in Moscow,' warned Yeltsin, 'will be suppressed.' On 3 October 1993, his commandos seized the TV station; the fighting raged all night. Yeltsin's tanks fired on the White House (watched in person by this author), as it was stormed by his commandos. The autocratic Yeltsin won out: 'Russia needs order.'

Yeltsin was determined to hold together the Russian Federation,†

---

* The expelled Hutus joined the mayhem in Congo. Kagame pursued them, backing a veteran revolutionary whose life personified the catastrophe of modern Congo. At twenty, Laurent-Désiré Kabila had embraced Marxism and backed the pro-Soviet faction, fighting with Che Guevara, but when the American ally, Mobutu, took power, Kabila had become a gold smuggler and Tanzanian brothel keeper. Only now was Kabila emerging to take power in Congo, backed by Kagame and the long-reigning Ugandan autocrat, Yoweri Museveni, with all sides using armies of *kadogos* (child soldiers). Once in power, Kabila, nicknamed *Mbongo* – the Bull – struggled to satisfy his backers in a new frenzy of mineral exploitation and murderous warfare. He fell out with Uganda and Rwanda, then embraced Zimbabwe and Angola, but losing control of the army he executed his once-loyal child soldiers, who now conceived Operation Mbongo Zero – Kill Bull – orchestrated by Rwanda. The children infiltrated the Marble Palace and, aided by a bodyguard, shot him dead. Kabila had named his son as heir: Joseph, aged twenty-nine, succeeded him, ruling for twenty years.
† And to claw back power in the newly independent republics, backing the armed secession of Abkhazia on Georgia's Black Sea shore: Shevardnadze defied Moscow but was almost killed in Sukhumi. As Russian tanks threatened Georgia and the ex-president

itself a honeycomb of ethnic republics. Its most contumacious people were the Islamic Chechens, deported to Siberia by Stalin in 1944. Now, led by an ex-Soviet air force general, this warrior people, controlled by clans and warlords, claimed a messy independence. Yeltsin surrounded Grozny, a feverish city where this author watched posses of militiamen cavort in surreal uniforms, some wearing spangled holsters, as they waited for the Russian assault. In December 1994, Yeltsin ordered the killing of the Chechen leaders by a car bomb to be followed by the storming of Grozny; his defence minister, Grachev, promised to take it in 'two hours with one airborne regiment'. Instead Russian troops were savaged by the Chechens, who ultimately retook the city. In 1996, Yeltsin was humiliatingly forced to withdraw.

By June that year, Yeltsin, drinking and sick with arteriosclerosis, was facing an election that the resurgent Communists were likely to win. General Korzhakov, who boasted that he had 'governed the country for three years', advised cancelling the elections. But Yeltsin's daughter Tatiana, a thirty-six-year-old engineer who had worked in the Soviet space industry, took control, calling in the oligarchs. These were led by a Jewish mathematician and engineer, Boris Berezovsky, who had made billions taking over AvtoVAZ car factories and Siberian oil companies. He had won the family's trust organizing the publication of Yeltsin's memoirs. Now he became Yeltsin's 'grey cardinal', nicknamed Rasputin. 'In history many times,' he told this author, 'financiers influenced states: aren't we like the Medici?' Even more trusted – and discreet – was Berezovsky's quiet young protégé, Roman Abramovich. Tatiana had left her husband for Yeltsin's ghostwriter, Valentin Yumachev, whom she later married. He was soon promoted to Yeltsin's chief of staff, forming this court around the president – the *Familia*.

It was not the only family in power. On 21 January 1994, Bassel al-Assad, heir to the presidency of Syria, accompanied by his first cousin Hafez Makhlouf, Republican Guard officer, was speeding to the airport in his Mercedes on the way to a ski holiday when he lost control.

KNIGHTS OF DAMASCUS, MARXIST MONSTER MOVIES AND KINGS OF DATA: IPHONES AND DAGGERS

Gamsakhurdia tried to rally his forces (he would be killed in the attempt), Shevardnadze flew to Moscow to bend the knee to the tsar, inviting this author to fly with him: 'There are at least two Russias,' he said: 'democratic and totalitarian; in ten years I hope Russia and Georgia will be democracies but in Russia the dark forces of empire are the wolves that are always waiting in the forest.'

Bassel was short, bearded, athletic and rugged, a winner of equestrian tournaments, friends with King Hussein's equestrienne daughter, an enthusiast for guns, sports cars and Lebanese girls. Trained in Russia, now commander of the Presidential Security, he was the beloved favourite of his father, Hafez al-Assad, whom he advised on Lebanon. The president portrayed him as the young Saladin, the Golden Knight, on horseback fighting Crusaders and Zionists. His companion in the car was also at the heart of the dynasty: Makhlouf's aunt was Anisa Assad, the first lady, his brother Rami already emerging as the family's business fixer.

Ailing with diabetes and arteriosclerosis, Assad based his dynasty on his alliance with Iran, which would protect him from his rival Saddam. But he was infuriated by the emergence of secret talks between Rabin, now Israeli prime minister, and Arafat, PLO chairman.

As successive US presidents, starting with Carter, tried to nurture peace, Israel had refused to negotiate with the terrorist organization for over twenty years. Now Rabin allowed his foreign minister, Shimon Peres, to start secret negotiations. The two – laconic Rabin, visionary Peres – hated each other. Peres orchestrated secret conversations in Oslo between an Israeli academic and a Palestinian official that developed into Israeli recognition of the PLO and vice versa, establishing a Palestinian Authority, the first step towards a state, and the sharing of Jerusalem. 'I said peace first, then the details,' Peres recalled. 'Peace is like love: first you have to trust.' To Assad this was betrayal, but for King Hussein, who had managed to appease his menacing Arab neighbours Saddam and Assad while secretly meeting with Rabin for decades, it was an opportunity: Hussein joined the process. On 13 September 1993, at the White House, Rabin and Arafat, accompanied by King Hussein, hosted by Clinton, signed the peace accords. A month later Hussein and Rabin signed their own treaty.

Watching this in Damascus, Assad ordered the assassination of King Hussein. He was not the only one reaching for his pistol. On 4 November 1995, Rabin was assassinated by a Jewish zealot. The killing started the disintegration of the Oslo Accords, exacerbated by Israeli nationalists and Palestinian extremists. When Rabin's successors offered a division of Jerusalem, Arafat rejected it. The two-state solution – the only hope for peace – remained frozen. 'We're not ashamed, nor are we afraid,' said Hussein at Rabin's funeral in Jerusalem, 'nor are we anything but determined to continue the legacy for which my friend fell, as did my grandfather in this very city when I was with him – and but a boy.' Hussein, warned by the CIA, avoided Assad's assassins, but secretly he was suffering from cancer. His brother Hassan was crown prince, but he started to groom his eldest son, Abdullah.

In Damascus, Bassel al-Assad was killed in that car crash, his cousin wounded. Hafez ordered mourning for the 'Martyr of the Nation'. Three children were left: the youngest, Maher, was a stocky trigger-happy officer with anger-management issues; the second youngest Madj had mental problems; and a middle brother, Bashar, was a doctor living in London under an assumed name. Anisa favoured Maher, but Assad summoned the twenty-eight-year-old Bashar, tall, lanky, chinless with a lisp and a liking for Phil Collins music – an unlikely candidate for dictator. He had become an ophthalmic surgeon because he hated blood, yet he was about to unleash a level of butchery even his father had never contemplated.

The Communist rulers who survived were those who combined dynasty with ideology. The Castro brothers endured in Cuba. In North Korea, Kim Il-sung curated his succession. On 8 July 1994, when Kim died aged eighty-two, he was not only embalmed* but also declared the immortal Eternal President, while his carefully laid plan for a hereditary Marxist dynasty smoothly raised his son, Kim Jong-il, to the throne. Born in Russia, named Yuri – the family called him Yura – he had been educated in China during the Korean War (sometimes holidaying secretly in Malta), while starting his rise quietly in the Party apparat, until 1980 when his father promoted him to Dear Leader and Supreme Commander.

Sporting a bouffant quiff and Stalinka tunics, Kim had been raised as a princeling, favouring Scotch whiskies, lobsters and sushi, but he was a shrewd power broker, learning from his father the essential rules of Kimite dynasty – survival depended on playing off the superpowers, promoting the family and liquidating any opposition. His two obsessions were western films and nuclear weapons. Father and son regarded themselves as being at perpetual war with South Korea and the capitalist states, and kidnapped over 3,000 citizens from South Korea and even Japan. Having started in the Agitprop department, Jong-il craved a sophisticated film industry. In 1978, he orchestrated the kidnapping from

---

* A special medical unit had long maintained Lenin's body and honed this special Soviet skill. Communist leaders, first Georgi Dmitrov of Bulgaria, then Marshal Choibalsan of Mongolia and Gottwald of Czechoslovakia, were all embalmed and displayed. When Stalin died, he joined Lenin in the Mausoleum, but in 1961 Khrushchev ordered his removal. That was far from the end of the embalming of Communist autocrats. In 1969, Ho Chi Minh was embalmed, followed by Mao and Neto of Angola. The embalmments of Forbes Burnham of Guyana and later Hugo Chávez of Venezuela were botched and they had to be buried. Lenin, Mao, two Kims, Ho and Neto remain on display.

Hong Kong of Choi Eun-hee, the beautiful actress ex-wife of the leading South Korean film director Shin Sangok; when he was lured to Hong Kong to find her, he too was kidnapped. After two years of indoctrination, they were taken to meet Kim, who showed them his collection of 15,000 movies, ordered them to remarry and produced their Marxist monster movie *Pulgasari*.

As for any monarch, the biology of succession was unremitting. Kim had first had a daughter in an arranged marriage, but while supervising North Korean films and theatre he naturally had access to a harem of official entertainers known as *Kippumjo*, the Joy Squad, said to be divided into Satisfaction, Happiness and Entertainment divisions for sex, wellbeing and dancing, according to Kenji Fujimoto, Kim's sushi chef and companion. A film star, married to someone else, gave birth to his first son Kim Jong-nam – but without the father's all-important blessing. Around 1972, he started an affair with a dancer Ko Yong-hui, who bore him three children, two sons – the second named Kim Jong-un – and a daughter Kim Yo-jong, who became his official family.

While maintaining a state with a million-strong military and 200,000 political prisoners, father and son sought the Bomb, but their Soviet and Chinese allies refused to help. The Kims scoured the world for technology to upgrade uranium and develop weapons, opening negotiations with Pakistan, which was trying to catch up with India. Pakistan's nuclear mastermind, A. Q. Khan – nicknamed Centrifuge Khan – handed over the technology during the 1980s when Benazir Bhutto, daughter of the executed premier of the 1970s, heiress of another south Asia family dynasty, was elected prime minister. First promoted by Benazir's father, A. Q. Khan had embarked on history's greatest criminal enterprise: the sale of Pakistani nuclear technology. He travelled the world to eighteen countries. Saddam was interested; in Iran, Syria and Libya, Khamenei, Assad and Qaddafi bought it. Khan delivered the Libyan package emblazoned 'Good Look Fabrics', disguised as a suit from an Islamabad tailor. When Kim bought it, Benazir Bhutto supposedly delivered it personally.

When America discovered the existence of North Korea's nuclear programme, Kim, whom American diplomats remembered as genial and masterful, conducted negotiations to squeeze maximum benefits for his dwindling economy while secretly procuring the Bomb. At the same time, he reviewed his sons for their suitability for the succession: the oldest was not of his official family; the second was too weak; but his third son, Kim Jong-un, nicknamed 'Jong Unny', whom he had sent to a Swiss school, was just like him.

In Moscow, reformers, oligarchs and the *Familia* feared that Yeltsin, fuddled and soused, was about to lose the election to the Communists: a heart attack had rendered him almost gaga. But Berezovsky raised $140 million and commandeered the TV stations to ensure that he was re-elected. The *Familia* fought Korzhakov for power: Lenin and Stalin had commandeered the criminal underworld for their murderous secret police; courtiers and oligarchs now threatened to kill each other. A bomb beheaded Berezovsky's driver. 'After the attempt on Berezovsky's life,' recalled Korzhakov, 'he always wanted to kill someone in return . . . telling me so calmly, as if I was the guy killing everyone.'

Yeltsin's *Familia* dismissed the overmighty bodyguard; the half-alive Yeltsin won the 1996 election. But in August Chechen warlords infiltrated Grozny and retook the city, expelling the Russian army. Yeltsin underwent quintuple coronary surgery. The Familia then ruled the floundering state.

America thrived as the unipower. The elation of Cold War victory dizzied American and European potentates; America and its system, liberal democracy, had triumphed. Success begets success: in Africa and south America, countries became US-style democracies. It was hard not to watch Russian implosion with a certain smugness.[*]

On 21 March 1997, Yeltsin, meeting Clinton in Helsinki, agreed that NATO could expand into the former Soviet empire, in return for $4 billion, but he warned that it was 'a mistake, a serious one' and 'a sort of bribe'. Clinton himself could not believe what Russia was conceding – and nor could many Russians. It was just the start of a blistering humiliation. It was not magnanimous of the US but, worse, it lacked foresight. America encouraged Yeltsin's reforms, but it could have offered a Marshall Plan to ease Russia's transformation and find a way to invite Russia into the western system. It was not just America's fault: Russian grandees still thought of Russia in terms of empire and autocracy. Moreover, America brushed aside Yeltsin's protests to bomb

---

[*] Yet just as it seemed that all human life was leading progressively to a freer world, the warnings from scientists who proved that human industry over two centuries was warming the planet became increasingly urgent. Few leaders had paid any attention to these warnings: one of the first to do so was a visionary prince of Wales, later Charles III, who, at twenty-two, in February 1970 warned against the 'horrific effects of pollution in all its cancerous forms', asking, 'Are we all prepared to accept price increases . . . to discipline ourselves to [accept] restrictions and regulations for our own good?' Only twenty years later, in June 1992, at a first UN Earth Summit in Rio did politicians start to debate how to limit this anthropogenic damage. This now became one of the most urgent challenges facing humanity. Yet to achieve meaningful change leaders, especially in surging industrial nations like China and India, would have to not only ignore but override the immediate interests of their nations and people in favour of a future benefit for all mankind.

Russia's ally Serbia. Poland, Czechoslovakia and Hungary joined the European Union and NATO, as did the three ex-Soviet republics on the Baltic. Ukraine and Georgia were next to apply.* Marxism had been defeated, Russia broken, and China was far behind. It looked as if the Leninist empire had fallen bloodlessly; in fact the fall of the USSR would extend over thirty years – and be far from bloodless: Russian resentment was felt viscerally by an ex-Chekist fallen, like his motherland, on hard times.

'We lived like everyone, but sometimes I had to earn extra money,' recalled an KGB colonel struggling to survive, 'as a taxi driver. It's not pleasant to speak about.' The taxi driver was Vladimir Putin, now unemployed in St Petersburg. 'What's the collapse of the Soviet Union?' he said. 'It's the collapse of historical Russia under the name of the Soviet Union.'† As such it was 'the greatest geopolitical disaster of the twentieth century'.

In March 1997, the *Familia* summoned Putin to Moscow. Putin, then aged forty-four, had attached himself to the liberal, if venal, mayor of Petersburg, becoming his omnipresent fixer and deputy. Revealingly his first TV interview highlighted his KGB past and played the Stierlitz theme tune. When the mayor lost an election, Putin was offered a minor job in the presidential apparat in Moscow. But just a year later, he was appointed deputy chief of the presidential staff at the time of Russia's deepest humiliation and America's triumph.

It was bizarre moment. Russia was stumbling; Yeltsin fired one premier after another; gangsters killed their rivals; oligarchs strutted; the Chechens were defiant. Yet Yeltsin, half visionary liberal, half clumsy autocrat, understood the lessons of history. 'We are all guilty,' he said on 17 July 1998 as he presided over the burial of the skeletons of the murdered Tsar Nicholas II and his family in the Romanov crypt in Petersburg, but 'the bitter lesson is that any attempts to change life by violence are doomed'. Now he considered his legacy: 'We must finish this century, which has become the century of blood and lawlessness

---

* One of the American successes was persuading Ukraine and Kazakhstan to give up nuclear weapons left after the fall of the Soviet Union in return for US aid. In 1991, Ukraine and Kazakhstan found themselves in possession of thousands of Soviet warheads, the world's third and fourth largest nuclear powers. In 1992, Kazakhstan gave up its nuclear arsenal. At Budapest in December 1994, Ukraine's 'territorial integrity' was guaranteed by Russia, the USA and Britain in return for giving up its nuclear weaponry – a decision that some now regard as a mistake.

† 'The dangerous timebomb,' that allowed the republics to secede, 'planted in the foundation of our state, exploded the moment the safety mechanism provided by the Communist Party was gone,' Vladimir Putin wrote later as president. 'A parade of sovereignties followed.'

for Russia, with repentance and reconciliation' but also strength. The *Familia* sought an heir.

Many claimed to have invented that heir. Berezovsky insisted he had first noticed Putin, but it was Yumashev who spotted him. In July 1998, they appointed this unknown as chief of the FSB, successor of the KGB. Swollen, dazed, yet imperious and mysterious, Yeltsin could not stop his authority from disintegrating; the opposition was preparing impeachment as the prosecutor-general investigated *Familia* corruption. In April 1999, Putin unveiled a grainy video of the prosecutor-general, paunchy and naked, cavorting flabbily with two prostitutes. The prosecutor-general was dismissed. Tatiana and Yumashev, guided by Abramovich, were impressed with Putin, young, tough, inscrutable. They made him an extraordinary offer – to be president, provided the *Familia* would not be prosecuted. 'How will I keep my wife and children safe?' Putin asked – he had two daughters. The *Familia* explained that the Kremlin would keep him safe. But how would he win? A short, victorious war.

On 9 August 1999, Yeltsin suddenly appointed Putin as premier. 'I wasn't just offering a promotion,' recalled Yeltsin. 'I wanted to hand him the Cap of Monomachos' – the tsar's crown.* In October, Putin invaded Chechnya, delighting Russians with his gangsterish swagger: 'We'll follow the terrorists everywhere; if we find them on the toilet, excuse me, yes, we'll kill them in the crapper.' Russia fought an unrestrained war against terrorists, and also against civilians, who were tortured, vanished and murdered at will. The army was a brutal, clumsy tool: Russian generals, said Putin admiringly, 'don't chew snot'. Yeltsin told Putin he was going to appoint him acting president. 'I'm not ready,' replied Putin. 'It's a difficult destiny.' Yeltsin was determined. 'I agree,' said Putin finally, remarking, 'It would be stupid to say, "No, I'd rather sell sunflower seeds."'

'Today I want to ask your forgiveness, because many of our hopes have not come true,' said Yeltsin, on New Year's Eve, 1999. 'I am standing down ... The country has a strong man, fit to be president.' He named this mysterious person as acting president.

The first decree Putin signed was entitled 'On guarantees for the former president and his family'.

On 26 March 2000, Putin won the presidency. Yeltsin showed him into Stalin's old office: 'It's your office now, Vladimir.' The *Familia*

---

* In September, three mysterious apartment bombings killed three hundred people. Blamed on Chechen terrorists, it was possibly the work of FSB agents creating the crisis for Putin to solve.

believed they would control this 'accidental' president. Yet Putin brought the focus and tactics of a judo blackbelt to the Kremlin. 'I toil,' he said, 'like a galley slave.' Proud to sit in Stalin's office, he invited visitors to open books from the former general secretary's library kept in the Little Corner. Absolute power crafts a new character. Initially awkward and clumsy, he quickly developed the ferocious vigilance needed to thrive in the Kremlin, his relish in deploying targeted violence and military hardware scarcely tempered by gallows humour. Revelling in his machismo, he posed bare-chested and gun-toting, cradling tigers and stalking bears. Questioned about his ruthless reputation, he joked, 'There's no one to talk to since Mahatma Gandhi died' – and on his birthday his courtiers gave him a bust of Gandhi. His favourite saying was, 'It's like shearing a piglet – too much squealing, too little wool.'

Putin swept the *Familia* aside and restored the power of the state, controlled elections, emasculated the Duma (parliament), broke the press and promoted a mix of liberals and KGB veterans. 'The government's undercover FSB team has completed its first assignment,' he joked to a gathering of secret policemen, often adding, 'There's no such thing as an ex-KGB man.'

He 'pacified' Chechnya, appointing a murderous princeling, the twenty-nine-year-old Ramzan Kadyrov, as ruler. Kadyrov became his loyalest courtier, vying with his secret police to be his most lethal grandee.* Putin then turned on the oligarchs, inviting them to Stalin's mansion, to warn them against meddling in politics. When they disobeyed, they were broken: one was arrested and sent to a labour camp. Berezovsky, outraged that his puppet had seized the sceptre, was driven out of Russia. Putin ordered his security forces to liquidate traitors: 'Enemies are right in front of you, you fight, you make peace, everything's clear. But a traitor must be destroyed' – even in England: Berezovsky died mysteriously – found hanged in his Surrey mansion; his associate ex-KGB Colonel Litvinenko was poisoned with polonium. 'I don't know who killed him but he was a traitor,' said Putin. 'It wasn't us, but a dog's death for a dog.' In the former imperium, he was determined to restore not the USSR – he was appalled by Lenin's creation of a Ukrainian Soviet republic out of Russian national lands – but its traditional empire. Russia, he believed, was a 'unique civilization', the mother of all Russias, and he espoused autocracy and an ethno-nationalism, envisioning an

---

* Putin's initial choice was an Islamic rebel warlord Akhmad Kadyrov, who had been the mufti of independent Chechnya but in 2000 changed sides and became Putin's Chechen president. On his assassination in 2004, Putin turned to his son Ramzan.

exceptionalist Orthodox Russian World, a Eurasian successor to Kyivan Rus and the Romanov empire, superior to the west, channelling the ideas of Slavophiles and White philosophers in the Russian civil war. As the other ex-Soviet republics developed their identities as nations, Russia, created as an empire, found no other vision of itself – except it was now an empire with a grievance.

Putin denounced American paramountcy. 'What's a unipolar world?' he asked. 'It's a world where there's one master. And that's pernicious not only for all those within this system but for the sovereign itself because it destroys itself from within.'

In November 2000, as Putin orchestrated the crushing of Chechen resistance, the Americans – after a near draw that led to a legal standoff – elected another inexperienced leader in his forties. While Putin grew up feral on a Leningrad housing estate, George W. Bush was sailing yachts at his family compound Kennebunkport.

Son of a president, grandson of a senator, a Yalie aristocratic fratboy who had remade himself as a swaggering Texan, making money in oil, owning the Texas Rangers baseball team, he won the presidency on his first attempt. The two Bush presidents – father and son, along with Clinton – presided over the climax of the American century. Simultaneously, US entrepreneurs spearheaded technical advances that dovetailed with America's global vision – and the globalized economy that it dominated.

'For the past thirty-three years,' said Steve Jobs, in remission from cancer and looking back on his life while talking to students in 2005, 'I have looked in the mirror every morning and asked myself: "If today were the last day of my life, would I want to do what I am about to do today?"' Jobs had changed the world: 'Of all the inventions of humans, the computer is going to rank near or at the top as history unfolds.' Intolerant and intolerable, unkind and often cruel, Jobs believed creativity was about following your instincts – 'connecting the dots'. Jobs was the son of two teachers – a Syrian and his Swiss lover – but 'my biological mother was a young, unwed graduate student, and she decided to put me up for adoption' – and he was adopted by an American coastguard. As a schoolboy he worked at the business-machine company Hewlett Packard, later travelled to India, embraced Zen Buddhism, dropped out of college (to take a calligraphy course), then at twenty founded a company in his parents' garage, where he started to design the first consumer computer. He called it Apple.

The idea of computers was not new.* Their development made inevitable the arrival of smartphones and computers facile and small enough to be used by ordinary people, but it took forty years to happen. In 1959, Robert Noyce at Fairchild Semiconductor invented a single piece – a monolithic integrated circuit, a chip – that made the revolution possible just at the same time as Paul Baran was developing his messaging network to function after a nuclear apocalypse. In 1968, Alan Kay at Xerox predicted a 'personal, portable information manipulator' that he called a Dynabook, just as the first active-matrix liquid-crystal display was developed. In 1975 IBM created its first portable device, the same year that a Seattle lawyer's son, Bill Gates, dropped out of Harvard to develop a system of instruction for computers to use – software – bought by IBM. Five years later, Gates launched a more sophisticated system, Windows.

In 1974, the Pentagon's ARPA communications, designed to connect the leadership after nuclear war, had been extended into academia by Vint Cerf and Bob Kahn, who called it the inter-network – internet. In 1980 ARPANET was closed, but the European nuclear research organization CERN started to use the system, which in 1989 inspired a thirty-four-year-old mathematics professor there, Tim Berners-Lee: 'I just had to take the hypertext idea and connect it to the Transmission Control Protocol and domain system idea and – ta-da! – the World Wide Web.' Like Edison or Watt before him, he did not claim to have invented it: 'Most of the technology involved in the web, like the hypertext, like the Internet, multi-font text objects, had all been designed already. I just had to put them together.' He invented a system of addresses – //www – that became so universal the internet almost became a groove of the

---

* In 1837, the poet Lord Byron's daughter, Ada, countess of Lovelace, and her friend Charles Babbage, partly inspired by the article of an Italian military engineer Luigi Menabrea, later premier of united Italy, had devised a programme for what they called an Analytical Engine. In 1843, Lovelace wrote instructions that she called algorithms, inspired by al-Khwarizmi of 820s Baghdad, but she also foresaw the perils of 'autocrats of information'. Babbage designed their Engine. Yet it was a century before such technology was invented by a German scientist Konrad Zuse who in 1941 built the first computer, Z3, in Berlin and devised the first programming language, *Plankalkül*. His Z3 was destroyed by an Allied air raid, but after the war Zuse founded the first tech company – and sold his patent to the American company IBM, which had also worked on tabulating vast quantities of personal data for the US government in Nazi Germany and the USA. Simultaneously, at Bletchley Park in Britain, a young mathematician, Alan Turing, who at twenty-four had defined a 'universal computing machine', was designing an electromagnetic machine to decrypt the German Enigma code. In 1946, he designed an Automatic Computing Engine and two years later he built one: it filled a room. Next he and a colleague created the first gaming programme, the chess-playing *Turochamp*. In January 1952, a series of accidents, involving his male lover and a burglary, led to Turing admitting a homosexual relationship, illegal under an 1885 law. Turing pleaded guilty to 'gross indecency' and he agreed to an atrocious treatment, chemical castration. At forty-one, Turing killed himself with cyanide.

human brain. 'I never foresaw how big the Net would become,' Berners-Lee told this author, 'but I had designed it to be totally universal. And there was a moment as it grew exponentially that I realized it would change the world.'

In 1984, Jobs, a visionary bundler of ideas, tweaker of inventions and crafter of exquisite designs, launched the Macintosh, a computer that a consumer could use to move between different facilities, adding a hand control that he called a mouse and the ability to choose new fonts, inspired by the course of calligraphy he had once taken. 'I was lucky,' he explained. 'I found what I loved to do early in life.' But 'Then I got fired. The heaviness of being successful was replaced by the lightness of being a beginner again.'

When Jobs returned to Apple he devised, starting in 1998, a series of devices beginning with an 'i' (standing for 'internet, individual, instruct, inform and inspire'). In 2007, his iPhone changed human behaviour, creating a fashionable but indispensable machine. By 2020, around 2.2 billion iPhones had been sold, 19 billion smartphones altogether – tiny mechanisms that forever changed human nature and behaviour in ways not yet clear. Smartphones became technologies so essential they became almost membral extensions. By 2005, at least 16 per cent of humans were using smartphones; by 2019, the figure was 53.6 per cent, 86.6 per cent in the west. The internet opened a mass of new knowledge to citizens, and many abandoned more laborious yet more trustworthy sources of information. The internet thickened society, adding new layers of discourse and power to give a dynamic to already pluralistic societies – a further shift from 'sovereign power', in Foucault's analysis, to 'disciplinary power'.

The new knowledge spread openness; but, like writing, printing and television, it could be controlled and manipulated: even in democracies, its panjandrums exercised vast secret power as despots of data, and there has never been a better tool for tyranny. Its tendency to create sequestered localities of the same-minded meant that it parochialized as many as it globalized. In many countries, mobile phones were used by people who still lived in iPhone and dagger societies, dominated by kin, tribe and sect, that could barely feed or heat their people. In some cases, terrorists were beheading people with swords while chatting via WhatsApp on their iPhones.

Less flashy but as important were the astonishing improvements in public health – reduced child mortality, smallpox vaccinations, chlorinated water. These are the result of interlinked developments high and low: the invention of the lavatory linked to sewers may have saved a billion lives since the 1860s. The doubling of human life expectancy in one century and the reduction of child mortality by a factor of ten are triumphs with no downside – except our own voracious success as a species, our population rising from a billion people in 1800 to eight billion in 2025. The industrial revolution combined with our medical revolution now threatens our own existence.

While the Net was invented by Brits and Americans and developed in Silicon Valley, where the new digital titans worked out how to make it profitable, it was the closed world that would really grasp its potential: the Chinese security services were quickest to appreciate its power of surveillance. The Russians harnessed its ability to amplify and justify rage and propagate lies in the open world. The autocracies understood quickly that their hackers could poison the delicate political anatomy of the democracies by using their very freedoms against them.

Bush was keen to meet Putin. On 16 June 2001, at a Slovenian summit, the new commande-in-chief of the unipower met the new Russian potentate. 'I looked the man in the eye,' said Bush, revealing the naivety of American paramountcy. 'I found him very straightforward and trustworthy – I was able to get a sense of his soul.' Putin, fighting an Islamic insurgency in Chechnya, warned Bush of the jihadi threat to the American homeland from a new Afghan force, the Taliban. The Communists had not lasted long after the Soviet withdrawal from Afghanistan, but a vicious civil war had discredited the warlords. In Kandahar, a coterie of ex-mujahedin Ghilzai *talibs* (madrassa students), under Omar, a one-eyed expert RPG-7 gunner who had returned to teaching, formed a vigilante band to stop crime and corruption. Adopted and funded by the Pakistani ISI, and backed by Haqqani, the Taliban quickly conquered the country, and invited Osama bin Laden back.

PRINCE OF THE TOWERS

'Those extremists are all being funded by Saudi Arabia,' Putin told Bush, 'and it is only a matter of time before it results in a major catastrophe.'

Bush was astonished. 'I was taken aback,' recalled Condoleeza Rice, daughter of a minister from Birmingham, Alabama, descended from slaves, who became a State Department Russianist, Stanford professor and now the first black national security advisor,* 'by Putin's alarm and

---

* After retiring as secretary of state, Rice researched her family history: 'My great-great-grandmother Zina on my mother's side bore five children by different slave owners,' she wrote. 'My great-grandmother on my father's side, Julia Head, carried the name of the slave owner and was so favored by him that he taught her to read.'

vehemence.' It was they decided sour grapes after the Soviet defeat in Afghanistan.

Putin was right. While W had been planning his presidential run, another entitled scion of privilege was planning his own momentous mission. The older Bush's Iraq war and protection of Saudi Arabia had horrified Osama bin Laden; he demanded an audience with King Fahd, though he was instead received by his brother Prince Sultan. Osama proposed that he reject American troops – present since the Gulf War – and let an Arab legion of mujahedin defend Mecca. Fahd trusted the bin Ladens, but dismissed Osama's quixotic fanaticism and expelled him. He in turn despised the debauched Saudi kings for whom his father had worked: the Prophet had banned infidels from Arabia; now American troops were stationed there, while the American ally, Israel, had attacked Lebanon. Bin Laden, who received a $7 million annual income from his family, refined both his ideology and his organization, setting up in Sudan, working on his own engineering business while also setting up a network of terrorist cells, fundraisers, bomb makers, undercover operatives and the essential cannon fodder of Islamic terror, young – often teenaged – suicidists.

When his plans were ready in early 1998, he procured a *fatwa* from a tame cleric to kill the Americans and their allies – civilians and military – and to 'liberate the al-Aqsa Mosque [Jerusalem] and the holy mosque of Mecca'. That August, bin Laden killed hundreds when his suicidists drove truck bombs into US embassies in Tanzania and Kenya. Clinton ordered missile attacks on bin Laden in Sudan, which was forced to expel the terrorist.

Bin Laden had lost his family income and was living on subscriptions from Saudi backers when he got Omar's invitation. He arrived on a private plane with wives and 300 mujahedin. Backed by Omar, now calling himself *Amir al-Mu'minin*, and Haqqani, justice minister, bin Laden declared war on the USA and started to train al-Qaeda volunteers. As Clinton secretly ordered his capture or assassination, Omar helped bin Laden set up headquarters, where he now considered a long-time ambition: an attack on American skyscrapers. In 1999, a trusted Pakistani henchman proposed a spectacular attack by suicidists piloting jet planes* into the Twin Towers, the prestigious Manhattan skyscrapers

---

* The idea of using planes as flying bombs was as old as flying itself, considered by Russian terrorists against the Romanovs in 1905 and used by Japanese kamikazes during the Second World War. Palestinian hijackers had proven both the vulnerability of civilian jet planes and the spectacular fear produced by attacking these hulking symbols of western comfort.

with which he was familiar because they had been abortively attacked by his nephew seven years earlier.

Suicide bombers had been invented by the Sri Lankan Tamil Tigers,* quickly copied by jihadis. Bin Laden grasped the power of attacking the homeland: 'to destroy towers in America so it could taste some of what we are tasting'. Although a US commando attack on al-Qaeda camps was cancelled, Clinton ordered missile strikes – just missing bin Laden, who was already personally selecting his team of suicidists, in particular a cell from Hamburg who spoke English, nineteen of whom were now dispatched to learn aviation in American flight schools. 'I was responsible for entrusting the nineteen brothers with the raids,' bin Laden later bragged. Fifteen of the nineteen were Saudi. Its date was chosen for the defeat of the Ottomans outside Vienna in 1683.

Although the CIA and FBI realized that bin Laden was planning an American attack, and although the two agencies collected shards of intelligence, including the bizarre revelation that there were Arab pilots who were only interested in studying take-off but not landing, they were, with a few stellar exceptions, too competitive to share information and too unimaginative to grasp the scale of bin Laden's ambition.

Three months after Putin's warning, on 11 September 2001 George W. Bush was listening to children reading *The Pet Goat* in a Floridian school when his chief of staff interrupted to whisper in his ear: 'A second plane hit the second tower. America is under attack.'

As Bush arrived at the school, nineteen mass murderers had seized four jet planes, filled with innocent civilians; at 8.46 a.m., the first plane, controlled by five terrorists, flew into the 110-storey North Tower of the World Trade Center; Bush was informed that a small plane had accidentally crashed into the tower; he then entered the schoolroom. At 9.03 a.m., the second plane flew into the South Tower. As terrified people jumped from the higher storeys, with the world watching on live TV, the towers collapsed – a vision of live pandemonic apocalypse. At 9.37 a.m. a third plane dived into the Pentagon in DC. Each plane was the scene of desperate yet unknown despair and heroism; in a fourth plane, assigned to the White House or the Capitol, brave passengers, after wishing loved ones goodbye in heartbreaking messages, cried

---

* That was how they killed Rajiv Gandhi. His premiership was overshadowed by an arms scandal, an environmental disaster and his intervention in the civil war between the Sinhalese government and the Tamil Tiger militia in Sri Lanka, initially to protect the Tamils, of whom there were many in southern India. But once in Sri Lanka, Indian troops found themselves fighting fanatical Tamil insurgents, the Tigers. Rajiv lost the 1989 election; and, on 21 May 1991, while campaigning, he was approached by a female Tamil Tiger suicide bomber – the first of a new phenomenon – who ignited her explosives.

'Let's roll!' and attacked the terrorists, who in the ensuing struggle crashed the plane into a Pennsylvanian field at 10.03. Altogether 2,977 were killed, as well as all the terrorists. Bin Laden had laid the bait, and already American potentates were considering whether to hit not just bin Laden and the Taliban but also Saddam Hussein. That afternoon, the defence secretary, Donald Rumsfeld, wondered if intelligence was 'good enough to hit SH at same time. Not only OBL . . . Need to move swiftly . . . Go massive . . . Sweep it all up. Things related or not.'

Amid panic and fear in the heartland, the fifty-five-year-old Bush, converted to his new mission, turned to his experienced vice-president Dick Cheney, a midwestern Yalie with a snarl who, as Bush senior's defence secretary, had supervised Desert Storm before making money chairing the oil service company Halliburton. 'I can hear you,' Bush told Americans through a bullhorn at a Ground Zero stinking of fire and death. 'So will the people who knocked down these buildings.' Soon afterwards he warned the Taliban to 'hand over the terrorists, or . . . share in their fate'. Cheney, the most powerful vice-president in US history, devised new domestic powers making it easier to find terrorists and unleashed the CIA to hunt them across the world and foil more atrocities. As he sanctioned the 'rendition' (seizure), 'enhanced interrogation' (torture) and imprisonment of suspects in secret 'black prisons' lent by sympathetic powers, Bush declared a worldwide War on Terror that encompassed a global anti-terror campaign and two land wars.

In October, American troops, aided by sympathetic northern warlords, many of them Tajiks, Hazaras and Uzbeks, invaded Afghanistan. Special units, Operational Detachment Alpha 574, rode south on horseback, taking part in history's last cavalry charges. The quick conquest and the establishment of a new president, Hamid Karzai, a Pashtun whose father had been shot by the Taliban, encouraged an exhilarating confidence in American paramountcy that called for a wider mission. Amir Omar escaped to Pakistan, as did bin Laden, both aided by the Haqqani terror dynasty led by the founder's son Sirajuddin.

Although there was no real connection between Saddam and al-Qaeda, in January 2002 Bush warned Americans of an Axis of Evil – the phrase a reference to the Hitler Axis of the Second World War – including North Korea, Iraq and Iran, which could not be permitted 'to threaten us with the world's most destructive weapons'. Cheney and Rumsfeld proposed an ambitious escalation: not only to destroy an unfinished enemy, Saddam Hussein, but to impose American democracy in west Asia.

Saddam had slaughtered rebel Kurds and Arabs to restore his power after Desert Storm, but in August 1995, his two sons-in-law – cousins, the brothers Hussein and Saddam Kamel, married to his daughters Raghad and Rana – suddenly fled Baghdad and drove in a convoy across the desert to Jordan, where they were given asylum. The loss of his daughters was humiliating, but the Kamels had clashed with the demented Uday, who dubbed himself Abu Sarhan – Son of the Wolf – and was once again terrorizing Baghdad: girls were raped, men beaten; a group of French tourists were forced to have sex with each other at gunpoint. All remembered not his mania but his 'eerie quietness'. He had recently rushed into a family party, fought with his brothers-in-law and, drawing his gun, accidently shot an uncle in the leg.

Hussein Kamel, who had helped procure Saddam's illegal weapons, had destroyed them after 1991 and now, debriefed by the CIA, he confirmed their destruction. But Saddam approached the brothers through his daughters, promising protection if they returned. Foolishly, in February 1996, they all went back to Baghdad, where, after being ordered to divorce their wives, they were attacked in their house by their clan and killed after a twelve-hour shootout. The sisters blamed their brother Uday for the killing. Soon afterwards, Uday's car was ambushed and he was wounded but survived. Blaming his sisters, he arrested them, claiming they had planned to kill him. Eventually Saddam restored some family order among his murderous spawn.

Saddam did not believe the Americans would attack him again. Like the Kims in North Korea, he felt vulnerable without weapons of mass destruction. A lifelong radical, he hated the supervision of the west, which he feared could embolden Iran. His policy was to destroy his weapons so as not to give America a pretext, while refusing to cooperate in order to maintain the menace towards Iran. It was the most catastrophic bluff in history.

Elated by the surgical American conquest of Afghanistan – the unipower at its maximal – Bush ordered the CIA to find the evidence of such weapons in Iraq. Meagre and misleading intelligence was soon sculpted to fit his policy, now backed by Tony Blair, the talented British prime minister. An attractive, well-spoken public-school boy and Oxford barrister, he disciplined his Labour party, possessing the encompassing charisma to win three elections on his own personal centre ground. He and Bush had little in common, but they shared a Christian faith and missionary vision. Drawn to America at its plenitude, despite soaring opposition and suspicion about the dubious intelligence, Blair committed Britain to the war.

On 20 March 2003, Bush ordered 130,000 American and 45,000

British troops into Iraq, defeating Iraqi troops in an awesome display of high-tech warfare and seizing Baghdad three weeks later: the unipower had taken just twenty-six days to conquer Iraq. But the US occupation was short-sighted and heavy-handed. All Baathists – most of the army and civil service – were dismissed. A frivolity was reflected in a most-wanted list in the form of playing cards: Saddam – the Ace of Hearts – had vanished with his sons. Three months later, Uday and Qusay and the latter's fourteen-year-old son Mustafa were betrayed by their host in Mosul for $30 million and killed in a three-hour shootout with the Americans. In May, Bush, standing on USS *Abraham Lincoln* in a bomber jacket, in front of a 'Mission Accomplished' banner, declared the 'end of major combat operations' that in fact marked the start of a creeping insurgency by a sinister gallimaufry of jihadist terrorists (led by al-Qaeda), Sunni and Shia militias (the latter backed by Iran) and the sacked Baathists. In December, at a remote farm, Saddam, shaggy and unkempt, was captured hiding in a manhole, but it made little difference. Using funds channelled by Saddam's wife Sajida and his daughter Raghad, the insurgents converted the American triumph into a dystopic pandemonium of bombings, assassinations and urban cauldron battles. If there had been no link to al-Qaeda before the US invasion, now its terrorists launched a spree of sectarian killings.

At dawn on 30 December 2006, a stooping grizzled figure, wearing a dark suit, was led on to a scaffold between two executioners in ski masks in front of an audience of his Shiite enemies, including several ministers in the new Iraq government, some of whom were filming with their mobiles. As a rope was tightened around his neck and he recited the *shahada*, voices cried out the names of Shiites he had killed. 'That's how you express your manhood?' growled the sixty-nine-year-old Saddam.

'Go to hell!' shouted the audience.

'The hell that's Iraq?' – and the trapdoor opened.

'The tyrant,' they chanted, 'is dead.'*

Bush finally embraced the new counter-insurgency tactics in Iraq, devised by a gifted general, David Petraeus, surging US troops and

---

* All this blood and treasure delivered one dividend: Qaddafi, fearful that he was next for the Saddam treatment, surrendered his nuclear programme: he was welcomed into the western family. The Americans were outraged to discover that Qaddafi had bought the technology from the Father of the Pakistani Bomb, A. Q. Khan. But the scientist was unchastened: 'I saved the country for the first time when I made Pakistan a nuclear nation and saved it again when I confessed and took the whole blame on myself.' Astonishingly the greatest criminal of the nuclear age was never investigated or prosecuted, dying in 2021 of Covid.

building Sunni alliances, to stem the mayhem – but 4,000 Americans and 500,000 Iraqis were killed. No weapons of mass destruction were found. The new Iraq, sectarian and corrupt, was far from a liberal democracy.

Moving between Afghan and Pakistani hideouts, hunted by American commandos, bin Laden could reflect that his gambit to bleed and degrade US power had worked. But he had not foreseen that the chief beneficiary was not his Sunni jihad but instead the resurgence of Shia Iran.

'So how's it feel?' W. Bush asked Barack Obama.

'It's a lot,' replied Obama. 'I'm sure you remember.'

'Yep, I do,' said W. 'It's a heck of a ride you're about to take . . .'

It was 20 January 2009: W and Laura Bush were welcoming the new president Obama and his wife Michelle to the White House. The polar opposite of Bush, Obama was a uniquely charismatic figure who attracted different segments of American society. Not only was he the first black commander-in-chief, the son of the maverick Kenyan economist who had come to Hawaii and Harvard on a scholarship, and the free-spirited white anthropologist. He was the most literary, cerebral president since Lincoln. This cool-blooded law professor, nicknamed No Drama Obama, was elected to soothe Americans after Iraq. Yet his background was not totally American – closer to Africa, further from the slavery experienced by most African-Americans. He described himself as 'a platypus or some imaginary beast', joking, 'I've got relatives who look like Bernie Mac, I've got relatives who look like Margaret Thatcher.'

Obama was obsessed by his Kenyan family: 'I only remember my father for one month my whole life.' In 1988, aged twenty-seven, before he started studying law at Harvard, he travelled to Kenya to research his book of family history – 'making peace', wrote his wife Michelle, 'with his phantom father'.*

Moving to Chicago after Harvard, he worked at a top law firm – 'Oh how earnest I was then, how fierce and humourless,' he wrote – where he met a stellar Princeton and Harvard alumna descended from slaves in South Carolina, Michelle Robinson. Daughter of a charismatic father who scarcely let MS cramp his style and died 'having given us absolutely everything', and from a family filled with strong women, she was ambitious: 'I assessed my goals, analyzed my outcomes, counted my wins . . . the life of a girl who can't stop wondering am I good enough?' She always remembered, 'There's an age-old maxim in the black community: you've got to be twice as good to get half as far.'

---

* Obama lost his mother early too: in November 1995, aged fifty-two, she died of cancer.

As the only two African-Americans in their law firm, they dated, finding in his adventurousness and her stability that 'opposites attract'. She thought him rare as a 'unicorn . . . this strange mix-of-everything man' – 'refreshing, unconventional and weirdly elegant'. He thought her 'an original . . . She was tall, beautiful, funny . . . and wickedly smart. I was smitten.' But she believed that 'the road to the good life was narrow and full of hazards. Family was all.' He had that characteristic of politicians: 'He was oddly free from doubt.'

Obama started community work and taught law at Chicago before at thirty-five winning election to the Illinois Senate in November 1996. Michelle laughed at his effect on white people: 'In my experience you put a suit on any half-intelligent black man and white people tended to go bonkers.' When Obama, who became a US senator in 2004, ran for the presidency four years later, Michelle 'avoided talking to me about the horse-race aspect of the campaign', until, her face 'pensive', she asked one night, 'You're going to win, aren't you?'

Obama had studied the darkness and the light within American society. America was the 'only great power made up of people from every corner of the planet', but the challenge was 'to see if we can do what no other nation has ever done. To see if we can actually live up to our creed.' He was an optimist. 'Maybe I can do some good,' he told Michelle. America was the 'place where all things are possible'. When he won the presidency, 'I felt,' wrote Michelle, 'like our family launched out of a cannon and into some strange underwater universe.'

Obama had campaigned for the White House on the slogan 'Yes we can', but in power things at home and abroad were less possible than he expected.

Yet 'The more pressure he was under,' noticed Michelle, 'the calmer he seemed to get.' That was just as well since he arrived in the middle of a world banking crisis caused by reckless investments in American property. Great financial houses crashed. Prompted and aided by Gordon Brown, ascetic and analytical British prime minister, Obama spent $626 billion on saving the economy and those banks too big to fail. Yet his election did not halt the trigger-happy racism of American society: on 26 February 2012, Trayvon Martin, seventeen years old, was shot in Florida by a vigilante; on 17 July 2014, Eric Garner, a gentle forty-two-year-old horticulturalist, was killed in a chokehold by a Staten Island policeman. Its filming by a witness with a mobile phone launched a new movement: Black Lives Matter.

As for 'my foreign policy?' he said. 'Don't do stupid shit.' He agonized over how to end the 9/11 wars and tried to reset the US relationship with

Putin. America's Iraqi catastrophe was an opportunity for Putin, who hated Obama, for him the personification of American humbug.

Putin waited for a chance to assert Russian power in his sphere, embracing the myth of the Broken Promise: Bush and Clinton had promised not to extend NATO eastwards and yet now Ukraine was moving towards membership. 'Not one inch to the east, they told us in the 1990s,' said Putin in December 2021. 'They cheated, just brazenly tricked us.'

It was only a matter of time before Belarus, ruled by a porcine tyrant, former director of a collective piggery, would return to the Muscovite fold, but huge, proud Ukraine, divided, ill led and beset by corruption, still had dangerous potential as a democracy that could undermine Putin's autocracy and his imperial millenarian vision of the Russian World. In 2004, a pro-western candidate, Viktor Yushchenko, keen for Ukraine to join NATO and the EU, was set to win presidential elections. Putin ordered FSB agents to poison the candidate, who only just survived, his face scarred. Then an attempt to rig the election for Putin's candidate, the corrupt, brutish Viktor Yanukovych, was foiled by 200,000 Kyivans who occupied central Kyiv in their Orange Revolution. To Putin, the Russian state was unthinkable without Ukraine. 'What is Ukraine?' Putin asked. 'Does it exist as a country?' He added, 'Whatever it has, is a gift from us.' He regarded Ukraine and Belarus as little Russias with no independent right of existence.*

Putin watched and waited. His first opportunity came in tiny but defiant Georgia. Putin despised Shevardnadze, who had given away the empire. When in 2003 the Grey Fox, by then seventy-five, faced a revolution led by the young, showy American-educated Mikheil Saakashvili, Putin refused to back the old leader. Shevardnadze retired.

Putin watched Saakashvili's posturings with contempt. When Saakashvili, encouraged by America, challenged the Russian clients in Ossetia, Putin snarled, 'Bring me Saakashvili's head,' and invaded, routing the Georgian forces.† America protested but did nothing.

---

* 'Russians, Ukrainians and Belorusians are all descendants of Ancient Rus,' Putin wrote in a historical essay in July 2021. 'Russians and Ukrainians are one people: a single whole,' while 'Modern Ukraine was entirely a product of the Soviet era . . . on the lands of historical Russia . . . One fact is crystal clear: Russia was robbed . . . The true sovereignty of Ukraine is only possible in partnership with Russia.' Putin and his new imperialists focused on the Muscovite and Russian conquests that suited him – and ignored the cosmopolitan multi-ethnic Ukraine, ruled by Ottomans, Habsburgs, Polish kings and Lithuanian dukes, and peopled by Cossacks, Tatars, Poles, Jews, Italians and Greeks, as well as Russians and Ukrainians.
† Putin was now premier, having served two presidential terms, the limit allowed by Yeltsin's constitution. He had pulled off a political chess move – *rokirovka* – in which a player switches king and castle, choosing a bland henchman to serve as president.

Now Obama flew in to see Putin. At his mansion at Novo-Ogarevo, Obama observed Putin: 'short and compact – a wrestler's build – with thin, sandy hair, a prominent nose, and pale, watchful eyes', exuding 'a practiced disinterest . . . that indicated someone who'd grown used to power'. He reminded Obama of a Chicago 'ward boss, except with nukes'.

Ironically Putin's view of American presidents was almost identical: he advised his henchmen to watch his favourite Netflix drama *House of Cards* to explain US politics. 'Don't harbour any illusions,' he later lectured Obama's vice-president Joe Biden. 'We're not like you, we may look like you but . . . inside we have different values.' Obama listened to Putin accuse America of being 'arrogant, dismissive, unwilling to treat Russia as an equal partner'. Putin worked to redress the balance: in 2010, his vassal Yanukovych won the Ukrainian elections, then, in the Arab world, he found a further opportunity.

BASHAR, THE BAYONET AND THE MONA LISA OF INDIA

On 6 March 2011, in the southern Syrian town of Deraa, fifteen school-children mocked the young dictator Bashar al-Assad in graffiti on the walls of their school, inspired by demonstrations against the dictators of Tunisia, and then of Egypt, Libya and Yemen, communicating by the exciting encoded medium of WhatsApp. In Deraa, the hated governor, a cousin of Assad, arrested the schoolchildren and tortured them. When their families protested, the army fired on them. The town rose in rebellion, which spread across Syria.

In 2000, when Hafez al-Assad died, the thirty-four-year-old ophthalmologist Bashar succeeded to the throne, marrying a British-Syrian surgeon's daughter, Asma, who was an unlikely recruit to the Mafia-style family – a private schoolgirl (then known as Emma) and French literature graduate. Anisa, Bashar's mother, had disapproved of the marriage: she wanted Bashar to marry a cousin. But the couple were in love. Asma gave Bashar the pet name Batta – Duck. When she arrived, the Assads isolated her.

She and Bashar promised reform and courted the west. *Vogue* magazine hailed Bashar as 'wildly democratic' and Asma as the 'rose of the desert . . . glamorous, young, and very chic – the freshest and most magnetic of first ladies . . . a thin, long-limbed beauty . . . breezy, conspiratorial, and fun'. *Vogue* was right about the conspiracy: in 2006 when the Lebanese billionaire Rafic Hariri, former and future premier, challenged Syrian power, Bashar ordered his killing in a car bombing, which so outraged the Lebanese that he was forced to withdraw his troops. Sensing 'a great conspiracy', Dr Assad sent tanks and troops against his own students, teenagers and Islamicists. 'My father was right,' he said. 'Thousands of deaths in Hama bought us three decades of stability . . .'

On 17 February 2011, Libyan cities rebelled against the Neronian dictator Qaddafi, who, assisted by his son Saif al-Islam, threatened that the rebels, these 'cockroaches', would be 'hunted down street by street, house by house until the country is cleansed of dirt and scum'. Obama was determined to avoid any interventions. In Egypt, Mubarak, who had been in power since Sadat's assassination, faced a popular revolution and looked to Obama for support. Obama refused: Mubarak resigned. In Libya, Qaddafi had lost half of the country, but he promised, 'Everything will burn.' David Cameron, fresh-faced young British prime minister, regarded Qaddafi as 'Mad Dog, a horrific figure who sold Semtex to the IRA' and 'ordered the downing of PanAm 103 over Lockerbie'. He called Nicolas Sarkozy, the diminutive, manic French president, to discuss an intervention. Obama was, recalled Cameron, 'unenthusiastic'. But now Qaddafi's forces were advancing on rebel Benghazi.

On 28 February, Cameron suggested a no-fly zone; NATO agreed to intervene to save lives, and Obama delivered air cover. Qaddafi threatened to kill Cameron and his family. Beginning on 20 March, NATO air forces, led by Britain and France, attacked Qaddafi's forces for months until the regime cracked. On 15 September, Cameron and Sarkozy visited Tripoli: 'we'd promised we'd go together . . . We wove through jubilant hordes to a stage in Freedom Square and gave speeches as 10,000 people chanted Cam-er-on and Sar-koz-y! Still we had no idea where Qaddafi was . . .'

Putin approved the NATO campaign, provided Qaddafi himself was not targeted. Anglo-French air strikes strafed the colonel's convoy. 'They say they don't want to kill him,' sneered Putin, 'so why are they bombing him? To scare the mice?' On 20 October, near Sirte, NATO got him. Qaddafi, wounded and hiding in a drainage pipe, was captured, wounded in the stomach, then, filmed on a smartphone, sodomized with a bayonet and finally shot dead. Watching the video of the tormented tyrant, Putin saw himself: 'You could end up losing Russia. Qaddafi thought he'd never lose Libya but the Americans tricked him.' So this was American freedom: 'All the world saw him being killed, all bloodied. Is that democracy?' He would not let it happen again: in Syria, Putin backed Assad.

As the revolution reached the suburbs of Damascus, Assad, backed by his brother Maher, his Alawite clan and secular Sunnis, treated his own country as enemy territory: 'Assad or We Burn the Country' was their slogan. He released Islamic jihadis from prison to taint the rebels; his secret police tortured and slaughtered many; he launched unrestrained bombing and chemical attacks. As pandemonium spread, Assad flirted with gushing girls in his office, and Asma spent $250,000 on new furniture online. While Maher led the 4th Armoured Division against the town of Homs, Asma reviewed Christian Louboutin shoes online. 'Does anything catch your eye?' she emailed a friend. When her friend, a Qatari princess, warned her she was in denial, Asma responded, 'Life's not fair, my friend, but ultimately there's a reality we all need to deal with.'

'If we're strong together we'll overcome this together. I love you,' she wrote to her Duck, even though she may have discovered Bashar's infidelities. He responded with a love heart and some country-and-western lyrics: 'I've made a mess of me / The person that I've been lately / Ain't who I wanna be.' In 2013, returning from an end-of-Ramadan party, Assad and Asma were attacked by rebels. They survived, but now Maher was unleashed to crush the rebels, while their sister Bushra gave advice and her husband Assef Shawkat, one of the intelligence chieftains, clashed with him. Maher shot and wounded him. Later Shawkat was killed in a rebel bomb attack. Maher lost his leg in another assassination attempt. Soon afterwards Bushra al-Assad, widowed by the killing of Shawkat, left for Dubai. But Asma stayed. After the death of the matriarch Anisa, Asma became official First Lady. 'The president is the president of all Syria,' she announced. 'The First Lady supports him.' The family held on, just as the greatest democratic dynasty was subsiding.

'She was a striking woman in her sixties,' was how Obama described Sonia Gandhi in November 2010, 'dressed in a traditional sari with dark, probing eyes and a quiet, regal presence.' Sonia Gandhi had recovered from the murder of her husband, Rajiv, to assume leadership of Congress, and Obama was impressed by her 'shrewd and forceful intelligence' in the service of 'the enduring . . . family dynasty'. After winning two elections, Sonia chose not to become premier herself, appointing an ex-finance minister, Manmohan Singh, India's first Sikh leader.

Nicknamed Mona Lisa, Sonia dominated from behind the scenes for a decade, but Obama was less impressed by her son, Rahul, the heir. Obama wondered if this was the end: 'Would the baton be successfully passed?'

Four years later, Rahul was routed by a Hindu nationalist from Gujarat, Narendra Modi, and his Bharatiya Janata Party (BJP). In an India long ruled by dynasty, Modi represented a self-made Hindu middle class; he liked to say he had once sold tea at Vadnagar railway station. As a boy he joined the paramilitary RSS, a believer in *Hindutva*. Joining its youth wing at eight, Modi became a full-time *pracharak* – organizer – so devoted that although he went through an arranged marriage as a boy, he never lived with his wife: politics was his sole passion. The Nehrus were declining thanks tó decades of corruption, entitlement and failure to confront India's inequalities.

The BJP's rise was accelerated by a campaign to raze the Babri Mosque at Ayodhya, supposedly built by the first Tamerlanian emperor at the site of a Hindu shrine believed to be the birthplace of Rama. Holiness is always infectious, the holier and more hallowed for one sect, the more so for its rival. In 1992, a national campaign had mobilized a Hindu crowd to attack the mosque and demolish it, sparking riots that killed 2,000 people.

In 1998, the BJP managed to form a coalition government. In February 2002, in Gujarat, where Modi was chief minister, elected after a campaign promoting *Hindutva*, a train bearing Hindu pilgrims to Ayodhya caught fire – probably after a Muslim mob set the coaches alight. Modi declared it a terrorist attack by Muslims and did little to defuse the tension. In the following days, Hindu mobs killed around 2,000 Muslims, some of them burned alive, women raped and mutilated, while police stood by. Promising free-market reforms, in 2014 Modi won the first of two general elections, but his autocratic style, bias against Muslims in his Citizenship Act and clumsy economic reforms revealed that he was as careless as the Nehrus, only less tolerant of minorities.

At 2 p.m. on 2 May 2011, as the Arab Spring gathered momentum, the calm of a walled mansion in north-eastern Pakistan, not far from the capital Islamabad, was broken by the distant whirl of helicopters.

WHERE LIONS AND CHEETAHS LURK

Two US Blackhawks bearing, in Obama's words, 'twenty-three members of the Seal team, a Pakistani American CIA translator and a military dog named Cairo' were taking part in Operation Neptune Spear. Obama joined his staff in the White House Situation Room as the choppers flew low over Pakistan. As they approached the mansion, one of the helicopters went down.

It was Obama's hardest decision. The CIA had informed him that at a mysterious fortified house, linked to Osama bin Laden by two of his couriers, they had been watching a tall man walk in the tiny garden. 'We call him the Pacer,' said the lead officer. 'We think he could be bin Laden.' Obama consulted his cohorts: Vice-President Biden 'weighed in against the raid, given the enormous consequences of failure'. But Obama approved the mission against bin Laden, tactlessly codenamed Geronimo.

At home, Michelle endured the stress of politics. 'I sensed an undercurrent of tension in her, subtle but constant,' recalled Obama, 'like the faint thrum of a hidden machine.' He saw 'part of her stayed on alert, waiting and watching for the next turn of the wheel, bracing herself for calamity'. Sometimes 'the lions and cheetahs started to lurk', wrote Michelle. 'When you're married to the president you come to understand quickly that the world brims with chaos . . .'

They sensed a coming darkness, a backlash against their liberal values – and they were right. In 2010, a tall, wide-hipped property developer with an auburn tan and a bright-yellow combover started to consider running for president against Obama. Donald Trump, then aged sixty-four, was already the personification of American illusion – grandson of a Bavarian immigrant and gold-rush brothel-keeper, son of a post-war Queens slum landlord. Using his billion-dollar inheritance, he became a developer of luxury Manhattan hotels and Atlantic City casinos, funded by junk bonds, constantly refinanced on the edge of bankruptcy and paying scarcely any tax on his loss-making ventures. In the 1980s, he had promoted the myth of this dealmaking with a bestselling book, *The Art of the Deal*, which in 2004 won him the job of presenting a TV reality show, *The Apprentice*. His new fame enabled him to reinvigorate his Trump franchise.

Husband of three glamorous women – a Czech skier, an American model and a Slovene model – patriarch of a business dynasty, lover of a bazzoon of *Playboy* centrefolds and porn performers, this bombastic bazooka of complex inferiority would put on a fake voice and, claiming to be his own publicist, ring newspapers to tell them that 'the Donald' was having affairs with supermodels and popstars. While having an affair with his future second wife, he had quoted her praise of his sexual virtuosity to give the *New York Post* one of its most memorable headlines: 'BEST SEX I'VE EVER HAD'. He was a fairground huckster, for whom the truth mattered less than the spectacle, and expertise or knowledge were contemptible, but he had a gift for articulating what millions were thinking. As a 'killer', never a 'loser', he had long coveted power: in 1987, he had taken out advertisements offering to negotiate arms limitation with Gorbachev. Steeped in the seamy dealmaking of New York property, with its hints of Mafia pay-offs, long mocked in New York high society, he had built a Monopoly set of golden tower buildings, altogether achieving much more than most politicians had ever attempted before they came to office.

In March 2011, to the Obamas' incredulity, Trump floated a racist conspiracy theory that Obama had not been born in the USA. 'Growing up, no one knew him,' he said. 'I want him to show his birth certificate ...' Obama, rattled and astonished, mocked him but realized that Trump 'was a spectacle and in the USA of 2011 that was a sort of power ... Far from being ostracized for the conspiracies he'd peddled, he had never been bigger.' Michelle felt that 'The whole thing was crazy and mean-spirited ... But it was also dangerous, deliberately meant to stir up the wingnuts and kooks.' Yet Trump still seemed to be a reality-show maven who posed no threat.

Now in the Situation Room in May 2011, as Obama watched the grainy image of the chopper making an emergency landing in Pakistan, he feared the worst, but the pilot managed to land: 'I saw ... grainy figures on the ground ... entering the main house' as the commandos worked their way up the three-storey house, passing groups of children, shooting three armed men who challenged them, a woman who was caught in crossfire, until they reached the top floor: they heard shots. But where was Geronimo?

THE KILLING OF GERONIMO

On the top floor of the mansion, the Seals encountered Osama bin Laden, 'the man who had directed the murder of thousands and set in motion a tumultuous period of world history'. They shot him in the forehead and chest. In the Situation Room, 'audible gasps'. Obama was 'glued to the video feed'. Then suddenly 'we heard ... words we'd been waiting to hear'.

'Geronimo ID'd ... Geronimo EKIA.' Enemy killed in action.

'We got him,' said Obama softly. A photo arrived of the dead terrorist: 'I glanced briefly ... it was him.'

Bin Laden's body was carried off by the Seals, and was later buried in the Arabian Sea. When Obama announced the hit, he linked it to his own mission. 'Americans can do whatever we set our mind to – that's the story of our history,' he said. 'We can do these things because of who we are.'

Geronimo had been a risk. The new technologies offered easier ways to wage surgical warfare. On 30 September 2011, Obama approved the killing by drone of a terrorist, Anwar al-Awlaki, in Yemen. It was far from being the first of these killings by US 'unmanned aerial vehicles', devices that heralded a new era of warfare.*

Trump did not run for the presidency in 2012. As Obama won his second term, an intrigue in Chongqing was settling the struggle of two princelings for the Chinese leadership. In November 2011, the body of an English financier, Neil Heywood, entangled in high Chinese politics via a powerful woman he called an 'empress', was discovered in a Chongqing hotel, destroying one candidate for the leadership – and opening the way for the other to be the all-powerful autocrat. The two rivals were both crown princes, sons of Mao's grandees, leaders and heirs of what the Party called 'lineages' of family power. Bo Xilai, flamboyant son of one of Deng's Eight Immortals, was an ambitious Politburo member, boss of what was later called the 'independent kingdom' of Chongqing, and candidate for the leadership.

His rival was Xi Jinping, son of Deng's ally Xi Zhongxun, who had fallen from power and then returned to the top. Xi junior, like many of those who had been rusticated, combined the entitlement of the princelings with the plain, harsh habits of the peasants. The trauma had made the family closer; it had toughened Xi but it had not put him off the Party. On the contrary, it was the Party that had restored order and safety after the Cultural Revolution. But it was only after Mao's death that Deng brought them back. When Xi senior retired, he arranged for his son to work at the Central Military Commission, the most important office after the Politburo's Standing Committee. In 1986, when he was

---

* The drones had been invented during the Yom Kippur War by an Iraqi-born Israeli designer, Abraham Karem, for reconnaissance. In 2001, after 9/11, Cofer Black, chief of the CIA's Counterterrorist Center, proposed arming the Predators to kill Osama bin Laden. The hunter-killer drones fired supersonic Hellfire missiles that hit targets before they could be heard. Keen to avoid hitting their own troops and causing other accidental deaths, Bush commissioned the CIA to run the targeted killing of terrorists using the Predators, later updated to Reapers. Kill lists were collated by the CIA and presented to the president, then the teams – 'mission intelligence coordinators', 'pilots' and 'sensor operators' – sitting in hangars at Creech Air Force Base in Nevada triggered the executions thousands of miles away in the mountains of the Hindu Kush or the deserts of Yemen. The drones were in the 'humane' tradition of the guillotine, but early strikes killed hundreds of innocent passers-by. A 2008 strike against Haqqani killed around twenty innocent people, but he survived. They became increasingly accurate, by 2015 used for assassinations by most sophisticated military powers. Artificial intelligence would soon enable drones or high-tech guns to kill targets identified by facial recognition. The future of war will encompass daggers and rifles but also robotic killing machines operated from satellites, and possibly reprogrammed to kill certain individuals on sight.

promoted to deputy secretary of Hebei province, he met someone who changed his destiny. Peng Liyuan was the most famous singer in China, a beautiful soprano who, sporting Red Army uniform, sang Party ballads. Xi, just emerged from an unhappy marriage to an ambassador's daughter, 'fell in love at first sight' – according to his official biography – and they had a daughter. His stolid climb up the Party was far from meteoric. In 1997, he joined the Central Committee as an alternate, becoming a full member in 2002, but he was on his way. He was appointed first secretary of Zhejiang province and in 2007 joined the Standing Committee as a future leader. But just behind him came the flashier Bo, who caught up fast.

Bo had a flaw – his wife, Gu Kailai, herself the daughter of a general. Together they had recruited Heywood as their fixer, in return for commissions. But Heywood, fluent in Chinese and married to a Chinese woman, got too close. When Gu demanded he divorce his wife and devote himself to her interests, he complained she was 'behaving like an old-fashioned Chinese aristocrat or empress'. Whether he had an affair with Gu or demanded a vast commission or both, Gu recruited the Chongqing police chief who entertained Heywood then poisoned him with cyanide, declaring later that his death was from alcohol poisoning. They cremated the body. When the police chief feared he was about to be killed himself and sought asylum in the US embassy, the murder was exposed.

In 2012, Bo and Gu were arrested and condemned, their patrons on the Standing Committee were purged and their rival Xi emerged as the leader. As Obama led the US in holding pattern, Xi directed what he called the 'resurrection' of China. But it was a more singular moment than that: America was starting a process of self-laceration that altered its world mission. As the bipolar system was a memory and American paramountcy was wavering, China, which many times had dominated its own region, would, for the first time, join the World Game.

ACT TWENTY-THREE
8 BILLION

Trumps and Xis, Sauds, Assads and Kims

THE CALIPHATE AND THE CRIMEA

On 21 August 2013, in the Damascus suburbs, Assad used sarin, a nerve gas, against his own people, some of whom were photographed suffocating and foaming – the first of several such atrocities. Obama had promised he would not tolerate chemical weapons; Cameron demanded action. Yet Obama was focused on a Nixonian grand deal with Iran. American hawks and allies led by Israel demanded bombing to stop Iran developing the Bomb. Obama negotiated a delay in Iranian production in return for lifting sanctions. Yet Iran's maestro of clandestine operations, General Qasem Solemeini, an elegant protégé of Supreme Leader Khamenei, ramped up his help for the Assads, recruiting militiamen from his Lebanese Hezbollah vassals. Assad also requested Russian assistance. Putin dispatched his air force as Kurdish *Peshmerga* militias carved out their own independent fiefs and much of the country was occupied by jihadist and secular militias.

Closer to home, Putin feared that Ukraine, keen to join the EU and NATO, was slipping from his grasp. In 2010, his thuggish ally, Yanukovych, had won the presidency and enjoyed a short kleptocratic fiesta, looting $70 billion. When, under Kremlin pressure, he withdrew from EU negotiations, 500,000 Ukrainians protested in Kyiv. Yanukovych's secret police shot seventy-seven protesters before he was driven out. On 22 February 2014, Putin sent troops to occupy Crimea.* On 18 March, he annexed the peninsula. He then sent his intelligence officers to incite rebellion and back pro-Russian separatist warlords in Donbas. In Russia his popularity soared, but he had missed the opportunity

* Crimea, home of Byzantine and Slavic, Genoese, Venetian and Ottoman entrepôts, was long the heartland of a Mongol khanate, ruled by the Giray dynasty, until 1783 when it was annexed to Russia by Potemkin. In 1853, Palmerston and Napoleon III invaded Crimea to challenge Nicholas I's aggressive Russian empire. Its fall in July 1942 was one of the successes of Hitler's summer offensive which almost won the war; but Stalin, suspecting that Crimean Tatars had welcomed the German invaders, ordered their deportation and replacement by Russian settlers. In 1954, Khrushchev transferred Crimea to Ukraine.

of his career: had he then launched a full invasion of Ukraine to support the legitimately elected Yanukovych, it is likely he would have succeeded. Instead, he tried to destroy Ukraine from within – actions that fostered the very thing he most feared: a passionate pro-western Ukrainian patriotism, backed by a large, committed and experienced military.

As Assad's survival began to look dubious, he was rescued by Putin but also something even more ghoulish. In neighbouring Iraq, the bullying by the Shiite rulers sparked a new Sunni insurgency, this time backed by a fundamentalist cabal of al-Qaeda jihadists and secular Baathists, a marriage made in American prisons and then organized into a force that aspired to rule actual territory.

On 10 June 2014, riding SUVs down Mesopotamian roads beneath their death-cult black banners, warriors of Islamic State – known to Arabs as *Daesh* – suddenly emerged out of nowhere to take Mosul in Iraq and then burst into Syria too. Led by Abu Bakr al-Baghdadi, *Daesh* combined medieval Wahhabi ideology with sophisticated internet communications, pragmatic oil financing and bold military manoeuvrability. It appealed digitally to credulous radicalized teenagers in British and French cities, and used spectacular televised beheadings and burnings of western hostages to advertise its surprising conquests. Baghdadi, commander of 30,000 warriors and soon ruler of an Iraqi–Syrian state of around ten million people, declared a caliphate, as *Daesh* slaughtered Yazidis and members of other sects regarded as heretics, offering their recruits captured women as sex slaves and blowing up ancient non-Muslim monuments.

The ultimate jeopardy of *Daesh* focused Putin's support: the mayhem was the fault of 'a single centre of domination [that] emerged in the world after the Cold War', he said in September 2015, meaning America. 'The export of revolutions, this time of so-called "democratic" ones, continues . . . Instead of the triumph of democracy and progress, we got . . . extremists and terrorists.' While America armed Kurdish *Peshmerga*, who began to fight *Daesh* on the ground, Putin bombed Assad's opponents.

As Obama finished his term, the confidence of the unipower America withered. America's world crusade, governed by rules and morals developed by the chastening struggle of the Second World War, confirmed by the victory of 1989, was the most ambitious programme in world history, backed by its most potent ever state. Yet even this massive and supreme technarchy could be foiled by bands of mountain warriors in an iPhone and dagger state. And despite it all, its twenty years as the unipower of a globalized world had failed to deliver peace abroad or prosperity at home.

In one of his last trips, Obama flew to London where Cameron was holding a referendum on British membership of the European Union, the trade organization with aspirations to become a federal state. If it left, he warned Britons, 'The UK is going to be in the back of the queue' for a US trade deal. But on 23 June 2016, rallied by a haystack-haired maverick, Boris Johnson, the British did just that.

In Syria, America joined the mayhem to bombard *Daesh*. But the winners were Assad and his backers Russia and Iran.

'We don't have victories any more,' said Trump on 15 June 2015, riding down the golden elevator in his eponymous auric tower that almost matched his hair, skin and style. 'We used to have victories, but we don't have them . . . We've got to make America great again!'

THE DYNASTS

Revelling in his outrages, Trump commandeered a populist disdain for the self-righteous, often illiberal orthodoxies of liberals and progressives in big cities, old universities and famous newspapers – and the venal networks in the 'swamp' of Washington. He was a coarse but effective communicator, gifted with comic timing, capable of speaking live for hours authentically playing himself and expressing the prejudices and rages of his white, lower-middle-class Christian base, convinced that somehow, someone had given away their American birthright. Many of them believed that Latinos and immigrants were stealing their jobs. Trump promised a Wall to seal the Mexican border and a ban on Muslim immigrants. He announced, 'The American carnage stops right here, right now. From this day forward, it's going to be only America first.'

No one senses the weakness of others as acutely as the man who fears his own. Trump's malice was implacably on target, his playground nicknames on the nail, as he brushed aside his Republican rival John Ellis Bush, Florida governor and brother of W, as 'Low-Energy Jeb' and forever tainted his Democratic opponent, wife of a former president, Hillary Clinton as 'Crooked Hillary'. Like Trump himself, she also personified the tiny, elderly circles of America's elites, wherein power was often passed via family links.

The Obamas were downhearted by Trump. 'Both of us', wrote the president, 'were drained' by the rise of 'someone diametrically opposed to everything we stood for'. They asserted the old decencies: 'When they go low,' said Michelle Obama, 'we go high.' But Trump was oblivious to such distinctions. Personality, wealth and television were all as serious for Trump as statecraft and geopolitics: projections of power.

Inadvertently he was promoted relentlessly and breathlessly by the very TV networks that despised him. Trump's bombast immediately created its exact opposite: his progressive opponents aped his mendacity and righteousness, printing unsubstantiated calumnies, endorsing untrue scandals and fabulistic conspiracies, redoubling intolerance in witch-hunts and ultimately even banning stories critical of their own candidate. The open world had never been richer or more secure, yet America – emulated by the other comfort democracies – started to consume itself in vicious, self-mutilating schisms about history and nation, virtue and identity, every bit as demented as the christological controversies of medieval Constantinople. Some of it was the result of the comfortable tedium of bourgeois existence. 'When we look at history,' Mao had written, 'we adore times of war; when we get to periods of peace and prosperity, we're bored.' Television and internet inevitably brought entertainment closer to politics: Trump channelled something of Nero, Commodus and Wilhelm II.

In November 2019, Trump won the presidency. No one so relished its autocratic regality. America's war presidency had developed not because it had built an empire abroad but because it had conquered a continent at home. Trump's White House was a disorganized, corrupt and nepotistic court, starring his entitled daughter Ivanka and son-in-law Jared Kushner, an effete property heir. But he was soon infuriated by the restraints of democracy.

The Russians had long had naive views about the power of US presidents, but now, watching Trump and the opposition to him, Putin saw America's self-laceration as decadence. 'There's a gap between the ruling elites and the people,' he said. 'The so-called Liberal Idea has come to the end of its natural life.' Facing sanctions for annexing Crimea and stalemate in Ukraine, Putin flaunted his power in Syria, where brutal Russian bombing had won the war for Assad. To compensate for Russian economic weakness, Putin deployed the potent disinformation of Russian hackers and bots to undermine American confidence in democracy. And the ex-Chekist, still popular at home, deployed calculated menace against opponents and traitors. At home, his Chechen vassal organized the shootings of liberal journalists and opposition politicians. In provincial Salisbury, in spring 2018, a British agent, Sergei Skripal, released from Russian jail in a spy swap, was poisoned with Novichok by the military intelligence agency GRU.*

Trump, who had grown up in Mafia-dominated Queens, talking about 'hits' and 'rats', envied the real trigger power of Putin. When challenged, he defended the Russian: 'There're a lot of killers. You think our country's innocent. Our country does a lot of killing.' In July 2018, when the two met in Helsinki, soon after Skripal's poisoning, Trump again defended Putin against accusations of interfering with US elections: 'President Putin says it's not Russia. I don't see any reason why it would be.'

Yet Trump did challenge exhausted policies abroad: he tried to confront China, attempted a personal approach to North Korea and revisited the frozen Israel–Palestine negotiations. But first, on 20 May 2017, his first foreign visit, he embraced America's oldest local ally.

A brash, ambitious young prince, Mohammed bin Salman – MBS – now controlled Saudi Arabia. The moment his aged father, Salman bin Abdulaziz, succeeded as king, MBS energetically commandeered the court and defence power centres. He launched a war against Iranian allies in Yemen and planned a reform of the Arabian economy, Vision 2030, a new city to be called Neom (meaning new in Greek, future in Arabic) and a new touristic industry around the Nabataean ruins of al-Ula. He also introduced the right to drive for Arabian women, the opening of cinemas and the trillion-dollar flotation of Aramco. These reforms delighted the west. Trump placed Kushner in charge of Arab relations, and the two princelings shared a dynastic view of the world. As Kushner worked on a peace plan for Israel and Palestine, MBS, infuriated by the Palestinians, hinted at recognizing Israel.

Yet there was another side of MBS. He was from Prince Salman's junior brood of sons, the fifth boy and not by his senior wife, a Saudi princess, but a second Bedouin wife. The eldest had been the first Arab into space; MBS, nicknamed Little Saddam in the family, had much to prove, both the common thing – a will to power – and that rare quality – a vision of what to do with it. As an ambitious young prince, he was nicknamed Stray Bear by his friends, always genial and playful with westerners, a modern millennial joking about his love of *Game of Thrones*, discussing the digital future at meetings with the tech

---

* In 2015, Boris Nemtsov, opposition leader and Yeltsin's deputy premier, was shot and killed near the Kremlin by Chechen assassins. In 2019, in provincial Tomsk, FSB agents poisoned opposition leader Andrei Navalny, again with Novichok; like Skripal, he barely survived.

plutocrats. But his visionary impatience dovetailed with brutal intolerance. Inheriting his father's aggressive intelligence, he was resentful
that other princes were much richer, that dynasties like the bin Ladens
received vast commissions and that the kingdom itself was too cautious
in confronting its enemies. Long before reaching power, he had sent a
bullet to a business rival, earning the nicknamed Abu Rasasa – Father
of the Bullet.

If he needed any lessons in policing a royal family, a young Kim
provided them. When Kim Jong-Il, seventy, died of a heart attack in
December 2011, he was declared immortal and his untried son, Kim
Jong-Un, twenty-seven, had succeeded him. Now, In February 2017, two
women, recruited by a TV station to take part in a reality-show prank,
an irresistible temptation to many, approached a plump, scruffy eastern
man at Kuala Lumpur airport and sprayed him in the face. Minutes
later, poisoned with the nerve agent VX and with his organs closing
down, Kim Jong-nam, exiled eldest son of Kim Jong-il and once crown
prince of North Korea, was dead, his assassination ordered by his younger half-brother, Kim Jong-un. Rapidly promoting himself to marshal,
Kim Jong-un, the image of his grandfather and father, orchestrated the
killings of his powerful uncle and family, messily shredded by firing
squads of anti-aircraft guns. He had targeted his brother, who, after
losing his rank for trying to escape to Japan, had been allowed to live
quietly in China, because he talked to journalists. 'Without reforms,'
Kim Jong-nam had said, 'North Korea will collapse.' Now that problem
was solved.

Closely advised by his younger sister Kim Yo-jong, the Marshal tested
a hydrogen bomb, defying America. After trading insults – Trump was
'the insane dotard', Kim 'little Rocket Man' (a reference to the song by
the president's favourite singer, Elton John) – the two met as equals in
Singapore, confirming the kudos of nuclear weapons. 'I don't think I
have to prepare very much,' boasted Trump, but Kim gave up no Bombs,
indulging instead in a correspondence that the president compared to
'love letters'.

'Even now I can't forget the moment I held your excellency's hand,'
wrote Kim to Trump on 25 December 2018, remembering their meeting
as being 'like the scene in a fantasy film'. It was a fantasy. While Rocket
Man returned home triumphant, Father of the Bullet was targeting his
own difficult insider.

In October 2018, members of MBS's secret retinue, known as the
Saudi Rapid Intervention Group, arrived on a private jet in Istanbul.

The Group was the vanguard of MBS's Centre for Studies and Media Affairs that dealt with special tasks. A first unit swept the consulate for bugs, finding none – even though it was riddled with Turkish listening devices. The staff were given a day off. Then fifteen retainers arrived, led by an intelligence officer who travelled with MBS in America and an Interior Ministry forensic surgeon, Colonel-Doctor Salah al-Tubaigy, with a bone saw in his luggage. While they waited tensely, the doctor told his colleagues that when dissecting bodies 'I listen to music – you should do that too.' Finally the chief myrmidon looked at his watch.

'Has the sacrificial animal arrived yet?' he asked.

Moments later, a sturdy man wearing a blazer and grey trousers entered the Saudi consulate, with an appointment to get papers so that he could marry his fiancée. Jamal Khashoggi was a journalist but also a court insider who believed he would be safe, unaware that all his digital communications were watched by MBS's team. He had hesitated to enter Saudi territory, arranging for his fiancée to wait outside, but he was not as suspicious as he should have been. This was because Khashoggi was a member of the Saudi elite, grandson of King Abdulaziz's doctor, nephew of the billionaire fixer Adnan Khashoggi and a journalist, writing Janus-like in the *Washington Post* embracing western pluralism and in the Arabic press criticizing the Saudi–American alliance. By bugging his telephones, MBS learned that Khashoggi was rallying dissidents. For MBS too was Janus-like, embracing western reforms yet tolerating no opposition.

In June 2017, he had seized his cousin Muhammad bin Nayef, fifty-seven, forcing him to cede his title, crown prince. He had kidnapped the Lebanese premier for getting too close to Iran-backed Hezbollah, hard to avoid in a Lebanon dominated by the Shia militia. He had blockaded Qatar. He had ordered the kidnap of the female activist and filmmaker Loujain al-Hathloul, who was tortured. He paid particular attention to criticism on Twitter, where Khashoggi had millions of followers, infiltrating Twitter itself to find out the details of critical accounts while investigating corruption in the royal family. 'You have a body that has cancer everywhere, the cancer of corruption,' he explained. 'You need the shock of chemo or the cancer will eat the body.'

In November 2017, MBS arrested a constellation of princes and billionaires including five bin Ladens, who were imprisoned in the Ritz-Carlton in Riyadh and forced to pay billions in fines. Soon afterwards MBS himself spent $300 million on a new yacht, $50 million on a holiday in the Maldives and then $400 million on a Leonardo da Vinci painting, *Salvator Mundi*.

As soon as he entered the consulate, Khashoggi was taken upstairs and must have seen the team waiting for him.

He was sedated, then suffocated with a plastic bag. After that the doctor, putting on earphones, dismembered him with his bone saw. The CIA reported MBS ordered the killing but this compulsive visionary and despotic reformer, dedicated to Saudi dynasty, personal autocracy, cultural liberalization and – a player of the *Call of Duty* videogame – millennial technology, weathered the storm.

Trump's unconventional approach could have solved problems, but every initiative was spoiled by his own unique mix of narcissistic braggadocio, racist undercurrent and clumsy autocracy. He delivered few of the promised victories.* In 2017, American and British air power obliterated *Daesh* from above as Kurdish Peshmerga and Iranian-backed Shiite militias rolled them back on the ground. Yet the *Daesh* threat had saved Assad, who was backed by the Iranians, Hezbollah and Russian air power. The death of the family matriarch Anisa, Bashar's mother, left her family exposed – her billionaire nephew Rami Makhlouf owned half the economy – and allowed Asma to emerge. Now Bashar, faced with rebuilding a ruined state, demanded that Rami hand back some of his riches; when he refused he was arrested. Asma herself was diagnosed with cancer. When she recovered, she started to approve government appointments and build her own smartphone and smartcard business-es, run by her brother and other henchmen, while her portraits – often inscribed 'The Lady of Jasmine' – appeared beside those of Bashar. Lady Jasmine had become a potentate of war.

Trump accelerated the withdrawal from the 9/11 wars, which had cost eyewatering quantities of treasure and blood. Yet Iraq was controlled by Shiite factions allied to Iran which enjoyed tormenting America. On 8 May 2018, Trump withdrew from Obama's Iran agreement, calling it 'the worst deal ever'.

On 3 January 2020, after Iranian militias had fired on American forces in Iraq, Trump ordered the assassination of Iran's 'shadow commander', Soleimani, liquidated by a drone at Baghdad airport. In

---

* Yet American ingenuity was still rich: in 2020, Elon Musk sent a crewed SpaceX rocket into space, the first such private mission. He was already a galactic entrepreneur, launching satellites for internet communications. He was the creative maverick of the digital titans, a modern combination of Edison and Rockefeller, spiced with a touch of Cagliostro – born in South Africa, son of an Afrikaner entrepreneur and a former model – who started writing programs while living on a sofa and showering at the local YMCA. His Tesla electric cars made him the world's richest man. Now he promised a 'space-bearing civilization', dreaming of 'a self-sustaining city on Mars. That's, I think, the critical thing for maximizing the life of human-ity.' This new galactic home for human families is far off – but no longer just science fiction.

August 2020, Trump delivered his 'Abraham Accords' between Israel and the Gulf monarchies, backed by MBS, aimed at the chief enemy, Iran. This dramatic alignment placed Israel, chief military power despite its chaotic democracy, at the centre of an Arab–Islamic affinity led by MBS, whose oil made him indispensable.

'We must become more unpredictable as a nation,' said Trump at one of his campaign rallies. 'We must immediately become more unpredictable.' In this, he had delivered.

THE EMPEROR, THE TSAR AND THE COMEDIAN

Several unpredictable – but frequently predicted – things were happening in the People's Republic. Trump confronted a rising China and a gaping trade deficit that he said was 'ripping off' America. Ever since Nixon, China had been a protected sector in foreign policy that was targeted against Russia. In the process, western leaders had been awed by the prosperity and wealth of China, appeasing its Party and letting its trade soar. Now Trump insisted, 'We can't let that continue.' His trade war hurt both economies, but when the two met Xi Jinping was as confident and vigilant as Trump was inconsistent and erratic. A man who had experienced a vertiginous downfall, who had been in prison himself, who had seen his sister commit suicide, was unmoved by Trump.

When he became leader in 2012, his view of power was unromantic and realistic. 'People with little contact with power always see these things as mysterious and novel,' he said in a rare moment of public reflection. 'But what I see aren't just the superficial things: the power, the flowers, the glory, the applause. I see the bullpens and how people can blow hot and cold.' His family came with him: his nonagenarian mother called a family meeting to warn them against exploiting his rise.[*] His wife Peng became the first leader's wife to be publicly prominent since Madame Mao, but she claimed, 'When he comes home, I've never felt as if there's some leader in the house . . .' His political 'lineage' rose with him too; he purged rivals and their 'lineages'.

Now his mission was simple. 'East, west, south, north and centre,' he said, 'the Party leads everything.' Deng ruled that the Chinese must 'bide their time and hide their strength'. But now Party rule was consolidated, the former British and Portuguese colonies Hong Kong and

---

[*] Not only had Xi visited America but his daughter Mingze was reading English and psychology at Harvard where she used a pseudonym but shared digs, cooked her own meals and attended lectures on Chinese history with a famed British professor.

Macau restored; only Taiwan remained unredeemed. As he was promoted to Core Leader without the usual term limit and with his own 'Xi
Jinping Thought', Xi promised a 'Chinese dream' for his people, with
'common prosperity' for all. China boasted the second largest GDP after
America, becoming the world's largest exporter. Now, Xi looked abroad.

'The Chinese nation has stood,' declared Xi, 'grown rich and become
strong – and now it embraces the new brilliant prospect of rejuvenation.'
This meant an expansion of Chinese power, military and economic, as
he offered loans, roads, ports and technology to extend his 'Belt and
Road' network of power, without having to conquer an empire. It was an
autocratic version of the Marshall Plan. The trajectory of the Xi era was
upwards: 'The great rejuvenation of the Chinese nation has entered an
irreversible process.' But it could be delivered only by the Party founded
by Mao. 'Don't forget the original intent,' warned Xi. That meant that
any resistance to the Party must be crushed. Xi, a harsh authoritarian,
cracked down on dissent, tightening police supervision of citizens and
internet using the new technologies of surveillance and face recognition, while in Xiangjing he conducted an ethnic purge of the Muslim
Uighurs, a million of whom were confined to education camps. But the
unification of China, meaning the conquest of Taiwan, was the spark
wheel of Xi's world mission, not just as Chinese nationalist and Maoist
heir but also given his father Xi Zhongxun's 'United Front' work. It was,
writes Jospeh Torigian, 'always both a national and a family affair'. As
Chinese growth faltered under his rigid autocracy, Xi surely pondered
a 'short, victorious war' – the risks of 'rolling the iron dice' to retake
Taiwan that could win him immortality or destroy his rule altogether.
Simultaneously, his natural ally, Putin, promoting his resurgent Russia,
was weighing up a similar gamble.

Putin had faced minor sanctions for annexing Crimea, but his war
in Ukraine was stalemated. His view of Ukrainian illegitimacy was
only confirmed when Ukraine elected a clown as president: Volodymyr
Zelensky, forty-year-old son of a mathematics professor, was a Russian-
speaking Jewish comedian from east Ukraine who had become the most
popular man in the country when he starred in a TV series, *Servant of
the People*, in which he played an everyman history teacher who becomes
president of Ukraine. When he decided to run for president, he called
his party Servant of the People. In March 2019, he won a landslide victory: in the era of Trump, the preposterous Neronian fusion of politics
and showbusiness seemed to confirm the decadence of democracy.
Indeed, Trump's corruption – his refusal to recognize the difference
between his interests and those of the state – soon tainted Ukraine.

He tried to withhold Ukrainian military aid unless Zelensky smeared his Democratic rival Joe Biden, a gambit that led to his impeachment. Trump survived his congressional trial. Zelensky emerged unscathed.

Diminutive, emotional and playful, Zelensky seemed too soft to handle his dictatorial antithesis, the lethal Putin, who believed that the actor personified Ukraine's failure. Zelensky had shown courage in entering this brutal arena, but he struggled to govern Ukraine and halt its rampant corruption. It looked as if his presidency might fail. In one of his movies, *Rzhevsky versus Napoleon*, Zelensky had played Napoleon invading Russia. But in real life the threat was from the east.

Yet, if ever a crisis came, the essential relationship in the tripolar World Game was between Xi and Putin, who had met thirty times. 'I've had closer interactions with President Putin than with any other foreign colleagues,' said Xi in June 2019 as Putin showed him the Romanov palaces of his home town, Petersburg. 'He's my best and bosom friend.' Xi boasted of their personal affinity: 'We've taken a high-speed train ride together, watched an ice-hockey friendly, celebrated his birthday and bantered about light-hearted matters, literature, art, and sport . . .' But while Russia's rigid dictatorship was still dependent on its oil income, its bigger brother China was at a historic zenith, a moment unique in its history. Then Xi faced that challenge: a pandemic.

The Party knew such a disease would one day come, but no one knew when and no one was prepared. On 17 November 2019, a man in China's Hubei Province was diagnosed with a new virus. On 31 December, Wuhan Municipal Health Commission announced a cluster of cases of pneumonia caused by an unknown germ. A thirty-three-year-old doctor at Wuhan Central Hospital, Li Wenliang, shared a report of a respiratory virus with his colleagues and was arrested for 'making false comments on the internet'. On 31 January 2020, two Chinese tourists in Italy fell ill. On 6 February, in the United States, the first patient died; on 7 February, Dr Li died of this new respiratory virus, Coronavirus 2019. The fast-moving twenty-first-century world, in which millions of people flew from city to city on cheap flights, spread the disease with unprecedented speed. For two years, fear and panic followed waves of the virus that, like every pandemic, inspired civil schisms, distrust of foreigners, wild conspiracy theories and strained governments, which by March 2020 were confining people to their homes. The lockdown started to reverse a century and a half in which the office – the working space – had occupied as much time and attention as family life. Thanks to smart computers, many people could work at home, as they had before the industrial revolution; ironically, the pandemic returned people to their families.* Fifteen million people – mainly older and poorer, and those with respiratory vulnerabilities – died.

Xi declared a 'dynamic zero-Covid' policy that treated the pandemic like 'a people's war against an invisible enemy', but such a disease was impossible to control and it exposed the vulnerability of China's prosperity and the rigidity both of its system and of its leader. In the open world, smaller war democracies – Taiwan, Israel – proved more efficient than larger comfort democracies, but its mitigation was most catastrophic in India where around five million (a third of the global Covid deaths) died, thanks in part to its government's incompetence.

Trump's bombast wilted amid the hysteria, his incompetence and insouciance exposed, and in November he decisively lost the election to Biden, who at seventy-eight became the oldest president with Kamala Harris as the first female, first African-American and first Asian-American vice-president. Even though Biden had won six million more votes, Trump, refusing to concede, espoused a conspiracy claiming that he had been robbed of the presidency. On 6 January 2021, encouraged and abetted by Trump, a mob of freakishly garbed Trumpians stormed the weakly defended Capitol to stop Congress's electoral vote count. It was fortunate that Trump lacked the backing and the acumen to organize a coup, but he now dominated the Republican party, hinting at a second presidency; America had not seemed so fragile since the civil war.

Every president had dreamed of extracting America from the 9/11 wars, above all from Afghanistan, where the corrupt pro-American rulers were maintained by a small NATO presence while the Taliban controlled much of the countryside. In the classic iPhone and dagger state, men in Toyota trucks with Kalashnikovs could still take towns and defy America's expensive technologies. Biden unwisely accelerated an exit, insisting that the Afghan army was 'better trained, better equipped, more competent' than the Taliban, whose victory was 'highly unlikely'. Instead, on 15 August, the Taliban, commanded by the terror lord Sirajuddin Haqqani, advanced, the regime collapsed and thousands fled to the airport where the Americans desperately evacuated their friends. Not even the fall of Saigon was such a self-inflicted blow.

---

* Lockdown did not stop conflicts outside Europe. In November 2020, in the latest skirmish in the disintegration of the Ethiopian empire, the high-handedness of the Ethiopian prime minister Abiy Ahmed alienated the Tigrayans, who had led the liberation from Mengistu in the 1990s. Abiy had fought Mengistu under the Tigrayans, rising to deputy intelligence chief. But now the Tigrayans returned to war. Abiy made an alliance with the Eritrean dictator Isaias Afwerki and attacked the Tigrayans, who counter-attacked and almost broke through to Addis before they were again pushed back.

One man was watching this from the isolation of his mansion outside Moscow. Now sixty-nine, Putin asked historians whom he met, 'How will history judge me?' Putin, spoiled by easy if blood-drenched successes in Chechnya, Syria and Crimea, limited in debate by his dominance and misinformed by his sycophantic secret police, came to believe that a *coup de main* at the opportune moment would restore the Russian imperium and destroy Ukraine as a nation. Russia's massive oil and natural gas production could fund a war and force dependent Europe to acquiesce. Putin sensed a felicitous conjunction offered a unique opportunity: the democracies were paralysed with culture wars; NATO, said President Macron, was 'brain-dead'; Britain, now led by the erratic Johnson, had undermined the EU; Biden, unlike the unpredictable Trump, personified western bewilderment; and Xi backed him. In February 2022, Putin flew to Beijing where Xi explained, 'We're working together to promote a truly multilateral world order,' pooling their 'efforts to uphold the real democratic spirit', code for a world of power spheres ruled by the autocrats of empire nations.

Putin massed 180,000 troops around Ukraine and demanded Ukrainian subjugation along with western withdrawal from eastern Europe. Biden warned against an invasion. Putin rolled 'the iron dice': on 24 February 2022, he announced a 'special military operation' against Ukraine: 'To anyone who'd consider interfering from the outside . . . you'll face consequences greater than any you have faced in history.'

Zelensky was asleep at home in the Ukrainian presidential compound when Russian rockets hit Kyiv. He and his wife Olena rushed to their two children. 'We woke them up. It was loud. There were explosions.' Zelensky decided to stay at any cost – and it was too dangerous to move his family as Russian commandos, landed by parachute, attacked the Triangle government district in a bid to assassinate him.

Moscow's tanks raced towards Kyiv. Western experts and Putin's epigones agreed on one thing: an era had closed, a new one had opened – and, within a few weeks, Ukraine would collapse . . .

CONCLUSION

There is such a thing as too much history. This may be a strange reflection for a historian who is just finishing a world history in a time of
pandemic and European war. But the fetishistic obsession with curated
versions of nations and empires in the past can blind one to the present
and what really matters: people living today, and how they and their
families wish to live. That is one of the reasons I chose to write this
book through families – the measure of happiness for what one wants
for one's family defines what one wants for the world. Yet it is a balance.
History matters: we long to know how we came to be who we are. 'Life
can only be understood backwards,' writes Søren Kierkegaard, 'but it
must be lived forwards.' History never dies; history is never history; it is
kinetic, mutating and dynamic, a deathless arsenal of stories and facts
to teach us how humans lived, but also to be deployed in the causes of
today, good and evil, a mission complicated by the internet – that cesspit,
treasure-trove and reliquary of hatreds and hobbies, truths, randomness
and revels, calumnies and conspiracies. Yet it is our reverence for the
legitimacy granted by history that gives it such lethal, propulsive power.

The Ukrainian war marks the end of an exceptional period: the
Seventy-Year Peace, divided into two phases – forty-five years of Cold
War, then twenty-five of American unipotency. If the first era was like
a chess tournament and the second like a game of solitaire, today is a
multi-player computer game.

Putin's invasion of Ukraine is not a new way of exerting and expanding power. Its flint-hearted ferocity is a return to normality in a way that
the dynasts in this book – warlords, kings and dictators – would find
routine: normal disorder has been resumed. Many of today's empire nations seem keen to expand spheres of influence that mimic old empires.
The wanton killing of Ukrainian civilians, the bodies in the streets and
the escape of families from the war, reminds us what much of history
was like in times when there were no mobile phones to record atrocities
and refugees, and court historians praised murderous conquerors as
heroes. We have met plenty of those in this book, and this is not the

only sign that human momentum is not just a march of progress but also a stuttering spasm of contingencies. It is a struggle not just between clashing states and ideologies but between contradictory facets of human nature. If nothing else, the Ukrainian invasion demonstrates the real difference between the open world of the liberal democracies and the closed world where the combination of traditional menace and digital surveillance increasingly allows control states to police their people in a way scarcely imaginable even by a Stalin.

Family power is also resurgent for it too is characteristic of our species. Dynastic reversion seems both natural and pragmatic when weak states are not trusted to deliver justice or protection and loyalties remain to kin not to institutions. Leaders who can trust no one usually trust family. In a growing number of Asian, Latin American and African states, from Kenya to Pakistan and the Philippines, demo-dynasties deliver some of the magical reassurance of family power; others from Nicaragua to Azerbaijan, Uganda to Cambodia, are becoming absolutist republican monarchies. It is certainly a bad way to run a country – even worse than democracy.

But today's dictators and dynasties are not a return to earlier centuries. Even in iPhone and dagger states, they are part of a new world where events move at unprecedented speed, where contenders and markets are interconnected and where the jeopardy of nuclear catastrophe is ever present.

This, coupled with Covid and global warming, foster fears of apocalypse. A sense of impending eschaton seems to be part of human character, perhaps a recognition of the miraculous but fragile conquest of earth by one species. But the stakes today make the End of Days ever more possible.

Yet in some senses *Homo sapiens* has never been so healthy, and is living longer and better than ever before; society may, in places, be more peaceful than it ever was. While our forefathers were likely to die of infections, violence or famine, today humans are dying of diseases – coronaries, cancer and neurodegeneration – because we live so long and often eat so much. Many of these diseases will soon be cured by new technologies of genetic modification. These improvements are so striking that even the poorest countries today have higher life expectancies than the richest empires of a century ago. Sierra Leone now has a life expectancy of 50.1 years, which is the same as France in 1910. In 1945, Indians lived until thirty-five; now their life expectancy is seventy. Naturally this has changed the shape of families: parents have many children when they expect most to die; now low child mortality, along with female education and contraception, encourages later marriage and smaller families.

In the next eighty years, the population of Europe and east Asia will plummet, that of Nigeria will quadruple to 800 million, making it larger than the entire EU, the second biggest country after India; Congo will triple to 250 million, Egypt will double, Russia will shrink and its Muslims will form a majority. China will halve, its power and economy possibly challenged by the drawbacks of its own autocracy; the US will remain much the same, its ingenious power, however flawed and fragile, likely to endure longer than doomsayers predict. The African giants, Nigeria, Egypt and Congo, could thrive, but it seems more likely that their rulers will be unable to manage or feed their peoples. It is not so much 'winter is coming', more like the interminable broiling of a world furnace: climate change – heat and flooding – will make it harder to produce enough food. Already many countries are iPhone and dagger dispolities, realms that barely protect or feed their populations; many states will subside, borders, drawn by imperial powers, will blur into exsurgent warlands – as is already happening in Sahel in perpetual wars for water and resources – or they will succumb to the protection of empire nations, keen to secure their rare earth elements – and old fashioned diamonds, gold and oil. Their peoples will migrate to northern comfort states on a scale unseen since the nomadic invasions. A book of this span has many themes but a key one is that all nations are formed by families in movement: the challenge for the open states is to absorb the migrants they need while being rich enough to sustain the comfort that makes them attractive.

Scale matters in the World Game, but one thing is certain: whoever wins will not win for long. If this history proves anything, it is that the human ability to self-mutilate is almost limitless. 'In individuals, insanity is rare,' wrote Nietzsche, 'but in groups, parties, nations and epochs, it is the rule.' It is easy to criticize politicians but this interconnected world makes it ever harder to govern: 'You philosophers . . . you write on paper,' Catherine the Great warned. 'Unfortunate Empress that I am, I write on the susceptible skins of living beings.'

One of the mysteries of such times of crisis is the absence of great leaders, but they are made by their opportunities: 'We're little men serving a great cause,' said Nehru, 'but because the cause is great something of the greatness falls on us also.' Kissinger mocked the very idea of greatness: 'In retrospect, all successful policies seem preordained. Leaders like to claim prescience for what has worked, ascribing planning to what usually starts as a series of improvisations.' History is driven as much by clowns as by visionaries. 'History likes to joke,' said Stalin; 'sometimes it chooses a fool to drive historical progress.'

'I've seen the future,' sang Leonard Cohen. 'It is murder.' Today's problems are deep and colossal. Globalization was part of the progressive development that raised living standards, ended most diseases and most famines, but its conveniences have a cost: some are left out of its bounty and some of its bounty requires perilous compromises with enemies. Covid pandemic and Ukrainian war show how fast its food and energy supply lines can fray. Even the miraculous health improvements could be corroding: US life expectancy fell in the three years up to 2020 – for the first time since the Spanish Flu. Microbial resistance to antibiotics could make routine operations much more risky. Covid is probably a dress rehearsal for a graver influenza pandemic.

Even though no empire nations have fought each other since 1945, the time will come when they do and they are developing new killing machines – intergalactic and thermobaric – as well as improving their traditional heavy metal. 'Never place a loaded rifle on the stage,' wrote Chekhov, 'if it isn't going to go off.' He was talking about theatre, but this is true in warfare too: ultimately all those weapons will be used. Thousands of tanks can still clash like steel cavalry as they did in the last century, but in this new world cheap gadgets – tank- and plane-smashing drones and portable missiles – mean that smaller countries can destroy the expensive toys of larger ones. This is wonderful if they are being used against an evil empire, less so if used against us. Before nuclear weapons, the west would have gone to war against Russia for invading Ukraine – as it did in the Crimean War – and the US–Chinese rivalry would most likely have led to war too. There are only nine nuclear powers – not a bad record – but actually around forty states could adapt their peaceful nuclear facilities to get nuclear weaponry in a few years. The use of tactical atomic weapons would perhaps be equivalent to the Chernobyl accident; the use of hydrogen bombs could destroy the world. Nuclear war on some scale is not just plausible but likely – and it is worth reflecting that, at the time of writing, no nuclear power has ever lost a war.

The number of autocracies is surging, that of democracies ebbing. It is impossible to define exactly what causes one state to fall and another to rise, but Ibn Khaldun, a character in this story and its presiding spirit, identified *asabiyya*, the cohesion essential for a society to thrive: 'Many nations suffered a physical defeat, but that's never marked their end. Yet when a nation becomes the victim of psychological defeat, that marks the end.'

Control states disdain but also fear and envy the gaudy, outrageous, ingenious, clamorous mess – part fairground, part farmyard – that is freedom in our open world. Dictatorships move faster under experienced leaders, but violence and control are wired into the closed world. The rigidity and delusions of tyrannies are incorrigible, their virtue-spirals end in executions, not just cancellations, their adventures end in devastation and slaughter. When they fail, autocrats take state and people down too.

The only leaders more buffoonish and lethal than the fairground hucksters elected in our flailing democracies are the omnipotent clowns of the tyranny. The challenge for open states is to channel their freedoms and pluralism creatively, rather than indulging in schisms about small differences. Democracies are built on invisible trust: over and over again, when anomie strikes, trust is lost and so is openness. 'As soon as any man says of the affairs of state, "What does it matter to me?"' wrote Rousseau, 'the state may be given up as lost.' The lesson of recent years is that the gains that were taken as won – the lessons of 1945, the evil of antisemitism, the crimes of genocide and war-making; the right to abortion and triumphs of the 1960s great liberal reformation – have to be fought for again.

But there is hope too: during the American ascendancy, US-style presidencies and elections became essential for legitimacy in old and new post-colonial states. If Theodore Parker's fashionable dictum that 'the arc of the moral universe . . . bends towards justice' seems over-optimistic, it says something that since 1945 even the most brazen tyrannies feel obliged to pretend to hold elections and respect laws and legislatures – even when they are 'cosplay democracies'. The open world is still the happiest and freest place to live.

Open societies are slow, their leaders amateurish, their policies inconsistent, but when they mobilize they are flexible, efficient and creative. Technology undermines democratic solidarity and aids tyranny and conspiracy, yet it also advances openness and justice. Its very facility means atrocities and wars can be instantly recorded and viewed everywhere in our new virtual-arena world. The immediate challenge of technology is to learn to control its addictiveness and surveillance while enjoying its benefits. The unelected, invisible power of the despots of data must be diminished. States and individuals have to work that out.

Population growth and climate change can only be solved by either catastrophic population decline – pandemic, natural disaster or thermonuclear war – or by cooperation on a titanic scale. And here too the tendency towards power blocs might actually be helpful: when the time comes – if it comes – a cabal of potentates could make those decisions.

'The real problem of humanity,' said Edward O. Wilson, 'is we have palaeolithic emotions, medieval institutions and godlike technology.' Just because we are the smartest ape ever created, just because we have solved many problems so far, it does not mean we will solve everything. Human history is like one of those investment warning clauses: past performance is no guarantee of future results. Yet the harshness of humanity has been constantly rescued by our capacity to create and love: the family is the centre of both. Our limitless ability to destroy is matched only by our ingenious ability to recover.

In this book I have written of the fall of noble cities, the vanishing of kingdoms, the rise and fall of dynasties, cruelty upon cruelty, folly upon folly, eruptions, massacres, famines, pandemics and pollutions, yet again and again in these pages the high spirits and elevated thoughts, the capacity for joy and kindness, the variety and eccentricity of humanity, the faces of love and the devotion of family run through it all, and remind me why I started to write.

Celebrate your joy with us!
Join if in the whole wide world there's
Just one soul to call your own! . . .
Be embracéd, all you millions,
Share this kiss with all the world!

Friedrich Schiller, 'Ode to Joy'

And you should have been cautious, better educated by the past,
The ancient bamboo books of history
Were there for you to study.
But you didn't see . . .
Times change, power passes;
It is the pity of the world.

Li Qingzhao

Human history is not the battle of good struggling to overcome evil. It is a battle fought by a great evil struggling to crush a small kernel of human kindness. But if what is human in human beings has not been destroyed even now, then evil will never conquer.

Vasily Grossman

Rulers, statesmen and nations are often advised to learn the lesson of historical experience. But what experience and history teach is that nations and governments have never learned anything from history.

Hegel

I gazed in every direction and all appeared wonderfully beautiful. There were stars which we never see from earth . . . all larger than we have ever imagined. The starry spheres were much greater than the earth; indeed the earth seemed so small I was scornful of our empire . . . If only you look on high and contemplate this eternal home and resting place you will no longer bother with the gossip of the common herd or put your trust in human reward . . . for what men say dies with them and is blotted out with the forgetfulness of posterity.

Cicero

The wine is heady, make haste!
And time is scarce, take all of it you can.
Who knows if next year's spring,
So sweet, will find you dust and ash or living man.

Saadi

Think of all the beauty still left around you and be happy.

Anne Frank

SELECT BIBLIOGRAPHY

This is a work of synthesis based on the widest reading and travels over thirty years. In a bid to lighten an already large book, the Select Bibliography is available online at: www.simonsebagmontefiore.com

For the sake of length, I have chosen the key works on which each section is based. Again, for the sake of length, I have not listed every book read on each subject nor annotated every fact and quotation. There is some primary research in this book: in my own lifetime, I have been lucky to talk to some of the characters about their lives. In those cases, I quote them 'as told to this author' in the text.

INDEX

Page numbers with the symbols *, † and ‡ attached refer to footnotes.

Beaufort Sea

Greenland
(Den.)

Jan Mayen

Russian
Federation

Alaska
(USA)

Norwegia

Iceland

Faroe Is. (Den.)

United
Kingdom

Ireland

Canada

NORTH
ATLANTIC
OCEAN

France

6

Portugal   Spain

2—○

United States
of America

○— Bermuda (UK)

Azores Is. (Port.)

Madeira (Port.)—○   Morocco

13—○

Canary Is. (Sp.)

Alge

Gulf of
Mexico

The Bahamas

Turks & Caicos Is. (UK)

Western
Sahara

Cayman Is. (UK)   Cuba

Dominican Rep.

Mauritania

Mali

Mexico   Belize

Jamaica   Haiti

see enlargement

Cabo Verde   Senegal

The Gambia

Burkina
Faso

Guatemala   Honduras

El Salvador   Nicaragua

Guinea-Bissau   Guinea

Costa Rica

Venezuela   Guyana

Sierra Leone   Ghana

Panama

Suriname

Liberia   C

French Guiana (Fr.)

Côte d'Ivoire   Togo

Colombia

Equatorial Guine

Hawaii (USA)

PACIFIC
OCEAN

Equator

São Tomé & Príncipe

Ga

C

Galápagos Is. (Ec.)   Ecuador

○— *Ascension (UK)*

French Polynesia (Fr.)

Peru   Brazil

Bolivia

St Helena (UK) ○

1 Albania	**18** Lebanon
2 Andorra	**19** Liechtenstein
3 Armenia	**20** Lithuania
4 Austria	**21** Luxembourg
5 Azerbaijan	**22** Malta
6 Belgium	**23** Moldova
7 Bosnia & Herzegovina	**24** Monaco
8 Croatia	**25** Montenegro
9 Cyprus	**26** Netherlands
10 Czech Republic	**27** North Macedonia
11 Denmark	**28** Palestine
12 Estonia	**29** San Marino
13 Gibraltar (UK)	**30** Serbia
14 Hungary	**31** Slovakia
15 Israel	**32** Slovenia
16 Kosovo	**33** Switzerland
17 Latvia	**34** Vatican City

Paraguay

SOUTH
ATLANTIC
OCEAN

Chile   Uruguay

Argentina

Falkland Is. (UK)

South Georgia (UK)

Enlargement (Caribbean)

Dominican
Republic

37   Anguilla

44   43

*Puerto Rico
(USA)*

42 ○   Antigua &
Barbuda

St Kitts & Nevis   41

39

Dominica

Caribbean Sea

40

St Lucia

35

38   36

St Vincent & the
Grenadines   Barbados

Grenada

Venezuela

Trinidad &
Tobago

35 Aruba (Neth.)	
36 Bonaire (Neth.)	
37 British Virgin Is. (UK)	
38 Curaçao (Neth.)	
39 Guadeloupe (Fr.)	
40 Martinique (Fr.)	
41 Montserrat (UK)	
42 Saba / St Eustatius (Neth.)	
43 St Martin (Fr./Neth.)	
44 US Virgin Is. (USA)	

Weddell Sea